MW01265460

BARRON'S
GUIDE TO
Distance Learning

SECOND EDITION

DEGREES • CERTIFICATES • COURSES

Pat Criscito

BARRON'S

All inquiries should be addressed to:
Barron's Educational Series, Inc.
250 Wireless Boulevard
Hauppauge, NY 11788
http://www.barronseduc.com

Library of Congress Catalog Card No. 2001037944

International Standard Book No. 0-7641-1791-2

Library of Congress Cataloging-in-Publication Data

Criscito, Pat, 1953–
    Barron's guide to distance learning : degrees, certificates,
courses / Pat Criscito.—2nd ed.
       p. cm.
    Includes indexes.
    ISBN 0-7641-1791-2
    1. Distance education—United States. 2. Distance education—
Canada. 3. Distance education—United States—Directories
4. Distance education—Canada—Directories.
I. Title: Guide to distance learning. II. Title.

LC5805.C75   2002
378.1'75'02573—dc21   2001037944

PRINTED IN THE UNITED STATES OF AMERICA
9 8 7 6 5 4 3 2 1

Contents

Preface

This book will provide you with all the information you need to find an accredited undergraduate, graduate, or doctoral program that will allow you to complete your course work without sitting in a traditional college classroom. Whether you want to begin a degree program from scratch, finish one you have already begun, earn continuing education credits, stay on the cutting edge of your profession, or take a single class to expand your personal growth, you have selected the right book. Here's what you will find in the following pages:

▸ An introduction to the concept of distance learning and its terminology.

▸ Information to help you discern an accredited program from a "diploma mill."

▸ Tools to assess whether or not you have the personality for nontraditional learning.

▸ Ways to earn credit for what you already know.

▸ Means to finance the cost of your education.

▸ Complete lists of degrees, certificates, and courses to help you evaluate the programs of nearly 900 colleges and universities.

▸ Indexes listing colleges by geographic location, type of programs offered, individual classes, or on-campus requirements.

Regionally accredited colleges and universities throughout the United States and Canada are profiled here, plus a few international colleges that are accredited by one of the six regional accreditation associations in the United States. Each profile provides contact information (including Web page and e-mail address), program availability (degrees, certificates, and individual classes), admission requirements, costs, teaching methods, financial aid information, and a brief description of the school. An extensive series of indexes follows with breakdowns by location, on-campus requirements, and fields of study.

This guide could not have been written without the cooperation of every college listed. My thanks to every person who took the time to complete the survey and to those who graciously answered questions and provided special information about their programs. The work would never have been finished without my dedicated assistants—Heather Florio, Melanie Carlston, and Teri Adams-Fjellman—and the researchers who spent months on the telephone and at computers sending e-mails, entering data, proofreading, and editing the profiles—George Kitkowski, David Huggins, Dana Ware, Robbie Smarr, Kathy Traxler, and Jill Mortellaro. Thanks to each of you and to Mike for your undying support.

Introduction to Distance Learning

1

You are just six classes short of a degree, but with a full-time job that requires you to travel two weeks every month, you can't possibly make the time to go back to school! Or so you think. In reality, if you have a computer with a modem, a television set, or a mailbox and a bit of self-discipline, a diploma may be closer than you think.

Online learning, televised classrooms, and home-study courses have revolutionized the way instruction is delivered, making it possible to earn college credits from the comfort of our homes or offices without regard for time and geographical barriers. Whether you are a professional who can study for a few hours on an airplane or during a lunch break at work, or a young mother who can "go to school" after the kids are asleep, distance learning may be your answer to completing a degree or acquiring certification.

What Is Distance Learning?

According to Webster, distance is "a measure of separation in space or time." Therefore distance learning is defined as a formal educational process where the majority of the instruction occurs when the learner and instructor are not in the same place and are often separated by time. Education is delivered to people instead of people to education. The definition is as simple as that, but here's a little something of what it means to you as a student.

- Instead of sitting in a lecture hall or attending a seminar, you participate in an online conference through your computer, watch a videotape on your home television set, or join a videoconference at a local teleconferencing center.

- Instead of a team project where a group of students meets together in the same place once a week, you collaborate via computer conferences, e-mail, or audioconferences.

- Instead of searching through the stacks in a dusty library, you surf the Net or use online databases and research librarians.

- Instead of sitting down with your faculty advisor over a cup of coffee, you use e-mail, telephone, or live computer chats.

- Instead of handing in your homework during class, you return your assignments electronically online or via e-mail, fax, or by mail.

- Instead of testing with your class, you go to a local testing center, find a proctor at your local high school or college, or take tests via e-mail, fax, or online.

Many terms in the academic world are used synonymously with distance learning, including distributed learning, nontraditional education, external degree program, innovative program, asynchronous learning, alternative education, independent study, online program, nonresidential program, faculty-directed courses, guided self-study, electronic classrooms, and correspondence study, among others. Each of these terms has subtle differences, and a college can choose to call its program whatever it likes, but for the sake of consistency, this book will use the words *distance learning* to describe all of them.

The History of Distance Learning

Distance learning dates back more than 100 years to Europe, Africa, and Asia, where open universities offered "external" degrees. In Australia, the University of Queensland offered an external degree program as early as the 1890s. Today, higher education institutions in Australia incorporate distance learning into many of their programs, making Australia a leader in distance education worldwide.

The well-known British Open University began in 1971 and now serves more than 200,000 undergraduate and graduate students worldwide. It is one of the largest distance learning schools in the world and is ranked among the top ten universities in the United Kingdom. At a speech in Ankara, Turkey, Sir John Daniel, the Vice Chancellor of the Open University, reported that his research had discovered eleven distance learning "mega-universities" around the world with more than 100,000 students each. Anadolu University in Turkey was the largest university in the world when measured by the number of degree-level students (570,000). The China TV University System is a close second with more than 550,000 degree-level students in its distance learning programs.

Canada is a world leader in distance education. Because of its vast expanse and sparsely populated areas, nearly all provinces have developed various media to bring university programs to remote areas that might not otherwise have access to a university education. In addition to the distance learning programs offered by conventional universities, Alberta, British Columbia, and Quebec have each developed an "open university" based on the British model. They have liberal admission policies and use home study, television, teleconferencing, printed materials, audiotapes, and videotapes, among other delivery methods.

Distance learning in the United States began in the late nineteenth century with correspondence courses, such as the one offered by Isaac Pitman in 1840 to teach his system of shorthand. Columbia University and other colleges offered radio courses in the 1920s and 1930s and televised courses in the 1960s. Since 1890, about 100 million Americans have taken courses at a distance, including such well-known people as Franklin D. Roosevelt, Walter P. Chrysler, Walter Cronkite, Barry Goldwater, and Charles Schulz.

The first exclusively distance degree program in the United States was developed by the University of the State of New York in 1970. Ewald B. Nyquist suggested the formation of the Regents External Degree Program sponsored by the university's Board of Regents. That program has awarded more than 56,000 degrees and was known as Regents College until changing its name to Excelsior College. In early 1998, Excelsior College became chartered as an independent member institution with the University of the State of New York.

Today, technology-based distance education has emerged as an increasingly important component of higher education in the United States. Many states have developed innovative distance learning programs that are on the cutting edge of technology. One good example is the Western Governors University (WGU). Formed by the governors of the states in the western United States, WGU is a "virtual university" with no campus and a heavy reliance on technology. It brings the resources of numerous colleges, universities, corporations, and other organizations together to provide degrees and certificates to students around the world.

Why Distance Learning?

When colleges and universities first began incorporating distance education into their programs, they thought they were tapping into a new market of underserved adult learners who were too busy or lived too far away to come to a traditional campus. It often didn't occur to them that many of their traditional on-campus students would be eager to ease their schedules by taking courses online or would use distance learning to get into courses that had already been closed on campus. Now there are just as many on-campus students taking advantage of distance learning as there are off-campus students. At the State University of New York's Learning Network, 80 percent of the students study full- or part-time on a SUNY campus. At Arizona State University, only 3 percent of the distance education students live in another state. In Canada, Lori Wallace, a senior instructional designer at the University of Manitoba, tracked the demographics of distance education students for more than a decade and found that 66 percent of the students were taking concurrent courses on campus. However, all distance education students have at least one of these things in common:

▸ They are trying to finish a degree to get a job or to advance to a better one,

▸ Or they need certification for their profession,

▸ Or they need continuing education units (CEUs) to stay current in their profession,

▸ Or they love learning and take college classes for personal enrichment, intellectual stimulation, socialization, or recreation,

▸ Or they want a chance to study with well-known teachers who have agreed to collaborate with certain distance learning programs or to complete a degree program at a prestigious college far from where they live,

▸ Or they are high school students wanting to get a jump on a college education,

▸ And they need the flexibility that distance learning offers because of where they live, their physical limitations, or the time constraints of work or family commitments.

This flexibility is why people elect to take courses via television, the Internet, or correspondence even when classrooms are just a few minutes away. Online courses are especially popular because students can log on day or night to check e-mail messages, discussion logs, and instructor assignments. Some online courses do require "attendance" at live chats, but this limits the school's market, so many online courses steer away from real-time activities that require a student to be somewhere at a set time.

Colleges and universities like distance learning because it allows them to accommodate growth without building new facilities and it helps them reach a wider student population. The University of Phoenix, for instance, added 2,500 students every month in 2001 to its online programs and is developing a new FlexNet program to accommodate even more students. Distance learning often helps fulfill the institution's mission of providing education to its students, regardless of their location, diversity, economic status, age, or experience.

For the student, continuing education is often the key to staying current in a rapidly changing job market. According to the Commission for a Nation of Lifelong Learners (CNLL), more than 80 percent of adults believe they need more education to advance their careers. William Hine, Ed.D., dean of the School of Adult and Continuing Education at Eastern Illinois University in Charleston, says:

> *The half-life of a college degree is three to five years. If you're not retooling or gaining new knowledge, your education is almost obsolete, especially in the sciences, health, and technology. Those who aren't committed to lifelong learning are unlikely to move ahead in their careers.*

In the next decade, 75 percent of the current work force will need significant retraining, and more than half of the new jobs will require higher education and training. In their November 1997 report, the CNLL says that education provides the critical margin of competitiveness in a worldwide economy and, without it, America will not be able to maintain its leadership in the global economy.

I like how Glenn Jones, the founder and chief executive officer of Jones International, defined *education* in his book, *Cyberschools:*

> *Education is a process. Education is how information becomes meaningful. Information without meaning is useless. Education converts information into knowledge, understanding, and wisdom much like changing temperature turns water into ice. Education is the loom through which information is woven into value systems, dignity, self-worth, freedom, and into civilization itself.*

With the emergence of today's "knowledge worker," that definition is more true now than at any other time in history. Companies are demanding that their workers be able to produce new designs and concepts instead of just following standard procedures and producing familiar products (Peter Drucker and Robert Reich). This demands effective education.

By developing a love for lifelong learning, you can boost your earning power and make your skills more marketable, giving you that competitive edge so necessary in today's cutthroat corporate world. It is no longer possible to take a job right out of high school, be trained by an employer, and work for the same company until retirement. There is no gold watch at the end of the rainbow, and this trend is unlikely to change. The baby boom generation has already embraced a philosophy of lifelong learning as a result of this dynamic global workplace, and distance learning is the perfect way to incorporate this philosophy into your schedule.

Let's take a look at the U.S. Census Bureau's 2000 mean earning statistics to get an idea of how lifelong learning translates into annual income:

Education Level	Men	Women
High School Diploma	$35,121	$23,498
Associate Degree	$44,706	$31,285
Bachelor's Degree	$62,543	$40,263
Master's Degree	$75,441	$49,635
Professional Degree	$130,711	$72,171
Doctoral Degree	$107,988	$69,085

According to the U.S. Department of Education's National Center for Education Statistics, the average college student today is over the age of 22 and works full time. According to their projections, by the year 2008, nearly 9 million students over the age of 22 will be enrolled in colleges and universities in the United States alone. The Distance Education and Training Council (DETC) surveyed the institutions it accredits and found that the typical student was 31 years old, 48 percent were male, 90 percent were employed, and 31 percent had their tuition paid by their employer. This shift in demographics increases the demand for education that is more accessible and more affordable.

Traditional campus-based universities are accepting the fact that higher education must change with the times. With this change have come distance learning options that meet the needs of adult learners and accept the realities of the new student demographic. These schools are delivering education based on the student's resources (computer, television, or mailbox) and not the resources of the university (manicured lawns and ivy-covered walls). John Sperling put it best when he said:

As we move to meet the educational needs of working adults in a mobile society, our concept of the university must extend beyond place and embrace process. An adult university cannot be campus bound; rather, its borders must be defined by the lives of its students.

Mike Leavitt, a former governor of Utah, has said:

For the twenty-first century, I believe there will be a basic change in higher education. It will move from mass production to mass customization. The educational system will be transformed into a competency-based, versus credit-based system, and higher education will revolve around the student. Where learning takes place will no longer be as important as what a student actually learns.

The majority of regionally accredited colleges and universities today either have distance learning programs now or are seriously considering them. Many have developed full-scale programs that incorporate virtual classrooms via the Internet, interactive computer conferencing, e-mail, newsgroups, LISTSERVs, bulletin boards, fax, videoconferencing, audioconferencing, videotapes, cable/satellite television, and/or correspondence study in various combinations. Others are just dipping their toes into the ocean of possibilities by offering a few classes. Research by the U.S. Department of Education's National Center for Education Statistics has shown that 39 percent of all colleges and universities were offering courses via distance learning in 1998, but that number grew to 54 percent in 2001.

According to a study by the National Center for Education Statistics, distance education is more likely to be conducted by public institutions rather than private colleges/universities. Their research found that 78 percent of public four-year and 62 percent of public two-year institutions offered distance learning courses, compared with 19 percent of private four-year and 5 percent of private two-year institutions. Private schools are more likely to offer graduate or first-professional level programs than public institutions. Distance education is also strongly related to institutional size—the larger the school, the more likely that it will offer distance education.

Some degree-granting institutions aren't even colleges at all, but are corporations or industry associations that have applied for accreditation to award academic degrees. More than $50 billion is spent on training by employers every year, and some experts estimate that as many as 1,000 corporate universities exist in the United States. Colleges and universities have even teamed up with corporations to form consortia to offer classes, degrees, and certificates.

Types of Distance Learning

Distance learning methods are as numerous as the technologies for delivering the instruction. The three primary delivery mediums are computer, television, and mailbox in various combinations. Let's look at them in more detail.

Correspondence Courses

Distance learning is not a novel concept. Correspondence study (also called home study or independent study) has been around for more than 100 years. The biggest difference between those programs and today's distance learning is technology. However, pure correspondence courses —without the use of technology in some form (e-mail, fax, videotapes, audiotapes, CD-ROMs, satellite/cable television, video/audioconferencing, etc.)—are quickly becoming dinosaurs. Correspondence study, regardless of its delivery method, is included in this book's definition of distance learning.

Accreditation of a correspondence course is critical since most colleges and universities will not accept transfer credits from a school that is not regionally accredited. You will find that the majority of correspondence courses are geared toward undergraduate rather than graduate-level study. Regardless of their level, correspondence courses generally work this way:

1. You complete an application and mail it to a designated address with a check or credit card number for your fees.

2. You receive the course, study guide, instructions, syllabus, etc., in the mail.

3. You order the textbooks listed in the instructions.

4. You receive your textbooks in the mail and begin completing lessons.

5. As each lesson is completed, you return it to your instructor where it is evaluated and graded.

6. The corrected and graded lesson is returned to you in the mail, along with comments from your instructor.

7. You may be required to take a mid-course examination and a final examination. These are usually given at a local testing center provided by the school, although you can make arrangements to pay a local proctor from a list approved by the school.

8. The proctor returns the completed examination to the school.

9. You receive a final grade in the mail.

Virtual Classrooms

If you were a student at the University of Phoenix Online Campus, you would dial into their system via modem, read the instructor's assignment and lectures, review your fellow classmates' comments about the current topic in a continuous newsgroup format, and then spend time responding to discussion questions. When you logged off, you would then complete your homework and prepare for the next assignment. Periodically, you would "meet" online with your group members to collaborate on group projects.

At the University of Denver, the faculty create their own Internet home pages for each class. These sites contain a wealth of information about the courses, including the syllabus, textbook requirements, detailed learning outcomes, full instructions for completing assignments, and relevant hyperlinks to other sites that the instructor has selected for the course. Students communicate with the instructor and other students via e-mail, and instructors create chat rooms and bulletin boards for idea exchanges and discussions about topics related to the assignments.

While some schools use private computer networks, others use the World Wide Web and bulletin board systems. Some teach entire courses online, and others only parts of courses. Some professors post extensive print materials, video clips, and graphics and use sophisticated messaging systems on their sites, while others use only e-mail. There is no universal approach to online learning, so you need to ask the college or university for more information about its technology before you apply. Most distance learning catalogs and brochures provide clear explanations of the technologies you will be required to use in each class.

Keep in mind, however, that technology is not infallible. Like the proverbial "My dog ate my homework," you are at the mercy of your instructor if your computer crashes! Always back up your files to a floppy disk and set your e-mail software to save any e-mail you send or receive to a "filing cabinet." Then periodically save that filing cabinet to a floppy disk.

This may all seem too "techie" for you, but you don't have to be a computer expert to travel the information superhighway. You will use basic computer skills that can be learned in a day. After all, what is school for if not to teach you what you need to know to be successful using computer-based learning? The university of your choice will have support staff available to walk you through the technology requirements of any class.

Video and Audioconferencing

Videoconferencing and audioconferencing (sometimes called teleconferencing) are now affordable for any school thanks to continuing advances in technology. In fact, a school can hook up a system that lets students and instructors talk to and see each other in remote locations for a few hundred dollars worth of equipment. The more money one spends on teleconferencing equipment, however, the higher the quality of both the video and audio connection, so colleges and universities are spending much more than a few hundred dollars! Unlike other distance learning teaching methods, unless you have a camera and other equipment on your computer, you will have to leave your home or office to join the conference from a location on another college campus or a commercial teleconferencing center.

Videoconferencing allows the class to hold face-to-face discussions and to display visual aids for all to see. It is possible to look at and modify designs on the screen or to make presentations using PowerPoint software. Some programs use teleconferencing to allow students to "sit in" on traditional on-campus classes. The students in class interact with the distance students as if they were sitting in the classroom and vice versa. Instructors use special electronic white boards instead of chalkboards, so the distance learning student can even see what is written on the board in the corner of his or her computer screen.

If you have a video camera on your computer, a full-duplex sound card, Internet access, and the necessary software (all of which come as standard equipment on many new high-end computers today), you already have your own computerized teleconferencing site. The biggest drawback to Internet-based teleconferencing is the small picture size and slightly jerky motion of the image. In the near future, however, more homes and offices will have access to DSL or ISDN telephone lines or cable modems, which allow data to move faster and therefore create better sound and picture quality.

A less frequently used medium of communication in distance learning classes is audioconferencing where only conversation is heard. There is no visual element. The students are either speaking individually from their home telephones via a conference call or several small groups of students are sitting around a table with a special speaker in the middle that picks up all of the conversations around the table.

Television

Televised courses were aired over public television stations for many years, but today's televised courses are usually broadcast over special cable channels (like the Learning Channel), via satellite, or from private television stations at universities. Television is a popular method of delivering education, since most homes in developed countries contain at least one television set.

This category of distance learning also includes videotapes of classes that were conducted in special classrooms set up like television studios. These videotapes are often included as a part of correspondence courses today and require only a television set and VCR.

What Is Available

Degree Programs

Most colleges and universities begin their distance learning experiments by offering only individual classes. As their experience with distance learning matures, these schools expand their programs to offer undergraduate, graduate, and sometimes doctoral degrees via this nontraditional format. For a look at the types of degrees available at colleges and universities listed in this guide, check the indexes by fields of study at the end of the book.

Certification Programs

Professional certification is required in many industries, such as teaching, medicine, computer science, hotel management, and quality control. Even where it is not required, certification can help you get a job or promotion, so it is well worth pursuing. Certification is offered in an incredibly diverse number of fields, including business, financial planning, computer networking, theology, human development, child psychology, chemical engineering, transportation planning, and construction management, to name a very few.

Credit Courses

If you are close to finishing a degree but lack a few credits, taking individual classes may help you reach your goal of graduation. Credits from a regionally accredited college or university may be applied toward a degree or transferred to your degree-granting institution, but you should always check first. Don't waste your valuable time and money on a class that won't transfer, if that is your goal.

For those who never attended college or who have earned only a few credits, distance learning classes give the student an opportunity to test the waters before enrolling in a full degree program. If an expensive college requires you to take only the "core courses" from that institution, then you can use community colleges and less-expensive alternatives to complete some of the prerequisite credits before enrolling in the degree program. Again, **always check with your degree-granting institution to make sure the credits you are about to earn are transferrable.**

Continuing Education Units (CEUs)

If you are a teacher, accountant, physician, nurse, or other licensed professional, most states require you to maintain your certification by continuing your education. Distance learning makes this convenient. A doctor can tape a show from cable television, watch it at her convenience, and then call to request that the short exam be faxed to her office the next morning. A teacher can take classes via the Internet during the summer instead of leaving his family behind while he spends six weeks at summer school in another city.

A single Continuing Education Unit (CEU) is granted for each ten contact hours spent participating in an organized continuing education setting. *Organized* means qualified instructors and responsible programs, which accredited college programs offer. Instead of earning college credits, check with the institution about earning CEUs instead.

Noncredit Courses for Self-Enrichment

If you love to learn but don't care whether you earn college credit for the classes you take, you can sometimes audit distance learning classes just like you can when they are offered on campus. Not all distance learning classes can be audited, however, so check with the school. Because you don't receive a grade for an audited class, you are not required to turn in homework or take final exams, although many students still do the work because it is part of the learning process.

Besides providing self-enrichment, noncredit courses can help you move ahead in your job as you increase your knowledge of specialized areas in your field. Distance learning is an efficient way to enhance your value as an employee in today's competitive work environment. Recognizing this, many corporations now collaborate with colleges and universities to offer classes at the work site, which benefits both the employer and the employee. If your employer doesn't offer this service, try suggesting it.

Student Services

Learning resources are critical to the success of a student in a distance learning environment. This includes access to tutoring, career counseling, research, technical support, online databases, and libraries. Good distance learning institutions pride themselves on their student-service offerings. They go out of their way to provide toll-free phone numbers for student questions and problems. They provide online or automated registration services, and library services and textbooks are just a phone call or an e-mail away.

The timely availability of research and library resources is very important. The more challenging the course, the more resources you will need. Make sure that you have access to on-campus librarians, databases, periodicals, and the complete library catalog. It should take no more than one to three days to receive requested materials, but you need to plan ahead. You can't procrastinate in distance learning programs!

Graduation

What about graduation? Do you yearn for that cap and gown? Universities understand that graduation is just as important for a distance learning student as it is for the traditional student. In order to provide a traditional finale to the nontraditional educational experience, most schools include their local distance learning students in traditional graduation ceremonies or provide televised or Internet-based ceremonies for students who are too far away to realistically travel to an on-campus event. For instance, International University in Denver held a small ceremony in its corporate offices with university administrators and professors in caps and gowns. Several students traveled to Denver for the ceremony, while the others connected via the Internet. The commencement speaker joined the ceremony via a separate video link.

Because distance learning students are traditionally older, this event becomes very important to both the students and their families. The sense of accomplishment that comes from completing a long-held dream and sharing it with your family is reinforced with a graduation ceremony, so don't miss it!

By the way, the diploma you will receive from a distance learning program will, in most cases, be identical to those received by students on campus. In fact, diplomas and transcripts rarely mention how a class was completed.

Is Distance Learning Just as Credible?

The answer is yes! When you choose a regionally accredited college or university for your distance education, the quality of the courses, instructors, materials, exams, papers, theses, and dissertations are the same as their on-campus counterparts. The way education is delivered (video, computer, correspondence) has little effect on a student's achievement, provided the delivery method is appropriate to the course.

It has long been held that educational quality is linked to the age of the institution, how much money it has at its disposal, how tough it is to get admitted, and how small the classes were. Those standards changed in the twentieth century. It is difficult to evaluate distance learning institutions by the same criteria. They are relatively new, very cost effective, and often offer open admission.

According to a study at California State University at Northridge, students learning in a virtual classroom tested 20 percent better across the board than their counterparts who learned in a traditional classroom. There was no significant difference between the sex, age, computer experience, or attitude toward the subject material of the two groups. All of the research published since 1920 indicates that correspondence/distance study students perform just as well as, and in most cases better than, their classroom counterparts. This success stems from several factors, including:

- ▸ Distance learners tend to be self-motivated, disciplined, and higher achievers.

- ▸ Generally, distance students are voluntarily seeking further education and have set goals for themselves that make success more likely.

- ▸ They are usually employed in a career where advancement can be readily achieved through academic achievement.

- ▸ Distance learners in virtual classrooms spend about 50 percent more time collaborating with each other than students in a traditional classroom, which reinforces the learning environment.

- ▸ The most successful students initiate calls to instructors for assistance and possess a more serious attitude toward their classes.

How Much Does Distance Learning Cost?

Tuition rates and textbook costs for distance learning classes are usually the same as their on-campus counterparts, although they are sometimes less and sometimes more. Your savings will not be related to what you pay the school. Instead, you save the costs of commuting, parking, child care, and lost work time. Depending on the teaching method used, you will, of course, need a computer with a modem, television, or a VCR. That means an additional cost if you don't already have these technologies or if you need to update your computer system. However, if you already own or have access to the technology you need, your only additional cost will be an occasional trip to a testing center or to a campus-based seminar or other on-campus meeting required by some programs.

When you think about the incredible amount of time and money it takes to develop these new teaching methods, you can appreciate the fact that the schools are not actually charging you *more* for your distance learning! Not only do colleges and universities pay the additional costs for the development of a new curriculum, but they also must hire computer programmers, Web site developers, videographers, site administrators, distribution clerks, online library resource personnel, specially trained counselors, and technical support staff. On top of that, they must maintain the computer systems, teleconferencing systems, and other equipment necessary to deliver distance learning to the students.

Teaching in front of a camera or via a computer is not the forte of every instructor. Universities must identify faculty members with outstanding presentation abilities and the willingness to consider flexible approaches toward student learning. Training of faculty in the use of technology is vitally important to the success of any distance learning program but, at the same time, it is very expensive. Instead of the traditional weekly office hours, distance learning instructors must give their students daily attention.

Glenn Jones, an innovator in cable television and distance education for more than 30 years, sees the solution to the cost of developing distance learning in "free market fusion" between nonprofit educational entities and private-sector companies. Massive consortia have already been formed between cable companies, four-year universities, community colleges, public broadcasting services, and other for-profit entities to make distance learning available to more students at a reasonable price.

Internet Resources

For more information about distance learning, peruse the following Web sites:

▸ Check under "distance learning," "alternative education," or "adult and continuing education" at Yahoo for related sites: http://www.yahoo.com/Education/Distance_Learning/Adult_and_Continuing_Education/

▸ A metasite for hyperlinks to Internet sites related to distance education: http://www.cisnet.com/~cattales/Deducation.html

▸ The Association of Learning Technologies promotes the use and development of learning technologies for higher education: http://www.csv.warwick.ac.uk/alt-E/

▸ The U.S. Distance Learning Association is a nonprofit group formed in 1987 to promote the development and application of distance learning for education and training: http://www.usdla.org

▸ The Distance Education Clearinghouse of the University of Wisconsin: http://www.uwex.edu/disted/home.html

▸ Educause, an extensive collection of higher education information and technology materials: http://www.educause.edu/

▸ Distance Learning Resources Network: http://www.dlrn.org

▸ Established in 1983, the Canadian Association of Distance Education (CADE) is a national association of professionals committed to excellence in the provision of distance education in Canada: http://www.cade-aced.ca/

▸ At the PBS home page, you will find a list of all community colleges participating in PBS's *Going the Distance* program: http://www.pbs.org/als/

▸ The Distance Education and Training Council has links to its member institutions as well as general information about distance learning: http://www.detc.org

▸ For lists of accredited college degrees through correspondence, check: http://collegeathome.com/

▸ The Interactive College Resource Center lists educational programs available to working adults in Southern California: http://www.icrc.com/

▸ The Commonwealth of Learning, a resource for international distance learning resources: http://www.col.org

▸ The University of Idaho's overview of distance learning: http://www.uidaho.edu/evo/distglan.html

▸ For the latest information on the Western Governors University and distance learning out West, check the Web site for the Western Interstate Commission for Higher Education (WICHE): http://www.wiche.edu

▸ The California Virtual University Foundation offers a central source of information on courses available in California via the Internet, television, or other technologies. It allows users to search the site by college (95 institutions), topic (more than 1,600 courses and 100 full degree or certificate programs), or by delivery method: http:// www.california.edu

▸ The official publication of the Federal Government Distance Learning Association: http://fgdla.org

▸ Distance education resources from Auburn University: http://www.auburn.edu/administration/horizon/sept_www.html

▸ The National Education Association: http://www.nea.org

▸ Adult Distance Education Internet Surf Shack: http://www.edsurf.net

- Consortium for Open Learning: http://www.distlearn.com
- University of Tennessee's distance learning LISTSERV: http://web.ce.utk.edu
- Distance learning newsgroup: alt.education.distance (check the frequently asked questions first at http://pages.prodigy.com/PAUM88A/)

2 ► *Is Distance Learning Right for You?*

Y ou might think that it will be easier to get better grades when taking distance courses because you will never miss a class or be late while fighting a traffic jam. Or you might think the classes themselves are inherently easier, but that isn't the case. In fact, distance education is often just as time consuming as traditional classroom work. The time you would have spent in class you will spend reading material and writing responses.

Distance learning was designed with highly motivated adults in mind—those who have a clear sense of their goals and can work autonomously. Many younger students seem to have a difficult time succeeding at distance learning. Although generalizations are not true for everyone, younger students frequently have a greater need to be with a live person, to feel the passion of the instructor, and to socialize with fellow students. They find the competition and camaraderie inherent in a classroom full of students motivating, and motivation is the key to success in distance learning. If you are such a student, look for distance learning classes with interactive media (chats, videoconferencing, group work, etc.).

If you are self-motivated and disciplined, regardless of your age, you will have an easier time succeeding in a distance learning setting. You will often be required to be resourceful in thinking through problems and researching solutions on your own. You must be able to set and achieve realistic goals and to work without the supervision or regulations of an instructor. You must be persistent when faced with the choice of watching your favorite television show or doing your homework, which can consume up to 20 hours of your time a week. You will find it a frequent challenge to balance your work, family, school, and recreation time. If you are a social animal who prefers not to be alone, or if you are a procrastinator who always puts off until tomorrow what should be done today, distance learning will be more difficult for you.

The Personality Evaluation

How do you know if you truly have the personality for distance learning? You might never know until you try taking a few classes. If you find that you just prefer to be in a classroom situation where you can bounce ideas off other people or that you need the interaction with a professor and other students in order to learn, then you might have to change course. Here's a little test that can help you determine whether you have the personality for distance learning before beginning, although you will never know until you try it.

The following evaluation is reproduced here with the permission of the Extended Learning Institute of Northern Virginia Community College. It is designed to determine whether a student's circumstances and lifestyles are compatible with distance learning. Choose one answer for each of the ten questions below. Then go to the answer section and assess how well distance learning would fit your needs.

1. My need to take this course now is:
   - ❑ a. High—I need it immediately for degree, job, or other important reason.
   - ❑ b. Moderate—I could take it on campus later or substitute another course.
   - ❑ c. Low—It's a personal interest that could be postponed.

2. Feeling that I am part of a class is:
   - ❑ a. Not particularly necessary to me.
   - ❑ b. Somewhat important to me.
   - ❑ c. Very important to me.

3. I would classify myself as someone who:
   - ❑ a. Often gets things done ahead of time.
   - ❑ b. Needs reminding to get things done on time.
   - ❑ c. Puts things off to the last minute.

4. Classroom discussions are:
   - ❑ a. Rarely helpful to me.
   - ❑ b. Sometimes helpful to me.
   - ❑ c. Almost always helpful to me.

5. When an instructor hands out directions for an assignment, I prefer:
   - ❑ a. Figuring out the instructions on my own.
   - ❑ b. Trying to follow directions on my own, then asking for help as needed.
   - ❑ c. Having the instructions explained orally.

6. I need faculty comments on my assignments:
   - ❑ a. Within a few weeks, since I can review what I did.
   - ❑ b. Within a few days or I forget what I did.
   - ❑ c. Right away or I get very frustrated.

7. Considering my professional and personal schedule, the amount of time I have to work on a course is:
   - ❑ a. More than enough for a campus or distance learning course.
   - ❑ b. The same as for taking a class on campus.
   - ❑ c. Less than for taking a class on campus.

8. When I am asked to use VCRs, computers, voice mail, or other technologies that may be new to me:
   - ❑ a. I look forward to learning new skills.
   - ❑ b. I feel apprehensive but try anyway.
   - ❑ c. I put it off and try to avoid it.

9. As a reader, I would classify myself as:
   - ❑ a. Good—I usually understand the text without help.
   - ❑ b. Average—I sometimes need help to understand the text.
   - ❑ c. Slower than average.

10. If I have to go on campus to take exams or complete lab work:
    ❑ a. I can go to campus anytime.
    ❑ b. I may miss some lab assignments or exam deadlines if campus labs are not open evenings and weekends.
    ❑ c. I will have difficulty getting to the campus even in the evenings or on the weekends.

Scoring

Add 3 points for each "a" that you chose, 2 points for each "b," and 1 point for each "c." If you scored more than 25, distance learning is a real possibility for you. If you scored between 15 and 24, distance learning may work for you, but you may need to make a few adjustments to your schedule to succeed. If you scored 15 or less, distance learning may not currently be a suitable option for you. Here's why:

1. Course work might be neglected because of personal or family circumstances unless there are compelling reasons for completing a course.

2. Some students prefer the independence of distance learning courses; others find it uncomfortable.

3. Distance learning courses give you greater freedom to schedule your work, but they also require more self-discipline.

4. Some people learn best by interacting with other students, but distance learning does not afford as much opportunity for this type of interaction.

5. Distance learning courses require you to work from written directions without face-to-face explanations by the instructor.

6. It may take as long as two weeks to get comments back from your instructor by mail.

7. Distance learning courses require at least as much time as attending classes and completing assignments for campus courses.

8. Distance learning courses frequently use technology for teaching and communication.

9. Print materials are the primary source of directions and information in distance learning.

10. Some distance learning courses require three or four trips to the campus for examinations, and some require lab and library trips. Since evening and weekend lab hours may be limited, schedule flexibility is important.

Reading and Writing Skills

Learning through reading is the primary focus of most distance learning programs. Whether it is a textbook, a Web page, a correspondence course, or an e-mail communication, the ability to read and to absorb facts and ideas from print are critical to the success of a distance learning student. If you have not studied in a while, or if it was never really easy for you, then you will want to find a good book on study skills and read it before you take your first class.

Some people try highlighting key words as they read, or they ask themselves questions about what they just read. Others read the material out loud or review the entire book multiple times. Find what method works best for you and hone it to a fine edge. Taking a study skills class might be very useful, too.

Writing skills are just as important, if not more so, than in traditional education. If you write well, you will find it easier to put your thoughts into writing via e-mail and mailed replies. If writing, spelling, and grammar aren't your strong suits, your written messages may lead your instructor and fellow students to draw inaccurate conclusions about your ability. One nice thing about distance learning in all of its forms is that you can spend more time thinking about and responding to questions from instructors than you can in a traditional classroom setting. And you can use the spell check and grammar features of your e-mail or word processing software to make your replies as correct as possible.

Communication at a Distance

You will find that, in most cases, you will receive more individual attention from your instructors in distance learning courses than in traditional on-campus classes. It is not unusual for a professor to lecture to more than 300 students at a time in an ivy-covered hall. In distance learning, the professor has no choice but to communicate with each student one-on-one.

The same goes for your classmates. Many students have actually found that they interact more via e-mail and take more time to introduce themselves than they would in a classroom. Remember, you can't use first impressions and body language to get to know your classmates, so what you write in your e-mail message is what you are to them.

One of the best things about the Internet is that it is a great social equalizer. You will find yourself communicating with fellow class members without regard for appearance, race, sex, ethnicity, or other common prejudices.

By working long distance on group projects, you will also learn important distance collaboration skills that are real-world necessities when telecommuting or videoconferencing in your job. According to Brian Mueller, Vice President of Distance Education at the University of Phoenix, "There's a lot of talk in the workplace about *virtual teams* working together to complete projects. Our programs really help students develop that skill."

Having the support of your family, friends, and employer is important when you begin a distance learning program. Examine your lifestyle, determine where you can make time for your studies, set aside a private study space with a door that can be closed, and then have a serious discussion with your loved ones. Hold a family meeting to lay the ground rules for your study time and to make sure your children and spouse know how important your studies are to you. Trying to cope with your new schedule may be difficult without that support. If you know where you are heading and how you will get there, then the rewards are a bit more tangible. This advance planning and development of a support structure will help you stick it out to the end. By taking one day and one challenge at a time, you will hold a degree in your hands before you know it.

Special Skills and Resources

If you are participating in online courses, you will need some basic computer skills with word processing, Internet browser, and e-mail software. Like a microwave oven, you don't have to understand how it works to make it work, but it helps if you become generally familiar with your computer's abilities. Some of these skills can be learned as you go, but you will feel more comfortable with online learning if you take some basic computer classes first. Classes in Microsoft Word or Microsoft Office, basic Internet skills, and Internet research using search engines will be the most helpful. Another option would be to ask a knowledgeable friend for help. It shouldn't take more than a day of one-on-one tutoring to get the basics under control. You may feel overwhelmed at first, but every computer expert began by pushing a computer power button the first time.

If you are registered for televised courses, you will need a television set, cable TV connection or satellite dish, and VCR. Take away the cable connection and you will have everything you need to take correspondence courses that include videotapes.

Student Profiles

As the wife of a career military noncommissioned officer, this author spent years living in exotic countries on remote Air Force bases that left few options for finishing a degree other than by distance learning. I know first hand how challenging it can be. In speaking with students all across the United States and Canada, I was inspired by their stories and wanted to share a few with you in the hopes that their experiences will help you understand just how distance learning works in the real world.

Christine M. Danner
Business and Marketing Teacher
Institute of Business and Entrepreneurship
Flanagan High School
Broward County, FL

I recently completed my Master of Education in Secondary Education/Computer Technology from the University of North Florida by taking online courses. I earned my undergraduate degree the traditional way at Michigan State University in 1986, which led to a career in marketing for six years. Then I began to wonder about the direction of my life. Something was missing and I began to look for a way to further my education and contribute to society.

I started by taking night courses and working as a full-time high school teacher and part-time waitress. Somehow I managed to juggle all of my responsibilities and still find time for a small social life, which is how I met my future husband. When I was only two courses away from finishing my graduate degree, we were married and moved 300 miles away from the campus. Finding a new teaching position in south Florida wasn't difficult, but I was worried about completing my degree. I had come so far and could not let my dream slip away.

At about the same time, my faculty advisor at the University of North Florida was piloting a distance learning course. At her recommendation, I was allowed to apply the course to my degree program. My first experience with online learning was very challenging and interactive. As a class, we conversed regularly through an online service called Nicenet. Our course requirements were submitted weekly via an online assignment verification form set up by our instructor. Each assignment used different resources and required a variety of learning techniques. During the course of the semester, we videotaped ourselves teaching, conversed with other teachers across the world, reported back to the class, researched topics online, and studied from a textbook.

Over the past year, more professors at the University of North Florida have begun teaching at a distance. I took my final course from a professor who was spending the summer in Wyoming. The students in this course were required to complete individual weekly assignments and submit them via e-mail.

Thanks to these technology advancements, I was able to continue my studies and achieve my goal of graduation.

Patrick A. Kelleher

Lieutenant Colonel
United States Marine Corps
Deputy Chief of Counter-Space Operations
U.S. Space Command
Peterson Air Force Base, CO

As a test pilot in the Marine Corps, I was often required to fly across the country for extended periods of time, making it very difficult to complete my master's degree. While I was attending the U.S. Naval Test Pilot School, I learned of a graduate program offered via distance learning by the University of Tennessee that allowed me to transfer the credits I had earned in test pilot school toward a Master of Science in Aviation Systems.

I had earned my undergraduate degree in mechanical engineering from Gonzaga University in 1980. During my career as a Marine aviator, I had flown nearly 3,000 hours in more than 36 different aircraft models and types, including two and a half years as a test pilot at the Patuxent River test facility in Maryland. Even though I was satisfied with my military career, I wanted to set my sights on a graduate degree, so I enrolled in the University of Tennessee graduate program. This program offered a quality curriculum that didn't conflict with my military responsibilities.

All of the lectures were provided on videotape, which meant I could watch them any time of the day or night even while traveling. The on-base faculty representative and reliable telephone contacts at the home campus made it easy to get the help I needed. Because of this flexibility, I graduated in 1992 without sacrificing any of the quality you would expect from such a program.

Jeanette LeBlanc, Ph.D.

Chief of Program Evaluation
Human Relations Division, Center for Character Development
United States Air Force Academy, CO
Faculty of the University of Phoenix and Central Michigan University
Independent trainer, consultant, and speaker

Distance learning changed my life! I earned my Bachelor of Liberal Arts with a concentration in psychology from Regents College, State University of New York, while living in Germany (1989). It took less than one year from enrollment to earn that degree because of the number of credits I was able to transfer from traditional college classes and earn through examinations such as CLEP, DSST, ACT-PEP, and the advanced GRE.

Completing my undergraduate degree at such a rapid pace empowered me to achieve an even bigger dream—a master's degree in counseling from Georgia State University (1991) through a semi-traditional format of evening and weekend classes. I worked full time as a counselor at a private psychiatric hospital and at a residential program for abused adolescent girls during the two years it took to earn my graduate degree.

Graduate school was challenging and thrilling in so many ways, and I was hooked on learning. Immediately after graduation, I applied to a distance doctoral program at Walden University and was accepted. I was able to condense my residency into "regional intensive sessions" and summer sessions and completed my entire doctoral progam in two years instead of the traditional three to five years. In 1994, I earned a Ph.D. in Administration/Management with a specialization in Psychology of Human Behavior and Organizational Development.

Because of my three college degrees and outstanding external degree programs, I have been able to create a career of my own design. I would recommend nontraditional means of completing a college education to any student who seeks an opportunity for advanced learning, greater self-awareness and discipline, and career advancement.

As the great counselor and educator Eda Le Shan once said, "Excellence in life seems to me to be the way in which each human being makes the most of the adventure of living and becomes most truly and deeply himself, fulfilling his own nature in the context of a good life with other people. . . . What he knows and what he feels have equal importance in his life." May your adventure in life allow you to become most truly and deeply who you are meant to be. Pursue your college dreams boldly as you expand your heart, mind, and sphere of positive influence.

Joseph S. Stanjones

Captain, United States Army
Special Forces Detachment Commander
10th Special Forces Group (Airborne)
Fort Carson, CO

As a Special Forces officer, I spend as many as 200 days per year deployed overseas. At one point in my career I was trying to choose between staying in the Army or taking another path and decided I needed a master's degree either way. After some research, I chose the University of Phoenix Center for Distance Education because it used only the Internet. I began working on my MBA in Global Management in September of 1997 and completed more than one-third of my studies during my travels abroad.

My battalion made annual rotations to Bosnia and Herzogovina and, knowing that I would be stationed in Eastern Europe for extended periods of time, I chose an international Internet provider. I was fortunate to be stationed with the British Multinational Division HQ in Banja Luka, Republika Srpska. I was able to use the first and only Internet server available in the Republic (INECCO) to continue my studies. Even though it was not the fastest server, I was able to maintain contact with my academic advisor to register for classes, conduct research, and contact instructors for submission of all assignments.

Whether I decide to continue with my military career or pursue an international management position in the civilian sector, completing my degree via distance learning has helped me to reach my goal.

3 ▶ *Accreditation of Distance Learning*

Accreditation is simply a recognition, after evaluation, that in the judgment of peers, an institution is providing the educational services at a level of quality that society and the educational world have a right to expect (from the policy statement of the Middle States Association of Colleges and Schools). The focus of accreditation, regardless of the method of instructional delivery or physical location of the learner or the instructor, is on the consistency, quality, and integrity of an institution's academic programs. Distance learning programs must meet the same standards as all other offerings of a college or university.

There are two types of accreditation in the United States—institutional accreditation and specialized accreditation. Institutional accreditation is granted by regional and national accrediting commissions, and specialized accreditation is awarded to professional programs within institutions or to occupational schools. Accreditation is a voluntary process, and those institutions that choose to apply for accredited status undergo a rigorous process of peer review and self-regulation that includes:

1. A self-study conducted by the institution itself over an extended period of time— sometimes years.

2. An evaluation visit by a team of experienced academic colleagues whose function is to review the institution and to give it an informed, searching analysis. The focus of the team's attention is inevitably the intellectual work of the institution. The institution's organization, administration, facilities, and resources are examined for their effect on teaching and learning.

3. The institution studies the team's evaluation and writes a formal response to the accrediting association.

4. The accrediting association studies all the evaluation materials so that it can form its own conclusions relating to the quality of the institution's performance. It examines the institution's self-study document, the evaluation team's report, and the institution's formal response to that report.

5. Accreditation is either granted or denied.

6. Following accreditation, the institution must agree to abide by the standards of its accrediting organization. It must regulate itself and make periodic follow-up reports to ensure the improvement of the institution.

One of the benefits of accreditation is the assurance that you will be able to attain the same educational outcomes as you would in traditional classroom-based programs. You also have the right to the same admissions, orientation, registration, advisement, counseling, tutoring, placement, financial aid, and other student services that are available to all other students of a university, regardless of the delivery method of your classes. Without accreditation by a nationally recognized accrediting organization, a school is not eligible to participate in government student assistance programs, which means you, as a student, are not eligible for federal grant or loan money. Those employers who offer tuition assistance to employees will generally insist that a school be regionally accredited before reimbursing a student. Accreditation is also an important factor in the transferability of credits from one institution to another, although it is less important if you are taking courses for self-enrichment.

Who Accredits the Accreditors?

Not all accreditation associations are legitimate. It is not unusual for a diploma mill to create its own accrediting authority and then grant itself "accreditation"! So, how do you know that a college or university is accredited by a legitimate authority? It's really quite easy. There are two oversight organizations that accredit the accreditors. The first is the Council for Higher Education Accreditation (CHEA), a voluntary, nongovernmental organization. The second is a branch of the United States government, the U.S. Department of Education. More than 70 accrediting associations in the United States are recognized by CHEA or the U.S. Department of Education, or both.

CHEA was established in 1996 as a result of the dissolution of its two predecessor organizations, the Council on Postsecondary Accreditation (COPA) and the Commission on Recognition of Postsecondary Accreditation (CORPA). CHEA was established through the efforts of a group of college and university presidents and is accountable to its member institutions of higher learning. CHEA acts as the national policy center and clearinghouse on accreditation for the higher education community.

In Canada, all schools are regulated by provincial governments; no pan-Canadian accrediting body evaluates the quality of general undergraduate university programs. However, a number of agencies do perform this function for some professional programs at both the undergraduate and graduate levels. Membership in the Association of Universities and Colleges of Canada is generally assumed as evidence that an institution is providing programs with acceptable standards. Besides *accreditation*, the terms *university* and *college* are different in Canada, too. Universities are degree-granting institutions. Colleges, community colleges, CEGEPs, and institutes of technology do not grant degrees and tend to be more vocationally oriented.

For more information on accreditation in the United States and Canada, contact:

▸ Council for Higher Education Accreditation (CHEA)
One Dupont Circle NW, Suite 510
Washington, DC 20036-1135
Phone: (202) 955-6126
Fax: (202) 955-6129
Web page: http://www.chea.org

- U.S. Department of Education
  Office of Postsecondary Education
  Washington, DC 20202-5171
  Phone: (202) 708-7417 or (800) 872-5327
  Fax: (202) 708-9469
  Web page: http://www.ifap.ed.gov/offices/OPE/index.html

- Council of Ministers of Education
  252 Bloor Street West, Suite 5-200
  Toronto, Ontario, Canada M5S 1V5
  Phone: (416) 954-2551
  Fax: (416) 964-2296
  Web page: http://www.cmec.ca/

Who Accredits Colleges and Universities?

Regional Accreditation

Six regional accrediting organizations are responsible for accrediting the majority of colleges and universities in the United States. These associations accredit entire institutions. All of these associations have been approved by both CHEA and the U.S. Department of Education:

- New England Association of Schools and Colleges
  (Connecticut, Maine, Massachusetts, New Hampshire, Rhode Island, and Vermont)
  209 Burlington Road
  Bedford, MA 07130-1433
  Phone: (781) 271-0022
  Fax: (781) 271-0950
  Web page: http://www.neasc.org

- Middle States Association of Colleges and Schools
  (Delaware, District of Columbia, Maryland, New Jersey, New York, Pennsylvania, Puerto Rico, and the Virgin Islands)
  3624 Market Street
  Philadelphia, PA 19104
  Phone: (215) 662-5606
  Fax: (215) 662-5950
  Web page: http://www.msache.org

- North Central Association of Colleges and Schools
  (Arizona, Arkansas, Colorado, Illinois, Indiana, Iowa, Kansas, Michigan, Minnesota, Missouri, Nebraska, New Mexico, North Dakota, Ohio, Oklahoma, South Dakota, West Virginia, Wisconsin, and Wyoming)
  30 North LaSalle, Suite 2400
  Chicago, IL 60602-2504
  Phone: (312) 263-0456
  Fax: (312) 263-7462
  Web page: http://www.ncahigherlearningcommission.org

- Northwest Association of Schools and Colleges
  (Alaska, Idaho, Montana, Nevada, Oregon, Utah, and Washington)
  11130 NE 33rd Place, Suite 120
  Bellevue, WA 98004
  Phone: (425) 827-2005
  Fax: (425) 827-3395
  Web site: http://www.cocnasc.org

- Southern Association of Colleges and Schools
  (Alabama, Florida, Georgia, Kentucky, Louisiana, Mississippi, North Carolina, South Carolina, Tennessee, Texas, and Virginia)
  1866 Southern Lane
  Decatur, GA 30033-4097
  Phone: (404) 679-4500 or (800) 248-7701
  Fax: (404) 679-4558
  Web page: http://www.sacscoc.org

- Western Association of Schools and Colleges
  (California, Guam, and Hawaii)
  3402 Mendocino Avenue
  Santa Rosa, CA 95403-2244
  Phone: (707) 569-9177
  Fax: (707) 569-9179
  Web page: http://www.wascweb.org

Canadian Accreditation

Since provincial governments control the accreditation of schools in Canada, you can contact the following departments and ministries for more information:

- Newfoundland Department of Education
  3rd Floor, Confederation Building, West Block
  P.O. Box 8700
  St. John's, Canada A1B 4J6
  Phone: (709) 729-5097
  Fax: (709) 729-5896
  Web page: http://www.gov.nf.ca/edu/

- Nova Scotia Department of Education and Culture
  P.O. Box 578
  Halifax, NS, Canada B3J 2S9
  Phone: (902) 424-5605 or (902) 424-5168
  Fax: (902) 424-0511
  Web page: http://www.ednet.ns.ca/

- Prince Edward Island Department of Education
  P.O. Box 2000
  Sullivan Building, 2/3 Floors

16 Fitzroy Street
Charlottetown, PE, Canada C1A 7N8
Phone: (902) 368-4600
Fax: (902) 368-4663 or (902) 368-4622
Web page: http://www2.gov.pe.ca/educ/

▸ New Brunswick Department of Education
P.O. Box 6000
Fredericton, NB E3B 5H1, Canada
Phone: (506) 453-3678
Fax: (506) 453-3325
Web page: http://www.gov.nb.ca/education

▸ Quebec Ministry of Education
Édifice Marie-Guyart
11e étage, 1035, rue de la Chevrotière
Quebec, QC G1R 5A5, Canada
Phone: (418) 643-7095
Fax: (418) 646-6561
Web page: http://www.meq.gouv.qc.ca/

▸ Ontario Ministry of Education and Training
Mowat Block
900 Bay Street
Toronto, ON M7A 1L2, Canada
Phone: (416) 325-2929 or (800) 367-5514
Fax: (416) 325-2934
Web page: http://www.edu.gov.on.ca/

▸ Manitoba Department of Education
Legislative Building
450 Broadway
Winnipeg, MB R3C 0V8, Canada
Phone: (204) 945-2211
Fax: (204) 945-8692
Web page: http://www.gov.mb.ca/educate/

▸ Saskatchewan Department of Education
Department of Post-Secondary Education and Skills Training
2220 College Avenue
Regina, SK S4P 3V7, Canada
Phone: (306) 787-6030
Fax: (306) 787-2280
Web page: http://www.sasked.gov.sk.ca/

▸ Alberta Department of Education
West Tower, Devonian Building
11160 Jasper Avenue
Edmonton, AB T5K 0L2, Canada

Phone: (403) 427-7219
Fax: (403) 427-0591
Web page: http://www.learning.gov.ab.ca

▸ British Columbia Ministry of Education
P.O. Box 9156, Stn. Prov. Govt.
Victoria, BC V8W 9H2, Canada
Phone: (250) 387-4611
Fax: (250) 356-5945
Web page: http://www.bced.gov.bc.ca/ or http://www.gov.bc.ca/aett

Ministry of Advanced Education, Training and Technology
Phone: (250) 356-2771
Fax: (250) 356-3000

▸ Northwest Territories Department of Education, Culture, and Employment
P.O. Box 1320
4501 50th Avenue
Yellowknife, NT X1A 2L9, Canada
Phone: (867) 920-6240
Fax: (867) 873-0456
Web page: http://www.learnnet.nt.ca

▸ Yukon Department of Education
P.O. Box 2703
Whitehorse, YT Y1A 2C6, Canada
Phone: (867) 667-5141
Fax: (867) 393-6339
Web page: http://www.gov.yk.ca/depts/education/

Even though it is not an accrediting organization, the following association represents most of the universities and university-level colleges in the country:

▸ Association of Universities and Colleges of Canada
350 Albert Street, Suite 600
Ottawa, Ontario K1R 1B1, Canada
Phone: (613) 563-1236
Fax: (613) 563-9745
Web page: http://www.aucc.ca

Specialized Accreditation

Some national accrediting bodies accredit only specific kinds of schools, such as religious schools, home study institutions, and some trade and technical schools. Others accredit individual programs or departments within a college. This is more common in the professions where it is sometimes more important that a program or department be accredited by the profession's accrediting body than it is for the entire institution to be accredited by a regional or national accrediting organization. For instance, some school districts hire only teachers who have earned their degrees from schools approved by the National Council for Accreditation of Teacher Education (NCATE).

The following agencies accredit entire schools:

Bible Colleges

‣ American Association of Bible Colleges
P.O. Box 1523
130 F North College Avenue
Fayetteville, AR 72701
Phone: (501) 521-8164
Fax: (501) 521-9202
Web page: http://www.gospelcom.net/aabc

Career and Technology Schools

‣ Accrediting Commission for Career Schools and Colleges of Technology (ACCSCT)
2101 Wilson Boulevard, Suite 302
Arlington, VA 22201
Phone: (703) 247-4212
Fax: (703) 247-4533
Web page: http://www.accsct.org

Distance Education

‣ Distance Education and Training Council (DETC)
1601 18th Street, NW
Washington, DC 20009-2529
Phone: (202) 234-5100
Fax: (202) 332-1386
Web page: http://www.detc.org

Health Education

‣ Accrediting Bureau of Health Education Schools (ABHES)
2700 South Quincy Street, Suite 210
Arlington, VA 22206
Phone: (703) 998-1200
Fax: (703) 998-2550
Web page: http://www.abhes.org

Independent Colleges

‣ Accrediting Council for Independent Colleges and Schools (ACISC)
750 First Street NE, Suite 980

Washington, DC 20002-4241
Phone: (202) 336-6780
Fax: (202) 842-2593
Web page: http://www.acics.org

Occupational Education

▸ Council on Occupational Education (COE)
41 Perimeter Center East, NE, Suite 640
Atlanta, GA 30346
Phone: (770) 396-3898 or (800) 917-2081
Fax: (770) 396-3790
Web page: http://www.council.org

Rabbinical and Talmudic Schools

▸ Association of Advanced Rabbinical and Talmudic Schools (AARTS)
175 Fifth Avenue, Room 711
New York, NY 10010
Phone: (212) 477-0950
Fax: (212) 533-5335

Theology

▸ Association of Theological Schools in the United States and Canada
10 Summitt Park Drive
Pittsburgh, PA 15275-1103
Phone: (412) 788-6505
Fax: (412) 788-6510
Web page: http://www.ats.edu

The following specialized and professional accrediting associations are responsible for evaluating specific programs within a college or university.

Acupuncture

▸ Accreditation Commission for Acupuncture and Oriental Medicine
Maryland Trade Center 3
7501 Greenway Center Drive, Suite 820
Greenbelt, MD 20770
Phone: (301) 313-0855
Fax: (301) 313-0912
Web page: http://www.acaom.org

‣ Accreditation Review Committee on Education for the Anesthesiologist's Assistant
Emory University School of Medicine
617 Woodruff Memorial Building
Atlanta, GA 30322
Phone: (404) 727-5910
Fax: (404) 727-3021
Web page: http://www.anesthetist.org

‣ Accrediting Bureau of Health Education Schools
803 West Broad Street, Suite 730
Falls Church, VA 22046
Phone: (703) 533-2082
Fax: (703) 533-2095
Web page: http://www.abhes.org

‣ Accrediting Commission on Education for
Health Services Administration (ACEHSA)
730 11th Street, NW, Fourth Floor
Washington, D.C. 20001
Phone: (202) 638-5131
Fax: (202) 638-3429
Web page: http://www.acehsa.org

‣ American Association of Blood Banks (AABB)
Committee on Accreditation of Specialists in Blood Bank Technology Schools
8101 Glenbrook Road
Bethesda, MD 20814-2749
Phone: (301) 215-6492
Fax: (301) 907-6895
Web page: http://www.aabb.org

‣ Commission on Accreditation of Allied Health Education Programs (CAAHEP)
(CAAHEP accredits the following disciplines: Anesthesiologist Assistant, Athletic Trainer, Cardiovascular Technology, Cytotechnology, Diagnostic Medical Sonography, EMT-Paramedic, Electroneurodiagnostic Technologist, Health Information Administration/Technician, Kinesiotherapy, Medical Assistant, Medical Illustrator, Ophthalmic Medical Technologist/Technician, Orthotic and Prosthetic Practitioner, Perfusion, Physician Assistant, Respiratory Therapy, Blood Bank Technology, Surgical Assistant, and Surgical Technology.)
35 East Wacker Drive, Suite 1970
Chicago, IL 60601-2208
Phone: (312) 553-9355
Fax: (312) 553-9616
Web page: http://www.caahep.org

‣ Cytotechnology Programs Review Committee
American Society of Cytopathology
400 West Ninth Street, Suite 201

Wilmington, DE 19801-1555
Phone: (302) 429-8802
Fax: (302) 429-8807
Web page: http://www.cytopathology.org

‣ Council on Accreditation (American Health Information Management Association)
233 North Michigan Avenue, Suite 2150
Chicago, IL 60601-5800
Phone: (312) 233-1100
Fax: (312) 233-1090
Web page: http://www.ahima.org

‣ Curriculum Review Board of the American Association of Medical Assistants'
Endowment
20 North Wacker Drive, Suite 1575
Chicago, IL 60606-2963
Phone: (312) 899-1500
Fax: (312) 899-1259
Web page: http://www.aama-ntl.org

‣ Accreditation Review Committee on Education for the Physician Assistant
Marshfield Clinic
1000 N. Oak Avenue
Marshfield, WI 54449-5788
Phone: (715) 389-3785
Fax: (715) 389-3131
Web page: http://www.arc-pa.org

‣ National Board for Respiratory Therapy Education
8310 Nieman Road
Lenexa, KS 66214-1579
Phone: (913) 599-4200
Fax: (913) 541-0156
Web page: http://www.nbrc.org

‣ Accreditation Review Committee on Education in Surgical Technology
7108-C South Alton Way
Englewood, CO 80112-2106
Phone: (303) 694-9262
Fax: (303) 741-3655
Web page: http://www.arcst.org

Architecture

‣ National Architectural Accrediting Board
1735 New York Avenue NW
Washington, DC 20006
Phone: (202) 783-2007

Fax: (202) 783-2822
Web page: http://www.naab.org

Art and Design

▸ National Association of Schools of Art and Design
11250 Roger Bacon Drive, Suite 21
Reston, VA 21090
Phone: (703) 437-0700
Fax: (703) 437-6312
Web page: http://www.arts-accredit.org

Business

▸ The Association to Advance Collegiate Schools of Business
600 Emerson Road, Suite 300
St. Louis, MO 63141-6762
Phone: (314) 872-8481
Fax: (314) 872-8495
Web page: http://www.aacsb.edu

▸ Association of Collegiate Business Schools and Programs (ACBSP)
7007 College Boulevard, Suite 420
Overland Park, KS 66211
Phone: (913) 339-9356
Fax: (913) 339-6226
Web page: http://www.acbsp.org

Chiropractic Education

▸ The Council on Chiropractic Education
8049 N. 85th Way
Scottsdale, AZ 85258-4321
Phone: (480) 443-8877
Fax: (480) 483-7333
Web page: http://www.cce-usa.org

Christian Education

▸ Transnational Association of Christian Schools
P.O. Box 328
Forest, VA 24551
Phone: (804) 525-9539
Fax: (804) 525-9538
Web page: http://www.tracs.org

Clinical Laboratory Science

▸ National Accrediting Agency for Clinical Laboratory Science (NAACLS)
8410 West Bryn Mawr Avenue, Suite 670
Chicago, IL 60631
Phone: (312) 714-8880
Fax: (312) 714-8886
Web page: http://www.naacls.org

Clinical Pastoral Education

▸ Association for Clinical Pastoral Education
1549 Claremont Road, Suite 103
Decatur, GA 30033-4611
Phone: (404) 320-1472
Fax: (404) 320-0849
Web page: http://www.acpe.edu

Computer Science

▸ Computing Sciences Accreditation Board
184 North Street
Stamford, CT 06901
Phone: (203) 975-1117
Fax: (203) 975-1222
Web page: http://www.csab.org

Construction Education

▸ American Council for Construction Education
1300 Hudson Lane, Suite 3
Monroe, LA 70201-6054
Phone: (318) 323-2816
Fax: (318) 323-2413
Web page: http://acce-hq.org

Continuing Education

▸ Accrediting Council for Continuing Education and Training
1722 N Street, NW
Washington, DC 20036
Phone: (202) 955-1113
Fax: (202) 955-1118
Web page: http://www.accet.org

Cosmetology

▸ National Accrediting Commission of Cosmetology Arts and Sciences
901 North Stuart Street, Suite 900
Arlington, VA 22203-1816
Phone: (703) 527-7600
Fax: (703) 527-8811
Web page: http://www.naccas.org

Counseling

▸ American Association for Counseling and Related Educational Programs (CACREP)
5999 Stevenson Avenue
Alexandria, VA 22304
Phone: (703) 823-9800
Fax: (703) 823-1581
Web page: http://www.counseling.org/cacrep

Culinary

▸ American Culinary Federation, Inc. (ACF)
10 San Bartola Drive
St. Augustine, FL 32085
Phone: (904) 824-4468
Fax: (904) 825-4758
Web page: http://www.acfchefs.org

Dance

▸ National Association of Schools and Dance
11250 Roger Bacon Drive, Suite 21
Reston, VA 20190
Phone: (703) 437-0700
Fax: (703) 437-6312
Web page: http://www.arts-accredit.org

Dentistry and Dental Auxiliary Programs

▸ American Dental Association
211 East Chicago Avenue, 18th Floor
Chicago, IL 60611
Phone: (800) 621-8099 or (312) 440-2500
Fax: (312) 440-2915
Web page: http://www.ada.org

Dietetics

▸ The American Dietetic Association
216 West Jackson Boulevard, Suite 800
Chicago, IL 60606-6995
Phone: (312) 899-4872
Fax: (312) 899-4817
Web page: http://www.eatright.org/cade

Engineering

▸ Accreditation Board for Engineering and Technology (ABET)
111 Market Place, Suite 1050
Baltimore, MD 21202
Phone: (410) 347-7700
Fax: (410) 625-2238
Web page: http://www.abet.org

Environment

▸ National Environmental Health Science and Protection Accreditation Council
National Environmental Health Association
720 South Colorado Boulevard, Suite 970-S
Denyer, CO 80246-1925
Phone: (303) 756-9090
Fax: (303) 691-9490
Web page: http://www.neha.org/accredcouncil.html

Family and Consumer Sciences

▸ American Association of Family and Consumer Sciences (AAFCS)
1555 King Street
Alexandria, VA 22314
Phone: (703) 706-4600
Fax: (703) 706-4663
Web page: http://www.aafcs.org

Forestry

▸ Society of American Foresters
5400 Grosvenor Lane
Bethesda, MD 20814-2198
Phone: (301) 897-8720 x119
Fax: (301) 879-3690
Web page: http://www.safnet.org

Funeral Service Education

▸ American Board of Funeral Service Education
13 Gurnet Road, #316
P.O. Box 1305
Brunswick, MA 04011
Phone: (207) 798-5801
Fax: (207) 798-5988
Web page: http://www.abfse.org

Industrial Technology

▸ National Association of Industrial Technology
3300 Washtenaw Avenue, Suite 220
Ann Arbor, MI 48104-4200
Phone: (734) 677-0720
Fax: (734) 677-2407
Web page: http://nait.org

Interior Design

▸ Foundation for Interior Design Education Research
146 Monroe Center NW, Suite 1318
Grand Rapids, MI 49503-2822
Phone: (616) 458-0400
Fax: (616) 458-0460
Web page: http://www.fider.org

Journalism

▸ Accrediting Council on Education in Journalism and Mass Communications
School of Journalism
University of Kansas
Stauffer-Flint Hall
Lawrence, KS 66045
Phone: (785) 864-3986
Fax: (785) 864-5225
Web page: http://www.ukans.edu/~acejmc/

Landscaping Architecture

▸ American Society of Landscape Architects
4401 Connecticut Avenue NW, Fifth Floor
Washington, DC 20008-2369
Phone: (202) 686-2752

Fax: (202) 686-1001
Web page: http://www.asla.org

Law

▸ American Bar Association
550 West North Street
Indianapolis, IN 46202
Phone: (317) 264-8340
Fax: (317) 264-8355
Web page: http://abanet.org/legaled

▸ Association of American Law Schools
1201 Connecticut Avenue NW, Suite 800
Washington, DC 20036-2605
Phone: (202) 296-8851
Fax: (202) 296-8869
Web page: http://www.aals.org

Liberal Education

▸ American Academy for Liberal Education
1700 K Street, N.W., Suite 901
Washington, DC 20006
Phone: (202) 452-8611
Fax: (202) 452-8620
Web page: http://www.aale.org

Librarianship

▸ American Library Association
50 East Huron Street
Chicago, IL 60611
Phone: (800) 545-2433, x2436
Fax: (312) 280-2433
Web page: http://www.ala.org

Management

▸ The International Association for Management Education
600 Emerson Road, Suite 300
St. Louis, MO 63141-6762
Phone: (314) 872-8481
Fax: (314) 872-8495
Web page: http://www.aacsb.edu

Marriage and Family Therapy

▸ American Association for Marriage and Family Therapy
1133 15th Street NW, Suite 300
Washington, DC 20005-2710
Phone: (202) 452-0109
Fax: (202) 223-2329
Web page: http://www.aamft.org

Medicine

▸ In odd-numbered years beginning each July 1, contact:
American Medical Association
515 North State Street
Chicago, IL 60610
Phone: (312) 464-4933
Fax: (312) 464-5830
Web page: http://www.lcme.org

▸ In even-numbered years beginning each July 1, contact:
Association of American Medical Colleges
2450 North Street, NW
Washington, DC 20037
Phone: (202) 828-0596
Fax: (202) 828-1125
Web page: http://www.lcme.org

Midwifery

▸ Midwifery Education Accreditation Council
220 West Birch
Flagstaff, AZ 86001
Phone: (520) 214-0997
Fax: (520) 773-9694
Web page: http://www.meacschools.org

Montessori Education

▸ Montessori Accreditation Council for Teacher Education
Commission on Accreditation
University of Wisconsin—Parkside, Tallent Hall
900 Wood Road, P.O. Box 2000
Kenosha, WI 53141-2000
Phone: (888) 446-2283 or (262) 595-3335
Fax: (262) 595-3332
Web page: http://www.macte.org

Music

  ‣ National Association of Music Schools
    11250 Roger Bacon Drive, Suite 21
    Reston, VA 22090
    Phone: (703) 437-0700
    Fax: (703) 437-6312
    Web page: http://www.arts-accredit.org

Naturopathic Medicine

  ‣ Council on Naturopathic Medical Education
    P.O. Box 11426
    Eugene, OR 97440-3626
    Phone: (541) 484-6028
    Web page: http://www.cnme.org

Nuclear Medicine

  ‣ Joint Review Committee on Educational Programs in
    Nuclear Medicine Technology (JRCNMT)
    One Second Avenue East, Suite C
    Polson, MT 59860-2107
    Phone: (406) 883-0003
    Fax: (406) 883-0022
    Web page: http://www.jrcnmt.org

Nurse Anesthesia

  ‣ Council on Accreditation of Nurse Anesthesia Educational Programs
    222 South Prospect, Suite 304
    Park Ridge, IL 60068-4010
    Phone: (847) 692-7050
    Fax: (847) 692-7137
    Web page: http://www.aana.com

Nurse Practitioners

  ‣ National Association of Nurse Practitioners in Women's Health
    Council on Accreditation
    503 Capital Court NE, Suite 300
    Washington, DC 20005
    Phone: (202) 543-9693
    Fax: (202) 543-9858
    Web page: http://www.npwh.org

- Nurse Practitioner Support Services
  10024 SE 240th Street, Suite 102
  Kent, WA 98031
  Phone: (253) 852-9042
  Fax: (253) 852-7725
  Web page: http://www.nurse.org

Nursing

- American College of Nurse-Midwives
  818 Connecticut Avenue NW, Suite 900
  Washington, DC 20006
  Phone: (202) 728-9860
  Fax: (202) 728-9897
  Web page: http://www.acnm.org

- National League for Nursing
  350 Hudson Street
  New York, NY 10014
  Phone: (800) 669-1656
  Fax: (212) 898-3710
  Web page: http://www.nln.org

- National League for Nursing Accrediting Commission, Inc. (NLNAC)
  61 Broadway
  New York, NY 10006
  Phone: (800) 669-1656 x451 or (212) 363-5555 x153
  Fax: (212) 812-0390
  Web page: http://www.nlnac.org

- American Nurses Credentialing Center
  600 Maryland Avenue SW, Suite 100 West
  Washington, DC 20024-2571
  Phone: (800) 284-2378
  Web page: http://www.nursingworld.org/ancc

- Commission on Collegiate Nursing Education
  1 Dupont Circle NW, Suite 530
  Washington, DC 20036-1120
  Phone: (202) 887-6791
  Fax: (202) 887-8476
  Web page: http://www.aacn.ncle.edu/accreditation/index.htm

Occupational Education

- Accreditation Commission of Career Schools and Colleges of Technology
  2101 Wilson Boulevard, Suite 302
  Arlington, VA 22201

Phone: (703) 247-4212
Fax: (703) 247-4533
Web page: http://www.accsct.org

▸ Council on Occupational Education
41 Perimeter Center East NE, Suite 640
Atlanta, GA 30346
Phone: (770) 396-3898 or (800) 917-2081
Fax: (770) 396-3790
Web page: http://www.council.org

Occupational Therapy

▸ Accreditation Council for Occupational Therapy Education
American Occupational Therapy Association (AOTA)
4720 Montgomery Lane
P.O. Box 31220
Bethesda, MD 20824-1220
Phone: (301) 652-2682
Fax: (301) 652-7711
Web page: http://www.aota.org

Opticianry

▸ Commission on Opticianry Accreditation
7023 Little River Turnpike, Suite 207
Annandale, VA 22003
Phone: (703) 941-9110 or (800) 443-8997
Fax: (703) 916-7996
Web page: http://www.COAaccreditation.com

Optometry

▸ American Optometric Association
243 North Lindbergh Boulevard
St. Louis, MO 63141
Phone: (314) 991-4100
Fax: (314) 991-4101
Web page: http://www.opted.org or http://www.aoanet.org

Osteopathic Medicine

▸ American Osteopathic Association
142 East Ontario Street
Chicago, IL 60611-2864

Phone: (312) 202-8000
Fax: (312) 202-8200
Web page: http://www.aoa.net

Pharmacy

▸ American Council on Pharmaceutical Education
311 West Superior Street
Chicago, IL 60610
Phone: (312) 664-3575
Fax: (312) 664-4652
Web page: http://www.acpe-accredit.org

Physical Therapy

▸ American Physical Therapy Association
1111 North Fairfax Street
Alexandria, VA 22314
Phone: (703) 706-3245
Fax: (703) 684-7343
Web page: http://www.apta.org

Planning

▸ American Institute of Certified Planners
Association of Collegiate Schools of Planning
Planning Accreditation Board
Merle Hay Tower, Suite 302
3800 Merle Hay Road
Des Moines, IA 50310
Phone: (515) 252-0729
Fax: (515) 252-7404
Web page: http://www.netins.net/showcase/pab-fi66/

Podiatry

▸ American Podiatric Medical Association
9312 Old Georgetown Road
Bethesda, MD 20814-2752
Phone: (301) 571-9200
Fax: (301) 581-9299
Web page: http://www.apma.org

Psychology

▸ American Psychological Association
750 First Street NE
Washington, DC 20002-4242
Phone: (202) 336-5979
Fax: (202) 336-5978
Web page: http://www.apa.org

Public Affairs and Administration

▸ National Association of Schools of Public Affairs and Administration
1120 G Street NW, Suite 730
Washington, DC 20005
Phone: (202) 628-8965
Fax: (202) 626-4978
Web page: http://www.naspaa.org

Public Health

▸ Council on Education for Public Health
800 I Street NW, Suite 202
Washington, DC 20001-3710
Phone: (202) 789-1050
Fax: (202) 789-1895
Web page: http://www.ceph.org

Radiologic Technology

▸ Joint Review Committee on Education in Radiologic Technology
20 North Wacker Drive, Suite 900
Chicago, IL 60606-2806
Phone: (312) 704-5300
Fax: (312) 704-5304
Web page: http://www.jrcert.org

Recreation and Parks

▸ National Recreation and Parks Association
American Association for Leisure and Recreation
22377 Belmont Ridge Road
Ashburn, VA 20148-4501
Phone: (703) 858-2150
Fax: (703) 858-0794
Web page: http://www.activeparks.org/education

Rehabilitation Counseling

‣ Council on Rehabilitation Education
1835 Rohlwing Road, Suite E
Rolling Meadows, IL 60008
Phone: (847) 394-1785
Fax: (847) 394-2108
Web page: http://www.core-rehab.org

Social Work

‣ American Art Therapy Association
1202 Allanson Road
Mundelein, IL 60060
Phone: (847) 949-6064
Fax: (847) 566-4580
Web page: http://www.arttherapy.org

‣ Council on Social Work Education
1600 Duke Street, Suite 300
Alexandria, VA 22314
Phone: (703) 683-8080
Fax: (703) 683-8099
Web page: http://www.cswe.org

Speech-Language Pathology and Audiology

‣ American Speech-Language-Hearing Association
10801 Rockville Pike
Rockville, MD 20852
Phone: (301) 897-5700
Fax: (301) 571-0457
Web page: http://www.asha.org

Teacher Education

‣ National Council for Accreditation of Teacher Education
2010 Massachusetts Avenue NW, Suite 500
Washington, DC 20036-1023
Phone: (202) 466-7496
Fax: (202) 296-6620
Web page: http://www.ncate.org

Theater

‣ National Association of Schools of Theatre (NAST)
11250 Roger Bacon Drive, Suite 21

Reston, VA 20190
Phone: (703) 437-0700
Fax: (703) 437-6312
Web page: http://www.arts-accredit.org

Veterinary Medicine

▸ American Veterinary Medical Association
1930 North Meacham Road, Suite 100
Schaumburg, IL 60173-4360
Phone: (847) 925-8070
Fax: (847) 925-1329
Web page: http://www.avma.org

Internet Resources

For more information on accreditation, check out the following Web sites:

▸ American Association of Community Colleges (AACC): http://www.aacc.nche.edu

▸ American Association of State Colleges and Universities (AASCU): http://www.aascu.org

▸ American Council on Education (ACE): http://www.acenet.edu/

▸ Association of Specialized and Professional Accreditors (ASPA): http://www.chea.org/

▸ Association of American Colleges and Universities: http://www.aacu-edu.org

▸ National Association of State Universities and Land Grant Colleges (NASULGC): http://www.nasulgc.org

Should You Consider an Unaccredited College?

The decision whether to charter a college or university is the responsibility of individual state governments. Some states are very strict when it comes to authorizing institutions that grant degrees and others are not. California and Louisiana were once famous for their lack of control over educational institutions, but they have improved their regulations within the past few years. At one time, a person could open a school in California for as little as $50,000 in assets and a quick, rubber-stamped government application. This, of course, led to a host of unaccredited schools, many of which were fraudulent. Hawaii now seems to have taken the place of California and Louisiana as the home to the most "diploma mills" in the United States.

On the other end of the spectrum, New York exercises tight control over all educational institutions in its state. Since 1784, the University of the State of New York has acted as an oversight organization to regulate all public and independent colleges and universities in New York. Its Board of Regents determines the state's educational policies and establishes standards for maintaining the quality of schools and the academic programs that lead to college degrees, licenses, and diplomas.

Once an educational institution has been chartered by a state, the school can operate legally without accreditation. As discussed previously in this chapter, regional accreditation is voluntary, and not all legitimate schools choose to go through the long process of accreditation. Remember, too, that all colleges and universities start out as unaccredited, so lack of accreditation does not necessary imply that a school is inferior. However, because of the uncertainty involved in listing unaccredited schools, this book includes only those colleges or universities that have been accredited by one of the six regional accreditation associations or the Distance Education and Training Council's Accrediting Commission.

If you decide that the best opportunity for you lies with an unaccredited college or university, look before you leap! Here are some steps you can take to ensure that you are dealing with a legitimate institution:

1. Speak with knowledgeable people in your industry about whether a degree or certification from the school would be acceptable. In fields such as nursing and law, you might not be able to get a license if you attend an unaccredited college or university, even if you have a degree.

2. Call the school and ask why it is not accredited. Perhaps it has applied with one of the approved oversight organizations but has not yet been accepted for accreditation. If so, ask for the name, address, and phone number of the organization. Then call the accrediting body to verify the school's standing.

3. Ask the school for references and talk with former students.

4. Contact one of these state agencies for more information on the school's chartered status and reputation:

Alabama

▸ Alabama Commission on Higher Education
Suite 205
3465 Norman Bridge Road
Montgomery, AL 36105-2310
Phone: (334) 281-1998
Web page: http://www.ache.state.al.us

▸ Alabama Department of Education
Gordon Persons Office Building
50 North Ripley Street
Montgomery, AL 36130-3901
Phone: (205) 242-8082
Web page: http://www.alsde.edu

▸ Department of Postsecondary Education
401 Adams Avenue

Montgomery, AL 36104
Phone: (334) 242-2900
Web page: http://www.acs.cc.al.us/acs/todpe.htm

Alaska

▸ Alaska Commission on Postsecondary Education
3030 Vintage Boulevard
Juneau, AK 99801-7100
Phone: (907) 465-2962
Web page: http://www.state.ak.us/acpe

▸ Alaska Department of Education
Goldbelt Place
801 West Tenth Street, Suite 200
Juneau, AK 99801-1894
Phone: (907) 465-2800
Web page: http://www.educ.state.ak.us/

Arizona

▸ Arizona Commission for Postsecondary Education
2020 North Central Avenue, Suite 275
Phoenix, AZ 85004-4503
Phone: (602) 229-2591
Web page: http://www.acpe.asu.edu

▸ Arizona Department of Education
1535 West Jefferson
Phoenix, AZ 85007
Phone: (602) 542-4361
Web page: http://www.ade.state.az.us

▸ Arizona Board of Regents
2020 North Central Avenue, Suite 230
Phoenix, AZ 85004-4593
Phone: (602) 229-2500
Web page: http://www.abor.asu.edu

Arkansas

▸ Arkansas Department of Higher Education
114 East Capitol
Little Rock, AK 72201-3818
Phone: (501) 371-2000
Web page: http://www.arscholarships.com

- Arkansas Department of Education
  4 State Capitol Mall
  Little Rock, AK 72201-1071
  Phone: (501) 682-4475
  Web page: http://arkedu.state.ar.us

California

- California Student Aid Commission
  P.O. Box 419026
  10834 International Drive
  Rancho Cordova, CA 95741-9026
  Phone: (916) 526-7994
  Web page: http://www.csac.ca.gov

- California Department of Education
  721 Capitol Mall
  Sacramento, CA 95814
  Phone: (916) 657-2451
  Web page: http://www.cde.ca.gov

- California, Postsecondary Education Commission
  1303 J Street, Suite 500
  Sacramento, CA 95814-2938
  Phone: (916) 445-7933
  Web page: http://www.cpec.ca.gov

- Bureau for Private Postsecondary and Vocational Education
  400 R Street, Suite 5000
  Sacramento, CA 95814
  Phone: (916) 445-3427
  Web page: http://www.dca.ca.gov/bppve/

Colorado

- Colorado Commission on Higher Education
  1380 Lawrence Street, Suite 1200
  Denver, CO 80204
  Phone: (303) 866-2723
  Web page: http://www.state.co.us/cche-dir/heeche.html

- Colorado Department of Education
  201 East Colfax Avenue
  Denver, CO 80203-1705
  Phone: (303) 866-6779
  Web page: http://www.cde.state.co.us/

Connecticut

▸ Connecticut Department of Higher Education
61 Woodland Street
Hartford, CT 06105-2326
Phone: (860) 947-1800
Web page: http://www.ctdhe.org

▸ Connecticut Department of Education
165 Capitol Avenue
Hartford, CT 06145
Phone: (860) 566-5497
Web page: http://www.state.ct.us/sde/

Delaware

▸ Delaware Higher Education Commission
Carvel State Office Building, Fourth Floor
820 North French Street
Wilmington, DE 19801
Phone: (302) 577-3240
Web page: http://doe.state.de.us/high-ed/

▸ Delaware Department of Education
John E. Townsend Building
401 Federal Street
Dover, DE 19903-1402
Phone: (302) 739-4601
Web page: http://www.doe.state.de.us

District of Columbia

▸ Department of Human Services
Office of Postsecondary Education, Research and Assistance
2100 Martin Luther King Jr. Avenue SE Suite 401
Washington, DC 20020
Phone: (202) 698-2400
Web page: http://www.dhs.washington.dc.us/office_of_postsecondaryeducat/

Florida

▸ Florida Department of Education
Turlington Building
325 West Gaines Street
Tallahassee, FL 32399-0400
Phone: (850) 488-4234
Web page: http://www.firn.edu/doe/

▸ State Board of Independent Colleges and Universities
Florida Department of Education
Koger Center, Turner Building, Suite 200
Tallahassee, FL 32301
Phone: (888) 224-6684
Web page: http://www.firn.edu/doe/sbicu

Georgia

▸ Georgia Student Finance Authority
State Loans and Grants Division
2082 East Exchange Place, Suite 200
Tucker, GA 30084
Phone: (770) 724-9000
Web page: http://www.gsfc.org

▸ Georgia Department of Education
2054 Twin Towers East
205 Butler Street
Atlanta, GA 30334-5001
Phone: (404) 656-2800 or (800) 311-3627

▸ Board of Regents of the University System of Georgia
270 Washington Street SW
Atlanta, GA 30334
Phone: (404) 656-6050
Web page: http://www.usg.edu

Hawaii

▸ Hawaii State Postsecondary Education Commission
2444 Dole Street, Room 209
Honolulu, HI 96822-2302
Phone: (808) 956-8213
Web page: http://www.hern.hawaii.edu/hern/

▸ Hawaii Department of Education
1390 Miller Street
Honolulu, HI 96813
Phone: (808) 586-3310
Web page: http://www.k12.hi.us

Idaho

▸ Idaho Board of Education
P.O. Box 83720
Boise, ID 83720-0027

Phone: (208) 334-2270
Web page: http://www.sde.state.id.us/osbe/board.htm

▸ State Department of Education
650 West State Street
Boise, ID 83720
Phone: (208) 332-6800 or (800) 432-4601
Web page: http://www.sde.state.id.us

Illinois

▸ Illinois Student Assistance Commission
1755 Lake Cook Road
Deerfield, IL 60015-5209
Phone: (847) 948-8500 or (800) 899-4722
Web page: http://www.isac-online.org

▸ Illinois State Board of Education
100 North First Street
Springfield, IL 62777
Phone: (217) 782-4321
Web page: http://www.isbe.net

Indiana

▸ State Student Assistance Commission of Indiana
150 West Market Street, Suite 500
Indianapolis, IN 46204-2811
Phone: (317) 232-2350 or (888) 528-4719
Web page: http://www.ssaci.state.in.us

▸ Indiana Department of Education
Room 229 – State House
Indianapolis, IN 46204-2798
Phone: (317) 232-6665
Web page: http://www.doe.state.in.us

▸ Indiana Commission for Higher Education
101 West Ohio Street, Suite 550
Indianapolis, IN 46204
Phone: (317) 464-4400
Fax: (317) 464-4410
Web page: http://www.che.state.in.us

▸ Commission on Proprietary Education (privately owned, vocational-technical schools)
302 West Washington Street, Room E-201
Indianapolis, IN 46204-2767
Phone: (317) 232-1320

Fax: (317) 233-4219
Web page: http://www.in.gov/cope/

Iowa

- ▸ Iowa College Student Aid Commission
  200 10th Street, Fourth Floor
  Des Moines, IA 50309-2824
  Phone: (800) 383-4222 or (515) 281-3501
  Web page: http://www.state.ia.us/collegeaid/

- ▸ Iowa Department of Education
  Grimes State Office Building
  East 14th and Grand
  Des Moines, IA 50319-0146
  Phone: (515) 281-3436
  Web page: http://www.state.ia.us/educate/

- ▸ Board of Regents, State of Iowa
  100 Court Avenue, Suite 203
  Des Moines, IA 50319-0001
  Phone: (515) 281-3934
  Fax: (515) 281-6420
  Web page: http://www2.state.ia.us/regents/info.html

Kansas

- ▸ Kansas Board of Regents
  700 SW Harrison, Suite 1410
  Topeka, KS 66603-3760
  Phone: (785) 296-3421
  Web page: http://www.kansasregents.org/

- ▸ Kansas Department of Education
  120 SE Tenth Avenue
  Topeka, KS 66612-1182
  Phone: (785) 296-3201
  Web page: http://www.ksde.org

Kentucky

- ▸ Kentucky Higher Education Assistance Authority
  1050 U.S. Highway 127 South
  Frankfort, KY 40601-4323
  Phone: (800) 928-8926 or (502) 696-7200
  Web page: http://www.kheaa.com

- Kentucky Department of Education
  500 Mero Street
  Frankfort, KY 40601
  Phone: (502) 564-4770
  Web page: http://www.kde.state.ky.us

- Council on Postsecondary Education
  1024 Capital Center Drive, Suite 320
  Frankfort, KY 40601
  Phone: (502) 573-1555
  Fax: (502) 573-1535
  Web page: http://www.cpe.state.ky.us

Louisiana

- Louisiana Office of Student Financial Assistance
  P.O. Box 91202
  Baton Rouge, LA 70821-9202
  Phone: (800) 259-5626 or (225) 922-1012
  Web page: http://www.osfa.state.la.us/

- Louisiana Department of Education
  P.O. Box 94064
  626 North Fourth Street
  Baton Rouge, LA 70704-9064
  Phone: (225) 342-4411 or (877) 453-2721
  Web page: http://www.doe.state.la.us

- Board of Regents
  150 Third Street, Suite 129
  Baton Rouge, LA 70804-9064
  Phone: (504) 342-4411

Maine

- Maine Education Assistance Division
  Finance Authority of Maine (FAME)
  5 Community Drive
  Augusta, ME 04332-0949
  Phone: (207) 623-3263 or (800) 228-3734
  Web page: http://www.famemaine.com

- Maine Department of Education
  23 State House Station
  Augusta, ME 04333-0023
  Phone: (207) 287-5800
  TDD/TTY for Hearing-Impaired: (207) 287-2550
  Web page: http://janus.state.me.us/education/homepage.htm

Maryland

▸ Maryland Higher Education Commission
Jeffrey Building, 16 Francis Street
Annapolis, MD 21401-1781
Phone: (800) 974-1024
Web page: http://www.mhec.state.md.us

▸ Maryland Department of Education
200 West Baltimore Street
Baltimore, MD 21201-2595
Phone: (410) 767-0462
Web page: http://www.msde.state.md.us

Massachusetts

▸ Massachusetts Board of Higher Education
One Ashburton Place, Room 1401
Boston, MA 02108
Phone: (617) 994-6950
Web page: http://www.mass.edu

▸ Massachusetts Department of Education
Educational Improvement Group
350 Main Street
Malden, MA 02148-5023
Phone: (781) 388-3300
Web page: http://www.doe.mass.edu

▸ Massachusetts Higher Education Information Center
700 Boylston Street, Boston Public Library
Boston, MA 20116
Phone: (800) 442-1171
Web page: http://www.adinfo.org

Michigan

▸ Michigan Higher Education Assistance Authority
Office of Scholarships and Grants
P.O. Box 30462
Lansing, MI 48909-7962
Phone: (517) 373-3394 or (888) 447-2687
Web page: http://www.MI-StudentAid.org/

▸ Michigan Department of Education
608 West Allegan Street
Hannah Building, Fourth Floor
Lansing, MI 48933

Phone: (517) 373-3324
Web page: http://www.mde.state.mi.us

Minnesota

▸ Minnesota Higher Education Services Office
1450 Energy Park Drive, Suite 350
St. Paul, MN 55108-5227
Phone: (800) 657-0866
Web page: http://www.mheso.state.mn.us

▸ Minnesota Department of Children, Families, and Learning
1600 Highway 36 West
Roseville, MN 55113-4266
Phone: (651) 582-8200
Web page: http://cfl.state.mn.us

Mississippi

▸ Mississippi Postsecondary Education, Financial Assistance Board
3825 Ridgewood Road
Jackson, MS 39211-6453
Phone: (800) 227-2980
Web page: http://www.ihl.state.ms.us

▸ Mississippi State Department of Education
359 North West Street, Suite 365
Jackson, MS 39201
Phone: (601) 359-3513
Web page: http://www.mde.k12.ms.us

Missouri

▸ Missouri Department of Higher Education
3515 Amazonas Drive
Jefferson City, MO 65109-5717
Phone: (573) 751-2361 or (800) 473-6757
Web page: http://www.mocbhe.gov

▸ Missouri State Department of Elementary and Secondary Education
P.O. Box 480
Jefferson City, MO 65102-0480
Phone: (573) 751-8613
Web page: http://www.dese.state.mo.us

Montana

▸ Montana University System
2500 Broadway, P.O. Box 203101
Helena, MT 59620-3103
Phone: (406) 444-6570
Web page: http://www.montana.edu/wwwoche/

▸ Montana Office of Public Instruction
P.O. Box 202501
Helena, MT 59620-2501
Phone: (406) 444-2082 or (888) 231-9393
Web page: http://www.metnet.state.mt.us

Nebraska

▸ Nebraska Coordinating Commission for Postsecondary Education
P.O. Box 95005
Lincoln, NE 68509-5005
Phone: (402) 471-2847
Web page: http://www.ccpe.state.ne.us

▸ Nebraska Department of Education
P.O. Box 94987
301 Centennial Mall South
Lincoln, NE 68509-4987
Phone: (402) 471-2295
Web page: http://www.nde.state.ne.us

Nevada

▸ Nevada State Department of Education
700 East Fifth Street
Carson City, NV 89701
Phone: (775) 687-9141
Web page: http://www.nsn.k12.nv.us/nvdoe/

▸ Commission on Postsecondary Education
1820 East Sahara Avenue, Suite 111
Las Vegas, NV 89104
Phone: (702) 486-7330

New Hampshire

▸ New Hampshire Postsecondary Education Commission
2 Industrial Park Drive
Concord, NH 03301-8512

Phone: (603) 271-2555
Web page: http://www.state.nh.us/postsecondary/

▸ New Hampshire Department of Education
State Office Park South
101 Pleasant Street
Concord, NH 03301
Phone: (603) 271-3144 or (800) 339-9900
Web page: http://www.ed.state.nh.us

New Jersey

▸ Higher Education Student Assistance Authority
P.O. Box 540
Quakerbridge Plaza, Building 4
Trenton, NJ 08625-0540
Phone: (800) 792-8670
Web page: http://www.hesaa.org/

▸ New Jersey Department of Education
P.O. Box 500
100 Riverview Place
Trenton, NJ 08625-0500
Phone: (609) 292-4469
Web page: http://www.state.nj.us/education/

▸ New Jersey Commission on Higher Education
P.O. Box 542
20 West State Street
Trenton, NJ 08625
Phone: (609) 292-4310
Fax: (609) 292-7225
Web page: http://www.state.nj.us/highereducation/

New Mexico

▸ New Mexico Commission on Higher Education
1068 Cerrillos Road
Santa Fe, NM 87501-4925
Phone: (505) 827-7383 or (800) 279-9777
Web page: http://www.nmche.org

▸ State Department of Education
Education Building
300 Don Gaspar
Santa Fe, NM 87501-2786
Phone: (505) 827-6516
Web page: http://www.sde.state.nm.us

New York

▸ New York State Higher Education Services Corporation
99 Washington Avenue
Albany, NY 12255
Phone: (518) 473-7087 or (888) 697-4372
Web page: http://www.hesc.com

▸ New York State Education Department
Education Building, Room 111
89 Washington Avenue
Albany, NY 12234
Phone: (518) 474-5844
Web page: http://www.nysed.gov

North Carolina

▸ North Carolina State Education Assistance Authority
P.O. Box 13663
Research Triangle Park, NC 27709-3663
Phone: (919) 549-8614 or (800) 700-1775
Web page: http://www.ncseaa.edu

▸ North Carolina Department of Public Instruction
Education Building
301 North Wilmington Street
Raleigh, NC 27601-2825
Phone: (919) 715-1299
Web page: http://www.ncpublicschools.org

▸ North Carolina System of Community Colleges
Caswell Boulevard
200 West Jones Street
Raleigh, NC 27603
Phone: (919) 733-7051
Fax: (919) 233-0680

North Dakota

▸ North Dakota University System
North Dakota Student Financial Assistance Program
600 East Boulevard Avenue, Dept. 215
Bismarck, ND 58505-0230
Phone: (701) 328-4114
Web page: http://www.nodak.edu

▸ North Dakota Department of Public Instruction
11th Floor, Dept. 201

600 East Boulevard Avenue
Bismarck, ND 58505-0440
Phone: (701) 328-2260
Web page: http://www.dpi.state.nd.us

Ohio

▸ Ohio Board of Regents
State Grants and Scholarships Department
P.O. Box 182452
Columbus, OH 43218-2452
Phone: (888) 833-1133 or (614) 466-7420
Web page: http://www.regents.state.oh.us/sgs/

▸ Ohio Department of Education
25 South Front Street
Columbus, OH 43215-4183
Phone: (877) 644-6338
Web page: http://www.ode.state.oh.us

Oklahoma

▸ Oklahoma State Regents for Higher Education
Oklahoma Guaranteed Student Loan Program
State Capitol Complex, 500 Education Building
Oklahoma City, OK 73105-4500
Phone: (405) 524-9120
Web page: http://www.okhighered.org

▸ Oklahoma State Department of Education
2500 North Lincoln Boulevard
Oklahoma City, OK 73105-4599
Phone: (405) 521-3301
Web page: http://sde.state.ok.us/

Oregon

▸ Oregon Student Assistance Commission
Suite 100, 1500 Valley River Drive
Eugene, OR 97401-2130
Phone: (541) 687-7400 or (800) 452-8807
Web page: http://www.osac.state.or.us/

▸ Oregon University System
P.O. Box 3175
Eugene, OR 97401
Phone: (541) 346-5700
Web page: http://www.ous.edu

- Oregon Department of Education
  255 Capitol Street NE
  Salem, OR 97310-0203
  Phone: (503) 378-3569
  Web page: http://www.ode.state.or.us

Pennsylvania

- Pennsylvania Higher Education Assistance Agency
  1200 North Seventh Street
  Harrisburg, PA 17102-1444
  Phone: (717) 720-2800
  Web page: http://www.pheaa.org

- Pennsylvania Department of Education
  333 Market Street, 10th Floor
  Harrisburg, PA 17126-0333
  Phone: (717) 787-5820
  Web page: http://www.pde.state.pa.us

Rhode Island

- Rhode Island Board of Governors for Higher Education and
  Rhode Island Office of Higher Education
  301 Promenade Street
  Providence, RI 02908-5748
  Phone: (401) 222-6560
  Web page: http://www.ribghe.org/riche.htm

- Rhode Island Higher Education Assistance Authority
  560 Jefferson Boulevard
  Warwick, RI 02886
  Phone: (800) 922-9855 or (401) 736-1100
  Web page: http://www.riheaa.org

- Rhode Island Department of Education
  255 Westminster Street
  Providence, RI 02903-3400
  Phone: (401) 222-4600
  Web page: http://www.ridoe.net

South Carolina

- South Carolina Department of Education
  1006 Rutledge Building
  1429 Senate Street
  Columbia, SC 29201

Phone: (803) 734-8492
Web page: http://www.sde.state.sc.us/sde/

‣ South Carolina Commission on Higher Education
1333 Main Street, Suite 200
Columbia, SC 29201
Phone: (803) 737-2260 or (877) 349-7183
Web page: http://www.che400.state.sc.us

South Dakota

‣ South Dakota Department of Education and Cultural Affairs
700 Governors Drive
Pierre, SD 57501-2291
Phone: (605) 773-3134
Web page: http://www.state.sd.us/deca/

‣ South Dakota Board of Regents
306 East Capitol Avenue, Suite 200
Pierre, SD 57501
Phone: (605) 773-3455
Web page: http://www.ris.sdbor.edu

Tennessee

‣ Tennessee Higher Education Commission
Parkway Towers
404 James Robertson Parkway
Suite 1900
Nashville, TN 37243-0830
Phone: (615) 741-3605
Web page: http://www.state.tn.us/thec/

‣ Tennessee State Department of Education
710 James Robertson Parkway
Nashville, TN 37243-0375
Phone: (615) 741-2731
Web page: http://www.state.tn.us/education

Texas

‣ Texas Higher Education Coordinating Board
P.O. Box 12788
Austin, TX 78711
Phone: (800) 242-3062 or (512) 427-6420
Web page: http://www.thecb.state.tx.us/

▸ Texas Education Agency
William B. Travis Building
1701 North Congress Avenue
Austin, TX 78701-1494
Phone: (512) 463-9734
Web page: http://www.tea.state.tx.us

Utah

▸ Utah State Board of Regents
355 West North Temple
#3 Triad Center, Suite 550
Salt Lake City, UT 84180-1205
Phone: (801) 321-7100
Web page: http://www.utahsbr.edu

▸ Utah State Office of Education
250 East 500 South
Salt Lake City, UT 84111
Phone: (801) 538-7500
Web page: http://www.usoe.k12.ut.us

Vermont

▸ Vermont Student Assistance Corporation
Champlain Mill
1 Main Street, Fourth Floor
Winooski, VT 05404-2601
Phone: (800) 642-3177 or (802) 655-9602
Web page: http://www.vsac.org/

▸ Vermont Department of Education
120 State Street
Montpelier, VT 05620-2501
Phone: (802) 828-3147
Web page: http://www.state.vt.us/educ/

▸ Vermont State Colleges
P.O. Box 359
Waterbury, VT 05676-0359
Phone: (802) 241-2520
Fax: (802) 241-3369
Web page: http://spider.vsc.edu

Virginia

▸ State Council of Higher Education for Virginia
  James Monroe Building, Ninth Floor
  101 North 14th Street
  Richmond, VA 23219
  Phone: (804) 225-2600
  Web page: http://www.schev.edu

▸ Virginia Department of Education
  P.O. Box 2120
  101 North 14th Street
  Richmond, VA 23218-2120
  Phone: (804) 225-2020 or (800) 292-3820
  Web page: http://www.pen.k12.va.us/go/VDOE/

Washington

▸ Washington State Higher Education Coordinating Board
  P.O. Box 43430, 917 Lakeridge Way
  Olympia, WA 98504-3430
  Phone: (360) 753-7800
  Web page: http://www.hecb.wa.gov/

▸ Office of Superintendent of Public Instruction
  Old Capitol Building 600 South Washington
  P.O. Box 47200
  Olympia, WA 98504-7200
  Phone: (360) 586-6904
  Web page: http://www.k12.wa.us

West Virginia

▸ West Virginia Department of Education
  Building 6
  1900 Kanawha Boulevard East
  Charleston, WV 25305-0330
  Phone: (304) 558-0304
  Web page: http://wvde.state.wv.us

▸ West Virginia Higher Education Policy Commission
  1018 Kanawha Boulevard East
  Charleston, WV 25301-2827
  Phone: (304) 558-2101
  Web page: http://www.hepc.wvnet.edu

Wisconsin

▸ Wisconsin Higher Educational Aids Board
131 West Wilson Street, Room 902
Madison, WI 53707-7885
Phone: (608) 267-2206
Web page: http://heab.state.wi.us

▸ Wisconsin Department of Public Instruction
125 South Webster Street
P.O. Box 7841
Madison, WI 53707-7841
Phone: (608) 266-3108 or (800) 441-4563
Web page: http://www.dpi.state.wi.us

▸ Wisconsin Association of Independent Colleges and Universities
16 North Carroll Street, Suite 200
Madison, WI 53703-2716
Phone: (608) 256-7065
Web page: http://www.marquette.edu/waicu

Wyoming

▸ Wyoming Department of Education
2300 Capitol Avenue, Second Floor
Cheyenne, WY 82002-0050
Phone: (307) 777-7675
Web page: http://www.k12.wy.us

▸ Wyoming Community College Commission
2020 Carey Avenue, Eighth Floor
Cheyenne, WY 82002
Phone: (307) 777-7763
Web page: http://www.commission.wcc.edu

American Samoa

▸ American Samoa Community College
Board of Higher Education
P.O. Box 2609
Pago Pago, AS 96799-2609
Phone: (684) 699-1141

▸ American Samoa Department of Education
Pago Pago, AS 96799
Phone: (684) 633-5237
Web page: http://www.government.as/education.htm

Guam

‣ Guam Department of Education
P.O. Box DE
Agana, GM 96932
Phone: (671) 475-0457

Commonwealth of the Northern Mariana Islands

‣ Northern Marianas College
Olympio J. Borja Memorial Library
AS-Terlaje Campus, P.O. Box 1250 CK
Saipan, MP 96950-1250
Phone: (670) 234-3690
Web page: http://www.nmcnet.edu

‣ Commonwealth of the Northern Mariana Islands Public School System
P.O. Box 501370
Saipan, MP 96950
Phone: (670) 664-3721
Web page: http://net.saipan.com/cftemplates/pss/index.cfm

Puerto Rico

‣ Puerto Rico Council on Higher Education
P.O. Box. 19900
San Juan, PR 00910
Phone: (787) 724-7100
Web page: http://www.ces.prstar.net

‣ Puerto Rico Department of Education
P.O. Box 190759
San Juan, PR 00919-0759
Phone: (809) 759-2000

Virgin Islands

‣ Virgin Islands Joint Boards of Education
P.O. Box 11900
St. Thomas, VI 00801
Phone: (340) 774-4546

‣ Virgin Islands Department of Education
44-46 Kongens Gade
St. Thomas, VI 00802
Phone: (340) 774-2810

Byrd Program Representatives for Marshall Islands, Micronesia, and Palau

- Adult Education Program
  Federated States of Micronesia
  P.O. Box P587
  Polikir, Pohnpei, FM 96941
  Phone: (691) 320-2609
  Web page: http://www.literacynet.org/micronesia

- Pacific/Southwest Regional Technology Consortium
  California State University, Long Beach
  Center for Language Minority Education and Research
  College of Education, Ed 1, Room 18
  1250 Bellflower Boulevard
  Long Beach, CA 90840-2201
  Phone: (562) 985-5806
  Web page: http://psretc.clmer.csulb.edu

- Republic of the Marshall Islands
  RMI Scholarship Grant and Loan Board
  P.O. Box 1436
  3 Lagoon Road
  Majuro, MH 96960
  Phone: (692) 625-3108

- Republic of Palau
  Ministry of Education Bureau
  P.O. Box 1346
  Koror, PW 96940
  Phone: (680) 488-1003

Shop! Shop! Shop!

You are spending big money. Potential students often spend more time shopping for a new suit than they spend evaluating their choice of college. It is a buyer's market, and serious students have the right to insist that programs meet their needs in terms of what is taught, when it is taught, and where it is taught. You should expect a school to be serious about the business of providing you with an education. You have the right to know whether a school has a good track record. To help ensure that you are getting value for your hard-earned dollars, following is a script you can use to question all the schools you are considering, whether accredited or not:

- Are you accredited and by whom?
- How many students are enrolled?
- How many students graduate each year? (If the attrition rate is 50 percent or more, beware!)
- What are the demographics of your student body?

- What are the job placement rates of students in my area of study?

- What are the credentials of your faculty in my area of study? (For instance, where did they earn their diplomas, how many years have they taught, and so on.)

- What is the average student-to-instructor ratio? (It should be no more than 20 students to each instructor, unless it is a one-time seminar.)

- Will I communicate with other students during the course of study in group projects, and if so, how will I communicate with them?

- Can I transfer credits from my previous college work?

- How many credits can I transfer to your college?

- Do you accept credits I have earned from examinations and experiential learning?

- Do you offer student services such as tutoring, financial aid, career placement, libraries, and so on?

- Does the program I am interested in have time limits for completion?

- How much does each credit cost?

- What other costs can I expect?

- Can I get a refund if I decide to withdraw from a course?

- Can I see work done by your students? (This will give you an idea about the quality of the school's instruction.)

- May I have the names of and contact information for three former students so I might call them for references?

Before you are finished, call the Better Business Bureau in the city where the school is located, or call the Consumer Protection Division of your state's Attorney General's office. Ask them whether the school has any unresolved complaints or a track record of negative reports. Now you are ready to begin earning credits.

4 ▶ *Earning and Transferring Credits*

Colleges and universities often grant credit for a wide range of prior learning, including standardized proficiency examinations, portfolio assessment of experiential learning, local challenge examinations, assessment by a panel of experts, correspondence courses, and courses offered in your workplace. They now recognize that learning takes place in many environments and not just in the classroom.

The concept of granting college credits for learning, regardless of where it was gained, is not new. Many very famous European universities have granted credits and degrees for centuries based on the knowledge a student demonstrates on examinations and not on the amount of time spent in a classroom.

Credit Banks

Many students do not need to enroll in a degree or certificate program but do need to consolidate their academic records for employment, continuing education, or professional certification purposes. Credit banks provide the means for certifying college-level credits accumulated at various institutions without enrolling in a degree program. Credit earned for examinations, experiential learning, and extrainstitutional learning can be consolidated at a credit bank as well. There is no guarantee, however, that the credits you have been granted elsewhere will be accepted by a credit bank. Those credits accepted by the credit bank will be consolidated on a single transcript with the name of the college or university that operates the credit bank, even though you may not have taken a single class at that school. There is, of course, a fee for this service, which can range anywhere from $75 to $335. Contact one of the following sources for more information:

▸ Excelsior College Credit Bank
7 Columbia Circle
Albany, NY 12203-5159
Phone: (518) 464-8500 or (888) 647-2388
Fax: (518) 464-8777
Web page: http://www.excelsior.edu

▸ Thomas Edison State College Credit Bank
101 West State Street
Trenton, NJ 08608-1176
Phone: (609) 984-1150 or (888) 442-8372
Fax: (609) 984-8447
Web page: http://www.tesc.edu

▸ Charter Oak State College
Credit Banking
55 Paul Manafort Drive
New Britain, CT 06053-2142
Phone: (860) 832-3800
Fax: (860) 832-3999
Web page: http://cosc.edu

Credits by Examination

In the 1950s, when experienced adults began returning to colleges and universities after several years of work, they discovered that they knew as much as, if not more than, their instructors. They became bored, lost their motivation, and either dropped out altogether or reluctantly trudged through course after course just to obtain a degree. The colleges were unable to meet their needs because they were teaching them what they already knew, so, during the late 1950s and early 1960s, examinations were developed to test a person's knowledge and equate it to college learning. Depending on the results achieved on these tests, the student could earn college credits and fulfill the requirements for a course without sitting in a single class. This was the first step in meeting the needs of adult learners. Today, these equivalency examinations include the CLEP, DANTES, and Excelsior College Examinations, among others. Credit can also be granted for completing the GRE, GMAT, LSAT, MSAT, and other proficiency examinations. The Proficiency Examination Program (PEP) offered by the American College Testing Program (ACT) was discontinued in 1998, but some colleges still grant credit for passing grades on previous exams.

Examinations are an inexpensive way to accumulate credit toward a degree by demonstrating knowledge gained outside the classroom. Earning credits through examination also allows the student to start studying at a higher level by earning credits for introductory classes, which saves valuable time in earning a degree.

The College-Level Examination Program (CLEP) is the most widely accepted credit-by-examination program in the United States: More than 2,800 accredited institutions of higher learning award credit for satisfactory scores on CLEP examinations in 5 general and 29 subject areas that cover courses typical of the first two years of college. The CLEP examinations include:

▸ *General Examinations:* College Mathematics, English Composition, Humanities, Natural Sciences, and Social Sciences and History.

▸ *Composition and Literature:* American Literature, Analyzing and Interpreting Literature, English Literature, and Freshman College Composition.

▸ *Foreign Languages:* College-Level French Language, German Language, and Spanish Language.

▸ *History and Social Sciences:* American Government, History of the United States I: Early Colonizations to 1877, History of the United States II: 1865 to the Present, Human Growth and Development, Introduction to Educational Psychology, Principles of Macroeconomics, Principles of Microeconomics, Introductory Psychology, Introductory Sociology, Western Civilization I: Ancient Near East to 1648, Western Civilization II: 1648 to the Present.

- *Science and Mathematics:* Calculus with Elementary Functions, College Algebra, College Algebra-Trigonometry, Trigonometry, General Biology, General Chemistry.

- *Business:* Information Systems and Computer Applications, Principles of Management, Principles of Accounting, Introductory Business Law, Principles of Marketing.

Your local bookstore or college library will have CLEP study guides to help prepare you for any of the tests. Barron's produces an excellent study guide, *How to Prepare for the CLEP— College-Level Examination Program, General Examination.*

Advanced Placement (AP) tests are a good way for motivated high school students to earn college credits before they ever set foot in a college classroom. They are offered every May in high schools across the United States in such subjects as biology, calculus, chemistry, English, European history, French, physics, Spanish, statistics, U.S. government and politics, and U.S. history. Check with your high school counselor for testing dates and preparation help. Barron's publishes a series of test preparation guides to help you succeed on these examinations. You can find them in your school library, bookstore, or online at http://www.barronseduc.com.

The Defense Activity for Non-Traditional Education Support (DANTES) serves as a clearing-house for information about training and testing in the military and Department of Defense. DANTES also provides educational testing and will help military personnel find suitable distance education programs that will minimize the loss of credit transfer. The DANTES Subject Standardized Tests (DSSTs) were developed by the Educational Testing Service under a contract with the Department of Defense. The tests are available to civilian as well as military personnel, and credits are granted for DSSTs at hundreds of colleges and universities in the United States.

You should contact the admissions and/or testing office of a college or university in your local area to determine where exams are being offered. You are not required to take these exams at the distance learning institution where you will be taking classes. The tests are standardized, and you can find convenient testing centers in your area. For instance, Regents College Examinations are given at Sylvan Technology Centers throughout the United States and Canada. The Educational Testing Service oversees most of the testing for CLEP, DANTES, TOEFL, GRE, GMAT, AP, SAT, and Praxis. Their Web site is a good place to start for study resources for all of the exams.

- Educational Testing Service (ETS)
  Rosedale Road
  Princeton, NJ 08541
  Phone: (609) 921-9000
  Fax: (609) 734-5410
  Web page: http://www.ets.org

- College-Level Examination Program (CLEP)
  The College Board
  45 Columbus Avenue
  New York, NY 10032-6992
  Phone: (212) 713-8000
  Web page: http://www.collegeboard.com

- DANTES, DSSTs
  The Chauncey Group International, Ltd
  664 Rosedale Road
  Princeton, NJ 08540-2218
  Phone: (609) 720-6500
  Fax: (609) 720-6550
  Web page: http://www.chauncey.com

- Regents College Examinations
  7 Columbia Circle
  Albany, NY 12203-5159
  Phone: (800) 466-1365
  Web page: http://www.regents.edu

Credits for Life Experiences

Besides testing, several other methods can be used to earn college credit for the knowledge you have gained outside a formal classroom. These include assessment of prior learning through essays, portfolio development, and expert panel interview. Whether your knowledge was gained through your work, travel, volunteering, hobbies, reading for personal development, or other activities, it can equate to college-level learning.

It is important, however, for you to differentiate between *learning* and *experience*. You can report for work every day for ten years, perform your job by rote, and never *learn* anything. Just because you experienced something doesn't necessarily mean you developed college-level learning from that experience. That learning must be at least equivalent to what other students have achieved in a comparable college class.

As an example, let's say you manufacture computer chips in a clean room. Every day you etch the same patterns, use the same chemicals, and inspect the finished products the same way. What have you learned besides the mechanics of your job? Probably not much. You have gained *experience*. Now let's say you are interested in getting ahead in your industry, so you grill your boss constantly with questions about the safe handling and disposal of the chemicals. You talk with the design engineers at every opportunity to find out about the functions of the patterns you are etching after they are installed in a computer. You read some books on quality control and develop a new procedure that salvages some of the defective chips. Now, what have you *learned*? You are beginning to master your craft and you are now ready to take a test, develop a portfolio, or be interviewed by a panel of experts.

Colleges and universities that assess experience for credit have developed extensive processes to ensure that students deserve that credit. Those processes are different for every school, so you must ask what each one requires for assessment of experiential learning. At the University of Phoenix, for example, a student can earn a maximum of 30 prior learning credits as a result of professional training (workshops, seminars, licenses, business and professional courses, and other institutionally sponsored course work). This learning must be documented in an "Experiential Learning Portfolio" that contains detailed evidence of learning outcomes, supporting documentation, and descriptions of personal and professional experience. This can include certifications (CPS, CPIM, CFM, CPCU, MSCE, ATC, PFSM, CPhT), diplomas, licenses (pilot, real estate, and so on), awards and citations, taped presentations, written speeches, manuscripts, photographs, newspaper articles, artwork, product samples, patents, musical scores, computer programs, printed programs, letters from third parties, and the list goes on, limited only by your imagination.

Once the portfolio is submitted, it is evaluated by faculty evaluators who hold advanced degrees in their respective disciplines. They are chosen for their educational and professional competence and are assigned according to their expertise. The quality of the evaluation process is assured through internal auditing of evaluations, comprehensive recordkeeping and tracking systems, and well-defined policies and procedures.

Most colleges and universities use the portfolio and essay methods to evaluate prior learning, but occasionally a student is required to undergo an oral interview instead. This is more likely to be required when demonstrating foreign language proficiency or presenting complex ideas. In such cases, an expert or group of experts questions the student, either in person or via audiotape or videotape. Even if the panel submits its questions in writing, the student is always required to respond to the questions orally. Avoid this type of assessment if you are uncomfortable with communicating orally.

Credits earned through portfolio development, essays, and expert panel interviews are often less expensive than taking an equivalent course. They can be as little as $25 or $50 per credit instead of $200 or more. Not only is it less expensive, but earning credit for experience also means you can achieve your degree goals faster. Since learning has already occurred, demonstrating that learning can take much less time, and you won't have to sit through a class covering information you already know.

For more information on assessment of prior learning, contact:

▸ Council for Adult and Experiential Learning (CAEL)
55 East Monroe Street, Suite 1930
Chicago, IL 60603
Phone: (312) 499-2600
Fax: (312) 499-2601
Web page: http://www.cael.org

Extrainstitutional Learning

The American Council on Education (ACE) has been granting academic credit for military training since the mid-1940s. In 1974, ACE began using the same process to evaluate courses provided by corporations, business associations, labor unions, professional organizations, government agencies, and nonprofit organizations, among others. Under PONSI (Program on Noncollegiate Sponsored Instruction), the American Council on Education has determined the value of thousands of extrainstitutional courses offered by organizations whose primary business is not education.

The Board of Regents of the University of the State of New York sponsors a similar program called the National PONSI (National Program on Noncollegiate Sponsored Instruction). They not only evaluate extrainstitutional programs for credit but also promote the use of those credits with colleges and universities nationwide.

In addition to earning credit for courses you have already taken, you might try participating in some of the courses approved in your area, if they are not restricted to employees or members. Try to get your hands on one of the directories available from any of the following organizations. Since most of these directories are nearly $50, you may want to look for them first at your local library or college admissions office.

- American Council on Education (ACE)
  One Dupont Circle NW
  Washington, DC 20036
  Phone: (202) 939-9300
  Fax: (202) 833-4760
  Web page: http://www.acenet.edu

- National Program on Noncollegiate Sponsored Instruction
  Education Building Addition, Room 960A
  89 Washington Avenue
  Albany, NY 12234
  Phone: (518) 486-2070
  Fax: (518) 486-1853
  Web page: http://www.nationalponsi.org

- Educational Testing Service (ETS)
  Rosedale Road
  Princeton, NJ 08541
  Phone: (609) 921-9000
  Fax: (609) 734-5410
  Web page: http://www.ets.org

Financing the Cost of Distance Learning

5

You can finance the cost of higher education in many ways, but not all of them can be used for distance learning. Your first stop should always be the college's financial aid office. The experienced staff will know exactly which degree and certificate programs qualify for what types of financial aid. The school's Web site might also provide some of that information. A simple phone call to the school to request further information can get you started. In the meantime, here is some general information about the types of financing available for your education.

Grants

A grant is an outright gift of money that doesn't have to be repaid. The federal government and most state governments offer grant programs that help pay for tuition, although they rarely pay 100 percent of a student's expenses. The amount of grant money a student receives is based on need. The fewer personal resources you have and the less income you make per year, the more money you can receive from grants.

Federal Pell Grants are awarded only to undergraduate students who have not earned a bachelor's or professional degree. For many students, Pell Grants form the foundation for other financial aid. They are limited to less than $3,000. You can receive only one Pell Grant in any award year. How much you get depends on financial need, expected family contributions, cost of attendance, and whether you are a full-time or part-time student. When you complete the Free Application for Federal Student Aid (FAFSA), you will automatically be considered for a Pell Grant.

The Federal Supplemental Educational Opportunity Grant (FSEOG) is for undergraduates with exceptional financial need. These grants are for students with the lowest expected family contributions and can range from $100 to $4,000 a year. Much depends on when you apply, your level of need, the funding level of the school you are attending, and the policies of the financial aid office of your school.

Although not a grant, per se, the Federal Work-Study program provides jobs both on and off campus for undergraduate and graduate students with financial need, allowing them to earn money to help pay education expenses. The program encourages community service and work related to a student's course of study. You must be paid at least the current federal minimum wage, but it may be higher depending on the type of work you do and the skills required. How many hours you are allowed to work is determined by your employer or financial aid administrator who will consider your class schedule and academic progress. The amount you earn cannot exceed your total Federal Work-Study award.

Federal and State Loans

The U.S. Department of Education makes available billions of dollars annually in financial aid to enable millions of students to attend college. Approximately two-thirds of all student financial aid in the United States comes from these federal programs. Individual states also administer grant and loan programs, generally under the oversight of the higher education agency in a student's home state. Even though these dollars are either provided by or guaranteed by the government, the financial aid administrator of your college is the person to contact for information.

Direct and FFEL (Federal Family Education Loan) Stafford Loans are the Department of Education's major form of student financial assistance for both undergraduate and graduate students who are enrolled at least half time. The major difference between these two types of loans is not their terms and conditions but the source of the loan funds. Under the Direct Loan Program, the funds are lent directly by the U.S. government. If a college does not participate in Direct Loans, then the funds are lent from a bank, credit union, or other lender that participates in the FFEL Program.

Direct and FFEL Stafford Loans are either subsidized or unsubsidized. Subsidized loans are interest deferred until you complete your education. The federal government determines your financial need and then pays the interest for you until you begin repayment. An unsubsidized loan is not based on need, and you pay the interest from the time the loan is disbursed until it is paid in full. If you allow the interest to accumulate while you are enrolled, it will be capitalized, meaning the interest will be added to the principal amount of the original loan. To prevent this, you can choose to pay the interest as it accumulates, which means you pay less in the long run.

PLUS Loans are available through both the Direct Loan and FFEL programs to parents of students. PLUS Loans enable parents with good credit histories to borrow money to pay the educational expenses of dependent children who are undergraduate students enrolled at least half time. PLUS Loans can fill in the gaps of other financial aid and make it possible for students to continue their education. Unlike student loans, which do not have to be repaid until you are out of school, parents must begin repaying a PLUS loan 60 days after the final loan disbursement for the academic year. There is no grace period for these loans.

A Federal Perkins Loan is a low-interest loan for undergraduate and graduate students with exceptional financial need. The school itself is the lender of government funds that are matched with school funds. You must repay this loan directly to the school beginning nine months after you graduate, leave school, or drop below half-time status. A student is allowed up to ten years to repay a Federal Perkins Loan.

Remember that these forms of financial aid are borrowed money that must be repaid. You will have to repay the loan even if you drop out or don't receive a passing grade. Defaulting on a school loan can affect your credit rating just like defaulting on any debt. There are ways to defer payment or to consolidate several federal student loans into one smaller payment. For more information, contact the U.S. Department of Education at 800-4-FED-AID (800-433-3243) or through their Web page at http://www.ed.gov. There are even a few cases where a loan can be cancelled if you meet the requirements (certain teachers, for instance).

The AmeriCorps program provides full-time educational awards in return for work in community service. You can work before, during, or after your postsecondary education and use the funds to pay current educational expenses or to repay federal student loans. For more information on this program, call 800-942-2677 or check their Web page at http://www.cns.gov/americorps/.

Veteran and Military Benefits

The Department of Veterans Affairs provides financial aid for veterans, reservists, and active duty military personnel and their families through several programs, including:

- Montgomery GI Bill

- Post-Vietnam Era Veterans Educational Assistance Program (VEAP)

- Old GI Bill

- Educational Assistance Test Program

- Educational Assistance Pilot Program

- Survivors' and Dependents' Educational Assistance Program

- Restored Entitlement Program for Survivors (REPS)

- Vocational Rehabilitation

- Military Tuition Assistance

The basic eligibility for these programs varies from one to the other and usually depends on when the student served on active duty. For instance, the Montgomery GI Bill is generally for military personnel—whether active duty, disabled, or honorably discharged—who entered military service on or after July 1, 1985. VEAP applies to persons who served on or after January 1, 1977, until July 1, 1985. In most cases, eligibility expires ten years from the date of discharge or release from active duty. However, only the Department of Veterans Affairs can determine an applicant's eligibility for educational assistance. Application forms are available at all VA offices, active duty stations, and American embassies. If you are serving on active duty, check with the Educational Service Office on your post, base, or ship. For the nearest VA office contact:

- Veterans Administration
  810 Vermont Avenue, NW
  Washington, DC 20420
  Phone: (800) 326-8276 (educational loans)
  or (800) 827-1000 (VA benefits)
  Web page: http://www.va.gov

State governments frequently set up their own educational benefit programs for veterans. In the state of New York, for instance, it is possible to receive financial assistance if you are a Vietnam or Persian Gulf veteran. However, you must also be a resident of New York State and attend an approved college of the University of the State of New York. Talk with your school's financial aid office to get information about programs in your state.

Scholarships

Many organizations offer scholarships and grants to students pursuing their educational goals. If you have access to the Internet, you can visit the Financial Aid Information page (FinAid) at http://www.finaid.org or the Free Scholarship Search and Information Service (FreSch!) at http://www.freschinfo.com/index.phtml or FASTaid's free scholarship search at http://www.fastaid.com. Be careful when surfing the Web for scholarship information. Nearly 95 percent of the scholarship-related sites on the Web are actually advertisements for scholarship search firms that charge anywhere from $30 to $150 for information you can actually find free.

Public and college libraries are good sources for information on scholarships, and don't neglect your college's financial aid office. If you are still in high school, your guidance counselor will also have multiple resources available. Check with foundations, religious organizations, civic groups, and such community organizations as the American Legion, YMCA, 4-H Club, Elks, Kiwanis, Jaycees, Chamber of Commerce, Girl Scouts, or Boy Scouts, among many others. Don't overlook aid from professional organizations such as the American Medical Association, the American Bar Association, and others.

Applying for a scholarship is a long and sometimes fruitless endeavor, but it is well worth attempting. Expect to complete lengthy applications; gather recommendation letters, transcripts, and test scores; write essays; and sometimes even complete personal interviews before being seriously considered for a scholarship. Even then, the award might be as small as $500 or $1,000. There are exceptions, though, so don't give up. Be persistent, and steel yourself to face some rejection.

Other Sources of Funds

Local banks and credit unions frequently offer private loans to students outside of federal and state programs. Family and friends might be willing to lend you money, as well.

Vocational rehabilitation assistance is offered through individual states. The Federal government provides funding to each state for retraining of individuals with disabilities. Contact a vocational rehabilitation counselor for information about the benefits available in your state.

Many employers and unions provide financial assistance to their employees and members who wish to earn college credits or complete a degree program. Your human resources office or union representative will have more information. If your employer does not currently offer tuition assistance, you might be the one to get the ball rolling.

Federal and state departments of labor sponsor numerous training and tuition assistance programs for displaced workers and others who wish to access higher education as they pursue career goals. Contact your local labor department to see if you are eligible for such programs.

For more information on loans, grants, scholarships, and other types of college financial aid, look for *Barron's Complete College Financing Guide* (ISBN 0-8120-9523-5) at your local bookstore or library or at http://www.barronseduc.com.

- The U.S. Department of Education's Web site is an excellent place to find information on financial aid: http://www.ed.gov/prog_info/SFA/StudentGuide/

- The Department of Education provides financial aid information and online application forms: http://www.ed.gov/offices/OSFAP/students

- Mark Kantrowitz's FinAid site includes a college cost projector, savings growth projector, savings plan designer, annual yield calculator, compound interest calculator, savings plan yield calculator, life insurance needs calculator, federal housing index calculator, and loan discounts calculator, among other valuable information: http://www.FinAid.org

- Graduate and Undergraduate School Guide: http://www.schoolguides.com/ or http://www.graduateguide.com

- CollegeSmart financial aid planning software: http://www.collegesmart.com

- The National Association of Student Financial Aid Administrators (NASFAA) site with information for students and parents: http://www.nasfaa.org

- Educaid, the student loan specialists: http://www.educaid.com

- KapLoan, the Kaplan student loan information program: http://www.kaplan.com/

- Sallie Mae gives information on graduate student loans: http://www.salliemae.com

- Nellie Mae is a large nonprofit provider of student and parent education loan funds: http://www.nelliemae.org/

- The Education Resources Institute (TERI) loan programs and services site: http://www.teri.org

- Vermont Student Assistance Corporation: http://www.vsac.org

- Access Group provides financial products and services for graduate and professional students: http://www.accessgroup.org/

- Citibank student loans: http://studentloan.citibank.com/slcsite/

- American Express educational loans: http://www.finance.americanexpress.com

- College Funding, Inc.: http://www.cfionline.com

- Chela Financial: http://www.chelafin.com/

- Education Assistant Corporation: http://www.eac-easci.org

- Educational Finance Group for medical students: http://www.efg.net/programs/

- FastWEB Scholarship Search offers a free computer search of more than 275,000 scholarships: http://www.fastweb.com

- FASTaid free scholarship service: http://www.fastaid.com/

- Free Scholarship Search and Information Service (FreSch!): http://www.freschinfo.com

- Scholarship Resource Network Express: http://www.srnexpress.com

- CollegeNET scholarship search: http://www.collegenet.com/

- Fulbright scholarships: http://www.iie.org/fulbright/

- The Chronicle of Higher Education's weekly list of fellowship and grant deadlines: http://chronicle.com/

- Citizen's Scholarship Foundation of America: http://www.csfa.org

- Cornell University Graduate School Fellowship Notebook: http://www.cornell.edu/student/GRFN

- A USENET newsgroup for exploring college financial aid issues: news:soc.college.financial-aid

- American Association of University Women (AAUW) fellowships and grants: http://aauw.org

- The Rotary Foundation scholarship program: http://www.rotary.org/foundation/educational_programs

- The Foundation Center for information on corporate fellowships: http://fdncenter.org

- Internet Nonprofit Center specializing in information about nonprofit organization: http://www.nonprofits.org/

- Go College, a college and financial aid search: http://www.gocollege.com

- College Board Online Scholarship Search: http://www.collegeboard.com

- The Gates Millennium Scholars: http://www.gmsp.org

- Yahoo's list of grants: http://dir.yahoo.com/education/financial-aid/grants

- Yahoo's list of scholarships: http://dir.yahoo.com/education/financial-aid/scholarship-programs

6 ▶ Get Ready, Get Set, Go!

Now that you know what distance learning is, it's time to move! You will need to examine your options (the get ready part), make a plan (get set), and then start the process of being accepted to the college or university of your choice (go!).

Examine Your Options

Look for schools that have the best programs and the best instructors for your area of interest. Does your industry require a prestigious school for success? Then make sure the school has a reputation you would be proud to announce on a bumper sticker. If you want to transfer your distance learning credits to a degree program at another school, make sure you contact that school in advance to ensure that they will accept your credits. Do you have the necessary credentials for admission? Make sure your previous degrees, class prerequisites, and minimum grade point average match the school's requirements. Does the school require that you live within a certain distance of the campus or reside in a certain state? Would a trade or vocational school be a better choice in your career field?

Some programs can be completed totally away from a college campus, while others will require that you attend seminars or other special programs on campus. Some courses will allow you to enroll whenever you want and work at your own pace. Others will be more traditional in structure and have stricter deadlines. So, review each college's catalog and policies closely before making a decision, then make sure you have the funds and commitment to complete the program.

Make a Plan

Once you have narrowed your choices, your first step will be to request an application from each college. Gather your transcripts, complete the application, write the essay (if required), and submit them to the school. You can complete your college application in two ways: (1) by filling out a paper application packet sent through the mail, or (2) by completing an online application form through a college's Web page or an application service like:

- CollegeLink: http://www.collegelink.com
- CollegeScape: http://www.collegescape.com/
- College Bound Network: http://www.collegebound.net

If you choose the electronic route, make sure you don't neglect the quality of your writing. Use your word processing software's spell check and grammar features to make your application as error free as possible. Print out a copy before e-mailing your application and then back up your e-mail to a floppy disk. For a hard-copy application, call the college directly and request a catalog, financial aid information, and application package.

To find help on the Internet for completing a graduate school application, check the Rensselaer Polytechnic University's online help with application essays at http://www.rpi.edu/dept/llc/writecenter/web/text/apply.html or the Applicant Support Network at http://www.iglou.com/asn/.

Once you are accepted, you will need to request and complete financial aid forms and take any entrance examinations required. Then you are ready to begin your classes.

Entrance Examinations

Undergraduate Exams

If you are a recent high school graduate with little work experience and no previous college credits, you will more than likely be required to submit SAT or ACT scores before admission to most of the schools in this book. Undergraduate distance learning programs will rarely require SAT or ACT testing for acceptance of working adults over the age of 25, but they will often require general aptitude tests in math and communication to assess the student's readiness for college-level learning. If you have difficulty passing these entrance examinations, most schools provide remedial classes that can qualify for your admission.

To help prepare for these examinations, find any of the following Barron's books in your local bookstore, library, or online at *www.barronseduc.com*:

- *How to Prepare for the SAT I*

- *Pass Key to SAT I*

- *SAT I Computer Study Program*

- *Barron's SAT I with CD-ROM*

- *Hot Words for the SAT I*

- *Barron's New Math Workbook for SAT I*

- *Verbal Workbook for SAT I*

- *14 Days to Higher SAT I Scores*

- *SAT I Wordmaster, Level I and Level II*

- SAT II subject preparation books in: American History and Social Studies, Biology, Chemistry, French, Japanese, Literature, Mathematics Level I/IC/IIC, Physics, Spanish, World History, and Writing

- *ACT Computer Study Program*
- *How to Prepare for the ACT*
- *Pass Key to the ACT*

Graduate Exams

Most graduate programs, on the other hand, generally require applicants to take an examination before acceptance. The GRE (General Aptitude Test of the Graduate Record Examination) is the most commonly used, but some schools also require a GRE Subject Test in a special area of study. The GMAT (Graduate Management Admissions Test) is usually required instead of the GRE for admission into graduate business schools. Speak with the prospective school about its requirements and about testing available in your area. For more information about the GRE and testing sites they sponsor all over the world, contact the Educational Testing Service:

Educational Testing Service (ETS)
Rosedale Road
Princeton, NJ 08541
Phone: (609) 921-9000
Fax: (609) 734-5410
Web page: http://www.ets.org

The General Aptitude Test of the GRE is not an achievement or intelligence test; instead it tests your verbal, quantitative, and analytical abilities. It takes three and one-half hours to complete and is usually given twice a year at test centers in major metropolitan areas.

Each Subject Test is also three and one-half hours long and tests your basic understanding of information in a specific field. Subject Tests are available in the following disciplines, depending on admission requirements: biology, chemistry, computer sciences, economics, education, engineering, French, geology, history, literature in English, mathematics, music, physics, political science, psychology, sociology, and Spanish.

The GMAT is a four-hour test that measures a student's ability to think systematically, as well as reading and analytical skills. A student need not have business experience to pass this test since it does not test knowledge in specific business subjects, although you should have a strong basic knowledge of algebra, geometry, and arithmetic.

If you are not a native English speaker or are applying from a country that does not speak English as its primary language, you will need to prove your ability to communicate in English before being accepted into most American schools. The Test of English as a Foreign Language (TOEFL) is the most frequently used examination for this purpose. For information about dates and locations of tests around the world, write:

TOEFL
P.O. Box 6151
Princeton, NJ 08541
Phone: (609) 771-7100
Fax: (609) 771-7500
Web page: http://www.ets.org

The Medical College Admission Text (MCAT) and the Law School Admission Test (LSAT) are required for admission to specialized medical or law schools. The LSAT does not measure special knowledge of law, but the MCAT is designed to measure your general knowledge of basic physics, chemistry, and biology. Both exams require good critical thinking skills.

Your local bookstore or library will have some great resources for preparing for the GRE, GMAT, LSAT, MCAT, PCAT, TOEFL, and other examinations. Barron's publishes several excellent study guides, including:

▸ *How to Prepare for the Graduate Record Exam* (with or without computer software)

▸ *Pass Key to the GRE*

▸ *GRE Computer Study Program*

▸ *How to Prepare for the GRE: Biology*

▸ *How to Prepare for the GRE: Psychology*

▸ *How to Prepare for the GMAT* (with CD-ROM)

▸ *Pass Key to the GMAT*

▸ *How to Prepare for the TOEFL*

▸ *TOEFL Strategies*

▸ *Essential Words for the TOEFL*

▸ *Practice Exercises for the TOEFL*

▸ *Pass Key to the TOEFL*

▸ *TOEFL Computer Study Program*

▸ *How to Prepare for the Law School Admission Test—LSAT*

▸ *Pass Key to the LSAT*

▸ *Law Dictionary*

▸ *How to Prepare for the MCAT, Medical College Admission Test*

▸ *How to Prepare for the PCAT, Pharmacy College Admission Test*

Learning Contracts

Some distance learning programs use learning contracts (or degree plans). The student negotiates the courses and work required to complete a degree and then writes a contract stating the educational goals, learning outcomes, and methods for acquiring that learning, including resources, educational activities, and evaluation procedures. This allows students to tailor a degree program to meet their exact needs.

This legal document is binding on both parties once accepted and signed. That means that, if you fail to complete your part of the bargain, you might forfeit your tuition and be forced to withdraw from the program. On the other hand, the school is equally bound by the contract, and if you satisfactorily complete all elements of the contract, you must be awarded the degree or credits agreed upon. Most learning contracts have a binding arbitration clause that protects both you and the school from breeches of contract.

This contract is extremely important to you and to your future, so don't take its preparation or signing lightly. Certain occasions might even require an attorney's expert eye to review the contract before it is finalized.

Transcripts and Grades

Whenever you complete a course at a college or university, the school records the grade on a transcript and sends a grade report to you for your records. Rarely does a transcript indicate how a course was completed—via distance learning or in a traditional classroom. You can request an official transcript in writing from any institution, although the transcript is not considered "official" if you open the envelope. In your letter, ask the college to send the transcript directly to the requesting institution to avoid any problems of legitimacy.

Course Materials

Every course will require some kind of study materials. Once you register for a course, you will automatically receive a study guide (or instructions for where to get one). This guide will tell you about your instructor, meeting times and places (if any), homework, and will contain an outline of the course. In most cases, you will be required to purchase a textbook and other materials, which might include a workbook, extra reading assignments, lab kits, videotapes, CD-ROMs, audiotapes, and other necessities. These additional costs should be figured into your budget, since they can become significant over time.

Internet Resources

Study and Testing Help

- Links to more than 2,000 Internet study resource sites: http://www.caso.com.
- Princeton Review's Graduate School and the GRE: http://www.review.com/
- Kaplan Educational Centers: http://www.kaplan.com/
- The Graduate Management Admission Council's MBA Explorer: http://www.gmac.org/
- GMAT percentile conversion table: http://haas.berkeley.edu/
- Eisenhower National Clearinghouse for science test preparation: http://www.enc.org

- National Science Teacher's Association site: http://www.nsta.org/

- Mathematics Archives: http://archives.math.utk.edu/

- Geometry: http://www.geom.umn.edu/apps/gallery.html

- Chemistry Web Elements: http://www.cchem.berkeley.edu/

- Microbiology: http://virtual.class.uconn.edu/MCB/index.html

Digital Libraries and General Research

- World Wide Web Virtual Library subject catalog: http://vlib.org/Overview.html

- The Library of Congress' National Digital Library Project: http://rs6.loc.gov/amhome.html

- National Library of Canada: http://www.nlc-bnc.ca/confed/e-1867.htm

- Online Computer Library Center, Inc.: http://www.oclc.org

- Alex catalog of electronic texts on the Internet: gopher://rsl.ox.ac.uk/11/lib-corn/hunter

- U.S. National Library of Medicine: http://www.nlm.nih.gov/

- Global Electronic Library: http://www.jec.edu/index.html

- The Voice of the Shuttle: http://humanitas.ucsb.edu/

- Tradewave Gallery Index for Science: http://www.galaxy.com

- Carnegie Mellon University history and historiography index: http://eserver.org/history/

- Classics Subject Guide: http://www.ualberta.ca/~slis/guides/classics/home.htm

- Economic History Services of the Cliometric Society: http://cs.muohio.edu/

- Historical documents: gopher://gopher.vt.edu:10010/10/33

- National Science Foundation: gopher://stis.nsf.gov/

- Search directory for women: http://www.wwwomen.com/

- Michigan State University's search engine for university and informational resources: http://writing.msu.edu/modules/research/engines/default.html

- Library support for learners: http://www.lis.uiuc.edu/~sloan/libdist.htm

- Resources: http://www.lib.odu.edu/services/disted/dersrcs.html

- World Wide Web Virtual library: http://www.cisnet.com/~cattales/Deducation.html

Search Engines

- ▸ Altavista: http://www.altavista.com
- ▸ Excite: http://www.excite.com/
- ▸ Hotbot: http://hotbot.lycos.com
- ▸ Lycos: http://www.lycos.com
- ▸ Yahoo: http://www.yahoo.com

Diversity Resources

- ▸ Minority Resources:
  - http://www.hanksville.org/NAresources/indices/NAhistory.html
  - http://lib.nmsu.edu/subject/bord/lagaia
  - http://www.sacnas.org/
  - http://www.unm.edu/~lananet/
  - http://www.nmu.edu/www-sam/multiculturallinks.htm
  - http://www.minoritystudents.org
- ▸ Resources for Asian American students:
  - http://www.ai.mit.edu/people/irie/aar/
  - http://www.umiacs.umd.edu/users/sawweb/sawnet
  - http://asianamculture.about.com/culture/asianamculture
  - http://www.naasu.org/eeasu/links.htm
  - http://www.mit.edu/activities/aar/aarframe.html
- ▸ Resources for women:
  - http://pencilboxmag.com
  - http://www.advancingwomen.com/college.html
  - http://www.bwni.com/college
- ▸ Resource for the sight and hearing impaired:
  - American Council of the Blind: http://www.acb.org/index.html
  - College and career programs for deaf students: http://gri.gallaudet.edu/ccg/

▸ Christina DeMello's College and University Home Page Directory: http://www.mit.edu-cdemello/www/geog.html

▸ Yahoo!'s list of universities: http://dir.yahoo.com/Education/Higher_Education/Colleges_and_ Universities

▸ List of American universities: http://www.clas.afl.edu/CLAS/american-universities.html

▸ Ecola's guide to U.S. colleges: http://www.ecola.com/college/

▸ Associated Western universities: http://www.awu.org/

▸ University of Texas' list of community colleges: http://www.utexas.edu/world/comcol/alpha/

▸ Community colleges Web search: http://www.mcli.dist.maricopa.edu/cc/search.html

▸ Internet College Exchange: http://www.collegenight.com/

▸ Shortcuts to American universities: http://www.emich.edu/ public/economics/links.htm

▸ University of Texas at Austin's list of colleges: http://www.utexas.edu/world/univ/

▸ Canadian universities: http://www.uwaterloo.ca/canu/

▸ Distance education institutions: http://distancelearn.about.com

▸ The College Information Handbook site with hyperlinks to more than 3,200 colleges and universities in the United States: http://www.collegeboard.org/

▸ CollegeNet college search: http://www.collegenet.com/

▸ College guide: http://www.mycollegeguide.org

▸ Edition XII, a U.K. site with a worldwide directory of schools with MBA programs: http://www.editionxii.co.uk/

▸ University of Minnesota's list of distance education programs: http://www.cee.umn.edu/disted/AL/delinks.html

▸ Distance learning on the Net: http://hoyle.com/distance.htm

▸ Higher education and distance learning site: http://members.tripod.com/~lepine/

▸ International Center for Distance Learning: http://www.icdl.open.ac.uk/icdl

▸ Benjamin Franklin Institute of Global Education: http://www.bfranklin.edu/de.html

▸ Online distance education learning resource for adult students: http://www.edsurf.net/

▸ Distance education guru: http://home.rmci.net/michael/index6.htm

▸ Distance education resources: http://www.tec.hkr.se/~chen/webresources/disted.html

- Distance education organization: http://ccism.pc.athabascau.ca

- Distance education WWW resources: http://info.aes.purdue.edu/acs/deit/links.html

- Distance learning opportunity sites: http://www.ph.utexas.edu/~ehyberts/dislrn.htm

- The Commonwealth of Learning: http://www.col.org/

- Distance Education and Training Council: http://www.detec.org

- United States Distance Learning Association: http://www.usdla.org/

- America's 100 Most Wired Colleges: http://www.zdnet.com/yil/content/college/colleges99.html

- Prominent diploma mills with a checklist of what to look for: http://cust3.iamerica.net/easywave/

- Help for reentry students from a UCSC faculty member: http://www.ucsc.edu/stars/reentry/index.html

Other Related Sites

- CSU Mentor to assist students and families in matching needs with colleges: http://www.csumentor.edu

- CollegeView: http://www.collegeview.com/

- U.S. News & World Report's College and Careers page: http:// www.usnews.com/usnews/edu/eduhome.htm

- Mapping Your Future: http://www.mapping-your-future.org/

- Best Education Sites Today (BEST): http://www.education-world.com/

- MBA Style Magazine: http://members.aol.com/mbastyle/

The Directory

7

The intent of this guide is to give you a general idea of the types of programs offered by regionally accredited colleges and universities throughout the United States and Canada. It is not an inexhaustible list of schools with distance learning programs. Because more and more distance learning programs will be developed by colleges and universities every month, what was complete yesterday will not be complete today. In addition, not every college that was surveyed chose to respond, although the vast majority of schools did respond. This book will give you enough information, however, to help you narrow down your choices to the programs best suited to your needs without overwhelming you with details.

This guide was current on the date it was published, but exact tuition rates, fees, course availability, entrance requirements, and other details will change often. Some distance learning courses are offered only at certain times of the year or only to students in certain geographic locations, so be sure to check with the school before making your final decision. The catalogs, brochures, and Web pages of colleges and universities are updated several times a year and are the best sources for current information. Remember to shop, shop, shop!

How to Read the Profiles

Each profile begins with *contact information*, including full address, phone number(s), fax number, division responsible for distance learning, Web site, and e-mail address. This information is more dynamic than you might expect, especially the e-mail addresses and Web site URLs (Universal Resource Locators). If you can't get through via e-mail, then the school's mail system has probably changed or the person who was the contact is no longer there. In such cases, simply call the phone number listed and ask for a new e-mail address. Web sites move often, so you will need to use a good Internet search engine to find new addresses when a college moves its site. Try http://www.altavista.com or http://www.yahoo.com. If a URL contains multiple / marks after the first //, then try to delete all of the extensions up to the primary domain name (for example, http://www.ctc.edu instead of http://www.ctc.edu/~distance).

Degree programs are divided into three categories: undergraduate (associate and bachelor's), graduate (master's), and postgraduate (doctoral). *Certificate programs* and individual *class titles* are listed in paragraph form, separated by commas. Remember, other classes might be available via distance learning besides those listed here. Look at the kinds of degree and certificate programs offered by the school and assume that classes are available in the same general subject areas. Ninety-eight percent of colleges allow students to take individual classes without being enrolled in a degree or certificate program, which is great news for those with a love of lifelong learning. You don't need to commit to a degree or certificate program to begin taking college courses now, and distance learning allows busy adults to work around their already-overcommitted time schedules.

Teaching methods (called delivery methods in the academic world) are the technologies used to deliver the classes. The Internet, real-time chats, asynchronous conferencing, electronic classrooms, e-mail, newsgroups, and LISTSERVs all require the use of a computer equipped with a modem. The faster your modem speed, the more satisfied you will be with the quality of your online experience, except for e-mail, of course, which is not as dependent on computer speed. Because each college uses these teaching methods in unique combinations, it is fruitless to give an example of how your class will be delivered. What is more important is that you determine whether you have the technology you need to take the class (computer, modem, VCR, television set, and so on) and then call the schools with programs that interest you to get the details of how they use those technologies.

Here are some of the definitions of the various teaching methods:

▸ *Internet:* The world's largest network of connected computers, linking government, military, businesses, organizations, educational institutions, and private individuals. The World Wide Web (WWW) is the software that links the information of the Internet, while the Internet is the physical collection of computers and cables by which Web files are transmitted. In order to access the Internet, you will need a computer, modem, browser software, and an Internet Service Provider (ISP). When you subscribe to a commercial online service such as America Online, CompuServe, Microsoft Network, or other ISP, the browser software is installed on your computer's hard drive automatically when you install the ISP software. Most colleges and universities today have a Web site that provides information about the school, much like the catalog that is published every semester. Distance learning programs often use the Internet for much more than just providing information. Professors will set up their own Web pages under the school's domain to give course outlines, assignments, and hyperlinks to related subjects.

▸ *Electronic classrooms:* By combining live transmission of video and audio, real-time conferencing, and hyperlinks to volumes of printed information on the Internet, electronic classrooms are the closest thing to traditional classroom environments that you will find in distance learning. Electronic classrooms can use the Internet or private networks. Some private networks use Lotus Notes to allow students to see graphics, watch video clips, and communicate with each other and the instructor.

▸ *Real-time chats:* These are computer conferences in which students and instructors exchange messages in real time. This is synchronous, two-way communication. Study groups will often use real-time chats to communicate about projects.

▸ *E-mail:* Electronic mail is an electronic message sent from one computer to another via the Internet or a commercial online service. E-mail is used to communicate back and forth between instructors and fellow students.

▸ *CD-ROM:* Similar to a music compact disc, CD-ROMs can store large volumes of data for access by computers. A single CD-ROM can hold the information from an entire textbook and still have plenty of room left for a set of encyclopedias with photographs.

Instructors are making use of this technology to provide valuable resource materials for students in their classes. In order to play a CD-ROM, however, a computer must have a special drive that usually comes standard on most of today's new computers.

▸ *Newsgroups:* Newsgroups offer students the opportunity to participate in "chats" that are not dependent on "real time." Instead of chatting with someone live, you read a continuous thread of discussion on a certain topic and add your comments whenever you like. Other students in the same class are adding their comments over a period of days or weeks until the discussion ends. Newsgroups can be accessed through the Internet or through a college's local network of computers.

▸ *LISTSERV:* A LISTSERV is really just a mailing list, an organized form of e-mail that you are sent automatically. You subscribe to a mailing list as part of your class, and mail is sent to you whenever the instructor or a student has something to say to all class members. Like e-mail, you read it at your convenience.

▸ *Television (videotape, cable, satellite, PBS):* Some correspondence courses are accompanied by videotapes that make the subject as alive as if the student were in a traditional classroom. To participate in such a course, you must, of course, have access to a videocassette player/recorder (VCR) and a television set. PBS, cable, and satellite television program are one-way video. In other words, the instruction is coming to you, but you can't interact with the instructor in real time. This is asynchronous communication, meaning the interaction between student and instructor occurs before and/or after, but not during, the instruction, usually by e-mail or telephone.

▸ *Videoconferencing:* This is interactive video in which the students and instructors can see and hear each other. As a general rule, video cameras and monitors are placed in the rooms, and operators in each classroom work the equipment. Students can see the teacher and any visual aids on one monitor and see students at other sites on the other monitors. The instructor can choose not to watch the classes when they are shown in multiple locations. Video allows students and instructors to pick up on the nuances of a discussion, including body language, movement, and personal interaction.

▸ *Audioconferencing:* Also known as teleconferencing, this technology allows students to use a telephone to listen to and join classes in real time, but the participants cannot see one another. A bridge operator sets up a telephone connection between all of the parties, like a party line. You should have a good telephone with a mute button and a speaker for audioconferencing.

▸ *Audiographics:* This type of audio-based technology uses telephone lines to transmit visual information such as charts and illustrations. Fax machines, electronic black boards, telewriters, electronic pens, compressed video, and freeze-frame video are good examples of this technology. Some of these technologies require computers or special equipment at the student's end of the telephone line and are more likely to be used in a group setting at a remote meeting place. These technologies are used when visual demonstrations are an important part of the learning, such as in mathematics, science, and art subjects, but they're not used as frequently as videoconferencing.

- *Radio Broadcast:* Prerecorded or live broadcasts are made using radio signals that can be picked up by anyone within broadcast range with a radio receiver. Radio broadcasts are more popular overseas than in the United States, but they are a great delivery method for highly verbal subjects like psychology or auditory subjects like music appreciation.

- *Audiocassette Tapes:* Audiotapes contain prerecorded instruction and are delivered to the student with the print study materials. Audiotapes are generally used when the number of students is too small to justify a radio broadcast or in cases where students are outside the range of a radio signal. Students with very visual or kinaesthetic learning styles may find it difficult to learn in an auditory learning environment.

- *Independent Study (also called Correspondence Study):* Traditional correspondence courses fall into this category. You are truly alone in this type of program; there is no classroom or group interaction. It is just you and your instructor, corresponding back and forth until the work is done. Correspondence isn't always via the post office anymore and includes such technologies as fax, e-mail, and telephone conferences with the instructor.

- *Learning Contracts:* You will find information about learning contracts at the end of Chapter 6 of this book.

Credits Granted for: Many colleges and universities grant credit for life experiences, examinations, and extrainstitutional learning (corporate and professional association seminars and workshops). These were discussed in detail in Chapter 4.

The *admission requirements* listed in this book are the bare essentials. They include age, employment status, prerequisites, and restrictions such as state residency and time limits for completion. Once you have narrowed down your choices, call each college to request a catalog or check the Web page for full details.

On-Campus Requirements: Some degree and certificate programs require that students spend a certain number of hours or percentage of study time in a traditional classroom setting, either on their campus, in an off-campus classroom, or at seminars. If you live a long distance from the campus, the requirement of on-campus time becomes a very important part of your decision-making process.

Tuition and fees will rarely be exactly what they are quoted in this guide because of the lead-time required in producing such a book and because of the shelf-life of the printed word. The real advantage of showing prices in this guide is that it helps you compare the relative price ranges of different schools. You will know whether a school offers the highest prices, the lowest prices, or prices in between. Always call the school or check the Web page before making a decision.

Credit by: The last item in the tuition and fees section of each profile indicates whether an institution's credits are measured by semester or quarter. Transferring credits earned under a quarter system to a college that awards credits by the semester can sometimes be difficult, since quarters equate to partial credits under a semester system. Speak with your admissions counselor about how these credits will appear on your transcript.

Financial Aid: Various financing options are listed for each college. Read more about financial aid in Chapter 5.

Accreditation is explained more fully in Chapter 3, but suffice it to say that every institution listed in this book has been accredited by one of the six regional accreditation associations or the Distance Education and Training Council.

Description: The last item in each profile is a brief description of the school in its own words. The number in parentheses in the first sentence of the profile is the year the school was founded.

Following the profiles is a series of indexes that cross-references schools by state/province, fields of study, and on-campus requirements. Use these indexes to narrow down your choice if location, subjects, or travel time are important to you.

The Profiles

Acadia University

38 Crowell Avenue	Phone: (902) 585-1434
Wolfville, NS, Canada B0P 1X0	(800) 565-6568
	Fax: (902) 585-1068

Division(s): Continuing and Distance Education
Web Site(s): http://conted.acadiau.ca
E-mail: continuing.education@acadiau.ca

Certificate Programs: Computer Science, Business Administration, Business Administration Diploma.

Class Titles: Accounting, Management, Managerial Finance, Marketing, Operations Management, Business Law, Computer Programming, Systems Programming, Digital Systems, Data Structures/File Processing, Object Oriented Systems, Economics, History of Education, Philosophy of Education, Literature, Reading/Writing Texts, Shakespeare, Romantics, 18th Century Novel, Short Story, Canadian Short Story, Frankenstein to Dracula, Oceanography, Atmosphere/Weather/Climate, Western Civilization, Canadian History, U.S. History, Maritime Provinces, Women in Modern World, Environmental Law, Latin Prose/Poetry, Math Functions, Nutrition, Politics/Government, Experimental Psychology, Applied Psychology, Drugs/Behaviour, Stress/Coping, Personality, Sociology, Sociology of Aging, Criminology, Spanish, Biology: Human Physiology and Anatomy, Algebra and Trigonometry, Physics: The Solar System, Stars, Galaxies, and the Universe, Sociology of Death and Dying, Secondary Science Education, Problems in Education: Computers in Education, Developmental Psychology, Advanced Business Research, Fundamental Chemistry.

Teaching Methods: *Computers:* Internet, electronic classroom, e-mail, CD-ROM, newsgroup, LISTSERV. *TV:* videotape. *Other:* videoconferencing, audiographics, correspondence.

Admission Requirements: *Undergraduate:* high school completion. *Certificate:* high school completion.

On-Campus Requirements: None.

Tuition and Fees: *Undergraduate:* $524/3-hour credit course. *Application Fee:* $25. *Other Costs:* $100 distance education fee. *Credit by:* open entry.

Financial Aid: Federal Student Loans, Provincial Student Loans.

Accreditation: Association of Universities and Colleges of Canada.

Description: Acadia University (1838) is a fully accredited institution with a long tradition of offering accessible post-secondary education. Every year, more than 2,000 students access Acadia University through its worldwide distance learning program, which began in 1965. Acadia offers credit courses toward degrees in all branches of university work. More than 200 curriculum combinations lead to degrees, diplomas, and certificates in Faculties of Arts, Pure and Applied Science, Professional Studies, and Theology.

Adams State College

208 Edgemont	Phone: (719) 587-7671
Alamosa, CO 81102	(800) 548-6679
	Fax: (719) 587-7974

Division(s): Extended Studies
Web Site(s): http://www.adams.edu
E-mail: ascextend@adams.edu/exstudies/

Class Titles: Education courses; vary by semester. Business, Economics, Education, English, Environmental Studies, Physical Education, Journalism, Math, Psychology, and Sociology.

Teaching Methods: *Computers:* Internet, real-time chat, e-mail, LISTSERV. *TV:* satellite broadcasting, PBS, videotape. *Other:* correspondence, independent study, individual study.

On-Campus Requirements: None.

Tuition and Fees: *Undergraduate:* $80–$100/credit independent study. *Graduate:* $100/credit. *Other Costs:* books extra. *Credit by:* semester.

Accreditation: North Central Association of Colleges and Schools, National Council for Accreditation of Teacher Education, National Association of School of Music, Council for Accreditation of Counseling and Related Education Programs.

Description: Adams State College was founded in 1921 by the Colorado General Assembly. Situated in the San Luis Valley, a valley the size of the state of Connecticut, located in southcentral Colorado, the campus is surrounded by the Sangre de Cristo and Juan Mountain ranges. The Division of Extended Studies coordinates distance learning opportunities at Adams State. It works closely with the academic deans to assist in fulfilling the college mission to provide educational opportunities to students in rural areas or who are otherwise unable to attend the residential campus.

Adelphi University

1 South Avenue　　　　　　　　Phone: (516) 877-4690
Garden City, NY 11530　　　　　Fax: (516) 877-4607

Division(s): School of Business
Web Site(s): http://Adelphi.Edu
E-mail: gupta@adelphi.edu

Undergraduate Degree Programs:

Bachelor Business Administration in Management (New York state approved)

Graduate Degree Programs:

Master of Business Administration in Management (New York state approved)

Teaching Methods: *TV:* 2-way audio/video room systems. *Other:* videoconferencing, Internet.

Admission Requirements: *Undergraduate:* application, ACT/SAT, high school graduate or equivalent, upper 1/3 of class, application fee, transfer transcripts. *Graduate:* bachelor's degree, transcripts, GMAT, application fee.

On-Campus Requirements: None.

Tuition and Fees: *Undergraduate:* $500/credit. *Graduate:* $540/credit. *Application Fee:* $35 undergraduate, $50 graduate. *Other Costs:* home computer required for video-enabled courses, costs for ISDN systems are student's responsibility. *Credit by:* semester.

Financial Aid: Federal Pell Grant, Supplemental Educational Opportunity Grant, Federal Work-Study, New York resident programs, Adelphi scholarships, awards, grants, loans.

Accreditation: Middle States Association of Colleges and Schools.

Description: Adelphi (1896) is a liberal arts institution chartered by the State Board of Regents in 1896. Initially located in Brooklyn with 57 students and 16 faculty members. In 1929, it moved to its current location in Garden City. It became a women's college in 1912 for 3 decades. The university, over the years, added several programs and schools besides the liberal arts courses of study including Nursing (1944), Social Work (1949), doctoral level Clinical Psychology (Derner Institute, 1951), and the Schools of Education, Business, and University College (in the 1960s and 1970s). In the 1990s, the Honors College and the Center for Health and Human Services were added to the university.

AIB College of Business

2500 Fleur Drive　　　　　　　Phone: (515) 244-4221
Des Moines, IA 50321　　　　　　　　(800) 444-1921
　　　　　　　　　　　　　　　　Fax: (515) 244-6773

Division(s): Online Education Department
Web Site(s): http://www.aib.edu
E-mail: dubucd@aib.edu

Undergraduate Degree Programs: Contact school.

Certificate Programs: The full first year of the Court Reporting program is offered online.

Class Titles: Computer Fundamentals, Microsoft Excel, Introduction to Composition, Steno I, Microsoft Word, Word Processing, Principles of Accounting I, Composition I, Microsoft Office 2000, Steno II, Technical Writing, Word Processing II.

Teaching Methods: *Computers:* Internet, real-time chat, electronic classroom, e-mail, CD-ROM, newsgroup, LISTSERV.

Credits Granted for: experiential learning, portfolio assessment.

Admission Requirements: *Undergraduate:* student must fill out the online education application, located on the web site and complete the online learning readiness questionnaire, also available on the web site. Student will receive an e-mail with the questionnaire results. Once the application is processed and payment is received, the student will receive another e-mail containing various information, including how the student can purchase books, when the student will need to attend orientation, if applicable, etc. Students will be contacted by instructor to start class.

On-Campus Requirements: some classes may require specific contact hours.

Tuition and Fees: *Undergraduate:* $205/credit hour. *Application Fee:* $25. Tech Support Fee: $50. *Credit by:* quarter.

Financial Aid: Federal Stafford Loan, Federal Perkins Loan, Federal PLUS Loan, Federal Pell Grant, VA, state programs for residents of Iowa, Federal Supplemental Educational Opportunity Grant.

Accreditation: North Central Association of Colleges and Schools, Commission on Institutions of Higher Education.

Description: AIB College of Business (1921) is an independent, coeducational, associate degree-granting college of business. The college offers associate degree and diploma courses of study. The college is dedicated to its mission of providing quality educational opportunities that prepare students to pursue careers in business. The high-tech campus is located in the heart of Des Moines, Iowa and spreads over 20 acres. AIB is a leader in computer education through partnerships with IBM and Microsoft. AIB will be offering online classes with the summer quarter to start June 4. Several phases have taken place to get online education in place at AIB. The most recent and valuable phase was a piloted online education course. This course was designed as a trial run and gave students and instructors a chance to overcome any obstacles that could and have occurred with online education. All went very well with the piloted class and AIB has decided to go online with selected courses.

Aims Community College

5590 W. 11th Street, P.O. Box 69	Phone: (888) 644-3451
Greeley, CO 80632	(970) 330-8008 ext. 6504
	Fax: (970) 339-6646

Division(s): Continuing Education
Web Site(s): http://www.aims.edu
E-mail: distance@aims.edu

Undergraduate Degree Programs:
Associate of Arts with an emphasis in:
　Telecommunications
　Computer Information Systems
　Mortgage Banking
Associate of Applied Science in:
　Computer Information Systems
Biomedical Electronic Technology
　Electronic Technology
　Sales and Customer Service

Certificate Programs: Telecommunications Certificate, Information Technology Certificate, Sales and Customer Service Certificate, Microsoft Certified Systems Engineer (MCSE).

Class Titles: Contact school and check web site for details.

Teaching Methods: *Computers:* Internet, threaded discussions (asynchronous chat), e-mail, CD ROM, LISTSERV. *TV:* videotape, cable program, satellite broadcasting, PBS. *Other:* correspondence, independent study.

Credits Granted for: experiential learning, portfolio assessment, extrainstitutional learning (corporate or professional association seminars/workshops), examination (CLEP, DANTES).

Admission Requirements: *Undergraduate:* courses are offered monthly so students may enroll anytime. Students have 10 weeks to complete a course. Students have access to instructors through e-mail, fax, and toll-free numbers.

On-Campus Requirements: None.

Tuition and Fees: *Undergraduate:* $140/credit (course materials are included in the cost of tuition with the exception of software for Microsoft Office Products). *Other Costs:* course materials are included in the cost of tuition. Materials are shipped to student's home via UPS, FedEx, and U.S. mail. *Credit by:* quarter.

Financial Aid: Federal Stafford Loan, Federal Perkins Loan, Federal PLUS Loan, Federal Pell Grant, VA, state programs for residents of (Colorado).

Accreditation: North Central Association of Colleges and Schools.

Description: Aims Community College (1967) is a 2-year, postsecondary institution dedicated to responding to the educational needs of the local, regional, and global communities. Aims has 3 campuses located in Greeley, Loveland, and Ft. Lupton, Colorado with approximately 17,000 students. In 1998 Aims entered the Distance Learning arena offering a Telecommunications Certificate designed by telecommunication industry experts at the request of U.S. West, now Qwest. Soon afterward, employees of many other telecommunication companies such as AT&T began requesting the courses for the purpose of enhancing employee skills. Now students may earn their degree via distance. Aims also entered into an agreement to offer courses to round off military training in biomedical technology. Aims awards college credit to military persons who have completed the military biomedical training and wish to earn an associate degree via Distance through Aims. There are approximately 4,000 distance enrollments at this time.

Alaska Pacific University

4101 University Drive	Phone: (907) 564-8222
Anchorage, AK 97508	Fax: (907) 564-8317

Division(s): RANA (Rural Alaska Native Adult) Program
Web Site(s): http://www.alaskapacific.edu
E-mail: tjohn@alaskapacific.edu

Undergraduate Degree Programs:
Accounting, Business Administration, Education (K–8), Human Services.

Graduate Degree Programs: Business Administration.

Teaching Methods: *Computers:* Internet, real-time chat, e-mail, CD-ROM, newsgroup, LISTSERV. *TV:* videotape, satellite broadcasting. *Other:* videoconferencing, audioconferencing, audiographics, audiotapes, fax, correspondence, independent study, individual study, learning contracts.

Credits Granted for: experiential learning, portfolio assessment, extrainstitutional learning, examination (CLEP, ACT-PEP, DANTES, GRE).

Admission Requirements: *Undergraduate:* RANA application.

On-Campus Requirements: Yes, one week residency at beginning of each semester.

Tuition and Fees: *Undergraduate:* $285/credit. *Credit by:* semester.

Financial Aid: Federal Stafford Loan, Federal PLUS Loan, Federal Pell Grant, Federal Work-Study, VA, Alaska resident programs.

Accreditation: Northwest Association of Schools and Colleges.

Description: Alaska Pacific University (1957) is a private, independent university that promotes the fullest development of its students through liberal arts and professional programs while emphasizing individual attention to students, the development of leadership abilities, and the nurturing of spiritual and moral values consistent with its Christian heritage, while still respecting the religious convictions of all. The university emphasizes personal growth through student-centered, experiential education using Alaska, the Arctic, and the Pacific Rim as laboratories for learning. The university develops and maintains academic excellence by combining the breadth, integrative understanding, and critical thinking of the liberal arts with practical and focused knowledge for professional careers. The Rural Alaska Native Adult Program, implemented in 1998, marks APU's advent into distance learning. RANA is designed to allow rural Alaskans to complete bachelor's degrees in several professional fields without lengthy absences from their home communities.

Albertus Magnus College

700 Prospect Street	Phone: (203) 773-8505
New Haven, CT 06511	Fax: (203) 773-5257

Division(s): Division of Continuing Education
Web Site(s): http://www.albertus.edu/ce
E-mail: ce_info@albertus.edu

Undergraduate Degree Programs:
Associate of Arts
Bachelor of Arts
Bachelor of Science
Bachelor of Fine Arts

Certificate Programs: Management Information Systems, Human Resource Management, Business Administration, The Stewart B. McKinney AIDS Counseling Certificate.

Class Titles: Contact school or check web site.

Teaching Methods: *Computers:* Internet, real-time chat, electronic classroom, e-mail, CD-ROM, newsgroup, LISTSERV.

TV: videotape, cable program, satellite broadcasting, PBS. *Other:* radio broadcast, videoconferencing, audioconferencing, audiographics, audiotapes, fax, correspondence, independent study, individual study, learning contracts.

Credits Granted for: portfolio assessment, examinations (CLEP, ACT-PEP, DANTES, AMC Challenge Exam).

Admission Requirements: *Undergraduate:* high school diploma or its equivalent, application and matriculation. *Certificate:* high school diploma or its equivalent, application and matriculation.

On-Campus Requirements: 40 classroom hours/3-credit course.

Tuition and Fees: *Undergraduate:* $816/3-credit course. *Application Fee:* $30 (one-time fee, nonrefundable). Computer Lab Fee: $50. Degree Completion Fee: $125. *Other Costs:* books (prices will vary). *Credit by:* The Division of Continuing Education has an accelerated format. There are 5 terms per academic year. Each term is 8 weeks in duration. Students who take 2 classes in each of our 5 terms will earn 30 credits in one academic year. Classes are offered at night, on Saturday, and online.

Financial Aid: Federal Stafford Loan, Federal Perkins Loan, Federal Pell Grant, Federal Work-Study, VA, State programs for residents of CT-Federal Supplemental Opportunity Grant, CT College Independent Student Grant (Residential, Minority, Community Service), Albertus Magnus College Scholarships, Direct Bill Contracts with several local employers.

Accreditation: New England Association of Schools and Colleges, Inc.

Description: From its founding in 1925 by the Dominican Sisters of Saint Mary of the Springs, Albertus Magnus College has placed strong emphasis on the liberal arts, preserving the long tradition of scholarly inquiry and the search for truth. The mission of Albertus Magnus College is to produce well-prepared, capable, forward-looking men and women, able to work productively in a career and live enriched and enriching lives. Since 1985 the Division of Continuing Education has helped working adults obtain a degree at an accelerated pace. Classes are small, no more than 25 students, and offered in the evening, on Saturday, and online to accommodate adults' busy schedules. We offer associate and bachelor's degrees in 13 different majors as well as 4 specialized certificate programs. Online courses were introduced into the Division of Continuing Education curriculum January 2001. The overwhelming positive response to these courses will undoubtedly lead to greater frequency and variety of online course offerings in the near future.

Alexandria Technical College

1601 Jefferson Street
Alexandria, MN 56308

Phone: (320) 762-4504
Fax: (320) 762-4501

Division(s): Academic Affairs
Web Site(s): http://www.alextech.org
E-mail: jillk@alx.tec.mn.us

Undergraduate Degree Programs: Contact school.

Certificate Programs: AS/400 Training.

Class Titles: AS/400 Training, Composition I, Multicultural Communication, Technical Writing.

Teaching Methods: *Computers:* Internet, real-time chat, electronic classroom, e-mail, CD-ROM, newsgroup, LISTSERV. *TV:* videotape, fax, correspondence, independent study, individual study, learning contracts.

Credits Granted for: experiential learning, portfolio assessment, examination (CLEP, ACT-PEP, DANTES, GRE).

Admission Requirements: *Undergraduate:* high school-graduate/GED. Open enrollment.

Tuition and Fees: *Undergraduate:* approximately $79/credit (currently awaiting board approval). *Application Fee:* $20. *Other Costs:* book and fee costs vary. *Credit by:* semester.

Financial Aid: Federal Stafford Loan, Federal Perkins Loan, Federal PLUS Loan, Federal Pell Grant, Federal Work-Study, VA, state programs for residents of Minnesota.

Accreditation: The Higher Learning Commission, and a member of the North Central Association of Colleges and Schools.

Description: Alexandria Technical College (1961) has established a solid reputation for quality instruction and service to its students. The college provides more than 40 program areas, has coordinated instructional programs with area high schools, and has an extensive workforce development program. Since the merger of Minnesota State Colleges and Universities in 1995, the college has achieved enrollment growth of more than 15%. The college's largest programs are law enforcement, carpentry, communication art and design, practical nursing, diesel mechanics, and computer technical support specialist. New programs include technical communications, e-commerce business management, e-commerce technical specialist, and wireless communications. The college's focus on technology has made it a leader not only in Minnesota, but nationally. The college has training partnerships with business and industry, including 3M and Caterpillar.

Allan Hancock College

800 S. College
Santa Maria CA 93454

Phone: (805) 922-6966 ext 3320

Division(s): Learning Resources
Web Site(s): http://www.hancock.cc.ca.us

Undergraduate Degree Programs: Contact school.

Certificate Programs: Contact school.

Class Titles: The college offers a wide variety of transfer and vocational courses via Distance Learning, such as classes in English, grammar, sociology; please see web site for full details.

Teaching Methods: *Computers:* Internet, real-time chat, electronic classroom, e-mail, CD-ROM, newsgroup, LISTSERV. *TV:* videotape, cable program, satellite broadcasting, PBS. *Other:* videoconferencing, audiotapes.

Admission Requirements: *Undergraduate:* courses are open to adults over 18. *Certificate:* courses are open to adults over 18.

On-Campus Requirements: varies by course; use web site for details.

Tuition and Fees: *Undergraduate:* $11/credit. *Credit by:* semester.

Financial Aid: Federal Pell Grant, Federal Work-Study, state programs for residents of California.

Accreditation: Western Association of Schools and Colleges.

Description: Allan Hancock College (1920) is an accredited California community college, part of the 107 college state system. The college is situated in the northern part of Santa Barbara County, in a semirural area. The college offers Distance Learning courses via a number of modalities. The list of courses is constantly expanding.

Allegany College of Maryland

12401 Willowbrook Road, SE
Cumberland, MD 21502-2596

Phone: (301) 784-5293

Division(s): Distance Learning
Web Site(s): http://www.ac.cc.md.us
E-mail: gbrooks-broadwater@ac.cc.md.us

Undergraduate Degree Programs:
AA/AS/AAS in:
   General Studies
   Education
   Business Administration

Computer Science
Forest Technology
Nursing
Dental Hygiene
Occupational and Physical Therapy Assistant
Medical Lab Technology
Radiologic Technology
Respiratory Therapy
Therapeutic Massage
Automotive Technology
Communication Arts
Human Services
Office Technologies
Hospitality Management
Culinary Arts
Arts and Science

Certificate Programs: Practical Nursing, Business Management, Office Technology, Computer Science, Travel/Tourism.

Class Titles: Contact school.

Teaching Methods: *Computers:* Internet, real-time chat, *TV:* videotape, cable program, satellite broadcasting, PBS. *Other:* videoconferencing, independent study.

Credits Granted for: experiential learning, portfolio assessment, extrainstitutional learning (PONSI, corporate or professional association seminars/workshops), examination (CLEP, ACT-PEP, DANTES, GRE).

Admission Requirements: *Undergraduate:* open door policy; all students over 16 with proven ability to benefit.

On-Campus Requirements: Students must earn at least 15 credits toward an associate degree on campus in direct classroom experience.

Tuition and Fees: *Undergraduate:* $85/credit for county residents, $167 for state residents, and $186/credit for non-state residents. *Other Costs:* course fees depend on program of choice. *Credit by:* semester.

Financial Aid: Federal Stafford Loan, Federal Perkins Loan, Federal Pell Grant, Federal Work-Study, VA, state programs for residents of Maryland.

Accreditation: Middle States Association of Colleges.

Description: Allegany College of Maryland (1961) is a community college serving about 2,800 credit students and 10,000 noncredit students set in a rural, western end of the state of Maryland.

Alliant International University (formerly California School of Professional Psychology and United States International University)

10455 Pomerado Rd	Phone: (858) 635-4772
San Diego, CA 92131	Fax: (858) 635-4739

Division(s): Department of Education
Web Site(s): http://www.alliant.edu
E-mail: admissions@usiu.edu

Undergraduate Degree Programs: No distance learning at this level.

Graduate Degree Programs: Master of Arts in Technology and Learning (available online).

Postgraduate Degree Programs: No distance learning at this level.

Certificate Programs: No distance learning at this level.

Teaching Methods: *Computers:* Internet, real-time chat, e-mail, on-line discussions, e-college, journals, document sharing. *TV:* None. *Other:* None.

Credits Granted for: experiential learning, portfolio assessment, extra-institutional learning (PONSI, corporate or professional association seminars/workshops), examination (CLEP, ACT-PEP, DANTES, GRE).

Admission Requirements: *Graduate:* Application, $40 application fee, official transcripts from all colleges attended with Bachelor's degree posted, two letters of recommendation, two page personal essay (International Applicants must submit proof of English proficiency and proof of financial support).

On-Campus Requirements: None.

Tuition and Fees: *Graduate:* $295 per credit. *Application Fees:* $40. *Software: Graduation Fee:* $50. *Other Costs:* Distance Learning Fee per class. *Credit by:* quarter.

Financial Aid: Federal Stafford Loan, Federal Work-Study, VA, APLE (Assumption Program of Loans for Education), GAPLE (Graduate Assumption programs of loans for Education), USIU Sibling Tuition Grant, USIU Legacy Grant, BITAP (Business and Industry Tuition Assistance Program) and FWS (Federal Work Study).

Accreditation: WASC (Western Association of Schools and Colleges).

Description: (1952) Founded in 1952, AIU provides a unique and remarkable institution of higher learning. Our concept, experienced by thousands of successful alumni around the globe, is simple: Gather students from diverse cultures at a small university located in beautiful surroundings and challenge them to learn. AIU is a private, independent, nonprofit university located in 60 acres of wooded land in the San Diego suburb of Scripps Ranch. The university also has campuses in Mexico City; Nairobi, Kenya; and six other locations in California.

Alvin Community College

| 3110 Mustang Road | Phone: (281) 756-3728 |
| Alvin, TX 77511 | Fax: (281) 756-3880 |

Division(s): Department of Distance Education
Web Site(s): http://www.alvin.cc.tx.us or http://www.alvin.cc.tx.us/de
E-mail: de@alvin.cc.tx.us

Undergraduate Degree Programs: Contact school.

Certificate Programs: Contact school.

Class Titles: Arts, Biology, Business, Math, Computer Science, Emergency Medical Technician, History, Management, Government, English, Nursing, Office Administration.

Teaching Methods: *Computers:* Internet, real-time chat, electronic classroom, e-mail, newsgroup, Bulletin Boards *TV:* videotape. *Other:* independent study, individual study.

Credits Granted for: class completion extrainstitutional learning (PONSI, corporate or professional association seminars/workshops), examination (CLEP, ACT-PEP, DANTES, GRE).

Admission Requirements: *Undergraduate:* students may be admitted to ACC if they are high school graduates, have passed the GED, or transfer from another college or university. High school students who have completed their junior year may also apply for admission. Call 281/756-3531 or visit a high school counselor for more information. *Certificate:* students may be admitted to ACC if they are high school graduates, have passed the GED, or transfer from another college or university. High school students who have completed their junior year may also apply for admission. Call 281/756-3531 or visit a high school counselor for more information.

On-Campus Requirements: None.

Tuition and Fees: *Undergraduate:* cost depends upon course load and residency status. *Credit by:* semester.

Financial Aid: Federal Stafford Loan, Federal Pell Grant, Federal Work-Study, VA, state programs for residents of Texas.

Accreditation: Southern Association of Colleges and Schools.

Description: Alvin Community College (1948) is a public, 2-year, comprehensive community college located in Alvin, Texas, approximately 50 miles southeast of Houston. Dedicated to promoting the dignity and worth of all individuals, ACC believes that learning is a lifelong process, and that all individuals should have opportunities for lifelong education.

American Academy of Nutrition

| 1204 Kenesaw | Phone: (800) 290-4226 |
| Knoxville, TN 37919 | Fax: (949) 760-1788 |

Other Campus: 3408 Sausalito, Corona Del Mar, CA 92625-1638
Web Site(s): http://www.nutritioneducation.com
E-mail: aantn@aol.com

Undergraduate Degree Programs:
Associate of Science in Applied Nutrition

Certificate Programs: Diploma in Comprehensive Nutrition.

Class Titles: Understanding Nutrition, Environmental Challenges/Solutions, Eating Disorders/Weight Management, Vegetarian Nutrition, Medicinal Herbs/Other Alternative Therapies, Nutrition Counseling Skills, Women's Special Health Concerns, Pregnancy, Pediatric/Adolescent Nutrition, Clinical Nutrition, Sports Nutrition, Community Nutrition, Managing Small Business, Direct Marketing (Selling) Skills, Child Development, Anatomy/Physiology, Human Biology, General Chemistry, Organic/Biochemistry, Psychology, English: Reading Enhancement, Public Speaking, Business Mathematics.

Teaching Methods: *TV:* videotape. *Other:* audioconferencing, audiotapes, fax, correspondence, independent study, individual study.

Credits Granted for: other college courses.

Admission Requirements: *Undergraduate:* age 18, high school graduate or equivalent, 15-month limitation for completion of diploma program, 12-month limitation for completion of each degree segment, 4-month completion for an individual course.

On-Campus Requirements: None.

Tuition and Fees: *Undergraduate:* $99/credit. *Other Costs:* $20/course fee for final exam (proctored).

Financial Aid: DANTES approval, employer paid tuition, group rates.

Accreditation: Distance Education and Training Council.

Description: For more than a decade, the American Academy of Nutrition (1984) has been dedicated to providing students from all walks of life with the most accessible, convenient, and comprehensive nutrition distance education in the world. We offer certificate, diploma, and degree programs that maintain the highest academic standards. Our faculty is comprised of respected nutrition educators providing the learning materials used by highly regarded universities. Our guided curriculum offers traditional and scientifically sound alternative approaches to thinking and nutrition. We are fully committed to helping people help others.

The American College

270 S. Bryn Mawr Avenue	Phone: (888) 263-7265
Bryn Mawr, PA 19010	Fax: (610) 526-1465

Division(s): Academics
Web Site(s): http://www.amercoll.edu
E-mail: studentservices@amercoll.edu

Graduate Degree Programs:
Master of Science in Financial Services.

Certificate Programs: Chartered Life Underwriter, Chartered Financial Consultant, Certified Financial Planner, Registered Health Underwriter, Registered Employee Benefits Consultant, Chartered Leadership Fellow.

Class Titles: Contact school or check web site for details.

Teaching Methods: *Computers:* Internet, e-mail, CD-ROM. *TV:* videotape, satellite broadcasting. *Other:* videoconferencing, audioconferencing, audiotapes, fax, correspondence, independent study, individual study.

Credits Granted for: transfer of credit, extrainstitutional learning (PONSI, corporate or professional association seminars/workshops), (CLEP, ACT-PEP, DANTES, GRE).

Admission Requirements: *Graduate:* bachelor's degree from accredited institution. *Certificate:* 3 years full-time business experience.

On-Campus Requirements: Only for graduate degree (2 one-week residency sessions).

Tuition and Fees: *Graduate:* total program: $9,095, *Other Costs:* Certificate: $300–$395/course.

Accreditation: The Commission on Higher Education of the Middle States Association of Colleges and Universities.

Description: The American College (1927) is the nation's oldest and largest Distance Education learning institution devoted exclusively to financial services education. The American College is accredited by the Commission on Higher Education of the Middle States Association of College and Schools. We offer professional designations, a Master of Science in Financial Services (MSFS) graduate degree, customized certificate programs, and numerous continuing education courses and seminars for those seeking career growth in life insurance and financial services. Our 35-acre, beautifully landscaped campus in suburban Philadelphia houses the Gregg Conference Center, a full-service educational complex, which features conference rooms, an auditorium with state-of-the-art technology, dining facilities, a business center, sophisticated audiovisual capabilities, and 50 overnight guest rooms. Our library, the Vane B. Lucas Memorial Library, is one of the finest resources of financial services information in the country. Our extensive collection contains materials on financial services, estate planning, insurance, taxation, management, pension planning, economics, and aging.

American College of Computer and Information Sciences (ACCIS)

2101 Magnolia Avenue, Suite 200	Phone: (800) 729-2427
Birmingham, AL 35205	Fax: (205) 328-2229

Division(s): ACCIS is a Distance Education College
Web Site(s): http://www.accis.edu/
E-mail: admiss@accis.edu

Undergraduate Degree Programs:
Bachelor of Science in:
    Computer Science
    Information Systems

Graduate Degree Programs:
Master of Science in:
    Computer Science
    Information Systems

Class Titles: All classes listed in the degree programs can be taken individually.

Teaching Methods: *Computers:* Internet, real-time chat, e-mail, CD-ROM, newsgroup, LISTSERV. *Other:* textbooks.

Credits Granted for: Transfer from other accredited colleges, experiential learning, portfolio assessment, examination (CLEP, DANTES).

Admission Requirements: *Undergraduate:* graduation from high school or satisfactory completion of the General Education Development (GED). *Graduate:* a bachelor's degree in computer science or a related discipline is a prerequisite for admission into the MS program.

On-Campus Requirements: None.

Tuition and Fees: *Undergraduate:* $105/credit. *Graduate:* $135/credit. *Application Fee:* $20. *Software:* purchased as needed; also available through Specialty Books. *Other Costs:* textbooks: purchased from Specialty Books. *Credit by:* semester.

Financial Aid: DANTES affiliated, VA Benefits, Sallie Mae, ACCIS finiancing.

Accreditation: Accrediting Commission of the Distance Education and Training Council (DETC) and licensed and approved by the Alabama State Department of Education.

Description: ACCIS (1988) was founded in 1988 as a Distance Learning educator. It is ACCIS' mission to serve the educational needs of students worldwide through the highest quality education in computer and information technology, thus meeting the global needs of industry, business, education, and government for highly skilled technical employees with the ability to think critically and solve problems creatively. As a Distance Learning college, ACCIS strives to be a student-centered community that responds to the intellectual, professional, and personal goals of individual students by offering self-paced programs that enable students to maintain their personal and professional responsibilities while pursuing a degree. ACCIS accomplishes its mission through active interaction among students and between students and their professors; through a strong curricula focused on applying the technical knowledge gained; by recognizing the interconnected global community in which we live; and by passing on the lower tuition costs inherent in Distance Education.

American College of Prehospital Medicine

7552 Navarre Parkway, Suite 1	Phone: (806) 939-0840
Navarre, FL 32566-7312	Fax: (806) 939-7713

Division(s): All
Web Site(s): http://www.acpm.edu
http://www.richardson.edu
E-mail: support@acpm.edu

Undergraduate Degree Programs:
Associate of Science in Emergency Medical Services
Bachelor of Science in Emergency Medical Services

Certificate Programs: Emergency Medical Technology; Effective Supervision.

Teaching Methods: *Computers:* Internet, electronic classroom, e-mail, CD-ROM, LISTSERV. *TV:* videotape. *Other:* audiotapes, fax, correspondence, independent study, individual study.

Credits Granted for: experiential learning, portfolio assessment, extrainstitutional learning, examination (PONSI, cor-

porate, or professional association seminars/workshops), (CLEP, ACT-PEP, DANTES, GRE).

Admission Requirements: *Undergraduate:* high school graduate, completion of EMT-Basic certification or military equivalent, RN or PA. *Certificate:* age 18, high school graduate.

On-Campus Requirements: The Certificate Course in Emergency Medical Technology requires 32 hours minimum of local seminar work for psychomotor skills and 10 hours of clinical exposure that will also be arranged by the Instructor/Coordinator appointed by the college.

Tuition and Fees: *Undergraduate:* $250/semester hour for single course enrollment, flat tuition for the 2 degree programs: $5,200 for the Associate of Science in Emergency Medical Services, $6,800 for the Bachelor of Science in Emergency Medical Services (we finance these amounts internally at 12% APR). *Application Fee:* $50. *Software:* $47.50. *Other Costs:* Students are required to have a CD-ROM equipped and Internet capable computer. Can be purchased locally or ACPM will refer them to the corporate sales department of PC Connection. Students who mail work to the college will incur postage expenses. No costs for telephone as all faculty have toll-free access for U.S./U.S.-possession students. No other costs. Tuition includes all course materials, books, software, videotapes, audiotapes, etc. *Credit by:* semester.

Financial Aid: VA, DANTES, military tuition assistance, Military TA Top-up program.

Accreditation: Distance Education and Training Council.

Description: ACPM (1991) was founded to provide a means for civilian and military emergency care providers to complete their undergraduate education.

American Graduate University

733 North Dodsworth Avenue	Phone: (626) 966-4576
Covina, CA 91724	Fax: (626) 915-1709

Division(s): Student Services
Web Site(s): http://www.agu.edu
Info@agu.edu

Graduate Degree Programs:
Master of Project Management
Master of Acquisition Management

Certificate Programs: Project/Program Management, Acquisition and Contracting, Financial Management and Pricing, Management.

Class Titles: Program Management, Government Program Management, Project Management, Technical Program

Management, Earned Value Management Systems, Contracting/Procurement for Project Managers/Technical Personnel, Project Scheduling Techniques, Risk Analysis/ Management, Building/Managing Project Teams, Marketing/ Pricing/Management of Government Contracts/Subcontracts, Pricing/Negotiation of Government Contracts/Subcontracts, Contract Management/Administration, Subcontract Management/Advanced Procurement Techniques, Government Contract Law, Price/Cost Analysis, Negotiation Principles/Practices, Government Contracting, Financial Management of Government Contracts, Essentials of Management, Law/Contracts, Business Research Methods, Management Accounting/Control, Organizational Behavior/ Human Resources, Financial Management, Management Economics.

Teaching Methods: *Computers:* e-mail. *Other:* correspondence, fax, live instruction.

Credits Granted for: transfer credits.

Admission Requirements: *Graduate:* accredited undergraduate degree, employed in subject area field. No requirements to take individual courses. *Certificate:* high school graduate, employed in subject area field.

On-Campus Requirements: None.

Tuition and Fees: *Graduate:* $550–$650/distance education course, $995–$1295/course for 3-day, 4-day, or 5-day live courses (12 courses in master's degree programs, 6 courses in professional certificate programs). *Credit by:* equivalent to semester; enrollment and completion take place continuously throughout the year.

Financial Aid: VA, DANTES.

Accreditation: Distance Education and Training Council.

Description: American Graduate University (1958) and its affiliate, Procurement Associates, Inc., have been developing and conducting public and distance education courses in all aspects of program/project management, contracts/ procurement, and business management. AGU's distance education courses, offered since 1969, have attracted 100,000 industry and government representatives worldwide. AGU presently offers Master of Project Management and Master of Acquisition Management degree programs; professional certificate programs in project/program management, acquisition and contracts management, financial management, and business management; and individual professional development. The university is accredited and has full institutional approval from the California Bureau for Private Postsecondary and Vocational Education to grant its degrees.

American Health Information Management Association

233 N. Michigan Avenue, Suite 2150	Phone: (312) 233-1106
Chicago, IL 60601-5519	Fax: (312) 233-1406

Division(s): Continuing Education and Training
Web Site(s): http://www.ahimacampus.org
E-mail: lana.vukovljak@ahima.org

Undergraduate Degree Programs: contact school.

Class Titles: Coding Assessment and Training Solutions (20 courses), Coding Basics Program (12 courses), Ambulatory Payment Classification (3 courses), How to Achieve HIPAA Compliance, Privacy Training Program (4 courses), Health Information Systems: Beyond the Basics (4 courses), National Convention Educational webcasts (7), Archived Interment Seminars (20).

Teaching Methods: *Computers:* Internet, real-time chat, electronic classroom, e-mail. *Other:* audioconferencing, audiotapes, fax, correspondence, independent study, individual study.

Credits Granted for: Continuing Education credit hours—CEs

Admission Requirements: *Undergraduate:* please contact school.

On-Campus Requirements: None.

Tuition and Fees: *Undergraduate:* please contact school. *Credit by:* 8–15 weeks.

Financial Aid: Federal Stafford Loan, Federal Perkins Loan, Federal PLUS Loan, Federal Pell Grant, Federal Work-Study, VA, state programs for residents of Illinois.

Accreditation: ACE, DETC, Illinois State Board of Education.

Description: The American Health Information Management Association (AHIMA) (1999) is a nonprofit professional association that represents more than 40,000 specially educated health information management professionals who work throughout the healthcare industry. As the membership organization, the American Health Information Management Association fosters the professional development of its members through education, certification, and lifelong learning, thereby promoting quality information to benefit the public, the healthcare consumer, providers, and other users of clinical data. AHIMA has as one of its goals the continual improvement of training services offered to its members. To that end, its Continuing Education and Training Department has developed a number of Internet training and communications initiatives over the past several years.

American Health Science University

1010 South Joliet, #107
Aurora, CO 80012

Phone: (800) 530-8079
Fax: (303) 367-2577

Division(s): None.
Web Site(s): http://www.ahsu.com
E-mail: cn@ahsu.edu; masters@ahsu.edu

Graduate Degree Programs: Master of Science in Nutritional Science.

Certificate Programs: Certified Nutritionist (CN).

Teaching Methods: *Computers:* e-mail. *Other:* fax, correspondence, independent study, individual study.

Credits Granted for: experiential learning, examination.

Admission Requirements: *Undergraduate:* Bachelor's degree from an accredited college or university recognized by the U.S. Department of Education with a cumulative GPA of 2.5 (on a 4.0 scale) and a grade of C or better in all required courses. Three semester hours of Anatomy and Physiology and three semester hours of Normal Nutrition. Basic computer proficiency and access to an Internet-ready computer. *Certificate:* Bachelor's degree or equivalent work experience.

On-Campus Requirements: None.

Tuition and Fees: *Graduate:* $450/credit. *Certificate:* $235/credit. *Application Fee:* $100. *Other Costs:* $5 per course for shipping of course materials; $30 administrative fee per course; $250 for Comprehensive Certification Exam (required for all students enrolled in the Certified Nutritionist program). *Credit by:* semester.

Accreditation: Distance Education and Training Council. Courses validated by the American Council on Education.

Description: American Health Science University was founded in 1980 to enable individuals to pursue high-quality education in the field of nutrition from the comfort of their own homes. The accredited Certified Nutritionist and Master's degree programs are designed for individuals interested in profitably meeting the needs of a new kind of health care consumer who is asking questions about nutrition, nutritional supplements, herbs, and diets, and who has other lifestyle concerns.

American Institute of Applied Science, Inc.

100 Hunter Place
Youngsville, NC 27596-0639

Phone: (919) 554-2500 or (800) 354-5134
Fax: (919) 556-6784

Division(s): Forensic Science
Web Site(s): http://www.aiasinc.com
E-mail: aias@mindspring.com

Diploma Programs:
Basic Forensic Science
Advanced Forensic Science

Class Titles: Fingerprint Classification and Identification, Modus Operandi, Criminal Investigation, Firearms Identification, Questioned Documents, Police Photography, several courses in crime scene processing, such as Trace Evidence, Drugs and Alcohol.

Teaching Methods: *Computers:* e-mail. *Other:* fax, correspondence, independent study, individual study.

Admission Requirements: *Certificate and Diploma:* High school diploma or GED only.

On-Campus Requirements: None.

Tuition and Fees: varies from $60 to $1,021 depending on course/program. *Credit by:* study hours—230 hours/per program.

Financial Aid: VA, DANTES, our own interest-free payment plans.

Accreditation: Accrediting Commission of the Distance Education and Training Council and the North Carolina Community College System (licensed by).

Description: The American Institute of Applied Science (1916) is internationally recognized for its comprehensive training of professionals in the field of forensic identification and investigation. The American Institute of Applied Science developed the home-study correspondence course expressly for students who work full time or are active in other full-time educational programs. Students have the opportunity to learn at their own pace, without strict deadlines. The courses offered are designed to teach, in an accessible format, the complexities of forensics to students who are new to the subject, or to experienced investigators who are interested in using the information to complement their on-the-job experiences. Consequently, more than 200,000 men and women have achieved a high degree of professional experience and personal achievement as a result of their graduation from the American Institute of Applied Science, which is the best correspondence course of its kind. Thousands of AIAS graduates are law enforcement professionals who hold important positions in the field of criminal identification and forensic science. And nearly 350 law enforcement agencies throughout the world accept or require this program for positions in identification bureaus and crime labs.

American Military University

9104-P Manassas Drive
Manassas Park, VA 20111

Phone: (703) 330-5398
Fax: (703) 330-5109

Division(s): Academic Department
Web Site(s): http://www.amunet.edu
E-mail: info@amunet.edu

Undergraduate Degree Programs:
Associate of Arts in General Studies
Bachelor of Arts in:
  American Military History
  World Military History
  Intelligence Studies
  Management
  Military Management
  Marketing
  Criminal Justice
  International Relations
  Interdisciplinary Studies

Graduate Degree Programs:
Master of Arts in:
  Military Studies
    Major in American Revolution Studies
    Major in Civil War Studies
    Major in Land Warfare
    Major in Air Warfare
    Major in Naval Warfare
    Major in Intelligence
    Major in Unconventional Warfare
    Major in Defense Management
  Management
  Transportation Management
  Criminal Justice
  National Security Studies

Certificate Programs: *Undergraduate:* Career Counseling, Corrections Management, Health Administration, Homeland Security, Human Resources, Information Technology Management, Security Management, United Nations. *Graduate:* Air Warfare, American Military History, American Revolution Studies, Ancient Military History, Civil War Studies, Coalition and Combined Arms Warfare, Homeland Security, Intelligence Studies, Land Warfare, Logistics Management, Military Leadership, Military Operations other than War, Military Philosophy and Strategy, Military Studies, Naval Warfare, Organizational Management, Peacekeeping Studies, Program and Acquisition Management, Regional Studies, Terrorism Studies, Unconventional Warfare, World War II Studies.

Class Titles: All classes may be taken individually.

Teaching Methods: *Computers:* Internet, real-time chat, electronic classroom, e-mail, newsgroup, LISTSERV. *Other:* independent study.

Credits Granted for: experiential learning, portfolio assessment, extrainstitutional learning, (PONSI, ACE), examination (CLEP, DANTES).

Admission Requirements: *Undergraduate:* high school diploma/GED, age 18, 10 years to complete program, must have Internet access. *Graduate:* accredited bachelor's degree, 7 years to complete program. *Undergraduate:* high school diploma or GED, must have Internet access. *Graduate:* must have bachelor's degree, must have Internet access.

On-Campus Requirements: None.

Tuition and Fees: *Undergraduate:* $250/credit. *Graduate:* $250/credit. *Graduation Fee:* $100. *Credit by:* semester.

Financial Aid: VA, Military Assistance, Undergraduate, Merit Scholarships, Undergraduate Book Grants.

Accreditation: Accrediting Commission of the Distance Education and Training Council.

Description: American Military University is an independent, nationally accredited private institution that offers its programs exclusively through distance education using state-of-the-art electronic classrooms to deliver its courses. The university's mission is to promote the development and application of knowledge, the acquisition of problem-solving skills, and the maturation of intellect and character. The AMU distance education model features mentored study that arises from a personal, one-on-one relationship between student and faculty. AMU started offering distance education courses in 1993 and now offers over 600 courses taught by a faculty of 175 members. The current student body numbers approximately 3,600 students and over 400 students have received their degrees through distance education.

American River College

4700 College Oak Drive
Sacramento, CA 95841

Phone: (916) 484-8456
Fax: (916) 484-8018

Division(s): Learning Resources
Web Site(s): http://www.arc.losrios.cc.ca.us/learnres/distance.html (credit) http://www.ed2go.com/arc (noncredit)
E-mail: ondricd@arc.losrios.cc.ca.us (credit), whitakn@arc.losrios.cc.ca.us (noncredit)

Class Titles: *Credit:* Biology, Business, Computer Information Science, English, Gerontology, Health Education,

Interdisciplinary Studies, Library, Management, Marketing, Sociology. *Noncredit:* Business, Internet courses, Computer courses, Personal Enrichment courses, Small-Business courses, Large-Business/Management courses, Nursing courses.

Teaching Methods: *Computers:* Internet, real-time chat, threaded discussion, e-mail, CD-ROM, LISTSERV. *TV:* videotape, cable program.

Credits Granted for: CLEP, DANTES.

Admission Requirements: *Undergraduate:* some Distance Education courses have prerequisites. Some courses require e-mail access, a computer, and necessary software. Noncredit courses have no residency requirements.

On-Campus Requirements: Telecourses require viewing of cable programs on local cable channels; courses have some required on-campus meetings. Telecourses meet on campus approximately 5 times during the semester for testing and lectures. Online courses require one on-campus orientation each semester. Web-assisted courses meet both online and on campus each week during the semester. Noncredit courses have no on-campus requirements. Contact American River College for further information.

Tuition and Fees: *Undergraduate:* $11/credit for California residents. Noncredit education classes costs range from $60 to $125. *Other Costs:* textbook costs may be required. *Credit by:* semester.

Financial Aid: Federal Stafford Loan, Federal Pell Grant, Federal Work-Study, Federal Supplemental Educational Opportunity Grant, VA, California resident programs, institutional scholarships. No financial aid available for noncredit classes.

Accreditation: Western Association of Schools and Colleges.

Description: American River College (ARC) (1955) is a public community college, offering instructional and support services and special programs during the day, evening, and weekends on campus and at a growing number of locations in the community. The college awards Associate in Arts or Science degrees, occupational certificates, and transfer credit to students who wish to continue their education at a 4-year college or university. ARC is among the 10 largest community colleges in the state and is looked upon as a leader in innovative programs and services. It transfers more students to UC Davis and CSU Sacramento than any other community college. ARC offers 4 types of Distance Education courses: courses by television, online courses, teleweb courses (using a combination of TV and online instruction), and web-assisted courses (requiring both on-campus and online meetings each week of class).

Andrew Jackson University

10 Old Montgomery Highway
Birmingham, AL 35209

Phone: (800) 429-9300
(205) 871-9288
Fax: (205) 871-9294

Division(s): Distance Learning
Web Site(s): http://www.aju.edu
E-mail: info@aju.edu

Undergraduate Degree Programs:
Bachelor of Arts in Communication
Bachelor of Science in Business
Bachelor of Science in Criminal Justice

Graduate Degree Programs:
Master of Business Administration
Master of Public Administration
Master of Science in Criminal Justice

Teaching Methods: *Computers:* e-mail, software, CD-ROM. *TV:* videotape. *Other:* audiotapes, fax, correspondence, independent study, individual study.

Credits Granted for: experiential learning, portfolio assessment, extrainstitutional learning, examination (CLEP, ACT-PEP, DANTES).

Admission Requirements: *Undergraduate:* high school diploma or equivalent. *Graduate:* accredited bachelor's degree.

On-Campus Requirements: None.

Tuition and Fees: *Undergraduate:* $3,350/30-credit module (equivalent of 2 semesters) includes $150 enrollment fee. *Graduate:* $4,950/entire 36-credit program includes $150 enrollment fee. *Application Fee:* $75 (applicable to enrollment fee). *Software:* optional for some courses. *Other Costs:* $850–$1,350 textbooks, $100 graduation fee. *Credit by:* semester.

Financial Aid: interest-free tuition payment plan, PLATO loans, VA, DANTES.

Accreditation: Distance Education and Training Council.

Description: Andrew Jackson University's (1994) degree programs are designed for those whose circumstances demand flexible study. Courses are available only through off-campus, directed learning. Students may enroll and begin their program at any time and proceed as quickly as their desire, time, and ability permit. Degree programs are textbook-based, and study guides include learning objectives, assignment description, and detailed instructions. Some course materials also include audiotapes or videotapes and software or CD-ROM exercises. Each lesson is submitted as completed to allow for frequent faculty feedback. Midterm and final exams are proctored.

Berrien Springs, MI 49104

Phone: (800) 471-6210
Fax: (616) 471-6236/6374

Division(s): A.U./H.S.I., undergraduate correspondence course, School of Education, Office of Instructional Support, graduate

Web Site(s): http://www.educ.andrews.edu/DLC
E-mail: graves@andrews.edu (undergraduate)
sedde@andrews.edu (Education, graduate)

Undergraduate Degree Programs:
Associate of Arts in General Studies, Personal Ministry emphasis
Bachelor of Arts in:
   Religion
   General Studies, Humanities emphasis
Bachelor of Science in General Studies:
   Cross-Cultural Relations emphasis
   Human Organization and Behavior emphasis

Graduate Degree Programs:
variable; contact school.

Class Titles: 50 courses in areas of: Behavioral Science, Psychology, Sociology, Communication, Composition, American Literature, Cultural Geography, World Civilization, American History, Church History, American Government, College Algebra, Statistics, Enjoyment of Music, Nutrition, Astronomy, Greek, Biblical Studies, Religion. Graduate titles: Managing Behavior in Diverse Classroom, Technology/Learning in Today's Classroom, Helping Students Become Self-Directed Learners, Learning Differences: Effective Teaching with Learning Styles/Multiple Intelligence, Building Your Repertoire of Teaching Strategies, Including Students with Special Needs in Regular Classroom, Motivating Today's Learner, Teaching Students to Get Along, Strategies for Preventing Conflict/Violence, Succeeding with Difficult Students, High-Performing Teacher, How to Get Parents on Your Side, Assertive Discipline/Beyond, Assessment to Improve Student Learning. General Studies/H.S.I. (undergraduate). *Graduate Courses:* Teacher Continuing Education and Recertification (Canter Correspondence and Online), Educational Administration and Leadership.

Teaching Methods: *TV:* videotape, satellite broadcast. *Other:* correspondence.

Credits Granted for: experiential learning, portfolio assessment, extrainstitutional learning, examination (CLEP, ACT-PEP, DANTES, GRE).

Admission Requirements: *Undergraduate:* official documentation of completion of secondary school studies with a minimum of 13 units of solid subjects. Minimum GPA and college-bound percentile on ACT/SAT of (a) 2.75 overall GPA (b) or 2.5 overall GPA and 35th percentile on ACT/SAT (c) or 2.25 overall GPA and 50th percentile on ACT/SAT. A GED certification with a minimum average score of 60 on 5 sections and no section lower than 50 will also meet minimum admission requirements. *Graduate:* Students complete the admissions forms for Andrews University and are processed as Permission to Take Classes students. Students are encouraged to have a study partner or partners or participate in the course activities. The regular standards for admission do not apply to PTC students at Andrews University on the main campus, extension campuses, or distance learning settings. If students subsequently wish to enroll in the university for degree programs, they are processed through regular admission channels and standards with a maximum of 32 credits PTC transferrable to a degree.

On-Campus Requirements: None.

Tuition and Fees: *Undergraduate:* $165/credit. *Graduate:* $350/course. Discounts offered for 2 or more registering for same course together. Call to verify current/discounted rates. *Application Fee:* $30, degree-seeking student. *Other Costs:* extra for shipping/handling of textbooks and study guides, $60 enrollment processing fee (one or more classes). *Credit by:* quarter basis: courses offered on semester basis but converted to quarter credits before they are transcripted. Most courses are 3 semester hours (4.5 quarter credits); 5 quarter credits (equal to 3.3 semester hours) per course.

Financial Aid: Students must be accepted into a degree-seeking program at Andrews University and be attending at least half-time. Eligibility is determined through the standard FAFSA process. Students must adhere to the same academic calendar as on-campus students. If students are Michigan residents and meet other eligibility requirements, state funding is available.

Accreditation: North Central Association of Colleges and Schools, National Council for Accreditation of Teacher Education.

Description: Andrews University (1874) is a Christian university in the Seventh-Day Adventist tradition. It was first established in 1874 in Battle Creek, Michigan as Battle Creek College. Andrews University is comprised of the College of Arts and Sciences, the College of Technology, the School of Business, the School of Education, the Seventh-Day Adventist Theological Seminary, and the Division of Architecture. Course and degree offerings through the undergraduate distance education program are primarily offered through College of Arts and Sciences. The university offers more than 180 education programs on campus with a general education component rooted in the strong liberal arts tradition. The undergraduate distance education program at Andrews University functions in partnership with Home Study

International, a distinguished and accredited distance education delivery institution since 1909. Our partnership is new, having established the AU/HSI Distance Education program in 1997. The graduate distance education program is housed in the School of Education and was established in 1989.

Angelina College

PO Box 1768	Phone: (409) 639-1301
Lufkin, TX 75902-1768	Fax: (409) 639-4299

Division(s): Registration
Web Site(s): http://angelina.cc.tx.us
E-mail: jcutting@angelina.cc.tx.us

Undergraduate Degree Programs:
Associate of Science in many areas
Associate of Arts in many areas
Associate of Applied Science in many areas

Certificate Programs: Business, some vocational programs.

Class Titles: Psychology, Sociology, Government, History.

Teaching Methods: *TV:* videotape, satellite broadcasting. *Other:* Off-site classrooms.

Credits Granted for: examination (CLEP, ACT-PEP, DANTES).

Admission Requirements: *Undergraduate:* application, transcripts, TASP test results.

On-Campus Requirements: None.

Tuition and Fees: *Undergraduate:* $19/credit in-district, $25/credit out-of-district, $30/credit out-of-state. *Other Costs:* $66 in fees. *Credit by:* semester.

Financial Aid: Federal Pell Grant, Federal Work-Study, VA.

Accreditation: Southern Association of Colleges and Schools.

Description: Angelina College opened the doors of its original 7 buildings to students in the fall of 1968. Distance learning programs began around 1993, allowing students to study off-campus. Credits earned at Angelina may be transferred to senior colleges throughout the nation.

Anne Arundel Community College

101 College Parkway	Phone: (777) 541-2464
Arnold, MD 21012	Fax: (777) 541-2691

Division(s): Distance Learning Center
Web Site(s): http://web.aacc.cc.md.us/diseduc
E-mail: pmmccarthyoneill@mail.aacc.cc.md.us

Undergraduate Degree Programs:
Associate of Science in Business Administration Transfer
Associate of Applied Science in Business Management
Associate of Arts in General Studies Transfer
Associate of Applied Science in Computer Information Systems Personal Computer Systems Technology Option

Certificate Programs: The following certificates can be earned entirely through Weekend College or a Combination of Weekend College and Distance Learning: Business Management (Concentration in Communications or Small Business), Computer Information Systems Personal Computer Specialist Option, Medical Assisting.

Teaching Methods: *Computers:* Internet, real-time chat, electronic classroom, e-mail, CD-ROM, LISTSERV. *TV:* videotape, cable program, PBS. *Other:* videoconferencing, fax, independent study.

Credits Granted for: examination (CLEP, DANTES).

Admission Requirements: *Undergraduate:* academic credentials, SAT, ACT, AACC assessment tests and/or equivalent college courses.

On-Campus Requirements: None.

Tuition and Fees: *Undergraduate:* $60/credit. *Other Costs:* $35/telecourse; telecourse tape rental $33.50. *Graduation Fee:* $20. $20 registration fee. *Credit by:* semester.

Financial Aid: Federal Stafford Loan, Federal PLUS Loan, Federal Pell Grant, Federal Work-Study, VA, Maryland resident programs.

Accreditation: Middle States Association of Colleges and Schools.

Description: Anne Arundel Community College began in 1961 with teaching as its central mission. It is an accredited, public, open-admission institution of higher learning located in the Washington-Baltimore-Annapolis triangle. In 2000, 50,474 credit and noncredit students were enrolled in more than 2,000 credit and noncredit courses on the centrally located 230-acre campus, at two off-campus centers, or other county locations. The distance learning program began in 1981 with telecourses. Its original charge was to serve students unable to attend traditional classroom courses because of scheduling conflicts, lack of transportation, home responsibilities, etc. In February 1995 the Going the Distance Agreement was signed, committing the college to develop degree and program completion pathways for its distance learning students. Currently, the distance learning program offers telecourses, on-line courses, and interactive courses.

Antelope Valley College

3041 West Avenue K
Lancaster, CA 93536-5426

Phone: (661) 722-6304
Fax: (661) 943-5573

Division(s): Academic Affairs
Web Site(s): http://www.avc.edu
E-mail: dredmayne@avc.edu

Undergraduate Degree Programs:
Associate in Arts
Associate in Science

Certificate Programs: 49 certificate programs.

Class Titles: Contact the school or check web site for details.

Teaching Methods: *Computers:* Internet, e-mail. *TV:* video-tape, PBS.

Credits Granted for: examination (CLEP).

Admission Requirements: Contact school.

Tuition and Fees: *Undergraduate:* $11/credit for California residents; $145/credit for non-California residents. *Credit by:* semester.

Financial Aid: Federal Stafford Loan, Federal Perkins Loan, Federal PLUS Loan, Federal Pell Grant, Federal Work-Study, VA, state programs for residents of California.

Accreditation: Western Association of Schools and Colleges.

Description: Antelope Valley College (1929) is a comprehensive community college serving the needs of people for more than 70 years. The college offers programs for students planning to transfer to 4-year universities, as well as those seeking entry-level job skills in technical areas. Antelope Valley College boasts small class sizes with the ability of students to have easy access to faculty members. Approximately 11,000 students are enrolled during the fall and spring semesters. Students can also enroll in courses during the summer term or winter intersession. Courses are offered days, evenings, and weekends. A full range of support services is provided including financial aid, counseling, career center, job placement, disabled student services, tutoring, and more. The college entered the Distance Learning field with television courses more than a decade ago. It has since expanded to courses on the Internet.

Antioch University McGregor

800 Livermore Street
Yellow Springs, OH 45387

Phone: (937) 769-1818
Fax: (937) 769-1805

Division(s): Individualized Master of Arts program
Web Site(s): http://www.mcgregor.edu
E-mail: rpaige@mcgregor.edu

Graduate Degree Programs:
Master of Arts

Certificate Programs: Graduate Certificate in Conflict Resolution, Graduate Certificate in the Constructive Engagement of Environmental Conflict.

Class Titles: Conflict Resolution—Management, Community College Specialization, Communication, Counseling Psychology, Community Development, Creative Writing, Education, Gender Studies, Humanities, Intercultural Studies, Liberal Studies, Literature, Management, Psychology, Studio Art, Theater or Performing Arts (individualized degree).

Teaching Methods: *Computers:* Internet, real-time chat, e-mail, LISTSERV. *Other:* fax, correspondence, independent study, individual study, learning contracts.

Credits Granted for: experiential learning, portfolio assessment.

Admission Requirements: *Graduate:* accredited bachelor's degree, letters of reference, clear sense of educational direction, ability to handle demands of a limited residency program *Certificate:* accredited bachelor's degree.

On-Campus Requirements: Two short-term sessions once or twice per year, depending on field of study.

Tuition and Fees: *Graduate:* $2,678/quarter: Conflict Resolution; $3,414/quarter: Management, Community College Specialization. *Application Fee:* $50. *Other Costs Graduation Fee:* $60, $75/quarter technology fee. *Credit by:* quarter.

Financial Aid: Federal Stafford Loan, Federal Work-Study.

Accreditation: North Central Association of Colleges and Schools.

Description: Antioch University McGregor, established in 1988, offers adults who are interested in furthering their education a diverse range of graduate, undergraduate, certificate, and continuing education programs that are responsive to emerging societal needs. Each program encourages critical thinking, provides opportunities for collaborative learning, emphasizes cultural diversity and an international perspective, and promotes the integration of life and work experience with academic knowledge. McGregor's approach to education stems from Antioch University's historical emphasis on intellectual, emotional, and ethical development and from its commitment to social justice. Distance education Master of Arts degrees are offered in conflict resolution; management, community college specialization; and a variety of individualized liberal and professional studies.

Arcadia University

| 450 South Easton Road | Phone: (888) 232-8373 |
| Glenside, PA 19038-3295 | Fax: (215) 572-4049 |

Division(s): Continuing Education
Web Site(s): http://www.arcadia.edu
E-mail: admiss@arcadia.edu
Arcadia University does not offer any degree programs in a distance learning format. However we do offer courses during the summer and occasionally during the academic year that utilize distance learning technologies (video courses, online courses, videoconferencing) for either entire courses or parts of courses. Courses that contain distance learning elements, either entirely or partially, are so indicated on our course selection materials.

Class Titles:
Online: Research Methods (Psychology)
Partially online: Introduction to Communications (Communications)
Video: Science Fiction Cinema (Communications)
   American Cinema (English)
   Interpreting Literature (English)
   Popular Cinema in the 1990s (Communications)

Teaching Methods: *Computers:* Internet, real-time chat, electronic classroom, e-mail, CD-ROM, newsgroup, LISTSERV. *TV:* videotape, cable program, PBS. *Other:* videoconferencing, audioconferencing, fax, correspondence, independent study, individual study, learning contracts.

Credits Granted for: experiential learning, extrainstitutional learning, examination (CLEP, ACT-PEP, DANTES, GRE).

Admission Requirements: *Undergraduate:* high school transcript, college transcript, recommendations. *Graduate:* undergraduate college transcript, recommendations, GRE. *Doctoral:* same. *Certificate:* official transcripts.

On-Campus Requirements: None.

Tuition and Fees: *Undergraduate:* $340/credit. *Graduate:* $420/credit. *Application Fee:* $30. *Credit by:* semester.

Financial Aid: Federal Stafford Loan, Federal Perkins Loan, Federal PLUS Loan, Federal Pell Grant, Federal Work-Study, VA, Pennsylvania resident programs.

Accreditation: Middle States Association of Colleges and Schools.

Description: Arcadia University, a small, comprehensive college, offers a wide array of liberal arts and professional programs in a personalized setting. Building on 143 years of academic achievement, this coeducational, independent institution is committed to forging a synthesis of liberal education and career preparation in its undergraduate programs. Recognizing the pluralism of our nation and the increasing internationalism in business and other institutions, the college also is committed to expanding students' horizons, and preparing them to prosper in a world of cultural diversity. Students may pursue undergraduate study at Arcadia University on a full-time or part-time basis; day, evening or weekend; for credit or not for credit. The college offers high quality, undergraduate degree programs in more than 30 fields of study, as well as graduate degrees and certificates of advanced study. History: Founded in Beaver, Pennsylvania, as Beaver College, Arcadia University was one of the country's first institutions to provide women with an education equivalent to that offered men in private schools. In 1972, the school became coeducational. Originally under the auspices of the Methodist Episcopal Church, Arcadia University is now one of the church-related colleges of the Presbyterian Church (USA), but it is independently controlled and ecumenical in spirit. In 1925, with the purchase of the property owned by the Beechwood School in suburban Philadelphia, the school moved to Jenkintown. In 1928, it acquired the former country estate of William Welsh Harrison in Glenside. After operating on 2 campuses for many years, the school consolidated all its activities in Glenside in 1962. The Arcadia University campus today takes its special character from the original buildings of the estate in a naturally beautiful setting. Above its wooded slopes and open, rolling lawns rise the massive towers of Grey Towers Castle, inspired by the famous Alnwick Castle in England. Winding, tree-lined drives lead to the smaller stone buildings of the original estate, now converted into classrooms and studios which preserve the old-world charm.

Arizona State University

| PO Box 870501 | Phone: (602) 965-6738 |
| Tempe, AZ 85287-0501 | Fax: (602) 965-1371 |

Division(s): Distance Learning Technology
Web Site(s): http://www.dlt.asu.edu
http://asuonline.asu.edu (Internet courses)
E-mail: distance@asu.edu

Graduate Degree Programs:
Master of Science in Engineering, Electrical Engineering major (available in metro Phoenix area over TV)

Class Titles: Change each semester.

Teaching Methods: *Computers:* Internet, real-time chat, electronic classroom, e-mail, CD-ROM, newsgroup, LISTSERV. *TV:* videotape, cable program, satellite broadcasting, PBS. *Other:* videoconferencing, audioconferencing, audiographics, audiotapes, fax, correspondence, independent study.

Credits Granted for: examination (CLEP, ACT-PEP, DANTES, GRE).

Admission Requirements: *Undergraduate:* high school graduate and/or sufficient ACT/SAT scores. *Graduate:* application to Graduate Admissions Office; visit http://www.asu.edu. *Certificate:* variable.

On-Campus Requirements: Students must complete 30 hours (may be at a distance) through ASU.

Tuition and Fees: *Undergraduate:* $125; other tuition/fees may apply. *Graduate:* $126; other tuition/fees may apply. *Application Fee:* $40 nonresident undergraduate, nonrefundable; $15 nondegree graduate, nonrefundable. *Other Costs:* $35 graduation application fee, $10 nondegree studies. *Credit by:* semester.

Financial Aid: Federal Stafford Loan, Federal Perkins Loan, Federal PLUS Loan, Federal Pell Grant, Federal Work-Study, VA, Arizona resident programs.

Accreditation: North Central Association of Colleges and Schools.

Description: Arizona State University (1885) began offering classes at a distance in 1935 with the introduction of correspondence study. In 1955, ASU offered the first telecourse in Arizona over a local TV station. In 1982 the Arizona Board of Regents adopted guidelines for developing educational telecommunications systems. In the fall of 1982, the Instructional Television Fixed Service (ITFS) system began sending engineering and business courses to corporate sites in Phoenix. The ITFS system also connects to various educational access channels, allowing students to receive some live interactive courses in their homes. Shortly after National Technological University (NTU) began in 1988, ASU contributed courses via satellite. The university also uses NAUNet, a microwave network connecting the 3 state universities. For several years ASU has offered CD-ROM courses and, since the spring of 1996, has offered courses via the Internet.

Art Instruction Schools

3309 Broadway Street NE	Phone: (612) 362-5075
Minneapolis, MN 55413	Fax: (612) 362-5260

Division(s): Art Education
Web Site(s): www.artists-ais.com
E-mail: info@artists-ais.com

Certificate Programs: Fundamentals of Art.

Teaching Methods: *Other:* correspondence, independent study, individual study, telephone, homeschool.

Credits Granted for: portfolio assessment for advanced college placement.

Admission Requirements: *Certificate:* review of personal artwork competence, 2-year completion limit.

On-Campus Requirements: None.

Tuition and Fees: *Undergraduate:* $2,285/28 lessons included in the Fundamentals of Art certificate program. *Credit by:* self-paced learning schedule.

Accreditation: Distance Education and Training Council.

Description: Art Instruction Schools (1914) began as an in-house training department for commercial artists in the Minneapolis printing industry. Today we enroll students throughout the U.S., Canada, and several other foreign countries, making AIS the premier home-study art school in the world. Some of our students just want to become more familiar with basic art concepts and techniques. But many others have gone on to become famous, supporting the Hollywood film industry, Disney, or their private careers, like Charles Schulz, creator of "Peanuts" cartoons. Many graduates work in commercial art or sell their work in galleries worldwide. Some use our training as a foundation for advanced placement into a college art program. Whatever your motivation, AIS instructors will guide you through the Fundamentals of Art—from shapes to shading, pencil to color, muscle structure to figure drawing, perspective to building your portfolio—you can learn it all at home, on your own schedule, as a class of one.

Ashland Community College, Kentucky Community and Technical College System

1400 College Drive	Phone: (606) 326-2142
Ashland, KY 41101	(606) 326-2169
	Fax: (606) 326-2186

Division(s): Mansbach Library
Web Site(s):
http://www.ashlandcc.org/DistanceLearning/default.htm
E-mail: carol.greene@kctcs.net

Undergraduate Degree Program:
Associate Degree

Teaching Methods: *Computers:* Internet, real-time chat, electronic classroom, e-mail, CD-ROM, *TV:* PBS. *Other:* Web-enhanced PBS courses.

Credits Granted for: experiential learning, examination (CLEP).

Admission Requirements: Ashland Community College has an "open door" admission policy mandated by the state legislature. To be admitted as a student at ACC, one must submit an application for admission, high school transcripts, and transcripts of all college work. Students may be asked to submit other documents. To be admitted into some technical programs (for example, Nursing) one needs to satisfy certain admission requirements.

The ACT test is required for full-time students. Placement tests are required before taking English or math courses. All applicants meeting the appropriate academic requirements and technical standards shall be considered equally for admission to a community college or to any academic program thereof regardless of race, color, religion, sex, marital status, national origin, sexual orientation, age, beliefs, mental, or physical disability. Students may apply online at the college's web site: http://www.ashlandcc.org/

On-Campus Requirements: Some online courses require on-campus meetings. Please see the course descriptions on the College's Distance Learning web site for specific information.

Tuition and Fees: *Undergraduate:* Kentucky residents, West Virginia—Cabell, Mingo, and Wayne counties, Ohio—Gallia, Lawrence, Scioto Counties: $61/credit hour. *Nonresident:* $183/credit hour. *Credit by:* semester.

Financial Aid: Federal Stafford Loan, Federal Perkins Loan, Federal Pell Grant, Federal Work-Study, VA, Kentucky resident programs.

Accreditation: Southern Association of Colleges and Schools.

Description: Located in the foothills of eastern Kentucky, Ashland Community College has been the 2-year college of choice for students in the Ashland area for more than 60 years. Ashland Junior College was founded in 1938. In 1997 ACC became part of the Kentucky Community and Technical College System. As part of KCTCS, Ashland Community College continues to offer university-parallel programs for transfer to 4-year institutions and career programs for advancement in professional fields. In addition, ACC responds to the needs of local business and industry for state-of-the-art workforce training. Thousands of people in the tri-state area of Kentucky, Ohio, and West Virginia visit the ACC campus throughout the year for life-long learning experiences and cultural programs.

The college offers a variety of online courses and, in cooperation with the Kentucky Educational Network, TV courses. Students may choose to take additional online courses through the Kentucky Virtual University, a cooperative venture by the public colleges and universities in the Commonwealth of Kentucky. Students who choose Ashland Community College as their home college can combine ACC courses with KVU courses to complete the associate degree in arts.

Assemblies of God Theological Seminary

1435 N. Glenstone Avenue Phone: (417) 268-1044
Springfield, MO 65802 Fax: (417) 268-1009

Division(s): Office of Continuing Education
Web Site(s): http://www.agts.edu
E-mail: rwalls@agseminary.edu

Graduate Degree Programs:
Master of Arts in Christian Ministries
Master of Divinity In-Service Track

Class Titles: Pastoral Epistles, Epistle to Romans, Greek 1A, Greek 1B, Hebrew 1A, Hebrew 1B, Sermon on the Mount, Pastoral Epistles, Life of Christ, The Parables of Jesus, The Epistles and Revelation, The Epistles to the Hebrews, Understanding OT, Christian/OT Theology, Pentateuch, Book of Psalms, The Book of Isaiah, The Post-Exilic Prophets, Theology of Jonathan Edwards, Survey of Church History, History of the Church to the Reformation, History of the Church Since the Reformation, Reformation Church History, The Ancient Church, The Radical Reformation, Theology of Martin Luther, Missionary Encounter, An Introduction To Muslim Evangelism, Intro to World Christian Missions, History of Missions, Theology of Liberation, Urban Missions/Ministry, Church Leadership/Administration, Interpersonal Communication and Conflict Management, Spiritual Formation, Christian Worldview, Christian Ethics, Exploring Approaches to Apologetics, Christian Worldview, Contemporary Theology I, Contemporary Theology II, Exploring Approaches to Apologetics.

Teaching Methods: *Computers:* Internet, e-mail, CD-ROM, LISTSERV. *TV:* videotape. *Other:* audiotapes, fax, correspondence, independent study, individual study, learning contracts.

Admission Requirements: *Graduate:* To be admitted, you must meet these requirements: 1. be a dedicated, born-again believer, 2. to be capable of rigorous academic discipline, 3. to be emotionally suited for Christian service, 4. to hold a 4-year bachelor's degree or its equivalent from an acceptable college (a limited number of mature applicants may be accepted without a bachelor's degree), 5. to have earned a GPA of at least 2.5 on a 4.0 scale (lower GPA's may be considered for admission on academic probation).

On-Campus Requirements: Our primary delivery is extension studies. Students may take only up to one-third of their degree hours through D.L.

Tuition and Fees: *Graduate:* $279/credit. *Application Fees:* $35. *Credit by:* semester.

Financial Aid: Federal Stafford Loan, Federal Perkins Loan, Federal PLUS Loan, Federal Pell Grant, Federal Work-Study, VA, state programs for residents of Missouri.

Accreditation: Association of Theological School in the United States and Canada and The Higher Learning Commission and a member of the North Central Association.

Description: AGTS (1972) is a fully accredited (regionally and nationally) seminary with a variety of resident and external studies degree programs. Our student population is a diverse mixture of national and international participants. Our external studies sites are located in Florida, Pennsylvania, Minnesota, and Washington.

Athabasca University

1 University Drive	Phone: (780) 675-6456
Athabasca, Alberta, Canada T9S 3A3	(800) 788-9041
	Fax: (780) 675-6145

Web Site(s): http://www.athabascau.ca
E-mail: auinfo@athabascau.ca

Undergraduate Degree Programs:
Bachelor of Administration with concentrations in Health Administration, Industrial Relations, and Human Resources; Management; Organization; Public Administration
Bachelor of Administration (Post Diploma) with concentrations in Health Administration; Industrial Relations, and Human Resources; Management; Organization
Three-year Bachelor of Arts degree with concentrations in Anthropology, English, French, History, Humanities, Information Systems, Labour Studies, Political Economy, Psychology, Sociology, Women's Studies
Three-year Bachelor of Arts general degree
Four-year Bachelor of Arts—Joint with Mount Royal College
Four-year Bachelor of Arts with majors in Anthropology, Canadian Studies, English, French, History, Humanities, Information Systems, Labour Studies, Political Economy, Psychology, Sociology, Women's Studies
Bachelor of Commerce
Bachelor of General Studies with designation in Arts and Science. Applied Studies
Bachelor of Nursing (Post Registered Nurse)
Bachelor of Professional Arts with majors in: Communication Studies, Criminal Justice, Human Services
Bachelor of Science with major in Human Science
Bachelor of Science (Post Diploma)
Bachelor of Science in Human Science (Post Diploma)
Bachelor of Science in Computing and Information Systems
Bachelor of Science in Computing and Information Systems (Post Diploma)

Graduate Degree Programs:
Master of Arts—Integrated Studies
Master of Business Administration
Master of Business Administration—Information Technology Management
Master of Business Administration—Agriculture
Master of Distance Education
Master of Health Studies
Master of Science—Information Systems
Advanced Graduate Diploma: Advanced Nursing Practice
Advanced Graduate Diploma in Distance Education (Technology)
Advanced Graduate Diploma in Management

Certificate Programs: Accounting, Advanced Accounting, Administration, Career Development, Computers and Management Information Systems, Counseling Women, English Language Studies, French Language Proficiency, Health Development Administration, Home Health Nursing, Computing and Information Systems, Industrial Relations and Human Resources, Labour Studies, Public Administration.

Diploma Programs: Arts, Inclusive Education.

Class Titles: Accounting, Administration, Administrative Studies, Anthropology, Applied Studies, Art History, Astronomy, Biology, Business Administration, Canadian Studies, Career Development, Chemistry, Commerce, Communications, Communication Studies (Humanities), Communication Studies (Social Science), Communication Studies (Applied Studies), Computers and Management Information Systems, Computer Science, Computing and Information Systems Master, Counselling, Cree Language, Criminal Justice, Distance Education, Graduate, Economics, Education (see also Distance Education), Educational Psychology, English, English as a Second Language (ESL), Environmental Studies, Entrepreneurship, Finance, First Nations Studies, French, Geography (Social Science), Geography (Science), Geology, German, Global Studies, Health, Health Development Administration, Health Studies, Undergraduate, Health Studies, Graduate, History, Humanities, Human Resources Management, Industrial Relations, Information Systems, Integrated Studies—Master of Arts, Labour Studies, Legal Studies, Management, Marketing, Mathematics, Music, Native Studies (Humanities), Nursing, Undergraduate, Nursing, Graduate, Nutrition, Organizational Behaviour, Philosophy, Physics, Political Economy, Political Science, Psychology, Public Administration, Religious Studies, Science, Small Business, Social Science, Sociology, Sociology/Anthropology, Spanish Taxation, Women's Studies (Humanities), Women's Studies (Social Science).

Teaching Methods: *Computers:* Internet, electronic classroom, e-mail, CD-ROM, newsgroup. *TV:* videotape, cable program, satellite broadcasting. *Other:* radio broadcast, videoconferencing, audiotapes, correspondence, independent study, individual study. Any particular course might use a combination of the above. Some courses are also available in the classroom taught in association with one of AU's partners. Students have support from professors, tutors, advisors, and service departments through contact by e-mail and telephone (toll-free in Canada and the U.S.)

Credits Granted for: experiential learning, portfolio assessment, extrainstitutional learning. Along with its Centre for Prior Learning Assessment, the university has collaboration and articulation agreements with several colleges, universities, and professional associations, often giving diploma-holders or members advanced standing in Athabasca via block transfer credit.

Admission Requirements: *Undergraduate:* age 18 (some exceptions). Some courses/programs have academic or geographic restrictions. *Graduate:* Call (800) 561-4650 or (800) 788-9041.

On-Campus Requirements: None.

Tuition and Fees: *Undergraduate:* $444/3-credit course (includes tuition, textbooks, materials/handling, student/alumni fees). *Graduate:* Fees vary between programs. *Application Fee:* $50 (one-time, nonrefundable, for undergraduates). *Credit by:* course (3- or 6-credit).

Financial Aid: Financial assistance is available to full- and part-time students from Alberta Students Finance or the financial aid agency where a student resides. The amount varies according to need. In-province students obtain a Financial Aid Package from Athabasca University. Out-of-province students would contact the financial aid agency in their locale. All students are automatically considered for academic awards and scholarships without application unless specified otherwise. Award recipients are announced twice per year at Convocation.

Accreditation: Association of Universities and Colleges of Canada, Association of Commonwealth Universities, International Council for Distance Education, Canadian Association for Distance Education, Canadian Association for Graduate Studies.

Description: Athabasca University was created in 1970 as a publicly funded and fully accredited university under the statutes of the Province of Alberta, Canada. Athabasca University's primary focus is the delivery of courses and programs by distance and online methods at both the undergraduate and graduate level. Students can pursue studies at their own pace, in their own home or workplace, completing a program or an individual course(s); 25,000 individuals access AU courses annually.

Atlantic Union College

338 Main Street
South Lancaster, MA 01561

Phone: (978) 368-2300
(800) 282-2030
Fax: (978) 368-2514

Division(s): Adult Degree Program
Web Site(s): http://atlanticuc.edu
E-mail: adp@atlanticuc.edu

Undergraduate Degree Programs:
Bachelor of Science
Bachelor of Arts

Graduate Degree Programs:
Master of Education

Teaching Methods: *Computers:* e-mail. *Other:* audiotapes, fax, correspondence, independent study, individual study, learning contracts.

Credits Granted for: prior learning credit portfolios, examination (CLEP).

Admission Requirements: *Undergraduate:* high school graduation or equivalent (GED with no score below 50 in any subtest or 5 GCE passes). Students who do not have high school equivalency may prepare portfolio to demonstrate the necessary competencies for college admission have been met. TOEFL score of 550 is required for applicants whose native language is not English. Completed application, essay, letter of recommendation, transcripts, application fee. *Graduate:* application, essay, recommendations, application fee, GRE scores, transcript of bachelor's degree.

On-Campus Requirements: 8–11 day seminars offered in January and July or each time they start a new unit of study.

Tuition and Fees: *Undergraduate:* $3,749/unit of study (16–18 credits). *Graduate:* $4,317/unit of study. *Application Fee:* $15 undergraduate, $25 graduate. *Other Costs:* $50 graduation fee, $40 student fees. *Credit by:* semester.

Financial Aid: Federal Stafford Loan, Federal Pell Grant.

Accreditation: New England Association of Schools and Colleges.

Description: Atlantic Union College is an accredited coeducational, liberal arts/professional institution. Founded in 1882 by the Seventh-Day Adventist Church for the purpose of preparing trained workers for its worldwide organization, the college now educates students for many professions and occupations in the church, community, and larger society. The campus welcomes qualified students who are interested in an education structured on Christian and liberal arts principles. The college draws its students from all over the world, encouraging a varied and cosmopolitan campus atmosphere. The Adult Degree Program is based on 2 beliefs held by the college faculty: that many adults whose college work has been interrupted by marriage, work, military service, or other personal circumstances should have the opportunity of completing their degrees, and that there are many ways of doing reputable academic work other than being enrolled in on-campus courses. The program was founded in 1972 for adults who wished to complete degrees started years before, for college graduates who are changing their professions, and for life-long learners.

Auburn University

204 Mell Hall	Phone: (334) 844-3103
Auburn, AL 36849	Fax: (334) 844-4731

Division(s): Distance Learning
Web Site(s): http://www.auburn.edu/outreach/dl
E-mail: audl@auburn.edu

Graduate Degree Programs:
Master of:
>   Business Administration
>   Aerospace Engineering
>   Chemical Engineering
>   Civil Engineering
>   Computer Science and Software
>   Electrical and Computer
>   Industrial/Systems Engineering
>   Materials Engineering
>   Mechanical Engineering
>   Hotel/Restaurant Management
>   Rehabilitation Counseling

Class Titles: Economics, Entomology, Film.

Teaching Methods: *Computers:* Internet, real-time chat, electronic classroom, e-mail, CD-ROM, LISTSERV. *TV:* videotape. *Other:* videoconferencing, audioconferencing, audiotapes, fax, correspondence, individual study.

Credits Granted for: examination (CLEP, ACT-PEP, DANTES, GRE).

Admission Requirements: *Graduate:* GRE, 5-year limit, etc.

On-Campus Requirements: Some days required for graduate degrees.

Tuition and Fees: *Undergraduate:* $82–$125/semester hour. *Graduate:* $185–$1,100 semester hour. *Application Fee:* $25 (graduate). *Software:* variable. *Other Costs:* materials, etc. *Credit by:* semester.

Financial Aid: Federal Stafford Loan, Federal Perkins Loan, Federal PLUS Loan, Federal Pell Grant, Federal Work-Study, VA, Alabama resident programs.

Accreditation: Southern Association of Colleges and Schools.

Description: Auburn University (1859) today enrolls 21,778 students, the largest on-campus enrollment in Alabama. The university's mission is to embrace the interrelation of instruction, research, and outreach. For instruction, Auburn offers the baccalaureate in more than 130 areas that span the disciplines, providing the state's only publicly supported programs in many fields. The graduate school provides master's level programs in more than 64 areas and the doctorate in more than 40. Auburn's successes in research within its 12 schools and colleges have been recognized by the National Science Foundation and the Carnegie Foundation, among others. Many outreach programs use the Auburn University Conference Center, with advanced audio/visual and computer technology. The Auburn University Satellite Uplink provides capabilities for national and international video programming. Through this comprehensive university instruction, research, and outreach, Auburn is having a positive impact on people's lives.

Austin Community College

7748 Highway 290 West	Phone: (512) 223-8026
Austin, TX 78736	Fax: (512) 223-8988

Division(s): Open Campus
Web Site(s): http://dl.austin.cc.tx.us
E-mail: dl@austin.cc.tx.us

Undergraduate Degree Program:
Associate of Arts in General Studies

Certificate Programs:
Certificate in Vocational Nursing

Teaching Methods: *Computers:* Internet, e-mail. *TV:* videotape, cable program. *Other:* videoconferencing, audioconferencing, audiotapes, fax, independent study.

Credits Granted for: examination (CLEP, ACT-PEP, DANTES, GRE).

Admission Requirements: *Undergraduate:* high school graduate.

On-Campus Requirements: Each class requires an orientation either in class or online.

Tuition and Fees: *Undergraduate:* $46/credit in-district, $98/credit Texas out-of-district, $214/credit out-of-state and international. *Credit by:* semester.

Financial Aid: Federal Stafford Loan, Federal Perkins Loan, Federal Pell Grant, Federal Work-Study, VA, Texas resident programs, Federal PLUS Loan.

Accreditation: Southern Association of Colleges and Schools.

Description: In 1973 Austin Community College offered its first classes to 2,363 students. Since then, ACC has grown to 6 campuses, a district administration office building, and numerous community sites throughout its service area. More than 26,000 students attended during the fall of 2001. ACC offered its first distance learning course in the spring of 1979. It now offers more than 200 courses each semester and generates approximately 6,600 enrollments each semester. Open Campus is rapidly expanding its offerings with online and interactive video classes.

Aviation and Electronic Schools of America

7940 Silverton Avenue, Suite 101	Phone: (619) 566-2184
San Diego, CA 92126	Fax: (619) 684-3583

Division(s): Jamie Doyle
Web Site(s): http://www.aesa.com
E-mail: aesa@aesa.com

Certificate Programs: FCC General Radiotelephone Operator's License, Airframe and Powerplant License, FCC General Telephone Operator's License.

Teaching Methods: *TV:* videotape. *Other:* correspondence, independent study, individual study.

On-Campus Requirements: Some programs require the student to attend a seminar portion that will be equal to 49% or less of the total course length.

Tuition and Fees: *Undergraduate:* Contact school. *Graduate:* Contact school. *Doctoral:* Contact school. *Application Fee:* Contact school. *Software:* Contact school. *Other Costs:* Contact school.

Financial Aid: VA (pending).

Accreditation: Distance Education and Training Council.

Description: Aviation and Electronic Schools of America (1988) specializes in short-term career advancement programs leading to certification or higher skills in the aviation maintenance, telecommunications, electronic, and computer fields. Originally founded by James P. Doyle, the school has grown to 55 current employees. To better serve our military and other frequently traveling students, the company developed the FCC General Radiotelephone Operator's License course in a distance format. Current plans call for the addition of a distance version of the Airframe and Powerplant License course as well as combination distance/seminar versions of the Airframe and Powerplant and FCC General Radiotelephone Operators license courses.

Babson College

Babson Park	Phone: (781) 239-4354
Wellesley, MA 02457	Fax: (781) 239-5266

Division(s): Babson School of Executive Education
Web Site(s): http://www.babson.edu/see
E-mail: exec@babson.edu

Postgraduate Degree Programs:
Building Business Acumen

Certificate Programs: Building Business Acumen Certificate.

Class Titles: Creating Competitive Advantage, Evaluating Market Opportunities, Maximizing Operational Performance, Building a Business Case, Managing in a Dynamic Environment, Capturing Global Markets, Enhancing Enterprise Value.

Teaching Methods: *Computers:* Internet, CD-ROM. *Other:* audiographics, audiotapes, independent study, individual study.

Credits Granted for: experiential learning, portfolio assessment, extrainstitutional learning (PONSI, corporate or professional association seminars/workshops).

Admission Requirements: *Postgraduate, Certificate:* Mid-to-senior level professionals seeking to enhance business management knowledge.

On-Campus Requirements: None.

Tuition and Fees: *Postgraduate:* $50,000 for entire program. Each of the 7 self-study modules are priced individually. *Credit by:* Certificate credit is granted upon completion of all 7 modules.

Financial Aid: Contact school.

Accreditation: The American Assembly of Collegiate Schools of Business and the New England Association of Schools and Colleges (AACSB).

Description: Babson College in Wellesley, Massachusetts (1919), recognized internationally as a leader in entrepreneurial management education, was founded by entrepreneur and financier Roger W. Babson. It grants BS, MBA, and custom MS degrees through its undergraduate program and the F.W. Olin Graduate School of Business at Babson College, and offers executive development programs to experienced managers worldwide through the Babson School of Executive Education. The college's newly launched for-profit venture, Babson Interactive LLC, develops Distance Learning programs and business simulations for executives and graduate students. For program and publicity information, please visit http://www.babson.edu.

Baker College Center for Graduate Studies and Baker College On-Line

1116 West Bristol Road	Phone: (800) 469-3165
Flint, MI 48507-9843	Fax: (810) 766-4399

Division(s): Undergraduate and Graduate Studies
Web Site(s): http://online.baker.edu
E-mail: gurden_c@corpfl.baker.edu

Undergraduate Degree Programs:
Associate of Business—General Business
Associate of Applied Science—Web Design
Bachelor of Business Administration:
    General Business Administration
    Health Care Administration
    Human Resource Management

Graduate Degree Programs:
Master of Business Administration:
    Accounting
    Computer Information Systems
    Finance
    Health Care Administration
    Human Resource Management
    Industrial Management
    International Business
    Leadership Studies
    Marketing

Certificate Programs: Certificate in Web Design.

Class Titles: Contact school for list.

Teaching Methods: *Computers:* electronic classroom, e-mail. *Other:* None.

Credits Granted for: experiential learning, portfolio assessment, examination (CLEP, ACT-PEP, DANTES, GRE).

Admission Requirements: *Undergraduate:* high school graduate, with work experience. *Graduate:* accredited bachelor's degree and 3 years of work experience. *Certificate:* high school graduate or equivalent.

On-Campus Requirements: None.

Tuition and Fees: *Undergraduate:* $155/credit. *Graduate:* $215/credit. *Application Fee:* $20; one time only. *Other Costs:* books. *Credit by:* quarter.

Financial Aid: Federal Stafford Loan, Federal Perkins Loan, Federal PLUS Loan, Federal Pell Grant, Federal Work-Study, VA, Michigan resident programs.

Accreditation: North Central Association of Colleges and Schools.

Description: Baker College (1888) is a private, nonprofit, educational institution. Currently Baker College has 13 campuses throughout Michigan and is currently the largest private school system in the state. Baker entered distance education through its graduate school in 1994. Since many MBA candidates are busy with work, family, etc., Baker designed a degree to fit their needs.

Baker University

8001 College Boulevard, Suite 100	Phone: (913) 491-4432
Overland Park, KS 66210	Fax: (913) 491-0470

Division(s): School of Professional and Graduate
Web Site(s): http://www.bakerspgs.edu
E-mail: kelly.belk@apollogrp.edu

Undergraduate Degree Programs:
Associate of Arts in Business
Bachelor of Science in Management
Bachelor of Business Administration

Graduate Degree Programs:
Master of Business Administration
Master of Science in Management
Master of Liberal Arts
Master of Arts in Education
Master of Arts in School Leadership

PROGRAM CANCELLED

Teaching Methods: *Computers:* Internet, real-time chat, e-mail. *Other:* None.

Credits Granted for: experiential learning, portfolio assessment, extrainstitutional learning, examination (CLEP, ACT-PEP, DANTES, GRE).

Admission Requirements: *Undergraduate:* AAB degree: one year of work experience; high school GPA minimum of 2.3 or GED minimum of 47 or college GPA minimum of 2.0 on minimum of 24 transferable credits; BSM/BBA degree: one year full-time work experience, college GPA minimum of 2.0 on minimum of 36 transferable credits. *Graduate:* a bachelor's degree from a regionally accredited college or university, two years of full-time work experience.

On-Campus Requirements: None.

Tuition and Fees: *Undergraduate:* $210/credit—AAB degree; $295/credit—BSM and BBA degrees. *Graduate:* $315/credit—MSM degree; $335/credit—MBA degree. *Application Fee:* $20. *Credit by:* semester.

Financial Aid: Federal Stafford Loan, Federal Perkins Loan, Federal PLUS Loan, Federal Pell Grant, Federal Work-Study, VA, Kansas resident programs.

Accreditation: The Higher Learning Commission and a member of the North Central Association.

Description: Baker University (1858) continued as a pioneer of higher education with the introduction of adult-centered programs in 1975. The formation of the School of Professional and Graduate Studies in 1988 formalized the commitment to the metropolitan communities throughout Kansas and Western Missouri. Also, it provided a vehicle for responsiveness to business and industry throughout the region in the form of graduate and undergraduate programs in business. In 1997, Baker offered the first online course to students who needed additional elective hours to complete their undergraduate degrees. The course provided feedback to the administration that gave direction to future forays into distance learning opportunities. Today, Baker provides online courses for both undergraduate and graduate students needing to complete their degrees. The future looks promising as Baker looks closely at providing online educational opportunities to students in more remote areas of Kansas and Missouri.

Bakersfield College

1801 Panorama Drive	Phone: (661) 395-4011
Bakersfield, CA 93305	Fax: (805) 395-4241

Division(s): Distance Learning Office
Web Site(s): http://www.bakersfieldcollege.org
E-mail: kloomis@bc.cc.ca.us

Undergraduate Degree Programs:
Associate of Arts
Associate of Science

Teaching Methods: *Computers:* Internet, electronic classroom, e-mail. *TV:* cable program.

Admission Requirements: *Undergraduate:* high school diploma or certificate of proficiency. Persons age 18+ without diploma may be admitted based on other experience. High school students may apply for the "Concurrent Enrollment" program. Students from foreign institutions may contact the International Education Research Foundation in Los Angeles.

On-Campus Requirements: Orientation, examinations, and review sessions held on campus. Only online courses are "geography free."

Tuition and Fees: *Undergraduate:* $11/unit. *Application Fee:* $134/unit nonresidents, up to 15 units/semester. *Other Costs:* It is estimated that the cost of books and supplies will be $250–$275/semester for a 15-unit schedule. *Credit by:* semester.

Financial Aid: Federal Stafford Student Loan, Federal PLUS Loan, Federal Pell Grant, Federal Work-Study, California resident programs-Board of Governor's Enrollment Fee Waiver,

CAL Grants, Extended Opportunities Programs Services, Cooperative Agencies Resources for Education, Federal Supplemental Educational Opportunity Grant.

Accreditation: Western Association of Schools and Colleges.

Description: Bakersfield College is one of the oldest 2-year community colleges in the nation. The initial program offered a one-year curriculum, and in 1915 the trustees of the Kern County High School and Junior College District authorized a second year of junior college and normal school courses. The college opened its present 153-acre campus on Panorama Drive in 1956. As a member of the INTELECOM, a consortium of 32 Southern California community colleges, Bakersfield offers a wide variety of telecourses. BC began offering online courses in the fall of 1997, and now offers numerous online courses.

Ball State University

Carmichael Hall, Room 200	Phone: (765) 285-1586
Muncie, IN 47306	or 1-800-872-0369
	Fax: (765) 285-7161

Division(s): School of Continuing Education and Public Service
Web Site(s): http://www.bsu.edu/distance/ispcourses.htm
E-mail: jburton@bsu.edu

Undergraduate Degree Programs:
Associate of Arts in General Arts

Class Titles: Principles of Accounting 1; Principles of Accounting 2; Introduction to Cultural Anthropology; Global Cultural Diversity; Introductory Astronomy: A Study of the Solar System and Beyond; Principles of Business Correspondence; Information Resources Management; Principles of Office Supervision; Principles of Business Law; Introduction to Business; Introduction to American Criminal Justice System; Introduction to Criminology; Research Methods in Criminal Justice; Data Analysis in Criminal Justice; Introduction to Policing; Introduction to Corrections; Introduction to Courts/Judiciary; Juvenile Justice and Delinquency; Race, Ethnic, and Gender Issues in Criminal Justice; Victimology; Decision Making and Ethics in Criminal Justice; Organized Crime; Crisis Intervention in Criminal Justice; Police Systems and Organization; Institutional Corrections; Community Corrections; Criminal Evidence; Criminal Law; Current Topics in Criminology; Current Topics in Policing; Current Topics in Corrections; Current Topics in Legal Aspects of Criminal Justice; Survey of Economic Ideas; Elementary Microeconomics; Elementary Macroeconomics; English Composition 1; English Composition 2; World Literature; Personal Finance; Independent Study in Family and Consumer Sciences; Earth, Sea, and Sky: A Geographic View; Global Geography; Elementary Meteorology; Global Climatology; Geography of

Indiana; Geomorphology; Introduction to the History of Business in the United States; The West in the World; World Civilization 1; World Civilization 2; American History, 1492–1876; American History, 1877 to Present; Introduction to Sport in American Life; The United States and the Vietnam War; Recent United States History: 1945 to the Present; Fundamentals of Human Health; Principles of Community Health; Alcohol Problems; Drug Dependency and Abuse; Consumer Health Issues; Death and Dying; Principles of Insurance; Mass Media in Society; Introduction to Advertising; Mathematics and Its Applications; Management Principles; Introduction to Athletic Training; Prevention and Care of Athletic Injuries; Therapeutic Modalities in Athletic Training; Practicum 1 in Athletic Training; Practicum 2 in Athletic Training; Introduction to Philosophy; Ethics; Conceptual Physics; American National Government; Introduction to Political Science; State and Local Politics; Urban Government in the United States; Public Administration; Public Opinion and Political Behavior; Metropolitan Problems; General Psychology; Statistics; Introduction to Biopsychology; Religions in American Culture; Religions of the World; Principles of Sociology; Deviance; Society and the Individual; Sociological Research Design; Applied Social Statistics; Leisure; Family; Social Gerontology; Introduction to Theatre.

Teaching Methods: *Other:* independent study by correspondence.

Admission Requirements: *Undergraduate:* students must be high school graduates or equivalent and in good standing at any previous institutions attended beyond high school.

On-Campus Requirements: None.

Tuition and Fees: *Undergraduate:* $132/credit hour. *Application Fees:* $25 (nonrefundable). *Other Costs:* any additional costs required for course materials are listed in the course description (in our correspondence catalog). *Credit by:* semester.

Financial Aid: Federal Stafford Loan, Federal Perkins Loan, Federal PLUS Loan, Federal Pell Grant (in most cases, students must be enrolled in on-campus hours in conjunction with correspondence hours to receive aid).

Accreditation: North Central Association of Colleges and Secondary Schools.

Description: Ball State University (1918), is a state-supported university. It is accredited by the North Central Association of Colleges and Secondary Schools. Correspondence courses have existed at Ball State since the 1920s and the program currently serves 1,200 students. Courses leading to an Associate of Arts in General Arts degree are offered by correspondence. Other degree programs are offered by Distance Education, however, they are restricted to Indiana at this time.

Barclay College

607 North Kingman	Phone: (620) 862-5252
Haviland, KS 67059	Fax: (620) 862-5242

Division(s): External Studies
Web Site(s): http://www.barclaycollege.edu
E-mail: griel@barclaycollege.edu

Undergraduate Degree Programs: Contact school.

Certificate Programs: Bible Knowledge Certificate (21 credit hours), Bible and Ministry Certificate (21 credit hours).

Class Titles: Contact school and check web site for details.

Teaching Methods: correspondence, independent study, directed research.

Credits Granted for: experiential learning, extra-institutional learning (PONSI), examination (CLEP, DANTES).

Admission Requirements: *Certificate:* high school diploma.

On-Campus Requirements: None.

Tuition and Fees: *Undergraduate:* $150/per credit hour. *Credit by:* semester.

Financial Aid: VA.

Accreditation: Accrediting Association of Bible Colleges (AABC).

Description: Barclay College (1917) is a 4-year, interdenominational Christian Bible College with an Evangelical Friends Church heritage. The college has an 80-year history of excellence in preparing students for the ministry and profession. The college's main campus is located in Haviland, Kansas. Barclay College is a multifaceted educational institution with a traditional on-campus program, on-campus continuing education opportunities, and the ADVANTAGE! program at various extension sites. Barclay College personnel and students are also active as speakers or musicians for churches, youth camps and rallies, or other special events.

Barstow College

2700 Barstow Road	Phone: (760) 252-2411 x7347
Barstow, CA 92311	Fax: (760) 252-1875

Division(s): Learning Resources and Distance Education Department
Web Site(s): http://www.bcconline.com
E-mail: jaclark@barstow.cc.ca.us

Undergraduate Degree Programs:
Associate in Science with an emphasis in Business, Computer Science, Management, and Administration of Justice. An Associate of Arts in Liberal Arts is also available.

Class Titles: Introduction to the Administration of Justice, Principles/Processes of the Justice System, Concepts of Criminal Law, Legal Aspects of Evidence, Community Relations, Concepts of Enforcement Services, Principles of Investigation, Juvenile Crime/Delinquency, Justice, Allied Health, Art History/Appreciation, Business Law I, Business Law II, Introduction to Business, Business English, Business Communications, Business Administration, Environmental Biology, Human Sexuality, Database Design and Management ACCESS, Exploring Information Superhighway, Spreadsheets: Microsoft Excel, Microsoft Word Essentials, Advanced Microsoft Word Essentials, Business Technology, Introduction to Computers, Information Networking, Systems Analysis and Design, Computer Science, Introduction to Online Courses, Introduction to Communicator, Occupational Work Experience, Principles of Economics-Macro, Principles of Economics Micro, Survey of English Literature, Introduction to Shakespeare, Creative Writing, English Composition and Reading, Introduction to Literature, Critical Thinking and Composition, Basic English, Introduction to Ethnic Studies, The Age of Dinosaurs, Health Education, Survey of Western Civilization, Survey of U.S. History, Introduction to Management, Elements of Supervision, Human Resource Management, Psychology of Management, Management Supervision, Introduction to Sport Psychology, American Political Institutions, Introduction to Psychology, Developmental Psychology, Child Growth and Development, Introduction to Career/Life Planning, Adult Development and Aging, Introduction to Drug/Alcohol Studies, Issues in Psychology, Introduction to Cultural Anthropology, Introduction to Archaeology, Introduction to Astronomy, Introduction to Biology, Consumer Economics, Introduction to Fire Technology, Business Math, Humanities through The Arts, Survey of Film, Introduction to Marine Environment, Introduction to Earth Science, Legal Aspects of Corrections, Control and Supervision in Corrections, Correctional Interviewing and Counseling, Introduction to Corrections, Marriage and Family, American Social Problems, Principles of Accounting.

Teaching Methods: *Computers:* Internet, real-time chat, electronic classroom, e-mail, newsgroup, LISTSERV. *TV:* videotape, cable program, PBS. *Other:* correspondence, independent study, individual study, learning contracts.

Credits Granted for: experiential learning, portfolio assessment, extrainstitutional learning, examination (CLEP, ACT-PEP, DANTES, GRE). Up to 30 credits may be earned through experiential learning and assessment. Another 30 credits may be earned through examination. Only 12 credits of residential course units is required for graduation and these may be earned strictly online. Military evaluations conducted upon receipt of all transcripts and completion of 6 units with the Institution.

Admission Requirements: *Undergraduate:* age 18 and application completion. No entrance exams (SAT, ACT, TABE) required. Transfer students must submit transcripts.

On-Campus Requirements: While a student must complete 12 units with the institution in order to establish residency, these can be accomplished strictly through online enrollments.

Tuition and Fees: *Undergraduate:* $11/unit for California residents or military personnel assigned to California. All others, $145/unit no application fees. *Credit by:* semester.

Financial Aid: Federal Pell Grant, Federal Work-Study, VA, California resident programs, Military Tuition Assistance (TA).

Accreditation: Western Association of Schools and Colleges.

Description: Barstow College (1962) is a public community college serving the Eastern Mojave Desert area. It is centrally located 2 hours from Los Angeles and the southern California beaches and $2^1/_2$ hours from Las Vegas. The college has 3,500 students, making it one of the state's smallest community colleges. Because of its proximity to surrounding military bases, Barstow has a long history of working closely with the military. It is a member of the Servicemembers' Opportunity College, actively supporting SOCAD, SOCMAR, and SOCNAV programs. About 60% of its annual graduates are soldiers, sailors, and marines stationed primarily in California. An early pioneer with ITV, the college has long been involved in nontraditional instruction. Ultimately, Barstow intends to offer online access to all of its associate degrees.

Barton County Community College

PO Box 2463	Phone: (877) 620-6606
Ft. Riley, Kansas 66442	Fax: (785) 784-7542

Web Site(s): http://www.bartonline.org
E-mail: butlew@barton.cc.ks.us

Undergraduate Degree Programs:
Associate of Arts
Associate of Science
Associate of Applied Science
Associate of General Studies
Areas of emphasis: Military Studies, Dietary Management and Hazardous Material

Certificate Programs: Dietary Management.

Class Titles: Database Management Systems, Information Super Highway, Multimedia Presentations, Spreadsheet Applications, Word Processing Applications, Advanced Word Processing Applications, Information Processing Systems Management, Total Quality Management, Process Management, Strategic Management, Business Ethics, Interpersonal Communications, Organizational Communications, Sanitation and Management of Food Systems, Nutrition Therapy, Human Resources Management, Field Experience in Sanitation and Management of Food Systems, Field Experience in Nutrition, Field Experience in Human Resources Management, Personal Finance, Technical and Report Writing, American West, Western Civilization to 1500, Western Civilization 1500 to Present, American Military History, Military History of the American Revolution, Military History of the Civil War, Military History of World War I, Military History of World War II, Supply in War, Basic Nutrition, Environmental Management, Environmental Protection Agency Regulations I, Treatment, Storage and Disposal of Hazardous Materials, Environmental Protection Agency Regulations II, Industrial Hygiene and Toxicology, OSHA Regulations, Contingency Plans, Department of Transportation Regulations, Environmental Science with Lab, Introduction to Literature, The Short Story, Introduction to Leadership Concepts, Introduction to Drama, Technical Mathematics, Elements of Statistics, Introduction to Philosophy, Introduction to Logic, Physical Geography, Introduction to Political Science, International Relations, Introduction to Counseling, Group Dynamics, Contemporary Social Problems, Cross Cultural Awareness, Leadership Training Techniques, Technical Problems (Military Logistic Planning).

Teaching Methods: *Computers:* Internet.

Credits Granted for: military experience, PONSI, corporate or professional association seminars/workshops, examination (CLEP, ACT-PEP, DANTES, GRE).

Admission Requirements: *Undergraduate:* open admission, high school graduate or GED.

On-Campus Requirements: None.

Tuition and Fees: *Undergraduate:* $125/credit hour. *Other Costs:* Books; cost varies between textbooks. *Credit by:* semester.

Financial Aid: Federal Stafford Loan, Federal Perkins Loan, Federal PLUS Loan, Federal Pell Grant, Federal Work-Study, VA, state programs for residents of Kansas.

Accreditation: North Central Association of Colleges and Schools.

Description: The bartonline program staff is located at the BCCC (1968) extension campus at Fort Riley, Kansas. Bartonline was founded in 1997 to provide a flexible method for adult students to complete associate degrees. We provide classes in 8- and 16-week formats. Our fall and spring semester each contain two 8-week and one 16-week session. The summer semester contains one 8-week session. Courses are organized in week-long blocks that allow students the flexibility to determine when they will attend class.

Bates Technical College

1101 South Yakima Avenue	Phone: (253) 680-7232
Tacoma, WA 98405	(888) 872-7221
	Fax: (253) 680-7231

Division(s): Paraeducation Training Program
Web Site(s): http://www.bates.ctc.edu
E-mail: jpearson@bates.ctc.edu
cbrewer@bates.ctc.edu

Class Titles: Beginning Sign Language, Education of Students with Disabilities, School Law, Child Growth and Development, Psychology—Understanding Human Behavior, Deafness—Implications for Learning and Life, Abuse and Neglect of Children.

Teaching Methods: *Computers:* e-mail. *TV:* videotape. *Other:* fax, toll-free phone number.

Admission Requirements: *Undergraduate:* contact department.

On-Campus Requirements: None.

Tuition and Fees: *Undergraduate:* $90/5 credits Sign Language, $65/3 credits Students with Disabilities, $65/3 credits School Law, $65/3 credits Child Growth/ Development, $90/5 credits Psychology, $20/1 credit Deafness—Learning and Life, $20/1 credit Child Abuse/ Neglect.

Accreditation: Northwest Association of Schools and Colleges.

Description: Bates Technical College (1948) has been in the business of training people for careers for more than 60 years. Bates is Washington state's largest technical college, with more than 25,000 class registrations per year. Bates Technical College offers distance learning opportunities for individuals currently working as paraeducators or those wishing to enter the field. Although the target audience is paraeducators, other school employees, people working with children in the private sector, or anyone interested in educa-tion would benefit. Courses are designed to meet the Washington State core competencies for paraeducators.

Bay Mills Community College

12214 West Lakeshore Drive	Phone: (906) 248-3354
Brimley, MI 49715	Fax: (906) 248-3351

Division(s): Nishnaabek Kinoomaadewin Virtual College
Web Site(s): http://www.bmcc.org
E-mail: register@bmcc.org
sbertram@bmcc.org

Class Titles: Art Appreciation, History of World Civilization, Business Math, College Composition, Head Start Performance Standards, Children's Literature, Evaluation/Continuous Improvement, Partners in Decision Making, Strategic Planning/Proposal Writing.

Teaching Methods: *Computers:* Internet, real-time chat, electronic classroom, e-mail. *Other:* None.

Admission Requirements: *Undergraduate:* open enrollment, placement testing.

On-Campus Requirements: None.

Tuition and Fees: *Undergraduate:* $85/credit. *Other Costs:* $50 registration fee (12 hours or more), $30 registration fee (1–11 hours), $50 computer fee (12 hours or more), $25 computer fee (1–11 hours), $20 student activity fee (12 hours or more), $20 building fee (12 hours or more). *Credit by:* semester.

Financial Aid: Federal Pell Grant, Federal Work-Study, VA.

Accreditation: North Central Association of Colleges and Schools.

Description: Bay Mills Community College (1984) is a tribally controlled community college. It is chartered by the Bay Mills Indian Community pursuant to the Tribally Controlled Community College Act of 1978. The college serves the tribes of Michigan and neighboring communities. A Board of Regents elects administrative officers and establishes policy. In 1994, BMCC was declared a land grant college. In 1996, Dr. Helen Scheirbeck, Chief of the American Indian Program Branch, held a series of brainstorming sessions in Washington, DC. Dr. Scheirbeck wanted to examine technology to see if training and educating American Indian Head Start employees could be done in an innovative way. Those sessions resulted in a plan that eventually became the Nishnaabek Kinoomaadewin Virtual College at Bay Mills Community College.

Beaufort County Community College

U.S. 5337 Highway 264 East	Phone: (252) 946-6194
Washington, NC 27889	Fax: (252) 946-9575

Division(s): Learning Resources Center
Web Site(s): http://www.beaufort.cc.nc.us
E-mail: pennys@email.beaufort.cc.nc.us

Undergraduate Degree Programs: Contact school.

Certificate Programs: see web site.

Class Titles: English, Nursing, Counseling, Business.

Teaching Methods: *Computers:* Internet, real-time chat, electronic classroom, e-mail, CD-ROM, newsgroup, LISTSERV. *TV:* videotape.

Credits Granted for: experiential learning.

Admission Requirements: *Undergraduate:* BCCC maintains an open door admission policy with selective placement in the different curriculums of the college for applicants who are high school graduates or who are at least 18 years of age.

On-Campus Requirements: None.

Tuition and Fees: *Undergraduate:* $27.50/credit. *Credit by:* semester.

Financial Aid: Federal Stafford Loan, Federal PLUS Loan, Federal Pell Grant, Federal Work-Study, VA.

Accreditation: Southern Association of Colleges and Schools.

Description: BCCC (1967) is a public comprehensive community college with a commitment to provide accessible and affordable quality education, relevant training, and lifelong learning opportunities for the people served by the college. Due to the rural service area of the college, educational opportunities for area citizens are greatly enhanced by using asynchronous and synchronous technology. BCCC was able to launch its Distance Education after receiving a grant from the USDA.

Bellevue Community College

3000 Landerholm Circle SE	Phone: (425) 564-2438
Bellevue, WA 98007-6484	Fax: (425) 564-6186

Division(s): Distance Education, Room D-261
Web Site(s): http://distance-ed.bcc.ctc.edu/
E-mail: landerso@bcc.ctc.edu

Undergraduate Degree Programs:
Associate of Arts and Sciences Transfer Degree in Business
General Studies Degree (nontransferable)
Media Communications and Technology
Web/Multimedia Authoring (nontransferable)

Certificate Programs: Media Communications and Technology, Web/Multimedia Authoring.

Class Titles: Written Expression, Programming, Mathematical Models/Applications, Exploring Digital Future, Global History: Neanderthal to Nukes, Techniques/Technology of Persuasion, Washington/Pacific Northwest, Accounting, Archeology, Economics (macro/micro), Psychology, Sociology, Ecology/Biosphere, Nutrition/Human Body, Weather/Climate/Vegetation/Soils, Grammar/Sentence Structure, Powerpoint, Internet, Multimedia Foundations,

Digital Imaging, Web Design, Web Tools, Web Multimedia, Animation for Multimedia, Internet Objects, Programming for Web Authors, Portfolio/Employment, Internship in Media. Contact the school or check web site for details.

Teaching Methods: *Computers:* Internet, real-time chat, electronic classroom, e-mail. *TV:* videotape, cable program.

Credits Granted for: Evaluation of academic transfer credit.

Admission Requirements: *Undergraduate:* high school diploma or age 18.

On-Campus Requirements: Weekly review sessions at instructor's discretion for telecourses; online courses require no on-campus attendance.

Tuition and Fees: *Undergraduate:* $63/credit (5-credit classes). *Other Costs:* $25/class distance education, lab. *Credit by:* quarter.

Financial Aid: Federal Stafford Loan, Federal Perkins Loan, Federal Pell Grant, Federal Work-Study, VA, Washington resident programs.

Accreditation: Northwest Association of Schools and Colleges Commission on Colleges.

Description: Bellevue Community College, founded in 1966, began offering Annenberg-funded telecourses in 1986, added PBS offerings as they became available, and began producing its own telecourses in 1992. BCC began offering the 90-credit transfer degree in 1993, adding online courses in 1997. Bellevue currently has an AAS Transfer Degree, an AAS Business Transfer Degree, a General Studies Degree (nontransferable), a Web/Multimedia Authoring Degree (nontransferable), and various certificate programs available completely online.

Bellevue University

1000 Galvin Road South	**Phone: (800) 756-7920**
Bellevue, NE 68005	**Fax: (402) 293-2020**

Division(s): Center for Distributed Learning
Web Site(s): http://www.bellevue.edu
E-mail: online-u@bellevue.edu

Undergraduate Degree Programs:
Online Undergraduate Degree Completion Programs are:
  Business Administration of Technical Studies
  Business Information Systems
  Criminal Justice Administration
  E-business
  Global Business Management
  Health Care Administration
  Leadership
  Management

Management of Human Resources
Management Information Systems

Graduate Degree Programs:
Master of Business Administration (with concentrations offered in: Accounting, Cyber Law, Finance, International Management, Management Information Systems)
Master of Science in Computer Information Systems
Master of Science in Health Care Administration
Master of Arts in Management
Master of Arts in Leadership

Special Programs:
Microsoft Certified Systems Engineer and Project Management

Class Titles: courses for accelerated undergraduate degree completion programs for bachelor of science degrees in criminal justice administration, management, global business management, business information systems, as well as for graduate degree programs listed above.

Teaching Methods: Internet, real-time chat, videotape, fax and learning contracts.

Credits Granted for: experiential learning, portfolio assessment, extrainstitutional learning, military training, examination (CLEP, ACT-PEP, DANTES, GRE).

Admission Requirements: *Undergraduate:* Associate's degree or 60 semester credit hours. *Graduate:* Must possess an undergraduate degree from a regionally accredited college or university; or a U.S. equivalent degree from a nationally or internationally accredited college or university; have maintained a GPA of 2.5 (2.75 for MSHS) or better from the most recent 60 credits of course work earned toward the bachelor's degree; have a cumulative GPA of 3.0 or better for prior graduate work.

On-Campus Requirements: None.

Tuition and Fees: *Undergraduate:* tuition for accelerated majors is $11,310 (excludes books, includes all fees). *Graduate:* tuition for online MBA courses is $295/credit hour (excludes books, excludes fees).
Undergraduate tuition for general education and elective courses is $165/credit hour (excludes books, excludes fees). *Application Fee:* $50 (graduate) or $25 (undergraduate)—nonrefundable.

Financial Aid: Federal Stafford Loan, Federal Perkins Loan, Federal PLUS Loan, Federal Pell Grant, Federal Work-Study, VA, Nebraska resident programs.

Accreditation: The Higher Learning Commission and a member of the North Central Association of Colleges and Schools—Commission on Institutions of Higher Education (NCA-CIHE).

Description: Bellevue University is an information-age institution of higher learning with progressive options for online graduate and undergraduate degrees. Graduate and undergraduate programs, online, on campus, and in centers throughout the region, prepare students for an ever-changing environment. Bellevue University is one of Nebraska's largest fully accredited independent colleges. Programs serve the needs of more than 3,400 students annually and cater to working adult students as well as traditional undergraduate students. Benefits include accelerated degree completion programs, online programs, an online library, and cooperative credit transfer agreements. Associate's degrees are accepted in full, and credit is given for corporate and military training.

Bemidji State University

1500 Birchmont Drive Northeast D-3D	Phone: (218) 755-2068
Bemidji, MN 56601-2699	Fax: (218) 755-4604

Division(s): Center for Extended Learning
Web Site(s): http://cel.bemidji.state.msus.edu/cel/
E-mail: cel@vax1.bemidji.msus.edu

Undergraduate Degree Programs:
Associate Degrees in Arts, Science (Criminal Justice)
Bachelor of Science in Criminal Justice

Teaching Methods: *Computers:* Internet, real-time chat, electronic classroom, e-mail, CD-ROM, newsgroup, LISTSERV. *TV:* videotape, cable program, satellite broadcasting, PBS. *Other:* radio broadcast, videoconferencing, audioconferencing, audiographics, audiotapes, fax, correspondence, independent study, individual study, learning contracts.

Credits Granted for: experiential learning, portfolio assessment, extrainstitutional learning (PONSI, corporate or professional association seminars/workshops), examination (CLEP, ACT-PEP, DANTES, GRE).

Admission Requirements: *Undergraduate:* U.S. citizen, high school diploma or GED.

On-Campus Requirements: None.

Tuition and Fees: *Undergraduate:* $122.33/credit. *Graduate:* $163.03/credit. *Application Fee:* $20.

Financial Aid: Federal Stafford Loan, Federal Perkins Loan, Federal PLUS Loan, Federal Pell Grant, Federal Work-Study, VA, state programs for residents.

Accreditation: North Central Association of Colleges and Schools.

Description: Bemidji State Normal School was chartered in 1919 by the Minnesota State Legislature in response to a growing need for public school teachers. In 1921 it became Bemidji State Teachers College and offered a 4-year degree. In 1975, in recognition of its growing role as a multipurpose educational institution, it became Bemidji State University. Bemidji established its External Studies Program in 1974 to provide university study and educational services to adults unable to participate in programs on campus in rural, northern Minnesota. The program, which offers most university courses, allows individuals who are place-bound or have barriers such as distance or work schedule to pursue their educational goals.

Bergen Community College

400 Paramus Road	Phone: (201) 447-9232
Paramus, NJ 07652	Fax: (201) 612-8225

Division(s): Instructional Support Services and Center for Instructional Technology
Web Site(s): http://www.bergen.cc.nj.us
E-mail: mkassop@bergen.cc.nj.us

Undergraduate Degree Programs:
11 undergraduate associate degrees are currently offered completely online, including Sociology, Business Administration, Management, Marketing, Psychology, History, Philosophy and Religion, Social Sciences, and Education. In addition, all General Education requirements may be fulfilled online.

Certificate Programs:
United States Studies

Class Titles: American Language Program, Anthropology, Art, Biology, Business, Chemistry, Criminal Justice, Economics, Education, Geography, History, Information Technology, Literature, Mathematics, Office Technology, Philosophy and Religion, Political Science, Psychology, Sociology, Speech, Theater, Health and Fitness, Writing.

Teaching Methods: *Computers:* Internet, real-time chat, electronic classroom, e-mail, CD-ROM, *TV:* videotape.

Credits Granted for: examination (CLEP, ACT-PEP, DANTES, GRE).

Admission Requirements: *Undergraduate:* high school junior or older; high school diploma or GED.

On-Campus Requirements: None.

Tuition and Fees: *Undergraduate:* $65/credit. *Application Fee:* $50. *Other Costs:* $10/credit general fee, $4/credit technology fee. *Credit by:* semester. All online courses are $80/credit with no additional fees.

Financial Aid: Federal Stafford Loan, Federal Perkins Loan, Federal PLUS Loan, Federal Pell Grant, Federal Work-Study, VA, New Jersey resident programs.

Accreditation: Middle States Commission on Higher Education.

Description: Bergen Community College (1965) registered its first class with day and evening students in 1968. Its first phase of expansive construction was completed in 1973. Since then, the college has expanded its facilities to include additional classrooms, laboratories, library space, a theater arts center, and a student center. Bergen Community College realizes the need to educate citizens to meet the varied demands of a complex society and to prepare people of all ages to undertake the obligation of intelligent citizenship and family life. To this end, the college offers diverse and useful educational experiences. The online program has been developed to provide busy adult students, who cannot attend classes on campus on a regular basis, with the opportunity to start or continue their college education in a fulfilling and flexible format. Online courses are demanding, but they provide students with a rich educational experience that emphasizes collaborative learning and highly responsive instructors.

Bethany College

800 Bethany Drive	Phone: (800) 843-9410
Scotts Valley, CA 95066	Fax: (831) 430-0953

Division(s): External Degree Program
Web Site(s): http://www.bethany.edu
E-mail: edp@fc.bethany.edu

Undergraduate Degree Programs:
Associate of Arts in:
    Early Child Development
    Church Ministries
    General Studies
Bachelor of Arts in:
    Addiction Studies
    Applied Professional Studies
    Biblical and Theological Studies
    Church Leadership
    Early Child Development
    General Ministries
    Liberal Arts
    Psychology
    Social Science

Certificate Programs: Addiction Counseling (CPAC).

Class Titles: Contact school or check web site for details.

Teaching Methods: *Computers:* Internet, real-time chat, electronic classroom, e-mail, CD-ROM, newsgroup, LISTSERV. *TV:* videotape. *Other:* audiotapes, fax, independent study, individual study, learning contracts.

Credits Granted for: experiential learning, portfolio assessment, examination (CLEP, Advanced Placement (AP) Examination, Bethany Challenge Examination Program (BCEP).

Admission Requirements: *Undergraduate:* GPA of 2.0 (4.0 scale) or better on all prior school work, SAT or ACT scores (transfer students with at least 24 college semester units may be exempt), high school diploma or the equivalent, at least 23 years of age, completion of all application materials, and sympathy with the college's doctrinal statement.

On-Campus Requirements: All students entering the program must come to the campus for a program orientation. Students return to the campus at the beginning of each subsequent semester for a progress review. The purpose of the progress review is to provide academic advising, achieve enrollment and financial registration, and meet with professors.

Tuition and Fees: *Undergraduate:* Contact School. *Application Fee:* $35 (waived for online applicants). *Graduation Fee:* $75. *Other Costs:* $85 for registration fee. *Credit by:* semester.

Financial Aid: Federal Stafford Loan, Federal Perkins Loan, Federal PLUS Loan, Federal Pell Grant, VA.

Accreditation: Western Association of Schools and Colleges.

Description: Bethany College (1919) was founded as the training school for Glad Tidings Temple, an inner-city ministry conducted by Robert and Mary Craig in San Francisco. Since 1947, Bethany has been operated as the official leadership preparation school of the Assemblies of God, Northern California and Nevada District. The school was moved to its present site in the Santa Cruz mountains in 1950 and became a 4-year degree-granting college in 1955. In 1992 the External Degree Program was launched to serve the adult Distance Learning community. Bethany College has the distinction of being the oldest accredited Assemblies of God College in the world. Because of its heritage and the continuing need for effective Pentecostal leadership, the college is committed to providing the finest environment for the spiritual, academic, and professional development of its students.

Bismarck State College

1500 Edwards Avenue	
PO Box 5587	Phone: (701) 224-5714
Bismarck, ND 58506-5587	Fax: (701) 224-5552

Division(s): General Instruction
Web Site(s): http://www.bsc.nodak.edu/online
E-mail: lahuber@gwmail.nodak.edu

Undergraduate Degree Programs:
Associate in Arts: Emphasis in Criminal Justice
Associate in Applied Science in:
    Power Plant Technology

Process Plant Technology
Electric Power Technology
Electrical Transmission Systems Technology.

Certificate Programs: Power Plant Technology, Process Plant Technology, Electric Power Technology, Electrical Transmission Systems Technology, Information Processing Specialist.

Class Titles: Accounting, Biology w/lab, Keyboarding, Computer Information Systems, Computer Science, Criminal Justice, English, History, Math, Philosophy, Psychology, Sociology, Communications.

Teaching Methods: *Computers:* Internet, real-time chat, electronic classroom, e-mail. *Other:* Interactive Video Network (IVN), Interactive Television (ITV).

Credits Granted for: extrainstitutional learning, examination (CLEP, ACT-PEP, DANTES) portfolio assessment (Fall 2002).

Admission Requirements: *Undergraduate:* application for admission ACT/COMPASS entrance scores for specific programs/students, dual credit offered to high school seniors, no residency requirements for online students. *Certificate:* Same as above.

On-Campus Requirements: None.

Tuition and Fees: *Undergraduate:* $110/credit. *Application Fee:* $25. *Credit by:* semester.

Financial Aid: Federal Stafford Loan, Federal Perkins Loan, Federal PLUS Loan, Federal Pell Grant, Federal Work-Study, VA, Federal Supplemental Grant, Alternative Loans.

Accreditation: North Central Association of Colleges and Schools.

Description: As a community college, Bismarck State College's (1993) purpose is to provide high-quality, student-centered learning opportunities. Students may earn college credits for transfer to a 4-year college, complete training in a vocational-technical program, keep job skills current, or take noncredit courses in subjects of personal interest. Bismarck has been involved in the distance learning field since its founding. Since that time, we have provided interactive video instruction and offered a variety of general education requirements. In 1995 we began offering online courses in general education. Currently BSC offers over 60 courses with online enrollments exceeding 1,000.

Black Hawk College

6600 34th Avenue	Phone: (309) 796-5004
Moline, IL 61265	Fax: (309) 792-8127

Division(s): Vice President of Instructional Services
Web Site(s): http://www.bhc.edu
E-mail: holdingh@bhc1.bhc.edu

Undergraduate Degree Programs:
Associate in Science
Associate in Arts

Certificate Programs: International Business.

Class Titles: Contact School or check web site for details.

Teaching Methods: *Computers:* Internet, real-time chat, electronic classroom, e-mail, CD-ROM, newsgroup, LISTSERV. *TV:* videotape, cable program, satellite broadcasting, PBS. *Other:* videoconferencing, audioconferencing, audiographics, audiotapes, fax, correspondence, independent study.

Credits Granted for: experiential learning, portfolio assessment, extrainstitutional learning (PONSI, corporate or professional association seminars/workshops), examination (CLEP, ACT-PEP, DANTES, GRE).

Admission Requirements: *Undergraduate:* open door policy that includes high school graduates or those with a GED certificate, anyone 18 years of age and older, transfer students from other colleges and universities. *Certificate:* same as above.

On-Campus Requirements: can be met through online classes.

Tuition and Fees: *Undergraduate:* $61/credit. *Graduation Fee:* $5 late fee. *Other Costs:* $4 auxiliary/material fee/credit hour. *Credit by:* semester.

Financial Aid: Federal Stafford Loan, Federal PLUS Loan, Federal Pell Grant, Federal Work-Study, Federal Supplemental Grants, VA, state programs for residents of Illinois, various institutional and privately funded awards.

Accreditation: Commission on Institutions of Higher Education—North Central Association of Colleges and Schools (NCA).

Description: Black Hawk College (1946) is one of 49 community colleges in Illinois. The College serves all or part of nine counties in northwestern Illinois with a population of more than 225,000 residents. The College's district office is located on the Quad-Cities campus in Moline, while the East Campus is located five miles south of Kewanee, Illinois. Operated as one college with two campuses and several outreach sites, Black Hawk offers more than 50 liberal arts and sciences curicula in the transfer area and more than 70 career track programs leading to degrees and certificates. In 1992, Black Hawk College became a member of the Western Illinois Education Consortium, one of ten distance learning consortia in Illinois. Member institutions share courses via compressed video in order to meet the needs of the underserved students in western Illinois. As member institutions began to develop online courses, the consortium sought NCA accreditation for

AA and AS degrees made up of shared courses offered online. NCA accreditation was granted in 2001. Black Hawk College is also an active member of Illinois Community Colleges Online.

Black Hills State University

Extended Services
1200 University Street Unit 9508   Phone: (605) 642-6771
Spearfish, SD 57799-9508   Fax: (605) 642-6031

Division(s): Extended Services
Web Site(s): http://www.bhsu.edu/academics/distlrn/index.html
E-mail: sheilaaaker@bhsu.edu

Undergraduate Degree Programs:
Various courses offered via distance education.

Graduate Degree Programs:
Complete degree of Master of Science in Curriculum and Instruction offered online.

Class Titles: Business Administration, Management, Economics, Education, English, Special Education, Human Experience, Geography, Psychology, Tourism, and Hospitality Management.

Teaching Methods: *Computers:* Internet, electronic classroom e-mail. *Other:* videoconferencing, correspondence independent study.

Credits Granted for: examination (CLEP, AP, DANTES).

Admission Requirements: *Undergraduate:* admission form/fees, course prerequisites, and completion limits. *Graduate:* admission form/fees, course prerequisites, and completion limits.

On-Campus Requirements: None.

Tuition and Fees: *Undergraduate:* Costs are reasonable; contact school for details. *Graduate:* Costs are reasonable; contact school for details. *Application Fee:* contact school. *Software:* contact school. *Other Costs:* contact School. *Credit by:* semester.

Financial Aid: Contact university for available distance learning assistance.

Accreditation: North Central Association of Colleges and Schools, National Council for Accreditation of Teacher Education, National Association of Schools of Music, International Assembly for Collegiate Business Education.

Description: Black Hills State University has served the citizens of South Dakota, the region, and beyond since 1885. The university is located in Spearfish, which is situated in a picturesque mountain valley near the Montana/Wyoming border. Distance education by correspondence and extension has been a major part of the school's delivery for many years. In 1992 BHSU began offering technology-based distance learning and is currently increasing this delivery via online courses and videoconferencing courses.

Blinn College

PO Box 6030   Phone: (979) 821-0403
Bryan, TX 77805   Fax: (979) 821-0208

Division(s): Distance Education
Web Site(s): http://www.blinncol.edu/disted
E-mail: cschaefer@acmailroom.blinncol.edu

Undergraduate Degree Programs:
Associate in Arts
Associate in Science

Class Titles: Anthropology, Business Law, Introduction to Business, Microcomputer Application, Microeconimics, Macroeconomics, Child Development, American History, World Geography, Arts Appreciation, Federal Government, State Government (Texas), Western Civilization, Psychology, Sociology, English Composition, Technical Writing, Speech, Philosophy, Personal Fitness.

Teaching Methods: *Computers:* Internet, electronic classroom. *TV:* videotape, cable program. *Other:* videoconferencing.

Credits Granted for: examination (CLEP).

Admission Requirements: open admissions, community college.

On-Campus Requirements: Some classes require occasional on-site meetings.

Tuition and Fees: Please contact school. *Credit by:* semester.

Financial Aid: Federal Pell Grant, VA state programs for residents of Texas.

Accreditation: Southern Association of Colleges and Schools.

Description: Blinn College (1883) is located in Brenham and serves a 13-county area with campuses in Bryan and Schulenburg. The school was founded by the Methodist denomination. In 1937 Washington County made Blinn the first county-owned junior college district in Texas. To further open its resources to immediate and prospective constituency, Blinn began a distance learning telecourse program in the spring of 1996. Currently Blinn offers telecourses and Internet courses for credit. Our distance learning program continues to grow.

Bluefield State College

219 Rock Street
Bluefield, WV 24701

Phone: (304) 327-4059
Fax: (304) 327-4106

Division(s): Center for Extended Learning
Web Site(s): http://www.bluefield.wvnet.edu
E-mail: tblevins@bscvax.wvnet.edu

Undergraduate Degree Programs:
Associate of Arts in Liberal Arts

Class Titles: Tests/Measurements, Business Law, Health Promotion/Protection, Composition. BSC offers various PBS and Interactive Video (2-way, audio/video, live instruction) courses each semester.

Teaching Methods: *Computers:* e-mail, Web materials. *TV:* videotape, PBS (in West Virginia), interactive video. *Other:* workbooks.

Credits Granted for: Prior education, life experience through portfolio assessment, CLEP scores.

Admission Requirements: *Undergraduate:* high school diploma, GED, or individual classes without formal enrollment.

On-Campus Requirements: Attendance at Bluefield, Beckley, or Lewisburg, West Virginia, required for interactive video.

Tuition and Fees: *Undergraduate:* $96/credit hour, $233/credit hour out-of-state. Several Distance Learning courses are available at in-state rates through the Southern Regional Electronic Campus. *Credit by:* semester.

Financial Aid: Federal Stafford Loan, Federal Perkins Loan, Federal Pell Grant, Federal Work-Study, VA, West Virginia resident programs.

Accreditation: North Central Association of Colleges and Schools (national organization accreditation for 12 specialty area degree programs).

Description: Bluefield State College was established as a black teachers' college by the West Virginia Legislature in 1895 and was integrated after 1954. By the 1960s, the college had a comprehensive 4-year program of teacher education, arts and sciences, and engineering technology. Today BSC focuses primarily on career and technical 2- and 4-year programs and secondarily on liberal arts offerings. The college offers baccalaureate and associate degrees, with instructional programs in engineering technologies, business, teacher education, arts and sciences, nursing and health science professions, and a variety of career fields. Students may also complete the nontraditional Regents Bachelor of Arts degree. BSC began offering instructional television courses in the mid-1970s through the West Virginia Higher Education ITV Consortium, which produced satellite-delivered courses on the West Virginia Satellite Network (SATNET) in the late 1980s. In 1996 the college installed an Interactive Video Network between its 3 campuses and created the Center for Extended Learning. This effort now includes asynchronous delivery of distance courses to the Southern Regional Education Board Virtual Campus.

Boise State University

1910 University Drive
Boise, ID 83709

Phone: (208) 426-5622
Fax: (208) 426-3467

Division(s): Division of Extended Studies—MS 1120
Web Site(s): http://boisestate.edu
http://boisestate.edu/extendedstudies
http://edtech.boisestate.edu/online/
http://coen.boisestate.edu/dep/ipt.htm
E-mail: eackerma@boisestate.edu

Graduate Degree Programs:
Master of Science in:
    Instructional/Performance Technology
    Educational Technology

Certificate Program: Educational Tecynology.

Class Titles: Accounting, Art, Biology, Chemistry, Communication, Education, Educational Technology, Electrical Engineering, Engineering, English, Geosciences, Geography, Health Sciences, History, Instructional and Performance Technology, Management, Mathematics, Modern Languages, Music, Nursing, Physics, Political Science, Psychology, Sociology, Theater Arts.

Teaching Methods: *Computers:* Internet, real-time chat, electronic classroom, e-mail, LISTSERV. *TV:* videotape, cable program, satellite broadcasting, PBS. *Other:* radio broadcast, videoconferencing, fax, independent study, individual study, learning contracts.

Credits Granted for: Experiential learning, portfolio assessment, examination (CLEP, ACT-PEP, DANTES, GRE).

Admission Requirements: *Undergraduate:* Regular university admission for full-time students. Part-time students must meet the course prerequisites. See information at: http://admissions.boisestate.edu. *Graduate:* Specific program admission requirements are listed at the following URLs: Instructional and Performance Technology—http://coen.boisestate.edu/dep/ipt.htm. Educational Technology—http://edtech.boisestate.edu/online/. *Postgraduate:* N/A. *Certificate:* Similar to those listed above.

On-Campus Requirements: Most undergraduate online classes do not have campus meetings. There are no on-campus requirements for either MS degree.

Tuition and Fees: *Undergraduate:* $135.25/credit for part-time resident students. *Graduate:* $220 (resident), $365 (nonresident)/credit for part-time students. *Postgraduate:* N/A. *Application Fee:* $20. *Software:* varies. *Other Costs:* $20–40 for additional distance fees on undergraduate classes. *Credit by:* semester.

Financial Aid: Federal Stafford Loan, Federal Perkins Loan, Federal PLUS Loan, Federal Pell Grant, Federal Work-Study, VA, state programs for residents of Idaho.

Accreditation: Northwest Association of Schools and Colleges.

Description: With humble beginnings as a junior college in 1932, Boise State University now enrolls over 16,000 students each semester in its undergraduate, graduate, and applied technology programs. BSU students come from every county in Idaho, nearly every state in the nation, and from numerous foreign countries. Boise State's 8 colleges offer 180 major fields, many of which have been offered through distance education since 1980. BSU started offering a master's degree through asynchronous computer conferencing in 1989 and has a long history of offering quality education at a distance. Students can now receive two Master of Science degrees completely online including one in Educational Technology and one in Instructional and Performance Technology. Additional distance education delivery methods include: telecourses; live classes broadcast on interactive television to sites and on cable television to student's homes; and videoconferencing around the state and to rural high school sites. BSU participates in the Idaho Electronic Campus.

Borough of Manhattan Community College

199 Chambers Street	Phone: (212) 346-8645
New York, NY 10007	Fax: (212) 346-8635

Division(s): Office of Academic Affairs
Web Site(s): http://bmcc.cuny.edu
E-mail: jpaznik@bmcc.cuny.edu

Undergraduate Degree Programs: Contact School.

Class Titles: Business, Computer Science, Critical Thinking, Early Childhood Education, English, Human Services, Math, Psychology, Office Administration (keyboarding), Spanish.

Teaching Methods: *Computers:* Internet, electronic classroom, e-mail, CD-ROM.

Credits Granted for: exams and class requirements.

Admission Requirements: *Undergraduate:* admission to Distance Learning courses is the same as admission to any of the college's courses; see college catalog online.

On-Campus Requirements: Many classes meet once or twice (per semester) in a classroom, and some courses have an in-class final. Check with professor.

Tuition and Fees: *Undergraduate:* $105/credit NYC matriculated students, $120/credit NYC nonmatriculated students, $105/credit NY residents with B-81 firm on file, $130/credit NY residents with no B-81 firm on file, $130/credit nonresidents; $130/credit foreign students, $130/credit nondegree students. *Application Fees:* $40 new students, $50 transfer students, $40 nondegree students. *Credit by:* semester.

Financial Aid: Federal Pell Grant, Federal Supplemental Educational Opportunity Grant, Federal Work-Study, Federal Perkins Loan, William D. Ford Direct Loan Program, Federal Direct Stafford Loans, Unsubsidized Federal Direct Stafford Loans, Federal Direct PLUS Loans, Federal Direct Consolidation Loans, Tuition Assistance Program, Aid for Part-time Study, NYC Council Acadmic Scholarship, College Discovery.

Accreditation: Middle States Association of Colleges and Schools.

Description: BMCC's (1963) mission is to provide general, liberal arts, and career education, including transfer programs, to a diverse urban population. The college is committed to offering quality education in a pluralistic urban environment, to fostering excellence in teaching, to facilitating the enhancement of learning, and to sustaining full access to higher education for those who seek fulfillment of personal, career or socioeconomic goals. BMCC began offering online learning courses in the spring, 2000 semester with a few pilot courses. In the fall, 2001 semester there are 20 courses online, and we expect to be increasing our online offerings each semester.

Boston University

15 Saint Mary's Street	Phone: (617) 353-2943
Brookline, MA 02446	Fax: (617) 353-5548

Division(s): Manufacturing Engineering
Web Site(s): http://www.bu.edu/MFG/
E-mail: esv@bu.edu

Graduate Degree Programs:
Master of Science in Manufacturing Engineering

Class Titles: Production Systems Analysis, Process Modeling and Control, Computational Problem Solving, Product Development, Intellectual Assets, Manufacturing Strategy, Materials and Processes in Manufacturing, Green

Manufacturing, Product Supply Chain Design, Product Management, Financial and Managerial Accounting, Operations Management, Simulation, Optimization Theory, Probability with Statistical Applications, Product Quality, Advanced Engineering Mathematics, Production Systems Design, Graduate Project (by petition only).

Teaching Methods: *Computers:* Internet, e-mail, CD-ROM. *TV:* videotape. *Other:* videoconferencing, fax, correspondence, independent study.

Admission Requirements: *Graduate:* GRE or GMAT, undergraduate engineering degree.

On-Campus Requirements: None.

Tuition and Fees: *Graduate:* $809/credit. *Application Fee:* $60. *Other Costs:* $40 for registration/per semester. *Credit by:* semester.

Accreditation: New England Association of Schools and Colleges.

Description: Founded in 1839 and incorporated in 1869, Boston University is an independent, coeducational, nonsectarian university open to women and all members of minority groups. The Department of Manufacturing Engineering offers BS, MS, and PhD degrees and was the country's first department with an ABET-accredited BS program in manufacturing engineering. The distance learning program (DLP) graduate program, also known as ICV, may be completed in about 3 years and leads to the Master of Science in Manufacturing Engineering. Concentrations are offered in Product Innovation and Management, Manufacturing Operations Management, and Manufacturing Systems and Operations Research. Students may take up to 3 courses before applying to the program. ICV permits the department to conduct synchronous instruction at industrial sites with complete 2-way video and audio interaction.

Bradley University

| 1501 W. Bradley Avenue | Phone: (309) 677-2820 |
| Peoria, IL 61625 | Fax: (309) 677-3321 |

Division(s): Continuing Education
Web Site(s): http://www.bradley.edu/continue
E-mail: continue@bradley.edu

Undergraduate Degree Programs: Contact school.

Graduate Degree Program:
Electrical Engineering
Mechanical Engineering

Class Titles: Course titles may vary by semester. Prospective students should contact our office to receive the latest information. We offer the following general subjects by videotape: Electrical Engineering, Mechanical Engineering. Bradley University also offers a limited number of online courses, which vary by term. For updated information, please check our website: http://www.bradley.edu/pubs/all.handbooks.html

Teaching Methods: *Computers:* Internet, real-time chat, electronic classroom, e-mail. *TV:* videotape. *Other:* fax, correspondence, independent study, individual study, learning contracts.

Credits Granted for: Examination (CLEP).

Admission Requirements: *Undergraduate:* see: http://www.bradley.edu/admissions/index2.html. *Graduate:* see: http://www.bradley.edu/academics/grad/admission.html.

On-Campus Requirements: The graduate programs in EE or ME may require an on-campus component to review projects. That requirement would be determined by the faculty members, graduate advisors, and department chairs.

Tuition and Fees: *Undergraduate:* $415/credit hour. *Graduate:* $515/credit hour (off campus engineering courses only). *Application Fee:* $40 for domestic applicants; $50 for international applicants. *Software:* cost depends on course. *Graduation Fee:* contact our office for information. *Other Costs:* $175 technology fee for video courses; additional shipping costs will be assessed for students located outside the continental United States. *Credit by:* semester.

Financial Aid: Federal Stafford Loan, Federal Perkins Loan, Federal PLUS Loan, Federal Pell Grant, Federal Work-Study, VA, state programs for residents of Illinois.

Accreditation: North Central Association of Colleges and Schools.

Description: Bradley University (1897) an independent, privately endowed, coeducational institution was founded as Bradley Polytechnic Institute by Lydia Moss Bradley as a memorial to her children and husband, Tobias. It became a 4-year college in 1920, and in 1946 became a university and began offering graduate programs. It is fully accredited. Bradley offers its undergraduate students over 90 programs among 5 colleges: Foster College of Business Administration; Slane College of Communications and Fine Arts; Education and Health Sciences; Engineering and Technology; and Liberal Arts and Sciences. More than 900 students are seeking master's degrees and doing graduate course work at Bradley, which offers 13 graduate degrees in 31 academic areas including an AACSB-accredited MBA program. Bradley's highest priority is excellent teaching supported by research, scholarship, and creative activities. Faculty not only provide personalized attention in learning and academic advising, but also serve as mentors and professional guides to their students. Bradley's full-time faculty number 317. As teachers and scholars, many are national authorities in their fields. The average class contains fewer than 24 students.

Brenau University

One Centennial Circle	Phone: (770) 718-5328
Gainesville, GA 30501	Fax: (770) 718-5329

Division(s): Online Education
Web Site(s): http://online.brenau.edu
E-mail: online@lib.brenau.edu

Undergraduate Degree Program:
Registered Nurse to Bachelor of Science in Nursing Bridge

Graduate Degree Programs:
Master of Business Administration in:
    Leadership Development
    Accounting
Master of Education in Early Childhood Education

Class Titles: Please contact school.

Teaching Methods: *Computers:* Internet, real-time chat, electronic classroom, CD-ROM, newsgroup, LISTSERV, e-mail. *Other:* radio broadcast, videoconferencing, audioconferencing, audiographics, audiotapes, fax, correspondence, individual study, learning contracts, independent study.

Credits Granted for: experiential learning, military credit, extrainstitutional learning, portfolio assessment, examination (CLEP, ACT-PEP, DANTES, GRE).

Admission Requirements: *Undergraduate:* application, transcripts from every institution attended, standardized test scores, $30 nonrefundable application fee, TOEFL. *Graduate:* application, transcripts from every institution attended, standardized test scores, $30 nonrefundable application fee, TOEFL.

On-Campus Requirements: program completion requires classroom course work. Contact school for information.

Tuition and Fees: *Undergraduate:* $350/credit. *Graduate:* same. *Application Fee:* $30. *Graduation Fee:* $75. *Other Costs:* minimal fees for lab courses. *Credit by:* semester.

Financial Aid: Federal Stafford Loan, Federal Perkins Loan, Federal Pell Grant, Federal PLUS Loan Federal Work-Study, VA, Georgia resident programs.

Accreditation: Southern Association of Colleges and Schools.

Description: Brenau University (1878) is an historic private comprehensive university located in Gainesville, Georgia. The university's 3 colleges—the Online College, the co-ed Evening and Weekend College (EWC), and the Women's

College—have complementary missions. The Online College serves a population of students who are unable or unwilling to attend campus-based classes. Faculty members who have been schooled in adult learning theory offer degree and certification programs, as well as individual courses, online. Instructional methods reflect a collaborative learning focus. Dialogue among students, using an asynchronous bulletin board system, is central to the collaborative learning goal. Online students bring with them varied life and work experiences that, when shared with classmates, enable them to synthesize and apply theory within the context of real world situations. Online classes are delivered via the Internet using the popular Blackboard platform. Other common application programs are also used to enhance delivery of course materials.

Brevard Community College

1519 Clearlake Road	Phone: (407) 632-1111 x6470
Cocoa, FL 32922	Fax: (407) 633-4565

Division(s): Dean of Distance Learning
Web Site(s): http://www.brevard.cc.fl.us
E-mail: harrisp@brevard.cc.fl.us

Undergraduate Degree Programs:
Associate of Arts
Associate of Science in Legal Assisting

Class Titles: All courses can be taken individually, without degree program enrollment.

Teaching Methods: *Computers:* Internet, electronic classroom, e-mail. *TV:* videotape, cable program, PBS. *Other:* correspondence and independent study (only with instructor consent).

Credits Granted for: experiential learning, portfolio assessment, examination (CLEP, ACT-PEP, DANTES).

Admission Requirements: *Undergraduate:* high school diploma or GED (USAFI accepted for individual classes, placement testing required for AA degree courses).

On-Campus Requirements: None.

Tuition and Fees: *Undergraduate:* $47.50/credit in-state, $172.11/credit out-of-state. *Application Fee:* $20. *Software:* Internet service provider fee; BCC technology fee. *Other Costs:* videotapes up to $50. *Credit by:* semester.

Financial Aid: Federal Stafford Loan, Federal Pell Grant, Federal Work-Study, VA, Florida resident programs.

Accreditation: Southern Association of Colleges and Schools.

Description: Established in 1960 by dedicated local citizens, Brevard Community College is a vital part of America's Space

Coast. BCC is recognized nationwide as one of America's leading community colleges in institutional excellence, financial management, student development, culture, equal opportunity, service to the community, and use of technology. BCC began offering telecourses in 1987 and online courses in 1995. Today the college offers 50 courses online and a full 2-year curriculum through TV. Its mission is to meet the educational needs of its students, area businesses, and industry through quality, affordable education.

Bridgewater State College

100 Burrill Avenue	Phone: (508) 279-6145
Bridgewater, MA 02325	Fax: (508) 279-6121

Division(s): Moakley Center
Web Site(s): http://www.bridgew.edu/DEPTS/MOAKLEY
E-mail: mfuller@bridgew.edu

Class Titles: Learners with Special Needs in School/Society, Seminar on Educational Leadership for Future, Research Methods, Selection/Development of Educational Personnel, Legal Issues in Special Education, Inclusion Classroom, Curriculum Development for Learners with Special Needs, Exceptional Child in School, Management, Irish Literature, Ethnic Experience in America.

Teaching Methods: *Computers:* Internet, e-mail. *TV:* videotape, PBS. *Other:* videoconferencing, fax.

Admission Requirements: *Undergraduate:* high school degree or equivalent, SAT or ACT. *Graduate:* bachelor's degree, 2.5 GPA, GRE, letters of recommendation. *Doctoral:* master's degree, 3.0 GPA, letters of recommendation. *Certificate:* undergraduate degree, GRE, letters of recommendation.

On-Campus Requirements: None.

Tuition and Fees: *Undergraduate:* $110/credit resident, $358/credit nonresident. *Graduate:* $136/credit resident, $358/credit nonresident. *Doctoral:* $137/credit resident. *Application Fee:* $20 (undergraduate), $25 (graduate). *Other Costs:* $12 (less than 12 semester hours) or $24 (12 semester hours or more) for student government association, $25 late registration fee; $50 distance learning fee. *Credit by:* semester.

Financial Aid: Federal Perkins Loan, Federal Pell Grant, Federal Work-Study, Federal Ford Direct Subsidized and Unsubsidized Loans, Federal Ford Direct Plus Loan, Mass Plan, Federal Supplemental Educational Opportunity Grant, BSC Tuition Waiver, BSC Tuition Grant, BSC Fee Grant, Massachusetts State Scholarship.

Accreditation: New England Association of Schools and Colleges.

Description: Bridgewater State College (1840) is one of America's oldest public colleges, rich in tradition and pride. Today, Bridgewater is a multipurpose liberal arts institution that enrolls 8,700 full- and part-time students, offers 100 undergraduate and graduate academic programs, has a full-time faculty of 256 teacher-scholars, and occupies a 235-acre campus with 29 academic and residential buildings. Distance learning programs began in the fall of 1997.

Brigham Young University

206 Harman Continuing Education Building	
Box 21514	Phone: (801) 378-2868
Provo, UT 84602-1514	Fax: (801) 378-5817

Division(s): Independent Study
Web Site(s): http://coned.byu.edu/is/
E-mail: roy_schmidt@byu.edu

Certificate Programs: Family History

Class Titles: call (801) 378-4351.

Teaching Methods: *Computers:* Internet, e-mail, CD-ROM. *Other:* correspondence, audiotapes, independent study.

Admission Requirements: *Undergraduate:* open-enrollment. *Certificate:* open-enrollment.

On-Campus Requirements: None.

Tuition and Fees: *Undergraduate:* $98/credit. *Other Costs:* $20/course extension, or transfer. *Credit by:* semester.

Financial Aid: limited independent study scholarships.

Accreditation: Northwest Association of Schools and Colleges.

Description: Brigham Young University's (1875) mission is to assist individuals in their quest for perfection and eternal life. The mission of the Division of Continuing Education is to help people improve their lives by offering quality educational programs. The mission of the Department of Independent Study is to make quality educational experiences available to all who can benefit from individualized learning.

Broome Community College

P.O. Box 1017	Phone: (607) 778-5001
Binghamton, NY 13902	Fax: (607) 778-5310

Web Site(s): http://www.sunybroome.edu
E-mail: guzzi_m@sunybroome.edu

Undergraduate Degree Programs: Contact school.

Class Titles: Understanding Electronic Commerce, Mastering the Internet and WWW, Basics of Website Creation, Computers and Communication, Designing Effective Web Pages, Accounting I, Marketing, Operations Management, Managerial Accounting, Advance Topics in Human Resources, Small Business Management, Business Reports and Computer Communications, Direct Marketing, Qualitative Marketing Research Methodologies, Introduction to Early Education, College Writing I, Healthcare Financing, the West and the World since 1500, U.S. History I, Elementary Algebra and Trigonometry, Statistics I, Calculus I, Calculus II, Pharmacology, Physical Science-Astronomy, Physical Science-Meteorology, Physical Science-Geology, Physics I, Physics II, Introduction to American Government, Human Development, Child Development, Intelligence and the Mentally Retarded, Behavior Modification, Psychology of Advertising, Introduction to Sociology.

Teaching Methods: *Computers:* Internet, real-time chat, electronic classroom, e-mail, CD-ROM, LISTSERV.

Credits Granted for: experiential learning, portfolio assessment, extrainstitutional learning (PONSI, corporate or professional association seminars/workshops), examination (CLEP, ACT-PEP, DANTES).

Admission Requirements: *Undergraduate:* for nonmatriculated students minimum age requirement of 16 for qualified students; nonmatriculated students (not officially admitted to a degree program) are not required to complete an application for admissions. All students (matriculated and nonmatriculated) must complete a registration form. Matriculated students at Broome Community College must have approval from an academic advisor prior to registration.

On-Campus Requirements: None.

Tuition and Fees: *Undergraduate:* $100/credit. *Software:* depends upon the course. *Other Costs:* Technology fee: $20 for part-time students, $30 for full-time students. *Credit by:* semester.

Financial Aid: Students must be matriculated to apply for financial aid. Federal Stafford Loan, Federal Perkins Loan, Federal Plus Loan, Federal Pell Grant, Federal Work-Study, VA, state programs for residents of New York State, Tuition Assistance Program (TAP) Aid for Part-Time Study (APTS) Educational Opportunity Program (EOP), Vietnam veterans tuition award supplement, child of veterans award supplement.

Accreditation: Middle States Association of Colleges and Schools.

Description: Broome Community College (1946) is a comprehensive community college supervised by the State University of New York and sponsored by Broome County, New York. It offers programs to prepare graduates for immediate employment (Associate in Applied Science Degrees), and for transfer to 4-year colleges and universities (Associate in Arts, Associate in Science Degrees). The college also sponsors a variety of certificate programs, short-term training programs, and noncredit community education courses. Broome Community College was chartered as the New York State Institute of Applied Arts and Sciences at Binghamton in 1946. Eventually, the college name was changed in 1971 to Broome Community College. Broome Community College strives to be a leader in anticipating and responding to diverse individual, community, and global needs for accessible lifelong educational opportunities. Broome Community College collaborates with others to create high-quality, innovative, student-centered learning environments guided by our shared values.

Brown University

| BOX G-BH | Phone: (401) 444-1862 |
| Providence, RI 02912 | Fax: (401) 444-1850 |

Division(s): Addiction Technology Transfer Center of New England
Web Site(s): http://www.caas.brown.edu/CED/coursecal.html
E-mail: monte_bryant@brown.edu

Certificate Programs: Addiction-related continuing education for CEUs.

Class Titles: Addictionology: A Systems Approach to Criminal Justice, Adolescent Chemical Dependency, Advanced Pharmacology—Staying Current with Drugs of Abuse, Alcohol and Other Drugs and Disabilities, Anabolic Steroids, Core Functions of Addictions Counseling, Criminal Justice: Addictionology, Cultural Awareness, Effective Substance Abuse Strategies for Offenders in the Criminal Justice System, In-Depth Study of the 12 Steps and 12 Traditions, Linking Substance Abuse and Interpersonal Violence, Motivational Interviewing: A New Approach to Behavior Change, Multicultural Policy: the Counselor as a Change Agent, Posttraumatic Stress Disorder and Addiction, Problem and Compulsive Gambling, Relapse Prevention: Theory and Practical Application, Spirituality and Addictions, Strategies to Deal with Individuals and Social Risks Associated with Substance Abuse and Dependence, Substance Abuse among Older Adults, Substance Use Issues in Gay and Lesbian Clients: Considerations for Effective Practice, Understanding and Utilizing 12 Step Programs, Dual Diagnosis—Advanced, Dual Diagnosis—Introduction, HIV and Addictions, Lifestyle and Stress Management: the Balancing Act, Overeating as a Response to Stress Management: Basic Behavior Change Strategies, Prevention Problem Gambling and the Impact on the Family, Suicide, Advanced Ethics, Basic Ethics, Clinical Supervision, Gambling and Women, Battered Women and Substance Abuse, Medical Aspects of AOD.

Teaching Methods: *Computers:* Internet, real-time chat, electronic classroom, e-mail, LISTSERV. *Other:* individual study.

Admission Requirements: *Certificate:* no requirements.

On-Campus Requirements: None.

Tuition and Fees: Contact school. *Other Costs:* $35 course. *Credit by:* Continuing Education Units (CEUs) for Professional Development.

Accreditation: National Association of Alcohol and Drug Abuse Counselors (NAADAC).

Description: Coordinated through Brown University's Center for Alcohol and Addiction Studies, this unique learning initiative first began in March 1997 and has continued to flourish ever since. By selecting instructors who are at the top of their field, or who have made major contributions to their communities or the body of addictions knowledge, this program has begun to attract participants from all over the world. The Online Education Program of the Addiction Technology Transfer Center of New England, funded by Substance Abuse and Mental Health Services Administration, Center for Substance Abuse Treatment, was chartered in order to extend the reach of addictions education to the World Wide Web. The primary purpose of this program is to provide addiction specialists and other interested persons throughout the world with convenient, and easy to access "cyber" classrooms in which they can be kept abreast with the latest advances in addiction treatment and prevention.

Bucks County Community College

434 Swamp Road	Phone: (215) 968-8000
Newtown, PA 18940	Fax: (215) 968-8148

Division(s): Distance Learning Office
Web Site(s): http://www.bucks.edu/distance
E-mail: learning@bucks.edu

Undergraduate Degree Programs:
Associate of Arts in Business Administration
Associate of Arts in Liberal Arts
Associate of Arts in Management/Marketing
Associate of Arts in Science

Certificate Programs: Entrepreneurship, Retailing, Microsoft Office, Web Designer.

Class Titles: Accounting, Art History, Business, Communication, Composition, Computer Science, Criminal Justice, Education, Foreign Language, History, Health, Law, Literature, Management, Marketing, Math, Medical Transcription, Music, Paralegal, Political Science, Psychology, Science, Sociology, Web Design, Women's Studies.

Teaching Methods: *Computers:* Internet, real-time chat, electronic classroom, e-mail, CD-ROM, LIST-SERV. *TV:* videotape, PBS. *Other:* audiotapes, fax, correspondence, independent study, individual study.

Credits Granted for: experiential learning, portfolio assessment, extrainstitutional learning, examination (CLEP, ACT-PEP, DANTES, GRE).

Admission Requirements: *Undergraduate:* Open admissions.

On-Campus Requirements: variable (see www.bucks.edu/distance).

Tuition and Fees: *Undergraduate:* varies by residency. $74/credit state residents in Bradford, Bucks, Pike, Wayne, Tioga counties. *Application Fee:* $30. *Credit by:* semester.

Financial Aid: Federal Stafford Loan, Federal Perkins Loan, Federal PLUS Loan, Federal Pell Grant, Federal Work-Study, VA, PHEA.

Accreditation: Middle States Association of Colleges and Schools.

Description: Bucks County Community College (1965) is one of the largest community colleges in Pennsylvania. The Distance Learning Program began in 1994 and involves 170 courses with 10 complete AA degrees in Business, Liberal Arts, and Science, as well as degree completions in many other areas.

Bunker Hill Community College

250 New Rutherford Avenue	Phone: (617) 228-2256, 2214, 2079
Charlestown, MA	Fax: (617) 228-2106

Division(s): BHCC's eCollege
Web Site(s): http://www.bhcc.state.ma.use-mail/
E-mail: onlinehelp@bhcc.state.ma.us or onlineadvising@bhcc.state.ma.us

Undergraduate Degree Programs:
Computer Science
Criminal Justice
General Concentration

Certificate Programs: Computer Science, Criminal Justice.

Class Titles: Call, write, or e-mail for comprehensive schedule.

Teaching Methods: *Computers:* Internet, real-time chat, electronic classroom, e-mail, CD-ROM. *TV:* videotape, satellite broadcasting, PBS, private college consortium network. *Other:* videoconferencing, audiotapes, correspondence, independent study, learning contracts.

Credits Granted for: experiential learning, portfolio assessment, extrainstitutional learning (PONSI, corporate or professional association seminars/workshops), examination (CLEP, ACT-PEP, DANTES).

Admission Requirements: *Undergraduate:* GED or high school diploma, placement test.

On-Campus Requirements: final and some midterm exams on campus or with off-campus proctor.

Tuition and Fees: *Undergraduate:* $65/credit, Massachusetts state resident, $271/credit nonresident and international students. *Application Fee:* $10 in-state, $35 out-of-state. *Credit by:* semester, with continuous enrollment for correspondence courses.

Financial Aid: Federal Stafford Loan, Federal Perkins Loan, Federal PLUS Loan, Federal Pell Grant, Federal Work-Study, VA, state programs for residents of Massachusetts.

Accreditation: New England Association of Schools and Colleges.

Description: BHCC (1973) is a comprehensive, urban 2-year college offering Associate in Arts, Associate in Science, and Certification programs in a variety of disciplines. The college has been involved in Distance Education since its inception in 1973.

Burlington College

| 95 North Avenue | Phone: (802) 862-9616 |
| Burlington, VT 05401 | Fax: (802) 658-0071 |

Division(s): Independent Degree Program
Web Site(s): http://www.burlingtoncollege.edu
E-mail: tkahan@burlcol.edu

Undergraduate Degree Programs:
Bachelor of Arts in:
  Writing and Literature
  Transpersonal Psychology
  Cinema Studies
  Fine Art
  Individualized Major

Certificate Programs: AA in General Studies.

Teaching Methods: *Computers:* e-mail, LISTSERV. *Other:* fax, independent study, correspondence, phone contacts and meetings, individual study, learning contracts.

Credits Granted for: experiential learning, portfolio assessment, extrainstitutional learning, examination (CLEP, ACT-PEP, DANTES).

Admission Requirements: *Undergraduate:* we require 45 previously earned college credits (C- or better) and demonstrated ability to study independently and write well.

On-Campus Requirements: IDP requires a weekend residency each term, there are 2 terms per year.

Tuition and Fees: *Undergraduate:* $2,330/semester part-time (6–9 credits), $3,965/semester full-time (12–15 credits). *Application Fee:* $50. *Graduation Fee:* $75. *Credit by:* semester.

Financial Aid: Federal Stafford Loan, Federal Perkins Loan, Federal PLUS Loan, Federal Pell Grant, Federal Work-Study, VA, Vermont resident programs.

Accreditation: New England Association for Schools and Colleges.

Description: Burlington College (1972) was founded by Dr. Stewart LaCasce as an alternative college for nontraditional students emphasizing individualized education and community involvement. From 1972–1992 the college was primarily oriented around its campus program though it had always had contract-based learning for students wanting to do independent study. In 1993 the Independent Degree Program was conceived and has operated ever since. The primary areas for study are in the liberal arts, specifically, Transpersonal Psychology, Psychology, and Writing and Literature. The program also works with what is called individualized majors, wherein each student's program is individually designed.

Burlington County College

| Route 530 | Phone: (609) 894-9311 x7790 |
| Pemberton, NJ 08068 | Fax: (609) 894-4189 |

Division(s): Office of Distance Learning/Noncredit Online Programs
Web Site(s): http://www.bcc.edu (credit); http://ed2go.com/bccenrich (noncredit)
E-mail: sespensh@bcc.edu

Undergraduate Degree Programs:
Associate of Arts
Associate of Science

Certificate Programs: A+ Certification, Basic Supervision, Customer Service, Purchasing, Total Quality, Project Management Principles.

Class Titles: *Credit:* Cultural Anthropology, Art, Biology/Human Affairs with Lab, Human Ecology, Business Administration, Management, Personal Finance/Money Management, Business Law, Marketing, Small Business Management, American Cinema, Computer Science, Internet Literacy, Microeconomics, Macroeconomics, Whole Child, College Composition, French, Earth Revealed, Geology with Lab, U.S. History, Ancient/Medieval Foundations, History of Modern East Asia, Children's Literature, Statistics, Music,

American Government/Politics, Project Universe, Oceanus, Psychology, General Psychology, Child Psychology, Developmental Psychology, Abnormal Psychology, Theater, Criminal Justice, Sociology, Spanish, Marriage/Family. *Noncredit:* Internet courses: Internet, Web Pages, Creating Web Graphics, Getting Organized with Outlook, Microsoft Front Page, Marketing Your Business or Organization on the Internet, Achieving Top Search Engine Positions for Your Web Site, Dreamweaver, CGI Programming for the Web, JAVA Programming for the Web, Javascript Programming for the Web, Using America Online. *Computer courses*: PC Troubleshooting, Windows File and Disk Management, Photoshop Basics, 101 Tips for iMac/Macintosh, Quickbooks, Windows 2000 Professional, Visual Basic 6.0, Quicken for Windows, Microsoft Word, Microsoft Excel, Microsoft Access, Microsoft Publisher, Microsoft PowerPoint, Microsoft Works-Word Processor, Making the Most of Windows Me, WordPerfect, Corel QuattroPro, Keyboarding, A+ Hardware/Operating Systems/OS II. *Personal Enrichment courses*: Fire Service, Medical Terminology, Magazine Writing, Creativity Training for Writers, Travel Writing, Speed Spanish, Grammar for ESL, Personal Financial Planning, A to Z Grantwriting, Debt Elimination Techiques that Work, GRE Preparation, Preparing for the LSAT, Preparing for the SAT/ACT, Preparing for the GMAT, Write Your Life Story, Natural Health/Healing. *Small Business courses*: Start Your Own Consulting Practice, Marketing for Small Business, Start and Operate Your Own Home-Based Business, Practical Financial Management for Small Business, Business Communications using E-mail. *Nursing courses*: Substance Abuse/Alcoholism, Preexisting Diabetes and Pregnancy, Antibiotic Resistant Infections. *Business/Management courses*: Transition to Managerial Work, Communication, Motivation, Conflict Resolution/Problem Solving, Interpersonal Skills for Managers, Marketing/Sales, Customer Identification/Definition/Expectations, Customer Service Techniques.

Teaching Methods: *Computers:* Internet, electronic classroom, e-mail, CD-ROM. *TV:* videotape, cable program, ETN, PBS. *Other:* radio broadcast, audioconferencing, videoconferencing, audiotapes, fax.

Credits Granted for: examination (CLEP, DANTES).

Admssion Requirements: *Undergraduate:* must be at least a high school junior and take New Jersey Basic Skills Test.

On-Campus Requirements: We offer optional but very helpful seminars and an orientation.

Tuition and Fees: *Undergraduate:* $60/credit plus $5.50/credit in general classes, $4/credit in technology, $25/course license fee (all for Burlington County residents, part time); $75 plus fees/credit out-of-county; $140 plus

fees/credit out-of-state. *Application Fee:* $20. *Noncredit: see web site. Credit by:* semester.

Financial Aid: Federal Stafford Loan, Federal Perkins Loan, Federal PLUS Loan, Federal Pell Grant, Federal Work-Study, VA, New Jersey resident programs.

Accreditation: Middle States Association of Colleges and Schools.

Description: Burlington County College (1969) is a community college that awards associate degrees and certificates. Many students go on to other colleges for a bachelor's degree after completing their work at BCC. Distance Education began in 1978 through telecourses. The program blossomed in 1995 when the college became a pilot school for PBS' *Going the Distance* program. The Distance Learning Department now offers 60 video, radio, and Internet courses each semester.

Butte Community College

3536 Butte Campus Drive	Phone: (530) 895-2434
Oroville, CA 95965	Fax: (530) 895-2380

Division(s): Center for Media and Distance Learning
Web Site(s): http://www.butte.cc.ca.us
E-mail: lemleyja@butte.cc.ca.us@bctv.net

Class Titles: Math, Science, Agricultural Science, History, Political Science, Anthropology, Latin, Business, Child Development, Administration of Justice, Telecommunications, Sociology, Economics, English, Reading, Education, Humanities, Psychology.

Teaching Methods: *Computers:* Internet. *TV:* videotape, cable program. *Other:* videoconferencing.

Admission Requirements: *Undergraduate:* age 18.

On-Campus Requirements: depends on course.

Tuition and Fees: *Undergraduate:* $11/credit. *Application Fee:* $40. *Other Costs:* out-of-state tuition. *Credit by:* semester.

Financial Aid: Federal Stafford Loan, Federal Perkins Loan, Federal PLUS Loan, Federal Pell Grant, Federal Work-Study, VA, California resident programs.

Accreditation: Western Association of Schools and Colleges.

Description: Butte Community College (1968) is located in northern California and serves a primarily rural, 2-county area. We began distance learning using telecourses in 1986 and have expanded into 2-way, live interactive and the Internet.

Cabrillo Community College

6500 Soquei Drive   Phone: (831) 479-6201
Aptos, CA 95003   Fax: (831) 479-5092

Division(s): Transfer Education
Web Site(s): http://www.cabrillo.cc.ca.us
E-mail: glgaring@cabrillo.cc.ca.us

Class Titles: *Online Courses:* Computer Accounting, Financial Accounting, Head and Neck Anatomy, Criminal, Criminal Courts and Procedures, CG54 Career Counseling, English 1A, College Composition, Information Research, Elements of Writing, Sentence Structure, United States History to 1865, Music Appreciation, World Music, Intro to Government. *Telecourses within Region:* Beginning French, Spanish, Introduction to Anthropology, Introduction to Government, World Regional Geography, Personal Health, Introduction to Elementary Statistics. *Live Interactive within Region:* Business Grammar.

Teaching Methods: *Computers:* Internet, real-time chat, discussion boards, electronic classroom, e-mail, CD-ROM, LISTSERV. *TV:* videotape, cable program satellite broadcasting, PBS. *Other:* videoconferencing, audiotapes, fax.

Admission Requirements: *Undergraduate:* Age 18; high school diploma, GED, or equivalent certificate.

On-Campus Requirements: Varies with course.

Tuition and Fees: *Undergraduate:* $11/credit.

Financial Aid: Federal Stafford Loan, Federal PLUS Loan, Federal Pell Grant, Federal Work-Study, VA, California resident programs: California Grant A, B, C, ELOPS/Care.

Accreditation: Western Association of Schools and Colleges.

Description: Cabrillo Community College (1959) is one of California's top 10 community colleges for number of students who transfer to the University of California system. Almost 70% of the courses offered to Cabrillo's 13,000 students are transferable. CCC began its distance education program in 1994. Detailed information about the distance education program is located at *www.cabrillo.cc.ca.us/instruct/distlearn*

Caldwell College

9 Ryerson Avenue   Phone: (973) 618-3285
Caldwell, NJ 07006   Fax: (973) 618-3660

Division(s): Continuing Education, External Degree Program
Web Site(s): http://www.caldwell.edu
E-mail: jalbalah@caldwell.edu

Undergraduate Degree Programs:
Bachelor of Science in:
    Accounting
    Business Administration
    Computer Information Systems
    International Business
    Marketing and Management
Bachelor of Arts in:
    Communications Art
    Criminal Justice
    English
    History
    Multidisciplinary Studies
    Political Science
    Psychology
    Religious Studies
    Sociology
    Social Studies

Class Titles: Contact school for complete listing of courses offered.

Teaching Methods: *Computers:* Internet, e-mail. *TV:* videotape. *Other:* audiotapes, fax, correspondence, independent study.

Credits Granted for: experiential learning, portfolio assessment, extrainstitutional learning, examination (CLEP, ACT-PEP, DANTES).

Admission Requirements: *Undergraduate:* 12 transferable college credits.

On-Campus Requirements: External degree students are required to be on campus. On a designated Saturday at the beginning of the semester, students registered for External Degree courses meet with the faculty member who is teaching the course.

Tuition and Fees: *Undergraduate:* $357/credit. *Application Fee:* $40. *Credit by:* semester.

Financial Aid: Federal Stafford Loan, Federal Perkins Loan, Federal PLUS Loan, Federal Pell Grant, Federal Work-Study, VA, New Jersey resident programs.

Accreditation: Middle States Association of Colleges and Schools.

Description: Caldwell College (1939) is a Catholic, coeducational, 4-year liberal arts institution committed to intellectual rigor, individual attention, and the ethical values of the Judeo-Christian academic tradition. Caldwell College offers a 12:1 student-faculty ratio, small classes, and individual attention. Professors know their students by name, challenge them to strive for excellence, and provide the support needed to achieve it. This close relationship between faculty members and students also leads to a spirit of friendship throughout the campus community. Caldwell College pioneered the external degree concept in 1979, becoming the first higher education institution in the state of New Jersey to offer students the option of completing their degrees without attending on-campus classes. The external degree program offers 16 majors.

Calhoun State Community College

Highway 31 North	Phone: (256) 306-2755
PO Box 2216	(256) 306-2729, (256) 306-2621
Decatur, AL 35609	Fax: (256) 306-2507

Division(s): Dean of Instruction, Distance Education Coordinator
Web Site(s): http://www.calhoun.cc.al.us
E-mail: registration: mwt@calhoun.cc.al.us
answer questions: cfb@calhoun.cc.al.us

Class Titles: Business, Chemistry, Computer Information Systems, Health, History, Math, Music, Philosophy, Physical Science, Psychology, Sociology, Spanish, French, Speech, Theatre Appreciation, English, Biology, Geography.

Teaching Methods: *Computers:* Internet, e-mail, CD-ROM. *TV:* videotape. *Other:* audiotapes, fax, correspondence.

Credits Granted for: examination.

Admission Requirements: *Undergraduate:* application, high school graduation or GED.

On-Campus Requirements: The distance education courses (college by cassette, college by CD, or Web-based) do require some visits to campus, either for exams, labs, etc.

Tuition and Fees: *Undergraduate:* $76/credit. *Credit by:* semester.

Financial Aid: Federal Stafford Loan, Federal Pell Grant, Federal Work-Study, VA, Alabama resident programs, Federal Supplemental Educational Opportunity Grant.

Accreditation: Southern Association of Colleges and Schools.

Description: Calhoun State Community College (1947) began as a technical college and expanded to academic offerings. In 1992 we began offering telecourses via cable broadcast, PBS, and college by cassette. The college by cassette was the preferred format by students. In the past year, we added Web-based college and college by CD courses.

California College for Health Sciences

2423 Hoover Avenue	Phone: (619) 477-4800
National City, CA 91950	Fax: (619) 477-4360

Division(s): Correspondence Institution
Web Site(s): http://cchs.edu
E-mail: cchsinfo@cchs.edu

Undergraduate Degree Programs:
Vocational Programs:
Medical Assisting
Pharmacy Technician
Physical Therapy Aide
EKG Technology
Home Health Aide
Associate of Science in:
Business
Respiratory Therapist
EEG
Medical Transcription
Allied Health
Early Childhood Education
Bachelor of Science in:
Health Services Management
Respiratory Care
Business

Graduate Degree Programs:
Master of Business Administration/Health Care
Master of Science in:
Health Services with Community Health or Wellness Promotion
Health Care Administration
Master of Public Health

Certificate Programs: Business Essentials, Community Health Education, Gerontology, Health Psychology, Health Care Ethics, Polysomnography.

Class Titles: English, Health Science, Sociology, Sciences, Math, Management, Business.

Teaching Methods: *Computers:* e-mail *Other:* fax, correspondence, independent study, individual study.

Credits Granted for: extrainstitutional learning, examination (CLEP, ACT-PEP, DANTES, GRE).

Admission Requirements: *Undergraduate:* Associate and Vocational: minimum of high school diploma. Entrance to Respiratory varies. BS degrees: 60 semester credits. *Graduate:* accredited BS degree. *Certificate:* 60 semester credits of lower-division work.

On-Campus Requirements: None.

Tuition and Fees: *Undergraduate:* EEG, Respiratory, Medical Transcription vary. *Other Costs*: $133/credit. *Graduate:* $133/credit. Shipping and handling fees and book charges are additional. *Credit by:* semester.

Financial Aid: VA.

Accreditation: Distance Education and Training Council.

Description: California College for Health Sciences (1975) is a private postsecondary institution originally founded as a resident campus for respiratory care education. In 1978 the school launched a distance education component in the field of respiratory care. Since that time, the distance education curriculum has expanded to include programs in medical transcription, EEG, health services management, wellness promotion, and early childhood education. Associate, bachelor's, and master's degrees are offered. The mission of the college is "to assist prospective and working health and human services professionals in the achievement of their individual career objectives with comprehensive, highly accessible and practical education that meets national professional academic standards." The independent study format of distance education enables students to design a study schedule that meets their individual needs, taking into consideration career and family obligations.

California National University for Advanced Studies

16909 Parthenia Street	Phone: (800) 782-2422
North Hills, CA 91343	(818) 830-2411
	Fax: (818) 830-2418

Division(s): Distance Learning
Web Site(s): http://www.cnuas.edu
E-mail: cnuadms@mail.cnuas.edu

Undergraduate Degree Programs:
Bachelor of Science in:
    Business Administration
    Engineering
Bachelor of Computer Science
Bachelor of Quality Assurance Science

Graduate Degree Programs:
Master of Business Administration
Master of Human Management Resources
Master of Science in Engineering

Teaching Methods: *Computers:* Internet, real-time chat, e-mail, CD-ROM. *Other:* audioconferencing, videotape, audiotapes, fax, telephone contact, correspondence, independent study, individual study.

Credits Granted for: transfer credits, challenge exams, portfolio assessment towards prerequisite requirements, extrainstitutional learning, examination (CLEP, ACT-PEP, DANTES, GRE).

Admission Requirements: *Undergraduate:* high school graduate or GED, Math Placement Test when appropriate, TOEFL when appropriate. *Graduate:* bachelor's degree, 3.0 cumulative undergraduate GPA, TOEFL when appropriate.

On-Campus Requirements: None.

Tuition and Fees: *Undergraduate:* $235/credit (U.S./Canadian residents), $255/credit (non U.S./Canadian residents). *Graduate:* $255/credit (U.S./Canadian residents), $305/credit (non U.S./Canadian residents). *Application Fee:* $50 U.S./Canadian, $100 non-U.S./non-Canadian. *Other Costs:* $150 registration fee nonrefundable of tuition/course, $25 extension program application, software/textbooks, shipping costs variable, $15 late payment, $100 change of degree program. *Credit by:* trimester (15 weeks).

Financial Aid: VA, DANTES tuition assistance, GI Bill, SALLIE MAE.

Accreditation: Distance Education and Training Council.

Description: California National University (1993) was founded to provide quality degree programs in a flexible environment so that midcareer professionals could meet contemporary challenges to re-think and re-tool. CNU has adopted an innovative approach to a traditional education: combining correspondence with direct personal contact and technology. A unique aspect to CNU programs is the one-on-one instruction students receive from a distinguished, national faculty. Although the university has taken advantage of advancements in technology to improve instruction, technology is regarded as an enhancement rather than a replacement for good teaching and relevant content. Students enjoy an educational climate typical of one found on a small traditional campus. This is accomplished at a distance through a centralized learning network that emphasizes committed student service and open communication. CNU offers bachelor's and master's degrees in business administration and engineering.

California State University, Bakersfield

| 9001 Stockdale Highway | Phone: (805) 664-2441 |
| Bakersfield, CA 93311-1099 | Fax: (805) 664-2447 |

Division(s): Extended University
Web Site(s): http://www.csub.edu/ExtUniversity
E-mail: rperezll@csub.edu, Marketing Director
torr@csubak.edu, Regional Program Coordinator
kbaird@csubak.edu, Certificate Program Coordinator

Undergraduate Degree Programs:
Liberal Studies
Environmental Resource Management
Communication.

Graduate Degree Programs:
Master of Arts in Education Technology
Master of Arts in Educational Administration
Master of Arts in Education: Curriculum and Instruction
Master of Science in Organizational Administration

Certificate Programs: Attorney Assistant, Drug and Alcohol Studies, Managing Human Resources, Safety and Risk Management, Workers' Compensation Law, Medical Procedure Coder, Substitute Teacher, Elementary Education Teaching Credential, E-Commerce, Professional Clear Teaching Credential, Preliminary and Professional Administrative Services Credential.

Class Titles: General education courses, Business Administration, Communicative Sciences/Disorders, Nursing, Master's Social Work.

Teaching Methods: *Computers:* Internet, real-time chat, electronic classroom, e-mail, CD-ROM, newsgroup, LISTSERV. *TV:* videotape, cable program.

Credits Granted for: experiential learning, portfolio assessment, extrainstitutional learning (PONSI, corporate or professional association seminars/workshops), examination (CLEP, ACT-PEP, DANTES, GRE).

Admission Requirements: *Undergraduate:* high school graduate, have a qualifiable eligibility index (see section of Eligibility Index in catalog) and have completed with grades of C or better each of the courses in the comprehensive pattern of college preparatory subject requirements (see subject requirements in catalog). Courses must be completed prior to the first enrollment in the California State University. *Graduate:* program-specific. *Certificate:* program-specific.

On-Campus Requirements: Yes. Varies by program.

Tuition and Fees: *Undergraduate:* $502/quarter, 6.1 or more units. *Graduate:* $306/quarter, 0.1 to 6.0 units, $528/quarter, 6.1 or more units. *Lecture:* $95/quarter unit. *Laboratory:* $115/quarter unit. *Internships:* $115/quarter unit. *Field Work:* $115/quarter unit. *Application Fee:* $55. *Credit by:* quarter.

Financial Aid: Federal Stafford Loan, Federal Perkins Loan, Federal PLUS Loan, Federal Pell Grant, Federal Work-Study, VA, California resident programs.

Accreditation: Western Association of Schools and Colleges.

Description: The individual California State Colleges were brought together as a system by the Donahoe Higher Education Act of 1960. In 1972 the system became The California State University and Colleges and in 1982 the system became The California State University.

California State University, Chico

Center for Regional and Continuing Ed	Phone: (530) 898-6105
Chico, CA 95929-0250	Fax: (530) 898-4020

Division(s): Center for Regional and Continuing Education
Web Site(s): http://rce.csuchico.edu/online
E-mail: jlayne@csuchico.edu

Undergraduate Degree Completion Programs:
Bachelor of Science in:
  Computer Science
  Liberal Studies
  Social Science
  Sociology
  Political Science
Minors available in:
  Business Administration
  Career and Life Planning
  Family Relations
  Political Science
  Psychology
  Sociology

Graduate Degree Programs:
Master of Science in Computer Science

Certificate Programs: Greater Avenues for Independence, Resource Specialist.

Class Titles: courses toward Bachelor of Science in Liberal Studies and toward Certificate in Paralegal Studies.

Teaching Methods: *Computers:* Internet, e-mail, video-streaming. *TV:* videotape, satellite. *Other:* None.

Credits Granted for: examination (CLEP).

Admission Requirements: *Undergraduate:* Chico Distance and Online Education students must meet the same university admissions requirements and deadlines as those students on-campus. Only students who have already been admitted to the university (prior to the beginning of classes) will be allowed to register for Chico Distance and Online Education classes. Early application to the university is encouraged. For more information, please contact the school. *Graduate:* same as undergraduate. *Certificate:* same as undergraduate.

On-Campus Requirements: None.

Tuition and Fees: *Undergraduate:* same as on-campus students. Fall 2001 fees were $715 for 0–6 units and $1,015 for 6.1 units or more. All fees are subject to change by action by the Board of Trustees of the California State University. *Graduate:* Please call the Center for Regional and Continuing Education for information regarding this corporate program. *Application Fee:* $55. *Credit by:* semester.

Financial Aid: Federal Stafford Loan, Federal Perkins Loan, Federal Pell Grant, VA, California resident programs (financial aid DOES NOT apply to the Computer Science degrees).

Accreditation: Western Association of Schools and Colleges.

Description: California State University, Chico (1887), is located in northern California, 99 miles north of the state capital of Sacramento. It was established as California's second State Normal School. CSU, Chico, is the second oldest institution in the 23-campus California State University System. The university has been active in distance education since 1975. CSU, Chico, offers 2 distinct distance education programs.

California State University, Fullerton

800 North State College Boulevard	Phone: (714) 278-4651
Fullerton, CA 92834	Fax: (714) 278-4169

Division(s): Distance Education
Web Site(s): http://distance-ed.fullerton.edu
E-mail: jkahrhoff@fullerton.edu

Undergraduate Degree Programs:
Bachelor of Science in Nursing
Partial degree program in Liberal Studies, Elementary Education, Special Education

Class Titles: Art, Business Administration, Communications, Comparative Religion, Economics, Elementary Education, History, Human Services, Math, Nursing, Sociology, Special Education, Physics.

Teaching Methods: *Computers:* Internet, real-time chat, electronic classroom, e-mail. *TV:* ITFS, videoconferencing.

Credits Granted for: experiential learning, portfolio assessment, extrainstitutional learning (PONSI, corporate or professional association seminars/workshops), examination (CLEP, ACT-PEP, DANTES, GRE).

Admission Requirements: *Undergraduate:* application. *Graduate:* same. *Doctoral:* same. *Certificate:* same.

On-Campus Requirements: Some classes are offered completely at a distance, while others require on-campus meetings.

Tuition and Fees: *Undergraduate:* $137/lecture unit, $175/activity unit, $217/laboratory unit. *Credit by:* semester.

Financial Aid: Federal Stafford Loan, Federal Perkins Loan, Federal PLUS Loan, Federal Pell Grant, Federal Work-Study, VA, California resident programs.

Accreditation: Western Association of Schools and Colleges.

Description: California State University, Fullerton (1957) boasts almost 29,000 students and is one of the fastest-growing campuses in the California State University system. University Extended Education (UEE) provides more than 50 professional development certificate programs, as well as individual courses, seminars, and workshops, with over 60,000 enrollments each year. In addition to our online offerings, classes are held at 5 Orange County locations, delivered by industry experts and university faculty. Distance Learning,

is part of UEE, and recalls its beginning to 1986, when CSU Fullerton delivered 4 classes to 6 high schools in Orange County on cable TV via the Titan Interactive Network. Distance Learning now offers numerous conferences and noncredit classes, in addition to over a dozen online courses and 50 ITVs. In the future, the university will be enhancing existing programs, as well as developing new distance degree courses and programs, to support the growing need for online education.

California State University, Northridge

18111 Nordhoff Street	Phone: (818) 677-2355
Northridge, CA 91330-8324	(800) 882-0128
	Fax: (818) 677-2316

Division(s): Creative Media Sciences
Web Site(s): http://www.csun.edu
E-mail: sheri.kaufmann@csun.edu
karen.j.green@csun.edu

Graduate Degree Programs:
Masters:
    Communicative Disorders
    Electrical Engineering

Teaching Methods: Telephones, TV, videotape, cable program, satellite broadcasting, fax, correspondence, independent study, individual study.

Credits Granted for: experiential learning, portfolio assessment, extrainstitutional learning, examination (CLEP, ACT-PEP, DANTES, GRE).

Admission Requirements: *Graduate:* GRE or MAT, bachelor's degree with prerequisite course work, letters of reference, writing sample for the Communicative Disorder degree. For the Electrical Engineering degree, the student should contact admission representative at (818) 677-3700.

On-Campus Requirements: attendance at designated receive sites for 2-way video for the Electrical Engineering degree.

Tuition and Fees: *Undergraduate:* Electrical Engineering tuition: 0–6 units $607 and 6.1–more units $907. Open university students pay $120/unit. N/A for the Communicative Disorders degree. *Graduate:* Electrical Engineering tuition: 0–6 units $631 and 6.1–more units $946. For Communicative Disorders degree, the tuition is $445/credit hour. *Application Fee:* For Electrical Engineering degree contact Admissions Office at (818) 677-3700; $55 application fee for the Communicative Disorders degree. *Software:* computer and software $1,200 for the Communicative Disorders degree. *Graduation Fee:* $30 for the Communicative Disorders degree. *Other Costs:* books $2,000 estimate for Communicative Disorders. Books and supplies costs for the Electrical Engineering Degree. *Credit by:* semester.

Financial Aid: Contact the Financial Aid office at (818) 677-3000 for the Electrical Engineering degree; FAFSA for the Communicative Disorders degree.

Accreditation: Western Association of Schools and Colleges, American Speech-Language Hearing Association.

Description: Electrical Engineering: The Creative Media Services program at California State University, Northridge (1958) is a university outreach program providing quality education for the distant learner. This is accomplished using multiple technologies including online-based courses, interactive ISDN-based 2-way video, and a 14,000-square mile 4-channel interactive microwave broadcasting system. The microwave system enables the university to establish an electronic network and to provide training and education to students in the Los Angeles, Orange, Kern, and Ventura counties. The Creative Media Services offers credit courses and extension courses from studio class rooms to telecommute centers, schools, and industrial corporations.

Communication Disorders and Sciences Distance Master's Degree Program: The extraordinary need for increased numbers of speech-language pathologists is demonstrated through national and state data. Accredited graduate programs in speech-language pathology operate at enrollment capacity. The small numbers of master's degree graduates annually falls short in fulfilling the present need, which does not take into account the estimated rise in the school age population. The initial target population for the online program was personnel already employed by school districts. Many of these people cannot attend a residential program because of geography. Many cannot attend because commuting is impractical due to congested freeways and inadequate public transportation in large urban areas. Other students must work and are unable to attend a "day" program. The planning for this program began in 1997. A feasibility analysis and survey was conducted in the state of California. The first cohort began in May of 1999 and the second class began in September of 2000.

California State University, San Marcos

Extended Studies	Phone: **(760) 750-4020**
San Marcos, CA 92096	Fax: **(760) 750-3138**

Division(s): Department of Distance Learning
Web Site(s): http://www.csusm.edu/es
E-mail: bre@host1.csusm.edu

Class Titles: History of California, Riding Information Superhighway, Sociology of Ethnicity/Racism, Sociology of

Law, Sociology: Postmodern Thought, Mainstreaming, Using Database Instruction in Special Education, Teaching Reading in K-8 Classroom.

Noncredit: MCSE, A+, Web Design, professional development courses.

Teaching Methods: *Computers:* Internet. *Other:* None.

On-Campus Requirements: None.

Tuition and Fees: *Undergraduate:* $105/unit tuition. No other costs. *Graduate:* same. *Credit by:* semester. *Noncredit:* $49–$180 total.

Financial Aid: No financial aid through extended studies.

Accreditation: Western Association of Schools and Colleges.

Description: California State University, San Marcos (1989) offers excellence in undergraduate and graduate education to a diverse citizenry in an increasingly interdependent world. As the 20th campus in the California State System, CSU San Marcos provides an academic environment in which students, taught by active scholars, researchers, and artists, can achieve a foundation in the liberal arts and sciences and acquire specific competencies appropriate to major disciplines or graduate/professional study. Noncredit distance learning courses now available for personal and professional development, starting at just $49.

California State University, Stanislaus

801 West Monte Vista Avenue	Phone: **(209) 667-3171**
Turlock, CA 95382-0299	Fax: **(209) 667-3356**

Division(s): Mediated and Distance Learning
Web Site(s): www.csustan.edu/TLC/dist_lrn.htm
E-mail: nbwright@stan.csustan.edu

Undergraduate Degree Programs:
Bachelor of Arts in Communications Studies
Bachelor of Arts in History (Stockton)

Graduate Degree Programs:
Master of Business Administration (Stockton)

Class Titles: Students must be regularly enrolled students at CSU Stanislaus in order to take a distance learning course. Accounting, Auditing, Computer in Accounting, Anthropology/Modern Social Issues, Cultures of Pacific, Native Americans, Comparative Religion, Folk Literature/Arts, American Art, Frontiers in Biology, Business Law, Child Abuse/Neglect, Chemicals in Your Life, Biochemistry, Computer Information Systems, Administration of Corrections, Language/Speech Development, Communications Research Methods, Communication Colloquium, Communication Theory, Organizational Communication, Persuasion/Social Influence, Mass Communication Perspectives, Public Relations, Personal Computing, Business/Economic Environment, Applied Writing, Rhetoric, Linguistic Theory, Masterpieces of World Literature, English Grammar, Contemporary World History, Medieval Europe, Renaissance/Reformation History, 19th Century Europe, 20th Century Europe, Great Teachings, Contemporary America, Women in American History, East Asia in Traditional Times, Islamic Civilization, Colonialism/States of Asia/Africa, European Intellectual History, Judaism/Jewish History, Hitler/Nazi Era, Directed Reading Seminar, Senior Thesis, History of Journalism, Applied Mathematical Models, Gerontology, International Business, Marketing, Health Assessment, Nursing Leadership/Management, Community Health Nursing, Nursing Research, Operations Management, Productivity Management, Psychological Testing, Behavior Genetics, Learning Disabilities, Cross-Cultural Social Issues, Treatment of Offender, Sociology of Death, Sociology of Mental Health, Social Science Interdisciplinary Seminar.

Teaching Methods: *Television:* All courses are live and interactive. CSU Stanislaus currently has 2 channels of Instructional TV Fixed Service microwave, which is 2-way audio and one-way video to all locations. We also have one channel of compressed video (CODEC) between Turlock and Stockton. That channel is both 2-way audio and 2-way video. The instructional TV rooms are computer-equipped. Some instructors use Web materials, but that is not standard. Some online courses.

Credits Granted for: All courses are for letter grade or pass/fail. They are all part of the regular degree programs of the University.

Admission Requirements: *Undergraduate:* high school graduate in top 1/3 of class. *Graduate:* bachelor's degree.

On-Campus Requirements: Except in Stockton, and then only for the programs mentioned above, most distance learners will take some or much of their course work on the Turlock campus. Stockton has a large site at which 200 courses/year are taught "live" in addition to the 80 or so ITV courses. At the Stockton Center, therefore, many degrees are offered.

Tuition and Fees: *Undergraduate:* $555.50 for in-state undergraduate for 0–6 units, $855.50 (fall and spring) for 7 or more units. Out-of-state undergraduates pay same as in-state PLUS $246/unit. *Graduate:* $575.50 for graduates carrying 0–6 units, $890.50 (fall and spring, so double that for the year) for 7 or more units. Out-of-state graduates pay same as above PLUS $246/unit. *Application Fee:* $55. *Software:* might vary and apply in certain courses. *Credit by:* We have a 4-1-4. This includes 2 13-week terms and a 1-month winter

term. All courses are regular 3- and 4-unit semester courses, meeting extra minutes during the 13-week terms to be the equivalent of a 15-week term.

Financial Aid: Federal Stafford Loan, Federal Perkins Loan, Federal PLUS Loan, Federal Pell Grant, Federal Work-Study, VA, California resident programs.

Accreditation: Western Association of Schools and Colleges.

Description: California State University, Stanislaus (1960) is located in the heart of the San Joaquin Valley and currently has a College of Arts, Letters, and Science; a School of Business; and a School of Education. It offers a full array of bachelor's and master's degrees in English, history, psychology, social work, education, business administration, and public administration. Stanislaus began offering live, interactive, distance learning courses to sites in its service area in the fall of 1981. It currently has 3 channels of operation that televise 75–95 courses/academic year.

Camden County College

Box 200 College Drive
Blackwood, NJ 08012

Phone: (609) 227-7200 x4271
Fax: (609) 374-5017

Division(s): Extended Education Services
Web Site(s): http://www.camdencc.edu/
E-mail: svasta@camdencc.edu

Undergraduate Degree Programs:
Associate in Arts/Liberal Arts and Sciences

Class Titles: American Cinema, American Federal Government, Anthropology, Business Law, Business Math, Business, Economics, Composition, Ethics, French, Health/Wellness, History of American Education, History of Western Civilization, U.S. History, Journalism, Literature, Management, Small Business Management, Marketing, Math Skills, Abnormal Psychology, Psychology, Child Psychology, Selling, Sociology of Family, Sociology, Spanish.

Teaching Methods: *Computers:* Internet, electronic classroom, e-mail, CD-ROM. *TV:* videotape, cable program, satellite broadcasting, PBS. *Other:* independent study, individual study, learning contracts.

Credits Granted for: experiential learning, portfolio assessment, extrainstitutional learning, examination (CLEP, ACT-PEP, DANTES, GRE).

Admission Requirements: *Undergraduate:* rolling admissions for accredited secondary or preparatory school graduates, State Equivalency Certificates, or age 18, plus application. Camden acceptance does not guarantee admission to restricted programs in Allied Health and Automotive Technology. CCC is authorized to issue I-20's and F-1 student visas with proper documentation and satisfactory academic progress.

On-Campus Requirements: None.

Tuition and Fees: *Undergraduate:* $59/credit in-county, $63/credit out-of-county, $111/credit foreign students. *Other Costs:* $19 general service fee 1–11 credits, $32 general service fee 12 or more credits, $25/course-$193/credit lab and material fees for applicable courses, $25/course distance learning course fee. *Credit by:* semester.

Financial Aid: Federal Stafford Loan, Federal Perkins Loan, Federal PLUS Loan, Federal Pell Grant, Federal Work-Study, New Jersey resident programs.

Accreditation: Middle States Association of Colleges and Schools.

Description: More than 30 years ago, the Salvatorian Fathers sold their Mother of the Savior Seminary and its 320 acres to Camden County College (1967). Today, Camden enrolls 13,000 credit students in 75 degree programs encompassing technical fields and liberal arts and sciences. A national leader in technology instruction with programs such as robotics, computer-integrated manufacturing, and laser/electro-optics technology, the college is also recognized as a vital resource for transfer education, customized training for business and industry, and community-based cultural arts programming. The campus in Cherry Hill focuses on undergraduate courses using state-of-the-art technology as well as delivering customized training for business and industry. Distance learning programming recognizes the need to serve those who have transportation, child-care, and employment-related issues that make it difficult or impossible to participate in the traditional college experience.

Canadian School of Management

335 Bay Street Suite 1120 **Toronto, Ontario M5H 2R3**	**Phone: (416) 360-3805** **Fax: (416) 360-6863**

Web Site(s): http://www.c-s-m.org/
E-mail: csm@c-s-m.org

Undergraduate Degree Programs:
Business Management
Health Management

Graduate Degree Programs:
Business Management
Health Management

Postgraduate Degree Programs:
Business Management
Health Management

Certificate Programs: Health Services Administration, Business Administration, Travel Counseling, and Management.

Class Titles: Contact school or check web site for details.

Teaching Methods: *Computers:* Internet, real-time chat, electronic classroom, e-mail, CD-ROM, newsgroup, LISTSERV. *Other:* correspondence.

Credits Granted for: experiential learning, portfolio assessment, extrainstitutional learning (PONSI, corporate or professional association seminars/workshops), examination (CLEP, ACT-PEP, DANTES, GRE), previous academic credits.

Admission Requirements: *Undergraduate:* 18 months of full-time general university education; prior formal or experiential learning is taken into consideration for credit; supervisory/administrative/managerial work experience with references. *Graduate:* bachelor's degree or equivalent; minimum 4 years management-related experience; plus required proficiency in certain management areas as per our catalog. *Postgraduate:* master's degree or equivalent as determined by registrar; minimum 4 years senior managerial experience; advanced understanding of areas of management together with demonstrated learning from managerial actions in which the applicant is or has been involved. *Certificate:* must have Grade 12 certificate, or be 24 years of age and be able to demonstrate the ability to cope with the work based on previous work experience.

On-Campus Requirements: None.

Tuition and Fees: Undergraduate: $575/course (3 credit) via Internet, $625/course correspondence. *Graduate:* same as above. *Postgraduate:* $1,350/5 credits plus other fees. *Application Fee:* $75. *Graduation Fee:* $105 for certificates and undergraduate degrees; $175 for master's degrees. *Other Costs:* intramural session as per brochure. *Credit by:* Our terms are every 3 months and students usually take 2–3 credit courses per term.

Financial Aid: Canadian government student assistance (for Canadian residents only).

Accreditation: University of Action Learning.

Description: CSM (1975) offers professional and academic qualifications for all levels of management. CSM uses Action Learning as its philosophy and methodology as we believe that workplace learning provides an important insight into management issues. Students build on existing knowledge and skills, adding breadth through contact with faculty, mentors, and fellow students. The Internet provides library resources and permits tutorial support as well as a forum for discussion.

Capella University

222 South 9th Street, 20th Floor
Minneapolis, MN 55402

Phone: (888) CAPELLA
Fax: (612) 337-5396

Web Site(s): http://www.capellauniversity.edu
E-mail: info@capella.edu

Undergraduate Degree Programs:
Bachelor of Science in Information Technology

Graduate Degree Programs:
Master of Business Administration (MBA)
Master of Science in Organization and Management
Master of Science in Training and Development
Master of Science in Education
Master of Science in Human Services
Master of Science in Psychology
Master of Science in Information Technology

Postgraduate Degree Programs:
Doctor of Philosophy in Organization and Management
Doctor of Philosophy in Education
Doctor of Philosophy in Human Services
Doctor of Philosophy in Psychology

Certificate Programs: Communications Technology Management, E-Business, Entrepreneurship, Finance, Human Resource Management, Information Technology Management, International Business, Leadership, Marketing and Brand Management, Adult Education, Distance Education, Educational Administration, Instructional Design for Online Learning, Teaching and Training Online, Training and Development, Addiction Counseling, Criminal Justice, Diversity Studies, Health Care Administration, Management of Non-Profit Agencies, Marriage and Family Services, Professional Counseling, Social Work and Community Services, Social Work, Urban School Services, Addiction Psychology, Clinical Psychology, Counseling Psychology, Family Psychology, Health Psychology, School Psychology, Sport Psychology, Post-Doctoral Certificate in Counselor Education and Supervision, Post-Doctoral Certificate in Clinical Psychology, Continuing Professional Education Certificate in Online Graduate Teaching and Training in Professional Psychology, E-Business Ventures, Graphics and Multimedia, Information System Quality Assurance, Network Technology, Web Application Development, Web Application Project Management, Web Application Security.

Teaching Methods: *Computers:* Internet, real-time chat, electronic classroom, e-mail, newsgroup, LISTSERV.

Credits Granted for: experiential learning, extra-institutional learning (PONSI, corporate or professional association seminars/workshops), examination (CLEP, ACT-PEP, DANTES, GRE). Please contact an Enrollment Counselor for more details.

Admission Requirements: *Undergraduate:* Admission requirements vary by program. *Graduate:* Admission requirements vary by program. *Postgraduate:* Admission requirements vary by program. *Certificate:* Admission requirements vary by program.

On-Campus Requirements: Residency requirements vary by program. Visit http://www.capellauniversity.edu to learn more.

Tuition and Fees: *Undergraduate:* ~$1,350 per course. *Graduate:* ~$575–1,475 per course. *Postgraduate:* Varies by program. *Application Fees:* $50 *Graduation Fee:* Varies by program. *Other Costs:* $50–400 for books, transcript evaluations, petition for credit and other services. *Credit by:* quarter.

Financial Aid: Federal Stafford Loan, Federal Pell Grant, VA, Minnesota SELF Loan, various alternative loans.

Accreditation: North Central Association of Colleges and Schools.

Description: Capella University's (1993) innovative, online course delivery format leverages the speed, convenience, and flexibility of the Internet to provide a quality education at a time and place most convenient for you. With more than 400 online courses and 80 specialized degree programs, Capella University is dedicated to helping working adults integrate advanced education into their busy lives. Our online curriculum enables you to learn at your own pace and schedule, while connecting you with an engaging, supportive community of expert faculty and fellow learners around the world. Programs are designed to be accessible from any web browser, anywhere, anytime, so your learning can fit into your personal and professional schedule. Programs can be customized to help achieve your career and personal goals, and you'll receive a level of personal attention and individualized support not found in many traditional programs.

Capitol College

11301 Springfield Road
Laurel, MD 20708

Phone: (301) 369-2800
Fax: (301) 953-3876

Division(s): Distance Education
Web Site(s): http://www.capitol-college.edu
http://www.capitol-online.edu
E-mail: admissions@capitol-college.edu

Undergraduate Degree Programs:
Bachelor of Science in Software and Internet Applications

Graduate Degree Programs:
Master of Science in:
    Information Architecture
    Information and Telecommunications
    Electronic Commerce
    Network Security

Certificate Programs: Preparation for CCNP, Preparation for CCNA, Object-Oriented Programming, Programming and Data Management, Web Programming, Web Site Development, Computer and Network Security, Software Engineering.

Teaching Methods: *Computers:* Internet, real-time audio real-time chat, electronic classroom, e-mail, CD-ROM, newsgroup. *Other:* None.

Credits Granted for: portfolio assessment, examination (CLEP, ACT-PEP, DANTES, GRE).

Admission Requirements: *Undergraduate:* high school diploma. *Graduate:* undergraduate degree. *Certificate:* high school diploma (undergraduate certificate), undergraduate degree (graduate certificate).

On-Campus Requirements: None.

Tuition and Fees: *Undergraduate:* $333–482/credit. *Graduate:* $333/credit. *Application Fee:* none if done online. *Software:* none. *Graduation Fee:* $150. *Credit by:* semester.

Financial Aid: Federal Stafford Loan, Federal Perkins Loan, Federal PLUS Loan, Federal Pell Grant, Federal Work-Study, VA, Maryland resident programs (must be degree-seeking).

Accreditation: Middle States Association of Colleges and Schools.

Description: Capitol College was founded in 1927 as Capitol Radio Engineering Institute (CREI), a correspondence school that offered electronics courses. A residence division was opened in Washington, D.C. in 1932 to develop training programs for the military. In 1946 CREI was accredited by the Engineer's Council for Professional Development. The license to confer the Associate of Applied Science (A.A.S.) degree came in 1954. In 1964 the Capitol Institute of Technology was founded in its present form as a private, nonprofit, nonsectarian institution of higher education. In 1965 the college was licensed to confer the bachelor of science degree in engineering technology. By 1983 the college had moved to its current location in Laurel, Maryland. The name change to Capitol College followed in 1987. By 1994 Capitol College had acquired a master's program and was offering a variety of engineering, engineering technology, computer, and management degrees. The online teaching program was started in 1997.

Carl Sandburg College

2400 Tom L. Wilson Boulevard	**Phone: (309) 344-2518**
Galesburg, IL 61401	**Fax: (309) 344-3526**

Division(s): Learning Resource Services
Web Site(s): http://www.csc.cc.il.us
E-mail: ckreider@csc.cc.il.us

Undergraduate Degree Programs:
Associate of Arts
Associate of Science
Associate of Fine Arts
Associate of Applied Science
Associate in General Education

Class Titles: Computer Information Systems, English, Health, Music, Secretarial, Auto Body Repair, Biology, Child Development, Chemistry, Economics, Math, Medical Terminology, Music, Political Science, Psychology, Radiology, Sociology.

Teaching Methods: *Computers:* Internet, real-time chat, electronic classroom, e-mail. *TV:* videotape. *Other:* videoconferencing, audioconferencing, independent study.

Credits Granted for: experiential learning, portfolio assessment, extrainstitutional learning (PONSI, corporate or professional association seminars/workshops), examination (CLEP, ACT-PEP, DANTES, GRE).

Admission Requirements: *Undergraduate:* Open admissions.

Tuition and Fees: *Undergraduate:* $57/credit hour in district; $313/credit hour out of state. *Credit by:* semester.

Financial Aid: Federal Stafford Loan, Federal Perkins Loan, Federal Pell Grant, Federal Work-Study, VA, Illinois resident programs.

Accreditation: North Central Accrediting Association.

Description: Carl Sandburg College (1966) is a comprehensive, 2-year community college. We offer selected courses in a variety of disciplines via distance learning; however, an entire program cannot be completed by distance.

Carroll College

100 N. East Avenue	**Phone: (262) 524-7216**
Waukesha, WI 53186	**Fax: (262) 650-4851**

Division(s): School of Professional Studies
Web Site(s): http://www.cc.edu
E-mail: pstudies@cc.edu

Undergraduate Degree Programs:
Bachelor of Arts
Bachelor of Science

Graduate Degree Programs:
Master of Software Engineering

Certificate Programs: Civil War, E-commerce, Marketing/Sales Promotion, Programmer Analyst, World Wide Web.

Class Titles: Business, Civil War, Computer Science, Math.

Teaching Methods: *Computers:* Internet, real-time chat, electronic classroom, e-mail, CD-ROM, newsgroup, LISTSERV.

Credits Granted for: experiential learning, portfolio assessment, examination (CLEP, DANTES, AP, IB).

Admission Requirements: *Undergraduate:* Contact college for details *Graduate:* Contact college for specific program requirements. *Certificate:* Undergraduate and Civil War Studies: open admissions.

On-Campus Requirements: Varies by course.

Tuition and Fees: *Undergraduate:* $198 per credit. *Graduate:* $385 per credit. *Graduation Fee:* $60 *Other Costs:* Books/supplies vary by course. *Credit by:* semester.

Financial Aid: Federal Stafford Loan, Federal Perkins Loan, Federal PLUS Loan, Federal Pell Grant, VA, Wisconsin resident programs.

Accreditation: North Central Association of Colleges and Schools.

Description: Nearly 2,700 students attend Carroll College (1846) and its partner school, Columbia College of Nursing in Milwaukee. The college, affiliated with the Presbyterian Church (U.S.A.), also collaborates with U.S. Speedskating, AFS, Quad Graphics, Quad/Tech, McHugh Software International, Northwestern Mutual Life, and Hawaiian Pacific University. Areas of undergraduate study include Accounting, Actuarial Sciences, Art, Athletic Training, Biology, Business Administration, Business and Information Technology, Chemistry, Communication, Computer Science, Criminal Justice, Education, English, Environmental Science, Exercise Science, Geography, Graphic Communication, History, Mathematics, Music, Nursing, Organizational Leadership, Physical Education, Politics, Psychology, Religious Studies, Social Work, Sociology, Spanish, and Theatre Arts. Graduate education at Carroll includes master's degrees in Education, Physical Therapy, and Software Engineering. The School of Professional Studies offers evening and Saturday classes on campus, in addition to a growing number of distance courses.

Carroll Community College

1601 Washington Road
Westminster, MD 21157

Phone: (410) 386-8100
Fax: (410) 876-5869

Division(s): Continuing Education and Training/Academic and Student Development
Web Site(s): http://www.carroll.cc.md.us
E-mail: kshattuck@carroll.cc.md.us

Class Titles: *Credit:* Advanced Math, Nutrition for Nursing, Computers, Sciences, Sociology, History, English, Psychology, Philosophy, Business. *Noncredit:* Vet Tech Assistant, RN Refresher, over 100 courses in Computer, Skills, Management and Supervison, Communications, and Personal Interest.

Teaching Methods: *Computers:* Internet, real-time chat, electronic classroom, e-mail. *TV:* videotape, cable program, satellite broadcasting, PBS. *Other:* videoconferencing, independent study, individual study, learning contracts.

Credits Granted for: portfolio assessment, examination (CLEP, DANTES).

Admission Requirements: *Undergraduate:* completed admission application, high school transcripts or GED scores, ACT/SAT results if available, and other transcripts if possible, completion of placement tests and meeting with an academic advisor. *Noncredit:* course prerequisites if required.

Tuition and Fees: *Undergraduate:* $75/credit. *Other Costs:* 15% of tuition college service fee; $2/billable hour student activity fee; $75/semester/1/2 hour applied music lab fee; $25/applicable life fitness course fee; $2/request transcript fee; $1/2$ course tuition credit-by-exam fee. *Noncredit:* tuition fees varied. *Credit by:* semester.

Financial Aid: Federal Pell Grant, Federal Work-Study, Federal Supplemental Educational Opportunity Grant, Maryland State Scholarships, Institutional Scholarships.

Accreditation: Middle States Association of Colleges and Schools.

Description: Carroll Community College (1976) began as a campus of Catonsville Community College, became an independent community college on July 1, 1993, and fully accredited in the spring of 1996. CCC entered into the distance education arena first with telecourses. In 1995, the college purchased a compressed video system as part of a grant awarded to 5 community colleges. This system is linked via a T-1 line and has ISDN capabilities. In 1997, the college added a second live interactive system that provides a statewide link via fiber to other colleges, universities, and public school systems. The college also provides noncredit courses for the professions via the live interactive video systems and the Internet. The college began offering courses via the Internet in 1997 throughout Maryland Community Colleges Teleconsortium.

Casper College

125 College Drive, Suite AD 298	Phone: (307) 268-2348
Casper, WY 82601	Fax: (307) 268-2224

Division(s): Academic Affairs
Web Site(s): http://www.cc.whecn.edu
E-mail: steinle@acad.cc.whecn.edu

Undergraduate Degree Programs:
Associate of Arts
Associate of Science
Associate of Applied Science
Associate of Applied Arts
Associate of Business

Certificate Programs: one-year certificates of completion.

Teaching Methods: *Computers:* Internet, real-time chat, e-mail, LISTSERV. *TV:* videotape, cable program, satellite broadcasting, PBS. *Other:* independent study, individual study.

Credits Granted for: extrainstitutional learning, examination (CLEP, ACT-PEP, DANTES, GRE).

Admission Requirements: *Undergraduate:* high school graduate or GED. No admission requirement if special nondegree student. *Certificate:* same as undergraduate.

On-Campus Requirements: None.

Tuition and Fees: *Undergraduate:* $55/credit resident, $131/credit nonresident. *Credit by:* semester.

Financial Aid: Federal Stafford Loan, Federal PLUS Loan, Federal Pell Grant, Federal Work-Study, VA, Wyoming resident programs.

Accreditation: North Central Association of Colleges and Schools.

Description: Casper College (1945) was established as Wyoming's first community college and has grown in size and reputation into one of the West's outstanding 2-year colleges. Casper offers 70 academic transfer degrees and 30 technical/career programs. Distance education classes were added to the curriculum 3 years ago to meet the needs of a sparsely populated geographic region. CC currently offers a wide variety of telecourses and Internet course offerings and continues to grow each year.

Catholic Distance University

120 E. Colonial Highway	Phone: (540) 338-2700
Hamilton, VA 20158	Fax: (540) 338-4788

Web Site(s): http://www.cdu.edu/
E-mail: masters@cdu.edu

Graduate Degree Programs:
Masters in Religious Studies
Master of Arts in Religious Studies

Certificate Programs: Catechetical Diploma (based on undergraduate courses).

Class Titles: Contact school or check web site for details.

Teaching Methods: *Computers:* chat room, e-mail. *TV:* cable program. *Other:* audiotapes, fax, correspondence, independent/individual study.

Credits Granted for: extrainstitutional learning (ACE/College Credit Recommendation Service, courses at accredited institutions).

Admission Requirements: *Undergraduate:* Continuing Education: no special requirements. Five months allowed to complete each course; high school diploma. Nine months allowed to complete each course. *Graduate:* bachelor's degree with undergraduate prerequisite courses in philosophy and the Catholic Catechism required unless waived based on prior education or appropriate experience. Seven years allowed for completing Master's in Religious Studies; 8 years for the Master of Arts in Religious Studies. *Certificate:* Catechetical Diploma requires successful completion of one undergraduate course rated at 3 semester hours. Twelve-course diploma program must be completed in 5 years.

On-Campus Requirements: No residency requirements.

Tuition and Fees: *Undergraduate:* Continuing Education: $85/course; $150/credit hour when course taken for college credit; $125/credit hour when not taken for college credit. *Graduate:* $215/credit hour. *Application Fee:* $100 for Master's Program; $75 for Catechetical Diploma. *Other Costs:* textbooks and other documents for master's program. *Credit by:* semester.

Financial Aid: VA (for master's program and related undergraduate prerequisite courses only). Department of Defense's DANTES Program for active duty military personnel (undergraduate and graduate courses).

Accreditation: Distance Education Training Council.

Description: The Catholic Distance University (1983) uses Distance Learning to educate adults worldwide in the teachings of the Roman Catholic Church.

CCCOnline

9075 East Lowry Boulevard	Phone: (303) 365-8888
Denver, CO 80230	Fax: (303) 365-8803

Web Site(s): http://www.ccconline.org
E-mail: john.schmahl@heat.cccoes.edu

Undergraduate Degree Programs:
Associate of Arts

Teaching Methods: *Computers:* Internet, electronic classroom, real-time chat, e-mail, CD-ROM, newsgroup, LIST-SERV. *TV:* videotape, cable program, satellite broadcasting, PBS. *Other:* radio broadcast, videoconferencing, audioconferencing, audiographics, audiotapes, fax, correspondence, independent study, individual study.

Credits Granted for: experiential learning, portfolio assessment, extrainstitutional learning, examination (CLEP, ACT-PEP, DANTES, GRE).

Admission Requirements: *Undergraduate:* age 16 and entrance exam, or prior college education.

On-Campus Requirements: None.

Tuition and Fees: *Undergraduate:* $120/credit. *Other Costs:* $25 for voice mail. *Credit by:* semester.

Financial Aid: Federal Stafford Loan, Federal PLUS Loan, Federal Pell Grant, Federal Work-Study, VA, Colorado resident programs.

Accreditation: North Central Association of Colleges and Schools.

Description: Colorado Electronic Community College (1995) is a unique and new college in the Colorado system. The school uses distance education methods and electronic technology to bring college courses to your home and place of work. We have the courses to deliver a full Associate of Arts degree for transfer to 4-year colleges and universities. These courses fulfill the typical requirements of Composition, Speech, Math, Sciences, Behavioral Sciences, Humanities, and Open Electives. Twenty courses are needed to graduate, representing about 60 semester-hour credits. Your degree plan might be much shorter if you have transfer credits.

Central Community College

PO Box 4903	Phone: (308) 398-7387
Grand Island, NE 68801	Fax: (308) 398-7398

Division(s): Extended Learning
Web Site(s): http://www.cccneb.edu
E-mail: scunningham@cccnet.edu

Undergraduate Degree Programs:
Associate of Arts
Associate of Applied Sciences

Teaching Methods: *Computers:* Internet, real-time chat, electronic classroom, e-mail, CD-ROM, newsgroup, LIST-SERV. *TV:* videotape, cable program, satellite broadcasting, PBS. *Other:* radio broadcast, videoconferencing, audioconferencing, audiographics, audiotapes, fax, correspondence, independent study, individual study, learning contracts.

Credits Granted for: experiential learning, portfolio assessment, extrainstitutional learning, examination (CLEP, ACT-PEP, DANTES, GRE).

Admission Requirements: *Undergraduate:* please contact school for information. *Graduate:* please contact school for information. *Doctoral:* please contact school for information. *Certificate:* please contact school for information.

On-Campus Requirements: None.

Tuition and Fees: *Undergraduate:* $44/credit. *Other Costs:* vary for special tools/supplies. *Credit by:* semester.

Financial Aid: Federal Stafford Loan, Federal Perkins Loan, Federal PLUS Loan, Federal Pell Grant, Federal Work-Study, VA, Nebraska resident programs.

Accreditation: North Central Association of Colleges and Schools.

Description: Central Community College (1973) as it exists today was formed with the enactment of legislation that established 6 technical community college areas in the state of Nebraska. This enabling legislation merged the Hastings campus (including its practical-nursing program in Kearney), which was established in 1966 as Nebraska's first vocational-technical college (serving a 17-county area), and the Platte campus, established at Columbus in 1969 as Nebraska's first county-supported community college. The Grand Island campus began offering courses in 1976. Central Community began offering courses at a distance through its learning centers almost from the beginning, with individualized curriculum offerings as its strength.

Central Methodist College

411 CMC Square	Phone: (660) 248-6286
Fayette, MO 65248	Fax: (660) 248-2622

Division(s): Academic Dean's Office
Web Site(s): http://www.cmc.edu
E-mail: aoberhau@cmc2.cmc.edu

Undergraduate Degree Programs:
Bachelor of Arts
Bachelor of Science

Graduate Degree Programs:
Master of Education

Class Titles: Nursing, Education, German, Religion. We offer noncredit courses/certificates as well, completely online.

Teaching Methods: *Computers:* Internet, LISTSERV. *Other:* videoconferencing, audioconferencing, fax, independent study, individual study.

Credits Granted for: examination (CLEP, ACT-PEP, DANTES, GRE).

Admission Requirements: *Undergraduate:* 2.5 GPA, 20 ACT. *Graduate:* 2.75 GPA.

On-Campus Requirements: yes, students cannot complete programs with distance learning only.

Tuition and Fees: *Undergraduate:* $500 and $125. *Graduate:* $165. *Application Fee:* $20–$25. *Credit by:* semester.

Financial Aid: Federal Stafford Loan, Federal Perkins Loan, Federal PLUS Loan, Federal Pell Grant, Federal Work-Study, VA, Missouri resident programs.

Accreditation: North Central Association of Colleges and Schools.

Description: Central Methodist College (1855) is located midway between St. Louis and Kansas City in a region of exceptional natural beauty. The 52-acre campus is a National Historic District distinguished by its majestic plantation of shade and ornamental trees. During the last decade, CMC began cooperative programs that allow regional citizens who have completed their AA degree (or who have 62 credits) to earn a bachelor's degree at nearby Mineral Area College and East Central College. In 1996 the college began offering its first master's degree program, the Master of Education, on all 3 campuses.

Central Missouri State University

Humphreys 403	**Phone: (660) 543-8480**
Warrensburg, MO 64093	**Fax: (660) 543-8333**

Division(s): Extended Campus—Distance Learning
Web Site(s): http://www.cmsu.edu/extcamp/
E-mail: bassore@cmsu1.cmsu.edu
ccampbell@cmsu1.cmsu.edu

Undergraduate Degree Programs:
Bachelor of Science in Crisis and Disaster Management

Graduate Degree Programs:
Master of Science in:
    Industrial Management
    Criminal Justice
    Library Information Technology

Doctoral Degree Programs:
Doctor of Philosophy in Technology Management

Certificate Programs: State certification requirements for teachers of the severely developmentally disabled.

Class Titles: Public Speaking, Early Childhood Nutrition/Health, Interactive TV Training, Cooperative Learning, Introduction to Crisis and Disaster Management, Principles of Teaching Industrial Education, Introduction to Electronic Information, Introduction to the Internet via the Internet, Introduction to Business, Teaching Reading in Secondary Schools, Investigating Conspiracy Theories, Computer Technology in Education, Nutrition, Educational Technology Leadership.

Teaching Methods: *Computers:* Internet, real-time chat, electronic classroom, e-mail, CD-ROM. *TV:* 2-way interactive TV, PBS. *Other:* videoconferencing.

Credits Granted for: extrainstitutional learning, examination (CLEP, ACT-PEP, DANTES, GRE).

Admission Requirements: *Undergraduate:* ACT of 20, high school diploma or GED, transcript. *Graduate:* GRE/GMAT, undergraduate degree, transcripts, 8-year completion time. *Doctoral:* master's degree, transcripts, 8-year completion time. *Certificate:* variable.

On-Campus Requirements: Varies.

Tuition and Fees: *Undergraduate:* $147/credit. *Graduate:* $210/credit. *Doctoral:* $192/credit. *Application Fee:* $25. *Other Costs:* vary for books plus $5/book mailing charge. *Credit by:* semester.

Financial Aid: Federal Stafford Loan, Federal Perkins Loan, Federal PLUS Loan, Federal Pell Grant, Federal Work-Study, VA, Missouri resident programs.

Accreditation: North Central Association of Colleges and Schools.

Description: Central Missouri State University (1871) is a state university offering 150 areas of study to 11,800 undergraduate and graduate students. The wide range of academic programs, people with varied backgrounds and experiences, a friendly and inviting environment, skilled professors, and excellent facilities combine to make Central Missouri State an outstanding institution of higher education. Central, charged with a statewide mission in professional technology, meets the needs of students physically located off campus through its commitment to distance education. Classes are conducted via 2-way interactive TV and the Internet. A charter member of one of Missouri's largest educational consortiums, Central currently offers master's degree programs, a variety of undergraduate and high school dual-credit classes, and specified courses of a cooperative doctoral degree using distance learning technologies.

Central Piedmont Community College

PO Box 35009
Charlotte, NC 28235

Phone: (704) 330-2722
(704) 330-5092
Fax: (704) 330-6945

Division(s): College Without Walls, a part of Instruction Development and Information Technology Division
Web Site(s): http://cww.cpcc.cc.nc.us
http://www.cpcc.cc.nc.us
E-mail: cww@cpcc.cc.nc.us

Undergraduate Degree Programs:
Associate of Arts
Associate in Health Information Technology
Associate in Early Childhood Education

Certificate Programs: Early Childhood Administration, Health Information Technology.

Teaching Methods: *Computers:* Internet, (using Blackboard delivery system), real-time chat, electronic classroom, e-mail, CD-ROM, *TV:* videotape, cable program, PBS. *Other:* None.

Credits Granted for: examination (CLEP).

Admission Requirements: *Undergraduate:* open-door policy.

On-Campus Requirements: Some of the Early Childhood Education courses may require a lab component.

Tuition and Fees: *Undergraduate:* $27.50/credit, NC residents; $169.50/credit, non-NC residents. *Other Costs: Student Activity Fee* $10–19; *Technology Fee* $0–48/semester. *Credit by:* semester.

Financial Aid: Federal Stafford Loan, Federal Perkins Loan, Federal PLUS Loan, Federal Pell Grant, Federal Work-Study, VA, North Carolina resident programs.

Accreditation: Southern Association of Colleges and Schools.

Description: Central Piedmont Community College (1963) is an innovative and comprehensive public 2-year college with a mission to advance the lifelong educational development of adults.

Central Virginia Community College

3506 Wards Road
Lynchburg, VA 24502

Phone: (804) 832-7600
Fax: (804) 386-4531

Division(s): Learning Resources Center
Web Site(s): http://www.cvcc.vccs.edu
E-mail: beasleys@cv.cc.va.us

Certificate Programs: Occupations/Technical areas.

Class Titles: Business, Health, Sociology, Biology, Economics, Math, Psychology, Marketing.

Teaching Methods: *Computers:* Internet, electronic classroom, e-mail, CD-ROM. *TV:* videotape, PBS. *Other:* videoconferencing, audioconferencing, audiotapes, fax, correspondence, independent study, individual study.

Credits Granted for: experiential learning, examination (CLEP, ACT-PEP, DANTES, GRE).

Admission Requirements: *Undergraduate:* please contact school for information.

On-Campus Requirements: Some courses have on-campus orientation sessions and on-campus proctored testing.

Tuition and Fees: *Undergraduate:* $37.12/credit in-state, $164.82/credit out-of-state. *Other Costs:* $10 general student fee. *Credit by:* semester.

Financial Aid: Federal Stafford Loan, Federal Perkins Loan, Federal PLUS Loan, Federal Pell Grant, Federal Work-Study, VA, Virginia resident programs.

Accreditation: Southern Association of Schools and Colleges.

Description: Central Virginia Community College (1967) is part of the Virginia Community College System. It offers associate degrees, diplomas, and certificate programs in Occupations/Technical areas as well as for college transfer. In 1987 the college began offering distance education courses in several disciplines. The program and course offerings have grown to include Web-based and compressed-video offerings.

Central Washington University

400 East 8th Avenue
Ellensburg, WA 98926

Phone: (509) 963-3001
Fax: (509) 963-3022

Division(s): Office of the Provost
Web Site(s): http://www.cwu.edu
E-mail: schwindt@cwu.edu

Undergraduate Degree Programs:
Business Administration
Education
Organization Development

Class Titles: Personal Finance via Internet, a variety of Professional Development, Education, Accounting, Business courses.

Teaching Methods: *Computers:* Internet, electronic classroom, e-mail, CD-ROM. *TV:* videotape, cable program, satellite broadcasting. *Other:* videoconferencing, fax, independent study, individual study.

Admission Requirements: *Undergraduate:* 1st-year students (under 45 credits): transcripts from high school or college (if attended), ACT/SAT scores that meet the mission index, required high school core (contact school for details). Transfer students (over 45 credits): all college transcripts, meet minimum GPA standard (alternate admission possible for low GPA). *Graduate:* official copies of all undergraduate and graduate study at other institutions, 3 recommendation letters, personal statement of education objectives and professional aims (500 words or less). For some programs, acceptable GRE, 3.0 GPA for last 90 quarter hours (60 semester hours).

On-Campus Requirements: Students are required to attend the satellite broadcast session or participate in an evening orientation for Internet course.

Tuition and Fees: *Undergraduate:* $100.80/credit (2-credit minimum). *Graduate:* $161.60/credit (2-credit minimum). *Application Fee:* $35. *Other Costs:* $25 technology fee, $35 athletic fee, $40 health and counseling fee, other software or lab-related fees may apply. Tuition and fees are always subject to change. *Credit by:* quarter.

Financial Aid: Federal Stafford Loan, Federal Perkins Loan, Federal PLUS Loan, Federal Pell Grant, Federal Work-Study, VA.

Accreditation: Northwest Association of Schools and Colleges.

Description: Central Washington University (1890) is one of 6 state-supported institutions offering bachelor's and graduate degrees. The words *Docendo Discimus*, "by teaching we learn," remain today as in the past the cornerstone of the university's mission. Central Washington University's mission is to prepare students for responsible citizenship, responsible stewardship of the earth, and enlightened and productive lives. Faculty, staff, students, and alumni serve as an intellectual resource to assist central Washington, the state, and the region in solving human and environmental problems. The university community values teaching as the vehicle to inspire intellectual depth and breadth, to encourage lifelong learning, and to enhance the opportunities of its students. The faculty develop and strengthen bachelor's and master's degree programs in the arts, sciences, and humanities; in teacher education; in business; in the social services; and in technological specializations. A strong liberal arts foundation; applied emphases; opportunities for undergraduate research, creative expression, and international study; and close working relationships between students and faculty are hallmarks of the undergraduate experience. Graduate programs develop partnerships between faculty and students to extend scholarship to important areas of research and practice. Central has 6 university-center programs in addition to on-campus programs. Distance learning originated a few years ago when we broadcast our Wenatchee Site to ensure that students met their degree requirements.

Central Wyoming College

2660 Peck Avenue
Riverton, WY 82501

Phone: (307) 855-2269
Fax: (307) 855-2065

Division(s): Distance Education
Web Site(s): http://www.cwc.cc.wy.us
E-mail: jmccoy@cwc.cc.wy.us

Undergraduate Degree Programs:
Associate of Arts
Associate of Science

Class Titles: several individual courses are offered every semester.

Teaching Methods: *Computers:* Internet, real-time chat, electronic classroom, e-mail, CD-ROM. *TV:* videotape, PBS. *Other:* audioconferencing, videoconferencing.

Credits Granted for: examination (CLEP, DANTES).

Admission Requirements: *Undergraduate:* under age 16 with permission; COMPASS/ACT; plans underway for open-entry, open-exit courses.

On-Campus Requirements: None.

Tuition and Fees: *Undergraduate:* $68/credit. *Other Costs:* $7/credit for computer-based courses. *Credit by:* semester.

Financial Aid: Federal Stafford Loan, Federal PLUS Loan, Federal Pell Grant, Federal Work-Study, VA, Wyoming resident programs.

Accreditation: North Central Association of Colleges and Schools.

Description: The Central Wyoming College (1966) campus is located in a city of 10,000 on the banks of Wind River. The campus and community lie in the Wind River Valley, bounded by mountains on 3 sides. Lakes and streams are abundant, and recreational opportunities are unlimited. Yellowstone National Park, Grand Teton National Park, Hot Springs State Park, and extensive forested lands are within easy driving distance. Outdoor activities include skiing, snowmobiling, snowshoeing, ice skating, hiking, backpacking, hunting, fishing, photography, horseback riding, golf, and swimming. The valley has a rich and varied history, with a large portion presently occupied by an Indian reservation housing Shoshone and Arapahoe tribes. CWC has offered distance education since 1983 through a campus-based PBS station and the student-run FM radio station. Recently the program has expanded to include courses via the Internet; CD-ROM; electronic classrooms; and live, 2-way, interactive audio/video connections.

Centralia College

| 600 West Locust | Phone: (360) 736-9391 |
| Centralia, WA 98531 | Fax: (360) 330-7502 |

Division(s): Distance Learning (Correspondence)
Web Site(s): http://www.centralia.ctc.edu or http://www.webmaster@centralia.ctc.edu
E-mail: freund@centralia.ctc.edu

Undergraduate Degree Programs:
A complete degree is not available through distance learning at this time; however, many transferable classes are offered.

Certificate Programs: Same as above.

Class Titles: *Correspondence Courses:* Accounting, Pharmacology/Physiology of Alcohol/Drugs, Astronomy, Business, Business Law, Transcription Fundamentals, Filing, Legal Terminology, Medical Terminology, Education, Physical Geography, Health/Wellness, Exercise/Nutrition, Nutrition, U.S. History, Pacific Northwest History, Algebra, Technical Mathematics, Probability/Statistics, Plane Trigonometry, Pre-Calculus, Survey of Calculus, Elementary Math Concepts, Oceanography, Philosophy, Political Science, American Government, Meteorology, Business Math, Technical Math, Western Civilization. *Online Courses:* Accounting, Four-Field Anthropology, General Chemistry, English Composition, Introduction to American Literature, Survey of Western Civilization, Mathematical Models and Applications, Philosophy, Logic, Psychology.

Teaching Methods: *Computers:* Internet, e-mail. *TV:* video-tape, satellite broadcasting, PBS. *Other:* videoconferencing, fax, correspondence, independent study, individual study.

Credits Granted for: examination (CLEP, Advanced Placement), military credit and experience, articulation agreements, law enforcement/fire protection training.

Admission Requirements: *Undergraduate:* age 18 and/or a high school (or GED program) graduate. Special considerations may be given to individuals not meeting these criteria. Some programs have additional requirements that must be met.

On-Campus Requirements: At this time, it is not possible to earn all credits for a degree off-campus, although many of a student's credits may be earned through correspondence courses.

Tuition and Fees: *Undergraduate:* $58.10/credit Washington state resident, $71.26/credit nonresident US citizens, $228.70/credit nonresident non-US citizens. *Graduation Fee:* $10.80. *Other Costs:* student activities fee $5, placement testing (ASSET) $10, Program fee for correspondence students $12.42 or $24.37 for video program fee. Technology fee $4/credit with $40 maximum/quarter, and other fees for

specialized programs. Fees and tuition subject to change; please check for current rates. Fees and tuition rates quoted above are effective for Fall 2001. *Credit by:* quarter.

Financial Aid: Federal Stafford Loan, Federal Perkins Loan, Federal PLUS Loan, Federal Pell Grant, Federal Work-Study, VA, Washington resident programs.

Accreditation: Northwest Association of Schools and Colleges, Washington State Board for Community College Education, State Approving Agency for the Training of Veterans, U.S. Department of Education.

Description: Centralia College (1925) is the oldest continuously operating community college in the state of Washington. It is located on the I-5 corridor in an area that is a combination of forest and farmland. The community is mostly rural, but also has 2 cities with a combined population of about 18,000 people. The service area of Centralia College covers 2,409 square miles which includes Lewis County and south Thurston County. Our Distance Learning Program began in 1976 in the form of video courses. It later progressed to other correspondence courses in 1980. This program was created in answer to requests by students for distance learning and individual study programs. It was modeled after a successful program at Everett Community College. The need for these classes has grown due to work schedules, cost and time of commuting, and convenience for the student. We currently offer 42 correspondence courses, with 2 additional courses on the Internet.

Cerro Coso Community College

| 3000 College Heights Boulevard | Phone: (888) 537-6932 |
| Ridgecrest, CA 93555 | Fax: (760) 934-6019 |

Division(s): Office of Instruction
Web Site(s): http://www.cc.cc.ca.us/cconline
E-mail: mhightow@cc.cc.ca.us

Undergraduate Degree Programs:
Associate of Arts
Associate of Science

Certificate Programs: Business Administration, Computer Information Systems.

Class Titles: dozens—see Web site for current class descriptions.

Teaching Methods: *Computers:* Internet, real-time chat, electronic classroom, e-mail, CD-ROM, newsgroup, LISTSERV. *Other:* None.

Credits Granted for: examination (CLEP, USAFI, DANTES).

Admission Requirements: *Undergraduate:* accredited high school graduates, holders of CHSPE or GED certificates, or age 18 and able to profit from college instructional programs.

On-Campus Requirements: None.

Tuition and Fees: *Undergraduate:* $11/credit. *Other Costs:* variable materials fees. *Credit by:* semester.

Financial Aid: Federal Stafford Loan, Federal Perkins Loan, Federal PLUS Loan, Federal Pell Grant, Federal Work-Study, VA, California resident programs.

Accreditation: Western Association of Schools and Colleges.

Description: Cerro Coso Community College (1973) is a comprehensive community college serving the eastern Sierra Nevada and eastern Kern County regions of California. Cerro Coso has 4 instructional sites that together form the largest geographical service area (12,000 square miles) of any community college in California, serving a population of approximately 85,000. A leader in distance learning online classes and degree programs, Cerro Coso offers 5 dozen online classes each semester leading to an Associate in Arts or Associate in Science in Administration of Justice, Social Sciences, Business Administration, Computer Information Systems, or Liberal Arts. Online classes serve students in other states and nations.

Chabot College

25555 Hesperian Boulevard   Phone: (510) 786-6758
Hayward, CA 94545   Fax: (510) 264-1506

Division(s): Distance Education Center
Web Site(s): www.chabotcollege.org
E-mail: mpeterson@clpccd.cc.ca.us

Undergraduate Degree Programs:
Various courses are offered, almost enough to complete an Associate of Arts Degree

Class Titles: Cultural Anthropology, General Chemistry, Astronomy: Stars and The Universe, The Solar System. Introduction to Music, World Music, Beginning Camera Use, Business Law, Business Management, General Economics, U.S. History Through Reconstruction, U.S. History Since Reconstruction, Stress Management/Health Psychology/Lab, General Psychology, Principles of Sociology, Cultural/Racial Minorities, Marriage/Family Relations.

Teaching Methods: *Computers:* Internet, real-time chat, electronic classroom, e-mail, LISTSERV. *TV:* videotape, cable program.

Admission Requirements: *Undergraduate:* high school diploma or GED equivalent.

On-Campus Requirements: Usually only for telecourses.

Tuition and Fees: *Undergraduate:* $13/semester unit. *Credit by:* semester units.

Financial Aid: Federal Stafford Loan, Federal Perkins Loan, Federal PLUS Loan, Federal Pell Grant, Federal Work-Study, VA, California resident programs.

Accreditation: Western Association of Schools and Colleges. The College is approved by the California State Department of Education and is a member of the American Association of Community and Junior Colleges and the Community College League of California.

Description: Chabot College (1961) has been serving southern Alameda County for more than 4 decades. It shares a diverse learning environment of 12,500 students, of which 27% are enrolled full time and 73% are enrolled part time. Almost 45% take courses only during the day, 22% take both day and evening, while 30% take evening or evening/Saturday courses. Clearly, our student population needs an alternative mode of accessing education in the midst of working full time in a very congested Bay Area. To meet this need, we began offering telecourses in 1990, having offered independent study for some time before then. We are increasing our online courses each semester.

Chadron State College

1000 Main Street   Phone: (800) 242-3766 or (308) 432-6376
Chadron, NE 69337   Fax: (308) 432-6473

Division(s): Extended Campus Programs
Web Site(s): http://www.csc.edu
E-mail: alangford@csc.edu

Undergraduate Degree Programs:
Bachelor of Science in Interdisciplinary Studies

Class Titles: Software Application/Aviation, Accounting Principles I, Accounting Principles II, Intermediate Accounting I, Business Law I, Records Management, Earth Science, Environmental Geology, Physical Geology, Historical Geology, Survey of Economics, Macroeconomics, Microeconomics, Principles of Marketing, Buyer Behavior, Parenting in a Contemporary Society, Program Management, Individualized Fitness, Foundations of P.E., Personal Health and Wellness, Theory and Readings in Elementary P.E., Introduction to Adapted P.E., U.S. History to 1877, U.S. History Since 1877, Western Civilization I, Traffic Safety I, Traffic Safety II, Computer Science Curriculum, Principles of Management, Introduction to Math, Intermediate Algebra, College Algebra, History and Foundations of Mathematics, Linear Algebra, Applied Statistics, American National Government, International Politics, Child Psychology, Developmental Adolescent Psychology, Psychopharmacology, Abnormal Psychology, Real Estate Principles, Introduction to Sociology, Principles of Information Systems, Human Resource Management, Introduction to Social Work,

Social Work Technologies, Fundamentals of School Administration, The Middle School, Human Relations.

Teaching Methods: Internet, satellite broadcasting, interactive audio/video conferencing, correspondence, independent study.

Credits Granted for: experiential learning, portfolio assessment, examination (CLEP).

Admission Requirements: *Undergraduate:* high school graduate or GED.

On-Campus Requirements: None.

Tuition and Fees: *Undergraduate:* $162.25/credit. *Application Fee:* $15. *Credit by:* semester.

Accreditation: North Central Association of Colleges and Schools, National Council for the Accreditation of Teacher Education, Council on Social Work Education, American Association of University Women.

Description: Founded as a teacher's college, Chadron State College (1911) now offers degrees in 21 areas to a student body of 2,800. The college has 50 correspondence courses, 10 online courses, approximately 35 courses per semester by ground line videoconferencing to selected sites, and 8 interactive satellite transmission courses per semester.

Chaminade University of Honolulu

| 3140 Waialae Avenue | Phone: (808) 735-4755 |
| Honolulu, HI 96816 | Fax: (808) 735-4766 |

Division(s): Accelerated Undergraduate Programs
Web Site(s): http://www.chaminade.edu
E-mail: online@chaminade.edu

Undergraduate Degree Programs: no complete degree programs are currently available on-line.

Class Titles: Anthropology, Business, Criminal Justice, English, History, Philosophy, Physics, Political Science, Psychology, Religion.

Teaching Methods: *Computers:* Internet, e-mail.

Credits Granted for: experiential learning, portfolio assessment, extrainstitutional learning (PONSI, corporate or professional association seminars/workshops), examination (CLEP, ACT-PEP, DANTES, GRE).

Admission Requirements: *Undergraduate:* completion of high school or equivalent.

On-Campus Requirements: None.

Tuition and Fees: *Undergraduate:* $100/credit hour for 100 and 200 level classes, $143/credit hour 300 and 400 level classes. *Application Fee:* $50. *Graduation Fee:* $85. *Other Costs:* $15/credit hour technology fee. *Credit by:* semester.

Financial Aid: Federal Stafford Loan, Federal Perkins Loan, Federal PLUS Loan, Federal Pell Grant, Federal Work-Study, VA, state programs for residents of Hawaii.

Accreditation: Western Association of Schools and Colleges/Accrediting Commmission for Senior Colleges and Universities.

Description: Chaminade University of Honolulu (1955) was founded by the Reverend Robert R. Mackey S.M. in 1955. The university is named for Father William Joseph Chaminade (1761–1850), a French Catholic priest who lived through the French Revolution and the rise and fall of Napoleon. Chaminade University campus is located on a hillside in Honolulu with a spectatular view extending from Diamond Head to downtown Honolulu. The university began offering accelerated evening and weekend programs for working people and members of the armed forces seeking degrees in 1967. Online courses were added as another option starting in 1996.

Champlain College

| 163 South Willard Street | Phone: (888) 545-3459 |
| Burlington, VT 05401 | Fax: (802) 865-6447 |

Division(s): Online Distance Learning Program
Web Site(s): http://www.champlain.edu
http://www.champlain.edu/ccol
E-mail: online@champlain.edu

Undergraduate Degree Programs:
Associate of Science: Accounting, Business, e-Business and Commerce, International Business, Management, Software Development, Telecommunications, Web Site Development and Management. Bachelor of Science: Computer Information Systems, Professional Studies.

Certificate Programs: Accounting, Business, e-Business and Commerce, International Business, Management, Software Development, Telecommunications, Web Site Development and Management.

Class Titles: Accounting, Art, Computers, Communications, Early Childhood Education, Economics, English, Geography, History, Hospitality, Legal Field, Management, Marketing, Math, Philosophy, Social Sciences, Telecommunications.

Teaching Methods: *Computers:* Internet real-time chat, electronic classroom, e-mail.

Credits Granted for: portfolio assessment, extrainstitutional learning, examination (CLEP, DANTES).

Admission Requirements: *Undergraduate:* graduation from a recognized secondary school or possession of a high school equivalency certificate (GED). TOEFL (Test of English as a Foreign Language) score for international students for whom English is not their first language, or equivalent English proficiency test, such as the ELPT. *Certificate:* Applicants to a Certificate program must also include a current résumé or outline of employment history in addition to the requirements listed above.

On-Campus Requirements: None.

Tuition and Fees: *Undergraduate:* $350/credit (2001–2002 academic year). *Application Fee:* $35. *Software:* Costs vary where applicable. *Other:* books, costs vary. *Credit by:* semester.

Financial Aid: Federal Stafford Loan, Federal Perkins Loan, Federal PLUS Loan, Federal Pell Grant, Federal Work-Study, VA, Vermont resident programs.

Accreditation: New England Association of Schools and Colleges.

Description: Champlain College was a pioneer in using the Internet for delivering education; we recognized the future when we saw it, so we began offering online courses 9 years ago, before most people had ever heard of the World Wide Web. Champlain has a long history as an innovative, energetic institution. Since 1878 we have been providing students with an education that makes a difference in their lives. We make it our mission to understand what is happening in the job market, to know which skills are important to employers, and we translate that understanding into programs bristling with relevant, workplace-savvy content.

Charter Oak State College

66 Cedar Street
Newington, CT 06111-2646

Phone: (860) 666-4595 x21
Fax: (860) 666-4852

Division(s): Academic
Web Site(s): http://cosc.edu
E-mail: sisrael@charteroak.edu

Undergraduate Degree Programs:
Associate in Arts
Associate in Science
Bachelor of Arts
Bachelor of Science

Video-Based Courses: Geography: World Regional Geography, Biology: Intro to Genetics, Biology: Cycles of Life, History: People's Century: Part 2 (1945–1999), Anthropology: Faces of Culture, Fine Arts: Art of Western World, Sociology: Sociology of the Diversity, Communication: Media Waves: An Introduction to Mass Communication, Sociology: Sociology of the Family, Economics: Introduction to Microeconomics, History: The Civil War, Mathematics: Contemporary Mathematics, Philosophy: Ethics in America, Business: Small Business Management, Film: Introduction to Film.

Online Courses: English: Power Writing, Mathematics: Contemporary Mathematics, English: World Literature for Children, Political Science: Ethics in International Relations, Business: Business Policy, Psychology: Cognitive Psychology, Psychology: Social Psychology, Sociology: Sociology of the City, IDS: Introduction to Adult Learning*, IDS: Service Learning*, IDS: Tools to Critical Thinking‡, Political Science: The Modern Presidency, Economics: The Economics of Health & Health Care, Sociology: Research Methods for the Behavioral Sciences Nursing-Nurse Refresher course (non credit)**.

Online Accelerated Courses (8 weeks): Management: Group & Organizational Dynamic, Communication: Organizational Communication, Criminal Justice: Selected Topics in Comparative Criminal Justice, Criminal Justice: Ethics & the Administration of Justice, IDS: Priciples of Leadership*, Social Science: Social Problems & Their Impact on the Workplace, Management: Systems Approach, Human Resource Management: Human Resource Management, Management: International Management, Management: Strategic Planning, Philosophy: Personal Values & Organizational Ethics, Psychology: Selected Topics in Social Psychology & Deviance.
*IDS is Interdisciplinary Studies.
‡The only course offered for no credit.

Teaching Methods: *Computers:* Internet, real-time chat, electronic classroom, e-mail, CD-ROM, newsgroup. *TV:* videotape. *Other:* learning contracts accelerated courses.

Credits Granted for: experiential learning, portfolio assessment, extrainstitutional learning, examination (CLEP, ACT-PEP, DANTES, GRE).

Admission Requirements: *Undergraduate:* age 16, must have completed 9 college credits.

On-Campus Requirements: None.

Tuition and Fees: *Undergraduate:* $74/video-based credit, resident; $110/video-based credit, nonresident. $107/online credit, resident; $146/online credit nonresident. Military personnel pay resident tuition/fees. *Application Fee:* $45. *Other Costs:* $20/semester nonresident nonrefundable course registration fee; $457 enrollment/technology fee/first-year advising fee, resident, $660 nonresident; $325 annual advising fee/records maintenance, resident; $467 nonresident; $250 baccalaureate concentration proposal review fee. *Credit by:* semester.

Financial Aid: Federal and state grants, federal loans, Cosc Foundation grants, institutional fee awards, and merit scholarships.

Accreditation: New England Association of Schools and Colleges.

Description: Charter Oak State College (1973) was established as a virtual university to provide an alternate way for adults to earn a degree. Charter Oak does not offer classroom instruction and has no residency requirements. Instead, students earn credits based on Charter Oak faculty evaluation of courses transferred from regionally accredited colleges and universities, distance courses offered by Charter Oak and other regionally accredited colleges and universities, noncollegiate-sponsored instruction, college-level exams, special assessment, contract learning, and portfolio review. Degrees are offered at the associate and bachelor's levels.

Chesapeake College

1000 College Avenue	
PO Box 23	Phone: (410) 822-5400
Wye Mills, MD 21679	Fax: (410) 827-7057

Division(s): Academic Support Services
Web Site(s): http://www.chesapeake.edu
E-mail: mcalexander@chesapeake.edu

Class Titles: Accounting, Business, Computer Information Systems, Early Childhood Development, Economics, English, History, Paralegal Studies, Math, Sociology, Psychology.

Teaching Methods: *Computers:* Internet, e-mail, LISTSERV, electronic classroom. *TV:* videotape, PBS, interactive video classroom. *Other:* audiotapes, correspondence, independent study, individual study, self-guided instruction.

Credits Granted for: examination (CLEP, ACT-PEP).

Admission Requirements: *Undergraduate:* open admissions, prerequisite testing for some classes.

On-Campus Requirements: most distance classes require attendance at 3 seminars during the semester.

Tuition and Fees: *Undergraduate* $65/credit. *Other costs:* $15 for distance education classes. Consolidated Fee (per credit hour) $10; $5 registration fee. *Credit by:* semester.

Financial Aid: Federal Stafford Loan, Federal Perkins Loan, Federal PLUS Loan, Federal Pell Grant, Federal Work-Study, VA, Maryland resident programs.

Accreditation: Middle States Association of Colleges and Schools.

Description: Chesapeake College (1965), a nonresidential community college serving the 5-county, mid-shore region on Maryland's eastern shore, was established as the state's first regional community college in 1965. Chesapeake offers career and transfer programs in a wide variety of fields, including accounting, business management technology and business administration, computer information systems and computer transfer, criminal justice, engineering, teaching education, nursing, and liberal arts and sciences. Chesapeake, which has always strived to be on the cutting edge of technology, opened its first distance learning classroom in 1994. The college's main campus in Wye Mills is networked with fully interactive, fiber-optic distance learning classrooms at 5 other mid-shore sites.

Christopher Newport University

1 University Place	Phone: (757) 594-7607
Newport News, VA 23606	Fax: (757) 594-7500

Division(s): CNU ONLINE
Web Site(s): http://www.cnuonline.cnu.edu
E-mail: online@cnu.edu

Undergraduate Degree Programs:
Bachelor of Science in Governmental Administration with concentrations in:
    Public Management
    Criminal Justice
    International Studies
Bachelor of Arts in Philosophy with concentration in
    Religious Studies

Class Titles: Accounting, Business, English, Government, Health, Philosophy, History, Mathematics, Physics, Religious Studies, Sociology.

Teaching Methods: *Computers:* Internet, World Wide Web, electronic classroom, e-mail.

Credits Granted for: examination (CLEP, ACT-PEP, GRE, DANTES).

Admission Requirements: *Undergraduate:* Admission to the university is required for CNU Online courses.

On-Campus Requirements: None.

Tuition and Fees: *Undergraduate:* $130/credit *Graduation Fee:* $25. *Application Fee:* $25. *Credit by:* semester.

Financial Aid: Federal Stafford Loan, Federal Perkins Loan, Federal PLUS Loan, Federal Pell Grant, Federal Work-Study, VA, Virginia resident programs.

Accreditation: Southern Association of Colleges and Schools.

Description: Christopher Newport University (1961), a state-supported comprehensive institution, first offered computer-based distance learning courses in 1993. In the fall of 2001, a total of 1000 students enrolled in approximately 50 distance learning courses.

Cincinnati Bible College and Seminary

2700 Glenway Avenue	Phone: (513) 244-8181
Cincinnati, OH 45204-3200	Fax: (513) 244-8140

Division(s): Distance Education
Web Site(s): http://www.cincybible.edu
Online Courses at http://disted.cincybible.edu
E-mail: College: evan.casey@cincybible.edu
Seminary: jeff.derico@cincybible.edu

Undergraduate Degree Programs:
Bachelor of Arts or Bachelor of Science:
 Bible
 Preaching Ministry
 General Ministry
 Urban & International Ministry
 Youth Ministry
 Christian Education Ministry
 Children's Ministry
 Worship Ministry
 Professional Child Care
 Early Childhood Teacher Education with Milligan College
  (includes Master's Degree)
 Elementary Teacher Education License with Milligan
  College (includes Master's Degree)
 Secondary Teacher Education License with Milligan
  College (includes Master's Degree)
 Inclusive Early Childhood License with College of Mt. St.
  Joseph
 Middle Childhood License with College of Mt. St. Joseph
 Adolescent to Young Adult License with College of Mt. St.
  Joseph
 Signing Interpreter Training with Cincinnati State
Bachelor of Music:
 Church Music
 Music Education
Bachelor of Science in Helping Professions:
 Professional Child Care
 Psychology
 Communication Arts
 Music
 Other in arrangment with student and other schools
Associate of Arts:
 Bible
 Christian Education Christian Vocations Early Childhood
  Education Communication Arts Church Music Psy-
  chology Deaf Studies

Teaching Methods: *Computers:* Internet, real-time chat, electronic classroom, e-mail, CD-ROM, newsgroup, LISTSERV. *TV:* videotape, cable program, satellite broadcasting, PBS. *Other:* radio broadcast, videoconferencing, audioconferencing, audiographics, audiotapes, fax, correspondence, independent study, individual study, learning contracts.

Credits Granted for: experiential learning, portfolio assessment, extrainstitutional learning, examination (CLEP, ACT-PEP, DANTES, GRE).

Admission Requirements: *Undergraduate:* Please contact school.

On-Campus Requirements: None.

Tuition and Fees: *Undergraduate:* $180/credit. *Other Costs:* textbooks/syllabus. *Credit by:* semester.

Flinancial Aid: Federal Stafford Loan, Federal Perkins Loan, Federal PLUS Loan, Federal Pell Grant, Federal Work-Study, VA, state programs for residents of Ohio.

Accreditation: North Central Association of Colleges and Schools, Accrediting Association of Bible Colleges.

Description: On September 23, 1924, Cincinnati Bible Seminary came into existence through the merging of 2 institutions who were similar in purpose and beliefs. CBS came into being to meet the pressing leadership needs of the Restoration Movement fellowship at that time. The founding principle and ultimate purpose of the school was to provide church leaders who were well-grounded in the word of God. In 1987 the corporate name of the school was changed to Cincinnati Bible College and Seminary. The undergraduate division was designated as Cincinnati Bible College, and the graduate division as Cincinnati Bible Seminary. Correspondence studies were developed to provide a home study opportunity for those who were not able to attend classes on campus.

Citrus Community College

1000 Foothill Boulevard	Phone: (626) 963-0323
Glendora, CA 91741	Fax: (626) 914-8574

Division(s): Distance Education
Web Site(s): http://www.citrus.cc.ca.us
E-mail: kguttman@citrus.cc.ca.us

Undergraduate Degree Programs:
General Education, Associate of Arts in fall 1999

Class Titles: Introduction to Cultural Anthropology, Native North Americans, Art History Appreciation—Fundamentals, Motion Picture Appreciation, Biology: Contemporary Topics, General Biology, Human Anatomy, Introduction to Business, Business Law and Legal Environment, Introduction to Management, Beginning General Chemistry, Introduction to Computers, Mass Media and Society, Reporting and Writing News, Principles of Economics, Fundamentals of Composition, Reading/Composition, Composition/Critical Thinking, Introduction to Technical Writing, Planetary Astronomy, California Geology, Cultural Geography, Effective

Family Day Care Practices, Administration of Early Childhood Education 1, Administration of Early Childhood Education 2, Political and Social History of the United States, History of World War I, History of the Vietnam War, Survey of Mathematics, Introduction to Statistics, College Algebra, History of Rock and Roll, Music Appreciation, Introduction to Health Occupations, Introduction to Nutrition/Vocational Nursing, Diet Therapy for the Vocational Nurse, Growth/Development of the Young, Adult, Elderly, Leadership in Nursing, Fitness for Life, Health Science, Introduction to Philosophy, Government of the United States, Introduction to Public Policy, Introductory Psychology, Physiological Psychology, Drug/Acohol Abuse, Introduction to Sociology, Contemporary Social Problems, Marriage/Family/Intimate Relations, Public Address, Writing Communication for Leaders, Budget/Cost Control for Managers, Water Industry Politics and Policy.

Teaching Methods: *Computers:* Internet, real-time chat, e-mail, CD-ROM, newsgroup, LISTSERV. *TV:* videotape, PBS. *Other:* audioconferencing, audiotapes, fax, correspondence, independent study, individual study, learning contracts.

Admission Requirements: *Undergraduate:* open enrollment.

On-Campus Requirements: per California regulations.

Tuition and Fees: *Undergraduate:* $12/credit. *Credit by:* semester (units).

Financial Aid: Federal Stafford Loan, Federal Perkins Loan, Federal PLUS Loan, Federal Pell Grant, Federal Work-Study, VA, California resident programs.

Accreditation: Western Association of Schools and Colleges.

Description: Citrus College (1915) is located in the foothills of the San Gabriel Mountains, 25 miles northeast of Los Angeles. The 104-acre campus has the distinction of being the oldest community college in Los Angeles County and the fifth oldest in the state. The college, which opened with 28 students, currently enrolls 10,000. Citrus offers transfer programs to 4-year colleges and universities, a 2-year college degree, and 30 career and technical training programs to prepare students for the job market. Distance education began in 1996 and has grown from one class of 17 students to more than 56 classes. An online AA degree in general education is available, as well as a partially online vocational nursing program.

City College of San Francisco

50 Phelan Avenue	Phone: (415) 239-3885
San Francisco, CA 94112	Fax: (415) 239-3241

Division(s): Telecourses/online
Web Site(s): None.
E-mail: online@ccsf.org

Class Titles: contact school for more information.

Teaching Methods: *Computers:* e-mail, LISTSERV-BBS. *TV:* cable program. *Other:* None.

Admission Requirements: *Undergraduate:* age 18.

On-Campus Requirements: 2-hour orientation, 2-hour midterm, 2-hour final.

Tuition and Fees: *Undergraduate:* $12/unit. *Credit by:* semester.

Financial Aid: Federal Stafford Loan, Federal Perkins Loan, Federal PLUS Loan, Federal Pell Grant, Federal Work-Study, VA, California resident programs.

Accreditation: Western Association of Schools and Colleges.

Description: City College of San Francisco is a 2-year community college that has offered distance education for more than 10 years. CCSF currently provides 19 telecourses each semester, with an average enrollment of 55.

City University

11900 NE First Street	Phone: (425) 637-1010
Bellevue, WA 98005	(800) 426-5596
	Fax: (425) 709-7699

Division(s): Admissions and Student Affairs
Web Site(s): http://www.cityu.edu
E-mail: info@cityu.edu

Undergraduate Degree Programs:
Associate of Science in:
    General Studies
    General Studies-Medical Lab-Lab Technology
    General Studies-Medical Office-Lab Technology
    Paralegal Studies
Bachelor of Arts in:
    Applied Behavioral Science-Applied
    Applied Behavioral Science-General
Bachelor of Science in:
    Accounting
    Business Administration-E-Commerce Emphasis
    Business Administration-Europe
    Business Administration-General Management Emphasis
    Business Administration-Human Resource Emphasis
    Business Administration-Individualized Emphasis
    Business Administration-Information Systems-Technical Emphasis
    Business Administration-Marketing Emphasis
    Business Administration-Project Management Emphasis
    Computer Systems-C & C++ Programming Emphasis
    Computer Systems-Individualized Emphasis
    Computer Systems-Networking-Telecommunications Emphasis

Computer Systems-Web Design Emphasis
Computer Systems-Web Development 3-Commerce Emphasis
General Studies
Mass Communication and Journalism

Graduate Degree Programs:
Master of Business Administration in:
  E-Commerce Emphasis
  Executive Accounting
  Financial Management Emphasis
  General Management Emphasis
  General Management-Europe
  Human Resource Management Emphasis
  Individualized Emphasis
  Information Systems Emphasis
  Managerial Leadership Emphasis
  Marketing Emphasis
  Personal Financial Planning
  Project Management Emphasis
Master of Education in:
  Curriculum and Instruction
  Guidance and Counseling
  Reading and Literacy
Master of Arts in:
  Counseling Psychology
  Management
Master of Science:
  Computer Systems-C++ Programming Emphasis
  Computer Systems-Individualized Emphasis
  Computer Systems-Web Development Emphasis
  Computer Systems-Web Programming Language Emphasis
  Project Management
Master of Public Administration in:
  Public Administration

Certificate Programs:
Undergraduate Certificate Programs:
  Accounting
  C & C++ Programming
  Human Resource Management
  Marketing
  Networking-Telecommunications
  Paralegal Studies
  Web Design
  Web Development E-Commerce
Graduate Certificate Programs:
  C++ Programming
  Financial Management
  General Management
  Human Resource Management
  Information Systems
  Managerial Leadership
  Marketing

Personal Financial Planning
Project Management
Public Administration
Teacher Credentialing-California
Web Development
Web Programming Language

Teaching Methods: Standard Distance Learning: e-mail, phone, fax, post.

Credits Granted for: Prior Learning Assessment (PLA), some continuing education portfolio assessment, examination (CLEP, ACT-PEP, DANTES, Challenge).

Admission Requirements: *Undergraduate:* age 18, high school or GED diploma, application. *Graduate:* accredited bachelor's degree or equivalent, application. The MEd and MA programs have additional requirements. *Certificate:* application.

On-Campus Requirements: None.

Tuition and Fees: *Undergraduate:* $182/credit (U.S.); $210/credit (Canada) *Graduate:* $324/credit (U.S.); $332/credit (Canada). *Application Fee:* $75. *Software:* variable. *Other Costs:* books. *Credit by:* quarter.

Financial Aid: Federal Stafford Loan, Federal PLUS Loan, Federal Pell Grant, Federal Work-Study, SEOG (Supplemental Education Opportunity Grant), VA, Scholarships, Private loans. (Federal Perkins Loan is not available).

Accreditation: Northwest Association of Schools and Colleges.

Description: City University (1973) is a private, nonprofit institution of higher education. Its mission is to provide educational opportunities worldwide, primarily to segments of the population not being fully served. In keeping with its mission of providing convenient, accessible education, the university offers most of its degree programs through distance learning. Students may earn degrees exclusively by distance learning or by combining traditional classroom courses with distance courses. Students may communicate with instructors by e-mail, phone, mail, or fax. Distance learning courses may be started on the first of any month as long as registration and payment take place by the 20th of the preceding month.

Clackamas Community College

19600 South Molalla Avenue
Oregon City, OR 97045

Phone: (503) 657-6958
Fax: (503) 655-8925

Division(s): Instructional Support Services
Web Site(s): http://www.clackamas.cc.or.us
E-mail: cyndia@clackamas.cc.or.us

Undergraduate Degree Programs: Contact school.

Class Titles: Child Abuse, Career Exploration, Computing, Reporting, Health GED, Marketing, Business, Anthropology, Autocad (Drafting), Print Reading, Geometric Dimensioning, Chemistry, Environmental Safety and Health, Waterworld, Social Science, Criminal Justice, Literature, Writing, Biology, Speech, Health.

Teaching Methods: *Computers:* Internet, electronic classroom, e-mail, CD-ROM, newsgroup, LISTSERV. *TV:* videotape, cable program, satellite broadcasting, PBS. *Other:* videoconferencing, audioconferencing, fax, correspondence, independent study, individual study, 2-way interactive TV.

Credits Granted for: experiential learning, extrainstitutional learning, examination (CLEP, ACT-PEP, DANTES, GRE).

Admission Requirements: *Undergraduate:* age 16, open-admission process, some programs have special admissions.

On-Campus Requirements: 12 credit hours required for full-time status, 3 classroom hours weekly for 11 weeks for 3 (term) credits.

Tuition and Fees: *Undergraduate:* $40/credit for 1–14 credits, $600 for 14–18 credits, $40/credit above 18 credits. *Other Costs:* general fee of $4/credit, distance learning fee $30/course/term. *Credit by:* quarter.

Financial Aid: Federal Stafford Loan, Federal Perkins Loan, Federal PLUS Loan, Federal Pell Grant, Federal Work-Study, VA, Oregon resident programs, Federal Supplemental Educational Opportunity Grants.

Accreditation: Northwest Association of Schools and Colleges.

Description: Clackamas Community College (1966) is a small, rural/suburban college offering transfer, technical, professional, and adult supplemental education. Located near the major metropolis city of Portland, Clackamas offers associate transfer degrees, several technical/professional programs, and a 2-year certificate Honors Program. The college's 4,700 full-time students can participate in athletics, student government, clubs, intramurals, and foreign student programs. Testing, advising, registration, and tutorial assistance are available, and some free special support services/accommodations are available for students with disabilities. Clackamas has offered distance learning telecourses since 1979 and online courses since 1997.

Clarion University of Pennsylvania

131 Harvey
Clarion University
Clarion, PA 16214-1232

Phone: (814) 393-2778
Fax: (814) 393-2779

Division(s): Office of Distance Learning and Extended Studies
Web Site(s):
http://www.clarion.edu/academic/distance/index.shtml
E-mail: cmuschweck@mail.clarion.edu, fleisher@clarion.edu

Undergraduate Degree Programs:
Real Estate

Graduate Degree Programs:
Library Science
Nursing

Class Titles: graduate classes in Library Science, undergraduate and graduate classes in Nursing, and undergraduate classes in Communication and various other departments. Course offerings vary by semester; visit Web site.

Teaching Methods: *Other:* videoconferencing, web-based.

Credits Granted for: examination (CLEP, ACT-PEP, DANTES, GRE).

Admission Requirements: *Graduate:* bachelor's degree, 2.75 undergraduate GPA.

On-Campus Requirements: None.

Tuition and Fees: *Undergraduate:* $158/credit resident, out-of-state $325. *Graduate:* $230/credit resident, out-of-state $346. *Application Fee:* $25. *Other Costs:* approximately 10% of student's tuition (support, health, activities, student center, etc.). *Credit by:* semester.

Financial Aid: Federal Stafford Loan, Federal Perkins Loan, Federal PLUS Loan, Federal Pell Grant, Federal Work-Study, VA, Pennsylvania resident programs.

Accreditation: Middle States Association of Colleges and Schools.

Description: Clarion University of Pennsylvania is a member of the State System of Higher Education of Pennsylvania. Clarion began offering distance education courses in 1996 using videoconferencing between the Clarion campus and the Venango campus in Oil City. In 1997–1998, Clarion offered 18 distance learning classes at 6 sites in western Pennsylvania and Harrisburg. Since that time the number of classes offered has steadily risen. Distance learning classes are offered only at specified sites including Clarion University campus, Venango campus, Clarion University Pittsburgh site, Slippery Rock University, and Dixon Center (Harrisburg). Classes are not available via the Internet.

Clarkson College

101 South 42nd Street
Omaha, NE 68131

Phone: (800) 647-5500
Fax: (402) 552-3575

Division(s): Distance Education
Web Site(s): http://www.clarksoncollege.edu
E-mail: admiss@clarksoncollege.edu

Undergraduate Degree Programs:
Bachelor of Science in:
   Health Care Business
   Nursing (for RNs only)
   Medical Imaging (for Radiographers only)

Graduate Degree Programs:
Master of Science in:
   Nursing (for BSNs only)
   Family Nurse Practitioner (post-master's certificate)
   Enrollment limited to residents of: Colorado, Iowa, Kansas, Maryland, Nebraska, South Dakota, Wyoming.

Teaching Methods: *Computers:* Internet, electronic classroom, discussion groups, e-mail. *Other:* audioconferencing, audiotapes, videotapes, fax, correspondence, independent study, individual study.

Credits Granted for: portfolio assessment, extrainstitutional learning, examination (CLEP, ACT-PEP, DANTES).

Admission Requirements: *Undergraduate:* high school transcripts, ACT/SAT scores, college transcripts, essay. *Graduate:* college transcripts, 3 letters of reference, admission essay.

On-Campus Requirements: 5 weekends for clinical evaluation for MSN students in Family Nurse Practitioner major and one day to defend thesis or for comprehensive exams for graduate students.

Tuition and Fees: *Undergraduate:* $289/credit. *Graduate:* $334/credit. *Application Fee:* $15. *Other Costs:* $75/semester for distance education courses. *Credit by:* semester.

Financial Aid: Federal Stafford Loan, Federal Perkins Loan, Federal PLUS Loan, Federal Pell Grant, Federal Work-Study, VA.

Accreditation: North Central Association of Colleges and Schools, National League for Nursing, International Assembly for Collegiate Business Education.

Description: Clarkson College (1888) is a private, nonprofit, coeducational institution that offers undergraduate and graduate health science degrees. Clarkson began as a School of Nursing before branching out into other areas of health care including business, patient information management, physi-cal therapist assistant, occupational therapy assistant, radiologic technology, and medical imaging. The distance program was started in 1989 when the college offered courses at satellite campuses in rural Nebraska. Today, distance courses are available to students in all 50 states. Our mission is to provide high-quality education to prepare competent, thoughtful, ethical, and compassionate health care professionals for service to individuals, families, and communities. We accomplish this mission by emphasizing teaching, research, and service.

Cleveland College of Jewish Studies

26500 Shaker Boulevard
Beachwood, Ohio 44122

Phone: (216) 464-4050
Fax: (216) 464-5827

Division(s): Dean's office
Web Site(s): http://www.ccjs.edu
E-mail: lrosen@ccjs.edu

Graduate Degree Programs:
Master of Judaic Studies

Class Titles: Contact school or check web site for details.

Teaching Methods: videoconferencing.

Credits Granted for: institutional learning (PONSI, corporate or professional association).

Admission Requirements: *Graduate:* application, application fee, 2 letters of recommendation, undergraduate transcripts, interview.

On-Campus Requirements: Only via videoconferencing classroom setting.

Tuition and Fees: *Graduate:* $400/credit. *Application Fees:* $50. *Graduation Fee:* $100. *Other Costs:* $25/year for registration fee. *Credit by:* semester.

Accreditation: Board of Regents of the State of Ohio, North Central Association of Colleges and Schools.

Description: Cleveland College (1963) is a pluralistic, nondenominational institution of higher Jewish learning whose core faculty is full-time academically trained scholars of Judaic studies dedicated to high-quality teaching within a community-oriented institution of higher Jewish learning. The college subscribes to a vision of Jewish renewal through the creative exploration of classical resources and their application to contemporary Jewish concerns.

Cleveland Institute of Electronics

1776 East 17th Street	Phone: (216) 781-9400
Cleveland, OH 44114	Fax: (216) 781-0331

Division(s): Entire School
Web Site(s): http://www.cie-wc.edu
E-mail: instruct@cie.wc.edu

Undergraduate Degree Programs:
Associate in Applied Science in Electronic Engineering Technology
Bachelor in Electronic Engineering Technology

Certificate Programs: 10 programs in Electronics/Computer Technology.

Class Titles: CET Exam Review, FCC Exam Review, Programmable Controllers, Television Diagnosis/Repair, Computers, Database Management, Computer Aided Design/Drafting, Oscilloscope Fundamentals, Automotive Electricity/Electronics, Mobile Equipment, Microprocessor Theory/Applications, AC/DC Basic Electronics with Lab, Fiber Optics, Soldering with Lab.

Teaching Methods: *Computers:* Internet, real-time chat, electronic classroom, e-mail, CD-ROM, newsgroup, LISTSERV *TV:* videotape, cable program, satellite broadcasting, PBS *Other:* independent study.

Credits Granted for: extrainstitutional learning (DANTES).

On-Campus Requirements: independent study.

Tuition and Fees: *Credit by:* Independent Study.

Financial Aid: VA.

Accreditation: Distance Education and Training Council.

Cleveland State University

2344 Euclid Avenue	Phone: (216) 687-2149
Cleveland, OH 44115	Fax: (216) 687-9399

Division(s): Continuing Education
Web Site(s): http://www.csuohio.edu/offcampus
E-mail: f.anthony@csuohio.edu

Graduate Degree Programs:
Master of Social Work (cooperative with University of Akron)
Master of Education in Educational Technology (at Lorain Community College)
Master of Science in Health Sciences.

Certificate Programs: Six Sigma, Clinical Bioethics, manufacturing.

Class Titles: for credit—Business, Education, English, Philosophy, Psychology, Sociology, Engineering; noncredit—Business, Computers, Hazardous Materials, Nursing/Health Professions.

Teaching Methods: *Computers:* Internet, electronic classroom, e-mail, LISTSERV. *TV:* videotape, cable program, satellite broadcasting, PBS. *Other:* videoconferencing, audioconferencing, fax, correspondence, independent study, faculty at remote site classroom.

Credits Granted for: portfolio assessment, examination (CLEP, ACT-PEP, DANTES, GRE), life experiences.

Admission Requirements: *Undergraduate:* application and fees, transcripts, appropriate test scores (SAT/ACT/others), special for international students. *Graduate:* 2.75 GPA or 50th percentile on standardized admission test (may include GRE, GMAT, MAT); additional requirements vary by colleges and departments.

On-Campus Requirements: programs generally include some on-campus residency.

Tuition and Fees: *Undergraduate:* $170.60/credit or $2,047.20/12–18 credits resident, $335.82/credit or $4,030.20/12–18 credits nonresident. *Graduate:* $227.35/credit or $2,962/13–16 credits resident, $450.35/credit or $5,854.55/13–16 credits nonresident. *Application Fee:* $25. *Credit by:* semester.

Financial Aid: Federal Stafford Loan, Federal Perkins Loan, Federal PLUS Loan, Federal Pell Grant, Federal Work-Study, Ohio resident programs, cooperative education, student employment, scholarships, grants.

Accreditation: North Central Association of Colleges and Schools.

Description: Established as a state-assisted university, Cleveland State University (1964) assumed a tradition for excellence when it adopted Fenn College. Five years later, the university merged with the Cleveland-Marshall College of Law. Today Cleveland State continues to grow, offering quality, diversity, and flexibility in its programs and course offerings. Courses leading to degrees are offered though CSU's 7 colleges—5 for undergraduates and 2 for graduates. The campus consists of 80 acres with 35 buildings used for teaching, research, housing, and recreation. CSU supports students, faculty, and staff use of computing, telecommunications, and electronic media for teaching, learning, and administration. University courses have been taught for a number of years at off-campus locations. Over the past several years, partnerships and cooperative agreements have been developed with area colleges and universities, community colleges, public schools, government agencies, and companies to provide an increasing number of courses using video and electronic distance learning technologies.

Clinton Community College

136 Clinton Point Drive
Plattsburgh, NY 12901

Phone: (518) 562-4200
Fax: (518) 562-4158

Web Site(s): http://clintoncc.suny.edu
E-mail: sloavl@clintoncc.suny.edu

Undergraduate Degree Programs: Contact school.

Certificate Programs: Contact school.

Class Titles: Accounting I, Business Communications, Introduction to Microcomputer Applications, Advanced Software Applications, Fundamental Economics, Literature and Composition, Technical Writing, Multicultural American Literature, Government and Politics in America, Introduction to Sociology.

Teaching Methods: *Computers:* Internet, real-time chat, electronic classroom, e-mail, CD-ROM, newsgroup, LISTSERV.

Credits Granted for: experiential learning, portfolio assessment, extrainstitutional learning (PONSI, corporate or professional association seminars/workshops), examination (CLEP, ACT-PEP, DANTES, GRE).

Admission Requirements: Contact school or check web site for details.

On-Campus Requirements: None.

Tuition and Fees: *Undergraduate:* $100/credit. *Other Costs:* $1.75/credit hour for activity fee. *Credit by:* semester.

Financial Aid: Federal Stafford Loan, Federal Perkins Loan, Federal PLUS Loan, Federal Pell Grant, Federal Work-Study, VA, state programs for residents of New York.

Accreditation: Middle States Association of Colleges and Schools.

Description: Clinton Community College (1967), an associate degree-granting institution, was chartered by the Clinton County Legislature in 1966 and first opened it's doors in 1969. Clinton is a branch campus of the State University of New York and participates in the SUNY Learning Network for Distance Learning. The campus is located in Plattsburgh, New York. The 100-acre campus is dramatically situated on a bluff overlooking Lake Champlain, surrounded by the Adirondack Mountains of New York and the Green Mountains of Vermont. Clinton offers associate degrees in both transfer and career areas. We have several plus 2 programs with 4-year colleges. We also offer certificate programs. Our most popular degrees are Nursing (RN), Liberal Arts, Business Administration, Criminal Justice, and Electrical Technology.

Clinton, Muscatine, and Scott Community Colleges

306 West River Drive
Davenport, IA 52801

Phone: (563) 336-3300
Fax: (563) 336-3350

Division(s): Academic Affairs
Web Site(s): http://www.eiccd.cc.ia.us
E-mail: eiccdinfo@eiccd.cc.ia.us

Undergraduate Degree Programs:
Associate of Arts in General Studies
Associate of Applied Science in Environmental Technology

Class Titles: wide variety of classes.

Teaching Methods: *Computers:* Internet, electronic classroom, e-mail, CD-ROM. *TV:* videotape, PBS. *Other:* audioconferencing, videoconferencing, correspondence, independent study, individual study.

Credits Granted for: experiential learning, examination (CLEP).

Admission Requirements: *Undergraduate:* open-admissions.

On-Campus Requirements: None.

Tuition and Fees: *Undergraduate:* $72/credit. *Other Costs:* variable. *Credit by:* semester.

Financial Aid: Federal Stafford Loan, Federal Perkins Loan, Federal PLUS Loan, Federal Pell Grant, Federal Work-Study, VA.

Accreditation: North Central Association of Colleges and Schools.

Description: Clinton, Muscatine, and Scott Community Colleges (1965) are located along the Mississippi River in the Iowa communities of Clinton, Muscatine, and Bettendorf. The colleges also have additional sites in Davenport and Maquoketa. The colleges offer 100 Associate in Arts and Associate in Applied Science programs as well as certificate and diploma options. Length of study ranges from one semester to 2 years.

Coastline Community College

11460 Warner Avenue, Third Floor
Fountain Valley, CA 92708

Phone: (714) 241-6216
Fax: (714) 241-6287

Division(s): Distance Learning Department
Web Site(s): http://pelican.ccc.cccd.edu/dl
E-mail: See web site.

Undergraduate Degree Programs:
Associate of Arts

Class Titles: Anthropology, Astronomy, Biology, Business, Chemistry, Communications, Computer, Computer Services Technology, Computer Science, Ecology, English, French, Geology, Health, History, Humanities, International Business, Management/Supervision, Marine Science, Math, Philosophy, Political Science, Psychology, Social Science, Sociology, Spanish.

Teaching Methods: *Computers:* Internet, real-time chat, discussion forums, chat-room, electronic classroom, e-mail, CD-ROM. *TV:* videotapes (pre-produced), cablecast programs, satellite broadcasting, PBS, KOCE. *Other:* codec-interactive videoconferencing, audiocassette tapes, fax, independent study, independent study-labs.

Credits Granted for: portfolio assessment, by examination (CLEP, ACT-PEP, DANTES, GRE) and professional credit (to be evaluated).

Admission Requirements: *Undergraduate:* individuals age 18+ who can profit from instructional qualify for admission. If under 18, you will qualify for admission if one of the following has been satisfied: graduated from high school, passed the California High School Certificate of Proficiency Test or equivalent, completed the 10th grade and received permission from your high school. (Note: students who have not completed the 10th grade may be eligible to enroll in certain advanced courses not available at their high schools. Permission of the dean of student services or designee, the parent and the high school principal or designee is required.)

On-Campus Requirements: All distance learning courses have examinations (midterm, essay exam and/or final exam). These examinations are administered on site by the instructor or administered at an on-site location by a department approved proctor. Some courses may require student attendance for workshops, review sessions or field trips. Students may transfer units from other accredited 2- or 4-year institutions; however, if the student wants to graduate from Coastline, the student would need to take 12 units from Coastline.

Tuition and Fees: *Undergraduate:* $11/unit resident, $134/unit nonresident, $140/unit international. *Software:* students enrolled in Internet or CD-ROM-based courses must have access to a multimedia computer with a full-service connection to an Internet provider to participate. Students who enroll in telecourse or cablecast courses must have access to a TV and/or access to the cable station carrier. For students who do not have access to a TV or cable station carrier, they can view video lessons at one of seven Coastline Viewing Centers located in the Coast Community College District. *Other Costs:* course materials ($75–$175), varies for shipping, approximately $60/semester course video rental, $7/semester mandatory health fee. Tuition and fees subject to change. *Credit by:* semester.

Financial Aid: Federal Pell Grant, Federal Supplemental Educational Opportunity Grant, Federal Perkins Loan, Federal Stafford Loan, Cal Grants A, B and C.

Accreditation: Western Association of Schools and Colleges.

Description: Coastline Community College (1976) is committed to accessible, flexible, student-centered education within and beyond the traditional classroom. Our distance learning combines technology—television, computers, fax/modems, telephone—with textbooks and printed materials to bring course content, instructor, and students together. With more than 20 years' experience in distance learning, Coastline offers a variety of college-credit course options to meet educational needs.

Coconino Community College

3000 North 4th Street, Suite 17	Phone: (520) 527-1222
Flagstaff, AZ 86003-8000	Fax: (520) 526-8693

Division(s): Education Services
Web Site(s): http://www.coco.cc.az.us
E-mail: smiller@coco.cc.az.us

Undergraduate Degree Programs:
Associate of Arts
Associate of Business
Associate of Science
Associate of Applied Science
Associate of General Studies

Certificate Programs: Accounting Technician, Alternative Energy Technician, Assisted Living, Carpentry Apprenticeship, Clerical, Computer Software Technology, Construction Technology, Drafting—Computer-Aided Drafting, Drafting—Architectural CAD Technician, Early Childhood Education, Electrical Construction Wiring Training, Employment Success, Fire Science, Hospitality, Legal Secretary, Manufacturing/Welding, Medical Insurance, Medical Transcription, Nursing Assistant, Phlebotomy, Pre-Professional Nursing, Psychiatric Technician, Sheet Metal Apprenticeship.

Teaching Methods: *Computers:* Internet, real-time chat, electronic classroom, e-mail, CD-ROM. *Other:* videoconferencing, fax, correspondence, independent study, individual study, learning contracts.

Credits Granted for: extrainstitutional learning, examination (currently under consideration).

Admission Requirements: *Undergraduate:* open campus, with minimal restrictions.

On-Campus Requirements: None.

Tuition and Fees: *Undergraduate:* $27/credit in-state, $42/credit out-of-state. *Other Costs:* vary/course. *Credit by:* semester.

Financial Aid: Federal Pell Grant, Federal Work-Study, VA, Arizona resident programs, Navajo Nation programs, Hopi Nation programs.

Accreditation: North Central Association of Colleges and Schools.

Description: The multicampus Coconino Community College (1991) primarily serves the residents of 18,000-square-mile Coconino County. We offer Web-based courses (since 1997). We also use PLATO courseware for delivery to our extension sites (Grand Canyon, Williams, Page, and others). The college's new Distance Learning initiatives and remote-site construction projects are funded by a district-wide referedum and a USDOE Title III grant award.

Cogswell Polytechnical College

1175 Bordeaux Drive	Phone: (408) 541-0100 x105
Sunnyvale, CA 94089-1299	(800) 264-7955 x105
	Fax: (408) 747-0764

Division(s): Degrees at a Distance Program for the Fire Service
Web Site(s): http://www.cogswell.edu
E-mail: olfs@cogswell.edu

Undergraduate Degree Programs:
Bachelor of Science Fire Administration science with concentrations in Fire Administration and Fire Prevention Technology

Certificate Programs: Fire Administration, Fire Prevention/Technology.

Class Titles: Core curriculum of upper division Fire Science courses, concentration courses in Fire Science.

Teaching Methods: *Computers:* Internet (one course, 1999–2000, with more to follow). *Other:* fax, correspondence, independent study.

Credits Granted for: extrainstitutional learning (professional association seminars/workshops), examination (CLEP, DANTES).

Admission Requirements: *Undergraduate:* 12 units of lower-division Fire Science and English Composition.

On-Campus Requirements: None.

Tuition and Fees: *Undergraduate:* $405/3-unit course. *Application Fee:* $50. *Other Costs:* vary, textbooks when required. *Credit by:* semester.

Financial Aid: modest scholarships.

Accreditation: Western Association of Schools and Colleges.

Description: Cogswell College (1887) was founded as a San Francisco polytechnical school. The college is now located in the Silicon Valley, between San Francisco and San Jose. Cogswell offers on-campus programs with degrees in Electrical Engineering, Software Engineering, and Computer and Video Imaging. The Degrees at a Distance Program with Bachelor of Science degree in Fire Science is the school's only distance learning. Cogswell is part of a consortium of 7 colleges and universities across the country that offer this program sponsored by the National Fire Academy.

College Misericordia

| 301 Lake Street | Phone: (570) 674-6451 |
| Dallas, PA 18612 | Fax: (570) 674-6232 |

Division(s): Adult Education and Community Service
Web Site(s): http://www.misericordia.edu
E-mail: lbrown@miseri.edu

Undergraduate Degree Programs:
Bachelor of Science in New Media

Graduate Degree Programs:
Master of Science in Organizational Management
Instructional Technology

Postgraduate Degree Programs: Contact school.

Certificate Programs: Management Information Systems, New Media.

Class Titles: Contact school or check web site for details.

Teaching Methods: *Computers:* Internet, real-time chat, electronic classroom, e-mail, LISTSERV. *Other:* videoconferencing, fax, correspondence, independent study, individual study, learning contracts.

Credits Granted for: experiential learning, prior learning assessment, portfolio assessment, extrainstitutional learning (PONSI, corporate or professional association seminars/workshops), examination (CLEP, ACT-PEP, DANTES, GRE).

Admission Requirements: *Undergraduate:* contact school. *Graduate:* MAT or GRE, baccalaureate degree, and evidence of ability to do graduate-level work, computer literacy. *Postgraduate:* prior academic performance and computer literacy. *Certificate:* ability to do appropriate academic work and computer literacy.

On-Campus Requirements: None.

Tuition and Fees: *Undergraduate:* $390/credit. *Graduate:* $450/credit. *Postgraduate:* $450/credit. *Application Fee:* $25. *Graduation Fee:* $125. *Other Costs:* textbooks and course materials. *Credit by:* semester.

Financial Aid: Federal Stafford Loan, Federal Perkins Loan, Federal PLUS Loan, Federal Pell Grant, Federal Work-Study, VA, state programs for residents of Pennsylvania.

Accreditation: Middle States Association of Colleges and Schools.

Description: Founded in 1924 as Luzerne County's first 4-year college, College Misericordia is one of 18 Mercy colleges and universities across the country. The college is dedicated to the values of the Sisters of Mercy: mercy, service, justice, and hospitality. These values can be found throughout our community, from programs of study to service projects. College Misericordia offers the benefits of a small college and the scope of a larger institution. It is rated among the top colleges and universities by *Time* magazine. The hallmark of College Misericordia is a dedicated faculty and a high-quality core liberal arts and sciences curriculum. Often referred to as our trinity of learning, a College Misericordia education combines quality academics, professional preparation, and service leadership. Together they help students prepare for a lifetime of learning and success. The faculty's dedication is manifested in our extraordinarily high retention rate, and 97% our graduates are employed in a career of their choice or are enrolled in graduate school 6 months after graduation.

College of DuPage

425 22nd Street	Phone: (630) 942-3326
Glen Ellyn, IL 60137	Fax: (630) 942-3764

Division(s): Centers for Independent Learning
Web Site(s): http://www.cod.edu/cil
http://www.cod.edu/online
E-mail: schiesz@cdnet.cod.edu

Undergraduate Degree Programs:
Associate in Arts
Associate in Science
Associate in Applied Science
Associate in General Studies
Associate in Engineering Science

Certificate Programs: 125 certificate programs.

Class Titles: 175 courses.

Teaching Methods: *Computers:* Internet, real-time chat, electronic classroom, e-mail, CD-ROM. *TV:* videotape, local cable broadcast, local radio broadcast. *Other:* telecourses using audiotape and videotape, independent study, individual study, learning contracts.

Credits Granted for: experiential learning, examination (CLEP, credit by proficiency examination through an instructor).

Admission Requirements: *Undergraduate:* open-door, age 18, high school graduate who can benefit from college-level instruction.

On-Campus Requirements: None.

Tuition and Fees: *Undergraduate:* $35/credit in-district, $113/credit out-of-district, $156/credit out-of-state. *Application Fee:* $10. *Other Costs:* $35/credit for all Internet-delivered courses, $50 science fee. *Credit by:* quarter (11 weeks in length).

Financial Aid: Federal Stafford Loan, Federal Perkins Loan, Federal PLUS Loan, Federal Pell Grant, Federal Work-Study, VA, Illinois resident programs.

Accreditation: North Central Association of Colleges and Schools.

Description: The College of DuPage (1966) is a comprehensive 2-year community college that serves a district population of 950,000 in the far-western suburbs of Chicago. The college has an overall enrollment of 34,000 students each fall term. The Centers for Independent Learning offer a variety of distance learning formats in 175 courses serving an enrollment of 5,000 distance learners each academic term.

College of Lake County

19351 West Washington	Phone: (847) 223-6601
Grayslake, IL 60030	Fax: (847) 223-0934

Division(s): Educational Affairs
Web Site(s): http://www.clc.cc.il.us/applic.htm
E-mail: cbulakowski@clc.cc.il.us

Undergraduate Degree Programs:
Associate in Arts
Associate in Applied Science in:
    Computer Information Systems
    Multimedia

Class Titles: Environmental Biology (BIO 120), U.S. History to 1876 (HST 221), U.S. History 1876 to Present (HST 222), Introduction to Psychology (PSY 121), Introduction to Sociology (SOC 121), Introduction to Anthropology (ANT 121), Introduction to Criminal Justice (CRJ 121), Internet Fundamentals (COM 115), Developing Web Pages (COM 116), Advanced Online Publishing (COM 216), Building Commercial Websites (COM 218), Fire Prevention Principles (FST 177), Oceanography (GEO 124), Elementary Concepts of Math (MTH 101), Basic Algebra (MTH 102), Intermediate Algebra (MTH 108), Elementary Statistics (MTH 222), Introduction to Math Analysis (MTH 224), Introduction to Business (BUS 121), Small Business Management (BUS 219), Business Law I (BUS 221), Introduction to Computers (CIS 120), Managing Microcomputer Systems (CIS 231),

English Composition I (ENG 121), English Composition II (ENG 122), Mass Communication (ENG 123), Advanced Composition: Scientific & Technical Communication (ENG 126), Linguistics and Society (ENG 128), Critical Thinking (HUM 127), Film and Society (HUM 222), Women and the Arts (HUM 226).

Teaching Methods: *Computers:* Internet, real-time chat, e-mail, CD-ROM, newsgroup. *TV:* videotape, satellite broadcasting, PBS. *Other:* videoconferencing, fax, independent study, individual study, learning contracts.

Credits Granted for: experiential learning, portfolio assessment, extrainstitutional learning, examination (CLEP, DANTES), AP.

Admission Requirements: *Undergraduate:* meet prerequisites for credit courses.

On-Campus Requirements: not for Internet courses, some telecourses may require an orientation.

Tuition and Fees: *Undergraduate:* $49/credit, $5 comprehensive fee, $177 out-of-district, $248 out-of-state. *Credit by:* semester.

Financial Aid: Federal Stafford Loan, Federal Perkins Loan, Federal PLUS Loan, Federal Pell Grant, Federal Work-Study, VA, Illinois resident programs.

Accreditation: North Central Association of Colleges and Schools.

Description: College of Lake County (1969) offers its students a variety of options. They can enroll as transfer students, career students, basic skills students, or as students interested in lifelong learning. CLC is committed to the needs of all students who can benefit from postsecondary instruction. The college understands that many students have busy schedules and live far from campus but want to take college courses. This commitment that learning need not be limited to constraints of time and place has been an important source of the commitment to distance learning.

The College of Saint Catherine

2004 Randolph Avenue	Phone: (877) 627-8347
St. Paul, MN 55105	Fax: (310) 578-4716

Division(s): Department of Education
Web Site(s): http://www.masters4teachers.net
E-mail: karla.wilkins@educate.com

Graduate Degree Programs:
Graduate: Master of Arts in Education via distance learning (MAED)

Class Titles: The Reflective Teacher, The Constructivist Curriculum, Student Centered Assessment, High Involvement Learning, Learner Responsive Classrooms: Integrating Learning Styles and Multiple Intelligences, Action Research: Inquiry into Classroom Practice, The Art of Teaching: Effective Models of Instruction, Creating Community: Reframing Behavior Management, Strategies for Effective Inclusion, Emerging Issues in Education.

Teaching Methods: *Computers:* Internet, e-mail. *TV:* videotape. *Other:* portfolio, faculty facilitator, collegial learning teams, audiotapes, fax, conference calls.

Credits Granted for: portfolio assessment, individual assignments, study team assignments.

Admission Requirements: *Graduate:* completed application for admission, nonrefundable application fee, official transcripts from each postsecondary institution attended, copy of your current teaching certificate, 2 letters of recommendation, GPA of 3.0 is required. Applicants with a GPA lower than 3.0 may be considered for admission if they take the GRE and receive an acceptable score.

On-Campus Requirements: None.

Tuition and Fees: *Graduate:* $212/credit. *Graduation Fee:* $75. *Other Costs:* $25 for one-time application fee, $70/course for materials fee. *Credit by:* semester.

Financial Aid: Federal Stafford Loan, Minnesota SELF Loan.

Accreditation: Commission on Institutions of Higher Education of the North Central Association of Colleges and Schools (NCA). The College of St. Catherine is approved by the National Council for the Accreditation of Teacher Education (NCATE).

Description: The College of St. Catherine (St. Kate's) (1905) is the largest Catholic college for women in the country. The St. Paul campus is dedicated to liberal arts education for women and graduate education for women and men. With beautiful campuses in both St. Paul and Minneapolis, the college has a total enrollment of over 4,300 students. St. Kate's professional programs prepare students for advanced graduate work. The college provides a learning environment conducive to the development of skills, attitudes, and competencies that foster growth. St. Kate's is committed to excellence and to providing challenging and relevant programs meeting the changing needs of students, the professional communities it serves, and society.

College of Saint Scholastica

1200 Kenwood Avenue
Duluth, MN 55811-4199

Phone: (218) 733-2236
(218) 723-6026/
(800) 888-8796 (MEDL)
(218) 723-6448 (HIM Graduate)
(218) 723-6709 (HIM ART)
(218) 723-6709 (MEDL)
Fax: (218) 723-6709/2239

Division(s): Education (MEDL)
Health Information Management (HIM)
Web Site(s): http://www.css.edu or http://www.css.edu/medl
E-mail: klutz@css.edu
seichenw@css.edu (HIM)
vvruno@css.edu (HIM ART)

Undergraduate Degree Programs:
Bachelor of Arts in Health Information Management/ Accredited Record Technician (ART) Progession Program

Graduate Degree Programs:
Master of Education in:
Curriculum and Instruction (MEDL)
Curriculum and Instruction via Distance Learning (MEDL)
Master of Arts in Health Information Management (HIM)

Class Titles: Chemistry, Computer Science/Information Systems, Education (undergraduate/graduate), Health Information Management (undergraduate/graduate), Management, Religious Studies.

Teaching Methods: *Computers:* Internet, real-time chat, electronic classroom, e-mail, CD-ROM. *TV:* videotape, electronic bulletin boards, cable program, satellite broadcasting. *Other:* audiotapes, fax, correspondence, independent study, individual study, learning contracts.

Credits Granted for: experiential learning, portfolio assessment, examination (CLEP, ACT-PEP, DANTES, GRE), transfer of 6 graduate credits.

Admission Requirements: *Undergraduate:* ART certification. *Graduate:* 2 years of professional experience in educational setting, undergraduate degree with transcripts, prior graduate course transcripts, 2 letters of recommendation, essay, letters of recommendation, interview, 2.8 cumulative GPA (MEDL).

On-Campus Requirements: Orientation Seminary and Colloquium at various sites including CSS campus, 2 weeks in June. For MEDL: 2 weekends (exploring alternatives at this time).

Tuition and Fees: *Undergraduate:* $312/quarter credit, $468/ semester credit. *Graduate:* $332/quarter credit, $498/ semester credit, $240/semester credit, $275/semester credit MEDL. *Application Fee:* $50. *Software:* variable. *Other Costs:* textbooks, etc. *Credit by:* semester.

Financial Aid: Federal Stafford Loan, Federal Perkins Loan, Federal PLUS Loan, Federal Pell Grant, Federal Work-Study, VA, Minnesota resident programs.

Accreditation: North Central Association of Colleges and Schools, Commission on Accreditation of Allied Health Education Programs, The Higher Learning Commission.

Description: The College of St. Scholastica (1912) is an independent, coeducational, comprehensive college with programs in the liberal arts and sciences and professional career fields. Founded in the Catholic intellectual tradition and shaped by the Benedictine heritage, the college stresses intellectual and moral preparation for responsible living and meaningful work. The college entered into Distance Education in 1996 and continues to explore expanding the programs offered via Distance Learning.

College of San Mateo

1700 West Hillsdale Boulevard
San Mateo, CA 94402-3784

Phone: (650) 524-6933
Fax: (650) 574-6345

Division(s): Office of Instruction/Distance Learning
Web Site(s): http://gocsm.net
E-mail: bianchig@smccd.net

Undergraduate Degree Programs:
Associate in Arts courses
Associate in Science courses

Class Titles: *T.V:* Archaeology, Art of the Western World, Astronomy, Contemporary American Business, Small Business Management, Marketing, Business Law, Career and Life Planning, Chemistry, Nutrition, Race to Save the Planet, American Cinema, French, Geology, General Health Science, Modern Latin America and the Caribbean, Italian, Business Management, Ethics in America, Fitness, Psychology, Courtship, Marriage and the Family, Abnormal Psychology, Child Psychology, Salesmanship Fundamentals, Sociology, Spanish, Speech. *Online:* Financial Accounting, HTML, Advanced HTML, Electronic Commerce, Basic Chinese Writing Skills, Computer and Information Science, Networks and Data Communications, Principles of Network Design and Management, Programming Methods I and II C++, Programming Methods I Java, Internet Programming: JavaScript/HTML, Composition and Reading, Composition, Literature, and Critical Thinking, Advanced Composition, Review of English Grammar for Nonnative Speakers, American Politics, California State and Local Government.

Teaching Methods: *Computers:* Internet, real-time chat, electronic classroom, e-mail, CD-ROM, newsgroup, LISTSERV. *TV:* videotape, cable program, satellite broadcasting, PBS. *Other:* audiotapes, fax.

Credits Granted for: *Military Service Credit:* Upon presentation of separation or discharge papers, veterans are exempted from the Health Science and P.E. requirements for the AA/AS degree. They are also granted 6 units of elective credit toward degree.

Admission Requirements: *Undergraduate:* age 18, high school graduate or passed California Proficiency Examinations. High school juniors or equivalent may be admitted concurrently with permission.

On-Campus Requirements: introductory meeting and exams for some classes.

Tuition and Fees: *Undergraduate:* $11/unit, California residents; $138/unit, nonresidents, (plus $11.00 per unit enrollment fee). *Other Costs:* $1 student representation fee, $5 refundable student body fee, no health fee if only registered in distance learning, parking permits. *Credit by:* semester.

Financial Aid: Federal Stafford Loan, Federal Perkins Loan, Federal PLUS Loan, Federal Pell Grant, Federal Work-Study, VA, Federal SOP grant, Cal Grant, EOPS, Board of Governors Enrollment Fee Waiver, local scholarships.

Accreditation: Accrediting Commission for Community and Junior Colleges of the Western Association of Schools and Colleges, an institutional accrediting body recognized by the Commission on Recognition of Postsecondary Accreditation and the U.S. Department of Education.

Description: College of San Mateo (1922), the oldest of the 3 colleges in San Mateo County Community College District, is located on a 153-acre site that provides a panoramic view of the north Bay Area. College of San Mateo, is a state and locally supported 2-year college. It is accredited by the Western Association of Schools and Colleges, Inc. Distance Learning courses were first offered in 1977. In 2001 we offered over 85 online and telecourse classes. Students may obtain a degree by taking a combination of distance learning courses.

College of Southern Maryland

8730 Mitchell Road, PO Box 910	Phone: (301) 934-2251
La Plata, MD 20646	Fax: (301) 934-7699

Division(s): Learning Technologies Team
Web Site(s): http://www.csm.cc.md.us
E-mail: pault@csm.cc.md.us

Undergraduate Degree Programs:
Business Administration
Management Development
Information Services Technology
General Studies
Arts and Sciences
Arts and Sciences: Arts and Humanities

Certificate Programs: Accounting—Basic, Accounting—Advanced, Computer Skills for Managers, Information Services Technology, Web Developer.

Class Titles: Contact school or check web site for details.

Teaching Methods: *Computers:* Internet, real-time chat, electronic classroom, e-mail, LISTSERV. *TV:* videotape, cable program, PBS, independent study.

Credits Granted for: transfer from regionally accredited colleges, portfolio assessment, examination (CLEP, A,P, DANTES).

Admission Requirements: *Undergraduate:* open-door admissions. *Certificate:* open-door admissions.

On-Campus Requirements: None.

Tuition and Fees: *Undergraduate:* Charles, Calvert, St. Mary's County (in Maryland) residents—$73/credit; other Maryland residents—$146/credit; out-of-state residents—$190/credit. Credit by examination—$20; portfolio assessment—$73; certification verfication—$20; combined fee—20% of tuition amount. *Graduation Fee:* (degrees/certificates) $20. *Other Costs:* telecourse/web-based course fee, $20/credit. *Credit by:* semester.

Financial Aid: Federal Stafford Loan, Federal PLUS Loan, Federal Pell Grant, Federal Work-Study, VA, state programs for residents of Maryland, Institutional scholarships and grants.

Accreditation: Middle States Association of Colleges and Schools.

Description: The CSM (1958) is a regionally accredited institution that prides itself on delivering quality higher education programs and services to more than 60% of Southern Maryland residents who attend higher education institutions. As an open-door, public institution, the staff and faculty at CSM work closely with a diverse student population regardless of past academic performance. In fall 2000, the college ranked top in the state for its student completion and transfer rates, and 91% of graduates are employed in full-time jobs related to their college program. CSM has a long history of offering a comprehensive telecourse program. Enrolling over 1,200 telecourse students each year, new telecourses and additional sections of popular ones are added regularly. Continuing this commitment to Distance Learning, CSM has developed a large inventory of online courses. For the fall 2001 semester, 48 unduplicated online courses are offered. Additional online courses are under development and will be available soon. CSM's commitment to Distance Learning is not only ongoing, but also is strengthened by a growing number of online programs.

College of the Canyons

26455 Rockwell Canyon Road   Phone: (661) 259-7800, x3600
Santa Clarita, CA 91355   Fax: (661) 259-3421

Division(s): Learning Resources
Web Site(s): http://www.coc.cc.ca.us
E-mail: drake_r_j@mail.coc.cc.ca.us

Undergraduate Degree Programs: Please contact school.

Class Titles: Anthropology, Astronomy, American Cinema, Business, Philosophy, Economics, Western World History, U.S. History, Health, Political Science, Psychology, Sociology. *Online:* Chemistry, Computer Tech, Economics, English, Hotel and Restaurant Management, Music, Philosophy, Psychology.

Teaching Methods: *Computers:* Internet, real-time chat, electronic classroom, e-mail, CD-ROM, newsgroup, LISTSERV. *TV:* videotape, cable program, satellite broadcasting, PBS.

Credits Granted for: experiential learning, examination (CLEP).

Admission Requirements: *Undergraduate:* age 18 or high school diploma.

On-Campus Requirements: *College by television classes:* Usually 5-6 two-hour face-to-face sessions on Saturdays. *Online classes:* There is a mandatory on-campus orientation for all classes. Other on-campus meetings are at the instructor's discretion.

Tuition and Fees: *Undergraduate:* $11/credit in-state, $133/credit out-of-state. *Application Fee:* $100 out-of-state only. *Other Costs:* annual Student Center Fee: $1/unit/$10 maximum; health fee: $12; parking: $40/semester, $20/summer. *Credit by:* semester.

Financial Aid: Federal Stafford Loan, Federal Pell Grant, Federal Work-Study, VA, California Community Colleges Board of Governors Fee Waiver, California CAL Grants A, B and C.

Accreditation: Western Association of Schools and Colleges.

Description: College of the Canyons (1969) in the Santa Clarita Community College District is a 2-year, public community college located 30 miles north of Los Angeles, California. Our College by TV program began in 1989 and our online program began in 1999.

College of the Sequoias

915 South Mooney Boulevard   Phone: (209) 730-3790
Visalia, CA 93277   Fax: (209) 730-3894

Division(s): Liberal Arts
Web Site(s): http://sequoias.cc.ca.us
E-mail: nancyf@cos.cc.ca.us

Undergraduate Degree Programs:
Associate of Arts
Associate of Science

Class Titles: English, Child Development, Nutrition, Math.

Teaching Methods: *Computers:* Internet, real-time chat, e-mail, LISTSERV. *TV:* videotape, cable program, satellite broadcasting, microwave, 2-way interactive TV. *Other:* None.

Admission Requirements: *Undergraduate:* English/math prerequisites.

On-Campus Requirements: 5 hours of face-to-face contact.

Tuition and Fees: California residents: $12/unit. Out-of-state and foreign students: $135/unit. *Credit by:* semester.

Financial Aid: Federal Stafford Loan, Federal Perkins Loan, Federal PLUS Loan, Federal Pell Grant, Federal Work-Study, VA, California resident programs.

Accreditation: Western Association of Schools and Colleges.

Description: College of the Sequoias, a community college in Visalia, was instituted in 1926 and is known for its academic excellence, high transfer rate, and award-winning vocational programs. Distance learning is new to this institution, beginning in the spring of 1997 with 2 online English courses. It has expanded to include television and other distance classes. The college has also begun broadcasting from its own TV studio.

College of the Siskiyous

800 College Avenue   Phone: (530) 938-5201
Weed, CA 96094   (530) 938-5520

Division(s): Office of Instruction/Information Technology
Web Site(s): http://www.siskiyous.edu/distancelearning/
E-mail: a_r@siskiyous.edu (Admissions and Records Office)

Undergraduate Degree Programs: Contact school.

Class Titles: Accounting, English, Math, Family and Consumer Science.

Teaching Methods: *Computers:* Internet, real-time chat, electronic classroom, e-mail, CD-ROM, newsgroup, LISTSERV. *Other:* videoconferencing, correspondence, independent study.

Admission Requirements: *Undergraduate:* contact school.

On-Campus Requirements: None.

Tuition and Fees: *Undergraduate:* $11/credit. *Other Costs:* health fee, nonresident fee (if applicable). *Credit by:* semester.

Financial Aid: Federal Stafford Loan, Federal Pell Grant, Federal Work-Study, VA, state programs for residents of California.

Accreditation: Western Association of Schools and Colleges.

Description: College of the Siskiyous (1959), one of the most beautiful community colleges campuses in California, is located at the base of majestic Mount Shasta. This 250-acre campus is easily accessible off both Interstate 5 and Highway 97 in the town of Weed. There are more than 3,000 students enrolled at College of the Siskiyous. Facilities include dormitories, a 600-seat theater, football stadium, and a spacious library and media center, as well as life science labs, vocational education and computer labs, and a number of general purpose classrooms. A staff of approximately 200 administrative, instructional, and classified personnel help students obtain the best education possible. Exceptional successes by COS students have been achieved in music, drama, science, engineering, and athletics during the history of the school. The college is widely recognized for its excellent programs in the humanities and arts, sciences and technology, and in athletics. The setting, a natural environment of mountains, forests, lakes, and streams, serves as an outdoor workshop for many classes such as art, geology, the life sciences, and physical and recreational education. Graduates repeatedly express their feelings regarding their experience at College of the Siskiyous in terms of the warmth and friendliness of the staff and the provision of quality instruction in a caring atmosphere.

College Universitaire de Saint-Boniface

200 Avenue de la Cathedrale	Phone: (204) 235-4408
Saint-Boniface, MB, Canada R2H OH7	Fax: (204) 235-4485

Division(s): Faculty of Arts
Web Site(s): http://www.ustboniface.mb.ca
E-mail: registra@ustboniface.mb.ca

Undergraduate Degree Programs:
Psychology, Translation

Class Titles: Psychology (French), Translation courses—Traduction (French).

Teaching Methods: *Computers:* Internet, LISTSERV. *TV:* videotape, cable program, satellite broadcasting, PBS. *Other:* radio broadcast, videoconferencing, audioconferencing, audiographics, audiotapes, fax, correspondence, independent study, individual study, learning contracts.

Credits Granted for: experiential learning, portfolio assessment, extrainstitutional learning, examination (CLEP, ACT-PEP, DANTES, GRE).

Admission Requirements: *Undergraduate:* high school diploma, entrance exams.

On-Campus Requirements: None.

Tuition and Fees: *Undergraduate:* $610/6-credit course. *Credit by:* semester.

Financial Aid: VA.

Accreditation: Association of Universities and Colleges of Canada.

Description: Then and now, excellence in French and English language skills has always been a College Universitaire de Saint-Boniface (1818) trademark. The bilingual skills and excellent liberal arts education of many CUSB alumni have made them natural candidates for important positions in Manitoba's and Canada's civil services and enterprises. The university's French-language and francophone literature programs have made it Manitoba's window on the world's francophone communities. BS programs and an honours BA in translation are also offered. The university's community college division, l'Ecole Technique et Professionnelle, offers one- and two-year programs in business administration, bilingual secretarial services, and in training French-language day care, health service, and business workers. CUSB's Department of Continuing Education offers courses to francophone adults and to adults wanting to learn French, Spanish, and German. Continuing Education and the University of Manitoba are now offering Spanish-language training to 2,000 volunteers of the 1999 Pan American Games. CUSB will soon offer a Bachelor of Business Administration program capitalizing on bilingual skills by stressing international/intercultural administration and acquiring another business language. The university began its distance learning program in 1996.

Colorado Christian University

180 S. Garrison Street	Phone: (303) 963-3357
Lakewood, CO 80226	Fax: (303) 274-7560

Division(s): Vice President for Academic Affairs
Web Site(s): http://www.ccu.edu
E-mail: rzwier@ccu.edu

Undergraduate Degree Programs: Contact school.

Graduate Degree Programs: Master of Business Administration.

Class Titles: Contact school or visit web site.

Teaching Methods: *Computers:* Internet, real-time chat, electronic classroom, e-mail, CD-ROM, LISTSERV.

Credits Granted for: experiential learning, portfolio assessment, examination (CLEP, ACT-PEP, DANTES, GRE).

Admission Requirements: Contact school or visit web site.

On-Campus Requirements: not in Distance Learning courses.

Tuition and Fees: *Undergraduate:* $225/credit. *Graduate:* $225–555/credit. *Credit by:* semester.

Financial Aid: Federal Stafford Loan, Federal Perkins Loan, Federal PLUS Loan, Federal Pell Grant, Federal Work-Study, VA.

Accreditation: North Central Association of Colleges and Schools.

Description: Colorado Christian University (1989) is a nondenominational university that was formed through the merger of other institutions in Colorado. It is a Christian educational institution offering associate, baccalaureate, and master's degrees in the arts, sciences, and professional fields. CCU began offering Distance Learning courses in 1999 and offers one program (the MBA) almost exclusively through this format.

Colorado State University

Spruce Hall	Phone: (970) 491-5288
Fort Collins, CO 80523-1040	(877) 491-4336
	Fax: (970) 491-7885

Division(s): Educational Outreach
Web Site(s): http://www.learn.colostate.edu/Depts/CE
E-mail: info@learn.colostate.edu

Undergraduate Degree Program:
Social Sciences (online format)
Fire Service

Graduate Degree Programs:
Master of Science in:
    Statistics
    Computer Science (online)
    Human Resource Development
    Bioresource and Agricultural Engineering
    Chemical Engineering
    Civil Engineering
    Electrical Engineering (online)

    Engineering Management
    Environmental Engineering
    Industrial Engineering
    Industrial Hygiene
    Mechanical Engineering
    Systems Engineering and Optimization
Master of Business Administration

Certificate Programs: Postsecondary Teaching, Telecommunications, Natural Resources and the Environment.

Online Certificate Programs: Paralegal, Legal Secretary, Victim Advocacy, Alternative Dispute Resolution, Legal Investigation, Travel Counselor.

Teaching Methods: *Computers:* Internet, e-mail, newsgroup, LISTSERV. *TV:* videotape, PBS. *Other:* fax, correspondence, independent study, individual study.

Credits Granted for: examination (CLEP, ACT-PEP, DANTES, GRE).

Admission Requirements: *Graduate:* residing in the U.S. or Canada or in the U.S. Military. For the MBA, must have 4 years of experience in management.

On-Campus Requirements: None.

Tuition and Fees: *Graduate:* $436/credit; MBA $448/credit. *Undergraduate Online:* $260–336/credit. *Independent Study:* $160/credit. *Credit by:* semester.

Financial Aid: Federal Stafford Loan, Federal Perkins Loan, Federal PLUS Loan, Federal Pell Grant, VA if admitted to a degree seeking program.

Accreditation: North Central Association of Colleges and Schools, American Assembly of Collegiate Schools of Business.

Description: Colorado State University (1879) has a unique mission in the state of Colorado. The land-grant concept of a balanced program of teaching, research, extension, and public service provides the foundation for the university's teaching and research programs, the Agricultural Experiment Station, Cooperative Extension, and the Colorado State Forest Service. The university has long been a leader in recognizing the rapidly changing global environments and has a commitment to excellence in international education in all its instructional, research, and outreach programs. The Distance Degree Program (formerly known as SURGE) was started in 1967. Since that time, more than 530 degrees have been conferred through the program, and numerous individual courses have been completed.

Columbia Basin College

2600 North 20th Avenue
Pasco, WA 99301

Phone: (509) 547-0511
Fax: (509) 546-0401

Division(s): Distance Learning
Web Site(s): http://www.cbc2.org/distance
E-mail: distance@cbc2.org

Undergraduate Degree Programs:
Associate of Arts and Sciences

Class Titles: Accounting, Business Law, Computer Science, Research Writing, Literature, Technical Writing, Math, History, Sociology, Anthropology, Economics, World Civilization, Psychology, Internet, Computer Applications, Business Technology, Literature, Health, Anthropology, Career Decisions, Introduction to Art.

Teaching Methods: *Computers:* Internet, real-time chat, electronic classroom, e-mail, CD-ROM, newsgroup, LISTSERV. *TV:* videotape, satellite broadcasting, PBS. *Other:* videoconferencing, correspondence, independent study, individual study.

Admission Requirements: *Undergraduate:* open-admission, placement testing. *Certificate:* open admission, placement testing.

On-Campus Requirements: None.

Tuition and Fees: *Undergraduate:* $514/10–18 credits, residential. *Other Costs:* $20 distance education fee; $2/credit technology fee. *Credit by:* quarter.

Financial Aid: Federal Stafford Loan, Federal Perkins Loan, Federal PLUS Loan, Federal Pell Grant, Federal Work-Study, VA, Washington resident programs.

Accreditation: Northwest Association of Schools and Colleges.

Description: Columbia Basin College (1955) is a 2-year, comprehensive community college that held its first classes in a temporary quarters at Pasco Naval Base. The first permanent building was completed in 1957, and ongoing capital construction has added an additional 21 buildings in southeastern Washington state. Enrollment has increased from 299 students in 1955 to nearly 12,000 students in 2001. The faculty includes 114 full-time and 300 part-time instructors. Columbia Basin has offered videotaped telecourses since 1985 and began providing classes on the Internet in 1997. In 2002, an AA degree, transferable to state institutions, will be available for students desiring to complete online course work leading to an Associate of Arts, and Sciences degree.

Columbia College

1301 Columbia College Drive
Columbia, SC 29203

Phone: (803) 786-3788
Fax: (803) 786-3393

Division(s): Evening College
Web Site(s): http://www.columbiacollegesc.edu,
http://www. csquareonline.net
E-mail: cbroome@colacoll.edu

Undergraduate Degree Programs: No degree programs are offered totally online.

Graduate Degree Programs: No degree programs are offered totally online.

Class Titles: Art History, Dance Appreciation, History, Health, Political Science, Religion.

Teaching Methods: *Computers:* Internet, real-time chat, electronic classroom, e-mail, newsgroup, LISTSERV. ECollege portal system and courseware. *Other:* independent study, individual study, learning contracts.

Credits Granted for: experiential learning, portfolio assessment, examination (CLEP, AP, IB).

Admission Requirements: *Undergraduate:* application, SAT scores and high school transcript (if within 5 years of high school graduation), 2 letters of recommendation, official transcripts from all other educational institutions. *Graduate:* application, official transcripts from all undergraduate and graduate institutions attended, bachelor's degree, 2 letters of recommendation, essay, and TOEFL score of 550 or above if first language is not English (an undergraduate or graduate degree from an English-speaking institution will substitute for TOEFL scores). Additional requirements may be required of specific programs.

On-Campus Requirements: not for online courses.

Tuition and Fees: *Undergraduate:* $275/credit. *Graduate:* $325/credit. *Application Fee:* $20. *Other Costs:* $150/ semester. *Credit by:* semester.

Financial Aid: Federal Stafford Loan, Federal Perkins Loan, Federal Pell Grant, Federal Work-Study, VA, state programs for residents of South Carolina.

Accreditation: Southern Association for Colleges and Schools (SACS).

Description: Columbia College (1854) is a private liberal arts college for women with a coeducational evening college for working adults and a graduate school attracting professionals from around the world. The college is ranked by *U.S. News and World Report* as one of the top 10 regional liberal arts colleges in the South. Enrollment is 1,300 students from 21 states and 13 countries, approximately half of whom live on campus. The college's undergraduate curriculum offers 38 majors, 23 minors, and a premedical program. The graduate school offers 2 master's programs. In 1996 Columbia College was one of only 5 colleges and universities in the United States to receive a prestigious Hesburgh Award for "innovative faculty development enhancing undergraduate learning." The college's Leadership Institute has been recognized by both the Kellogg Foundation and the Women's College Coalition. Columbia College is affiliated with the United Methodist Church.

Columbia International University

7435 Monticello Road	Phone: (803) 735-8343 x3710
Columbia, SC 29203	(800) 777-2227 x3710
	Fax: (803) 754-9119

Division(s): Columbia Extension
Web Site(s): http://www.ciuextension.com
E-mail: extoff@ciu.edu

Certificate Programs: Graduate Certificate in Biblical Studies.

Class Titles: *Undergraduate:* Christian Evidences, Old Testament Survey, Galatians, Living Your Faith: Studies in Amos, Mark: Cross in Our Lives, Ephesians, Philippians: How to Study/Teach, Colossians/Philemon, Bible Interpretation, Progress of Redemption, New Testament Survey, Introduction to World Christian Movement, Biblical Counseling by Encouragement, Bible Doctrine, Bibliology: Inerrancy/Authority, Ethics/Sanctification; *Graduate:* Genesis-Poetical Books, Prophetic Books, Gospels/Life of Christ, Acts—Revelation, Biblical Hermeneutics, Psalms, Upper Room Discourse, Acts in Perspective, Progress of Redemption, Christian/Old Testament Theology, Romans, Leadership/Administration, Role of Women in Ministry, Personal Evangelism, Field Education: Personal Evangelism, Greek Exegesis of Romans, Early/Medieval Church: 30 AD–1517, Reformation/Modern Church: 1517–Present, American Christianity, Cultural Anthropology, Social Anthropology for Missionaries, Women in Islam, China/Chinese Ministry, Ministry of Encouragement, Christian Life, Introduction to Islam, Nature of the Learner, Field Education: Foundations of Ministry, Missions, History of Missions, Biblical Theology of Missions, Folk Religions, Theologies of Liberation, Doctrine: Survey, Theology of Jonathan Edwards.

Teaching Methods: *Computers:* Internet, CD-ROM, e-mail. *TV:* videotape. *Other:* audiotapes, fax, bulletin boards, independent study.

Credits Granted for: examination (CLEP, DANTES, GRE).

Admission Requirements: *Undergraduate:* independent learning credit courses (undergraduate and graduate): admittance to Columbia International University. Special nondegree student: application and fee; may earn 12 Independent Learning semester credits before completing full application. *Graduate:* see undergraduate. *Certificate:* see undergraduate.

On-Campus Requirements: *Undergraduate:* Columbia International University requires bachelor's degree students to complete a minimum of 32 semester hours in residence including a minimum of 2 consecutive regular semesters in which they are registered for at least 6 semester hours credit. Of the remaining hours, up to 30 credit hours earned through IDL may be applied toward a bachelor's degree from CIU. Up to 15 credit hours earned through IDL may be applied toward an Associate of Arts degree. Consult the College Admissions Office for more information on earning a CIU degree. *Graduate:* Columbia Biblical Seminary requires at least half of any seminary degree to be earned while on campus. Intensive 2–3 week courses offered on campus during January or the summer months are applied toward satisfying this residency requirement. Because of the many options available to help you complete a CBS degree, and because of varying limits on the number of credits earned through IDL which may be applied toward a degree, begin planning your academic program with counsel from the Seminary Admissions Office.

Tuition and Fees: *Undergraduate:* $135/credit. *Graduate:* $175/credit. *Application Fee:* $10. *Other Costs:* materials (textbooks, lectures, study guides, etc.). *Credit by:* semester.

Financial Aid: only for resident study.

Accreditation: Southern Association of Colleges and Schools, Accrediting Association of Bible Colleges, Association of Theological Schools.

Description: Columbia International University (1923) is a multidenominational, biblically based, Christian institution with one of the leading missionary training programs in the world. Although CIU is denominationally unaffiliated, it serves students from many denominations and independent churches. CIU is the parent company encompassing the Bible College Division and Graduate School Division of CIU, as well as Columbia Biblical Seminary and School of Missions, Ben Lippen Schools, and Christian radio stations WMHK (Columbia, SC) and WRCM (Wingate/Charlotte, NC).

Columbia Southern University

24847 Commercial Avenue	Phone: (334) 981-3771
Orange Beach, AL 36561	(800) 977-8449
	Fax: (334) 981-3815

Division(s): Development/Academic Affairs
Web Site(s): http://www.columbiasouthern.edu
E-mail: poche@columbiasouthern.edu

Undergraduate Degree Programs:

Bachelor of Science in:

    Business Administration

    Criminal Justice Administration

    Occupational Safety and Health

    Environmental Management

    Health Care Administration

    Business Administration majors, which include Marketing, Human Resource Management, Finance, Accounting and others

Graduate Degree Programs:

Master of Science in:

    Occupational Safety and Health

    MBA—MBA concentrations include Marketing, Management, E-Commerce, Human Resource Management, and others

Certificate Programs: Certified Environmental Compliance Manager (CECM), Certified Ergonomics Compliance Director (CECD), Industrial Hygiene Manager, Certified Pharmacy Technician (CPT), Certified Human Resource Manager (CHRM), Certified Employment Law Specialists (CELS).

Class Titles: Contact the school or check web site for details.

Teaching Methods: *Computers:* Internet, real-time chat, electronic classroom, e-mail, CD-ROM, newsgroup, LISTSERV. *TV:* videotape, cable program, satellite broadcasting, PBS. *Other:* radio broadcast, videoconferencing, audioconferencing, audiographics, audiotapes, fax, correspondence, independent study, individual study, learning contracts.

Credits Granted for: experiential learning, portfolio assessment, extrainstitutional learning (PONSI, corporate or professional association seminars/workshops), examination (CLEP, ACT-PEP, DANTES, GRE).

Admission Requirements: *Undergraduate:* high school diploma. *Graduate:* bachelors degree from an accredited school. *Certificate:* high school diploma.

On-Campus Requirements: None.

Tuition and Fees: *Undergraduate:* $93.75/credit. *Graduate:* $131.25/credit. *Graduation Fee:* $75. *Credit by:* quarter.

Financial Aid: VA.

Accreditation: The Distance Education and Training Council.

Description: Columbia Southern University (1993) was established as a comprehensive academic institution of higher learning. The university's mission is to education students in Business Administration, Criminal Justice Administration, Occupational Safety and Heath, Environmental Management, and Health Care Administration. CSU dates back to July 1993, when the University of Environmental Sciences was established to formally recognize training programs in environmental and safety compliance that were designed to be completed through Distance Education. Response to these programs was overwhelming. UES developed its first degree programs in 1994. In 1996 it was decided to offer degree programs in Business Administration, Criminal Justice Administration, and Health Care Administration, and to change the name to Columbia Southern University. In January 2001 Columbia Southern University became an accredited member of the Distance Education Training Council. DETC is listed by the U.S. Department of Education as a nationally recognized accrediting agency.

Columbia State Community College

PO Box 1315   Phone: (931) 540-2665

Columbia, TN 38402-1315   Fax: (931) 540-2795

Division(s): Extended Services

Web Site(s): http://www.coscc.cc.tn.us

E-mail: shuler@coscc.cc.tn.us

Undergraduate Degree Programs:

Associate of Arts

Associate of Science

Associate of Applied Science

Certificate Programs: Business Management, Commercial Performance, Customer Service, Dance Studio Management, Early Childhood Education, Electronics Engineering Technology, EMT-Paramedic, Industrial Technology, Musical Instrument Digital Interface, Workforce Preparedness.

Class Titles: Psychology, Business, Computer Information Systems, Medical Terminology, Humanities Seminar, Composition, Mass Communications, Office Administration, Literature, Art Appreciation, Philosophy.

Teaching Methods: *Computers:* Internet. *TV:* videotape.

Credits Granted for: experiential learning, portfolio assessment, extrainstitutional learning, validated by examinations.

Admission Requirements: *Undergraduate:* high school diploma or GED; ACT for degree-seeking students under age 21 and for selected programs; placement exams in math, reading, and writing for students with ACT scores under 19. Dual enrollment for exceptional high school students. *Certificate:* high school diploma or GED.

On-Campus Requirements: Associate degrees and certificates cannot be earned entirely at a distance from Columbia State. However, students may select Columbia State as their home institution to pursue a complete Associates degree via the Tennessee Board of Regents online Regents Degree Program. Associate of Applied Science in Information Technology, Associate of Arts in General Studies, and

Associate of Science in General Studies are available through Columbia State. Information on the Regents Degree Program is available at www.tn.regentsdegrees.org.

Tuition and Fees: *Undergraduate:* $56/semester hour in-state ($647 maximum/semester), $224/semester hour out-of-state ($2,585 maximum/semester). *Application Fee:* $5 payable on first registration. *Credit by Exam Fee:* $15/semester hour. *Technology Access Fee:* $5.50/semester hour ($62.50 maximum/semester). *Student Activity Fee:* $3/semester. *Graduation Fee:* $25.00. Credit by semester.

Financial Aid: Federal Stafford Loan, Federal Perkins Loan, Federal PLUS Loan, Federal Pell Grant, Federal Work-Study, VA, Tennessee resident programs.

Accreditation: Southern Association of Colleges and Schools.

Description: Columbia State Community College (1966) is located in south-central Tennessee and serves a 9-county area. It is an open-door commuter institution with one main campus and 4 off-campus sites dedicated to enhancing the region's educational, cultural, economic, and social life. The college has established for its constituents: a university-parallel general transfer program with a strong core curriculum, industrial and business programs with a strong emphasis on computer technologies to serve the growing business and industrial community, nursing and allied health programs to serve the need for health care professionals, a strong developmental studies program to serve the needs of open-admission students, and noncredit and community service programs to provide lifelong personal and professional development. The college began distance education in 1990 with an interactive TV system connecting the main campus with a branch site. Videotape courses were added in 1994, and compressed video was introduced in 1995. An average of 30 courses per semester are offered via distance learning.

Columbia Union College

7600 Flower Avenue	Phone: **(800) 782-4769**
Takoma Park, MD 20912	**(301) 891-4119**
	Fax: **(301) 891-4121**

Division(s): Home Study International
Web Site(s): http://www.cuc.edu
E-mail: enrollmentservices@hsi.edu

Undergraduate Degree Programs:
Associate of Arts
Associate of Science
Bachelor of Arts
Bachelor of Science

Class Titles: at least 50 classes in general areas of Health, Nutrition, History, Business, Business Administration, Psychology, Theology/Religion, General Studies, Respiratory Program, French, Spanish, Greek, Biology, Communications, Computer Science, Education, English, Fine Arts (Music Appreciation), Math, Sociology.

Teaching Methods: *Computers:* Internet, real-time chat, electronic classroom, e-mail, CD-ROM, newsgroup, LISTSERV. *TV:* videotape, satellite broadcasting. *Other:* audiotapes, fax, correspondence, independent study, individual study, learning contracts.

Credits Granted for: experiential learning, portfolio assessment, extrainstitutional learning, examination (CLEP, ACT-PEP, DANTES, GRE).

Admission Requirements: *Undergraduate:* high school graduate or equivalent, 2.5 high school GPA, 2.0 college GPA (if attended), must finish distance education courses within one year or pay to extend. No requirements for nondegree seeking students.

On-Campus Requirements: if degree requires.

Tuition and Fees: *Undergraduate:* $190/credit. *Application Fee:* $50. *Other Costs:* $60 enrollment fee, supplies vary. Maryland sales tax on supplies. If delivered in Maryland, shipping and handling fee. *Credit by:* semester.

Accreditation: Middle States Association of Colleges and Schools, Maryland Higher Education Commission, Accrediting Association of Seventh-day Adventist Schools, Colleges, and Universities.

Description: Columbia Union College is a Christian institution operated by the Seventh-Day Adventist Church. The heart of Columbia Union College is a Christocentric vision, with its affirmation of the goodness of life, the sacredness of earth, and the dignity of all people and cultures. The mission of the college, carried out in the spirit of this vision, is: to make learning a pleasure and a joy, to embrace the adventure of truth, to link scholarship and service, to develop talent through an ethos of excellence, to seize the challenge and opportunity of the nation's capital, and to produce graduates who bring competence and moral leadership to their communities. Columbia's External Degree Program, established in 1969, meets the needs of adult students who find it difficult to finish a college degree during traditional, weekday hours or within fixed class schedules. It is not intended to replace traditional, on-campus learning; approximately half of all credits should be earned in the classroom. Students may pursue a degree or supplement a program elsewhere without being confined to class schedules or to a campus. They can live anywhere, move anytime, start anytime during the year, and study on their own time at their own pace without interfering with their course work.

Columbia-Greene Community College

4400 Route 23
Hudson, NY 12534
Phone: (518) 828-4181
Fax: (518) 822-2015

Division(s): Academic Programs
Web Site(s): http://www.sunycgcc.edu
E-mail: carito@sunycgcc.edu

Class Titles: contact school.

Teaching Methods: *Computers:* Internet, electronic classroom, e-mail, LISTSERV. *TV:* cable program. *Other:* None.

Credits Granted for: experiential learning, examination (CLEP, DANTES).

Admission Requirements: *Undergraduate:* proof of prerequisite skill/knowledge. Contact school for complete information.

On-Campus Requirements: None.

Tuition and Fees: *Undergraduate:* $100/credit. *Credit by:* semester.

Accreditation: Middle States Association of Colleges and Schools.

Description: Columbia-Greene Community College (1969) is a small, rural, public community college. Columbia-Greene is a unique college, large enough to offer a broad array of dynamic programs in the technologies, the humanities and the arts, yet small enough to nurture students. We are a comprehensive, 2-year college offering a variety of transfer and career programs leading to associate degrees.

Columbus State Community College

550 East Spring Street
Columbus, OH 43215
Phone: (614) 287-5353
Fax: (614) 287-5123

Division(s): Instructional Technologies and Distance Learning
Web Site(s): http://www.cscc.edu and http://global.cscc.edu
E-mail: global@cscc.edu

Undergraduate Degree Programs:
Associate of Science in Business Management
Associate of Arts

Class Titles: Accounting, Organizational Behavior, Management Decisions, Case Studies in Business Seminar, Visual Basic, Economics (micro/macro), Technical Writing, Writing About American Experience, Images of Men/Women in Literature, Shakespeare, Survey of British Literature, Business Finance, Managed Care Trends, Medical Terminology, Human Resource Management, Labor Relations, Civilization, Computer Literacy, Internet, Nursing Skills, Gerontological Nursing, Business Grammar Usage, Business, Management, Business Ethics, Small Business Development, Small Business Operations, Speech, Composition, Essay/Research, Business Communication, French, Personal Finance, Nutrition, Business Law, Legal Environment of Business, Marketing, Business Math, Natural Science, Spanish.

Teaching Methods: *Computers:* Internet, real-time chat, electronic classroom, e-mail, CD-ROM, newsgroup, LISTSERV. *TV:* videotape, cable program, satellite broadcasting, PBS. *Other:* videoconferencing, audioconferencing, audiotapes, fax, independent study, individual study.

Credits Granted for: experiential learning, portfolio assessment, extrainstitutional learning.

Admission Requirements: *Undergraduate:* open. *Certificate:* open.

On-Campus Requirements: None.

Tuition and Fees: *Undergraduate:* $2,461/credit. *Credit by:* quarter.

Financial Aid: Federal Stafford Loan, Federal Perkins Loan, Federal PLUS Loan, Federal Pell Grant, Federal Work-Study, VA, Ohio resident program.

Accreditation: North Central Association of Colleges and Schools.

Description: As a comprehensive community college, Columbus State (1963) has a strong commitment to technical education, offering the Associate of Applied Science and the Associate of Technical Studies degree programs in business, health, public service, and engineering technologies to prepare graduates for immediate employment. The transfer programs, Associate of Arts and Associate of Science, meet the majority of freshman and sophomore course requirements of bachelor's degree programs offered by 4-year colleges and universities in central Ohio and throughout the state. Columbus State has been offering distance learning for more than 2 decades in the area of TV and video-based learning. The college began its Web-based course offering in 1996.

Columbus State University

4225 University Avenue
Columbus, GA 31907
Phone: (706) 568-2410
Fax: (706) 565-3529

Division(s): Computer Science
Web Site(s): http://csuonline.edu
E-mail: cleveland.art@colstate.edu

Graduate Degree Programs:
MS in Applied Computer Science

Class Titles: Computer Science: Programming Languages, Computer Networks, Operating Systems, Databases, Object-Oriented Design, Graphical User Interfaces, Software Design.

Teaching Methods: *Computers:* Internet, real-time chat, electronic classroom, e-mail, CD-ROM, newsgroup, LISTSERV. *Other:* None.

Admission Requirements: *Graduate:* accredited undergraduate degree, 2.75 undergraduate cumulative GPA, 800 on GRE (verbal and math), or undergraduate degree in computer science or closely related field or 50 percentile on computer science of GRE.

On-Campus Requirements: None.

Tuition and Fees: *Graduate:* contact school for more information. *Credit by:* semester.

Accreditation: Southern Association of Colleges and Schools.

Description: Columbus State University (1998) is a public, comprehensive, senior university that serves 6,000 students on its 132-acre main campus and many more on its off-campus centers. CSU is located 100 miles southwest of Atlanta and serves diverse educational needs with a mixture of liberal arts and professional programs leading to associate, bachelor's, and graduate degrees. The university fosters several programs that have achieved a national reputation of excellence. Columbus State has also received national acclaim for its programs in computer education, economic development, and regional services. The university has educated more than 500 computer professionals for local corporate partners. The first degree program to be delivered on online is the Master of Science in Applied Computer Science. CSU Online will continuously strive to keep this program and all additional programs academically sound and pertinent to the changing needs of today's workplace.

Community College of Philadelphia

| 1700 Spring Garden Street | Phone: (215) 751-8702 |
| Philadelphia, PA 19130 | Fax: (215) 972-6391 |

Division(s): Office of Distance Education, Division of Educational Support Services
Web Site(s): http://www.ccp.cc.pa.us
E-mail: distance@ccp.cc.pa.us

Class Titles: Anthropology, Chemistry, Economics, French, History, Marketing, Management, Philosophy, Psychology, Sociology, Spanish, Geography, Algebra.

Teaching Methods: *Computers:* Internet, CD-ROM, e-mail. *TV:* videotape, cable program, PBS. *Other:* video-conferencing.

Credits Granted for: experiential learning, extrainstitutional learning, portfolio assessment, examination (CLEP, ACT-PEP, APP).

Admission Requirements: *Undergraduate:* open admission for all who may benefit; accredited secondary school diploma or state equivalency.

On-Campus Requirements: Most courses require a few meetings for reviews, exams, and labs (in some cases).

Tuition and Fees: *Undergraduate:* $76/credit. *Application Fee:* $20 for new students; additional $5/semester for distance courses. *Software:* $6/credit technology fee. *Other Costs:* $3/credit general fee. *Credit by:* semester.

Financial Aid: Federal Stafford Loan, Federal Perkins Loan, Federal PLUS Loan, Federal Pell Grant, Federal Work-Study, VA, Pennsylvania resident programs, Federal Supplemental Educational Opportunity Grant.

Accreditation: Middle States Association of Colleges and Schools.

Description: An urban community college in Philadelphia, the college opened for classes in 1965 in a former department store at 34 S. 11th Street while a permanent campus was being sought. In 1971 the college acquired from the federal government the building at 1700 Spring Garden Street that had housed the third Philadelphia Mint and eventually would become the centerpiece of its permanent campus. We joined in a consortium of other local colleges under WHYY, our local PBS affiliate offering telecourses, and have just recently begun expanding offerings to Internet-based courses.

Community College of Rhode Island

| One Hilton Street | Phone: (401) 455-6113 |
| Providence, RI 02905-2304 | Fax: (401) 455-6047 |

Division(s): Instructional Technology and Distance Education
Web Site(s): http://www.ccri.cc.ri.us
E-mail: webadmissions@ccri.cc.ri.us

Class Titles: Biology, Business, English, Math, Law, Social Science, Psychology, Liberal Arts, Justice Studies, History, Computer Studies, Nursing.

Teaching Methods: *Computers:* Internet, real-time chat, e-mail, electronic bulletin board. *TV:* videotape, cable program, satellite broadcasting, PBS. *Other:* None.

Credits Granted for: experiential learning, portfolio assessment, cooperative education, examination (CLEP, GRE).

Admission Requirements: *Undergraduate:* age 18. *Certificate:* age 18.

On-Campus Requirements: final exam.

Tuition and Fees: *Undergraduate:* $73/credit. *Application Fee:* $20. *Other Costs:* $25 for general fees. *Credit by:* semester.

Financial Aid: Federal Stafford Loan, Federal Perkins Loan, Federal PLUS Loan, Federal Pell Grant, Federal Work-Study, VA, Rhode Island resident programs.

Accreditation: New England Association of Schools and Colleges, National League of Nursing, National Accrediting Agency for Clinical Laboratory Sciences, Commission on Dental Accreditation, Joint Review Committee on Education in Radiologic Technology, Committee for Accreditation of Respiratory Care Programs, Commission on Accreditation in Physical Therapy Education, American Chemical Society, Granted Developing Program Status by the American Council of Occupational Therapy Education.

Description: Community College of Rhode Island (1964) is the largest public, 2-year, degree-granting college in New England. It provides a variety of career, technical, and academic programs at campuses in Warwick (1972), Lincoln (1976), and Providence (1990) and offers courses at satellite facilities in East Providence, Middletown, Newport, and Westerly. From its modest beginning with 325 students to its present enrollment of 15,000, CCRI has grown to meet the goals of its founders. In 1987, CCRI began offering distance education courses delivered by TV, using the local cable companies. CCRI's telecourses, with enrollment around 1,000, offer accessibility and flexibility to learners who have personal or professional challenges and responsibilities that prohibit travel to a campus on a regular basis for traditional classes.

Community College of Southern Nevada

6375 West Charleston W3D	Phone: (702) 651-5619
Las Vegas, NV 89146	Fax: (702) 651-5741

Division(s): Community Education
Web Site(s): http://www.ccsn.nevada.edu/distanceed
E-mail: distanceed@ccsn.nevada.edu

Undergraduate Degree Programs:
Associate of Arts in:
    General Studies
    English
    Sociology

Certificate Programs: Cardio-Respiratory Therapy, Veterinary Technology.

Class Titles: American Sign Language, Astronomy, Business, Education, English, History, Library Skills, Mathematics, Music, Philosophy, Political Science, Psychology, Sociology, Study Skills, Marketing, Health, Art, Biology, Speech, Accounting, Health Information Technology, Computer Science, Fire Science, Environmental Science, Phlebotomy.

Teaching Methods: *Computers:* Internet, real-time chat, e-mail. *TV:* videotape, PBS. *Other:* videoconferencing, fax.

Admission Requirements: *Undergraduate:* application and fees, age 16 with signature of parent or legal guardian, placement tests for math and English.

On-Campus Requirements: None.

Tuition and Fees: *Undergraduate:* $44/credit for certificate or associate degree. *Other Costs:* $4 tech fee/credit. *Application Fee:* $5. *Credit by:* semester.

Financial Aid: Federal Stafford Loan, Federal Perkins Loan, Federal PLUS Loan, Federal Pell Grant, Federal Work-Study, VA, Nevada resident programs.

Accreditation: Western Association of Schools and Colleges.

Description: The Community College of Southern Nevada consists of 4 distinct campuses: Charleton Campus (1988), Cheyenne Campus (1974), Henderson Campus (1981), and Summerlin Center (1998). The mission of Nevada's community colleges as institutions of the university and community college system of Nevada is to provide superior student-centered educational opportunities for the citizens of the state within designated service areas of each college. The community college mission encompasses a belief that education and training are the chief means of developing human capital for investment in the economic health of the state of Nevada.

Community College of Vermont

1197 Main Street, Suite 3	Phone: (802) 748-6673
St. Johnsbury, VT 05860	Fax: (802) 748-5014

Division(s): Office of On-line Learning
Web Site(s): http://online.ccv.vsc.edu/welcome.html
E-mail: wardc@mail.ccv.vsc.edu

Class Titles: vary with term: Abnormal Psychology, Creative Writing Poetry, America Between Wars, Critical Issues of Holocaust, Foundations of Western Civilization, Bioethics, Environmental Science, Philosophy, Programming in C++, Mythology, Current Issues in Management, Word Processing, Criminology/Criminal Behavior, Modern Poetry, Women's Utopian Literature, Elementary Statistics, Sociology, Principles of Accounting, Women in Management, Web Site Design/Management, Internet.

Teaching Methods: *Computers:* Internet, real-time chat, electronic classroom, e-mail, CD-ROM, newsgroup, LISTSERV.

Credits Granted for: experiential learning, portfolio assessment, extrainstitutional learning, examination (CLEP, ACT-PEP, DANTES, GRE).

Admission Requirements: *Undergraduate:* high school diploma, on-site assessment of basic skills.

On-Campus Requirements: None.

Tuition and Fees: *Undergraduate:* $117 (in-state) $236 (out-of-state)/credit. *Other Costs:* $10/credit academic services, varying materials fees. *Credit by:* semester.

Financial Aid: Federal Stafford Loan, Federal Perkins Loan, Federal PLUS Loan, Federal Pell Grant, Federal Work-Study, VA, Vermont resident programs.

Accreditation: Northeast Association of Colleges and Schools.

Description: Community College of Vermont (1970) began offering online courses via web crossing in 1995. CCV's courses—online and traditional—are designed for students residing in Vermont or in nearby areas of New York, Massachusetts, and New Hampshire.

Community Colleges of Colorado Online

9075 East Lowry Boulevard, Building 965   Phone: (800) 841-5040
Denver, CO 80230

Web Site(s): http://ccconline.org
E-mail: john.schmahl@heat.cccoes.edu

Undergraduate Degree Programs:
Associate of Arts in:
    General Education
Associate of Applied Science in:
    Agricultural Business
    Business
    Construction Technology with an Emphasis in Construction Electrician
    Convergent Technology
    Emergency Management and Planning
    Library Technician
    Occupational Safety and Health Technology
    Construction Technology with an Emphasis in Power Technology
    Associate of Arts with an Emphasis in Public Administration

Certificate Programs: Agricultural Business, Computer Networking, Convergent Technologies, Emergency Management and Planning, Library Technician, Microsoft Certified System Engineer (MCSE): Occupational Safety and Health Technology.

Class Titles: Contact school or check web site for details.

Teaching Methods: *Computers:* Internet, real-time chat, electronic classroom, e-mail, CD-ROM, newsgroup, LISTSERV. *TV:* videotape, cable program, satellite broadcasting, PBS. *Other:* radio broadcast, videoconferencing, audioconferencing, audiographics, audiotapes, fax, correspondence, independent study, individual study, learning contracts.

Credits Granted for: experiential learning, portfolio assessment, extrainstitutional learning (PONSI, corporate or professional association seminars/workshops), examination (CLEP, ACT-PEP, DANTES, GRE).

Admission Requirements: *Undergraduate:* open enrollment.

On-Campus Requirements: None, for most degrees. Convergent Technologies has a lab requirement.

Tuition and Fees: *Undergraduate:* $122.70/credit. *Credit by:* semester.

Financial Aid: Federal Stafford Loan, Federal Perkins Loan, Federal PLUS Loan, Federal Pell Grant, Federal Work-Study, VA, state programs for residents of Colorado.

Accreditation: North Central Association of Colleges and Schools.

Description: (Online degrees consortium formed in 1997.) The Community Colleges of Colorado Online is comprised of the 14 colleges in the Community Colleges of Colorado, Dawson Community College, and Northwest Missouri State University. Through CCCOnline, you can now earn fully accredited associate of arts degrees, associate of applied science degrees, and certificates, in various disciplines.

Concordia University

7400 August Street   Phone: (708) 209-3024
River Forest, IL 60305   Fax: (708) 209-3176

Division(s): University College
Web Site(s): http://www.curf.edu
E-mail: crfconted@curf.edu

Class Titles: Theology, Psychology, Education.

Teaching Methods: *Computers:* Internet, e-mail, LISTSERV. *TV:* interactive TV. *Other:* videoconferencing, audioconferencing, audiotapes, fax, correspondence, independent study.

Credits Granted for: experiential learning, portfolio assessment, extrainstitutional learning, examination (CLEP, ACT-PEP, DANTES, GRE).

Admission Requirements: *Undergraduate:* high school diploma.

On-Campus Requirements: None.

Tuition and Fees: *Undergraduate:* variable. *Credit by:* semester.

Financial Aid: Federal Stafford Loan, Federal Perkins Loan, Federal PLUS Loan, Federal Pell Grant, Federal Work-Study, VA, Illinois resident programs.

Accreditation: North Central Association of Colleges and Schools.

Description: Concordia University (1864) is a church-related (Lutheran) liberal arts institution offering bachelor's and master's degrees. Concordia has offered courses via correspondence since 1950 and is now in the process of making these courses available on the Web.

Concordia University, Austin

3400 IH35 North	**Phone: (512) 452-7661**
Austin, TX 78705-2799	**Fax: (512) 459-8517**

Division(s): College of Adult Education
Web Site(s): http://www.concordia.edu
E-mail: adp@concordia.edu

Undergraduate Degree Programs:
Bachelor of Arts in:
    Early Childhood Education
    Accounting
    Behavioral Sciences
    Business
    Management
    Church Music/Conducting
    Church Music/Organ
    Communications
    Elementary Education
    Secondary Education
    English
    Environmental Science
    Liberal Arts
    Mexican American Studies
    History
    Pre-Seminary Spanish

Graduate Degree Programs:
Master in Education

Class Titles: Communications/Human Communication Theory, Mass Media History/Theory, English/Short Story, Government/American Government, History/Western Civilization from 1715, Math/Finite Math, Psychology/Personality Theory, Religion/New Testament, Religion/Old Testament, Religion/History/Philosophy of Reformation, Religion/American Christianity.

Teaching Methods: *TV:* videotape, cable program, satellite broadcasting. *Other:* None.

Credits Granted for: experiential learning, portfolio assessment, extrainstitutional learning, examination (CLEP, ACT-PEP, DANTES, GRE).

Admission Requirements: *Undergraduate:* high school graduation or equivalent, ACT/SAT scores.

On-Campus Requirements: attend orientation.

Tuition and Fees: *Undergraduate:* $440/credit distance learning; validated prior learning, administrative fee $85; evaluation fee/semester hour requested $60. *Application Fee:* $25. *Other Costs:* adult degree program modules $995/$1,800. *Credit by:* semester.

Financial Aid: Federal Stafford Loan, Federal Pell Grant, Federal Work-Study, VA, Texas resident programs.

Accreditation: Southern Association of Colleges and Schools.

Description: Concordia University at Austin (1926) opened as Concordia Academy to train young men for ministry in the Lutheran Church. The junior college department, added in 1951, became coeducational in 1955. Concordia received authorization to implement a 4-year liberal arts program in 1979, and its first BA students graduated in 1982. The current student population includes various cultural, religious, and ethnic backgrounds. Distance learning was started in 1992 to help students reach their educational goals by providing more convenient access and flexibility to classes off campus. ADP sites now in Dallas, Houston, and San Antonio.

Concordia-New York

171 White Plains Road	**Phone: (914) 337-9300**
Bronxville, NY 10708	**Fax: (914) 395-4500**

Web Site(s): http://www.concordia-ny.edu
E-mail: meb@concordia-ny.edu

Undergraduate Degree Programs:
Bachelor of Liberal Arts
Bachelor of Science in:
    Education
    Social Work
    Business

Class Titles: call (914) 337-9300 ×2103 or e-mail blanco@concordia-ny.edu.

Teaching Methods: *TV:* videoconferencing (compressed video).

Credits Granted for: portfolio assessment, extrainstitutional learning, examination (CLEP, ACT-PEP, DANTES, GRE).

Admission Requirements: *Undergraduate:* high school graduate with strong college-prep curriculum, application, SAT/ACT scores, official transcripts from high school and all colleges or universities, recommendations. *Certificate:* variable.

On-Campus Requirements: one year in residence.

Tuition and Fees: *Undergraduate:* $444/credit. *Credit by:* semester.

Financial Aid: Federal Stafford Loan, Federal PLUS Loan, Federal Pell Grant, Federal Work-Study, VA, New York resident programs.

Accreditation: Middle States Association of Colleges and Schools, Council on Social Work Education.

Description: Concordia-New York (1881) is a liberal arts, church-related college that offers majors in the liberal arts as well as in education, social work, and business. The college is small (600), located in a beautiful NYC suburb, and two-thirds of its students are residential. Distance learning at Concordia began in 1996 as part of the Concordia University System, a group of 10 schools nationwide. It allows member schools to send and receive classes via compressed video.

Concordia University

275 N Syndicate	Phone: 800-211-3370;
St Paul, MN 55104	Fax: (651) 603-6144

Division(s): College of Graduate and Continuing Studies (School of Human Services School of Accelerated Learning)
Web Site(s): http://www.cshs.csp.edu
E-mail: cshs@csp.edu

Undergraduate Degree Programs:
BA in Marketing (CSAL)
CSHS:
  BA in School age care
  BA in Criminal Justice
  BA in Youth Development
  BA in Management of Human Services organizations
  BA in Child development
  Fast Track (34 gen ed credits)

Graduate Degree Programs:
  MA in Education Early Childhood
  MA in Education in Schoolage care
  MA in Education, Youth Development
  MA in Human Services, Family Studies
  MA in Human Services, Leadership

Certificate Programs: School Age care, Early Childhood.

Class Titles: Anthropology, sociology, psychology, history, computer, math, English, child development, leadership, human development, http://www.cshs.csp.edu/brochures/online/descriptions.htm.

Teaching Methods: *Computers:* Internet, real-time chat, electronic classroom, e-mail, CD-ROM, bulletin board (asynchronous discusssion group), textbooks, handouts, audio tape *TV:* videotape *Other:* independent study.

Credits Granted for: experiential learning, CLEP.

Admission Requirements: *Undergraduate:* 50 credits transferred, 2 reference letters, resume, 4-day residency for distance education. *Graduate:* BA degree; 4 day residency for distance education, portfolio, 2 reference letters. *Certificate:* High school diploma.

On-Campus Requirements: the 4-day residency is required at the beginning of the program.

Tuition and Fees: *Undergraduate:* $228 per credit *Graduate:* $264 per credit *Application Fees:* $25 *Graduation Fee:* $100 *Credit by:* Semester.

Financial Aid: Federal Stafford Loan, Federal Perkins Loan, VA.

Accreditation: Higher learning commission (NCA).

Description: Since 1994, The Concordia School of Human Services (1893) has offered several programs. All of the programs are offered by distance education, and all are designed for working adults. The distance education program begins with a four-day residency at the Concordia University campus in St. Paul. At the residency, students learn the technology they will be using, and begin their first class. They will meet the instructors and have a chance to ask questions about specific courses. Students will also meet the department staff and learn the support services that are available. Finally, the residency is a time to meet the other members of the cohort. The distance education cohorts are very interactive; there is a great deal of communication that goes back and forth between learners and between learners and professors. The distance education process relies heavily on e-mail. Like the traditional on-campus cohorts, the distance education process is reading intensive and writing intensive. The mission of the School of Human Services is to create and deliver outstanding education programs that will prepare professionals for enlightened care—facilitating their continued growth and development in fields that serve children, youth, and adults.

Concordia University, Wisconsin

12800 North Lake Shore Drive   Phone: (262) 243-4442
Mequon, WI 53097   (800) 665-6564
                                          Fax: (262) 243-4459

Division(s): Distance Learning Programs
Web Site(s): http://www.cuw.edu
E-mail: sarah.weaver@bach.cuw.edu

Graduate Degree Programs:
Nursing
Education Administration
Curriculum and Instruction
Reading
Education-Counseling
Business Administration

Teaching Methods: *Computers:* Internet, e-mail. *TV:* videotape. *Other:* videoconferencing, fax, correspondence, independent study, individual study.

Admission Requirements: *Graduate:* 3.0 GPA undergraduate degree, official transcripts, 2 letters of recommendation, letter of intent, current résumé. Student must complete the program in 5 years.

On-Campus Requirements: Students must come to campus to take one course on campus to fulfill their residency requirement. The courses are one to two weeks in length depending on the program.

Tuition and Fees: *Graduate:* $325–375 per credit. *Application Fee:* $35. *Graduation Fee:* $80. *Other Costs:* approximately $70–150 for textbooks. *Credit by:* semester. *Other Requirements:* There is open enrollment and registration. Once a student registers, he or she has four week to turn in the first assignment. All courses are designed to be completed in 8–10 weeks. However, a student has up to 16 weeks to complete each course.

Financial Aid: Federal Stafford Loan, Federal Perkins Loan, Federal Pell Grant, Federal Work-Study, VA, Wisconsin resident programs.

Accreditation: North Central Association of Colleges and Schools. National League for Nursing, Commission on Collegiate Nursing Education, Lutheran Church Missouri Synod. We are also approved by the Wisconsin Department of Public Instruction and by the State of Wisconsin, Department of Regulation and Licensing for licensure as a Professional Counselor.

Description: Concordia University Wisconsin (1881) was founded as a school of the Lutheran Church, Missouri Synod. Concordia gained university status in 1989. The stated mission of the university is to prepare individuals for service to Christ in the Church and the world. In fulfillment of that mission, the university has itself chosen to serve a select number of professions. Among them are Education, Business, and Nursing, as well as others. Serving these professions means offering education for them, which fully meets the contemporary demands of those professions. Recognizing that a bachelor's degree is no longer appropriate as the terminal education point for most of the professions served by the university, Concordia offers graduate education in those fields where it has the requisite expertise, and where graduate education is, increasingly, a must for professionals in those fields.

Connecticut State University System

39 Woodland Street   Phone: (860) 493-0000
Hartford, CT 06105-2337   Fax: (860) 493-0120

Division(s): OnlineCSU
Web Site(s): http://www.onlinecsu.ctstateu.edu
E-mail: kaputr@sysoff.ctstateu.edu or OnlineCSU@sysoff.ctstateu.edu

Undergraduate Degree Programs: Contact school.

Graduate Degree Programs:
Master of Science in:
    Library Science
    Educational Technology
    Data Mining
    Accounting

Certificate Programs: Certificate in Data Mining.

Class Titles: Accounting, Anthropology, Business, Communication, Computer Science, Data Mining, Economics, Education, Educational Psychology, Educational Technology, English, History, Justice and Law Administration, Industrial Technology, Information and Library Science, Management, Marketing, Mathematics, Nursing, Philosophy, Political Science, Psychology, Social Work, Sociology, Spanish, Statistics, Theater.

Teaching Methods: *Computers:* Internet, real-time chat, electronic classroom, e-mail, CD-ROM, newsgroup. *TV:* videotape. *Other:* videoconferencing, audioconferencing, audiotapes, fax.

Credits Granted for: Please contact the individual university and department for credit-based questions.

Admission Requirements: Please visit the web site for admission requirement details.

On-Campus Requirements: There is no on-campus requirement. Should a particular class request on-campus participation, provisons will be made for those unable to visit the university.

Tuition and Fees: *Undergraduate:* $220/credit as of fall 2001, for both in and out-of-state residents. *Graduate:* $260/credit as of fall 2001, for both in and out-of-state residents. *Other Costs:* online fee: $32/class. *Credit by:* semester.

Financial Aid: please contact the offering Connecticut State University institution for information regarding financial aid.

Accreditation: New England Association of Schools and Colleges, Connecticut Department of Higher Education. Individual programs are accredited as appropriate.

Description: OnlineCSU, the virtual classroom for the four Connecticut State University institutions, was created in 1998. The Connecticut State University System was created in 1983, with its orgins going back to the founding of a school for teachers in 1849. OnlineCSU is the virtual classroom of the 4 Connecticut State University (CSU) institutions—Central, Eastern, Southern, and Western Connecticut State Universities. OnlineCSU ensures that the education traditionally available only in the classroom is now available online day or night, at home or at work, on business trips or vacation. CSU is a comprehensive, fully accredited university system; as such, all graduate and undergraduate courses taught through OnlineCSU are approved for credit and applicable toward a degree or for continuing education. In addition, OnlineCSU offers full graduate degree programs online, including a master of science in library science, with several other graduate degree programs in development. OnlineCSU distinguishes itself from other online learning providers by ensuring that the faculty who develop the course also teach the course. This means no "canned" courses from freelance educators.

Connors State College

RR 1, Box 1000	Phone: (918) 463-2931
Warner, OK 74469	Fax: (918) 463-6314

Division(s): Director, Distance Education
Web Site(s): http://www.connors.cc.ok.us
E-mail: rramming@connors.cc.ok.us

Class Titles: Agriculture, Math, History, Spanish, Criminal Justice, Geography, Political Science, Psychology, Computer Science, Business.

Teaching Methods: *Computer:* Internet. *TV:* interactive video, videotape, PBS. *Other:* None.

Credits Granted for: examination (CLEP, departmental, Advanced Placement), military credit evaluation.

Admission Requirements: *Undergraduate:* open-admission; testing (ACT/CPT) for advising/course placement. *Certificate:* same as undergraduate.

On-Campus Requirements: None.

Tuition and Fees: *Undergraduate:* $43.25/credit Oklahoma resident. *Other Costs:* $5/semester student ID, $10/semester parking permit, $3–$20/course instructional fees/lab fees. *Credit by:* semester.

Financial Aid: Federal Stafford Loan, Federal Perkins Loan, Federal Pell Grant, Federal Work-Study, VA, Oklahoma resident programs.

Accreditation: North Central Association of Colleges and Schools, National League of Nursing, Oklahoma State Board of Nursing Registration and Nursing Education.

Description: Connors State College (1908) is a rural, 2-year college in eastern Oklahoma. It has campuses in Warner and Muskogee. Connors provides general education curricula consistent with the first 2 years of a baccalaureate program, developmental education for college preparation, and occupational and continuing education. Connors State College has offered telecourse for many years and began offing interactive television courses in the spring of 1997, and is continuously expanding its distance education offerings.

Contra Costa College

2600 Mission Bell Drive	Phone: 510 235-7800
San Pablo, CA 94806	

Web Site(s): http://www.contracosta.cc.ca.us/
E-mail: jmoore@contracosta.cc.ca.us
or egeringer@contracosta.cc.ca.us

Undergraduate Degree Programs: Contact school.

Class Titles: Cultural Anthropology, Survey of General Chemistry, Theater Appreciation, Writing: Expository, Physical Geography, Education for Healthful Living, History of the U.S., History of Western Civilization, Introduction to Humanities, Introduction to Philosophy, Goverment of the U.S., General Psychology, Introduction to Sociology, Applied Vocational Skills Lab, Retailing, Introduction to Web Page Design, Composition and Reading, Composition and Reading, Global English on the Internet, Finding Information Online and in Print, Interpersonal Communication.

Teaching Methods: *Computers:* Internet, real-time chat, electronic classroom, e-mail, CD-ROM, newsgroup, LIST-SERV. *TV:* videotape, cable program, satellite broadcasting, PBS. *Other:* radio broadcast, videoconferencing, audioconferencing, audiographics, audiotapes, fax, correspondence, independent study, individual study, learning contracts.

Admission Requirements: *Undergraduate:* prospective students must be 18 years old or older or have completed high school equivalent. All new students are required to participate in the college matriculation process.

Tuition and Fees: *Undergraduate:* $11/unit, resident, $147/unit, nonresident *Credit by:* semester.

Financial Aid: Direct Loans, Federal Pell Grant, Federal Work-Study, State Programs for residents of California.

Accreditation: Western Association of Schools and Colleges.

Description: Contra Costa College is a comprehensive community college located in San Pablo, California. We serve primarily the residents of west Contra Costa County. We are the first of 3 colleges in the district, established in Richmond in 1949. Originally named West Contra Costa Junior College, the college is located on 83 acres in the rolling hills of San Pablo overlooking the San Pablo Bay. Program accreditation includes the California Board of Registered Nursing, the California Board of Vocational Nurse Examiners, and the American Dental Association. The college is approved for the training of veterans, and for the education of foreign students by the United States Department of State and the United States Immigration and Naturalization Services. Our, vision, beliefs, values, mission, and goals are all focused on the needs of all students.

Cornell University

| 115 Warren Hall | Phone: (607) 266-7656 |
| Ithaca, NY 14852-4320 | Fax: (607) 254-5122 |

Division(s): Agricultural Resources and Managerial Economics and Food Industry Management Distance Education Program
Web Site(s): http://distance-ed.arme.cornell.edu
E-mail: distance-ed@cornell.edu

Certificate Programs: Food Industry Management Distance Education.

Class Titles: 40 courses in Supermarket, Convenience Store/ Distribution Series.

Teaching Methods: *Computers:* e-mail, CD-ROM. *TV:* videotape. *Other:* fax, correspondence, independent study, workshops.

Credits Granted for: articulation agreements with some colleges—our students' transcripts are evaluated by outside schools for credit. Cornell college credit is not awarded.

Admission Requirements: *Undergraduate:* open enrollment. *Certificate:* open enrollment.

On-Campus Requirements: None.

Tuition and Fees: *Undergraduate:* $60–95/course certificate program (students work at their own pace).

Accreditation: Middle States Association of Colleges and Schools.

Description: The Cornell University (1964) Food Industry Management Distance Education Program serves the food industry, supermarkets, wholesalers, and convenience stores. This certificate program offers 40 courses in an independent study format. Companies often teach our courses in-house in a workshop format. The program offers bachelor's, master's, and PhDs on campus, executive development programs on campus and globally, applied research for the food industry, and the Distance Education Program.

Cossatot Community College of the University of Arkansas

P.O. Box 960	Phone: (870) 584-4471
De Queen, AR 78132	and (800) 844-4471
	Fax: (870) 642-3320

Division(s): Distance Education Department
Web Site(s): http://ctc.tec.ar.us
E-mail: dpark@ctc.tec.ar.us

Undergraduate Degree Programs:
Associate of General Studies Degree.

Class Titles: Contact school or check web site for details.

Teaching Methods: *Computers:* Internet, real-time chat, electronic classroom, e-mail, CD-ROM, newsgroup, LISTSERV. *TV:* videotape, cable program, PBS, *Other:* videoconferencing, audioconferencing, audiographics, audiotapes, fax, correspondence, independent study, individual study, learning contracts.

Credits Granted for: experiential learning, portfolio assessment, extrainstitutional learning (PONSI, corporate or professional association seminars/workshops), examination (CLEP, ACT-PEP, DANTES, GRE).

Admission Requirements: *Undergraduate:* high school diploma or equivalent, ACT or ASSET test.

On-Campus Requirements: None.

Tuition and Fees: *Undergraduate:* $40/credit in-state; $120/credit out-of-state. *Other Costs:* $22 registration fee, $15 technology fee, $10 Internet course. *Credit by:* semester.

Financial Aid: Federal Pell Grant, Federal Work-Study, VA, state programs for residents of Arkansas.

Accreditation: North Central Association of Colleges and Schools.

Description: Cossatot Community College of the University of Arkansas is a small rural college that focuses on student learning and service to students. Established in 1991 as Cossatot Technical College, it has grown from 100 to almost 900 credit-seeking students. The development of the

Distance Education program is a response to the ever-growing needs of adults for improved educational opportunities designed to fit into their increasingly busy lives. Cossatot Distance Education courses are designed and taught by the college's regular faculty and reflect the same learning objectives and outcomes as the on-campus classes. Currently over half of the on-campus students take one or more Distance Education classes. These classes are most appropriate to highly motivated, self-directed students. Classes include a variety of interactive elements including bulletin boards, private mail, chat rooms, and toll-free access to the instructor.

County College of Morris

214 Center Grove Road	Phone: (973) 328-5184
Randolph, NJ 07869-2086	Fax: (973) 328-5082

Division(s): Distance Education
Web Site(s): http://www.ccm.edu
E-mail: mroman@ccm.edu

Undergraduate Degree Programs:
Associate in:
Arts
Science
Applied Science

Certificate Programs: college credit programs of varying lengths that lead to certificates.

Teaching Methods: *Computers:* Internet, real-time chat, electronic classroom, e-mail, CD-ROM. *TV:* videotape, cable program, satellite broadcasting, PBS. *Other:* videoconferencing, audioconferencing, audiographics, audiotapes, fax, correspondence, independent study, individual study.

Credits Granted for: experiential learning, extrainstitutional learning, examination (CLEP, ACT-PEP, DANTES, GRE).

Admission Requirements: *Undergraduate:* high school diploma or GED.

On-Campus Requirements: None.

Tuition and Fees: *Undergraduate:* $77/credit. *Application Fee:* $25. *Software:* variable. *Credit by:* semester.

Financial Aid: Federal Stafford Loan, Federal Perkins Loan, Federal PLUS Loan, Federal Pell Grant, Federal Work-Study, VA, New Jersey resident programs.

Accreditation: Middle States Association of Colleges and Schools.

Description: County College of Morris (1968) is located on 218 acres of rolling terrain. The college is dedicated to meeting the needs of area residents and employers for educational advancement and career training and to fostering social and cultural enlightenment within the community it serves. The college believes that enlightened self-interest and the public good are synonymous, and that all citizens are worthy of the opportunity to develop their potential to the fullest. CCM Online brings the college to you through classes in your own home on days and times convenient for you. You'll find no physical boundaries or limitations with CCM Online. We're as close as your home or office computer!

Covenant Theological Seminary

12330 Conway Road	Phone: (800) 264-8064
Saint Louis, MO 63141	(314) 434-4044
	Fax: (314) 434-4819

Division(s): Access
Web Site(s): http://www.covenantseminary.edu
E-mail: admissions@covenantseminary.edu

Graduate Degree Programs:
Master of Arts in:
Theological Studies
Doctor of Ministry

Certificate Programs: All are graduate certificates. Please contact school.

Teaching Methods: *Computers:* Internet, e-mail, CD-ROM. *TV:* videotape. *Other:* correspondence, individual study, audioconferencing, audiotapes, fax.

Admission Requirements: *Graduate:* Bachelor of Arts or its equivalent. *Postgraduate:* Master of Divinity and 3 years practical experience.

On-Campus Requirements: For the MATS: 3 one-week residencies on main campus.

Tuition and Fees: *Graduate:* $195/credit (2001–2002). *Postgraduate:* $260/credit (2001–2002). *Application Fee:* $25. *Graduation Fee:* $50. *Other Costs:* tape rental fees vary for video or audio; costs for books. *Credit by:* semester.

Financial Aid: Federal Stafford Loan, VA.

Accreditation: North Central Association of Colleges and Schools, Association of Theological Schools.

Description: Covenant was established in 1956 by men who recognized that their denomination needed a strong theological school to firmly root its future leaders in the doctrines of grace for leadership. In 1989 the school recognized the growing numbers of men and women who were in nonordained ministry throughout the church and who were recognizing the need to be more firmly rooted in these doctrines. The seminary responded by establishing the Access program, making the MATS entirely available in 2001.

Crowder College

601 Laclede Avenue
Neosho, MO 64850

Phone: (417) 451-3223
Fax: (417) 451-9669

Division(s): Distance Education Information Technology
Web Site(s): http://www.crowdercollege.net
E-mail: admissions@crowdercollege.net

Undergraduate Degree Programs:
Associate in Arts Degree
Associate in Science Degree
Associate in Applied Science Degree
Nursing Program
Environmental Resource Center

Certificate Programs: Auto Body, Auto Mechanics Professional, Agriculture Equipment/Diesel Technology, Environmental Health Technology, Fire Science, Industrial Maintenance, Office Assistant, and Safety Management.

Teaching Methods: *Computers:* Internet, electronic classroom, e-mail, CD-ROM. *TV:* videotape, cable program, satellite broadcasting, PBS. *Other:* videoconferencing, audioconferencing, audiographics, audiotapes, fax, correspondence, independent study, individual study, learning contracts.

Credits Granted for: experiential learning, portfolio assessment, extrainstitutional learning (PONSI, corporate or professional association seminars/workshops), examination (CLEP, ACT-PEP, DANTES, GRE).

Admission Requirements: *Undergraduate:* must have either a diploma from an accredited high school, a certificate of high school equivalency through the General Education Development test, and copies of their ACT test scores or SAT scores. Special admissions are handled for the following individuals; International students, non-degree-seeking students, dual-credit students, and senior citizens. *Certificate:* same as undergraduate.

On-Campus Requirements: None.

Tuition and Fees: *Undergraduate:* $44/credit hour for district resident. $64/credit hour for Missouri resident. $84/credit hour for out-of-district resident; $84/credit hour for international students. *Nursing Program Tuition:* in-district resident $58/credit hour, out-of-district $68/credit hour. *Environmental Resource Center Tuition:* Water/Wastewater Semester $68/credit hour, Hazardous Materials Semester $68/credit hour. *Application Fee:* $25. *Technology/Facilites Use Fee:* $6/credit hour. *Graduation Fee:* $35. *Other Costs:* Room and Board $1,850 per semester *Nursing Clinical Fees:* $125/semester. (Additional nursing lab fees may vary.) *Credit by:* semester.

Financial Aid: Federal Stafford Loan, Federal Pell Grant, Federal Perkins Loan, Federal PLUS Loan, Federal Work-Study, VA, Missouri resident programs.

Accreditation: Missouri Department of Elementary and Secondary Education and the Coordinating Board of Higher Education. Crowder College is also fully accredited by the North Central Association of Colleges and Secondary Schools. Program accreditations are in the Missouri State Board of Nursing, Teacher Education Certification, through the Department of Elementary and Secondary Education, and the National Institute for Automotive Excellence (ASE).

Description: In the 37 years of its history, Crowder College (1963) has gone from 400 to 1,800 students. In addition, to extensive renovation of existing buildings, 8 new buildings have been added. New programs, notably alternative energy, teacher education, and industrial technology, have added dimensions to Crowder's opportunities. From the remnants of a military camp, Crowder has grown to show that it's a college that is "big in attitude, big in aptitude." Crowder College's Distance Education program has been in effect for 5 years now. Each year has brought improvements and growth to the program with an approximate count of 500+ students enrolled. Crowder College Online is an exciting new way to learn. Crowder College delivers online, flex-time courses to students while expanding opportunities for those who find it difficult to attend on-campus classes. Current online offerings include: Business, Diesel Mechanics, Electronics, General Studies, and Environmental Health.

Crown College

6425 State Road 30
St. Bonifacius, Minnesota 55375

Phone: (952) 446-4153
Fax: (952) 446-4149

Division(s): Distance Education Department
Web Site(s): http://www.crownonline.org
E-mail: cconline@crown.edu

Undergraduate Degree Programs:
Associate of Science in Christian Ministries
Bachelor of Science in Christian Ministries

Graduate Degree Programs:
Master of Arts in Ministry Leadership
Master of Arts in Intercultural Studies

Class Titles: Contact school or check web site for details.

Teaching Methods: *Computers:* Internet, real time chat, electronic classroom, e-mail, CD ROM, newsgroup, LISTSERV.

Credits Granted for: experiential learning, portfolio assessment, extrainstitutional learning (PONSI, corporate or professional association seminars/workshops), examination (CLEP, ACT PEP, DANTES, GRE).

Admission Requirements: *Undergraduate:* adult (25 plus age)/agree with lifestyle covenant/pastoral reference/ (AS) diploma or equivalent/(BS), associate degree or equivalent prior to enrollment *Graduate:* agree with lifestyle covenant/pastoral reference/bachelor's degree prior to enrollment.

On-Campus Requirements: None.

Tuition and Fees: *Undergraduate:* $289/credit. *Graduate:* $289/credit. *Application Fees:* $20. *Graduation Fee:* $75. *Credit by:* semester.

Financial Aid: Federal Stafford Loan, Federal Perkins Loan, Federal PLUS Loan, Federal Pell Grant, Federal Work Study, VA, state programs for residents of Minnesota.

Accreditation: North Central Association of Colleges and Schools (NCA) and Accrediting Association of Bible Colleges (AABC).

Description: Crown College (1916) is the midwestern regional college of The Christian and Missionary Alliance, an extensive missionary denomination with national offices in Colorado Springs, Colorado. Crown College is situated on a beautiful 193-acre campus about 10 miles west of the Minneapolis suburbs between the communities of St. Bonifacius and Waconia. The college determined about $3^1/_2$ years ago to enter the Distance Learning field. It began to organize its intended program with Real Education, which is now eCollege. In the fall of 2000, the first online courses were offered with 4 students enrolled. Since that time, the program has grown and beginning this fall a total of 4 degrees will be offered online. Crown College Online is primarily designed to provide training for those interested in church ministry, missions, or Christian public service organizations.

Cuesta College

Highway 1	Phone: (805) 546-3122
San Luis Obispo, CA 93403	Fax: (805) 546-3966

Division(s): Instructional Services
Web Site(s): http://www.cuesta.cc.ca.us
E-mail: cuestainfo@bass.cc.ca.us

Class Titles: Chemistry, Health Education, Business, Computer Information Systems, Economics, Electronics Technology, English, Fashion/Design/and Merchandising, Interior Design, Library Information, Learning Skills, Math, Emergency Care, Nutrition.

Teaching Methods: *Computers:* Internet, e-mail, CD-ROM. *Other:* None.

On-Campus Requirements: varies by course.

Tuition and Fees: *Undergraduate:* $11/credit in summer, $11/credit in fall (California residents), $146/credit in summer, $146/credit in fall (nonresident tuition). *Other Costs:* varies for material fees. *Credit by:* semester.

Financial Aid: Board of Governor's Fee Waiver (BOGFW), Federal Pell Grant, Federal Stafford Loan program, Federal SEOG grant, Federal Work Study, Cal Grant B and C, campus-based scholarships, recommend use of the Free Application for Federal Student Aid.

Accreditation: Western Association of Schools and Colleges.

Description: The original junior college was initiated as a postgraduate division of San Luis Obispo High School in 1916 and was terminated when the U.S. entered World War I. The district again formed a junior college in 1936, which remained in operation until 1959. The San Luis Obispo County Junior College District was established by the electorate of the county in 1963. In the fall of 1998, the college opened its North County campus, serving approximately 2,000 students in day and evening classes. Cuesta College offered its first distance education classes in 1998.

Cumberland County College

College Drive, PO Box 1500	Phone: (856) 691-8600
Vineland, NJ 08362-0517	Fax: (856) 691-9489

Division(s): Information Technology
Web Site(s): http://cccnj.net
E-mail: dfotid@cccnj.net

Undergraduate Degree Programs:
Associate in:
    Arts
    Fine Arts
    Applied Science
    Science

Certificate Programs: 18 academic, 22 career, and 6 short-term. Contact school for details.

Class Titles: English Composition, Spanish, Statistics, Economics, Psychology, Sociology, Human Growth/ Development, Child Psychology. Gerontology, U.S. History, Western Civilization, Mass Media, Business, Marketing, Management.

Teaching Methods: *Computers:* Internet, real-time chat, electronic classroom, e-mail, CD-ROM, LISTSERV. *TV:* videotape, cable program, *Other:* radio, videoconferencing, audioconferencing, audiotapes, fax.

Credits Granted for: examination (CLEP, ACT-PEP, DANTES, GRE).

Admission Requirements: *Undergraduate:* open admission.

On-Campus Requirements: Please contact school.

Tuition and Fees: *Undergraduate:* $70/credit. *Application Fee:* $25. *Graduation Fee:* $40. *Other Costs:* $5/credit technology fee. *Credit by:* semester.

Financial Aid: Federal Stafford Loan, Federal PLUS Loan, Federal Pell Grant, Federal Work-Study, VA, New Jersey resident programs.

Accreditation: Middle States Association of Colleges and Schools.

Description: Cumberland County College was the first community college in New Jersey to open its own campus in October 1966. Today, the college is dedicated to preparing students and community members for success in the ever-changing global environment. Cumberland's motto—*Pride, Service, Excellence*—drives its attitude toward delivering outstanding academic and career education programs, and it summarizes CCC's role as a community asset. The college's reputation for quality flows from innovative professors who teach in well-equipped classrooms and laboratories. And the campus is a community center that stimulates the county's social cultural and recreational environment. The college's 100-acre campus, featuring nine buildings, provides an excellent educational and social atmosphere. New facilities include a modern academic support laboratory, the state's first aquaculture training center, and centralized science laboratories adjacent to the Phillip Alampi Agriculture Building. Dedicated in 1995, the 38,000-square-foot Frank Guaracini Jr. Fine and Performing Arts Center is the cultural hub of the region. Other buildings include the administration building, the academic building, the computer technology center, the library-distance learning center, the Frank Wheaton Industrial Technology Building, and the Dr. Charles Cunningham Student Center, with a recently renovated gymnasium.

Cumberland University

One Cumberland Square	**Phone: (800) 339-0529**
Lebanon, TN 37087-3554	**Fax: (310) 578-4716**

Division(s): Special Programs
Web Site(s): http://www.masters4teachers.net
E-mail: eleanor.jones@educate.com

Graduate Degree Programs:
Master of Arts in Education Degree via Distance Learning (MAE)

Class Titles: Advanced Educational Psychology, Advanced Studies in Classroom Management, Innovative Instructional Technologies, Education: The Profession and the Professional, Curriculum Design and Assessment, Strategies for the 21st Century Classroom, Educational Research Methods, Contemporary Issues in Education, Strategies for Reading Comprehension OR Literacy and Learning Strategies for Middle and Secondary Students, School Public Relations and Communication, Diverse Populations in Teaching and Learning, School Law and Its Effect Upon Teachers

Teaching Methods: *Computers:* Internet, e-mail. *TV:* videotape. *Other:* faculty facilitator, collegial study team, audiotapes, fax, conference calls.

Credits Granted for: final exam for each course, comprehensive exam at the end of the 2-year program.

Admission Requirements: *Graduate:* completed application for admission, nonrefundable, one-time application fee, official transcripts from each postsecondary institution attended for bachelor's degree and graduate course work, 3 completed recommendation forms, scores from one of the following: Miller Analogies Test, National Teacher Exam, Praxis II (PLT), or Graduate Record Examination (GRE), copy of teaching license.

On-Campus Requirements: Students must come to the campus once each term for the final course exams. They must also come to campus to take the comprehensive exam at the conclusion of the 2-year program.

Tuition and Fees: *Graduate:* $199/credit. *Application Fees:* $50 one-time, nonrefundable. *Other Costs:* $70/course for materials fee. *Credit by:* semester.

Financial Aid: Federal Stafford Loan.

Accreditation: Commission on Colleges of the Southern Association of Colleges and Schools (SACS).

Description: Founded in Lebanon, Tennessee in 1842, Cumberland University is respected throughout the state for providing innovative educational programs that adhere to the highest academic standards. The history of Cumberland University reflects the school's desire to meet the changing educational needs of its students. Cumberland has designed its Master of Arts in Education program to promote a quality graduate education experience with the convenience and flexibility of Distance Learning.

Cuyahoga Community College

2900 Community College Avenue	**Phone: (216) 987-4257**
Cleveland, OH 44114	**Fax: (216) 987-3675**

Division(s): Distance Learning Center
Web Site(s): http://dlc.tri-c.cc.oh.us
E-mail: distance@tri-c.cc.oh.us

Class Titles: Business Administration, English, Medical Terminology, Philosophy, Psychology, Information Literacy,

Marketing, Sociology, Information Technology, Anthropology, Biology, Court Reporting, Economics, Environmental Health, Geography, French, Spanish, German, History, Math, Political Science, Plant Science.

Teaching Methods: *Computers:* Internet, real-time chat, e-mail, CD-ROM, newsgroup, LISTSERV. *TV:* videotape, cable program, PBS. *Other:* videoconferencing, independent study, individual study.

Credits Granted for: experiential learning, portfolio assessment, examination (CLEP, ACT-PEP, DANTES, GRE).

Admission Requirements: *Undergraduate:* high school graduates or GED equivalent or age 18. In some instances, certain courses may be restricted to program majors. Admission to a specific program may be competitive or require specific minimum qualifications. Some students may be requested to enroll in special courses to eliminate deficiencies in academic preparation.

On-Campus Requirements: Vary.

Tuition and Fees: *Undergraduate:* $58.40/credit Cuyahoga County resident, $77.55/credit Ohio resident, $159.90/credit nonresident. *Other Costs:* $25 additional fee for some distance learning courses. *Credit by:* semester.

Financial Aid: Federal Stafford Loan, Federal Perkins Loan, Federal PLUS Loan, Federal Pell Grant, Federal Work-Study, VA.

Accreditation: North Central Association of Colleges and Schools.

Description: Cuyahoga Community College (Tri-C)(1963) is Ohio's first and largest public community college. Since its founding, the college has served more than 500,000 county residents. Today, Tri-C serves nearly 58,000 credit and non-credit students at its Eastern, Metropolitan and Western campuses, off-campus sites located throughout the county, and through multiple distance learning options. The college offers 70 career/technical options, and its arts and science courses transfer to state universities and private colleges throughout the U.S.

Daemen College

4380 Main Street	Phone: (716) 836-3900
Amherst, New York, 14226	(716) 839-8571
	Fax: (716) 839-8261

Web Site(s): http://www.daemen.edu
E-mail: tklejna@daemen.edu

Undergraduate Degree Programs:
(Post Basic) Bachelor of Nursing

Graduate Degree Programs:
Master of Science In Executive Leadership and Change (videoconferenced select sites)
Graduate Physical Therapy (videoconferenced select sites and web-based classes in development may require a weekend on-campus seminar session)

Certificate Programs: Leadership and Change.

Class Titles: Concepts of Professional Nursing, Professional Issues (Nursing), Holistic Perspectives (Nursing), Health Assessment (Nursing), Clinical Applications of Structural and Mechanical Properties of Biological Tissues (Physical Therapy), Comprehensive Wound Management (Physical Therapy), Clinical Instructor Basics.

Teaching Methods: *Computers:* Internet, real-time chat, electronic classroom, e-mail *TV:* videotape, videoconferencing, video streaming, audio conferencing. *Other:* audiotapes, fax, correspondence, independent study.

Credits Granted for: experiential learning through Credit for Learning from Life Experience (CLIE) program, portfolio assessment, extrainstitutional learning at the discretion of individual departments, credit by examination for enrolled students who score successfully on select college proficiency examinations offered by the New York State Education Department or the College Board, examination (CLEP).

Admission Requirements: *Undergraduate:* must possess or be a candidate for a high school diploma or have gained high school equivalency. *Graduate:* graduate nurse status or current licensure registration. *Postgraduate:* program in physical therapy in development. *Certificate:* contact school.

On-Campus Requirements: varies per program; additional information of college web site through admissions.

Tuition and Fees: *Undergraduate:* $440/credit hour. *Graduate:* $505/credit hour. *Application Fee:* $25. *Other Costs:* Continuing Education and Certificate Courses: varies by event. *Credit by:* semester.

Financial Aid: Federal Perkins Loan, Federal Supplemental Educational Opportunity Grant, Federal Pell Grant, Federal Work-Study, VA, state programs for residents of New York State, Daemen Programs.

Accreditation: Board of Regents of the State of New York, Commission on Higher Education of the Middle States Association of Colleges and Schools. Business by The International Assembly for Collegiate Business Education, Nursing Program by the National League for Nursing, Physical Therapy by The American Physical Therapy Association, Physician Assistant Program by the Commission on Accreditation of Allied Health Education Programs. Social Work by the Council on Social Work Education.

Description: Daemen (1947) is a small private liberal arts college in the Buffalo area of New York state. Daemen offers undergraduate and graduate degree programs as well as continuing education programs. Beyond the Liberal Arts programs Daemen has strong programs in business, education, fine arts, nursing, physical therapy, and physician assistants. Daemen has been delivering Distance Education programs since 1998. Initial Distance Education offerings have been focused in the health disciplines.

Dakota State University

201A Karl Mundt Library	Phone: (605) 256-5049
Madison, SD 57042-1799	(800) 641-4309
	Fax: (605) 256-5208

Division(s): Office of Distance Education
Web Site(s): http://www.departments.dsu.edu/disted/
E-mail: dsuinfo@pluto.dsu.edu

Undergraduate Degree Programs:
Information Systems and Health Information Administration

Graduate Degree Programs:
Master of Science in Information Systems (MSIS)
Master of Science in Computer Education and Technology (MSCET)

Class Titles: Basic Programming, Principles of Programming, COBOL, Composition, Career Planning, Sociology, Fund Raising, Health Care Courses, Literature, Native American Studies, Psychology, Information Systems.

Teaching Methods: *Computers:* Internet, e-mail. *Other:* None.

Credits Granted for: experiential learning, examinations, etc.

Admission Requirements: *Undergraduate:* must meet prerequisites; international students must have a TOEFL of 550. *Graduate:* same.

On-Campus Requirements: None.

Tuition and Fees: *Undergraduate:* $142.25/credit. *Graduate:* $181.60/credit. *Credit by:* semester.

Accreditation: North Central Association of Colleges and Schools, National Council on Accreditation of Teacher Education.

Description: The primary purpose of Dakota State University (1881) is to provide instruction in computer management, computer information systems, electronic data processing, and other related undergraduate and graduate programs. Secondarily, the school offers authorized 2-year, one-year, and short courses for application and systems training, and elementary and secondary teachers are trained to use computers and information processing. Distance courses have been offered online since 1991, and DSU is planning to expand its distance programs soon by offering degrees online.

Dalhousie University

Registrar's Office	
Arts and Administration Building,	Phone: (902) 494-2450
University Avenue	Fax: (902) 494-1630
Halifax, NS, Canada B3H 4H6	

Division(s): various departments
Web Site(s): http://www.dal.ca/de
E-mail: de@dal.caregistrar@dal.ca

Undergraduate Degree Programs:
Bachelor of Science in Nursing
Bachelor of Social Work

Graduate Degree Programs:
Master of Business Administration (Financial Services)
Master of Information Technology Education
Master of Science (Occupational Therapy)
Master in Nursing
Master of Social Work

Certificate Programs: Business Management, Disability Management (Diploma), Emergency Health Services Management (Diploma), Employee Benefit Specialist, Financial Management, Fire Service Administration, Fire Service Leadership, Human Resource Management, Local Government Administration, Police Leadership, Small Business Management, Software Management and Development.

Class Titles: Anatomy and Neurobiology, Continuing Medical Education, Physiology and Biophysics.

Teaching Methods: *Computers:* Internet, custom www, web CT, E-education, real-time chat, electronic classroom, e-mail, CD-ROM, newsgroup, LISTSERV. *TV:* videotape, cable program, television broadcast. *Other:* radio broadcast, videoconferencing, computer conferencing, audioconferencing, audiographics, audiotapes, fax, correspondence, face to face, independent study, individual study, learning contracts, print materials, tutorials.

Credits Granted for: experiential learning, portfolio assessment, extrainstitutional learning, examination (CLEP, ACT-PEP, DANTES, GRE).

Admission Requirements: *Undergraduate:* contact registrar's office for specific requirements.

On-Campus Requirements: variable; contact registrar.

Tuition and Fees: *Undergraduate:* variable, contact registrar or Henson College directly. *Credit by:* semester.

Financial Aid: Dalhousie has a leading student assistance program, for enrolled students.

Accreditation: Association of Universities and Colleges of Canada, Atlantic Association of Universities, and the Association of Commonwealth Universities.

Description: Dalhousie University (1818) is a comprehensive teaching and research university located in Halifax, the provincial capital of Nova Scotia and a major regional center for Atlantic Canada. Dalhousie offers 3,600 courses in over 182 undergraduate, graduate, and professional degree programs, to 13,700 full- and part-time students. Professional programs are available in architecture, dentistry, engineering, law, and medicine. The university is proud of its excellent students and alumni who consistently attract awards from other prestigious external agencies as demonstrated by the 72 Rhodes Scholars since 1904. Dalhousie's 180 years of history provide a solid foundation for the development of exciting new learning opportunities for the 21st century.

Dallas Baptist University

| 3000 Mountain Creek Parkway | Phone: (214) 333-6893 |
| Dallas, TX 75211 | Fax: (214) 333-5373 |

Division(s): Online Education
Web Site(s): http://www.dbuonline.org
E-mail: online@dbu.edu

Undergraduate Degree Programs:
Bachelor of Business Studies in Management
Bachelor of Business Studies in Business Administration

Graduate Degree Programs:
Master of Business Administration in:
Management e-commerce

Certificate Programs: e-Commerce.

Class Titles: Over 50 classes offered online for the specific degree programs.

Teaching Methods: *Computers:* Internet, real-time chat, e-mail, CD-ROM. *Other:* fax, independent study.

Credits Granted for: experiential learning, portfolio assessment, extrainstitutional learning (PONSI, corporate or professional association seminars/workshops), examination (CLEP, ACT-PEP, DANTES, GRE).

Admission Requirements: *Undergraduate:* go to http://www.dbu.edu/admissions/undergrad.html *Graduate:* go to http://www.dbu.edu/Graduate/admissions.html Adult Degree: http://www.dbu.edu/adulted/ *Certificate:* http://www.dbu.edu/Graduate/admissions.html

On-Campus Requirements: None.

Tuition and Fees: *Undergraduate:* $365/credit. *Graduate:* $375/credit. *Application Fee:* $25 *Credit by:* semester.

Financial Aid: Federal Stafford Loan, Federal Perkins Loan, Federal PLUS Loan, Federal Pell Grant, Federal Work-Study, VA, state programs for residents of Texas.

Accreditation: Commission on Colleges of the Southern Association of Colleges and Schools for associate, bachelor's, and master's degrees. The College of Business is accredited by the Association of Collegiate Business Schools and Programs (ACBSP).

Description: Dallas Baptist University (1998) has offered fully accredited degree programs via the Internet, creating a rich online environment where students and faculty members can collaborate and interact. Our online campus features a dynamic combination of the newest Internet technologies from streaming media to threaded discussions. Online courses offer students a convenient way to learn subject material, do research, take tests, and communicate with professors and other students in a rich learning environment.

Dallas TeleCollege of the Dallas Community Colleges

9596 Walnut Street	Phone: (972) 669-6400
Dallas, TX 75243	(888) 468-4268
	Fax: (972) 669-6409

Division(s): R. Jan LeCroy Center for Education Communications
Web Site(s): http://telecollege.dcccd.edu
E-mail: as+8552@dcccd.edu

Undergraduate Degree Programs:
Associate of Arts
Associate of Science

Class Titles: All courses can be taken independent of a degree program.

Teaching Methods: *Computers:* Internet, electronic classroom, real-time chat, e-mail, CD-ROM. *TV:* videotape, cable program, satellite broadcasting PBS. *Other:* audioconferencing, fax, independent study, individual study, correspondence.

Credits Granted for: portfolio assessment, examination (CLEP, ACT-PEP, DANTES, GRE).

Admission Requirements: *Undergraduate:* 18 years of age, assessment required for verbal and math.

On-Campus Requirements: 25% of the degree must be from DCCCD, not inclassroom requirements. Degree can be earned from a distance.

Tuition and Fees: *Undergraduate:* depends on residency. *Credit by:* semester.

Financial Aid: Federal Stafford Loan, Federal Perkins Loan, Federal PLUS Loan, Federal Pell Grant, VA, Texas resident programs.

Accreditation: Southern Association of Colleges and Schools.

Description: The DCCCD (1965) has been a pioneer in distance education for three decades. Our telecourse products are used by 1,500 colleges and universities around the world and have generated over 1 million enrollments. TeleCollege, our virtual campus, offers over 150 courses each semester in a variety of distance learning formats.

Dallas Theological Seminary

3909 Swiss Avenue	Phone: (800) 992-0998
Dallas, TX 75204	Fax: (214) 841-3565

Division(s): External Studies
Web Site(s): http://www.dts.edu
E-mail: External_Studies@dts.edu

Graduate Degree Programs:
Master of Arts in Biblical Studies

Certificate Programs: Graduate Studies

Teaching Methods: *Computers:* Internet, e-mail, LISTSERV. *TV:* videotape. *Other:* audiotapes, fax, correspondence, independent study, individual study.

Credits Granted for: graduate transfer, experiential learning, portfolio assessment, extrainstitutional learning, examination (on-site Advanced Standing).

Admission Requirements: *Graduate:* regionally accredited bachelor's degree. *Certificate:* regionally accredited bachelor's degree.

On-Campus Requirements: students must complete at least 50% of their program either at the main campus (Dallas) or one of the extension sites (San Antonio, TX; Houston, TX; Tampa, FL; or Chattanooga, TN/Atlanta, GA regional site).

Tuition and Fees: *Graduate:* $235-310/credit. *Application Fee:* $30. *Graduation Fee:* $100. *Credit by:* semester.

Financial Aid: Grants (San Antonio, Houston, Tampa), VA (Texas only).

Accreditation: Southern Association of Colleges and Schools, Association of Theological Schools.

Description: Dallas Theological Seminary (1924) entered the distance learning field in 1987 when the first extension site was launched. Since then, extension sites in Houston, Tampa, Austin, San Antonio, and Chattanooga/Atlanta have grown into fully accredited sites offering the Master of Arts degree in Biblical Studies with more than 350 students enrolled. Helping to fulfill the mission of the school, the extension program seeks to deliver graduate theological education to lay-oriented ministers and professional ministers desiring a Bible-centered curriculum and to encourage students toward professional programs offered on the main campus in Dallas (1,450 students).

Daniel Webster College

20 University Drive	Phone: (603) 577-6500
Nashua, NH 03060	Fax: (603) 577-6503

Division(s): Continuing Studies
Web Site(s): http://www.dwc.edu/abetterplace
E-mail: ocs@dwc.edu

Undergraduate Degree Programs:
Organizational Behavior Degree Completion Program (50% online)

Certificate Programs: Web Master Technology.

Class Titles: Introduction to Database, Visual Basic, Introduction to UNIX, Marketing, Introduction to Networks, WWW Technology, Film and Culture, Programming in C and Java.

Teaching Methods: *Computers:* Internet, real-time chat, electronic classroom, e-mail.

Credits Granted for: experiential learning, portfolio assessment, extrainstitutional learning (PONSI, corporate or professional association seminars/workshops), examination (CLEP, ACT-PEP, DANTES, GRE).

Admission Requirements: *Undergraduate:* through continuing studies, proof of high school graduation.

On-Campus Requirements: Yes, for the degree completion program; 50% on campus.

Tuition and Fees: *Undergraduate:* $224/credit for individual courses. Degree Completion Program: Organizational Management: $11,920 for the 18-month program. *Graduation Fee:* $60. *Credit by:* semester.

Financial Aid: Federal Stafford Loan, Federal Perkins Loan, Federal PLUS Loan, Federal Pell Grant.

Accreditation: New England Association of Schools and Colleges.

Description: Daniel Webster College (1972) began its history as an aviation institution. A few years after the college's inception, it opened its evening program and began servicing adult professionals in the areas of management, computer science, and it's newest major software development. Over the past several years, it has also begun to offer a series of cutting-edge certificate programs. Most recently, the FAA supported the college's first efforts to begin a Distance Education program by awarding it a grant that resulted in the creation of its Eaton-Richmond Center. This academic multimedia center offers students and faculty access to cutting-edge technology and has encouraged the college to move quickly into the creation of a series of innovative programs.

Danville Area Community College

| 2000 East Main Street | Phone: (217) 443-8577 |
| Danville, IL 61832 | Fax: (217) 443-3178 |

Division(s): Instructional Media
E-mail: jspors@dacc.cc.il.us

Undergraduate Degree Programs:
Associate and Transfer Associate

Class Titles: About 75 different courses are offered through alternative delivery at Danville Area Community College. In addition, collaborative arrangements with many other institutions and organizations allow a much wider selection of approved course offerings.

Teaching Methods: *Computers:* Internet, CD-ROM, Web CT Online, real-time chat, electronic classroom, e-mail, newsgroup, LISTSERV. *TV:* videotape, cable program, satellite broadcasting, PBS. *Other:* videoconferencing, interactive video.

Credits Granted for: experiential learning, porfolio assessment, corporate or professional association seminars/workshops, examination ACT-PEP.

Admission Requirements: *Undergraduate:* asset or ACT/SAT test scores.

On-Campus Requirements: None.

Tuition and Fees: *Undergraduate:* $48/credit in-district, $89/credit (out of district). *Credit by:* semester.

Financial Aid: Federal Stafford Loan, Federal Perkins Loan, Federal PLUS Loan, Federal Pell Grant, Federal Work-Study, VA, Illlinois and Indiana resident programs.

Accreditation: North Central Association of Colleges and Schools, The Higher Learning Commission.

Description: Danville Area Community College (1946) has been actively involved with providing alternatively delivered

instruction since 1994. Providing Access with Excellence continues to be our goal.

Danville Community College

| 1008 South Main Street | Phone: (434) 797-8454 |
| Danville, VA 24541 | Fax: (434) 797-8415 |

Division(s): Learning Resources
Web Site(s): http://www.dcc.vccs.edu
E-mail: wdey@dcc.vccs.edu

Certificate Programs:
Webmaster

Class Titles: FrontPage 2000, Automotive Air Conditioning Certification, Introduction to Business, Principles of Supervision, Introduction to Exceptional Children, Web Page Design I, Survey of Repro. Processes, Mathematics for Graphic Communications, Safety and Health Issues in Printing and Graphic Communications, Personal Wellness, Technical Writing, Job Search Strategies, Drafting and Design, Computer Animation, Writing for Web Pages, E-Commerce, Graphic Design for Web Pages, Word 2000.

Teaching Methods: *Computers:* Internet, CD-ROM, LIST-SERV, electronic classroom, e-mail. *TV:* videotape, PBS. *Other:* videoconferencing, fax, individual study learning contracts.

Admission Requirements: *Undergraduate:* high school diploma or equivalent.

On-Campus Requirements: None.

Tuition and Fees: *Undergraduate:* $40.12/credit in-state, $172/credit out-of-state. *Other Costs:* None. *Credit by:* semester.

Financial Aid: Federal Perkins Loan, Federal Stafford Loan, Federal PLUS Loan, Federal Pell Grant, Federal Work-Study, VA, Virginia resident programs.

Accreditation: Southern Association of Colleges and Schools.

Description: Danville Community College (1967) is a 2-year institution of higher education established under a statewide system of community colleges. The college operates on the semester system and offers 2 summer sessions. The faculty of 65 full-time and 100 part-time instructors provides a faculty-student ratio of 1:27. DCC began offering distance learning classes in 1995. Distance learning students use videos, the Internet, textbooks, study guides, and interactive television to complete their course work and earn college credits.

Darton College

2400 Gillionville Road	Phone: (229) 430-6938
Albany, GA 31707	Fax: (229) 430-6910

Division(s): Instructional Technology and Distance Learning
Continuing Education
Web Site(s): http://itdl3.dartnet.peachnet.edu/~distlrn/
http://dartnet.peachnet.edu
E-mail: Admissions@mail.dartnet.peachnet.edu

Class Titles: Medical Terminology, Accounting I, Environmental Biology, Keyboarding/Formatting, Document Processing, WordPerfect/Word with Medical, WordPerfect/Word, Desktop Publishing, Financial Planning/Investment Management, Business, Computer Concepts/Software Applications, Public Speaking, Special Problems in Computer Systems, Critical Thinking, Macroeconomics, Microeconomics, English Composition, American Literature, British Literature, Western Civilization, U.S. History, Health Record Content and Structure, College Algebra, Statistics, Pharmacology and Mathematics for Medical Transcription, Physical Science, American Government, Psychology, Spanish, Japanese.

Teaching Methods: *Computers:* Internet, real-time chat, electronic classroom, e-mail, CD-ROM, newsgroup. *TV:* live television, videotape, cable program, satellite broadcasting. *Other:* GSAMS (Georgia Statewide Academic and Medical System), a 2-way interactive video conferencing network.

Credits Granted for: examination (CLEP, AP (Advanced Placement), DANTES).

Admission Requirements: *Undergraduate:* entering freshmen must provide SAT I or ACT scores, a transcript of secondary school credits showing graduation or GED, immunization certificate. For complete details and for nontraditional students requirements check catalog (online at http://dartnet.peachnet.edu).

On-Campus Requirements: If student lives within 50 miles of the campus, *may* be asked to come on campus for orientation, tests, or labs. Testing, proctoring, and other arrangements are made for students outside the immediate service area.

Tuition and Fees: *Undergraduate:* $53/semester hour. *Application Fee:* $20. *Technology Fee:* $25. *Other Costs:* see catalog for nonresidents and other special fees. *Credit by:* semester.

Financial Aid: Federal Stafford Loan, Federal Perkins Loan, Federal PLUS Loan, Federal Pell Grant, Federal Work-Study, VA, Georgia HOPE scholarship.

Accreditation: Southern Association of Colleges and Schools.

Description: Darton College (1963), part of the University System of Georgia, is a community college that offers 2-year degrees in transfer and career programs. Distance Learning courses were first offered in 1993 as a delivery tool for outreach to high schools, for workforce development, and for providing educational access in rural areas. The courses are multimedia-enriched, interactive learning experiences. These are instructor-led classes, not independent study or correspondence courses. Darton College is a recognized leader in distance learning and its distance learning program has received national recognition from the National Council of Instructional Administrators for exemplary initiatives in the use of technology. It is also ranked 50th among the "Most Wired Two-Year Institutions" in a 2001 survey done by Yahoo! Internet Life and Peterson's.

Davenport University

415 East Fulton Street	Phone: (616) 742-2080
Grand Rapids, MI 49503	Fax: (616) 742-2076

Division(s): Davenport University Online
Other colleges: Davenport College, Detroit College of Business, Great Lakes College
Web Site(s): http://online.davenport.edu
E-mail: DU online

Undergraduate Degree Programs: Associate's, Bachelor's

Graduate Degree Program:
Master of Business Administration

Certificate Programs: Technical Specialties and Certification Preparations.

Class Titles: Management, Marketing, International Business, Computer Information Systems, Healthcare Administration, Business Law, Communications, Social Sciences.

Teaching Methods: *Computers:* Internet, real-time chat, electronic classroom, e-mail, net meeting. *Other:* None.

Credits Granted for: experiential learning, portfolio assessment, extrainstitutional learning, examination (CLEP, ACT-PEP, DANTES, GRE).

Admission Requirements: *Undergraduate:* Open Admissions—high school completion or equivalent. *Graduate:* undergraduate degree w/GPA, work experience, current résumé, case analysis, professional recommendations.

On-Campus Requirements: None.

Tuition and Fees: *Undergraduate:* $830/course. *Graduate:* $952/course. *Application Fee:* $25 undergraduate.

Graduation Fee: $50 application fee. *Other Costs:* $25 technology fee/term. *Credit by:* quarter.

Financial Aid: Federal Stafford Loan, Federal Perkins Loan, Federal PLUS Loan, Federal Pell Grant, Federal Work-Study, VA, Michigan resident programs.

Accreditation: North Central Association of Colleges and Schools.

Description: Davenport Online is a chance to be connected to a university with a rich heritage in higher education. Our foundation stems from more than 134 years of quality, career-focused instruction. Davenport University (1866) is the system of choice for more than 15,000 degree-seeking students. Your online degree will carry the same prestige as a degree completed at any of our 27 campuses spread throughout Michigan and northern Indiana.

What began as the founding of Grand Rapids Business College in 1866 has turned into a distinct university with a wealth of opportunities for today's business professional. While our focus has always been to train and educate students for careers in business, we have expanded our mission to include an array of academic programs in a variety of careers. Davenport Online provides another option for taking advantage of our many programs. Perhaps that's why we've become the perfect balance of business and education.

De Anza College

21250 Stevens Creek Boulevard   Phone: (408) 864-8969
Cupertino, CA 95014   Fax: (408) 864-8245

Division(s): Distance Learning Center
Web Site(s): http://dadistance.fhda.edu
E-mail: information@dadistance.fhda.edu

Undergraduate Degree Programs:
Associate of Arts in Liberal Arts

Certificate Programs: Business Administration.

Class Titles: Accounting, Algebra, American Government/ Politics, Anatomy/Physiology, Biology, Business, Business Law, Child Development, Computers/Data Processing/ Applications, Economics, English Literature, English Writing, Health, History, Humanities, Intercultural Studies, Library Skills, Management, Marketing, Mass Communication, Medical Terminology/Common Diseases, Microsoft Windows NT Administration, Music, NCLEX Practice/Analysis, Newswriting, Nutrition, Parenting, Philosophy, Psychology, Religion, Sociology, Statistics, World Wide Web Page Development

Teaching Methods: *Computers:* Internet, chat rooms, bulletin boards, e-mail, CD-ROM, LISTSERV, Web pages. *TV:* videotape, cable programs, PBS. *Other:* None.

Admission Requirements: *Undergraduate:* age 18 or high school graduate, younger students allowed with permission of high school and guardian. *Certificate:* same as undergraduate.

On-Campus Requirements: Business certificate program requires one course on campus. Some courses require on-campus testing.

Tuition and Fees: *Undergraduate:* $7/credit California residents, $87/credit nonresidents, $94/credit foreign citizens. *Other Costs:* $23/quarter term. *Credit by:* quarter.

Financial Aid: Federal Stafford Loan, Federal Perkins Loan, Federal PLUS Loan, Federal Pell Grant, Federal Work-Study, VA, California resident programs, Federal Supplemental Educational Opportunity Grant Program, Extended Opportunity Program Grant, Bureau of Indian Affairs, Board of Governors Fee Waivers, Cal Grant A, Cal Grant B, Cal Grant C, De Anza College Book loans.

Accreditation: Western Association of Schools and Colleges.

Description: De Anza College (1967), located in the Silicon Valley area of northern California, is one of more than 100 public community colleges in the state and has gained a national reputation for its responsiveness to community needs, including students with physical and learning disabilities, minorities, re-entry students, and distance learning students. De Anza offers educational opportunities in a range of programs including the first 2 years of 4-year degree programs that parallel the requirements of the University of California, California State University, and private colleges and universities. The distance learning program at De Anza has been in operation since 1974 and offers courses via TV, video, Internet, and mixed media. All distance courses are equivalent to the on-campus courses and are taught by De Anza College instructors. The Distance Learning Center offers more than 85 lower-division courses per term in a variety of subject areas.

Delaware County Community College

901 South Media Line Road   Phone: (610) 359-5158
Media, PA 19063   Fax: (610) 325-2828

Division(s): Distance Learning
Web Site(s): http://www.dccc.edu/dl
E-mail: ewelling@dcccnet.dccc.edu

Undergraduate Degree Programs:
Associate

Class Titles: Biological Science, Business, Small Business Management, Management, Marketing, Business Law, Business Math, Economics (micro/macro), Composition, American History, Western Civilization, American Cinema, Contemporary Moral Problems, American National Government, Psychology, Abnormal Psychology, Child Psychology, Sociology, Sociology of Marriage/Family, Cultural Anthropology, Spanish.

Teaching Methods: *Computers:* Internet, real-time chat, electronic classroom, e-mail, CD-ROM, newsgroup, LISTSERV. *TV:* videotape, cable program, satellite broadcasting, PBS. *Other:* videoconferencing, audiotapes, fax, correspondence, independent study, individual study.

Credits Granted for: portfolio assessment, extrainstitutional learning, examination (CLEP).

Admission Requirements: *Undergraduate:* contact school. *Graduate:* contact school. *Doctoral:* contact school. *Certificate:* contact school.

On-Campus Requirements: orientation and testing only.

Tuition and Fees: *Undergraduate:* $63/credit sponsoring school district, $126/credit nonsponsoring school districts, $189/credit out-of-state. *Application Fee:* $20. *Other Costs:* $9/credit instructional support fee, $15/semester records fee. *Credit by:* semester.

Financial Aid: Federal Stafford Loan, Federal Perkins Loan, Federal PLUS Loan, Federal Pell Grant, Federal Work-Study, VA, Pennsylvania resident programs.

Accreditation: Middle States Association of Colleges and Schools.

Description: Delaware County Community College (1967) is dedicated to providing high-quality, low-cost educational opportunities that meet the needs of our students. Programs include college and university parallel programs equivalent to the first 2 years of a bachelor's degree, career programs to prepare graduates for employment, and short-term certificate programs in specific occupational fields. DCCC's competency-based curriculum ensures that our students are really prepared for employment or further education. Our faculty, from instructors to full professors, are committed to being there for their students. Counselors, tutors, librarians, and the entire DCCC staff are dedicated to providing the support and services our students need. DCCC has an extensive distance learning program with courses offered online and through TV and independent study. The true measure of DCCC's value can be gauged only by what happens to DCCC students when they leave. They meet their goals—98% seeking jobs are employed within 3 months after graduation and 89% of those who intend to transfer do.

Delaware Technical and Community College

PO Box 897
Dover, DE 19903

Phone: (302) 857-1810
Fax: (302) 857-1815

Division(s): Academic Affairs
Web Site(s): http://www.dtcc.edu
E-mail: mmills@college.dtcc.edu

Class Titles: Algebra, College Algebra/Trigonometry, College Math/Statistics, Calculus, Math for Behavioral Sciences, Biomedical Statistics, Math of Finance, Precalculus, Business Statistics, Business Law, Business, Customer Service, Consumer Behavior, Economics (macro/micro), Principles of Management, Principles of Marketing, Salesmanship, Medical Terminology, Electricity, Composition, Technical Writing, Critical Reading/Thinking, Oral Communications, Post-Industrial American Literature, American History, History of Technology, Health Careers, Political Science, General Psychology, Industrial Psychology, Child Development, Human Development, Psychology of Aging, Abnormal Psychology, Family Structures, Sociology, Adult Learner Success Strategies.

Teaching Methods: *Computers:* Internet, electronic classroom, e-mail, newsgroup. *TV:* videotape, satellite broadcasting, fiber-optic cable, PBS. *Other:* videoconferencing, audioconferencing, fax.

Credits Granted for: experiential learning, extrainstitutional learning, examination (CLEP, ACT-PEP, DANTES, GRE).

Admission Requirements: *Undergraduate:* open admissions. *Certificate:* open admissions.

On-Campus Requirements: orientation is conducted on campus, via videotape, and via interactive classroom. Tests are scheduled with the instructor, in a test center, or through a proctor at a distant location.

Tuition and Fees: *Undergraduate:* $66/credit hour instate and $165/credit hour out of state. *Application Fee:* $10. *Other Costs:* $4 per credit/hour technology support fee; plus appropriate lab fees, textbooks/materials, and student services fees. *Credit by:* semester.

Financial Aid: Federal Stafford Loan, Federal Perkins Loan, Federal PLUS Loan, Federal Pell Grant, Federal Work-Study, VA, Delaware resident programs.

Accreditation: Middle States Association of Colleges and Schools.

Description: Delaware Technical and Community College (1966) is a statewide institution of higher education providing basic, technical, and industrial training opportunities and continuing education to every resident of Delaware at 4 conveniently located campuses. Several degree programs are offered online, and the Associate in Applied Science degree is granted upon successful completion of specific curriculum requirements. The college is committed to using distance learning to enhance the instructional processes at all of its campus locations. Telecourses developed by various community college networks and by Delaware Tech faculty are recorded in our 2 state-of-the-art TV studios.

Delgado Community College

615 City Park Avenue	**Phone: (504) 483-4173**
New Orleans, LA 70119-4399	**Fax: (504) 483-4895**

Division(s): Community Campus
Web Site(s): http://www.dcc.edu
E-mail: tstamm@dcc.edu

Class Titles: Psychology, Philosophy, History, Business, Speech, Sign Language, Allied Health.

Teaching Methods: *TV:* videotape, cable program. *Other:* compressed video, Internet.

Credits Granted for: experiential learning, portfolio assessment, examination (CLEP, ACT).

Admission Requirements: *Undergraduate:* placement test, immunization form, transfer transcript.

On-Campus Requirements: varies with class.

Tuition and Fees: *Undergraduate:* $240/1–3 credits, $282/4 credits, $324/5 credits, $366/6 credits, $408/7 credits, $450/8 credits, $492/9 credits, $534/10 credits, $576/11 credits, $618/12 or more credits. *Application Fee:* $15. *Credit by:* semester.

Financial Aid: Federal Stafford Loan, Federal PLUS Loan, Federal Pell Grant, Federal Work-Study, VA, Louisiana resident programs (TOPS, merit scholarships).

Accreditation: Southern Association of Colleges and Schools.

Description: Delgado Community College (1929) is a comprehensive, multicampus, public community college with strong undergraduate programs as well as occupational and technical programs. The college is dedicated to providing educational opportunities for all people in a free and open society. Through an open-door admissions policy, the college welcomes students from diverse racial, religious, economic, educational, and cultural backgrounds. Central to the college curriculum is a commitment to the integration of arts and sciences, career education, and technology. In recognition of the diverse needs of the individual and the demands of a democratic society, the college provides a comprehensive educational program that helps students clarify values and develop skills in critical thinking, self-expression, communication, decision making, and problem solving.

Delta College

1961 Delta Road	**Phone: (989) 686-9398**
University Center, MI 48710	

Division(s): Distance Learning
Web Site(s): http://www.delta.edu
E-mail: jmadams@alpha.delta.edu

Undergraduate Degree Programs: Contact school.

Class Titles: Economics, Business Math, Business Law, Small Business MGT, Intro to Business, Principals of Marketing, Principals of Management, History, Humanities/Arts, Lifelong Wellness, Philosophy, Ethics, Political Science, Psychology, Sociology, Anthropology, Spanish, Oral Communication.

Teaching Methods: *Computers:* Internet, real-time chat, electronic classroom, e-mail, CD-ROM. *TV:* videotape, cable program, satellite broadcasting, PBS. *Other:* audiotapes.

Credits Granted for: CLEP, ACT-PEP, DANTES, GRE.

Admission Requirements: Contact school.

On-Campus Requirements: All testing is on campus.

Tuition and Fees: *Undergraduate:* $61.40/credit. *Other Costs:* $10–25 for course fee. *Credit by:* semester.

Financial Aid: Federal Stafford Loan, Federal Perkins Loan, Federal PLUS Loan, Federal Pell Grant, Federal Work-Study, VA, state programs for residents of Michigan.

Accreditation: North Central Association of Colleges and Schools.

Description: Delta (1961) College is a comprehensive community college offering programs and couses in 3 major areas: Academic Division (16,000 full- and part-time students, 70 associate degree programs, and 26 certificate degree programs), Corporate Services Division (35,000 workers trained in 1999), Community Service Division (5,000 enrollment annually).

Delta State University

Box C-1	**Phone: (601) 846-3125**
Cleveland, MS 38733	**Fax: (601) 846-4313**

Division(s): Continuing Education
Web Site(s): http://www.deltast.edu
E-mail: mataylor@dsu.deltast.edu

Class Titles: 25 courses in areas of art, music, English, speech communication, history, social sciences, business, education, all by correspondence.

On-Campus Requirements: None.

Tuition and Fees: *Undergraduate:* $110/credit for correspondence. *Graduate:* $144/credit for correspondence. *Credit by:* semester.

Accreditation: Southern Association of Colleges and Schools.

Description: Delta State University (1924) was created as Delta State Teachers College. Delta State is a public institution, receiving primary funding from the state; however, it also seeks and receives support from private and federal sources, as well as tuition revenue. The university provides a comprehensive undergraduate curriculum, offering 15 bachelor's degrees in 45 majors. It also seeks to meet the need for advanced training in certain fields by providing programs of study for 9 master's degrees, the Educational Specialist degree and the Doctor of Education degree.

Denver Seminary

3401 South University Boulevard	Phone: (303) 761-2482
Englewood, CO 80110	Fax: (303) 761-8060

Division(s): Distance Education
Web Site(s): http://www.gospelcom.net/densem/
E-mail: davidb@densem.edu

Graduate Degree Programs:
Master of Arts
Master of Divinity

Certificate Programs: Theology, Leadership, Christian Studies.

Teaching Methods: *Computers:* Internet, e-mail. *Other:* audiotapes, fax, correspondence, independent study, individual study.

Admission Requirements: *Graduate:* undergraduate degree.

On-Campus Requirements: one-third of degree must be taken on the Denver campus.

Tuition and Fees: *Graduate:* $340/credit; but $235/credit for distance students. *Application Fee:* $5 short application, $25 full application. *Other Costs:* $75–$125/course materials. *Credit by:* semester.

Financial Aid: Federal Stafford Loan, Federal Perkins Loan, Federal PLUS Loan, Federal Pell Grant for regular students, but not for specials.

Accreditation: North Central Association of Colleges and Schools, Association of Theological Schools, Council for Accreditation of Counseling and Related Education Programs (MA Counseling—Licensure only).

Description: Denver Seminary (1950) is a graduate theological seminary in the evangelical Christian tradition educating men and women for a variety of ministries in this country and abroad. Our mission is "To glorify God in partnership with his church to equip leaders to know the truth, practice godliness and mobilize ministry." Started by a group of Baptist churches, the seminary now serves students from 50 Christian denominations. In the mid-1990s, the seminary began offering audio courses in a distance education mode. Plans are currently underway to expand the distance offerings and modes to capitalize on new technologies. The Distance Learning Institute has been founded as a subsidiary of Denver Seminary to expand the seminary's presence in this arena.

DeSales University

2755 Station Avenue	Phone: (610) 282-1100
Center Valley, PA 18034-9568	Fax: (610) 282-0673

Division(s): Academic Affairs
Web Site(s): http://www.desales.edu
E-mail: rosemarie.giltrap@desales.edu

Undergraduate Degree Programs:
Accounting.

Graduate Degree Programs:
Master of Business Administration.

Class Titles: Contact school or check web site for details.

Teaching Methods: *Computers:* Internet, real-time chat, electronic classroom, e-mail, CD-ROM, newsgroup, LISTSERV. *TV:* videotape, PBS. *Other:* videoconferencing, independent study, individual study.

Credits Granted for: portfolio assessment and CLEP.

On-Campus Requirements: None.

Admission Requirements: *Undergraduate:* an open admissions policy is in effect at DeSales University for ACCESS students with the exception of education programs that have specific admissions criteria. *Graduate:* A baccalaureate degree from an accredited college or university under conditions substantially equivalent to the undergraduate program at DeSales University; an acceptable level of academic quality in undergraduate work. Normally, this is defined as having achieved an undergraduate GPA of at least 3.0; computer literacy and familiarity with basic, business-oriented software; an acceptable score on the Graduate Management Admission Test (GMAT).

Tuition and Fees: *Undergraduate:* $250/credit. *Graduate:* $450/credit. *Application Fee:* Graduate $35, undergraduate $30. *Graduation Fee:* $105. *Credit by:* semester.

Financial Aid: Federal Stafford Loan, Federal Perkins Loan, Federal PLUS Loan, Federal Pell Grant, Federal Work-Study, VA, state programs for residents of Pennsylvania.

Accreditation: Middle States Association of Colleges and Universities.

Description: DeSales University (1965) is a Catholic liberal arts institution established by the Oblates of St. Francis de Sales. The school is located on a suburban 400-acre campus in Center Valley, Pennsylvania, and offers 31 bachelor's degrees including 10 preprofessional programs, and 5 graduate programs. Current enrollment is 2,549 students including traditional, nontraditional, and graduate students. For the past 25 years, DeSales University's ACCESS program has helped individuals earn degrees or certificates through flexible 8-week courses, weekend, daytime, and nighttime courses, summer courses and most recently, online courses. Graduate programs include the Master of Business Administration, which is the only MBA in the area and the only one of a handful nationwide that can be earned fully online and features some of the most progressive programming anywhere including an online e-commerce concentration.

Diablo Valley College

321 Golf Club Road	Phone: (510) 685-1230
Pleasant Hill, CA 94523	Fax: (510) 687-2527

Division(s): All academic departments
Web Site(s): http://www.dvc.edu
E-mail: fmarce@dvc.edu

Undergraduate Degree Programs:
Associate of Arts in Liberal Arts

Certificate Programs: Administration of Justice, Alcohol and Drug Studies, Architecture Technology, Accounting, Office Professional, Real Estate, Real Estate—Salesperson's License (license only), Real Estate—Broker's License (license only), Retailing, Small Business Management, Computer and Information Science, Computer Hardware Support, Microcomputer Hardware Support, Construction and Building Inspection, Construction Supervision and Superintendency, Construction Management, Dental Assisting, Dental Hygiene, Dental Laboratory Technology, Early Childhood Assistant–Basic, Early Childhood Assistant–Children's Center Instruction, Early Childhood Assistant–Family Day Care Provider/Foster Care Provider, Electronic Service Technology, Advanced Electronic Technology, Civil Drafting, Mechanical Drafting, General Drafting, Materials Testing, Surveying, Environmental Hazardous Materials Technology, Facilities Maintenance Technology, Horticulture—Basic, Landscape Construction, Landscape Design, Landscape Maintenance, Hotel and Restaurant Management: Baking and Pastry, Culinary Arts, Restaurant Management, Hotel Administration; Library and Information Technology, Machine Technology, Management Studies, Multimedia, Music Industry Studies, Respiratory Therapy, TV Arts, Women's Programs and Services.

Teaching Methods: *Computers:* Internet, real-time chat, electronic classroom, e-mail, CD-ROM, newsgroup, LISTSERV. *TV:* videotape. *Other:* videoconferencing, audioconferencing, audiotapes.

Credits Granted for: experiential learning, examination (CLEP, ACT-PEP, DANTES).

Admission Requirements: *Undergraduate:* open admission, 2 hours of study required for every hour of instruction.

On-Campus Requirements: None.

Tuition and Fees: *Undergraduate:* $12/unit. *Credit by:* semester.

Financial Aid: Federal Stafford Loan, Federal Perkins Loan, Federal PLUS Loan, Federal Pell Grant, Federal Work-Study, VA, CalWorks.

Accreditation: Western Association of Schools and Colleges.

Description: Diablo Valley College (1949), located in Contra Costa County, is a California community college. The college offers an Associate of Arts Degree in Liberal Arts and Certificates of Achievement in various occupational programs. The publicly supported college offers low-cost access to quality higher education. Diablo Valley serves 25,000 students of all ages each year and remains the college of choice for students seeking transfer to the University of California and the California State University systems.

Dickinson State University

1679 6th Avenue West	Phone: (701) 483-2166
Dickinson, ND 58601	Fax: (701) 483-2028

Division(s): Office of Extended Campus
Web Site(s): http://www.dsu.nodak.edu
E-mail: Marty_Odermann_Gardner@dsu.nodak.edu

Undergraduate Degree Programs:
Bachelor of University Studies Degrees
Associate in Arts Degree
Associate in Applied Science Degree

Teaching Methods: *Computers:* Internet, real-time chat, electronic classroom, e-mail, newsgroup. *TV:* videotape. *Other:*

videoconferencing, audioconferencing, fax, correspondence, independent study, individual study, learning contracts.

Credits Granted for: experiential learning, portfolio assessment, extrainstitutional learning, examination (CLEP, DANTES).

Admission Requirements: *Undergraduate:* Contact school for complete admission requirements.

Tuition and Fees: *Undergraduate:* $110/credit. Resident tuition includes all fees. *Application Fee:* $25. *Credit by:* semester.

Financial Aid: Federal Stafford Loan, Federal Perkins Loan, Federal PLUS Loan, Federal Pell Grant, Federal Work-Study, VA, North Dakota resident programs.

Accreditation: North Central Association of Schools and Colleges.

Description: Dickinson State University (1918) is a regional 4-year institution within the North Dakota University System, whose primary role is to contribute to intellectual, social, economic, and cultural development, especially in western North Dakota. The university's mission is to provide high quality accessible programs; to promote excellence in teaching and learning; to support scholarly and creative activities; and to provide service relevant to the economy, health, and quality of life of the citizens of North Dakota.

Dixie State College of Utah

225 South 700 East	Phone: (435) 652-7500
St. George, UT 84770	Fax: (435) 652-4080

Division(s): Continuing Education
Web Site(s): http://www.dixie.edu
E-mail: brings@dixie.edu

Undergraduate Degree Programs:
Associate of Arts
Associate of Science
Bachelor of Science

Certificate Programs: Diesel Mechanic, Health Science, Computer Information.

Class Titles: English, Music, Math, Computer Science, Economics.

Teaching Methods: *Computers:* Internet, real-time chat, electronic classroom, e-mail, CD-ROM. *TV:* videotape. *Other:* independent study.

Credits Granted for: corporate or professional association seminars/workshops, examination (CLEP, ACT-PEP, DANTES, GRE).

Admission Requirements: *Undergraduate:* high school transcripts, ACT or SAT. *Graduate:* same as undergraduate.

On-Campus Requirements: None.

Tuition and Fees: *Undergraduate:* $54/credit. *Graduate:* $90/credit. *Application Fee:* $25. *Other Costs:* Student fees per semester $146. *Technology Fee:* $30. *Credit by:* semester.

Financial Aid: Federal Stafford Loan, Federal Perkins Loan, Federal PLUS Loan, Federal Pell Grant, Federal Work-Study, VA, Utah resident programs.

Accreditation: Northwest Association of Schools and Colleges.

Description: Dixie College (1911) is a state-supported, comprehensive community college located 300 miles south of Salt Lake City and 110 miles northeast of Las Vegas. The combination of a semitropical climate and cotton-raising efforts by the first colonizers in 1861 caused the early settlers to refer to the area as Utah's Dixie—hence the name Dixie College. Dixie offers academic instruction for the completion of associate degree programs as well as certificates in vocational/technical programs. The college offered an Internet-based course in 1995 and has continued to add online courses and other distance learning options including cable TV and video-based courses.

Dodge City Community College

2501 North 14th Avenue	Phone: (316) 227-9325
Dodge City, KS 67801	Fax: (316) 227-9113

Division(s): None
Web Site(s): http://www.dccc.cc.ks.us
E-mail: None

Class Titles: Medical Terminology, Computer Science, Furniture Refinishing, Education, Emergency Medical Technician, English, History, Spanish, Math, Philosophy, Psychology, Speech, Zoology, Art, Geography, Government, Political Science, Mass Communications, Physical Education, Sociology, Child Care, French, Administration Assistant, Technology, Business, Developmental Studies, Electives, Health, Human Development, Social Work; also noncredit courses.

Teaching Methods: *Other:* live, full-motion interactive TV.

Credits Granted for: examination (CLEP).

Admission Requirements: *Undergraduate:* open admission.

On-Campus Requirements: 100% in ITV.

Tuition and Fees: *Undergraduate:* $32. *Other Costs:* $5/credit for incidental fees. *Credit by:* semester.

Financial Aid: Federal Stafford Loan, Federal Perkins Loan, Federal PLUS Loan, Federal Pell Grant, Federal Work-Study, VA.

Accreditation: North Central Association of Colleges and Schools.

Description: As a student, every day will be an opportunity for you to develop new skills, new knowledge, and new relationships. Working with competent caring faculty and staff, you can achieve your personal, academic, and career goals. What you accomplish will depend primarily on the effort you make, but there are great people here to work with you. We are committed to learning, personal growth, and community development.

Drake University

| 2507 University | Phone: (515) 271-4985 |
| Des Moines, IA 50311 | Fax: (515) 271-4985 |

Division(s): Office of the Provost (Web-based)
Web Site(s): http://www.multimedia.drake.edu/summer/
E-mail: onlinelearning@drake.edu

Undergraduate Degree Programs: Contact school.

Graduate Degree Programs: Contact school.

Postgraduate Degree Programs: Contact school.

Class Titles: Accounting, Adult Learning (Performance and Development), Business, Chemistry, Computer Science, Cultural Studies, Economics, Teaching and Learning, English, Fine Arts, History, Journalism and Mass Communication, Law, Management, German, Pharmacy, Politics and International Relations, Psychology, Public Administration, Rhetoric and Communication Studies, Sociology, Statistics, Women's Studies.

Teaching Methods: *Computers:* Internet, real-time chat, electronic classroom, e-mail, CD-ROM, newsgroup, LISTSERV.

Admission Requirements: Students from other institutions are welcomed to register in courses for which the student is qualified as non-degree-seeking students. *Postgraduate:* Some of our postgraduate programs are limited to current Drake students while other students are welcome to register in courses for which the student is qualified upon receiving a letter of good standing from degree-granting institution.

On-Campus Requirements: None.

Tuition and Fees: *Undergraduate:* $230/credit. *Graduate:* $260, $340 (MBA), $625 (Law)/credit. *Credit by:* semester.

Financial Aid: Federal Stafford Loan, Federal Perkins Loan, Federal PLUS Loan, Federal Pell Grant, Federal Work-Study, VA.

Accreditation: North Central Association of Schools and Colleges (charter member).

Description: Drake (1881) began offering web-based courses in 1997, and since then students from throughout the United States and the world have taken summer web courses from Drake. Drake began offering web courses to provide its students a quality alternative to on-campus courses and typically offers over 50 web courses each summer. Drake's web courses meet the same high teaching and instructional standards as its on-campus courses with the added flexibility of not tying the student to a classroom, which affords students the opportunity to both work and take courses from Drake during the summer. Drake's commitment to developing rigorous and innovative online courses taught by full-time faculty is your assurance of excellence. Your instructor determines the schedule of course work and assignments and is available to help you. Drake also has developed an extensive support network for its online courses. Enrollment is limited to ensure quality learning and maximum interaction between students and instructors.

Drury University

| 900 N. Benton Avenue | Phone: (417) 873-7406 |
| Springfield, MO 65802 | Fax: (417) 873-7529 |

Division(s): College of Graduate and Continuing Studies
Web Site(s): http://www.drury.edu
E-mail: grader@drury.edu

Undergraduate Degree Programs:
Associate of Science in Environmental Studies, Management Concentration

Class Titles: Political Science, History, Business, Economics, Criminology, Sociology, Religion, Psychology, English, Biology, Environmental Science, Physics, Communications, Education, Philosophy, Global Studies.

Teaching Methods: *Computers:* Internet, real-time chat, electronic classroom, e-mail, CD-ROM.

Admission Requirements: *Undergraduate:* high school diploma or GED. *Graduate, Postgraduate:* Contact school.

On-Campus Requirements: currently 15 hours of seated courses are required before enrolling for an online course. This requirement will be dropped in 2002.

Tuition and Fees: *Undergraduate:* $142/credit. *Graduate:* $214–280/credit. *Postgraduate:* $214–280/credit. *Application Fee:* $20. *Graduation Fee:* $60 for graduate students. *Other Costs:* undergraduate student fee $15. *Credit by:* semester.

Financial Aid: Federal Stafford Loan, Federal Perkins Loan, Federal PLUS Loan, Federal Pell Grant, Federal Work-Study, VA, state programs for residents of Missouri.

Accreditation: North Central Association of Colleges and Schools, National Council for the Accreditation of Teacher Education, National Architecture Accrediting Board, Association of Collegiate Business Schools and Programs.

Description: Drury University (1873) is an institution of higher education offering master's, baccalaureate and associate degrees. The university enrollment is 4,500 students. Programs are characterized by a focus on preparing students for professional careers through careful attention to a liberal arts education and the interaction of liberal arts education into professional preparation. Drury is distinctive in its attention to the comprehensive preparation of graduates competent to assume leading roles in their professions and in their communities. The online program at Drury University began in the spring semester of 1999 through the College of Graduate and Continuing Studies. The Drury online program reflects the Drury mission in all of its aspects.

Dunwoody Institute

818 Dunwoody Boulevard	Phone: (612) 374-5800
Minneapolis, MN 55403	Fax: (612) 374-8931

Division(s): Continuing Education
Web Site(s): http://www.dunwoody.tec.mn.us
E-mail: forsberg@dunwoody.tec.mn.us

Undergraduate Degree Programs:
Associate of Applied Science

Class Titles: Introduction to Computer Information Systems, Macroeconomics, Principles of Marketing, Introduction to Psychology, Strategies for Success, Business Law I, Principles of Management, Interpersonal Professional Communications, Spreadsheets for Windows, Microeconomics, Direct Marketing, Electronic Marketing, Intro-

duction to Humanities, Strategies for Success, Business Law II, Introduction to Meteorology, Operations Management, Business Ethics, Organizational Communications, Introduction to CIS, Database for Windows, Microeconomics, Macroeconomics, Principles of Selling, Marketing Management, Introduction to Psychology, Strategies for Success, Ecology, Entrepreneurship, Composition.

Teaching Methods: *Computers*: Internet, electronic classroom, e-mail. *TV*: videotape, cable program, satellite broadcasting, PBS. *Other*: radio broadcast, videoconferencing, audioconferencing, audiographics, audiotapes, fax, correspondence, independent study, individual study, learning contracts.

Tuition and Fees: varies by class.

Accreditation: North Central Association of Colleges and Schools.

Description: Dunwoody Institute (1914) is a private, nonprofit institution of higher education offering diplomas and associate degrees focused on industry and technology. Dunwoody prepares men and women for highly skilled and professional careers in technology and entrepreneurial pursuits. The institute, offering an intense-structured approach to education that facilitates the learning and development of the individual, entered the field of Distance Learning in the year 2000.

Duquesne University

600 Forbes Avenue	Phone: (412) 396-6200
Pittsburgh, PA 15212	Fax: (412) 396-5144

Division(s): Center for Distance Learning
Web Site(s): http://www.duq.edu/Distance Learning
E-mail: virtualcampus@duq.edu

Undergraduate Degree Programs:
Bachelor of Science in Nursing

Graduate Degree Programs:
Master of Science in Nursing
Master of Music Education
Master of Science Environmental Science Management
Master of Arts in Leadership and Liberal Studies

Doctoral Degree Programs:
Doctor of Pharmacy—Nontraditional
Doctor of Philosophy in Nursing

Certificate Programs: Instructional Technology, Post-BSN, Post-MSN.

Undergraduate Class Titles: Imag Lit & Critical Writing, Basic Philosophical Questions, Christian Understanding Human Personality, Mediating Org Disputes, Creating High Performance, Research Process in Nursing, Nursing Leadership/Mgmt, Transcultural Nursing, Trends & Issues in Nursing, Ethics of Interpersonal Relationships, Abnormal Psychology, Cultural Anthropology, Shaping of the Modern World, Leadership Trends—Info Technology, Basic Pharmacology, Nutrition for Health Promotion, Media Pop Culture, Irish Literature, Social Psychology.

Graduate Class Titles: Mgmt of Instructional Technology, Valuing Diverse Workforce, Legal Issues for Leaders, Lead & Liberal Studies, Decision Making and PS, Conflict Resolution, Gender & Society, Ethics/Spiritual Values, Nursing Research Methods, Bioethics, Advanced Pharmacology, Physical Assessment, Nutrition Sup Pharm & Dis Mgt, Pharmacotherapy in Elderly, Nursing Theory, Adv Practice Role Devel, Transcultural Nursing, Adv Pharmacology Nurs, Mgmt of Childbearing Family, Family Counseling, Theory Devel in Nursing, Quant Methods in Nur Res, Survey of Environmental Technology, Environmental Mgmt, Workup of Drug Therapy, Drug Lit Evaluation & Statistics, Cardiovascular I—Pharmacotherapy, Endocrine II—Phar & Disease Mgt, Oncology & Immun I—Ph & DM, Psychiatry & Neurology I—Ph & DM, Critical Issues w/Herbal Product Info, Psychology of Music Teaching, Music Research, Digital Imaging for MM, Web Development.

Teaching Methods: *Computers:* Internet, real-time chat, electronic classroom, e-mail, CD-ROM, newsgroup, LISTSERV. *Other:* videoconferencing, audioconferencing.

Credits Granted for: experiential learning, portfolio assessment, examination (CLEP).

Admission Requirements: *Graduate:* accredited RN certificate for BSN degree. *Doctoral:* accredited bachelor's degree. *Certificate:* accredited bachelor's degree.

On-Campus Requirements: vary according to program. Most graduate level programs require some on-campus residency.

Tuition and Fees: *Undergraduate:* $425–$598/credit. *Graduate:* $479–$622/credit. *Application Fee:* $25–$50. *Software:* variable. *Other Costs:* $30/course technology fee. *Credit by:* semester.

Financial Aid: Federal Stafford Loan, Federal Perkins Loan, Federal PLUS Loan, Federal Pell Grant, Federal Work-Study, VA, Pennsylvania resident programs.

Accreditation: Middle States Association of Colleges and Schools.

Description: Duquesne University (1878) first opened its doors as the Pittsburgh Catholic College of the Holy Ghost with an enrollment of 40 students and a faculty of 7. Today Duquesne is a progressive educational facility that was recently named one of the top ten Catholic universities in the U.S. The university's academics are recognized both nationally and internationally. As a result of its worldwide academic excellence, Duquesne has signed agreements with institutions in Belgium, Germany, France, Spain, Ireland, England, China, Japan, and Italy, as well as the new Commonwealth of Independent States. To support these international collaborations and to extend the opportunity for access to the same rigorous Duquesne quality education to prospective students from more remote regional and national sites, Duquesne initiated distance learning activities in 1995. The programs and offerings expand each year.

Dutchess Community College

53 Pendell Road	Phone: (845) 431-8000
Poughkeepsie, NY 12601	Fax: (845) 431-8993

Division(s): Academic Affairs
Web Site(s): http://www.sunydutchess.edu
E-mail: registrar@www.sunydutchess.edu

Undergraduate Degree Programs:
Associate of Arts
Associate of Science
Associate of Applied Science

Teaching Methods: *Computers:* Internet, electronic classroom, e-mail, CD-ROM. *TV:* videotape, cable program, satellite broadcasting. *Other:* videoconferencing, audiotapes, fax, correspondence, independent study.

Credits Granted for: experiential learning, portfolio assessment, extrainstitutional learning, examination (CLEP, ACT-PEP, DANTES, GRE).

Admission Requirements: *Undergraduate:* high school diploma or GED.

On-Campus Requirements: None.

Tuition and Fees: *Undergraduate:* $89/credit resident, $178/credit nonresident. *Credit by:* semester.

Financial Aid: Federal Stafford Loan, Federal Perkins Loan, Federal PLUS Loan, Federal Pell Grant, Federal Work-Study, VA, New York resident programs.

Accreditation: Middle States Association of Colleges and Schools.

Description: Dutchess Community College (1958) began distance learning in the mid-1970s with telecourses.

Approximately 8 courses are offered each semester. In the mid-1990s, the college began offering asynchronous courses and currently offers 5 different courses each semester utilizing this computer technology. Dutchess Community College is a founding member of the SUNY Learning Network.

D'Youville College

320 Porter Avenue	Phone: (716) 881-7607
Buffalo, NY 14201	Fax: (716) 881-7760

Division(s): None
Web Site(s): http://ddl.dyc.edu
E-mail: jtm@ddl.dyc.edu

Undergraduate Degree Programs: Contact school.

Graduate Degree Programs: Contact school.

Class Titles: Education, Business, Occupational Therapy, Physical Therapy, Health Services Administration, Chemistry, Physics, English, History, Information Technology.

Teaching Methods: *Computers:* Internet, real-time chat, e-mail, CD-ROM, LISTSERV. *TV:* videotape, cable program. *Other:* audioconferencing, correspondence, independent study, individual study, learning contracts.

Credits Granted for: examination (CLEP, ACT-PEP, DANTES, GRE).

Admission Requirements: *Undergraduate:* SAT or ACT, 80 grade average, top 25% of class. *Graduate:* 30 transfer credits.

On-Campus Requirements: None unless stated by course instructor.

Tuition and Fees: *Undergraduate:* $380/credit hour. *Graduate:* $430/credit hour. *Credit by:* semester.

Financial Aid: Federal Stafford Loan, Federal Perkins Loan, Federal PLUS Loan, Federal Pell Grant, Federal Work-Study, VA, New York resident programs.

Accreditation: Middle States Association of Colleges and Schools; other programs accredited by their own governing bodies.

Description: D'Youville College (1908) is an independent, urban, coeducational college providing liberal arts and professional programs for 1,900 graduate and undergraduate students through day, evening, weekend, and summer sessions. D'Youville was founded by the Grey Nuns as the first college for women in western New York. It became coeduca-

tional in 1971, and a graduate program in Community Health Nursing was introduced in 1983. Since then, other graduate programs have been developed in Elementary Education, Secondary Education, Special Education, Health Services Administration, and Family Nurse Practitioner. Additionally 5-year programs leading to BS/MS degrees have been established in Dietetics, International Business, Nursing, Occupational Therapy, and Physical Therapy. An RN-BS/MS degree is also offered in Nursing.

East Carolina University

Erwin Building	Phone: (800) 398-9275
Greenville, NC 27858	(252) 328-6109
	Fax: (252) 328-6540

Division(s): Continuing Studies
Web Site(s): http://www.options.ecu.edu/
E-mail: des@mail.ecu.edu

Undergraduate Degree Programs:
Bachelor of Science in Information Technologies
Bachelor of Science in Industrial Technology

Graduate Degree Programs:
MAEd Instructional Technology
MLS Library Science
MS in Speech, Language, and Auditory Pathology
MS in Nutrition and Dietetics
MSN in Nursing
MSIT Manufacturing
MSIT Digital Communications
MSOS Occupational Safety
In development:
  MA in English / Concentration in Technical and Professional Communication
  MAEd in Art
  MAEd in Special Education

Certificate Programs:
Graduate: Computer Network Professional, Professional Communications, Tele-Learning, Virtual Reality in Education, Website Developer.

Teaching Methods: *Computers:* Internet, real-time chat, electronic classroom, e-mail, LISTSERV. *Other:* videoconferencing, audioconferencing, independent study.

Credits Granted for: examination (CLEP).

Admission Requirements: *Undergraduate:* submit application and fee, transcripts from high school and colleges attended. *Graduate:* submit application and application fee, transcripts. *Postgraduate:* submit application and application fee, transcripts. *Certificate:* submit application and application fee, transcripts.

On-Campus Requirements: None.

Tuition and Fees: *Undergraduate, Graduate, Postgraduate:* varies according to residence. *Application Fee:* $45. *Software:* variable. *Credit by:* semester.

Financial Aid: Federal Stafford Loan, Federal Perkins Loan, Federal PLUS Loan, Federal Pell Grant, Federal Work-Study, VA, North Carolina resident programs.

Accreditation: Southern Association of Colleges and Schools.

Description: East Carolina University is the third largest of the 16 institutions that comprise the University of North Carolina system. The university has offered distance learning programs for more than 50 years. With the advent of the Internet, ECU has expanded its offerings and now serves students from North Carolina, the United States and all over the world. In 1998, ECU was ranked 25 in *Yahoo Internet Life* magazine's top 100 most wired schools, a fact that reflects the university's commitment to technology. Currently, ECU offers a number of degrees and courses via distance learning, taught mostly on the Internet. New programs are in development. Visit www.options.ecu.edu for the latest information.

East Central College

1964 Prairie Dell Road	Phone: (314) 583-5193
Union, MO 63084	Fax: (314) 583-1897

Division(s): Media Services
Web Site(s): http://www.ecc.cc.mo.us
E-mail: klosk@ecmail.ecc.cc.mo.us

Undergraduate Degree Programs:
Associate of Arts
Associate of Science
Associate of Applied Science

Certificate Programs: One-Year Certificate, Two-Year Certificate. Visit web site for more details.

Class Titles: General Education, Technical Education, and Remedial Education courses offered. Visit web site for current course listings.

Teaching Methods: *Computers:* web-based courses. *TV:* videotape, cable program, PBS. *Other:* independent study, individual study, ITV videoconferencing.

Credits Granted for: portfolio assessment, examination (CLEP, ACT).

Admission Requirements: *Undergraduate:* high school transcript or GED scores, math/English assessment, proof

of immunity to measles and rubella if born after 1956. *Certificate:* same as undergraduate.

On-Campus Requirements: orientation session at beginning of each telecourse and web-based course. Arrangements can be made for special circumstances.

Tuition and Fees: *Undergraduate:* $48/credit in-district, $65/credit out-of-district, $95/credit out-of-state. *Software:* variable. *Other Costs:* vary for field trips, tickets, supplies, usage fees for special courses. *Credit by:* semester.

Financial Aid: Federal Stafford Loan, Federal SEOG, Federal PLUS Loan, Federal Pell Grant, Federal Work-Study, VA, Missouri State Grants, A+ Program, college and community scholarships.

Accreditation: North Central Association of Colleges and Schools.

Description: East Central College (1968) was established to provide a postsecondary educational resource for the people of East Central Missouri. The college held its first classes in 1969 in temporary quarters. That same year a 114-acre campus site was purchased. An additional 92 acres were purchased in 1994 to accommodate expansion and growth. District voters have approved $14.7 million in bonds to build the administration building in 1971, the multipurpose building in 1973, the vocational-technical building in 1978, the classroom building in 1985 and the auditorium/classroom building in 1998. A regional training center opened in 2001. Since 1968, East Central College has helped 80,000 area residents prepare for jobs and careers, begin work on college degrees, and take part in enrichment programs and cultural activities.

East Central Community College

Broad Street	Phone: (601) 635-2111
Decatur, MS 39327	Fax: (601) 635-4060

Division(s): Adult and Continuing Education
Web Site(s): http://www.eccc.cc.ms.us
E-mail: jk.llens@eccc.cc.ms.us

Undergraduate Degree Programs:
Associate of Arts
Associate of Science
Associate of Applied Science

Class Titles: Art, Government, Sociology, Nutrition, Psychology, Philosophy, Spanish.

Teaching Methods: *Computers:* electronic classroom. *TV:* PBS. *Other:* None.

Credits Granted for: examination (CLEP, DANTES).

Admission Requirements: *Undergraduate:* high school diploma or equivalent. *Certificate:* same as undergraduate.

On-Campus Requirements: None.

Tuition and Fees: *Undergraduate:* $50/credit. *Credit by:* semester.

Financial Aid: Federal Stafford Loan, Federal PLUS Loan, Federal Pell Grant, Federal Work-Study, VA, Mississippi resident programs.

Accreditation: Southern Association of Colleges and Schools.

Description: East Central Community College (1928) is a public 2-year college with a credit enrollment of more than 2,100 students. We offer university transfer curricula and terminal vocational/technical curricula. Our distance education program is several years old and is mainly via educational TV in Mississippi.

East Los Angeles College

| 1301 Avenida Cesar Chavez | Phone: (323) 265-8774 |
| Monterey Park, CA 91754 | |

Division(s): Online Education
Web Site(s): http://www.elaconline.nete-mail/
E-mail: Kerrin_M._McMahan@laccd.cc.ca.us

Undergraduate Degree Programs: Contact school.

Class Titles: Accounting, Computer Science, English Composition, Nutrition, Health, History, Mathematics, Office Administration, Philosophy, Psychology, Speech, Theater.

Teaching Methods: *Computers:* Internet, real-time chat, e-mail, CD-ROM.

Admission Requirements: *Undergraduate:* any high school graduate or any other person over 18 years of age is eligible for admission to East Los Angeles College. K-12 students may be admitted if ELAC determines they may benefit from college instruction.

On-Campus Requirements: None.

Tuition and Fees: *Undergraduate:* $11/credit. *Software:* varies with course(s) taken. *Other Costs:* textbooks and materials—costs vary with course(s) taken. *Credit by:* semester.

Financial Aid: Federal Perkins Loan, Federal PLUS Loan, Federal Pell Grant, Federal Work-Study, VA, state programs for residents of California.

Accreditation: Western Association of Schools and Colleges.

Description: ELAC (1945) is one of the 9 public 2 year colleges within the Los Angeles Community College District. It enrolls more than 25,000 students. ELAC began offering online courses in 1998, and joined the California Virtual Campus system in spring 2001.

Eastern Kentucky University

| 521 Lancaster Avenue | Phone: (606) 622-2001 |
| Richmond, KY 40475 | Fax: (606) 622-1177 |

Division(s): Office of Extended Programs
Web Site(s): http://www.eku.edu
E-mail: richard boyle@eku.edu

Class Titles: Accounting, Algebra, Art, Biology, Business, Computer Information Systems, Economics, Education, English, Environmental Health Science, Finance, Geography, Health, History, History of Science, Insurance, Library Science, Loss Prevention/Safety, Management, Marketing, Mass Communications, Music, Nursing, Occupational Therapy, Philosophy, Police Studies, Political Science, Psychology, Real Estate, Religion, Sociology, Spanish, Special Education, Theater, Trigonometry.

Teaching Methods: *Computers:* Internet, real-time chat, electronic classroom, e-mail, LISTSERV. *TV:* cable program, satellite broadcasting, PBS. *Other:* audiotapes, correspondence.

Credits Granted for: examination (CLEP, ACT-PEP, DANTES, GRE).

Admission Requirements: *Undergraduate:* high school diploma or GED, ACT, precollege curriculum. *Graduate:* bachelor's, GRE scores, letters of recommendation.

On-Campus Requirements: yes for television courses, no for correspondence and Web-based courses.

Tuition and Fees: *Undergraduate:* $106/credit *Graduate:* $145/credit. *Credit by:* semester.

Financial Aid: Federal Stafford Loan, Federal Perkins Loan, Federal PLUS Loan, Federal Pell Grant, Federal Work-Study, VA, Kentucky resident programs.

Accreditation: Southern Association of Colleges and Schools.

Description: Eastern Kentucky University (1906), originally founded as a teacher's college, is a regional, coeducational, public institution of higher education offering general and liberal arts program, preprofessional and professional training in education, and various other fields at the undergraduate and graduate levels. It currently enrolls 15,000 students and continues to prepare quality teachers for the elementary and secondary schools of the state. However, a strong liberal arts curriculum leading to appropriate degrees, together with preprofessional courses in several areas and graduate programs, enable Eastern to serve Kentucky as a regional university. For 60 years the university has offered distance learning through correspondence courses. In the past few years it has used modern technology to deliver telecourses through the statewide public TV network and its own cable-linked network. Web-based courses on the Internet were first offered in 1998.

Eastern Michigan University

100 Boone Hall	Phone: (734) 487-1081
Ypsilanti, MI 48197	Fax: (734) 487-6695

Division(s): Continuing Education
Web Site(s): http://www.ce.emich.edu
E-mail: distance.learning@emich.edu

Graduate Degree Program:
Master of Science in Engineering Management

Postgraduate Degree Program:
Second Bachelor's Degree in Dietetics

Certificate Programs:
Graduate Certificate in Legal Administration

Class Titles: Course titles vary by semester; refer to www.ce.emich.edu for specific information.

Teaching Methods: *Computers:* Internet, real-time chat, electronic classroom, e-mail, CD-ROM, newsgroup, LISTSERV. *TV:* videotape, cable program, satellite broadcasting, PBS. *Other:* videoconferencing, fax, correspondence, independent study.

Credits Granted for: experiential learning, portfolio assessment, extrainstitutional learning, examination (CLEP, ACT-PEP, DANTES, GRE).

Admission Requirements: *Undergraduate:* open-admission. *Graduate:* Open. *Postgraduate:* Open. *Certificate:* Open.

On-Campus Requirements: None.

Tuition and Fees: Tuition costs vary; refer to www.ce.emich.edu for specific information. *Credit by:* semester.

Financial Aid: Federal Stafford Loan, Federal Perkins Loan, Federal PLUS Loan, Federal Pell Grant, Federal Work-Study, VA, state programs for residents of Michigan.

Accreditation: North Central Association of Colleges and Schools.

Description: Eastern Michigan University (1849) is a public, comprehensive, metropolitan university that offers programs in the arts, sciences, and professions. The university is composed of more than 24,000 students who are served by 680 full-time faculty as well as 1,200 staff, both on campus, off campus, and electronically. EMU offers undergraduate, graduate, specialist, doctoral, and certificate programs in its colleges of arts and sciences, business, education, health and human services, and technology.

Eastern Oregon University

1410 L Avenue	Phone: (800) 544-2195
La Grande, OR 97850-2899	Fax: (541) 962-3627

Division(s): Distance Education
Web Site(s): http://www.eou.edu/dde
E-mail: dde@eou.edu

Undergraduate Degree Programs:
Associate of Science in Office Administration
Bachelor of Arts/Bachelor of Science in:
    Liberal Studies
    Business/Economics
    Politics/Philosophy/Economics
    Physical Education/Health
    Fire Services Administration

Graduate Degree Programs:
Master of Teacher Education (not available outside Oregon)

Class Titles: 300 courses in a variety of subject areas including Business, Economics, English, Geography, Philosophy, Political Science, Psychology, Science, Writing.

Teaching Methods: *Computers:* Internet, real-time chat, electronic classroom, e-mail, CD-ROM, newsgroup, LISTSERV. *TV:* videotape, cable program, IPTU, PBS. *Other:* videoconferencing, audioconferencing, audiotapes, fax, correspondence, independent study, individual study.

Credits Granted for: experiential learning, portfolio assessment, agency-sponsored learning, examination (CLEP).

Admission Requirements: *Undergraduate:* high school diploma, SAT (recommended). *Graduate:* undergraduate diploma.

On-Campus Requirements: Master of Teacher Education and Fire Services Administration require some on-campus training.

Tuition and Fees: *Undergraduate:* $95/credit. *Graduate:* $132/credit. *Software:* $15. *Other Costs:* $50 admission fee, $4/credit tech fee. *Credit by:* quarter.

Financial Aid: Federal Stafford Loan, Federal Perkins Loan, Federal PLUS Loan, Federal Pell Grant, Federal Work-Study, VA, Oregon resident programs.

Accreditation: Northwest Association of Schools and Colleges.

Description: Eastern Oregon University (1929) has been involved in distance learning programs since 1978 as part of its mission to provide education to the eastern half of the state. Currently Eastern is Oregon's pilot provider to the Western Governors University and is involved in creating a model virtual institution through the Eastern Oregon Collaborative Colleges Center. Eastern does not charge out-of-state tuition to non-Oregon residents. The emphasis of the distance learning program is on helping students obtain degrees; however, students can take up to 8 quarter credits per term without being admitted to Eastern. Admission is required to pursue a degree at Eastern and to be eligible for financial aid.

Eastern Washington University

526 Fifth Street, HAR 217	Phone: (509) 359-2268
Cheney, WA 99004	Fax: (509) 359-2220

Division(s): Distance and Extended Learning
Web Site(s): http://deo.ewu.edu/dcesso/oce/del.html
E-mail: gothedistance@ewu.edu

Class Titles: General education core requirement courses, Black Culture, African American History, Literature, Modern Government in American Context, Western Heritage: Origins to 18th Century, Western Heritage: 18th Century to Present, American Experience: Survey, Great World Views, Attention Deficit/Hyperactivity In Schools, Child Abuse: Recognition/Intervention Strategies, Accounting, Personnel Management, Creative Writing, Short Story Writing, Writing Poetry, Thematic Teaching, Literature of Bible, American Literature to Whitman, American Literature: Twain to Dreiser, 20th Century American Literature, Facts About HIV/AIDS, Adolescent Health, History/Government of Pacific Northwest, Women in American History, Finite Math, Sport Psychology, Physical Education, Time Management, Psychology, Abnormal Psychology, Social Psychology.

Teaching Methods: *Computers:* Internet, e-mail. *Other:* independent learning, correspondence.

Credits Granted for: portfolio assessment, examination (CLEP).

On-Campus Requirements: None.

Tuition and Fees: *Undergraduate:* $93 (resident), $319/credit (nonresident). *Graduate:* $199/credit (resident). *Software:* student will need software to access the Internet for online classes. *Other Costs:* $87/credit independent learning/correspondence. *Credit by:* quarter.

Financial Aid: Federal Stafford Loan, Federal Perkins Loan, Federal PLUS Loan (if enrolled as a degree seeking student), Federal Pell Grant, Federal Work-Study, VA (www. ewu.edw).

Accreditation: Northwest Association of Schools and Colleges.

Description: Eastern Washington University (1882) is a comprehensive regional university with educational facilities in Cheney and Spokane. The university serves a large traditional and nontraditional student population. EWU provides high-quality liberal arts and professional education and maintains a strong commitment to excellence in instruction. Distance education in the form of correspondence courses have been offered at EWU since the 1930s, tele-courses for the past decade, and online Internet courses since 1998. In the fall of 1998, the university joined in a consortial arrangement with other state institutions to offer a distance learning degree in business. This consortium will allow the Washington state higher education institutions to join resources to provide multiple statewide degrees in coming years.

Edison Community College

8099 College Parkway SW	Phone: (941) 489-9455
Ft. Myers, FL 33919	Fax: (941) 433-8000

Division(s): Distance Learning
Web Site(s): http://www.edison.edu
E-mail: lbronder@edison.edu or mroth@edison.edu

Undergraduate Degree Programs:
General Education Degree
Associate in Arts
Associate in Science

Certificate Programs: Accounting Applications, Small Business Management, Computer Programming/Applications, Crime Scene Technology, Dental Assisting, Emergency Medical Technician, Emergency Medical Services, Network Specialist, Turf Equipment Technology.

Class Titles: Courses toward associate degrees in: Agriculture, Anthropology, Art, Astronomy, Biology, Business, Chemistry, Criminal Justice, Ecology, Economics, Education, Engineering, English, Geology, Pre-Medical Technology, Pre-Nursing, Pre-Physical Therapy, Pre-Occupational Therapy, Health/Wellness, History, Hospitality, Human Services, Humanities, Languages, Literature, Music, Philosophy, Physics, Political Science, Pre-Law, Pre-Medicine, Pre-Dentistry, Psychology, Radio/TV, Sociology, Speech, Theater Arts, Accounting, Technology, Business Administration/Management, Banking/Finance, Customer Service Technology, Hospitality/Tourism Management, International Business, Marketing/Management, Small Business/Entrepreneurship, Cardiovascular Technology, Citrus Production Technology, Computer Programming Applications, Networking, Programming, Criminal Justice Technology, Management, Dental Hygiene, Drafting/Design Technology, CAD, Civil Engineering/Land Surveying, Electronics Engineering Technology, Emergency Medical

Services Technology, Fire Science Technology, Golf Course Operations, Legal Assisting, Nursing RN, Nursing Advanced Placement Option, Radiologic Technology, Respirator Care; and toward certificates in Accounting Applications, Business Data Processing, Small Business Management, Emergency Medical Services-Basic, Emergency Medical Services-Paramedic, Fire Apparatus Operator, Fire Officer, Fire Safety Inspector, Special Fire Safety Inspector, Arson Investigator.

Teaching Methods: *Computers:* Internet, real-time chat, electronic classroom, e-mail. *TV:* videotape. *Other:* video-conferencing, audioconferencing, audiotapes, fax, correspondence, independent study, individual study.

Credits Granted for: examination (CLEP).

Admission Requirements: *Undergraduate:* Degree-seeking students must contact their high school for an official transcript and/or our GED office for official GED scores. Their Social Security number should be included on all documents. These must be on file in the Admissions Office before they register for their second term. If they have taken the ACT or SAT in the last 2 years, they must submit their scores to the Counseling Center. If they have not, they will need to take the FCELPT (placement test) at Edison. They must schedule an orientation and advising session at the Counseling Center. This session is required of all new degree-seeking students. They must arrange to have each college/university they have attended send an official transcript directly to Edison Admissions Office on the Lee County campus. All transcripts should include their Social Security number. CLEP and AP scores are official transcripts and must be sent from The College Board. Nondegree Seeking Students: Orientation is strongly recommended; students are limited to a maximum academic load of 18 semester hours during the fall/spring sessions and 9 semester hours during the summer A/B sessions; testing is required for most English and math courses. Students who are college graduates or who have completed college-level math or English classes with a grade of C or higher may be exempt from testing. Early admission, accelerated, and dual-enrollment high school students: Part-time and full-time dual-enrollment high school students must complete testing before registering; must submit completed/signed dual-enrollment forms indicating which courses are approved by the high school for dual enrollment or early admission and test scores. Early admission students must also submit a letter of recommendation for college-campus early admission; accelerated students are admitted by letter of recommendation from their high school principal and counselor. The letter must specify the course(s) requested. Testing is required for most English and math courses; parents/guardians must co-sign the admissions applications if students are under age 18. *Certificate:* see undergraduate.

On-Campus Requirements: None.

Tuition and Fees: *Undergraduate:* $50.45/credit in-state, $187.95/credit out-of-state. *Other Costs:* $6–$112 health and science fees, $26.50 or $32.50 health technologies fee ($15 one-time program application fee), $50 or $100 applied music fees, $35 telecourse fee, $5–$100 workforce programs fees, $30 or $35 visual arts fee, $15 or $100 health and wellness fees, $10 Department of Learning Assistance fee. All fees are subject to change if approved by the Florida Legislature. *Credit by:* semester.

Financial Aid: Federal Stafford Loan, Edison Community College Short-Term loan, Federal Pell Grant, Federal Work-Study, VA, Florida Student Assistance Grant, Federal Supplemental Education Opportunity Grant, state programs for residents of Florida.

Accreditation: Southern Association of Colleges and Schools.

Description: Edison Community College (1962) celebrates 39 years of service to southwest Florida this year. Since the first students were admitted to Edison, the college has enrolled more than 175,000 students in credit courses. Associate in Art and Associate in Science degrees are offered at Edison as well as one-year certificate programs. Edison's 3 campuses—Lee County, Charlotte County, and Collier County—bring higher education within reach of the entire 5-county district. As a student-centered learning college, we recognize the importance of Distance Education. Our Department of Distance Learning has been active for 20 years. We continually expand educational opportunities for students in outlying areas of southwest Florida as well as nontraditional students in our immediate area. At this time a student may earn a General Education Degree completely through Distance Learning telecourses.

Edison Community College

1973 Edison Drive	Phone: (937) 778-8600
Piqua, OH 45356	Fax: (937) 778-1920

Division(s): Learning Information Systems
Web Site(s): http://www.edison.cc.oh.us
E-mail: eccreg@edison.cc.oh.us

Undergraduate Degree Programs:
Associate of:
   Arts
   Science
   Applied Science
   Applied Business
   Technical Study

Class Titles: English Composition, Literature, Humanities, Technical Writing, Economics, Psychology, Desktop Publishing, Archaeology, Art, Business, Sociology, Speech.

Transition LPN to ADN, Calculus, Advanced Technical Writing, Great Books, Technical Editing, Introduction to the Internet.

Teaching Methods: *Computers:* Internet, e-mail, CD-ROM. *TV:* videotape, videoconference. *Other:* independent study, individual study, learning contracts.

Credits Granted for: experiential learning, portfolio assessment, extrainstitutional learning, examination (CLEP, ACT-PEP, DANTES, GRE).

Admission Requirements: *Undergraduate:* open admissions.

On-Campus Requirements: None.

Tuition and Fees: *Undergraduate:* $81/credit in-state, $162/credit out-of-state. *Application Fee:* $15. *Software:* variable. *Credit by:* semester.

Financial Aid: Federal Stafford Loan, Federal Perkins Loan, Federal PLUS Loan, Federal Pell Grant, Federal Work-Study, VA, Ohio resident programs.

Accreditation: North Central Association of Colleges and Schools.

Description: Edison Community College (1973) is a comprehensive community college serving western Ohio. Learning is our business. Because we are learner-centered, we provide multiple opportunities for students to succeed. Edison uses a combination of online, cassette, and flexibly scheduled courses to serve students with time and place barriers. Whether students are dealing with family, work, or community activities, Edison's schedule fits students' schedules. Students currently may receive telephone advising, and online advising is planned. Registration is possible in person, by phone, or by mail, and the bookstore will mail books to online students. Faculty, Learning Lab, and Student Development professionals will work with students to meet their other distance learning needs. Edison's courses transfer to 4-year colleges and universities. Member of Ohio Learning Network.

Edmonds Community College

20000 68th Avenue West	Phone: (425) 640-1098
Lynnwood, WA 98036	Fax: (425) 640-1704

Division(s): Distance Learning Office
Web Site(s): Edmonds Community College: http://www.edcc.edu/
Distance Learning: http://online.edcc.edu/
E-mail: ttorres@edcc.edu

Undergraduate Degree Programs:
Associates of Arts (AA) Degree
Bachelor's (BA) Degree in Business Administration—general Business

Certificate Programs: Case Management.

Class Titles: Contact school or check web site for details.

Teaching Methods: *Computers:* Internet, electronic classroom, e-mail, LISTSERV. *TV:* videotape, cable program.

Credits Granted for: experiential learning, portfolio assessment, extrainstitutional learning (PONSI, corporate or professional association seminars/workshops), examination (CLEP, ACT-PEP, DANTES, GRE).

Admission Requirements: *Undergraduate:* English and math placement test.

Tuition and Fees: *Undergraduate:* $58.10/credit. *Application Fee:* $15. *Graduation Fee:* $20 (cap and gown). *Other Costs:* $2.05/credit for Assessment Fee (up to 10 credits or a fraction thereof), $2/credit for Technology Fee (up to 10 credits). *Credit by:* quarter.

Financial Aid: Federal Stafford Loan, Federal Pell Grant, Federal Work-Study, Federal Supplemental Educational Opportunity Grant, ECC Grant, Worker Retraining Grant, Work-based Learning Grant, VA, WA State Need Grant.

Accreditation: Northwest Association of Schools and Colleges.

Description: Edmonds Community College (1967) is a leader in providing quality opportunities for learning and service, responding to the dynamic needs of our diverse community. Edmond Community College is the community's place to learn. We strive to provide the best in teaching and learning, in the services we offer our students and community, and in our many innovative partnerships. Our goal is helping students take the first step to a 4 year degree, take the next step to a great job, or take a path that makes life better for them and their families. Edmonds Community College was an early pioneer in online learning and currently offers one of the largest Distance Learning programs in Washington State. We offer over 130 courses online and several complete certificates and degrees are now available completely at a distance.

El Camino College

16007 Crenshaw Boulevard	Phone: (310) 660-6453
Torrance, CA 90506	Fax: (310) 660-3513

Division(s): Instructional Services
Web Site(s): http://www.elcamino.cc.ca.us
E-mail: jshannon@admin.elcamino.cc.ca.us

Class Titles: courses toward Associate of Arts, Associate of Science, and toward Certificate of Completion and Certificate of Competence in a variety of fields, including anthropology, astronomy, child development, computer information systems, contemporary health, English, English as a second language, history, humanities, music, political science, psychology, sociology, Japanese, philosophy, real estate.

Teaching Methods: *Computers:* Internet, real-time chat, e-mail, LISTSERV. *TV:* videotape, cable program, PBS. *Other:* None.

Admission Requirements: *Undergraduate:* age 18. Students under age 18 may qualify if graduated from high school or passed the California High School Certificate of Proficiency Test. El Camino College may admit anyone in grades K-12 who, in the opinion of the college president, may benefit from instruction taken.

On-Campus Requirements: varies at discretion of instructor.

Tuition and Fees: *Undergraduate:* $11/unit. *Software:* Required for some online courses; cost varies. *Other Costs:* textbooks, cost varies. *Credit by:* semester.

Financial Aid: Federal Stafford Loan, Federal Pell Grant, Federal Work-Study, Federal Supplemental Educational Opportunity Grant, Federal Parents Loans, VA, Board of Governors Waiver, California Grants B and C, Aid for American Indians.

Accreditation: Western Association of Schools and Colleges.

Description: El Camino College (1947) has taken its mission most seriously since its founding more than a half-century ago. Recognizing the ever-changing population of the South Bay area along with the diversity of educational needs and advances in technology, the college continually refocuses its courses and programs to stay in the vanguard of America's higher education.

Elizabethtown Community College

600 College Street Road	Phone: (270) 769-2371
Elizabethtown, KY 42701	Toll-Free (877) 246-2ECC
	Fax: (270) 769-0736

Division(s): Distance Learning Programs
Web Site(s): www.elizabethtowncc.com
E-mail: ruth.williams@kctcs.net, gwyn.sutherland@kctcs.net

Undergraduate Degree Programs:
Associate in Arts
Associate in Applied Science

Graduate Degree Programs:
Through the University of Kentucky and Western Kentucky University.

Class Titles: History, Psychology, Business, Sociology, Music, French, English, Speech, Nursing.

Teaching Methods: *Computers:* Internet, e-mail, CD-ROM. *TV:* videotape, cable program, satellite broadcasting, PBS, KET. *Other:* videoconferencing.

Credits Granted for: examination (CLEP, ACT-PEP, DANTES, GRE).

Admission Requirements: *Undergraduate:* open-admission.

On-Campus Requirements: exams usually administered on campus.

Tuition and Fees: *Undergraduate:* $61/credit resident, $183/credit nonresident. *Other Costs:* $20/TV course KET fee (nonrefundable). *Credit by:* semester.

Financial Aid: Federal Stafford Loan, Federal Perkins Loan, Federal PLUS Loan, Federal Pell Grant, Federal Work-Study, VA, Kentucky resident programs.

Accreditation: Southern Association of Colleges and Schools.

Description: Elizabethtown Community College (1963) is one of 13 community colleges in the Kentucky Community and Technical College System. Formerly a branch of the University of Kentucky, the school was founded in 1963, offering transfer programs, associate degree programs, and community service and education. Those areas of focus remain today, along with the addition of local workforce training and development. ECC has partnered with the University of Kentucky and Kentucky Educational TV since the late 60s to provide distance learning to students in the area. Earlier access was achieved via microwave transmissions and open-air broadcasts. Today, students are served using cable, computers, interactive TV, satellite delivery, as well as the traditional open-air broadcasts. ECC is currently exploring all possible avenues to provide quality educational opportunities to all potential students.

Embry-Riddle Aeronautical University

600 South Clyde Morris Boulevard	Phone: (386) 226-4953
Daytona Beach, FL 32114	(386) 226-7627

Division(s): Department of Distance Learning
Web Site(s): http://www.embryriddle.edu
E-mail: whittumt@db.erau.edu

Undergraduate Degree Programs:
Associate in Science in Aviation Business Administration
Associate of Science in Professional Aeronautics
Bachelor of Science in Professional Aeronautics
Bachelor of Science in Management of Technical Operations

Graduate Degree Programs:
Master in Aeronautical Science
Master of Business Administration/Aviation

Class Titles:
All classes offered can be taken by nondegree-seeking students. For a complete list of courses see *http://www.ec. erau.edu/ddl/course.htm*

Teaching Methods: *Computers:* Internet, electronic classroom, e-mail, CD-ROM.

Credits Granted for: portfolio assessment, examination (CLEP, DANTES, GRE).

Admission Requirements: *Undergraduate:* nontraditional student, some programs require experience in aviation. *Graduate:* bachelor's degree.

On-Campus Requirements: None.

Tuition and Fees: *Undergraduate:* $145/credit. *Graduate:* $315/credit. *Application Fee:* $30. *Credit by:* semester.

Financial Aid: Federal Stafford Loan, Federal Pell Grant, VA.

Accreditation: Southern Association of Colleges and Schools.

Description: At Embry-Riddle Aeronautical University, what we do—and do best—is teach the science, practice, and business of the world of aviation and aerospace. Since it was founded just 22 years after the Wright brothers' first flight, the university and its graduates have built an enviable record of achievement in every aspect of aviation and aerospace. Embry-Riddle is the world's oldest, largest, and most prestigious university specializing in aviation and aerospace. The curriculum at Embry-Riddle covers the operation, engineering, research, manufacturing, marketing, and management of modern aircraft and the systems that support them.

Emporia State University

1200 Commercial Street	
Campus Box 4052	Phone: (620) 341-5385
Emporia, KS 66801	Fax: (620) 341-5744

Division(s): Office of Lifelong Learning
Web Site(s): http://www.lifelong.emporia.edu
E-mail: lifelong@emporia.edu

Undergraduate Degree Completion Program:
Bachelor of Integrated Studies—Internet

Graduate Degree Programs:
Master of Science in:
  Business Education—Internet
  Instructional Design and Technology—Internet
  Health, Physical Education, and Recreation

Certificate Programs:
Graduate Certificate in Geospatial Analysis—Internet
Graduate Certificate Series: The Internet—Internet
Endorsement in Early Childhood Special Education—Internet
Endorsement in English as a Second Language—Internet

Class Titles: Using the World Wide Web, BIS Online Seminar, BIS Online Assessment, BIS Capstone Project, Ethics in the Modern World, Coordination of Business/Education Partnerships, Industrial Technology Selection and Facility Design, Business and Society, Supervision and Evaluation, Brain-Based Learning for Educators, Analysis of Research, Methods of Early Childhood Special Education, Reading Theory and Literacy Practice: Elementary Teachers, Teaching Reading to Diverse Learners, Psychology of the Adult Learner, Essentials of Spanish Grammar, Curriculum for Individuals with Emotional and Behavior Disorders, Introduction to Social Welfare, Applied Computer Concepts, Internet Uses in K-12 Education, Foundations of Instructional Technology, Internet Resources and Tools for Educators, Instructional Design, Multimedia Design, Current Developments in Physical Education, Advanced Technology in HPER, Analysis of Teaching/Coaching, Advanced Exercise Physiology, Introduction to Geospatial Analysis, Field Geomorphology, Geoliterature and Geowriting, Remost Sensing, Urban Geography, History of Geology.

Teaching Methods: *Computers:* Internet, real-time chat, electronic classroom, e-mail, CD-ROM, newsgroup, LISTSERV. *TV:* videotape. *Other:* desktop, videoconferencing, Interactive TV.

Credits Granted for: experiential learning, portfolio assessment, extrainstitutional learning, examination (CLEP, ACT-PEP, DANTES, GRE).

Admission Requirements: Please contact ESU for details.

On-Campus Requirements: Please contact ESU for details.

Tuition and Fees: *Undergraduate:* $89/credit. *Graduate:* $121/credit. *Application Fee:* $25 undergraduate, $30 graduate. *Other Costs:* Out-of-state library courses have additional costs. *Credit by:* semester.

Financial Aid: Federal Stafford Loan, Federal Perkins Loan, Federal PLUS Loan, Federal Pell Grant, Federal Work-Study, VA, Kansas resident programs.

Accreditation: North Central Association of Colleges and Schools.

Description: Emporia State University (1863) was established as the state's first school for training teachers. With an enrollment of 5,400 students, the university is a public, comprehensive university which confers bachelor and master, degrees in the College of Liberal Arts and Sciences, and the School of Business. In addition, a specialist degree is available in the Teachers College, and a doctorate in the School of Library and Information Science.

Evangel University

1111 North Glenstone Avenue
Springfield, MO 65802

Phone: (417) 865-2815
Fax: (417) 865-9599

Division(s): Office of Academic Affairs
Web Site(s): http://www.evangel.edu
E-mail: sandersb@evangel.edu

Undergraduate Degree Programs: Contact school.

Graduate Degree Programs:
Master's degrees

Class Titles: Government, History, General Education.

Teaching Methods: *Computers:* Internet, real-time chat, electronic classroom, e-mail, discussion boards. *Other:* independent study, individual study.

Admission Requirements: Contact school.

Tuition and Fees: *Undergraduate:* $253–$375/credit depending on course load. *Graduate:* $250/credit. *Other Costs:* vary. *Credit by:* semester.

Accreditation: North Central Association of Colleges and Schools among others.

Description: Evangel University (1955) offers more than 80 academic programs on the cutting edge of today's professional fields. Our standards of excellence attract students who have a strong commitment to academics and who tend to have above average ACT and SAT scores. Evangel's theme, "Christ is Lord," touches every aspect of campus life—spiritual, intellectual, social, and physical. Our staff, curriculum, and campus activities center around helping students integrate their Christian faith into their chosen career fields. Evangelical. Boldly Christian. Unquestionably academic.

Everett Community College

2000 Tower Street
Everett, WA 98201

Phone: (425) 388-9501
Fax: (425) 388-9144

Division(s): Library-Media Services
Web Site(s): http://www.evcc.ctc.edu
E-mail: distance@evcc.ctc.edu

Undergraduate Degree Programs:
Associate in Arts and Sciences
Associate in Technical Arts
Associate of Science

Certificate Programs: various.

Class Titles: Computer Science, English, Literature, Geology, Early Childhood Education, Nutrition, History, Music, Psychology, Business Technology, Social Sciences, Art, Theater.

Teaching Methods: *Computers:* Internet, real-time chat, e-mail, newsgroup, LISTSERV. *TV:* telecourse. *Other:* correspondence.

Credits Granted for: experiential learning, portfolio assessment, extrainstitutional learning, examination (CLEP, ACT-PEP, DANTES, GRE).

Admission Requirements: *Undergraduate:* accredited high school graduate, age 18, or apply for options program. Skills assessment test if taking more than 7 credits.

On-Campus Requirements: None.

Tuition and Fees: *Undergraduate:* $55/credit resident, $215/credit nonresident. *Application Fee:* $20. *Other Costs:* telecourse tape rental, online services, lab fees. *Credit by:* quarter.

Financial Aid: Federal Stafford Loan, Federal Perkins Loan, Federal PLUS Loan, Federal Pell Grant, Federal Work-Study, VA, Washington resident programs.

Accreditation: Northwest Association of Schools and Colleges.

Description: Everett Community College (1941) has grown from modest beginnings in a converted elementary school to become an institution of stature in the community and within the Washington state community college system. Everett offers programs for students who intend to transfer to a college or university as well as a variety of occupational and professional-technical programs. The college has offered distance learning opportunities for many years to provide students with flexibility in scheduling and increased access to college programs.

Everglades College

1500 NW 49th Street
Fort Lauderdale, FL 33309

Phone: (888) 772-6077
Fax: (954) 772-2695

Division(s): eCampus (Department of Online Education)
Web Site(s): www.evergladescollege.edu
www.evergladescollege.org
E-mail: susanz@evergladescollege.edu

Undergraduate Degree programs:
Bachelor of Science with majors in:
    Business Administration
    Information Technology
    eCommerce
    Applied Management
    Professional Aviation
    Aviation Management
Associate of Science with concentrations in:
    Professional Aviation
    Aviation Management

Class Titles: Contact school or visit web site for details.

Teaching Methods: *Computers:* Internet, real-time chat, electronic classroom, e-mail, CD-ROM, newsgroup, LISTSERV.

Credits Granted for: examination (CLEP, ACT-PEP, DANTES, GRE).

Admission Requirements: *Undergraduate:* high school diploma/GED, Everglades entrance exam.

On-Campus Requirements: None.

Tuition and Fees: *Undergraduate:* $4,450/semester. *Application Fee:* $52. *Other Costs:* registration fee: $145, varies for textbooks. *Credit by:* semester.

Financial Aid: Federal Stafford Loan, Federal Perkins Loan, Federal PLUS Loan, Federal Pell Grant, Federal Work-Study, VA.

Accreditation: Accrediting Commission of Career Schools and Colleges of Technology (ACCSCT).

Description: Everglades College's (1990) Online Programs are web-based courses, designed by qualified faculty and staff to create an interesting, interactive learning environment. Everglades' virtual classroom is comfortable, and courses can be taken easily by anyone with access to the World Wide Web. Lesson plans, assignments, and class schedules are posted online, while student/teacher interaction and student/student interaction also occur over the Internet. Scheduled discussions, e-mail messages, live chats, and real-time group discussions are a few of the opportunities for interacting during your online course.

Excelsior College

7 Columbia Circle	**Phone:** Toll free (888) 647-2388
Albany, NY 12203-5159	and (518) 464-8500
	Fax: (518) 464-8777

Division(s): All (Excelsior College is a distance education institution.)
Web Site(s): http://www.excelsior.edu
E-mail: admissions@excelsior.edu

Undergraduate Degree Programs: Business, Liberal Arts, Nursing, and Technology.

Graduate Degree Programs:
Master of Arts in Liberal Studies (MLS)
Master of Science in Nursing (MSN)

Certificate Programs: Home Health Care Nursing (undergraduate); Health Care Informatics (graduate).

Teaching Methods: *Computers:* Internet, real-time chat, electronic classroom, e-mail, CD-ROM, LISTSERV. *TV: Other:* audioconferencing, audiotapes, fax, correspondence, independent study, individual study, learning contracts.

Credits Granted for: college-level proficiency examinations (Excelsior College Examinations, CLEP, DANTES, GRE), transfer credit from regionally accredited colleges and universities, experiential learning, portfolio assessment, extra-institutional learning, ACE-evaluated military training.

Admission Requirements: *Undergraduate:* Open admission except nursing. MLS: bachelor's degree, admissions essay; MSN: BSN degree, RN licensure, and GRE or Miller Analogies Test. *Certificate:* Home Health Care Nursing Certificate Program (undergraduate): active RN licensure; Health Care Informatics Certificate Program (graduate): bachelor's degree in a health care discipline or bachelor's degree and work experience in a health care organization.

On-Campus Requirements: None.

Tuition and Fees: *Undergraduate:* $725 associate enrollment fee first year, $875 bachelor's enrollment fee first year, $340/$380 each additional year plus other program-specific fees. Student Information Services Fee $40 per year; other fees vary per program. MSN: $315 per credit plus program fees; MLS: $870/$1740 3/6-credit core course fees plus fees for learning contracts, thesis, etc. Both programs assess $150 annual Graduate Student Fee. *Application Fees:* $40 undergraduate programs (optional preenrollment credit assessment); $100 graduate programs. *Graduation Fee:* $430 associate (less for military students); $465 bachelor's; $100 graduate programs *Other Costs:* Vary per program. *Credit by:* semester.

Financial Aid: VA, New York resident programs, institutional scholarships, private grants/scholarships, private (alternative) loans.

Accreditation: Commission on Higher Education of the Middle States Association of Colleges and Schools, National League for Nursing Accrediting Commission, Technology Accreditation Commission (TAC) of the Accreditation Board for Engineering and Technology (ABET).

Description: Founded on the philosophy that "What you know is more important than where or how you learned it," Excelsior College (1971) began as the external degree program of the New York State Board of Regents. In 1998, the Board of Regents granted the college (then known as Regents College) a charter to operate as a private, independent college. The college is governed by a board of trustees comprised of individuals from across the United States who are prominent in the fields of business, education, and the professions. An assessment and evaluation institution with more than 89,000 graduates, Excelsior College awards degrees in 30 programs at the associate and baccalaureate levels in business, liberal arts, nursing, and technology as well as master's-level degrees in liberal studies and nursing. An MBA program is also being developed. With no residency requirement, the college provides students high-quality, accessible, convenient, and fairly priced evaluation services, which efficiently translate college-level learning into academic credit. While remaining open to all, the college ensures academic quality through rigorous programs, student-centered advisement, and careful assessment. It works in partnership with other colleges and universities, employers, and organizations to remove barriers to educational opportunity.

Ferris State University

410 Oak Street, Alumni 113	Phone: (231) 591-2340
Big Rapids, MI 49307-2022	Fax: (231) 591-3539

Division(s): The University Center for Extended Learning
Web Site(s): http://www.ferris.edu/ucel
E-mail: hardmanc@ferris.edu
ucel@ferris.edu

Undergraduate Degree Programs:
None completely distance education; some courses available online.

Graduate Degree Programs:
None completely distance education; some courses available online.

Certificate Programs: Heating, Ventilating, and Air Conditioning; Environmental Health and Safety Management; Geographic Information Systems.

Class Titles: Business to Business Advertising, Business to Consumer E-Commerce Marketing, Data Communications Management, Direct Marketing, English Literature, Environmental Regulations, Geographic Information Systems, Internet as an Instructional Resource, JAVA for C++ Programmers, JAVA Programming, Marketing, Micro Classroom Applications, Midrange SQL & DB Trig Program Development, PC: Strategic and Operational Management Issues, Placing Materials on the Internet, Project Management, UNIX, Using JAVA Script in the Classroom, World of Information Systems.

Teaching Methods: *Computers:* Internet, real-time chat, electronic classroom, e-mail, CD-ROM newsgroup. *Other:* fax, correspondence, independent study, individual study, learning contracts, videoconferencing.

Credits Granted for: experiential learning, portfolios, transfer credits, examination (CLEP, ACT-PEP, DANTES, GRE)—all depending on program.

Admission Requirements: *Undergraduate:* program-specific. *Graduate:* program-specific. *Certificate:* program-specific.

On-Campus Requirements: For most programs, 30 credits must be from Ferris State University.

Tuition and Fees: Tuition rates for the upcoming academic year are set by the Board of Trustees each July. *Undergraduate:* 1–6 credits = $180/credit; 7+ credits = $190 (2000/2001 resident rates). *Graduate:* $250/credit (2000/2001 resident rate). *Postgraduate:* $4,720/semester (2000/2001 resident rate). *Application Fee:* $20 (returning students and alumni are free).

Financial Aid: Pell Grant, Supplemental Educational Opportunity Grant (SEOG), Perkins Loan, College Work Study (CWS), Nursing Loan, Health Professions Loan, Federal Direct Subsidized and Unsubsidized Loans, Federal Direct PLUS Loan, Robert Byrd Honors Program, Michigan Adult Part-Time Grant, Michigan Competitive Scholarship, Michigan Educational Opportunity Grant (MEOG), Michigan Merit Award (MEAP), Michigan Work Study, Postsecondary Access Student Scholarship (PASS), Tuition Incentive Program.

Accreditation: North Central Association of Colleges and Schools.

Description: Ferris State University (1884) is a national leader in providing opportunities for innovative teaching and learning in career-oriented, technological, and professional education. Distance education technologies and modes of delivery are used most frequently to support and enhance existing on-campus and off-campus course certificate and degree offerings.

Fielding Graduate Institute

2112 Santa Barbara Street	Phone: (800) 340-1099
Santa Barbara, CA 93105	Fax: (805) 687-9793

Division(s): None.
Web Site(s): http://www.fielding.edu
E-mail: admissions@fielding.edu

Graduate Degree Programs:
Master of Arts in Organizational Management
Master of Arts in Organizational Development

Doctoral Degree Programs:
Doctorate in Clinical Psychology (PhD)
Doctorate in Human and Organization Development (PhD)
Doctorate in Educational Leadership and Change (EdD)

Certificate Programs: Neuropsychology

Teaching Methods: *Computers:* Internet, electronic classroom, e-mail, LISTSERV. *Other:* networked learning, individual study, learning contracts, faculty mentoring, array of face-to-face academic and research seminars throughout the year.

Credits Granted for: competency-based assessment.

Admission Requirements: *Doctoral:* accredited bachelor's degree, professional and academic experience in desired field, interest and ability in graduate-level research and writing, critical thinking skills. Applicants to Psychology Program must reside within the 48 contiguous states.

On-Campus Requirements: one-week orientation session; other face-to-face opportunities at various times and locations.

Tuition and Fees: *Graduate:* $14,100 Psychology and Human and Organizational Development, $13,200 Educational Leadership and Change, $13,400 Organizational Management, $16,000 Neuropsychology (all annual tuitions). *Doctoral:* same as undergraduate. *Application Fee:* $75. *Other Costs:* variable. *Credit by:* semester.

Financial Aid: Federal Stafford Loan.

Accreditation: Western Association of Schools and Colleges, American Psychological Association.

Description: Fielding Graduate Institute (1974) was founded on the principles of adult learning and the best practices of distance education. Its scholar-practitioner model serves midcareer professionals by offering opportunities for self-directed, mentored study with the flexibility of time and location that enables students to maintain commitments to family, work, and community. An active, geographically dispersed learning community is formed from dynamic scholarly and intellectual interactions by means of electronic communication combined with an annual schedule of face-to-face events at various locations.

Finger Lakes Community College

4255 Lake Shore Drive	**Phone: (716) 394-3500**
Canandaigua, NY	**Fax: (716) 394-5005**

Division(s): Academic Affairs
Web Site(s): http://www.flcc.edu/

Undergraduate Degree Programs:
Associate in Arts
Associate in Science
Associate in Applied Science.

Certificate Programs: Contact school.

Class Titles: Offerings vary from term to term. In the last year we have offered: English, Philosophy, Business Communications, Economics, Science, Biology courses.

Teaching Methods: *Computers:* Internet, real-time chat, electronic classroom, e-mail. *TV:* videotape, cable program. *Other:* independent study, individual study, learning contracts.

Credits Granted for: experiential learning, extrainstitutional learning (PONSI, corporate or professional association seminars/workshops), examination (CLEP, ACT-PEP, DANTES, GRE).

Admission Requirements: *Undergraduate:* Basic Skills Assessment Testing.

On-Campus Requirements: students must complete a minimum of 32 credits and complete a minimum of 50% of their program major in residence for an Associate Degree.

Tuition and Fees: *Undergraduate:* $91/credit, NY State Resident; $182/credit, non NY State Resident. *Credit by:* semester.

Financial Aid: Federal Stafford Loan, Federal Perkins Loan, Federal PLUS Loan, Federal Pell Grant, Federal Work-Study, VA, state programs for residents of New York.

Accreditation: Middle States Association of Colleges and Schools.

Description: Finger Lakes Community College (1965) is a small, caring community dedicated to helping students reach their career and educational goals. Located in Canandaigua, New York, the 250-acre campus overlooks beautiful Canandaigua Lake. Additionally, the college offers extension centers in Geneva, Newark, and Victor. FLCC is one of 30 two-year community colleges within the State University of New York System. Finger Lakes Community College offers degrees in Associate in Arts, Associate in Science, Associate in Applied Science and several one-year certificate programs. Finger Lakes offers a small college environment where teachers really care about teaching and students really care about learning. Faculty and staff at Finger Lakes will know you by name. FLCC has approximately 4,000 students, and the average class section size is approximately 18. FLCC students are a diverse group, representing a wide variety of ages and life experiences.

Fisher College

118 Beacon Street	**Phone: (508) 998-6679**
Boston, MA 02116	**Fax: (508) 998-6685**

Division(s): Division of Continuing Education/Home Campus Division
Web Site(s): http://homecampus.fisher.edue-mail/
E-mail: homecampus@fisher.edu

Undergraduate Degree Programs:

Certificate Programs: Contact school.

Class Titles: Accounting, Computer Applications, Computer Technology, Web Design, e-Commerce, Management, Marketing, Economics, Organizational Behavior, Business

Policy, Legal Studies, Criminal Justice, Early Childhood Education, Psychology, Sociology, Literature, Humanities, Ethics, Finance, History of Art, American Legal System, Medical Terminology, Sciences, Preparatory Mathematics, Women's Studies.

Teaching Methods: *Computers:* Internet, real-time chat, asynchronous discussion forum, e-mail, CD-ROM, newsgroup.

Credits Granted for: examination (CLEP, ACT-PEP, DANTES, GRE).

Admission Requirements: *Undergraduate:* open admission to all, with a high school diploma or GED. *Certificate:* open admission to all, with a high school diploma or GED.

On-Campus Requirements: None.

Tuition and Fees: *Undergraduate:* $155/credit. *Software:* no fees; however, student needs appropriate software for some specific computer-type courses, such as MS Excel, Word, or Frontpage. *Graduation Fee:* $50. *Credit by:* semester.

Financial Aid: Federal Stafford Loan, Federal Perkins Loan, Federal PLUS Loan, Federal Pell Grant, Federal Work-Study, VA, state programs for residents of Massachusetts.

Accreditation: New England Association of Schools and Colleges.

Description: Fisher College (1903) is an independent college, located in downtown Boston, Massachusetts, offering curricula that integrate a liberal education with career and preprofessional programs designed to meet the changing needs of both traditional and nontraditional learners. Fisher's Division of Continuing Education, established in 1975 offers a Bachelor of Science in Management, associate degrees, and certificate programs at a number of locations in Massachusetts. Home Campus@Fisher College, the Distance Education division, began offering courses over the web in 1998, to meet the needs of busy adult students not able to attend regularly scheduled courses and degrees on campus. Course offerings quickly grew to approximately 70 credit courses and students take classes from all over the United States as well as in other countries.

Flathead Valley Community College

777 Grandview Drive	**Phone: (406) 756-3822**
Kalispell, MT 59901	**Fax: (406) 756-3815**

Division(s): Educational Services
Web Site(s): http://fvcc.cc.mt.us
E-mail: mstoltz@fvcc.cc.mt.us

Class Titles: World Regional Geography.

Teaching Methods: *TV:* TV broadcast, videotape. *Other:* None.

Credits Granted for: experiential learning, examination (CLEP), military credits, advanced placement, service learning, Tech Prep.

On-Campus Requirements: None.

Tuition and Fees: *Undergraduate:* $63/credit county resident, $97/credit Montana resident, $207/credit nonresident. *Other Costs:* $25 for equipment, $3/credit computer fee. *Credit by:* semester.

Financial Aid: Federal Stafford Loan, Federal Perkins Loan, Federal PLUS Loan, Federal Pell Grant, Federal Work-Study, VA, Montana resident programs.

Accreditation: Northwest Association of Schools and Colleges.

Description: Flathead Valley Community College (1967) is a comprehensive community college, providing college transfer, vocational, and community service classes for residents of northwestern Montana. In 1984–85 the college added the Glacier Institute program in Glacier Park and the Lincoln County Center, which provides classes to the residents of Lincoln County. In the fall of 1998 we began offering World Regional Geography via local TV broadcast. Students can also come into our instructional media center and view the tapes. We are planning to develop courses to be offered over the Internet.

Florence-Darlington Technical College

2715 West Lucas Street	**Phone: (843) 661-8031**
Florence, SC 29501	**Fax: (843) 661-8358**

Division(s): Distance Learning
Web Site(s): http://www.fdtc.org
E-mail: younginerl@flo.tec.sc.us

Undergraduate Degree Programs:
Associate in Arts

Certificate Programs: Business.

Class Titles: More than 105 online courses.

Teaching Methods: *Computers:* Internet, e-mail. *TV:* videotape, satellite broadcasting. *Other:* videoconferencing, audioconferencing, audiotapes, fax, correspondence, independent study.

Credits Granted for: examination (CLEP, ACT-PEP, DANTES).

Admission Requirements: *Undergraduate:* age 18 or high school diploma or GED certificate, college entrance requirements, SAT/ACT or computerized placement tests.

On-Campus Requirements: None.

Tuition and Fees: *Undergraduate:* $55/credit. *Application Fee:* $15. *Credit by:* semester.

Financial Aid: Federal Stafford Loan, Federal Perkins Loan, Federal PLUS Loan, Federal Pell Grant, Federal Work-Study, VA, South Carolina resident programs.

Accreditation: Southern Association of Colleges and Schools.

Description: Founded to attract industry to the state to provide employment for South Carolinians, the South Carolina Technical Education System began with legislation enacted in 1961 to create the South Carolina Advisory Committee for Technical Education. The committee identified strategic locations throughout the state for technical education training centers to train people for industrial employment. The Florence-Darlington Technical Education Center was established in 1963 and presently serves Florence, Darlington, and Marion counties. In 1974, the Florence-Darlington Technical Education Center received accreditation from the Southern Association of Colleges and Schools and changed its name to Florence-Darlington Technical College. The college's initial enrollment of 250 students now stands at 3,000 curriculum students. Its original campus of 10 acres has expanded to 100 acres with a modern complex of 7 major buildings totaling 300,000 square feet. The college also operates sites in Hartsville and Lake City and will soon open a large medical education complex in downtown Florence.

Florida Atlantic University

777 Glades Road	Phone: (561) 297-0160
Boca Raton, FL 33431	Fax: (561) 297-3668

Division(s): Distance Education and Instructional Technology (DEIT)
Web Site(s): http://www.deit.fau.edu
E-mail: marlene@fau.edu

Graduate Degree Programs:
Virtual Master's of Business Administration (VMBA)
M.S. Engineering

Certificate Programs: Gerontology.

Teaching Methods: *Computers:* Internet, newsgroup, LIST-SERV, real-time chat, electronic classrooms, e-mail, CD-ROM. *TV:* videotape, cable program, satellite broadcasting.

Credits Granted for: experiential learning determined by assessment and examination (CLEP, etc.).

Admission Requirements: *Undergraduate:* SAT or ACT. *Graduate:* GRE, GMAT.

On-Campus Requirements: None.

Tuition and Fees: *Undergraduate:* $80/credit resident, $324/credit nonresident. *Graduate:* $157/credit resident, $535/credit nonresident. *Postgraduate:* $157/credit resident, $535/credit non-resident. *Application Fee:* $20. *Credit by:* semester.

Financial Aid: Federal Stafford Loan, Federal Perkins Loan, Federal PLUS Loan, Federal Pell Grant, Federal Work Study, VA, Florida resident programs.

Accreditation: Southern Association of Colleges and Schools, AACSB.

Description: Florida Atlantic University (1961) ranks among the top universities in the nation in *U.S. News and World Report* and is one of the top 100 college buys in the country, according to *America's 100 Best College Buys R-2000*. Florida Atlantic University is a mid-size comprehensive university located in the heart of a rapidly expanding metropolitan area, encompassing cities and towns from Fort Lauderdale to Port St. Lucie. The original campus is located in Boca Raton, and the university has expanded to 6 other campuses in South Florida: Dania Beach (SeaTech), Davie, Fort Lauderdale (2 locations—Reubin O'D. Askew Tower and Commercial Boulevard), Jupiter Campus, and Port St. Lucie (Treasure Coast). FAU offers personal attention from a top-notch faculty and staff, small classes, (20-to-1 student/faculty ratio), a wide choice of majors, state-of-the-art labs, 100+ clubs and organizations including sororities, fraternities, and intramural sports, and a Division I athletics program. At FAU, more than 22,000 students enjoy a campus life that's as busy as they make it and a location just minutes away from South Florida's sunny beaches and attractions.

Florida Atlantic University College of Business

220 SE 2nd Avenue	Phone: (954) 762-5248
Fort Lauderdale, FL 33301	

Web Site(s): http://www.fau.edu/cibit/gsb
E-mail: smith@fau.edu

Graduate Degree Programs:
MBA

Class Titles: Contact school or check web site for details.

Teaching Methods: *Computers:* Internet, real-time chat, electronic classroom, e-mail, CD-ROM, newsgroup, LISTSERV. *TV:* videotape, cable program, satellite broadcasting, PBS. *Other:* radio broadcast, videoconferencing, audioconferencing, audiographics, audiotapes, fax, correspondence, independent study, individual study, learning contracts.

Admission Requirements: *Graduate:* GMAT, 3.0 GPA.

On-Campus Requirements: None.

Tuition and Fees: *Graduate:* $157/credit (in-state tuition). *Credit by:* semester.

Financial Aid: Federal Stafford Loan, Federal Perkins Loan, Federal PLUS Loan, Federal Pell Grant, Federal Work-Study, VA, state programs for residents of Florida.

Accreditation: AACSB, Southern Association of Colleges and Schools.

Description: As a fully accredited member of the American Assembly of Collegiate Schools of Business, students at Florida Atlantic University (1961) are assured of receiving a quality education from some of the world's most renowned faculty. FAU MBA students receive a well-rounded education in which analytical, logical, and communication skills are stressed. The mission of the FAU College of Business is to be one of the nation's preeminent regional business schools by consistently creating and delivering the most relevant global business and economics higher education teaching, leadership and research programs for the strategic industries in our South Florida service area, as well as for the business and not-for-profit administrative professions in the region.

Florida Community College at Jacksonville

Deerwood Center	Phone: (904) 997-2654
9911 Old Baymeadows Road	Fax: (904) 997-2727
Jacksonville, FL 32202	

Division(s): Distance Learning Office/Virtual College
Web Site(s): http://distancelearning.org
E-mail: kdobson@fccj.org

Undergraduate Degree Programs:
Associate of Arts
Associate of Science
Associate in Applied Science

Teaching Methods: *Computers:* Internet, real-time chat, e-mail, electronic classroom, WebCT, and Blackboard Learning Management Systems. LISTSERV. *TV:* videotape, cable program satellite broadcasting, PBS. *Other:* videoconferencing (ITV), fax, correspondence, independent study, individual study, learning contracts.

Admission Requirements: *Undergraduate:* Individuals seeking general admission to Florida Community College must meet the following minimum criteria: 1. The individual must be a U.S. citizen, 2. The individual must be 18 years of age or older, 3. The individual must have earned a standard or college-ready high school diploma or the equivalency of a high school diploma.

On-Campus Requirements: Some Distance Learning courses require on-campus testing and/or orientation. Please check the schedule each semester for more information.

Tuition and Fees: *Undergraduate:* $51.45/credit. *Application Fee:* $15. *Other Costs:* $10/course for Telecourses. *Credit by:* semester.

Financial Aid: All students: Federal Stafford Loan, Federal Perkins Loan, Federal PLUS Loan, FSEOG, Federal Pell Grant, Federal Work-Study, VA, Scholarships, Talent Grants, Florida State Residents: Bright Futures Scholarship Program, Florida Student Assistance Grant (FSAG).

Accreditation: Southern Association of Colleges and Schools.

Description: FCCJ (1963) is one of 28 public 2-year colleges of the Florida Community College System, and is second largest in the state and the ninth largest in the United States. Distance Learning through telecourses has been available to FCCJ students since 1979. Online courses via the Internet were introduced in 1996, and live 2-way, interactive television (ITV) courses were first offered in January 2000. FCCJ offers a robust Distance Learning program with 33–35 telecourses, 50–60 online courses, and 20–30 ITV courses each semester. FCCJ's Distance Learning program was selected as one of 10 community college programs in the country to be included in the 1996 League for Innovation Publication, "Learning without Limits: Model Distance Learning Programs in Community Colleges." In 1997 the college received the Telecourse People Award for the most outstanding telecourse program in the country. FCCJ became a member of the Florida Community College Distance Learning Consortium (FCCDLC) in 1996 and a member of the Southern Regional Electronic Campus (SREC) in 1997.

Florida State University

3500-C, University Center	Phone: Toll-Free (877) 357-8283
Tallahassee, FL 32306-2550	Fax: (850) 644-5803

Division(s): Office for Distributed and Distance Learning
Web Site(s): http://www.fsu.edu/~distance
E-mail: inquiries@oddl.fsu.edu

Undergraduate Degree Programs:
Computer and Information Science, with a major in Computer Science or Software Engineering
Information Studies
Interdisciplinary Social Science, with a concentration in Economics, Geography, or Sociology
Nursing (open only to licensed Registered Nurses in certain areas of Florida)

Graduate Degree Programs:
Criminology, with a major in Criminal Justice Studies

Library and Information Studies
Mechanical Engineering
Instructional Systems, with a major in Open and Distance Learning
Risk Management/Insurance

Class Titles: Computer Applications in Criminal Justice, Criminal Justice Administration, Crime and Delinquency, Crime Detection and Investigation, Child Growth and Development, New Communication Technology, Gender and Society in Ancient Greece, Ancient Mythology, East and West, Family Resource Management, Global Changes/Local Places, Sociology of Health Care, Policy Planning for the Aged.

Teaching Methods: *Computers:* Internet, real-time chat, e-mail, CD-ROM. *TV:* videotape.

Credits Granted for: portfolio assessment, extrainstitutional learning, examination (CLEP, ACT-PEP, DANTES, GRE).

Admission Requirements: *Undergraduate:* Florida Associates Degree or equivalent. At least 2 semesters of foreign language (high school credit may substitute). *Graduate:* at least a 3.0 GPA or have a minimum score of 1,000 on the combined verbal and quantitative portions of the Graduate Record Examinations General Test.

On-Campus Requirements: only for Nursing (RN to BSN) degree program.

Tuition and Fees: Please contact school. *Credit by:* semester.

Financial Aid: Federal Stafford Loan, Federal Perkins Loan, Federal PLUS Loan, Federal Pell Grant, Federal Work-Study, VA, Florida Student Assistance Grant (FSAG) and Bright Futures Scholarship.

Accreditation: Southern Association of Colleges and Schools.

Description: Since its founding 150 years ago, Florida State University (1851) has been guided by its mission to meet the higher education needs of the people of Florida and the U.S. The University remains rooted in its tradition of encouraging critical inquiry, promoting lifelong learning, and responding to radical transformations within professions and society—most recently the technological revolution.

FSU's distance programs integrate student/teacher collaboration, comprehensive student support, and current technology to deliver a university learning experience. Students develop a core of intellectual tools that enable them to learn efficiently and adapt quickly to new settings and challenges, long after earning their degree.

Students learning from a distance receive the same high-quality education and degrees as those students who complete on-campus programs. No distinction is made on transcripts.

Floyd College

3175 Cedartown Highway   Phone: (706) 802-5000
Rome, GA 30161   Fax: (706) 295-6610

Division(s): Instructional Technology Support
Web Site(s): http://www.fc.peachnet.edu
E-mail: marsha_welch@fc.peachnet.edu

Class Titles: Chemistry, Geology, English Literature, English Composition, American History, Political Science, Pre-Calculus, Math I, American Sign Language Interpreter Training, Economics, Psychology, Medical Terminology, Clinical Calculations.

Teaching Methods: *Computers:* Internet, real-time chat, electronic classroom, e-mail, CD-ROM, LISTSERV, digital video. *TV:* videotape, cable program. *Other:* videoconferencing.

Credits Granted for: examination (CLEP, ACT-PEP).

Admission Requirements: *Undergraduate:* traditional freshman: application, high school transcript, SAT/ACT, immunization for MMR, possible entrance exam, college prep curriculum recommended. Nontraditional freshman: application, high school diploma or GED, MMR immunization, entrance exam. Transfers: application, official transcripts and good standing from all colleges/universities, MMR immunization; might need: high school transcripts, SAT/ACT, entrance exam; must live in Georgia for one year prior to registration for resident rate (some waivers may be allowed). *Certificate:* high school transcript or GED.

On-Campus Requirements: No; however, students must compete 20 semester hours of Floyd College credit level course work in order to receive a degree.

Tuition and Fees: *Undergraduate:* $49/hour. *Software:* $75 technology fee for computer access or lease required of all students. *Other Costs:* $23 student activity fee, $17 data card fee, $2 parking fee, various courses may have lab or course participation fees required. *Credit by:* semester.

Financial Aid: Federal Pell Grant, Work-Study, Stafford Loans, Supplemental Educational Opportunity Grant, Veterans' Assistance, Georgia Student Incentive Grant, Regents' Scholarship, HOPE Scholarships, Vocational Rehabilitation, Service Cancelable Loans.

Accreditation: Southern Association of Colleges and Schools.

Description: Floyd College (1970) has 4 ways to deliver courses at a distance. FCTV, GSAMS videoconferencing, college by cassette, and online. FCTV telecourses air on the college's local cable station. GSAMS courses use 2-way audio/video inteactive videoconferencing technologies. Students must attend all sessions in a GSAMS classroom.

College by Cassette courses are contained on a series of videotapes that can be checked out from the library. Students watch these videotaped lectures and travel to campus for reviews, exams, etc. Online courses vary in their on-campus attendance requirements. In addition, the college operates 3 off-campus centers: Cartersville, Haralson County, and Acworth at North Metro Technical Institute.

Fond du Lac Tribal and Community College

2101 14th Street	Phone: (218) 879-0800
Cloquet, MN 55720	(800) 657-3712
	Fax: (218) 879-0814

Division(s): Instructional Services—Interactive TV Network
Web Site(s): http://www.fdl.cc.mn.us
E-mail: admissions@asab.fdl.cc.mn.us

Undergraduate Degree Programs:
Associate in Arts
Associate in Science
Associate in Applied Science

Certificate Programs: Anishinaabe, Child Development, Customer Service, Management Development, Microcomputer Software Specialist, Office Technology.

Class Titles: Anishinaabe Language, Federal Laws/American Indian, Survey of Bilingual American Indian Education, Chippewa of Lake Superior, Contemporary Indian Concerns, American Indian Studies, Chemical Dependency/Addiction, Chemical Dependency Counseling/Assessment, College Writing, American Indian Literature, American Indian History, Family Counseling, American Indian Philosophy, Transition to College.

Teaching Methods: *Computers:* Internet, electronic classroom. *TV:* Interactive TV Network, satellite broadcasting. *Other:* independent study, individual study by arrangement.

Credits Granted for: examination (CLEP, Advanced Placement Program), International Baccalaureate program, Evaluation of Educational Experiences in the Armed Services.

Admission Requirements: *Undergraduate:* open-door institution; all individuals, regardless of prior academic preparation, have the opportunity to advance their education at Fond du Lac Tribal and Community College. *Certificate:* same as undergraduate.

On-Campus Requirements: The Interactive TV Network is a collection of off-campus interactive classrooms. Broadcasts originate from the main campus but can be delivered to many locations.

Tuition and Fees: *Undergraduate:* $74/credit. *Application Fee:* $20. *Other Costs:* $35–$45 average textbook(s) cost/course. *Credit by:* semester.

Financial Aid: Federal Stafford Loan, Federal PLUS Loan, Federal Pell Grant, Federal Work-Study, VA, Minnesota State Grant for Minnesota residents, American Indian College Fund, Alliss Grant, Supplemental Educational Opportunity Grants, Child Care Grant.

Accreditation: North Central Association.

Description: When you walk in the door at Fond du Lac Tribal and Community College (1987), you feel like you're home. The campus is nestled among 60-foot-tall red pines, making you feel like you're in your own private forest. As part of the Minnesota State College and University system, FDLTCC awards 2-year AA, AS, and AAS degrees, plus fully transferrable degree program credits that meet the lower-division and general education requirements in most 4-year programs in the state. Several occupational and certificate options are available, including computer-related careers. As one of the newest and most technologically advanced campuses in Minnesota, the school boasts a student-computer ratio of only 6 to 1, with Internet and individual e-mail accounts available to all students. FDLTCC also offers continuing education for credit and noncredit courses, workshops, and seminars in business, communications, human services, public service, social science, arts, and recreation. FDLTCC will be adding on-campus housing and more classroom and office space. The U.S. Department of Agriculture has designated FDLTCC a Center of Excellence to provide education, employment, and research opportunities in soil science and related areas. Without a doubt, FDLTCC is a comfortable and affordable place to start a college program. With approximately 700 students, you won't get lost in the crowd.

Foothill College

12345 El Monte Road	Phone: (650) 949-7614
Los Altos, CA 94022	Fax: (650) 949-7123

Division(s): Distance and Mediated Learning
Web Site(s): http://www.foothillglobalaccess.org
E-mail: turmelle@fhda.edu

Undergraduate Degree Programs:
Associate of Arts in:
  Economics
  History
  Psychology
  Social Sciences
  General Studies

Class Titles: Please go to: www.foothillglobalaccess for complete listings of over 90 courses.

Teaching Methods: *Computers:* Internet, real-time chat, electronic classroom, e-mail, CD-ROM, newsgroup, LIST-

SERV. *TV:* videotape, cable program, satellite broadcasting, PBS. *Other:* radio broadcast, videoconferencing, audioconferencing, audiographics, audiotapes, fax, correspondence, independent study, individual study, learning contracts.

Credits Granted for: DANTES, GRE.

Admission Requirements: *Undergraduate:* see http://www.foothillglobalaccess.org/main/registration_process.htm.

On-Campus Requirements: None.

Tuition and Fees: *Undergraduate:* $7/credit. *Credit by:* quarter.

Financial Aid: Federal Stafford Loan, Federal Perkins Loan, Federal PLUS Loan, Federal Pell Grant, Federal Work-Study, VA, state programs for residents of California.

Accreditation: Western Association of Schools and Colleges.

Description: Foothill College has offered classes at community-based sites for over 20 years. A rewarding career starts with an ambitious student, expert faculty, and an innovative curriculum. Foothill College is your on ramp to a career in today's competitive job market. Today, more than 5,000 students take classes at the Middlefield Campus and 60 other locations in Palo Alto, Mountain View, Los Altos, Menlo Park, Moffett Field, and other surrounding communities. We strive to offer online courses that meet the same high academic standards as traditional classes. The main difference is the delivery method. Through our program, you can now earn associate degrees in general studies/social science, economics, or history. These degrees are fully transferable and can be completed mostly online. A few courses, such as speech, English, and math, may require occasional meetings or proctored exams. Students who complete an intensive career training program at Foothill are aggressively recruited for hot, in-demand jobs. Employers value Foothill graduates and recognize our nationwide reputation for quality training. Foothill offers more than 40 career choices. When you enroll in a career program at Foothill College, you're guaranteed expert instruction and value. At Foothill, you, "our student," are the most important person on campus.

Fort Hays State University

600 Park Street   Phone: (800) 628-FHSU
Hays, KS 67601   Fax: (785) 628-4037

Division(s): Virtual College
Web Site(s): http://www.fhsu.edu/virtual_college
E-mail: v_college@fhsu.edu

Undergraduate Degree Programs:
Bachelor of General Studies
Bachelor of Science in Justice Studies

Graduate Degree Programs:
Master of Liberal Studies

Certificate Programs: Cisco On-line Certification Prep Program for Cisco Certified Network Associate (CCNA), Leadership, Gerontology, Ethnic Studies, more than 100 professional development and salary enhancement courses for teachers, 13 three-credit-hour, award-winning business courses, 26 one-credit-hour organizational leadership training courses.

Class Titles: Leadership Studies, Speech Language Pathology, Institute in Education: Assistive Technology, Agriculture, Art, Biology, Business Administration, General Business, Management, Accounting, Marketing, Communication, Information Networking and Telecommunications, Computer and Information Systems, Business Communications, Economics and Finance, Educational Administration and Counseling, Counseling, Educational Administration, English, Geography, Geology, Health and Human Performance, History, Interdisciplinary Studies, Modern Language, Music, Nursing, Justice Studies, Political Science, Psychology, Sociology, Social Work, Special Education, Teacher Education, Elementary Education, Library Science.

Teaching Methods: *Computers:* Internet, real-time chat, electronic classroom, e-mail, CD-ROM, newsgroup, LISTSERV. *TV:* videotape, cable program, satellite broadcasting, PBS. *Other:* videoconferencing, audioconferencing, audiographics, audiotapes, fax, correspondence, independent study, individual study.

Credits Granted for: examination (CLEP, ACT-PEP, DANTES, GRE).

Admission Requirements: *Undergraduate:* under 21 years of age, must meet qualified admissions (information available from Virtual College); no residency requirement. *Graduate:* must be admitted to graduate school before taking classes (information available from Virtual College).

On-Campus Requirements: None.

Tuition and Fees: *Undergraduate:* $112/credit hour. *Graduate:* $224/credit hour. *Application Fee:* $25. *Other Costs:* $30 for media fee for 1-credit hour course, $35 for media fee for 2-credit hour course, $40 media fee for 3-credit hour course. *Credit by:* semester.

Financial Aid: Federal Stafford Loan, Federal Perkins Loan, Federal PLUS Loan, Federal Pell Grant, Federal Work-Study, VA, state programs for residents of Kansas, TA for Navy sailors.

Accreditation: North Central Association of Colleges and Schools.

Description: FHSU (1902) was established as a public institution of higher education in western Kansas. The campus includes more than 40 beautiful limestone-faced buildings that are wired for the latest technology. FHSU is comprised of 4 academic colleges: Arts and Sciences, Business and Leadership, Education, and Health and Life Sciences. The university also has a growing graduate school. FHSU has vigorously embraced technology over the past decade. Students all over the world are relying on FHSU's Virtual College to deliver a quality education. Many scholars and specialists are among the more than 300 full-time faculty members at FHSU who couple superb teaching with a warm and caring attitude. Your professors continually interact with you, encouraging you to succeed with new content and concepts. Faculty also work as advisors to help students reach their academic goals.

Fort Peck Community College

PO Box 398, Highway 2	Phone: (406) 768-3231
Poplar, MT 59255	Fax: (406) 768-5475

Division(s): Academics
Web Site(s): Search for Fort Peck Community College
E-mail: donnab@fpcc.cc.mt.us

Undergraduate Degree Programs:
Bachelor of Science in:
  Elementary Education—Rocky Mountain College and Montana State University-Northern Applied Business Management (Degree Completion Program)—Rocky Mountain College
  Information Technology—Three College Consortium (Rocky Mountain is the degree granting Institute)
Associate of Arts Degrees:
  American Indian Studies
  Business Administration
  Business Administration—
    Management Option
  Business Administration—
    Entrepreneur Option
  Education
  Early Childhood Education
  Visual Arts
  Human Services
  Psychology
Associate of Science:
  Computer Operator/
    Service Technician
  Hazardous Material/
    Waste Technology
  Human Services—
    Wellness Option
  Science—Biomedical
  Science—Environmental
  Science—Education
Associate of Applied Science:
  Agricultural Technology
  Automotive Technology
  Building Trades
  Electronics Technology
  Hazardous Material/Waste
    Technology
  Internetworking

Business—E-Commerce
Chemical Dependency
  Counseling
Specialist/Professional—
  Service
Technician
Office Technology
Surveying

Graduate Degree Programs:
Education (Learning Development)—Montana State University—Northern

Certificate Programs: Contact school or check web site.

Class Titles: Select agricultural courses available from Montana State University-Bozeman on demand.

Teaching Methods: *Computers:* Internet, real-time chat, e-mail. *TV:* videotape, cable program, satellite broadcasting, PBS. *Other:* videoconferencing, audioconferencing, fax, independent study, individual study, and 2 interactive television systems (PictureTel and Vision Net).

Credits Granted for: directed study, independent study, and special topics.

On-Campus Requirements: None.

Tuition and Fees: determined by degree-granting institution. *Credit by:* semester.

Financial Aid: Federal Pell Grant, Federal Work-Study, VA, Montana resident programs.

Accreditation: Northwest Association of Schools and Colleges.

Description: Fort Peck Community College (1969) is a tribally-controlled institution chartered by the governments of the Fort Peck Assiniboine and Sioux tribes. Although FPCC does not deny anyone the opportunity for higher education, the school's primary purpose is to serve the Indian population of the Fort Peck Reservation. To preserve Indian culture, history, and beliefs and to perpetuate them among all Indian people are important functions of the college. Since many of the people choose not to leave their homeland, education must be brought to them. FPCC's programs enable students to earn transferrable college credits. The college also maintains occupational programs based on the needs of the local people and on local employment opportunities.

Fort Scott Community College

2108 South Horton	Phone: (316) 223-2700
Fort Scott, KS 66701	Fax: (316) 223-4927

Division(s): Dean of Instruction and Interactive Distance Learning Facilitator
Web Site(s): http://www.ftscott.cc.ks.us
E-mail: beckyme@ftscott.cc.ks.us

Class Titles: English, Sociology, Algebra, History, Psychology, Music Appreciation, varies with semester.

Teaching Methods: *TV:* interactive TV. *Other:* fax, telephone, U.S. postal services.

Admission Requirements: *Undergraduate:* open-enrollment; high school juniors/seniors with principal's permission.

On-Campus Requirements: None.

Tuition and Fees: *Undergraduate:* $31/credit resident, $59/credit nonresident, border states, Missouri, Oklahoma, Nebraska, Colorado, $87/credit nonresident other states, $109/credit international. *Other Costs:* $14/credit fees.

Financial Aid: Federal Stafford Loan, Federal Plus Loan, Federal Pell Grant, Federal Work-Study, VA, Single Parent, Supplemental Educational Opportunity Grants, endowed and institutional scholarships.

Accreditation: North Central Association of Colleges and Schools.

Description: Fort Scott Community College (1919) is the oldest community college in Kansas, founded as Fort Scott Junior College. In 1965, we became a separate institution and were renamed Fort Scott Community College. We moved to the present 147-acre site in 1967. Early in 1982, the college completed Arnold Arena. One side is an agricultural and rodeo arena with earth floor and welded pipe pens. The other half contains a basketball gym, weight training area, athletic dressing rooms, classrooms, and athletic offices. N. Jack Burris Hall was built in 1989 for the Environmental Water Technology program. It also houses our Interactive Distance Learning Lab where we teach ITV college courses to area high school students and other community colleges, including our own Paola, Kansas extension site. The IDL lab began operation in 1996. We also receive courses from Pittsburg State University, and the lab is used by the community for satellite downlinks and videoconferences. We can interact with 3 sites simultaneously through the use of video cameras, microphones, monitors, and asynchronous transmission over fiber optic cables.

Fox Valley Technical College

1825 North Bluemound Drive	Phone: (920) 735-5600
Appleton, WI 54923-2277	(800) 735-FVTC (3882)
	Fax: (920) 735-2582

Division(s): Instructional Support Services
Web Site(s): www.foxvalley.tec.com
E-mail: admissions@foxvalley.tec.wi.us

Undergraduate Degree Programs: more than 70 associate degree and technical diploma programs

Certificate Programs: more than 70 short-term certificate offerings

Teaching Methods: *Computers:* Internet, real-time chat, electronic classroom, e-mail, CD-ROM. *TV:* videotape, cable program, satellite broadcasting. *Other:* videoconferencing, audioconferencing, fax, correspondence, independent study, individual study, learning contracts.

Credits Granted for: portfolio assessment, seminars/workshops, examination (CLEP, ACT-PEP, DANTES, GRE).

Admission Requirements: *Undergraduate:* for career programs—high school graduate or demonstrated ability to master subject matter, academic assessment or ACT scores. Some programs have additional requirements. High school students can begin applying in February of their junior year.

On-Campus Requirements: None.

Tuition and Fees: *Undergraduate:* $77–$80/credit. *Application Fee:* $30. *Credit by:* semester.

Financial Aid: Federal Stafford Loan, Federal PLUS Loan, Federal Pell Grant, Federal Work-Study, VA, Wisconsin Higher Education Grant, Talent Incentive Program Grant, Indian Student Assistance, Fox Valley Technical College Foundation Scholarships.

Accreditation: North Central Association of Colleges and Schools.

Description: Established in 1967 as one of 16 districts in the Wisconsin Technical College System, the Fox Valley Technical College district encompasses a 5-county area in northeastern Wisconsin. Each year more than 50,000 people enroll in at least one course through FVTC. The college has been actively involved with distance learning since the mid-1980s. The two main campuses and 5 Regional Centers have been connected by Interactive Television for nearly 20 years. Additionally, partnerships have been established with the following networks:

Wisconsin Technical College Network (WTCN) established in 1998, a consortium of the 16 technical colleges making up the Wisconsin Technical College System; Wisconsin Overlay Network for Distance Education Resources (WONDER) established in 1992, a consortium of 12 educational institutions: 5 University System schools, 4 technical colleges, and 3 high schools; K-12 Schools/College Alliance for Distance Education (KSCADE) established in 1998, a consortium comprised of 29 high school districts, 1 University System school, and 2 technical colleges. Fox Valley Technical College currently has 65 Internet courses available on the Internet.

Franciscan University of Steubenville

1235 University Boulevard
Steubenville, OH 43952

Phone: (740) 283-6517
(800) 466-8336
Fax: (740) 284-7037

Division(s): Distance Learning
Web Site(s): www.franuniv.edu
E-mail: distance@franuniv.edu

Graduate Degree Programs:
Master of Arts in Theology and Christian Ministry.

Class Titles: Theology, Philosophy.

Teaching Methods: *Other:* audiotapes with corresponding study guides.

Admission Requirements: *Undergraduate:* official copies of high school transcript and all college work. *Graduate:* undergraduate degree, official copies of college transcripts, 3 recommendations, and possible undergraduate prerequisites.

On-Campus Requirements: 6 credits.

Tuition and Fees: *Undergraduate:* $175/credit. *Graduate:* $175/credit. *Application Fee:* $20. *Other Costs:* $50 for media package audiotapes and study guide. Shipping and textbooks are extra. *Credit by:* Each course is worth 3 semester credits.

Accreditation: North Central Association of Colleges and Schools.

Description: Over the years, Franciscan University of Steubenville (1946) has received numerous requests for distance learning courses in Catholic theology, philosophy, and history. Under the persevering leadership of Fr. Michael Scanlan, TOR, now serving as Chancellor of the university, we have responded to those requests by establishing Franciscan University Distance Learning. In 1994 Distance Learning began recording graduate theology courses live in the classroom. Several undergraduate theology and philosophy courses were also recorded to provide background requirements for applicants with undergraduate degrees in other fields of study. Franciscan University of Steubenville received approval to offer the Master of Arts in Theology and Christian Ministry degree through Distance Learning in March 1999.

Franklin University

201 South Grant Avenue
Columbus, OH 43215-5399

Phone: (888) 341-6237
Fax: (614) 341-6366

Division(s): Distance Education
Web Site(s): http://www.alliance.franklin.edu
E-mail: alliance@franklin.edu

Undergraduate Degree Programs:
Completion degrees in:
    Business Administration
    Technical Management
    Computer Science
    Management Information Sciences
    Health Care Management
    Public Safety Management
    Digital Communication
Subsequent degrees in:
    Computer Science
    Management Information Systems

Teaching Methods: *Computers:* Internet, real-time chat, electronic classroom, e-mail, CD-ROM, newsgroup, LISTSERV. *Other:* audioconferencing, fax.

Admission Requirements: *Undergraduate:* completion programs—accredited associate degree or 60 credit hours, 2.5 GPA, enrollment in an Alliance Partnership. Subsequent degree programs—accredited bachelor's degree.

On-Campus Requirements: students enrolled in a completion degree program will complete some of their required course work through a local Alliance Partner that may include a traditional classroom setting. Students enrolled in the subsequent degree programs can complete all of the required course work outside of the traditional classroom setting.

Tuition and Fees: *Undergraduate:* $212/credit, standard courses; $258/credit, Computer Science and MIS (management information sciences) courses. *Credit by:* semester.

Financial Aid: Financial Aid, Federal Stafford Loan, Federal PLUS Loan, Federal Pell Grant, Federal Work-Study, VA, Federal Supplemental Educational Opportunity Grant, Franklin University Transfer Grant, Ohio resident programs, Lifetime Learning Credit.

Accreditation: North Central Association of Colleges and Schools.

Description: Franklin University (1902) has served 20,000 alumni since 1902. Annually, nearly 7,000 students pursue programs leading to Bachelor of Science degrees. Franklin University is a student-centered, independent institution of lifelong higher education, working in partnership with central Ohio's business, Alliance Partnerships nationwide, and the professional business community in a global context. The university promotes excellence in teaching and the use of appropriate technology to deliver accessible, innovative, measurably effective learning, which integrates theory and develops the ability of students to become lifelong learners. To accomplish this goal, Franklin University's Distance Education program is designed and faculty are prepared to develop the following skills and abilities of students: problem finding and problem solving, active researcher, collaborative thinker/worker/team member, strategist, leader, communicator and critical thinker. Students will discover that online courses are interactive, inquiry-based, focused on real-world learning and taught by faculty who are experienced practitioners.

Friends University

2100 University Avenue
Wichita, Kansas 67213

Phone: (316) 295-5881
Fax: (316) 295-5060

Division(s): Academic Affairs
Web Site(s): http://friends.edu
E-mail: doveb@friend.edu

Undergraduate Degree Programs:
Organizational Management and Leadership
Electronic Commerce Management

Graduate Degree Programs:
Master of Arts in Teaching

Class Titles: Contact school or check web site for details.

Teaching Methods: *Computers:* Internet, electronic classroom, e-mail, CD-ROM, LISTSERV.

Credits Granted for: experiential learning, portfolio assessment, extrainstitutional learning (PONSI, corporate or professional association seminars/workshops), examination (CLEP, ACT-PEP, DANTES, GRE).

Admission Requirements: *Undergraduate:* 62 hours of credit from an accredited institution, 25 years of age, Writing 1 and 2. *Graduate:* teaching certificate, bachelor's degree from an accredited college.

On-Campus Requirements: All courses are partly on ground and partly by Distance delivery. No course or program is more than 40% by Distance delivery.

Tuition and Fees: *Undergraduate:* $308.25/credit. *Graduate:* $360.25/credit. *Application Fees:* $20, Undergraduate, $45. *Software:* $15/term, undergraduate only. *Other Costs:* curriculum fee. $40/credit hour, undergraduate only, *Portfolio* fee: $40/credit hour, undergraduate only. *Credit by:* semester.

Financial Aid: Federal Stafford Loan, Federal Perkins Loan, Federal PLUS Loan, Federal Pell Grant, Federal Work-Study, VA, state programs for residents of Kansas. Graduate: Loan Programs only.

Accreditation: The Higher Learning Commission of the North Central Association of Colleges and Schools, National Council for Accreditation of Teacher Education.

Description: Friends University (1898) is an independent comprehensive university founded by the Society of Friends

(Quakers) more than 100 years ago. We currently have more than 3,000 students in Wichita and throughout Kansas. Online instruction was begun 4 years ago and is done primarily as a support to adult cohort bachelor's and graduate programs.

Front Range Community College

3645 West 112th Avenue
Westminster, CO 80031

Phone: (303) 404-5513
Fax: (303) 404-5156

Division(s): Technology Based Learning Center
Web Site(s): http://frontrange.rightchoice.org
E-mail: adrienne.calvo@wc.frcc.cccoes.edu

Undergraduate Degree Programs:
Associates of Arts
Associates of Applied Sciences in Business Administration
Associates of General Studies

Certificate Programs: Legal Assisting (Paralegal).

Class Titles: Anthropology, Biology, Business and Management, Chemistry, Computer Information Systems, Computer Programming, Computer Applications, Web Authoring, Economics, English Composition and Creative Writing, Technical Writing, Journalism, Speech and Communications, Early Childhood Professions, Geography, Geology, History, Humanities, Marketing, Math, Paralegal, Philosophy, Physics, Political Science, Psychology, Sociology.

Teaching Methods: *Computers:* Internet, *TV:* videotape, PBS.

Credits Granted for: portfolio assessment, examination (CLEP, ACT-PEP, DANTES, GRE).

Admission Requirements: *Undergraduate:* All degree- or certificate-seeking students and those taking more than one course must take an assessment test before enrolling for courses.

On-Campus Requirements: None.

Tuition and Fees: *Undergraduate:* $60.05/resident, 291.35 nonresident. *Credit by:* semester.

Financial Aid: Federal Stafford Loan, Federal PLUS Loan, Federal Pell Grant, Federal Work-Study, VA, Colorado resident programs.

Accreditation: North Central Association of Colleges and Schools.

Description: Front Range (1970) is the leader in distance education in Colorado. We have offered distance courses since 1979 and have more than 100 different courses online or in telecourse format. We offer a paralegal certificate completely online and are just finishing developing the courses for a complete associates degree in business. Most of our students are in Colorado, but we have successful students from as far away as Japan and Eastern Europe.

Frostburg State University

101 Braddock Road   Phone: (301) 687-4353
Frostburg, MD 21532   Fax: (301) 687-3025

Division(s): Instructional Technology Support Center
Web Site(s): http://www.fsu.umd.edu
E-mail: fsuweb@fre.fsu.umd.edu

Class Titles: Accounting, Business Administration, Criminal Justice, Education, Engineering, English, French, Political Science, Recreation

Teaching Methods: *Computers:* Internet, real-time chat, electronic classroom, e-mail. *TV:* videotape. *Other:* audiotapes, fax, independent study, extended classroom using compressed and full motion video.

Credits Granted for: pass-by-examination.

Admission Requirements: *Undergraduate:* see Web site: (http://www.fsu.umd.edu/ungrad/unadmiss.htm). *Graduate:* see Web site: (http://www.fsu.umd.edu/grad/gradmiss.htm).

On-Campus Requirements: Combination of distance learning and traditional to complete degrees.

Tuition and Fees: *Undergraduate:* $142/credit in-state part-time, $252 out-of-state part-time, $1,722 full-time in-state, $4,471 full-time out-of-state. *Graduate:* $170/credit in-state, $217/credit out-of-state. *Application Fee:* $30 graduate application. *Other Costs:* vary for athletic fee, Student Union operating fee, auxiliary facilities fee, transportation fee, and optional activity fee depending on status as full/part-time, in-state/out-of-state, undergraduate/graduate. *Credit by:* semester.

Financial Aid: Federal Stafford Loan, Federal Perkins Loan, Federal PLUS Loan, Federal Pell Grant, Federal Work-Study, VA, Maryland resident programs.

Accreditation: Middle States Association of Colleges and Schools, Council on Social Work Education, Interorganizational Board of Master's in Psychology Programs.

Description: Frostburg State University (1898) is a comprehensive constituent of the University System of Maryland. Originally established to train elementary school teachers, Frostburg now offers 35 undergraduate programs to 4,430 undergraduates and 17 master's degree programs to 918 graduate students. FSU consists of a main campus in Frostburg and off-campus centers in Hagerstown and

Frederick. A recently established program site in Catonsville provides a master's degree in Parks and Recreation Resource Management through traditional classes and distance education. Since 1970, FSU has sponsored off-campus courses and programs at various sites in the state. Distance education emerged in 1995 when faculty applied technology that linked classrooms at different locations. In 1998, FSU added to its array of alternative delivery mechanisms through online courses.

Fuller Theological Seminary

135 North Oakland Avenue   Phone: (626) 584-5266
Pasadena, CA 91182   Fax: (626) 304-3740

Division(s): Distance Learning
Web Site(s): http://www.fuller.edu
E-mail: idl@fuller.edu

Certificate Programs: Christian Studies, Youth and Family Ministries.

Class Titles: courses toward certificates and degrees in our School of Theology MA and MDiv programs and our School of World Mission (MA and ThM programs).

Teaching Methods: *Computers:* Internet, real-time chat, electronic classroom, e-mail, CD-Rom. *TV:* videotape. *Other:* audiotapes, fax, correspondence, independent study, individual study.

Credits Granted for: accredited graduate level credit.

Admission Requirements: *Graduate:* accredited bachelor's degree or equivalent. Admission is granted to a specific program, not to Fuller Seminary or its schools at large. Fuller depends on factors beyond applicant's academic record, including theological development, Christian experience, spiritual growth, call to service, and gifts for ministry. Men and women of God are qualified for Christian ministry by faith, moral character, experience, and academic achievement. *Doctoral:* see graduate requirements. *Certificate:* see graduate requirements; see Fuller's catalog for complete details.

On-Campus Requirements: Residency requirements vary by degree program. Consult Fuller's catalog.

Tuition and Fees: *Graduate:* consult catalog or contact Admissions Department, (800) 238-5537. *Doctoral:* see graduate. *Credit by:* quarter.

Financial Aid: Federal Stafford Loan, Federal Perkins Loan, Federal Work-Study, VA, California resident programs.

Accreditation: Association of Theological Schools (ATS), Western Association of Schools and Colleges.

Description: Fuller Theological Seminary is the product of the vision and work of radio evangelist Charles E. Fuller and pastor/writer Harold John Ockenga. Started just after the end of World War II, Fuller has grown to be the largest seminary in the United States. Its Schools of Theology, Psychology, and World Mission are characterized by an evangelical, multidenominational, international, and multiethnic commitment. Its mission is to prepare men and women for the manifold ministries of Christ and His Church. For more than a quarter century, Fuller has been involved in Distance Learning. Today, the use of Internet and other technologies as well as more traditional approaches are employed to bring the classroom to students anywhere at any time. Courses offered include those from the Schools of Theology World Mission. Starting in the fall of 2001, students can earn a master's degree from Fuller Theological Seminary at a distance.

Fullerton College

321 East Chapman Avenue	Phone: (714) 992-7487
Fullerton, CA 92832-2095	Fax: (714) 879-3972

Division(s): Distance Education
Web Site(s): http://wwwmedia.fullcoll.edu
E-mail: admiss.reg@fullcoll.edu

Class Titles: History, Oceanography, Business, Psychology, Stress Management, Sociology, Cinema, Geography, English as Second Language.

Teaching Methods: *Computers:* Internet, real-time chat, electronic classroom, e-mail, CD-ROM, newsgroup, LISTSERV. *TV:* videotape, cable program, PBS. *Other:* videoconferencing, audiotapes, fax, correspondence, independent study, individual study, VHS tapes.

Credits Granted for: examination.

Admission Requirements: *Undergraduate:* please see catalog on Web site.

On-Campus Requirements: orientation and testing (usually).

Tuition and Fees: *Undergraduate:* $11/credit (maximum $60/semester). *Credit by:* semester.

Financial Aid: Federal Stafford Loan, Federal Perkins Loan, Federal PLUS Loan, Federal Pell Grant, Federal Work-Study, California resident programs.

Accreditation: Western Association of Schools and Colleges.

Description: Fullerton College (1913) is a Southern California community college with a history as the oldest existing college in the state. Fullerton began distance education in 1981 with the cablecasting of telecourses to the North Orange County area. We now serve 165,000 households in 8 cities.

Fulton-Montgomery Community College

2805 State Highway 67	Phone: (518) 762-4651
Johnstown, NY 12095	Fax: (518) 762-4334

Division(s): Business and Technology Department
Web Site(s): http://www.fmcc.suny.edu
E-mail: schristi@fmcc.suny.edu

Undergraduate Degree Programs:
Associate in:
  Arts
  Sciences
  Applied Sciences
  Occupational Studies

Certificate Programs: contact school.

Class Titles: Economics, Health/Nutrition, Statistics, Computers, Multimedia Technology, Accounting, Library Resources, Physical Education, Political Science, English.

Teaching Methods: *Computers:* Internet, real-time chat, electronic classroom, e-mail. *TV: Other:* fax, independent study.

Credits Granted for: experiential learning, portfolio assessment, extrainstitutional learning (PONSI, corporate or professional association seminars/workshops), examination (CLEP, ACT-PEP, DANTES).

Admission Requirements: *Undergraduate:* admission is open to any individual who has earned a high school diploma or GED and whose academic records, potential, and personal qualifications meet with the deadlines and requirements established by the college in its admissions procedures. Applicants, 18 years of age or older, who do not have a high school diploma or GED, will be considered for admission based on demonstrated ability to benefit from college-level work determined by scores on the college's placement test. SAT or ACT tests are not required. High school students wishing to supplement their high school education must contact the Admissions Office to determine eligibility for college study. Non-NYS residents pay out-of-state tuition charges.

On-Campus Requirements: None.

Tuition and Fees: *Undergraduate:* $99/credit (NYS resident), $198/credit (non-NYS residents). *Application Fees:* Free. *Graduation Fee:* $30. *Other Costs: Technology Fee:* 9 or more credits: $60, 8 or fewer credits: $38, *Student Activity Fee:* 12 credits: $65, Part-time: $2/CR *Credit by:* semester.

Financial Aid: Federal Stafford Loan, Federal Perkins Loan, Federal PLUS Loan, Federal Pell Grant, Federal Supplemental Educational Opportunity Grant, Federal Work-Study, VA, state programs for residents of New York: New York State Tuition Assistance Program, Educational Opportunity Program.

Accreditation: Middle States Association of Colleges and Schools.

Description: Fulton-Montgomery Community College (1963), a unit of the State University of New York, is dedicated to providing quality educational opportunities through affordable, accessible, comprehensive services and a commitment to excellence and integrity. Situated in the foothills of the Adirondack Mountains just 40 miles from Albany, New York, capital, FMCC has newly renovated facilities, state-of-the-art technology, and beautifully landscaped grounds. The college has over 50 academic programs leading to associate degrees in Arts, Sciences, Applied Sciences, Occupational Studies, as well as college certificates. FMCC began offering Distance Learning Opportunities in strategically selected program areas in 1999 and is in the process of developing its first on-line degree program in Business Administration (AS degree). The college has joined the SUNY Learning Network and plans to gradually expand its on-line course offerings.

Fuqua School of Business, Duke University

| One Towerview Drive | Phone: (919) 660-7804 |
| Durham, NC 27708-0120 | Fax: (919) 660-8044 |

Division(s): Executive MBA Programs
Web Site(s): http://www.fuqua.duke.edu
E-mail: cross-continent-info@fuqua.duke.edu

Graduate Degree Programs:
Master of Business Administration

Teaching Methods: *Computers:* Internet, real-time chat, e-mail, CD-ROM, newsgroup, bulletin board discussions. *Other:* fax, correspondence phone.

Admission Requirements: *Graduate:* 3 to 9 years' professional work experience, bachelor's degree or equivalent, GMAT, TOEFL (non-native English speakers), recommendations, company sponsorship letter.

On-Campus Requirements: Students attend 9 weeks of residential sessions (8 one-week sessions plus one week of orientation during the first residency). They can attend residencies in either Durham, N.C. or Frankfurt, Germany. Students switch campuses in order to co-mingle with their counterparts from the other continent one to three times during the program. A residency occurs approximately once every 10 weeks.

Tuition and Fees: *Graduate:* $74,000 or equivalent in euros covers the full 20 months of the program. Tuition includes books and other class materials, and lodging and meals while attending the 8 residential sessions. Tuition does not include travel to and from the residential sessions, a laptop computer, or a personal Internet service provider (ISP). A nonrefundable deposit is due upon admission to the program. *Application Fee:* $150 (nonrefundable). There are 8 terms of 10 weeks duration each comprising the 20-month program. Students take 2 classes per term, for a total of 16 classes (48 credits): 11 required courses, 4 electives, and one integrative capstone course.

Financial Aid: Federal Stafford Loan, International Student Loans (Duke administered).

Accreditation: American Association of Collegiate Schools of Business.

Description: The Fuqua School of Business (1970) is the youngest of the top-tier U.S. business schools and has a current annual enrollment of approximately 1,000 in its degree programs. In 1980 Atlanta entrepreneur J. B. Fuqua provided a generous financial gift that allowed the school to rapidly rise in stature. Fuqua's online learning debuted in 1996 as part of the Duke MBA-Global Executive program. This program pioneered the use of significant online learning combined with more traditional classroom teaching in a model Duke calls "place and space." In October, 1999 Duke University announced the establishment of the Fuqua School of Business Europe in Frankfurt, Germany. This campus serves as European headquarters for a portion of the students in the Duke MBA-Cross Continent program, which enrolled its first class in August, 2000. Cross Continent also combines classroom teaching with on-line, Internet-enabled learning, balancing one week of face-to-face interaction with 6 weeks on online activity. In 2001 *US News & World Report* ranked Fuqua's executive MBA programs #2 nationally.

Garland County Community College

101 College Drive
Hot Springs, AR 71913-9174

Phone: (501) 760-4155
Fax: (501) 760-4100

Division(s): Community Services/Continuing Education
Web Site(s): http://www.gccc.cc.ar.us
http://www.edzgo.com/gccc
E-mail: rjeffery@admin.gccc.cc.ar.us

Class Titles: a variety of computer classes and supervisory management classes for noncredit. For-credit telecourses: Small Business Management, Geography, Health/Safety, Psychology, Sociology, History, Literature, Art Appreciation, others. Schedule changes each semester, and we offer more telecourses each semester.

Teaching Methods: *Computers:* Internet, real-time chat, electronic classroom, e-mail, CD-ROM, newsgroup, LISTSERV. *TV:* videotape, cable program, satellite broadcasting, PBS. *Other:* videoconferencing, audioconferencing, audiotapes, fax, correspondence, independent study, individual study, learning contracts.

Credits Granted for: experiential learning (corporate or professional association seminars/workshops), portfolio assessment, examination (CLEP, ACT-PEP, DANTES, GRE).

Admission Requirements: *Undergraduate:* application, high school transcript or GED, proof of immunization, ASSET/ACT/SAT. *Certificate:* same as undergraduate.

On-Campus Requirements: 18 hours.

Tuition and Fees: *Undergraduate:* contact school or visit Web site (costs are per class and include books, etc.). *Credit by:* semester.

Financial Aid: Federal Stafford Loan, Federal Perkins Loan, Federal PLUS Loan, Federal Pell Grant, Federal Work-Study, VA, Arkansas resident programs, Emergency Secondary Education Loan Program, Garland County Community College Scholarships, JTPA, Single Parent/Homemaker Program.

Accreditation: North Central Association of Colleges and Schools, National League for Nursing Accrediting Commission, Commission on the Accreditation of Allied Health Educational Programs, Joint Review Committee in Education on Radiologic Technology, Association of Collegiate Business Schools and Programs, National Accrediting Agency for Clinical Laboratory Sciences.

Description: Garland County Community College (1973) was established as a public 2-year college to provide postsecondary educational opportunities to the citizens of Garland County and surrounding areas. The college is located in Mid-American Park, just outside the city limits of Hot Springs, America's oldest national park. The average enrollment is 1,800 per semester at this commuter college. While the majority of our students are Garland County residents, many students from surrounding counties also enroll. A profile shows that 44.4% of all students attend full time. Some 65% are female, 7.13% are minority, and 5.4% are dual-enrolled high school/college students. A majority (61.9%) receive some form of financial aid. The average age of our graduates is 30. Since 80% of our students work and attend college, many of them find the early morning, evening, and weekend classes an advantage. As an integral part of this community GCCC recognizes the necessity of providing services to meet the needs of the area's business, industry, and schools. Distance Education at GCCC is relatively new, but our goal is to work toward providing courses any time and any place to meet the needs of our students.

Gateway Community College

60 Sargent Drive
New Haven, CT 06511

Phone: (203) 285-2108
Fax: (203) 285-2038

Division(s): Department of Instructional Design
Web Site(s): http://www.gwctc.commnet.edu
E-mail: gw_samberg@commnet.edu

Undergraduate Degree Programs: Contact school.

Certificate Programs: Contact school.

Class Titles: American Public Policy, Sociology, English, English As A Second Language (ESL), Business, Biology.

Teaching Methods: *Computers:* Internet, real-time chat, electronic classroom, e-mail, CD-ROM. *TV:* videotape, cable program, satellite broadcasting, PBS. *Other:* radio broadcast, videoconferencing, audioconferencing, audiographics, audiotapes, fax, correspondence, independent study, individual study, learning contracts.

Credits Granted for: experiential learning, portfolio assessment, extrainstitutional learning (PONSI, corporate or professional association seminars/workshops), examination (CLEP, ACT-PEP, DANTES, GRE).

Admission Requirements: *Undergraduate:* open enrollment, community college.

Tuition and Fees: *Undergraduate:* $70/credit. *Credit by:* semester.

Financial Aid: Federal Stafford Loan, Federal Perkins Loan, Federal PLUS Loan, Federal Pell Grant, Federal Work-Study, VA, state programs for residents of Connecticut.

Accreditation: Connecticut Board of Governors for Higher Education and accredited by the New England Association of Schools and Colleges.

Description: Gateway Community College adopted the following mission statement in 1997: to offer high-quality instruction and comprehensive services in an environment conducive to learning. We respond to the changing academic, occupational, technological, and cultural needs of a diverse population. Gateway is located on 2 campuses, the Long Wharf Campus in New Haven and the North Haven Campus. The college offers over 70 academic programs or program options that lead to either Associate in Arts, Science, or Applied Science degrees, or certificates, and the faculty ranks among the finest educators in Connecticut.

Gavilan College

5055 Santa Teresa Boulevard	Phone: (408) 848-4705
Gilroy, CA 95020-9578	Fax: (408) 848-3077

Division(s): Learning Center
Web Site(s): http://gavilan.cc.ca.us
E-mail: vestrada@gavilan.cc.ca.us

Class Titles: Telecourses: Child Development, English, Humanities, Archaeology, Anthropology.

Teaching Methods: *Computers:* Internet, real-time chat, electronic classroom, e-mail, CD-ROM, newsgroup, LISTSERV. *TV:* videotape, cable program. *Other:* audioconferencing, videoconferencing, audiotapes, fax, independent study, individual study, learning contracts.

Credits Granted for: examination (CLEP, ACT-PEP, DANTES, GRE).

Admission Requirements: *Undergraduate:* age 18, high school graduate, or able to profit from instruction. *Certificate:* varies.

On-Campus Requirements: Telecourse orientations, exams.

Tuition and Fees: *Undergraduate:* $12/credit. *Other Costs:* $10 Health Fee, $5 Campus Center Use. *Credit by:* semester.

Financial Aid: Federal Pell Grant, Federal Work-Study, VA.

Accreditation: Western Association of Schools and Colleges.

Description: Gavilan College is a small community college founded in 1919. It has offered telecourses each semester since 1994, and now offers a limited number of online classes. San Jose State University also conducts some upper division and graduate courses, especially in education, by microwave through the Gavilan campus.

Gemological Institute of America

5345 Armada Drive	Phone: (760) 603-4000
Carlsbad, CA 92008	(800) 421-7250 x4001
	Fax: (760) 603-4003

Division(s): Distance Education
Web Site(s): http://www.gia.edu
E-mail: admissions@gia.edu

Certificate Programs: Diamonds, Diamond Grading, Colored Stones, Colored Stone Grading, Gem Identification, Diamond Essentials, Insurance Replacement Appraisal, Pearl and Bead Stringing, Counter Sketching, Gemologist Diploma, Graduate Gemologist Diploma.

Class Titles: Diamonds, Diamond Grading, Colored Stones, Gem Identification, Colored Stone Grading, Pearls, Pearl and Bead Stringing, Counter Sketching, Insurance Replacement Appraisal, Jewelry Essentials, Colored Stone Essentials, Diamond Essentials.

Teaching Methods: *Computers:* Internet, real-time chat, e-mail, CD-ROM, newsgroup. *TV:* videotape. *Other:* individual study.

On-Campus Requirements: 3 extension classes to earn Graduate Gemologist Diploma—these classes travel to various cities throughout the U.S. annually.

Tuition and Fees: *Undergraduate:* [program tuitions] $3,150 or $3,750 w/audiotapes Gemologist Program (5 courses), $1,195 or $1,550 w/audiotapes Diamonds Program (2 courses), $2,095 or $2,395 w/audiotapes Colored Stones Program (3 courses); [course tuitions] $655 or $845 w/audiotapes Diamonds, $755 or $945 w/audiotapes Diamond Grading, $755 or $1,055 w/audiotapes Colored Stones, $655 Colored Stones Grading, $955 Gem Identification, $525 Pearl and Bead Stringing, $525 Counter Sketching, $349 Diamond Essentials, $525 Insurance Replacement Appraisal.

Accreditation: Distance Education Training Council.

Description: Gemological Institute of America (1931) is the leading education, research, and information source for the international gem and jewelry industry. Since its founding, GIA has provided gemological and jewelry manufacturing arts training to 200,000 jewelers with classes and programs offered at its 12 campuses around the world, through distance education programs, and through traveling extension classes. GIA's mission is to ensure the public trust by educating and serving the jewelry industry worldwide.

Genesee Community College

College Road
Batavia, NY 14020-9704

Phone: (716) 343-0055 x6595
Fax: (716) 343-0433

Division(s): Distance Learning
Web Site(s): http://www.genesee.suny.edu
E-mail: jwcianfrini@sunygenesee.cc.ny.us

Class Titles: Accounting, Anthropology, Art, Biology, Business, Marketing, Management, Sales, Writing, English, Creative Writing, Technical Writing, Cinema, History, Western Civilization, Personal Health, Gerontology, Literature, Algebra, Medical Terminology, Paralegal, Psychology, Sociology, Physics, Coaching, Retailing.

Teaching Methods: *Computers:* Internet, electronic classroom, e-mail. *TV:* videotape, cable program. *Other:* videoconferencing, audioconferencing, audiotapes, fax, correspondence.

Admission Requirements: *Undergraduate:* open-door; some specific majors do have restrictions, i.e., allied health fields, paralegal, etc. *Certificate:* same as undergraduate.

On-Campus Requirements: one optional orientation visit to main campus. Optional orientations to off-campus support sites recommended.

Tuition and Fees: *Undergraduate:* $97–$108/credit, lower division. *Other Costs:* $25 technology fee, full-time (prorated for part-time). *Credit by:* semester.

Financial Aid: Federal Stafford Loan, Federal Perkins Loan, Federal Pell Grant, Federal Work-Study, VA, New York resident programs, Tuition Assistance Plan.

Accreditation: Middle States Association of Colleges and Schools.

Description: Genesee Community College (1967) is a comprehensive community college with 3,000 full-time students in a rural area of western New York state, serving a 4-county area and beyond, with 45 certificate, AAS, AS and AA degrees. The main campus in Batavia, 4 campus centers in towns 25–50 miles distant, and distance learning offerings serve both traditional age college students and working adults. The distance learning program is exemplified by a wide diversity of delivery media, course design parameters, support infrastructure and curricula. Student support services (advising, tutoring, technical training and support, etc.) are centrally administered but decentrally provided. Over 70 course sections serve 1,800 students/year in both synchronous and asynchronous delivery modes (telecourses, online courses, live interactive video courses) and an on-time student course completion rate of better than 80% is consistently maintained.

George Washington University

2134 G Street NW, Suite B-06 (GSEHD)
2300 I St. NW, Ross Hall,
Suite 720 (HSP)
Washington, DC 20052
(GSEHD)/20037 (HSP)

Phone: (202) 994-8808 (GSEHD)
(202) 994-8528 (HSP)
Fax: (202) 994-2145 (GSEHD)
(202) 994-0870 (HSP)

Division(s): Graduate School of Education and Human Development/Health Sciences Program
Web Site(s): http://www.gwu.edu/~etl or http://www.gwumc.edu/healthsci/
E-mail: etladmin@gwu.edu or hsphora@gwu.edu

Undergraduate Degree Programs:
Bachelor of Science in Health Sciences with a major in:
  Clinical Management and Leadership
  Clinical Research Administration
  Emergency Health Services Management

Graduate Degree Programs:
Master of Arts in Educational Technology Leadership
Master of Science in Health Sciences with a major in:
  Clinical Leadership with a concentration in Clinical Medicine and Therapeutics
  Clinical Leadership with a concentration in End-of-Life Care
  Clinical Leadership with a concentration in Practice Management
  Clinical Leadership with a concentration in Clinical Research Administration

Certificate Programs: Distance Learning, Clinical Research Administration, Adult to Family Nurse Practitioner, End-of-Life Care.

Class Titles: *Required courses:* Managing Computer Applications, Educational Hardware Systems, Applying Educational Media/Technology, Computers in Education/Human Development, Design/Development of Educational Software, Instructional Design, Power/Leadership/Education, Education Policy, Quantitative Methods/Research Methods. *Elective Courses:* Needs Assessment, Program Evaluation, Managing Multimedia Production, Critical Issues in Distance Education, Effective Presentations for Education/Training, Technology/Disabilities, Technology/Organizations, Telecommunications in Education, History of Media/Technology, Human Computer Interaction in Education, Health Sciences.

Teaching Methods: *Computers:* Internet, asynchronous asu conferencing, streaming audio and video, e-mail, LISTSERV, real-time chat, electronic classroom, CD-ROM, newsgroup. *TV:* videotape. *Other:* audiotapes, fax, independent study, individual study.

Credit Awarded For: examination (CLEP, DANTES).

Admission Requirements: *Undergraduate:* AS degree or equivalent in a health care profession including 6 credits in English Composition and 3 credits in College Algebra. Individual programs may have additional prerequisite requirements. *Graduate: For GSEHD:* bachelor's degree with 2.75 GPA, 2 letters of recommendation, résumé, statement of purpose GRE or MAT. *For HSP:* bachelor's degree from an accredited institution, 3.0 GPA, 2 letters of recommendation, and a statement of purpose. *Certificate:* for GSEHD: same as graduate. for HSP: Adult to Family Nurse Practitioner: current certification as an Adult Nurse Practitioner.

On-Campus Requirements: None except for Adult to Family Nurse Practitioner program (check with program for specifics).

Tuition and Fees: *Undergraduate:* $292/credit. *Graduate:* GSEHD: $298/credit. HSP: $376/credit (Nurse Practitioner $742.50/credit). *Application Fee:* GSEHD: $50, HSP: $60. *Software:* GSEHD: variable. *Graduation Fee:* HSP: $100. *Other Costs:* $35 registration fee. *Credit by:* semester (and a summer session).

Financial Aid: Federal Stafford Loan, Federal Perkins Loan, Federal PLUS Loan, Federal Pell Grant, Federal Work-Study.

Accreditation: Middle States Association of Colleges and Schools.

Description: The George Washington University (1821) is a private, nonsectarian, coeducational institution located in the heart of the nation's capital. The Educational Technology Leadership (ETL) program at The George Washington University was the first educational technology-oriented Master of Arts program to be delivered at a distance throughout the United States. The program has remained at the forefront of communications technology (including satellite, cable, Internet, multimedia) in delivering Distance Learning to students throughout North America and the world. The ETL program is also available in a Distance Learning-supported face-to-face environment in Alexandria, Virginia. The faculty and staff of ETL believe that Distance Education offers unparalleled opportunities in high-quality graduate study for self-motivated high-potential students. The ETL program has been in existence for 9 years and graduates find jobs in various education and training arenas in public agencies and the private sector. ETL students are very competitive and regularly report that they are hired because of their degree or simply their participation in the ETL program. Highly motivated students with basic computer skills will find the ETL program worth their time and energy. The Health Sciences Programs have developed innovative educational programs to meet the needs of health care professionals as they assume positions of leadership and pursue career pathways in this era of rapid change and advancing technologies. The programs provide "anytime and anyplace" opportunities for working profes-

sionals to advance their education and careers. Health Sciences Distance Learning Programs, which evolved from 20 years of experience providing off-campus health sciences education to Navy health care professionals, utilizes advancements in communications technology to provide access for health sciences professionals throughout the world to the school's internationally renowned faculty, researchers, and practitioners.

Georgia Institute of Technology

CDL 620 Cherry Street, ESM Room G-6	Phone: (800) 225-4656
Atlanta, GA 30332-0240	Fax: (404) 894-8924

Division(s): Center for Distance Learning
Web Site(s): http://www.conted.gatech.edu/distance
E-mail: brenda.morris@conted.gatech.edu

Graduate Degree Programs:
Master's Degrees in:
   Electrical and Computer Engineering
   Industrial Systems Engineering
   Mechanical Engineering
   Health Physics
   Environmental Engineering

Class Titles: Contact school or visit web site for details.

Teaching Methods: *Computers:* Internet, real-time chat, electronic classroom, e-mail, CD-ROM, newsgroup, LISTSERV. *TV:* videotape. *Other:* videoconferencing, audioconferencing, fax.

Admission Requirements: *Graduate:* student is required to submit application, applicaton fee, GRE score, TOEFL score if applicable, undergraduate transcripts, letters of recommendation, biography.

On-Campus Requirements: None.

Tuition and Fees: *Graduate:* Tuition for the 2001/2002 academic year is $560/semester hour. *Application Fee:* $50. *Graduation Fee:* $25. *Credit by:* semester.

Financial Aid: Distance Learning students are able to apply for student loans through GT financial aid office.

Accreditation: Southern Association of Colleges and Schools.

Description: The Georgia Institute of Technology, founded in 1885, has over 14,000 students from 110 countries. The Distance Learning program has approximately 400 students from the United States and abroad. GT's graduate engineering program ranks fourth in the nation according to U.S. *News and World Report.* In the Distance Learning program, video cameras record instructor presentations during the regular semester Georgia Tech graduate classes.

The tapes and supporting materials are sent to off-campus students. Some courses are now being offered via the Internet. Students enrolled in the program communicate with their professor by telephone, fax, and/or electronic mail. Students have access to all Georgia Tech services including library and computer system.

Georgia Perimeter College

555 North Indian Creek Drive	Phone: (404) 294-3494
Clarkston, GA 30021-2396	Fax: (404) 294-3492

Division(s): Center for Distance Learning
Web Site(s): http://www.gpc.peachnet.edu/~dl
E-mail: richard@gpc.peachnet.edu

Undergraduate Degree Programs:
Associate of Science in General Studies
Associate of Science in Business Administration

Teaching Methods: *Computers:* Internet, real-time chat, electronic classroom, e-mail, CD-ROM, newsgroup, LISTSERV. *TV:* videotape, cable program, satellite broadcasting, PBS. *Other:* radio broadcast, videoconferencing, audioconferencing, audiographics, audiotapes, fax, correspondence, independent study, individual study, learning contracts.

Admission Requirements: *Undergraduate:* ACT/SAT, immunization.

On-Campus Requirements: None.

Tuition and Fees: *Undergraduate:* $53/credit. *Application Fee:* $20. *Other Costs:* $38 technology fee $50 telecourse fee. *Credit by:* semester.

Financial Aid: Federal Stafford Loan, Federal PLUS Loan, Federal Pell Grant, Federal Work-Study, VA, Georgia resident programs, Georgia Hope Scholarships.

Accreditation: Southern Association of Colleges and Schools.

Description: A regional multi-campus unit of the university system of Georgia, Georgia Perimeter College (1964) strives to meet the changing expectations of our diverse collegiate and community constituencies by providing effective, innovative, lifelong educational opportunities. We are committed to diversity, continuous improvement, high academic standards, and the efficient use of the resources. In decision making at all levels, the enhancement of our students' lives is our first priority. GPC supports one of the oldest and largest distance learning programs in the state, serving over 4,000 distance learners every year.

Glen Oaks Community College

62249 Shimmel Road	Phone: (888) 994-7818
Centreville, MI 49032	Fax: (616) 467-9068

Division(s): E-Learning Department
Web Site(s): http://www.glenoaks.cc.mi.us
E-mail: dtaylor@glenoaks.cc.mi.us

Undergraduate Degree Programs: contact school.

Certificate Programs: Social Work Technician, Banking and Finance.

Class Titles: Introduction to Management, Principles of Accounting, Sociology.

Teaching Methods: *Computers:* Internet, real-time chat, electronic classroom, e-mail, newsgroup, LISTSERV.

Admission Requirements: see web site for more information about admissions requirements.

Tuition and Fees: *Undergraduate:* in district $48/credit, $58/credit. *Technology Fee:* $5. *Graduation Fee:* $11. *Other Costs:* Internet Course Fee: $75. *Credit by:* semester.

Financial Aid: Federal Stafford Loan, Federal Perkins Loan, Federal PLUS Loan, Federal Pell Grant, Federal Work-Study, VA, state programs for residents of Michigan.

Accreditation: North Central Higher Learning Commission.

Description: Glen Oaks Community College (1967) is situated in a rural area 30 miles south of Kalamazoo, Michigan. The character of the college, its communities, and its people is shaped by its pristine rural location, the nearby influence of one of the Midwest's largest Amish populations, a widespread acceptance of a traditional work ethic, a history of solid community support for the college, and continual opportunities for educational and community services that have presented themselves. Glen Oaks is preparing for the 21st century by offering flexible educational opportunities that fit today's learners.

Glendale Community College

1500 North Verdugo Road	Phone: (818) 240-1000
Glendale, CA 91208	Fax: (818) 549-9436

Division(s): Various
Web Site(s): www.glendale.cc.ca.us
E-mail: info@glendale.cc.ca.us

Undergraduate Degree Programs:
Associate of Arts
Associate of Science

Certificate Programs: Yes.

Teaching Methods: *Computers:* Internet, electronic classroom, e-mail, CD-ROM, newsgroup. *TV:* videotape, cable program, PBS. *Other:* independent study.

Credits Granted for: examination (CLEP, ACT-PEP, DANTES, GRE).

Admission Requirements: *Undergraduate:* age 18 and/or ability to benefit.

On-Campus Requirements: None.

Tuition and Fees: *Undergraduate:* $11 residents, $130 out-of-state. *Other Cost options:* $10 technology fee, other fees $30 (first time student). *Credit by:* Semester.

Financial Aid: Federal Pell Grant, Federal Work-Study, California resident programs.

Accreditation: Western Association of Schools and Colleges.

Description: Glendale Community College (1927) has long served Glendale, Burbank, Pasadena, and Los Angeles with quality academic and career education. The college has extensive credit and noncredit programs. Contract education and an extensive array of software courses are provided through the Professional Development Center. Glendale is implementing a carefully designed plan to expand facilities and renovate existing structures in response to the increased demands of technology and enrollment. Students currently have access to more than 20 specialized computer laboratories for subjects from business to science as well as for general use. The college has a long-standing telecourse program and added Internet-based instruction in 1998. GCC expects to have a breadth of Internet-based courses available within the year.

Global University

1211 S. Glenstone
Springfield, MO 65804

Phone: (417) 862-9533
or 1-800-443-1083
Fax: (417) 862-0863

Division(s): Institution is Entirely Distance Learning
Web Site(s): http://www.globaluniversity.edu
E-mail: info@globaluniversity.edu

Undergraduate Degree Programs:
Bible/Theology
Religious Education
Missions
Pastoral Ministries
Ministerial Studies

Graduate Degree Programs:
Biblical Studies
Ministerial Studies

Certificate Programs: The Christian Communicator, The Pentecostal Message, The Christian Doctrine, The Christian Mission, The New Testament Interpreter, The Old Testament Interpreter, The Christian Educator, The Christian Counselor, Church Ministry, The Christian Message, The Bible Message, The Work of the Church.

Class Titles: Contact the school or check web site for details.

Teaching Methods: *Computers:* Internet. *Other:* audiotapes, correspondence, independent study, individual study.

Credits Granted for: experiential learning, examination (CLEP).

Admission Requirements: *Undergraduate:* high school graduation. *Graduate:* B.A. degree (15 hours Bible courses).

On-Campus Requirements: None.

Tuition and Fees: *Undergraduate:* $75/credit. *Graduate:* $139/credit. *Application Fees:* $35 for undergraduate, $45 for graduate. *Graduation Fee:* $25 plus cap and gown. *Other Costs:* texts and study guides. *Credit by:* semester.

Financial Aid: VA.

Accreditation: Distance Education and Training Council.

Description: Global University is the result of a merger between Berean University and ICI University (2000) serving students in more than 160 countries. Courses are offered on evangelism/discipleship, adult continuing education, undergraduate, and graduate levels. Many courses are available in multiple languages. Students may take courses via print media or online.

Gloucester County College

1400 Tanyard Road
Sewell, NJ 08080

Phone: (856) 415-2241
Fax: (856) 468-1988

Division(s): Instructional Technology
Web Site(s):
http://www.gccnj.edu/distance_learning/index.htm
E-mail: kmomballou@gccnj.edu

Undergraduate Degree Programs: Contact school.

Certificate Programs: Contact school.

Class Titles: Medical Terminology, Photography, Environmental Science, Accounting, Managerial Accounting, Intro to the Internet, Computer Literacy, Intro to Computers, Concepts of Information Technology, Web Page Design and Development, English Composition, Children's Literature, History of Western Civilization, Elementary Algegra, Intermediate Algebra, College Algebra.

Teaching Methods: *Computers:* Internet. *TV:* videotape.

Credits Granted for: experiential learning, portfolio assessment, extrainstitutional learning (PONSI, corporate or professional association seminars/workshops), examination (CLEP, DANTES, GRE).

Admission Requirements: *Undergraduate:* as an open-enrollment institution, a completed admissions application and official documentation of high school graduation (or equivalent) are all that's required to be accepted. The only programs with additional requirements are the selective admissions programs. Students will be scheduled for the COMPASS Basic Skills Test that is used for placement purposes.

Tuition and Fees: *Undergraduate:* $62.50 for county residents, $63.50 for out-of-county, $250 for out-of-state, and $80 for online courses. *Application Fee:* $20. Technology Fee: $7.50/credit. *Graduation Fee:* $40. Student Activity Fee: $2.50/credit. *Credit by:* semester.

Financial Aid: Federal Stafford Loan, Federal Perkins Loan, Federal PLUS Loan, Federal Pell Grant, Federal Work-Study, VA, state programs for residents of New Jersey.

Accreditation: Middle States Association of Colleges and Schools.

Description: Gloucester County College (1968) is a comprehensive, coeducational, 2-year college sponsored by the residents of Gloucester County through the Board of Chosen Freeholders. Situated on a 270-acre campus, the college offers more than 70 degree programs leading to the AA, AS and AAS degrees. More than 20 certificate programs are offered. GCC's Distance Learning program consists of ITV, telecourse, and online courses. Telecourses have been offered by the college for more than a decade while online courses were first offered in 1999. Distance Learning courses meet the needs of students for a flexible, convenient way to attend GCC. Distance Learning students have a full range of academic and support services available to them including library resources, academic advising, tutoring, counseling, and the convenience of registering, obtaining grades, and purchasing textbooks online.

Goddard College

123 Pitkin Road	**Phone: (802) 454-8311**
Plainfield, VT 05667	**(800) 468-4888**
	Fax: (802) 454-1029

Division(s): Admissions Office
Web Site(s): http://goddard.edu
E-mail: tinat@goddard.edu

Undergraduate Degree Programs:
Bachelor of Arts in:
　Education
　Psychology
　Liberal Arts
　Individualized Study
　Health Arts and Sciences

Graduate Degree Programs:
Master of Arts in:
　Education
　Psychology
　Health Arts and Sciences
Master of Fine Arts in:
　Creative Writing
　Interdisciplinary Arts

Teaching Methods: *Computers:* Internet, real-time chat, e-mail, newsgroup, LISTSERV. *Other:* fax, correspondence, independent study, individual study, learning contracts.

Credits Granted for: experiential learning, portfolio assessment, examination (CLEP, ACT-PEP, DANTES).

Admission Requirements: *Undergraduate:* adult students, high school diploma or GED. *Graduate:* adult students, accredited undergraduate degree.

On-Campus Requirements: 7-day residency at beginning of each semester.

Tuition and Fees: *Undergraduate:* B.A. Off-Campus Tuition: $4,030, Board $184, Room $142. M.A. Off-Campus Tuition: $4,779, Board $184, Room $142. M.A./Psychology Fee Extra $250. M.F.A. Tuition: $4,871, Board $184, Room $142. *Application Fee:* $40. *Credit by:* semester.

Financial Aid: Federal Stafford Loan, Federal Perkins Loan, Federal PLUS Loan, Federal Pell Grant, Federal Work-Study, VA.

Accreditation: New England Association of Schools and Colleges.

Description: As an heir to Goddard Seminary, Goddard College (1938) was chartered as an experimental and progressive institution of higher learning. In 1959 Goddard was accredited by the New England Association of Schools and Colleges. We have consistently shown a commitment to education of adults as well as younger students, a recognition that education and vocation are inseparable, and the understanding of learning as an individual process. In 1963 Goddard pioneered the first low-residency undergraduate program, acknowledging the need of working adults to be served by a workable program. In the 1970s, graduate programs were also developed in this mode.

Gogebic Community College

E4946 Jackson Road
Ironwood, MI 49938

Phone: (906) 932-4231 x343
Fax: (906) 932-2129

Division(s): Dean of Instruction's Office
Web Site(s): http://gogebic.cc.mi.us
E-mail: nancyk@admin1.gogebic.cc.mi.us

Undergraduate Degree Programs:
Certificate and Associate Degree

Class Titles: vary with semester; call or e-mail for current offerings.

Teaching Methods: *Computers:* Internet, real-time chat, electronic classroom, e-mail, CD-ROM, newsgroup, LISTSERV. *TV:* videotape, cable program, satellite broadcasting, PBS. *Other:* videoconferencing, audioconferencing, fax, correspondence, independent study.

Credits Granted for: in exceptional circumstances: experiential learning, portfolio assessment, extrainstitutional learning, examination (CLEP, ACT-PEP, DANTES, GRE).

Admission Requirements: *Undergraduate:* open-door policy. *Certificate:* same as undergraduate.

On-Campus Requirements: None.

Tuition and Fees: *Undergraduate:* $47/credit in-district, $63/credit out-of-district, $67/credit out-of-state reciprocity area, $90/credit out-of-state. *Other Costs:* $220 estimated total annual fees based on full-time load of 31 credits. *Credit by:* semester.

Financial Aid: Federal Stafford Loan, Federal Perkins Loan, Federal PLUS Loan, Federal Pell Grant, Federal Work-Study, VA, Michigan resident programs.

Accreditation: North Central Association of Colleges and Schools.

Description: Gogebic Community College (1932) is a small, rural, full-service community college located in Michigan's western Upper Peninsula. The college offers liberal arts, technical, and community service programming. GCC's primary service district is Gogebic County, but it also serves the western 6 counties in the Upper Peninsula. Because this large service area is rural, the barriers of time and distance are often a hindrance to those pursuing a college education. The college initially entered distance learning as a way of addressing these barriers, and over time has broadened its offerings.

Golden Gate University

536 Mission Street
San Francisco, CA 94105

Phone: (888) 874-2923
(415) 369-5250
Fax: (415) 227-4502

Division(s): CyberCampus
Web Site(s): http://cybercampus.ggu.edu
E-mail: cybercampus@ggu.edu

Undergraduate Degree Programs:
Bachelor of Public Administration

Graduate Degree Programs:
Master of Accountancy
Master of Science in Marketing
Executive Master of Public Administration
Master of Science in Healthcare Administration
Master of Science in Taxation
Master of Business Administration (MBA)
Master of Science in Finance
Master of Science Financial Planning
Master of Science in Telecommunications Management

Certificate Programs: *Undergraduate:* Finance, Technology Management. *Graduate:* Accounting, Arts Administration, Finance, Information Systems, Marketing, Personal Financial Planning, Healthcare Administration, Tax.

Class Titles: Business Law, Consulting Small Business Planning, Consulting: The Role of the Accountant, Intermediate Accounting III, Introductory Management Accounting, Contemporary Arts & Culture, Beginning Web Pages & HTML, Management Info Systems, Business Writing, Expository Writing, Research Writing, Business Development in Financial Services, Financial Management, Investments, Quantitative Analysis for Managers, Statistics, Doing Business in Asia, Management Principles, The Manager as Communicator, Project Management, Public Sector Labor Relations, Introduction to Philosophy, American Government, Networking Protocols, Fund-Raising in Arts Administration, Accounting for Managers, Auditing, Consulting: Small Business Planning, Consulting: The Role of the Accountant, Advanced HTML & Juvascript, Architecture of the Internet & WWW, Computer Programming for Managers, Database Management Systems, Designing Storefronts for E-Commerce, Distributed Systems, Info Systems Planning & Project Control, Intro to Web Page Design & HTML, Management Information Systems, Systems Analysis & Design I, Economics for Managers, Financial Markets & Institutions, Graduate Research Project in Public Management, Graduate Research, Writing & Presentation, Public Policy Analysis & Program Evaluation, Public Service & the Law, Capital Budgeting & Long Term Financing, Derivative Markets, Estate Planning, Financial Management, Insurance Planning, Investments, Personal Financial Planning, Technical Analysis of Securities, Venture

Capital & Start-Up Financing, Healthcare Admin Grad Research Project, Internship: Healthcare Administration, Long Term Care Systems & Social Policy, Business Policy & Strategy, Effective Decision Making & Communications, Informational Business Management, Managing the Electronic Business, Small Business Management, Business-to-Business Marketing, Consumer Behavior, Marketing for E-Commerce, Marketing Management, Operations & Supply Chain Mgt for E-Commerce, Operations Management, Purchasing & Supply Management, Advanced Federal Income Taxation, Estate & Gift Taxation, Estate Planning, Federal Income Tax of Corps & Shareholders, Federal Income Tax of Partners & Partnerships, Federal Tax Procedure, International Taxation, Limited Liability Companies & Corps: A Choice of Entity, Property Transactions, Tax Research & Decision Making, Tax Timing, Tax of Foreign Persons with U.S. Activities, Advanced Switching Systems, Architecture of the Internet & WWW for E-Commerce, Customer Service & Call Center Technologies, E-Commerce Industry & Technology, E-Commerce Systems & Technology, Global Communications, Local Area Networks, Telecommunications Management, The Futures of Telecommunications.

Teaching Methods: *Computers:* Internet, electronic class-room, e-mail, interactive discussion conference. *Other:* None.

Credits Granted for: examination (CLEP, ACT-PEP, DANTES, GRE).

Admission Requirements: *Graduate:* MBA programs—statement of purpose, official GMAT score report, official transcript. Other master's degree programs—statement of purpose, undergraduate GPA of 2.5 (except MAC requires 3.0 and MS Taxation requires 3.2). *Certificate:* An official transcript documenting the equivalent of a college/university degree from an approved institution. Some certificate programs have prerequisite courses that students must meet. Admitted certificate-program students must maintain normal academic standards, including GPA. All units applied to a certificate program must be earned at Golden Gate University. Transfer credit is not applicable.

On-Campus Requirements: The student never has to attend a class meeting. The course is taught entirely over the Internet. All courses require at least one supervised exam. The student must select an exam supervisor for this exam. Some examples of supervisors are employers, local librarians, other universities or any GGU campus location.

Tuition and Fees: *Undergraduate:* $1,149/course. *Graduate:* $1,749/School of Taxation course; $1,590/School of Business and School of Technology course; $1,260/Executive Master of Public Administration course. *Application Fee:* $55 degree, $25 certificate, $70 degree or certificate for international students. *Credit by:* quarter.

Financial Aid: Federal Stafford Loan, Federal Perkins Loan, Federal PLUS Loan, Federal Pell Grant, Federal Work-Study, VA, California resident programs.

Accreditation: Western Association of Schools and Colleges.

Description: Golden Gate University (1853) has been a leader in quality, practical training for working professionals for more than a century. The university is dedicated to providing an educational environment and curricula that simulate the professional workplace. This dedication inspired Cyber-Campus, the university's Online Campus. In existence since the fall of 1997, the online university began with 13 courses. Now it offers 30 courses and, by the fall of 1998, will offer almost 50. The program's success is a reflection of a thorough development cycle and a commitment to quality.

Gonzaga University

East 502 Boone Avenue   Phone: (800) 533-2554 x5912
Spokane, WA 99258-0001   Fax: (509) 323-5965

Division(s): Off-Campus Education Services
Other Contacts: Nursing: (800) 533-2554 x5542
Organizational Leadership: (800) 533-2554 x6645
Fax for Nursing and Organizational Leadership:
    (509) 323-5827
Web Site(s): http://www.gonzaga.edu
E-mail: aruff@soe.gonzaga.edu (Off-Campus Education)
norwood@gu.gonzaga.edu (Nursing)
albert@gu.gonzaga.edu (Organizational Leadership)

Graduate Degree Programs:
Master of Initial Teaching (includes teacher certification)
Master of Arts in:
    Administration and Supervision (Canada only)
    Teaching: Teaching At-Risk Kids
    Curriculum and Instruction
    Counseling (Canadian program only)
    Organizational Leadership
Master of Science in Nursing

Certificate Programs: Postgraduate Family Nurse Practitioner.

Teaching Methods: *Computers:* Internet, electronic class-rooms, e-mail, CD-ROM, LISTSERV. *TV:* videotape. *Other:* audioconferencing, fax, correspondence, independent study, individual study, learning contracts, face-to-face instruction.

Credits Granted for: portfolio assessment.

Admission Requirements: *Graduate:* program-specific, written statement of purpose, 2 letters of recommendation, transcripts, GRE or Miller Analogies Test. *Doctoral:* same as graduate.

On-Campus Requirements: Off-Campus Education: Our programs are comprised of face-to-face instruction offered in a community over a 2-year period. Classes typically meet twice a week every other week. Our Master of Arts in Counseling program (Canadian only) requires on-campus residency the first year for one summer session (4 weeks). All other programs are offered in the community year-round. Nursing and FNP Certificate: 2 days/month. Organizational Leadership: no on-campus requirement.

Tuition and Fees: *Graduate:* $365/credit Off-Campus Education, $465/credit Nursing and Organizational Leadership. *Application Fee:* $40. *Other Costs:* $60 Miller Analogies Test, $100–$250 practicum fee (for supervisor honorarium), $40 orals fee, $40 readers travel fee, $25 summer session administrative fee, $10 technology fee/semester. *Credit by:* semester.

Financial Aid: Federal Stafford Loan, Federal PLUS Loan.

Accreditation: National Council of Accreditation for Teacher Education, National League for Nursing, Private Postsecondary Education Commission of British Columbia, Advanced Education and Career Development.

Description: Gonzaga University (1968) has provided distance graduate degrees to 1,800 students from northern Canada to the Hawaiian Islands in its 30 years of extended service. The university will continue to offer its graduate program as long as a need exists for Jesuit-inspired education. The mission of the university is to develop knowledgeable and competent professionals. Gonzaga is committed to providing excellence without elitism, to blending contemporary and innovative theory and practice, and to appreciating wide-range views and ideologies. The School of Education offers graduate-level, off-campus programs in teacher certification, administration and curriculum, teaching at-risk kids, educational technology, and sports administration. Counseling programs are offered only in Canada and require a summer residency. Programs are designed around a typical work schedule, through weekly courses or through evening courses twice every other week over a 2-year period. The School of Professional Studies offers a blend of distant and on-campus study and experiences for the nursing programs. This format combines videotapes of current campus classes and student interaction by region with campus attendance periods. The student can proceed at his or her own pace in this format. The organizational leadership program is offered in an evening and/or weekend class format.

Gordon-Conwell Theological Seminary

130 Essex Street
South Hamilton, MA 01982

Phone: (877) 736-5465 (toll free)
Fax: (978) 468-1791
(978) 646-4565

Division(s): Ockenga Institute
Web Site(s): http://www.gcts.edu/semlink
E-mail: semlink@gcts.edu

Certificate Programs: Ockenga Institute Diploma—nondegree program in which a diploma is awarded for the completion of 6 courses.

Class Titles: Christian Ethics, Christian/Old Testament Theology, Church History to Reformation, Church History Since Reformation, Church History Survey, Church Leadership/Administration, Epistle to Romans, Christian Apologetics, Pastoral Care/Counseling, Marriage Counseling, Modern Theology, New Testament Survey, Pastoral Epistles, Reformation Church History, Systematic Theology, Spiritual Formation for Ministry, Tentmaking Witness at Home/Abroad, Theology of Jonathan Edwards, Theology Survey, Urban Mission/Ministry.

Teaching Methods: *Computers:* Internet, CD-ROM. *TV:* videotapes. *Other:* audiotapes.

Admission Requirements: *Graduate:* accredited bachelor's degree, recommendations. *Certificate:* application, recommendations.

On-Campus Requirements: a student may complete up to a third of a master's degree (10 of 30 courses towards a Master of Divinity and 6 of 20 courses towards a Master of Arts degree) through the Semlink distance education program. The degree must then be completed in residence. Gordon-Conwell does not offer correspondence degrees.

Tuition and Fees: *Graduate:* $495/3-credit course. *Application Fee:* $25. *Credit by:* semester.

Financial Aid: Semlink students may be eligible to defer prior loans or be eligible for a federal loan if taking 2 courses simultaneously.

Accreditation: Association of Theological Schools in the U.S. and Canada, New England Association of Schools and Colleges.

Description: Gordon-Conwell Theological Seminary (1987) has a rich, century-long heritage. The school's roots are founded in 2 institutions which have long provided evangelical leadership for the Christian church in a variety of ministries. The Conwell School of Theology was founded in Philadelphia in 1884 by the Rev. Russell Conwell, a prominent Baptist minister who was well known for his famous sermon and book, *Acres of Diamonds*. The Conwell School later developed into Temple University in Philadelphia. In

1889, out of a desire to equip "men and women in practical religious work and to furnish them with a thoroughly biblical training," the Boston Missionary Training School was founded by another prominent Baptist minister, the Rev. A. J. Gordon. Based in Boston, Massachusetts, the school shared Gordon's deep concern for missions abroad and in New England urban centers. Upon his death, the institution was given his name, and the Gordon Divinity School eventually moved to Boston's North Shore. The Conwell School of Theology and Gordon Divinity School merged in 1969 through the efforts of philanthropist J. Howard Pew, Dr. Harold J. Ockenga, and Dr. Billy Graham. Their vision was for an institution "established within a strong evangelical framework, an independent, interdenominational seminary whose constituents are united in the belief that the Bible is the infallible, authoritative Word of God . . . consecrated to educating men and women in all facets of gospel outreach." Semlink is a personalized learning method which allows you to study at your own pace when and where it is most convenient for you. Each course is structured around cassette-taped lectures with a course syllabus and study guide supplemented by textbooks, reference materials and, in some cases, video, Internet, and CD-ROM formats. If taken for credit, you will receive individual attention from both a Gordon-Conwell mentor and faculty advisor as you proceed through each course. Inviting friends to join you in regular sessions enriches your experience and adds accountability.

Goucher College

1021 Dulaney Valley Road	Phone: (410) 337-6200
Baltimore, MD 21204	(800) 697-4646
	Fax: (410) 337-6085

Division(s): Center for Graduate and Professional Studies
Web Site(s): http://goucher.edu/
E-mail: nmack@goucher.edu

Graduate Degree Programs:
Master of Arts in:
    Historic Preservation
    Arts Administration
Master of Fine Arts in Creative Nonfiction

Teaching Methods: *Computers:* Internet, real-time chat, electronic classroom, e-mail, CD-ROM, newsgroup, LISTSERV. *Other:* fax, correspondence, independent study, individual study, learning contracts.

Admission Requirements: *Graduate:* accredited bachelor's degree, 2 years of paid or volunteer post-graduate work experience.

On-Campus Requirements: 2-week summer residencies.

Tuition and Fees: *Graduate:* varies; contact school for details. *Credit by:* varies; contact school for details.

Financial Aid: Federal Stafford Loan

Accreditation: Middle States Association of Colleges and Schools.

Description: Since its founding in 1885, Goucher College has been known for its commitment to excellence in liberal arts and sciences education. The limited-residency, distance-learning graduate programs began in 1995. These programs offer an opportunity to students, living anywhere, to earn further knowledge and credentials which will make them valuable in their fields. The limited-residency format allows the programs to include nationwide experts in the fields.

Governors State University

Stuenkel Road	Phone: (800) 478-8478
University Park, IL 60486	Fax: (708) 534-8458

Division(s): Extended Learning
Web Site(s): http://www.govst.edu.bog
E-mail: gtvstudy@govst.edu
gsubog@govst.edu

Undergraduate Degree Programs:
Board of Governors Bachelor of Arts

Class Titles: Financial Accounting, Alcoholism: Study of Addiction, Substance Abuse: Current Concepts, Addictions Counseling: Multicultural Perspective, Managing Health Behaviors, Adolescent Substance Abuser: School/Family/Treatment/Prevention Strategies, Alcoholism: Employee Assistance in Business/Industry, Beliefs/Believers, Anthropology in Film, Worlds of Art, Human Evolution, Models of Intervention for Substance Abusing Offender, Concepts in Communication, Communication Workshop: Family Communication, Macroeconomics, Foundations of Education, Living Literature: Classics/You, Composition: Structure/Style, Writing, Modern American Poetry: Voices/Visions, Shakespeare's Plays, Native American Authors, World Regional Geography, Key Issues in State/Federal Constitutional Government, History of Illinois/Its Constitution, Modern Chinese History, Russia in 20th Century, Hispanic Experience in U.S., Ethnicity/Culture/Politics, African Civilizations, Latin American Culture/Society, American Cinema, Management Strategies, Production Management, Organizational Behavior, Marketing Management, Public Administration, Religion, Urban Politics, Psychology, Personality Theories, Social Psychology, Child Development, Adulthood, Seasons of Life, Cognitive Development Through Life Cycle, Urban Studies, Family History: Legacies, Women/Social Action, Urban Dynamics, Survey of Social Science, Dealing with Diversity, Survey of Exceptional Students, Statistics.

Teaching Methods: *Computers:* Internet, electronic classroom, e-mail, CD-ROM. *TV:* videotape, cable program, PBS. *Other:* audioconferencing, audiotapes, correspondence.

Credits Granted for: experiential learning, portfolio assessment, extrainstitutional learning, examination (CLEP, ACT-PEP, DANTES, USAFI), ACE-approved training.

Admission Requirements: *Undergraduate:* Governors State University is an upper-division and graduate public university in Illinois. The Board of Governors BA degree completion program is a program for adult learners that can be completed at a distance. It is not organized by traditional academic disciplines. Students may design their own degree program to fit their career goals. Students with 60 semester hours from a regionally accredited institution will be readily admitted into the program. Students with 30–59 semester credit hours and substantial experiential learning may be admitted on a conditional basis until they reach 60 hours. Students must have a GPA of 2.0 or better. The BOG program accepts transfer credit with passing grades from any regionally accredited college or university in the U.S. There are no time limits to when the credits were earned. Students may transfer up to 80 hours of lower division credit into the program.

On-Campus Requirements: students must take 24 semester hours of course work from Governors State. Students may select course work from the 55 media-based distance learning courses that are offered by GSU (TV, correspondence, Internet, CD-ROM) to fulfill this requirement.

Tuition and Fees: *Undergraduate:* $108/credit. *Graduate:* $115/credit. *Software:* variable. *Other Costs:* fee for portfolio assessment. *Credit by:* trimester (semester).

Financial Aid: Federal Direct Loan, Federal Perkins Loan, Federal Pell Grant, Federal Work-Study, VA, Illinois resident programs.

Accreditation: North Central Association of Colleges and Schools.

Description: Governors State University (1969), located in the southern suburbs of Chicago, serves 9,000 adult students each year. GSU, an upper-division and graduate-level university, has 4 colleges (Arts and Sciences, Business and Public Administration, Education, and Health Professions) with 172 full-time faculty. GSU is known for its adult-oriented Board of Governors BA degree program, which can be completed at a distance, as well as its production of TV courses. There are 12,000 graduates of the BOG BA degree program. The average age is 40; 95% of BOG BA graduates in the job market are employed; and 42% of BOG alumni enroll in a graduate program after completing their BOG BA degree.

Grace University

1311 South 9th Street
Omaha, NE 68108

Phone: (402) 449-2999
Fax: (402) 341-9587

Division(s): Grace College of Continuing Education
Web Site(s): http://www.graceu.edu
E-mail: guconed@graceu.edu

Class Titles: I Corinthians, Romans, Philosophy, Apologetics, Church History, Biblical Counseling, Gospels, Computer Applications, Psychology.

Teaching Methods: *Computers:* Internet, e-mail. *Other:* correspondence, independent study.

Credits Granted for: experiential learning, portfolio assessment, examination (CLEP).

Admission Requirements: *Undergraduate:* application, references, transcripts, health form, ACT scores.

On-Campus Requirements: None.

Tuition and Fees: *Undergraduate:* $260/credit. *Application Fee:* $25. *Credit by:* semester.

Financial Aid: Federal Stafford Loan, Federal PLUS Loan, Federal Pell Grant, VA, state programs for residents of all states, institutional scholarships and grants, alternative loans.

Accreditation: North Central Association of Colleges and Schools, AABC.

Description: Originally founded as Grace Bible Institute, then renamed as Grace College of the Bible, Grace University (1943) adopted its new identity by adding 2 more colleges in 1995. Grace College of the Bible continues to be the university's primary undergraduate college, offering associate's and bachelor's degrees. Grace is a distinctly Christian university with an interdenominational identity and a curriculum shaped by the university's conservative, evangelical heritage. All undergraduates complete a double major: the first in Biblical Studies and the second in a chosen major field. For students completing a degree at a different college or university, Grace's Independent Studies program offers "electives" required by most colleges. Taking a couple of Christ-centered courses and transferring them into another program is an ideal way to inject some biblical learning into your overall college experience.

Graceland University

University Place
Lamoni, IA 50140

Phone: (515) 784-5324
Fax: (515) 784-5405

Division(s): Continuing Education/Distance Learning
Web Site(s): http://graceland.edu/home.html
E-mail: cps@graceland.edu

Undergraduate Degree Programs:
Bachelor of Arts in:
    Accounting
Bachelor of Science in:
    Business Administration
    Elementary Education
    Information Technology
    Sociology/Criminal Justice

Graduate Degree Programs:
Master of Science in Nursing

Teaching Methods: *Computers:* Internet, CD-ROM, e-mail. *TV:* videotape, Iowa Communication Network (interactive fiberoptic cable). *Other:* audioconferencing, fax, correspondence, independent study, individual study, by arrangement.

Credits Granted for: experiential learning, extrainstitutional learning, examination (CLEP, ACT-PEP, DANTES, GRE).

Admission Requirements: *Undergraduate:* associate degree or 60 college credits. *Graduate:* varies.

On-Campus Requirements: variable.

Tuition and Fees: *Undergraduate:* $190/credit. *Graduate:* varies. *Application Fee:* $30. *Other Costs:* varies. *Credit by:* semester.

Financial Aid: Federal Stafford Loan, Federal Perkins Loan, Federal PLUS Loan, Federal Pell Grant, Federal Work-Study, VA, Iowa Tuition Grant, Canadian Student Loan Plan.

Accreditation: North Central Association of Colleges and Schools, National Council for Accreditation of Teacher Education.

Description: Graceland University (1895), delivering distance education for more than a decade, is committed to lifelong learning. Graceland's curriculum, firmly rooted in the liberal arts tradition and enhanced by career-oriented practical experiences, is ideally suited to the distance learner. The majority of the college's continuing and distance education students participate in the Partnership Program between Graceland and 4 regional community colleges. A student with the equivalent of an associate degree takes day, evening, or weekend classes delivered traditionally by Graceland faculty or through the innovative medium of live, interactive fiberoptic TV at one of these partnership sites. Independent study courses and courses scheduled by arrangement with the instructor allow students to tailor a program of study to their modern lifestyle. This structured yet flexible approach allows students to complete their bachelor's degree in as few as 2 years. (Nursing degrees may be obtained from the Outreach Program in Independence, MO. Phone (800) 833-0524 for information.)

Grand Canyon University

3300 W Camelback Road
Phoenix, AZ 85017

Phone: (800) 800-9776, ext.2029
(800) 339-0183
Fax: (602) 589-2010

Division(s): College of Education
Web Site(s): http://www.grand-canyon.edu
http://www.masters4teachers.net
E-mail: mat4u@grand-canyon.edu
carmie.rehor@educate.com

Graduate Degree Programs:
Masters of Arts in Teaching

Class Titles: Overcoming Challenges Facing Professional Educators: The High-Performing Teacher, Effective Classroom Management, Collaborative Action Research, Motivating Today's Learner, Learning Styles and Multiple Intelligences, Models of Effective Teaching, Curriculum and Assessment, Current Issues: Technology in the Classroom, Helping Students Become Self-Directed Learners, Teaching Reading in the Elementary Grades or Teaching Reading at the Secondary Level, Capstone Project.

Teaching Methods: *Computers:* Internet, real-time chat, e-mail. *TV:* videotape. *Other:* fax, correspondence, independent study, individual study, faculty facilitator, collegial study teams, audiotapes, fax, conference calls.

Credits Granted for: capstone project, individual assignments, study team assignments.

Admission Requirements: *Graduate:* bachelor's degree, cumulative GPA of at least 2.8 on a 4.0 scale for all college work, copy of your current state-approved teaching credential or Association of Christian Schools International (ACSI) credentials, a minimum of one year of teaching experience, access to a classroom or group of students, access to a computer and TV/VCR, official transcripts from each postsecondary institution attended, one recommendation from an individual who knows you professionally, copy of your most recent teaching evaluation from your school administrator, completed and signed application form, signed credit agreement form, one-time application fee.

On-Campus Requirements: None.

Tuition and Fees: *Graduate:* $225/credit. *Application Fee:* $50. *Graduation Fee:* $25. *Other Costs:* $70 for supplies per course. *Credit by:* semester.

Financial Aid: Federal Stafford Loan, Federal Perkins Loan, VA.

Accreditation: North Central Association of Colleges and Schools.

Description: Since 1949, Grand Canyon University (GCU) has been known throughout the Southwest for providing innovative and quality education programs for teachers that adhere to the highest academic standards. Located in Phoenix, Arizona, GCU has grown into an active and thriving campus. In utilizing a Distance Learning format, the program's goal is to bring GCU to you. The GCU College of Education provides "professional degree programs that emphasize academic excellence." It is the faculty's desire to provide a learning environment for the professional teacher in which collaborative efforts between college faculty and practicing teachers positively affect students in the classroom. Over the past 5 years, *U.S. News and World Report* has recognized GCU in its annual ranking of "Best Colleges and Universities."

Grand Rapids Baptist Seminary

1001 East Beltline NE	Phone: (616) 222-1422
Grand Rapids, MI 49525	Fax: (616) 222-1414

Division(s): Academic Office
Web Site(s): http://www.grbs.edu
E-mail: grbs@cornerstone.edu

Class Titles: Biblical Hermeneutics, Old Testament Biblical Theology, Acts of Apostles, Pastoral Epistles, Hebrews, Life of Christ, Gospel of Luke, Post-Exilic Prophets, Parables of Jesus, Historical Theology: Ancient Church, Historical Theology: Reformation Church, Historical Theology: Christianity in America, Theologies of Liberation, Radical Reformation, Doctrine of Man/Sin, Christian Worldview, Christian Ethics, Theology of Jonathan Edwards, Theology of Martin Luther, Doctrine of Salvation, Contemporary Theology, Doctrine of Trinity, Apologetics, Spiritual Formation, Role of Women in Ministry, Adult Ministries in Church, Urban Mission/Ministry, History/Philosophy of Christian Missions, Missionary Encounter with World Religions, Muslim Evangelism, Interpersonal Conflict Management, Administration/Care of Church, History/Philosophy of Christian Education.

Teaching Methods: *Computers:* e-mail. *Other:* audiotapes, fax, correspondence, independent study, individual study, learning contracts.

Credits Granted for: transfer credit, advanced standing by exam.

Admission Requirements: *Graduate:* admission into the degree programs requires a bachelor's degree from a regionally accredited college with a 2.5 cumulative GPA, statement of Christian faith commitment, and fulfillment of all other application requirements as outlined in the Grand Rapids Baptist Seminary academic catalog. Contact school.

On-Campus Requirements: currently all the degree programs at Grand Rapids Baptist Seminary are designed as resident programs, with the exception of the Doctor of Ministry degree program. The resident degree programs do allow up to 15% completion through distance education.

Tuition and Fees: *Graduate:* $295/credit. *Application Fee:* $25. *Other Costs:* $60/set of lecture tapes (estimated). *Credit by:* semester.

Financial Aid: institution grants and scholarships, Federal Stafford Loan, Federal PLUS Loan, Federal Work-Study, VA.

Accreditation: North Central Association of Colleges and Schools, Associate Member of Association of Theological Schools.

Description: Grand Rapids Baptist Seminary (1949) is a graduate school of biblical studies, theology, and ministry which serves individuals preparing for vocational ministry. The seminary is located in Grand Rapids, Michigan. Currently some 260 students are enroled in residence and through distance education in the various graduate degree programs. Grand Rapids Baptist Seminary maintains a strong commitment to its Baptistic theological heritage and historical biblical Christianity, while seeking to serve the broader evangelical community with a distinctively conservative theological education.

Grantham College of Engineering

34641 Grantham College Road	Phone: (800) 955-2527
Slidell, LA 70460	Fax: (985) 649-4183

Division(s): Distance Education (100%)
Web Site(s): http://www.grantham.edu
E-mail: admissions@grantham.edu

Undergraduate Degree Programs:
Associate and Bachelor of Science in:
    Computer Science (tracks in Web Design)
    Internet Engineering
    Management Information Systems
    Computer Programming.
Associate and Bachelor of Science in:
Computer Engineering Technology and Electronics Engineering Technology.

Class Titles: all classes offered by school; check catalog.

Teaching Methods: *Computers:* Internet, real-time chat, e-mail, CD-ROM. *Other:* fax, correspondence, independent study, individual study.

Credits Granted for: experiential learning, portfolio assessment, examination (CLEP, ACT-PEP, DANTES, GRE).

Admission Requirements: *Undergraduate:* high school diploma, GED, or equivalent, TOEFL score of 500 for international students.

On-Campus Requirements: None.

Tuition and Fees: *Undergraduate:* $2,600/semester. *Application Fee:* $150. *Other Costs:* $60 for 3-month extension to semester. (Students have 12 months to complete each semester). *Credit by:* semester. Semesters range from 13–17 credit hours depending on degree program and semester.

Financial Aid: VA, DANTES, employer tuition assistance, Sallie Mae Loans.

Accreditation: Distance Education and Training Council.

Description: For 50 years Grantham has designed its degree programs to meet the needs of working adults by providing a quality, accredited college education on a flexible schedule. Thousands of students have discovered the benefits of the Grantham distance education model. Grantham College of Engineering shapes its courses and degree programs to ensure our students learn the latest technologies and the underlying fundamental principles.

Information technology has transformed the economy, and created an enormous demand for expertise in computer science and engineering technology. If you are one of the many adults seeking advancement but held back by the lack of a formal education, Grantham gives you the opportunity to earn a college degree. And if you are planning for a future in information technology or engineering technologies, then you should consider the degree programs described on our web site.

Gratz College

7605 Old York Road   Phone: (800) 475-4635
Melrose Park, PA 19027   or (215) 635-7300
   Fax: (215) 635-7320

Division(s): Education
Web Site(s): http://www.gratzcollege.edu
E-mail: admission@gratz.edu

Undergraduate Degree Programs: Contact school.

Graduate Degree Programs: Contact school.

Class Titles: Essential Rabbinic Beliefs, Judaism's Encounter with Modernity, Eastern European Jewish Civilization, Y.L. Peretz: Creating a Modern Jewish Culture.

Teaching Methods: *Computers:* Internet, real-time chat, electionic classroom, e-mail, *TV:* satellite broadcasting. *Other:* videoconferencing.

Admission Requirements: *Undergraduate:* high school graduate or GED recipient, application, personal statement. *Graduate:* college graduate, application, personal statement, references.

On-Campus Requirements: None.

Tuition and Fees: *Undergraduate:* $382/Credit. *Graduate:* $466/Credit. *Credit by:* quarter.

Financial Aid: Federal Stafford Loan, Federal PLUS Loan, Federal Pell Grant, VA.

Accreditation: Middle States Association of Colleges and Schools.

Description: Gratz College (1895) is the oldest independent, nondenominationally affiliated college of Jewish Studies in the Western Hemisphere. The college awards bachelor's degrees, professionally and nonprofessionally oriented master's degrees in Jewish education, Jewish music, Jewish communal service, and Jewish studies. Gratz College's highly qualified faculty of full- and part-time professors, supplemented by distinguished visiting faculty from other leading institutions, share a primary commitment to Jewish studies and to teaching. Gratz College developed a commitment to bring Jewish studies to a wider audience by entering the Distance Learning arena in 2000.

Grays Harbor College

1620 Edward P. Smith Drive   Phone: (360) 532-9020
Aberdeen, WA 98520   Fax: (360) 538-4293

Division(s): Continuing Education
Web Site(s): http://ghc.ctc.edu
E-mail: admissions@ghc.ctc.edu

Undergraduate Degree Programs:
Associate of Arts
Associate of Science
Associate of Science (transfer)
Associate of Applied Science or Technology
Associate of General Studies

Certificate Programs: Accounting/Bookkeeping, Aquaculture Technician, Business Management, Corrections, Criminal Justice, Geographic Information Systems, Medical Office Assistant, Microcomputer Maintenance and Service Technician, Network Technician, Office Technology, Pharmacy

Technician, Practical Nursing, Related Welding, Small Business/Entrepreneurship, Software Applications, Trim Carpentry, Watershed Restoration, Welding Technology.

Teaching Methods: *Computers:* Internet, real-time chat, electronic classroom, e-mail, LISTSERV. *TV:* videotape. *Other:* videoconferencing, independent study.

Credits Granted for: examination (CLEP).

Admission Requirements: *Undergraduate:* age 18 with high school diploma or GED, complete a placement exam. *Certificate:* same as undergraduate.

On-Campus Requirements: None.

Tuition and Fees: *Undergraduate:* $55/credit in-state. *Other Costs:* $60 parking, technology, and lab fees. *Credit by:* quarter.

Financial Aid: Federal Stafford Loan, Federal PLUS Loan, Federal Pell Grant, Federal Work-Study, VA, Washington resident programs, scholarships.

Accreditation: Northwest Association of Schools and Colleges.

Description: Grays Harbor College (1930) continues to operate quality programs at an affordable price. We offer classes in several formats and many areas of interest. Classes can be delivered via Internet, video, and teleconferencing. Our Internet site is constantly being updated as we upgrade and adapt our courses with new technology and methods.

Green River Community College

12401 Southeast 320th Street
Auburn, WA 98092   **Phone: (253) 288-3354**

Division(s): Office of Distance Learning
Web Site(s): http://www.grcc.ctc.edu
E-mail: schapman@grcc.ctc.edu

Undergraduate Degree Programs:
Associate of Arts

Class Titles: Anthropology, Aviation, Interpersonal Relations, Career Explorations, Human Sexuality, Stress Management, Word for Windows, Drama Appreciation, Art of the Film, Early Childhood Education, Education, Spelling Improvement, Introductory Composition, Practical College Writing, Medical Terminology, Writing, Geography, History, Mathematics, Psychology, Sociology.

Teaching Methods: *Computers:* Internet, real-time chat, electronic classroom, e-mail, CD-ROM, newsgroup, LISTSERV. *TV:* videotape, cable program, satellite broadcasting, PBS.

Credits Granted for: examination (CLEP, DANTES), enlisted military experience, advanced placement.

Admission Requirements: *Undergraduate:* age 18, high school diploma; state residency requirements waived for distance courses only. *Certificate:* same as undergraduate.

On-Campus Requirements: None.

Tuition and Fees: *Undergraduate:* $54.70/credit. *Software:* $20–40/class, for some classes. *Graduation Fee:* $10. *Other Costs:* $2/credit, technology fee. *Credit by:* quarter.

Financial Aid: Federal Stafford Loan, Federal PLUS Loan, Federal Pell Grant, Federal Work-Study, VA, Washington resident programs.

Accreditation: Northwest Association of Schools and Colleges.

Description: Green River Community College (1964) began offering distance learning courses in earnest in 1998. The distance offering has grown to over 40 courses, enrolling over 1,000 students per quarter. More courses are being developed by faculty every quarter.

Greenville Technical College

506 South Pleasantburg Drive   **Phone: (864) 250-8098**
Greenville, SC 29606-5616   **Fax: (864) 250-8085**

Division(s): Distance Learning
Web Site(s): http://www.college-online.com
http://www.greenvilletech.com
E-mail: moreinfo@college-online.com

Undergraduate Degree Programs:
A variety of one-year diploma and 2-year associate degree programs in a wide choice of fields including industrial/ engineering technologies, nursing/allied health sciences, business, criminal justice, and culinary arts. Associate in Sciences and Associate in Arts degrees are available through the University Transfer program.

Certificate Programs: Programs in a wide choice of fields including industrial and engineering technologies, nursing and allied health sciences, business, criminal justice, and culinary arts.

Class Titles: Accounting, Art History/Appreciation, Astronomy, Biology, Chemistry, Computers/Programming, English Composition, English Literature, Ethics, History, Hospitality, Internet Communications, Logic, Math, Management, Marketing, Microcomputer Applications, Office Systems Technology, Operating Systems Psychology, Public Speaking, Sociology, Spanish, Total Quality Management.

Teaching Methods: *Computers:* Internet/online, e-mail. *TV:* videotape, cable program. *Other:* videoconferencing.

Admission Requirements: *Undergraduate:* open admission policy. This does not mean, however, that there are no entrance requirements. The state of South Carolina imposes general restrictions governing all admissions practices. Various residency requirements exist. See online catalog.

On-Campus Requirements: Some video courses and College Online courses have on-campus requirements.

Tuition and Fees: *Undergraduate:* full-time tuition/semester (12 hours or more): Greenville County Resident $850, out-of-county South Carolina Resident $925. *Credit by:* semester.

Financial Aid: Federal Stafford Loan, Federal PLUS Loan, Federal Pell Grant, Federal Work-Study, Federal HOPE Tax Credit, VA, South Carolina Resident Needs-based Grant, South Carolina Resident Palmetto Life Scholarships.

Accreditation: Southern Association of Colleges and Schools.

Description: Greenville Technical College (1963) is a comprehensive community college offering a wide variety of educational opportunities to the citizens of the upstate region of South Carolina. For-credit enrollment during fall semester 1998 totaled just more than 9,400 students. For 35 years the college has continuously updated and tailored educational programs to meet the needs of the students and the needs of local business and industry. The college has played a major role in the rapid and diverse economic growth in the upstate region of South Carolina. The college is dedicated to an aggressive distance learning program in an effort to provide students with as much class scheduling flexibility as possible. The college began offering distance learning telecourses in 1991 and courses via the Internet in 1997. Fall semester 1998 found more than 1,600 students taking advantage of the various distance learning course offerings.

Hadley School for the Blind

700 Elm Street	Phone: (847) 446-8111
Winnetka, IL 60093	Fax: (847) 446-0855

Division(s): All departments
Web Site(s): http://www.hadley-school.org
E-mail: info@hadley-school.org

Undergraduate Degree Programs:
High school level courses/diploma
Continuing adult education.

Graduate Degree Programs:
Continuing Education Units or Carnegie units

Class Titles: 6 core course areas: Academic/High School Studies, Braille/Other Communication Skills, Technology, Independent Living/Life Adjustment, Recreation/Leisure Time, Parent/Family Education

Teaching Methods: *Computers:* e-mail. *Other:* audiotapes, fax, correspondence, individual study.

Credits Granted for: course work.

Admission Requirements: *Undergraduate:* proof of legal blindness, family member of a legally blind person, or a professional or paraprofessional in the field of blindness/visual impairment.

On-Campus Requirements: None.

Tuition and Fees: *Undergraduate:* All of Hadley's services are tuition-free. *Credit by:* year-round; credit is awarded upon completion of a course.

Accreditation: Distance Education and Training Council, North Central Association of Colleges and Schools.

Description: The Hadley School for the Blind (1920) was founded by William A. Hadley and Dr. E. V. L. Brown as a distance education institution to teach braille to blind adults. Today, Hadley offers more than 90 tuition-free courses in 6 core course areas to more than 11,000 blind/visually impaired students, their families, and professionals throughout the world. The mission of The Hadley School for the Blind is to enable blind persons during all stages of life to acquire specialized skills, attitudes, and knowledge needed to enhance their participation in personal, family, and community life. The school accomplishes this mission by providing lifelong learning opportunities in a home setting through distance education with the support of family, friends, and blindness professionals.

Hamilton College

1924 D Street SW	Phone: (319) 363-0481
Cedar Rapids, IA 52404	Fax: (319) 363-3812

Division(s): Center for Distance Learning
Web Site(s): http://www.hamiltonia.edu
E-mail: hamiltoninfo@hamiltonia.edu

Undergraduate Degree Programs:
Associate of Science in Applied Management
Associate of Science in Interdisciplinary Studies
Bachelor of Science in Management

Class Titles: All courses can be found in our catalog.

Teaching Methods: *Computers:* Internet, real-time audio and text chat, electronic classroom, e-mail, CD-ROM, peer group projects, research components, interactive Web sites to supplement texts. *Other:* audioconferencing, audiotapes are used to supplement other course materials.

Credits Granted for: extrainstitutional credit (work or life experiences and/or participation in formal courses, following guidelines of ACE, DANTES, SOC), other college or university transfer credit, nationally standardized exams (CLEP, ACE).

Admission Requirements: *Undergraduate:* official high school transcript or GED scores; brief essay describing work, educational experiences, and objectives for enrollment; and brief essay demonstrating how the student will succeed in a distance course or program. International students must demonstrate a 490 TOEFL score in written English.

On-Campus Requirements: None.

Tuition and Fees: *Undergraduate:* $210/credit. *Application Fee:* $25 one-time fee. *Software:* $30/semester technology fee. *Other Costs:* books and supplies are additional. Evaluation of transfer credit or extrainstitutional credit; fees are available in the catalog. *Credit by:* quarter.

Financial Aid: Federal Stafford Loan, Federal Perkins Loan, Federal PLUS Loan, Federal Pell Grant, Federal Work-Study, VA, Iowa resident programs.

Accreditation: North Central Association of Colleges and Schools.

Description: Hamilton College (1900) has been a leader in private education for almost a century. Residentially, the 4-campus system provides educational and career training to Iowa residents. Nationally, the Center for Distance Learning was established early in 1998 after several years of development, research, and planning. The college believes in the learner-centered model of instruction and in the use of multimedia in delivering course content. Students are empowered through this model by being active participants in their educational success. The combination of highly credentialed, extensively trained faculty and students involved in their own educational goals form a strong and innovative distance education program.

Hamline University

| 1536 Hewitt Avenue A1710 | Phone: (651) 523-2900 |
| Saint Paul MN 55104-1284 | Fax: (651) 523-2987 |

Division(s): Graduate School of Education
Web Site(s): http://web.hamline.edu/graduate/graded/gcs/online.html
E-mail: gradprog@gw.hamline.edu

Undergraduate Degree Programs: Contact school.

Graduate Degree Programs: Contact school.

Class Titles: Exploring Archaeology Online, Becoming Better Classroom Managers, Language and Society, Linguistics for Language Teachers, Testing and Evaluation of ESL Students, Minnesota's Own Civil War, The Writing Process in Action in the Primary and Intermediate Grades, Implementing Strategic

Reading, Brain Compatible Teaching and Learning, Minnesota's Own Civil War, The Writing Process in Action in the Primary and Intermediate Grades.

Teaching Methods: *Computers:* Internet, real-time chat, electronic classroom, e-mail, LISTSERV. *TV:* videotape, cable program, satellite broadcasting, PBS. *Other:* videoconferencing, audioconferencing, independent study, individual study, learning contracts.

Credits Granted for: experiential learning, portfolio assessment, examination (CLEP).

Admission Requirements: *Undergraduate:* ACT or SAT, high school diploma. *Graduate:* graduate degree. *Certificate:* graduate degree

On-Campus Requirements: Orientation only

Tuition and Fees: *Undergraduate:* $501/credit. *Graduate:* $174/credit. *Software:* varies. *Other Costs:* varies. *Credit by:* semester.

Financial Aid: Federal Stafford Loan, Federal Perkins Loan, Federal PLUS Loan, Federal Pell Grant, Federal Work-Study, VA, state programs for residents of Minnesota.

Accreditation: North Central Association of Colleges and Schools.

Description: Hamline University (1854), Minnesota's first university, is a high-quality, nationally ranked comprehensive university with more than 3,000 students in its College of Liberal Arts, School of Law, Graduate School of Education, Graduate School of Public Administration and Management, and Graduate Liberal Studies Program. In the mid-1990s, Hamline's Distance Learning programs began in the Graduate School of Education, with an innovative Learning Community program that allows students to pursue graduate degrees without traveling to campus. That innovative tradition is currently exemplified by the nationally recognized Center for Global Environmental Education (CGEE), which specializes in combining environmental education with Distance-Learning technology.

Harcourt, Learning Direct

Student Service Center	Phone: (570) 342-7701
925 Oak Street	Fax: (570) 343-0560
Scranton, PA 18515	

Division(s): Education
Web Site(s): http://www.harcourt-learning.com
E-mail: info@harcourt-learning.com

Undergraduate Degree Programs:
Associate in Specialized Business (ASB) in:
Accounting

Business Management, with Marketing and Finance options
Applied Computer Science
Hospitality Management
Associate in Specialized Technology (AST) in Mechanical, Electrical, Electronics, Industrial, and Civil Engineering Technology

Class Titles: Contact school or check web site for details.

Teaching Methods: *Computers:* Internet, e-mail, CD-ROM. *Other:* fax, correspondence, independent study, individual study.

Credits Granted for: extrainstitutional learning (PONSI), examination (CLEP, ACT-PEP, DANTES, GRE).

Admission Requirements: *Undergraduate:* high school diploma or equivalency.

On-Campus Requirements: The only resident requirement is an 11-day Resident Lab held at Penn State/Harrisburg each year. The lab is required for Engineering Technology students only.

Tuition and Fees: *Undergraduate:* $789/Semester. *Credit by:* semester.

Financial Aid: No financing; monthly payment plan.

Accreditation: Distance Education and Training Council.

Description: The history of Harcourt Learning Direct (1890) begins when newspaper publisher Thomas J. Foster set out to train miners in better mining and safety techniques. He started the Colliery Engineering School of Mines and designed a distance training program in Mine Safety. The program was offered through the mail via advertising in his (and other) newspapers, and the first student was officially enrolled on October 16, 1891. By the end of the first year, 500 men had enrolled in Foster's program. In 1901 the name of the school was changed to International Correspondence Schools (ICS), reflecting its expanded scope and direction. Foster's revolutional approach to education was a success. By 1945 more than 5 million men and women had enrolled. In June 1997 ICS was purchased by Harcourt, Inc., a leading global multimedia publisher. Rechristened Harcourt Learning Direct, the company had entered a new period of expansion and innovation. Today, Harcourt Learning Direct offers more than 66 Distance Education programs, as well as a highly successful high school program. The Center for Degree Studies offers 11 specialized associate degree programs in business and technology.

Harford Community College

401 Thomas Run Road	**Phone: (410) 836-4145**
Bel Air, MD 21015-1698	**Fax: (410) 836-4198**

Division(s): Library and Information Services
Web Site(s): http://www.harford.cc.md.us/DistLearn/
E-mail: cvonders@harford.cc.md.us

Undergraduate Degree Programs:
Associate of Arts in:
General Studies
Business
Computer Information Systems

Class Titles: all classes listed on the web page may be taken individually if prerequisites are met.

Teaching Methods: *Computers:* Internet, real-time chat, electronic classroom, e-mail, CD-ROM, newsgroup, LISTSERV. *TV:* videotape, cable program, PBS.

Admission Requirements: *Undergraduate:* open enrollment.

On-Campus Requirements: some exams are administered in testing centers (on campus or off); varies from course to course.

Tuition and Fees: *Undergraduate:* $65 (county residents), $130 (Maryland Residents), $195 (out-of-state). An additional $40/course is assessed for online courses. *Graduation Fee:* $15. *Credit by:* semester.

Financial Aid: Federal Stafford Loan, Federal Pell Grant, Federal Work-Study, VA, state programs for residents of Maryland.

Accreditation: Middle States Association of Colleges and Schools.

Description: Harford Community College (HCC) (1957) provides high-quality, accessible, and affordable educational opportunities and services that promote professional competence, economic development, and improve the quality of life in a multicultural community. The Distance Learning program encompasses online courses and telecourses. The online program began in the spring of 1999. The college now offers 3 degree programs and 50+ courses online; HCC is a member of MCCT (Maryland Community College Teleconsortium) and MOL (Maryland Online), which provide an additional pool of courses to HCC's students.

Harold Washington College

30 East Lake Street	**Phone: (312) 553-5975**
Chicago, IL 60615	**Fax: (312) 553-5987**

Division(s): Center for Distance Learning
Web Site(s): http://www.ccc.edu/cdl
E-mail: cdl@ccc.edu

Undergraduate Degree Programs:
Associate Degree

Teaching Methods: *Computers:* Internet, e-mail, CD-ROM (for programs for military). *TV:* broadcast video, video-cassette, satellite broadcasting. *Other:* videoconferencing, audioconferencing.

Credits Granted for: experiential learning, portfolio assessment, examination (CLEP, ACT-PEP, DANTES, GRE).

Admission Requirements: *Undergraduate:* age 18, high school graduate or GED, college entrance exam; prerequisites may apply depending on course.

On-Campus Requirements: Some courses may have on-campus requirements for lab, orientation, and/or testing.

Tuition and Fees: *Undergraduate:* current tuition rate for Chicago residents and for Internet courses is $50/credit hour. This fee is subject to change and varies for out-of-district students and for international students living in Chicago. *Other Costs:* $25 nonrefundable registration fee, $30/course licensing fee. *Credit by:* semester.

Financial Aid: Federal Stafford Loan, Federal Perkins Loan, Federal PLUS Loan, Federal Pell Grant, Federal Work-Study, VA, Illinois resident programs.

Accreditation: North Central Association of Colleges and Schools.

Description: The Center for Distance Learning (CDL) coordinates college-credit Distance Learning courses for the City Colleges of Chicago and is headquartered at Harold Washington College. CDL offers more than 70 college credit courses, including courses in business, computer science, economics, science, English, foreign language, political science, psychology, and sociology. Distance Learning courses have the same prerequisites as well as the same academic requirements and transferability as traditional college credit courses. In the Distance Learning model, students learn through the Internet, television, videocassette, and/or computer-assisted instruction, allowing them to work independently but with the guidance of faculty. Students log on to the course web site, view weekly television or video programs, read required textbooks, submit homework assignments, and take exams. The college believes in the learner-centered model of instruction and in the use of multimedia in delivering course content. Students are empowered through this model by being active participants in their educational success.

Harper College

1200 Algonquin Road	Phone: (847) 925-6000
Palatine, IL 60067	Fax: (847) 925-6037

Division(s): Resources for Learning/Department of Instructional Technology
Web Site(s): http://www.harper.cc.il.us
E-mail: mmoten@harper.cc.il.us (registrar)

Undergraduate Degree Programs:
Associate of:
    Arts
    Science
    Applied Science

Class Titles: Astronomy, Career Development, Chemistry, Computer Information Systems, Dietetic Technician, English, Geography, History, Management, Marketing, Math, Music Appreciation, Pharmacology, Physical Science, Accounting, Economics, Political Science, Psychology.

Teaching Methods: *Computers:* Internet, e-mail, CD-ROM, LISTSERV. *TV:* videotape, cable program, satellite broadcasting, PBS. *Other:* interactive video, independent study.

Credits Granted for: examination (CLEP, ACT-PEP).

Admission Requirements: *Undergraduate:* assessment testing after 6 credit hours.

On-Campus Requirements: None.

Tuition and Fees: *Undergraduate:* $58/credit hour. *Application Fee:* $25. *Other Costs:* Activity Fee: $32 (part-time $16). Registration Fee: $10. *Telecourse Fee:* $20. *Other Fees:* $5.25/credit hour. *Credit by:* semester.

Financial Aid: Federal Stafford Loan, Federal Perkins Loan, Federal PLUS Loan, Federal Pell Grant, Federal Work-Study, VA, Illinois resident programs.

Accreditation: North Central Association of Colleges and Schools.

Description: Founded in 1965, Harper College has been offering telecourses since 1982 and is expanding into Web-based offerings.

Harrisburg Area Community College

One HACC Drive	Phone: (717) 780-2541
Harrisburg, PA 17110-2999	Fax: (717) 780-1925

Division(s): Distance Education
Web Site(s): http://www.hacc.edu
E-mail: distance@vm.hacc.edu

Class Titles: Accounting, Anthropology, Biology, Business, Economics, Composition, Finance, Geology, Geography, Government/Politics, Health, History, Nutrition, Humanities, Management, Marketing, Math, Philosophy, Physical Science, Psychology, Sociology, Computer Information Systems, Computer Science, Criminal Justice, General Technology, and WEB.

Teaching Methods: *Computers:* Internet, real-time chat, electronic classroom, e-mail, CD-ROM. *TV:* videotape. *Other:* videoconferencing, audiotapes, fax, correspondence.

Credits Granted for: extrainstitutional learning (corporate or professional association seminars/workshops), examination (CLEP, ACT-PEP, DANTES, GRE).

Admission Requirements: *Undergraduate:* entrance exams for math and English. *Certificate:* same as undergraduate.

On-Campus Requirements: attend course orientation meeting or watch a copy in our library on tape, 3 exams.

Tuition and Fees: *Undergraduate:* $77.50–$150/credit depending on residency. *Application Fee:* $30. *Software:* variable. *Other Costs:* $20 videotape rental, $18 copyright fee (videocourses). *Credit by:* semester.

Financial Aid: Federal Stafford Loan, Federal Perkins Loan, Federal PLUS Loan, Federal Pell Grant, Federal Work-Study, VA, Pennsylvania resident programs.

Accreditation: Middle States Association of Colleges and Schools.

Description: Established in 1964 as the first community college in Pennsylvania, Harrisburg Area Community College welcomed its first class of 426 students on September 21. In seeking to fulfill its mission of "providing educational and cultural opportunities to the community it serves," HACC has become one of the largest undergraduate colleges in Pennsylvania, with 11,000 students enrolling in credit programs and courses each semester. Our programs consist of both videocourses and online offerings. Our distance education courses award the same academic credit as traditional classroom sections. No distinction is made on a student's transcript. These credits can be applied to college degree programs and transfer the same as on-campus sections of the same course.

Harvard University Extension School

51 Brattle Street
Cambridge, MA 02138

Phone: (617) 495-9414
Fax: (617) 495-9176

Division(s): Extension School
Web Site(s): http://extension.harvard.edu
E-mail: randi_ellingboe@harvard.edu

Undergraduate Degree Programs:
Distance Education may be used to complete some but not all courses in Extension School programs.
  Associate in Arts
  Bachelor of Liberal Arts

Graduate Degree Programs:
Master of Liberal Arts in:
  Information Technology
  Liberal Studies

Certificate Programs: Applied Science, Special Studies in Administration and Management, Environmental Management, Museum Studies, Public Health, Publishing and Communications, Technologies of Education.

Class Titles: Personal Computers and the Internet, Website Development, Communications Protocols and Internet Architectures, Computer Networks and Network Programming, Java for Distributed Computing, Information Technology for Museums, Programming in Perl, Algorithms and Data Structures, Developing Windows Applications Using Visual C++, UNIX Systems Programming, Environmental Management, American Constitutional History, Genomics and Computational Biology, Environmental Ethics and Land Management, Sustainable Development.

Teaching Methods: *Computers:* streamed video lectures, course web sites, e-mail, online bulletin boards, chat rooms.

Admission Requirements: *Undergraduate:* successful completion of 3 courses in program, TOEFL. Extension School courses are open enrollment. There are requirements for admission to programs. *Graduate:* undergraduate degree, successful completion of 3 courses in program, TOEFL. *Certificate:* undergraduate degree, TOEFL.

On-Campus Requirements: Students who wish to complete the ALM in IT program via Distance Education must complete a mandatory minimum of one semester in residency to attend one or more courses on campus. At this time, it is not possible to complete other programs via Distance Education. The required semester of residency can be fall, spring, or the 8-week summer session available through the Harvard Summer School. Only the Summer School offers on-campus housing.

Tuition and Fees: *Undergraduate:* approximately $500–$1400/course. Each course is priced individually. Tuition is per course, not per credit. *Graduate:* approximately $1,200–$1,700/course. *Application Fee:* $75 one-time fee. *Other Costs:* $35 once per semester. Cost of books and other supplies is not included in tuition. *Credit by:* semester.

Financial Aid: Federal Pell Grant, VA, state programs.

Accreditation: New England Association of Schools and Colleges.

Description: The Extension School (1909) is one of 12 degree-granting schools at Harvard University. The Extension School was created to serve working adults. Since then, the Extension School continues to offer part-time study in the evenings to an increasingly diverse and international population. Extension School courses are open enrollment to students who feel they meet the stated course prerequisites. Students who choose to do so may enroll in a degree or certificate by fulfilling the admissions requirements of that program. Since the fall of 1997, the Extension School has made an increasing number of its courses available to distance learners through our Distance Education program. Students participating in a course via Distance Education do the same work and receive the same credit as students attending the course on campus.

Hawkeye Community College

1501 East Orange Road	Phone: (319) 296-4022
Waterloo, IA 50704	Fax: (319) 296-9140

Division(s): Academic Telecommunications
Web Site(s): http://www.hawkeye.cc.ia.us/academic/distance
E-mail: distance@hawkeye.cc.ia.us or rrezabek@hawkeye.cc.ia.us

Undergraduate Degree Programs:
Associate in Arts

Class Titles: Intro to Business, General Psychology, Intro to Sociology, Principles of Marketing, Composition, Calculus, Western Civilization, Non-parenteral Med Aide (continuing ed), Intro to Criminal Justice, Human Growth/Development.

Teaching Methods: *Computers:* Internet, real-time chat, electronic classroom, e-mail, CD-ROM, newsgroup, LISTSERV. *TV:* videotape telecourse, cable program, satellite broadcasting, PBS, live interactive TV, videoconferencing. *Other:* independent study, individual study, learning contracts.

Credits Granted for: examination (CLEP, ACT-PEP, DANTES, GRE).

Admission Requirements: *Undergraduate:* high school diploma or GED.

On-Campus Requirements: None.

Tuition and Fees: *Undergraduate:* $170/credit in-state, $132/credit out-of-state or international. *Other Costs:* $9/credit for student activities, registration, and computers. *Credit by:* semester.

Financial Aid: Federal Stafford Loan, Federal PLUS Loan, Federal Pell Grant, Federal Work-Study, VA, SEOG, Iowa resident programs.

Accreditation: North Central Association of Colleges and Schools.

Description: Hawkeye Community College (1966) was originally founded as a Vocational/Technical School. The college serves Black Hawk County and all or part of 10 other counties in northeast Iowa. The student population has doubled during the past 5 years to 4,000 students. Hawkeye's distance learning program and its Telecommunications System were established in 1993. Live interactive TV courses are provided over the state's DS-3 fiber-optics system (the Iowa Communications Network) and a 5-county Instructional TV Fixed Service (ITFS) system. In addition, Hawkeye offers credit telecourses that can be viewed on Iowa Public TV or by videocassette lease, and online courses are provided over the Internet. The distance learning Web site was established in 1996.

Hebrew College

160 Herrick Road	Phone: (617) 278-4929
Newton Centre, MA 02459	Fax: (617) 264-9264

Division(s): Center for Information Technology
Web Site(s): http://hebrewcollege.edu
http://hebrewcollege.edu/online
http://hebrewcollege.edu/online/degree
E-mail: online-courses@hebrewcollege.edu, onlineMA@hebrewcollege.edu

Graduate Degree Programs:
Master of Arts in Jewish Studies

Class Titles: Introduction to Jewish Studies, Study of Judaism, Genres of Biblical Literature, Philosophies of Classical Judaism, Introduction to Rabbinic Literature, Modern Jewish Thought, Modern Hebrew.

Teaching Methods: *Computers:* Internet, real-time chat, electronic classroom, e-mail, CD-ROM, LISTSERV, videoconferencing, audioconferencing, audiotapes.

Admission Requirements: *Graduate:* Undergraduate degree in any field.

On-Campus Requirements: two 1-week summer seminars.

Tuition and Fees: *Undergraduate:* $525/credit. *Graduate:* $525/credit. *Noncredit:* $450. *Guided study:* Range $600–$900. *Registration fee:* $75/semester. *Credit by:* semester.

Financial Aid: Several means of assistance are available through the college, including grants, scholarships, and tuition discounts for those working in the Jewish community. In addition, there are a variety of community scholarships available.

Accreditation: New England Association of Schools and Colleges.

Description: Hebrew College (1921) has been providing outstanding undergraduate and graduate training in Jewish studies and education since it began at its campus near Boston, Massachusetts. A leader in the field of online Jewish education, Hebrew College began offering a wide range of online courses in 1995 and launched the first online Master of Arts in Jewish Studies in 2000. This is a unique opportunity to join a learning community that features a full offering of master's-level courses, ongoing interaction with other students, one-to-one mentoring by faculty (not teaching assistants), and expert technical assistance. We believe that this program—including learning via the Internet, e-mail, interactive video, summer on-site programs, and other forums—represents a new chapter in Jewish studies and education. We invite you to find out more about this exciting new way to earn a master's degree, advance professionally, and deepen your knowledge of Jewish texts and Hebrew language.

Heriot-Watt University

1330 Avenue of the Americas	**Phone: (800) 622-9661**
New York, NY 10019	**or (212) 641-6616**

Division(s): Edinburgh Business School
North American Division
Web Site(s): www.hwmba.edu
E-mail: MBAinquiries@nyif.com

Graduate Degree Programs:
Master of Business Administration

Teaching Methods: *Other:* independent study, individual study. Online. Available September 2001.

Credits Granted for: Professional credentials such as CPA; graduate-level business courses, undergraduate degree in business; or a series of single subject, undergraduate business courses. Up to 2 compulsory courses may be waived for prior learning.

Admission Requirements: *Graduate:* accredited bachelor's degree or passing exams for 2 courses.

On-Campus Requirements: One final exam/course at local testing center for distance learning.

Tuition and Fees: *Graduate:* $825/course. *Other Costs:* $100/course exam registration fee. *Credit by:* successful exam completion.

Accreditation: Royal Charter, the highest level of British accreditation, equivalent to full U.S. accreditation.

Description: Heriot-Watt University was originally established in 1821 as an engineering college. Now located on a modern, 280-acre campus in Edinburgh, Scotland, the school is well-established as a premier business and technical university. Each year 2,500 graduates earn degrees in science, engineering, business, and technology. The Edinburgh Business School is Heriot-Watt University's graduate school of business. EBS administers the closely linked, on-campus and distance learning MBA programs. Students can pursue the MBA on campus, entirely by distance learning, or in combination, making it one of the most flexible programs available. MBA students must successfully complete 7 compulsory courses and 2 electives. Currently the Heriot-Watt MBA by distance has 9,000 students in 140 countries. The Heriot-Watt office opened in 1991 to serve North American students.

Herkimer County Community College

100 Reservoir Road	**Phone: (315) 866-0300 x211**
Herkimer, NY 13350	**Fax: (315) 866-0876**

Division(s): Internet Academy
Web Site(s): http://www.hcccia.com
E-mail: lamble@hccc.suny.edu

Undergraduate Degree Programs:
Associate in Science
Associate in Applied Science

Teaching Methods: *Computers:* Internet, electronic classroom, e-mail.

Credits Granted for: examination (CLEP, ACT, GRE).

Admission Requirements: *Undergraduate:* open admissions.

On-Campus Requirements: minimum of 30 hours credit from Herkimer County Community College required for associate degree. All may be via distance learning.

Tuition and Fees: *Undergraduate:* $80/credit, $7/credit online fee. *Other Costs:* variable, but minimal. *Credit by:* semester.

Financial Aid: Federal Stafford Loan, Federal Perkins Loan, Federal PLUS Loan, Federal Pell Grant, Federal Work-Study, VA, New York resident programs.

Accreditation: Middle States Association of Colleges and Schools.

Description: Herkimer County Community College (1967) is a full-service, open-door college. We are affiliated with the State University of New York and have a population of about 2,500 students. Our distance learning opportunities are extensive, with both closed-circuit videoconferencing for local students and Internet-based classes for anytime/anyplace student access.

Highland Community College

2998 West Pearl City Road	Phone: (815) 235-6121 x3457
Freeport, IL 61032	Fax: (815) 235-1366

Division(s): Learning Resource Center
Web Site(s): http://highland.userworld.com/telecour
E-mail: ewelch@admin.highland.cc.il.us

Class Titles: History, Accounting, Business, Nutrition, Photography, Psychology, Poetry, Statistics, Literature, Economics.

Teaching Methods: *Computers:* electronic classroom. *TV:* videotape, cable program, satellite broadcasting. *Other:* None.

Credits Granted for: examination (CLEP, ACT-PEP, DANTES, GRE).

Admission Requirements: *Undergraduate:* high school graduate.

On-Campus Requirements: None.

Tuition and Fees: *Undergraduate:* $50/credit. *Other Costs:* assorted fees. *Credit by:* semester.

Financial Aid: Federal Stafford Loan, Federal Pell Grant, Federal Work-Study, VA, Illinois resident programs.

Accreditation: North Central Association of Colleges and Schools.

Description: Highland Community College (1963) is a small student-oriented, publicly funded community college in northwestern Illinois that serves a 4-county district. Distance learning courses are self-paced, videotape-based, or via interactive video classes.

Highline Community College

2400 South 240th	Phone: (206) 878-3700 x3011
Des Moines, WA 98000	Fax: (206) 870-3776

Division(s): Distance Education
Web Site(s): http://flightline.highline.ctc.edu/distanced
E-mail: dsteussy@hcc.ctc.edu

Undergraduate Degree Programs:
Associate Degree

Certificate Programs: Occupational Programs—Accounting, Administration of Justice/Law Enforcement, Administrative Assistant, Bookkeeping, Business, Career Transition, Child Care Provider, Chiropractic Technician, Client-Server Specialist, Dental Assistant, Drafting/Design Technology, Education: Early Childhood, Special Ed/Ed Paraprofessional, Freight Forwarding, Hotel/Tourism, Interactive Media, Interior Design, Internet Business, Library Technician, Legal Secretary, Legal Word Processor, Manufacturing Engineering Technology, Marketing/Selling, Medical Assistant, Medical Secretary and Receptionist, Medical Transcriptionist/Word Processor, Microcomputer Information Specialist, Network Specialist, Nursing, Nursing Articulation (Ladder), Office Assistant, Offset Printing, Paralegal, Parent Education, Physical Education, Plastics Manufacturing, Production Illustration, Respiratory Care, Retailing, Small Business Entrepreneurship, Transportation Agent, Travel/Transportation, Word Processing Operator, Word Processing Specialist.

Class Titles: Biology, Business, General Science, History, Education, Literature, Social Science, Humanities, Mathematics, Computer Programming.

Teaching Methods: *Computers:* Internet, real-time chat, electronic classroom, e-mail, CD-ROM, newsgroup, LISTSERV. *TV:* videotape, cable program, PBS. *Other:* videoconferencing, correspondence, independent study, individual study, learning contracts.

Credits Granted for: experiential learning, portfolio assessment, extrainstitutional learning, examinations (CLEP, ACT-PEP, DANTES, GRE).

Admission Requirements: *Undergraduate:* Advisors help with this process. Contact Denny Steussy at (206) 878-3710 x3534. For the 2-year associate degree: high school graduate or age 18; U.S. citizen, refugee, or immigrant; foreign students are enrolled through the admissions office; prerequisites for all classes; time limits for completion.

On-Campus Requirements: Vary with course type. None for online.

Tuition and Fees: *Undergraduate:* $54.70/credit. *Other Costs:* $20/quarter for e-mail accounts. *Credit by:* quarter.

Financial Aid: Federal Pell Grant, Supplementary Educational Opportunity Grant, Federal Work-Study, Federal Stafford Loan, Stafford Student Loan Program, student employment, State Need Grant, State Work Study, Highline Community College Grant, and Tuition Waiver.

Accreditation: Northwest Association of Schools and Colleges.

Description: Highline Community College (1961) offers high-quality transfer, occupational, and continuing education programs to a diverse campus population and a wide array of community residents. Highline has offered distance courses for more than 20 years. The college offers a wide variety of programs designed to teach the technical, professional, and personal skills needed for employment in today's competitive world. Faculty are joined by representatives of business and labor in their specific fields to develop and review curricula to maintain high quality.

Hillsborough Community College

39 Columbia Drive	
PO Box 31127	Phone: (813) 253-7574
Tampa, FL 33631-3127	Fax: (813) 259-6018

Division(s): eCampus Department
Web Site(s): http://www.hcc.cc.fl.us/eCampus
E-mail: ltrombly@hcc.cc.fl.us

Class Titles: American History, Florida History, American Government, Art Appreciation, English, Humanities, Astronomy, Biology, Earth Science, Child Development, Psychology, Sociology, Marriage/Family, Economics (micro/macro), Personal Finance, Business, Management, Marketing, College Algebra, Algebra, Computers/Technology, Internet.

Teaching Methods: *Computers:* Internet, real-time chat, electronic classroom, e-mail, CD-ROM. *TV:* videotape, cable program, PBS. *Other:* videoconferencing, audiotapes, fax, correspondence, independent study, audioconferencing.

Credits Granted for: examination (CLEP, DANTES).

Admission Requirements: *Undergraduate:* high school diploma; college-level reading, writing, and math for most distance learning courses.

On-Campus Requirements: 5 meetings (optional) each term. The majority of work that determines student's grades must be completed in the presence of the instructor or an approved proctor. Some 75% of Associate of Arts and 75% of Associate of Science degrees earned at a distance; the other 25% are on site.

Tuition and Fees: *Undergraduate:* $52.70/credit resident, $196.36/credit nonresident. *Other Costs:* $20 lab fee for all eLearning courses. *Credit by:* semester.

Financial Aid: Federal Stafford Loan, Federal Perkins Loan, Federal PLUS Loan, Federal Pell Grant, Federal Work-Study, VA, Florida resident programs.

Accreditation: Southern Association of Colleges and Schools.

Description: Hillsborough Community College (1968) is embarking on its 33rd year of providing contemporary educational programs to a highly diverse population. HCC's facilities include campuses in Tampa, Brandon, Plant City, and Ybor City. Courses are also offered at many off-campus sites throughout Hillsborough County. More than 45,000 students attend HCC each year. Of Florida's 28-member community college system, HCC ranks 7th in size. Students at HCC embody the spirit of diversity. In addition to a multitude of ethnic backgrounds and age groups, HCC students include individuals who are pursuing a college degree for the first time to those returning to college to increase their knowledge and skills. Because there is no "typical" HCC student, newcomers quickly fit right in. HCC is committed and continuously strives to anticipate technological, economic, and demographic trends to ensure that its graduates are well prepared to achieve success in their next ventures.

Hocking College

3301 Hocking Parkway	Phone: (740) 753-3591
Nelsonville, OH 45764	Fax: (740) 753-4097

Division(s): Academic Affairs
Web Site(s): http://www.hocking.edu
E-mail: dabelko_e@hocking.edu

Class Titles: Human Organism, Job Communications, Technical Writing, Communications II, Communications III/IV, Job Search, Basic Math, Pre-Algebra, Medical Terminology, Front Office Procedures, Housekeeping Management, Hospitality Supervision, Managing for Quality, Hospitality Industry Training, Hospitality Industry Computer Systems, Security Management, Contemporary Club Management, Hospitality Human Resources, Tourism and Hospitality Industry, Bar and Beverage Management, Convention Management, Food and Beverage Controls, Statistical Process and Quality Control.

Teaching Methods: *Computers:* e-mail. *Other:* videoconferencing.

Credits Granted for: experiential learning, portfolio assessment.

Admission Requirements: *Undergraduate:* high school diploma or GED. Some programs have special admission requirements.

On-Campus Requirements: 30 credit hours.

Tuition and Fees: *Undergraduate:* $60/credit part-time in-state, $120/credit out-of-state, $717/12–18 credits in-state, $1,434/12–18 credits out-of-state, additional for international. *Application Fee:* $15. *Other Costs:* varying lab fees. *Credit by:* quarter.

Financial Aid: Federal Stafford Loan, Federal PLUS Loan, Federal Pell Grant, Federal Work-Study, VA, Ohio Instructional Grant.

Accreditation: North Central Association of Colleges and Schools.

Description: Hocking College (1968) is a 2-year technical college in which the accent is on "learning by doing." Located in southeastern Ohio about 60 miles from Columbus, the college offers associate degrees and certificates in more than 30 programs. It also provides the state-approved Transfer Module for students planning to transfer to a 4-year college. The 6,000 students are diverse in age, background, geographic origin, and interests and represent 88 Ohio counties, 20 states, and 47 foreign countries. Students may enroll in day or evening classes and may choose traditional classroom or self-paced instruction. Hocking's 2-way, interactive, audio-video distance learning program was established with funding from the Rural Utilities Services in 1994. Additionally, new, asynchronous, online distance learning offerings are being developed.

Holy Apostles College and Seminary

33 Prospect Hill Road	Phone: (860) 632-3022
Cromwell, CT 06415	Fax: (860) 632-3075

Division(s): International Catholic University
Web Site(s): http://www.catholicity.com/school/icu
E-mail: icu@sicugnet.net

Graduate Degree Programs:
Master of Arts in:
   Theology
   Philosophy

Class Titles: Contact school or check web site for details.

Teaching Methods: *Computers:* Internet, e-mail. *Other:* fax, correspondence.

Admission Requirements: *Graduate:* Bachelor of Acts degree with 3.0 GPA.

On-Campus Requirements: None.

Tuition and Fees: *Graduate:* $165/credit. *Credit by:* semester.

Accreditation: New England Association of Schools and Colleges.

Description: Holy Apostles (1956) was founded in Cromwell, Connecticut, by The Very Reverend Eusebe M. Menard, O.F.M., to provide a college-level program of education and formation especially for adults who sought to answer God's call to the priesthood later in life, with an academic and seminary environment suited to their age and background. Holy Apostles Seminary was then a college-level preparatory seminary, which Fr. Menard entrusted to the Missionaries of the Holy Apostles. In 1972, in accordance with both the directives of Vatican Council II and its responsibilities in the larger Christian community, Holy Apostles broadened its purpose to include undergraduate degrees for men and women who were not seminarians. This began Holy Apostles College division. In 1978 the focus of the seminary program was broad-

ened to include a graduate degree program in addition to the undergraduate seminary program. For the first time, seminarians were able to earn the Master of Divinity degree and complete the entire program of priestly formation. The aim of ICU is to make the Catholic intellectual, cultural, and literary patrimony available to those unable to attend a traditional campus.

Holy Names College

3500 Mountain Boulevard	Phone: (510) 436-1321
Oakland, CA 94619-1699	(800) 430-1321
	Fax: (510) 436-1325

Division(s): Nursing
Web Site(s): http://www.hnc.edu
E-mail: None

Undergraduate Degree Programs:
Bachelor of Science in Nursing; RN to BSN Program

Teaching Methods: *Computers:* computer software, e-mail, CD-ROM. *TV:* interactive TV. *Other:* videoconferencing, telephone, fax, print, mail. Adjunct faculty are at each videoconferencing site.

Credits Granted for: examination (CLEP), ACE/PONSI evaluated military training programs, ACE/PONSI evaluated business training programs, transfer credits.

Admission Requirements: *Undergraduate:* for transfer students, good standing at last institution, 2.2 GPA in 30 transferable units, Associate Degree in Nursing or hospital school of nursing diploma, currently licensed as RN in California or eligibility for NCLEX, completion of lower-division prerequisites including Anatomy/Physiology, Microbiology, Sociology or Anthropology, Psychology, and freshman English Composition.

On-Campus Requirements: classes are telecast to multiple sites at selected hospital facilities throughout California on Wednesdays and Thursdays from 6:00 to 9:00 P.M.

Tuition and Fees: *Undergraduate:* $335/credit. *Application Fee:* $35. *Credit by:* semester.

Financial Aid: Federal Stafford Loan, Federal Pell Grant, VA, Cal Grant, Employer Tuition Reimbursement.

Accreditation: National League for Nursing, Western Association of Schools and Colleges, Collegiate Commission on Nursing Education.

Description: Holy Names College (1868) is a cosmopolitan institution of innovative higher learning offering men and women of all faiths and ages the opportunity to obtain an outstanding education in liberal arts, preparation for many careers, and an enriched life. A leader in providing degree completion opportunities for working adults, Holy Names has offered a campus-based nursing program for Registered Nurses seeking BSN degrees since 1971. Since 1995 the college has offered its accredited NLN program via teleconferencing and in partnership with California hospitals.

Home Study International (Griggs University)

12501 Old Columbia Pike	Phone: (800) 782-4769
Silver Spring, MD 20904-6600	Fax: (301) 680-5157

Division(s): entire school
Web Site(s): http://www.griggs.edu
E-mail: enrollmentservices@griggs.edu

Undergraduate Degree Programs:
Bachelor of Science in:
    Church Business Management
    Religious Education
Bachelor of Arts in:
    Religion
    Theological Studies

Class Titles: all classes are available via distance learning. Call university for complete list.

Teaching Methods: *TV:* videotape. *Other:* audiotapes, correspondence.

Credits Granted for: experiential learning, portfolio assessment, examination (CLEP, ACT-PEP, DANTES, GRE).

Admission Requirements: *Undergraduate:* accredited secondary school graduate or equivalent, completion of adequate pattern of high school subjects, 2.0 high school GPA; if native language is not English, must submit exam results for TOEFL or Michigan Test for English Language Proficiency with scores of 550 (TOEFL), 213 (CTOEFL), or 90 (Michigan).

On-Campus Requirements: None.

Tuition and Fees: *Undergraduate:* $140/credit. *Enrollment Fee:* $60. *Other Costs:* varies for textbooks, supplies, materials. *Credit by:* semester.

Accreditation: Accrediting Commission of the Distance Education and Training Council.

Description: Since 1909 Home Study International has helped students achieve their educational goals through distance learning. The mission of HSI is to provide students with a well-balanced education that will enrich the quality of their lives and their church.

Hope International University

2500 East Nutwood Drive	Phone: (714) 879-3901 x1228
Fullerton, CA 92831	Fax: (714) 992-0274

Division(s): Distance Learning
Web Site(s): http://www.hiu.edu
E-mail: dl-info@hiu.edu

Graduate Degree Programs:
Master of Business Administration
Master of Ministry Intercultural Studies

Class Titles: Theology of Ministry, Life of Christ, World Civilization, Violent Encounters in Family, History of Hebrew People (in Spanish only), Intercultural Studies, Marriage/Family/Child Counseling, Biblical Interpretation (Theology/Hermeneutics), Bible Survey, Cross Cultural Mores/Values, World Christian Movement, Missiological Exegesis.

Teaching Methods: *Computers:* Internet, real-time chat, electronic classroom, e-mail. *TV:* videotape. *Other:* audiotapes, fax, correspondence, independent study, individual study, learning contracts.

Credits Granted for: experiential learning.

Admission Requirements: *Graduate:* bachelor's degree, 3.0 GPA for full admission, TOEFL.

On-Campus Requirements: None.

Tuition and Fees: *Undergraduate:* $475/unit. *Graduate:* $1,005/class. *Application Fee:* $30. *Other Costs:* $100 videotape deposit (refunded upon videotape's return). *Credit by:* semester.

Financial Aid: Federal Stafford Loan, Federal Perkins Loan, Federal PLUS Loan, Federal Pell Grant, Federal Work-Study, CAL Grant, FEOG.

Accreditation: Western Association of Schools and Colleges.

Description: Hope International University (1928) is built upon the historic and solid foundations of Pacific Christian College, which was called Pacific Bible Seminary at its inception. The university is composed of 3 schools: Pacific Christian College—the traditional undergraduate college; the School of Professional Studies—with an adult degree completion program and international programs; and the School of Graduate Studies—which offers several graduate programs to enhance professional and church-related management careers. Distance Learning began in 1994 with individual courses delivered via videotape; student progress is monitored by university faculty. The program has grown to include 2 complete online degree programs at the graduate level. The Master of Business Administration and the Master of Intercultural Studies are offered online to students worldwide.

Hospitality Training Center

220 North Main Street	Phone: (330) 653-9151
Hudson, OH 44236	Fax: (330) 650-2833

Certificate Programs: Medical Office Computer Specialist, Motel Management Home-based Travel Agent.

Teaching Methods: *Other:* correspondence, independent study, individual study, learning contracts.

Credits Granted for: experiential learning, portfolio assessment, extrainstitutional learning, examination (CLEP, ACT-PEP, DANTES GRE).

Admission Requirements: *Certificate:* open enrollment.

On-Campus Requirements: None.

Tuition and Fees: *Undergraduate:* $1,995 Motel Management, $2,395 Medical Office Computer Specialist (includes software), $1,282 Home-Based Travel Agent. *Credit by:* hours.

Accreditation: Distance Education and Training Council.

Description: Hospitality Training Center (1961) was founded by Dr. Robert W. McIntosh at Michigan State University. In 1963, Duane Hills purchased the school, originally known as Modern School, and changed the name to Motel Managers School. This name was changed in 1985 to Hospitality Training Center to better reflect what the school is doing. Currently 3 courses are being offered and are accredited by DETC. The school is now over 40 years old. It is the only school in the U.S. to train for Motel Management by Distance Learning. Duane Hills was the president of DETC and served on the Board of Trustees.

Houston Community College

3100 Main, MC 1740	Phone: (713) 718-5275
Houston, TX 77002	Fax: (713) 718-5388

Division(s): Distance Education
Web Site(s): http://distance.hccs.cc.tx.us
E-mail: paul_c@hccs.cc.tx.us

Undergraduate Degree Programs:
Associate Degree

Class Titles: Accounting, Anthropology, Art, Biology, Business, Chemistry, Child Development, Criminal Justice, Computer Science, Drafting, Economics, Electronic Engineering Technology, English, Geography, Geology, Government, History, Human Services, Math, Marketing, Philosophy, Photography, Physical Education, Psychology, Real Estate, Records Management, Sociology, Spanish.

Teaching Methods: *Computers:* Internet, real-time chat, electronic classroom, e-mail, CD-ROM, technical communication. *TV:* videotape, cable program, PBS. *Other:* videoconferencing, audiotapes, fax, correspondence, independent study, print based.

Credits Granted for: examination (CLEP).

Admission Requirements: *Undergraduate:* open door, high school graduate or GED, TASP/ASSET testing, see catalog for exemptions.

On-Campus Requirements: Some classes have weekly on-campus labs.

Tuition and Fees: *Undergraduate:* $117 credits in-district, $204 credits out-of-district, $369 credits out-of-state. *Other Costs:* $24/course distance education fee. *Credit by:* semester.

Financial Aid: Federal Stafford Loan, Federal Pell Grant, Federal Work-Study, VA, Texas resident programs.

Accreditation: Southern Association of Colleges and Schools.

Description: The Houston Community College System (1971) was created as a public open-admission institution of higher education offering associate degrees, certificates, workforce training, and lifelong learning opportunities for all people in the communities it serves. In an effort to make education more accessible to all students, HCCS has offered a regular schedule of telecourses since 1985, and in 1987 it introduced the first computer-modem course. The distance education department currently offers 120 courses to 3,000 students each semester: telecourses airing on PBS-TV, HCCS cable, and Stafford cable, videocassette courses, print-based (textbook only) courses, and Internet courses.

Husson College

One College Circle	Phone: (207) 941-7079
Bangor, ME 04401	

Division(s): Information Technology
Web Site(s): http://www.husson.edu

Undergraduate Degree Programs:
RN
BSN

Class Titles: Contract school or check web site for details.

Teaching Methods: *Computers:* Internet, electronic classroom, e-mail. *TV:* videotape. *Other:* videoconferencing, audioconferencing, fax, correspondence, independent study, individual study, learning contracts.

Credits Granted for: examination (CLEP, ACT-PEP, DANTES, GRE).

Admission Requirements: *Undergraduate:* high school transcripts, RN license.

On-Campus Requirements: None.

Tuition and Fees: *Undergraduate:* $328/credit. *Application Fee:* $25. *Other Costs:* $125 for tuition deposit. *Credit by:* semester.

Financial Aid: Federal Stafford Loan, Federal Perkins Loan, Federal PLUS Loan, Federal Pell Grant, Federal Work-Study, VA, state programs for residents of Maine.

Accreditation: National League for Nursing, New England Association of Schools and Colleges.

Description: Husson College (1899) has had a baccalaureate nursing program since 1984. In 1988 that program established a special program for RNs with associate degrees or diplomas to study for a BSN. In 1997 this on-campus program offered a Distance Learning track.

Hypnosis Motivation Institute

18607 Ventura Boulevard, Suite 310	Phone: (800) 682-4464
Tarzana, CA 91356	Fax: (818) 344-2262

Division(s): Extension School
Web Site(s): http://www.HypnosisMotivation.com
E-mail: None

Certificate Programs: Hypnotherapy.

Class Titles: Hypnotherapy

Teaching Methods: *TV:* videotape. *Other:* audiotapes, fax, correspondence, tutorial.

Admission Requirements: *Undergraduate:* age 18.

On-Campus Requirements: None.

Tuition and Fees: *Undergraduate:* $4,400/300 clock hours. *Credit by:* clock hour.

Accreditation: Distance Education and Training Council.

Description: Hypnosis Motivation Institute (1968) is America's only accredited college of hypnotherapy.

Illinois Eastern Community Colleges
Frontier Community College
Lincoln Trail College
Olney Central College
Wabash Valley College

233 East Chestnut Street	Phone: (618) 393-2982
Olney, IL 62450	Fax: (618) 392-4816

Division(s): Information Technology
Web Site(s): http://www.iecc.cc.il.us
E-mail: hubblee@iecc.cc.il.us

Class Titles: Sign Language, Speech, Music Appreciation, Composition, Statistics, Spanish, Economics, Sociology

Teaching Methods: *TV:* videotape, videoconferencing. *Other:* correspondence, independent study, individual study.

Credits Granted for: experiential learning, portfolio assessment, examination (CLEP, ACT-PEP, DANTES, GRE).

Admission Requirements: *Undergraduate:* ASSET test.

On-Campus Requirements: None.

Tuition and Fees: *Undergraduate:* $40/credit. *Application Fee:* $10. *Credit by:* semester.

Financial Aid: Federal Stafford Loan, Federal Perkins Loan, Federal PLUS Loan, Federal Pell Grant, Federal Work-Study, VA, Illinois resident programs.

Accreditation: North Central Association of Colleges and Schools.

Description: The mission of Illinois Eastern Community Colleges District (1967) is to provide educational opportunities and public services to the citizens of southeastern Illinois. IECC is a system of 4 public institutions of higher education supported by a district office. By offering quality educational and public service programs, the colleges work together to better the cultural, social, and economic futures of the citizens of southeastern Illinois.

Indiana College Network

714 North Senate Avenue	Phone: (800) 426-8899
Indianapolis, IN 46202	Fax: (812) 855-9380

Division(s): Student Services Center
Web Site(s): http://www.icn.org
E-mail: info@ihets.org

Undergraduate Degree Programs:
Associate of Applied Science in:
    Accounting
    Business Administration (Management Specialty)

Business Administration (Marketing Specialty)
Design Technology (Architecture Specialty)
General Studies
Law Enforcement
Associate of Arts in:
    Behavioral Sciences
    Biblical Studies
    General Arts
    Justice Administration (Ministry Concentration)
    Justice Administration (Public Policy Concentration)
    Liberal Arts (General Studies)
Associate of General Studies
Associate of Science in:
    Behavioral Sciences
    Business Administration
    Business Administration (Management Option)
    Communications
    General Aviation Flight Technology
    General Studies
    Histotechnology
    Labor Studies
    Law Enforcement
Bachelor of General Studies
Bachelor of Science in:
    Business Administration
    Community Health
    Criminology
    Electronics Technology
    General Industry Technology
    Health Services
    Human Resource Development
    Industrial Supervision
    Insurance
    Labor Studies
    Mechanical Technology
    Nursing
    Vocational Trade-Industrial-Technical Education

Graduate Degree Programs:
Master of Arts in:
    Criminology
    Education in Educational Administration and Supervision
    Education in Elementary Education
    Education in Special Education
    Executive Development and Public Service
    Health and Safety (Specialization in Occupational Safety Management)
Master of Business Administration
Master of Business Administration in Food and Agricultural Business
Master of Science in:
    Adult Education
    Computer Science
    Criminology
    Education in Language Education

Electrical and Computer Engineering
Health and Safety (Specialization in Occupational Safety Management)
Human Resource Development
Industrial Engineering
Interdisciplinary Engineering
Mechanical Engineering
Nursing (Adult/Family Nurse Practitioner)
Nursing (Nurse Educator)
Recreation (Therapeutic Recreation Emphasis)
Student Affairs Administration

Certificate Programs: Behavioral Sciences—Community Rehabilitation, Christian Worker, Corrections, Digital Signal Processing, Distance Education, Driver Education, General Studies, Information Technology, Justice and Ministry, Labor Studies, Law Enforcement, Library/Media Services, Office Software Specialist, Private Security, Public Administration, Recreation Activities Leadership, School Administration.

Teaching Methods: *Computers:* Internet, e-mail, CD-ROM, newsgroup, LISTSERV. *TV:* videotape, cable TV, satellite broadcasting, PBS. *Other:* videoconferencing, audioconferencing, correspondence, independent study.

Credits Granted for: variable.

Admission Requirements: *Undergraduate:* variable. *Graduate:* variable. *Certificate:* variable.

On-Campus Requirements: some courses may require a student to attend a specific number of on-campus sessions; most courses do not.

Tuition and Fees: *Undergraduate:* tuition and fees are established independently by each participating institution. *Software:* variable. *Credit by:* Most participating institutions are on the semester system, although many are offering courses with open enrollment throughout the year.

Financial Aid: Financial aid is determined independently by each participating institution, and may include the Federal Stafford Loan, Federal Perkins Loan, Federal PLUS Loan, Federal Pell Grant, Federal Work-Study, VA, etc.

Accreditation: All participating institutions are accredited.

Description: The Indiana College Network (ICN) (1992) is a not-for-profit service of the Indiana Higher Education Telecommunication System, a unique state-funded consortium of 39 public and private universities and colleges. The network's Student Services Center serves prospective students as a clearinghouse for information about admissions, registration, career counseling, and financial aid. It is the students' first stop in registering for distance education courses. Partnership institutions include: Ball State University, Independent Colleges of Indiana, Inc., Indiana State University, Indiana University, Ivy Tech State College,

Purdue University, University of Southern Indiana, and Vincennes University.

Indiana Institute of Technology

1600 East Washington Boulevard	Phone: (888) 666-8324
Fort Wayne, IN 46803	(219) 422-5561
	Fax: (219) 422-1518

Division(s): Extended Studies Division
Web Site(s): http://www.indtech.edu
E-mail: stahl@indtech.edu

Undergraduate Degree Programs:
Associate of Science in:
 Business Administration
 Concentrations in Management of Finance
Bachelor of Science in:
 Business Administration
 Concentrations in Management, Marketing, Accounting, or Human Resources

Class Titles: Accounting, Business, English, Humanities or Social Science classes.

Teaching Methods: *Computers:* e-mail. *Other:* fax, correspondence, independent study, individual study.

Credits Granted for: experiential learning, portfolio assessment, extrainstitutional learning, examination (CLEP, ACT-PEP, DANTES, GRE).

Admission Requirements: *Undergraduate:* application fee, official copy of high school transcript/GED.

On-Campus Requirements: None.

Tuition and Fees: *Undergraduate:* $206/credit. *Application Fee:* $50. *Credit by:* semester.

Financial Aid: Federal Stafford Loan, Federal PLUS Loan, Federal Pell Grant, VA.

Accreditation: North Central Association of Colleges and Schools.

Description: Indiana Institute of Technology (1930) is a private, not-for-profit institution offering undergraduate degrees in engineering, computer science, and business. The Extended Studies Division was founded in 1981 to deliver the traditional, quality business education. Indiana Tech has become known for its emerging number of adult students. ESD offers students 2 degree programs: the Accelerated Degree Program (classroom environment) and the Independent Study Program (self-study). The Independent Study Program offers you the opportunity to complete your entire college degree without attending formal classes. Via mail, you are provided with the detailed materials to guide

you through the course work at your own pace. The established completion period for courses is 6 months.

Indiana University

P.O. Box 1345	(800) 334-1011
Bloomington, IN 47402	Phone: (317) 274-4178
	Fax: (317) 274-4513, (812) 855-8680

Division(s): Office of Distributed Education
Web Site(s): http://www.indiana.edu/~iude/
E-mail: scs@indiana.edu

Undergraduate Degree Programs:
Associate of General Studies
Associate of Science in Histotechnology
Associate of Science in Labor Studies
Bachelor of General Studies
Bachelor of Science in Labor Studies

Graduate Degree Programs:
Master of Science in Adult Education
Master of Science in Language Education
Master of Business Administration
Master of Science in Instructional Systems Technology
Master of Science in Music Technology
Master of Science in Therapeutic Recreation

Certificate Programs: Labor Studies, Distance Education, Histotechnology.

Diploma Program:
Through the IU School of Continuing Studies students can also pursue the fully accredited Indiana University High School Diploma.

Class Titles: Accounting, African Studies, American Studies, Anthropology, Astronomy, Biology, Business, Classical Studies, College of Arts/Sciences, Communication/Culture, Computer Science, Criminal Justice, Economics, Education, English, Fine Arts, French, Geological Sciences, Health/Physical Education/Recreation, History, Journalism, Labor Studies, Mathematics, Music, Nursing, Philosophy, Physics, Political Science, Psychology, School of Public/Environmental Affairs, Sociology, Spanish, Telecommunications.

Teaching Methods: *Computers:* Internet, e-mail, CD-ROM. *TV:* videotape, cable program, satellite broadcasting. *Other:* Indiana Higher Education Telecommunication System (IHETS), IU's two-way interactive Virtual Indiana Classroom (VIC) network, fax, correspondence, independent study.
 IU's "insite" service provides students with access to university admissions, advising, course financial aid, transcript and scheduling information via the World Wide Web. During

their degree, students can regularly access updated advising reports online to plan their current or proposed course of study.

Credits Granted for: experiential learning, portfolio assessment, examination (CLEP, DANTES), military service, accredited transfer credits.

Admission Requirements: Admission, course, and exam requirements vary for each program. Students are encouraged to consult web sites for individual program requirements.

On-Campus Requirements: Select programs may require on-campus attendance. Course delivery requirements are outlined on individual program web sites and can be accessed through the Office of Distributed Education web site (http://www.indiana.edu/~iude).

Tuition and Fees: Varies by program. Students are encouraged to visit program web sites for details.

Financial Aid: Varies by program. Students are encouraged to visit program web sites for details.

Accreditation: North Central Association of Colleges and Schools.

Description: One of the oldest state universities west of the Allegheny Mountains, Indiana University was founded in Bloomington in 1820 and today has 8 campuses statewide. Indiana University (IU) has offered distance instruction to learners worldwide since 1912. In spring 1999, it created an Office of Distributed Education to support the university's distributed education efforts; in June 2000, the university released a Strategic Plan for Distributed Education, demonstrating its commitment to taking the next bold step: to integrate information technology into the mainstream of teaching and learning. IU has had 116 of its degree programs ranked among the nation's top 20 by the Gourman Report, *U.S. News & World Report*, and the National Research Council. The university's largest campus, IU Bloomington, has been named among the nation's top 10 "wired" campuses by Yahoo! *Internet Life Magazine* and *PC Week* have ranked IU among the top public institutions for information technology innovation.

Indiana University of Pennsylvania

390 Pratt Drive	Phone: (724) 357-2228
Indiana, PA 15705	Fax: (724) 357-7597

Division(s): Continuing Education
Web Site(s): http://www.iup.edu/contin/
E-mail: ce-ocp@grove.iup.edu

Undergraduate Degree Programs:
Associates Degree in General Studies (with Clarion University of Pennsylvania).
We do offer an expanding list of undergraduate level courses (Criminology, Food and Nutrition, Geoscience, Mathematics, Physics, Political Science, Safety Sciences).

Certificate Programs: Web-based instruction for Physics Certification (Graduate credit) Certificate of Recognition in Safety Sciences.

Class Titles: Criminology, Food and Nutrition, Geoscience, History, Mathematics, Physics, Political Science, Safety Sciences.

Teaching Methods: *Computers:* Internet, electronic classroom, e-mail, LISTSERV, CD-ROM, newsgroup. *Other:* radio broadcast, videoconferencing, audioconferencing, audiographics, audiotapes, fax, correspondence, independent study, individual study.

Admission Requirements: *Undergraduate:* state certification in science or math, 8 credits of physics at introductory college level, math background including calculus. NOTE: state requirements also include one course in biology, 2 in chemistry, and one course in geoscience. *Certificate:* Certificate of Recognition in Safety Sciences—minimum 2.6 GPA in bachelor's degree, transcripts, application, and fee. Web-based instruction for Physics Certification (WINPC)—minimum 2.6 GPA in bachelor's degree, transcripts, Level I Certificate, application, and fee, prior teaching certification in the sciences.

On-Campus Requirements: For some programs. Certificate of Recognition in Safety Sciences does not require on-campus classes. Web-Based Instruction for Physics Certification (WINPC) requires summer on-campus laboratories.

Tuition and Fees: These tuition figures are subject to change for Fall 2001 approximately August 2001. *Undergraduate:* $158/credit. *Graduate:* $230/credit. *Application Fee:* $30 *Other Costs:* registration fee $20/person +10% of tuition for off-campus instructional fee. *Credit by:* semester.

Financial Aid: Federal Stafford Loan, Federal Perkins Loan, Federal PLUS Loan, Federal Pell Grant, Federal Work-Study, VA, Pennsylvania resident programs.

Accreditation: Middle States Association of Colleges and Schools.

Description: Indiana University of Pennsylvania (1875) is recognized for its combination of academic excellence with affordable prices. IUP provides an intellectually challenging experience to more than 13,000 students at the university's 3 campuses, all easily accessible from Pittsburgh and the

Middle Atlantic region. IUP's primary campus is located in a safe, friendly community in easy reach of a wide range of outdoor activities. The Distance Education Program at IUP has experienced exponential growth in the last 3 years and constantly expanding the opportunities for all students. The DE programs are primarily Web-based with added features such as CD-ROMS, Streamed Video, WebCT, and other multimedia products.

Indiana University, South Bend

1700 Mishawaka Avenue
South Bend, IN 46634-7111

Phone: (219) 237-4488
Fax: (219) 237-6550

Division(s): Office of Information Technology/Instructional Media Services
Web Site(s): http://www.iusb.edu
E-mail: kweidner@iusb.edu

Class Titles: History, Psychology, Communications, General Studies, Philosophy, Labor Studies, Chemistry, Education, Personal Finance.

Teaching Methods: *TV:* 2-way audio/video interactive, PBS. *Other:* IHETS, satellite broadcast.

Admission Requirements: *Undergraduate:* good standing at another higher education institution. Please contact school for complete information.

On-Campus Requirements: programming is available only at TV receive sites in Indiana.

Tuition and Fees: *Undergraduate:* $109.25/credit Indiana resident. *Other Costs:* $25/3 credits technology fee. *Credit by:* semester.

Financial Aid: Federal Stafford Loan, Federal Perkins Loan, Federal PLUS Loan, Federal Pell Grant, Federal Work-Study, VA, Indiana resident programs.

Accreditation: North Central Association of Colleges and Schools.

Description: Indiana University at South Bend (1966), with 100 certificate, associate, bachelor's, and master's degree programs, is northern Indiana's primary resource for lifelong learning. Approximately 7,500 students are enrolled in degree and certificate programs in South Bend and at off-campus sites in Elkhart and Plymouth. Graduate students comprise 20% of enrollment, and some 9,000 area residents enroll in IUSB's Continuing Education programs. For the past 7 years, IUSB has offered distance education classes through the Virtual Indiana Campus, a 2-way, interactive audio/video system connecting IU campuses and centers throughout the state. Some additional programming is offered through PBS to the local service area.

Indiana Wesleyan University

4301 South Washington Street
Marion, IN 46953

Phone: (800) 621-8667 x2866
Fax: (765) 677-2380

Division(s): Center for Distributed Learning
Web Site(s): http://IWUonline.com
E-mail: dshutt@indwes.edu

Undergraduate Degree Programs:
Online Bachelor of Science in Business Information Systems (completion, 52 credits)
Online Bachelor of Science in Management (completion, 40 credits)

Graduate Degree Programs:
Online Master of Business Administration
Online Master of Education

Class Titles: Biblical Literature, Methods in Bible Study, Ethics, Composition, Earth Science, Career Development, Mathematics, American History, Music Appreciation, Drivers' Ed on Information Superhighway, Internet Tools, Personal Computing.

Teaching Methods: *Computers:* Internet, electronic bulletin board, real-time chat. *Other:* None.

Credits Granted for: experiential learning, portfolio assessment, examination (CLEP, ACT-PEP, DANTES), extrainstitutional learning, American Council on Education Guide to the Evaluation of Educational Experiences in Armed Services.

Admission Requirements: *Undergraduate:* high school graduate or GED, 60 accredited transferable credits (40 hours may be equivalent training), 2.0 overall GPA, minimum of 2 years of full-time work experience beyond high school. *Graduate:* online MBA: bachelor's degree; 2.5 overall college GPA; 3 years of full-time, related work experience; prerequisites in math, economics, finance, and accounting. *Online Master of Education:* bachelor's degree; 2.75 overall college GPA; valid teacher's license; 1 year of K-12 teaching experience.

On-Campus Requirements: None.

Tuition and Fees: *Electives:* $225/credit. *Bachelor of Science in Business Information Systems:* $295/credit. *Bachelor of Science in Management:* $250/credit. *Master of Business Administration:* $375/credit. *Master of Education:* $285/credit. *Application Fee:* $25. *Graduation Fee:* $70 (undergraduate) $80 (graduate). *Other Costs:* educational resource fee: $200 (undergraduate, U.S.), $400 (undergraduate, outside U.S.), $300 (graduate, U.S.), $600 (graduate, outside U.S.); $25/credit examination transcription fee, $150 portfolio application fee plus $40/credit transcription fee. *Credit by:* semester.

Financial Aid: Federal Stafford Loan, Federal Pell Grant, Indiana resident programs, VA.

Accreditation: North Central Association of Colleges and Schools.

Description: Indiana Wesleyan University (1890) is a Christian, liberal arts, coeducational university related to The Wesleyan Church. The original campus was well known in Indiana for teacher education before it annexed the Fairmount Bible School. Today the university prepares students for service and leadership roles in teacher education, health care, social work, business, industry, government, Christian ministries, and other areas. Indiana Wesleyan was the fastest-growing college in Indiana over the past 5 years. More than 2,000 students are enrolled in traditional programs on the Marion campus, and 5,000 working men and women take College Adult and Professional Studies classes throughout the state. In 1997 we began offering online, elective courses within the APS undergraduate programs. We began the Online Master of Business Administration program in 1998. The other online degree program began early 2001.

Institute of Transpersonal Psychology

| 744 San Antonio Road | Phone: (650) 493-4430 |
| Palo Alto, CA 94303 | Fax: (650) 493-6835 |

Division(s): Global Program
Web Site(s): http://www.itp.edu
E-mail: itpinfo@itp.com

Graduate Degree Programs:
Master of Arts in Transpersonal Studies
Master of Transpersonal Psychology

Certificate Programs: Transpersonal Studies, Spiritual Psychology, Women's Spiritual Development, Creative Expression, Wellness Counseling and Bodymind Consciousness.

Teaching Methods: *Computers:* Internet, real-time chat, electronic classroom, e-mail, CD-ROM, newsgroup, LISTSERV. *Other:* fax, correspondence, independent study, individual study, learning contracts.

Admission Requirements: *Graduate:* Master of Transpersonal Psychology: bachelor's degree from an accredited school, with 8 semester (12 quarter) credits in basic psychology course work (see ITP web site for details), with a passing grade of B or better. Master of Arts in Transpersonal Studies: Bachelor's degree from an accredited school, 8 semester (12 quarter) credits in general social sciences courses, with a passing grade of B or better. Emotional maturity and experience in self-exploration are essential factors for admission into any program. *Certificates:* high school diploma.

On-Campus Requirements: for each certificate, 4–5-day seminars are required at the beginning and end of each year.

Tuition and Fees: $9,116 per year for Regular Certificates, $9,992 for Online Certificates, $7,304 per year for Master's in Transpersonal Studies, $10,084 for Masters of Transpersonal Psychology, $1,013 for 3-units course. *Application Fee:* $55. *Software:* $740 per year for Certificates, $1,248 for Master of Transpersonal Psychology. *Acceptance Fee:* $100. *Credit by:* quarter.

Financial Aid: Federal Stafford Loan.

Accreditation: Western Association of Schools and Colleges.

Description: The Institute of Transpersonal Psychology, founded in 1975, is a private, nonsectarian graduate school. Transpersonal psychology is a branch of psychology that studies the whole person through an integrated approach of mind, body, and spirit. ITP offers whole-person learning with traditional and nontraditional psychological and spiritual models of learning and teaching. Course work integrates experiential work with theory and research. Campus programs offer a PhD in Transpersonal Psychology, a Master of Arts in Counseling Psychology (MFT), and a Master of Arts in Transpersonal Psychology. The Global Program gives students the opportunity to study at any location in the world. Each certificate and master's degree is designed to allow maximum flexibility to mature students who have the desire, ability, and motivation to work independently and in relationship with the support of a Global faculty mentor.

Inter-American University of Puerto Rico

| 500 Road 830 | Phone: (787) 279-1912 |
| Bayamon, PR 00957 | Fax: (787) 279-2205 |

Web Site(s): http://bc.inter.edu
E-mail: http://mail.bc.inter.edu

Undergraduate Degree Programs:
Associate of Science in:
　Secretarial Sciences
　Accounting
　Business Administration
　Audiovisual Communications Technology
　Computer Sciences
　Telecommunications Technology
　Installation and Repair of Computer Systems
Bachelor of Arts in:
　Mathematics
　Secretarial Sciences
　　Information Processing
　　Executive Secretary

Bachelor of Business Administration in:
- Accounting
- Managerial Economics
- Management
- Human Resources Management
- Industrial Management
- Marketing
- Computer Management Information Systems

Bachelor of Science in:
- Industrial Engineering
- Electrical Engineering
- Mechanical Engineering
- Airway Sciences
  - Management
  - Electronic Systems
  - Computer Sciences
  - Aircraft Management
- Computer Sciences
  - Commercial
  - Systems
  - Scientific Applications
- Communications Technology
- Mathematics
- Biology
  - General
  - Microbiology
  - Public Health
  - Environmental Sciences
  - Environmental

Class Titles: all courses (ask for list).

Teaching Methods: *Computers:* Internet, e-mail, CD-ROM. *TV:* videotape. *Other:* audioconferencing, videoconferencing, audiotapes, independent study, learning contracts, portfolio assessment, individual research, seminar, special topics, COOP Program.

Credits Granted for: portfolio assessment (3–9 credits/portfolio submitted), learning contracts (maximum 15 credits for associate degrees, maximum 25 credits for bachelor degrees), independent study (maximum 6 credits for associate degrees, maximum 12 credits for bachelor degrees), individual research (maximum 3 credits for associate degrees, maximum 6 credits for bachelor degrees), seminar (1–6 credits/course), special topics (1–6 credits/course), COOP Program (maximum 4 credits for associate degrees, maximum 7 credits for bachelor degrees).

Admission Requirements: *Undergraduate:* evidence of graduation from an accredited secondary school or its equivalent with a minimum GPA of 2.00, present scores of the College Entrance Examination Board Test, Scholastic Aptitude Test (English language students) or the "Prueba de Aptitud Académica" (Spanish language students), obtain a minimum admission index of 800, interview (if necessary), application,

transcript of secondary school record, nonrefundable fee of $19, an updated certificate of vaccination (if the student is under 21 years old), medical form completed by a licensed physician (before May 1 for admission in August).

On-Campus Requirements: to obtain a degree, at least 50% of the credits must be taken at the campus.

Tuition and Fees: *Undergraduate:* $105/credit. *Application Fee:* $19. *Credit by:* semester.

Financial Aid: Federal Stafford Loan, Federal Perkins Loan, Federal Pell Grant, Federal Work-Study, VA.

Accreditation: Middle States Association of Colleges and Schools.

Description: Inter-American University of Puerto Rico (1912) is a private, nonprofit organization founded as the Polytechnic Institute of Puerto Rico by Rev. John W. Harris. In 1944, the IAUPR was accredited by the Middle States Association. It was the first 4-year liberal arts college to be accredited outside the USA. It is also the largest private university of Puerto Rico, with an enrollment of 41,300 students in 1997. The Bayamon campus was established in 1956 as an extension of the San German campus. In 1984, the Bayamon University College (former name) was converted into an independent academic unit of the entire system. In 1991 its name was changed to Inter-American University of Puerto Rico, Bayamon campus and its mission also changed to a focus on science and technology programs. In January 1997, the Bayamon campus was moved to its new facilities in Southern Bayamon. The engineering programs were established and the campus was inaugurated in October 1997.

International Aviation and Travel Academy

4846 South Collins	**Phone: (817) 784-7000**
Arlington, TX 76018-1110	**Fax: (817) 784-7022**

Division(s): Travel and Tourism
Web Site(s): http://www.iatac.com
E-mail: info@iatac.com

Certificate Programs: Airline/Travel Industry Extension/Residency Program.

Class Titles: Careers in Travel Industry, Professional Development/Career Planning, Airport Related Operations, Lodging Industry, Travel Agency Operations/Sales/Marketing, Rail/Bus/Rent-a-Car/Cruises, Customer Service Skills/Telephone Sales Techniques, Selling Domestic/International Travel, U.S. Travel Geography/Airlines of North America, World Travel Geography/International Airlines, How To Use Official Airline Guides/Travel Planners, Domestic/International Tariff Skills, Ticket Writing/Travel Industry

Automation, Basic Sabre Computer Skills/Travel Project/Review.

Teaching Methods: *Computers:* Internet, e-mail. *Other:* correspondence.

Admission Requirements: *Certificate:* high school diploma prior to residency.

On-Campus Requirements: None.

Tuition and Fees: *Credit by:* program.

Accreditation: Distance Education and Training Council.

Description: At International Aviation and Travel Academy (1971), training makes the difference. With state-of-the-art equipment, experienced staff, and a broad-ranged curriculum, we are committed to providing industry employers with high-caliber personnel. Our graduates have been recruited by more than 300 airline and service companies. IATA's mission is to recognize and fulfill the needs of the aviation and travel industry and those pursuing careers in these industries. IATA's educational mission is to meet the training need for entry-level skills required in the travel and transportation industry. Our perspective includes personal as well as career and professional growth. Standards are high and they match the levels of success our graduates are trained to achieve. Working in this thriving industry, you'll have the chance to meet fascinating people, go places you've always dreamed of, and enjoy the personal and professional rewards that are unique to this career path.

Iowa State University

102 Scheman Building	Phone: (515) 294-6222
Ames, IA 50011-1112	Fax: (515) 294-6146

Division(s): Continuing Education and Communication Services
Web Site(s): http://www.lifelearner.iastate.edu
E-mail: lspicer@iastate.edu

Undergraduate Degree Programs:
Bachelor of Science in Professional Agriculture

Graduate Degree Programs:
Master of Agriculture
Master of Engineering in Systems Engineering
Master of Family and Consumer Sciences
Master of Science in:
    Agronomy
    Computer Engineering
    Electrical Engineering
    Statistics

Certificate Programs: Financial Counselor.

Teaching Methods: *Computers:* Internet, real-time chat, e-mail, CD-ROM, LISTSERV. *TV:* videotape, satellite broadcasting, fiber optic 2-way videoconferencing. *Other:* independent study.

Credits Granted for: examination (CLEP, ACT-PEP, AP, IB, GRE and departmental exams).

Admission Requirements: *Undergraduate:* high school diploma or GED. *Graduate:* vary by degree. *Doctoral:* vary by degree. *Certificate:* vary by certificate.

On-Campus Requirements: None.

Tuition and Fees: *Undergraduate:* $130/credit. *Graduate:* $176/credit. *Doctoral:* $206/credit. *Application Fee:* $20. *Software:* variable. *Other Costs:* various. *Credit by:* semester.

Financial Aid: Federal Stafford Loan, Federal Perkins Loan, Federal PLUS Loan, Federal Pell Grant, Federal Work-Study, VA, Iowa resident programs.

Accreditation: North Central Association of Colleges and Schools.

Description: Outreach at Iowa State University (1859) has its history as far back as 1904 when agriculture agents traveled by train to several sites in Iowa offering short courses and lectures on topics ranging from plant breeding to manure management. Today, Iowa has a dedicated fiber optic video system connecting ISU with more than 600 towns and cities. Within our rich heritage of outreach, we have a strong vision for the future, keeping ISU at the forefront of educational excellence for the 21st century.

Iowa Valley Community College District

3700 S. Center Street	Phone: (641) 752-7106
Marshalltown, IA 50158	Fax: (641) 752-5909

Division(s): Distance Learning Facilitator
Web Site(s): http://www.iavalley.cc.ia.us
E-mail: gebaker@iavalley.cc.ia.us

Undergraduate Degree Programs: Contact school.

Class Titles: Introduction to Biology, Introduction to Broadcasting, Radio/TV Writing, Principles of Management, Principles of Supervision, Methods of Guiding Behavior (Limited Options, Contact Instructor), Human Growth and Development, Educational Psychology, English Composition, Technical Writing, Mass Communication, General Psychology, Abnormal Psychology.

Teaching Methods: *Computers:* Internet, e-mail, LISTSERV.

Admission Requirements: *Undergraduate:* none for one class; more classes require admission to college.

On-Campus Requirements: None.

Tuition and Fees: *Undergraduate:* $82.50/credit. *Credit by:* semester.

Financial Aid: Federal Stafford Loan, Federal Perkins Loan, Federal PLUS Loan, Federal Pell Grant, Federal Work-Study, VA, state programs for residents of Iowa.

Accreditation: North Central Association of Colleges and Schools.

Description: IVCCD (1967) was organized as one of 15 community college districts in Iowa. The district includes Ellsworth Community College in Iowa Falls, Marshalltown Community College, and Iowa Valley Continuing Education. In the fall of 1998, Iowa Valley Community College District initiated a program of offering college credit courses over the Internet. Since that small beginning with one class, the Iowa Valley offerings expanded to 13 classes in the fall of 1999. As part of an ongoing project with the Consortium of Iowa Community Colleges, these courses, along with others at other Iowa community colleges may be available in a coordinated offering. Eventually, the student will be able to obtain an AA degree solely over the Internet. At Iowa Valley, each class instructor writes his or her own course web sites that are part of the courses, or use customizable sites provided by the textbook publisher. Individual lesson plans are adapted to the Internet format, offering specialized tools that are appropriate for the class offered. The advantage to this format is that class instructors are not tied down to what they are provided by the book or off-site course developer, but rather create living web page courses that are easily adapted on the fly to differing needs of the students. Each class offers a variety of tools suited to the particular needs of the class.

Iowa Wesleyan College

601 N Main Street	Phone: (319) 385-6247
Mt. Pleasant, IA 52641	Fax: (319) 385-6296

Division(s): Office of Extended Learning
Web Site(s): http://www.iwc.edu
E-mail: exl@iwc.edu

Undergraduate Degree Programs:
Bachelor of Arts
Bachelor of Science

Class Titles: Organizational Behavior, Life Health, Art Appreciation, Sociology, Modern World Religions, Abnormal Psychology, General Psychology, Human Resource Management, Management Accounting, Expository Writing.

Teaching Methods: *Computers:* Internet, e-mail. *TV:* PBS. *Other:* videoconferencing, fax, independent, study.

Credits Granted for: experiential learning, extrainstitutional learning, examination (CLEP, ACT-PEP, DANTES, GRE).

Admission Requirements: *Undergraduate:* high school equivalency.

On-Campus Requirements: None.

Tuition and Fees: *Undergraduate:* $220/credit. *Credit by:* semester.

Financial Aid: Federal Stafford Loan, Federal Perkins Loan, Federal PLUS Loan, Federal Pell Grant, Federal Work-Study, VA, Iowa resident programs.

Accreditation: North Central Association of Colleges and Schools.

Description: Iowa Wesleyan College (1842) is the oldest coeducational liberal arts college west of the Mississippi River. It serves southeast Iowa and the bordering areas in Illinois and Missouri. A distinctive program of required service-learning, field experience, and emphasis on lifeskills (communication, reasoning, valuing, and social effectiveness) characterizes the curriculum. Many graduates enter the teaching, business, social services, and nursing professions. Distance learning began in the early 1990s.

ISIM University

501 South Cherry Street, Room 350	Phone: (303) 333-4224
Denver, CO 80246	Fax: (303) 336-1144

Division(s): Admissions
Web Site(s): http://www.isim.edu
E-mail: admissions@isim.edu

Graduate Degree Programs:
Master of Business Administration
Master of Science in Information Management
Master of Science in Information Technology

Certificate Programs: Project Management and Project Management for Information Systems Professionals, Fundamentals of Information Systems, Business Management, Finance.

Class Titles: All courses can be taken individually through ISIM's executive education program. Visit http://www.isim.edu for course information.

Teaching Methods: *Computers:* Internet-based electronic classroom, e-mail. *Other:* guided self-study program via fax, correspondence, e-mail, independent study.

Credits Granted for: experiential learning, portfolio assessment, examination, transfer credit.

Admission Requirements: *Graduate:* evidence of bachelor's degree (20 years of experience may qualify candidates for ISIM's MBA program), all official college transcripts, resume, goals statement, 3 letters of recommendation.

On-Campus Requirements: None.

Tuition and Fees: *Graduate:* $415/credit. *Application Fee:* $75. *Other Costs:* $1,500–$2,000 for books, shipping (based on completion of 36 credits). *Credit by:* 5 terms/year.

Accreditation: Distance Education and Training Council.

Description: Founded in 1987, ISIM University, formerly known as the International School of Information Management, serves both individuals and organizations in providing its distance education offerings worldwide. ISIM is accredited by the Distance Education and Training Council and recognized by Colorado Commission of Higher Education to offer graduate degree programs and continuing education. ISIM is also a member of the U.S. Distance Learning Association and a member of the American Association of Collegiate Registrars and Admissions Officers. ISIM brings education and training curriculum to individuals over the Internet and through guided self-study. Three times in the last 8 years, ISIM has earned top industry honors. In 1991, 1994, and 1996, the U.S. Distance Learning Association conferred on ISIM its "Best Distance Learning Program in Higher Education" award. ISIM offers graduate degrees in Business Administration, Information Management, and Information Technology as well as certificate and executive education programs to students worldwide with an eye on the global marketplace.

Ivy Tech State College

7999 U.S. Highway 41 South	Phone: (800) 377-4882
Terre Haute, IN 47802	Fax: (812) 299-8770

Division(s): Information Technology, Academic & Information Systems Division
Web Site(s): http://ivytech7.cc.in.us
E-mail: cwymer@ivy.tec.in.us

Undergraduate Degree Programs:
Undergraduate: Accounting Technology, Drafting/Design Technology, Business Management, Administrative Office Technology.

Certificate Programs: Administrative Office Technology.

Class Titles: Accounting, Business, Physics, Physical Science, Algebra, English, CAD, Speech, Design, Drafting, Fiber Optics, Psychology.

Teaching Methods: *Computers:* Internet.

Credits Granted for: experiential learning, portfolio assessment extrainstitutional learning, (PONSI, corporate or professional association seminars/workshops), examination (CLEP, ACT-PEP, DANTES, GRE).

Admission Requirements: *Undergraduate:* a completed application for admissions, proof (transcripts) of a high school diploma or GED results or demonstrated "ability to benefit" based upon assessment by the college, participation in assessment administered by the college. This is required for all students who are seeking the associate degree or the technical certificate and students who wish to take general education courses. *Special Note for Distance Education Students:* If you do not live near an Ivy Tech Campus, you may make arrangements for taking the assessment at a college near you. For information on taking our admissions assessment at another college please contact Jan Dykstra of ACT at 319-337-1376. ACT will locate the closest institution that provides either the COMPASS or ASSET. When you contact the host institution, let them know that you are a distance education student and need to complete the assessment for admission requirements at your home institution. There may or may not be a minimal charge. Send your results to Ivy Tech State College, Admissions Office, 7999 US Hwy 41 South, Terre Haute, IN 47802. If you have any questions, contact the Ivy Tech CETS office at *mfisher@ivy.tec.in.us* or 800-377-4882.

Also required: completion of specific program requirements as needed.

On-Campus Requirements: Anatomy and Physiology I and II and Microbiology require on-campus lab time (usually 1 session per semester).

Tuition and Fees: *Undergraduate:* $65/credit. *Other Costs:* Beginning fall semester, 2001, out-of-state students will be assessed slightly higher tuition (TBA). *Credit by:* semester.

Financial Aid: Federal Stafford Loan, Federal Perkins Loan, Federal PLUS Loan, Federal Pell Grant, Federal Work-Study, VA, Indiana resident programs.

Accreditation: North Central Association of Colleges and Schools.

Description: Ivy Tech State College is a 2-year, associate degree college. Ivy Tech consists of 14 regional campuses with more than 60,000 students in the state of Indiana. The Wabash Valley Region of Ivy Tech State College has been offering online courses and degrees since 1996, and was the first 2-year college in the United States accredited to offer online degrees by the North Central Association of Colleges and Schools. We offer more than 100 courses online in addition to degrees in Accounting, Business, Drafting/CAD, and Administrative Office.

J. Sargeant Reynolds Community College

1636 East Parham Road
PO Box 85622
Richmond, VA 23285-5622

Phone: (804) 371-3612
Fax: (804) 371-3822

Division(s): Center for Distance Education
Web Site(s): http://www.jsr.cc.va.us
E-mail: smarshall@jsr.cc.va.us

Undergraduate Degree Programs:
Liberal Arts
Business Administration
Management
Respiratory Therapy (at selected sites in Virginia)

Certificate Programs: Management Development.

Class Titles: Accounting, African-American Literature, Business, Creative Writing, Developmental Biology, Developmental Chemistry, Computer Science, Economics, English, Finance, French, History, Information Systems, Mathematics, Medical Terminology, Political Science, Psychology, Sociology.

Teaching Methods: *Computers:* Internet, real-time chat, forums, e-mail, LISTSERV. *TV:* videotape, cable program. *Other:* videoconferencing, audiographics, audiotapes, fax, correspondence, independent study.

Admission Requirements: *Undergraduate:* high school diploma or equivalent, or age 18 and able to benefit from a program at the college. See catalog for more information. *Certificate:* Same as undergraduate.

On-Campus Requirements: Some courses may require labs to be completed on campus. Most courses offer the opportunity for an on-campus orientation meeting with the instructor.

Tuition and Fees: *Undergraduate:* $50/credit for Virginia residents; $174/credit for out-of-state residents. *Software:* technology fee included in undergraduate tuition fee listed above. *Other Costs:* lab fees for selected courses. *Credit by:* semester.

Financial Aid: FFEL Stafford Loans, FFEL Federal PLUS Loans, FFEL Consolidation Loans, Federal Pell Grant, FSEOG, Federal Work-Study, VA, Virginia resident programs, various private scholarships.

Accreditation: Southern Association of Colleges and Schools.

Description: J. Sargeant Reynolds Community College (1972) is a 3-campus institution and the third-largest college in the Virginia Community College System. The college offers 30 degree programs (including 6 transfer programs); 13 one-year certificate programs; and 54 career studies certificate programs requiring less than one year of full-time study. JSRCC has been delivering print-based, distance education courses since 1980, with its first telecourse in 1984. Audiographics, compressed video, and computer-based deliveries were added in 1994.

Jacksonville State University

700 Pelham Road N
Jacksonville, AL 36265

Phone: (256) 782-5346
Fax: (256) 782-5169

Division(s): Department of Distance Education
Web Site(s): http://www.jsu.edu/depart/distance/
E-mail: DLInfo@jsucc.jsu.edu

Graduate Degree Program:
Master of Public Administration with a concentration in Emergency Management

Class Titles: Accounting, Anthropology, Statistics, Technology, Business, Data Processing, Computer Operating Systems, Management Information Systems, Software Engineering, Database Systems, Education (Education Administration, Early Childhood Education, Elementary Education, Secondary Education, Physical Education, Special Education), Management, Economics, Psychology, English, Emergency Management, Human Development, Finance, Geology, Geography, Western Civilization, American History, Human Resources, Algebra Nursing, Health, American Government, Public Administration, Social Work, Sociology Technology.

Teaching Methods: *Computers:* Internet, synchronous chat, asynchronous discussion board, e-mail, CD-ROM. *TV:* videotape, cable program, satellite broadcasting, PBS. *Other:* videoconferencing; many of these methods are combined into hybrid formats, such as videoconferencing courses supplemented with online coursework.

Credits Granted for: examination (CLEP, ACT/SAT, GRE, MAT).

Admission Requirements: For information on admission requirements, please go to the following address: http://www.jsu.edu/depart/admissions/attend.html.

On-Campus Requirements: This is dependent upon the format of the class. Online courses do not require on-campus visits; videoconferencing and College by Cassette courses may require on-campus visits.

Tuition and Fees: *Undergraduate:* $110/credit. *Graduate:* $132/credit. *Postgraduate:* $132/credit. *Application Fee:* $20. *Other Costs:* $20 undergraduate/graduate degree fee. *Software:* dependent upon course. *Other Costs:* various fees, from $5–$20. Note: information subject to change without prior notice to individual students. *Credit by:* semester.

Financial Aid: Federal Stafford Loan, Federal Perkins Loan, Federal Plus Loan, Federal Pell Grant, Federal Work Study, VA.

Accreditation: Southern Association of Colleges and Schools.

Description: Jacksonville State University (1883) began the early stages of Distance Learning with compressed video in 1994. As interest in the program increased from the surrounding areas, more sites were added in and out of state, and the videoconferencing system grew to now encompass more than 15 sites. Concurrently, an agreement with PBS and a local community college allowed the College by Cassette program to offer discounted-tuition on 100–200 level courses taught via videocassette. The newest and largest area of our Distance Education program today is by far the online system, which serves students all over the nation and now offers an entire MPA in one area that is unique to online learning. As more requests for courses are being offered, Jacksonville State University continues to meet the demands of all of its students.

Jamestown Community College

525 Falconer Street	Phone: (716) 665-5220
Jamestown, NY 14702-0020	Fax: (716) 665-5518

Division(s): Hultquist Library
Web Site(s): http://www.sunyjcc.edu

Class Titles: Music, Computer Science, Business, Sociology, SUNY Learning Network/Computer Courses.

Teaching Methods: *Computers:* Internet, real-time chat, electronic classroom, e-mail, LISTSERV. *TV:* videotape, cable program, satellite broadcasting, PBS. *Other:* videoconferencing, independent study, individual study, learning contracts.

Credits Granted for: experiential learning, portfolio assessment.

Admission Requirements: *Undergraduate:* age 18 or high school diploma.

On-Campus Requirements: None.

Tuition and Fees: *Undergraduate:* $92 resident, $162 out-of-state. *Other Costs:* various fees $20–$50. *Credit by:* semester.

Financial Aid: Federal Stafford Loan, Federal Perkins Loan, Federal PLUS Loan, Federal Pell Grant, Federal Work-Study, VA, New York resident programs.

Accreditation: Middle States Association of Colleges and Schools.

Description: Jamestown Community College (1950) began distance learning in 1996. JCC is also a receive site for the Pennsylvania State MBA program, the SUNY Fredonia BS in Business, and the SUNY University, Buffalo, BS in Nursing.

Jefferson College

1000 Viking Drive	Phone: (314) 789-3000
Hillsboro, MO 63050	Fax: (314) 789-4012

Division(s): Extended and Nontraditional Learning
Web Site(s): http://www.jeffco.edu
E-mail: lbigelow@gateway.jeffco.edu

Class Titles: Algebra, Biology, Business, Children's Literature, Economics, English, French, History, Personal Health, Psychology, Sociology, Spanish, Geography.

Teaching Methods: Web-based courses, e-mail, bulletin board. *TV:* videotape, cable program, satellite broadcasting, PBS, ITV.

Credits Granted for: examination (CLEP, ACT-PEP, departmental proficiency exams), military experience.

Admission Requirements: *Undergraduate:* Official high school graduate transcript or GED (high school equivalency) scores, completion of COMPASS or official ACT scores for placement purposes.

On-Campus Requirements: None.

Tuition and Fees: *Undergraduate:* $45/credit in-district, $67/credit out-of-district/in-state, $90/credit out-of-district/out-of-state (Tuition and fees are subject to change without prior notice.). *Application Fee:* $20 (one-time fee for new students only). *Other Costs:* $7/credit facilities use fee, $2 (first-time-student only) student identification fee, $25 lab fees (vary by course), $40/course telecourse fee. *Credit by:* semester.

Financial Aid: Federal Stafford Loan, Federal Perkins Loan, Federal PLUS Loan, Federal Pell Grant, Federal Work-Study, VA, Missouri resident programs, Missouri Art Program.

Accreditation: North Central Association of Colleges and Schools.

Description: Jefferson College (1963) is a student-centered, comprehensive community college on 450 beautifully wooded acres located 25 miles south of St. Louis. Jefferson offers its 4,000 students Associate of Arts and Associate of Science degrees, along with an Associate of Applied Science degree in more than 20 vocational-technical programs.

Jewish Theological Seminary

3080 Broadway
New York, NY 10027

Phone: (212) 678-8897
Fax: (212) 749-9085

Division(s): Kaminer Center for Distance Learning
Web Site(s): http://www.jtsa.edu
http://courses.jtsa.edu
E-mail: dlp@jtsa.edu

Graduate Degree Programs:
Master of Arts in Jewish Education
Master of Arts in Interdepartmental Studies (Jewish Studies)

Class Titles: Hebrew, Bible, Talmud, Jewish Philosophy, Jewish Education, Jewish Literature, Jewish History.

Teaching Methods: *Computers:* Internet, real-time chat, electronic classroom, e-mail. *Other:* None.

Admission Requirements: *Graduate:* GRE or MAT, undergraduate transcript, letters of recommendation. Some applicants may need to show work experience in the field of Jewish communal service.

On-Campus Requirements: 15 credits (5 courses) must be taken on site; typically completed during 2 intensive 4-week summer sessions.

Tuition and Fees: *Undergraduate:* $500/credit. *Graduate:* $620/credit. *Application Fee:* $50. *Graduation Fee:* $240. *Other Costs:* registration fee. *Credit by:* semester.

Financial Aid: Federal Stafford Loan, Federal Perkins Loan, Federal PLUS Loan, Federal Pell Grant, Federal Work-Study, VA, state programs for residents of New York (TAP and ATP), institutional fellowships.

Accreditation: Middle States Association of Colleges and Schools.

Description: The Jewish Theological Seminary (1886) is the center of an international network of academic, research, education, and community programs at the service of world Jewry; the premier North American center for the academic study of Judaism; and the spiritual center of Conservative Judaism worldwide. Its New York City campus houses the undergraduate Albert A. List College of Jewish Studies, the Graduate School, the Rabbinical School, the William Davidson Graduate School of Jewish Education, the H. L. Miller Cantorial School and College of Jewish Music. JTS faculty constitutes the largest assembly of Judaica scholars in North America; the renowned JTS library houses the largest collection of Judaica and Hebraica outside Israel. JTS began its distance learning program in 1996 thanks to a generous grant from the Kaminer Family Foundation. Currently, JTS offers courses for academic credit, professional development, adult education (degree and non-degree).

John Tracy Clinic

806 West Adams Boulevard
Los Angeles, CA 90007

Phone: (213) 748-5481
Fax: (213) 749-1651

Division(s): Academy for Professional Studies
Web Site(s): http://www.jtc.org
E-mail: gragusa@jtc.org

Class Titles: Typical/Atypical Infant/Child Development, Methods of Auditory Learning/Teaching Speech to Children with Hearing Loss, Professional as Facilitator: Working with Children with Hearing Loss Infancy–Preschool (Methods), Public Policy/Service Delivery Systems for Infants/Toddlers with Special Needs, Working with Families of Children with Special Needs: Parent-Professional Teams, Audiology for Teachers of Children with Hearing Loss, First Language: It's Nature/Acquisition/Development in Typical Children, Language Evaluation and Intervention with Young Deaf Children, Methods of Auditory Learning and Teaching Speech to Children with Hearing Loss, Adapting Elementary and Secondary Curriculum for Children with Hearing Loss, Advanced Methods, Practicum, and Research in Speech for Children with Hearing Loss, Topics in Deafness, Master's Seminar: Development of Thematic Instruction, Master's Seminar: Development of an Ethnographic Study.

Teaching Methods: *Computers:* Internet, asynchronous discussion forum, e-mail. *TV:* audiotapes and videotapes. *Other:* commercial texts, syllabus.

Admission Requirements: *Graduate:* bachelor's degree, working in or access to educational setting with young deaf children.

On-Campus Requirements: None.

Tuition and Fees: *Graduate:* $700/course. *Application Fee:* $35. *Other Costs:* vary for texts, materials, postage. *Credit by:* semester.

Accreditation: Distance Education and Training Council.

Description: In 1942, Mrs. Spencer (Louise Treadwell) Tracy and 12 other mothers of young deaf children established a place where such parents could receive information and support. The nonprofit institution was officially named "John Tracy Clinic" (1943) for the deaf son of Mr. and Mrs. Spencer Tracy. Mrs. Tracy and the Board of Directors understood the need to have well-trained teachers to work with the children and to demonstrate to parents how to facilitate a positive learning environment for their children. For this reason, John Tracy Clinic and the University of Southern California soon began a joint master's-level, resident program in teacher education in the area of deaf and hard-of-hearing. In 1996, John Tracy Clinic Academy for Professional Studies was established to offer distance education courses for professionals who work with deaf and hard-of-hearing children.

Johns Hopkins Bloomberg School of Public Health

615 North Wolfe Street	Phone: (410) 223-1830
Baltimore, MD 21205	Fax: (410) 223-1832

Division(s): Professional Education and Programs
Web Site(s): http://distance.jhsph.edu
E-mail: alentz@jhsph.edu

Graduate Degree Programs:
Master of Public Health

Certificate Programs: Graduate Certificate Program in Public Health

Teaching Methods: *Computers:* Internet, real-time chat, electronic classroom, e-mail, CD-ROM.

Admission Requirements: *Graduate: Application Fee:* $60. Personal statement of experience and goals, current résumé or curriculum vitae, 3 recommendations (submitted on our paper form), official academic records (transcripts or mark sheets) from each college or university attended beyond the secondary level, GRE test scores.

On-Campus Requirements: 20 credits (25% of degree).

Tuition and Fees: *Graduate:* $540/credit. *Application Fee:* $60. *Credit by:* quarter.

Financial Aid: Federal Stafford Loan, Federal Perkins Loan, Federal PLUS Loan, Federal Pell Grant, Federal Work-Study, VA, Maryland resident programs.

Accreditation: Council on Education for Public Health, Middle States Association of Colleges and Schools.

Description: Johns Hopkins School of Public Health is the oldest, largest, and most academically acclaimed school of public health in the country. Founded in 1916 with a grant from the Rockefeller Foundation, the school has grown exponentially to become an international resource in health research and education. Our faculty comprise one quarter of all faculty of U.S. schools of public health and awards one-sixth of all public health doctoral degrees. The school created the first academic departments of statistics, epidemiology, and virology. Research at the school led to the discovery of vitamins, vaccines, oral rehydration therapy, and other tools that prevent death and disability of millions of people every year. Our work in water purification systems has been adopted and used by every major municipal and industrial water system in the United States. Pioneering research on the polio virus opened the door to effective vaccines, and leadership was provided for eradicating smallpox worldwide. Major research and educational programs now include chronic diseases; organization, financing, and management of health services; violence and substance abuse; injury prevention; the molecular basis of disease; and many other pressing health concerns touched upon in the material contained on this web site. Our first class had 16 students. Today we teach 1,800 students a year from 80 different countries. We have 400 full-time faculty working across departmental lines in alliances of research and action aimed at solving society's most pressing health problems.

Johnson County Community College

12345 College Boulevard	Phone: (913) 469-8500
Overland Park, KS 66210	

Division(s): Computer Instruction and Media Resources
Web Site(s): http://www.jccc.net
http://web.jccc.net/academic/dl/help.htm

Undergraduate Degree Programs:
Associate of Arts

Class Titles: Accounting, Agribusiness, Astronomy, Automotive Technology, Biology, Business Office Technology, Chemistry, Child Development, Computer Personal Applications, Computer Information Systems, Drafting, Economics, English/Literature, Environmental Science, Fashion Merchandising, Geology, History, Information Technology, Law, Library Skills, Marketing, Marriage and the Family, Mathematics, Music, Oceanography, Philosophy, Photography, Political Science, Psychology, Sociology, Speech.

Teaching Methods: *Computers:* Internet, real-time chat electronic classroom, e-mail, CD-ROM, newsgroup, LISTSERV. *TV:* videotape, cable program. *Other:* videoconferencing, independent study, audioconferencing, audiographics, audiotapes, fax, correspondence, individual study, learning contracts.

Credits Granted for: experiential learning, portfolio assessment, examination (CLEP, ACT-PEP, DANTES, GRE) extra-institutional learning.

Admission Requirements: *Undergraduate:* high school graduate, or GED, or 18 years or older. May have to complete an assessment exam.

On-Campus Requirements: None.

Tuition and Fees: *Undergraduate:* $50/credit (county resident), $60/credit (state resident), $126/credit (nonstate resident). *Credit by:* semester.

Financial Aid: Federal Stafford Loan, Federal Perkins Loan, Federal PLUS Loan, Federal Pell Grant, Federal Work-Study, VA, KS resident programs.

Accreditation: North Central Association of Colleges and Schools.

Description: Johnson County Community College (1969) has emerged as one of the premier community colleges in the U.S. and earned a reputation for high-quality, comprehensive and flexible programming to meet the needs of the citizens of Johnson County. The college began its distance learning programming in 1976 with the introduction of telecourse instruction. These offerings continue as other courses are being developed and delivered in a Web-based environment.

Joliet Junior College

1215 Houbolt Road	Phone: (815) 773-6613
Joliet, IL 60431	Fax: (815) 773-6603

Division(s): Distance Education
Web Site(s): http://www.jjc.cc.il.us
E-mail: rsterlin@jjc.cc.il.us
lorsini@jjc.cc.il.us

Class Titles: Astronomy, Biology, Business, Economics, History, Marketing, Math, Political Science, Psychology, Sociology, English, General Studies Development, Horticulture, Hotel/Restaurant Management, Spanish, Speech, Agriculture, Art, Career/Lifestyle Planning, Chemistry, Computer Information Systems, Electronics, Nursing.

Teaching Methods: Computers: Internet. *TV:* videotape. *Other:* videoconferencing.

Credits Granted for: portfolio assessment, examination (CLEP).

Admission Requirements: *Undergraduate:* open door policy, high school graduate/GED, college transfer student, gifted high school student.

On-Campus Requirements: Mandatory orientation.

Tuition and Fees: *Undergraduate:* $44/credit, $171/credit out-of-district, $210/credit out-of-state, $242/credit out-of-country. *Other Costs:* $3/credit course fee, $4/credit technology fee, $3/credit student fee, $20/Distance Education course fee. *Credit by:* semester.

Financial Aid: Federal Stafford Loan, Federal PLUS Loan, Federal Pell Grant, Federal Work-Study, VA.

Accreditation: North Central Association of Colleges and Schools.

Description: Joliet Junior College (1901) is committed to providing a quality education that is affordable and accessible to the diverse student population it serves. Through a rich variety of educational programs and support services, JJC prepares its students for success in higher education and employment. As part of this college's commitment to lifelong learning and services to its community, it also provides a broad spectrum of transitional, extension, adult, continuing and work force education.

Jones International University

9697 East Mineral Avenue	Phone: (303) 784-8045
Englewood, CO 80112	Fax: (303) 784-8547

Division(s): Jones International University
Web Site(s): http://www.jonesinternational.edu
E-mail: info@jonesinternational.edu

Undergraduate Degree Programs:
Bachelor of Arts in Business Communication
Bachelor of Science in Information Technology

Graduate Degree Programs:
Master in Business Administration with majors in:
    E-Commerce
    Global Enterprise Management
    Entrepreneurship
    Health Care Management
    Information Technology Management
    Negotiation and Conflict Management
    Project Management (MBA program is also available in Spanish)
Master of Arts in:
    Business Communication
    Education in e-Learning
Master of Education with majors in:
    Research and Assessment
    Corporate Training and Knowledge Management
    Global Leadership and Administration
    Library and Resource Management
    Technology and Design
    Generalist

Certificate Programs: Financial Management in the Digital Age, Mastering e-Commerce, Managing the Global Enterprise, Health Care Administration, Successful Entrepreneurship, Information Technology Management, Successful Negotiation and Conflict Resolution, Project Management, Using the Internet in K-12 Education, Using the Internet in Higher Education, e-Learning Research and Assessment, Corporate e-Training Management, Leading the Global Learning Organization, e-Library Management, e-Learning Instructional Design, e-Learning Design and Production, Facilitating Online Learning, Creating and Managing e-Learning, Using the Internet in Corporate Training, Advanced Public Relations for the Wired World, Marketing Fundamentals in Today's Electronic Business

Environment, Public Relations Fundamentals for the New Media Manager, Cyber Marketing—The Competitive Advantages of Using the Internet, Essential Oral and Written Communication Skills for Managers, Human Resource Management for Changing Environments, Practical Communication Technology Tools for Managers, The Productive Organization Communication Skills for Management, Using Human Communication Skills to Motivate Performance, Leadership and Influence Through the Spoken and Written Word, Management Skills with a Human Directive, Team Strategies for the Effective Manager, Communications Management for the Global Marketplace, Applied Fundamentals for Telecommunications in Business, Telecommunications Applications for Managers, New Business Solutions Through Communications Technology.

Class Titles: Contact the school or check web site for details.

Teaching Methods: *Computers:* Internet, real-time chat, electronic classroom, e-mail, LISTSERV, electronic bulletin boards.

Credits Granted for: experiential learning, portfolio assessment, examination (CLEP, ACT-PEP, DANTES).

Admission Requirements: *Undergraduate:* Associate degree or 60 credits earned from a regionally accredited college or university, 2.5 GPA on all previous course work. Admission process: admission application form, $75 nonrefundable application fee, 3 letters of professional references, current résumé or curriculum vitae, official confirmation of earning a high school diploma, a sample of your writing, and official transcripts of all previous course work from each regionally accredited college or university attended. International students need to have their transcripts evaluated by AACRAO. *Graduate:* Bachelor's degree from a regionally accredited higher education institution, 2.5 GPA on all previous course work. Admission process: complete admission application form, $75 nonrefundable application fee, 3 letters of professional references, current résumé or curriculum vitae, a sample of your writing (MA students), or a statement describing your professional experience, educational, and professional goals (MBA and M.Ed. students), official transcripts from all the schools attended where a bachelor's degree was earned. MBA and M.Ed. programs require at least one year of managerial or professional experience. International students need to have their transcripts evaluated by AACRAO. *Certificate:* admissions applications are not required for professional and executive certificate programs or for enrollment in JIU courses. Admission applications are required only for degree-seeking students.

On-Campus Requirements: None.

Tuition and Fees: *Undergraduate:* $690/credit. *Graduate:* $825/credit. *Application Fees:* $75. *Graduation Fee:* $50. *Other Costs:* books, materials. *Credit by:* semester.

Financial Aid: VA Benefits, Military Tuition Assistance, Sallie Mae Loans, Plato Loans.

Accreditation: The Higher Learning Commission, a member of North Central Association (NCA).

Description: Founded in 1993 and launched in 1995, JIU is the first fully online accredited university. JIU received its accreditation from the Higher Learning Commission, a member of North Central Association (NCA) on March 5, 1999. JIU's unique educational programs take full advantage of the power of the Internet to foster communication, learning, and skill acquisition. These online programs are an exciting opportunity for adult learners looking to either complete their advanced degrees or explore new fields of interest. JIU courses are designed by content experts, who are leading authorities in their field of knowledge, and who teach at the most respected universities in the United States and around the world. JIU is dedicated to giving adult learners, whose lives can't always accommodate a classroom schedule, the same access to education as more traditional students. To learn more about JIU, visit http://www.jonesinternational.edu.

Judson College

1151 North State Street   Phone: (847) 695-2500 x2227
Elgin, IL 60123-1498   Fax: (847) 695-4880

Division(s): Continuing Education
Web Site(s): http://www.judsononline.org
E-mail: sdeck@judson-il.edu

Undergraduate Degree Programs:
Bachelor of Arts in Management and Leadership

Class Titles: Ecology and Environmental Problems, Biblical Studies: Old Testament, Biblical Studies: New Testament, History of Christianity I, History of Christianity II, Gospel of Luke, Romans, Advertising, Business Writing for Professionals, Expository Writing, Critical Thinking and Writing, Multicultural Perspectives in American Women Writers, Cultural Diversity, Career Studies, Art Appreciation, Music Appreciation, Spanish, Employee and Labor Relations, Employee Benefits and Compensation Management, Word Processing, Spreadsheets, Presentation Graphics, Database, Business Systems Analysis and Design, Database Communications, Visual Basic, Social Deviance, Human Resource Management, Astronomy, American Government, Psychology, Sociology, Judicial Process in America, Criminal Procedure: Law and Practice.

Teaching Methods: *Computers:* Internet, real-time chat, electronic classroom, e-mail, CD-ROM, LISTSERV. *TV:* videotape, cable program, satellite broadcasting, PBS. *Other:* video-conferencing, fax, correspondence, independent study, individual study, learning contracts.

Credits Granted for: experiential learning, portfolio assessment, examination (CLEP, DANTES).

Admission Requirements: *Undergraduate:* 3-year full-time employee verification, minimum 40 accredited transferable credits, age 23 years or older, minimum 2.0 GPA, writing sample.

On-Campus Requirements: 3-day weekend at start of program.

Tuition and Fees: *Undergraduate:* 3 Terms at $5,950/term, books included. *Application Fee:* $30. Individual courses priced separately. *Credit by:* semester.

Financial Aid: call for information.

Accreditation: North Central Association of Colleges and Schools, Coalition for Christian Colleges and Universities.

Description: Founded in 1963, Judson College is a fully accredited, 4-year, evangelical Christian college with campuses in Elgin, Illinois, and Rockford, Illinois. Serving approximately 700 traditional students and about 500 adult learners, the college began offering online classes in the spring semester of 1999. Those 3 initial online courses have now expanded to over 50 courses and an online degree completion program (AIM Online) beginning in the fall of 2001. The online degree in management and leadership is based upon the popular face-to-face AIM (Accelerated Instructional Model) program started at Judson College 1995. In AIM Online, a group of working adults called a cohort takes a sequence of 14 classes together, one online course at a time. Including holidays, the cohort lasts approximately 18 months.

Juniata College

1700 Moore Street	Phone: (814) 641-3620
Huntingdon, PA 16652	Fax: (814) 641-3685

Division(s): Information Technology
Web Site(s): http://departments.juniata.edu/it/it110/sp01 description.htm
E-mail: rhodes@juniata.edu

Class Titles: It 110—Principles of Information Technology, Communication, Music, Technical Writing, International Business.

Teaching Methods: Real-time chat, electronic classroom, e-mail, CD-ROM, newsgroup, LISTSERV. *TV:* cable program, satellite broadcasting, PBS. *Other:* radio broadcast, audio-conferencing, audiographics, audiotapes, fax, correspondence, independent study, individual study, learning contracts.

Admission Requirements: *Undergraduate:* same as college.

On-Campus Requirements: None.

Tuition and Fees: *Undergraduate:* please call. *Credit by:* semester.

Financial Aid: Federal Stafford Loan, Federal Perkins Loan, Federal PLUS Loan, Federal Pell Grant, Federal Work-Study, Pennsylvania resident programs.

Accreditation: Middle States Association of Colleges and Schools.

Description: Juniata College (1876) is an independent, co-educational college of liberal arts and sciences committed to providing an education that awakens students to the empowering richness of the mind and enables them to lead fulfilling and useful lives. Located in the small town of Huntingdon in the scenic central Pennsylvania mountains, the college occupies 110 acres with 31 buildings. Additional land holdings include a 365-acre Environmental Studies Field Station, the 315-acre Baker-Henry Nature Preserve, and the 70-acre Juniata College Conference Center. Primarily residential, Juniata maintains an enrollment of 1,250 students. To supplement its regular programs, Juniata began to use distance learning technology in 1995. Through the Consortium for Agile Pennsylvania Education, the college exchanges video-conference courses with CAPE members. Online instruction is also offered. Future plans include increasing the number of courses imported and exported and further collaboration with international sites.

Kankakee Community College

River Road	
PO Box 888	Phone: (815) 933-0345
Kankakee, IL 60901	Fax: (815) 933-0217

Division(s): Instruction and Workforce Development
Web Site(s): http://www.kcc.cc.il.us
E-mail: rmanuel@kcc.cc.il.us

Class Titles: Psychology, Managerial Accounting, Legal Environment in Business, Calculus, Transition for LPNs, Humanities, Business.

Teaching Methods: *TV:* videotape. *Other:* videoconferencing, audiotapes, independent study.

Admission Requirements: *Undergraduate:* contact school.

On-Campus Requirements: None.

Tuition and Fees: *Undergraduate:* $42/credit. *Credit by:* semester.

Financial Aid: Federal Stafford Loan, Federal Perkins Loan, Federal PLUS Loan, Federal Pell Grant, Federal Work-Study, VA, Illinois resident programs.

Accreditation: North Central Association of Colleges and Schools.

Description: Kankakee Community College (1966) serves as an educational, vocational, and recreational center for 130,000 residents of an area encompassing all or part of Kankakee, Iroquois, Ford, Grundy, Livingston, and Will counties. Kankakee County is located only 50 miles south of Chicago. For several years, KCC has offered a limited number of videotaped courses. Four years ago, the college began offering courses via interactive TV as a member of a network with 9 other institutions. The network has now expanded to include some high schools and medical centers. Although KCC does not offer a complete degree via distance, an increasing number of distance courses are being offered.

Kansas City, Kansas Community College

| 7250 State Avenue | Phone: (913) 288-7660 |
| Kansas City, KS 66112 | Fax: (913) 288-7663 |

Division(s): Continuing Education/Community Services
Web Site(s): http://www.kckcc.cc.ks.us
E-mail: ltrumbo@toto.net

Undergraduate Degree Programs:
Associate of Arts
Associate of Science
Associate of Applied Science
Associate in General Studies

Certificate Programs: Business, Child Care, Education, Engineering Technology, Fire Science, Law Enforcement, Long-Term Care Administration, Recreation Therapy, Special Education for Paraprofessionals, Victim/Survivor, Wellness/Fitness, Women's Studies, Addiction Counseling.

Teaching Methods: *Computers:* Internet, electronic classroom, e-mail, CD-ROM, newsgroup, LISTSERV. *TV:* videotape, cable program, satellite broadcasting, PBS. *Other:* videoconferencing, audiotapes, fax, correspondence, independent study, individual study, learning contracts.

Credits Granted for: experiential learning, portfolio assessment, examination (CLEP, ACT-PEP, DANTES, GRE), service learning.

Admission Requirements: *Undergraduate:* high school graduate or age 18 and GED. *Certificate:* high school graduate or age 18 and GED.

On-Campus Requirements: telecourses require some on-campus hours, online courses do not.

Tuition and Fees: *Undergraduate:* $45/credit resident, $119/credit out-of-state. *Other Costs:* additional fees are required in some classes. *Credit by:* semester.

Financial Aid: Federal Stafford Loan, Federal Perkins Loan, Federal PLUS Loan, Federal Pell Grant, Federal Work-Study, VA, Kansas resident programs.

Accreditation: North Central Association of Colleges and Schools.

Description: Kansas City, Kansas Community College (1923) is a public, 2-year institution located in northeast Kansas. Our college serves more than 6,000 students annually. The average age of students at the college is 30 (60% female, 39% male). Culturally, 63% are white, 21% African American, 5% Hispanic, 2% Asian/Pacific Islander, 1% American Indian, 8% are other. Students are 28% full time, 72% part time.

Kansas State University

13 College Court Building	Phone: (785) 532-5687
Manhattan, KS 66506	(800) 622-2KSU
	Fax: (785) 532-3779

Division(s): Division of Continuing Education
Web Site(s): http://www.dce.ksu.edu
E-mail: info@dce.ksu.edu

Undergraduate Degree Programs:
Bachelor of Science in:
    Interdisciplinary Social Sciences
    Animal Sciences and Industry
    Food Science and Industry
    General Business
Bachelor in Dietetics

Graduate Degree Programs:
Master of Engineering in:
    Electrical and Computer Engineering
    Civil Engineering
    Chemical Engineering
    Software Engineering
    Engineering Management
Master of Agribusiness
Master of Industrial/Organizational Psychology
Master of Family Financial Planning

Certificate Programs: Food Science

Class Titles: Farm/Ranch Management, Range Management, Animal Science, Food Science, Food Processing, Nutrition, Meat Science, Food Chemistry, Problems: Food Microbiology, Meat Selection/Utilization, Quality Assurance of Food Products, Food Analysis, Food Science Seminar, Food Science Problems, Cereal Science, Human Dimensions in Horticulture, Horticulture for Special Populations, Dealing with Diversity, Earth in Action, Earth Through Time, Geology Lab, College Algebra, General Calculus/Linear Algebra, Political Thought, World Politics, International Relations, Latin American Politics, Ideologies: Their Origins/Impact, Why Big Government?, Women's Studies.

Teaching Methods: *Computers:* Internet, real-time chat, electronic classroom, e-mail, CD-ROM, newsgroup, LISTSERV. *TV:* videotape, cable program, satellite broadcasting, PBS. *Other:* audioconferencing, videoconferencing, audiographics, audiotapes, fax, correspondence, independent study, individual study.

Credits Granted for: experiential learning, portfolio assessment, extrainstitutional learning, examination (CLEP, ACT-PEP, DANTES, GRE).

Admission Requirements: *Undergraduate:* contact Division of Continuing Education. *Graduate:* contact Ellen Stauffer, Engineering Program Coordinator at (785) 532-2562 or e-mail, engineering@dce.ksu.edu or see Web site at http://www.dce.ksu.edu/dce/engg. *Certificate:* contact Division of Continuing Education.

On-Campus Requirements: None.

Tuition and Fees: *Undergraduate:* $102/credit. *Graduate:* $146/credit. *Application Fee:* $55 for bachelor degree programs. *Other Costs:* media fees vary with course, textbooks, and materials. *Credit by:* semester.

Financial Aid: Federal Stafford Loan, Federal Perkins Loan, Federal PLUS Loan, Federal Pell Grant, Federal Work-Study, VA.

Accreditation: North Central Association of Colleges and Schools.

Description: Kansas State University (1863) was founded as a land-grant institution under the Morrill Act. It was initially located on the grounds of the old Bluemont Central College, which was chartered in 1858. The university moved to its present site in 1875. The 664-acre campus is in Manhattan, 125 miles west of Kansas City via Interstate 70 in the rolling Flint Hills of northeast Kansas. The campus is convenient to both business and residential sections of the city. Under an enactment of the 1991 Kansas Legislature, the Salina campus, 70 miles west of Manhattan, was established through a merger of the former Kansas College of Technology with the university. Additional university sites include 18,000 acres in the 4 branch locations of the Agricultural Experiment Station (Hays, Garden City, Colby, and Parsons) and 8,600 acres in the Konza Prairie Research Natural Area jointly operated by the AES and the Division of Biology. One of the 6 universities governed by the Kansas Board of Regents, Kansas State University continues to fulfill its historic educational mission in teaching, research, and public service.

Keiser College

1500 NW 49th Street **Phone: 1(800) 749-4456**
Fort Lauderdale, FL 33309 **Fax: (954) 351-4030**

Division(s): eCampus (Department of Online Education)
Web Site(s): http://www.keisercollege.cc.fl.us/ecampus.htm
http://www.keisercollege.org
E-mail: ecampus@keisercollege.cc.fl.us

Undergraduate Degree Programs:
Associate of Arts with concentrations in:
    Business Administration
    Accounting
    Paralegal
    eCommerce
    Health Services Administration
Associate of Science with a Concentration in Computer Network Administration

Class Titles: Contact school or visit web site for details.

Teaching Methods: *Computers:* Internet, real-time chat, electronic classroom, e-mail, CD-ROM, newsgroup, LISTSERV. *TV:* videotape, cable program, satellite broadcasting, PBS.

Credits Granted for: examination (CLEP, ACT-PEP, DANTES, GRE).

Admission Requirements: *Undergraduate:* high school diploma/GED, Keiser entrance exam.

On-Campus Requirements: None.

Tuition and Fees: *Undergraduate:* $4,450/semester. *Application Fee:* $52. *Other Costs:* registration fee: $145, varies for textbooks. *Credit by:* semester.

Financial Aid: Federal Stafford Loan, Federal Perkins Loan, Federal PLUS Loan, Federal Pell Grant, Federal Work-Study, VA.

Accreditation: Commission on Colleges of the Southern Association of Colleges and Schools (SACS).

Description: Keiser College's (1977) Online Programs are web-based courses, designed by qualified faculty and staff to create an interesting, interactive learning environment. Keiser's virtual classroom is comfortable, and courses can be taken easily by anyone with access to the World Wide Web. Lesson plans, assignments, and class schedules are posted online, while student/teacher interaction and student/student interaction also occur over the Internet. Scheduled discussions, e-mail messages, live chats, and real-time group discussions are a few of the opportunities for interacting during your online course.

Kellogg Community College

450 North Avenue
Battle Creek, MI 49017
Phone: (616) 965-3931 x2383
Fax: (616) 965-4133

Division(s): Educational Services
Web Site(s): http://www.kellogg.cc.mi.us
E-mail: parkerc@kellogg.cc.mi.us

Class Titles: Anthropology, Art History, General Business, Business Statistics, Business Management, Business Law, Marketing, Economics (Macro/Micro), American History, World History, Political Science, Psychology, Environmental Science, Sociology, International Business, Calculus, Cost Accounting, Criminal Justice Management, French, Information Processing, Organic Chemistry, World Literature, Electronic Devices.

Teaching Methods: *Computers:* Internet, real-time chat, electronic classroom, e-mail, CD-ROM. *TV:* videotape, cable. *Other:* videoconferencing, independent study.

Credits Granted for: experiential learning, portfolio assessment, extrainstitutional learning, examination (CLEP, ACT-PEP, DANTES, GRE).

Admission Requirements: *Undergraduate:* open admissions. *Doctoral:* open admissions. *Certificate:* open admissions.

On-Campus Requirements: None.

Tuition and Fees: *Undergraduate:* $55/credit for residents, $88/credit for nonresidents, $134.85/credit for international students. *Other Costs:* lab fees for some courses. *Credit by:* semester.

Financial Aid: Federal Pell Grant, Federal Work-Study, VA, Michigan resident programs, Ford Direct Loan, Direct PLUS Loan.

Accreditation: North Central Association of Colleges and Schools.

Description: Kellogg Community College (1956) is a public institution of higher learning that provides academic, occupational, general, and lifelong learning opportunities for all people in its district and contiguous service area. The institution offers a comprehensive range of curricula, courses, activities, and services while maintaining open-door admissions. Current enrollment is approximately 11,000. The institution has offered telecourses since 1990, and in 1997 it began interactive video courses via a fiber optic loop linking 23 secondary and postsecondary sites in a 2-county area. In the fall of 1998, Kellogg began offering interactive-video courses to additional sites via compressed video technology. Kellogg began offering Internet-delivered courses in 1998 with two online courses.

Kent State University

Moulton Hall
Kent, OH 44242
Phone: 330-672-9586
Fax: 330-672-9588

Division(s): Distributed Learning
Web Site(s): http://www.dl.kent.edu
E-mail: info@dl.kent.edu

Undergraduate Degree Programs: Contact school.

Graduate Degree Programs: Contact school.

Postgraduate Degree Programs: Contact school.

Certificate Programs: 15 programs; see *www.kent.edu.*

Class Titles: Nursing, Technology, English, Psychology, Math, Business, Education, Chemistry, Philosophy (see www.dl.kent.edu).

Teaching Methods: *Computers:* Internet, real-time chat, electronic classroom, e-mail, CD-ROM, LISTSERV. *TV:* Desktop Synchronous (LearnLinc—home or classroom): Interactive video/audioconferencing, application viewing/sharing, chat, videotape, synchronized web browsing, shared Whiteboard, e-mail, Listserv. *Other:* Videoconferencing Synchronous (VTEL) (Classroom): Interactive videoconferencing, computer, tape, e-mail, LISTSERV.

Admission Requirements: *Undergraduate:* see *www.admissions.kent.edu.* *Graduate:* see *www.admissions.kent.edu.* *Postgraduate:* see *www.admissions.kent.edu.* *Certificate:* see *www.admissions.kent.edu.*

On-Campus Requirements: entire degree programs are not available via distance, and classes that are may have an orientation session or a final exam session or both.

Tuition and Fees: *Undergraduate:* see *www.admissions. kent.edu.* *Graduate:* see *www.admissions.kent.edu.* *Postgraduate:* see *www.admissions.kent.edu.* *Application Fee:* see *www.admissions.kent.edu.* *Software:* see *www.admissions.kent.edu.* *Graduation Fee:* see *www.admissions.kent.edu.* *Other Costs:* see *www.admissions.kent.edu.* *Credit by:* semester.

Financial Aid: Federal Stafford Loan, Federal Perkins Loan, Federal PLUS Loan, Federal Pell Grant, Federal Work-Study, VA, state programs for residents of Ohio (see www. admissions.kent.edu).

Accreditation: Too many to list (see *www.kent.edu*).

Description: Kent State University (1910) is the third largest university in Ohio and one of the 40 largest in the United States. It is a mostly residential university with 8 regional campuses throughout northeast Ohio. Kent has been offering distance courses for more than 5 years, with offerings increasing dramatically each year. Distance education is simply an alternative way to take classes; it's not our way of life. It's meant to add flexibility to a normal course of study, not to be used exclusively to obtain a degree, at least this year. Visit www.kent.edu for more information.

Kentucky Community and Technical College System (KCTCS)

2624 Research Park Drive
P.O. Box 14092
Lexington, Kentucky 40512-4092

Phone: (859) 246-3100
Fax: (859) 246-3153

Division(s): Colleges under the umbrella of (KCTCS) offering online-courses:

Ashland Community College
Bowling Green Technical College
Central Kentucky Technical College
Elizabethtown Community College
Elizabethtown Technical College
Henderson Community College
Hopkinsville Community College
Hazard Community College
Jefferson Community College
Madisonville Community College
Madisonville Technical College
Maysville Community College
Owensboro Community College
Paducah Community College
Prestonsburg Community College
Somerset Community College
Southeast Community College
Western Kentucky Technical College

Web Site(s): http://www.kctcs.net/distancelearning/
E-mail: robert.johnson@kctcs.net

Undergraduate Degree Programs:
Associate of Arts Degree
Associate in Applied Science Degree

Certificate Programs: Office Systems Technology, Information Technology Fundamentals, Microsoft Certified System Engineer, A+.

Class Titles: Contact schools or check web site for details.

Teaching Methods: *Computers:* Internet, real-time chat, electronic classroom, e-mail, CD-ROM, LISTSERV. *TV:* videotape, cable program, satellite broadcasting, PBS. *Other:* radio broadcast, videoconferencing, audioconferencing, audiographics, audiotapes, fax, correspondence, independent study, individual study, learning contracts.

Credits Granted for: experiential learning, portfolio assessment, extrainstitutional learning (PONSI, corporate or pro-

fessional association seminars/workshops), examination (CLEP, ACT-PEP, DANTES, GRE).

Admission Requirements: *Undergraduate:* all of the KYVU courses listed in the course catalog are offered at participating KYVU institutions. These institutions determine academic requirements and/or prerequisites on a course by course basis.

On-Campus Requirements: It varies by college, class, and instructor.

Tuition and Fees: *Undergraduate:* $61/credit. *Credit by:* semester.

Financial Aid: Federal Stafford Loan, Federal Perkins Loan, Federal PLUS Loan, Federal Pell Grant, Federal Work-Study, VA, state programs for residents of Kentucky.

Accreditation: Southern Association of Colleges and Schools, Commission on Occupational Education.

Description: In May 1997 Governor Paul E. Patton signed the Kentucky Postsecondary Education Improvement Act of 1997, which created the Kentucky Community and Technical College System. KCTCS includes 13 community colleges and 25 postsecondary technical institutions (which later was reorganized to 15 technical colleges). In July 1997 the governor appointed the first 8 citizen members of the KCTCS Board of Regents. In November 1998 the Council on Postsecondary Education launched the Kentucky Virtual University. Five of 9 pilot projects involve KCTCS. KCTCS began implementation of its information technology project, later called Project Unity. In December 1998 the Board of Regents hired Dr. Michael B. McCall of South Carolina as the founding president of KCTCS.

Kettering University

1700 West Third Avenue
Flint, MI 48504-4898

Phone: (810) 762-7494
Fax: (810) 762-9935

Division(s): Office of Graduate Studies
Web Site(s): http://www.kettering.edu
E-mail: bbedore@kettering.edu

Graduate Degree Programs:
Master of Science in:
Manufacturing Management
Engineering
Operations Management

Teaching Methods: *Computers:* Internet, e-mail. *TV:* videotape. *Other:* fax, correspondence.

Admission Requirements: *Graduate:* application, transcripts, 2 letters of recommendation. International requirements include TOEFL.

On-Campus Requirements: None.

Tuition and Fees: *Graduate:* $465/credit. *Credit by:* quarter.

Financial Aid: Federal Stafford Loan, Graduate Access Loan, Michigan Tuition Grant.

Accreditation: North Central Association of Colleges and Schools.

Description: Founded in 1919, General Motors Corporation agreed to underwrite the school in 1926, and General Motors Institute, a totally cooperative undergraduate school was born. In 1982 GMI became independent of General Motors and the private corporation "GMI Engineering and Management Institute" was established. In January 1998, GMI changed its name to Kettering University. Kettering continues to maintain a close affiliation with industry, as it has throughout its history. In the fall of 1982 Kettering began a video-based, distance learning graduate program leading to a Master of Science in Manufacturing Management degree. In 1990 the Master of Science in Engineering degree was initiated and in 1998 the Master of Science in Operations Management degree was implemented.

Kirkwood Community College

6301 Kirkwood Boulevard SW	Phone: (319) 398-4974
Cedar Rapids, IA 52406-2068	Fax: (319) 398-5492

Division(s): Distance Learning and Learning Initiatives
Web Site(s): http://www.kirkwood.cc.ia.us
E-mail: jeadie@kirkwood.cc.ia.us

Undergraduate Degree Programs:
Associate of Arts

Class Titles: Composition, Literature, Humanities, Music Appreciation, Sociology, Anthropology, Psychology, History, Math, Chemistry, Accounting, Business, Medical Terminology, Nutrition, Keyboarding, MS Word, Water Treatment, Fire Science, Criminal Justice, Computer, Disability Services, Communications Media.

Teaching Methods: *Computers:* Internet, e-mail, CD-ROM, newsgroup. *TV:* videotape, cable program, satellite broadcasting, PBS, live interactive instructional TV. *Other:* audiotapes, correspondence.

Credits Granted for: examination (CLEP).

Admission Requirements: *Undergraduate:* open door. *Certificate:* open door.

On-Campus Requirements: Students must complete 16 credits from Kirkwood. These may be in distance delivered formats.

Tuition and Fees: *Undergraduate:* $73/credit. *Other Costs:* textbooks and other course materials. *Credit by:* semester.

Financial Aid: Federal Stafford Loan, Federal Perkins Loan, Federal PLUS Loan, Federal Pell Grant, Federal Work-Study, VA, Iowa resident programs.

Accreditation: North Central Association of Colleges and Schools.

Description: Kirkwood Community College (1966) is a publicly supported, 2-year college with a current enrollment of 11,643 credit students. The college offers diplomas, certificates, and degrees including associate of arts, associate of science, and associate of applied science degrees. Kirkwood pioneered interactive TV instruction in the early 1980s and has offered classes in asynchronous distance learning formats since 1984. Twenty percent of our students each semester are enrolled in one or more distance-delivered courses. Student support services such as advising, counseling, and tutoring for selected classes are available through the college's Web site.

Kirtland Community College

10775 North St. Helen Road	Phone: (989) 275-5000
Roscommon, MI 48653	Fax: (989) 275-6789

Division(s): None.
Web Site(s): http://kirtland.cc.mi.us
E-mail: loseed@kirtland.cc.mi.us

Undergraduate Degree Programs:
25 vocational (technical career oriented) associate degree programs and
Associate in (transfer programs):
    Arts
    Business Administration
    Computers
    Criminal Justice, General
    Fine Arts
    Science

Certificate Programs: contact school.

Class Titles: contact school.

Teaching Methods: *Computers:* Internet. *TV:* videotape. *Other:* None.

Credits Granted for: examination (CLEP, ACT-PEP, DANTES).

Admission Requirements: *Undergraduate:* high school graduate or GED completer.

On-Campus Requirements: 15 credits.

Tuition and Fees: *Undergraduate:* $54.10/credit in-district plus fees. *Credit by:* semester.

Financial Aid: Federal Stafford Loan, Federal Perkins Loan, Federal PLUS Loan, Federal Pell Grant, Federal Work-Study, VA, Michigan resident programs.

Accreditation: North Central Association of Colleges and Schools.

Description: On March 7, 1966, in accordance with provision of Public Act 188 of the Michigan Public Acts of 1955, Kirtland Community College was created by a vote of the electorate from 6 local K–12 school districts (Crawford-AuSable, Fairview Area, Gerrish-Higgins, Houghton Lake, Mio-AuSable and West Branch-Rose City). With this approval, the largest Michigan Community College District was formed. The college's district totals 2,500 square miles and consists of all or part of 9 counties.

Knowledge Systems Institute

3420 Main Street	Phone: (847) 679-3135
Skokie, IL 60076	Fax: (847) 679-3166

Division(s): None.
Web Site(s): http://www.ksi.edu; distancelearning.ksi.edu
E-mail: office@ksi.edu, dlearn@ksi.edu

Graduate Degree Programs:
Master of Science in Computer and Information Sciences

Certificate Programs: Computer and Information Sciences.

Teaching Methods: *Computers:* Internet, e-mail, multimedia audio and video. *Other:* None.

Admission Requirements: *Graduate:* BS degree or equivalent, open-admission for individual courses (see Web site: http://www.ksi.edu). *Certificate:* same as undergraduate.

On-Campus Requirements: All courses offered through distance learning.

Tuition and Fees: *Graduate:* $295/credit (all graduate courses are 3 credits). *Application Fee:* $40. *Credit by:* semester.

Financial Aid: Federal Stafford Loan, VA, Federal Work-Study.

Accreditation: North Central Association of Colleges and Schools.

Description: Knowledge Systems Institute (1978) is a Graduate School of Computer and Information Sciences dedicated to the training and education of professional people in the fields of computers and management information systems. KSI offers an MS degree in Computer and Information Sciences and an MS degree with specialization in Management Information Systems, Computer Networks, Software Engineering, E-commerce, and other areas. Most of

KSI's courses can be taken on campus or via the Internet. This approach greatly facilitates working professionals completing their education. For further information please consult our web site distancelearning.ksi.edu, or send e-mail message to: dlearn@ksi.edu.

Kutztown University

PO Box 700	Phone: (610) 683-4212
Kutztown, PA 19530	Fax: (610) 683-4398

Division(s): Academic Affairs
Web Site(s): http://www.kutztown.edu
E-mail: admission@kutztown.edu

Class Titles: American Literature, Current Health Issues, Personal Fitness.

Teaching Methods: *Computers:* Internet, real-time chat, e-mail, CD-ROM, newsgroup, LISTSERV, Web. *TV:* videotape, cable program, PBS. *Other:* audioconferencing, videoconferencing, audiotapes, fax, correspondence.

Credits Granted for: examination (CLEP, ACT-PEP, DANTES, GRE).

On-Campus Requirements: per instructor basis.

Tuition and Fees: *Undergraduate:* $167/credit in-state, $418/credit out-of-state. *Graduate:* $256/credit in-state, $420/credit out-of-state. *Credit by:* semester.

Financial Aid: Federal Stafford Loan, Federal Perkins Loan, Federal PLUS Loan, Federal Pell Grant, Federal Work-Study, VA, state grant programs for Pennsylvania, Delaware, Ohio, Rhode Island, Maine, Virginia, Massachusetts, Vermont, West Virginia residents. Private loans are also available.

Accreditation: Middle States Association of Colleges and Schools, Pennsylvania Department of Education, State System of Higher Education, National Council for Accreditation of Teacher Education, National League for Nursing, Inc., Council on Social Work Education.

Description: Kutztown University (1866) began as Keystone State Normal School in response to a local need for more teachers. Since those early times, KU has grown into a university that serves 7,900 students in 5 colleges: Business, Education, Liberal Arts and Sciences, Visual and Performing Arts, and Graduate Studies and Extended Learning. The campus sits on 326 acres of rural countryside near Kutztown (population 4,500), in the heart of the state's southeastern "Pennsylvania Dutch" area. Kutztown University first offered distance learning classes in 1996 and plans to expand its offerings in the future. The first classes used Internet technology, and a videoconferencing classroom and conference room have since been added. Kutztown, as a member of the Pennsylvania State System of Higher Education, collaborates with its sister institutions as well as with the community colleges, school districts, and various consortiums to enhance academic offerings and access.

Labette Community College

200 South 14th Street	Phone: (620) 820-1224
Parsons, KS 67357	Fax: (620) 421-4881

Division(s): Dean of Instruction
Web Site(s): http://labette.cc.ks.us
E-mail: chrisb@labette.cc.ks.us

Undergraduate Degree Programs:
Associate in:
    Arts
    Science
    Applied Science
    General Studies

Certificate Programs: Business, Technology, Paraprofessional, and more.

Class Titles: English Composition, Sociology, Art Appreciation, American History, World Regional Geography, General Psychology, Developmental Psychology, Medical Terminology, College Algebra, Computer Information Systems, C++ Programming, American Government, Economics, various allied health continuing education classes.

Teaching Methods: *Computers:* Internet, real-time chat, CD-ROM, newsgroup, LISTSERV, electronic classroom, e-mail. *TV:* videotape, *Other:* videoconferencing, audiotapes, independent study, individual study, learning contracts.

Credits Granted for: experiential learning, extrainstitutional learning (PONSI, corporate or professional association seminars/workshops), examination (CLEP, ACT-PEP, DANTES, GRE).

Admission Requirements: *Undergraduate:* high school graduate or GED, age 18 as a special student, high school juniors and seniors with permission of principal, "gifted" students (with copy of IEP).

On-Campus Requirements: None.

Tuition and Fees: *Undergraduate:* $47/credit. *Other Costs:* $15 Graduation Fee, $15 Technology Fee, $5 copies. *Credit by:* semester.

Financial Aid: Federal Stafford Loan, Federal Perkins Loan, Federal PLUS Loan, Federal Pell Grant, Federal Work-Study, VA, private scholarships, public scholarships.

Accreditation: The Higher Learning Commission of the North Central Association of Colleges and Schools.

Description: Labette Community College (1923) is a public, comprehensive community college with a variety of academic, vocational-technical, continuing education, lifelong learning, and workforce training programs and services. It is located in Parsons, Kansas, in the southeast corner of the state. The college has been active in Distance Learning since the 1980s and has a well-established online program.

Lackawanna Junior College

501 Vine Street	Phone: (570) 961-7853
Scranton, PA 18509	Fax: (570) 961-7858

Division(s): Distance Learning
Web Site(s): http://www.ljc.edu
E-mail: lewisg@ljc.edu

Class Titles: Classes vary by semester depending on demand from our satellite centers (see description). For example, an accounting course was offered from Scranton to Towanda via distance learning. It usually is not known until the beginning of a semester what courses may be offered via teleteaching.

Teaching Methods: videoconferencing.

Credits Granted for: experiential learning, portfolio assessment, extrainstitutional learning, examination (CLEP, ACT-PEP, DANTES, GRE).

Admission Requirements: *Undergraduate:* open-admission. *Certificate:* open-admission.

On-Campus Requirements: None.

Tuition and Fees: *Undergraduate:* $270/credit. *Application Fee:* $25. *Credit by:* semester.

Financial Aid: Federal Stafford Loan, Federal Perkins Loan, Federal PLUS Loan, Federal Pell Grant, Federal Work-Study, VA, Pennsylvania resident programs.

Accreditation: Middle States Association of Colleges and Schools.

Description: Lackawanna Junior College (1894) is an accredited, private, nonprofit, educational institution providing opportunities for career and personal development within selected associate degree, certificate, and continuing education programs. Degree programs are accredited by the Commission on Higher Education of the Middle States Association of Colleges and Schools. Lackawanna Junior College is an Equal Opportunity/Affirmative Action educational institution. Distance Learning at Lackawanna began in 1993. They have offered courses to satellite centers in Towanda, Honesdale, and Hazleton (all in Pennsylvania). In addition, they have teletaught courses to Monument Valley High School in Arizona. Lackawanna is a member of the Northern Tier (PA) Distance Learning Consortium.

Lake Region State College

1801 College Drive North | Phone: (701) 662-1510
Devils Lake, ND 58301-1598 | Fax: (701) 662-1570

Division(s): Office of Continuing Education
Web Site(s): http://www.lrsc.nodak.edue-mail/
E-mail: LRSC_Continuing_Education@lrsc.nodak.edu

Undergraduate Degree Programs:
Associate of Applied Science:
    Legal Assistant
    Early Childhood Education
    Practical Nurse
    Associate of Arts—Liberal Arts

Class Titles: German, Spanish, Agriculture.

Teaching Methods: *Computers:* Internet, real-time chat, electronic classroom, e-mail. *TV:* satellite broadcasting. *Other:* videoconferencing.

Credits Granted for: experiential learning, portfolio assessment, examination (CLEP, ACT-PEP, DANTES, GRE).

Admission Requirements: *Undergraduate:* application, application fee, high school or GED transcript, college transcripts, ACT score for those under 25 years of age.

On-Campus Requirements: None.

Tuition and Fees: *Undergraduate:* $85.04/credit/resident rate. *Application Fee:* $25. *Other Costs:* $25/credit Distance Education access fee and $35/credit for online course access fee. *Credit by:* semester.

Financial Aid: Federal Stafford Loan, Federal Perkins Loan, Federal PLUS Loan, Federal Pell Grant, Federal Work-Study, VA, state programs for residents of North Dakota.

Accreditation: North Central Association of Colleges and Secondary Schools.

Description: Located in Devils Lake, North Dakota, Lake Region State College (1941) is a 2-year comprehensive community college. The campus is situated on the northern edge of the city of Devils Lake, 3 miles from Devils Lake, North Dakota's largest natural body of water. On July 1, 1984, the college joined the state system of higher education. LRSC now reports directly to the State Board of Higher Education. LRSC began its involvement with Distance Education in 1990, when we were granted 2 dedicated Interactive Video Network rooms, in affiliation with the North Dakota Interactive Video Network. Since then, the college has added another video-conferencing unit. We began online courses in 1998 and have doubled our course listing since then. We are proud to be involved with the ND University System Online, which will offer the liberal arts degree online for the first time in fall 2001.

Lake-Sumter Community College

9501 Highway 441 | Phone: (352) 365-3566
Leesburg, FL 34788 | Fax: (352) 365-3501

Division(s): Television Studio and V.P. Educational Services
Web Site(s): http://www.lscc.cc.fl.us
E-mail: huntp@lscc.cc.fl.us

Class Titles: Marine Science, Earth Revealed, Business/Law, Business, Psychology, Psychology of Child Development, Basic Nutrition, Trends/Issues in Health, American National Government, Microcomputer Applications, Intro/Info Comtec, Intro Pharmacology.

Teaching Methods: *Computers:* Internet, electronic classroom, e-mail, CD-ROM. *TV:* videotape, satellite, broadcasting, PBS. *Other:* videoconferencing, audiotapes, fax, correspondence, independent study, individual study.

Credits Granted for: examination (CLEP, ACT-PEP, DANTES, GRE).

Admission Requirements: *Undergraduate:* high school diploma or GED. GPA of 2.5 or better, application.

On-Campus Requirements: students, logistically, must spend time on campus in a traditional classroom setting.

Tuition and Fees: *Undergraduate:* $39/credit resident, $145/credit nonresident. *Application Fee:* $20. *Software:* $15. *Other Costs:* $20 late registration, $16 nursing fee (insurance), $20/credit exemption exam fee, $20 international student processing fee. *Parking Fee:* $1/credit hour. *Credit by:* semester.

Financial Aid: Federal Stafford Loan, Federal Perkins Loan, Federal PLUS Loan, Federal Pell Grant, Federal Work-Study, VA, Florida resident programs.

Accreditation: Southern Association of Colleges and Schools.

Lake Superior College

2101 Trinity Road | Phone: (218) 733-7690
Duluth, MN 55811 | Fax: (218) 733-7690

Division(s): Dean of Technology and Distance Learning
Web Site(s): http://www.lsc.mnscu.edu/online/
E-mail: b.dahl@lsc.mnscu.edu (Barry Dahl)

Undergraduate Degree Programs:
Associate of Arts

Certificate Programs: Professional Bookkeeper (30 credits).

Class Titles: Accounting, Administrative Support, Allied Health, Art, Civil Engineering, Computer Information, English, Psychology, Physical Therapy, Sociology, Speech.

Teaching Methods: *Computers:* Internet, real-time chat, electronic classroom, e-mail, CD-ROM. *TV:* videotape. *Other:* independent study.

Credits Granted for: experiential learning, examination (CLEP, ACT-PEP, DANTES, GRE).

Admission Requirements: *Undergraduate:* online courses follow same start and stop dates as regular semesters.

On-Campus Requirements: None.

Tuition and Fees: *Undergraduate:* approximately $90/credit. *Application Fee:* $20, for admission to a program. *Graduation Fee:* $10. *Credit by:* semester.

Financial Aid: Federal Stafford Loan, Federal Perkins Loan, Federal Pell Grant, Federal Work-Study, VA, Post-secondary Child Care Loans, State loan programs for residents of Minnesota.

Accreditation: North Central Association (NCA).

Description: LSC (1950) began offering Internet-based, Distance Learning courses during 1997. From one class with 8 students, we have grown to more than 50 online courses with more than 1,000 students per year. New courses and program offerings are being added each semester.

Lake Superior State University

| 650 West Easterday | Phone: (906) 635-2802 |
| Sault Ste. Marie, MI 49783 | Fax: (906) 635-2762 |

Division(s): Continuing Education
Web Site(s): http://www.lssu.edu
E-mail: scamp@gw.lssu.edu

Undergraduate Degree Programs:
Bachelor of Arts/Bachelor of Science in:
    Business Administration
    Engineering Management
    Accounting
    Criminal Justice
    Nursing, BSN Completion

Teaching Methods: Live classes at off-campus regional center, which include interactive TV, videotape, and the Web.

Credits Granted for: previous academic work.

Admission Requirements: *Undergraduate:* average high school GPA: 2.88, ACT 21.

On-Campus Requirements: At the present time the majority of our distance education courses are offered at one of 4 distant sites (located in Alpena, Escanaba, Petoskey, and Traverse City, Michigan). Some classes require participation in concentrated labs on the campus of LSSU.

Tuition and Fees: *Undergraduate:* $172/credit. *Application Fee:* $20 undergraduate. *Credit by:* semester.

Financial Aid: Federal Stafford Loan, Federal Perkins Loan, Federal PLUS Loan, Federal Pell Grant, Federal Work-Study, VA, Michigan resident programs.

Accreditation: North Central Association of Colleges and Schools.

Description: Lake Superior State University (1946) is located in the beautiful and rugged, eastern upper peninsula. Distance education at Lake Superior State consists of interactive TV courses and degree programs available at 4 community colleges in northern Michigan in Alpena, Escanaba, Petoskey, and Traverse City. A variety of degrees are available at these sites, including bachelor's degrees in accounting, business administration, criminal justice, engineering management, and BSN nursing completion. Each degree can be completed entirely by distance at those off-campus locations.

Lakehead University

| RC 0009, 955 Oliver Road | Phone: (807) 346-7730 |
| Thunder Bay, ON, Canada P7E 5E1 | Fax: (807) 343-8008 |

Division(s): Part-Time Studies
Web Site(s): http://www.lakeheadu.ca/~disedwww/menu.html
E-mail: parttime@lakeheadu.ca

Undergraduate Degree Programs:
Bachelor of Arts (General)
Bachelor of Science in Nursing for Registered Nurses
Honors Bachelor of Social Work (1- and 4-year program)

Graduate Degree Programs:
Master of Forestry

Certificate Programs: Environmental Assessment, Environmental Management, Interdisciplinary Palliative Care.

Teaching Methods: *Computers:* Internet, e-mail, CD-ROM. *Other:* audioconferencing, videoconferencing, audiotapes, fax, independent study, videotapes.

Admission Requirements: *Undergraduate:* see university calendar. *Graduate:* see university calendar. *Certificate:* see university calendar.

Tuition and Fees: *Undergraduate:* $797.60/full-credit course. *Other Costs:* $8–$120 for manuals. *Credit by:* semester.

Financial Aid: Ontario Student Assistance Program.

Accreditation: Association of Universities and Colleges of Canada.

Description: At Lakehead University (1965), our faculty, staff, programs, and services team up to provide an extensive range of learning choices and alternatives. The university evolved from Lakehead Technical Institute, which was established in 1946. Lakehead serves a dual role with the responsibility for bringing knowledge and an understanding of a broad range of the basic disciplines to Northwestern Ontario, while striving to be a good general university for the purpose of regional accessibility.

Lakeland College

| W3718 South Drive, CTH "M" | Phone: (920) 565-2111 |
| Plymouth, WI 53073 | Fax: (920) 565-1206 |

Division(s): Lakeland College Online
Web Site(s): http://www.lakeland.edu

Undergraduate Degree Programs:
Bachelor of Arts

Graduate Degree Programs:
Masters in Business Administration

Certificate Programs: American Humanics Certificate Program.

Class Titles: Contact school or check web site for details.

Teaching Methods: *Computers:* Internet, real-time chat, electronic classroom, e-mail, CD-ROM, newsgroup.

Credits Granted for: examination (CLEP, DANTES).

Admission Requirements: *Undergraduate:* must have above a 2.0 GPA to be considered for admission. *Graduate:* official transcript from an accredited institution with a minimum GPA of 2.75 on a 4.00 scale *or* a minimum 3.00 GPA in the last 60 semester hours of undergraduate study.

On-Campus Requirements: None.

Tuition and Fees: *Undergraduate:* $195/credit. *Graduate:* $275/credit. *Credit by:* semester.

Financial Aid: Federal Stafford Loan, Federal Perkins Loan, Federal PLUS Loan, Federal Pell Grant, Federal Work-Study, VA, state programs for residents of Wisconsin.

Accreditation: North Central Association of Colleges and Schools.

Description: Lakeland College (1997) is an educational community where students and faculty share academic goals and join in a common intellectual quest. Teaching and learning—the search for knowledge and understanding and the critical examination of ideas, values, and actions—are central activities of the college. Lakeland College is also a global community, drawing students of varied ages, religious backgrounds, and cultural traditions, from areas around the world, building community out of the rich diversity of its members, in a climate of civility, respect, and free expression. It is within this context that the Lakeland College Bachelor of Arts degree program is offered online. The program, especially designed with the working adult in mind, provides a broad-based education consisting of course work that integrates research, case studies, technology, and other learning processes.

Lakeland Community College

| 7700 Clocktower Drive | Phone: (440) 953-7000 |
| Kirtland, OH 44094 | Fax: (440) 953-9710 |

Division(s): Instructional Technologies
Web Site(s): http://www.lakeland.cc.oh.us
E-mail: wryan@lakeland.cc.oh.us

Undergraduate Degree Programs:
Associate of:
    Arts
    Science
    Applied Business
    Applied Science
    Technical Studies

Certificate Programs: can be earned in any program.

Class Titles: American Visions, Cycles of Life, Race to Save the Planet, Dollars and Sense, It's Strictly Business, Entrepreneurship, Marketing, Taking the Lead, Microeconomics, Macroeconomics, American Cinema, Power of Place, Western Traditions, By the Numbers, Elementary Statistics, World of Music, Healthy Living, Voices in Democracy, Sociological Imagination, Portrait of a Family, Faces of Culture, English Composition, International Business, Business Law, Computers and Information Processing, Business Telecommunications, Network Essentials, Word Processing, Spreadsheets, Database, Presentation Graphics, Introduction to Technology, Medical Terminology.

Teaching Methods: *Computers:* Internet, e-mail, CD-ROM newsgroup, LISTSERV, real-time chat, electronic classroom. *TV:* videotape, cable program, satellite broadcasting, PBS. *Other:* videoconferencing, fax, correspondence, independent study, individual study, learning contracts.

Credits Granted for: certification, examination (CLEP), experience, articulation.

Admission Requirements: *Undergraduate:* application, official high school transcript, college transcripts if applicable.

On-Campus Requirements: class orientation for telecourses and online courses.

Tuition and Fees: *Undergraduate:* $62.95/credit in-county, $53/credit out-of-county, $77.20/164.95/credit out-of-state. *Other Costs:* $25 telecourse fee. *Credit by:* quarter (converting to semester in 2000).

Financial Aid: Federal Stafford Loan, Federal Perkins Loan, Federal PLUS Loan, Federal Pell Grant, Federal Work-Study, VA, Ohio resident programs, scholarships, grants, loans, work-study.

Accreditation: North Central Association of Colleges and Schools.

Description: Lakeland Community College's (1967) mission is to provide transfer programs to begin studies toward a 4-year degree, career programs leading to immediate employment, and training and retraining programs to update job skills. Lakeland offers more than 1,000 classes in 76 degree and certificate programs.

Lamar University

PO Box 10008, LU Station	Phone: (409) 880-8431
Beaumont, TX 77710	Fax: (409) 880-8683

Division(s): Continuing Education
Web Site(s): http://www.lamar.edu/academics
E-mail: adultstudies@hal.lamar.edu

Class Titles: Nutrition/Diet, U.S. History, American Government, Microcomputers/Business, Humanities, Communications, Economics, Pedagogy, Philosophy, Education Leadership, Nursing, Engineering.

Teaching Methods: *Computers:* Internet, e-mail. *TV:* videotape, cable program, PBS. *Other:* videoconferencing, fax.

Credits Granted for: experiential learning, portfolio assessment, extrainstitutional learning, examination (CLEP, SATII, DANTES, Subject Exams/Advanced Placement).

Admission Requirements: *Undergraduate:* accredited high school graduate, SAT/ACT, TASP, college transcripts if transfer student. *Graduate:* contact school. *Doctoral:* contact school.

On-Campus Requirements: exams only.

Tuition and Fees: *Undergraduate:* $350/credit. *Graduate:* $350/credit. *Doctoral:* $350/credit. *Web Fee:* $50/credit hour. *Other Costs:* additional Distance Learning fees are $10/credit hour. *Credit by:* semester.

Financial Aid: Federal Stafford Loan, Federal Perkins Loan, Federal PLUS Loan, Federal Pell Grant, Federal Work-Study, VA, Texas resident programs.

Accreditation: Southern Association of Colleges and Schools.

Description: Lamar University (1923) opened as "a Junior College of the first class" with 125 students and a faculty of 14. In 1932 the name of the institution was changed to Lamar College, to honor Mirabeau B. Lamar, second president of the Republic of Texas and the "Father of Education" in Texas. Lamar was the first junior college in Texas to become a 4-year, state-supported college. Lamar continued to grow, building strong programs in engineering, the sciences, business, and education. In 1962, a graduate school was established offering master's degrees in several fields. The Doctorate in Engineering was established in 1971, at which time Lamar boasted an enrollment of 10,874. New programs were added, including Technical Arts, Allied Health, Office Technology, and Restaurant/Institutional Food Management. The Doctorate of Education in Deaf Education was established in 1993. Lamar's growth has been steady and progressive, anticipating the evolving needs of its students.

Laney College

900 Fallon Street	Phone: (510) 446-7368
Oakland, CA 94607	Fax: (510) 464-3231

Division(s): Distance Learning
Web Site(s): http://www.peralta.cc.ca.us
E-mail: mgoldstein@peralta.cc.ca.us

Undergraduate Degree Programs:
Associate in Arts
General Curriculum

Class Titles: Anthropology, Astronomy, Biology, Business, Health Education, History, Humanities, Journalism, Philosophy, Psychology, Sociology, Spanish.

Teaching Methods: *Computers:* Internet, e-mail, CD-ROM. *TV:* videotape, cable program, PBS. *Other:* audiotapes, fax, correspondence, learning contracts, project-based learning, portfolio assessment.

Credits Granted for: all except computer classes over the Internet.

Admission Requirements: *Undergraduate:* all over age 18 admitted.

On-Campus Requirements: None.

Tuition and Fees: *Undergraduate:* $11/credit resident. *Credit by:* semester.

Financial Aid: Federal Stafford Loan, Federal SEOG, Federal Pell Grant, Federal Work-Study, VA, California resident programs (California educational grants).

Accreditation: Western Association of Schools and Colleges.

Description: Laney College (1953) is the largest of the 4 colleges in the Peralta Community College District. Laney offers a positive view of what is right about a diverse America. The college offers intense academic learning, modern occupational training, and a sophisticated, dedicated faculty whose teaching and caring are the heart of the college. Laney is well known for its outstanding student newspaper, *The Laney Tower*, its Transfer Opportunity Center, and its array of quality academic and vocational course offerings.

Lansing Community College

528 North Capitol Avenue	Phone: (517) 483-9940
Lansing, MI 48933	Fax: (517) 483-9750

Division(s): Distance Learning
Web Site(s): www.lcc.edu/distancelearning
E-mail: advising_vcollege@lansing.cc.mi.us

Undergraduate Degree Programs:
Business Administration Associate in Business
Criminal Justice, Law Enforcement Associate in Business
Computer Graphics, Multimedia Associate in Applied Arts Degree
Computer Programmer/Analyst Associate in Business
General Associate Degree
Microcomputer Database Specialist Associate in Business

Certificate Programs: Internet for Business, Microcomputer Database Specialist.

Class Titles: Accounting, Anatomy, Art, Astronomy, Biology, Business, Chemistry, Computer Applications, Community Health Services, Computer Information Systems, Computer Science, Criminal Justice, Economics, History, Humanities, Labor Relations, Legal Assistant/Law, Management, Math, Microbiology, Nursing, Physical Fitness: Health/Fitness Wellness, Philosophy, Political Science, Psychology, Sociology, Spanish, Speech, Statistics, Student Development, Theater, Writing.

Teaching Methods: *Computers:* Internet, Blackboard, chat, electronic classroom, e-mail, CD-ROM, LISTSERV, bulletin board. *TV:* videotape, cable program, interactive TV. *Other:* fax, correspondence.

Credits Granted for: experiential learning, portfolio assessment, extrainstitutional learning, examination (CLEP, ACT-PEP, DANTES, GRE).

Admission Requirements: *Undergraduate:* open-enrollment: age 18, high school diploma or GED, dual enrollment for high school students, TOEFL for international students.

On-Campus Requirements: None.

Tuition and Fees: *Undergraduate:* $50/credit in-district, $79/credit out-of-district, $109/credit out-of-state and international. *Application Fee:* $10. *Other Costs:* $10 virtual college course fee, $20 registration fee. *Credit by:* semester.

Financial Aid: Federal Stafford Loan, Federal PLUS Loan, Federal Pell Grant, Federal Work-Study, VA, Michigan resident programs.

Accreditation: North Central Association of Colleges and Schools.

Description: Lansing Community College (1957) has been committed to excellence in education for more than 40 years. We've grown from a small technical college to one of the largest, most comprehensive community colleges in the nation. We offer classes year-round on our 28-acre campus in the heart of Michigan's capital. You can choose from 150 degree and certificate programs and 2,500 courses, or complete the first 2 years of a liberal arts education. LCC first offered distance learning in 1979 through telecourses, later adding a Child Development Series on a cable TV access channel. Lansing was the first community college in Michigan to offer a full degree online, and continue to be a leader in distance learning by now offering more online degrees than any other community college in Michigan. Currently, students may choose from over 100 online courses.

Laramie County Community College

1400 East College Drive	Phone: (307) 778-5222
Cheyenne, WY 82007	Fax: (307) 778-1344

Division(s): Instruction
Web Site(s): http://www.lccc.cc.wy.us
E-mail: jjohns@lccc.cc.wy.us

Class Titles: Accounting, American Studies, Anthropology, Astronomy, Biology, Business, Communications, Computer Application, Computer Science, Economics, Education, English, Geography, Geology, History, Humanities, Management, Mathematics, Music, Nursing, Philosophy, Political Science, Psychology, Sociology.

Teaching Methods: *Computers:* Internet, real-time chat, e-mail. *TV:* telecourses, videotape. *Other:* independent study (instructor approval only), compressed video and videoconferencing to branch campus only.

Credits Granted for: departmental examination program, military service credits.

Admission Requirements: *Undergraduate:* high school graduate, age 18, or can benefit from a college's programs. Degree-seeking students need high school diploma or equivalent. All new students, unless otherwise exempted, must undergo assessment in reading, writing, and math prior to class registration. Prerequisites must be passed with a C or exempted through a higher-level course or through placement scores. *Certificate:* same as undergraduate.

On-Campus Requirements: To receive a degree from Laramie County Community College, a student must complete 15 semester hours in residence (distance education courses can count) at Laramie County Community College.

Tuition and Fees: *Undergraduate:* $68.50/credit resident, $161.50/credit out-of-state. *Application Fee:* $20. *Other Costs:* $20/telecourse and online course. *Credit by:* semester.

Financial Aid: Federal Stafford Loan, Federal PLUS Loan, Federal Pell Grant, Federal Work-Study, VA, Wyoming resident programs.

Accreditation: North Central Association of Colleges and Schools.

Description: The main campus of Laramie County Community College (1968) consists of 20 modern buildings. Outreach programs/facilities are also available at the Albany County Campus in Laramie, the Eastern Laramie County Campus in Pine Bluffs, and at F.E. Warren Air Force Base in Cheyenne. LCCC serves 4,600 credit and noncredit students each semester and has an annualized full-time enrollment of 2,556. The college first offered telecourses in 1982 and consistently offers 10–12 telecourses each semester. Internet courses were offered for the first time in the fall of 1996. Twenty-nine Internet courses are presently offered.

Las Positas College

3033 Collier Canyon Road	Phone: (925) 373-5800
Livermore, CA 94550-7650	Fax: (925) 373-4967

Division(s): Technology
Web Site(s): http://www.laspositas.cc.ca.us
E-mail: LPCdistEd@clpccd.cc.ca.us

Class Titles: Philosophy, Astronomy, Biology, Computer Information Systems, Computer Science, English, Health, History, Math, Physics, Sociology, Psychology, Religious Studies.

Teaching Methods: *Computers:* Internet. *TV:* videotape, PBS. *Other:* videoconferencing.

Admission Requirements: *Undergraduate:* high school graduate or equivalent or 18 years of age or older.

On-Campus Requirements: Telecourses might require an on-campus meetings. Instructors for web-based courses have the option of proctored exams.

Tuition and Fees: *Undergraduate:* $11/credit; out-of-state and international tuition set annually. *Credit by:* semester.

Financial Aid: Federal Stafford Loan, Federal Pell Grant, Federal Supplemental Educational Opportunity Grants, Cal Grants, Extended Opportunity Program Grants, Bureau of Indian Affairs loans and grants.

Accreditation: Western Association of Schools and Colleges.

Description: Las Positas College (1975) is a 2-year community college enrolling about 6,300 students. The college has a Distance Education program that offers telecourses, teleweb courses, videoconferenced courses, and a growing number of web-based and partially web-based courses.

Laurentian University

935 Ramsey Lake Road	Phone: (705) 673-6569
Sudbury, ON, Canada P3E 2C6	Fax: (705) 675-4897

Division(s): Continuing Education
Web Site(s): http://www.laurentian.ca/cce/index.htm
E-mail: cce_l@nickel.laurentian.ca

Undergraduate Degree Programs:
Bachelor of Arts in:
    Gerontology
    Law and Justice
    History
    Native Studies
    Psychology
    Religious Studies
    Sociology
    Women's Studies
Bachelor of Social Work (Native Human Services)
Bachelor of Liberal Science
Bachelor of Arts (in French):
    Droit et justice
    Folklore et Ethnologie de l'Amérique française
    Français (Langue et linguistique)
    Psychologie
    Sciences religieuses
Baccalauréat en service social

Certificate Programs: Family Life Studies and Human Sexuality, Gerontology, Law and Justice, Folklore et Ethnologie de l'Amérique Française (in French).

Teaching Methods: *Computers:* Internet, e-mail, LISTSERV, Web CT. *TV:* videotape. *Other:* audioconferencing, videoconferencing, audiotapes, fax, correspondence, individual study.

Credits Granted for: examination (CLEP, ACT-PEP, DANTES, GRE).

Admission Requirements: *Undergraduate:* contact school for information. *Certificate:* contact school for information.

On-Campus Requirements: 3 hours/week winter, 6 hours/week summer.

Tuition and Fees: *Undergraduate:* $862.40 focal-credit course (2001). *Application Fee:* $35. *Credit by:* semester.

Financial Aid: Ontario Student Assistance Program, Part-time Canada Student Loan, Special Opportunity Grants, Laurentian University Bursaries.

Accreditation: Association of Universities and Colleges of Canada.

Description: Laurentian University was founded in 1960. Its distance education program, Envision, was launched in September 1972 to reach the 600,000 northeastern Ontario students scattered in an area twice the size of France. Courses are designed to respond to students' needs for autonomous learning along with student and faculty inter-action. The first courses were TV-based, with subsequent productions through audiocassette, teleconferencing, and computer-based systems. All courses include a strong print component and utilize media according to stated learning objectives. Complete degree programs include 11 bachelor's in English, 5 in French. Laurentian offers Canada's largest bilingual distance education program, with a greater degree selection than most open universities. Laurentian University is a founding member of the Canadian Association for Distance Education and a member of the International Council for Distance Education. The university is also involved with the Commonwealth of Learning and provides all distance education courses free of charge to developing nations. Most recently, Laurentian University became a founding member of the CVU, the Canadian Virtual University, and developed a series of bilingual online modules, called *Cardiac Care on the Web*, for registered nurses to learn more about cardiac nursing.

Laval University

Pavillon J.-A.-Desève (1153)
Louis-Jacques-Casault (4731)
Quebec City, Quebec, Canada G1K 7P4

Phone: (418) 656-3202
Fax: (418) 656-5538

Division(s): Continuing Education Division
Web Site(s): http://www.ulaval.ca/dgfc
E-mail: dgfc@dgfc.ulaval.ca

Undergraduate Degree Programs:
Diploma in:
    Personal Financial Planning
    Computer Science
    Horticulture and Landscape Management
    Food Science and Quality Control

Graduate Degree Programs:
Diploma in Business Administration
Master's Degree in Managing Food Production, M.B.A.

Certificate Programs: Certificate in Food Distribution and Merchandizing, Certificate in Horticulture and Landscape

Management, Certificate in Computer Science, Certificate in Personal Financial Planning, Certificate in Food Science and Quality Control, Diploma in Insurance and Financial Products, Microprogramme in Entrepreneurship and Small and Medium-Sized Enterprises.

Teaching Methods: *Computers:* Internet, electronic class-room, e-mail, newsgroup. *TV:* videotape, cable program. *Other:* audioconferencing, videoconferencing, audiotapes, fax, correspondence, individual study.

Admission Requirements: *Undergraduate:* high school certificate.

On-Campus Requirements: None.

Tuition and Fees: *Undergraduate:* $62.35/credit (Quebec res-ident). *Application Fee:* $30. *Other Costs:* $ = FD100 for study material. *Credit by:* semester.

Accreditation: Association of Universities and Colleges of Canada, American Assembly of Collegiate Schools of Business.

Description: Laval University (1663) holds the distinction of being Canada's first university and the oldest French-speaking university in North America. Today it is recognized in program assessment and strategic planning. Laval is a leading learning institution of higher education that offers more than 350 programs to more than 34,000 students. Laval's reputation is known worldwide with more than 300 agreements with more than 50 countries.

Lehigh University

205 Johnson Hall
36 University Drive
Bethlehem, PA 18015

Phone: (610) 758-5794
Fax: (610) 758-6269

Division(s): Office of Distance Education
Web Site(s): http://www.distance.lehigh.edu
E-mail: mak5@lehigh.edu

Graduate Degree Programs:
Master of Science in:
    Chemistry
    Chemical Engineer
    Pharmaceutical Chemistry
    Polymer Science/Engineering
    Molecular Biology
    Quality Engineering
Master of Business Administration

Teaching Methods: *Computers:* Some programs online, Internet access, real-time chat, electronic classroom bulletin boards, e-mail, newsgroup, LISTSERV. *TV:* satellite broad-casting (live via digital KU-band satellite transmission into corporate sites). *Other:* None.

Admission Requirements: *Graduate:* accredited bachelor's degree. MBA requires GMAT scores. Each department has its own criteria.

On-Campus Requirements: Students must view classes live at their work site. MBA requires 2 Saturday campus participations.

Tuition and Fees: *Graduate:* $610/credit (2001/2002). *Application Fee:* $30 one-time. *Other Costs:* textbooks. *Credit by:* semester.

Financial Aid: Federal Stafford Loan.

Accreditation: Middle States Association of Colleges and Schools. MBA by AACSB.

Description: Lehigh University was founded in 1865 in Bethlehem, Pennsylvania, by industrialist and philanthropist Asa Packer, whose vision for the university—"a classical education for a useful life"—is still adhered to today. An independent, coeducational university with programs in the arts and humanities, business, education, engineering, and the natural and social sciences, Lehigh is small enough to be personal, yet large enough to provide stimulating diversity and to play important national and international roles. Lehigh is known for its integration of teaching, research, and service to industry. The integrating element of that teaching, research, and service is learning, which is the principal mission of all members of the Lehigh community. Whether serving students on campus or at off-site locations, Lehigh is an intellectually unified community of learners. Since 1992, the Lehigh Educational Satellite Network has aspired to provide educational opportunities at locations accessible for students and cost-effective for their employers. LESN-Online now offers selected courses and programs on the Internet. Distance education students are as important to the university as traditional students, and the program strives to maintain the high quality and character of education found on the Lehigh campus. The Office of Distance Education and its staff view distance students and their employers as clients of the university, deserving the best efforts in all areas, including technology, programming, academic support, and customer service. In short, the guiding principles of Lehigh University distance education are convenience, cost-effectiveness, academic excellence, and client satisfaction.

Lesley University

29 Everett Street
Cambridge, MA 02138

Phone: (617) 349-8421
Fax: (617) 349-8169

Division(s): Technology in Education, School of Education
Web Site(s): http://www.lesley.edu
E-mail: myoder@mail.lesley.edu

Graduate Degree Programs:
Master of Education

Class Titles: Computers/Technology/Education, Telecommunications: Curriculum In Global Context, Teaching/Learning with Multimedia, Integrating Technology into School Curriculum, Microworlds/Models/Simulation, Computer Structure, Technology/Special Needs, Technology: Impact on Society/Schools, Technology in Mathematics Curriculum, Technology in Language Arts Curriculum, Authoring with HTML—Weaving World Wide Classroom Webs, Video as Educational Technology.

Teaching Methods: *Computers:* Internet, e-mail, CD-ROM, newsgroup, LISTSERV.

Credits Granted for: students may transfer up to 6 graduate credits from other institutions, provided they meet our criteria.

Admission Requirements: *Graduate:* 7-year completion limit for master's degree.

On-Campus Requirements: None.

Tuition and Fees: *Graduate:* $400/credit. *Application Fee:* $45. *Software:* variable. *Other Costs:* $30–$60 materials fees, $15/semester registration fee. *Credit by:* 33 credits (11 3-credit courses, fall, spring, and summer semesters).

Financial Aid: Federal Stafford Loan, Federal Perkins Loan, Federal PLUS Loan, Federal Pell Grant, Federal Work-Study, VA, Massachusetts resident programs.

Accreditation: New England Association of Schools and Colleges.

Description: Lesley University's (1909) Technology in Education program, founded in 1979, is one of the oldest in the country. The program provides state-of-the-art technology courses with a mixture of practical classroom applications and educational theory. Our distance learning program began in 1997 and has a diverse student body from all over the world. Classes are small, under 20 students, and students are encouraged to work collaboratively. Most students are K–12 classroom teachers and administrators. Classes are rigorous and students rarely take more than 6 credits per semester. Eleven 3-credit courses are required, though students can transfer up to 6 approved graduate credits.

Lewis and Clark Community College

5800 Godfrey Road
Godfrey, IL 62035

Phone: (618) 468-2610
Fax: (618) 466-1294

Division(s): Technology Enhanced Learning
Web Site(s): http://www.lc.cc.il.us
E-mail: mhales@lc.cc.il.us

Undergraduate Degree Programs: Contact school.

Certificate Programs: Geriatric Case Management.

Class Titles: Accounting, Biology, Anatomy-Physiology, Human Sexuality, E-Commerce, Personal Investments, Child Development, Introduction to Unix, Introduction to Microcomputers, Computer Literacy, Criminal Justice, Microeconomics, Macroeconomics, Medical Terminology, Job Seeking Skills, Elementary Algebra, Keyboarding, Office Technology courses, Microsoft Office 2000, Astronomy, Career Development, General Psychology, Public Speaking, Industrial Supervision, Industrial Safety.

Teaching Methods: *Computers:* Internet, real-time chat, e-mail. *TV:* videotape, cable program, satellite broadcasting, PBS.

Credits Granted for: experiential learning, portfolio assessment, examination (CLEP, ACT-PEP, DANTES, GRE).

Admission Requirements: *Undergraduate:* open Enrollment. *Certificate:* open Enrollment.

On-Campus Requirements: None.

Tuition and Fees: *Undergraduate:* $53/credit hour indistrict; Online courses out-of-state and out-of-district: $80/credit hour. *Graduation Fee:* $25. *Other Costs:* $10/online course technology fee. *Credit by:* semester.

Financial Aid: Federal Stafford Loan, Federal Perkins Loan, Federal PLUS Loan, Federal Pell Grant, Federal Work-Study, VA, state programs for residents of Illinois.

Accreditation: North Central Association of College and Secondary Schools, Illinois Board of Higher Education National Accreditation Agency of Clinical Laboratory Sciences, American Dental Association, Commission on Dental Accreditation, National League of Nursing, National Automotive Technicians Education Foundation (NATEF).

Description: Lewis and Clark's first class began in the fall of 1970, after a public vote in November, 1969 approved the funds for a much-needed community college. Initial enrollment was 440 students. L and C was fortunate in being able to purchase the campus of Monticello College, an institution whose rich heritage dates back to 1838. The campus, centrally located in Godfrey, is renowned for its beauty. Occupying 215 acres of manicured lawns and majestic trees, L and C is housed in several stately buildings, most built from the limestone that is native to this area. L and C continues to improve and add to the facilities. It has grown with the area, and today attracts a student population of more than 6,000 students. We began offering online courses in 1998 and currently offer both online and videocassette courses, as well as our traditional on-campus classes.

Lewis-Clark State College

500 Eighth Avenue
Lewiston, ID 83501

Phone: (208) 792-2239
Fax: (208) 792-2444

Division(s): Distance Learning Technologies
Web Site(s): http://www.lcsc.edu/dlt
E-mail: dlt@lcsc.edu

Undergraduate Degree Programs:
Associate of Arts in Liberal Arts
Bachelor of Science in:
    Interdisciplinary Studies
    Business/Communication

Class Titles: Biology, Business, Communications, Computer/Information Sciences, Education, English Language/Literature, History, Math, Physical Sciences, Psychology, Social Sciences, Visual/Performing Arts.

Teaching Methods: *Computers:* Internet, real-time chat, electronic classroom, e-mail, CD-ROM, newsgroup, LISTSERV. *TV:* videotape, satellite broadcasting, PBS. *Other:* audioconferencing, videoconferencing, audiotapes, fax, correspondence, individual study, compressed video.

Credits Granted for: experiential learning, portfolio assessment, extrainstitutional learning, examination, military training.

Admission Requirements: *Undergraduate:* high school transcripts or GED; ACT, SAT, or CPT scores if degree-seeking.

On-Campus Requirements: limited for some classes.

Tuition and Fees: *Resident Undergraduate:* $110/credit part-time, $1,122 full-time. *Application Fee:* $20 degree-seeking. *Credit by:* semester.

Financial Aid: Federal Stafford Loan, Federal Perkins Loan, Federal PLUS Loan, Federal Pell Grant, Federal Work-Study, VA, Idaho resident programs.

Accreditation: Northwest Association of Schools and Colleges.

Description: Lewis-Clark State College (1893) is a regional undergraduate institution providing an alternative learning environment. An integral part of the college's mission is to provide outreach courses and programs to meet the educational and training needs of a diverse population. Since 1995, the college's flexible distance learning program has offered credit courses for students with time and geographic constraints. While many courses have required due dates for assignments and exams, they usually have no structured class meeting times. Course offerings follow the same academic calendar dates and registration procedures as on-campus classes. Some of the 50 distance courses offered include the general education core, electives, and major concentrations in business and communications, with additional courses developed annually. Most courses require e-mail and Internet access to complete assignments, participation in individual and group discussions with the instructor, and participation in peer group activities.

Liberty University

1971 University Boulevard	Phone: (804) 424-9595
Lynchburg, VA 24502	Fax: (800) 582-2617

Division(s): External Degree/Distance Education Program
Web Site(s): http://www.liberty.edu
E-mail: edpadmissions@liberty.edu

Undergraduate Degree Programs:
Associate of Arts in General Studies
Associate of Arts in Religion
Bachelor of Science in:
 Multidisciplinary Studies
 Religion
 Business
 Psychology

Graduate Degree Programs:
Master of Arts in Religion
Master of Arts in Counseling
Master of Divinity
Master of Business Administration
Master of Education
Doctor of Education
Doctor of Divinity

Teaching Methods: *Computers:* Internet, e-mail. *TV:* videotape. *Other:* correspondence, independent study, individual study.

Credits Granted for: experiential learning, portfolio assessment, extrainstitutional learning, examination (CLEP, ACT-PEP, DANTES, GRE).

Admission Requirements: *Undergraduate:* high school diploma or accredited bachelor's degree, SAT, ACT. *Graduate:* bachelor's from accredited institution and prerequisites appropriate to desired course.

On-Campus Requirements: *Undergraduate:* None. *Graduate:* Must spend one week on campus.

Tuition and Fees: *Undergraduate:* $130/credit. *Graduate:* $215/credit. *Application Fee:* $35. *Software:* varies. *Other Costs:* books and videos. *Credit by:* semester.

Financial Aid: Federal Stafford Loan, Federal Pell Grant, Federal Work-Study, VA, Virginia resident programs.

Accreditation: Southern Association of Colleges and Schools, Transnational Association of Christian Schools.

Description: Founded in 1971 as a liberal arts institution of higher learning, Liberty entered the field of distance education in 1985. Since then, more than 90,000 students have benefitted from its programs. Liberty's distance education program currently has more than 6,000 students enrolled in video-based curricula in associate, bachelor's, master's, and doctoral degrees.

LIFE Bible College

1100 Covina Boulevard	Phone: (909) 599-5433 x359
San Dimas, CA 91773	Fax: (909) 599-6690

Division(s): School of Distance Learning
Web Site(s): http://www.lifebible.edu
E-mail: sdl@lifebible.edu

Undergraduate Degree Programs:
Associate of Arts Degree

Teaching Methods: *Computer:* Internet. *Other:* correspondence, independent study.

Admission Requirements: *Undergraduate:* high school diploma or GED, must be a Christian for at least one year.

On-Campus Requirements: None.

Tuition and Fees: *Undergraduate:* $65/unit. *Application Fee:* $35 (for AA program). *Credit by:* semester.

Financial Aid: VA.

Accreditation: AABC, ACCESS, UCEA.

Description: Aimee Semple McPherson, founder of the Foursquare Denomination, established the School of Correspondence Studies at LIFE Bible College in 1924. She believed that every dedicated person should have an opportunity to study God's Word even if separated from the college by great distances. Today her vision is allowing people worldwide to study the Word of God through LIFE. LIFE Bible College provides flexible college-level training, providing students the freedom to set their own schedule and pace. After recently expanding its program, LIFE now offers an AA in Biblical Studies.

Lifetime Career Schools

101 Harrison Street	Phone: (717) 876-6340
Archbald, PA 18403	Fax: (717) 876-8179

Division(s): Distance Education
Web Site(s): http://lifetimecareerschools.com
E-mail: LCSLEARN@aol.com

Diploma and Certificate Programs: Landscaping, Flower Arranging and Floristry, Sewing/Dressmaking, Doll Repair,

Secretarial/Administrative Assistant, Bookkeeping, Cooking, Small Business Management, Personal Computers/Home Use, PC Specialist, Medical Transcription.

Teaching Methods: Distance Education lessons, audiocassettes, work projects, learning aids, Internet, and e-mail.

Admission Requirements: varies by program; 10th grade, high school, or GED.

On-Campus Requirements: None.

Tuition and Fees: *Undergraduate:* varies by program. $300–$700/program.

Accreditation: Distance Education and Training Council, Affiliations: International Council for Open and Distance Education, United States Distance Learning Association, Pennsylvania Department of Education, State Board of Private Licensed Schools, BBB of Northeastern Pennsylvania, Greater Scranton Chamber of Commerce.

Description: From its beginning, Lifetime Career Schools' (1944) charter has been to offer time and cost-efficient Distance Education programs designed for adult skills training. Using an open-enrollment philosophy, the institution offers programs that cater to the needs of working men and women desiring to change careers, upgrade workplace-related skills, or simply to learn more about a hobby. Beginning in 1998, LCS established a Web site and began supplementing traditional course material and student support with various forms of electronic publishing and communications.

Lima Technical College

4240 Campus Drive
Lima, OH 45804

Phone: (419) 995-8870
Fax: (419) 995-8096

Division(s): Alternative Learning Systems
Web Site(s): http://www.ltc.tec.oh.us
E-mail: als@ltc.tec.oh.us

Undergraduate Degree Programs:
Associate of Technical Studies in:
    Business Studies
    Emergency Medical Services Technology
Associate of Applied Science in Industrial Engineering
Associate of Applied Business in Business Administration
Associate of Applied Science in Concrete Technology

Certificate Programs: Distribution/Logistics Methods Study, Facilities Planning, Production Planning, Industrial Relations, Advance Topics, Distribution/Logistics Management (all part of Industrial Engineering Technology program).

Class Titles: Accounting, English, Developmental Writing, Economics, Sociology, Psychology, Childhood Development, Community Health/Safety, Phlebotomy, Intravenous Line Insertion, Quality Assurance in Health Care, Patient Education, Legal Issues in Health Care, Sanitation/Safety, Management, Marketing, Pre-algebra, Business Math, Fundamentals of Quality, Office Administration, Computer Applications, Law Enforcement, Corrections, Industrial Engineering, Blueprint Reading, Retail/Fashion Merchandising, Medical Terminology, Psychology, Sociology.

Teaching Methods: *Computers:* Internet, real-time chat, e-mail, CD-ROM, LISTSERV. *TV:* videotape, cable program, PBS. *Other:* videoconferencing, audiotapes, fax, correspondence, independent study, individual study.

Credits Granted for: experiential learning, portfolio assessment, extrainstitutional learning, examination (CLEP, ACT-PEP, DANTES, GRE).

Admission Requirements: *Undergraduate:* open-door; application, $25 nonrefundable fee, official high school transcript from each high school attended or certificate of GED score report along with the official high school transcripts showing work completed, sent directly to the Student Advising and Development Center; official college, university, or any other postsecondary institution transcript, sent directly from previous institution to the SAD; evidence of ACT scores (required of all students who seek admission to health programs except EMP P certification candidates); any other material required for admission to a specific program; finally, applicants to the college are required to take the ASSET and/or Compass Placement Test; Ohio high school students may earn credit applied toward graduation in the Postsecondary Enrollment Options Program—specific enrollment and application requirements are listed in the catalog.

On-Campus Requirements: testing for some distance learning courses.

Tuition and Fees: *Undergraduate:* $68/credit. *Application Fee:* $25. *Other Costs:* $20/quarter registration fee, lab fee for selected courses, $6/telecourse credit fee. *Credit by:* quarter.

Financial Aid: Federal Stafford Loan, Federal PLUS Loan, Federal Pell Grant, Federal Work-Study, VA, Ohio resident programs, Ohio Instructional Grant Program, academic scholarship, BVR, JTPA, Hauss-Helms Foundation.

Accreditation: North Central Association of Colleges and Schools.

Description: In 1971 Lima Technical College was chartered as a state, public-assisted associate degree granting institution of higher education. LTC has served 40,000 students in the area. Distance learning was initiated with the creation of an Office Administration self-paced program in 1990; in 1993 the distance learning initiative was taken a step further with the creation of the Alternative Learning Systems. Through the years the original self-paced program has continued to expand beyond its original program area; telecourses are broadcast via local cable channels; a videotape take-home program is available for those students not receiving the cable channel; numerous online courses are available through the college's Virtual College, and ALS is now venturing into the realm of online interactive classrooms. ALS students are supported in the ALS Center located on campus, with instructor support and multimedia computers for their use. E-mail accounts with Internet access are also provided upon registration.

Linfield College

900 SE Baker Street	Phone: (503) 434-2447
McMinnville, OR 97128	Fax: (503) 434-2215

Division(s): Continuing Education
Web Site(s): http://www.linfield.edu/dce
E-mail: dce@linfield.edu

Undergraduate Degree Programs:
Bachelor of Arts in Arts and Humanities
Bachelor of Science or Bachelor of Arts in:
Accounting
Business Information Systems
International Business
Management
Social and Behavioral Sciences

Certificate Programs: Accounting, Computer Information Systems, Human Resource Management, Marketing.

Teaching Methods: *Computers:* web-based courses. *Other:* videoconferencing, correspondence, independent study, individual study.

Credits Granted for: experiential learning, portfolio assessment, extrainstitutional learning, examination (CLEP, ACT-PEP, DANTES, GRE).

Admission Requirements: *Undergraduate:* high school completion, 2.0 college GPA.

On-Campus Requirements: 30 semester credits of Linfield course work.

Tuition and Fees: *Undergraduate:* $190/credit. *Application Fee:* $100. *Credit by:* semester.

Financial Aid: Federal Stafford Loan, Federal Pell Grant, VA, Oregon resident programs.

Accreditation: Northwest Association of Schools and Colleges.

Description: Linfield College (1849) is an independent, 4-year, liberal arts institution with an active off-campus

program for working adults. Distance learning technologies are used effectively to enhance opportunities for site-bound students and for traditional on-campus students as well.

Lock Haven University of Pennsylvania

Fairview Street	Phone: (570) 893-2072
Lock Haven, PA 17745	Fax: (570) 893-2638

Division(s): Continuing and Distance Education
Web Site(s): http://www.lhup.edu/cde
E-mail: poharama@lhup.edu

Undergraduate Degree Programs:
Early Admission Program for high school students
AS Nursing program to local hospitals (ITV)
AAS Management Information Systems (ITV)
AS/BS Criminal Justice (ITV)

Graduate Degree Programs:
Masters of Health Science
Masters of Education
Physician Assistants (ITV)
Concentrations in Curriculum and Instruction (ITV and Online) and Alternative Education (Online)

Postgraduate Degree Programs:
Continuing Professional Education for K12 Teachers (Online)
Continuing Medical Education for Physician Assistants (Online)

Certificate Programs (Noncredit): Paralegal Certificate, Legal Investigation, Alternative Dispute Resolution, Victim Advocacy, Legal Secretary, other programs under development.

Class Titles: English, Math, Sociology, Psychology, Music.

Teaching Methods: *Computers:* Interactive online courses and programs that include videostreaming, audiostreaming, chat, and threaded discussion, private video network to consortia members, interactive multipoint videoconferencing.

Credits Granted for: experiential learning, portfolio assessment examination (CLEP).

Admission Requirements: *Undergraduate:* high school diploma, GPA of 3.0, and SAT test scores above (1000). (Students who graduated from high school 5 years prior to applying for admissions do not need SAT test scores.) *Graduate:* baccalaureate degree, certified teacher (may be completed as a part of the program), GPA of 3.0 for regular admissions (applicants with less than 3.0 undergraduate GPA may be admitted conditionally). *Postgraduate:* no prerequisites. *Certificate:* no prerequisites.

On-Campus Requirements: None.

Tuition and Fees: *Undergraduate:* $158/credit resident, $312/credit out-of-state, $395/credit international. *Graduate:* resident $230/credit, out-of-state $390/credit, $390/credit international. *Postgraduate:* costs vary with program, visit the web site for more details. *Application Fee:* $25. *Educational Service Fee:* undergraduate 10%, graduate 15%. *Credit by:* semester.

Financial Aid: Federal Stafford Loan, Federal Perkins Loan, Federal PLUS Loan, Federal Pell Grant, Federal Work-Study.

Accreditation: Middle States Association of Colleges and Schools, The National Council for Accreditation of Teacher Education Programs, American Association for Physician Assistants.

Description: Lock Haven University (1870) is one of 14 institutions that make up the Commonwealth's State System of Higher Education. The university emphasizes active learning, individual attention from faculty, and the development of technological skills to enhance the twenty-first-century learner. Students experience the multicultural and global dimensions of our changing society and are provided with opportunities to acquire, clarify, and demonstrate those skills and values that are necessary for active participation in a democracy.

Long Beach City College

4901 East Carson Street	Phone: (562) 938-4025
Long Beach, CA 90808	Fax: (562) 938-4814

Division(s): Distance Learning program, School of Learning Resources, Teaching, and Technologies
Web Site(s): http://de.lbcc.cc.ca.us
E-mail: mhedberg@lbcc.cc.ca.us

Undergraduate Degree Programs:
Distance learning classes count toward the Associate of Arts and Associate of Science degrees.

Class Titles: International Business, Child Development, Computer/Information Science, Office Technologies, Computer and Business Information Systems, Counseling, English, Film, Food and Nutrition, Library, Geography, Math, Music, Philosophy, Anthropology, Astrology, Biology, History, Political Science, Psychology, Sociology.

Teaching Methods: *Computers:* Internet, e-mail, real-time chat, electronic classroom. *TV:* videotape, cable program, PBS. *Other:* None.

Credits Granted For: experiential learning.

Admission Requirements: *Undergraduate:* 18 years of age or older or high school graduate or under 18 but have a written permission from the high school counselor.

On-Campus Requirements: All TV courses require a few on-campus meetings at this time. Some online courses require on-campus meeting for orientation or exams.

Tuition and Fees: *Undergraduate:* $11/credit for California residents, $130/credit for out-of-state U.S. residents, $137/credit for international students. *Other Costs:* $7 for health fee, $15 parking fee plus material fees when applicable. *Credit by:* semester.

Financial Aid: Board of Governors Enrollment Fee Waiver Application, California State Grants, Federal Pell Grants, Federal Perkins Loan, William D. Ford Federal Direct Loan, Federal Supplemental Educational Opportunity Grants and Extended Opportunity Program and Services.

Accreditation: Western Association of Schools and Colleges.

Description: Since 1927 Long Beach City College has been an institution of higher education within the California Community College System. As a comprehensive college, Long Beach City College provides quality, affordable educational programs and related student services to those who can benefit from the programs the college offers. Through a collegiate experience and with an open door admission policy, the college fosters the development of individual potential and is responsive to the diverse educational needs of the community it serves. The primary purposes of the education program are to prepare students for transfer to baccalaureate-granting institutions, entry into work or career development, to support business and vocational education at the lower division level, and transitional instruction and those support services that promote student success—remedial education, adult noncredit courses, and students support services. College programs and services educate citizens to enrich the quality of life in the community. *Distance Learning:* TV courses have been offered at LBCC for over 20 years. Online courses have been offered for the last 4 years. Online course offering has grown more than 1,000% in the last few years; about 50 courses in various disciplines are currently offered online.

Lorain County Community College

1005 Abbe Road North	Phone: (440) 366-7582
Elyria, OH 44035	Fax: (440) 366-4150

Division(s): Distance Learning Center
Web Site(s): http://www.lorainccc.edu
E-mail: distance@lorainccc.edu

Undergraduate Degree Programs: Associate of Arts Degree

Class Titles: Accounting; Word for Windows; Art Appreciation; Web Design, Business; Microcomputer Applications; Tourism; Marketing; Mathematics; Health;

Nursing; English; Humanities; Philosophy; Spanish; French; Theater History; History.

Teaching Methods: *Computers:* Internet, real-time chat, electronic classroom, e-mail, CD-ROM, LISTSERV. *TV:* videotape, cable program, satellite broadcasting, PBS. *Other:* radio broadcast, videoconferencing, audioconferencing, audiographics, audiotapes, fax, correspondence, independent study, individual study.

Credits Granted for: experiential learning, portfolio assessment, proficiency testing, examination (CLEP, ACT-PEP, DANTES).

Admission Requirements: *Undergraduate:* at least 18 years of age, high school diploma or GED, placement assessment.

On-Campus Requirements: None.

Tuition and Fees: *Undergraduate:* $72.50/credit hour (in county), $87.50 (out-of-county), and $178 (out-of-state). *Graduation Fee:* $20. *Credit by:* semester.

Financial Aid: Federal Stafford Loan, Federal Perkins Loan, Federal PLUS Loan, Federal Pell Grant, Federal Work-Study, VA, state programs for residents of Ohio.

Accreditation: North Central Association of Colleges and Schools.

Description: LCCC (1963) is a comprehensive, open enrollment community college that offers pre-baccalaureate/ transfer degree programs, career/technical programs, developmental education, workforce training, continuing education, and community service programming. LCCC serves approximately 7,000 students each term in credit classes, and an additional 4,000 students enrolled in noncredit continuing education programs. In 1978 LCCC began to offer its first Distance Learning courses by prepackaged video tapes on a local television network. The Distance Learning effort was expanded during the 1990s to offerings on LCCC's cable channel, which included live interactive courses. In the summer of 1995, LCCC offered its first Internet course. Today, LCCC offers over 50 Internet courses. In the fall, the college will begin to offer courses via videoconferencing (IDVL) to local high schools and businesses. In 2000 LCCC's Associate of Arts degree was accredited by NCA for online delivery.

Los Angeles Harbor College

1111 Figueroa Place	Phone: (310) 522-8216
Wilmington, CA 90744	Fax: (310) 522-8404

Division(s): Academic Affairs
Web Site(s): http://www.lahc.cc.ca.us
E-mail: chingdm@lahc.cc.ca.us

Undergraduate Degree Programs:
Associate in Arts
Associate in Science

Certificate Programs: Please check web site for a complete list: www.lahc.cc.ca.us.

Class Titles: Contact school or check web site for details.

Teaching Methods: *Computers:* Internet *TV:* cable program, PBS. independent study.

Credits Granted for: examination (CLEP, ADVANCED PLACEMENT).

Admission Requirements: *Undergraduate:* open enrollment to anyone 18 years of age or older with the ability to benefit. *Certificate:* open enrollment to anyone 18 years of age or older with the ability to benefit.

On-Campus Requirements: Traditional classroom attendance standards for non-Internet or independent study courses.

Tuition and Fees: *Undergraduate:* $11/credit for California residents. Check LAHC web site for other fees. *Other Costs:* Parking Fee, Associated Students Fee, Representation Fee, Printing Fee; check web site. *Credit by:* 16-week semester.

Financial Aid: Federal Stafford Loan, Federal Perkins Loan, Federal PLUS Loan, Federal Pell Grant, Federal Work-Study, VA, state programs for residents of California.

Accreditation: Western Association of Schools and Colleges.

Description: (1949) Please check web site: www.lahc. cc.ca.us.

Lower Columbia College

1600 Maple Street	Phone: (360) 577-1428
Longview, WA 98632	Fax: (360) 577-3400

Division(s): Distance Education
Web Site(s): http://www.lcc.ctc.edu
E-mail: akaneko@lcc.ctc.edu
distance_ed@lcc.etc.edu

Undergraduate Degree Programs:
Associate in Arts and Science
Associate in Applied Science

Class Titles: Astronomy, Geology, Spanish, Music, English, Computer Science, Health, Business, Fire Science.

Teaching Methods: *Computers:* Internet, e-mail, CD-ROM. *TV:* videotape, cable program. *Other:* videoconferencing, correspondence, independent study.

Credits Granted for: examination (CLEP, AP).

Admission Requirements: *Undergraduate:* open-door; special admissions for nursing (RN) and medical assisting.

On-Campus Requirements: Some courses have lab requirements.

Tuition and Fees: *Undergraduate:* $51/credit. *Application Fee:* $11. *Other Costs:* various lab fees. *Credit by:* quarter.

Financial Aid: Federal Stafford Loan, Federal Perkins Loan, Federal PLUS Loan, Federal Pell Grant, Federal Work-Study, VA, Washington resident programs.

Accreditation: Northwest Association of Schools and Colleges.

Description: Lower Columbia College (1934) is a comprehensive community college serving Cowlitz and Wahkiakum counties in Washington. Programs at the college include 2-year transfer and vocational degrees as well as community and basic adult education. Our distance education program began 2 years ago with correspondence and videotape courses and has expanded to include online, Web-based, and interactive CD courses.

Loyola College, Maryland

4501 North Charles Street Baltimore, MD 21210	Phone: (410) 617-2000 Fax: (410) 617-5130

Division(s): Information Services
Web Site(s): http://www.loyola.edu/
E-mail: admissions@mailgate.loyola.edu

Undergraduate Degree Programs:
Bachelor of Science in Business

Graduate Degree Programs:
Master of Science in Education
Master of Business Administration

Class Titles: Accounting, Education, MBA courses.

Teaching Methods: *Computers:* Internet, real-time chat, electronic classroom, e-mail, CD-ROM, newsgroup, LISTSERV. *TV:* videotape. *Other:* videoconferencing, audioconferencing, independent study.

Credits Granted for: extrainstitutional learning, $342/credit part-time undergraduate (less than 12 credits).

Admission Requirements: *Undergraduate:* applications are evaluated according to their academic qualifications. The most important academic criteria include the secondary school record and performance on the SAT-I Reasoning Test, which is the required college entrance examination. *Graduate:* application form, nonrefundable fee, official transcripts from all postsecondary institutions that have awarded the applicant a degree or advanced certification. Additional requirements may be determined necessary based on specific program requirements.

On-Campus Requirements: vary by professor.

Tuition and Fees: *Undergraduate:* $18,200/annual full-time, $342/credit part-time. *Graduate:* $222/credit Education, $365/credit Engineering Science, $222/credit Modern Studies, Pastoral Counseling—contact Dept. Chair, $278/credit Psychology (MA/MS/CAS), $365/credit School of Business and Management, $278/credit Speech-Language Pathology (part-time CAGS students), Speech-Language Pathology (full-time students)—contact Dept. Chair. *Doctoral:* Psychology (PsyD)—contact Dept. Chair. *Application Fee:* $30 undergraduate. *Credit by:* semester.

Financial Aid: Federal Stafford Loan (Federal Direct Loan Participant), Federal Perkins Loan, Federal PLUS Loan, Federal Pell Grant, Federal Supplemental Educational Opportunity Grant, Federal Work-Study, VA, Maryland, Massachusetts, Vermont and Rhode Island resident programs.

Accreditation: The International Association of Management Education, American Association of Pastoral Counselors, American Speech-Language-Hearing Association, Middle States Association of Colleges and Schools, Council for Accreditation of Counseling and Related Educational Programs, U.S. Catholic Conference, Accreditation Board for Engineering and Technology (BSES Program only), American Chemical Society, Computer Science Accreditation Commission.

Description: Loyola College in Maryland (1852) is a comprehensive, liberal arts, Jesuit university comprised of a College of Arts and Sciences and a School of Business and Management. Loyola teaches its approximately 3,200 undergraduates and approximately 3,000 graduates to lead and serve in a diverse and changing world. In 1996 Loyola received its first grant for the flagship campus in Baltimore to join the Maryland Interactive Video Distance Learning Network, a full-motion, 2-way interactive video distance learning delivery system based on digital fiber-optic technology. In 1997 and 1998, Loyola received 2 additional grants to connect its graduate campuses in Columbia and Timonium. Loyola College students access course materials on the Web to supplement in-person instruction on campus. The expanding reach of the Internet has presented new opportunities to extend Jesuit education to learners across the nation and around the world. Loyola College is a member of the Jesuit Distance Education Network (JesuitNET). Through the newly created JesuitNET, the Association of Jesuit Colleges and Universities (AJCU) seeks to meet the diverse, growing needs of learners, both traditional and nontraditional, by providing a flexible and convenient way to learn, and complementing the classroom learning on Jesuit campuses.

Loyola University Chicago

6525 N. Sheridan Road
Skyscraper Building Room 201
Chicago, IL 60626

Phone: (773) 508-8000
Fax: (773) 508-8008

Division(s): Mundelein College
Web Site(s): http://online.luc.edu
http://www.luc.edu/online/
E-mail: advising@online.luc.edu

Undergraduate Degree Programs: Contact school.

Certificate Programs: Certificate in Computer Science: Web Development, Certificate in Computer Science: Networks and Telecommunication, Certificate in Computer Science: Database Applications, Professional Certificate in Computer Science.

Class Titles: Biology, Computer Science, Math, Philosophy, Physics, Statistics.

Teaching Methods: *Computers:* Internet, real-time chat, e-mail, threaded discussion.

Admission Requirements: *Undergraduate:* high school diploma, good academic standing at previous schools. *Certificate:* high school diploma, good academic standing at previous schools.

On-Campus Requirements: None.

Tuition and Fees: *Undergraduate:* $371/credit. *Application Fee:* $25. *Other Costs:* university services and programs fee varies by enrollment load. *Credit by:* semester.

Financial Aid: Federal Stafford Loan, Federal Perkins Loan, Federal PLUS Loan, Federal Pell Grant, VA, state programs for residents of Illinois is available to students enrolled in degree programs.

Accreditation: North Central Association of Colleges and Schools.

Description: Loyola University Chicago's (1870) Mundelein College serves nontraditional students in a variety of ways. Our online program began in the fall of 1999 and has expanded steadily. Students may now complete any of 4 computer science certificates entirely through online study. They may also take individual online courses as part of a degree program, for professional development, to fulfill prerequisites for graduate study or for personal enrichment. All of the online courses and certificate programs are also offered on campus and the faculty teaching online are the same faculty who teach on campus.

Loyola University Chicago

2160 S. First Avenue
Building 105 Office 2853
Maywood, IL 60153

Phone: (708) 216-9553
Fax: (708) 216-9555

Division(s): Niehoff School of Nursing
Web Site(s): http:// www.luc.edu/online/
http://www.luc.edu/schools/nursing
E-mail: Lgroves@luc.edu

Undergraduate Degree Programs: Contact school.

Graduate Degree Programs: Contact school.

Class Titles: Advanced Nursing Care of Patients with Respiratory Problems, Chest X-ray Interpretation for Advanced Practice Nursing, ECG Interpretation for Advanced Practice Nursing, Suturing/Invasive Procedures for Advanced Practice Nursing, Principles of Trauma Nursing, Management of Common Health Problems of the Adult.

Teaching Methods: *Computers:* Internet, real-time chat, electronic classroom, e-mail, CD-ROM, newsgroup, LISTSERV, online testing, electronic reserves. *TV:* videoconferencing.

Admission Requirements: Contact school.

On-Campus Requirements: Two of the above 6 courses require 2 face-to-face meetings; one at the beginning of the course and the other at the end of the course.

Tuition and Fees: *Undergraduate:* $371/credit. *Graduate:* $529/credit. *Application Fee:* $25. *Other Costs:* $160 for continuing education credit in lieu of college credit for postgraduate nurses and other RNs who qualify. *Credit by:* semester.

Financial Aid: Federal Stafford Loan, Federal Perkins Loan, Federal PLUS Loan, Federal Pell Grant, Federal Work-Study, VA, state programs for residents of Illinois.

Accreditation: North Central Association of Colleges and Schools.

Description: Loyola University Chicago (1870) is dedicated to developing knowledge in the service of humanity. Loyola is a coeducational Jesuit and Catholic university that is committed to excellence in teaching and research and community service. Loyola University Medical Center is one of the nation's leaders in treating the acutely ill, and provides a superior learning environment for nursing education. The Marcella Niehoff School of Nursing, founded in 1935, is the oldest university nursing program in Illinois. The school is fully accredited by the National League for Nursing, and offers a full range of majors for clinical nurse specialties and nurse practitioner programs across the continuum of care, from neonate through adult.

Loyola University, New Orleans

6363 St. Charles Avenue, Box 14
New Orleans, LA 70118

Phone: (504) 865-3250
Fax: (504) 865-3883

Division(s): City College
Web Site(s): http://www.loyno.edu/City College
E-mail: scheuer@loyno.edu

Undergraduate Degree Programs:
Bachelor of Criminal Justice
Bachelor of Nursing Science

Graduate Degree Program:
Masters of Science in Nursing

Teaching Methods: *TV:* videotapes.

Credits Granted for: experiential learning, portfolio assessment, extrainstitutional learning, examination (CLEP, ACT-PEP, DANTE, GRE).

Admission Requirements: *Undergraduate:* to enter the RN-to-BSN program, you must be a registered nurse and live in the state of Louisiana.

On-Campus Requirements: must attend one class on-campus; contact school for information.

Tuition and Fees: *Undergraduate:* $238. *Graduate:* $464. *Application Fee:* $20.

Financial Aid: Federal Stafford Loan, Federal Perkins Loan, Federal PLUS Loan, Federal Pell Grant, General Work-Study, VA, Louisiana resident programs.

Accreditation: National League for Nursing.

Description: Created in 1991, the Off-Campus Learning Program at Loyola University, New Orleans (1912) provides access for Louisiana adult residents who, because of their work schedules or distance from campus, cannot attend on-campus classes. The off-campus groups, located within the state, meet regularly to view classes on videotape at a location and time of their choosing. All assignments, exams, and papers correspond exactly to those of the on-campus students. Students have access to the campus professor through telephone conferences via our 800 line and through individual meetings. Off-campus students complete courses in the same semester as campus students.

Luna Community College

P.O. Box 1510
Las Vegas, NM 87701

Phone: (505) 454-5333
Fax: (505) 454-2588

Division(s): Learning Resource Center
Web Site(s): http://luna.cc.nm.us
E-mail: atrujillo@luna.cc.nm.us

Undergraduate Degree Programs: Contact school.

Class Titles: Nutrition, Trigonometry, Freshman Composition, Web Design, Chemistry, Pathophysiology.

Teaching Methods: *Computers:* Internet, real-time chat, electronic classroom, e-mail, CD-ROM, newsgroup, LISTSERV. *TV:* cable program, videoconferencing.

Admission Requirements: *Undergraduate:* prerequisites—entrance exam, technical exam, any course prerequisites.

On-Campus Requirements: None.

Tuition and Fees: *Undergraduate:* $23/credit hour. *Application Fees:* $10 for Distance Learning fee. *Credit by:* semester.

Financial Aid: Federal Stafford Loan, Federal Perkins Loan, Federal PLUS Loan, Federal Pell Grant, Federal Work-Study, VA, state programs for residents of New Mexico.

Accreditation: North Central Association of Colleges and Schools.

Description: Luna Community College (LCC) (1970), changed its name from Luna Vocational Technical Institute and expanded its scope in 2000. LCC now offers Associate of Applied Science and Associate of Arts Degrees in addition to many vocational certificate programs in the areas of health, business, technologies, and early childhood. The college was awarded a U.S. Dept. of Education Title V Grant in 1999 to develop a Distance Education program. Located in historic Las Vegas, New Mexico, where the Great Plains meet the Rocky Mountains, LCC has a beautiful, state-of-the-art campus serving approximately 1,200 students.

Luther Seminary

2481 Como Avenue
St. Paul, MN 55108

Phone: (651) 641-3456
(800) LUTHER-3
Fax: (651) 641-3425

Division(s): Cross-Cultural Education
Web Site(s): http://www.luthersem.edu
E-mail: rdolson@luthersem.edu

Graduate Degree Programs:
Master of Arts
Master of Theology
Master of Sacred Music
Master of Divinity

Doctoral Degree Programs:
Doctor of Philosophy
Doctor of Ministry

Certificate Programs: Islamic Studies.

Teaching Methods: *Computers:* Internet, electronic classroom, e-mail, CD-ROM, LISTSERV. *TV:* videotape, cable program, satellite broadcasting, PBS. *Other:* radio broadcast, videoconferencing, audioconferencing, audiographics, audiotapes, fax, correspondence, independent study, individual study, learning contracts. Listed teaching methods are subject to discretion of instructor.

Credits Granted for: For detailed information, call: (651) 641-3456 or toll-free: (800) LUTHER-3.

Admission Requirements: *Graduate:* accredited bachelor's degree or equivalent, 2.8 GPA. *Doctoral:* Doctor of Philosophy: bachelor's degree in divinity, accredited master's degree in arts or divinity (or equivalent), and 3.25 GPA. Doctor of Ministry: master of divinity degree, 3.0 GPA, transcripts of professional graduate degree(s). *Certificate:* accredited bachelor's degree (or equivalent), 2.8 GPA.

On-Campus Requirements: One full academic year or equivalent.

Tuition and Fees: *Graduate:* $7,150 full-time annual tuition for Master of Arts, Master of Divinity, Master of Sacred Music, Nondegree Students/Certificate Students/Auditors, $715/part-time full course, $351.50/part-time half course, $35 application fee. $275 applied lessons (for master of sacred music). $5,280 full-time annual tuition for Master of Theology, Post-Master of Divinity Nondegree Students, $880/part-time full course, $440/part-time half course, $35 application fee, $150 continuation fee. *Doctoral:* $10,600 full-time annual tuition for Doctor of Philosophy, $1,590/course part-time, $35 application fee, $500 annual continuation fee. $5,850 basic tuition for Doctor of Ministry (summer program), $50 application fee, $400 confirmation fee, $600 thesis fee. *Application Fee:* see specific degree categories. *Other Costs:* contact school. *Credit by:* semester (2 semesters and one January term).

Financial Aid: Federal Stafford Loan, Federal Perkins Loan, Federal PLUS Loan, Federal Pell Grant, Federal Work-Study, Presidential Scholarships (full tuition for first year of study for Master of Arts, Master of Religious Education, Master of Sacred Music, and Master of Divinity students who have recently graduated from college); Leadership Scholarships (full tuition for first year of study for Master of Divinity students seeking ordination through ELCA); Heritage Scholarships (full tuition awards for first year of study for Master of Sacred Music or Master of Divinity students); Quest Scholarship (partial tuition for first year of study for second career students); Spectrum Scholarships (for students of color).

Accreditation: North Central Association of Colleges and Schools, Association of Theological Schools in the U.S. and Canada, affiliated with the Evangelical Lutheran Church in America.

Description: Luther Seminary (1869), through a series of mergers covering more than half a century, represents the consolidation of 6 institutions. Today the Minnesota-based seminary is the largest of 8 Evangelical Lutheran Church in America seminaries in the U.S. providing theological education to equip people for ministry. The seminary's campus grounds consist of more than 40 acres of rolling wooded land in the small-town atmosphere of St. Anthony Park, one of the Twin Cities' oldest and most pleasant residential neighborhoods. The seminary's mission is to educate leaders called and sent by the Holy Spirit to witness salvation through Jesus Christ and to serve in God's world. LS supports a wide spectrum of distance study opportunities and programs designed to help students pursue areas of special interest and/or gain experience directly related to their ministry.

Lutheran Theological Seminary at Philadelphia

7301 Germantown Avenue	Phone: (215) 248-6378
Philadelphia, PA 19119	Fax: (215) 248-4577

Division(s): Director of Distance Learning
Web Site(s): http://www.ltsp.edu
E-mail: Registrar@ltsp.edu or MKyrch@ltsp.edu

Graduate Degree Programs:
Master of Divinity
Master of Arts in Religion

Doctoral Degree Programs:
Master of Theological Studies
Doctor of Ministry

Certificate Programs: Social Ministry and Church.

Class Titles: Communication in Congregation, Christian Education, Theology, Evangelism, Stewardship.

Teaching Methods: *Computers:* Web-based instruction, Internet (using Convene Software), real-time chat, electronic classroom, e-mail, CD-ROM, newsgroup, LISTSERV. *TV:* videotape, videoconferencing. *Other:* audioconferencing, audiographics, audiotapes, fax, correspondence, independent study, individual study, learning contracts.

Credits Granted for: examination.

Admission Requirements: *Graduate:* bachelor's degree, completion limits, credits older than 10 years not accepted for degree completion. *Doctoral:* Master of Divinity or Master of Arts in Religion. *Certificate:* bachelor's degree.

On-Campus Requirements: No full degree completion via Distance Learning.

Tuition and Fees: *Graduate:* $874/unit (3 semester hours). *Doctoral:* $924/unit (3 semester hours). *Application Fee:* $25. *Software:* $11/month Ecunet Access, Netscape Navigator/Internet Explorer (free). *Other Costs:* $1,250 health insurance for full-time students. *Credit by:* semester.

Financial Aid: Federal Stafford Loan, VA.

Accreditation: Middle States Association of Colleges and Schools, Association of Theological Schools.

Description: Lutheran Theological Seminary at Philadelphia's (1864) roots go back to 1747 with the colonial church and the first Lutheran Synod. Lutheran leaders like the notable Franklin Clark Fry and the current ELCA Bishop, H. George Anderson, are a part of the Philadelphia tradition. The first Lutheran graduate school was begun at Philadelphia in 1913. In 1938, "Mt. Airy" seminary, as it was then dubbed, was one of the first three Lutheran schools accredited by the American Association of Theological Schools. The first full-capacity TV studio was inaugurated in 1965. In 1998–1999, distance learning capabilities will be fully functional, increasing opportunities for learning at the campus and away from it. In partnership with the Eastern Cluster of Seminaries, opportunities for theological education will be made available to areas up and down the East Coast.

Madison Area Technical College

3550 Anderson Street	Phone: (608) 246-6282
Madison, WI 57704	Fax: (608) 246-6880

Division(s): Instructional Medical Services/Distance Education
Web Site(s): http://www.madison.tec.wi.us

Class Titles: variable: Abnormal Psychology, Anthropology, Corporate Finance, Drawing Interpretation, Effective Listening, Insurance, Real Estate Appraisal, Small Business, Spanish, Tax, Time Management, Accounting, Center Director, Cost Accounting, Employee Involvement, Psychology, Making Meetings Work, Morale/Work Place Ethics, OSHA/Hazardous, Real Estate Brokerage, Real Estate Law, Statistics, Business Statistics, Communication Skills, Speech, Contemporary American Society, Dealing with Diversity, Developmental Psychology, Economics, International Economics, Management Techniques, Mathematics of Finance, Small Business Management, GED via TV.

Teaching Methods: *Computers:* Internet, e-mail, LISTSERV. *TV:* videotape, interactive TV. *Other:* None.

Credits Granted for: experiential learning, portfolio assessment, extrainstitutional learning, examination (CLEP, ACT-PEP, DANTES, GRE).

Admission Requirements: *Undergraduate:* age 16, assessment test if joining a program; certain programs have higher requirements.

On-Campus Requirements: contact school.

Tuition and Fees: *Undergraduate:* $95/credit (college transfer). *Other Costs:* textbooks. *Credit by:* semester.

Financial Aid: Federal Stafford Loan, Federal Perkins Loan, Federal PLUS Loan, Federal Pell Grant, Federal Work-Study, VA, Wisconsin resident programs.

Accreditation: North Central Association of Colleges and Schools.

Description: Madison Area Technical College (1912) offers 2-year transfer associate degrees, along with job training to meet the demands of area employers. We also offer adult basic education.

Maharishi University of Management

1000 North 4th Street	Phone: (641) 472-1135
Fairfield, IA 52557	Fax: (641) 472-1137

Division(s): Continuing Education
Web Site(s): http://www.mum.edu
E-mail: cont_ed@mum.edu

Graduate Degree Programs:
Master of Business Administration

Class Titles: Business Economics, Managerial Communication Skills, Data Analysis for Managers, Accounting for Decision Making, Marketing Management, Operations Management, Legal Environment of Business, Human Resource Management, Financial Management, Organizational Excellence, Corporate Finance, International Finance, International Business, Marketing Research, Strategic Marketing, International Marketing.

Teaching Methods: *Computers:* Internet, e-mail, *TV:* videotape. *Other:* independent study, individual study.

Credits Granted for: experiential learning, extrainstitutional learning, prior work experience (based on examination).

Admission Requirements: *Graduate:* undergraduate degree and telephone interview with professional.

On-Campus Requirements: None.

Tuition and Fees: *Graduate:* $260/credit. *Credit by:* semester.

Financial Aid: Federal Stafford Loan, Federal Perkins Loan, university scholarships.

Accreditation: North Central Association of Colleges and Schools.

Description: Maharishi University of Management (1971) was founded by Maharishi Mahesh Yogi as Maharishi International University to make education complete, so that every student enjoys great success and fulfillment in life. In 1995 the name was changed to emphasize the importance for students to gain the knowledge and experience they need to successfully manage the personal and professional areas of their lives. Academic programs include bachelor's, master's, and doctoral programs in a broad range of disciplines, including programs in Management, Physics, Physiology, and Neuroscience (the science of creative intelligence). The educational approach in each discipline—in the sciences, applied sciences, humanities, arts, government, and business—applies the knowledge of the field to practical, professional values.

Manatee Community College

| PO Box 1849 | Phone: (941) 755-1511 x4267 |
| Bradenton, FL 34206 | Fax: (941) 727-6050 |

Division(s): Academic Affairs
Web Site(s): http://www.mcc.cc.fl.us

Undergraduate Degree Programs:
Associate of Arts
Associate of Science

Certificate Programs: numerous, contact school for more information.

Teaching Methods: *Computers:* Internet, electronic classroom, e-mail, CD-ROM, newsgroup, LISTSERV. *TV:* videotape, cable program, PBS. *Other:* videoconferencing, independent study, individual study, learning contracts.

Credits Granted for: experiential learning, portfolio assessment, examination (CLEP, ACT-PEP, DANTES, GRE).

Admission Requirements: *Undergraduate:* high school diploma or GED, placement tests. *Certificate:* high school diploma or GED, placement tests.

On-Campus Requirements: None.

Tuition and Fees: *Undergraduate:* $52.53/credit resident, $196.19/credit out-of-state. *Application Fee:* $20. *Other Costs:* varying textbooks costs and lab fees. *Credit by:* semester.

Financial Aid: Federal Stafford Loan, Federal Perkins Loan, Federal PLUS Loan, Federal Pell Grant, Federal Work-Study, VA, Florida resident programs.

Accreditation: Southern Association of Schools and Colleges.

Description: Manatee Community College (1958), a public, multicampus institution, is accredited by the Commission on Colleges of the Southern Association of Colleges and Schools to award Associate in Art and Associate in Science degrees. Manatee's enrollment exceeds 8,000 students, with individuals attending classes at 2 campuses and at many sites in the community. The college offers parallel programs for those seeking a bachelor's degree or higher; occupational-technical programs to prepare students to enter the job market or continue their education; and responsive, noncredit courses and activities for continuing education, upgrading skills, and enriching personal and cultural life.

Mansfield University

Clinton Street	Phone: (717) 662-4244
Mansfield, PA 16933	(800) 661-3640
	Fax: (717) 662-4120

Division(s): Center for Lifelong Learning
Web Site(s): http://www.mnsfld.edu
E-mail: knorton@mnsfld.edu

Class Titles: varies by semester—examples: Microcomputers, Composition, General Psychology, Accounting, Nursing Research, Biology, Geology, Criminal Justice, Macroeconomics, Nutrition. *Graduate Program:* Total online master's program in School Library and Information Technologies.

Teaching Methods: *Computers:* Internet, electronic classroom, e-mail, CD-ROM, LISTSERV. *TV:* videotape, satellite broadcasting. *Other:* audioconferencing, videoconferencing, audiographics, fax, correspondence, independent study, individual study.

Credits Granted for: examination (CLEP), credit by exam.

Admission Requirements: *Undergraduate:* high school diploma or GED, SAT. *Graduate:* GRE, official transcripts.

On-Campus Requirements: As we offer no complete undergraduate programs through distance education, all students take traditional classes on- or off-campus in addition to distance education classes.

Tuition and Fees: *Undergraduate:* $158/credit state residents, $395/credit nonresidents. *Graduate:* $230/credit state residents, $389/credit nonresidents. *Application Fee:* $25. *Other Costs:* $16/credit education fee for undergraduate state residents, $23/credit education fee for graduate state residents. Other fees may apply. *Credit by:* semester.

Financial Aid: Federal Stafford Loan, Federal Perkins Loan, Federal PLUS Loan, Federal Pell Grant, Federal Work-Study, VA, Pennsylvania resident programs.

Accreditation: Middle States Association of Colleges and Schools.

Description: Mansfield University (1857) is located in north-central Pennsylvania and has an enrollment of approximately 3,000 students. The university serves the region and the national and international communities by developing human and material resources. Mansfield is committed to providing optimum learning opportunities for students of a variety of ages, backgrounds, and needs. Distance education courses were instituted in 1995 to meet the needs of learners who were geographically isolated from the university or who could not, for a number of reasons, attend traditional classes. All distance course work meets academic, departmental standards and earns Mansfield University credits.

Marist College

3399 North Road	Phone: (845) 575-3225
Poughkeepsie, NY 12601-1387	Fax: (845) 575-3640

Division(s): School of Management
Web Site(s): http://www.marist.edu/graduate
E-mail: Jean.Theobald@Marist.edu

Graduate Degree Programs:
Master of Business Administration
Master of Public Administration

Teaching Methods: *Computers:* Internet, real-time chat, electronic classroom, e-mail.

Credits Granted for: acceptable transfer credits.

Admission Requirements: *Graduate:* admissions is based upon an applicant's previous academic record, past work experience, and/or achievement on the Graduate Management Admission Test (GMAT). Generally applicants with at least 10 years of professional work experience or an advanced degree are not required to take the GMAT. Applicants must have earned at least a bachelor's degree in any major from a regionally accredited school. Students have 7 years to complete the program from time of admittance.

On-Campus Requirements: None.

Tuition and Fees: *Graduate:* $480/credit for the Master of Business Administration Degree program, $330/credit for the Master of Public Administration Degree program. *Application Fee:* $30. *Registration Fee:* $30. *Credit by:* semester.

Financial Aid: Federal Stafford Loan, New York State Tuition Assistance Program (TAP), part-time graduate scholarships, Federal Work-Study.

Accreditation: Middle States Association of Colleges and Schools.

Description: Marist College (1960) is a private, independent college with 4,800 undergraduate and 800 graduate students enrolled in both on-campus and online programs. The MBA and MPA programs are designed primarily as a part-time program for working adults. The School of Management has offered the MBA and MPA degree programs since the 1970s and introduced an online option in 1999. Marist College was the first school in New York State to gain approval to offer both the online MBA and MPA programs. The online option is offered in an accelerated format to assist working adults to complete their degree requirements as quickly as possible. All courses required to earn a degree are currently available online and almost all graduate courses are taught by full-time faculty with earned doctorates and/or professional experience.

Marshall University

400 Hal Greer Boulevard	Phone: (304) 696-6387
Huntington, WV 25755	Fax: (304) 696-6419

Division(s): School of Extended Education
Web Site(s): http://www.marshall.edu/itvs
http://muonline.marshall.edu/aee/
E-mail: thill@marshall.edu

Undergraduate Degree Programs:
Regents Bachelor of Arts (for adults)
Bachelor of Business Administration

Graduate Degree Programs:
Masters in Educational Leadership—"T" course based
Masters in Adult and Technical Education (MS)—Distance Learning, text

Certificate Programs: There is a Statewide IT Program (Associate Degree) with which our Community and Technical College participates. Also, there is a HIT (Health Information Technology) Associate Degree program currently being developed through our Community and Technical College. This degree should be available in 2 years.

Class Titles: Keyboarding I, Applied Professional Math, Principles of Management, General Psychology, Academic Skills Review, Unified Principles of Biology, Basic Economics, Developmental Communications, Developmental Writing, Communications I, Communications II, Business Correspondence/ Report Writing, Technical Report Writing, Computers and Data Processing, Internet Fundamentals, Medical Terminology, General Chemistry I, Principles of Business Finance, Twentieth-Century World, American History to 1877, Developmental Mathematics, Developmental Algebra, Developmental Geometry, Business Mathematics I, Technical Mathematics I, Technical Mathematics II, West Virginia History, Principles of Management Information Systems, Principles of Marketing, Methods of Teaching Middle Grades, Symposium Elementary/Secondary Education I, Symposium Elementary/Secondary Education II,

Computing and Instructional Design, Teaching Math to Early Adolescent, Children's Literature, Current Issues and Problems Reading, General Special Education Programming, Special Education Research I, Social and Cultural Foundation, Pharmacology in Counseling, Human Development and Adjustment, Counseling Theories, Theory and Practice of Human Appr, Career and Lifestyle Development, Interv Current Issues School, Organization and Administration of School Counseling Programs, Internship in School Counseling, Psychology of the Mid Childhood Student, MAT Level I Clinical Experience, Sem III Educational Evaluation, Advanced Studies of Human Development, Educational Psychology, Educational Research and Writing, MAT Level II Clinical Experience, Sociology of American Schools, Expository Writing for Research, Introduction to School Leadership, Planning Resources and Evaluation for School Leadership, Curriculum Leadership, Human Relation Skills for Leaders, Technology and Classroom/Theory and Practice, Leadership in the Public Sector, The School and the Community, Intern: Portfolio Assessment, The Attendance Director, Higher Education Governance, Higher Education Politics, Biological Bases of Behavior, Advanced Developmental Psychology.

Teaching Methods: *Computers:* Internet, real-time chat, electronic classroom, e-mail, CD-ROM, newsgroup, LISTSERV. *TV:* videotape, satellite broadcasting, real-time interactive classrooms (compressed video). PBS. *Other:* videoconferencing, audioconferencing, audiotapes, fax, independent study, individual study, text-based instruction.

Credits Granted for: experiential learning, military education and experience (ACE), portfolio assessment, extra-institutional learning (PONSI, corporate or professional association seminars/workshops-ACE), examination (CLEP, ACT-PEP, DANTES).

Admission Requirements: *Undergraduate:* high school curriculum, application, official high school transcript or GED scores or 2.0 GPA or ACT/SAT-I verbal and math 810, transfer transcripts. *Graduate:* bachelor's degree, official undergraduate transcripts, application, information sheet, GRE/GMAT, department-specific requirements.

On-Campus Requirements: Only those online courses defined as T require any synchronous participation. T is defined as no more than 20% of the course taught in any synchronous mode (for example, video link, chat room at a particular time, classroom). Compressed video courses require participation at a remote classroom.

Tuition and Fees: *Undergraduate:* (estimated) $109.25/credit hour. *Undergraduate Online Course:* $108/credit hour (an additional $25.50 per course technology fee for Lewis College of Business courses only). *Graduate:* $123.50/credit hour. *Graduate Online Course:* $143/credit hour (an additional $33.75 per course technology fee for Lewis College of Business courses only). *Postgraduate:* $123.50/credit. *Application Fee:* $15/$20 resident; undergraduate/graduate; $30 nonresident; undergraduate/graduate. *Graduation Fee:* $30. *Other Costs:* $30/credit hour off-campus fee except for online course, which does not have this fee; *Portfolio Evaluation Fee:* $200; *Transfer Credit Evaluation Fee:* $50. *Transcript Fee:* $5. *Credit by:* semester.

Financial Aid: Federal Stafford Loan (direct loan), Federal Perkins Loan, Federal PLUS Loan, Federal Pell Grant, Federal Work-Study, VA, West Virginia resident programs.

Accreditation: North Central Association of Colleges and Schools, Accreditation Board for Engineering Technology, Accreditation Council for Continuing Medical Education, Accreditation Council for Graduate Medical Education, AACSB/The International Association for Management Education.

Description: Marshall University has developed a 21st-century campus by developing the infrastructure, policy, training paradigm, assessments, collaborative agreements, and institutional vision to create a campus that has no boundaries. This learning revolution presents challenges and incredible opportunities to our university. Implementation of online courses was developed with special consideration for educational decisions based on deepening understanding of the way in which face-to-face communications, telecommunications, and independent work can fit together for the best learning and teaching. Marshall University has developed a curriculum of fully remotely accessible E-Courses and technology enhanced T-Courses. An E-Course requires no seat time and no physical campus presence, whereas a T-course integrates 20% of the course with face-to-face interaction. Students can apply for admission, register for classes, retrieve financial aid data on their own schedules, and access full-text and multimedia library resources via a web browser. To further support online courses, an integrated, seamless student support office is essential. Traditional campus-based processes are often not suitable for distance education students. Currently, MU has over 900 courses that use the course delivery tool WebCT. As an SREC member, we currently post 25 active online courses. Over 2,000 students are served via compressed video to 13 locations. SatNET is a statewide satellite consortium of 16 institutions with 35 courses serving 1,500 students. HEITV is another statewide initiative supplying 18 courses and serving 1,800 students. Flashlight Project is used as the assessment tool for all distributed educational programs. Multiple forms of video are supported via our Accord and Video Server MCU. Streaming video (Real and Microsoft Media) are used within many courses. Videoconferencing is used extensively via the statewide ATM network. Cisco IP/TV is support on all our local and regional campuses. Over the summer of 2001, we will be implementing Pipeline educational portal with the WebCT integrator product. Annually, our online library subscriptions exceed 1.4 million hits. We are actively working with the K12 community integration for online dual credit statewide IT curriculum, telemedicine, online programs in workforce development, forensic science, manufacturing, and a seniors program.

Marygrove College

8425 W. McNichols Road	Phone: (800) 339-0736
Detroit, MI 48221-2599	Fax: (310) 578-4716

Division(s): Master in the Art of Teaching Distance Learning Degree Program
Web Site(s): http://www.masters4teachers.net
E-mail: rebecca.sekulich@educate.com

Graduate Degree Programs:
Master in the Art of Teaching (MAT) Distance Learning Degree Program

Class Titles: The High-Performing Teacher, Learning Styles/Multiple Intelligences, Motivating Today's Learner, Technology in the Classroom, Effective Classroom Management, Models of Effective Teaching, Collaborative Action Research, Inclusion, Curriculum Design and Authentic Assessment, Parents on Your Side.

Teaching Methods: *Computers:* Internet, e-mail. *TV:* videotape. *Other:* portfolio, audiotapes, fax, conference calls.

Credits Granted for: portfolio assessment, individual assignments, study team assignments.

Admission Requirements: *Graduate:* Completed application form, nonrefundable application fee, official transcripts of all undergraduate and graduate courses, 3.0 cumulative GPA OR 2 letters of recommendation indicating the applicant's ability to succeed in the program, copy of current teaching certificate, career plan essay of one typed page in length. Must be currently teaching in a regular position.

On-Campus Requirements: No.

Tuition and Fees: *Graduate:* $249/credit. *Application Fees:* $50. *Other Costs:* $20 for Registration fee per semester and $70 materials fee per course. *Credit by:* semester.

Financial Aid: Federal Stafford Loan, Federal Unsubsidized Stafford Loan, State of Michigan Tuition Grants (MI residents only).

Accreditation: The Higher Learning Commission and the North Central Association (NCA).

Description: Marygrove College (1905) is an independent, comprehensive (Master's I) college. Known for excellence in teacher education since 1914, Marygrove was one of the first colleges to offer the convenience and flexibility of a Distance Learning master's program. Within the first 5 years of its program, the college awarded more than 7,200 MAT degrees and enrolls over 4,600 current students. The high-quality outcomes the program yields have been the subject of several recent journal articles.

Marylhurst University

17600 Pacific Highway	
(Highway 43)	Phone: (503) 699-6319
Marylhurst, OR 97036-0261	Fax: (503) 697-5597

Division(s): Web-based Learning
Web Site(s): http://online.marylhurst.edu
E-mail: www.marylhurst.edu
mdie/schneider@marylhurst.edu

Undergraduate Degree Programs:
Business and Management
Communications
Cultural and Historical Studies
English Literature and Writing
Human Studies
Interdisciplinary Studies
Music
Organizational Communication
Psychology
Real Estate Appraisal and Finance
Religious Studies
Social Sciences
Science

Graduate Degree Programs:
Master of Business Administration

Certificate Programs: Business Studies, Conflict and Culture, Public Relations, Training and Development.

Class Titles: Psychology, Biology, Business Finance, Economics, History of Film, Selling.

Teaching Methods: *Computers:* Internet, real-time chat, e-mail, CD-ROM, newsgroup, LISTSERV. *TV:* videotape. *Other:* audioconferencing, audiotapes, fax, correspondence, independent study, individual study, learning contracts.

Credits Granted for: experiential learning, portfolio assessment, extrainstitutional learning (PONSI, corporate or professional association seminars/workshops), examination (CLEP, ACT-PEP, DANTES, GRE).

Admission Requirements: *Undergraduate:* No residency restrictions. First-time ACT/SAT, high school diploma, or GED; 2.5, recommendation transfer students-transcripts, 2.0, recommendation. *Graduate:* bachelor's degree, application and fee, official transcripts, additional material as requested by program. *Certificate:* open enrollment.

On-Campus Requirements: Program dependent.

Tuition and Fees: *Undergraduate:* $249/credit. *Graduate:* $293/credit. *Application Fee:* Undergraduate: $20. Graduate: $40. International Students: $50. *Other Costs:* Student Services Fee: $17/term, Technology Fee: $4/credit, International Student Fee: $300/quarter. *Credit by:* quarter.

Financial Aid: Federal Stafford Loan, Federal Perkins Loan, Federal PLUS Loan, Federal Pell Grant, Federal Work-Study, VA, Marylhurst specific scholarships.

Accreditation: Northern Association of Schools and Colleges.

Description: Marylhurst University (1893) is a dynamic educational institution serving students who want to be actively engaged in the learning process. The institution's collaborative learning environment fosters student development at all levels. Educational programs are constructed and taught with the intention of assisting students in becoming active learners who embrace not only the knowledge and skill competencies mastered, but also the process of continual change. Marylhurst has been a pioneer in innovative education methods, from credit-for-life experience to Internet-based courses. Marylhurst has been offering distance learning since 1996. Our newest offerings include a degree completion program with a Bachelor of Science in Management, a Bachelor of Arts in Organizational Communication, a Bachelor of Science in Real Estate Appraisal and Finance, and an online MBA program. *U.S. News & World Report*'s 2001 college rankings ranked Marylhurst University "in the Western Region's top tier and #1 with classes under 20 students."

Marywood University

| 2300 Adams Avenue | Phone: (570) 348-6235 |
| Scranton, PA 18509 | Fax: (570) 961-4751 |

Division(s): Off-Campus Degree Program
Web Site(s): http://www.marywood.edu
E-mail: ocdp@marywood.edu

Undergraduate Degree Programs:
Bachelor of Science in:
    Accounting
    Business Administration with concentrations in:
        Management
        Marketing
        Financial Planning

Certificate Programs: Professional Communications, Comprehensive Business Skills, Office Administration.

Teaching Methods: *Computers:* Internet, real-time chat, electronic classroom, e-mail, CD-ROM, newsgroup, LISTSERV. *Other:* videoconferencing, audioconferencing, audiographics, audiotapes, fax, correspondence, independent study, individual study.

Credits Granted for: experiential learning, portfolio assessment, extrainstitutional learning, examination (CLEP, ACT-PEP, DANTES, GRE).

Admission Requirements: *Undergraduate:* each person who wishes to enroll in the off-campus Degree Program completes and submits to the School of Continuing Education a Marywood application for admission. Rolling admission.

On-Campus Requirements: 12 credits for degree programs.

Tuition and Fees: *Undergraduate:* $312/credit. *Application Fee:* $40. *Other Costs:* $50/3 credits, registration; $100/4–11 credits, registration; $300/12+ credits, registration; $95 text and material fee/course. *Credit by:* semester.

Financial Aid: Federal Stafford Loan, Federal Perkins Loan, Federal PLUS Loan, Federal Pell Grant, Federal Work-Study, VA, Pennsylvania resident programs.

Accreditation: Middle States Association of Colleges and Schools.

Description: Marywood University (1915) is an independent, comprehensive Catholic university owned and sponsored by the Congregation of the Sisters, Servants of the Immaculate Heart of Mary, and collaboratively staffed by lay and religious personnel. Its mission is the education of men and women of all ages in undergraduate, graduate, and continuing education programs. The university serves a wide range of students, both nationally and internationally, while maintaining a concern for the education of women, culturally diverse persons, and first generation students. Committed to spiritual, ethical, and religious values and a tradition of service, Marywood University provides a framework that enables students to develop fully as persons and to master the professional and leadership skills necessary for meeting human needs on regional and global levels.

Massachusetts Institute of Technology

77 Massachusetts Avenue	
Building 9-268	Phone: (617) 253-1346
Cambridge, MA 02139	Fax: (617) 253-1566

Division(s): Center for Advanced Educational Services
Web Site(s): http://caes.mit.edu
E-mail: janetw@mit.edu

Class Titles: Programs that exist through the Center for Advanced Educational Services range from entirely asynchronous independent learning to entirely synchronous group-based learning. At present, there is no degree-granting program offered through CAES. However, some of the courses can be taken for MIT credit that may later be applied toward a degree-granting program. There is a 4-course program in System Dynamics that is offered asynchronously over the Web via videostreaming and CD-ROM. A certificate is awarded upon successful completion of this off-campus program. Many of the courses offered are taken for professional development, and Continuing Education Units (CEUs) are available upon request. In addition, participants can take professional development courses at their home organizations synchronously through satellite broadcast, asynchronously through videostreaming, CD-ROM, videotapes.

The Advanced Study Program (ASP) provides lifelong learning opportunities for working professionals to be a part of the MIT experience. ASP courses delivered via distance learning technologies allow learners to participate remotely instead of coming to the MIT campus. Participants in the off-campus courses benefit through interaction with other learners in different locations by sharing concepts and ideas through online study groups, and direct e-mail contact with faculty members. Presentation of program content is through videostreaming over the World Wide Web and is supplemented by print, CD-ROM, and Internet activity. More information on these programs can be found at http://caes.mit.edu/asp/off_campus/index.html.

Professional development (noncredit) courses that are offered through a joint venture with NTUC/PBS The Business and Technology Network provide continuous improvement opportunities for managers, consultants, engineers, and other knowledge workers. More information on these programs can be found at http://www-caes/programs/index.html.

The Professional Institute (PI) can bring its intensive, one-week, professional development courses to groups in organizations from industry, government, and academia. Taught by MIT faculty, topics cover a span of engineering, science, management, and technology. For a full course listing visit http://web.mit.edu/professional/summer/. Distance Learning programs with the Professional Institute are currently being developed.

Teaching Methods: Off-campus learners use a combination of communication technologies for course delivery, including videostreaming, satellite broadcast, the Internet, videotapes, CD-rom, e-mail, and voicemail. The design of MIT's Distance Learning programs recognizes the benefits of student-professor and student-student interaction. Depending upon the specific programs, students may need access to one or more of the following: an e-mail account, the Internet, a videotape player, a satellite downlink, and/or a voicemail account. At a minimum, the Web-based portion of the programs requires a Pentium or Power Macintosh computer with a web browser.

Credits Granted for: Both credit and noncredit courses are offered through CAES. Distance learners participating in the Advanced Study Program are eligible to receive MIT credit, in addition to certificates of completion, for course work that is successfully completed. Students enrolled in professional development (noncredit) courses are eligible for certificates of participation after course requirements are met, and they may also receive Continuing Education Units (CEUs) upon request.

Admission Requirements: Applicants seeking noncredit courses will be accepted based upon their academic training and professional experience. In order to maintain the highest standards, CAES reserves the right to select those applicants whose qualifications and experiences suggest that they will receive the most benefit from a given program.

On-Campus Requirements: None.

Tuition and Fees: Tuition in MIT's distance learning programs is based on the type of academic credit provided. For-credit courses, delivered live through the Advanced Study Program, carry full MIT tuition for qualified candidates. Tuition for professional development courses, delivered through Strategic Partner Relationships and the Professional Institute, is based on tuition arrangements established by those institutions. *Credit by:* semester.

Accreditation: Northeast Association of Schools and Colleges.

Description: Since 1995 the Center for Advanced Educational Services (CAES) offers various undergraduate, graduate, and professional development educational programs via multimodal distance learning. These programs follow the independent learning model of distance learning delivery. Students are provided with a variety of materials, including a course guide and detailed syllabus, and access to a faculty member who provides guidance, answers questions, and evaluates their work. These programs are most often delivered in an asynchronous manner. Several of our Independent Learning programs may also be redistributed through CAES partnerships with leading universities and organizations around the world.

McCook Community College

1205 East 3rd	Phone: (308) 345-6303 x223
McCook, NE 69001	Fax: (308) 345-3305

Division(s): Distance Learning
Web Site(s): http://www.mccook.cc.ne.us/mcc/
E-mail: haney@mpcca.cc.ne.us

Undergraduate Degree Programs:
Individual courses

Class Titles: Contact school for complete course listing.

Teaching Methods: *Computers:* Internet, real-time chat, electronic classroom, e-mail, CD-ROM, newsgroup, LISTSERV. *TV:* videotape, cable program, satellite broadcasting, PBS. *Other:* radio broadcast, videoconferencing, audioconferencing, audiographics, audiotapes, fax, correspondence, independent study, individual study, learning contracts.

Credits Granted for: experiential learning, portfolio assessment, extrainstitutional learning, examination (CLEP, ACT-PEP, DANTES, GRE).

Admission Requirements: *Undergraduate:* open enrollment.

On-Campus Requirements: None.

Tuition and Fees: *Undergraduate:* $48/credit. *Credit by:* semester.

Financial Aid: Federal Stafford Loan, Federal Perkins Loan, Federal PLUS Loan, Federal Pell Grant, Federal Work-Study, Nebraska resident programs.

Accreditation: North Central Association of Colleges and Schools.

Description: McCook Community College (1926) is the oldest 2-year institution in the state of Nebraska. We are primarily a transfer institution with a light offering of vocational courses. We have a fiber-optic system that is connected to all of the public schools in southwestern Nebraska plus Mid-Plains community colleges and NCTA in Curtis. We are in the process of developing courses to be offered via Internet. These will be available by fall 2001.

McDowell Technical Community College

Route 1, Box 170	Phone: (828) 652-6021
Marion, NC 28752	Fax: (828) 652-1014

Division(s): Educational Programs
Web Site(s): http://www.mcdowelltech.cc.nc.us
E-mail: KmL@mail.mcdowell.cc.nc.us

Class Titles: Business, Economics, Psychology, History.

Teaching Methods: *Computers:* Internet, electronic class room. *TV:* videotape, cable program, satellite broadcasting, PBS. *Other:* videoconferencing, fax, correspondence, independent study, individual study.

Admission Requirements: *Undergraduate:* open-door policy, GED or high school diploma, placement test.

On-Campus Requirements: Yes, student must maintain course work as traditional student does which includes video, readings, written papers/research, etc.

Tuition and Fees: *Undergraduate:* $27–50/credit. *Other Costs:* activity fee $8, full time insurance $1, part time $4. *Credit by:* semester.

Financial Aid: Federal Pell Grant, General Work-Study, VA, North Carolina resident programs, local scholarships.

Accreditation: Southern Association of Colleges and Schools.

Description: McDowell Technical Community College (1964) offered its first distance learning course in the 1991–1992 academic term with one telecourse. We now offer a variety of telecourses and information highway classes, and we have just begun online classes.

McHenry County College

8900 US Highway 14	Phone: (815) 455-8778
Crystal Lake, IL 80012-2761	Fax: (815) 455-4930

Division(s): Distance Learning Department
Web Site(s): http://www.mchenry.cc.il.us
E-mail: jgiulian@mchenry.cc.il.us

Undergraduate Degree Programs: Contact school.

Certificate Programs: International Business Certificate.

Class Titles: Accounting, Business, English Composition, International Business, International Marketing, Political Science, College Success, History, Computer Ethics.

Teaching Methods: *Computers:* Internet, real-time chat, electronic classroom, e-mail, CD-ROM. *TV:* videotape, cable program, satellite broadcasting, PBS. *Other:* videoconferencing, audioconferencing, audiographics, audiotapes, fax, correspondence, independent study, individual study, learning contracts.

Credits Granted for: experiential learning, portfolio assessment, extrainstitutional learning (PONSI, corporate or professional association seminars/workshops), examination (CLEP, ACT-PEP, DANTES, GRE).

Admission Requirements: *Undergraduate:* transcript from high school.

Tuition and Fees: *Undergraduate:* $46/credit hour. *Software:* $5–15. *Credit by:* semester.

Financial Aid: Feberal Stafford Loan, Federal Perkins Loan, Federal PLUS Loan, Federal Pell Grant, Federal Work-Study, VA, state programs for residents of Illinois.

Accreditation: North Central Association of Colleges and Schools.

Description: For McHenry County College, Distance Learning began almost 20 years ago with the introduction of

Telecourses. What started as a few basic general education Telecourses blossomed into over 40 different Telecourses currently being offered at MCC. Over 30,000 students have been enrolled in Telecourses over the past two decades. In addition to Telecourses, in the late 1980's, McHenry County College became involved with 2-way videoconferencing and satellite broadcasting. MCC downlinks a variety of satellite programs sponsored by the Public Broadcasting System and Illinois Satellite Network. Also, as a result of a federal HECA grant, MCC designed and constructed 2 interactive videoconferencing classrooms, enabling MCC classes to be exchanged with local and regional high schools, colleges, universities, government agencies, and businesses via TV monitors, cameras, and microphones. The latest Distance Learning addition has been the advent of MCC online courses. Currently, MCC offers a wide variety of general education classes, as well as a complete International Business certificate online. By spring 2002, MCC plans to extend its online course offerings to include: College Success, Computer Ethics, and History. McHenry County College is a member of the Illinois Virtual Campus, Illinois Community Colleges Online and Illinois Online Network.

Memorial University of Newfoundland

| E2000, G.A. Hickman Building | Phone: (709) 737-8700 |
| St. John's, NF, Canada A1B 3X8 | Fax: (709) 737-7941 |

Division(s): School of Continuing Education
Web Site(s): http://www.ce.mun.ca; http:mun.ca
E-mail: cstudies@mun.ca

Undergraduate Degree Programs:
Business Administration
Maritime Studies (only bachelor of maritime studies degree offered in Canada)
Nursing (post-RN)
Social Work (2nd degree)
Technology

Graduate Degree Programs:
Master of Education (Information Technology)
Master of Nursing

Certificate Programs: Career Development, Criminology, Library Studies, Municipal Administration, Public Administration, Business Administration, Newfoundland Studies.

Class Titles: 100 courses in arts, science, or professional studies.

Teaching Methods: *Computers:* Internet, e-mail, newsgroup, asyncronous conferencing, LISTSERV. *TV:* videotape, satellite broadcasting. *Other:* audioconferencing, audiographics, audiotapes, fax, correspondence, videoconferencing.

Credits Granted for: Please contact registrar for details (709) 737-4425 or www.mun.ca/regoff//

Admission Requirements: *Undergraduate:* high school diploma, official high school/college transcripts, letters of recommendation. *Graduate:* admission requirements and applications deadlines vary by program. Please contact the School of Graduate Studies for details (709) 737-2445 or www.mun.ca/sgs/ Students may apply via Web site www.mun.ca

On-Campus Requirements: Please contact registrar for details (709) 737-4425 or *www.mun.ca/regoff//*

Tuition and Fees: *Undergraduate:* $110/credit Canadian citizens/residents, $220/credit non-Canadians. *Graduate:* Please contact School of Graduate Studies (709) 737-2445. *Application Fee:* $40 Canadians ($80 transfers, non-Canadians). *Other Costs:* varies. *Credit by:* semester.

Financial Aid: Federal/Provincial Canada Student Loan Program.

Accreditation: Association of Universities and Colleges of Canada.

Description: Memorial University College was established in 1925 as a memorial to Newfoundlanders who had lost their lives during World War I. Memorial University then became a degree-conferring institution in 1949. In 1969 Memorial first offered distance education courses around the province. Its 30-year history in distance education has resulted in more than 13,000 student registrants a year at home and around the world. Memorial's unique feature is that it provides learning opportunities in areas with low media support, and uses the latest technologies in areas with high-speed access. This allows Memorial to service a wide variety of learners, regardless of location and technical resources. Memorial offers more than 250 undergraduate and graduate degree-credit distance courses annually, representing 22 disciplines in 8 faculties/schools, with 143 courses delivered in whole or in part, via the Internet.

Mercer University

| 1400 Coleman Avenue | Phone: (478) 301-2356 |
| Macon, GA 31207 | Fax: (478) 301-2241 |

Division(s): Technical Communication
Web Site(s): http://www.mercer.edu/mstco
E-mail: Reynolds_jd@mercer.edu, or davis_mt@mercer.edu

Graduate Degree Programs:
Master of Science in Technical Communication Management

Certificate Programs: Technical Communication Management (graduate-level modules).

Class Titles: Contact school or check web site for details.

Teaching Methods: *Computers:* Internet, real-time chat, e-mail, LISTSERV, WebCT. *TV:* videotape when needed. *Other:* occasional audioconferencing, audiotapes, fax; interactive group projects.

Admission Requirements: *Graduate:* at least 3 years experience as a technical communicator; minimum 3.0 undergraduate GPA from accredited institution; GRE scores; TOEFL scores if applicable; letters of reference and/or portfolio may be required, 7 years time limit for completion.

On-Campus Requirements: None.

Tuition and Fees: *Graduate:* $411.75/credit, plus any required university fees. *Application Fee:* $35 ($50 international). *Credit by:* semester.

Financial Aid: Contact school.

Accreditation: Southern Association of Colleges and Schools.

Description: Mercer University (1833) is a church-related institution of higher learning that seeks to achieve excellence and scholarly discipline in the fields of liberal learning and professional knowledge. The university is guided by the historic principles of religious and intellectual freedom, while affirming religious and moral values that arise from the Judeo-Christian understanding of the world. The MS in Technical Communication Management is designed for working professionals who expect to assume leadership roles in their organizations. The MS was the first degree program to be offered by Distance Learning, beginning in 1995. The program resides within the School of Engineering, Department of Technical Communication. In addition to the MS degree, Mercer University offers the BS degree in Technical Communication on the Macon, Georgia, campus only. See M. L. Keene, *Education in Scientific and Technical Communication: Academic Programs That Work* (STC, 1997).

Mercy College

555 Broadway
Dobbs Ferry, NY 10522

Phone: (914) 674-7521
Fax: (914) 674-7518

Division(s): Distance Learning
Web Site(s): http://mercynet.edu/merlin
E-mail: kcayenne@mercynet.edu

Undergraduate Degree Programs:
Associate of Arts in Liberal Arts
Associate of Science in Information Systems
Bachelor of Science in:
    Computer Information Systems
    Business
Bachelor of Arts in Psychology

Graduate Degree Programs:
Master of Science in:
    Banking
    Direct Marketing
    Internet Business
    Health Service Management
    Master of Business Administration

Certificate Programs: Direct Marketing, Continuing Education Unit (CEU) for Licensed Acupuncturists.

Class Titles: Behavioral Science, Civic/Cultural Studies, Economics, Education, Literature, Mathematics, Psychology, Science, Sociology Computers, Writing.

Teaching Methods: *Computers:* Internet, real-time chat, electronic classroom, e-mail LISTSERV, whiteboard *Other:* None.

Credits Granted for: experiential learning, portfolio assessment, extrainstitutional learning.

Admission Requirements: *Undergraduate:* application form, interview, placement exam (Individual programs may have additional requirements). *Graduate:* application form, résumé, 2 letters of reference. (Individual programs may require GMAT, GRE, or MAT.) *Certificate:* Contact school.

On-Campus Requirements: None.

Tuition and Fees: *Undergraduate:* Full-time per semester (12–18 credits)—$4,475. Part-time (1–11 credits)—$375/credit. Life achievement portfolio submission fee—$100. *Graduate:* all subjects except Banking—$435/credit. Banking—$525/credit. Graduate application fee—$35 to $60 depending on course of study. Thesis or Capstone Advisement fee—$435. *Application Fee:* $35. *Credit by:* quarter or semester.

Financial Aid: Federal Stafford Loan, Federal Perkins Loan, Federal PLUS Loan, Federal Pell Grant, Federal Work-Study, VA, New York resident programs.

Accreditation: Middle States Association of Colleges and Schools, New York State Board of Education.

Description: Mercy College (1950) is a comprehensive college offering both undergraduate and graduate degrees. Founded by the Sisters of Mercy, the college became independent in 1969. The guiding principles of the college are service to the community through education of both traditional and nontraditional students, reliance on the foundation of education, and dedication to teaching and the advancement of knowledge.

Metropolitan Community College

PO Box 3777
Omaha, NE 68103-0777

Phone: (402) 457-2416
Fax: (402) 457-2255

Division(s): Student and Instructional Services
Web Site(s): http://www.mccneb.edu
E-mail: Bnicks@metropo.mccneb.edu

Undergraduate Degree Programs:
Programs lead to:
  Associate in Applied Science
  Associate of Arts
  Associate of Science in Nursing

Certificate Programs: Certificate of Achievement

Teaching Methods: Online courses and telecourses.

Credits Granted for: experiential learning, portfolio assessment, extrainstitutional learning (PONSI, corporate or professional association seminars/workshops), examination (CLEP, ACT-PEP, DANTES, GRE).

Admission Requirements: *Undergraduate:* age 18, assessment testing.

On-Campus Requirements: None.

Tuition and Fees: *Undergraduate:* $28/credit residents, $35/credit nonresidents. *Graduation fee:* $25. *Other Costs:* $2/credit technology fee. *Credit by:* quarter.

Financial Aid: Federal Stafford Loan, Federal Perkins Loan, Federal PLUS Loan, Federal Pell Grant, Federal Work-Study, VA, Nebraska resident programs.

Accreditation: North Central Association of Colleges and Schools.

Description: Meteropolitan Community College is a comprehensive, full-service public community college supported by the taxpayers of Dodge, Douglas, Sarpy, and Washington counties. Its purpose is to provide high-quality educational programs and services, primarily in career preparation and general education, to people of all ages and educational backgrounds. Metro offers more than 40 telecourses and 38 online courses each term. Content areas include; English, Math, Social Sciences, History, Philosophy, Management and Accounting. With a 1999–2000 credit enrollment of 26,659 students, Metropolitan Community College has been one of the fastest-growing postsecondary institutions in Nebraska. This enrollment compares with 2,430 credit students in 1974–75, the college's first year.

Metropolitan State College of Denver

11990 Grant Street #102
Northglenn, CO 80233

Phone: (303) 450-5111
Fax: (303) 450-9973

Division(s): Extended Campus
Web Site(s): http://clem.mscd.edu/~options
E-mail: juergens@mscd.edu

Class Titles: Survey of African History, Ecology for Nonmajors, Chicano Studies, Private Security, Constitutional Law, Juvenile Law, Probation/Parole, Penology, Crime Prevention/Loss Reduction, Computers, Survey of American History, Issues in European History—Spain, Women in European History, Western Heroes/Villains, American Revolution, Modern Middle East, World War II 1939–1948, Pharmacology Drugs/Alcohol, Educational Exceptionality/Human Growth, Exceptional Learner in Classroom, Diversity, Disability/Education, Spanish, Communication Disorders, Voice Science—Pathology/Technology, Boundary Law, Women in Transition.

Teaching Methods: *Computers:* CD-ROM, *TV:* videotape, PBS. *Other:* audiotapes, fax, correspondence, independent study, individual study, learning contracts.

Credits Granted for: extrainstitutional learning, examination (CLEP, ACT-PEP, DANTES, GRE).

On-Campus Requirements: None.

Tuition and Fees: *Undergraduate:* $110/credit. *Other Costs:* tapes/slides $100. *Credit by:* semester.

Financial Aid: Federal Stafford Loan, Federal Perkins Loan, Federal PLUS Loan, Federal Pell Grant, Federal Work-Study, VA, Colorado resident programs.

Accreditation: North Central Association of Colleges and Schools.

Description: With no class meetings, correspondence courses at Metropolitan State College of Denver (1963) allow students to set an independent learning pace at home. Students may register for correspondence courses at any time and are given one calendar year to complete a course (unless they are financial aid recipients). Note that registration, financial aid processes, and tuition are different for correspondence courses. Please call for a registration form and a "Student Guide for Taking Correspondence Courses." Applicability of correspondence courses to majors may vary with department.

Michigan State University

| 216 Administration Building | Phone: (800) 500-1554 |
| East Lansing, MI 48824 | Fax: (517) 432-2069 |

Division(s): Vice Provost University Outreach
Web Site(s): http://www.vu.msu.edu
E-mail: gotomsu.edu@msu.edu

Undergraduate Degree Programs:
Bachelor of Science in Nursing (Completion Program)
Bachelor of Science in Interdisciplinary Social Science (Completion Program)

Graduate Degree Programs:
The following are degrees offered off-campus at regional offices in Birmingham, Grand Rapids, Kalamazoo, Marquette, Midland, Novi, Traverse City, Michigan:
Master of Arts in:
    K–12 Leadership
    Educational Technology and Instructional Design
    Child Development
    Advertising
    Curriculum and Teaching
    Public Relations
    Telecommunications
    Social Work
    Adult and Continuing Education
    Community Services
    Family Studies
Master of Science in:
    Nursing
Master of Business in Administation
The following are full programs offered via the Internet:
Master of Arts in:
    Criminal Justice/Security Management Specialization
    Criminal Justice/International Specialization
    Education
Master of Science in:
    Packaging
    Physics/Specialization in Beam Physics

Certificate Programs: Applied Plant Science (in-state-only), Chemical Engineering (Internet), Computer Aided Design (Internet), Criminal Justice-Security Management (Internet), Criminal Justice-International Focus (Internet), Educational Technology (in-state-only), Facilities Management (Internet), International Food Law (Internet), Landscape Management (in-state-only), Medical Technology (in-state-only), Social Work (Internet), and Watershed Management (Internet).

Class Titles: Material/Energy Balance, Law Enforcement, Pro-seminar in Criminal Justice, Design/Analysis in CJ Research, Security Management, Security Administration, Independent Study, Internship/Practicum, Home Computing, Concept of Learning Society, Computer/Technology, CAD for Design, Applied Pharmacology, APN in Managed Health, Aging/Health in U.S., Issues in Health Care, Physics, Beam Physics, Topics in Beam Physics, Social Psychology, Applied SW Research, Special Needs Children in School Settings, Social Work in Schools, Testing/School Social Work, Information Society, Telecommunication Applications, Telecommunication Network Management, Special Topics in TC: Policy. All courses via Internet.

Teaching Methods: *Computers:* Internet, real-time chat, e-mail, LISTSERV. *TV:* satellite, interactive TV (CODEC). *Other:* None.

Credits Granted for: examination (CLEP, Advanced Placement tests).

Admission Requirements: *Undergraduate:* grades, tests scores, caliber of high school program, principal and counselor comments, leadership qualities, exceptional talents, citizenship record, and high school achievement. *Graduate:* academic record, experience, personal qualifications, and proposed program of study.

On-Campus Requirements: Required for the satellite programs, some certificate programs, and CODEC programs. Not required for Internet courses or programs.

Tuition and Fees: *Undergraduate:* $152.25/credit (plus $301 matriculation fees/semester) lower-level undergraduates, $169.75/credit (plus $301 matriculation fees/semester) upper-level undergraduates. *Graduate:* $237/credit (plus $301 matriculation fees/semester). *Application Fee:* $30 for degree programs. *Other Costs:* all costs are from the 2000–01 school year. *Credit by:* semesters.

Financial Aid: Federal Stafford Loan, Federal Perkins Loan, Federal PLUS Loan, Federal Pell Grant, Federal Work-Study, VA, Michigan resident programs (financial aid available for degree-seeking students only, if they qualify).

Accreditation: Association of American Universities.

Description: Michigan State University (MSU), founded in 1855, is a research-intensive, land-grant university, offering more than 200 programs at the bachelor's through doctoral levels. It is one of the 58 members of the prestigious American Association of Universities and is a member of the Big Ten Conference. The core of MSU's land-grant tradition is the belief that educational opportunities should be available to the widest possible audience. Six guiding principles reflect the land-grant tradition at MSU: access to quality education, active learning, the generation of new knowledge, problem solving, diversity, and making people matter. A recently announced technology guarantee ensures students an intensive, quality-based technological experience (with increased interactive instruction) and lifelong access to MSU technology. The university's outreach mission, involving all 14 of its colleges, emphasizes the extension of knowledge to serve the needs of individuals, groups, and communities.

Michigan Technological University

1400 Townsend Drive
Houghton, MI 49931-1295

Phone: (906) 487-3170
Fax: (906) 487-2463

Division(s): Extended University Programs
Web Site(s): http://www/admin.mtu.edu/eup
E-mail: disted@mtu.edu

Undergraduate Degree Programs:
Bachelor of Science in:
Engineering (Mechanical Design)*
Engineering (Manufacturing)*
Surveying

Graduate Degree Programs:
Master of Science in Mechanical Engineering*
Doctor of Philosophy in Mechanical Engineering-Engineering
Mechanics*
*corporate sponsorship required

Teaching Methods: *Computers:* Internet, e-mail, LISTSERV.
TV: videotape. *Other:* audioconferencing, videoconferencing,
fax, independent study.

Credits Granted for: examination (CLEP, ACT-PEP, DANTES,
GRE).

Admission Requirements: *Undergraduate:* transcripts from
high school, C+ GPA. *Graduate:* MS: undergraduate degree,
transcripts, essay or personal statement, letter(s) of recommendation. PhD: graduate degree, transcripts, essay or
personal statement, letter(s) of recommendation.

On-Campus Requirements: BS in Surveying has some lab
assignments.

Tuition and Fees: *Undergraduate:* $320–$405/credit
Graduate: $750–$1,000/credit *Application Fee:* $30 ($35
international). *Credit by:* semester.

Financial Aid: Federal Stafford Loan, Federal Perkins Loan,
Federal PLUS Loan, Federal Pell Grant, VA.

Accreditation: Accreditation Board of Engineering and
Technology (BSE degrees) RAC of ABET (surveying).

Description: Michigan Technological University was founded
in 1885. As the demand for engineers grew, so did MTU's
reputation as a leader among technology-oriented educational institutions. Today, students from many states and foreign
countries pursue degrees in science, engineering, forestry,
business, liberal arts, social sciences, and technology.
Considered one of the four Michigan research institutions
(with MSU, UM, and WSU), Michigan Tech offers one of the
largest engineering programs in the nation. Based on undergraduate engineering enrollment, MTU recently ranked 11th
nationwide in BS degrees granted. Tech has offered individual courses via distance education for many years. A large

corporation interested in furthering its employees' education
initiated MTU's first BSE degree program in 1989. Today MTU
is also offering distance BSS, MS, and PhD programs.

Mid-America Bible College

3500 Southwest 119th Street
Oklahoma City, OK 73170

Phone: (405) 691-3800
Fax: (405) 692-3165

Division(s): Distance Education
Web Site(s): http://www.mabc.edu
E-mail: mbcok@cris.com
dmowry@mabc.edu

Undergraduate Degree Programs:
Bachelor of Science in Pastoral Ministry

Graduate Degree Programs:
Master of Arts in:
Ministry
Programming

Class Titles: New Testament, Old Testament, Gospel of John,
Acts, Romans, Life of Jesus, Psychology, Sociology,
American Literature, U.S. History, World History.

Teaching Methods: *Computers:* Internet, real-time chat,
e-mail, interactive educational television. *Other:* correspondence, independent study, individual study, learning
contracts.

Credits Granted for: experiential learning, portfolio assessment, extrainstitutional learning, examination (CLEP, ACT-
PEP, DANTES, GRE).

Admission Requirements: *Undergraduate:* if degree seeking,
approximately 2 years previous college with transcripts, 22
years of age. *Graduate:* BS or BA, at least 15 hours accredited Bible courses including 3 hours in systematic theology,
3 hours New Testament, and 3 hours Old Testament,
recommendations from pastor, friend, and former teachers,
2.7 CGPA.

On-Campus Requirements: None.

Tuition and Fees: *Undergraduate:* $500/3-hour course.
Graduate: $250/credit hour. *Application Fee:* $20. *Other
Costs:* Semester Registration Fee: $50. *Technology Fee:*
$5/credit hour, books. *Credit by:* semester.

Financial Aid: Federal Stafford Loan, Federal Perkins Loan,
Federal PLUS Loan, Federal Pell Grant, VA, Oklahoma resident programs.

Accreditation: North Central Association of Colleges and
Universities.

Description: Mid-America Bible College was founded in 1953
in Houston, Texas. The college moved to Oklahoma City, OK

in 1985 and became the first 4-year private college to move across state lines and keep its accreditation. In 1991, we started a distance learning program to go along with our already successful correspondence program. We chose the area of Pastoral Ministry and Specialized Ministry because of the many ministers who are unable to leave their present churches to pursue a college degree. Many of our graduates from the TELOS program go on to pursue master's and doctoral programs. For more information about our programs please call or write.

Mid-State Technical College

500 32nd Street North	Phone: (715) 422-5463
Wisconsin Rapids, WI 54494	Fax: (715) 422-5466

Division(s): Technology Center
Web Site(s): http://midstate.tec.wi.us/

Undergraduate Degree Programs: Contact school.

Certificate Programs: Contact school.

Class Titles: Machine Calculation, Management and Leadership Principles, Introduction to Computer courses, Marketing Principles, Communication, Social and Behavioral Sciences.

Teaching Methods: *Computers:* Internet *TV:* videotape, cable program. *Other:* correspondence, independent study.

Credits Granted for: experiential learning, portfolio assessment, extrainstitutional learning (PONSI, corporate or professional association seminars/workshops), examination (CLEP, ACT-PEP, DANTES).

Admission Requirements: *Undergraduate:* high school diploma, GED, or demonstration of ability to benefit. *Certificate:* high school diploma, GED, or demonstration of ability to benefit.

On-Campus Requirements: may vary depending on a given course.

Tuition and Fees: *Undergraduate:* $64, plus fees (varies by course)/credit. *Application Fee:* $30. *Graduation Fee:* students cannot complete an entire degree via distance education. *Credit by:* semester.

Financial Aid: Federal Stafford Loan, Federal Perkins Loan, Federal PLUS Loan, Federal Pell Grant, Federal Work-Study, VA, state programs for residents of Wisconsin.

Accreditation: North Central Association of Colleges and Schools.

Description: Mid-State Technical College (1967) is a publicly supported, regional, 2-year postsecondary institution that

is part of the Wisconsin Technical College System. MSTC develops, improves, and enhances the Central Wisconsin Workforce, fosters economic development, and helps area residents reach personal and career goals.

Middle Tennessee State University

1301 East Main Street	Phone: (615) 898-5611
Murfreesboro, TN 37132	Fax: (615) 898-8108

Division(s): Continuing Studies and Public Service
Web Site(s): Division web site: http://www.mtsu.edu/learn
Correspondence web site: http://www.mtsu.edu/~corres
Online courses web site: http://www.mtsu.edu/netcourse
Telecourse web site: http://www.mtsu.edu/~tlcourse
E-mail: dzeh@mtsu.edu

Online Degree Programs (Undergraduate):
Bachelor of Science in Professional Studies: Major in Information Technology
Bachelor of Science in Professional Studies: Major in Organizational Leadership
Bachelor of Science in Liberal Studies
Web Site(s): *www.tn.regentsdegrees.org*

Online Completion Degree: Program (Undergraduate):
Bachelor of Science: Undergraduate Completion Degree for Registered Nurses Web Site(s): *www.mtsu.edu/-nursing*

Graduate Degree Program:
Masters of Science: Teaching Mathematics (offered via videoconferencing in the middle Tennessee area)

Class Titles: Accounting, African-American Studies, Aging Studies, Algebra, Art, Astronomy, Business, Communication, Computer Literacy, Criminal Justice, Developmental Studies, Economics, Education, English Composition, Geography, Geology, Health and Nutrition, Human Sciences, Industrial Technology, Information Technology, International Relations, Journalism, Literature, Management, Mathematics, Marketing, Nursing, Political Science, Psychology, Radio/TV, Recording Industry, Religious Studies, Science, Social Work, Sociology, Theater Appreciation, Women's Studies, University Seminar.

Teaching Methods: *Computers:* Internet, real-time chat, electronic classroom, e-mail, newsgroup, LISTSERV. *TV:* videotape, cable program, satellite broadcasting, PBS. *Other:* videoconferencing, audioconferencing, audiotapes, fax, correspondence, independent study, individual study.

Credits Granted for: military service and training based on ACE Guide, extrainstitutional learning, examination (CLEP, ACT-PEP, DANTES, GRE).

Admission Requirements: Students entering as new freshmen are guaranteed admission if they have a 2.8 GPA or a 20

ACT. If a new freshman is 21 years old, he or she will not have to provide ACT scores, but may have to take a placement test. Transfer students are guaranteed admission if they have a 2.0 GPA with at least 9 semester hours of college credit. If they have less than 60 hours of college credit, we will also need to see official high school transcripts to check for deficiencies. More detailed information regarding admission requirements and procedures can be found at http://www.mtsu.edu/~admissn/admmenu.html

On-Campus Requirements: maximum amount of correspondence allowed is 1/4 the total number of credits for the degree. No more than 66 hours awarded by correspondence, credit by exam.

Tuition and Fees: *Undergraduate:* $97/credit hour. *Graduate:* $157/credit hour. *Application Fee:* $15. *Debt Service Fee:* $8/credit hour. *General Access Fee:* $27 + $11/credit hour. *Postal Service Fee:* (only for full-time students) $8. *Recreation Activity Fee:* $15. *Credit by:* semester.

Financial Aid: Federal Stafford Loan, Federal Perkins Loan, Federal PLUS Loan, Federal Pell Grant, Federal Work-Study, VA, Tennessee resident programs.

Accreditation: Southern Association of Colleges and Schools.

Description: Middle Tennessee State University (1911) opened with a 2-year program for training teachers. It evolved into a 4-year teacher's college in 1925. In 1965 the institution was granted university status, and in 1992 its 6 schools—5 undergraduate and one graduate—became colleges. MTSU began distance learning in 1994 with compressed video courses. Soon after, telecourses, correspondence courses, and online courses followed. In academic year 2000–2001, more than 4,500 students were served by distance learning.

Midland College

| 3600 North Garfield | Phone: (915) 685-4500 |
| Midland, TX 79705 | Fax: (915) 685-6401 |

Division(s): Distance Learning
Web Site(s): http://www.midland.cc.tx.us
E-mail: cduchesne@midland.cc.tx.us

Undergraduate Degree Programs:
Associate of Arts
Associate of Science
Associate of Applied Science

Certificate Programs: Accounting; Air Conditioning, Heating and Refrigeration Technology; Alcohol and Drug Abuse Counseling; Automotive Technology; Aviation Maintenance—Airframe and Powerplant; Building Science Technology; Child Care and Development; Coding; Computer Graphics Tech-

nology; Computer Information Systems with Business and Electronic Emphasis; Electronics Technology; Environmental Technology; Emergency Medical Services; Horticulture Technology; Law Enforcement; Legal Assistant; Management; Medical Imaging; Medical Transcription; Nursing-Vocational; Office Systems Technology; Respiratory Care; Welding.

Teaching Methods: *Computers:* Internet, e-mail. *Other:* videoconferencing, fax.

Credits Granted for: experiential learning, portfolio assessment, examination (CLEP, ACT-PEP, DANTES, GRE).

Admission Requirements: *Undergraduate:* open-door, high school graduate or GED, TASP. *Certificate:* same as undergraduate.

On-Campus Requirements: 25% of major course work.

Tuition and Fees: Contact school for all tuition and fee information. *Credit by:* semester.

Financial Aid: Federal Pell Grant, Federal Work-Study, VA, Texas resident programs.

Accreditation: Southern Association of Colleges and Schools.

Description: Midland College (1972) is an open-door, comprehensive, public community college committed to educational excellence. The college strives to provide citizens of its region with the opportunity to learn through diverse and flexible programs. The faculty is committed to instruction that provides students with occupational and professional skills, encourages creative and critical thinking, and promotes individual development. In 1996, distance learning became a reality at Midland College with the development of both an interactive videoconferencing classroom and computer communication-based instruction. Since that time, course offerings and enrollments have increased, and Web-based instruction is now available. Indeed, Midland College strives to enhance the quality of life in its "community."

Milwaukee School of Engineering

| 1025 North Broadway | Phone: (414) 277-7252 |
| Milwaukee, WI 53202 | Fax: (414) 277-7479 |

Division(s): Rader School of Business
Web Site(s): http://www.msoe.edu/
E-mail: papp@msoe.edu

Graduate Degree Programs:
Master of Science in Engineering Management
Master of Science in Medical Informatics

Class Titles: Principles of Research/Writing, Medical Informatics Journal Club.

Teaching Methods: *Computers:* Internet, e-mail, LISTSERV.

Credits Granted for: examination (CLEP)

Admission Requirements: *Graduate:* college degree, 2.80 GPA.

On-Campus Requirements: Courses taken via distance education must be less than 50% of the total program credits.

Tuition and Fees: *Graduate:* $440/credit *Application Fee:* $30 (waived when applying online) *Credit by:* quarter.

Financial Aid: Federal Stafford Loan, Federal Perkins Loan, Federal Work-Study, VA.

Accreditation: North Central Association of Colleges and Schools.

Description: Founded in 1903, MSOE is a private, coeducational, nonsectarian university located in a metropolitan center. It provides a balanced education—undergraduate and graduate in areas such as engineering, technical communication, business, management information systems, construction management, and nursing. Today, MSOE offers 16 bachelor's degrees and 6 master's degrees. Guidance from professors can be obtained through multiple communication techniques. Online courses have been offered since 1996. Only select graduate courses are available in their entirety via distance education. At MSOE, theory is brought to life and reinforced for students through extensive integration of laboratory experimentation. Understanding theoretical concepts and knowing how to apply them is key to the success of MSOE graduates.

Minnesota State University—Moorhead

1104 7th Avenue South	Phone: (218) 236-2392
Moorhead, MN 56563	Fax: (218) 287-5030

Division(s): Continuing Studies
Web Site(s): http://www.mnstate.edu/continue/
E-mail: contstdy@mnstate.edu

Undergraduate Degree Programs: Contact school.

Graduate Degree Programs: Contact school.

Class Titles: All courses are undergraduate unless otherwise noted. Introduction to Creative Writing, Personal Health, Disease Prevention, History of U.S. I, History of U.S. II, Scandinavian Humanities, Principles of Management, Indian Education, General Psychology, Developmental Psychology, Developmental Psychology (Web and CD-ROM), Personality (Psych), Abnormal Psychology, Sociology of Family, Sociology of Gender, Statistics in Educational Research

(graduate), Methods of Research (graduate), Electronic Resources: Issues and Practice (undergraduate and graduate).

Teaching Methods: *Computers:* Internet, electronic classroom, e-mail, CD-ROM, LISTSERV. *Other:* correspondence, independent study, individual study.

Credits Granted for: experiential learning, portfolio assessment, extrainstitutional learning (PONSI, corporate or professional association seminars/workshops), examination (CLEP, ACT-PEP, DANTES, GRE).

Admission Requirements: *Undergraduate:* high school graduation proof; high school trancript or GED. *Graduate:* proof of completed bachelor's degree, transcript. *Certificate:* same as undergraduate and graduate above.

On-Campus Requirements: None.

Tuition and Fees: *Undergraduate:* $110/credit. *Graduate:* $160/credit. *Application Fee:* $20. *Credit by:* semester.

Financial Aid: Federal Stafford Loan, Federal Perkins Loan, Federal PLUS Loan, Federal Pell Grant, Federal Work-Study, VA.

Accreditation: North Central Association of Colleges and Secondary Schools.

Description: The mission of Minnesota State University Moorhead (1887) is to foster excellence in teaching and learning. Founded as the Moorhead Normal School, the university evolved over the years but continually strives to provide an educational environment that supports intellectual development, that welcomes diversity and that develops the skills and talents of women and men so that they have the capacity to live usefully, act responsibly and be learners all their lives. The university provides baccalaureate-level programs in the liberal arts, natural and social sciences, teacher education, business and technology, the fine arts, and professional areas. MSUM also provides selected graduate programs and noncredit education programs in response to regional needs. In order to better serve the needs of students in the region, MSUM began to offer courses via distance in a packaged, correspondence-type format in the 1970s. MSUM later added courses offered via ITV and via the Web to increase access to our courses.

Minot State University

500 University Avenue W	Phone: (800) 777-0750 x3822
Minot, ND 58707	Fax: (701) 858-4343

Division(s): Center for Extended Learning
Web Site(s): http://online.minotstateu.edu
E-mail: conted@minotstateu.edu

Class Titles: Accounting, Cultural Studies, Business, Business Administration/Management, Business Information/Technology, Composition, English Language/ Literature, History, Human Resources Management, Math, Philosophy, Sociology, Teacher Education, Psychology, Special Education.

Teaching Methods: *Computers:* Internet, real-time chat, e-mail. *TV:* satellite broadcasting. *Other:* correspondence, independent study.

Credits Granted for: extrainstitutional learning (seminars/ workshops), examination (CLEP, ACT-PEP, DANTES, GRE).

Admission Requirements: *Undergraduate:* immunization records, ACT, high school diploma, official high school transcripts or GED. *Graduate:* bachelor's degree, official college/university transcripts, 3 letters of recommendation, immunization records, autobiography.

On-Campus Requirements: None.

Tuition and Fees: *Undergraduate:* $115/credit IVN/ Correspondence, $139/credit online courses. *Graduate:* $140/credit IVN/Correspondence, $161/credit online courses. *Application Fee:* $25 online study. *Credit by:* semester.

Financial Aid: Federal Stafford Loan, Federal Perkins Loan, Federal PLUS Loan, Federal Pell Grant, Federal Work-Study, VA, North Dakota resident programs.

Accreditation: North Central Association of Colleges and Schools.

Description: Founded in 1913, Minot State University is a comprehensive, public university whose twofold mission is to foster the intellectual, personal, and social development of its students, and to promote the public good through excellence in teaching, research, scholarly activity, and public service. Minot State is an integral part of the state and region it serves, and its mission is linked inextricably to the needs, aspirations, and commonwealth of the people of North Dakota. Since its founding, MSU has evolved steadily in serving North Dakota and creating opportunities for its citizens. In the late 1970s, Minot saw a need for students to take nontraditional courses. The school then developed the Office of Continuing Education and offered correspondence courses. Continuing Education expanded its distance program in 1996 by offering courses via the Internet through MSU Online.

Mississippi Delta Community College

| PO Box 668 | Phone: (662) 246-6392 |
| Moorhead, MS 38761 | Fax: (662) 246-6327 |

Division(s): Distance Learning Coordinator
Web Site(s): http://academicweb. mdcc.cc.ms.us/vccweb/ default.htm
E-mail: rstrawbridge@mdcc.cc.ms.us

Undergraduate Degree Programs:
Associate of Arts

Class Titles: courses toward Associate of Arts and Associate of Applied Science degrees.

Teaching Methods: *Computers:* Internet, real-time chat, electronic classroom, e-mail, CD-ROM. *TV:* videotape. *Other:* fax, independent study, individual study, learning contracts.

Credits Granted for: examination (CLEP).

Admission Requirements: *Undergraduate:* complete application, complete health form, and transcripts from all colleges attended or if no college credit, then high school transcript. Course prerequisites are listed in the catalog. It is available online at www.mdcc.cc.ms.us.

On-Campus Requirements: None.

Tuition and Fees: *Undergraduate:* $60/credit. *Other Costs: Software:* may vary by course. *Graduation Fee:* $35. *Credit by:* semester.

Financial Aid: Federal Stafford Loan, Federal Perkins Loan, Federal PLUS Loan, Federal Pell Grant, Federal Work-Study, VA, Mississippi resident programs.

Accreditation: Southern Association of Colleges and Schools.

Description: Mississippi Delta Community College was founded in 1926 as Sunflower Junior College. From the beginning in 1926, the college has achieved distinction among the junior/community colleges of the state. Its alumni are scattered throughout the United States in positions of trust and leadership. It is the philosophy of MDCC to provide quality educational experiences that include intellectual, academic, vocational, technical, social, cultural, and recreational learning opportunities, at a nominal cost, to those who qualify for the courses of study and programs offered. The college ventured into online instruction in 2000. We are partnered with the other community colleges in Mississippi to form the Mississippi Virtual Community College. We are committed to delivering quality educational experiences over the Internet, and welcome inquiries from all qualified students.

Modesto Junior College

| 435 College Avenue | Phone: (209) 575-6893 |
| Modesto, CA 95350 | Fax: (209) 575-6025 |

Division(s): Dean of Instructional Services
Web Site(s): http://gomjc.org
E-mail: davidsonm@yosemite.cc.ca.us

Undergraduate Degree Programs:
Associate of Arts
Associate of Science

Certificate Programs: Many available.

Class Titles: Chemistry, Nursing, English, Statistics, Psychology, Group/Organizational Communication, History, Humanities, Music.

Teaching Methods: *Computers:* Internet, real-time chat, electronic classroom, e-mail, CD-ROM, newsgroup, LISTSERV. *TV:* videotape, cable program, satellite broadcasting, direct broadcast (interhome network). *Other:* audioconferencing, videoconferencing, fax, correspondence, independent study, individual study, learning contracts.

Credits Granted for: experiential learning, portfolio assessment, extrainstitutional learning, examination (CLEP, ACT-PEP, DANTES), credit by examination.

Admission Requirements: *Undergraduate:* age 18 or high school graduate (permission needed if not a graduate).

On-Campus Requirements: None.

Tuition and Fees: *Undergraduate:* $11/unit residents, $125/unit nonresidents. *Other Costs:* Books, supplies, etc. *Credit by:* semester.

Financial Aid: Federal Perkins Loan, Federal Pell Grant, Federal Work-Study, VA, California resident programs.

Accreditation: Western Association of Schools and Colleges.

Description: Since 1921 Modesto Junior College has aspired to meet diverse educational, cultural, student, and community needs by offering open access to excellence in higher education and cultural activities. To accomplish this, college staff are committed to helping students with responsive and diverse career preparation, personal development, and lifelong learning opportunities. Modesto strives to provide excellence in instruction and support services, creating an intellectually and culturally stimulating atmosphere for students, staff, and the community. To aid continuing personal and professional development for all employees, Modesto offered telecourses in 1986, then entered the field of online instruction (Internet) in 1994.

Monroe Community College

1000 East Henrietta Road	**Phone:** (716) 292-2196
Rochester, NY 14623	**Fax:** (716) 292-3862

Division(s): Curriculum and Program Development
Web Site(s): http://www.monroecc.edu
E-mail: SLNregistration@monroecc.edu

Undergraduate Degree Programs:
Associate in Science, Business Administration; Associate in Science, Criminal Justice; Applied Associate in Science, Criminal Justice: Corrections Administration; Applied Associate in Science, Criminal Justice Police; Associate in Science, Physical Education Studies.

Certificate Programs: Dental Assisting.

Class Titles: Accounting, Biology, Nutrition, Business, Retailing, Law and Criminal Justice, Communication, Dental Assisting, English (composition, writing, literature), Building Construction, Health, Physical Education, Golf Management, Fitness Theory, Sports Management, Stress Management, Medical Transcription, History, Basic Refrigeration Theory, Mammography, Mathematics, Music, Nursing, Philosophy, Psychology, Sociology, Spanish, Travel and Tourism.

Teaching Methods: *Computers:* Internet, chat, e-mail, CD-ROM. *TV:* videotape, cable program, satellite broadcasting, PBS. *Other:* independent study.

Credits Granted for: experiential and adult learning, portfolio assessment, extrainstitutional learning, examination (CLEP, ACT-PEP, DANTES), community service learning, cooperative education.

Admission Requirements: *Undergraduate:* high school diploma or equivalent, degree-specific. *Certificate:* high school diploma or equivalent; each degree has specific academic entrance requirements.

On-Campus Requirements: None.

Tuition and Fees: *Undergraduate:* $105/credit, New York State residents; $210/credit, nonresidents; $1,250 full-time, New York State residents; $2,500 full-time, nonresidents. *Application Fee:* $20. *Laboratory/Service Fee:* $12 to $138 depending on course/credit hours. *Graduation Fee:* $35. *Other Costs:* $2 to $80.50 Student Association Fee depending on number of credit hours taken. Other fees may apply. *Credit by:* semester.

Financial Aid: Federal Stafford Loan, Federal Perkins Loan, Federal PLUS Loan, Federal Pell Grant, Federal Work-Study, VA, New York resident programs.

Accreditation: Middle States Association of Colleges and Schools.

Description: Monroe Community College (1961) is a comprehensive college offering a full variety of technical, business, health, and transfer curricula. The college enrolls 28,000 students annually in credit and noncredit courses. Distance learning courses currently include more than 100 Internet courses, offered in conjunction with the State University of New York (SUNY) Learning Network, as well as a dozen telecourses offered on PBS and cable TV.

Montana State University—Bozeman

128 EPS Building
PO Box 173860
Bozeman, MT 59717-3860

Phone: (406) 994-6812
Fax: (406) 994-7856

Division(s): Burns Telecommunications Center/individual departments
Web Site(s): http://btc.montana.edu
http://btc.montana.edu/nten
http://btc.montana.edu/ceres
http://btc.montana.edu/msse
http://www.math.montana.edu/mathed/distance
E-mail: kboyce@montana.edu

Graduate Degree Programs:
Master of Science in:
   Science Education
   Mathematics, Math Education Option
   Nursing, Family Nurse Practitioner
   Technology Education

Class Titles: Mountain Streams/Lakes, Infection/Immunity, Agricultural/Medical Biotechnology, Designing Technology-Based Solutions, 12 Principles of Soil Science, Exploration of Food Biotechnology, Internet-Based K-14 Earth System Science Instruction, Nutrition for Fitness/Performance, Special Relativity, Astronomy for Teachers, Comparative Planetology: Establishing Virtual Presence in Solar System, Demystifying Quantum Mechanics, Science/Photography, Studying Universe with Space Observatories, Visualization/Communication Tools for Mathematics/Science Teaching, General Relativity, Plains Landscape, Life in Streams/Ponds of Northern Great Plains, Hydrology of Streams/Ponds of Northern Great Plains, Conceptual Physics, Biology of Riparian Zones/Wetlands, Terrestrial Ecology of Plains/Prairies, Chemistry Concepts, Mountains/Plains Riparian Processes, Electronic Snow, Advanced Mathematical Modeling for Teachers, Physics of Energy, Water Quality.

Teaching Methods: *Computers:* Internet, real-time chat, electronic classroom, e-mail, CD-ROM. *TV:* videotape, cable program, satellite broadcasting, PBS. *Other:* videoconferencing, audioconferencing, audiotapes, fax.

Credits Granted for: extrainstitutional learning, examination (CLEP, ACT-PEP, DANTES, GRE).

Admission Requirements: *Graduate:* call school for details.

On-Campus Requirements: most individual courses are delivered entirely at a distance. Program-specific.

Tuition and Fees: *Graduate:* variable; call school for details. *Credit by:* semester.

Financial Aid: Federal Stafford Loan, Federal Perkins Loan, Federal PLUS Loan, Federal Pell Grant, Federal Work-Study, VA, Montana resident programs.

Accreditation: Northwest Association of Colleges and Schools.

Description: Montana State University, Bozeman (1893) is a 4-year public, comprehensive, land-grant university with undergraduate and graduate programs in liberal arts, basic sciences, the professional areas, agriculture, architecture, business, nursing, education and engineering. Founded in 1893 as Montana's land-grant institution, MSU-Bozeman is a multipurpose research university with 11,600 students. Its affiliated campuses are MSU-Billings, MSU-Northern in Havre, and MSU College of Technology-Great Falls. As a land-grant institution, Montana State University has a long history of outreach and distance learning experience. Courses and programs have been delivered throughout the state for more than a decade using videotape, public TV broadcast, satellite uplink and downlink, audioconferencing and face-to-face delivery. More recently MSU distance learning reaches beyond state borders and includes videoconferencing and Internet-based course delivery.

Montana State University Great Falls College of Technology

2100 16th Avenue South
Great Falls, MT 59405

Phone: (406) 771-4300
(800) 446-2698
Fax: (406) 771-4317

Division(s): Outreach
Web Site(s): http://www.msugf.edu
E-mail: outreach@msugf.edu

Certificate Programs:
Medical Transcription Certificate, Health Information Coding Specialist Specialized Endorsement.

Class Titles: Accounting Procedures, Healthcare Delivery, Disease Concepts, Alternative Medicines, Medical Terminology, Fitness for Life, Pharmaceuticals, Medical Science, Anthropology, Human Biology, Introduction to Business, Global Marketing, Public Speaking, Introduction to Computers, Internet Basics, Introduction to Programming, Database Management, Excel Spreadsheets, Composition, World Literature, Business/Technical Communications, Health Information Processes, ICD Coding, Introductory Algebra, Math for Liberal Arts, Fundamentals of Health Insurance, Medical Transcription, Microsoft Word, Physical Science, General Psychology, Lifespan Development, Introduction to Sociology.

Teaching Methods: *Computers:* Internet, real-time chat, electronic classroom, e-mail. *TV:* compressed video. *Other:* fax.

Credits Granted for: examination (CLEP, DANTES).

Admission Requirements: *Undergraduate:* after 7 credits, education assessment, immunization documents.

On-Campus Requirements: None.

Tuition and Fees: *Undergraduate:* $300/3-credit course Montana resident, $721/3-credit course nonresident. *Application Fee:* $30. *Other Costs:* $45/course distance learning fee. *Credit by:* semester.

Financial Aid: Federal Stafford Loan, Federal PLUS Loan, Federal Pell Grant, Federal Work-Study, VA, Montana resident programs.

Accreditation: Northwest Accreditation of Schools and Colleges.

Description: Montana State University—Great Falls College of Technology (1969) offers students several instructional formats: (1) 2-year Associate of Applied Science degrees, as well as associate degrees; (2) a Specialized Endorsement option for those who wish to move rapidly into the job market with a core of job skills; (3) short-term training in seminars and workshops, as well as customized training to fit the specific needs of companies; and (4) courses and programs through distance technologies, such as compressed video and computer-mediated instruction, that provide learning opportunities for those without access to regular college courses.

Montana State University, Northern

300 West 11th Street	Phone: (406) 265-3747
PO Box 7751	(800) 662-6132
Havre, MT 59501	Fax: (406) 265-3570

Division(s): Extended University
Web Site(s): http://nmclites.edu
E-mail: oveson@msun.nmclites.edu

Class Titles: general education classes and courses leading to the following degrees: Associate of Science in Business Technology, Bachelor of Science in Business Technology, Bachelor of Science in Nursing—Nursing Completion Program, Master of Education in Learning Development.

Teaching Methods: *Computers:* Internet, e-mail, CD-ROM. *TV:* videotape, interactive TV. *Other:* fax, individual study.

Credits Granted for: experiential learning/portfolio assessment, corporate or professional association seminars/workshops, work experience, examination (CLEP, DANTES).

Admission Requirements: *Undergraduate:* placement exams; measles, mumps, rubella immunizations, see catalog. *Graduate:* see undergraduate.

On-Campus Requirements: None.

Tuition and Fees: *Undergraduate:* $138/credit resident, $338/credit nonresident. *Graduate:* $164/credit resident, $363/credit nonresident. *Application Fee:* $30. *Credit by:* semester.

Financial Aid: Federal Stafford Loan, Federal Perkins Loan, Federal PLUS Loan, Federal SEOG, Federal Work-Study, Federal Pell Grant, VA, Montana resident programs.

Accreditation: Northwest Association of Schools and Colleges.

Description: Montana State University, Northern (1929) is a state-supported, coeducational university with affiliate campuses in Bozeman, Billings, and Great Falls. Northern serves a vast area of 32,000 square miles, including 4 Indian reservations. Constituencies include undergraduate students with traditional goals, students seeking specific knowledge or skills, and graduate students seeking master's degrees. Northern is a statewide resource for technology education and economic development, and it functions as a cultural resource and continuing education center for north central Montana. Through NorthNet, MSU–Northern is the primary provider of higher education to rural place-bound Montana residents in its 53 service communities. During the day, public schools use VisionNet to share teachers and special classes. Then MSU–Northern uses the system for college courses at night. Also, through MSU–Northern's QuickStart program, high school students may take our college-level courses during their school day.

Montana Tech of the University of Montana

1300 West Park Street	Phone: (406) 496-4311
Butte, MT 59701	Fax: (406) 496-4116

Division(s): Continuing Education and Extended Studies
Web Site(s): http://www.mtech.edu
E-mail: kburgher@mtech.edu
suanderson@mtech.edu

Undergraduate Degree Programs:
Occupational Safety/Health
Project Engineering and Management

Class Titles: Industrial Hygiene, Engineering/Tech, Sampling/Evaluation of Health Hazards, Safety Administration, Construction Safety, Industrial Toxicology, Fire Protection, Hazardous Material Management, Business/Professional Writing, Web-Based Accel Introduction to Computer Science, Microcomputer Software, Medical Terminology, Computer Concepts, Nursing Concepts, Transition to Registered Nursing, Web Page Design, Writing, Pollution Prevention, Management Economics/

Accounting, Entrepreneurship/Economic Feasibility, Financial Management of Technological Enterprises, Hazardous Waste Engineering, Information Technology for Managers, Application/Design of Industrial Experiments, Energy Conversion, Project Engineering/Management, Computer Applications in Engineering, Management Seminar, Legal Issues Related to PE & M.

Teaching Methods: *Computers:* Internet, electronic classroom, e-mail. *Other:* videoconferencing, fax, correspondence, independent study.

Credits Granted for: examination (CLEP, DANTES), ACE/PONSI military training program, ACE/PONSI business training program.

Admission Requirements: *Undergraduate:* application and fee, high school transcript. *Graduate:* same as undergraduate.

On-Campus Requirements: Currently under review.

Tuition and Fees: *Undergraduate:* resident lower level $176.95/credit, resident upper level $187.95/credit, out-of-state lower level $436.65/credit, out-of-state upper level $474.65/credit. *Graduate:* resident $195.70/credit, out-of-state $522.95/credit. *Application Fee:* $30. *Software:* variable. *Other Costs:* all OSH classes: $850/class, Master of Project Engineering and Management $1,280/class, lab fee: variable. *Credit by:* semester.

Financial Aid: Federal Stafford Loan, Federal Perkins Loan, Federal PLUS Loan, Federal Pell Grant, Federal Work-Study, VA, Montana resident programs.

Accreditation: Northwest Association of Schools and Colleges, ABET, ACS.

Description: Montana Tech of the University of Montana (1881) is one of 6 institutions that comprise the Montana University System. Montana Tech enrollment remains on a steady upward track, currently approaching 2,000 students, Three quarters of the student body receive some form of financial aid. Montana Tech features a 15:1 student-to-faculty ratio, providing ample opportunity for individual attention. Classes are taught by professors who possess a unique blend of academic and industrial experience. Graduates traditionally enjoy a 95% placement rate and garner starting salaries that exceed national averages in their respective degree areas.

Monterey Peninsula College

| 980 Fremont Street | Phone: (831) 646-4000 |
| Monterey, CA 93940 | Fax: (831) 655-2627 |

Division(s): Community Education
Web Site(s): http://www.mpc.edu

Undergraduate Degree Programs:
Associate of Arts
Associate of Science

Certificate Programs: Contact school for more information.

Class Titles: Contact school for more information.

Teaching Methods: *Computers:* Internet, CD-ROM. *TV:* videotape. *Other:* independent study.

Credits Granted for: experiential learning, examination (CLEP, ACT-PEP, DANTES, GRE).

Admission Requirements: *Undergraduate:* contact school for more information. *Certificate:* contact school for more information.

On-Campus Requirements: 12 units in residency.

Tuition and Fees: *Undergraduate:* $11/unit in state; $134/unit out of state. *Credit by:* semester.

Financial Aid: Federal Stafford Loan, Federal Perkins Loan, Federal PLUS Loan, Federal Pell Grant, Federal Work-Study, VA, California resident programs.

Accreditation: Western Association of Colleges and Schools.

Description: Monterey Peninsula College (1947), one of 107 colleges in the California Community College System, is the focal point for learning beyond secondary school. The college offers courses to prepare students for transfer to 4-year institutions, to prepare for the workplace, to update their work skills or prepare for a new career, to provide students with a general education, and to improve their basic skills.

Montgomery College

| 7362 Calhoun Drive | Phone: (240) 315-3030 |
| Rockville, MD 20855 | Fax: (240) 315-3007 |

Division(s): Office of Distance Learning
Web Site(s): http://www.montgomerycollege.org
E-mail: DL@mc.cc.md.us

Undergraduate Degree Programs:
Associate of Arts (AA)
Associate of Science (AS)
Associate of Applied Science (AAS)

Certificate Programs: Most of Montgomery College's departments offer a certificate program.

Class Titles: Contact the school or check web site for details.

Teaching Methods: *Computers:* Internet, real-time chat, e-mail, CD-ROM. *TV:* videotape, cable program, PBS. *Other:* videoconferencing.

Credits Granted for: experiential learning, portfolio assessment, examination (CLEP, ACT-PEP, DANTES, GRE).

Admission Requirements: *Undergraduate:* 18 years old or high school graduates. Those not meeting these criteria will be considered on an individual basis.

On-Campus Requirements: There are no collegewide requirements for on-campus attendance. Individual faculty may include such requirements.

Tuition and Fees: *Undergraduate:* $72/credit (for Montgomery County residents), $150/credit (for Maryland residents outside Montgomery County), $196/credit (for out-of-state residents). *Application Fees:* $25. *Other Costs:* consolidated fee 20% of total tuition, with a $50 minimum. *Facilities Fee:* $1/credit hour. *Credit by:* semester.

Financial Aid: Federal Stafford Loan, Federal Perkins Loan, Federal PLUS Loan, Federal Pell Grant, Federal Work-Study, VA, state programs for residents of Maryland.

Accreditation: Middle States Association of Colleges and Schools.

Description: Montgomery College (1946) is an open-access, public education community college dedicated to academic excellence and committed to student success. With 3 campuses and a Distance Learning presence, Montgomery College is integrally involved in the community and offers broad-based, high-quality educational opportunities to meet the needs of a diverse population. The college entered the field of Distance Learning more than 20 years ago with courses offered on television. More recently, a variety of courses have been offered on the Internet. Currently, the college offers approximately 50 courses in disciplines such as advertising art computer applications, English, history, management, psychology, and sociology on the Internet each semester.

Montgomery County Community College

340 Dekalb Pike, PO Box 400	Phone: (215) 641-6593
Blue Bell, PA 19422	Fax: (215) 619-7182

Division(s): Office of Distance Learning
Web Site(s): http://www.mc3.edu
E-mail: For Questions re Distance Learning: aconnoll@mc3.edu
For Registration Information: jleaver@mc3.edu

Undergraduate Degree Programs:
Associate in General Studies
Associate in Science in:
    Liberal Studies
    Business Administration

Certificate Programs: International Studies, Specialty Certificate in Computer Systems.

Class Titles: Accounting, Anthropology, Biology, Business Management, Career Development, Computer Science, Criminal Justice, Dental Hygiene, Economics, Earth Science, Education, Engineering, English (Writing and Literature), Foreign Languages, History, Marketing, Mathematics, Nursing, Philosophy, Physical Education and Health, Political Science, Psychology, Sociology.

Teaching Methods: *Computers:* Internet, electronic classroom, e-mail, newsgroup, LISTSERV. *TV:* videotape. PBS. *Other:* videoconferencing, independent study.

Credits Granted for: experiential learning, portfolio assessment, extrainstitutional learning, examination (CLEP, ACT-PEP, DANTES, GRE).

Admission Requirements: *Undergraduate:* as a community college, MCCC welcomes all students, including high school students, transfer students, adult learners, and international students.

On-Campus Requirements: There is no on-campus requirement for any Distance Learning course, but students may be required to enlist an approved proctor for some course assessments.

Tuition and Fees: *Undergraduate:* $75/credit in-county, $150/credit out-of-county, $225/credit, out-of-state. *Application Fee:* $25. *Other Costs:* Technology, Student Activity, Comprehensive fees: $7/credit. *Credit by:* semester.

Financial Aid: Federal Stafford Loan, Federal Perkins Loan, Federal PLUS Loan, Federal Pell Grant, Federal Work-Study, VA, Pennsylvania resident programs.

Accreditation: Middle States Association of Colleges and Schools.

Description: Founded in 1964, MCCC is a comprehensive community college, offering more than 70 associate degrees and certificates as well as numerous continuing education opportunities and cultural experiences. The college has been involved in distance education since the early 1990s and currently offers approximately 80 courses online, over the air, and through videoconferencing.

Moraine Valley Community College

10900 South 88 Avenue	Phone: (708) 974-5288
Palos Hills, IL 60465	Fax: (708) 974-1184

Division(s): Academic affairs
Web Site(s): http://www.mv.cc.il.us
E-mail: grund@moraine.cc.il.us

Class Titles: See web site.

Teaching Methods: *Computers:* Internet, electronic classroom. *TV:* videotape. *Other:* None.

Credits Granted for: experiential learning, examination (CLEP).

Admission Requirements: *Undergraduate:* placement tests for math and English.

On-Campus Requirements: None.

Tuition and Fees: *Undergraduate:* see web site. *Credit by:* semester.

Financial Aid: Federal Pell Grant, Federal Work-Study, VA, Illinois resident programs.

Accreditation: North Central Association of Colleges and Schools.

Description: Moraine Valley Community College (1967) is a public community college located in the southwest suburbs of Chicago. Selected courses are available via the Internet and videotape.

Morehead State University

213D Bert T. Combs Building	Phone: (606) 783-2183
Morehead, KY 40351	Fax: (606) 783-5025

Division(s): MBA Program
Web Site(s): http://www.moreheadstate.edu/colleges/business/mba
E-mail: msu-mba@morehead-st.edu

Graduate Degree Programs:
Master of Business Administration

Class Titles: Contact school or check web site for details.

Teaching Methods: *Computers:* Internet, real-time chat, electronic classroom, e-mail, CD-ROM, newsgroup, LISTSERV. *TV:* videotape, satellite broadcasting. *Other:* independent study.

Admission Requirements: *Graduate:* bachelor's degree from accredited institution and GMAT exam.

On-Campus Requirements: None.

Tuition and Fees: *Graduate:* $163/credit. *Other Costs:* $90 for technology fee. *Credit by:* semester.

Financial Aid: Federal Stafford Loan, Federal Perkins Loan, Federal PLUS Loan.

Accreditation: Association of Collegiate Business Schools and Programs.

Description: Morehead State University (1922) has about 8,300 students from 100 Kentucky counties, 40 other states, and 32 nations. Morehead State was the first institution in Kentucky to offer a complete degree program, the Master of Business Administration (MBA), totally through the World Wide Web.

Mortgage Bankers Association of America

1919 Pennsylvania Avenue, NW	Phone: (202) 557-2785
Washington, DC 20006	Fax: (202) 721-0194

Division(s): CampusMBA—The Learning Center for Real Estate Finance
Web Site(s): http://www.campusmba.org
E-mail: campusmba@mbaa.org

Class Titles: CampusMBA currently offers over 60 courses in the following subject areas: residential loan production, residential loan administration, secondary marketing, quality assurance and risk analysis, commercial real estate finance, and mortgage industry leadership.

Teaching Methods: *Computers:* Internet (Web-based training), videotape (video-based training). *Other:* print-based training, self-study learning.

Credits Granted for: Forty-four of CampusMBA's courses have been reviewed and recommended for college credit by the American Council on Education (ACE) College Credit Recommendation Service (CREDIT), formerly PONSI. For more information, visit http://www.campusmba.org/ and click on "College Credit." Credit acceptance or transfer of ACE CREDIT recommended courses is largely determined by the policy of the dean or registrar of the receiving college or university. ACE's CREDIT recommendation of courses is not a guarantee that credit will transfer to any college or university.

Admission Requirements: *Undergraduate:* no prerequisites.

On-Campus Requirements: None.

Tuition and Fees: *Undergraduate:* $185/Web-based course, $290/print-based courses, $260/video-based courses. Some courses require purchase of additional textbook. Students employed by a company that is a member of the Mortgage Bankers Association of America receive substantial discounts.

Accreditation: Distance Education and Training Council.

Description: The Mortgage Bankers Association of America (MBAA) is the only national association representing the real estate finance industry. Established in 1914, its membership of over 3,000 companies includes all elements of real estate finance: residential and commercial mortgage lenders, mortgage brokers, commercial banks, and others in the mortgage lending field. CampusMBA is the main educational arm for the Mortgage Bankers Association. The association began training mortgage banking professionals in 1948, later offering correspondence courses in the 1960s. For more than 30 years, mortgage banking professionals have gained the necessary knowledge and skills required to stay on top of their field without leaving the home or office. CampusMBA, specifically created to house MBA's Distance Learning curriculum, offers affordable training in web-based, print-based, or video-based Distance Learning formats. CampusMBA educates the real estate finance community with the highest standards of quality, value, and convenience, 24 hours a day, 7 days a week.

Mott Community College

1401 East Court Street　　**Phone:** (800) 398-2715
Flint, MI 48503　　　　　　(810) 762-5686
　　　　　　　　　　　　　　　Fax: (810) 762-0282

Division(s): College in the Workplace
Web Site(s): http://edtech.mcc.edu/cwp
E-mail: lfrance@edtech.mcc.edu

Undergraduate Degree Programs:
Associate in Arts
Associate in Science
Associate in General Studies
Associate in Applied Science:
　　General Business
　　Computer Occupations Technology

Certificate Programs: Computer Programming.

Teaching Methods: *Computers:* Internet, e-mail, CD-ROM, LISTSERV. *TV:* videotape, broadcasting, PBS. *Other:* videoconferencing, audiotapes, fax, independent study.

Credits Granted for: transfer credits from regionally accredited colleges only.

Admission Requirements: *Undergraduate:* registration forms are online at http://edtech.mcc.edu/cwp/start.html or call 800-398-2715.

On-Campus Requirements: None.

Tuition and Fees: *Undergraduate:* $450/course regardless of credit hours. *Other Costs:* $35/semester registration fee. *Credit by:* semester.

Financial Aid: Federal Stafford Loan, Federal PLUS Loan, Federal Pell Grant, Federal Work-Study, VA, Michigan resident programs.

Accreditation: North Central Association of Colleges and Schools.

Description: Mott Community College (1923) began its distance learning offerings in 1981, expanding into the College in the Workplace program in 1992 in order to better serve employees of manufacturing companies by delivering distance learning degrees totally campus-free. This program offers associate degrees through video-based and online courses. Convenient home study with flexible worksite testing allows students to earn their degrees while working full-time.

Mount Hood Community College

26000 Southeast Stark Street　　**Phone:** (503) 491-6953
Gresham, OR 97030　　　　　　　**Fax:** (503) 491-7389

Division(s): Distance Education Program
Web Site(s): http://www.mhcc.cc.or.us
http://www.oregoncolleges.online.org
E-mail: vogtc@mhcc.cc.or.us

Class Titles: Medical Terminology, Psychology, Health, Speech, Science, Management, Accounting, Computer Concepts, Literature, Keyboarding, Nutrition, Stress Management, Weight Management, Report Writing, Study Skills, Child Abuse, Medical Coding, Economics.

Teaching Methods: *Computers:* Internet, e-mail, LISTSERV. *TV:* videotape, cable program, satellite broadcasting, PBS. *Other:* audioconferencing, videoconferencing, audiotapes, fax, correspondence, independent study, individual study, learning contracts.

Admission Requirements: *Undergraduate:* placement exams, state identification showing residency and birth date, social security number. *Certificate:* same as undergraduate.

On-Campus Requirements: some meetings for telecourses, proctored tests for online classes arranged throughout the community.

Tuition and Fees: *Undergraduate:* $42.50/credit in-state, $138.50/credit out-of-state. *Other Costs:* $20 distance education course fees. *Credit by:* quarter.

Financial Aid: Federal Stafford Loan, Federal Perkins Loan, Federal PLUS Loan, Federal Pell Grant, Federal Work-Study, VA, Oregon resident programs.

Accreditation: Northwest Association of Schools and Colleges.

Description: Mount Hood Community College (1966) offers classes to its 30,000 students at the 200-acre main campus in Gresham, the MHCC Maywood Park Center, the Thompson Center, and at evening education centers in district public schools. MHCC offers general education instruction that permeates each of the college's 3 degrees: AAS, AGS, and AAOT, plus a variety of vocational certificates. The college strives to maintain effective, quality education within a comprehensive range of learning experiences that include traditional and nontraditional offerings. In the early 1980s, MHCC began offering distance education through telecourses over the local cablecast access channel and now offers courses online. With the growing demand placed on colleges to offer alternatives to the traditional way of learning, MHCC has dedicated itself to expanding and strengthening its distance education program.

Mount St. Vincent University

166 Bedford Highway	Phone: (902) 457-6437
Halifax, NS, Canada B3M 2J6	(800) 665-3838 (in Canada)
	Fax: (902) 457-6455

Division(s): Distance Learning/Continuing Education
Web Site(s): http://www.msvu.ca or http://www.msvu.ca/distance
E-mail: distance@msvu.ca

Undergraduate Programs:
Arts
Sciences
Tourism and Hospitality Management
Business Administration
Gerontology

Graduate Degree Programs:
Master of Education in Literacy Education
Master of Adult Education

Certificate Programs: Proficiency in French, Marketing, Tourism and Hospitality Management, Gerontology, Business, Information Management, Human Ecology, Accounting.

Class Titles: over 50 courses offered in general fields of English, Gerontology, Marketing, Math, French, History, Business, Tourism/Hospitality, Psychology, Adult Education, Literacy Education.

Teaching Methods: *Computers:* Internet, real-time chat, electronic classroom, e-mail, CD-ROM, newsgroup, LISTSERV. *TV:* videotape, cable program, satellite broadcasting. *Other:* audioconferencing, audiographics, fax, correspondence, independent study, individual study, learning contracts.

Credits Granted for: experiential learning, portfolio assessment, extrainstitutional learning, examination (CLEP, ACT-PEP, DANTES, GRE), transfer from other institutions.

Admission Requirements: *Undergraduate:* high school graduate or mature admission. *Graduate:* undergraduate degree. *Certificate:* similar to other undergraduate admission requirements; i.e., high school completion, or mature admission if out of school for more than 5 years. We are very flexible; pro-

fessors can choose to admit students at their discretion, even if the above criteria are not met.

On-Campus Requirements: None.

Tuition and Fees: Please contact school. *Application Fee:* $30. *Other Costs:* varies for books and course materials. *Credit by:* semester.

Financial Aid: scholarships and bursaries.

Accreditation: Association of Universities and Colleges of Canada.

Description: Mount St. Vincent University (1873) currently offers more than 50 distance education courses, many that lead to certificates, degrees, and diplomas. These courses are delivered through several modes, including TV broadcast, videotapes, audiographics, and recently via the Web. All distance courses include print materials, and sophisticated technology allows abundant interaction between students and professors. The university pioneered distance education in Maritime Canada, and for nearly 20 years has been expanding its offerings, employing increasingly user-friendly technology and reaching students ever further afield. Today, distance enrollment exceeds 1,000 and includes students from across Canada, the U.S., the Caribbean, the Middle East, and Africa. The language of instruction is English.

Mount Wachusett Community College

| 444 Green Street | Phone: (978) 632-6600 x275 |
| Gardner, MA 01440 | Fax: (978) 632-6155 |

Division(s): Division of Continuing Education and Community Services
Web Site(s): http://www.mwcc.mass.edu
E-mail: m_howlett@mwcc.mass.edu

Undergraduate Degree Programs:
Associate of Science in:
    Business Administration Transfer
    Business Administration Career
    Criminal Justice
    General Studies
    General Human Services

Teaching Methods: Web-based classes using Blackboard delivery software that incorporates discussion groups, online testing, and e-mail. *TV:* videotapes; PBS telecourses.

Credits Granted for: experiential learning, portfolio assessment, extrainstitutional learning, examination (CLEP, DANTES).

Admission Requirements: *Undergraduate:* application, official high school transcript or copy of GED certificate.

On-Campus Requirements: Web-based classes have no on-campus requirements, Telecourses may require on-campus orientation and testing, depending upon instructor.

Tuition and Fees: Tuition/credit hour: $25; college fees/credit hour: $62. *Application Fee:* $10 (nonrefundable). *Registration Fee:* $20/semester; Masspirg (optional): $7/semester. *Technology Access Fee:* $35/semester. *Health insurance:* $525 (September-August). *LEM* (laboratory, equipment, and materials). *Fee:* $10/credit. *Student Activity Fee:* $20/semester for students taking 9 credits or more per semester. *Audit Fee:* DCE evening course audit fee equals the cost of a credit course. Books (estimated: $50–$100/course). *Credit by:* semester.

Financial Aid: Federal Stafford Loan, Federal Perkins Loan, Federal PLUS Loan, Federal Pell Grant, Federal Work-Study, VA.

Accreditation: New England Association of Schools and Colleges.

Description: Mount Wachusett Community College (1963) is an accredited, public 2-year institution serving 29 cities and towns in North Central Massachusetts. The 269-acre main campus is located in Gardner, Massachusetts; satellite sites are located in Leominster, Fitchburg, Athol, and Devens. The college offers over 50 associate degree and certificate programs, as well as adult basic education/GED programs, education and training for business and industry, and noncredit community service programs. MWCC's corporate training programs are offered through the Leominster Campus and Corporate Training Center. MWCC students enjoy many support services and resources including the Fitness and Wellness Center, the Academic Support Center, and the 555-seat Theater at the Mount. Courses are offered in the day, evening, and on weekends, and via the Internet. Distance learning programs began in 1997 to sustain a learning environment responsive to the needs of a population diverse in culture and life experiences. The college continues to develop innovative methods to deliver its services to students who cannot physically attend classes and lectures.

Mountain State University (formerly The College of West Virginia)

609 South Kanawha Street	Phone: (304) 253-7351
PO Box 9003	(888) 915-2915
Beckley, WV 25802-9003	Fax: (304) 253-9059

Division(s): School of Extended and Distance Learning
Web Site(s): http://www.cwv.edu/saell
E-mail: saell@cwv.edu

Undergraduate Degree Programs:
Associate of Science in:
  Aviation Technology (must be a licensed pilot)
  Banking and Finance
  Business Administrations (concentrations in Accounting, Business Law, General Business, Management, and Office Management)
  Computer Information Technology*
  Computer Networking Technology*
  Criminal Justice
  Environmental Studies
  Marketing
  Medical Assisting
  Secretarial Science (concentrations in Administrative, Legal, and Medical) Travel
Associate of Arts in:
  Elementary Teacher Preparation
  Secondary Teacher Preparation
Associate of Science, Associate of Arts in General Studies
Bachelor of Science in:
  Business Administration (concentrations in Accounting, Business Law, General Business, Management, Office Management)
  Computer Networking*
  Criminal Justice
  Health Care Management (concentrations in Administration and Medical Informatics)
  Internet and E-Commerce*
  Marketing
  Bachelor of Science, Bachelor of Arts in Interdisciplinary Studies (concentrations in Biology, Environmental Studies, Health Services Management, Natural Sciences, Psychology, Pre-Medicine, Social and Behavioral Sciences)
  RN-BSN Pathway
* Offered via partnership with SMARTFORCE

Certificate Programs: Aviation Technology (must be a licensed pilot), Business, General Business, Office Technology (Secretarial, Word Processing), Travel.

Class Titles: Accounting, Art, Astronomy, Banking, Biology, Business Law, Chemistry, Computer Information Systems, Communications, Criminal Justice, Economics, English, Environmental Studies, Finance, Geography, Geology, Gerontology, Health Care Administration, Health Care Medical Informatics, History, Health Sciences, Hospitality, Health Science Education, Humanities, Interdisciplinary Studies, International Business, Legal Studies, Medical Assisting, Mathematics, Meteorology, Management, Marketing, Nursing, Office Management, Philosophy, Physical Science, Physics, Political Science, Psychology, Secretarial Science, Sociology, Social Work, Social Sciences, Travel, and Word Processing.

Teaching Methods: *Computers:* Internet, e-mail CD-ROM. *TV:* videotape. *Other:* fax, correspondence, independent study, individual study.

Credits Granted for: experiential learning, portfolio assessment, extrainstitutional learning, examination (CLEP, ACT-PEP, DANTES, GRE).

Admission Requirements: *Undergraduate:* open admission policy, high school diploma or equivalency. *Admissions process:* application, application fee of $25, official transcripts from all schools previously attended. *Certificate:* Same.

On-Campus Requirements: None. Students must complete a minimum of 12 hours if pursuing an associate degree and a minimum of 18 hours if pursuing a baccalaureate degree of coursework at MSU before earning their degree. Coursework can be completed through traditional (on-campus) courses or independent study courses (distance learning).

Tuition and Fees: *Undergraduate:* $180/credit beginning Fall 2001. *Application Fee:* $25. Graduation Fee: $35. *Credit by:* semester.

Financial Aid: Federal Stafford Loan, Federal PLUS Loan, Federal Pell Grant, Federal Work-Study, VA. West Virginia resident programs.

Accreditation: North Central Association of Colleges and Schools.

Description: Mountain State University is a private, not-for-profit institution located in southern West Virginia. The institution began as Beckley College in 1933. Founded as a 2-year institution during the Great Depression, Beckley College sought to provide affordable and quality education in marketable business skills for the youth of southern West Virginia. Today, Mountain State University (MSU) offers baccalaureate programs as well as graduate degree programs. MSU continues to provide programs that will lead to gainful employment for its graduates. MSU remains committed to the founding philosophy of Beckley College that every individual should have the opportunity to obtain an education and maximize his/her potential.

The School of Extended and Distance Learning (formerly The School of Academic Enrichment and Lifelong Learning) began as a separate school within the institution in 1995. The School of Extended and Distance Learning (SEDL) offers many progressive degree programs specifically designed for individuals who wish to begin and/or complete a college degree but find it difficult or impossible to attend traditional classes. By providing diverse and alternative methods for learning and earning college-level credit, SEDL is uniquely suited to meet the educational needs of busy adults with varied degree needs and lifestyles.

Mt. San Antonio College

| 1100 North Grand Avenue | Phone: (909) 594-5611 x5658 |
| Walnut, CA 91789 | Fax: (909) 468-3992 |

Division(s): Learning Resources
Web Site(s): http://vclass.mtsac.edu/distance/
E-mail: kstern@mtsac.edu

Class Titles: Business Organization/Management, Small Business Management, Principles of Business, General Psychology, Sociology, Marriage/Family, Physical Anthropology, General Cultural Anthropology, Child Growth/Development, Creative Writing-Poetry, Philosophy, Accounting, Biology.

Teaching Methods: *Computers:* Internet, e-mail, newsgroup, LISTSERV. *TV:* videotape, cable program, PBS. *Other:* fax.

Admission Requirements: *Undergraduate:* some courses have prerequisites. Must complete within a semester.

On-Campus Requirements: Students must be on campus for midterms and finals.

Tuition and Fees: *Undergraduate:* $11/unit in-state, $130/unit out-of-state. $154/unit Nonresident F-1 Visa Foreign Students. *Application Fee:* $30. *Credit by:* semester.

Financial Aid: Federal Perkins Loan, Federal Pell Grant, Federal Work-Study, VA, California resident programs.

Accreditation: Western Association of Schools and Colleges.

Description: Mt. San Antonio College opened in 1946. The 421-acre college site was originally part of the 48,000-acre La Puente Rancho. With an enrollment of 38,544, MSAC is the ninth largest overall district and largest single-campus, 2-year college district in California. The distance learning program began with televised courses in 1993 and introduced Internet courses in the fall of 1997.

Mt. San Jacinto College

| 1499 North State Street | Phone: (909) 487-6752 |
| San Jacinto, CA 92583 | Fax: (909) 487-1903 |

Web Site(s): http://www.msjc.cc.ca.us/dlearning
E-mail: dhelms@msjc.cc.ca.us

Undergraduate Degree Programs:
Associate of Arts
Associate of Science

Certificate Programs: multiple; contact school for details.

Class Titles: Health Science, Nutrition, Communication.

Teaching Methods: *Computers:* Internet, real-time chat, electronic classroom, e-mail. *TV:* videotape, cable program, PBS. *Other:* videoconferencing.

Credits Granted for: examination (CLEP).

Admission Requirements: *Undergraduate:* 18 years of age or high school diploma.

On-Campus Requirements: Telecourses require attendance at 5 class meetings. Each class meeting is 3 hours.

Tuition and Fees: *Undergraduate:* $11/credit. *Other Costs:* book costs vary. *Credit by:* semester.

Financial Aid: Federal Stafford Loan, Federal Perkins Loan, Federal PLUS Loan, Federal Pell Grant, Federal Work-Study, VA, California resident programs.

Accreditation: Western Association of Schools and Colleges.

Description: The college enrolled its first students in the fall of 1963, holding classes in rented facilities. The San Jacinto Campus was opened in 1965 with 2 buildings and has grown into a comprehensive college campus serving the needs of students and the community. In 1975 the residents of Temecula, Lake Elsinore, Perris, and adjacent areas voted to join the Mt. San Jacinto Community College District, increasing the college's area to the present 1,700 square miles. Although the boundaries have remained stable since 1975, the district has changed dramatically, especially since the 1980s. In recent years, unprecedented population growth has fostered the highest rate of enrollment increase of all 107 community colleges. In response to this intense growth, Mt. San Jacinto College opened its Menifee Valley Campus in October 1990. By the end of its first year, there were 2,100 students attending classes at the Menifee Valley Campus. MSJC began offering telecourses in 1996 and online courses in 2001.

Murray State University

303 Sparks Hall	Phone: (800) 669-7654
Murray, KY 42071	Fax: (502) 762-3593

Division(s): Continuing Education and Academic Outreach
Web Site(s): http://murraystate.edu
E-mail: kendra.marsh@murraystate.edu

Undergraduate Degree Programs:
Bachelor of Independent Studies

Class Titles: Correspondence Study, Animal Science, Poultry Science, World Civilizations, Personal Health, American Experience to 1865, American Experience Since 1865, New Technologies, Business Law, College Algebra, Records Management, Office Administration, Logic, American National Government, International Relations, Recreation/Leisure Services. *Internet courses:* Over 60 offered.

Teaching Methods: *Computers:* Internet, real-time chat, electronic classroom, e-mail, CD-ROM, newsgroup, LISTSERV.

TV: videotape, cable program, satellite broadcasting, PBS. *Other:* radio broadcast, videoconferencing, audioconferencing, audiographics, audiotapes, fax, correspondence, independent study, individual study, learning contracts.

Credits Granted for: portfolio assessment, extrainstitutional learning, examination (CLEP, ACT-PEP, DANTES, GRE) experiential learning.

Admission Requirements: *Undergraduate:* application for admission, official transcripts from all colleges attended, complete BIS 101 or BIS 300, introductory courses for the program, official high school transcript or GED test score. If you already have more than 24 semester hours college credits, you need not submit high school transcripts or ACT test score. You can be admitted to the Bachelor of Independent Studies degree program only if you have 12 semester hours of college credits. The purpose of these courses is to provide students with enough information to decide whether the BIS degree will meet their educational goals. Gain admission to Murray State University from the Admissions and Registrar's Office. Please note that your application must include the application form, required transcripts, and report of ACT scores if required. The Admissions Office will admit you only after your application is complete. At that time you may register for classes.

On-Campus Requirements: degree requirements: 128 semester hours required, 32 hours at Murray State, 40 upper-division hours, 61 4-year college hours. Persons who can schedule on-campus classes can usually complete the 32 hours of Murray State courses in almost any subject, but students at a greater distance will find their choice of courses limited. BIS advisers will provide information by telephone to prospective students.

Tuition and Fees: Please contact the Bursar's Office at (270) 762-4226 for current tuition rates. *Application Fee:* $25. *Credit by:* semester.

Financial Aid: Federal Stafford Loan, Federal Perkins Loan, Federal PLUS Loan, Federal Pell Grant, Federal Work-Study, VA, Kentucky resident programs.

Accreditation: Southern Association of Colleges and Schools.

Description: Murray State University (1922) recognizes its responsibilities to its designated service regions and to non-traditional students who desire educational opportunities. The function of the Center for Continuing Education and Academic Outreach is to organize all extended campus courses, correspondence, educational TV activities, workshops, conferences, noncredit courses, community education, military programs and adult outreach programs. Murray State University is a member of the Association for Continuing Higher Education.

Naropa University

2130 Arapahoe Avenue	Phone: (303) 444-0202
Boulder, CO 80302	Fax: (303) 245-4749

Division(s): Department of Distance Learning
Web Site(s): http://www.ecampus.naropa.edu
E-mail: registrar@ecampus.naropa.edu

Undergraduate Degree Programs: Contact school.

Graduate Degree Programs:
Masters in Contemplative Education.

Postgraduate Degree Programs: Contact school.

Certificate Programs: Graduate Certificate in Ecopsychology.

Class Titles: Psychology, Environmental Studies, Religious Studies, Buddhist Studies, Tibetan Language, Writing and Poetics.

Teaching Methods: *Computers:* Internet, real-time chat, electronic classroom, e-mail, fax.

Credits Granted for: experiential learning, portfolio assessment.

Admission Requirements: *Undergraduate:* Application form, $35 fee, 2–4-page statement of interest, 2 letters of recommendation, official postsecondary transcripts, high school transcript or GED (for less than 30 college credits), and supplemental departmental application. *Graduate:* application form, $50 fee, 3–5-page statement of interest, 3 letters of recommendation, résumé, official transcript indicating BA from accredited institution; prerequisites depend on department, and supplemental departmental application. *Certificate:* same as graduate.

On-Campus Requirements: individual courses require no on-campus meetings; however, short residency components in Boulder or other locations are required for completion of degree and certificates.

Tuition and Fees: *Undergraduate:* $483/credit. *Graduate:* $489/credit. *Postgraduate:* $489/credit. *Application Fee:* $50. *Other Costs:* $40/credit hour for technology for online classes. *Credit by:* semester.

Financial Aid: Federal Stafford Loan, Federal Perkins Loan, Federal PLUS Loan, Federal Pell Grant, Federal Work-Study, VA, state programs for residents of Colorado.

Accreditation: North Central Association of Schools and Colleges.

Description: Naropa University (1976) is a private, nonprofit, fully accredited liberal arts college offering undergraduate and graduate degrees in transpersonal psychology, contemplative psychology, Buddhist studies, writing, environmental studies, gerontology, somatic psychology, early childhood education, and more. Naropa is nonsectarian and characterized by its unique Buddhist educational heritage. Naropa's community embraces diversity; all are encouraged to apply.

Nassau Community College

One Education Drive	Phone: (516) 572-7883
Garden City, NY 11530-6793	Fax: (516) 572-0690

Division(s): College of the Air
Web Site(s): http://www.sunynassau.edu
E-mail: friedma@sunynassau.edu

Undergraduate Degree Programs:
Associate

Class Titles: Accounting, Art History, Business, Communications, Economics, English Literature, Film History/Appreciation, History, Italian, Business Law, Mathematics, Marketing, Music Appreciation, Health, Psychology, Sociology, Spanish, French, Social Problems, Physical Science.

Teaching Methods: *Computers:* Internet, e-mail. *TV:* videotape, PBS. *Other:* radio broadcast, audiotapes, fax, correspondence, independent study.

Credits Granted for: experiential learning, portfolio assessment, examination.

Admission Requirements: *Undergraduate:* high school graduate (GED).

On-Campus Requirements: Yes, for degree.

Tuition and Fees: *Undergraduate:* $92/credit. *Application Fee:* $20. *Other Costs:* $6/credit student fee (maximum = $60/semester). *Technology Fee:* $25 (full time), $10 (part time). *Credit by:* semester.

Financial Aid: Federal Stafford Loan, Federal Perkins Loan, Federal PLUS Loan, Federal Pell Grant, Federal Work-Study, VA, New York resident programs.

Accreditation: Middle States Association of Colleges and Schools.

Description: Nassau Community College (1959) is a comprehensive full-opportunity institution of higher education created as part of the State University of New York. The college is dedicated to high-quality, low-cost education and career preparation. The college offers Associate of Arts, Associate of Science, and Associate of Applied Science degrees, certificates, and continuing education programs. The 225-acre campus is located in central Nassau County. Nassau Community College has a long history in distance learning activities, beginning with its participation in the University of the Air program in the early 1970s. Course offerings at off-campus sites and the development of the

College of the Air program in 1991 continue this tradition. Additional courses have been added to the program each semester. In the 1999–2000 academic year, distance learning registrations exceeded 1,800 units.

National Genealogical Society

4527 17th Street N	Phone: (703) 525-0050 x223
Arlington, VA 22207-2399	(800) 473-0060 x223
	Fax: (703) 525-0052

Division(s): Learning Center
Web Site(s): http://www.ngsgenealogy.org
E-mail: education@ngsgenealogy.org

Class Titles: American Genealogy (correspondence), Introduction to Genealogy (online).

Teaching Methods: *Computers:* Internet, e-mail. *Other:* fax, correspondence.

On-Campus Requirements: None.

Tuition and Fees: *Undergraduate:* $295/correspondence course if member, $375 if nonmember; $60/online course if member, $75 if nonmember.

Accreditation: Distance Education and Training Council.

Description: The National Genealogical Society (1903) is a nonprofit national, membership organization for those interested in genealogy and family history. The society's programs and services include a library, library loan program, quarterly journal, bimonthly newsletter, bimonthly computer interest group digest, distance education courses, annual conference, and publications sales. Its first distance education course, American Genealogy: A Basic Course, was launched in 1981. The society will offer a short course for beginners on its Web site in late 1998.

National Tax Training School

4 Melnick Drive	Phone: (800) 914-8138
Monsey, NY 10952	Fax: (845) 352-8138

Division(s): Education
Web Site(s): http://www.nattax.com
E-mail: info@nattax.com

Certificate Programs: Federal Income Tax Course, Higher Course in Federal Taxation, California CPE, Tax Relief Act of 2001 CPE.

Class Titles: Contact school or check web site for details.

Teaching Methods: correspondence.

Admission Requirements: *Certificate:* 2 years high school recommended.

On-Campus Requirements: None.

Tuition and Fees: Certificate: $274.75, shipping and handling $26.50. *Credit by:* hours.

Accreditation: Distance Education and Training Council (DETC).

Description: National Tax Training School (1952) is the oldest accredited and foremost specialized correspondence school of tax training and offers the only course that was especially prepared for home study. The courses are written in a clear, concise manner using language that is understood even by students who do not have an accounting background. Since NTTS is a publishing house of tax books and tax newsletters, it remains in contact with its former students who have established their own tax preparation firms. Many of these firms send NTTS their trainees to prepare them for their new duties. Many state governments, which require licenses for their tax preparers, recommend the NTTS courses to their applicants. The NTTS courses are more than study courses. They offer manuals to guide the trainees in establishing their practices and a 5-year updating service to keep the students aware of tax law changes.

National Technological University

700 Centre Avenue	Phone: (800) 582-9976
Fort Collins, CO 80526	Fax: (970) 498-0601

Division(s): Academic Division
Web Site(s): http://www.ntu.edu
E-mail: Rhonda@ntu.edu

Graduate Degree Programs:
Masters in:
 Business Administration
 Chemical Engineering
 Computer Engineering
 Computer Science
 Electrical Engineering
 Engineering Management
 Environmental Systems Management
 Information Systems
 Management of Technology
 Manufacturing Systems Engineering
 Materials Science and Engineering
 Mechanical Engineering
 Microelectronics and Semiconductor Engineering
 Optical Science
 Project Management
 Software Engineering
 Systems Engineering

Telecommunication
Special Majors Program

Certificate Programs: Available for NTU's Fast Track Program in Computer Science, undergraduate.

Teaching Methods: *Computers:* Internet, real-time chat, e-mail, CD-ROM, threaded discussion, pdf documents. *TV:* videotape, satellite broadcasting. *Other:* fax, correspondence, telephone.

Admission Requirements: cumulative grade point average (CGPA) of no less than 2.90 on a 4.00 scale in appropriate major. Special major applicants, however, need a GCPA of no less than 3.00. For complete admission requirements, please go to http://www.ntu.edu/. *Certificate:* varies.

On-Campus Requirements: None.

Tuition and Fees: *Graduate:* $625–$1,162/credit. *Application Fee:* $50. *Credit by:* semester.

Financial Aid: VA.

Accreditation: North Central Association of Colleges and Schools, The Higher Learning Commission.

Description: National Technological University is a private, nonprofit institution founded in 1984 to serve the advanced educational needs of today's busy, highly mobile engineers, scientists, and technical managers. NTU awards 19 master's degrees and various certificates of completion via 4 delivery methods, including satellite, online, CD-ROM, and videotape. Since its inception, NTU has granted more than 1,600 master's degrees to individuals who have completed their programs of study while working as full-time technical professionals and managers. NTU's master's degree programs offer curricula instructed by faculty from more than 50 universities and no disruption for part-time students whose jobs require travel.

National Training, Incorporated
National Truck Drivers School
National Heavy Equipment Operator School

188 College Drive	**Phone: (904) 272-4000**
Orange Park, FL 32065	**Fax: (904) 272-6702**

Division(s): Student Services
Web Site(s): http://www.truckschool.com
E-mail: http://www.earthmoverschool.com
http://www.truckschool.com
inforequests@nationaltrainingschools.com

Certificate Programs: Heavy Equipment Operator Program, Commercial Driver's License Preparation, Accelerated Commercial Driver's License Preparation, CDL Prepared Independent Trucker's program.

Teaching Methods: *Other:* independent study, individual study, resident training.

Credits Granted for: Confirmed Tractor Trailer Driving classes at an accredited institution.

Admission Requirements: *Certificate:* See Course Catalog, for individual programs, pass DOT physical examination.

On-Campus Requirements: Resident training requires 3 to 6 weeks of hands on training and some classroom hours.

Tuition and Fees: *Undergraduate:* $2,845–$5,045 (tuition prices can be subject to change). *Credit by:* year-round.

Financial Aid: VA/Dantes tuition assistance available; Workforce Investment Act (WIA); vocational rehabilitation; outside and in-house financing available based on credit criteria.

Accreditation: Distance Education and Training Council.

Description: National Training was established in 1978. It is a proprietary postsecondary vocational education school designed to serve individuals desiring basic year-round skills training, to prepare individuals with no (or limited) experience in the operation of heavy construction equipment operations and combination tractor-trailer for entry-level positions within their chosen industry. Instills in our students an awareness of all factors that will enable them to accomplish, maintain, and continue to enhance their skills. This is accomplished through our combination Homes Study and Resident Training (practical experience). Graduates in our programs will be knowledgeable and able to intelligently converse with both industry and enforcement personnel with regard to Department of Transportation safety rules and regulations as stated in the code of Federal Regulations and as defined by the Occupational Safety and Health Act.

National University

11255 North Torrey Pines Road	**Phone: (760) 642-8210**
La Jolla, CA 92037	**Fax: (760) 642-8709**

Division(s): Online Student Services
Web Site(s): http://www.nu.edu
E-mail: onlineadmissions@nu.edu

Undergraduate Degree Programs:
Associate of Arts
Bachelor of Business Administration
Bachelor of Science in:
    Criminal Justice
    Global Studies
    Nursing

Graduate Degree Programs:
Global Master of Business Administration
Master of Science in Electronic Commerce
Master of Arts in Teaching
Master of Science Educational Technology
Master of Science in:
 Educational Administration
 Instructional Technology
 Nursing
Master of Education in Cross-cultural Teaching
Master of Forensic Sciences

Certificate Programs: Multiple Subject Teaching Credential, Single Subject Teaching Credential, Cross-Cultural Language Academic Development Certificate, Criminal Justice, Educational Technology, Electronic Commerce.

Teaching Methods: *Computers:* Internet, threaded discussion, real-time chat, e-mail, CD-ROM. *TV:* videoteleconferencing. *Other:* videoconferencing, independent study with special approval.

Credits Granted for: extrainstitutional learning, examination (CLEP, ACT-PEP, DANTES, GRE).

Admission Requirements: *Undergraduate:* 5 years work experience. Transfer students must have a cumulative GPA of 2.0 or higher. *Graduate:* 2.5 GPA from a regionally accredited university. *Certificate:* varies for undergraduate or graduate programs.

On-Campus Requirements: Most programs can be completed in their entirety in an online format. Some of the California credential programs require some meetings and professional field experience.

Tuition and Fees: *Undergraduate:* $190/quarter unit or $855/course. *Graduate:* $213.33/quarter unit or $960/course/credit. *Graduation Fee:* $100. *Other Costs:* $25 to $85/course for textbooks. *Application Fee:* $60. *Credit by:* quarter.

Financial Aid: Federal Stafford Loan, Federal Perkins Loan, Federal PLUS Loan, Federal Pell Grant, Federal Work-Study, VA, California resident programs.

Accreditation: Western Association of Schools and Colleges.

Description: Founded in 1971, as an independent, nonprofit institution of higher learning, National University was among the first to recognize and focus on the unique needs of adult learners. National University is dedicated to making lifelong learning opportunities accessible, challenging, and relevant to a diverse population of adult learners. Its distinctive and intensive one-course-per-month format, multiple locations, flexible programs, and online degrees enable adults to complete graduate and undergraduate programs in an accelerated

time frame, while maintaining family and work responsibilities. National University is the second-largest private university in California. National offers 80 to 100 online courses per month representing undergraduate and graduate course work in business, technology, education, criminal justice, and liberal studies. National University students have access to the library's extensive online resources, which include more than 31,000 electronic books and 4,000 electronic journals and full-text periodical databases.

Native American Educational Services College

2838 West Peterson	Phone: (773) 761-5000
Chicago, IL 60659	Fax: (773) 761-3808

Division(s): Chicago Campus
Web Site(s): www.naes.edu
E-mail: chicagonaes@aol.com

Undergraduate Degree Programs:
Public Policy

Class Titles: Internet: Finding American Indian-Related Resources, Literature, Cinema, History, Law, Public Policy, Lakota, Ojibwe.

Teaching Methods: *Computers:* Internet, real-time chat, electronic classroom, e-mail. *Other:* videoconferencing, fax, correspondence, independent study, individual study, learning contracts.

Credits Granted for: experiential learning, examination (CLEP).

Admission Requirements: *Undergraduate:* involvement in American Indian community; degree candidates must make special request to enroll if under age 23 with no college experience. *Graduate:* involvement in American Indian community, accredited bachelor's degree.

On-Campus Requirements: 54 credits in residency for degree candidates.

Tuition and Fees: *Undergraduate:* $208/credit. *Graduate:* $225/credit. *Other Costs:* $70/semester. *Credit by:* semester.

Financial Aid: Federal Pell Grant; Federal Work-Study; Illinois, Wisconsin, Montana, Minnesota resident programs; tribal programs for tribal members (depends on tribe).

Accreditation: North Central Association of Colleges and Schools.

Description: Native American Educational Services College (1974) is the only private, American-Indian-controlled, BA-granting institution in the U.S. We have 2 urban campuses, in the Chicago and Minneapolis Indian communities, and 2 reservation campuses, at Menominee in Wisconsin and Fort Peck in eastern Montana. We offer one degree: a BA in Public Policy. The focus of instruction is community building, which is accomplished by understanding the community's history and culture, understanding how public policy works in the local arena, understanding social change, and working to make it happen. The liberal-arts education is project based in a majority of the course work. We are constantly trying to find the balance between incorporating traditional tribal knowledge and conventional, Western-based knowledge into the curriculum. Though the students work in small communities, their knowledge base must spread far beyond those communities to include the problems, solutions, and situations of other communities throughout Indian country in the U.S., in indigenous communities throughout the hemisphere, and indeed throughout the world. We entered distant learning in the spring of 1998 to help our students learn modern technology and to offer our courses at several campuses simultaneously.

Neumann College

One Neumann Drive
Aston, PA 19014-1298

(800) 9-NEUMANN
Phone: (610) 558-5616
Fax: (610) 558-5652

Division(s): Academic Affairs
Web Site(s): http://www.neumann.edu
http://www.neumannonline.org
E-mail: neumann@neumann.edu

Certificate Programs: Spirituality for Leadership Development (designed in association with Catholic Health Associates to assist leaders in religious and values-based institutions).

Class Titles: Art, Business, Education, English, Information Management, Literature, Nursing, Philosophy, Politics and Psychology, as well as accelerated 6-credit continuing adult and professional studies courses.

Teaching Methods: *Computers:* Internet electronic classroom, e-mail. *TV:* cable program, PBS. *Other:* videoconferencing via PictureTel, fax, independent study.

Credits Granted for: experiential learning, portfolio assessment, examination (CLEP, ACT-PEP, DANTES, GRE).

On-Campus Requirements: Dependent upon program; usually none (e.g. except for Spirituality for Leadership Development Certificate).

Tuition and Fees: *Undergraduate:* $350/credit. *Graduate:* $440/credit ($590/credit for Physical Therapy). *Application Fee:* Undergraduate $35, Graduate $50. *Credit by:* semester.

Financial Aid: Federal Stafford Loan, Federal Perkins Loan, Federal PLUS Loan, Federal Pell Grant, Federal Work-Study, VA, Pennsylvania resident programs.

Accreditation: Middle States Association of Colleges and Schools.

Description: Neumann College (1965) is a Catholic, Franciscan College delivering distance education, online and through videoconferencing. Programs include a Spirituality for Leadership Development concentration, and a Certificate developed in collaboration with Catholic Health Association incorporating competencies for Mission Leadership, applicable toward master's degree or Graduate Certificate. Unique 6-credit undergraduate courses are applicable toward bachelor's degree.

New College of California

50 Fell Street
San Francisco, CA 94102

Phone: (415) 241-1377

Division(s): Media Studies and Teleducation
Web Site(s): http://www.newcollege.edu/mediastudies/
E-mail: dcaploe@newcollege.edu

Graduate Degree Programs:
Master of Arts in Media Studies

Class Titles: Theory, Political Economy—Theory, Ideologies, and History from the Peloponnesian War to the Present; Western Cultural History from the Renaissance to MTV; Special Area; Concentration; Final Project.

Teaching Methods: *Computers:* Internet, lectures on Audio CD-ROM, instant messaging, real-time chat, e-mail. *TV:* videotape. *Other:* telephone, audiotapes, fax, correspondence, independent study, individual study.

Admission Requirements: *Undergraduate:* high school transcripts, letters (SAT is optional). *Graduate:* accredited BA or BS, GRE strongly recommended, essay, transcripts.

On-Campus Requirements: Weekly seminars over the Internet after having done the reading and listened to the lectures on CD-ROMs.

Tuition and Fees: *Graduate:* ~$17,000 for entire degree program. *Application Fee:* $50. *Software:* $200 for first 4 terms for CD ROMs. *Other Costs:* books. *Credit by:* trimesters, 6 credits/course, one or two courses per trimester.

Financial Aid: Federal Stafford Loan, Federal Perkins Loan, Federal PLUS Loan, Federal Pell Grant, Federal Work-Study, VA, California resident programs.

Accreditation: Western Association of Schools and Colleges.

Description: The purpose of the Media Studies/Teleducation program is to link an innovative, humanities-based approach to the study of all forms of communication media with the concerns and technologies of the 21st century "global media society."

New England Institute of Technology

2500 Post Road	Phone: (401) 739-5000
Warwick, RI 02886	Fax: (401) 738-5122

Division(s): Center for Distributed Learning
Web Site(s): http://blackboard.neit.edu (password protected)
E-mail: neit.@neit.edu

Undergraduate Degree Programs: Contact school.

Class Titles: Technical Communications, Understanding Your PC, Time Management, Academic Writing, World Literature, Physics.

Teaching Methods: *Computers:* Internet, real-time chat, electronic classroom, e-mail, CD-ROM, newsgroup, LISTSERV.

Admission Requirements: Contact school.

On-Campus Requirements: for degree programs the majority of classrooms are on campus. Midterm and final exams are required to be taken on campus.

Tuition and Fees: Contact school. *Credit by:* quarter.

Financial Aid: Federal Stafford Loan, Federal PLUS Loan, Federal Pell Grant, Federal Work-Study, Federal SEOG, VA, state programs for residents of Rhode Island, Connecticut, Massachusetts.

Accreditation: New England Association of Schools and Colleges.

Description: For over 60 years, New England Institute of Technology (1940) has met the challenge of preparing its graduates to enter an increasingly competitive workplace. Founded as the New England Technical Institute, the present college began as a certificate-granting trade school. When the Board of Regents of the State of Rhode Island granted the institution the authority to offer associate in science degree programs in 1977, its name was changed to New England Institute of Technology (NEIT). In 1982 NEIT was accredited by the New England Association of Schools and Colleges (NEASC). The original educational programs have increased to 22 associate and 6 bachelor degree programs. The dynamic alterations to its program offerings and physical plant symbolize NEIT's vanguard journey into the 21st century and its response to the radical transformation that new technologies have brought to the workplace. The Distance Learning component was added to service on-campus requirements.

New Jersey City University

2039 Kennedy Boulevard	Phone: (201) 200-3449
Jersey City, NJ 07305-1597	Fax: (201) 200-2188

Division(s): Continuing Education
Web Site(s): http://newlearning.njcu.edu/dl/
E-mail: conted@njcu.edu

Class Titles: Using Internet in Education, Using Integrated Software Across Curriculum, Hypermedia, Publishing on Web: Design/Theory/Application, Technology in Social Studies Curriculum, Learning Theories, Introduction to Educational Technology, Technology in the English/Language Arts Curriculum, Nursing, Business, Travel and Tourism, Accounting, Physics, U.S. Politics, Pre-Calculus, Economics, Human & Intercultural Relations, Driver Education, Early Childhood, Grant Proposal Writing, Health Education, Advanced Epidemiology, Special Education, Health Care Management.

Teaching Methods: *Computers:* Internet, real-time chat, electronic classroom, e-mail, LISTSERV, WebCT courseware. *TV:* videotape, cable program, satellite broadcasting. *Other:* radio broadcast, videoconferencing, audioconferencing, audiographics, audiotapes, fax, correspondence, independent study, individual study, learning contracts.

Admission Requirements: *Undergraduate:* official high school transcript or copy of GED with official GED scores and scores from SAT I. *Graduate:* official transcripts from all colleges attended and a minimum cumulative average of 2.5 as an undergraduate.

On-Campus Requirements: None.

Tuition and Fees: *Undergraduate:* $156.75/credit in-state and online. *Graduate:* $262.75/credit in-state and online. *Application Fee:* $35 undergraduate, no application fee for graduate. *Other Costs:* in some courses, textbooks. *Credit by:* semester.

Financial Aid: Federal Stafford Loan, Federal Perkins Loan, Federal PLUS Loan, Federal Pell Grant, Federal Work-Study, VA, New Jersey resident programs.

Accreditation: Middle States Association of Colleges and Schools.

Description: Since 1929 New Jersey City University, an urban public institution, has provided academic excellence and access to students who often are the first in their families to attend college. Now, over 70 years later, more than 8,500 students and 350 faculty enjoy the 17-acre campus, which features 10 buildings including the state-of-the-art Recreation, Sports and Fitness Center and the Professional Studies Building, which contains one of the finest electronic learning laboratories in the country. The newest addition to the campus, will be a Fine Arts Building, scheduled for construction beginning in the fall of 2001. Presently, the university offers 28 undergraduate and 15 graduate degree programs. In 1997, through the efforts of the Continuing Education Department, the first online courses were offered in the graduate area in the Masters of Educational Technology. The Distance Learning program continues to grow. In the fall 2001 semester, 36 courses will be offered online, 23 graduate and 13 undergraduate.

The New Jersey Institute of Technology

| University Heights | Phone: (800) 624-9850 |
| Newark, NJ 07102 | Fax: (973) 596-3288 and (973) 596-3203 |

Division(s): Continuing Professional Education
Web Site(s): http://cpe.njit.edu
E-mail: cpe@njit.edu

Undergraduate Degree Programs:
Bachelor of Science in Computer Science
Bachelor of Arts in Information Systems

Graduate Degree Programs:
Master of Science in:
    Engineering Management
    Information Systems
    Professional Technical Communication

Certificate Programs: Biomedical Processing and Measurement, Computer Networking, E-Commerce, Information Systems Design and Development, Internet Applications Development, New! Internet Systems Engineering, New! Management of Technology, Object-Oriented Design, Practice of Technical Communications, Programming Environment Tools, Project Management, Telecommunications Networking.

Teaching Methods: *Computers:* Internet, real-time chat, electronic classroom, e-mail, CD-ROM, LISTSERV. *TV:* videotape, satellite broadcasting. *Other:* radio broadcast, videoconferencing, audioconferencing, audiotapes, fax, correspondence, independent study, individual study, learning contracts.

Admission Requirements: *Undergraduate:* the average composite SAT score for our enrolling freshmen is 1130. That means there are some students who have scored lower than that, and some who have scored higher. However, if your SAT scores are below 1000, we recommend you retake the test in an effort to raise your score. Your class rank should be in the top 30%; if your school does not rank, you should have at least a B average. You need to submit a completed application for admission, either online or a hard copy. You must have the following items sent to the admissions office: Your official high school transcript, official SAT I or ACT scores (if

the scores are posted on your official high school transcript we will consider them official; otherwise have the ETS send us your score report), $35 application fee, or a College Board waiver form signed by your guidance counselor. *Transfer Undergraduate:* official college transcript, list of courses in progress, $35 application fee. *Graduate:* The TOEFL is required for all international students. Applicants to a master's program must show a TOEFL of at least 550 on the paper exam or 213 on the computer-based examination. Applicants with scores below 550 or 213 are not considered for admission. You need to submit a completed application, either online or a hard copy. You must have the following items sent to the Office of Graduate Admission: $50 nonrefundable application fee, official transcripts, and proof of degree completion from all colleges and universities attended, official GRE/GMAT/TOEFL results (all test scores must be sent directly to the Office of Graduate Admission from ETS), one letter of recommendation in a sealed envelope. *Certificate:* original transcript, résumé, nonmatriculated application.

Tuition and Fees: *Undergraduate:* $216/credit. *Graduate:* $406/credit. *Application Fee:* $35 for undergraduate, $50 for graduate. *Software:* $25 for CD-ROM. *Graduation Fee:* $70. *Credit by:* semester.

Financial Aid: Federal Stafford Loan, Federal Perkins Loan, Federal PLUS Loan, Federal Pell Grant, Federal Work-Study, VA, state programs for residents of New Jersey.

Accreditation: American Assembly of Collegiate Schools of Business, Computer Science Accreditation Commission of the Computing Sciences Accreditation Board, Engineering Accreditation Commission of the Accreditation Board for Engineering and Technology, National Architectural Accrediting Board, National League for Nursing Accrediting Commission, Technology Accreditation Commission of the Accreditation Board for Engineering and Technology.

Description: Lifelong learning is a choice. For individuals who choose to advance their studies, for either professional or personal reasons, the convenience of Distance Learning is an ideal solution to continuing education. NJIT recognized this back in the early 1980s when NJIT pioneered Distance Education and both coined and trademarked the term, Virtual Classroom. Since the time, NJIT has been a leading supporter and developer of Distance Education. Utilizing a variety of methods, NJIT extends its classrooms to serve students who cannot attend campus classes. Students choose when they want to log into the Virtual Classroom (whether it is morning, afternoon, or night). They communicate online with the class at their own pace throughout the academic semester, fitting the learning process into their lives (vs. their lives into the learning process.) The focus of Distance Education is on students and how they can contribute to the learning experience.

New Mexico Highlands University

Ford Hall, NMHU
Las Vegas, NM 87701

Phone: (505) 454-3521
Fax: (505) 454-3066

Division(s): Educational Outreach Services, School of Business
Web Site(s): http://www.nmhu.edu/business
E-mail: glorialopez@nmhu.edu

Undergraduate Degree Programs:
Management
Management Information Systems
Accounting

Graduate Degree Programs:
Master's in Business Administration-Information Technology and Entrepreneurship Emphasis

Certificate Programs: Certificate in Entrepreneurial and Technology Firm Management, Certificate in Information Systems Development.

Class Titles: Accounting, Marketing, Management Information Systems, MBA core courses, Information Technology.

Teaching Methods: *Computers:* Internet, real-time chat, electronic classroom, e-mail, CD-ROM, newsgroup, LISTSERV. *TV:* videotape, cable program, satellite broadcasting. *Other:* videoconferencing, audioconferencing, audiographics, fax, correspondence.

Credits Granted for: examination (CLEP, ACT-PEP, DANTES, GRE).

Admission Requirements: *Undergraduate:* open enrollment. *Graduate:* 3.0 GPA, bachelor's degree. Work experience preferred. *Certificate:* bachelor's degree.

On-Campus Requirements: Each course in the MBA-IT sequence has an on-campus component. Students meet with their class over a weekend to complete the final 10 hours of contact time, or would participate in a one-week seminar with online components prior to the class. BBA programs are not full Distance Learning programs, but many courses are available.

Tuition and Fees: *Undergraduate:* $87.50/credit. *Graduate:* $450/course. *Application Fee:* $15. *Graduation Fee:* $30. *Other Costs:* computer usage fee: $5/credit. *Credit by:* semester.

Financial Aid: Federal Stafford Loan, Federal Perkins Loan, Federal PLUS Loan, Federal Pell Grant, Federal Work-Study, VA, state programs for residents of New Mexico.

Accreditation: Association for Collegiate Business Schools and Programs.

Description: In 1893 New Mexico Highlands University was founded as New Mexico Normal School and opened in 1898 under the guidance of a young educator and anthropologist, Edgar Lee Hewett, who was to take a prominent place in New Mexico history as founder of both the Museum of New Mexico and the Institute of American Archaeology in Santa Fe. NMHU is committed to providing educational opportunities to residents of northern New Mexico. Our Distance Learning program covers the northern half of New Mexico and started in 1996. The School of Business is the only school offering a degree completion program through Distance Education.

New Mexico State University

Box 3WEC
Las Cruces, NM 88003

Phone: (505) 646-5837
Fax: (505) 646-2044

Division(s): Office of Distance Education
Web Site(s): http://www.nmsu.edu/~distance/
E-mail: tenevare@nmsu.edu

Graduate Degree Programs:
Master of Arts in Education
Master of Science in Engineering
Master of Criminal Justice

Teaching Methods: *Computers:* Internet, e-mail, LISTSERV. *TV:* videotape, satellite broadcasting. *Other:* videoconferencing, independent study.

Credits Granted for: examination (CLEP, ACT-PEP, DANTES).

Admission Requirements: *Undergraduate:* high school graduate or GED, ACT. *Graduate:* accredited bachelor's degree.

On-Campus Requirements: None.

Tuition and Fees: *Undergraduate:* $134/credit. *Graduate:* $145/credit. *Application Fee:* $15. *Credit by:* semester.

Financial Aid: Federal Stafford Loan, Federal Perkins Loan, Federal Pell Grant, Federal Work-Study, VA, New Mexico resident programs.

Accreditation: North Central Association of Colleges and Schools.

Description: New Mexico State University, which began in 1888 as an agricultural college and preparatory school, is a comprehensive institution dedicated to teaching, research, and service. The main campus is in the southern New Mexico city of Las Cruces, population 75,000. With a current enrollment of nearly 15,000 and a regular faculty of about 700, the faculty/student ratio is 1 to 18.2. Almost 80% of the full-time faculty hold PhDs. The university offers 75 bachelor's, 50 master's, 4 specialists in education, and 20 doctoral degrees. NMSU is a Carnegie Foundation Level One research institution, anchoring the southern end of the Rio Grande Research Corridor. The campus has 2 of the state's 5 Centers for Excellence—in computing and in plant genetics—as well as a Physical Science Laboratory.

The New School

66 West 12th Street　　　　　　　**Phone:** (800) 319-4321
New York, NY 10011　　　　　　　　　　(212) 229-5630
　　　　　　　　　　　　　　　　　　　Fax: (212) 989-3887

Division(s): New School Online University
Web Site(s): http://www.dialnsa.edu
E-mail: nsadmissions@newschool.edu

Undergraduate Degree Programs:
Bachelor of Arts in Liberal Arts

Graduate Degree Programs:
Master of Arts in Media Studies

Class Titles: over 300 courses each year; examples: Foundations of Feminism, Decadent Feminist–Rethinking Feminism for 1990s, Political Theory for 21st Century, Multiculturalism in American Politics, Bill of Rights/Supreme Court, Situating Victim–Study of Crimes Against Women, Economic Theory/Transformation, Pacific Century, 1920s–Emergence of Modern America, Sociology–Tools for Understanding World, Ethics/Family, Foundations of Psychology, Depression/Melancholia–Humorous History, Theorizing Intellect, Social Psychology, Understanding Gender, Hysteria–Her Story, Jung, Insanity/Psychiatry/Society, Mother Earth/Father Sky–Feminine/Masculine in Native America, Society/Rights of Animals, Crime/Punishment, Borders of Identity, Celebrating Differences–Disability Culture, William Blake, 4 American Classics, 4 European Classics, Women's Autobiographical Writing, 7 Visionary Poets, Race/Sex in American Life: 6 African-American Women Writers, Psychoanalysis/Literature–Plumbing Literary Unconscious, D.H. Lawrence/Language of Love, Forbidden Literature, Secrets of South, Buddhas/Bards/Beatniks–Buddhist Influences in American Literature, Memorializing Vietnam, Lesbian Literary Tradition, Seeking (M)other–Mother/Daughter Theme in Literature, Environmental Geology, Observing Night Sky–Astronomy, Statistics for Everyone, Italian for Italian Speakers, Graduate Reading Course, Linguistics, Learner Assessment, Family Literacy, Methods/Techniques of Teaching ESL/EFL, English Grammar for ESL Teachers, Teaching Sound System of English, Teaching Writing, Published ESL/EFL Materials, Teaching ESL Writing Online, Business Writing (ESL), Fundamentals of English, Grammar of Business Writing, Fundamentals of Copy Editing, Elements of Business Writing, Preparatory Writing, Writing with Power–Language as Listening Tool, Silence to Poem, Rendering Ordinary Extraordinary–Poetry Workshop, Fiction Writing–Memory/

Imagination/Desires, Accidental Realities–Writing Experimental Fiction, Harlem Writers Guild Online Fiction Workshop, Writing Creative Nonfiction, Family Narrative–How/Why My Family Came to This Country, Playwriting, Documentary Fiction–Multigenre Writing from Multicultural Roots, Hypertext Poetry/Fiction, Electronic Studio–Photoshop for Artists, Drawing–Online Workshop for Beginners, Basic Photography–Critique/Response, Intermediate Photography–Critique/Response, Electronic Studio–Photoshop for Photographers, Whose Story Is It? Media in Developing Countries, How To Do Research Online, Screenwriting–Fundamentals, Screenwriting–Facing Blank Page, Business Management, Investment Basics, Fundamental Principles of Financial Freedom, UNIX Operating System, C Language Programming, Microsoft PowerPoint, MS Word (Windows 95), QuarkXPress (Macintosh), Adobe Illustrator (Macintosh), Photoshop 4.0 (Macintosh), Live Picture, World Wide Web Page Design/Construction Mac Platform, PC Platform, Webmaster, Trouble-shooting Web Graphics, MacroMedia DreamWeaver, How to Open a Restaurant, Marcus Apicius to Julia Child–Culinary History.

Teaching Methods: *Computers:* Internet, CD-ROM. *Other:* None.

Credits Granted for: experiential learning, portfolio assessment.

Admission Requirements: *Undergraduate:* for a distance, liberal arts BA: 60 transferable credits, application, official college transcripts, 2 related essays, and an interview. No graduate programs are currently available fully online; however, students with undergraduate degrees may be allowed to take a graduate DIAL course with department permission.

On-Campus Requirements: None.

Tuition and Fees: *Undergraduate:* $588/credit for degree students. A typical 12-week course costs $420. *Graduate:* $660/credit. *Other Costs:* $100 university services fee/semester for degree students. *Credit by:* semester.

Financial Aid: Federal Stafford Loan, Federal Perkins Loan, Federal PLUS Loan, Federal Pell Grant, Federal Work-Study, VA, New York resident programs.

Accreditation: Middle States Association of Colleges and Schools.

Description: The New School (1919) was established as a center for discourse and learning for adult students. It is the leader in American adult education. Established in 1994 with only 7 courses, New School Online University (NSOU) has grown to more than 300 courses annually, ranging from music and writing to business and communications. The New School is one of the few accredited universities that offers credit, noncredit, and degree courses that can be taken anytime, anywhere through the Internet. "Using any personal computer with Internet access, students can enter the classroom whenever they choose; it's open 24 hours a day, 7 days a week," notes Ann-Louise Shapiro, Dean of The New School. "Online education is one of the great advents in education, and we have worked hard to be on the cutting edge of the movement." The NSOU environment is very much like a traditional university. Each NSOU course is taught by a New School faculty member who provides lectures, asks and answers questions, gives assignments, assesses student work, and gives feedback in class or privately. Students discuss topics by posting comments, questions, and observations which become part of the ongoing text-based seminar instruction.

New York City College of Technology

300 Jay Street   Phone: (718) 260-5250
Brooklyn, NY 11201

Division(s): Instructional Technology
Web Site(s): http://www.nyctc.cuny.edu/
E-mail: connect@citytech.cuny.edu

Undergraduate Degree Programs: Contact school.

Certificate Programs: Stage Technology.

Class Titles: Biology, English, Local Area Networks, Microcomputers, Database Systems and Programming, LAN Concepts, AutoCad, Hospitality Management, Technology for Hospitality Management, Marketing, Legal Assistant Studies, Typography, African American Studies, World Wide Web Design, Digital Video.

Teaching Methods: *Computers:* Internet, electronic classroom, e-mail, CD-ROM. *Other:* videoconferencing.

Admission Requirements: *Undergraduate:* high school diploma or the high school equivalency diploma. The latter should be accompanied by proof of satisfactory final score and a statement of diploma issuance.

On-Campus Requirements: Residency requirements.

Tuition and Fees: *Undergraduate:* resident part-time matriculated $135/credit, nonresident part-time matriculated $275/credit. *Application Fee:* $40 fee (freshmen) or $50 fee (transfer). *Credit by:* semester.

Financial Aid: Federal Stafford Loan, Federal Perkins Loan, Federal Pell Grant, Federal Work-Study, VA.

Accreditation: Middle States Association of Colleges and Schools.

Description: We are the senior-level college of technology of the City University of New York and the only state-assisted college of technology in New York City. City Tech is the one college within the CUNY system that provides comprehensive training and education in more than 30 of the 21st-century technologies essential to the development and maintenance of the urban economic infrastructure that keeps New York City vibrant and growing. We trace our roots back to 1881, the year that Voorhees Technical Institute was founded. City Tech merged with Voorhees in 1971. In keeping with our tradition of exploring new technologies, Distance Learning is a rapidly growing area at the college, and more courses are continually being added.

New York Institute of Technology

PO Box 9029   Phone: (800) 873-NYIT (6948)
Central Islip, NY 11722-9029   Fax: (631) 348-0912

Division(s): Online Campus
Web Site(s): http://www.nyit.edu
E-mail: olc@nyit.edu

Undergraduate Degree Programs:
Bachelor of Science in:
    Behavioral Sciences
    Business Administration
Bachelor of Professional Studies in:
    Hospitality Management
Bachelor of Arts, Sciences, or Professional Studies in:
    Interdisciplinary Studies

Graduate Degree Programs:
Master of Science in Energy Management

Teaching Methods: *Computers:* Internet, e-mail. *Other:* None.

Credits Granted for: experiential learning, portfolio assessment, extrainstitutional learning, examination (CLEP, ACT-PEP, DANTES, GRE).

Admission Requirements: *Undergraduate:* high school diploma or equivalent. *Graduate:* bachelor's degree.

On-Campus Requirements: None.

Tuition and Fees: *Undergraduate:* $470/credit. *Graduate:* $545/credit. *Application Fee:* $50. *Credit by:* semester.

Financial Aid: Federal Stafford Loan, Federal PLUS Loan, Federal Pell Grant, VA, New York State programs (TAP), institutional scholarships and grants.

Accreditation: Middle States Association of Schools and Colleges.

Description: New York Institute of Technology's Online Campus offers students the opportunity to earn an undergraduate or graduate degree from NYIT, consistently ranked among the nation's finest colleges and universities by major publications, via the Internet. Only a computer, modem, and Internet service provider are required. This convenient option brings the advantages of an NYIT education to those for whom on-campus attendance is impossible—working professionals, parents caring for children, people who live too far from NYIT's 3 physical campuses, or those who require the flexibility or "attending" class on their own schedules. The school year is divided into two 15-week semesters (fall and spring), plus summer and January intersessions. All Online Campus courses, academic policies, and procedures are the same as those offered to on-campus students.

Newman University

3100 McCormick Avenue	Phone: (316) 942-4291 x241
Wichita, KS 67060	Fax: (316) 942-4483

Division(s): Adult and Professional Studies
Web Site(s): http://www.newmanu.edu
E-mail: cornelln@newmanu.edu

Undergraduate Degree Programs:
Bachelor of Science in:
   Business Management
   Nursing, RN completion
   Teacher Education

Graduate Degree Programs:
Master of Science Education in:
   Adult Education
   Elementary Education
   Middle Level Education
   English as a Second Language
   Leadership

Certificate Programs: Pastoral Ministries (in conjunction with the Diocese of Dodge City), Catholic Building Leadership (in conjunction with the Diocese of Oklahoma City).

Teaching Methods: *Computers:* e-mail. *TV:* videotape. *Other:* videoconferencing.

Credits Granted for: portfolio assessment, extrainstitutional learning, examination (CLEP, ACT-PEP, DANTES, GRE).

Admission Requirements: *Undergraduate:* contact school for specific requirements. *Graduate:* contact school for specific requirements. *Certificate:* contact Sr. Margaret Knoeber, Director of the Pastoral Ministry program at (316) 227-9616.

On-Campus Requirements: Certain components of these programs are taught in a traditional classroom setting at our outreach sites as well as on campus. Consult school for program specifics.

Tuition and Fees: *Undergraduate:* please consult with the school for specific program costs. *Credit by:* semester.

Financial Aid: Federal Stafford Loan, Federal Perkins Loan, Federal PLUS Loan, Federal Pell Grant, Federal Work-Study, VA, Kansas resident programs.

Accreditation: North Central Association of Colleges and Schools.

Description: Newman University (1933 as Sacred Hearts College) is an independent, coeducational Catholic college which incorporates career-oriented disciplines within its liberal arts curriculum. As an institution of higher learning, the university challenges individuals to come to an ever expanding awareness of themselves and their world through reason and experience.

Nichols College

P.O. Box 5000, Center Road	Phone: (508) 213-2207
Dudley, MA 01571	Fax: (508) 213-2490

Division(s): Graduate and Professional Studies
Web Site(s): http://www.nichols.edu
E-mail: joe.symock@nichols.edu

Undergraduate Degree Programs: Contact school.

Graduate Degree Programs: Contact school.

Class Titles: Accounting, Marketing, MIS Management, Web Page Design, Sociology, Psychology.

Teaching Methods: *Computers:* Internet, real-time chat, electronic classroom, e-mail. *TV:* videotape, cable program, PBS. *Other:* fax, correspondence, independent study, individual study, learning contracts.

Credits Granted for: experiential learning, portfolio assessment, extrainstitutional learning, examination (CLEP, ACT-PEP, DANTES), ACES.

Tuition and Fees: *Undergraduate:* $187/credit. *Graduate:* $392/credit. *Application Fee:* $25. *Graduation Fee:* $100. *Credit by:* semester.

Financial Aid: Federal Stafford Loan, Federal Perkins Loan, Federal PLUS Loan, Federal Pell Grant, Federal Work-Study, VA, state programs for residents of Massachusetts.

Accreditation: Northeast Association of Schools and Colleges.

Description: Nichols College (1815) traces its roots to Amasa Nichols, a wealthy Dudley industrialist, who founded Nichols

Academy, a private coeducational preparatory school. With the growth of public education, the academy closed in 1911. In 1931 the Trustees of Nichols Academy decided to put the academy property to use as an educational institution again. James Conrad was invited to to head a new school, which soon developed into a men's junior college of business with the authority to grant an Associate in Business Administration degree. In 1958 Nichols was granted authority to become a 4-year college and to confer the degree of Bachelor of Business Administration. Nichols continues to develop and expand its academic and social programs and maintains its long tradition and mission of service.

North Arkansas College

1515 Pioneer Drive	Phone: (870) 391-3217
Harrison, AR 72601	Fax: (870) 391-3250

Division(s): Vice President of Instruction
Web Site(s): http://pioneer.northark.cc.ar.us
E-mail: bgood@northark.cc.ar.us

Class Titles: courses toward Associate of Arts, Associate of Science, Associate of Applied Science, and toward certificates in Business: Computerized Data Processing (Web), English Composition I (Web/ITFS), English Composition II (Web/ITFS), Technical Report Writing (Web), Intermediate Algebra (teleweb), College Algebra (ITFS), English Composition II (Web/ITFS), Art Appreciation (ITFS), General Psychology (ITFS), Western Civilizations I (ITFS/teleweb), Western Civilizations II (ITFS), US History I (ITFS), Introduction to Sociology (ITFS), Macroeconomics (Web), Business Communications (Web), Computerized Accounting (Web), Nutrition (teleweb).

Teaching Methods: *Computers:* Internet, e-mail. *TV:* videotape, cable program, 2-way interactive TV, PBS. *Other:* independent study.

Credits Granted for: extrainstitutional learning, examination (CLEP, ACT-PEP, DANTES, GRE).

Admission Requirements: *Undergraduate:* application, ACT/COMPASS Test scores.

On-Campus Requirements: None.

Tuition and Fees: *Undergraduate:* $40/credit in-county, $50/credit out-of-county, $102/credit out-of-state. *Other Costs:* $3/credit activity fee; $2 student fee. *Credit by:* semester.

Financial Aid: Federal Stafford Loan, Federal Perkins Loan, Federal PLUS Loan, Federal Pell Grant, Federal Work-Study, VA, Arkansas resident programs.

Accreditation: North Central Association of Colleges and Schools, Commission on Institute of Higher Education.

Description: North Arkansas College (1974) is a public, comprehensive community college serving 7 counties in Northern Arkansas. The college offers 2-year transfer and technical degree programs, one-year technical certificates, certificates of proficiency, customized business and industry training, ABE-GED classes, and noncredit community education courses. Since 1995, Northark has expanded its distance learning program to include the following: college level courses offered to area high schools via interactive TV, bachelor's degrees in nursing and human resource development, master's degrees in adult and vocational education, master's level courses in nursing and education via interactive TV from AR universities, and Internet-based courses.

North Carolina State University

218 McKimmon Center	
Campus Box 7401	Phone: (919) 515-9030
Raleigh, NC 27695	Fax: (919) 515-6668

Division(s): Distance Education
Web Site(s): http://www2.ncsu.edu/oit/
E-mail: de_admin@ncsu.edu

Certificate Programs: Training and Development

Class Titles: Accounting, Adult/Community College Education (graduate level), Biology, Business, Calculus, Chemistry, Communication, Economics, Engineering (graduate level), English, French, History, Horticulture, Logic, Mathematics, Music, Nutrition, Parks/Recreation/Tourism Management, Philosophy, Physical Education, Physics, Political Science, Psychology, Spanish, Statistics, Textiles.

Teaching Methods: *Computers:* Internet. *TV:* videotape, cable program. *Other:* NC Network.

Admission Requirements: *Undergraduate:* high school diploma or GED, or admissions office permission. *Graduate:* bachelor's degree. *Certificate:* bachelor's degree.

On-Campus Requirements: Many courses completed without campus visits; lab courses require campus attendance.

Tuition and Fees: *Undergraduate:* $411/3-credit video course. *Graduate:* $624/3-credit course. *Other Costs:* textbooks. *Credit by:* semester.

Financial Aid: Available for students in degree programs or admittance courses.

Accreditation: Southern Association of Colleges and Schools.

Description: Founded in 1887, North Carolina State University serves the people of the state and nation under the provisions of the national Land Grant Act. As part of its commitment to public education, the university began offering distance education in 1976 to those unable to enroll in on-campus courses due to time, schedule, location, or other constraints. Students complete their degree or other educational goals through a diverse course selection offered via cable, Internet, and video.

North Central State College

2441 Kenwood Circle	Phone: (888) 755-4899
Mansfield, OH 44906	Fax: (419) 755-4750

Division(s): Vice President for Academic and Student Services
Web Site(s): http://www.ncstate.tec.oh.us
E-mail: mcollins@ncstate.tec.oh.us

Undergraduate Degree Programs:
Associate Degrees in Business, Health Sciences, Engineering Technologies. College also partners with many 4-year universities to offer bachelor's degrees to students, many through online classes.

Certificate Programs: Various certificates offered in Business, Health Sciences, Engineering Technologies.

Class Titles: Accounting, Business Computer Programming, Business Management, Criminal Justice (and Peace Officer Option), Early Childhood Education/Management Financial Management, Business Data Communications, Office Administration, Paralegal Studies, Digital Arts, Web/Tech Communications, Broadcast Journalism Communications, Human Services, Massage Therapy, Pharmacy Technology, Physical Therapist Assistant, Practical Nursing, Radiological Sciences, Registered Nursing, Respiratory Therapy, Therapeutic Recreation, Drafting and Design, Electrical Utility Technology, Electrical Maintenance, Electronic Engineering Technology, Heating/Ventilation/AC, Manufacturing Engineering Technology, Mechanical Engineering Technology, Tool & Die, Welding, and more.

Teaching Methods: *Computers:* Internet, e-mail, CD-ROM, LISTSERV. *TV:* videotape. *Other:* videoconferencing, independent study.

Credits Granted for: portfolio assessment, examination (CLEP, ACT-PEP).

Admission Requirements: *Undergraduate:* open admission with placement testing; some programs have limited enrollment. *Certificate:* same as undergraduate.

On-Campus Requirements: Contact school for more information.

Tuition and Fees: *Undergraduate:* $55.65/credit. *Other Costs:* variable lab fees. *Credit by:* quarter.

Financial Aid: Federal Stafford Loan, Federal Perkins Loan, Federal PLUS Loan, Federal Pell Grant, Federal Work-Study, VA, Ohio resident programs and other funding sources for those who qualify.

Accreditation: North Central Association of Colleges and Schools.

Description: North Central State College (1969), a public institution of higher education, is committed to providing comprehensive, occupationally oriented associate degree programs, certificate programs, customized business and industry training, noncredit courses, and other educational and community services. The primary mission of the college is to respond with continued excellence to the varied educational needs and interests of the citizens in the communities we serve. Since this is an ever-changing condition, we are constantly reviewing, improving, and expanding our programs, services, activities, and structure in order to maintain relevancy and responsiveness. Currently the course offerings via distance learning are increasing. Call for a listing of the available courses.

North Central University

910 Elliot Avenue S	Phone: (800) 446-1176
Minneapolis, MN 55404	(612) 343-4400
	Fax: (612) 343-4435

Division(s): Carlson Institute
Web Site(s): http://www.ncbc.edu; www.northcentral.edu
E-mail: info@northcentral.edu

Undergraduate Degree Programs:
Associate of Arts in:
    Bible/Theology
    Christian Education
    Ministerial Degree Program
Bachelor of Arts/Science in:
    Christian Education
    Christian Studies
    Church Ministries

Certificate Programs: One-Year Bible.

Teaching Methods: *TV:* videotape. *Other:* audiotapes, textbooks, study guides, individual study.

Credits Granted for: portfolio assessment, examination (CLEP).

Admission Requirements: *Undergraduate:* age 22, live outside the 100-mile radius of our campus, high school diploma or GED. *Certificate:* same as undergraduate.

On-Campus Requirements: None.

Tuition and Fees: *Undergraduate:* $99/credit. *Application Fee:* $30. *Other Costs:* $50 orientation fee. *Credit by:* semester (students may enroll at any time through our distance education program).

Financial Aid: VA benefits, GI Bill.

Accreditation: North Central Association of Schools and Colleges.

Description: Carlson Institute is the distance education department of North Central University (1930), formerly the North Central Bible College. The institute is named in honor of G. Raymond Carlson, former general superintendent of the Assemblies of God, our school's affiliation. Reverend Carlson is also a past president of North Central University. Since 1991, the purpose of the Carlson Institute has been to contribute to the overall mission of NCU by providing nontraditional programs of adult education with a Christian world view for those who cannot participate on the main campus, thus equipping them for ministry in the church and marketplace through excellence in curricula and services.

North Dakota State College of Science

800 N. 6th Street	Phone: (701) 671-2967
Wahpeton, ND 58076-0002	Fax: (701) 671-2570

Division(s): Nursing
Web Site(s): http://www.ndscs.nodak.edu
E-mail: Marlys_Baumann@ndscs.nodak.edu

Undergraduate Degree Programs:
Associate of Science Degree in Practical Nursing.

Class Titles: Nursing.

Teaching Methods: *Computers:* Internet, electronic classroom, e-mail, CD-ROM, newsgroup, LISTSERV. *TV:* videotape, cable program. *Other:* videoconferencing, audioconferencing, fax, correspondence, independent study, individual study.

Credits Granted for: examination (CLEP).

On-Campus Requirements: Labs and at clinical sites.

Tuition and Fees: *Undergraduate:* $100/credit. *Application Fees:* $25. *Credit by:* semester.

Financial Aid: Federal Stafford Loan, Federal Perkins Loan, Federal PLUS Loan, Federal Pell Grant, Federal Work-Study, VA, state programs for residents of North Dakota.

Accreditation: The Higher Learning Commission, National League for Nursing Commission on Accreditation.

Description: The North Dakota State College of Science (1903) is a state-supported 2-year comprehensive college. It is the second oldest junior college in the nation. It's motto, "Where Students Learn by Doing," is a way of life in studies at NDSCS. The college has 2 divisions: the transfer Arts,

Science, and Business Division and the Technologies and Services Division. The college provides a full college environment with an atmosphere of instruction and extracurricular activities. The college prides itself in excellence in teaching and positive student relationships.

North Dakota State University

1320 Albrecht Boulevard	Phone: (701) 231-7100
Fargo, ND 58105	(701) 231-1090/8944
	Fax: (701) 231-7016/8520

Division(s): Continuing Education, Information Technology Services, Extension
Web Site(s): http://www.ndsu.nodak.edu/conted
http://www.ndsu.nodak.edu/ndsu/resources/infores/ivn.html
http://www.ag.ndsu.nodak.edu/
E-mail: Continuing_Ed@ndsu.nodak.edu

Graduate Degree Programs:
Master of Business Administration
Master of Education Administration

Class Titles: Math, Computer Science, Counseling, Education, Child Development/Family Science, Speech/Communications, Business, University Studies, Health/Physical Education, Animal/Range Science, English, Physics, Engineering, Food/Nutrition, Anthropology, Nursing, Pharmacy, Zoology, Botany, Geology, Architecture, Art, Music.

Teaching Methods: NDSU supports a variety of distance delivery systems including online, video- and print-based individual study, videoconferencing, and any combination of these technologies. Technological support is available to individuals participating in courses. Students may interact with instructors via mail, telephone, e-mail, or fax. Students should have reasonably current computers, software, and browsers.

Credits Granted for: experiential learning, portfolio assessment, examination (CLEP, ACT-PEP, DANTES, GRE).

Admission Requirements: All students enrolling in a course must be admitted to the university, either as degree-seeking or non-degree-seeking student. Requirements will differ, so please contact NDSU for more information.

On-Campus Requirements: None.

Tuition and Fees: Tuition and fees vary. Generally, distance-based courses carry one fee. There is also an application fee of $25 for undergraduate students and $30 for graduate students. All fees are subject to change without notice. *Credit by:* semester.

Financial Aid: Students may apply for financial aid by completing and submitting the Free Application for Federal

Student Assistance (FAFSA). Other forms of financial aid may come from scholarships, loans, grants, or the student's employer.

Accreditation: North Central Association of Colleges and Schools.

Description: North Dakota State University (1890), a land-grant institution, provides instruction, research, and public service through its colleges, experiment station, and extension service. People are educated and served by the discovery, communication, application, and preservation of knowledge. The personal growth of individuals is fostered by creating an environment that nurtures intellectual, social, and cultural development. Academic and professional programs are offered that lead to bachelor's through doctorate degrees. NDSU assumes a coordinating role in the North Dakota University System for academic computing and economic development. Mission values include people, scholarship, the idea of a university, and the land-grant ideal. As a land-grant institution, NDSU has offered outreach programs throughout most of its history. This effort is broadening as technologies develop to provide quality educational opportunities.

North Georgia College & State University

329 West Main Street	Phone: (706) 864-1535
Dahlonega, GA 30597	(706) 864-1844
	Fax: (706) 864-1886

Division(s): Distance Learning Services I.I.T. (Information and Instructional Technologies) Division
Web Site(s): http://www.ngc.edu/
E-mail: bcmccrary@ngcsu.edu
tmccracken@ngcsu.edu

Degree Programs: None directly at this time from NGCSU, check out Georgia G.L.O.B.E. at http://www.georgiaglobe.org/

Certificate Programs: Reading Endorsement Sequence School of Education (Dr. Toni Bellon tbellon@ngcsu.edu)

Class Titles: Education, Nursing, Political Science.

Teaching Methods: *Computers:* Internet, electronic classroom, e-mail, LISTSERV. *TV:* videotape. PBS. *Other:* audioconferencing, videoconferencing, fax, independent study, individual study.

Credits Granted for: extrainstitutional learning, examination (CLEP).

Admission Requirements: *Undergraduate:* For complete information, request a catalog from the Director of Admissions, NGCSU, Dahlonega, GA 30597 / 706-864-1800 and/or visit our web site at: http://www.ngcsu.edu/, click

on Admissions, click on Admission Requirements, click on applicable links to read full information. Application, official high school, college or university transcripts; SAT or ACT test score. Age 16 with good moral character, approved high school graduate.

On-Campus Requirements: Situational—contact should be made to specific school and/or department for an explanation of their requirements.

Tuition and Fees: *Undergraduate:* Please contact school. *Credit by:* semester.

Financial Aid: Federal Pell Grants, Grants, Federal Supplemental Educational Opportunity Grant, Student Incentive Grant, Regent's Opportunity Grant, North Georgia College and State University Music Scholarships, Gloria Shott Scholarship, Georgia Military Scholarship, North Georgia College and State University Scholarships, Gordon Elwood Crowfoot Rotary Scholarship, Eugene C. Patterson Scholarship, Regents' Scholarship, Federal Perkins Loan, Brown Loan Fund, Federal Family Education Loan SGS and Class of '62 Loan Fund, Service-Cancellable Loan, Pickett and Hatcher Education Federal Work-Study Program, and more.

Accreditation: Southern Association of Colleges and Schools, National Council for Accreditation of Teacher Education, Georgia Professional Standards Commission.

Description: North Georgia College and State University (1873) is a traditional liberal arts college nestled in the Blue Ridge Mountains and is one of an elite group of publicly supported, coeducational, military, liberal arts colleges. NGCSU currently offers Distance Learning mostly via live videoconferencing technologies with WebCT as a support tool. We do have a School of Education Reading Endorsement Program completely available online using WebCT. We are in the process of expanding our live videoconferencing connections outside of Georgia and the United States to support our campus programs when we locate interested parties who will supply connection information. The State of Georgia offers system-wide web-based core courses (eCore), continuing education and training, college degree programs, IT and professional certification (offerings expanding every day) via the Georgia G.L.O.B.E. Project (Global Learning Online for Business and Education) accessible at http://www. georgiaglobe.org/. This project focuses on college-credit classes and/or degree programs, professional development, and/or industry certification training. Georgia GLOBE is not a college or university. Students who enroll in courses or degree programs marketed by Georgia GLOBE earn their credits and degrees from one of the 34 colleges and universities that comprise the University System of Georgia. Georgia GLOBE connects you to your lifelong learning needs. You may request information online or call Georgia G.L.O.B.E. at 1-800-404-2740.

North Idaho College

1000 West Garden Avenue
Coeur d'Alene, ID 83814

Phone: (877) 404-4536
Fax: (208) 769-7805

Division(s): Office of Distance Education
Web Site(s): http://www.nic.edu/disted
E-mail: distance@nic.edu

Undergraduate Degree Programs:
80% of course work for Associate of Science and Associate of Arts degree.

Certificate Programs: Child Development Associate course work, Practical Nursing.

Class Titles: Principles Accounting, Social and Cultural Anthropology, Native Peoples, History of Western Art, Fundamentals of Biology, Human Biology, Introduction to Computers, Basic Keyboard, Keyboard Speed, General Chemistry, Introduction to Speech, Interpersonal Communications, College Study Skills, Economics, English Composition, Introduction to Literature, Contemporary World Cultures, Geology, History of Civilization, History after 1876, Introduction Humanities, Basic Math, Elementary Algebra, Intermediate Algebra, College Algebra, Survey of Music, Fundamentals of Music, Officiating Soccer, Logic and Critical Thinking, Introduction to Psychology, Developmental Psychology, Introduction to Sociology, Child Health and Safety, Infancy to Middle Child, Pharmacy Technical Math, Practical Nursing, Finite Math, Legal Environments in Business, Early Childhood, History to 1500, State and Local Government.

Teaching Methods: *Computers:* Internet, real-time chat, electronic classroom, e-mail, CD-ROM, newsgroup, LISTSERV, interactive videoconferencing. *TV:* videotape. *Other:* videoconferencing, fax to complement independent study.

Credits Granted for: experiential learning, portfolio assessment, extrainstitutional learning, examination (CLEP, ACT-PEP, DANTES, GRE).

Admission Requirements: *Undergraduate:* open enrollment.

On-Campus Requirements: Many of the Internet courses require some on-campus activities; for example, the biology course has a weekly lab on campus.

Tuition and Fees: *Undergraduate:* $97/credit. *Other Costs:* $10/course for Internet fee. *Credit by:* semester.

Financial Aid: Federal Stafford Loan, Federal Perkins Loan, Federal PLUS Loan, Federal Pell Grant, Federal Work-Study, VA, state programs for residents of Idaho, Leverage Education Assistance Program, Federal Supplemental Educational Opportunity Grant, Idaho Work Study.

Accreditation: Northwest Association of Schools and Colleges.

Description: Founded in 1933, North Idaho College is a comprehensive community college serving Idaho's 5 northern counties. Located on the spectacular shores of Lake Coeur d'Alene and the Spokane River, North Idaho College offers the best of all worlds for learning and living. Quality instruction, small classes and a caring, talented faculty and staff, are the driving forces behind NIC's success. NIC offers associate degrees in more than 35 transferable academic majors and associate of applied science/certificates of completion in 25 applied technology programs. NIC's enrollment in credit courses is approximately 4,000 students with the classes averaging 15–20 students.

North Iowa Area Community College

500 College Drive
Mason City, IA 50401

Phone: (515) 422-4326
Fax: (515) 423-1711

Division(s): Academic Affairs/Telecommunications
Web Site(s): http://www.niacc.cc.ia.us
E-mail: mozaclar@niacc.cc.ia.us

Undergraduate Degree Programs:
Associate in Arts

Class Titles: Communication, Geography of Non-Western World, Ethics, Human Growth/Development, Management, Statistics, Psychology, U.S. Government, American History to 1865, American History 1865—Present, Cultural Anthropology, Chemistry, Medical Terminology, Psychology, Speech.

Teaching Methods: *Computers:* Internet, real-time chat, electronic classroom, e-mail, CD-ROM, newsgroup, LISTSERV. *TV:* videotape, cable program, satellite broadcasting, PBS. *Other:* radio broadcast, audioconferencing, videoconferencing, audiographics, audiotapes, fax, correspondence, independent study, individual study, learning contracts.

Credits Granted for: experiential learning, portfolio assessment, examination (CLEP, ACT-PEP, DANTES, GRE).

Admission Requirements: *Undergraduate:* Open-door policy.

On-Campus Requirements: None.

Tuition and Fees: *Undergraduate:* $89.95/credit. *Credit by:* semester.

Financial Aid: Federal Stafford Loan, Federal Perkins Loan, Federal PLUS Loan, Federal Pell Grant, Federal Work-Study, VA, Iowa resident programs.

Accreditation: North Central Association of Colleges and Schools.

Description: Founded in 1918, North Iowa Area Community College is the first public 2-year college in Iowa and one of the first in the country. The college has long been an innovator in 2-year higher education. NIACC has offered distance education since 1980 utilizing telecourses, directed study (correspondence), interactive TV, and most recently the Internet.

Northampton Community College

3835 Green Pond Road	Phone: (610) 861-5300
Bethlehem, PA 18020	Fax: (610) 861-5373

Division(s): Instructional Services/Distance Learning
Web Site(s): http://www.northampton.edu
E-mail: Bjohnson@northampton.edu

Undergraduate Degree Programs:
Associate Degree in:
    Accounting
    Business Administration
    Business Management
    General Studies
    Individualized Transfer Studies

Certificate Programs: Specialized diplomas in Library Technical Assistant and Family Child Care.

Class Titles: contact school.

Teaching Methods: *Computers:* Internet, Tele-web. *TV:* videotape, cable program, PBS. *Other:* videoconferencing, correspondence.

Credits Granted for: experiential learning, portfolio assessment, CLEP.

Admission Requirements: *Undergraduate:* open admission.

On-Campus Requirements: None.

Tuition and Fees: *Undergraduate:* $83 county, $167 out-of-county. *Application Fee:* $25 county. *Credit by:* semester.

Financial Aid: Federal Stafford Loan, Federal Perkins Loan, Federal PLUS Loan, Federal Pell Grant, Federal Work-Study.

Accreditation: Middle States Association of Colleges and Schools.

Description: Northampton Community College (1965) began distance education 30 years ago with correspondence courses. Today more than 100 courses open every month. Ten years ago telecourses were added. Today there are 20 telecourses. One hundred Internet courses and Tele-webs will join the offerings. Five degree and two specialized diplomas may be achieved through distance learning.

Northeastern Oklahoma A&M College

200 I Street NE	Phone: (918) 540-6296
Miami, OK 74354	

Division(s): Distance Education Office
Web Site(s): http://www.neoam.org/
E-mail: distanceed@neoam.cc.ok.us

Undergraduate Degree Programs: Contact school.

Class Titles: Economics, English, History, Political Science, Music Appreciation, History of Film, Geography, Psychology, Business.

Teaching Methods: *Computers:* Internet, real-time chat, electronic classroom, e-mail, CD-ROM. *TV:* videotape, cable program, PBS. *Other:* videoconferencing, fax, correspondence, independent study, individual study.

Admission Requirements: *Undergraduate:* visit http://www.neoam.cc.ok.us/~neoadmission/ for complete instructions.

On-Campus Requirements: Varies.

Tuition and Fees: *Undergraduate:* $48.85/credit hour. *Application Fees:* $25. *Graduation Fee:* $20. *Credit by:* semester.

Financial Aid: Federal Stafford Loan, Federal Perkins Loan, Federal PLUS Loan, Federal Pell Grant, Federal Work-Study, state programs for residents of Oklahoma.

Accreditation: North Central Association of Colleges and Schools.

Description: At Northeastern Oklahoma A&M College (1919), you will be treated as an individual. Small class sizes allow for personalized attention from instructors. Our open door policy allows NEO to accept students with any GPA or ACT scores, and we offer courses ranging from college preparatory through honors classes. NEO has been providing quality Distance Education since 1989.

Northeastern State University

600 North Grand	Phone: (918) 456-5511 x2060
Tahlequah, OK 74464	Fax: (918) 458-2061

Division(s): Office of Academic Affairs
Web Site(s): http://www.nsuok.edu
E-mail: nowlin@cherokee.nsuok.edu

Undergraduate Degree Programs:
Courses only

Class Titles: Accounting, Business Law, Marketing, Management, Meetings/Destination Management, Nursing (+2), Education.

Teaching Methods: *Computers:* e-mail, Internet, real-time chat. LISTSERV. *Other:* videoconferencing, audioconferencing.

Credits Granted for: examination (CLEP, ACT-PEP, DANTES, GRE).

Admission Requirements: *Undergraduate:* high school graduate or GED; high school GPA of 2.70; ranked in upper 50% of graduating class, or ACT composite of 20. Need 15 units of required high school courses (4 English, 2 Lab Science, 3 Math, 2 History, 1 Citizenship, 3 other subjects). *Graduate:* bachelor's degree, scores no more than 5 years old on appropriate aptitude test (Miller Analogies Test or GRE), undergraduate GPA of 2.5 (or 2.75 in the last 60 hours), proof of citizenship for U.S. citizens born outside U.S. and for resident aliens, TOEFL score of 550 for all U.S. citizen applicants or international applicants for whom English is a second language.

On-Campus Requirements: 30 hours of residency with Northeastern State University.

Tuition and Fees: *Undergraduate:* $76/credit, lower division; $160/credit, nonresident lower division; $77/credit, upper division; $170/credit, nonresident upper division. *Graduate:* $93/credit, resident; $202/credit, nonresident. *Other Costs:* $25 records fee, $2 cultural scholastic fee, $20/credit remedial course fee. *Credit by:* semester.

Financial Aid: Federal Stafford Loan, Federal Perkins Loan, Federal PLUS Loan, Federal Pell Grant, Federal Work-Study, VA, Oklahoma resident programs.

Accreditation: North Central Association of Colleges and Schools.

Description: Northeastern State University (1909) is one of six regional universities in Oklahoma. It offers 65 undergraduate degrees, 13 graduate degrees, and one doctoral degree in Optometry. Northeastern State University began offering distance education courses to limited sites in Oklahoma by interactive videoconferencing in the fall of 1997.

Northern State University

1200 South Jay Street   Phone: **(605) 626-2568**
Aberdeen, SD 57401   Fax: **(605) 626-2542**

Division(s): Continuing Education
Web Site(s): http://www.northern.edu
E-mail: geierj@northern.edu
exten@northern.edu

Class Titles: Basic Algebra, Intermediate Algebra, College Algebra, Finite Mathematics, Trigonometry, Calculus III, Math Concepts for Teachers I & II, United States History I and II, State and Local Government, Principles of Sociology, Courtship and Marriage, The Family, Technological Literacy, Occupational and Safety Education, Special Problems in Metric Measurement, Survey of Business, Mathematics for Business, Personal Finance, Supervisory Management, Marketing, Human Resources Management, Organizational Behavior, Retail Management, Educational Psychology, Methods of Bibliographic Instruction, Instructional Technologies, Selection of Library Media, Library Media Administration, Cataloging and Classification, Reference, Wellness, Business and Society, Ornithology, Composition, Introduction to Computers, Criminology, Survey of Physics, Introduction to Theater.

Teaching Methods: *Computers:* Internet, e-mail. *TV:* videotape, cable program, satellite broadcasting. *Other:* fax, correspondence.

Credits Granted for: examination (CLEP, ACT-PEP, DANTES, GRE).

Admission Requirements: *Undergraduate:* high school diploma or GED.

On-Campus Requirements: yes for regular degrees.

Tuition and Fees: *Undergraduate:* $142.25/credit. *Credit by:* semester.

Accreditation: North Central Association of Colleges and Schools, National Council for Accreditation of Teacher Education, institutional member of University Continuing Education Association.

Description: Northern State University (1901) is a multipurpose regional institution of higher education founded as a normal and industrial school to serve the northern part of the state. The university has since diversified its offerings to address the emerging needs of the students, community, and region. Teacher preparation remains an important feature of the institutional mission, as do programs in the arts and sciences, business, and fine arts. Through undergraduate and graduate programs, the university provides quality teaching and learning. Offering students a breadth and depth in the liberal arts and in professional studies, NSU develops effective and productive professionals and citizens. Further, the university creates and nurtures a community of students, faculty, and staff, supporting communication, student and faculty research, and professional growth. Northern State has designed programs to meet academic, social, cultural, and economic needs of the community and area, providing lifelong learning opportunities, a center for the arts and recreation, and support for regional development.

Northern Virginia Community College

8333 Little River Turnpike
Annandale, VA 22003-3796

Phone: (703) 323-3368
(800) 627-5443
Fax: (703) 323-3392

Division(s): Extended Learning Institute
Web Site(s): http://eli.nv.cc.va.us
E-mail: Jtownend@nv.cc.va.us

Undergraduate Degree Programs:
Associate Degree in:
    Business Administration
    Business/Public Management
    Engineering
    General Studies
    Information Systems Technology
    Liberal Arts

Certificate Programs: Certificate, Professsional Writing for Business, Government, and Industry, Career Studies Certificate in Medical Transcription, Certificate in Audio Visual Technology.

Class Titles: see web site for all courses offered.

Teaching Methods: *Computers:* Internet, e-mail, CD-ROM, computer conferencing. *TV:* videotape, satellite broadcasting, PBS, compressed video (only in Virginia). *Other:* voice-mail conferencing, audiotapes, fax, correspondence, independent study, individual study.

Credits Granted for: experiential learning, portfolio assessment, extrainstitutional learning (military service school courses), examination (CLEP, ACT-PEP, DANTES, GRE).

Admission Requirements: *Undergraduate:* high school diploma or equivalent, age 18, specific requirements to each individual curriculum.

On-Campus Requirements: Average of 3 proctored activities (e.g., exams, laboratories); local proctoring possible.

Tuition and Fees: *Undergraduate:* $39.45/credit in-state, $173.33/credit out-of-state. *Credit by:* semester.

Financial Aid: William D. Ford Federal Direct Loan, Federal Perkins Loan, Federal Pell Grant, Federal Work-Study, Federal Supplemental Educational Opportunity Grant, VA, Virginia residents (CSAP, VCCS grants).

Accreditation: Southern Association of Colleges and Schools.

Description: Northern Virginia Community College, founded in 1964, began its Extended Learning Institute in 1975, making it one of the nation's oldest, largest, and most successful distance education programs. ELI's purpose was to extend educational opportunities to the northern Virginia community. Since then, ELI has enrolled more than 160,000 students nationwide, and it currently offers 120 courses with 10,000 students annually. ELI provides courses for those who cannot or prefer not to attend regular classes on campus. Instruction includes TV, computers, audiocassettes, videocassettes, and printed materials designed especially for independent study. ELI also offers continuous enrollment for most courses; students can register any day the college is open.

Northland Pioneer College

P.O. Box 610, First Avenue at Hopi Drive
Holbrook, AZ 86025-0610

Phone: (800) 266-7845
Fax: (928) 532-6112

Division(s): Division of Business and Technology—Computer Technology Department
Web Site(s): http://www.northland.cc.az.us/
E-mail: wclrp@northland.cc.az.us

Undergraduate Degree Programs:
Associate of Applied Science
Associate of Arts
Associate of Science
Associate of Business
Associate of General Studies

Certificate Programs: Certificate of Applied Science; Certificate of Proficiency.

Class Titles: Legal Assistant (a complete program leading to an Associate of Applied Science degree is now available), Political Science, Early Childhood Development, Creative Writing, Environmental Biology, Computer Science (Networking; Windows NT; UNIX), Music Appreciation, Administrative Information Systems, Macro and Microeconomics.

Teaching Methods: *Computers:* Internet, e-mail. *TV:* video-conferencing, audioconferencing, learning contracts.

Credits Granted for: experiential learning, portfolio assessment.

Admission Requirements: *Undergraduate:* admissions form.

On-Campus Requirement: None.

Tuition and Fees: *Undergraduate:* see tuition and fee schedule on web site; $28/credit in-state, $50/credit out-of-state. *Graduation Fee:* $20. *Credit by:* semester.

Financial Aid: Federal Pell Grant, Federal Work-Study, VA.

Accreditation: North Central Association.

Description: (1974) NPC is a comprehensive, 2-year community college, serving a 21,000-square-mile area in rural and remote northeastern Arizona. The college is a nation-wide leader in Distance Learning using audio and video technologies, which it implemented in the early 1980s as a means of overcoming the time and distance constraints of its unique service area. In the past 3 years, NPC has added Internet courses to its Distance Learning offerings, now reaching an audience that is limited only by the breadth of the Internet.

NorthWest Arkansas Community College

One College Drive	Phone: (501) 619-4382
Bentonville, AR 72712	Fax: (501) 619-4383

Division(s): Distance Learning Department (in the Learning Department)
Web Site(s): http://www.nwacc.net/disted
E-mail: cbrooks@nwacc.net

Undergraduate Degree Programs: Contact school.

Class Titles: Beginning Algebra, College Algebra, Western Civilization, Business Communications, Database Management, World Literature, Psychology, Sociology, American History, Accounting, Web Page Design, Art Appreciation, English Composition, Internet Resourcing, Networking, Chemistry.

Teaching Methods: *Computers:* Internet, real-time chat, electronic classroom, e-mail, CD-ROM, discussion lists, WebCT, WWW. *TV:* videotape, satellite broadcasting, PBS, public and cable broadcast programs. *Other:* videoconferencing, fax, independent study, self-directed learning.

Credits Granted for: experiential learning, portfolio assessment, extrainstitutional learning (corporate or professional association seminars/workshops), examination (CLEP, DANTES) concurrent/step ahead; TAP (technical advanced placement); AP (advanced placement); Youth Apprenticeship; departmental examinations; Veterans (PE credit only); Interdisciplinary Honors; Public Service; Cooperative Vocational training.

Admission Requirements: *Undergraduate:* high school graduate or GED; complete application; placement test scores (within past 5 years); immunization for students born after January 1, 1957, official high school transcript or GED scores; proof of past 6 months residency; international students; high school students.

On-Campus Requirements: not for individual classes as a requirement. Asynchronous classes except for WWW-Based have at least 3 built-in campus times (testing, review session) at the discretion of the instructor.

Tuition and Fees: *Undergraduate:* $42 (in-district), $84 (out-of-district), $105 (out-of-state), and $155 (interna-

tional)/credit. *Application Fees:* $10. *Software:* varies. *Graduation Fee:* $20 Associates level; $10 Certificates. *Other Costs:* $22/class for Distance Learning fee. $1/credit hour co-curricular/students services fee. Various fees for certain classes. *Credit by:* semester.

Financial Aid: Federal Stafford Loan, Federal Pell Grant, Federal Work-Study, Federal Supplemental Educational Grant, VA, state programs for residents of Arkansas.

Accreditation: North Central Association of Colleges and Schools.

Description: NorthWest Arkansas Community College (NWACC) (1989) was established to serve and strengthen the community through learning for living. NWACC is located in Bentonville, Arkansas, serving 4 rural areas: Benton, Carroll, Madison, and Washington counties. The college receives revenues from the state of Arkansas and a mil levy from the Bentonville and Rogers school districts. General enrollment has tripled since 1990 (from 1,200 to 4,058 students), while the median age has dropped from 27 to 21 years of age. By 1999, 37% were in the 18–24 year group. Another changing demographic is reflected in enrollment; Hispanic students now comprise 4% of the student population. NWACC entered Distance Learning in 1997 with compressed interactive videoconferencing. We added telecourses in 1998, self-directed study in 1998, and WWW in 2000.

Northwest Indian College

2522 Kwina Road	Phone: (360) 676-2772 x4295
Bellingham, WA 98226-9217	or x4264
	Fax: (360) 676-0475

Division(s): Division for Business, Distance Learning, and Vocational Education Business/Technology
Web Site(s): http://www.nwic.edu
E-mail: lsantana@nwic.edu or lwoodtrost@nwic.edu

Undergraduate Degree Programs:
Two-year degree programs including transfer
Associate of Arts and Sciences in:
    General Direct transfer Degree
    Allied Health
    Business Administration
    Education
    Fine Art
    Native American Studies
    Tribal Environmental and Natural Resource Management
Associate of Technical Arts in:
    Chemical Dependency Studies
    Computer Maintenance and Networking
    Early Childhood Education
    Entrepreneurship
    Hospitality Management

Individualized Programs
Office Professions
Public and Tribal Administration
Tribal Environmental and Natural Resource Management
Associate of Science Transfer
Life Sciences
In Conjunction with Washington State University, a 4-year Bachelor of Education (for Native Teacher Preparation Program).

Certificate Programs: Computer Repair Technician (two-quarters and one-year); Construction Trades (one-year and two-year); Document Imaging Specialist; Early Childhood Education; Entrepreneurship; Harvest Diving; Hospitality Management; Individualized Program; Native American Art; Nutrition Assistant; Office Assistant; Paraeducation; Public and Tribal Administration; Shellfish Management.

Teaching Methods: *Computers:* Internet, electronic classroom, real-time chat, e-mail, CD-ROM. *TV:* videotape, cable program, satellite broadcasting, interactive video (Washington K-20) System. *Other:* videoconferencing, audioconferencing, audiotapes, fax, correspondence, independent study, individual study, learning contracts.

Credits Granted for: experiential learning, portfolio assessment, extra-institutional learning (corporate or professional association seminars/workshops), examination (CLEP).

Admission Requirements: *Undergraduate:* Open enrollment. The college programs are designed to meet the needs of Native American students. Assessment/Placement Instrument. *Certificate:* Assessment/Placement Instrument.

On-Campus Requirements: None.

Tuition and Fees: *Undergraduate:* $58 per credit (1–12 credits; $696 for 12–18 credits; plus $58 for 19+ credits) for students who are enrolled members of a federally recognized tribe or Alaska Native Corporation or who are covered by the Jay Treaty, and who have provided Northwest Indian College with such documentation. $156.50 per credit (1–12 credits; $1,878 for 12–18 credits; plus $156.50 for 19+ credits) for all others. *Application Fees:* None. *Software:* None. *Graduation Fee:* Varies according to cap and gown rental rates. Otherwise, none. *Credit by:* Quarter for all associate degrees and certificate programs. Semester for Bachelor's Degree in Education in cooperation with Washington State University.

Financial Aid: Federal Pell Grant, Federal Work-Study, VA, state programs for residents of Washington and many scholarship programs.

Accreditation: Northwest Association of Schools and Colleges, Commission on Colleges and Universities.

Description: Northwest Indian College (1983) is a tribally controlled institution chartered by the Lummi Indian Business Council. It is a public, nonprofit, comprehensive community college for the purpose of providing postsecondary education services to the Native American communities in Northwest Washington. The college broadcasts telecourses via satellite to sites on reservations in the Northwest. The college also offers Independent Learning courses, which combine print materials with videos, e-mail, or teleconferencing. Online courses are being developed.

Northwest Iowa Community College

603 West Park Street
Sheldon, IA 51201

Phone: (712) 324-5061
Fax: (712) 324-4136

Division(s): Iowa Communications Network
Web Site(s): http://nwicc.cc.ia.us
E-mail: cscott@nwicc.cc.ia.us

Undergraduate Degree Programs:
Associate of:
    Arts
    Science
    Technical Programs

Certificate Programs: Contact school for program list.

Teaching Methods: *TV:* satellite broadcasting, PBS. *Other:* independent study, individual study, learning contracts, videoconferencing via the fiber optic Iowa Communications Network.

Credits Granted for: corporate or professional association seminars/workshops, examination (CLEP, ACT-PEP, DANTES, GRE).

Admission Requirements: *Undergraduate:* high school or other transcripts, ASSET test, ACT or SAT.

On-Campus Requirements: None.

Tuition and Fees: *Undergraduate:* $56/credit. *Other Costs:* $3/credit Student Fee. *Credit by:* semester.

Financial Aid: Federal Stafford Loan, Federal PLUS Loan, Federal Pell Grant, Federal Work-Study, VA, Iowa Vocational Technical grants, SEOG grants.

Accreditation: North Central Association of Colleges and Schools.

Description: NCC is a 2-year community college providing a wide range of services to the communities and citizens of northwest Iowa. The college offers a comprehensive educational program, including many vocational-technical programs and a solid core of academic offerings that help develop a broadly educated person.

Northwest Missouri State University

800 University Drive	Phone: (800) 633-1175
Maryville, MO 64468	Fax: (660) 562-1121

Division(s): Northwest Online
Web Site(s): http://www.northwestonline.org
E-mail: admissions@northwestonline.org

Undergraduate Degree Programs:
Bachelor of Science in Accounting (degree completion program)
Bachelor of Science in Business Management (degree completion program)

Teaching Methods: *Computers:* World Wide Web, chat, threaded discussion, electronic classroom, e-mail, CD-ROM.

Credits Granted for: experiential learning, portfolio assessment, extrainstitutional learning, examination (CLEP, ACT-PEP, DANTES, GRE).

Admission Requirements: A participating student must have previously earned an associate in applied science degree from an articulated community college program in accounting or business. These programs will then provide that student with the opportunity to complete a bachelor of science in accounting or business management through Northwest.

On-Campus Requirements: None.

Tuition and Fees: *Undergraduate Online:* $15 application fee, $197.25/credit resident and nonresident, $5/credit technology access fee. *Credit by:* semester.

Financial Aid: Federal Direct Loan (subsidized), Federal Direct Loan (unsubsidized), Federal Perkins Loan, Federal PLUS Loan, Federal Pell Grant, Federal Work-Study, Missouri resident programs.

Accreditation: North Central Association of Colleges and Schools.

Description: Northwest Missouri State University has distinguished itself among American universities in at least 2 areas: our electronic campus and our "Culture of Quality" initiative to continuously improve every aspect of our institution. Northwest Missouri State University is a moderately selective, learner-centered, regional university offering a focused range of undergraduate and graduate programs.

Northwest Technical College

2022 Central Avenue NE	Phone: (218) 773-4575
East Grand Forks, MN 56721	Fax: (218) 773-4502

Division(s): Distance Education
Web Site(s): http://www.ntc-online.com/
E-mail: thompsonl@mail.ntc.mnscu.edu

Undergraduate Degree Programs:
Accounting, AAS
Accounting, Diploma
Practical Nursing, AAS
Microcomputer and Network Technology, AAS
Information Resource Specialist, AAS
Medical Transcriptionist, Certificate
Legal Secretary Technology, Certificate

Class Titles: Accounting, Computers, Information Resource, Medical Transcription, Legal, Nursing, General Education.

Teaching Methods: *Computers:* Internet, e-mail, CD-ROM, instructional management software. *Other:* fax, correspondence.

Credits Granted for: experiential learning, portfolio assessment.

Admission Requirements: *Undergraduate:* entrance exam. *Certificate:* entrance exam.

On-Campus Requirements: None.

Tuition and Fees: *Undergraduate:* $125/credit (resident or nonresident). *Application Fee:* $20. *Other Costs:* $5.75 state fees. *Credit by:* semester.

Financial Aid: Federal Stafford Loan, Federal Perkins Loan, Federal Pell Grant, Federal Work-Study, VA, Minnesota resident programs.

Accreditation: North Central Association of Colleges and Schools.

Description: Northwest Technical College (1992) is a regional technical college with 5 campuses serving northwestern Minnesota. Its primary mission is to provide quality occupational education to individuals, business, industry, and society in response to a changing world. The college provides industry-validated technical and general education curricula that are designed to meet a variety of career choices and that lead to the award of certificates, diplomas, or associate in applied science degrees. Distance Education was born in 1995 out of our changing societal needs and the rural area we live in. Knowing students would travel 2 hours round trip to attend classes everyday, we needed to find a better way. We began by writing general education curriculum in correspondence delivery. In 1997 we then upgraded to Internet delivery. Last year we began implementing virtual classroom software. Our course offerings now include 58 courses, and we are slated to deliver 3 AAS programs by the fall of '99.

Northwestern College

3003 Snelling Avenue North
Saint Paul, MN 55113-1598

Phone: (651) 631-5494
(800) 308-5495
Fax: (651) 631-5133

Division(s): Center for Distance Education
Web Site(s): http://www.nwc.edu/disted/ or
www. distance.nwc.edu
E-mail: distance.@nwc.edu

Undergraduate Degree Programs:
Intercultural Ministries

Certificate Programs: Bible.

Teaching Methods: *Computers:* Internet, real-time chat, e-mail. *TV:* videotape. *Other:* audiotapes, fax, correspondence, independent study.

Credits Granted for: (ICM only) experiential learning, portfolio assessment, examination (CLEP, ACT-PEP, DANTES, GRE).

Admission Requirements: *Undergraduate:* Evidence of new birth in Jesus Christ, willingness to subscribe to the patterns of life and conduct of the Northwestern community, likelihood of academic success at Northwestern, high school diploma or GED certificate, ACT/SAT scores, financial capability to meet college expenses.

On-Campus Requirements: None.

Tuition and Fees: *Undergraduate:* $200/credit. *Application Fee:* $25 one-time. *Other Costs:* $60/course materials fee. *Credit by:* semester.

Financial Aid: Federal Stafford Loan, Federal Perkins Loan, Federal PLUS Loan, Federal Pell Grant, Federal Work-Study, VA, Minnesota resident programs.

Accreditation: North Central Association of Colleges and Schools.

Description: Northwestern College (1902) is the only nondenominational private college in Minnesota. The college is an independent enterprise that takes a biblically Christian ethical and moral position with a theologically conservative doctrine. The alumni and its growing radio audience are the college's primary constituencies. The Center for Distance Education provides Christ-centered education and training at college and professional levels. NC's mission is to meet the needs of all students who aspire to an intellectual, reasoned, and healthy Christian worldview, and to help them prepare for productive ministry and occupational performance.

Northwestern Community College

500 Kennedy Drive
Rangely, CO 81648

Phone: (970) 675-3273
Fax: (970) 675-3330

Division(s): Distance Learning
Web Site(s): http://www.cncc.cc.co.us
E-mail: klangston@cncc.cc.co.us

Class Titles: Criminal Justice, Composition, Spanish, Math/Calculus, Forestry, Psychology, Statistics, Computer Science, Economics, Education, Business, Child Development, Sociology, Geography, Anthropology.

Teaching Methods: *Computers:* electronic classroom, e-mail. *TV:* videotape, cable program, satellite broadcasting, PBS. *Other:* videoconferencing, audioconferencing, fax, correspondence, independent study, Individual study.

Credits Granted for: experiential learning, portfolio assessment, examination (CLEP, ACT-PEP).

Admission Requirements: *Undergraduate:* GED or high school graduate, dual enrollments. *Certificate:* interview.

On-Campus Requirements: orientation and testing, some courses have associated labs.

Tuition and Fees: *Undergraduate:* In-state tuition $60.05/credit. Out-of-state tuition $230.85/credit. *Other Costs:* $45/Distance Learning course. *Credit by:* semester.

Financial Aid: Federal Stafford Loan, Federal Perkins Loan, Federal PLUS Loan, Federal Pell Grant, Federal Work-Study, VA, Colorado resident programs.

Accreditation: North Central Association of Colleges and Schools.

Description: Colorado Northwestern Community College (1967) is a small district community college serving the northwest region of Colorado. We anticipate joining the state community college system in early 1999. The college began distance learning activities in the form of audio bridge and telecourses. Recently we became a member of the WestCel Consortium and began delivering interactive video courses via a compressed video network. We also distribute Utah State University satellite courses to our campuses and communities via a cable TV educational and community access channel.

Northwestern Michigan College

1701 East Front Street
Traverse City, MI 49686

Phone: (231) 995-1076/1965
Fax: (231) 995-1080

Division(s): Academic/Media Technologies
Web Site(s): http://www.nmc.edu/flo
E-mail: joliver@nmc.edu or jwinowiecki@nmc.edu

Class Titles: Art Appreciation, Intro to Business, Western Civilization, US History, Principles of Marketing, Mechanics of Business Writing, Intro to Philosophy, Intro to Psychology, Intro to Sociology, Intro to Cultural Anthropology, Aircraft Turbine Engines, Instrument Ground, Human Biology, Business Law I, Intro to Computers in Business, UNIX Operating Systems, Internet Publishing I, Intro to Criminal Justice, English Composition, Children's Literature, Interpersonal Relations, Intermediate Algebra, Music Appreciation, Intro to Legal Assisting, Contemporary Ethical Dilemmas Abnormal Psychology, American Government, Michigan History, Business Math, Intro to Nursing, Fundamentals of Nursing-Lecture, Pharmacology, Lifespan Nursing Lecture, Adv. Maternal Child Nursing, Adv. Nursing of Adults-Clinical, Mental Health Nursing, Nursing Mgmt. Issues & Trends. Contact the school or check the web site (www.nmc.edu/flo) for more offerings and details.

Teaching Methods: *Computers:* Internet, real-time chat, electronic classroom, e-mail, CD-ROM, newsgroup, LISTSERV. *TV:* videotape, cable program, PBS. *Other:* videoconferencing.

Credits Granted for: experiential learning, portfolio assessment, extrainstitutional learning, examination (CLEP).

Admission Requirements: *Undergraduate:* Open access enrollment—must take ASSET test.

On-Campus Requirements: For online courses there is a 2-hour orientation before the course begins. For telecourses there are between 3–6 on-campus sessions through the semester. For ITV courses there are no requirements to come on campus.

Tuition and Fees: *Undergraduate:* $56/contact hour (in-district), $93.25/contact hour (in-state), $106/contact hour (out-of-state). *Application Fee:* $15 one time only. $15–$45/delivery-technology fee. *Other Costs:* $8/semester registration fee, $5/semester campus maintenance fee, $11/semester health fee for anyone taking 6 or more credits, $3/contact hour general fee (student government) up to a maximum of 12 contact hours. *Credit by:* semester.

Financial Aid: Federal Stafford Loan, Federal Perkins Loan, Federal PLUS Loan, Federal Pell Grant, Federal Work-Study, VA, Michigan resident programs.

Accreditation: North Central Association of Colleges and Schools.

Description: Northwestern Michigan College (1951) is a comprehensive community college founded by local citizens who wanted to provide an affordable college education for area residents. Starting out in temporary headquarters at the Traverse City airport terminal, NMC now has a spacious,

80-acre main campus. From 65 students and a staff of 6, NMC has grown to 4,000 students and 100 full-time faculty. In 1981 NMC began its distance education program with one telecourse, and now it offers courses in 4 delivery methods including telecourses, online courses, open entry/open exit independent courses, and Interactive TV that connects the main campus to the surrounding 16 high schools with a fiber optic network for voice, video, and data.

Notre Dame College

2321 Elm Street
Manchester, NH 03104

Phone: (603) 222-7183
Fax: (603) 222-7101

Division(s): Graduate Theology
Web Site(s): http://www.notredame.edu
E-mail: ministry.institute@notredame.edu

Class Titles: Bible, Systematics, Ethics, Ministry (all graduate courses). Graduate certificate available.

Teaching Methods: *Computers:* Internet, real-time chat, e-mail. *Other:* fax.

Admission Requirements: *Graduate:* apply as special student for online courses. Students must be able to access AOL. Contact school for more information.

On-Campus Requirements: None.

Tuition and Fees: *Graduate:* $325/credit. *Other Costs:* $75 late registration fee. *Credit by:* semester and 6-week summer sessions.

Financial Aid: Federal Stafford Loan, Federal Perkins Loan, Federal PLUS Loan, Federal Pell Grant, Federal Work-Study, VA, New Hampshire resident programs.

Accreditation: New England Association of Schools and Colleges.

Description: Notre Dame College (1950) is a 4-year, Catholic, coeducational liberal arts college, founded and sponsored by the Sisters of Holy Cross. The college community includes approximately 1,400 full- and part-time, graduate, undergraduate, and life-long learning students and more than 100 full- and part-time faculty. The mission of the college is education of the whole person, mind, heart, body, spirit. This holistic education is geared toward preparing students for leadership and service to their profession, their local community, their church, and society-at-large. Since its beginnings in 1950, the college has been a leader in teacher preparation, and, more recently, in programs in health science. It was the first and remains the only college in New Hampshire with a program in Graduate Theology. The college initiated distance education in fall 1997 when it began to offer Graduate Theology courses online.

Nova Southeastern University

6100 Griffin Road
Ft. Lauderdale, FL 33314-4416

Phone: (800) 986-2247 x2005
Fax: (954) 262-3915

Division(s): School of Computer and Information Sciences
Web Site(s): http://www.scis.nova.edu
E-mail: scisinfo@nova.edu

Graduate Degree Programs:
Master of Science in:
    Computer Science
    Computer Information Systems
    Management Information Systems
    Computing Technology in Education

Doctoral Degree Programs:
PhD in:
    Computer Science
    Computer Information Systems
    Information Systems
    Information Science
PhD or EdD in Computing Technology in Education

Certificate Programs: Information Resources Management.

Teaching Methods: *Computers:* Internet, real-time chat, electronic classroom, e-mail, electronic assignment submission, electronic forums, and bulletin boards. *Other:* None.

Admission Requirements: *Graduate:* application and fee, 500-word essay, portfolio or GRE (minimum score of 550/exam area, no more than 5 years old), 3 letters of recommendation, official transcripts of all graduate and undergraduate work with a 2.5 undergraduate GPA (3.0 in a major field), minimum of accredited bachelor's degree with appropriate major. Applicants whose native language is not English must pass the Test of English as a Foreign Language with a minimum 550 score. *Doctoral:* application and fee, 500-word essay, portfolio or GRE (minimum score of 550/exam area; no more than 5 years old), 3 letters of recommendation, official transcripts of all graduate and undergraduate work with a minimum 3.25 graduate GPA and an accredited master's degree with appropriate major. Applicants whose native language is not English must pass the Test of English as a Foreign Language with a minimum 550 score. *Certificate:* Application and fee, official transcripts of all graduate and undergraduate college credits, 2.8 GPA in a major field or a 3.0 graduate GPA, accredited bachelor's degree.

On-Campus Requirements: The master's degree can be done completely online with no on-campus requirement. The doctoral degree has a residency requirement. The student chooses between the Cluster or Institute format. Cluster format requires that the student attend classes at the campus 2 extended weekends per semester of classwork. The Institute format requires the student to attend classes at the campus one week per semester of classwork.

Tuition and Fees: *Graduate:* $395/credit. *Doctoral:* $445/credit. *Application Fee:* $50. *Other Costs:* $30 for registration. *Credit by:* semester.

Financial Aid: Federal Stafford Loan, Federal Perkins Loan, Federal PLUS Loan, Federal Pell Grant, Federal Work-Study, VA, Florida resident programs.

Accreditation: Southern Association of Colleges and Schools.

Description: The School of Computer and Information Sciences at Nova Southeastern University (1964) is a major force in educational innovation, distinguished by its ability to offer both traditional and nontraditional choices in educational programs and formats that enable professionals to pursue advanced degrees without career interruption. SCIS offers programs leading to the Master of Science, Doctor of Philosophy, and Doctor of Education in several disciplines to its 1400 graduate students from across the U.S. and other countries. The school pioneered online graduate education and has been offering programs with an online component since 1983. *Forbes* and the *Wall Street Journal* have recognized NSU as one of the top universities offering distance learning programs.

Oakland University

205 Wilson Hall
Rochester, MI 48326

Phone: (248) 370-2191
Fax: (248) 370-4475

Division(s): Academic Units
Web Site(s): http://www.oakland.edu/
E-mail: gilroy@oakland.edu

Undergraduate Degree Programs:
Bachelor of Arts in:
    Communications
    Music
Bachelor of General Studies
School of Nursing—Completion Degree

Teaching Methods: *TV:* videotape, cable program, satellite broadcasting. *Other:* audioconferencing, videoconferencing.

Credits Granted for: examination (CLEP).

Admission Requirements: *Undergraduate:* ACT for freshmen. If out of school for 3 years, sustained employment record; recommendations from employers, educators, or other professionals; and/or standardized tests.

On-Campus Requirements: undergraduate must complete 32 credits at Oakland University, which includes any of its locations.

Tuition and Fees: *Undergraduate:* $122/lower-division credit, resident; $135/upper-division credit, resident; $357/lower-division credit, nonresident; $385/upper-division credit, non-resident. *Graduate:* $237/credit resident, $490/credit nonresident. *Other Costs:* variable. *Credit by:* semester.

Financial Aid: Federal Stafford Loan, Federal Perkins Loan, Federal PLUS Loan, Federal Pell Grant, Federal Work-Study, VA, Michigan resident programs, William D. Ford Federal Direct Loan, Federal Supplemental Educational Opportunity Grant, Michigan Competitive Scholarships, Michigan Educational Opportunity Grants, Michigan Adult Part-Time Grants, Michigan Work-Study, Oakland University grants, Oakland University Institutional Scholarships.

Accreditation: North Central Association of Colleges and Schools.

Description: Oakland University (1957) currently offers its 15,235 students 71 undergraduate degree programs and 45 graduate programs. It includes the College of Arts and Sciences, School of Business Administration, School of Education and Human Services, School of Engineering and Computer Science, School of Health Sciences, and the School of Nursing. About 95% of OU's undergraduate students were employed within 4 months after graduation in 1996. OU firsts: The Network Management Program, which upgrades the skills of information system professionals, a health care/academic alliance with the Beaumont System to prepare nurses for a rapidly changing health care environment and an Advanced Technology in Business program. OU is Division I and is a member of the Mid-Continent Conference in Intercollegiate Athletics. The university is an equal opportunity and affirmative action institution. We started distance learning in 1995.

Oakton Community College

1600 E.Golf	Phone: (847) 635-1640
Desplaines, IL 60016	Fax: (847) 635-1887

Division(s): Library/Media Services
Web Site(s): http://www.oakton.edu/online
E-mail: sandy@oakton.edu

Undergraduate Degree Programs: Contact school.

Class Titles: Business, Marketing, Computer Science, Mathematics, Accounting, French, Biology, Earth Sciences, Physical Education, Anthropology, Computer Information Systems, English, Communications, History, Humanities, Management, Physics, Psychology, Political Science, Sociology, Social Sciences, Economics.

Teaching Methods: *Computers:* Internet, real-time chat, electronic classroom, e-mail, CD-ROM. *TV:* videotape, cable program, PBS. *Other:* radio videoconferencing, audiotapes, independent study, individual study, learning contracts.

Credits Granted for: examination (CLEP, ACT-PEP, DANTES, GRE).

Admission Requirements: Contact school.

On-Campus Requirements: None.

Tuition and Fees: *Undergraduate:* $50/credit. *Application Fee:* $25. *Other Costs:* $50/course. *Credit by:* semester.

Financial Aid: Federal Stafford Loan, Federal Perkins Loan, Federal PLUS Loan, Federal Pell Grant, Federal Work-Study, VA, state programs for residents of Illinois.

Accreditation: North Central Association of Colleges and Schools.

Description: Oakton Community College (1969) is an institution of higher education located in Des Plaines and Skokie, Illinois. Its superb faculty and state-of-the-art facilities provide affordable, quality education to residents of northern suburban Cook County. Oakton offers a full range of educational programs and community services including associate degrees for students intending to transfer to baccalaureate programs, career programs, and training courses to meet business needs. Oakton expanded its educational offerings in January 1999 with the establishment of courses taught on the World Wide Web. With this move Oakton joined colleges and universities worldwide that offer online education as part of their Distance Learning programs. Since then, Oakton has not only broadened its selection of web-centric online classes such as these, it has also created many "hybrid" and "web-enhanced" courses—more traditional classroom-based courses that make use of much of the same technology. Oakton builds minds and helps students shape their futures.

Ohio University

302 Tupper Hall	Phone: (740) 593-2910
Athens, OH 45701	(800) 444-2910
	Fax: (740) 593-2901

Division(s): Independent and Distance Learning Programs
Web Site(s): http://www.ohiou.edu/independent
E-mail: independent.study@ohio.edu

Undergraduate Degree Programs:
Associate of Arts
Associate of Science
Associate of Individualized Studies
Bachelor of Specialized Studies

Class Titles: see catalog.

Teaching Methods: *Computers:* Internet, e-mail, LISTSERV. *TV:* videotape. *Other:* audiotapes, fax, correspondence, independent study, individual study, learning contracts.

Credits Granted for: experiential learning, portfolio assessment, extrainstitutional learning, examination (CLEP).

Admission Requirements: *Undergraduate:* Enrollment in independent study courses is open to anyone who can profit from the learning. Enrollment in a course does not constitute formal admission to Ohio University or any of its degree programs. Degree-seeking students must have a high school diploma to be admitted to the External Student Program; transfer students must have a minimum 2.0 cumulative GPA. Admission to the External Student Program does not guarantee admission to any on-campus degree program.

On-Campus Requirements: None.

Tuition and Fees: *Undergraduate:* $85/credit. *Credit by:* quarter.

Financial Aid: VA.

Accreditation: North Central Association of Schools and Colleges.

Description: Ohio University (1804) was the first institution of higher learning in the Northwest Territory. Today it enrolls 20,000 students in 10 colleges, offering degrees in 325 subject areas. The university holds membership in several professional organizations, and many of its programs are individually accredited by their respective associations. The Independent and Distance Learning programs, begun in 1924, serves students at a distance through correspondence courses, course credit by examination, and individual learning contracts. Course materials may be presented via print, audiotape or videotape, computer disk, or Internet site. Assignments may be submitted by postal mail, fax, or e-mail. Credit earned through any of these options is considered resident credit. Almost 4,000 students take 300 courses annually through independent study. Advising and degree-planning services are offered through the External Student Program and the College Program for the Incarcerated.

Ohio University Eastern

45425 National Road W.	Phone: (740) 695-1720
St Clairsville OH 43950	Fax: (740) 695-7079

Division(s): Media Center
Web Site(s): http://www.eastern.ohiou.edu
E-mail: lorimor@ohio.edu

Undergraduate Degree Programs:
Communication in Human Services
Community Health Services
Early Childhood Education
Exercise Physiology
Food Service Management
General Business Administration

Health Services Administration
Middle Childhood Education
Organizational Communication
Specialized Studies
Nursing
Criminal Justice

Certificate Programs: Gerontology.

Class Titles: Human Biology, Chemistry, Computer Science, Film, Ohio History, Chinese History, Japanese History, Early Christianity, Castles and Cathedrals, Health, Humanities, Journalism, Math, Political Science, Physical Science, Psychology, Sociology, Telecommunications.

Teaching Methods: *Computers:* Internet, real-time chat, electronic classroom, e-mail, CD-ROM, LISTSERV. *TV:* videotape. *Other:* videoconferencing, audiotapes, fax, correspondence, independent study, individual study.

Credits Granted for: experiential learning, portfolio assessment.

Admission Requirements: *Undergraduate:* high school diploma or equivalent.

Tuition and Fees: *Undergraduate:* $94 lower division/$106 upper division/credit. *Application Fee:* $20. *Graduation Fee:* 50. *Credit by:* quarter.

Financial Aid: Federal Stafford Loan, Federal Perkins Loan, Federal PLUS Loan, Federal Pell Grant, Federal Work-Study, VA, state programs for residents of Pennsylvania and West Virginia.

Accreditation: North Central Association of Colleges and Schools.

Description: Ohio University Eastern (1957) is a regional campus of Ohio University. O.U. Eastern has developed Distance Learning courses since 1984. Our student body is rural, commuter-based and close to 50% nontraditional. It was the goal of the regional campus to reach our student body through Distance Learning to make college education more accessible and flexible for our student body.

Ohlone College

43600 Mission Boulevard	Phone: (510) 659-6160
Fremont, CA 94539	Fax: (510) 659-6265

Division(s): Learning Resources and Instructional Technology Division
Web Site(s): http://www.ohlone.cc.ca.us/
E-mail: mtamburello@ohlone.cc.ca.us

Class Titles: Anthropology, Computer Studies, English, English as Second Language, American Government,

Nutrition, Photography, Art, Business, Economics, Fitness for Life, Career Planning.

Teaching Methods: *Computers:* Internet, real-time chat, e-mail, CD-ROM, newsgroup, LISTSERV. *TV:* videotape, cable program. *Other:* videoconferencing.

Credits Granted for: examination (CLEP, ACT-PEP, DANTES, GRE), military service, noncollege courses.

Admission Requirements: *Undergraduate:* high school graduate or equivalency certificate, or age 18, or meets high school special admission requirements.

On-Campus Requirements: varies by class.

Tuition and Fees: *Undergraduate:* $11/credit California residents, $134 or $142/credit all others. *Credit by:* semester.

Financial Aid: Federal Stafford Loan, Federal Perkins Loan, Federal PLUS Loan, Federal Pell Grant, Federal Work-Study, VA, California resident programs.

Accreditation: Western Association of Schools and Colleges.

Description: Ohlone College (1966) is a 2-year, public, coed community college. Ohlone is a commuter, suburban campus located on a 534-acre hillside site (300 acres are reserved for open space) that is only 15 miles from San Jose and 40 miles from San Francisco. The college is on a semester calendar with a limited summer session that offers both general education and occupational education classes; extensive evening and early morning classes are available. Degrees offered by the college include AA and AS; more than 469 associate degrees were awarded in 1997. The college library has 65,000 books, an online catalog, and 9 CD-ROM periodical databases. Plus, there are 800 microcomputers located in the library, classrooms, computer centers, and learning/tutoring centers. The college has a state-of-the-art fine/performing arts center.

Oklahoma City University

2501 North Blackwelder	**Phone: (405) 521-5265**
Oklahoma City, OK 73106	**Fax: (405) 521-5447**

Division(s): Prior Learning and University Studies (PLUS)
Web Site(s): http://www.okcu.edu/plus
E-mail: plus@okcu.edu

Undergraduate Degree Programs:
Bachelor of Science in Technical Management
Bachelor of Arts in:
    Liberal Arts
    Business

Teaching Methods: *Other:* correspondence, independent study.

Credits Granted for: experiential learning, portfolio assessment (ACE), extrainstitutional learning, examination (CLEP, ACT-PEP, DANTES).

Admission Requirements: *Undergraduate:* high school diploma or GED, no minimum number of credit hours, appropriate for age 22.

Tuition and Fees: *Undergraduate:* $177.50/credit plus fees for most distance studies. *Application Fee:* $25. *Other Costs:* $20/semester enrollment fee. $25/term record maintenance. *Credit by:* semester.

Financial Aid: Federal Stafford Loan, Federal Perkins Loan, Federal PLUS Loan, Federal Pell Grant, VA, Federal Work-Study.

Accreditation: North Central Association of Colleges and Schools.

Description: Oklahoma City University (1904) is an independent institution affiliated with the United Methodist Church. The university is committed to a strong education in the liberal arts tradition. The PLUS program is an alternative way for busy, working adults to complete a bachelor of science or bachelor of arts degree. PLUS allows individuals the opportunity to earn course credit for knowledge students have already gained and helps them in attaining credits without spending unnecessary hours in the classroom. While the PLUS curriculum is as rigorous as traditional degree programs, it operates differently in that students may achieve credit through a variety of methods.

Oklahoma State University

470 Student Union	**Phone: (405) 744-6390**
Stillwater, OK 74078	**Fax: (405) 744-7793**

Division(s): Independent and Correspondence Study and University Extension
Web Site(s): http://www.okstate.edu/outreach/ics (for I&CS)
http://www.okstate.edu/outreach (for University Extension)
E-mail: ics-inf@okstate.edu

Graduate Degree Programs:
Master of Business Administration
Master of Science in:
    Electrical and Computer Engineering
    Electrical and Technology Management
    Fire and Emergency Management Administration
    Mechanical/Aerospace Engineering
    Natural/Applied Sciences Specialization in Health Care
        Administration
    Telecommunications Management
    Environmental Science
    Control Systems Engineer

Certificate Programs: Fire Protection Technology, Assistive Technology

Class Titles: all; see web site or request current catalog.

Teaching Methods: *Computers:* Internet, real-time chat, e-mail, CD-ROM, LISTSERV. *TV:* videotape, cable program, satellite broadcast. *Other:* videoconferencing, compressed video, audiotapes, ISDN/BRI desktop video, fax, correspondence, independent study, individual study, extrainstitutional learning, examination (CLEP, ACT-PEP, DANTES, GRE).

Admission Requirements: *Undergraduate:* variable. *Graduate:* variable.

On-Campus Requirements: None.

Tuition and Fees: *Undergraduate:* $79/credit for most correspondence courses, $99/credit for correspondence web courses. *High School:* $85/course. *Graduate:* $155–195/credit hour for most Distance Learning courses. (Check with individual department before enrolling). *Application Fee:* $15–25. *Other Costs: Record Maintenance:* $5; *Shipping Fees:* UPS $15, First Class (APO and FPO) $20, outside U.S. $55, Express varies, *Credit by:* semester.

Financial Aid: Federal Stafford Loan, Federal Perkins Loan, Federal PLUS Loan, Federal Pell Grant, Federal Work-Study, VA, Oklahoma resident programs.

Accreditation: North Central Association of Colleges and Schools.

Description: Oklahoma State University (1890) was founded as Oklahoma Agricultural and Mechanical College just 20 months after the Land Run of 1889. OSU is now a modern, comprehensive land-grant university that provides exceptional academic experiences, conducts scholarly research and other creative activities, and disseminates knowledge to the people of Oklahoma and throughout the world through its extension endeavors. Distance learning opportunities are coordinated by University Extension and offered by Independent and Correspondence Study and the various college extension units. More than 130 undergraduate distance courses are available, along with 12 accredited graduate-level degree and certificate programs. With technology changing daily, we aggressively stay on the cutting edge with delivery methods that utilize state-of-the-art equipment and the most advanced technology currently available.

Oklahoma State University, Oklahoma City

900 North Portland	Phone: (405) 945-3240
Oklahoma City, OK 73107	Fax: (405) 945-3325

Division(s): Academic Affairs
Web Site(s): http://www.osuokc.edu
E-mail: lindae@osuokc.edu

Undergraduate Degree Programs:
Associate of Applied Science in:
   Quality Management
   Nursing
   Interpreter Training
   Crime Victims Survivor Services
Associate of Science in:
   Drug and Alcohol Abuse
   Fire Protection Technology
   Public Service

Class Titles: Mathematics, English, Political Science, Computer Information Science, Quality Assurance.

Teaching Methods: *Computers:* Internet, real-time chat, electronic classroom, e-mail, CD-ROM, newsgroup, LISTSERV. *TV:* videotape, cable program. *Other:* videoconferencing, fax, correspondence.

Credits Granted for: experiential learning, extrainstitutional learning, examination (CLEP, ACT-PEP, DANTES, GRE).

Admission Requirements: *Undergraduate:* application, high school transcript (college transcript for transfer students), and ACT (or similar battery).

On-Campus Requirements: None.

Tuition and Fees: *Undergraduate:* $61.35/credit resident, $148.55/credit nonresident. *Other Costs:* $10/credit development course fee. *Credit by:* semester.

Financial Aid: Federal Stafford Loan, Federal Perkins Loan, Federal PLUS Loan, Federal Pell Grant, Federal Work-Study, VA, Oklahoma resident programs.

Accreditation: North Central Association of Colleges and Schools, Oklahoma State Regents for Higher Education, National League for Nursing.

Description: Oklahoma State University, Oklahoma City (1961) is a state-assisted, public, 2-year college serving 4,500 students each semester in one of the fastest growing metropolitan cities in the country. The mission of the institution is to provide collegiate-level career and transfer educational programs and supportive services to prepare individuals to live and work in an increasingly technological and global community. OSU-OKC offers more than 30 certificate and degree programs including Nursing, Fire Protection Technology, Alcohol and Substance Abuse Counseling, Interpreter Training, and Quality Management. The distance learning program, which began in 1996, has grown to include courses and programs online, via interactive TV, and through Western Governors University.

Olivet Nazarene University

One University Avenue	Phone: (800) 339-1149
Bourbonnais, IL 60914-2271	Fax: (310) 578-4716

Division(s): School of Graduate and Adult Studies
Web Site(s): http://www.masters4teachers.net
E-mail: michael.byron@educate.com

Graduate Degree Programs:
Master of Education Degree via Distance Delivery

Class Titles: The High-Performing Teacher, Effective Classroom Management, Motivating Today's Learner, Current Issues: Technology in the Classroom, Learning Styles and Multiple Intelligences, Collaborative Action Research, Instructional Strategies: Models of Effective Teaching, Curriculum Design and Assessment, Parents on Your Side, Including Students with Special Needs in the Regular Classroom.

Teaching Methods: *Computers:* Internet, e-mail. *TV:* videotape. *Other:* portfolio, faculty mentor, collegial study teams, audiotapes, fax, conference calls.

Credits Granted for: portfolio assessment, reflective paper, individual assignments, study team assignments.

Admission Requirements: *Graduate:* completed application for admission, $200 one-time registration fee (applied toward your first term tuition upon your acceptance into the program), copy of your current, valid teaching certificate, recent photo (passport type), valid e-mail address, letter of employment verification from your current employer (needed only if your teaching certificate has expired or if you teach in a private school), official transcripts from all undergraduate coursework.

On-Campus Requirements: None.

Tuition and Fees: *Graduate:* ONU requires that students go through Tuition Management Systems (TMS) to make monthly payments for the Master of Education Degree via distance delivery. Following is a summary of the fees required: *Registration:* $200, *Service Fee:* $95, 1st installment: $401.10, 2nd-19th installment: $401.05, *Total program cost:* $7,915. *Graduation Fee:* $100 (already included in the total program cost of $7,915). *Credit by:* semester.

Financial Aid: Subsidized and/or unsubsidized GSL/Stafford Loans.

Accreditation: North Central Association of Colleges and Schools (NCA).

Description: Founded in 1907, Olivet Nazarene University (ONU) is known throughout the Midwest for providing innovative educational programs that adhere to the highest academic standards. ONU has designed this Master of Education program to promote a quality graduate education experience with the convenience and flexibility of distance delivery.

Open Learning Agency

4355 Mathissi Place	Phone: (604) 431-3300
Burnaby, BC,	(Toll-free, Canada) (800) 663-9711
Canada V5G 4S8	Fax: (604) 431-3381

Division(s):
BC Open University and Open College (postsecondary)
OLA Skills Centres (IT training)
Knowledge Network (educational TV)
Open School (K–12)
Canadian Learning Bank (credit review services)
Web Site(s): http://www.ola.bc.ca
E-mail: student@ola.bc.ca

Undergraduate Degree Programs:
Bachelor of Arts, General Program
Bachelor or Arts, General Studies
Bachelor of Arts, Major Program
Bachelor of Business Administration
Bachelor of Business Administration (Public Sector Management)
Bachelor of Business in Real Estate
Bachelor of:
  Fine Art
  Design
  General Studies
  Health Science (Physiotherapy)
  Health Science (Psychiatric Nursing)
  Health (Science) (Respiratory Therapy)
  Music Therapy
  Music (Jazz Studies)
  Music (Performance)
  Science (General Program)
  Science (Major Program)
  Technology (Technology Management)
  Technology (Computing)
  Tourism Management

Certificate Programs: Business Skills, Management of Workplace Instruction, Workplace Leadership Foundation, Management Studies, General Studies, Certified Dental Assisting, Home Support Attendant, Nurse Refresher, Practical Nurse Refresher, Social Service Worker, Adult Basic Education, College Basic Education/Career Preparation Courses: Intermediate (Adult Grade 10), Advanced (Adult Grade 11).

Class Titles: Accounting, Administration, Agricultural Studies, Animal Science, Anthropology, Apiculture, Applied Science, Archaeology, Asian Studies, Astronomy, Biological Sciences, Business/Management, Calculus, Canadian

Studies, Career Planning, Certified Dental Assisting, Chemistry, Child Care, Commerce, Communication, Community Economic Development, Computer Applications, Computer Science, Computer Studies, Counseling, Criminology, Economics, Education, Adult Education, Curriculum Development, Early Childhood Education, Law for Teachers, Educational Psychology, Engineering, English, English as Second Language, Environmental Studies, Film, Finance, Fine Art, First Nations Studies, Food Science, Forestry, French, Geography, Geology, German, Gerontology, Health, History, Home Care Nursing, Home Support Attendant, Humanities, Japanese, Kinesiology, Languages Education, Law, Library Studies, Linguistics, Literature, Math, Museum Studies, Music, Nursing, Oceanography, Philosophy, Physics, Plant Science, Political Science, Practical Nursing, Psychology, Science, Social Sciences, Social Service, Soil Science, Spanish, Statistics, Urban Studies, Women's Studies, Workplace Leadership.

Teaching Methods: *Computers:* Internet, computer conferencing, e-mail. *TV:* broadcast, videotape. *Other:* independent study, some face-to-face and classroom-based methods, fax, telephone, audioconferencing, audiotapes, videotape.

Credits Granted for: experiential learning, portfolio assessment, extrainstitutional learning, transfer credit.

Admission Requirements: *Undergraduate:* open-admission. Students may register at any time throughout the year. For some programs, students must meet specific criteria and apply for admission. *Certificate:* same as undergraduate.

On-Campus Requirements: None.

Tuition and Fees: *Undergraduate:* Canadian $51/credit for 100 and 200 level courses, Canadian $64/credit for 300 and 400 level courses. *Graduate:* TBA. *Application Fee:* Canadian $45/course. *Other Costs:* textbooks/supplies, long distance costs (outside BC and the Yukon Territory). *Credit by:* course, although continuous registration is offered.

Financial Aid: Adult Basic Education Student Assistance Program (part-time bursaries and grants), British Columbia Student Assistance Program (full-time student loans), student loans, BC Grant and Loan Remission, private bursaries and scholarships.

Accreditation: BC Public Post-Secondary System, Association of Universities and Colleges of Canada, Association of Community Colleges of Canada.

Description: The government of British Columbia established the "Open Learning Institute" (1978) to develop and deliver distance education to British Columbians living outside urban centers. In 1988 the OLI merged with Knowledge Network (BC's educational broadcaster) and formed the Open Learning Agency. In the fall of 1998, this organization incorporated OLA Skills Centres, Open School (K–12), Knowledge Network, and BC Open University and Open College. As part of the Open Learning Agency, both BC Open University and Open College are committed to providing innovative learning opportunities for British Columbians, Canadians, and others around the world. Through flexible admissions policies, established distance learning methods, and new educational technologies, BC Open University students may earn credits toward associate and bachelor's degrees, or for transfer to other institutions. Through the same range of services, Open College students may pursue a range of certificates and diplomas, many of which may be applied to BC Open University programs.

Oral Roberts University

7777 South Lewis Avenue
Tulsa, OK 74171

Phone: (800) 643-7976
(918) 495-6236
Fax: (918) 495-7965

Division(s): Adult Learning Service Center
Web Site(s): http://www.oru.edu
E-mail: alsc@oru.edu
dschnacker@oru.edu (Darby Schnacker, Director of Distance Education)

Undergraduate Degree Programs:
Bachelor of Science in:
    Business Administration
    Christian Care/Counseling
    Church Ministries
    Elementary Education with state certification
    Liberal Studies

Graduate Degree Programs:
Master of Management
    Non-Profit Concentration
Master of Arts in Education with concentrations in:
    Christian School Administration
    Christian School Postsecondary Administration
    Christian School Curriculum
    Christian School Teaching
    Early Childhood Education
    Teaching With Certification
    Public School Administration
    Teaching English as a Second Language
Master of Arts in Practical Theology
Master of Divinity

Doctoral Degree Programs:
Doctor of Education in Educational Leadership
Doctor of Ministry

Certificate Programs: (Noncredit Certificate of Theology). Oral Roberts University provides correspondence courses at the certificate level to motivate Christians who seek further knowledge of the Bible, theology, and ministry. Individuals who take certificate-level courses receive a Certificate of Completion suitable for framing after each course. In addition, individuals who complete 12 certificate courses receive a Certificate of Theology from Oral Roberts University. Contact the Adult Learning Service Center for course information and enrollment.

Class Titles: Contact the Adult Learning Service Center at 918-495-6989 or view the course catalog online at www.oru.edu.

Home School College Program: College-level courses through correspondence for home-educated high school students. Courses include: Basic Drawing; Principles of Biology; Principles of Biology Lab; College Reading and Writing; Reading and Writing in the Liberal Arts; Study Skills; American History; Introduction to Humanities I; Introduction to Humanities II; Introduction to College Mathematics; College Algebra; Mathematics and Society; Charismatic Life and the Healing Ministry.

Teaching Methods: *Computers:* Internet, threaded discussion, chat rooms, e-mail, CD-ROM. *TV:* videotape. *Other:* audiotapes, fax, correspondence, independent study, modules.

Credits Granted for: portfolio assessment (undergraduate only), examination, transfer credits from approved institutions.

Admission Requirements: *Undergraduate:* application, high school transcripts, signed Honor Code, Minister's recommendation, essay, age 22+. *Graduate:* application, college transcripts, signed Honor Code, Minister's recommendation, two academic recommendations, essay, GRE/MAT/GMAT. *Doctoral:* application: college transcripts; signed Honor Code; Minister's recommendation; 2 academic recommendations; essay; GRE/MAT/GMAT; writing sample required for Ed.D.

On-Campus Requirements: No residency required for degrees through the School of LifeLong Education, Home School College Program, or Noncredit Certificate of Theology Program. Residency Requirements vary for programs in the schools of Theology and Missions, Business, and Education. Residency requirements are met through short, on-campus modules. Contact the Adult Learning Service Center at (918) 495-6989 for specific information.

Tuition and Fees: *Undergraduate:* $125/credit, $5/course administrative fee. Home School College Program $75/credit. *Graduate:* $299/credit for Business and Education; $262/credit for Theology; $90/term administrative fee. *Doctoral:* $299/credit for Doctor of Education; $2,425/year for Doctor of Ministry; $90/term administrative fee. *Application Fee:* $35. *Other Costs:* $15/course proctor fee. *Credit by:* semester.

Financial Aid: Federal Stafford Loan, Federal PLUS Loan, Federal Pell Grant, VA. Aid available only for degrees.

Accreditation: North Central Association of Colleges and Schools. The ORU School of Theology and Missions is accredited by the Association of Theological Schools in the United States and Canada. ORU is recognized by the Oklahoma State Regents for Higher Education. Its Teacher Education programs are approved by the State Department of Education, and it is a member of both the American Association of Colleges of Teacher Education and the Association of American Colleges.

Description: Founded in 1963, Oral Roberts University has been offering distance courses since 1974. In 1992 the School of LifeLong Education became a school within the University offering degree programs fully by correspondence. ORU's School of Education began offering the Bachelor of Science in Education with state certification through distance education in the Spring 2000 semester and it is the only program of its kind being offered in the state of Oklahoma. ORU's graduate programs through distance education offer professionals the opportunity to continue their education in a Christ-centered environment without leaving their homes and jobs. Oral Roberts University is a charismatic liberal arts university fully accredited and recognized by applicable professional societies.

Ottawa University, Kansas City

10865 Grandview Drive
Overland Park, KS 66210

Phone: (913) 451-1431
(888) 404-6852
Fax: (913) 451-0806

Division(s): Individual Departments
Web Site(s): http://www.ottawa.edu
E-mail: ottawainfo@aol.com

Undergraduate Degree Programs:
Bachelor of Arts in Management of Health Services

Graduate Degree Programs:
Master of Arts in Human Resources
Master of Business Administration

Teaching Methods: *Computers:* Internet, real-time chat, electronic classroom, e-mail. *Other:* correspondence, independent study.

Credits Granted for: experiential learning, portfolio assessment, extrainstitutional learning, examination (CLEP, ACT-PEP, DANTES).

Admission Requirements: *Undergraduate:* allied health service background and education. *Graduate:* accredited bachelor's degree. *Graduate MBA:* accredited bachelor's degree with accounting and economic course work.

On-Campus Requirements: undergraduate Friday and Saturday sessions 4 times/year in Overland Park, Kansas; Wilmington, Delaware; or New Orleans, Louisiana. Graduate Thursday through Sunday sessions 3 times/year in Overland Park, Kansas.

Tuition and Fees: *Undergraduate:* $260/credit. *Graduate:* $340/credit. *Application Fee:* $50. *Credit by:* semester.

Financial Aid: Federal Stafford Loan, Federal PLUS Loan, Federal Pell Grant, VA.

Accreditation: North Central Association of Colleges and Schools.

Description: Established as the university's first nonresidential campus, Ottawa University, Kansas City (1974) serves the educational needs of adults. Its programs, consistent with those of the residential campus, include individual educational planning, full-time faculty advisors, interdisciplinary approaches, and resources for lifelong learning. Additionally, these programs are directed to the unique circumstances of adult learners who must balance their quests for higher education with competing claims of work and family responsibility.

Owens Community College

| PO Box 10000 | Phone: (419) 661-7355 |
| Toledo, OH 43699-1947 | Fax: (419) 661-7662 |

Division(s): Academic Affairs
Web Site(s): http://www.owens.cc.oh.us
E-mail: mkaramol@owens.cc.oh.us

Undergraduate Degree Programs:
Associate of Arts
Associate of Applied Business in E-Business

Teaching Methods: *Computers:* Internet, real-time chat, electronic classroom, e-mail, CD-ROM telecourses, software—Blackboard, Web CT. *TV:* videotape, cable program, satellite broadcasting, PBS. *Other:* videoconferencing, audiotapes, fax, correspondence, independent study, individual study, learning contracts.

Credits Granted for: Education, work experience, etc.

Admission Requirements: *Undergraduate:* open-admission.

On-Campus Requirements: None.

Tuition and Fees: *Undergraduate:* $75/credit. *Software:* varies. *Other Costs:* $10 registration fee/semester, $25 waivers/course. *Lab fees:* vary by course. *Credit by:* semester.

Financial Aid: Federal Stafford Loan, Federal Perkins Loan, Federal Pell Grant, Federal Work-Study, VA, Ohio resident programs.

Accreditation: North Central Association of Colleges and Schools.

Description: Owens Community College began in 1965 as a technical institute. Its mission is to provide quality technical and general education for students and employers in its service area. The college is committed to preparing every graduate to succeed in the world of technical service, to make a positive contribution to society, and to support—as well as survive—change. As part of the Owens mission, distance learning began in the early 1990s through a partnership with Ameritech, which provided a fiber optic link between the 2 campuses and a number of businesses in Toledo and Findlay. Since then, the Board of Regents has approved a grant to expand that technology capability.

Ozarks Technical Community College

| 933 East Central | Phone: (417) 895-7107 |
| Springfield, MO 65802 | Fax: (417) 895-1328 |

Division(s): Academic Services
Web Site(s): http://www.otc.cc.mo.us
E-mail: slawler@otc.cc.mo.us

Class Titles: English, Humanities, Political Science, Jump Start Math, Lifetime Wellness, Pathophysiology.

Teaching Methods: *Computers:* e-mail. *TV:* online courses, Internet, real-time chat, electronic classroom.

Admission Requirements: None.

On-Campus Requirements: Some online courses are "blended." The student will attend 2–4 lab sessions on campus.

Tuition and Fees: *Undergraduate:* $56/credit. *Credit by:* semester.

Financial Aid: Federal Stafford Loan, Federal Pell Grant, Federal Perkins Loan, Federal PLUS Loan, Federal Work-Study, VA, Missouri resident programs (A+).

Accreditation: North Central Association of Colleges and Schools.

Description: Ozarks Technical Community College (1991) offered its first classes in the fall of 1991. It has since grown from 1,200 students to 7,300, making it the fastest growing community college in Missouri. The primary purpose of Ozarks Technical Community College is to provide technical education programs supported by essential foundation and basic skills courses, which are responsive to the education needs of the community and its industrial, commercial, and service organizations. In 2000 OTC began to offer web-based courses making it possible for students to take courses anywhere, anytime. There are currently several general education courses being offered by the college.

Pacific Oaks College

5 Westmoreland Place	Phone: (800) 684-0900
Pasadena, CA 91103	Fax: (626) 577-6144

Division(s): Distance Learning
Web Site(s): http://www.pacificoaks.edu
E-mail: admissions@pacificoaks.edu

Undergraduate Degree Programs:
Bachelor of Arts in Human Development

Graduate Degree Programs:
Master of Arts in Human Development

Certificate Programs: Human Development/Early Childhood (postgraduate), California Early Childhood Education Credential.

Class Titles: Early Childhood Themes/Life Cycle Issues, Communication for Empowerment, Leadership in Education, Working with Adults, Administration/Supervision: Fieldwork, College Teaching: Fieldwork, Parent/Community Work: Fieldwork, Reflective Teaching, Parent Involvement, Observation, Emergent Curriculum, Cognitive Development, Earliest Years, Working with Children, Anti-Bias Curriculum, Developmental Assessment/Program Planning, Assessment of Experience, Thesis Development, Advanced Studies in Human Development, Research Seminar, Development of Bicultural Children. Play, Language, and Literacy, Young Child with Special Needs, Early Childhood Special Education Curriculum.

Teaching Methods: *Computers:* Internet, e-mail, LISTSERV. *Other:* None.

Credits Granted for: experiential learning, portfolio assessment, examination (CLEP).

Admission Requirements: *Undergraduate:* 70 acceptable semester credits. *Graduate:* accredited bachelor's degree, OR 60 credits and age 35, with 5 years of leadership experience. *Certificate:* master's degree.

On-Campus Requirements: 2 classes in a week-long intensive or weekend format at Southern CA, Northern CA, or Seattle campus.

Tuition and Fees: *Undergraduate:* $550/credit. *Graduate:* $550/credit. *Application Fee:* $55. *Software:* included. *Other Costs:* $30/semester Student Activity. $25/semester online fee. *Credit by:* semester.

Financial Aid: Federal Stafford Loan, Federal Perkins Loan, Federal PLUS Loan, Federal Pell Grant, Federal Work-Study, VA, California resident programs.

Accreditation: Western Association of Schools and Colleges.

Description: Pacific Oaks College (1945) began as a community education center and nursery school and soon added a teacher education program, out of which the college grew. Upper division and graduate programs available to distance students lead to BA and MA degrees in Human Development, with specializations in Early Childhood Education, Bicultural Development, and Leadership in Education and Human Services. The college also offers on-campus, elementary teacher and family counselor certification programs. Online, as on campus, experiential learning is at the heart of Pacific Oaks' curriculum for adults as well as for children. Pacific Oaks believes people learn both theory and practice through action and interaction; thus the college encourages its students to work together and learn from each other. Through e-mail "meetings," lively discussion-in-writing involves students and faculty. Distance learning online has been available since 1996, and the course offerings are growing steadily.

Palo Alto College

1400 West Villaret Boulevard	Phone: (210) 921-5103
San Antonio, TX 78224-2499	Fax: (210) 921-5412

Division(s): Distance Learning
Web Site(s): http://www.accd.edu/pac/pacmain/pachp.htm
E-mail: robogarz@accd.edu

Undergraduate Degree Programs:
Associate

Certificate Programs: Personal Computer Skills, Entry Level Supervision, Total Quality Management, Customer Service Representative, Web Authoring, General Office—Level I, General Office—Level II, Administrative Assistant—Level III, Administrative Computer Technology—Tech-Prep Enhanced Skills, Business Communications, Data Entry Technician, Environmental Regulations Management—Level I, Environmental Compliance Management—Level II, Water Resource Management, Horticulture Business Management, International Logistics Management, Warehouse Management, Logistics Management, Product Marketing Specialist, Animal Health Specialist, Agribusiness Management—Enhanced Skills Certificate.

Class Titles: Accounting, Art, Business Computer Applications, Biology, Nutrition, Man and His Environment, Anatomy and Physiology, Business, Chemistry, Computer Science: Computer Literacy, Introduction To Computer and Information Systems, Fundamentals of Programming, Structured Programming, Communications, Criminal Justice,

Economics (Macro and Micro), English: Freshman Composition I and II, Literature: American Literature, British Literature, Geology, Government (National/State/Local and Problems/Policies), History of the U.S. I and II, Humanities, Information Studies, Information Systems: Integrated Software Applications, Internet/Web Page Development, Introduction To Visual Basic Programming, Special Topics: Java Programming, Presentation Media Software, Advanced Spreadsheets, Advanced Database, Math: College Algebra and Business Calculus, Music, Orientation, Physical Education, Philosophy, Psychology, Sociology, Speech.

Teaching Methods: *Computers:* Internet, real-time chat, electronic classroom, e-mail, CD-ROM, LISTSERV. *TV:* videotape, cable program, satellite broadcasting, PBS. *Other:* videoconferencing, audiotapes, fax.

Credits Granted for: examination (CLEP, DANTES, Subject Examination, Advanced Placement, standardized, departmental challenge), Army/ACE Registered Transcripts System through Service Members Opportunity Colleges for Active Army, military training, transfer transcripts. Credit by nontraditional methods must be applicable to a Palo Alto degree program.

Admission Requirements: *Undergraduate:* high school graduate with official transcript, GED, or transcript of last school attended if transferring; placement test scores; meet minimum scholastic standards of Palo Alto; TASP scores if taken. Contact the school for international student requirements. Conditional admission with permission. High school students may apply for Dual-Credit Program and earn college credit while in high school. No admission credentials needed for audit status. *Certificate:* same as undergraduate.

On-Campus Requirements: variable.

Tuition and Fees: *Undergraduate:* $120/1–6 hours, $168/7 hours, $192/8 hours, $216/9 hours, $240/10 hours, $264/11 hours, $288/12 hours, $312/13 hours, $336 14/hours, $360/15 hours, $384/16 hours, $408/17 hours, $432/18 hours, $456/19 hours, $480/20 hours, $504/21 hours in-district. Out-of-district Texas residents: $230/1–6, $322/7, $368/8, $414/9, $460/10, $506/11, $552/12, $598/13, $644/14, $690/15, $736/16, $782/17, $828/18, $874/19, $920/20, $966/21. Nonresidents and international: $460/1–6, $644/7, $736/8, $828/9, $920/10, $1,012/11, $1,104/12, $1,196/13, $1,288/14, $1,380/15, $1,472/16, $1,564/17, $1,656/18, $1,748/19, $1,840/20, $1,932/21. *Other Costs:* $3/credit instructional technology fee, $40 general summer fee, $60–$65 general fall/spring fee, $10 library fee, $6 summer registration fee, $10 fall/spring registration fee, $4 insurance fee except for international student, $10 auditing fee, lab and special fees depend on individual courses, $25 late registration fee, $5–$10 vehicle registration and parking permits (depending on time of year), $10 returned check fee, $4/schedule change. Note: summer tuition differs from fall/ spring tuition given above; contact school if interested. *Credit by:* semester.

Financial Aid: Federal Stafford Loan, Federal PLUS Loan, Federal Pell Grant, Federal Work-Study, VA, Texas Public Educational Grant, State Student-Incentive Grant.

Accreditation: Southern Association of Colleges and Schools.

Description: Palo Alto College (1983) is one of four colleges in the Alamo Community College District. It serves students from an immediate service area in the southern sector of San Antonio, other parts of Bexar County, and the outlying rural counties south of Bexar County. Palo Alto is one of the fastest-growing institutions of higher education in Texas. The college is an open-admission, public, 2-year college dedicated to the pursuit of excellence in its educational programs and services. PAC provides the foundation skills and workplace competencies that empower students to pursue their goals of entering the workforce, continue formal education at other colleges and universities, develop additional skills for their chosen occupations, or acquire learning for personal enjoyment and satisfaction. Palo Alto began distance learning 6 years ago via telecourses.

Palomar Community College

1140 County Mission Road
San Marcos, CA 92069-1487

Phone: (760) 744-1150 x2431
Fax: (760) 761-3519

Division(s): Educational TV
Web Site(s): http://www.ETV.palomar.edu
E-mail: shargrav@palomar.edu

Undergraduate Degree Programs:
Associate of Arts
Intersegmental General Transfer program

Certificate Programs: Certificate of Achievement.

Class Titles: Financial Accounting, Race/Class/Ethnic Groups in America, Cultural Anthropology, Art, American Sign Language, Business, Business Math, Business Law, Personal Finance, Small Business Management, Child Development, College Success Skills Career Search, English As Second Language, Humanities, Fundamentals of Music, Contemporary Legal Issues, Psychology, Marriage/Family, Abnormal Psychology, Refrigeration/Heat/Air Conditioning—Electric, Refrigeration/Heat/Air Conditioning—Mechanical, Sociology, Beginning Conversation, Intermediate Conversation, General Biology, Children's Literature, Career/Life Planning, Mass Media in America, Digital Imaging with Photoshop, Knowledge and Reality, Nutrition Pathways.

Teaching Methods: Computer: Internet *TV:* videotape, cable program, satellite broadcasting, PBS. *Other:* videoconferencing.

On-Campus Requirements: None.

Tuition and Fees: *Undergraduate:* $11/unit, California resident one year. *Credit by:* semester.

Financial Aid: Federal Stafford Loan, Federal Perkins Loan, Federal PLUS Loan, Federal Pell Grant, Federal Work-Study, VA, California resident programs.

Accreditation: Community and Junior Colleges of the Western Association of Schools and Colleges.

Description: The history of Palomar College (1946) is rich in tradition, educational achievements, and personalities. Exactly 100 persons showed up on the first day of classes. Enrollment has grown steadily over the last half century, with more than 25,000 full- and part-time students currently studying on Palomar's 200-acre campus. The college provides the first 2 years of regular 4-year college course work, a 2-year liberal arts AA, and training programs in semiprofessional and vocational fields. Outreach locations now include 4 high schools and 3 centers at the Pauma Indian Reservation.

Park University

8700 River Park Drive
Parkville, MO 64152

Phone: (816) 741-2000 x6240
Fax: (816) 741-6138

Division(s): School for Extended Learning
Web Site(s): http://www.park.edu
http://www.park.edu/dist/default.htm
E-mail: carolh@mail.park.edu

Class Titles: The courses offered online are on http://www.park.edu/dist/dist/courseoffering.htm. There are 76 available.

Teaching Methods: *Computers:* Internet, Conference Threads, e-mail, CD-ROM, Internet Service Provider.

Credits Granted for: experiential learning, portfolio assessment, examination (CLEP, ACT-PEP, DANTES, GRE).

Admission Requirements: *Undergraduate:* high school graduate.

On-Campus Requirements: None.

Tuition and Fees: *Undergraduate:* $128/credit. *Other Costs:* $10/credit fee. *Credit by:* semester.

Financial Aid: Federal Stafford Loan, Federal Perkins Loan, Federal PLUS Loan, Federal Pell Grant, Federal Work-Study, VA.

Accreditation: North Central Association of Colleges and Schools.

Description: The School for Extended Learning is the outreach arm of Park University (1875). It is dedicated to serving learners with quality educational programs whenever need is demonstrated. The service is accomplished through these extended learning programs: (1) the Resident Center Program delivers degree completion programs on U.S. military and federal installations, (2) a Community College cooperative program allows students to obtain a bachelor's degree, and (3) Distance Learning provides students access to current educational technologies. The School for Extended Learning takes very seriously the task of educating persons to use knowledge beneficially for economic, social, and moral purposes. It regards cultivating literary and critical intelligence, understanding human cultural context, and developing artistic and moral sensibilities as important education purposes. The school is also dedicated to sound innovation and experimentation in its programs to meet people's needs in extended learning settings. Finally, since it views education as both the acquisition and utilization of knowledge, the school recognizes verifiable educational accomplishment regardless of how or where it was acquired. (See http://www.park.edu/acad/catalog/mission.htm)

Parkland College

2400 West Bradley Avenue
Champaign, IL 61821

Phone: (217) 351-2542
Fax: (217) 353-2241

Division(s): Distance Education and Virtual Learning
Web Site(s): http://online.parkland.cc.il.us
E-mail: heastin@parkland.cc.il.us

Undergraduate Degree Programs:
Parkland College currently offers 9 degrees that can be completed at a distance:
 Associate in Arts
 Associate in General Studies
 Business Administration Associate in Science
 Business Education Associate in Science
 History Associate in Arts, Liberal Arts, and Sciences
 Mass Communications: Advertising/Public Relations Associate in Arts
 Mass Communications: Journalism Associate in Arts
 Psychology Associate in Arts
An additional 7 degrees have 95% of the course work offered at a distance:
 Business Management Associate in Applied Science
 Early Childhood Education Associate in Arts
 Elementary Education Associate in Arts
 Mass Communication: Integrated Associate in Arts
 Political Science Associate in Arts
 Secondary Education Associate in Arts
 Special Education Associate in Arts

Certificate Programs: 95% of the course work for the Business Independent Business Management Certificate can be completed at a distance.

Class Titles: Pathophysiology, Intro Chemistry, News Writing, Basic Web Page Design, Composition, Nursing, Sports Psychology, Physics, Biology, Mathematics, Marketing, Agriculture, Accounting, Anthropology, Art, Business, Computer Information Systems, Communications, Computer Science, Computer Technology Center, Economics, Education, History, Literature, Management, Music, Physical Education, Political Science, Theater.

Teaching Methods: *Computers:* Internet, real-time chat, electronic classroom, e-mail, CD-ROM, newsgroup, LISTSERV. *TV:* videotape, cable program, satellite broadcasting. *Other:* videoconferencing, audioconferencing, fax, correspondence, independent study, individual study.

Credits Granted for: experiential learning, portfolio assessment, extrainstitutional learning, examination (CLEP, ACT-PEP, DANTES, GRE).

Admission Requirements: *Undergraduate:* please call for information.

On-Campus Requirements: None.

Tuition and Fees: *Undergraduate:* $95/credit for online courses. *Credit by:* semester.

Financial Aid: Federal Stafford Loan, Federal Perkins Loan, Federal PLUS Loan, Federal Pell Grant, Federal Work-Study, VA, state programs for residents of Illinois.

Accreditation: North Central Association of Colleges and Schools.

Description: Parkland College (1965) is dedicated to providing for the comprehensive educational needs of its students with accessible and flexibly scheduled programs and high-quality services. Further, the college values and works toward the economic and cultural well-being of the local residents. Parkland recognizes the dignity and worth of each person, the contributions of diverse cultures, the value of creativity, and the need to rely on reason and cooperation to achieve our goals. The college's mission includes guiding and assisting students in becoming active, responsible, self-disciplined citizens; providing up-to-date technical-vocational and career education for students, business, and industry; providing developmental programs, courses, and services to prepare students for college-level work; preparing students for transfer to 4-year colleges/universities; assisting the district economically through services to the public, business, industry, agriculture, and labor; providing lifelong opportunities that include continuing and adult education; engaging students actively in developing a perspective on and an appreciation for cultural diversity; providing support services that enhance students' personal growth and supply employment informa-

tion and placement; and expanding students' global awareness through international studies and experiences.

Pasadena City College

1570 East Colorado Boulevard   **Phone: (626) 585-7108/7608**
Pasadena, CA 91106-2003   **Fax: (626) 585-7916**

Division(s): Learning Resources/Telecourse Administration
Web Site(s): http://paccd.cc.ca.us
E-mail: bnshimasaki@paccd.cc.ca.us

Undergraduate Degree Programs:
Associate of Science
Associate of Arts

Teaching Methods: *Computers:* Internet. *TV:* videotape, cable program, satellite broadcasting, PBS. *Other:* independent study (part of ITV).

Credits Granted for: extrainstitutional learning.

On-Campus Requirements: Courses meet on campus 19 hours/semester.

Tuition and Fees: $11/unit. *Nonresident:* $130/unit *Other Costs:* student representation fee, health fee. *Credit by:* semester.

Financial Aid: Federal Stafford Loan, Federal Perkins Loan, Federal Pell Grant, Federal Work-Study, VA, California resident programs, Supplemental Educational Opportunity grant; EOP.

Accreditation: Western Association of Schools and Colleges.

Description: Pasadena City College (1924) is the third-largest single-campus community college in the U.S., currently enrolling 24,114 credit and 4,660 noncredit students. PCC is located on a 53-acre campus in a district of 370,000, though the college draws 60% of its students from outside the district. The new Community Education Center, just a few miles from the campus, serves 11,000 clients per year, and Continuing Education offers courses to 7,500 students. Pasadena also owns and operates a Child Development Center within a few blocks of the campus. The District employs 419 faculty, librarians, counselors, and administrators and 367 maintenance, trade, professional, clerical, and management workers.

Passaic County Community College

One College Boulevard   **Phone: (973) 684-5790**
Paterson, NJ 07505-1179   **Fax: (973) 684-4079**

Division(s): Academic Affairs/Coordinator of Instructional Technology
Web Site(s): http://www.pccc.cc.nj.us
E-mail: rperdew@pccc.cc.nj.us

Undergraduate Degree Programs:
Associate in Arts
Associate in Science
Associate in Applied Science

Certificate Programs: Certificates in care specializations.

Class Titles: Communications, English, Health Information Technology, Math, Science, Criminal Justice and Fire Science.

Teaching Methods: *Computers:* Internet, Web CT. *TV:* satellite broadcasting (downlinks), Interactive Television Classes.

Credits Granted for: previous college transcripts, examination (CLEP, ACT-PEP, DANTES, GRE).

Admission Requirements: *Undergraduate:* high school diploma, GED.

On-Campus Requirements: None.

Tuition and Fees: *Undergraduate:* $80/credit (online courses). *Credit by:* semester.

Financial Aid: Federal Stafford Loan, Federal Perkins Loan, Federal PLUS Loan, Federal Pell Grant, Federal Work-Study, VA, state programs for residents of New Jersey.

Accreditation: Commission of Higher of Education, Middle States Association of Colleges and Schools.

Description: Passaic County Community College (1977) is a publicly supported 2-year college offering associate in arts and associate in science degree programs. We also offer associate in applied science degrees and certificates in career specializations. The college provides more than 40 degree and certificate programs to over 5,000 students. PCCC's main campus is in the lower portion of Passaic County, New Jersey, in the heart of one of the nation's most historic industrial cities, Paterson, New Jersey. The campus serves an extremely diverse population. In 1999 PCCC began to offer courses over the Internet. We did so to extend our reach across traditional boundaries, serving students at any time and any place. PCCC offered 4 web-based courses during the fall of 1999. In the September of 2001 we will offer our students over 20 web-based courses. To increase our students accessibility to courses we are part of the New Jersey Community College Consortium, which offers over 300 courses to students throughout the state of New Jersey. Starting in the fall of 2001 our students will be able to take courses from other NJVCCC institutions.

Peirce College

1420 Pine Street
Philadelphia, PA 19102

Phone: (877) 670-9190
Fax: (215) 546-5996

Division(s): Academic Advancement
Web Site(s): http://www.peirce.edu
E-mail: Info@peirce.edu

Undergraduate Degree Programs:
Business Administration
Information Technology

Class Titles: Contact school or check web site for details.

Teaching Methods: *Computers:* Internet, real-time chat, electronic classroom, e-mail, CD-ROM, newsgroup, LISTERV. *TV:* videotape, PBS. *Other:* fax, correspondence, independent study, individual study, learning contracts.

Credits Granted for: experiential learning, portfolio assessment, extrainstitutional learning (PONSI, corporate or professional association seminars/workshops), examination (CLEP, ACT-PEP, DANTES, GRE).

Admission Requirements: *Undergraduate:* high school diploma, GED.

On-Campus Requirements: None.

Tuition and Fees: *Undergraduate:* $325/credit. *Graduation Fee:* $50. *Other Costs:* $60/3 credits Technology Fee. *Credit by:* semester.

Financial Aid: Federal Stafford Loan, Federal PLUS Loan, Federal Pell Grant, Federal Work-Study, VA, state programs for residents of Pennsylvania.

Accreditation: Middle States Association of Colleges and Schools.

Description: "Peirce means Business" has been our credo since 1865. The college's mission and specialized 4-year curriculua are just as relevant today in support of workforce and economic development as prior programs were, dating back to the founding of the institution. Peirce is a welcoming place for working adult learners, including the first generation to attend college. Peirce Online was launched in fall 2000 and is the latest example of the strategic decision to "reach out" to students.

Penn State University

207 Mitchell Building
University Park, PA 16802-3601

Phone: (814) 865-5403
(800) 252-3592
Fax: (814) 865-3290

Division(s): Distance Education/World Campus
Web Site(s): www.worldcampus.psu.edu
E-mail: Distance Education: psude@cde.psu.edu
World Campus: psuwd@psu.edu

Undergraduate Degree Programs:
Bachelor of Arts in Letters, Arts, and Sciences—Emphasis in Organizational Leadership or Workplace Dynamics
LionHawk (a joint bachelor's degree program between Penn State and the University of Iowa)
Associate Degrees in:
   Letters, Arts, and Sciences
   Business Administration
   Human Development and Family Studies
   Dietetic Food Systems Management
LionHawk (joint bachelor's program between Penn State and University of Iowa)

Graduate Degree Programs:
Master of Education in Adult Education

Certificate Programs: *Credit:* Writing Social Commentary, Business Management, Small Business Management, Advanced Business Management, Retail Management I, Retail Management II, General Business, Marketing Management, Human Resources, Adult Development and Aging Services, Children, Youth, and Family Services, Community and Economic Development, Counselor Education-Chemical Dependency, Customer Relationship Management, Dietary Manager, Dietetics and Aging, Food Service Supervision, Educational Technology Integration, Hospitality Management, Logistics and Supply Chain Management, Noise Control Engineering, Reliability Engineering, Turfgrass Management. *Noncredit:* Supervisory Leadership, Geographic Information Systems, Webmaster, Digital Office, Paralegal, Legal Issues for Business Professionals, Legal Issues for those Dealing with the Elderly.

Teaching Methods: Primarily print-based courses with optional Web sites and e-mail lesson submission. Some courses are completely Web based. Audio- and videotapes are used in some courses.

Credits Granted for: selected CLEP and DANTES exams, AP exams, ACE reviewed military and nontraditional educational experiences.

Admission Requirements: *Undergraduate:* high school diploma or GED, SAT, or ACT. *Certificate:* high school diploma or GED for most; more education for some baccalaureate, postbaccalaureate, and graduate certificates.

On-Campus Requirements: None.

Tuition and Fees: Courses 000–299 $133/semester hour: Courses 300–499 $252/semester hour; graduate courses and some World Campus courses $291/semester hour. $30 processing fee per course. *Degree Application Fees:* $50. Software: varies for courses. *Credit by:* semester.

Financial Aid: Federal financial aid isn't available for rolling enrollment courses; may be available for courses with a specific start and end date depending on students' degree status and course load.

Accreditation: Middle States Association of Colleges and Schools.

Description: Penn State University was chartered in 1855 as the Farmer's High School. In 1953 the name was changed to The Pennsylvania State University to recognize that the school had become one of the nation's leading universities. Since 1892 Penn State has been a pioneer and international leader in distance education. Today, more than 20,000 adults choose Penn State to begin or continue their college education or to find personal enrichment.

Pensacola Junior College

1000 College Boulevard
Pensacola, FL 32504

Phone: (850) 484-1238
Fax: (850) 484-1838

Division(s): Distance Learning
Web Site(s): http://www.distance.pjc.cc.fl.us
E-mail: dlearn@pjc.cc.fl.us

Class Titles: American History, Humanities Art, Descriptive Astronomy, Biological Principles for Non Majors, Child Development, Human Growth/Development, Economics, English Composition, Marriage/Family Living, Personal Finance/Money Management, Business, Earth Science, Nutrition, Algebra, Trigonometry, Principles of Management, Psychology, Public Speaking, Statistics, Sociology, Social Problems, Music Appreciation, Internet Research.

Teaching Methods: *Computers:* Internet, real-time chat, electronic classroom, e-mail, CD-ROM, LISTSERV. *TV:* videotape, cable program, PBS. *Other:* videoconferencing, audiotapes, fax, correspondence.

Credits Granted for: examination (CLEP, departmental exemption, CPS), military credit, Prior Learning Assessment, Servicemembers Opportunity College, transfer correspondence college credit, CPS Examination.

Admission Requirements: *Undergraduate:* official high school transcript with graduation date, or official GED score report with diploma issue date.

On-Campus Requirements: 5–10 hours/term covering reviews and testing.

Tuition and Fees: *Undergraduate:* $48.50/credit state residents, $180.85/credit nonresidents. *Application Fee:* $30. *Other Costs:* $20–30 for lab fees; fees subject to change at the discretion of the Board of Trustees. *Credit by:* semester.

Financial Aid: Federal Stafford Loan, Federal PLUS Loan, Federal Pell Grant, Federal Work-Study, VA, Florida resident programs.

Accreditation: Southern Association of Colleges and Schools.

Description: Pensacola Junior College (1948) is a student-centered, comprehensive community college dedicated to providing educational opportunities that develop its students' personal, academic, career, and aesthetic capabilities so they may achieve self-fulfillment and participate fully and positively in a democratic society. PJC began offering telecourses in 1968 through the school's PBS station. Distance learning courses, using a variety of delivery modes, continue to increase as the college seeks to be flexible in meeting the needs of adult learners.

Peralta Community College District Alameda, Laney, Merritt, and Vista Colleges

| 333 East Eighth Street | Phone: (510) 466-7268 |
| Oakland, CA 94606 | Fax: (510) 466-7304 |

Division(s): Information Technology Management Information Systems
Web Site(s): http://www.peralta.cc.ca.us
E-mail: hperdue@peralta.cc.ca.us or lmnelson@mail.metro.net

Undergraduate Degree Programs:
Associate

Certificate Programs: numerous; call for listing.

Class Titles: Astronomy, Biology, Human Nutrition, Geology, Marine Environment, Physics, Archaeology, Social/Cultural Anthropology, Business, Economics USA (macro/micro), Cultural Geography, Health Issues, History of U.S. to 1877, History of U.S. Since 1865, History of Mexico, Media/Mass Society, Government/Politics in U.S., Psychology, Psychology of Childhood, Sociology, Minority Groups, Sociology of Family, Poetry, French, Human Values/Ethics, Arts/Ideas of West Culture, Religions of World, Destinos (Spanish course), Composition, Statistics, Math for Liberal Arts Students, Elementary Algebra, College Algebra, Computer Literacy, Speech.

Teaching Methods: *Computers:* Internet. *TV:* videotape, cable program, satellite broadcasting, PBS. *Other:* None.

Admission Requirements: *Undergraduate:* age 18.

On-Campus Requirements: None.

Tuition and Fees: *Undergraduate:* $11/credit. *Credit by:* semester.

Financial Aid: California Community Colleges Board of Governor's Enrollment Fee Waiver, Federal Pell Grant, Federal Supplemental Educational Opportunity Grant, Federal Work-Study, Student Loan Cal Grants B and C, Extended Opportunity Programs and Services.

Accreditation: Western Association of Colleges and Schools.

Description: The Peralta Community College District (1953), comprised of 4 colleges, is one of 71 community college districts in California. The colleges serve 23,000 students and offer the first 2 years of undergraduate education as well as numerous certificates. The mission of the colleges is to meet the educational needs of their communities by providing comprehensive and flexible programs that will enable students to transfer to 4-year institutions, to earn degrees and certificates in selected academic and occupational fields, to prepare for entry-level positions in specific careers, to improve their basic learning skills, and to expand their general knowledge. The distance education program was started in 1995.

Philadelphia University

| School House Lane and Henry Avenue | Phone: (215) 951-2943 |
| Philadelphia, PA 19144 | Fax: (215) 951-2907 |

Division(s): Office of Graduate Admissions
Web Site(s): http://www.philau.edu/graduate/index.html
E-mail: gradadm@philau.edu

Graduate Degree Programs:
Master of Science with Concentration in Midwifery
MBA in Textile and Apparel Marketing

Teaching Methods: *Computers:* Internet, real-time chat, electronic classroom, e-mail, CD-ROM, newsgroup, LISTSERV. *Other:* None.

Admission Requirements: *Graduate:* application, 2 recommendations, résumé, transcripts, standardized test.

On-Campus Requirements: Students in MS in Midwifery attend a 4-day orientation in Philadelphia. Students in the MBA in Textile and Apparel Marketing are not required to travel to Philadelphia.

Tuition and Fees: *Graduate:* $517/credit for Midwifery; TBA for MBA program. *Application Fee:* $35. *Credit by:* semester.

Accreditation: Middle States Association of Schools and Colleges.

Description: In 1884 a group of textile manufacturers, led by Theodore Search, established the Philadelphia Textile School and began a formal educational program for America's textile workers and managers. In 1961 the school changed its name to Philadelphia College of Textiles and Science. As Philadelphia College of Textiles and Science, the institution offered its first graduate degree, the Master's of Business Administration, in 1976. To better reflect the institution's breadth and depth and its successful growth, the college applied for and was granted university status by the Commonwealth of Pennsylvania in 1999, and, in a historic move, the Board of Trustees voted to change the college's name to Philadelphia University, the first private university to be named exclusively after the city of Philadelphia. The name Philadelphia University became effective on July 13, 1999. The MS in Midwifery was the first distance education program offered, and began in 1998. In 2001, the university launched the online MBA in Textile and Apparel Marketing.

Piedmont College

PO Box 10	Phone: (706) 778-3000
Demorest, GA 30535	Fax: (706) 776-2811

Division(s): Undergraduate and Graduate Admissions
Web Site(s): http://www.piedmont.edu
E-mail: ugrad@piedmont.edu
grad@piedmont.edu

Class Titles: vary each semester. Check the web site link for the Registrar for current information.

Teaching Methods: *Computers:* Internet, real-time chat, e-mail, LISTSERV. *Other:* videoconferencing, independent study, individual study, learning contracts.

Credits Granted for: experiential learning, portfolio assessment, examination (CLEP, ACT-PEP, DANTES).

Admission Requirements: *Undergraduate:* high school diploma or GED limited transfer credits, all official transcripts, SAT, 2.0 GPA. *Graduate:* varies by degree. Check the web site for the specific admissions criteria.

On-Campus Requirements: depends on course.

Tuition and Fees: *Undergraduate:* $437.50/credit. *Graduate:* $230/credit. *Credit by:* semester.

Financial Aid: Federal Stafford Loan, Federal Perkins Loan, Federal PLUS Loan, Federal Pell Grant, Federal Work-Study, VA, Georgia resident programs limited graduate assistantships.

Accreditation: Southern Association of Colleges and Schools.

Description: Piedmont (1897) is an independent, private, liberal arts college that awards Bachelor of Arts, Bachelor of Science, and Bachelor of Science in Nursing degrees in 22 major areas, and Master of Arts in Teaching and Master of Arts degrees in Early Childhood Education, Secondary Education in Math, Broad-field Science, Broad-field Social Science, and English, Special Education: Emotional/Behavior Disorders, Music Education, Art Education, Education Specialist, and Master in Public Administration, and Master in Business Administration. Enrollment is 1,900 in its Demorest, Athens, and off-campus locations. In 1994 Piedmont installed an interactive distance learning lab under the Georgia Statewide Academic and Medical System. Through its use, the college offers courses to local and distant high schools, and today provides classes between the college's Demorest campus and Athens center. In 1997 the college began offering classes on the Web, with many more offerings planned.

Pierce College

9401 Farwest Drive SW	Phone: (253) 964-6244
Lakewood, WA 98498-1999	Fax: (253) 964-6713

Division(s): Extended Learning
Web Site(s): http://www.pierce.ctc.edu
E-mail: distedu@pierce.ctc.edu

Class Titles: Social Anthropology, Survey of Anthropology, Human Anatomy/Physiology, Composition/Exposition, Computer Information Systems, Composition-Argumentation/Research, Literature, Poetry, Creative Writing, Environmental Science, French, Physical Geology, Wellness, Introduction to the Far East, Arithmetic, Algebra, Contemporary Moral Problems, Physical Science, Survey of Physics, Psychology, Human Development, Abnormal Psychology, General Astronomy, Business and Society, American Literature, World Literature, Earth Science, History of Civilization, Introduction to Contemporary Math, Introduction to Music, Introduction to Philosophy, Introduction to Logic, Social Service Mental Health, Alcohol Dependency, Environmental Biology.

Teaching Methods: *Computers:* Internet, e-mail. *TV:* videotape, PBS. *Other:* correspondence, independent study, individual study.

Admission Requirements: *Undergraduate:* application, assessment testing and/or transcripts from other institutions.

On-Campus Requirements: Vary—most require none.

Tuition and Fees: *Undergraduate:* Please visit www.pierce.ctc.edu for the most current tuition rates. *Other Costs:* varies for books, study guides, videotape rentals. *Credit by:* quarter.

Financial Aid: Federal Stafford Loan, Federal Perkins Loan, Federal PLUS Loan, Federal Pell Grant, Federal Work-Study, VA, Washington resident programs.

Accreditation: Northwest Association of Schools and Colleges.

Description: Pierce College (1967) is a public 2-year community college district with colleges in Lakewood and Puyallup and sites at Fort Lewis and McChord Air Force Base. Pierce is the state's third-largest district, serving more than 40,000 full-time and part-time students each year.

Pikes Peak Community College

5675 South Academy Boulevard	Phone: (719) 540-7539
Colorado Springs, CO 80906	Fax: (719) 540-7532

Division(s): Office of Distance Education
Web Site(s): http://www.ppcc.cccoes.edu
E-mail: Distance.Ed@ppcc.cccoes.edu

Undergraduate Degree Programs:
Associate of General Studies

Class Titles: Accounting, Business Math, Business, Biology, Developmental English, Composition, Technical Writing, Writing for Radio/TV, U.S. History, U.S. Government, Psychology, Developmental Mathematics, Algebra, Statistics, Criminal Justice, Spaceflight, Satellite Communication.

Teaching Methods: *Computers:* Internet, real-time chat, electronic classroom, e-mail, CD-ROM, newsgroup, LISTSERV. *TV:* videotape, cable program, satellite broadcasting, PBS. *Other:* correspondence, independent study, individual study, learning contracts.

Credits Granted for: experiential learning, portfolio assessment, examination (CLEP, ACT-PEP, DANTES).

Admission Requirements: *Undergraduate:* Age 16, high school diploma or GED, assessment tests in English, reading, math/study skills (college work or ACT/SAT may allow test exemptions).

On-Campus Requirements: None.

Tuition and Fees: *Undergraduate:* $60/credit. *Other Costs:* $33 Student Fee (fewer than 4 credits), $62 (4 or more); $9/term registration. *Credit by:* semester.

Financial Aid: Federal Stafford Loan, Federal Perkins Loan, Federal PLUS Loan, Federal Pell Grant, Federal Work-Study, VA, Colorado resident programs, PPCC Foundation Scholarships.

Accreditation: North Central Association of Colleges and Schools.

Description: Pikes Peak Community College (1968) is a 2-year public institution that provides occupational and liberal arts curricula allowing students to obtain employment in technical and vocational fields and/or transfer to 4-year colleges and universities. It also provides personal and avocational curricula to allow students throughout the community to pursue individual areas of interest for personal growth. Independent study opportunities have been available since the school opened, but distance learning that employs technology began in 1990 with interactive televised courses. The current program also includes telecourses and Internet courses.

Pine Technical College

900 Fourth Street, SE	Phone: (320) 629-5100
Pine City, MN 55063	(800) 521-7463
	Fax: (320) 629-5101

Division(s): Distance Education
Web Site(s): http://www.ptc.tec.mn.us
E-mail: schroedp@ptc.tec.mn.us

Degree Programs: see Description.

Class Titles: UNIX, Legal Secretary, English Composition, and others.

Teaching Methods: *Computers:* Internet, real-time chat, electronic classroom, e-mail, CD-ROM, newsgroup, LISTSERV. *Other:* fax.

Admission Requirements: *Undergraduate:* application and fees, contact information@ptc.tec.mn.us or call (800) 521-7463 for specific programs.

On-Campus Requirements: None.

Tuition and Fees: *Undergraduate:* MN, SD, ND, WI, Manitoba $94/credit plus one-time application fee—$20. MI, MO, NE $134/credit plus one-time application fee—$20. All other states $174/credit plus one-time application fee—$20.

Accreditation: North Central Association of Colleges and Schools.

Description: Pine Technical College (1965) is a nationally accredited 2-year college of approximately 1,000 students nestled at the edge of the St. Croix River valley, about an hour north of Minneapolis/St. Paul. PTC offers certificates, diplomas, and AAS degrees in more than 40 majors, several of which are unique to Minnesota and the upper Midwest. They range from traditional instruction in classic trades such as Gunsmithing and Taxidermy to high-tech educational programs in Virtual Reality, Web Applications, and other computer careers. PTC has become a national model for integrating high technology in a rural college campus.

Pitt Community College

PO Drawer 7007
Greenville, NC 27835

Phone: (252) 321-4608
Fax: (252) 321-4613

Division(s): Distance Learning Department
Web Site(s): http://www.pitt.cc.nc.us
E-mail: tkemen@pcc.pitt.cc.nc.us or krouse@pcc.pitt.cc.nc.us

Undergraduate Degree Programs:
Business Administration
Information Systems Generalist
Information Systems Programming
Health Information Technology

Certificate Programs: Management Applications and Principles, Information Systems Networking, Information Systems Generalist, Information Systems Programming, Object Oriented Programming, Administrative Managers, Home Office Computing, Computer Software Applications, Medical Office Administration, Medical Office Receptionist, Healthcare Leadership and Management, Starting Your Own Business.

Class Titles: General Biology, Business, Business Law, Computers, Programming/Logic, Spreadsheet, Survey of Operating Systems, Operating System-Windows, Database Concepts/Applications, Technical Support Functions, Internet, Network Theory, Trends in Technology, Systems Analysis/Design, Systems Project, Visual BASIC Programming, Advanced C, Internet Programming, Expository Writing, Health Law/Ethics, Coding/Classification, Quality Management, Medical Terminology, Data Comm/Networking, History of Philosophy, Sociology, Sonographic Physics, Abdominal Sonography, Gynecological Sonography. Several in Information Systems, Arts, Sciences, Health Sciences.

Teaching Methods: *Computers:* Internet, real-time chat, electronic classroom, e-mail. *Other:* videoconferencing.

Credits Granted for: experiential learning, examination (CLEP, ACT-PEP, DANTES, GRE).

Admission Requirements: *Undergraduate:* 16 years of age, entrance exam. *Certificate:* 16 years of age, entrance exam.

On-Campus Requirements: None.

Tuition and Fees: *Undergraduate:* $27.50/credit in-state, $169.75/credit out-of-state. *Software:* as needed. *Other Costs:* Maximum of $16 activity fee and $1.25 insurance fee. *Credit by:* semester.

Financial Aid: JTPA, Federal Stafford Loan, Federal PLUS Loan, Federal Pell Grant, Federal Work-Study, VA, private scholarships, Pitt Community College scholarships, Day Care Grant for eligible students who are parents of day care age children.

Accreditation: Southern Association of Colleges and School.

Description: Pitt Community College (1961) can trace its roots back to Pitt Technical Institute, which opened in 1964 with 96 students in 9 curricula. Since then, the school has added 2-year college transfer programs. The Learning Resources Center, which provides 33,000 square feet of Individualized Instruction Center services, opened in 1987. Then in 1990 a vocational education and lab/shop building opened to house these programs: Machinist, Electronic Servicing, Electronic Engineering Technology, Architectural Technology, Manufacturing Engineering Technology, and Industrial Construction Technology. PCC began Distance Education with the mission to educate additional students without regard to time or space and inform the workforce about the technology used in day-to-day business operations.

Plattsburgh State University of New York

101 Broad Street
Sibley Hall 418A
Plattsburgh, NY 12901

Phone: (518) 564-4234
Fax: (518) 564-4236

Division(s): Center for Lifelong Learning/Distance Learning Office
Web Site(s): http://www.plattsburgh.edu
E-mail: marshaca@splava.cc.plattsburgh.edu

Undergraduate Degree Programs:
Bachelor of Science major in Nursing/RN completion program

Class Titles: upper-level nursing courses, general education courses which vary by semester.

Teaching Methods: *Computers:* Internet. *Other:* videoconferencing—limited to sites in northern New York State.

Credits Granted for: Examination (CLEP, ACT-PEP, DANTES).

Admission Requirements: *Undergraduate:* for RN-BSN must be licensed RN, GPA 2.5.

On-Campus Requirements: Students must complete 36 Plattsburgh credits delivered by videoconferencing to sites across northern New York State.

Tuition and Fees: *Undergraduate:* $137/credit. *Graduate:* $213/credit. *Application Fee:* $30. *Other Costs:* $.85/credit College Fee; $7/credit Technology Fee. *Credit by:* semester.

Financial Aid: Federal Stafford Loan, Federal Perkins Loan, Federal PLUS Loan, Federal Pell Grant, VA, New York resident programs, Tuition Assistance Program (TAP).

Accreditation: Middle States Association of Colleges and Schools.

Description: Plattsburgh State University (1889) is a state-supported comprehensive institution. Its nursing programs are accredited by the National League for Nursing. It first offered distance learning courses in 1994 and currently offers courses in northern New York state by live, interactive video-conferencing and by Internet. In 2000, Plattsburgh offered 15 courses at a distance, and 250, students enrolled in distance learning courses.

Porterville College

100 East College Avenue	Phone: (559) 791-2220
Porterville, CA 93257	Fax: (559) 791-2487

Division(s): Office of Instruction
Web Site(s): http://www.pc.cc.ca.us
E-mail: yschultz@pc.cc.ca.us

Undergraduate Degree Programs:
Associate of Art
Associate of Science

Class Titles: Speech, Political Science, Economics, History, Math, Psychology, Health.

Teaching Methods: *Computers:* Internet, real-time chat, electronic classroom, e-mail. *Other:* independent study.

Admission Requirements: *Undergraduate:* admission application form online.

On-Campus Requirements: None.

Tuition and Fees: *Undergraduate:* $11/credit. *Credit by:* semester.

Financial Aid: Federal Stafford Loan, Federal Perkins Loan, Federal PLUS Loan, Federal Pell Grant, Federal Work-Study, VA, California resident programs.

Accreditation: Western Association of Schools and Colleges.

Description: Porterville College (1927) is a 2-year community college situated in the rural foothills of the Sierra Nevada Mountains in central California. This is Porterville's fourth year of offering online courses to make education more accessible to nontraditional students.

Portland State University

1633 Southwest Park Avenue	Phone: (503) 725-4865
Portland, OR 97201	(800) 547-8887 x4865
	Fax: (503) 725-4880

Division(s): Independent Study
Distance Learning
School of Extended Studies
Web Site(s): http://extended.pdx.edu/istudy
E-mail: xsis@ses.pdx.edu

Class Titles: Criminal Justice Process, Juvenile Justice Process, Criminal Law/Legal Constitutional Criminal Procedures, Court Procedures, Drawing, Accounting, Cost Accounting, Accounting for Not-For-Profit Organizations, Auditing, Nutrition, Principles of Economics (micro/macro), Shakespeare, Survey of American Literature, American Fiction, Contemporary Literature, Contemporary Literature (Drama), Corrective English (noncredit), English Composition, Geography, Geology, History of U.S., Algebra (noncredit), College Math, Calculus for Management/Social Sciences, Calculus, Probability/Statistics, Psychology as Natural Science, Psychology as Social Science, Human Development, Psychopathology, Quests for Meaning—World Religions, Sociology.

Teaching Methods: *Other:* correspondence, independent study.

Admission Requirements: *Undergraduate:* open enrollment.

On-Campus Requirements: None.

Tuition and Fees: *Undergraduate:* $80/credit plus a nonrefundable $20 registration fee *Other Costs:* textbook and/or additional course materials. Prices vary. *Credit by:* quarter.

Financial Aid: students must check whether or not correspondence study will be funded by their financial aid package.

Accreditation: Northwest Association of Schools and Colleges.

Description: Independent Study at Portland State University (1907) offers 60 courses that earn college credit in an array of 12 areas of study ranging from Business Administration to Sociology through correspondence providing a one-to-one learning experience for students who wish to set their own pace for course completion within a 12-month (maximum) time frame. Enrollment is open; students may register any day in any term; they do not need to be admitted by Portland State University to take Independent Study courses. The credits earned by students through Independent Study are held in the student's permanent record in the Portland State University Registrar's Office and may be transferred to the school of the student's choice.

Pratt Community College and Area Vocational School

348 North East S.R. 61
Pratt, KS 67124

Phone: (316) 672-5641
Fax: (316) 672-2519

Division(s): Instruction
Web Site(s): http://www.pcc.cc.ks.us
E-mail: donh@pcc.cc.ks.us

Teaching Methods: *Computers:* Internet, e-mail, newsgroup, LISTSERV. *TV:* videotape, cable program, PBS video courses. *Other:* audioconferencing, videoconferencing, audiographics, audiotapes, fax, correspondence, independent study, individual study, learning contracts.

Credits Granted for: experiential learning, portfolio assessment, extrainstitutional learning, examination (CLEP, ACT-PEP, DANTES, GRE).

Admission Requirements: *Undergraduate:* ASSET placement test or ACT exemption for degree student.

On-Campus Requirements: some campus time required.

Tuition and Fees: *Undergraduate:* $47/credit. *Credit by:* semester. *Other Costs:* Edukan Internet courses: $115/credit hour.

Financial Aid: Federal Stafford Loan, Federal Perkins Loan, Federal PLUS Loan, Federal Pell Grant, Federal Work-Study, VA, Kansas resident programs.

Accreditation: North Central Association of Colleges and Schools.

Description: Pratt Community College (1938) installed its first ITV studio in the fall of 1995. Interactive TV is the most readily used means of distance education at the school. A second studio was added in the fall of 1996. Audio and video signals from all sites are generally live and interactive, although filmed lessons, as well as commercial and educational films, can also be presented over ITV. PCC also has a Coder-Decoder system that allows the school to receive audio and video signals and to transmit such signals over telephone lines. Other distance education services available at PCC include satellite downlinks, which provide a one-way audio and video feed to several of the school's classrooms. PCC is also connected to Telenet 2, a statewide audio/video network connecting computers at various sites across Kansas. Edukan provides the Internet coursework.

Prescott College

220 Grove Avenue
Prescott, AZ 86301

Phone: (520) 778-2090
Fax: (520) 776-5151

Division(s): Adult Degree Programs
Web Site(s): http://www.prescott.edu
E-mail: admissions@prescott.edu

Undergraduate Degree Programs:
Adult Degree Program

Graduate Degree Programs:
Master of Arts Program

Class Titles: ADP Arts and Letters, ADP Community Development, ADP Education; ADP Environmental Studies, ADP Human Potential, ADP Integrative Studies, ADP Liberal Arts; MAP Adventure Education, MAP Counseling Psychology, MAP Education, MAP Environmental Studies, MAP Humanities.

Teaching Methods: *Computers:* e-mail. *Other:* liberal arts seminars, fax, independent study, individual study, learning contracts.

Credits Granted for: experiential learning, portfolio assessment, examination (CLEP, DANTES).

Admission Requirements: *Undergraduate:* personal essays, letters of recommendation; admission interview; recommended minimum 30 credits prior college. *Graduate:* résumé, personal statement and proposed study plan, letters of recommendation; required bachelor degree.

On-Campus Requirements: Undergraduates must attend a 3-day on-campus new student orientation, and weekend on-campus liberal arts seminar during second enrollment term. Graduate students must attend a 2-day on-campus new student orientation, and 2 weekend colloquia per term.

Tuition and Fees: *Undergraduate:* $210/credit; $3,825/term full-time *Graduate:* $280/credit; $5,050/term full-time. *Application Fees:* undergraduate, $25; graduate, $40. *Graduation Fee:* $75. *Credit by:* quarter.

Financial Aid: Federal Stafford Loan, Federal Perkins Loan, Federal PLUS Loan, Federal Pell Grant, Federal Work-Study, VA).

Accreditation: North Central Association of Colleges and Schools.

Description: Designed for working adults to obtain degrees on year-round basis. Prescott College (1966) programs are experiential and self-directed.

Presentation College

1500 North Main
Aberdeen, SD 57401

Phone: (605) 225-1634
Fax: (605) 229-8518

Division(s): Academic Dean
Web Site(s): http://www.presentation.edu
E-mail: admit@presentation.edu

Undergraduate Degree Programs:
Bachelor of Science in:
  Business
  Nursing
  Social Work

Teaching Methods: *Computers:* Internet, e-mail, LISTSERV. *TV:* videotape, closed-circuit cable program. *Other:* videoconferencing, audioconferencing, fax, correspondence, independent study, learning contracts.

Credits Granted for: portfolio assessment, examination (CLEP, ACT-PEP, DANTES, GRE).

Admission Requirements: *Undergraduate:* completed application form with $20 nonrefundable application fee, official high school transcript or GED, all official college and/or vocational technology transcripts, placement test scores, and ACT or SAT scores. *Certificate:* same as undergraduate.

On-Campus Requirements: None.

Tuition and Fees: *Undergraduate:* $4,254/block (12–18 credits), $280/credit regular tuition. *Application Fee:* $20. *Other Costs:* $40 technology fee. *Credit by:* semester.

Financial Aid: Federal Stafford Loan, Federal Perkins Loan, Federal PLUS Loan, Federal Pell Grant, Federal Work-Study, VA, South Dakota resident programs.

Accreditation: North Central Association of Colleges and Schools, National League for Nursing Accrediting Commission, Commission on Accreditation of Allied Health Education Programs, Council on Social Work Education.

Description: Presentation College (1922) is an independent, Catholic educational institution conducted by the Sisters of the Presentation of the Blessed Virgin Mary. The college has a satellite nursing program, the Cheyenne River Lakota Nursing School at Eagle Butte, South Dakota, that began in 1980. Presentation College's mission is to offer women and men the opportunity of education toward self-actualization, professional excellence, and lifelong learning. As a Catholic-Christian community, Presentation College challenges its members in the pursuit of Christian values and in responsive relationships with the human community and with God. Distance learning was initiated in response to rural education needs. Many individual courses are offered via videoconferencing. A Bachelor of Science Nursing completion program

is offered almost in its entirety over the system. Dual-enrollment credit courses are offered to area high schools.

Pueblo Community College

900 West Orman Avenue
Pueblo, CO 81004

Phone: (719) 549-3343
Fax: (719) 549-3453

Division(s): Educational Technology and Telecommunications
Web Site(s): http://www.pcc.cccoes.edu; www.cccconline.org
E-mail: kippie@pcc.cccoes.edu (for Distance Learning), admissions@pcc.cccoes.edu (for online courses at PCC-Admissions).

Undergraduate Degree Programs:
AAS in Business (CCC Online)

Class Titles: Course offerings vary each semester and may have prerequisites. Check web site for current listings. Courses may include: U.S. Cinema, Race to Save Planet, Nutrition Pathways, Child Development, Economics USA, Writer's Exchange, Power of Place, Earth Revealed, Literary Visions, Voices/Visions, College Algebra, Discovering Psychology, Sociological Imagination, Spanish, Biology, Human Anatomy/Physiology, Pathophysiology, Chemistry, Creativity/Young Child, Guidance Strategies for Young Children, Conceptual Physics, Clinical Nutrition, Language/Cognitive Development, Health Information Technology, Coding, Management of Health Information Systems, Medical Terminology, CP4m UCD9 Coding, Nutrition/Young Child, Health Statistics, Legal Aspects, Pharmacology.

Teaching Methods: *Computers:* Internet. *TV:* videotape, cable program, satellite broadcasting, PBS. *Other:* radio broadcast, audioconferencing, videoconferencing, audiotapes, fax, independent study, individual study.

Credits Granted for: portfolio assessment, examination (CLEP, ACT-PEP, Post-Secondary Enrollment Options, Advanced Vocational Education Program).

Admission Requirements: *Undergraduate:* age 18, admission application, high school graduate or GED, or ability to benefit demonstrated by examination.

On-Campus Requirements: Student must attend semester orientations to receive class syllabi and meet with course instructor. Telecourses require some lab work and testing and on-campus meetings.

Tuition and Fees: *Undergraduate:* $74.90/credit resident, $299.60/credit nonresident. *Other Costs:* $118/credit online courses, $45/course Telecourse Fee, $10 Student ID, $8, $9.25 Registration. *Credit by:* semester.

Financial Aid: Federal Stafford Loan, Federal Perkins Loan, Federal PLUS Loan, Federal Pell Grant, Federal Work-

Study, VA, Colorado resident programs, scholarships. See www.financialaid@pcc.cccoes.edu

Accreditation: North Central Association of Colleges and Schools.

Description: Pueblo Community College (1933) is located in the city of Pueblo, Colorado, population 102,000. PCC provides educational programs at its Pueblo campus, its Fremont County campus in Canon City, and at its Southwest Center, which serves Cortez and Durango. The mission of the college is to develop and support lifetime learning that leads to positive change in individuals, families, and communities. PCC's Educational Technology and Telecommunications Division provides telelearning to Pueblo and Southern Colorado through interactive TV, telecourses, and CBC (College by Cassette). Pueblo Community also offers high quality educational programming via the college's educational cable channel. This channel carries standard academic courses to students and teletraining programs to industry. These training programs can be delivered to work stations, corporate training centers, or to students' homes. PCC is also helping provide an Internet degree through Colorado Community College and Occupational Education System's (CCCOES) CCC Online. Currently, faculty from all Colorado community colleges collaborate through CCC Online to offer an AAS in Business via the Internet.

Pulaski Technical College

| 3000 West Scenic Drive | Phone: (501) 812-2200 |
| North Little Rock, AR 72118 | Fax: (501) 812-2391 |

Web Site(s): http://www.ptc.tec.ar.us
E-mail: abaldwin@mail.ptc.tec.ar.us

Undergraduate Degree Programs: Contact school.

Class Titles: Composition, literature, psychology, computer information systems, biology, journalism, business, microapplications, networking.

Teaching Methods: *Computers:* Internet, real-time chat, electronic classroom, e-mail, CD-ROM.

Admission Requirements: *Undergraduate:* open admission.

On-Campus Requirements: None.

Tuition and Fees: *Undergraduate:* $50/credit. *Graduation Fee:* $20. *Credit by:* semester.

Financial Aid: Federal Stafford Loan, Federal Perkins Loan, Federal PLUS Loan, Federal Pell Grant, Federal Work-Study, VA.

Accreditation: North Central Association of Colleges and Schools.

Description: Pulaski Technical College (1991) provides high-quality, accessible educational opportunities at the freshman and sophomore level in associate degree and technical certificate programs, a college-transfer curriculum, continuing education, and industry-specific training to support individual and community needs in central Arkansas. PTC has been training and educating students since 1969, but changed to a 2-year technical college in 1991. It has been offering Distance Education courses, primarily through the Internet, since 1999.

Purdue University

| 1589 Stewart Center Room 116 | Phone: (765) 496-5474 |
| West Lafayette, IN 47907-1589 | Fax: (765) 496-7696 |

Division(s): Distributed Learning Services
Web Site(s): http://www.purdue.edu/distance
E-mail: cmlawson@purdue.edu

Graduate Degree Programs:
Master of Science in Engineering

Doctoral Degree Programs:
Cohort Doctoral Program in Educational Administration

Certificate Programs: Digital Signal Processing

Teaching Methods: *Computers:* Internet, real-time chat, electronic classroom, e-mail, CD-ROM, newsgroup, LISTSERV. *TV:* videotape, cable program, satellite broadcasting, PBS. *Other:* videoconferencing, audioconferencing, audiotapes, fax, correspondence, independent study, individual study, learning contracts.

Credits Granted for: experiential learning, portfolio assessment, extrainstitutional learning, examination (CLEP, ACT-PEP, GRE), credit by exam, credit established/awarded on the basis of CEEB Match Achievement test score or Purdue Composite Score, transfer credit.

Admission Requirements: *Undergraduate:* SAT/ACT unless over age 25 with 12 credits, rank in or near upper half of high school class. Permission needed for high school student or younger. Contact individual schools for high school classes required.

On-Campus Requirements: determined on a course-by-course basis.

Tuition and Fees: *Undergraduate:* resident $145/credit, nonresident $454/credit. *Graduate:* resident $145/credit, nonresident $454/credit. *Doctoral:* resident $145/credit, nonresident $454/credit. *Application Fee:* resident $30, nonresident $30. *Other Costs:* $4.50/credit technology fee; $100–$2,518 differential fees depending on program; some courses assess a special fee ranging from $40–$4,130 depending on course.

Full fees at 8+ hours $2,082 (resident) and $6,936 (nonresident). 1–7 credits/semester assessed at the above rates. *Credit by:* semester.

Financial Aid: Federal Stafford Loan (subsidized and unsubsidized), Federal Perkins Loan, Federal PLUS Loan, Federal Pell Grant, Federal Work-Study, VA, Indiana resident programs, Lilly Awards, Purdue Loans, University Fee Remissions, Supplemental Grants, State awards, 4-H and other scholarships, ROTC, Merit Scholars, 21st Century Scholars, Hoosier Scholars, Special Education Services Scholarship, Minority Teachers Scholarship, Nursing Scholarship, Higher Education Award, Presidential Scholarship, departmental scholarships.

Accreditation: North Central Association of Colleges and Schools.

Description: Purdue University (1922) already has a significant track record in technology-enhanced distance learning. In 1922, Purdue's WBAA—Indiana's first radio station—began broadcasting electronic engineering courses. Since then, more schools and departments have provided educational opportunities to learners across Indiana and beyond. And today, the innovative use of distance learning to enhance teaching, learning, research, and outreach has become an institutional strategic priority. The office of Distributed Learning Service was established in 1997.

Queen's University

F1 Mackintosh-Corry Hall	Phone: (613) 533-2471
Kingston, ON, Canada K7L 3N6	Fax: (613) 533-6805

Division(s): Continuing and Distance Studies
Web Site(s): http://www.queensu.ca/cds
E-mail: cds@post.queensu.ca

Undergraduate Degree Programs:
Bachelor of Arts with minor concentrations in:
   History
   Psychology
   German
   English
   Political Studies
   Women's Studies

Class Titles: Drama, Economics, English Language/Literature, French Studies, Geography, German Language/Literature, History, Math/Statistics, Microbiology/Immunology, Pharmacology/Toxicology, Philosophy, Political Studies, Psychology, Religious Studies, Sociology, Spanish/Italian Languages/Literatures, Women's Studies, Effective Writing.

Teaching Methods: *Computers:* Internet, e-mail, CD-ROM. *TV:* videotape. *Other:* audioconferencing, audiotapes, fax, correspondence.

Admission Requirements: *Undergraduate:* high school diploma (university preparation program) or equivalent.

On-Campus Requirements: None.

Tuition and Fees: *Undergraduate:* Canadian (Cdn) $826/credit domestic, Cdn $2,264 international. *Application Fee:* Cdn $30. *Software:* variable. *Credit by:* semester and quarter.

Accreditation: Association of Universities and Colleges of Canada.

Description: The Queen's University (1841) main campus is located on the shores of Lake Ontario in historic Kingston, Ontario, Canada. The university was established by Royal Charter and has the oldest distance education program in North America, with the first correspondence courses being offered in 1889. Our students include those wanting to complete a degree or take university courses for interest, personal enrichment, or upgrading purposes. Print-based and CD-ROM/Internet-based correspondence courses provide students who are unable to attend classes an opportunity to complete Queen's degree credit courses from anywhere in the world. Each course consists of a series of assignments and either a final examination or final term paper. Queen's has more than 1,000 established exam centers around the globe, and if there is not a center within 60 miles of your home, one will be established for you.

Red Rocks Community College

13300 West 6th Avenue	Phone: (303) 914-6704
Lakewood, CO 80228	Fax: (303) 914-6716

Division(s): Learning and Resource Center
Web Site(s): http://www.rrcc.cccoes.edu

Undergraduate Degree Programs:
Online degrees through Red Rocks Community College in partnership with ccconline include:
   Associate of Applied Science in Business
   Power Technology
   Emergency Management and Planning
   Public Administration

Class Titles: *General Education/Core classes:* There is a wide variety of distance options available in classes in the Arts, Communication, Early Childhood, Humanities, Math, and Natural and Social Sciences. For a comprehensive listing of distance options, please visit our web site at http://www.rrcc.cccoes.edu

Online Computer/programming/Web classes: There are over 30 computer classes available online including Productivity Office suite tools, Multimedia software (Adobe, Macromedia), and various programming classes. See our web site for a complete listing.

Teaching Methods: *Computers:* Internet, e-mail, CD-ROM. *TV:* videotape, PBS. *Other:* audioconferencing, videoconferencing, fax, individual study, self-paced online instruction. RRCC is also a consortium partner in ccconline (see http://www.ccconline.org for more information).

Credits Granted for: experiential learning, portfolio assessment, examination (CLEP, DANTES).

Admission Requirements: *Undergraduate:* open-entry; assessment test for new students.

On-Campus Requirements: None.

Tuition and Fees: *Undergraduate:* $57.75/credit. *Other Costs:* $9.25 registration, $7.55/credit student fees. *Credit by:* semester.

Financial Aid: Federal Stafford Loan, Federal Perkins Loan, Federal PLUS Loan, Federal Pell Grant, Federal Work-Study, VA, Colorado resident programs.

Accreditation: North Central Association of Colleges and Schools.

Description: The mission of Red Rocks Community College (1971) is to develop and support lifelong learners so they may live fuller lives and add value to the communities in which they live and work. Providing learning options is essential for our students. We began offering self-paced courses 20 years ago to meet the needs of students. In 1991 we began offering videoconferencing courses to one site. We now offer an AA degree through videoconferencing to 3 sites. We also offer a variety of courses achieved through online instruction, including the AAS in Business.

Reformed Theological Seminary, Virtual Campus

2101 Carmel Road	Phone: (800) 227-2013
Charlotte, NC 28226	Fax: (704) 366-9295

Division(s): Distance Education
Web Site(s): http://www.rtsvirtual.org
E-mail: distance.education@rts.edu

Graduate Degree Programs:
Master of Arts in Religion

Certificate Programs: Missions, Biblical Studies, Historical Studies, Theological Studies, General Studies.

Class Titles: all courses.

Teaching Methods: *Computers:* Internet, e-mail, CD-ROM. *Other:* audiotapes, notebooks, fax, correspondence, learning contracts.

Credits Granted for: transfer credits from other institutions.

Admission Requirements: *Graduate:* accredited bachelor's degree.

On-Campus Requirements: Students pursuing the Master of Arts degree are required to complete 2 one-week seminars on an RTS residential campus.

Tuition and Fees: *Graduate:* $250/credit. *Application Fee:* $35. *Credit by:* semester.

Financial Aid: Individual and local scholarships are available.

Accreditation: Southern Association of Colleges and Schools, Association of Theological Schools in the U.S. and Canada.

Description: Obligations to family, church, and work make it impossible for many people to attend seminary classes on a traditional campus. The Virtual Campus (1991) offers RTS (1966) courses through tapes, notebooks, and the Internet, making it possible for students to pursue seminary training from home. Students in the MA/Distance program earn up to 90% of a fully accredited master's degree through the distance education courses offered by the Virtual Campus. Some students take courses to earn a certificate, and many take courses for personal enrichment.

Regent University

1000 Regent University Drive	Phone: (800) 373-5504
Virginia Beach, VA 23464	Fax: (757) 226-4381

Division(s): The Individual Schools run their Distance Learning Programs
Web Site(s): http://www.regent.edu
E-mail: admissions@regent.edu

Undergraduate Degree Programs:
Bachelor of Science in Organizational Leadership and Management

Graduate Degree Programs:
Master of Arts in Communication
Master of Arts in Journalism
Master of Arts in Organizational Leadership
Master of Arts in Management
LLM in International Taxation
Master of International Taxation
Master of Education/Individualized Degree
Master of Education/TESOL
Master of Education/Christian School Program
Master of Education/School-Based Security and Community Policing
Master of Education/Master Educator Program
Master of Arts in Biblical Studies

Master of Arts in Practical Theology
Master of Divinity

Doctoral Degree Programs:
Doctorate in Organizational Leadership
Doctorate in Communication
Doctor of Strategic Leadership
Doctorate in Education

Certificate Programs: Graduate Studies in Leadership, Advanced Graduate Studies in Leadership, Graduate Certificate Programs in Business, TESOL Certificate, and Worship and Renewal Studies Certificate.

Teaching Methods: *Computers:* Internet, real-time chat, electronic classroom, e-mail, CD-ROM, newsgroup, LIST-SERV. *Other:* audiotapes, videotapes, correspondence, independent study, individual study, field-based ministry programs, learning contracts.

Credits Granted for: bachelor's degree completion program—portfolio assessment, examination (CLEP, ACT-PEP, DANTES, GRE).

Admission Requirements: *Undergraduate:* at least 3 years of professional work experience, at least 45 transferable undergraduate credits with a minimum 2.0 GPA, $20.00 fee, writing sample, Community Life Form, 2 professional recommendations. *Graduate:* accredited 4-year bachelor's degree (nonaccredited degrees considered on an individual basis), cumulative undergraduate GPA of 2.75 (3.0 in desired area), submission of test scores (MAT, GMAT, GRE, etc., depending on school requirement), maturity in spiritual and/or character qualities, personal goals consistent with Regent's mission and goals and additional admissions criteria as determined by the individual schools. Accelerated Scholars and Professionals Program allows some students with at least 90 undergraduate credits and significant life experience in professional area to enter a master's program. *Doctoral:* same as graduate. *Certificate:* varies by program.

On-Campus Requirements: Some programs require a minimal residency or on-campus course. Contact the individual school of interest for information.

Tuition and Fees: *Undergraduate:* $295/credit. Graduate: Master of Arts in Communcation, Master of Arts in Journalism, PhD in Communication: $450/credit; Master of Arts in Organizational Leadership: $375/credit; PhD in Organizational Leadership, Doctor of Strategic Leadership: $500/credit: Master of Business Administration: approximately $25,000/program; Master of Arts in Management: $350/credit; LLM in International Taxation, Master of International Taxation: $624/credit; Master of Education: $357/credit; Doctorate in Education: $456/credit; Master of Arts in Biblical Studies, Master of Arts in Practical Theology, Master of Divinity: $295/credit. *Certificates:* Certificate of Graduate Study in Leadership: $375/credit; Certificate of Advanced Graduate Study in Leadership: $500/credit; Graduate Certificates in Business: $240/credit, Worship and Renewal Studies Certificate: $295/credit; TESOL Certificate: $375/credit. *Application Fee:* varies by program. *Software:* varies by program. *Graduate Fee:* varies by program. *Other Costs:* vary by program. *Credit by:* semester.

Financial Aid: Federal Stafford Loan, school-specific scholarships and grants, VA.

Accreditation: Southern Association of Colleges and Schools, Association of Theological Schools, American Bar Association, Council for accreditation of Counseling and Related Educational Programs.

Description: In 1991 Regent University introduced its online Worldwide Campus distance learning program, and now offers more than 20 graduate programs and a bachelor's degree completion program online. Each professional area of study is approached from a moral and ethical perspective founded in Judeo-Christian tradition, within a rigorous, scholarly framework. In addition to the online Worldwide Campus, Regent has a main campus in Virginia Beach and a Graduate Center in Northern Virginia/D.C. Regent offers a total of 27 master's and doctoral degrees, an undergraduate degree completion program, 14 graduate certificate programs, and alternative licensure program in education. The schools of Regent University consist of the: Graduate School of Business, College of Communication and the Arts; Center for Leadership Studies; School of Divinity; School of Education; Robertson School of Government; School of Law; School of Psychology and Counseling; and Degree Completion Program. Regent University currently has an enrollment of more than 2,400 students.

Rensselaer Polytechnic Institute

110 8th Street—CII 4011	Phone: (518) 276-8351
Troy, NY 12180-3590	Fax: (518) 276-8026

Division(s): Office of Professional and Distance Education
Web Site(s): http://rsvp.rpi.edu
E-mail: rsvp@rpi.edu

Graduate Degree Programs:
Business Administration (MBA)
Computer and Systems Engineering
Computer Science
Electrical Engineering (concentration in Microelectronics)
Electric Power Engineering
Information Technology—IT applications in Database Systems Design, Human-Computer Interaction, Information Systems Engineering, Networking, Software Engineering/Design, and E-Business

382 ▸ ▸ ▸

Engineering Science (concentrations in Management of Technology, Manufacturing Systems Engineering, and Microelectronics Manufacturing Engineering)

Management (concentrations in Human-Computer Interaction, MIS/IT, Production and Operations Management, Technology Management, Service Systems, and E-Business)

Mechanical Engineering

Industrial and Management Engineering (concentrations in Quality Engineering and Service Systems)

Technical Communication

Certificate Programs: Bioinformatics, Computer Graphics and Data Visualization, Computer Networks, Computer Science, Database Systems Design, Electric Power Engineering, Graphical User Interfaces, Human-Computer Interaction, Management and Technology, Manufacturing Systems Engineering, Mechanical Engineering, Microelectronics Manufacturing Engineering, Microelectronics Technology and Design, Quality and Reliability, Service Systems, Software Engineering.

Class Titles: 30 courses per semester, specific to degree program offered.

Teaching Methods: *Computers:* Internet videostreaming (live and on-demand), OnLine Conferencing, real-time chat, electronic classroom, e-mail, CD-ROM. *TV:* videotape, satellite broadcasting. *Other:* videoconferencing (ISDN).

Credits Granted for: approved transfer of college credit.

Admission Requirements: *Graduate:* completed graduate application, bachelor's degree, 3.0 undergraduate GPA, brief statement of background and goals, 3 letters of recommendation, official transcripts from all colleges and universities. *Certificate:* application form, prerequisites for all courses, transcript of bachelor's degree (or highest degree earned), bachelor's degree with 3.0 undergraduate GPA.

On-Campus Requirements: None.

Tuition and Fees: *Graduate:* $700/credit. *Application Fee:* $45. *Software:* varies. *Other Costs:* $35 for transcripts. *Credit by:* semester.

Financial Aid: VA.

Accreditation: Middle States Association of Colleges and Schools.

Description: Founded in 1824, Rensselaer is America's oldest private technological university. Internationally regarded as a leader in innovation and a prominent research institution with strong ties to industry, Rensselaer offers graduate and undergraduate degree programs in engineering, science, management, architecture, and humanities and social science. Recent media rankings in *U.S. News & World Report* and *Success* magazines have given high marks to Rensselaer in the areas of engineering, management information systems, and entrepreneurship. *Yahoo Internet Life* has ranked Rensselaer among the top "Most Wired Campuses" in the United States for the past 3 years. Rensselaer's distance education program, RSVP, has been delivering quality graduate courses, certificates, and degree programs to remote students since 1987. More than 1,000 professionals—many from leading corporations, others as individuals—pursue their courses at the workplace, at home, or on the road. Twice, the program has received national recognition: the US Distance Learning Association has named it "Best Distance Education Program—Higher Education," and *Teleconference* magazine acclaimed it "Outstanding Partnership with a Corporation" for RSVP's educational collaboration with General Motors.

Renton Technical College

3000 NE 4th Street	Phone: (425) 235-2352
Renton, WA 98126	Fax: (425) 235-7832

Division(s): Technology
Web Site(s): http://www.renton-tc.ctc.edu
E-mail: cdaniels@rtc.ctc.edu

Class Titles: English, Math, Technical Writing, Psychology, Computer Sciences, Medical Insurance Billing, Emergency Communications.

Teaching Methods: *Computers:* Internet, real-time chat, electronic classroom, e-mail, CD-ROM, newsgroup, LISTSERV. *TV:* videotape, cable program, satellite broadcasting, PBS. *Other:* radio broadcast, videoconferencing, audioconferencing, audiographics, audiotapes, fax, correspondence, independent study, individual study, learning contracts.

Credits Granted for: experiential learning, portfolio assessment, extrainstitutional learning (PONSI, corporate or professional association seminars/workshops), examination (CLEP, ACT-PEP, DANTES, GRE).

On-Campus Requirements: None.

Tuition and Fees: *Credit by:* quarter.

Financial Aid: Federal Stafford Loan, Federal Perkins Loan, Federal Pell Grant, Federal Work-Study, VA, Washington resident programs.

Accreditation: Northwest Association of Schools and Colleges.

Description: For more than 55 years, Renton Technical College (1941) has made dreams a reality for students training, retraining, and upgrading their skills for rewarding careers. As the community has grown and changed, Renton

Technical College has followed suit, offering exciting new programs and keeping abreast of cutting edge technologies that have reshaped the workplace. As we stand on the cusp of the 21st century, what remains constant is our commitment to service the community and help make dreams come true.

The Richard Stockton College of New Jersey

PO Box 195	Phone: (609) 652-4580
Pomona, NJ 08240-0195	Fax: (609) 748-5562

Division(s): Office of Distance Learning
Web Site(s): http://loki.stockton.edu/
E-mail: mark.jackson@stockton.edu

Class Titles: Ethnic/Cultural Studies, Business, Communications, Conservation/Natural Resources, Education, English Language/Literature, Literature, Health Professions/Related Sciences, History, Family Studies, Mathematics, Philosophy/Religion, Physical Sciences, Psychology, Social Sciences, Visual/Performing Arts.

Teaching Methods: *Computers:* Internet, electronic classroom, e-mail. *Other:* audiotapes, fax, correspondence, independent study, individual study, videotape.

Admission Requirements: *Undergraduate:* for fewer than 16 accepted credits: application, SAT/ACT, 16 units college preparatory, assessment tests in writing and reading, mathematics, and critical thinking; Transfer students: transcripts, 16 accepted credits, application; nonmatriculating student: application for nonmatriculating status. Can take up to 8 credits/term.

On-Campus Requirements: Varies, but all students must attend an in-person orientation.

Tuition and Fees: *Undergraduate:* $149.50/credit. *Application Fee:* $35 nonmatriculating students. *Other Costs:* $50 Technology Fee. *Credit by:* semester.

Financial Aid: Federal Stafford Loan, Federal Perkins Loan, Federal PLUS Loan, Federal Pell Grant, Federal Work-Study, VA, New Jersey resident programs.

Accreditation: Middle States Association of Colleges and Schools; Social Work: Council on Social Work Education; Education: New Jersey Department of Education and the National Association of State Directors of Teacher Education and Certification; Nursing: National League for Nursing, New Jersey Board of Nursing; Chemistry: American Chemical Society; Physical Therapy: American Physical Therapy Association; Environmental Health track: National Environmental Health Sciences and Protection Accreditation Council.

Description: The Richard Stockton College of New Jersey (1969) is an undergraduate college of arts and sciences and professional studies, providing distinctive undergraduate programs that combine traditional and alternative approaches to education, along with some graduate programs. The Office of Distance Learning (1995) provides access to quality and affordable higher education through alternative delivery methods.

Richland Community College

One College Park	Phone: (217) 875-7200
Decatur, IL 62521	Fax: (217) 875-6961

Division(s): Learning Resource Center
Web Site(s): http://www.richland.cc.il.us
E-mail: ncooper@richland.cc.il.us

Undergraduate Degree Programs:
Associate in Arts
Associate in Science
Associate in Engineering Science
Associate in Liberal Studies
Associate in Applied Science (occupational training programs)

Certificate Programs: basic certificate and 2-year degrees.

Teaching Methods: *Computers:* Internet, electronic classroom, e-mail. *TV:* videotape, satellite broadcasting. *Other:* videoconferencing, audiotapes, fax, correspondence, learning communities, independent study, extended learning program.

Credits Granted for: Examination (CLEP, APP), Proficiency Examination, Proficiency by Advanced Course.

Admission Requirements: *Undergraduate:* High school graduate or GED equivalent, or may qualify as high school student or "gifted" high school student. Possible placement testing in English, math, foreign language, or other areas. *Certificate:* same as undergraduate.

On-Campus Requirements: None.

Tuition and Fees: *Undergraduate:* $50*/hour (in-district students), $171*/hour (out-of-district students), $260*/hour (out-of-state students) (*includes academic fee). *Other Costs:* $10 semester registration fee (nonrefundable and payable at time of registration); lab fees vary depending on type of class and are payable at time of registration). *Credit by:* semester.

Financial Aid: Grants: Pell Grant, Supplemental Educational Opportunity Grant (SEOG). Illinois State Monetary Award Program Scholarships: Merit Recognition Scholarship, National Guard/Naval Militia Program, Policeman/Fireman

Scholarship, Correctional Workers' Scholarship, MIA/POW Scholarship, Illinois Veterans' Grant, Department of Rehabilitation Services, Richland Community College Foundation, Private, and institutional scholarships.

Accreditation: North Central Association of Colleges and Schools.

Description: The primary purpose of Richland Community College (1972) is to improve the quality of life in Central Illinois by actively serving the educational needs of its people, organizations, and institutions. Richland offers bachelor's, technical, continuing education, and community service programs. In 1994 Richland first offered its Distance Learning Program to enable students to take classes from several district sites through an interactive-video system. Area universities and other community colleges also use Richland's distance program.

Rio Salado College

2323 West 14th Street	Phone: (800) 729-1197
Tempe, AZ 85281	(480) 517-8000
	Fax: (480) 517-8129

Division(s): Academic Programs
Web Site(s): http://www.rio.maricopa.edu/
E-mail: admissions@email.rio.maricopa.edu

Undergraduate Degree Programs:
AA GR: Associate in Arts Degree, General Requirements
AS GR: Associate in Science, General Requirements
AGS: Associate in General Studies
AAS: Associate in Applied Science
   Chemical Dependency
   Computer Technology
   Organizational Leadership
   Programming and System Analysis

Certificate Programs:
CCL Certificates of Completion:
   Business Office Technology
   Chemical Dependency Level I
   Chemical Dependency Level II
   Computer Technology
   Desktop Publishing
   Networking
   Office User Specialist Prep
   Organizational Leadership
   Programming
   Programming and System Analysis
   Quality Customer Service
   Quality Process Leadership
   Technology Helpdesk Support
   Technology Troubleshooting
   Water Distribution and Collection
   Wastewater Treatment
   Water Treatment
   Web Master

Class Titles: Accounting, Anthropology, Biology, Business, Child/Family Studies, Communication, Computers, Counseling/Personal Development, Education, English, English Humanities, Geography, Geology, Health Science, History, Humanities, Integrated Studies, Management/Supervision, Mathematics, Medical Terminology, Office Automation Systems, Philosophy, Political Science, Psychology, Reading, Small Business, Sociology, Spanish, Theater, Total Quality Management, Water/Wastewater Management.

Teaching Methods: *Computers:* Internet, e-mail, CD-ROM. *Other:* audioconferencing, videoconferencing, audiotapes, correspondence.

Credits Granted for: experiential learning, portfolio assessment extrainstitutional learning, examination (CLEP, ACT-PEP, DANTES, GRE).

Admission Requirements: *Undergraduate:* open enrollment.

On-Campus Requirements: None.

Tuition and Fees: *Undergraduate:* $43/credit state Graduation Fee: $15. *Other Costs:* $5/semester registration fee. *Credit by:* semester.

Financial Aid: Federal Pell Grant, VA.

Accreditation: North Central Association for Colleges and Schools.

Description: Rio Salado College (1978), one of the 10 Colleges and 2 Skill Centers in the Maricopa Community College District (MCCD), is located throughout Maricopa County, Arizona. Established in 1978 with the population growing at an unprecedented rate, Rio Salado was designed to be the college that would provide educational services to the underserved and unserved geographic areas and special populations of the county. In order to be flexible and responsive to short-term as well as long-term community needs, Rio was charged to rent or lease facilities (instead of owning them) and provide instruction using primarily part-time faculty. By design, Rio was to be the vanguard college of the district, piloting the use of technology for delivery of instruction and services as well as challenging educational traditions in format and delivery plans. Governed mainly by a service-oriented administration, Rio focused on quick delivery of instruction and custom designed services. Now, 23 years later, Rio Salado remains true to its original charge, as evidenced in its mission statement. Our Mission Statement is as follows:

As an institution of higher education, Rio Salado College creates convenient, high-quality learning opportunities for diverse populations. We specialize in customized, unique programs and partnerships, accelerated formats, and distance delivery. In all that we do, we pursue continuous improvement and innovation, and we challenge the limits of tradition.

Riverside Community College

4800 Magnolia Avenue	Phone: (909) 222-8561
Riverside, CA 92506	Fax: (909) 222-8091

Division(s): Open Campus/Distance Education
Web Site(s): http://www.rccd.cc.ca.us; http: opencampus.com
E-mail: gbrady@rccd.cc.ca.us

Class Titles: Anthropology, Art, Astronomy, Business, Childhood Studies, Computer Information Systems, Graphics Technology, Guidance, Humanities, History, Management, Mathematics, Music, Oceanography, Philosophy, Physical Education, Political Science, Psychology, Reading, Sociology, Spanish, Telecommunications.

Teaching Methods: *Computer:* Internet, e-mail, electronic classroom. *TV:* videotape, cable program. *Other:* hybrid courses: more than 50% on campus.

Admission Requirements: *Undergraduate:* open admission. *Certificate:* open admission.

On-Campus Requirements: Telecourses: up to 5 on-campus sessions. Online courses: none. Hybrid courses: more than 50% on campus.

Tuition and Fees: *Undergraduate:* $11/credit residents; $145/credit nonresidents; $10/credit international student fee. *Credit by:* semester.

Financial Aid: Federal Pell Grant, Federal Work-Study, VA, state and institutional aid.

Accreditation: Western States Association of Schools and Colleges.

Description: Riverside Community College (1916) is an accessible, comprehensive school committed to providing an affordable postsecondary education (including student and community services) to a diverse student body. Located 60 miles east of Los Angeles, the RCC District has 3 campuses—Riverside, Moreno Valley, and Norco—serving 29,000 students. RCCD's values are expressed in student centeredness, teaching excellence, learning environment, and tradition.

Rochester Community and Technical College

851 30th Avenue SE	Phone: (507) 285-7256
Rochester, MN 55904	Fax: (507) 285-7108

Division(s): Academic Affairs
Web Site(s): http://www.roch.edu
E-mail: nancy.schumaker@roch.edu

Certificate Programs: online certificate in Digital Arts: Computer Graphics.

Class Titles: English Composition, French, History, Physics for Nonmajors, Technical Math, Graphic Design, Spanish, Child Development.

Teaching Methods: *Computers:* Internet, real-time chat, electronic classroom, e-mail, newsgroup, LISTSERV. *TV:* videotape, cable program, satellite broadcasting, PBS. *Other:* independent study.

Credits Granted for: examination (CLEP), Advanced Placement high school courses.

Admission Requirements: *Undergraduate:* high school diploma, basic skills testing and placement in developmental courses if needed (developmental courses not available as distance education at this time).

On-Campus Requirements: 25% of credits at this institution, but no restrictions on how many credits must be on-campus as opposed to distance-earned. No complete degree programs via distance learning, currently.

Tuition and Fees: *Undergraduate:* per credit for 1 to 11 credits; flat fee for 12 to 18 credits; per credit for 19 or more credits. *Credit by:* semester.

Financial Aid: Federal Stafford Loan, Federal Perkins Loan, Federal PLUS Loan, Federal Pell Grant, Federal Work-Study, VA, Minnesota resident programs.

Accreditation: North Central Association of Colleges and Schools.

Description: Rochester Community and Technical College (1915) is one partner in the University Center Rochester, which also houses sites for the University of Minnesota and Winona State University. The 2 universities deliver bachelor's and graduate programs in Rochester, with substantial portions of the curriculum delivered via ITV. The ITV mode is also used by RCTC to share delivery of courses in foreign languages, law enforcement, and mathematics with a nearby community college and area high schools. All 3 institutions are currently developing courses, and eventually degree programs, for delivery online.

Rochester Institute of Technology

Bausch and Lomb Center
58 Lomb Memorial Drive
Rochester, NY 14623-5604

Phone: (716) 475-2229
(800) 225-5748
Fax: (716) 475-7164

Division(s): Part-time and Graduate Enrollment Services
Web Site(s): http://online.rit.edu
E-mail: OPES@rit.edu

Undergraduate Degree Programs:
Bachelor of Science in:
- Applied Arts and Science, concentrations in:
  - Applied Computing
  - Disaster and Emergency Management
  - E-business
  - Environmental Management
  - Health Systems Administration Management
  - Manufacturing Management Technology
  - Mechanical Technology
  - Technical Communications
  - Telecommunications
  - Safety and Health Technology
  - Structural Design
- Electrical/Mechanical Engineering Technology
- Safety Technology
- Telecommunications Engineering Technology

Graduate Degree Programs:
Master of Science in:
- Applied Statistics
- Environmental, Health and Safety Management
- Graphic Arts Publishing
- Health Systems Administration
- Imaging Science
- Information Technology
- Microelectronics Manufacturing Engineering
- Software Development/Management
- Cross-Disciplinary Professional Studies

Certificate Programs: Disaster and Emergency Management, E-business, Industrial Environmental Management, Health Systems Administration, Basic Quality, Quality Implementation, Safety and Health Technology, Structural Design, Basic Technical Communications, Advanced Technical Communications, Data Communications, Voice, Communications, Network Management, Health Systems Finance (Graduate), Integrated Health Systems (Graduate), Statistical Quality (Graduate).

Teaching Methods: *Computers:* Internet, real-time chat, electronic classroom, e-mail, CD-ROM, LISTSERV. *TV:* videotape, cable program. *Other:* audioconferencing, videoconferencing, audiographics, audiotapes, fax.

Credits Granted for: experiential learning, portfolio assessment, extrainstitutional learning examination (CLEP, ACT-PEP, DANTES, GRE).

Admission Requirements: *Undergraduate:* 2-year degree or equivalent in credit for E/MET degree, TOEFL: 550. *Graduate:* accredited BS/BA/BTech, TOEFL: 550 or above.

On-Campus Requirements: Labs for E/MET program completed at predetermined site or in summer residence.

Tuition and Fees: *Undergraduate:* $286/credit hour (100, 200, 300 courses); $294/credit hour (400, 500, 600 courses). *Graduate:* $587/credit. *Application Fee:* $40 undergraduate/graduate degrees (nonmatriculation study accepted). *Other Costs:* books. *Credit by:* RIT—quarter, bachelor's degrees—180 quarter credits hours, graduate degrees—48 quarter credits, certificates vary.

Financial Aid: Federal Stafford Loan, Federal Perkins Loan, Federal PLUS Loan, Federal Pell Grant, Federal Work-Study, VA, New York resident programs (TAP, APTS).

Accreditation: Middle States Association of Colleges and Schools, New York State Education Department Office of Higher Education and the Professions. (Other programs hold individual, professional accreditations.)

Description: RIT is one of the nation's top comprehensive universities and sets the national standard for career-oriented, professional education. As a pioneer of distance learning education, RIT has offered innovative courses using electronic forms of communication since 1979. Each year, more than 2,000 students around the world enroll in RIT's online learning programs, working entirely off campus toward undergraduate and graduate certificates and degrees. RIT boasts one of the largest online learning programs in the country and was included in *Yahoo! Internet Life* magazines' Top 100 Wired Universities and *Barron's Best Buys in College Education.*

Rockland Community College

145 College Road, Room 4104
Suffern, NY 10901

Phone: (914) 574-4713
Fax: (914) 356-5811

Division(s): Instructional Technology
E-mail: rechevarria@sunyrockland.edu

Undergraduate Degree Programs:
Associate of Liberal Arts
Associate of Science

Teaching Methods: *Computers:* e-mail. *TV:* videotape, cable program, satellite broadcasting, PBS. *Other:* audiotapes, correspondence, independent study, individual study, learning contracts.

Credits Granted for: experiential learning, work, volunteer and community service, military, portfolio assessment, examination (CLEP).

Admission Requirements: *Undergraduate:* after completing 11 credits, an English and Math Placement Exam is required.

On-Campus Requirements: None.

Tuition and Fees: *Undergraduate:* $97/credit. *Application Fee:* $25 first-time student. *Other Costs:* $20/course for supplies, $3/credit activity fee. *Credit by:* semester.

Financial Aid: Federal Stafford Loan, Federal Perkins Loan, Federal PLUS Loan, Federal Pell Grant, Federal Work-Study, VA, New York resident programs, RCC institutional scholarships.

Accreditation: Middle States Association of Colleges and Schools.

Description: Rockland Community College (1959) is located on a 175-acre campus, with extension sites in Nyack, Haverstraw, and Spring Valley. The Rockland experience includes mingling with a diverse student population and studying with an experienced, award-winning faculty. The college pays special attention to individual needs through small class sizes, alternate learning modes, and a variety of student services. In addition, flexible scheduling enables many of the 5,000 Rockland students to earn credits or a degree through the Distance Learning program.

Roger Williams University

150 Washington Street
Providence, RI 02903

Phone: (401) 254-3530
Fax: (401) 254-3560

Division(s): Open College
Web Site(s): http://www.rwu.edu
E-mail: jws@alpha.rwu.edu

Undergraduate Degree Programs:
Bachelor of Science in:
   Business Management
   Criminal Justice
   Industrial Technology
   Public Administration
Bachelor of Arts in:
   Social Science

Class Titles: Biology, Financial Accounting, Enterprise, Business Ethics, Economics (micro/macro), Money/Banking, Management, Human Resource Management, Small Business Management, Business Policy, Marketing, Sales Management, Insurance, Investments, Financial Management, Stock Market, Computers, Spreadsheets (Excel), Computers Applications in Business, Criminal Justice, Policing in America, Substantive Criminal Law, Criminal Procedure, Constitutional Law, Evidence, Police Community Relations, Drugs/Society/Behavior, Criminology, Courts/Criminal Justice, Corrections in U.S., Correctional Administration, Community-Based Corrections, Juvenile Justice, Organized Crime, Law in Contemporary Society, Law of Contracts, Law of Business Organization, Man/Technology, Environment/Technology, ISO 9000, TQM, World Class MFG, Time/Motion, Production Planning, Manufacturing Processes, Workplace Safety, Quality Control, Facilities Plan/Design, Evolution of Jazz, Psychology, Psychology of Stress Management, American Government/Politics, Public Administration, State/Local Government, Public Policy, Public Personnel Administration, Public Financial Administration, Organizational Theory/Management, City Management, Social Science Research Methods, Perspectives on Peace, Sociology, Juvenile Delinquency, Theater.

Teaching Methods: *Computers:* Internet, e-mail. *TV:* videotapes, audiotapes. *Other:* fax, correspondence, independent study, individual study, internships, etc.

Credits Granted for: Up to 3 years (90 credits) allowed for experiential learning, portfolio assessment, extrainstitutional learning, examination (CLEP, ACT-PEP, DANTES, GRE); up to 3 years (90 credits) allowed for transfer credit, military service and training.

Admission Requirements: *Undergraduate:* high school diploma/GED. Advanced standing based on college credits, military training, creditable employment experiences, and/or CLEP exams. (Note: 60 credits required for Criminal Justice degree program.) Possible access to libraries, local college courses, local proctors, potential sites for internship placements, computers, etc.

On-Campus Requirements: No campus residency is required. In addition to academic and program requirements, students in the Open College must complete 30 credits at the university, although these do not need to be completed in the classroom or on campus. Normally, students need to meet with advisors and complete some activities on the main campus. These activities may include assisting in developing an educational plan, submitting student record materials, reviewing credit documentation, meeting with adjunct faculty, etc. However, the on-campus visit may be waived for distance students by an academic advisor.

Tuition and Fees: *Undergraduate:* $235–$400/credit. *Application Fee:* $35. *Credit by:* semester.

Financial Aid: Federal Stafford Loan, Federal Perkins Loan, Federal PLUS Loan, Federal Pell Grant, VA, military tuition assistance programs, some adult education scholarships.

Accreditation: New England Association of Schools and Colleges.

Description: Roger Williams University (1948) is a comprehensive, coeducational, private university offering degrees at the bachelor's and first professional levels. It has a waterfront campus in Bristol and an educational center in Providence. Roger Williams also offers undergraduate degree programs in liberal arts, engineering, architecture, business management, and other areas of professional studies, along with its new school of law. RWU's Open College began in 1974 as a comprehensive external degree program enabling working adults to study with minimal interference to family or job commitments; distance students have been enrolled since the program's beginning. It is a time-shortened degree program available part- or full-time, with continuous advisement services throughout the year. Special programs exist for students affiliated with the military.

Rogers State University

1701 West Will Rogers Boulevard	**Phone: (918) 341-7510**
Claremore, OK 74017	**Fax: (918) 343-7595**

Division(s): Distance Learning
Web Site(s): http://www.rsuonline.edu
http://www.rsu.edu
E-mail: online@rsu.edu

Undergraduate Degree Programs:
Associate of Arts in:
    Liberal Arts
    Business Administration
Associate of Science in Computer Science
Associate of Applied Science—Applied Technology
Bachelor of Arts—Liberal Arts
Bachelor of Science—Business Information Technology
Bachelor of Technology in Applied Technology

Class Titles: Financial Accounting, Managerial Accounting, Accounting Information Systems, Communications Graphics, Western Art History, General Environmental Biology, Principles of Management, Marketing Information and Decision Support Systems, Leadership and Change Dynamics, Introduction to Mass Communication, Introduction to Business, Communication Skills for Managers & Professionals, Fundamentals of Supervision, Emerging Technologies, Industrial Psychology, Introduction to Risk and Safety Management. Computer and Telecommunications Tools for Managers and Professionals, Government Regulation of Business, Business Law, Calculus I for Business, Business Statistics, Systems Analysis, Microcomputer Applications, Introduction to Computer Programming, Web Site Design & Development, Advanced Web Systems Development, Programming I, Java Programming, Programming II (C++), Software Engineering, Integrated Applications, Multimedia Development, Intro to Networking, Network Operating Systems, Data Modeling, Distributed Systems Development, Cross-Platform Development, Macro Economics, Micro Economics, International Relations, Basic

Writing Composition I & II, American Literature. Cinema, World Literature, Fiction Writing, Technical Writing, Intro to Philosophy, Humanities I & II, Seminar in Humanities, Earth Science, US History to 1865, US History From 1865, Music Appreciation, Computer Architecture, Elementary Algebra, Intermediate Algebra, Mathematics for Critical Thinking, College Algebra Introduction to Philosophy, Introduction To Astronomy, American Federal Government, Psychology, Introduction to Sociology, Social Problems Seminar, Social Ethics, Foundations of World Languages, Beginning Spanish I & II.

Teaching Methods: *Computers:* Internet, discussion format, real-time chat, electronic classroom, e-mail. *TV:* live broadcast and telecourses over broadcast and cable. *Other:* video-conferencing over IP (H.323).

Credits Granted for: examination (CLEP, APP).

Admission Requirements: *Undergraduate:* High school transcripts (or GED or equivalent) and ACT scores for students with no college course work, all college transcripts. Students over age 21 do not need to submit ACT scores. *Certificate:* Same as undergraduate.

On-Campus Requirements: None.

Tuition and Fees: *Undergraduate:* $68–$105/credit in-state, $152–$194/credit out-of-state. *Credit by:* semester.

Financial Aid: Federal Stafford Loan, Federal Perkins Loan, Federal PLUS Loan, Federal Pell Grant, Federal Work-Study, VA, Oklahoma resident programs.

Accreditation: North Central Association of Colleges and Schools, The Oklahoma State Regents for Higher Education.

Description: Rogers State University's history is nearly as old as Oklahoma. The institution began as prep school, changed to the Oklahoma Military Academy in 1919, then became a community college in 1972. In addition to providing a traditional classroom experience, Rogers State University offers academic programs designed to fit the busiest schedule by providing classes live from its own KRSC-TV or through RSU Online. In 1993 the university designed a program to bring the best distance learning to students across Oklahoma, the U.S., and the world. This program gives RSU students access to all important student services and classroom learning strategies online. No matter what degree program or learning option is chosen, Rogers State University students receive high-quality education that is convenient, flexible, and affordable. Rogers State University has been accredited since 1950.

Roosevelt University

430 South Michigan Avenue
Chicago, IL 60605-1394

Phone: (312) 281-3129
Fax: (312) 281-3132

Division(s): Distance Learning
Web Site(s): http://www.roosevelt.edu/distance-learning
http://www.roosevelt.edu (RU Online)
http://blackboard.roosevelt.edu
E-mail: kgersten@roosevelt.edu
areichle@roosevelt.edu

Certificate Programs: Training and Development (graduate); e-learning (graduate); Organizational Leadership (undergraduate).

Class Titles: Computer Science, Humanities, Economics, English, Finance, Geography, History, Hospitality Management, Psychology, Business, General Education for accelerated adult degree program, Education, Information Systems, Training and Development.

Teaching Methods: *Computers:* Internet electronic classroom e-mail. *Other:* fax, correspondence, individual study.

Admission Requirements: *Undergraduate:* high school diploma and be in good standing at Roosevelt or another institution. *Graduate:* varies by program.

On-Campus Requirements: None.

Tuition and Fees: *Undergraduate:* $380. *Application Fee:* $100 registration fee. *Credit by:* semester

Financial Aid: Federal Stafford Loan, Federal Perkins Loan, Federal PLUS Loan, Federal Pell Grant, Federal Work-Study, VA, Illinois resident programs, university programs.

Accreditation: North Central Association of Colleges and Schools.

Description: Roosevelt University (1945) was founded to provide opportunities for learning and teaching in conditions of freedom and equality. Since 1947, the home of Roosevelt's Chicago campus has been the famous auditorium building overlooking Grant Park and Lake Michigan. The Schaumburg Campus has become the largest and most comprehensive university in the northwest suburban area of Chicago. The Center for Professional Advancement opened on Michigan Avenue this year to focus on technology-based academic programs including Distance Learning. Roosevelt serves over 7,300 students at the baccalaureate, master's, and doctoral levels and offers classes during the day, at night, and on weekends to meet the needs of a diverse population. Through a generous grant from the McCormick Tribune Foundation, Roosevelt has added fully online courses to its wide array of course and program offerings.

Rose State College

6420 Southeast 15th Street
Midwest City, OK 73110

Phone: (405) 733-7393
Fax: (405) 736-0339

Division(s): Academic Affairs
Web Site(s): http://www.rose.cc.ok.us
E-mail: bbrown@ms.rose.cc.ok.us

Undergraduate Degree Programs:
Library Technical Assistant

Certificate Programs: Library Technical Assistant

Class Titles: 38 courses. Current semester offerings provided upon request.

Teaching Methods: *Computers:* Internet, real-time chat, electronic classroom, e-mail, LISTSERV. *TV:* videotape, cable program, PBS Affiliate Station. *Other:* videoconferencing, independent study.

Credits Granted for: extrainstitutional learning, examination (CLEP, ACT-PEP, DANTES, GRE).

Admission Requirements: *Undergraduate:* open-door policy.

On-Campus Requirements: None.

Tuition and Fees: *Undergraduate:* $48.70 resident, $122.25 out of state. *Application Fee:* $15. *Software:* $3/credit. *Credit by:* semester.

Financial Aid: Federal Stafford Loan, Federal Perkins Loan, Federal PLUS Loan, Federal Pell Grant, Federal Work-Study, VA, Oklahoma resident programs.

Accreditation: North Central Association of Colleges and Schools, Oklahoma State Regents for High Education.

Description: Rose State College (1970) is a public, 2-year institution located a short distance from downtown Oklahoma City. The college, originally named Oscar Rose Junior College, accepted its first students in September 1970. Curriculum consists of both terminal and transfer programs. Degrees granted include the Associate in Arts, Associate in Applied Science, and Associate in Science. The college provides opportunities for students outside traditional service areas through telecourses, Internet courses, and courses delivered through an interactive state telecommunications network. Semester schedules for both traditional and distance learning courses are provided upon request.

Rutgers, The State University of New Jersey

| 83 Somerset Street | Phone: (732) 932-5935 |
| New Brunswick, NJ 08901-1281 | Fax: (732) 932-9225 |

Division(s): Continuous Education and Outreach
Web Site(s): http://ce1766.rutgers.edu/online
E-mail: Rnovak@rci.rutgers.edu

Class Titles: Nursing, Youth Literature and Technology, Chinese, Education, Biomaterials, Human Resource Management, Business.

Teaching Methods: *Computers:* Internet, real-time chat, electronic classroom, e-mail, CD-ROM, newsgroup, LISTSERV. *TV:* videotape. *Other:* 2-way interactive videoconferencing, fax.

Admission Requirements: *Undergraduate:* vary according to discipline and school. No special admission requirements for distance learning students.

On-Campus Requirements: The majority of the distance learning courses are interactive videoconferenced courses between campuses or between campus and an off-campus site. Online courses are being developed in selected areas. See web site for details.

Tuition and Fees: *Undergraduate:* $6,500/academic year, New Jersey residents; $13,000/academic year, nonresidents. Tuition for the College of Engineering, College of Pharmacy, and Cook College (our school of life, environmental, marine, and agricultural sciences) is about 10% higher. These costs do not include books, travel, recreation, and personal expenses. Yearly tuition increases over the past 3 years have averaged 5%. *Graduate:* Total estimated educational and living expenses for the 2000–2001 academic year (excluding costs for the schools of management and law) are $18,700 for New Jersey residents and $22,000 for out-of-state residents. Expenses for international students are approximately $21,800 for the calendar year. *Application Fee:* $50, non-refundable. *Other Costs:* $168–$816 student fee (depending on school and part-time/full-time status), $40–$150 computer fee (part-time/full-time), $257 major medical insurance (mandatory for foreign students), $1,014 average fees residents/nonresidents. Contact school for details of tuition and fees. *Credit by:* semester.

Financial Aid: university, governmental, corporate, and individual sources—merit-based financial aid; university fellowships, scholarships, assistantships; Rutgers Excellence Fellowship Awards; special programs for students of underrepresented populations (Minority Advancement Program, Ralph Johnson Bunche Fellowships); part-time employment; New Jersey State Grants, Educational Opportunity Fund Grants, Federal Perkins Loans, Federal Stafford Loans, Federal Supplemental Educational Opportunity Grant, Federal Work-Study.

Accreditation: Middle States Association of Colleges and Schools.

Description: Established as Queen's College to train ministers for the Dutch Reformed Church, today Rutgers, the State University of New Jersey (1766) is one of the largest educational institutions in the U.S., with 3 campuses, 29 degree-granting schools, and 48,000 students. As New Jersey's land-grant institution and home to a host of centers, bureaus and institutes, Rutgers serves the evolving needs of the state and its citizens. Rutgers began offering distance learning courses several years ago to provide access to its many resources for students throughout the state. Most of the distance learning courses are offered through state-of-the-art, interactive video classrooms. Various courses are shared among the 3 campuses as well as with off-campus sites. In addition, the School of Communication, Information, and Library Science offers a 5-course, Internet-based certificate in Youth Literature and Technology (for details, consult http://scils.rutgers.edu/ac/pds/litandtech).

Sacramento City College

| 3835 Freeport Boulevard | Phone: (916) 558-2288 |
| Sacramento, CA 95822-1386 | Fax: (916) 558-2482 |

Division(s): Learning Resources
Web Site(s): http://www.scc.losrios.cc.ca.us/de
E-mail: phillije@www.scc.losrios.cc.ca.us

Undergraduate Degree Programs: Contact school.

Class Titles: Cultural Anthropology, American Cinema, Business, College Composition and Literature, Elementary French, Regional Geography, Sociology of Aging, Health Education, American History, Journalism, Library, Music Appreciation, Nursing, Philosophy, Psychology, Sociology, Speech, Work Experience.

Teaching Methods: *Computers:* Internet, real-time chat, electronic classroom, e-mail, CD-ROM, newsgroup, LISTSERV. *TV:* videotape, cable program, satellite broadcasting. *Other:* videoconferencing, audioconferencing, audiotapes, fax, correspondence, independent study, individual study, learning contracts.

Admission Requirements: Contact school.

On-Campus Requirements: On-campus meetings are required but this varies as to instructor and class.

Tuition and Fees: *Undergraduate:* $11/credit. *Graduate:* *Credit by:* semester.

Financial Aid: Federal Stafford Loan, Federal Perkins Loan, Federal PLUS Loan, Federal Pell Grant, Federal Work-Study, VA, state programs for residents of California

Accreditation: Western Association of Schools and Colleges.

Description: Sacramento City College (1916) is a part of the Los Rios Community College District and serves the educational needs of Sacramento and Yolo Counties. Our mission is to serve students by working together to pursue excellence and inspire achievement. The faculty and staff of the college will join with students to help them identify their educational needs, provide personal, financial, and educational planning and support, and explore and pursue a wide array of learning opportunities. The staff and faculty of the college are committed to the worth, dignity, and potential for growth in every person. We will challenge our students to imagine and pursue a future that stimulates us to the limits of our capacities to achieve. Along with our regular class schedule, the Distance Education Program offers telecourse classes, interactive and online classes designed to provide high-quality course work to those students who are unable to attend on-campus classes.

Sacred Heart University

| 5151 Park Avenue | Phone: (203) 371-7831 |
| Fairfield, CT 06432 | Fax: (203) 365-7500 |

Division(s): University College
Web Site(s): http://uc.sacredheart.edu
E-mail: godou@sacredheart.edu

Undergraduate Degree Programs:
Nursing—Leadership Studies.

Certificate Programs: Educational Technology at Graduate Level.

Class Titles: Leadership, English Composition, Literature, Chemistry, Computer Science, Media Studies, Sport Management, Nursing, Economics, Finance, Education, Accounting, Statistics Management, E-Commerce, History.

Teaching Methods: *Computers:* Internet, real-time chat, e-mail, CD-ROM, newsgroup, LISTSERV. *Other:* fax, correspondence, independent study, individual study.

Credits Granted for: experiential learning, portfolio assessment, extrainstitutional learning (PONSI, corporate or professional association seminars/workshops), examination (CLEP, DANTES, Regents).

Admission Requirements: *Undergraduate:* high school degree. *Graduate:* baccalaureate degree. *Certificate:* baccalaureate degree.

On-Campus Requirements: None.

Tuition and Fees: *Undergraduate:* $330/credit. *Graduate:* $375 to $435, depending on program. *Application Fee:* $65. *Graduation Fee:* $100. *Credit by:* semester.

Financial Aid: Federal Stafford Loan, Federal Perkins Loan, Federal PLUS Loan, Federal Pell Grant, Federal Work-Study, VA, state programs for residents of Connecticut.

Accreditation: New England Association of Schools and Colleges.

Description: Sacred Heart University (1963) was founded by the Most Reverend Walter W. Curtis, Bishop of the Diocese of Bridgeport. It was established to provide an affordable, quality education at a local Catholic university. From its outset, the university bore the mark of innovation. Charting a new direction within American Catholicism, the university was to be led and staffed by the laity, independent and locally oriented, serving the needs of the diocese and of southwestern Connecticut. The university consists of 4 colleges: College of Arts and Sciences, College of Business, College of Education and Health Professions, and University College. The latter is committed to the adult learner and provides continuing education programs. Its evening, weekend, and accelerated courses earn praise for their diversity and relevance to changing lifestyles. Located on 56 suburban acres in Fairfield, Connecticut, the main campus is just minutes from Exit 47 off the Merritt Parkway (Route 15), about one hour north of New York and 2 hours south of Boston. The university is a coeducational, independent, comprehensive institution of higher learning in the Catholic intellectual tradition. Its primary objective is to prepare men and women to live in and make their contributions to the human community.

Saddleback College

| 28000 Marguerite Parkway, AGB126 | Phone: (949) 582-4515 |
| Mission Viejo, CA 92692 | Fax: (949) 347-0438 |

Division(s): Office of Instruction
Web Site(s): http://www.saddleback.college.net
E-mail: snelson@saddleback.cc.ca.us

Class Titles: Accounting, Cultural Anthropology, Business, Business Management, Marketing, Salesmanship, Small Business Management, American History, Music Appreciation, History of Rock (music), American Government, Psychology, Developmental Psychology, Real Estate, Sociology, Marriage/Family, Marine Science, Creative Writing, Computer/Information Systems.

Teaching Methods: *Computers:* Internet, e-mail, CD-ROM. *TV:* videotape, cable program. *Other:* radio broadcast (broadcast area restricted).

Credits Granted for: experiential learning.

Admission Requirements: *Undergraduate:* high school diploma.

On-Campus Requirements: Some courses require on-campus meetings and computer lab work. Real estate courses are on campus at students' convenience. All courses must be completed within the semester offered.

Tuition and Fees: *Undergraduate:* $11/credit residents and military; $143/credit nonresidents. *Graduate:* same. *Doctoral:* same. *Application Fee:* $46 for citizens and residents of a foreign country. *Other Costs:* $3–$14 for health and material fees, as applicable. *Credit by:* semester.

Financial Aid: Federal Stafford Student Loans, Federal Perkins Loan, Federal Pell Grant, Federal Work-Study, Federal Supplemental Educational Opportunity Grant, Saddleback Emergency Loan Funds, Board of Governors Fee Waiver, California Student Aid Commission Program, Saddleback College Scholarships.

Accreditation: Western Association of Schools and Colleges, Accrediting Commission for Community and Junior Colleges.

Description: Saddleback College (1967) is committed to providing a high-quality, postsecondary education to all people, with nondiscriminatory recognition of the dignity and worth of the individual in a free society. To that end, Saddleback provides rigorous degree and certificate curricula in lower-division arts and sciences and in vocational and occupational fields. In addition, personal attention is extended through tutoring, remedial instruction, English as a second language, and support services such as counseling, career guidance, and assistance for the disabled. Finally, the college provides lifelong learning through Community Education seminars, credit and noncredit courses, workshops, etc., to support nontraditional community needs.

Saginaw Valley State University

7400 Bay Road
University Center, MI 48710-0001

Phone: (989) 790-4093
Fax: (989) 790-0180

Division(s): Academic Affairs
Web Site(s): http://www.svsu.edu
E-mail: jcl@svsu.edu

Undergraduate Degree Programs: Contact school.

Graduate Degree Programs: Contact school.

Postgraduate Degree Programs: Contact school.

Class Titles: Counseling Skills, Core Phenom and Nursing Intervention, Retail Management.

Teaching Methods: satellite broadcasting.

Admission Requirements: Contact school for details.

On-Campus Requirements: Classes can be taken at a remote site or at other campus locations.

Tuition and Fees: *Undergraduate:* $109.65/credit. *Graduate:* $173.65/credit. *Postgraduate:* $173.65/credit. *Application Fee:* $25. *Graduation Fee:* $30. *Other Costs:* $100. *Credit by:* semester.

Financial Aid: Federal Stafford Loan, Federal Perkins Loan, Federal PLUS Loan, Federal Pell Grant, Federal Work-Study, VA, state programs for residents of Michigan. Too many additional to list.

Accreditation: North Central Association of Colleges and Schools.

Description: Saginaw Valley State University (1963) is a comprehensive, coeducational, 4-year, state-supported university offering bachelor's and master's degrees. Chartered as a private institution to meet higher education needs in east-central Michigan, it became state-assisted in 1965. The name was changed to Saginaw Valley State University in 1987. Minimal classes are offered in Distance Education.

Saint Ambrose University

1950 E. 54th Street
Davenport, IA 52807

Phone: (563) 441-9500
Fax: (563) 441-9875

Division(s): Adult Education and Professional Development Division
Web Site(s): http://www.sau.edu/aepd
E-mail: gpetry@sau.edu

Certificate Programs: Business Management.

Class Titles: Human Resource Management; Business Ethics, Legal Environment of Business, Principles of Management, Principles of Marketing, Diversity in the Workplace, Organizational Theory, Mediation, International Business (all have an 8-week window for completion); Graduate: Human Resource Management Strategic Marketing Management (all have an 8-week window for completion).

Teaching Methods: *Computers:* Internet, real-time chat, electronic classroom, e-mail, CD-ROM, LISTSERV. *Other:* video-conferencing, audiotapes, fax, correspondence, independent study.

Credits Granted for: experiential learning, portfolio assessment, examination (CLEP, ACT-PEP, DANTES, GRE).

Admission Requirements: *Undergraduate:* all prerequisites apply, 23 years old or older, 3 years full-time work experience, high school graduate with 24 credit hours from an accredited college or university. *Graduate:* college graduate with prerequisites. *Certificate:* prerequisites.

On-Campus Requirements: None.

Tuition and Fees: *Undergraduate:* $312/credit. *Graduate:* $456/credit. *Application Fees:* $25. *Software:* $30. *Credit by:* semester.

Financial Aid: Federal Stafford Loan, Federal Perkins Loan, Federal PLUS Loan, Federal Pell Grant, Federal Work-Study, VA, state programs for residents of Iowa.

Accreditation: North Central Association of Colleges and Schools.

Description: "The St. Ambrose University Adult Education and Professional Development Division continually strives to be a quality-driven, multifaceted resource serving the lifelong learning needs of our vastly growing adult community through a variety of progressive and innovative delivery methods." St. Ambrose has come a long way since it began as a seminary and school of commerce for young men in 1882. In 1968 St. Ambrose became fully coeducational, although women had been taking classes on campus ever since the 1930s. St. Ambrose began offering graduate classes in 1977 with the Master of Business Administration program. Its graduate programs have expanded to 11 master's degrees, and a Doctorate of Business Administration was inaugurated in 1999. On April 23, 1987, St. Ambrose College became St. Ambrose University at the direction of the Board of Directors. The university was divided into the Colleges of Business, Human Services, and Arts and Sciences, a distinction that stands today.

Saint Charles County Community College

4601 Mid Rivers Mall Drive	Phone: (314) 922-8470
St. Peters, MO 63376-0975	Fax: (314) 922-8433

Division(s): Instructional Resources
Web Site(s):
http://www.stchas.edu/academics/distance/dlmain.htm
E-mail: arandazzo@scccc.stchas.edu

Class Titles: Anthropology, Art, Biology, Business, Criminal Justice, English, History, Health, Psychology, Sociology, Theater.

Teaching Methods: *Computers:* Internet, e-mail, LISTSERV. *TV:* videotape, PBS. *Other:* interactive video.

Credits Granted for: experiential learning, portfolio assessment, examination (CLEP, ACT-PEP, DANTES, GRE).

Admission Requirements: *Undergraduate:* high school diploma or a GED certificate, age 18 and demonstrate the ability to benefit through the student assessment process. *Certificate:* same as undergraduate.

On-Campus Requirements: None.

Tuition and Fees: *Undergraduate:* $45/credit in-district, $65/credit out-of-district in-state; $100/credit out-of-state/international. *Other Costs:* $5/credit service fee, $38/video/telecourse. *Credit by:* semester.

Financial Aid: Federal Stafford Loan, Federal Pell Grant, Federal Work-Study, VA, Missouri resident programs, A+, SCOG, VR, JTPA.

Accreditation: North Central Association of Colleges and Schools.

Description: St. Charles County Community College (1986) is an open-admission institution dedicated to providing accessible postsecondary educational programs and community services at a reasonable cost. By incorporating academic excellence and technological advancements, we prepare our students to achieve their educational, professional, and personal goals and enhance their cultural experiences. The college began offering courses through distance learning in 1992.

Saint Cloud State University

720 4th Avenue South	Phone: (320) 255-3081
Saint Cloud, MN 56301	Fax: (320) 654-5041

Division(s): Center for Continuing Studies
Web Site(s): http://www.stcloudstate.edu/~ccs
E-mail: ccs@condor.stcloudstate.edu

Undergraduate Degree Programs:
Bachelor of Elective Studies, Major in Community Psychology
Bachelor of Applied Science, Major in Aviation Maintenance Management

Graduate Degree Programs:
Master of Science in:
    Mass Communications
    Applied Economics
    Environmental and Technological Studies
    Educational Media
    Master of Business Administration

Certificate Programs: Certificate in Instructional Technology; Community Education Licensure.

Class Titles: Art, Anthropology, Child and Family Studies, Business and Computer Information Systems, Biology, Chemistry, Criminal Justice, Economics, Educational Administration, Educational Research, English, Environmental and Technological Studies, History, Leadership, Microcomputer Studies, Philosophy, Psychology, Reading, Sociology, Speech, Special Education, Social Science.

Teaching Methods: *Computers:* Internet, electronic classroom, e-mail, CD-ROM. *TV:* videotape, interactive television. *Other:* videoconferencing, audioconferencing, audiotapes, correspondence, independent study.

Credits Granted for: examination (CLEP, ACT-PEP, DANTES, GRE).

Admission Requirements: *Undergraduate:* high school diploma/GED; official high school or postsecondary transcripts, admissions application, GPA, ACT/SAT scores. *Graduate:* admission application, official undergraduate transcripts, graduate entrance exam (GRE/GMAT, etc.)

On-Campus Requirements: None.

Tuition and Fees: *Undergraduate:* off-campus: $112.50/credit; on-campus: $92.30/credit. *Graduate:* off-campus: $162.20/credit; on-campus: $141.65/credit. *Application Fees:* $20. *Graduation Fee:* $15. *Other Costs:* $20 for self-paced/online courses; $75 for off-campus and interactive television courses. *Credit by:* semester.

Financial Aid: Federal Stafford Loan, Federal Perkins Loan, Federal PLUS Loan, Federal Pell Grant, Federal Work-Study, VA, state programs for residents of Minnesota.

Accreditation: North Central Association of Colleges and Schools, North Central Association of Colleges and Schools, National Council for Accreditation of Teacher Education, American Association of Collegiate Schools of Business, International Association of Management Education, National Association of Schools of Arts and Design, American Speech-Language Hearing Association, Computer Science Accreditation Commission of the Computing Sciences Accreditation Board, Council of Education in Journalism and Mass Communications, National Association of Schools of Music, International Association of Counseling Services, Council on Rehabilitaiton Education, National Council for Accreditation of Teacher Education, Council for Exceptional Children.

Description: SCSU (1869) is a comprehensive university serving more than 14,000 traditional, on-campus students and 1,500 distance students each year. SCSU began Distance Learning offerings with correspondence study and off-campus courses around the state of Minnesota. In the past 15 years, we have developed a strong infrastructure in interactive television and are now adding online learning.

Saint Francis Xavier University

West Street, P.O. Box 5000	Phone: (902) 867-3906
Antigonish, NS, Canada B2G 2W5	Fax: (902) 867-5154

Division(s): Continuing and Distance Education
Web Site(s): http://www.stfx.ca
E-mail: cjones@stfx.ca

Undergraduate Degree Programs:
Bachelor of Science in Nursing, Post R.N.

Certificate Programs: Diploma in Ministry, Gerontological Nursing.

Class Titles: Nursing, Religion.

Teaching Methods: *Computers:* real-time chat, e-mail, CD-ROM, LISTSERV.

Admission Requirements: *Undergraduate:* high school certification, registered nurse certification. *Certificate:* open admission.

On-Campus Requirements: None.

Tuition and Fees: *Undergraduate:* $510/credit. *Credit by:* semester.

Accreditation: Association of Universities and Colleges of Canada.

Description: St. Francis Xavier University (1853) is a small liberal-arts institution in Atlantic Canada, highly ranked among Canadian universities for academic quality. Its distance education programs are learner-centered, with a strong emphasis on student support systems.

Saint Gregory's University

1900 West MacArthur	Phone: (405) 878-5100
Shawnee, OK 74804	Fax: (405) 878-5198

Division(s): Academic Advising
Web Site(s): http://sgc.edu
E-mail: kddavidson@sgc.edu

Undergraduate Degree Programs: Cannot currently complete a degree on line.

Class Titles: Theology, Sacred Scripture, Christ and the Human Person, Church History I, Christian Trinitarian Theology, Microeconomics, Macroeconomics, College Algebra.

Teaching Methods: *Computers:* Internet, e-mail, CD-ROM.

Credits Granted for: portfolio assessment, extrainstitutional learning (PONSI, corporate or professional association seminars/workshops), examination (CLEP, ACT-PEP, DANTES, GRE).

Admission Requirements: *Undergraduate:* time limit for completion is 16 weeks.

On-Campus Requirements: None.

Tuition and Fees: *Undergraduate:* $292/credit for 2001–2002 academic year. *Application Fee:* $25. *Software:* depends on the course. *Credit by:* semester.

Financial Aid: Federal Stafford Loan (minimum enrollment of 6 hours required), Federal Perkins Loan (minimum enrollment of 6 hours required), Federal PLUS Loan (minimum enrollment of 6 hours required), Federal Pell Grant, VA.

Accreditation: North Central Association of Colleges and Secondary Schools, Oklahoma State Regents for Higher Education, the U.S. Department of Justice for the admission of international students, State Accrediting Agency for the admission of eligible veterans, and U.S. Department of Education for federal financial aid programs.

Description: Established in 1875 by the Benedictine predecessors of St. Gregory's Abbey, St. Gregory's University is Oklahoma's oldest institution of higher education and its first laptop university. SGU has experienced unprecedented growth during the past several years and was named the state's fastest-growing college or university 4 times in the past 6 years. SGU offers a unique and academically rigorous curriculum that allows students to design a degree especially for their career interests. SGU students learn about the workplace firsthand through an aggressive internship and job-shadowing program. The university boasts small classes and a close-knit community nurtured by St. Gregory's Abbey and a caring faculty and staff. SGU prides itself on preparing students for a life of success and service as "A Community for Life." Each year the list of Distance Learning opportunities has grown upon the needs of our students and the community.

Saint Joseph's College of Maine

278 Whites Bridge Road	**Phone: (800) 752-4723**
Standish, ME 04084-4263	**Fax: (207) 892-7480**
	or (207) 892-7841

Division(s): Graduate and Professional Studies
Web Site(s): http://www.sjcme.edu/gps
E-mail: admiss@sjcme.edu
lrobinso@sjcme.edu

Undergraduate Degree Programs:
Business
Criminal Justice
General Studies
Health Care Administration
Liberal Studies
Long-Term Care Administration
Nursing
Professional Studies
Radiologic Science (degree completion)
Respiratory Care (degree completion)

Graduate Degree Programs:
Master of Science in:
    Health Services Administration
Nursing
Education
Pastoral Studies

Certificate Programs: Business Administration, Christian Tradition, Criminal Justice, General Studies, Health Care Management, Lay Ministry, Long-Term Care, Pastoral Studies (Graduate), Professional Studies.

Class Titles: Practically all of our undergraduate courses can be taken individually by students.

Teaching Methods: *Computers:* Internet, real-time chat, electronic classroom, e-mail, CD-ROM, newsgroup, LISTSERV. *Other:* independent study, individual study.

Credits Granted for: experiential learning, portfolio assessment, extrainstitutional learning (PONSI, corporate or professional association seminars/workshops), examination (CLEP, ACT-PEP, DANTES, GRE).

Admission Requirements: *Undergraduate:* high school graduate or GED equivalent. *Graduate:* bachelor's degree, GRE for Master's Nursing. *Certificate:* high school graduate or GED equivalent.

On-Campus Requirements: Most degree programs require student to attend one 2-week session at our lakeside campus in Maine during the course of study.

Tuition and Fees: *Undergraduate:* $200/credit. *Graduate:* $240/credit. *Application Fee:* $50. *Graduation Fee:* $50. *Credits by:* semester.

Financial Aid: Federal Stafford Loan, Federal Perkins Loan, Federal PLUS Loan, Federal Pell Grant, Federal Work-Study, VA, Maine resident programs.

Accreditation: New England Association of Schools and Colleges, nursing programs also accredited by Commission on Collegiate Nursing and Maine State Board of Nursing, Long-Term Care programs also accredited by National Association of Boards of Examiners of Long-Term Care Administrators.

Description: Saint Joseph's College of Maine (founded by the Sisters of Mercy in 1912) is a community of people inspiring each other to learn, serve, risk, and grow. This year (2001) marks our 25th year of offering degrees through distance education, a program established to provide a quality college education for working adults living anywhere in the world. Maine's only Catholic college, we provide academic opportunities to more than 4,000 students from all 50 states and 22 countries through our distance education programs, and to 900 undergraduate students at our campus in Maine. Courses are available in a variety of delivery modes to provide the flexibility that adult students need to succeed.

Saint Louis Community College

300 So. Broadway	Phone: (314) 539-5056
St. Louis, MO 63102	Fax: (314) 539-5005

Division(s): Telelearning Services
Web Site(s): http://stlcc.cc.mo.us
E-mail: lsterman@stlcc.cc.mo.us, jcampbell@stlcc.cc.mo.us, bdevoti@stlcc.cc.mo.us

Undergraduate Degree Programs:
Associate of Arts
Associate of Applied Science

Certificate Programs: Contract school.

Class Titles: Financial Accounting I, Medical Terminology, Stenocaptioning, Introductory Biology I, Introduction to Business Administration, Preparation for Chemistry, Fundamentals of Chemistry I, Freshman Academic Orientation, Public Speaking, Machine Shorthand I, Developmental English, Developmental English Lab, Introduction to College Writing, Introduction to College Writing Lab, English for Non-native Speakers II, College Composition I, College Composition II, Introduction to Fiction, American Literature After 1865, Information Systems for Business, S/P Programming With Visual C++ (I), S/P Programming With Visual C++ (II), S/P Programming With Visual C++ (III), S/P Internet Literacy, S/P FrontPage 2000, Computers and the Law, Web Site Design, Intermediate Algebra, College Algebra, Introduction to American Politics, General Psychology, Human Growth and Development, Abnormal Psychology, Introduction to Astronomy I, Meteorology, Introduction to Quality Control, Introduction to Sociology.

Teaching Methods: *Computers:* Internet, real-time chat, electronic classroom, e-mail, CD-ROM, newsgroup, LISTSERV, mailing list, FAQ's, projects, group projects, practicums, portfolios. *TV:* videotape, cable program, satellite broadcasting, PBS. *Other:* broadcast, videoconferencing, audioconferencing, audiotapes, fax, correspondence, independent study, individual study, learning contracts.

Credits Granted for: experiential learning, portfolio assessment, extrainstitutional learning (corporate or professional association seminars/workshops). All are class specific, examination (ACCUPLACER).

Admission Requirements: *Undergraduate:* Contact school. *Certificate:* ACCUPLACER test, transcripts, ability to pay, temporary residency visa or citizenship, passed test results for proficiency in English examination.

Tuition and Fees: *Undergraduate:* $42/credit residency, out-of-county $53/credit hour, $67/credit hour, out-of-state residency. *Other Costs:* $2.50/credit hour for student fees. Late registration fee: $10. Various miscellaneous charges pertaining to outside costs for a number of different classes. *Credit by:* semester.

Financial Aid: Federal Stafford Loan, Federal Perkins Loan, Federal PLUS Loan, Federal Pell Grant, Federal Work-Study, VA, state programs for residents of Missouri.

Accreditation: North Central Association of Colleges and Schools.

Description: SLCC's (1961) first Distance class was a television class in 1973. "Western Civilization" was aired twice a week on KETC, Channel 9 and had an enrollment of 140 students. In January 1991 the first SLCC computer class premiered. "English Composition" served student instruction through use of a modem for instruction, e-mail, bulletins, and library research. In January 1992 the first interactive television course, "Math for Chemistry Majors" debuted with 75 enrolled students. Enrollees were located at all 3 SLCC campus locations and received the instruction remotely via interactive television. Fall 2000 enrollment in distance education classes demonstrates the growth and expansion of this type of instruction all across the district. There are 32 web-based courses with an enrollment of 397. There are 10 interactive classes in session fall 2000 semester with an enrollment of 240 students. Twenty-nine telecourses are in session fall 2000 with an enrollment of 2,650 students.

Saint Louis University

3525 Caroline Mall	Phone: (314) 577-8993
St. Louis, MO 63104-1099	Fax: (314) 577-8949

Division(s): School of Nursing
Web Site(s): http://nursing.slu.edu
http://nursing.slu.edu/online
E-mail: SLUnurse@slu.edu

Graduate Degree Programs:
Master of Science in Nursing in the following specialties:
    Adult Nurse Practitioner
    Family Nurse Practitioner
    Gerontological Nurse Practitioner
    Pediatric Nurse Practitioner
    Adult Clinical Nurse Specialist/Case Manager
    Gerontological Clinical Nurse Specialist/Case Manager

Certificate Programs: Post-Master's Certificate in Nursing in the following specialties: Adult Nurse Practitioner, Family Nurse Practitioner, Gerontological Nurse Practitioner, Pediatric Nurse Practitioner.

Class Titles: Contact school or check web site for details.

Teaching Methods: *Computers:* World Wide Web, electronic classroom, e-mail, CD-ROM, Web streaming media (RealAudio, RealVideo).

Credits Granted for: Master's students may petition to transfer up to 6 credits of graduate study from another college or university.

Admission Requirements: *Graduate:* baccalaureate degree in nursing from a program accredited by a nationally recognized accrediting agency. (The School of Nursing will consider applications from registered nurses who have a non-nursing baccalaureate degree.) Cumulative credit point average of 3.0 (B) in a 4.0 system for admission as a Classified student. Probationary student status may be given if less than 3.0. Recommendations from 3 people (preferably master's or doctorally prepared nurses) who can speak to your potential for success in a master's level nursing program of study. Registered nurse licensure in the state in which you will complete your clinical practice. Proof of licensure must be on file with the School of Nursing. Submission of a current completed Student Health Record. In addition to required immunizations, the Hepatitis B immunization is strongly recommended. Students are required to submit proof of a TB screening when beginning clinical practica in some agencies. Completion of a beginning level health assessment course or the equivalent thereof is required for all nurse practitioner tracks. One year of nurse practice experience within the last 3 years is strongly recommended for all nurse practitioner tracks. Personal interview may be required. *Certificate:* an earned master's degree in an appropriate nursing specialty.

On-Campus Requirements: For master's students, 2 one-week residencies are required at specified periods according to your study plan. For post-master's students, 1 one-week residency is required prior to the final clinical practicum course.

Tuition and Fees: *Graduate:* graduate/post-Master's, $630/credit. *Application Fee:* $40. *Graduation Fee:* $50. *Other Costs:* $20/credit for nursing surcharge. *Student Activity Fee:* $19/semester. *Credit by:* semester.

Financial Aid: Federal Stafford Loan, VA, state programs for residents of Missouri, Saint Louis University scholarships, Federal traineeship funds through the School of Nursing for full-time students, U.S. Public Health Service, loans from professional nursing organizations.

Accreditation: National League for Nursing, American Association of Colleges of Nursing Commission on Collegiate Nursing Education, Higher Learning Commission of the North Central Association, Missouri State Board of Nursing.

Description: Saint Louis University was founded in 1818. The School of Nursing began in 1928. Saint Louis University is built on a 450-year Jesuit tradition of education, innovation, and exploration. The Master of Science in Nursing program at the School of Nursing prepares registered nurses as advanced practice nurses through comprehensive course work and practical experience in clinical settings. Distance

Learning via the World Wide Web at the School of Nursing in 1997 was established to provide opportunities for excellence in education to those nurses who are unable to attend the traditional classroom. The program offers the flexibility that most working nurses require. The program helps students make the most of their prior nursing education and work experience.

Saint Mary College

4100 S. Fourth Street
Leavenworth, KS 66048

Phone: (913) 758-6118
877-277-6257
Fax: (913) 758-6140
877-490-6844

Division(s): Education
Web Site(s): http://www.smcks.edu
E-mail: murphyn@hub.smcks.edu

Graduate Degree Programs:
Master of Arts in Teaching

Class Titles: Contact school or check web site for details.

Teaching Methods: *Computers:* Internet, e-mail. *TV:* videotape.

Admission Requirements: *Graduate:* must be teaching; must have a bachelor's degree with a minimum grade point average of 2.75 on a 4.0 scale; 2 letters of recommendation (one from a current school administrator), an essay.

On-Campus Requirements: None.

Tuition and Fees: *Graduate:* $230/credit. *Application Fees:* $25. *Graduation Fee:* $50. *Other Costs:* $75/semester for books, videos, study guides. *Credit by:* semester.

Financial Aid: Federal Stafford Loan.

Accreditation: North Central Association of Colleges and Schools.

Description: A 30-credit Master of Arts in Teaching (MAT) with an emphasis in Curriculum and Instruction is offered by Saint Mary College (1999), to practicing teachers. The program is designed to be a catalyst for positive change in education organizations by improving classroom practices. This program provides professionals seeking advancement and improved skills the opportunity to enhance personal growth and strengthen performance. The MAT curriculum includes professionally developed videotapes and interactive communication by e-mail. Each 3-credit course includes, along with the videotapes, study guides that include and describe the problem-based method used. College instructors interact with participants and provide coaching, feedback, and evaluation.

Saint Mary-of-the-Woods College

Guerin Hall
Saint Mary-of-the-Woods, IN 47876

Phone: (800) 926-7692
(812) 535-5106
Fax: (812) 535-4900

Division(s): Women's External Degree Admission
Web Site(s): http://www.smwc.edu
E-mail: wedadms@smwc.edu

Undergraduate Degree Programs:
Associate in Arts/Associate in Science in:
  Accounting
  Early Childhood Education
  General Business
  Gerontology
  Humanities
  Paralegal Studies
Bachelor of Arts/Bachelor of Science in:
  Accounting
  Accounting Information Systems
  Business Administration
  Computer Information Systems
  Digital Media Communication
  Education, including:
    Early Childhood
  Elementary Education
  Secondary Education:
    English
    Mathematics
    Social Studies
  English
  Gerontology
  History/Political Science/Prelaw
  Human Resource Management
  Human Services
  Humanities
  Journalism
  Marketing
  Mathematics
  Not-for-Profit:
    Childcare Administration
    Financial Administration
    Human Services
    Public Relations
  Occupational Therapy Applications
  Paralegal Studies
  Professional Writing
  Psychology
  Social Science and History
  Theology

Graduate Degree Programs:
Master of Arts in:
  Pastoral Theology

Earth Literacy
Music Therapy
Art Therapy

Certificate Programs: Gerontology, Paralegal Studies, Theology.

Class Titles: Almost all courses for above majors and general studies may be taken individually at a distance.

Teaching Methods: *Computers:* Internet, real-time chat, electronic classroom, e-mail, CD-ROM. *Other:* audiotapes, independent study, individual study.

Credits Granted for: experiential learning, portfolio assessment, extrainstitutional learning, examination (CLEP, DANTES).

Admission Requirements: *Undergraduate:* high school diploma/GED, academic history/work experience considered. Education majors must reside within 200 miles of campus. *Graduate:* bachelor's degree. *Certificate:* English Composition required if not previously taken.

On-Campus Requirements: Minimal residency each semester, or every other semester with approval. Education majors must reside within 200 miles of campus.

Tuition and Fees: *Undergraduate:* $294/credit. *Graduate:* $335/credit. *Application Fee:* $30. *Credit by:* semester.

Financial Aid: Federal Stafford Loan, Federal Perkins Loan, Federal PLUS Loan, Federal Pell Grant, Federal Work-Study, Indiana resident programs.

Accreditation: North Central Association of Colleges and Schools, through The Higher Learning Commission.

Description: Since 1973, the Women's External Degree program at Saint Mary-of-the-Woods College (1840) has provided the curriculum for contemporary adult women who juggle multiple responsibilities yet need or want a college degree. This structured but flexible independent study program of 5-month semesters leads to a degree in one of more than 25 majors. Beginning with an in-person appointment, faculty and students communicate by telephone, voice mail, e-mail, and postal service. (Computers with modems are required only for accounting and CIS majors, but computer/word processor access is strongly recommended.) Full-time faculty members serve as academic advisers, and WED staff provide additional support, advocacy, registration assistance, and information, including a quarterly newsletter for distance learners. Students may also take on-campus, independent study courses with intensive weekend seminars.

Saint Peter's College

| 2641 Kennedy Boulevard | Phone: (201) 915-9022 |
| Jersey City, NJ 07643 | Fax: (201) 432-4997 |

Division(s): School of Professional and Continuing Studies
Web Site(s): http://www.spc.edu
E-mail: hamilton_r@spc.edu

Certificate Programs: Master of Urban Education

Class Titles: undergraduate courses.

Teaching Methods: *Computers:* Internet, real-time chat, electronic classroom, e-mail, LISTSERV. *TV:* videotape, satellite broadcasting. *Other:* interactive TV, fax, correspondence, independent study, individual study, learning contracts.

Credits Granted for: experiential learning, portfolio assessment, extrainstitutional learning.

Admission Requirements: *Undergraduate:* honors high school senior or college freshman, resident of New Jersey.

On-Campus Requirements: 9 hours in workshops for graduate education courses; undergraduate students meet live with professor at their sites or the college several times a semester.

Tuition and Fees: *Undergraduate:* $400/credit. *Graduate:* $585/credit. *Application Fee:* $30. *Credit by:* semester and trimester.

Financial Aid: Federal Stafford Loan, Federal Perkins Loan, Federal PLUS Loan, Federal Pell Grant, Federal Work-Study, VA, New Jersey resident programs.

Accreditation: Middle States Association of Colleges and Schools.

Description: Saint Peter's College (1876) is a Jesuit college dedicated to *cura personalis* in an urban environment. Traditionally the typical undergraduate student has been a first-generation student, although recently the entering classes are more of a cross-section. Saint Peter's entered the field of Distance Learning in 1991 under a state Challenge Grant via satellite delivery. Since then the college has expanded its efforts to include interactive TV, the Web, videotape, satellite, fax, correspondence, independent study, individual study, and learning contracts. Saint Peter's uses Blackboard as its course management software. The on-campus requirements reflect the college's determination to maintain *cura personalis* in whatever teaching methodology is utilized.

Saint Petersburg College

| 9200 113th Street North | Phone: (727) 394-6116 |
| Seminole, FL 33772 | Fax: (727) 394-6124 |

Division(s): Telecourses and Online Course Campus
Web Site(s): http://e.spjc.edu
E-mail: womerl@spjc.edu

Undergraduate Degree Programs:
Associate of Arts
Associate of Science in Veterinary Technology

Class Titles: Biological Science, Biological Issues, Composition, Motion Picture Writing, Motion Picture Writing East-West Synthesis of Humanities, Developmental Mathematics, Algebra, Studies in Applied Ethics, Statistics, Emergency Management, Public Policy in Emergency Management, Emergency Technical Applications, EM Leadership, Disaster Recovery Operations, the entire Veterinary Technology Program, History of U.S., Cultural Anthropology, Accounting, Understanding Art, Universe: Infinite Frontier, Biological Science, Criminal Justice, Constitutional Law/Rules, Computer Concepts, Child Development, Principles of (Macro) Economics, Composition, Western Civilization, Environmental Science, Personal Finance, French, Business, Earth Revealed, Personal Wellness, Personal/Community Health, Western Humanities, Earth Science/Planet Earth, College Algebra, Small Business Management, Principles of Management, Principles of Marketing, Salesmanship, Oceanography, Applied Ethics, American National Government, General Psychology, Public Speaking, Spanish, Statistics, Sociology, Marriage/Family, and more.

Teaching Methods: *Computers:* Internet, real-time chat, electronic classroom, e-mail, CD-ROM, LISTSERV. *TV:* videotape, cable program, satellite broadcasting, PBS. *Other:* videoconferencing.

Credits Granted for: experiential learning, examination (CLEP).

Admission Requirements: *Undergraduate:* completed application, high school graduate with certain criteria or college can assist (or GED), eligible transfer students, early admission and dual-credit students, credit bank students, nondegree students not intending to pursue a formal degree, transient students, or students from other countries who have been admitted or are contemplating admittance to the U.S. to pursue their education (international students please call for details).

On-Campus Requirements: Presently, students may obtain an entire associate of arts degree through our telecourse program. On-campus requirements include an orientation session, a midterm review session, a midterm exam, a final review session, and a final exam.

Tuition and Fees: *Undergraduate:* $52/credit (in-state resident), $142/credit (out-of-state resident). *Application Fee:* $25. *Other Costs:* lab fees vary by course. *Credit by:* semester.

Financial Aid: Federal Stafford Loan, Federal Perkins Loan, Federal PLUS Loan, Federal Pell Grant, Federal Work-Study, VA, Federal Supplemental Educational Opportunity Grant, Student Assistant Program, Florida resident programs.

Accreditation: Southern Association of Colleges and Schools.

Description: St. Petersburg College (1927) is recognized as one of America's best community colleges. Until 1942, SPC was a private, nonprofit institution in downtown St. Petersburg, but today its campuses span Pinellas County. College sites now include 4 traditional campuses in Clearwater, St. Petersburg, Seminole and Tarpon Springs, plus a health education center in Pinellas Park and corporate and criminal justice/law enforcement training facilities in St. Petersburg. In addition, SPC offers classes at various offsite locations as well as via TV and computer. The Telecourse program, which began in 1980, is the largest in the Florida Community College system.

Salem International University

223 W. Main Street	Phone: (304) 782-5241
Salem, WV 26426	Fax: (304) 782-5306

Division(s): Provost's Office
Web Site(s): http://www.salemiu.edu
E-mail: Admissions Office, see our web site for on-line registration

Undergraduate Degree Programs:
Business
Computer Science

Graduate Degree Programs:
Teacher Education

Class Titles: Graduate Education Core Courses, general education undergraduate courses, and a limited number of courses in business and computer science.

Teaching Methods: *Computers:* Internet, real-time chat, e-mail, CD-ROM, LISTSERV.

Credits Granted for: experiential learning, portfolio assessment, extrainstitutional learning (PONSI, corporate or professional association seminars/workshops), examination (CLEP, ACT-PEP, DANTES, GRE).

Admission Requirements: *Undergraduate:* high school diploma or GED with a 2.0 or equivalent grade point average *Graduate:* in Teacher Education, an undergraduate degree.

On-Campus Requirements: No additional on-campus time is required for the courses offered online.

Tuition and Fees: *Undergraduate:* $249.50/credit hour. *Graduate:* $170/credit hour. *Application Fee:* $25. *Software:* $10/module. *Graduation Fee:* $100. *Credit by:* semester.

Financial Aid: Federal Stafford Loan, Federal Perkins Loan, Federal PLUS Loan, Federal Pell Grant, Federal Work-Study, VA, state programs for residents of West Virginia and Pennsylvania.

Accreditation: North Central Association of Colleges and Schools.

Description: SIU (1888) is a private institution granting associate, bachelor's, and master's degrees. Its mission is "to educate a world citizen who acquires wide knowledge without prejudice and makes decisions with an international point of view." On campus, SIU offers programs in the liberal arts, humanities, and sciences, as well as unique programs. Interaction with classmates is an important part of each student's personal growth. In 2000–2001, a third of SIU's students were from one of 30 countries outside of the United States. SIU is entering the Distance Learning field to serve the needs of current students and provide outreach to others. Salem is focusing on graduate teacher education, and undergraduate liberal arts, business, and computer science/information technology courses.

Salt Lake Community College

9750 S. 300 W.	Phone: (801) 957-3406
Sandy, UT 84070	Fax: (801) 957-5333

Division(s): Distance Education Services
Web Site(s): http://ecampus.slcc.edu
E-mail: johanswe@slcc.edu

Undergraduate Degree Programs:
Associate of Science:
General Studies
Business
Criminal Justice
Railroad Operation

Certificate Programs: Railroad Operations.

Class Titles: Business, Art, Accounting, Physical Science, Communication, English, History, Economics, Math, Environmental Science, Criminal Justice, Health Sciences, Humanities, Learning Enhancement, Non-Destructive

Testing, Philosophy, Physical Therapy Assistant, Sociology.

Teaching Methods: *Computers:* Internet, real-time chat, electronic classroom, e-mail, CD-ROM. *TV:* videotape, cable program, satellite broadcasting, PBS. *Other:* videoconferencing, audioconferencing, audiotapes, fax.

Admission Requirements: *Undergraduate:* open enrollment, CPT assessment test, ACT.

On-Campus Requirements: None.

Tuition and Fees: *Undergraduate:* $80 (approximately)/credit. *Application Fee:* $25. *Credit by:* semester.

Financial Aid: Federal Stafford Loan, Federal Perkins Loan, Federal PLUS Loan, Federal Pell Grant, Federal Work-Study, VA, state programs for residents of Utah.

Accreditation: Northwest Accreditation Association.

Description: Salt Lake Community College (1950) offers a variety of options for students desiring to take Distance Education courses. The most comprehensive way to succeed is by being connected to the Internet. All distance courses require an Internet connection. All distance courses offered by SLCC are taught by talented and credentialed faculty who respond to e-mail, voicemail, and conference calling. Our future will be in more and more credit and noncredit offerings to better serve our community and business partner needs.

San Antonio College

1300 San Pedro Avenue	Phone: (210) 733-2045
San Antonio, TX 78212	(210) 733-2181
	Fax: (210) 785-6494

Division(s): Distance Education Unit
Web Site(s): www.accd.edu/SAC/distance

Class Titles: General Biology, Child Growth/Development, Freshman Composition, American Government-National, American Government-Problems/Policy, History of U.S., Child Psychology, Sociology, Marriage/Family, Conversational Spanish, Nutrition, Mass Communication, Psychology, Business, Astronomy, Geography of World, Earth Sciences, Geographic Information Systems, Architectural Design, Data Communications, Criminal Justice, Legal/Research, Management, Public Administration, American/Texas Government, Crime in America, British Literature, American Literature, Reading in World Literature, Philosophy, Humanities.

Teaching Methods: *Computers:* Internet, real-time chat, electronic classroom, e-mail, newsgroup, LISTSERV. *TV:* videotape, cable program, satellite broadcasting, PBS. *Other:* videoconferencing, educational on-site contracts with business and industry.

Credits Granted for: extrainstitutional learning, examination (CLEP, ACT-PEP, DANTES, GRE).

Admission Requirements: *Undergraduate:* contact Admissions for information.

On-Campus Requirements: most students register for combined courses: telecourses, Internet, and on-campus courses.

Tuition and Fees: *Undergraduate:* contact school for complete tuition and fee information. *Credit by:* semester—16 weeks and flex term semesters.

Financial Aid: Federal Stafford Loan, Federal Perkins Loan, Federal PLUS Loan, Federal Pell Grant, Federal Work-Study, VA, Texas resident programs.

Accreditation: Southern Association of Colleges and Schools.

Description: San Antonio College (1925), a college of the Alamo Community College District, began Distance Education courses in the 1980s by offering telecourses. In 1992, the college expanded its off-campus course offerings to area businesses, and the surrounding cities of Seguin, New Braunfels, and Kerrville. In 1996, a Distance Education Director was hired and several off-campus coordinators were hired to coordinate and manage course offerings at various off-campus sites. The Distance Education Program at San Antonio College has been expanded since 1996 to include: telecourses, Internet courses, off-campus courses in area high schools and at military bases, interactive videoconferencing, contract education (on-site education at area businesses), and dual credit instruction (eligible high school students earn high school and college credit for approved courses). These flexible instructional delivery methods are available at 13 off-campus sites. The Distance Education Program serves approximately 3,000 distance education students per fall/spring semesters. San Antonio College has an annual enrollment of approximately 21,500 students (which includes the distance learners) and approximately 18,000 continuing education students. The mission of the Distance Education Unit is to provide high quality academic courses/programs to students when and where they want it using time-and-place independent learning options.

San Diego Community College District City, Mesa, and Miramar Colleges

3375 Camino del Rio South	Phone: (619) 388-6965
San Diego, CA 92108-3883	Fax: (619) 388-6523

Division(s): Instructional Services
Web Site(s): http://www.sdccd.net
E-mail: kfawson@sdccd.net

Class Titles: Descriptive Astronomy, Business Law, Business Math, Principles of Child Development, Economics, Health/Life Style, History of U.S., Mass Communications, Biology, Managing the Small Business, Keyboarding, Windows 98, Microsoft Excel, Learning the Internet, Microsoft Office, Quicken, Critical Thinking, Competition, Geology.

Teaching Methods: *Computers:* Internet, electronic classroom, e-mail, CD-ROM, newsgroup, LISTSERV. *TV:* videotape, cable program, satellite broadcasting, PBS. *Other:* radio broadcast, videoconferencing, audioconferencing, individual study, learning contracts.

Credits Granted for: examination (CLEP, ACT-PEP, DANTES, GRE).

Admission Requirements: *Undergraduate:* ability to benefit.

On-Campus Requirements: for orientation.

Tuition and Fees: *Undergraduate:* $12/credit. *Credit by:* semester.

Financial Aid: Federal Stafford Loan, Federal Perkins Loan, Federal PLUS Loan, Federal Pell Grant, Federal Work-Study, VA, California resident programs.

Accreditation: Associate of Community and Junior Colleges (Western Association of Schools and Colleges).

Description: The San Diego Community College District (1970) serves 100,000 students each semester through 3 two-year colleges and 6 continuing education centers. The colleges—San Diego City (1914), Mesa (1964), and Miramar (1969)—offer associate degrees and certificates in occupational programs that prepare students for entry-level jobs, plus arts and sciences programs that transfer to 4-year colleges and universities. The Continuing Education Centers allow adults to renew their learning experiences through noncredit vocational, basic skills, life skills, and enrichment classes at sites throughout the city. Shared governance activities involve faculty, students, and staff in the development of solutions to key policy and budget issues.

San Diego State University

5500 Campanile Drive   Phone: (619) 594-0919
San Diego, CA 92182-8010

Division(s): Office of Distributed Learning, Academic Affairs
Web Site(s): http://www.sdsu.edu/dl
E-mail: dl@mail.sdsu.edu

Class Titles: Geology, Education Technology, Exercise, Nutritional Sciences, Teacher Education, Business, History, Art, Political Science, Regulatory Affairs.

Teaching Methods: *Computers:* Internet, e-mail. *TV:* videotape, cable program, satellite broadcasting, PBS. *Other:* None.

Credits Granted for: completion of course work as outlined in class syllabus.

Admission Requirements: *Undergraduate:* for details, go to http://www.sdsu.edu/dl

On-Campus Requirements: None.

Tuition and Fees: *Undergraduate:* varies with each class, go to www.sdsu.edu/dl for fee information. *Credit by:* semester.

Accreditation: Western Association of Schools and Colleges.

Description: San Diego State University (1897), designated "Doctoral/Research University-Intensive" by the Carnegie Foundation, is ranked among the top 6.7 percent of higher education institutions in the United States. Course work is offered in 135 bachelor's and master's programs and 13 joint doctoral programs. SDSU offers a select number of quality distributed learning courses and programs, emphasizing highly interactive online courses distributed through the Internet. We also offer compressed video (2-way video/audio) courses and televised courses on San Diego's local cable channels.

San Joaquin Delta College

5151 Pacific Avenue   Phone: (209) 954-5039
Stockton, CA 95207   Fax: (209) 954-5600

Division(s): Instructional Development and Regional Education
Web Site(s): http://www.deltacollege.org
http://www.deltaonline.org
E-mail: kcampbell@sjdccd.cc.ca.us

Undergraduate Degree Programs:
Associate in Business

Certificate Programs: Supervision and Management, Merchandising, Early Childhood Educational Assistant.

Class Titles: Accounting, Business, Advertising, Transportation, Chinese, English, Algebra, Sociology, Computer Science.

Teaching Methods: *Computers:* Internet, real-time chat, electronic classroom, e-mail, CD-ROM, newsgroup, LISTSERV. *Other:* videoconferencing.

Credits Granted for: experiential learning, examination (CLEP).

Admission Requirements: *Undergraduate:* assessment/placement for first-time students.

On-Campus Requirements: None.

Tuition and Fees: *Undergraduate:* $11/credit residents, $130/credit nonresidents/international. *Credit by:* semester.

Financial Aid: Federal Pell Grant, Federal Work-Study, VA, California resident programs.

Accreditation: Western Association of Schools and Colleges.

Description: San Joaquin Delta is a public, 2-year community college founded in 1935. The college offers courses leading to transfer to the University of California and California State University systems and to other colleges and universities, associate degrees in Arts and in Science, and nearly 70 certificate programs. Its 165-acre campus is in Stockton, with other centers in nearby communities. The college operates a 157-acre educational farm, a 93-acre forestry field study area, and conducts evening classes in most district communities. Since its founding, San Joaquin has provided distance education to surrounding communities. The college offers courses through videoteleconferencing to centers in Jackson, San Andreas, Manteca, and Tracy. San Joaquin Delta College is committed to providing educational access and support through its online program, Deltaonline, which offers a variety of courses, an Associate of Arts degree, and certificates.

San José City College

2100 Moorpark Avenue
San Jose, CA 95128

Phone: (408) 298-2181 X3947

Division(s): Instructional Technology
Web Site(s): http://www.sjcc.edu
E-mail: dnorris@sjeccd.cc.ca.us

Undergraduate Degree Programs: Contact school.

Certificate Programs: Educational Technology.

Class Titles: First-Year Composition, Introduction to Literature (second semester composition), American Literature to 1865, American Literature from 1865, Gay and Lesbian Literature, Women in Literature, English as a Second Language, Financial Accounting, Managerial Accounting, E-Commerce and Technology, Introduction to Marketing, Introduction to Business, Internet Research Skills, Visual Basic Programming, Creative Writing, Introduction to Teaching Online, Developing Curriculum for Online Courses. More courses are being developed for the spring of 2002.

Teaching Methods: *Computers:* Internet, real-time chat, electronic classroom, e-mail, CD-ROM.

Admission Requirements: *Undergraduate:* open enrollment.

On-Campus Requirements: Students living within 150 miles of the campus must attend an on-campus final. All others must make arrangements with the instructor for a proctored final at a nearby institution.

Tuition and Fees: *Undergraduate:* $11/credit for in-state students, $148 for out-of-state students. High school students with R-40 on file, free tuition. *Credit by:* semester.

Financial Aid: Federal Stafford Loan, Federal Perkins Loan, Federal PLUS Loan, Federal Pell Grant, Federal Work-Study, VA, state programs for residents of California.

Accreditation: Accrediting Commission for Community and Junior Colleges and approved by the California State Department of Education.

Description: San José City College (1921) offers a 2 year lower-division college program paralleling 4-year colleges and universities. For students who plan to pursue a baccalaureate degree, the college provides a strong core of general education and majors' courses required for transfer. The college also offers a variety of one- and two-year technical, occupational, and preprofessional courses of study, leading to employment. The college began offering online courses in the summer of 2000. The program continues to grow each semester with the goal of offering an entire AA degree online.

San Jose State University

One Washington Square
San Jose, CA 95192-0135

Phone: (408) 924-2670
Fax: (408) 924-2666

Division(s): Continuing Education
Web Site(s): http://online.sjsu.edu
E-mail: de@cemail.sjsu.edu
szlotolo@conted.sjsu.edu

Graduate Degree Programs:
Master of Science in Occupational Therapy for OTRs
Transportation Management Graduate Program

Certificate Programs: Professional Instructional Technology Certificate, Mild to Moderate Special Education Credential.

Class Titles: *Online Classes:* Business, Child Development, Communications, Economics, English, Instructional Technology, Teacher Education, Special Education, Health Professions, Hospitality Management, Linguistics and Language Development, Mechanical Engineering, Meteorology, Politcal Science, Psychology, Radio Television Film. *Interactive Television Classes:* Counselor Education, Educational Leadership and Development, Teacher Education, Health Professions, Nursing. For information on individual classes, contact the school.

Teaching Methods: *Computers:* Internet, real-time chat, electronic classroom, e-mail, CD-ROM, newsgroup, LISTSERV. *TV:* videotape, cable program, satellite broadcasting, videoconferencing.

Credits Granted for: extrainstitutional learning (PONSI, corporate or professional association seminars/workshops), (CLEP, ACT-PEP, DANTES, GRE).

Admission Requirements: *Undergraduate:* Matriculated Students: refer to SJSU's Web page for information on admission. Nonmatriculated Students: no formal admission required. *Graduate:* Matriculated Students: refer to the Web page. *Certificate:* Formal university admission is not required to enroll.

On-Campus Requirements: depending on the program residence credit is required.

Tuition and Fees: *Undergraduate, Graduate, Application Fee, Graduation Fee:* refer to http://www.sjsu.edu. *Other Costs:* Continuing Education students: $155/unit. *Credits by:* semester.

Financial Aid: Federal Stafford Loan, Federal Perkins Loan, Federal PLUS Loan, Federal Pell Grant, Federal Work-Study, VA, California resident programs.

Accreditation: Western Association of Schools and Colleges.

Description: San Jose State University is the first public institution of higher education on the West Coast. The history of San Jose State began with Minns' Evening Normal School in San Francisco in 1857. This school became the California Normal School, created by the California legislature in 1862. Things have indeed changed. In 1857, the Normal School's purpose was to train teachers. Today, San Jose State offers more than 130 undergraduate and graduate degree programs, but training of K-12 teachers is a significant part of the university's activities. In 1870, the population of the City of San Jose was about 9,000 people. Today, the city has a population exceeding 900,000 and San Jose State University has more than 26,000 students. San Jose State University is a major, comprehensive public university located in a center of San Jose and in the heart of Silicon Valley. The On-line Master of Science in Occupational Therapy program was developed in 1998. Since that time, the main campus has increased its distance program. In 2000, the Center for Distributed Education was created to meet the Distance/online needs of the university.

San Juan College

4601 College Boulevard	Phone: (505) 566-3426
Farmington, NM 87402	Fax: (505) 566-3385

Division(s): Distance Education
Web Site(s): http://sjc.cc.nm.us
E-mail: degner@sjc.cc.nm.us

Undergraduate Degree Programs:
Associate of Science
Associate of Arts

Class Titles: Math, English, ECON, Child Care, Computer Technology, History, Criminal Justice.

Teaching Methods: *Computers:* Internet, electronic classroom, e-mail. *TV:* videotape, cable program, satellite broadcasting. *Other:* videoconferencing.

Credits Granted for: experiential learning, corporate or professional association seminars/workshops, examination (CLEP, ACT-PEP, DANTES, GRE).

Admission Requirements: *Undergraduate:* GED or high school graduate.

On-Campus Requirements: None.

Tuition and Fees: *Undergraduate:* $15/credit. *Application Fee:* $10. *Credit by:* semester.

Financial Aid: Federal Stafford Loan, Federal Perkins Loan, Federal PLUS Loan, Federal Pell Grant, Federal Work-Study, VA, programs for New Mexico residents and Indian Tribes.

Accreditation: North Central Association of Colleges and Schools.

Description: San Juan College (1965) serves northwestern New Mexico and the surrounding Four Corners region by providing a quality 2-year education at minimal cost. The college's mission is to provide educational opportunities and supportive services to its regional citizens to increase the productivity and efficiency of the surrounding business area.

Sandhills Community College

3395 Airport Road	Phone: (910) 692-6185
Pinehurst, NC 28374	Fax: (910) 695-1823

Division(s): Coordinator of Distance Learning
Web Site(s): http://www.sandhills.cc.nc.us/
E-mail: swansonr@email.sandhills.cc.nc.us

Undergraduate Degree Programs:
Associate in Arts general education courses

Class Titles: Principles of Management, Western Civilization, Early Childhood, Freshman English, Professional Research and Reporting, Developmental English, Introduction to Literature, World Geography, Introduction to Film, General Psychology, Introduction to Sociology, Nutrition, Developmental Mathematics.

Teaching Methods: *Computers:* Internet, real-time chat, e-mail, CD-ROM. *TV:* videotape, PBS. *Other:* independent study.

Credits Granted for: experiential learning, examination.

Admission Requirements: *Undergraduate:* high school graduate or equivalent; 16 or older.

On-Campus Requirements: identity verification and proctored tests in most cases.

Tuition and Fees: *Undergraduate:* $28/credit in-state, $170/credit out-of-state, subject to change. *Credit by:* semester.

Financial Aid: Federal Stafford Loan, Federal PLUS Loan Federal Perkins Loan, Federal Pell Grant, Federal Work-Study, VA, North Carolina resident programs, state/local scholarships.

Accreditation: Southern Association of Colleges and Schools.

Description: Sandhills Community College (1963) is a 2-year, public, postsecondary institution offering over 50 technical or vocational programs and 3 college-transfer degrees. Long known for excellence in college-transfer programs, nursing and health sciences, and engineering, transportation, and cosmetology technologies, Sandhills is rapidly estabilshing a reputation for cutting-edge computer, networking, and Internet technologies as well as quality Internet-based course offerings.

Santa Ana College

| 1530 W. Seventeenth St | Phone: (714) 564-6728 |
| Santa Ana, CA 92706 | Fax: (714) 647-0761 |

Division(s): Distance Education
Web Site(s): http://www.sacollege.org
E-mail: olea_jacque@rsccd.org

Undergraduate Degree Programs:
Associate of Arts
Associate of Science

Class Titles: Anthropology, Astronomy, Biology, Business Applications, Business, Computer Science, Fire Technology, Geology, History, Human Development, Interdisciplinary Studies, Nursing, Nutrition, Occupational Therapy Assistant, Philosophy, Psychology, Sociology.

Teaching Methods: *Computers:* Internet, real-time chat, electronic classroom, e-mail, CD-ROM, newsgroup, LISTSERV *TV:* videotape, cable program, satellite broadcasting, PBS *Other:* videoconferencing, audiotapes, fax, correspondence.

Credits Granted for: examination.

Admission Requirements: *Undergraduate:* 18 years of age.

On-Campus Requirements: Most courses require on-campus exams.

Tuition and Fees: *Undergraduate:* $11/credit. *Credit by:* semester.

Financial Aid: Federal Stafford Loan, Federal Perkins Loan, Federal PLUS Loan, Federal Pell Grant, Federal Work-Study, VA, state programs for residents of California.

Accreditation: WASC.

Description: (1915) Santa Ana College opened in 1915 as an upward extension of Santa Ana High School. Of California's 107 public community colleges, it is the fourth oldest. The mission of Santa Ana College is to be a leader and partner in meeting the academic, cultural, and work force and economic development needs of a diverse community. SAC prepares students for transfer, employment, and careers.

Santa Barbara City College

| 721 Cliff Drive | Phone: (805) 965-0581 ext. 2949 |
| Santa Barbara, CA 93109-2394 | Fax: (805) 963-7222 |

Division(s): Online College
Web Site(s): http://online.sbcc.net
E-mail: online@sbcc.net

Undergraduate Degree Programs:
Associate of Arts Degree in Liberal Studies

Certificate Programs: Medical Reimbursement, Medical Coding Specialist, Cancer Information Management, Cisco Networking Associate (Skills Competency Award).

Class Titles: Accounting, Administration of Justice, Art, Biology, Bio-Medical Sciences, Business Administration, Chicano Studies, Computer Network Engineering and Electronics, Computer Applications and Office Management, Earth and Planetary Sciences, Early Childhood Education, English, Graphic Design Photography, Health Education, History, Multimedia Arts and Technologies, Mathematics, Music, Physical Education, Personal Development, Philosophy, Spanish, Theater Arts.

Teaching Methods: *Computers:* Internet, real-time chat, electronic classroom, e-mail, CD-ROM, newsgroup.

Credits Granted for: experiential learning, portfolio assessment, extrainstitutional learning (PONSI, corporate or professional association seminars/workshops), examination (CLEP, ACT-PEP, DANTES, GRE).

Admission Requirements: *Undergraduate:* Santa Barbara City College is open to anyone who holds a high school diploma or equivalent, or is at least 18 years old or older and shows evidence of being able to benefit from instruction, or is currently enrolled in a local high school. (Local high school student may attend as special part-time students. Applications are available from the high school or the SBCC Counseling Center and Admissions Office).

On-Campus Requirements: Some courses require on-campus attendance. For complete course description, visit our web site at http://online.sbcc.net.

Tuition and Fees: *Undergraduate:* California residents $11/unit, out-of-state tuition $134/unit, international tuition $148/unit *Credit by:* semester.

Financial Aid: Federal Stafford Loan, Federal Perkins Loan, Federal PLUS Loan, Federal Pell Grant, Federal Work-Study, VA, state programs for residents of California.

Accreditation: Western Association of Schools and Colleges.

Description: One of the oldest community colleges in California, Santa Barbara City College (1909) has experienced rapid growth since founded, both in enrollments and course offerings. More than 13,000 students are currently enrolled in day and evening credit classes, and some 36,500 are enrolled in the Continuing Education Division. Students at SBCC are privileged to live in one of the most beautiful cities in the world. Nearly half of Santa Barbara's streets terminate at one of the nation's loveliest white sand beachfronts. A mild climate, early California architecture, abundant flora, combined with mountain, sea, and sand, constitute a unique atmosphere in which to live and study.

Santa Fe Community College

6401 Richards Avenue	**Phone: (505) 428-1000**
Santa Fe, NM 87505	**Fax: (505) 428-1237**

Division(s): Instructional Technology
Web Site(s): http://www.santa-fe.cc.nm.us; http://www2. santa-fe.cc.nm.us/
E-mail: kstubbs@santa-fe.cc.nm.us

Class Titles: Business, Office and Information Technologies, Computer Science, English, Environmental Science, Math, Nutrition.

Teaching Methods: *Computers:* Internet/Web, real-time chat, electronic classroom, e-mail, CD-ROM, discussion board. *TV:* videotape, cable program.

Credits Granted for: experiential learning, examination (CLEP, ACT).

Admission Requirements: *Undergraduate:* open admission. *Certificate:* open admission.

On-Campus Requirements: None.

Tuition and Fees: *Undergraduate:* $25.50–$61/credit, depending on residency. *Other Costs:* $20/credit distance learning fee. *Credit by:* semester.

Financial Aid: Federal Stafford Loan, Federal Pell Grant, Federal Work-Study, New Mexico State Lottery Scholarship.

Accreditation: North Central Association of Colleges and Schools.

Description: Santa Fe Community College's mission is a commitment to helping students succeed. The college's comprehensive system of support services, from tutoring to career counseling, is designed to help students achieve their educational and career goals. The college is equally committed to serving the community. Educational and job-training programs are tailored to the needs of individuals and business, industry, and government. SFCC's low tuition and open admission policy make higher education an option for everyone. In recent years, SFCC has successfully trained workers located throughout the Southwest with its Web-based distance course delivery system. Our distance learning methodologies are expanding to include streaming media and CD-ROM production and our offerings will soon include degree and certificate programs.

Santa Monica College

1900 Pico Boulevard	**Phone: (310) 434-3761**
Santa Monica, CA 90405	**Fax: (310) 434-3769**

Division(s): Department of Distance Education
Web Site(s): http://smconline.org
E-mail: stone_winniphred@smc.edu

Undergraduate Degree Programs: Contact school.

Certificate Programs: Business, Accounting, Marketing, Management, Computer Information Systems, Certified Public Accountant, Accounting Clerk.

Class Titles: Business, Business Law, Accounting, Marketing, Computer Information Systems, Computer Science, English, ESL, Political Science, Biology, Botony, Chemistry, Economics, Philosophy, History of Animation, Career Exploration in Entertainment, Computer-Aided Drafting, Music, General Education.

Teaching Methods: *Computers:* online via the Internet utilizing chat rooms, threaded discusssions, and interactive multimedia.

Admission Requirements: *Undergraduate:* high school diploma, or 18 years of age or older, 16 years of age or older with Student Score Report. *Certificate:* same as above.

On-Campus Requirements: Some of the courses may require student to enter a scheduled online chat room or that students attend a portion of the course in a traditional classroom.

Tuition and Fees: *Undergraduate:* $11/credit for California resident. *Credit by:* semester.

Financial Aid: Federal Stafford Loan, Federal Perkins Loan, Federal PLUS Loan, Federal Pell Grant, Federal Work-Study, VA, California state programs.

Accreditation: Western Association of Schools and Colleges.

Description: Santa Monica College (1917) is the leading job trainer and nation's undisputed leader in transfers to the University of California system, including UCLA. Additionally, SMC's reputation for quality attracts students from more than 100 countries around the world, and currently, more international students choose SMC to begin their higher education than any other community college in America. SMC opened its Virtual Campus, SMCONLINE.org in 1999. SMCONLINE.org now makes it easy to access the high-quality education afforded by SMC. The same award-winning faculty who teach on-campus work closely with online students to ensure their success. SMCONLINE.org offers classes for transfer, certificates, and skill building. In addition, enrollment, registration, payment, academic advisement, books, and library resources are available online to students.

Sauk Valley Community College

| 173 Illinois Route 2 | Phone: (815) 288-5511 |
| Dixon, IL 61021 | Fax: (815) 288-5958 |

Division(s): Instructional Deans
Web Site(s): http://www.svcc.edu
E-mail: Breedt@svcc.edu

Undergraduate Degree Programs:
Associate of Science
Associate of Arts

Class Titles: English, Humanities, Math, Criminal Justice.

Teaching Methods: *Computers:* Internet, real-time chat, e-mail, CD-ROM, LISTSERV. *TV:* videotape. *Other:* videoconferencing, audioconferencing, audiotapes, fax, correspondence, independent study.

Credits Granted for: experiential learning, examination (CLEP, ACT-PEP, DANTES, GRE).

Admission Requirements: *Undergraduate:* open policy.

On-Campus Requirements: some classes have test requirements that must be taken on campus or proctored.

Tuition and Fees: *Undergraduate:* $51/credit. *Other Costs:* out-of-state Internet $85.22/hour. *Credit by:* semester.

Financial Aid: Federal Stafford Loan, Federal Perkins Loan, Federal PLUS Loan, Federal Pell Grant, Federal Work-Study, VA, Illinois resident programs.

Accreditation: North Central Association of Colleges and Schools.

Description: Sauk Valley Community College (1965) provides opportunities in the traditional transfer areas, plus vocational-technical, adult and continuing education, community service, and career education. Sauk has taken a lead role in Internet classes and is teamed with the University of Illinois for the Illinois Virtual Campus. SVCC is authorized to confer the associate of arts, associate of science, associate of engineering science, and associate of fine arts degrees to students completing requirements in the university transfer programs. The college confers the associate of applied science degree and certificates to students completing requirements in career education programs. The associate of liberal studies degree is available to students desiring a nonspecialized degree.

Saybrook Graduate School and Research Center

| 450 Pacific Avenue, Third Floor | Phone: (415) 433-9200 |
| San Francisco, CA 94133 | Fax: (415) 433-9271 |

Division(s): Entire School
Web Site(s): http://www.saybrook.edu
E-mail: mmeyers@saybrook.edu

Graduate Degree Programs:
Master of Arts
Doctor of Philosophy

Class Titles: 94 classes available in Psychology, Human Science, and Organizational Systems.

Teaching Methods: *Computers:* Internet, electronic classroom, e-mail. *Other:* correspondence, independent study, individual study.

Admission Requirements: *Graduate:* accredited bachelor's degree, 3.0 GPA (some exceptions possible), degrees completed in under 7 years. *Doctoral:* same as graduate.

On-Campus Requirements: 3-day orientation to begin, 2 one-week conferences yearly.

Tuition and Fees: *Graduate:* $13,800/year (2001/2002). Fees for attending two Residential Conferences (RC) per year are also required. These fees include the cost of registration, lodging, meals, conference materials, and meeting space. *Credit by:* credits awarded/class.

Financial Aid: Federal Stafford Loan, VA.

Accreditation: Western Association of Schools and Colleges.

Description: Since 1971, Saybrook has been educating mid-career professionals in humanistic values relevant to the work place and the community. Saybrook Graduate School and Research Center's graduate education prepares scholar/practitioners to take effective leadership roles, develop the consciousness to realize the immense possibilities of these times, and minimize the potential for social and individual suffering. Saybrook provides a unique learner-centered environment based in an emancipatory humanistic tradition. Advanced studies in psychology are offered. Programs are designed for adult, mid-career professionals seeking an opportunity to engage in serious scholarly work, and who wish to develop the necessary research skills, scope of knowledge, and intervention skills to become more effective in their chosen sphere of work.

Approximately 425 students are currently enrolled at Saybrook, ranging in age from mid-'20s to '60s, and representing more than 36 states and several foreign countries. Saybrook Graduate School and Research Center (1971) offers master's and doctoral degrees in Psychology, Human Science, and Organizational Systems, based in a humanistic tradition. Areas of concentration include Clinical Inquiry, Consciousness Studies, Creativity/the Arts, Health Studies, Humanistic/Transpersonal Studies, Organizational Systems, and social trust. Saybrook's programs, designed for adult professionals, blend the humanistic and transpersonal psychology studies with critical and creative methods of inquiry. Using learning guides, students complete course work in independent study encouraged and evaluated by faculty who communicate by phone, letter, fax, or computer. Saybrook faculty serve as advisors, mentors, and tutors rather than as traditional "teachers." While much of the student's intellectual work is done independently, the relationship between faculty and student allows for support, commentary, and analysis that exceed traditional classroom situations.

Schoolcraft College

18600 Haggerty Road	Phone: (734) 462-4532
Livonia, MI 48152	(734) 462-4801
	Fax: (734) 462-4589

Division(s): Instruction
Web Site(s): http://www.schoolcraft.cc.mi.us/
E-mail: edoinidi@schoolcraft.cc.mi.us

Undergraduate Degree Programs:
Associate of Arts
Associate of General Studies
Bachelor of Science in Business Administration

Graduate Degree Programs:
Master of Science in Business Administration
(online degrees offered in connection with Madonna University)

Class Titles: Art Appreciation, Business Law, Intermediate Algebra, Business English, State and Local Government, Geography/International Economics, College Success, Health Education, Organization of Small Businesses, Advertising, Multimedia Lingo, Creative Writing, Environmental Science, Cultural Anthropology, Nutrition, Business, Business Math, Business Statistics, Business Management, Marketing, Child Development, Computer Systems, Office 2000, Speech, Economics, Composition, Literature/Short Fiction, Literature/Poetry, French, World Geography, Ancient World, Early Modern World, Early America (U.S. History), Contemporary America (U.S. History), Humanities through Arts, Math, Philosophy, Ethical Problems, Astronomy, Survey of American Government, Psychology, Child Psychology, Sociology, Spanish.

Teaching Methods: *Computers:* Internet, electronic classroom, e-mail, CD-ROM. *TV:* videotape, PBS. *Other:* audioconferencing, videoconferencing, audiotapes, fax, independent study.

Credits Granted for: examination (CLEP, ACT-PEP, DANTES, GRE).

Admission Requirements: *Undergraduate:* high school and college transcripts, ACT or placement tests in math, reading, and English.

On-Campus Requirements: None.

Tuition and Fees: *Undergraduate:* $54/credit (in-district) plus $20 fee, $195/credit online degree program (includes materials). *Application Fee:* $25. *Other Costs:* laboratory/course fees. *Credit by:* semester.

Financial Aid: Federal Stafford Loan, Federal PLUS Loan, Federal Pell Grant, Federal Work-Study, VA, Michigan resident programs.

Accreditation: North Central Association of Colleges and Schools.

Description: Schoolcraft College is a fully accredited community college founded in 1961 and located in northwestern Wayne County. Schoolcraft strongly emphasizes service to the community conducive to pursuing a quality education. The college provides corporate training programs and business services for companies exploring new world markets through its prototype "export resource center." The continued demand for excellence will lead us to monitor, improve, and expand to all markets.

Seabury-Western Theological Seminary

2122 Sheridan Road	Phone: (847) 328-9300 x28
Evanston, IL 60201	Fax: (847) 328-9624

Division(s): Academic Affairs
Web Site(s): http://www.seabury.edu
E-mail: swts@nwu.edu
seaburyadmissions@seabury.edu

Graduate Degree Programs:
Master of Divinity
Master of Theological Studies
Doctor of Ministry

Certificate Programs: Study, Advanced Study.

Teaching Methods: *Computers:* Internet, electronic classroom, e-mail, CD-ROM, LISTSERV. *TV:* videotape, cable program, satellite broadcasting, PBS. *Other:* audiotapes, fax, correspondence, independent study, individual study, learning contracts.

Admission Requirements: *Graduate:* bachelor's degree. *Certificate:* bachelor's degree and/or first professional degree.

On-Campus Requirements: 4 quarters/degree, 3 quarters/ certificate.

Tuition and Fees: *Graduate:* $1,455. *Application Fee:* $25. *Other Costs:* room/board, insurance, books. *Credit by:* quarter.

Financial Aid: Federal Stafford Loan, Federal Perkins Loan, Federal PLUS Loan, Federal Pell Grant, Federal Work-Study, VA, Illinois resident programs.

Accreditation: North Central Association of Colleges and Schools, Association of Theological Schools.

Description: Seabury-Western Theological Seminary is one of 11 accredited seminaries of the Episcopal Church. It was created in 1933 by merging Seabury Divinity School (1858) and Western Theological Seminary (1883). Since its initial fusion of Evangelical and Anglo-Catholic traditions, Seabury-Western has continued to respect and nurture the historic and evolving diversities in the Episcopal Church and Anglican Communion. In 1994 the seminary created the Seabury Institute ministry as a partnership with parishes exercising leadership for Church mission. The seminary's mission is to educate priests and lay leaders for Episcopal Church ministry. To that end, Seabury-Western is committed to all aspects of technology for enhanced teaching and learning. Beginning with e-mail and the Internet, Seabury now uses electronic reserves in most classes and offers at least one Internet class/year.

Seattle Central Community College

1701 Broadway, BE1148	Phone: (206) 587-4060
Seattle, WA 98122	(800) 510-1724
	Fax: (206) 287-5562

Division(s): Distance Learning Program
Web Site(s): http://distantlearning.net
E-mail: dislrn@sccd.ctc.edu

Undergraduate Degree Programs:
Associate of Arts

Class Titles: Cultural Anthropology, Composition, Literature, Geography, Intercultural Communication, American Cinema, Ethics in America, General Psychology, Developmental Psychology, Abnormal Psychology, Mass Media, Poetry, Astronomy, Environmental Issues/Problems, Spanish, Business/Economic Statistics, Far East History, Financial Accounting, Introduction to Business, Keyboarding/ Skillbuilding, Microeconomics, Macroeconomics, Introduction to Fiction, American Literature, U.S. History, History of Mathematics, Introduction to Microcomputer Applications, HTML and Web Page Designs, History of Jazz, History of Rock & Roll, Nutrition, Sociology.

Teaching Methods: *TV:* videotape, cable program, online, correspondence. *Other:* None.

Credits Granted for: work experience, examination (CLEP, ACT-PEP, ASSET, DANTES, GRE).

Admission Requirements: *Undergraduate:* age 18 or high school graduate (special consideration may be given to persons not meeting these conditions); fill out application to school (see https://admissions.ctc.edu/applicant/welcome. cfm) all official transcripts from higher education schools; placement tests. To qualify for in-state (resident) tuition, you must have lived in Washington State, for one year for reasons other than educational purposes.

On-Campus Requirements: None.

Tuition and Fees: *Undergraduate:* depending on number of credits registered: for in-state students, $370/5-credit class plus supplemental materials for out-of-state students. *Other Costs:* varies for supplemental materials. *Credit by:* quarter.

Financial Aid: Federal Pell Grant, Federal Supplemental Educational Opportunity Grant, Washington State Need Grant (state residency status required).

Accreditation: Northwest Association of Schools and Colleges.

Description: In its 30-year history, Seattle Central Community College (1968) has established a reputation for educational excellence and innovation. It is one of the largest colleges in Washington state, with an enrollment of 10,000 students. More than 60% of Seattle Central's students are taking freshman- and sophomore-level classes with plans to complete a bachelor's degree. Each year, the college transfers one of the largest number of students in the state to 4-year institutions.

Seattle Pacific University

3307 Third Avenue W
Seattle, WA 98119

Phone: (800) 482-3848
Fax: (206) 281-2271

Division(s): Continuing Education
Web Site(s): http://www.spu.edu/connection
E-mail: dlaack@spu.edu

Class Titles: Art Instruction for Elementary Classroom, Behavior is Language, Motivating At-Risk Learners, Proactive Classroom Management, Anger Control for Children/Teens, Advanced School Counseling, Emotional Intelligence, Moving from Teaching to Learning, Linking Language/Arts/Mathematics, Transformational Teaching, Standards-Based Teaching, Teaching Early Literacy, Medieval Europe, Great War/Shaping of 20th Century, U.S. History Since 1877, Civil War, History of Pacific Northwest, Disabilities, Classroom Strategies, Gifted Students, Strategies for ADD/Active Learners, Native American Art of Pacific Northwest Coast, Washington History, History of Puget Sound, Media Literacy, Impact of TV/Video, Assessment Literacy, Integrated Teaching, Survival Kit for New Elementary Teachers. Information & Interventions, American Revolution, American West, Beyond School Walls: Philosophy & Methods of Charlotte Mason, Child Abuse Issues for Educators, Classroom Management, Connections Across Cultures: Inviting Multiple Perspectives into Math/Science, Counseling Techniques for Teachers, Drugs & Alcohol in Schools, Families, Professionals & Exceptional Children, Integrating Children's Literature into Science & Social Studies, Learning Disabilities, Learning Styles, Making the Best Use of the Internet, Multicultural Children's Literature, Sexual & Other Forms of Harassment, Strategies for Teaching Abused/Traumatized Students, Students At-Risk, Taking Action Against Media Violence, Multiple Intelligences, Teaching Reading in the Content Areas, Teaching Research Skills, Tools for Working with Oppositional Students, Using Picture Books with Grades 4–12, Violence in Schools, Working with Special Needs Students in the Regular Classroom.

Teaching Methods: *Computers:* Internet, some software programs. *TV:* videotape, PBS. *Other:* audiotapes, correspondence, extensive course study guides, textbooks.

Admission Requirements: *Graduate:* bachelor's degree, no formal admission or requirements. Teachers take most graduate-level, professional development courses.

On-Campus Requirements: None.

Tuition and Fees: *Graduate:* approximately $75/credit. *Other Costs:* $20–$150 course materials. *Credit by:* quarter.

Accreditation: Washington State Board of Education, Northwest Association of Schools and Colleges, National Council for Accreditation of Teacher Education. SPU credits recognized by various regional association members and leading graduate schools throughout the country.

Description: For more than a decade, Seattle Pacific University's (1891) distance learning program has primarily served K–12 educators desiring quality professional development course work. SPU does not currently offer a complete degree program via distance learning. However, many individual courses may apply toward graduate degree requirements or toward fulfilling school district, endorsement-related, or other professional development needs.

Seminary Extension

901 Commerce Street, Suite 500
Nashville, TN 37203-3631

Phone: (615) 242-2453
Fax: (615) 782-4822

Division(s): Independent Study Institute
Web Site(s): None.
E-mail: seisi@compuserve.com

Class Titles: Theology, Pastoral Ministries, Religious Education, Biblical Study

Teaching Methods: *Computers:* Internet, real-time chat, e-mail. *TV:* videotape. *Other:* audiotapes, fax, correspondence, independent study, individual study.

Credits Granted for: extrainstitutional learning.

Admission Requirements: *Undergraduate:* age 16.

On-Campus Requirements: None.

Tuition and Fees: *Undergraduate:* Cost on course by course basis. Course cost variable according to cost of textbooks. *Credit by:* semester.

Accreditation: Distance Education and Training Council; course transfer credit recommended by American Council on Education (ACE).

Description: Seminary Extension (1951) has been offering quality distance education for more than 50 years. Courses in Theology, Christian Education, Biblical Studies, Pastoral Ministry, Church History, Music, and Church Growth are offered for those who feel the call to ministry. Class offerings have grown over the years and continue to grow today. We strive to provide a quality education at a very affordable price. Beginning with a few students taking courses through correspondence, Seminary Extension has grown to more than 5,000 students taking courses either through independent study or through a classroom network in more than 500 locations in the continental U.S. and abroad. We are expanding into online computer classes and currently deliver about 19 courses in this manner.

Seminole State College

2701 Boren Boulevard
Seminole, OK 74818

Phone: (405) 382-9243
Fax: (405) 382-9511

Division(s): Library
Web Site(s): http://www.ssc.cc.ok.us
E-mail: bunyan_j@ssc.cc.ok.us

Undergraduate Degree Programs: Contact school.

Class Titles: College Algebra, Pharmacology.

Teaching Methods: *Computers:* electronic classroom. *TV:* videotape.

Credits Granted for: examination (CLEP, ACT-PEP, DANTES, GRE).

Admission Requirements: *Undergraduate:* community college, college admission required before enrolling, ACT scores of 19 required in reading, English, mathematics, and science to enroll in college-level courses, scores below 19 in these content areas will require assessment testing and placement in remedial courses.

On-Campus Requirements: None.

Tuition and Fees: *Undergraduate:* $49.70/credit (includes all fees). *Application Fee:* $10. *Credit by:* semester.

Financial Aid: Federal Stafford Loan, Federal Perkins Loan, Federal PLUS Loan, Federal Pell Grant, Federal Work-Study, VA, state programs for residents of Oklahoma.

Accreditation: North Central Association of Colleges and Schools.

Description: Seminole State College (1931) is 2-year community college providing accessible and affordable postsecondary educational programs to the residents of eastcentral Oklahoma.

Sessions.edu

476 Broome St
New York, NY 10013

Phone: (212) 966-2270
Fax: (212) 966-5190

Division(s): Fully Online School of Design and New Media
Web Site(s): http://www.sessions.edu
E-mail: Admissions@sessions.edu

Undergraduate Degree Programs:
Graphic Design
Web Design
Digital Design
Multimedia
New Media Marketing
Combined Certificate

Class Titles: Introduction to Web Design, FrontPage I, Photoshop Basics, Interface Design, Color Theory, Web Type Design, Photoshop by Example, Illustrator by Example, Web Design I, Information Design, Web Animation, Digital Imaging Using Photoshop, Introduction to New Media, Writing Javascript, Flash Basics, Flash and Typography, HTML Basics, Dreamweaver I, Sound for the Web, Banner Advertising, Screenwriting for Multimedia, Intro to Digital Video, Digital Editing, 3D Modeling Using FormZ, Sex in Media, Web Portfolio Design, Intro to Graphic Design, Graphic Design, Quark Basics, Intro to Drawing, Branding and Identity, Managing Your Mac Fonts, Logo Design, Design for Non-Designers, Director Basics.

Teaching Methods: *Computers:* Internet, e-mail. Student work is posted on Internet bulletin boards for group and instructor review.

Credits Granted for: Courses listed for ACE credit equivalency beginning fall 2001.

Admission Requirements: *Undergraduate:* if the student is under 18 years old, he or she must have parental permission and a note from his or her principal if the student is enrolling during the school year.

On-Campus Requirements: None.

Tuition and Fees: *Undergraduate:* $1,599. *Other Costs:* individual courses range from $99 to $399. *Credit by:* Courses are not for credit, students work at their own pace.

Financial Aid: Payment plans, Sallie Mae private student loans, DANTES, state programs for residents of New York.

Accreditation: Distance Education and Training Council (DETC).

Description: Sessions.edu (1997) is the first online school in design and new media. Founded by designers and educators from 3 continents, Sessions.edu challenges traditional ideas about learning. Sessions.edu prepares students in over 90 countries for design and new media careers. Our goal is to allow you to study design at your own pace, wherever you are, free from the constraints of time and space.

Seton Hall University

400 South Orange Avenue
South Orange, NJ 07079

Phone: (888) SETON-WW
Fax: (973) 761-9325

Division(s): Seton Worldwide
Web Site(s): http://www.SetonWorldWide.net
E-mail: SetonWorldWide@shu.edu

Undergraduate Degree Programs:
Bachelor of Science in Nursing for Registered Nurses

Graduate Degree Programs:
Masters of Counseling:
Master of Healthcare Administration
Master of Strategic Communication and Leadership
Master of Educational Administration and Supervision
Master of Nursing (Nurse Practitioner)

Teaching Methods: *Computers:* Internet, real-time chat, electronic classroom, e-mail, CD-ROM, *TV:* videotape, cable program, satellite broadcasting, PBS. *Other:* videoconferencing audioconferencing, audiographics, audiotapes, fax, correspondence, independent study, individual study, learning contracts.

Admission Requirements: *Undergraduate:* Diploma from an accredited Associate or Diploma Nursing Program. *Graduate:* accredited BA/BS degree, MAT, or GRE exams.

On-Campus Requirements: 3 required on-site residencies during the program.

Tuition and Fees: *Application Fee:* $50 Please visit our web site or contact us for tuition information. *Credit by:* semester.

Accreditation: Middle States Association of Colleges and Schools.

Description: In October 1998 SetonWorldWide inaugurated the online Master of Healthcare Administration Program and Master of Communication and Strategic Leadership Program. The first class of students from these programs graduated in May 2000. Since October 1998, four other online degree programs have become operational: the Master of Education in Administration and Supervision Program, the Master of Counseling Program, the Master of Nursing (Nurse Practitioner), and the Bachelor of Science in Nursing for Registered Nurses. Currently over 350 students are enrolled in SetonWorldWide online programs. Plans are underway to inaugurate an online Executive Master of Business Administration 2002. SetonWorldWide serves the educational aspirations and professional needs of students from across the country and around the globe. Seton Hall (1986) is committed to utilizing the technological advantages that Internet-based delivery affords for the benefit of our students and the advancement of the teaching and learning process.

Shasta College

| 11555 Old Oregon Trail | Phone: (530) 225-4814 |
| Redding, CA 96049 | Fax: (530) 225-4983 |

Division(s): Extended Education and Telecommunications
Web Site(s): http://www.shastacollege.edu
E-mail: jpoulsen@shastacollege.edu

Class Titles: Physical Sciences, Natural Sciences, Math, English, Psychology, Sociology, Political Science, History, Speech, Humanities.

Teaching Methods: *Computers:* Internet, real-time chat, electronic classroom, e-mail, CD-ROM, newsgroup, LISTSERV. *TV:* videotape, cable program, PBS. *Other:* videoconferencing, audioconferencing, audiographics, audiotapes, fax, correspondence, independent study, individual study, learning contracts.

Credits Granted for: examination (CLEP, ACT-PEP, DANTES, GRE).

Admission Requirements: *Undergraduate:* high school graduate or age 18.

On-Campus Requirements: None.

Tuition and Fees: *Undergraduate:* $11/credit. *Credit by:* semester.

Financial Aid: Federal Stafford Loan, Federal Perkins Loan, Federal PLUS Loan, Federal Pell Grant, Federal Work-Study, VA, California resident programs.

Accreditation: Western Association of Schools and Colleges.

Description: Shasta College (1948) is one of 107 community colleges serving the educational needs of students. Programs are offered for the first 2 years of work designed for transfer to a college or university, vocational programs, and remedial education. Located in the far northern part of California surrounded by lakes, streams, and mountains, the college serves a geographical area of 10,000 square miles. Due to the rural nature of the college district, Shasta College has been involved in distance education for many years.

Shawnee Community College

| 8364 Shawnee College Road | Phone: (618) 634-2242 |
| Ullin, IL 62992 | Fax: (618) 634-9711 |

Division(s): Learning Resources/Instructional Services
Web Site(s): http://www.shawnee.cc.il.us
E-mail: deeb@shawnee.cc.il.us

Class Titles: African-American Literature, Spanish, Philosophy, Anthropology, Accounting-Managerial Concepts, Advanced Medical Terminology, Microsoft Access, Microsoft Excel, Word Perfect, American Literature, Anthropology, Art Appreciation, Bookkeeping, Business/Law, Business Organization, Calculus for Business/Social Science, Career Development, Algebra, Developmental Math, Dynamics, Economics (micro/macro), Exceptional Children, Composition, Finite Mathematics, French, Zoology, Government, Health, Human Growth/Development, Astronomy, Biology, Circuit Analysis, Health Information, Literature, Psychology, Sociology, Math for Liberal Arts, Medical Terminology, Modern Fiction, Nutrition, Microsoft Word, Reading Improvement, Thermodynamics, Trigonometry, World Literature, Business Management, Astronomy.

Teaching Methods: *Computers:* Internet, e-mail. *TV:* videotape, PBS. *Other:* videoconferencing, fax, correspondence, independent study.

Credits Granted for: all courses are for college credit.

Admission Requirements: *Undergraduate:* open-door policy for high school diploma/GED, with preference given to District #531 residents.

On-Campus Requirements: Class participation at designated sites for interactive video, on-campus midterm/finals for telecourses.

Tuition and Fees: *Undergraduate:* $40/hour, plus applicable fees, for in-district students. *Other Costs:* lab fees. *Credit by:* semester.

Financial Aid: Federal Pell Grant, Federal Work-Study, VA, Illinois resident programs, institutional scholarships.

Accreditation: North Central Association of Colleges and Schools.

Description: The main campus of Shawnee Community College (1967) is located 7 miles east of the Interstate 57 Ullin exit, southern Illinois. SCC operates extension centers in Anna, Cairo, and Metropolis, Illinois. The college entered into distance learning by offering telecourses. In 1994, SCC installed interactive video classrooms at the Ullin campus and the Metropolis extension center. This video network now includes 12 classrooms located at extension centers, high schools, and in one business in the Shawnee Community College district. Through participation in the Southern Illinois Telecommunications Network and the Illinois Virtual Campus. SCC students can access classes offered by other state community colleges, colleges, and universities. SCC offers English Composition and Microsoft application software courses online.

Shawnee State University

940 Second Street	Phone: (740) 355-2378
Portsmouth, OH 45662	

Division(s): Department of Nursing
Web Site(s): http://www.shawnee.edu
E-mail: To_SSU@shawnee.edu

Undergraduate Degree Programs:
Bachelor of Science—Nursing

Class Titles: BSNR—courses are taught with a combination of distance, on-site, or alternative methods.

Teaching Methods: *Computers:* Internet, e-mail. *TV: Other:* independent study, individual study.

Credits Granted for: experiential learning, examination (CLEP, ACT-PEP, DANTES, GRE).

Admission Requirements: *Undergraduate:* High School diploma or GED; ACT required for Allied Health programs.

Tuition and Fees: *Undergraduate:* $88 per credit. (in-state). *Credit by:* Quarter.

Financial Aid: Federal Stafford Loan, Federal PLUS Loan, Federal Pell Grant, Federal Work-Study, VA, state programs for residents of Ohio.

Accreditation: North Central.

Description: Shawnee State University was established in 1975.

Shoreline Community College

16101 Greenwood Avenue N	Phone: (206) 546-4663
Shoreline, WA 98133	Fax: (206) 546-4604

Division(s): Library Media Center
Web Site(s): http://oscar.ctc.edu/shoreline
E-mail: lcheng@ctc.edu

Class Titles: History, Math, Geology, Physics, Psychology, English, Library Science/Music, Biology, Business, Communications, French, Spanish, Wellness, Social Sciences, Geography, Applied News Writing, Women of Power, Information Competency, others.

Teaching Methods: *Computers:* Internet, real-time chat, electronic classroom, e-mail, CD-ROM, newsgroup, LISTSERV. *TV:* videotape, cable program, satellite broadcasting, PBS, Coast, Dallas, Jones, Thompson. *Other:* videoconferencing (Interactive TV), audioconferencing, audiotapes, fax, correspondence, independent study, individual study, learning contracts.

Credits Granted for: experiential learning, portfolio assessment, extrainstitutional learning, examination (CLEP, ACT-PEP, DANTES, GRE).

Admission Requirements: *Undergraduate:* accredited high school graduate or GED or age 18. *Certificate:* same as undergraduate.

On-Campus Requirements: up to 3 for telecourses.

Tuition and Fees: *Undergraduate:* $101/1–2 credits, $151/3 credits, $202/4 credits, $505/full-time (10–18 credits), residents. *Application Fee:* $10 nonrefundable. *Other Costs:* $30 lab fees if student wants to use Shoreline's computer lab for Internet access. *Credit by:* quarter.

Financial Aid: Federal Stafford Loan, Federal Perkins Loan, Federal PLUS Loan, Federal Pell Grant, Federal Work-Study, VA, Washington resident programs.

Accreditation: Northwest Association of Schools and Colleges.

Description: Shoreline Community College (1964) offers excellent academic, professional/technical, and work force training programs to meet the lifelong learning needs of its community. Dedicated faculty and staff are committed to the educational success of all students. Located 10 miles north of downtown Seattle, Shoreline is one of the most strikingly beautiful college campuses in the state. Twenty-seven buildings constitute the 83-acre campus. These include a state-of-the-art automotive training center and visual arts building, computer centers, laboratories, a student center, theater, a well-equipped gymnasium, child care center, a state-of-the-art multimedia center, and a library/media center. Shoreline's satellite, the Northshore Center, is conveniently located in Bothell and provides academic transfer courses and customized training. The college is a member of the American Association of Community Colleges and the Association of Community College Trustees.

Simpson College

701 North C Street   **Phone: (800) 362-2454 x1614**
Indianola, IA 50125   **Fax: (515) 961-1498**

Division(s): Adult Learning
Web Site(s): http://www.simpson.edu/dal
E-mail: adultlrn@simpson.edu

Undergraduate Degree Programs:
Bachelor of Arts

Class Titles: Criminal Justice, Communications.

Teaching Methods: *Computers:* Internet, electronic classroom, e-mail, LISTSERV. *Other:* None.

Credits Granted for: experiential learning, portfolio assessment, extrainstitutional learning, examination (CLEP, ACT-PEP, DANTES, GRE).

Admission Requirements: Contact school.

On-Campus Requirements: the majority of our studies are in-class. A limited number of courses are offered online or in a combination of online and in person.

Tuition and Fees: *Undergraduate:* $205/credit. *Credit by:* semester.

Financial Aid: Federal Stafford Loan, Federal Perkins Loan, Federal PLUS Loan, Federal Pell Grant, Federal Work-Study, VA, Iowa resident programs.

Accreditation: North Central Association of Colleges and Schools.

Description: Simpson College (1860) is a private, selective liberal arts college located in the Des Moines area. We have 1,300 full-time students and 650 part-time students who are served by the Division of Adult Learning. Simpson has served adult students for more than 20 years with adapted class schedules and locations.

Sinclair Community College

444 West Third Street   **Phone: (937) 512-2694**
Dayton, OH 45402   **Fax: (937) 512-2891**

Division(s): Distance Learning Division
Web Site(s): http://www.sinclair.edu/distance
E-mail: dlinfo@sinclair.edu

Undergraduate Degree Programs:
Associate of Arts in Liberal Arts/Sciences
Associate of Science in Business Administration

Class Titles: Abnormal Psychology, Accounting, Adolescent and Adult Psychology, Algebra, Business Law, Business Ownership, Cardiopulmonary Rehabilitation, Career Selection, Child Development, Comparing Cultures, Computer Applications, Consumer Law, Cultural Diversity, Dietetics, Economics, English, English as a Second Language, Environmental Law, Exercise Physiology, Family Violence, Family Violence, Fine Arts, General Psychology, Health Care Delivery and Management, History of Rock Music, HIV/AIDS, Human Relations and Organizational Behavior, Humanities, Juvenile Delinquency, Life Span Human Development, Linguistics, Literature, Living with Loss, Death, and Grief, Logic, Logistics, Love and Personal Growth, Mammographic Equipment and Applications, Management, Marketing, Mathematics, Medical Office Coding, Medical Terminology, Medical Terminology, Mental Health, MRI Applications, MRI Principles, Personal Finance, Personal Law, Pharmacology, Pharmacology for Radiographers, Photography, Prior Learning Portfolio Development, Probation and Parole, Psychology of Aging, Purchasing, Quality Management in Radiography, Remedial Reading, English, Arithmetic, Rural Communities, Safety Risk Management, Sociology, Software Applications (Word, PowerPoint, Excel, Access, Desktop Publishing, WordPerfect), Stress Management, Study Skills, Travel and Tourism, U.S. History, Western Civilization.

Teaching Methods: *Computers:* Internet, asynchronous chat, electronic classroom, e-mail, CD-ROM. *TV:* videotape, PBS.

Other: audioconferencing, videoconferencing, audiotapes, fax, correspondence, independent study, individual study, learning contracts.

Credits Granted for: experiential learning, portfolio assessment, extrainstitutional learning (PONSI), examination (CLEP, ACT-PEP, DANTES, GRE).

Admission Requirements: *Undergraduate and Certificate:* English/math/reading placement test.

On-Campus Requirements: None.

Tuition and Fees: *Undergraduate:* $29.45/credit Montgomery County, $48.45/credit outside Montgomery County in-state, $81.45/credit out-of-state. *Application Fee:* $10 (one time). *Graduation Fee:* $10 for degree. *Other Costs:* $20/quarter late registration fee. *Credit by:* quarter.

Financial Aid: Federal Stafford Loan, Federal Perkins Loan, Federal PLUS Loan, Federal Pell Grant, Federal Work-Study, VA, Ohio resident programs.

Accreditation: North Central Association of Colleges and Schools.

Description: Sinclair Community College is a comprehensive, 2-year, public institution offering educational opportunities to Miami Valley (Ohio) citizens for more than 100 years. Sinclair is Dayton's largest institution of higher education, serving 21,000 students and accounting for one-third of local enrollment. It is also among the 20 largest, single-campus, community colleges in the U.S., with 1,800 courses in nearly 100 disciplines and 46 association degrees in 25 areas. Not only does Sinclair prepare students for transfer into upper-division baccalaureate university programs and technical schools, it also offers them extensive opportunities to update technical knowledge needed in today's global economy. The college first offered distance learning in 1979 through local public service TV programs. Sinclair quickly realized that these nontraditional courses helped students with career and family commitments acquire a college education. Currently, the Sinclair Distance Learning Catalog contains more than 150 courses in online, videotape, audiotape, CD-ROM, and print formats.

Skagit Valley College

2405 East College Way	Phone: (360) 416-7603 or 7770
Mount Vernon, WA 98273-5899	Fax: (360) 416-7838

Division(s): Distance Education
Web Site(s): http://www.svc.ctc.edu
E-mail: veljkov@skagit.ctc.edu

Undergraduate Degree Programs:
Associate in Arts University and College Transfer

Certificate Programs: Microcomputers

Class Titles: Technical Writing, Math, Employer/Employee Roles/Perspectives, Computer Science C++, Computer Science Visual BASIC, Cultural Anthropology, Business, Chemical Concepts, Geology, Composition, History of World Civilization, Arts in Humanities, Literature, Film, Basic Arithmetic, Algebra, Applied Mathematics, Contemporary Mathematics, Probability/Statistics, Environmental Science, Nutrition, Ethics, Wellness for Life, Physical Fitness, General Psychology, Abnormal Psychology, Career Development, Sociology, Job Search Techniques, Spanish, Interpersonal Communication, Art/Craft of Social Structures, Perceptions of Earth's Geological Influences on Human Behavior, Information Age, Computer Science, Visual BASIC Programming, Microcomputers, Using Windows 95, Spreadsheets, Databases, Internet, Creating Web Pages, Microsoft Word, Wordperfect, Integrated Software Basics, Presentation Software.

Teaching Methods: *Computers:* Internet, electronic classroom, e-mail, newsgroup, LISTSERV. *TV:* videotape, satellite broadcasting, PBS. *Other:* audioconferencing, videoconferencing, audiotapes, fax, correspondence, independent study, individual study.

Credits Granted for: experiential learning, portfolio assessment, examination (DANTES).

Admission Requirements: *Undergraduate:* high school graduate or more than age 18.

On-Campus Requirements: for testing purposes only.

Tuition and Fees: *Undergraduate:* $46/credit. *Other Costs:* $25/course telecourses fee, $30/course tape rental fee rented during a specific quarter (optional), $25/quarter network user fee (mandatory for students taking computer-based courses). *Credit by:* quarter.

Financial Aid: Federal Stafford Loan, Federal PLUS Loan, Federal Pell Grant, Federal Work-Study, VA, Washington resident programs.

Accreditation: Northwest Association of Schools and Colleges.

Description: Skagit Valley College (1926) is the 2nd oldest, 2-year community college in the state, operating in Skagit, Island, and San Juan counties. In 1955 a 35-acre site was purchased and a complex of 6 buildings was soon completed. SVC now operates campuses in Mount Vernon, Oak Harbor, Clinton (South Whidbey Center), and Friday Harbor (San Juan Center). The college has taken an ever-increasing role in meeting the educational needs of the community. SVC enrolls more than 7,000 students, with full-time equivalents of 4,150. A strong international program attracts students from more than a dozen countries. Distance education is helping a growing number of students overcome the obstacles of time and geography. Half of the students attend SVC transfer to 4-year colleges or universities, while another one-third pursue vocational and technical training in 24 programs.

Slippery Rock University of Pennsylvania

200 Maltby Center	Phone: (724) 738-4484
Slippery Rock, PA 16057	Fax: (724) 738-4483

Division(s): Lifelong Learning
Web Site(s):
http://www.sru.edu/academics/distance_ed/index. html
E-mail: academic.records@sru.edu

Undergraduate Degree Programs:
Bachelor of Science in Nursing

Graduate Degree Programs:
Master of Science in:
Nursing (Family Nurse Practitioner)
Park Resource Management

Certificate Programs: Accounting.

Class Titles: Contact school or check web site for details.

Teaching Methods: *Computers:* Internet, real-time chat, electronic classroom, e-mail, CD-ROM, newsgroup, LISTSERV. *TV:* videotape, compressed video. *Other:* videoconferencing, fax, correspondence, independent study, individual study, voice mail.

Credits Granted for: examination (CLEP, ACT-PEP, DANTES, GRE).

Admission Requirements: Contact school for details.

On-Campus Requirements: None.

Tuition and Fees: *Undergraduate:* $161/credit. *Graduate:* $161/credit. *Application Fee:* $25. *Graduation Fee:* $20. *Credit by:* semester.

Financial Aid: Federal Stafford Loan, Federal Perkins Loan, Federal PLUS Loan, Federal Pell Grant, Federal Work-Study, VA, state programs for residents of Pennsylvania, SEOG, private scholarships, university gift aid from institutional funds.

Accreditation: Commission on Higher Education of the Middle States Association of Colleges and Schools.

Description: Slippery Rock University (1889) opened its doors as Slippery Rock State Normal School. Its first president was James E. Morrow, great-grandfather of Anne Morrow Lindbergh, and the enrollment for the first session was 168 students. Limited to a singular mission in teacher education, the normal school over the years fulfilled its mandate well, graduating thousands of students to staff the public schools in Pennsylvania and throughout the nation. In 1926, the institution was purchased by the Commonwealth, became a 4-year teachers' college, and continued the tradition of teacher training. While the curricular preparations were in elementary education and in a number of secondary education subjects, the area of academic focus that was assigned at that time by the Pennsylvania Department of Education was in health and physical education. And it was in that concentration that the institution soon achieved a national reputation for excellence. As part of the State System of Higher Education, Slippery Rock University enjoys an enrollment of some 7,000 students in more than 60 degree programs. Students are enrolled from 33 states and 60 countries. As one of the largest campuses in western Pennsylvania, SRU is situated on 600 acres in 48 buildings, and is located just 50 minutes north of downtown Pittsburgh. Slippery Rock University entered into the field of Distance Learning in 1995. The Master of Science in Nursing degree program, offered jointly by Clarion and Slippery Rock Universities, was originally established in order to reach out to rural communities in the areas surrounding the respective schools. Over time, this program and other new programs have expanded and now reach much of Western Pennsylvania.

South Arkansas Community College

300 South West Avenue	Phone: (870) 864-7155
El Dorado, AR 71730	Fax: (870) 864-7104

Division(s): Instruction
Web Site(s): http://southark.cc.ar.us
E-mail: pbuletza@southark.cc.ar.us

Undergraduate Degree Programs: No complete programs are offered.

Certificate Programs: Microsoft Certified Systems Engineer (MCSE).

Class Titles: Office Systems; Computer Information Systems.

Teaching Methods: *Computers:* Internet, electronic classroom, e-mail, newsgroup, LISTSERV. *TV: Other:* Videoconferencing, independent study.

Credits Granted for: experiential learning, portfolio assessment, extrainstitutional learning (PONSI, corporate or professional association seminars/workshops), examination (CLEP, ACT-PEP, DANTES).

Admission Requirements: Contact school for details.

On-Campus Requirements: Not for on-line courses.

Tuition and Fees: *Undergraduate:* $50/credit. *Other Costs:* cost for MCSE certificate will not exceed $5,000 for the entire package. *Credit by:* semester.

Financial Aid: Federal Stafford Loan, Federal Perkins Loan, Federal PLUS Loan, Federal Pell Grant, Federal Work-Study, VA, state programs for residents of Arkansas.

Accreditation: North Central Association of Colleges and Schools.

Description: South Arkansas Community College (1992) is a comprehensive institution located in El Dorado, Arkansas. Formed from the merger of Southern Arkansas University—El Dorado Branch and the Oil Belt Technical College, the college's root go back to 1967. The college offers college transfer courses, and programs in accounting, computer information technologies, business, office technology, sales and marketng, early childhood education, criminal justice, emergency medical technology, medical laboratory technology, occupational therapy assistant, physical therapist assistant, practical nursing radiology technology, chemical technology, environmental technology, industrial technology, automotive service technology, electronics technology, welding ands truck driving. Distance Learning courses were initiated 2 years ago by several faculty who wished to develop online courses.

South Central Technical College

1920 Lee Boulevard	Phone: (507) 389-7200
North Mankato, MN 56003	800-722-9359
	Fax: (507) 388-9951

Division(s): Department of Instructional Technology
Web Site(s): http://www.sctc.mnscu.edu/learnon
http://www.sctc.mnscu.edu/
E-mail: LearnOn@SCTC.MnSCU.edu

Undergraduate Degree Programs: Contact school.

Certificate Programs: ITV certificates: Child Development. ITV courses: Beginning and Intermediate Accounting courses. Online certificates: e-Commerce, Phlebotomy, Commercial Art. Online courses: Farm Business Management.

Class Titles: Contact school or check web site for details.

Teaching Methods: *Computers:* Internet, real-time chat, electronic classroom, e-mail, CD-ROM, newsgroup, LISTSERV. *TV:* Interactive Television.

Admission Requirements: *Certificate:* MnSCU application.

On-Campus Requirements: Phlebotomy Certificate requires on-site lab time.

Tuition and Fees: *Undergraduate:* ITV $85, Online $135.25/credit. *Application Fee:* $20. *Credit by:* semester.

Financial Aid: Federal Stafford Loan, Federal Perkins Loan, Federal PLUS Loan, Federal Pell Grant, Federal Work-Study, VA, and Minnesota state grants.

Accreditation: North Central Association of Colleges and Schools.

Description: South Central Technical College (1946), with campuses in Faribault and North Mankato/Mankato, is learner-focused, community-based, and technology driven. It is the ideal size to provide diversity in the programs offered, yet small enough to give students the personal attention they need to succeed. South Central offers more than 50 program majors in agribusiness, health and safety, business and marketing, and technical and industrial areas. In addition to regularly scheduled classes and an array of program majors, South Central Technical College provides educational programs specifically designed to meet the training needs of business and industry throughout the southcentral region of Minnesota. Special services include: career counseling and assessment, financial aid, supplemental support services, placement assistance and on-campus child care. The Foundations that support South Central Technical College have provided over $150,000 annually in the form of student scholarships. SCTC provides both flexible evening options and online learning opportunities. South Central Technical College responds to the needs of southern Minnesota with new programs including: Wireless Communications Technician, E-Commerce, Web Developer, Network Administrator, Medical Transcriptionist, and Coding Specialist, to name a few.

South Puget Sound Community College

2011 Mottman Road S.W.	Phone: (360) 754-7711
Olympia, WA 98512	Fax: (360) 664-0780

Division(s): Instruction
Web Site(s): http://www.spscc.edu
E-mail: lsmith@spscc.ctc.edu

Undergraduate Degree Programs: Contact school.

Certificate Programs: Contact school.

Class Titles: Anthropology, History, Sociology, Psychology, Purchasing, Early Childhood Education.

Teaching Methods: *Computers:* Internet, real-time chat, electronic classroom, e-mail, CD-ROM, LISTSERV. *TV:* videotape, cable program. *Other:* videocaonferencing, audioconferencing, audiographics, audiotapes, fax, correspondence, independent study, individual study, learning contracts.

Credits Granted for: PONSI, corporate or professional association seminars/workshops, examination (CLEP, ACT-PEP, DANTES, GRE).

On-Campus Requirements: Must complete at least 15 credits of AA program on campus.

Tuition and Fees: *Undergraduate:* $58.10/credit and fees. *Other Costs:* student fees. *Credit by:* quarter.

Financial Aid: Federal Stafford Loan, Federal Perkins Loan, Federal PLUS Loan, Federal Pell Grant, Federal Work-Study, VA, state programs for residents of Washington.

Accreditation: Northwest Association of Schools and Colleges.

Description: South Puget Sound Community College (1970), consisting of 100 forested acres, is located in Olympia, Washington, the state capitol. We have over 3,000 full-time students, and 7,000 individual students. Programs offered include Associate of Arts, Associate of Science, and over 20 Associate of Technical Arts degree and certificate programs. Caring faculty and supportive staff provide high-quality learning and student services. Facilities include a new student union, fitness lab, extensive library services, and beautiful surroundings.

South Suburban College

15800 S. State Street	**Phone: (708) 596-2000**
South Holland, IL 60473	**Fax: (708) 210-5776**

Web Site(s): http://www.ssc.cc.il.us
E-mail: pschmitt@ssc.cc.il.us

Undergraduate Degree Programs:
Associate in Arts
Associate in Science
Associate in Fine Arts in Art
Associate in Fine Arts in Music
Associate in Engineering Science

Certificate Programs: Accounting, Banking/Finance, Computer Information Science, Equine Operations, Management, Marketing, Materials Production Control, Office Administration and Technology, Corporate Records, Real Estate, Diagnostic Medical Sonography, Emergency Medical Technician (Paramedic), Mammography, Medical Assistant, Registered Nurse, Practical Nurse, Occupational Therapy, Medical Transcriptionist, Pharmacy Technician, Phlebotomy, Radiologic Technology, Court Reporting, Paralegal, Child Development, Fire Science, Human Services, Teacher Aide, Nanny, Building Code Enforcement, Building Construction Technology, Computer Aided Design, Electronics Engineering, Machine Tool, Publishing and Printing Technology, Coach Maintenance, Business Evening Express, Massage Therapy, Fitness Professional, Tax Preparer Certificate, Webmaster, Professional Golf Management.

Class Titles: Aviation, Business Law, Computer Literacy, English, Music, MS Office, HTML, Paralegalism, Publishing and Printing, and more.

Teaching Methods: *Computers:* Internet, real-time chat, electronic classroom, e-mail, CD-ROM. *TV:* videotape, cable program, satellite broadcasting, PBS. *Other:* radio broadcast, videoconferencing, audioconferencing, audiotapes, fax, correspondence, individual study.

Credits Granted for: experiential learning, portfolio assessment, examination (CLEP, ACT-PEP, DANTES, GRE).

Admission Requirements: *Undergraduate:* To be admitted to the college, an applicant needs to have received a high school diploma, a high school equivalency certificate (GED), or be assessed as "ability to benefit" per federal guidelines in placement testing. Degree-seeking students must be tested for placement in English, math, and reading. *Certificate:* Certificate-seeking students must be tested for placement in English, math, and reading.

On-Campus Requirements: None.

Tuition and Fees: *Undergraduate:* $53/credit in-district (for online courses, in-district tuition applies to all Illinois residents). *Software:* as needed. *Graduation Fee:* $20. *Other Costs: Student Activity Fee:* 1 to 5.9 hours: $2.75/hour, 6 or more hours: $300/hour. *Technology Fee:* 0 to 15 hours: $3.50/hour. Over 15 hours: $52.50. *Registration Fee* (one-time assessment): $20. *Internet Courses:* additional $10/course. *Credit by:* semester.

Financial Aid: Federal Stafford Loan, Federal Perkins Loan, Federal PLUS Loan, Federal Pell Grant, Federal Work-Study, VA, state programs for residents of Illinois.

Accreditation: North Central Association of Colleges and Schools.

Description: SSC (1927) has a 75-year history as an educational institution. The school is a comprehensive community college, offering classes in both traditional transfer areas and career areas. We have been actively developing our Distance Learning offerings since the mid-90s.

Southeast Arkansas College

1900 Hazel Street	**Phone: (870) 543-5900**
Pine Bluff, AR 71603	**Fax: (870) 543-5927**

Division(s): Dean of Instruction, General Studies Coordinator
Web Site(s): http://seark.org
E-mail: kbrown.king@stc.seark.tec.ar.us

Class Titles: English Composition, U.S. History to 1877, U.S. History Since 1877, U.S. Government, Geography, Personal Health/Safety, Art Appreciation, Sociology, Psychology, Anthropology, Small Business Management Intro to Business, Business Math.

Teaching Methods: *Computers:* Internet. *TV:* videotape, cable program, satellite broadcasting, PBS. *Other:* None.

Credits Granted for: experiential learning, portfolio assessment, extrainstitutional learning (corporate or professional association seminars/workshops), examination (CLEP, locally developed challenge exams).

Admission Requirements: *Undergraduate:* Please contact school for details.

On-Campus Requirements: Orientation, midterm, final. Access to videotaped broadcast during 8- to 16-week schedule. The Internet is used for orientation; all testing is on line.

Tuition and Fees: *Undergraduate:* $36/credit. *Other Costs:* $20 Telecourse, $5 Assessment, $2 per credit technology fee. *Credit by:* semester.

Financial Aid: Federal Stafford Loan, Federal PLUS Loan, Federal Pell Grant, Federal Work-Study, VA, JTPA.

Accreditation: North Central Association of Colleges and Schools.

Description: Southeast Arkansas College was transformed from a vocational-technical school to a 2-year comprehensive technical college in 1992. Previously, SeArk College was the state's oldest vocational-technical school. Enrollment has grown 148%, with course offerings at the Associate of Arts and Associate of Applied Science degree levels. SeArk has offered telecourses since 1994, compressed interactive video since 1998, and leads the state in number of courses offered and students enrolled. Internet courses have been offered since 1999. These courses help students maintain flexible hours around work, family, and classtime.

Southeast Community College

8800 O Street	Phone: (402) 437-2705
Lincoln, NE 68520	Fax: (402) 437-2541

Division(s): Academic Education
Web Site(s): http://www.college.sccm.cc.ne.us
E-mail: rhiatt@sccm.cc.ne.us

Undergraduate Degree Programs:
Associate of Applied Science degrees available via Internet in:
  Business Administration
    Radiologic Technology (with approved clinical training site)
    Surgical Technology (with approved clinical training site)

Class Titles: Business, Small Business Management, Principles of Management, Composition, Nutrition, Physical Geology, American History, Psychology, Sociology, Diversity, Geography.

Teaching Methods: *Computers:* electronic classroom, Internet, telecourses. *TV:* videotape, fiber optic, satellite broadcasting, PBS, videoconferencing.

Admission Requirements: *Undergraduate:* Under age 16 with permission, COMPASS assessment or ACT or SAT for Composition and Math.

On-Campus Requirements: None.

Tuition and Fees: *Undergraduate:* $30/quarter credit in-state, $35 out-of-state; $45/semester credit in-state, $50 out-of-state. *Other Costs:* Student Fees: $1/quarter credit, $4/semester credit. *Credit by:* Beatrice campus is semester, Lincoln campus is quarter.

Financial Aid: Federal Stafford Loan, Federal Perkins Loan, Federal PLUS Loan, Federal Pell Grant, Federal Work-Study, VA.

Accreditation: North Central Association of Colleges and Schools.

Description: Southeast Community College (1973) is a 2-year institution offering academic transfer and vocational programs. It provides distance learning through telecourses, satellite NEB*SAT (Nebraska Educational Television), Internet, and a fiber optic network in southeast Nebraska.

Southeast Missouri State University

One University Plaza	Phone: (573) 651-2189
Cape Girardeau, MO 63701	Fax: (573) 651-2827

Division(s): Office of Off-Campus Programs
Web Site(s): http://www.semo.edu
E-mail: sschapman@semovm.semo.edu

Undergraduate Degree Programs:
Business
Nursing
Elementary Education
Industrial Technology
Horticulture/Agribusiness

Graduate Degree Programs:
Educational Administration
Elementary and Secondary Education
Educational Counseling

Teaching Methods: *Computers:* Internet, real-time chat, e-mail. *TV:* videotape, ITV. *Other:* videoconferencing, fax.

Credits Granted for: examination (CLEP), early college credit.

Admission Requirements: *Undergraduate:* High school diploma or equivalent, ACT score if within 3 years of high school graduation, ASSET scores (administered locally) for returning adult learners. *Graduate:* Accredited BA/BS degree with 3.0 GPA cumulative, GRE score in upper 50%, letters of recommendation, plus additional requirements/department.

On-Campus Requirements: Approved undergraduate degree completion programs may by completed entirely via off-campus courses including those delivered by electronic means; other undergraduate programs and graduate programs require that 50% of work be completed on campus, however, ITV and Web-based courses will apply.

Tuition and Fees: *Undergraduate:* approximately $104/credit. *Graduate:* approximately $113/credit. *Application Fee:* $20 for undergraduates. *Software:* varies. *Other Costs:* varied lab and course support fees. *Credit by:* semester.

Financial Aid: Federal Stafford Loan, Federal Perkins Loan, Federal PLUS Loan, Federal Pell Grant, Federal Work-Study, VA, Missouri resident programs.

Accreditation: North Central Association of Colleges and Schools.

Description: Southeast Missouri State University (1873) was a teacher's college and a state college before becoming a university in 1972. Southeast is a regional institution of higher education serving the interests of the nation and Missouri while maintaining a strong focus on the needs of the 23 counties of southeast Missouri. The university achieves its multipurpose goals by offering programs at the associate, bachelor's, master's, and specialist levels. As an institution with a large, mostly rural service region, Southeast has a keen interest in developing and maintaining an innovative distance learning program. In addition to an expanding evening program on campus, the university operates off campus via fixed-site centers and community-college-based sites, utilizing on-site instruction, ITV delivery, and a growing number of Web-based courses.

Southeastern Community College

1500 West Agency Road	Phone: (319) 752-2731 x8261
West Burlington, IA 52655-0605	Fax: (319) 752-4957

Division(s): Distance Learning
Web Site(s): http://www.secc.cc.ia.us
E-mail: cchrisman@secc.cc.ia.us

Undergraduate Degree Programs:
Associate of Arts

Teaching Methods: *Computers:* Internet, e-mail, real-time chat, electronic classroom, CD-ROM, *TV:* videotape.

Admission Requirements: *Undergraduate:* high school diploma.

On-Campus Requirements: None.

Tuition and Fees: *Undergraduate:* $85/credit. *Credit by:* semester.

Financial Aid: Federal Stafford Loan, Federal Perkins Loan, Federal PLUS Loan, Federal Pell Grant, Federal Work-Study, VA, Iowa resident programs.

Accreditation: North Central Association of Colleges and Schools.

Description: Burlington Junior College (1920) and Keokuk Community College (1953) merged to become the North and South campuses of today's Southeastern Community College (1965). Southeastern is dedicated to the philosophy that individuals should have access to educational opportunities from which they can appropriately benefit. As an integral part of the regional society, the college has a major responsibility to support the economic and social development of the area. The college dedicates its resources to the realization of this philosophy by providing educational opportunities and services that promote personal, intellectual, economic, and social growth. SCC offers courses in 30 academic programs and 20 occupational disciplines. Southeastern offers a full range of credit courses that, if satisfactorily completed, will lead to a diploma or an associate degree. In addition, the college's Center for Business and Industry Services provides customized training for the region.

Southeastern Illinois College

3575 College Road	Phone: (618) 252-5400
Harrisburg, IL 62946	Fax: (618) 252-2713

Division(s): Distance Learning
Web Site(s): http://sic.cc.il.us/virtual.htm
E-mail: gjones@sic.cc.il.us

Undergraduate Degree Programs: Contact school.

Class Titles: Art Appreciation, Business Communications, Microeconomics, English Rhetoric and Composition I, English Rhetoric and Composition II, Modern Literature, Introduction to Psychology, Introduction to Criminal Justice, Interpersonal Communications, Statistics, American History I, American History II, Government, Personal Health, Child Psychology, Family In Society, Small Business Management, Business Organization and Management, Business Law, Mass Media, Introduction to Philosophy.

Teaching Methods: *Computers:* Internet, electronic classroom, e-mail. *TV:* videotape, PBS. *Other:* videoconferencing.

Admission Requirements: *Undergraduate:* Asset Test, high school diploma, or GED.

On-Campus Requirements: Telecourses require an on-campus visit at the beginning of the semester. In addition, some online courses require an on-campus visit for testing; however, a proctor can be arranged for students not living in the college district.

Tuition and Fees: *Undergraduate:* $39/credit. *Graduate: Graduation Fee:* $10. *Other Costs:* $10 for technology fee. *Credit by:* semester.

Financial Aid: Federal Stafford Loan, Federal Perkins Loan, Federal PLUS Loan, Federal Pell Grant, Federal Work-Study, VA, state programs for residents of Illinois.

Accreditation: North Central Association of Colleges and Schools.

Description: Southeastern Illinois College (1960) is a public 2-year community college committed to excellence in education. Southeastern takes pride in offering the highest-quality academic programs while lending guidance and assistance to students, businesses, and our community. Southeastern Illinois College offers Baccalaureate Transfer Programs, Career Education Programs, Adult and Continuing Education Programs, and Business and Industry Services. Southeastern is committed to offering quality Distance Learning opportunities for students. In 1986 the college began offering telecourses, added interactive video courses in 1996, and has offered a variety of online Internet-based courses for the past 4 years.

Southern Arkansas University Tech

100 Carr Road	Phone: (870) 574-4500
Camden, AR 71701	Fax: (870) 574-4520

Division(s): Center for Web-Based Learning
Web Site(s): http://www.sautech.edu
E-mail: psindle@sautech.edu

Undergraduate Degree Programs:
Under development.

Certificate Programs: Under development.

Class Titles: Business, History, Philosophy, Computers Physical Science, Biology, Literature, Algebra, Technical Writing, Speech, Wastewater Treatment, Solid Waste Management, Environmental Safety, CADD, Engineering Graphics.

Teaching Methods: *Computers:* Internet, e-mail, CD-ROM, newsgroup, LISTSERV. PBS. *Other:* videoconferencing, fax,

correspondence, independent study, individual study radio broadcast, audioconferencing, audiographics, audiotapes, learning contracts.

Credits Granted for: experiential learning, portfolio assessment, examination (CLEP, ACT-PEP, ASSET, SAT, DANTES, GRE) extrainstitutional learning.

Admission Requirements: *Undergraduate:* contact admissions at 870-574-4558.

On-Campus Requirements: None.

Tuition and Fees: *Undergraduate:* $50/credit. *Other Costs:* $20/credit up to 12 hours, $15 one-time transcript fee. *Credit by:* semester.

Financial Aid: Federal Stafford Loan, Federal Perkins Loan, Federal PLUS Loan, Federal Pell Grant, Federal Work-Study, VA, Arkansas resident programs.

Accreditation: North Central Association of Colleges and Schools.

Description: Since 1967 the college has moved from a major residential, dorm-filled, 2-year technical campus in south Arkansas to a 2-year comprehensive technical college serving 2 groups of students—local students who enroll in a combination of technical and college programs, and statewide students who participate in high-tech degree and advanced certificate programs. The college is committed to providing quality educational programs delivered through various technologies and methodologies to meet the need of its service area. In fall 1997 Chancellor Roger Worsley made the decision that SAU Tech should begin offering Internet courses. Summer 1998, 4 courses were offered online. Today SAU Tech now offers 22 courses online with plans to more than double this number in the next 2 years. With the addition of these courses, the college will have the associate of arts degree online.

Southern Christian University

1200 Taylor Road	Phone: (800) 351-4040
Montgomery, AL 36117	Fax: (334) 387-3878

Division(s): Extended Learning Department
Web Site(s): http://www.southernchristian.edu
E-mail: admissions@southernchristian.edu

Undergraduate Degree Programs:
Bachelor of Arts in Biblical Studies
Bachelor of Science in:
    Ministry/Bible
    Liberal Studies
    Management Communication
    Human Development
Associates Degrees (in development)

Graduate Degree Programs:
Master of Arts in Biblical Studies
Master of Science in:
   Counseling/Family Therapy
   Christian Ministry
Master of Science in Organizational Leadership
Master of Divinity in:
   Christian Ministry
   Family Therapy

Doctoral Degree Programs:
Doctor of Ministry in:
   Christian Ministry
   Family Therapy
PhD in Family Therapy (in development)
PhD in Bible (in development)

Certificate Programs: in development.

Class Titles: Examples include Counseling Studies, Organizational Leadership Studies, Professional Studies, Foundation Studies, Research Studies, Old Testament Studies, New Testament Studies, Missions Studies, Clinical Counseling, Pastoral Counseling, Family Therapy, and Doctor of Ministry courses. Visit *http://www.southernchristian.edu* for complete listing.

Teaching Methods: *Computers:* Web-based.

Credits Granted for: College Level Examination Program (CLEP), Defense Activity for Nontraditional Education Support (DANTES), Subject Standardized Testing Program (DSST), Regents College Examinations (formerly ACT/PEP), experiential learning, military experience.

Admission Requirements: *Undergraduate:* placement, exam, application, and fee. *Graduate:* Graduate Admissions Test, bachelor's degree, application, and fee.

On-Campus Requirements: None.

Tuition and Fees: *Undergraduate:* $320/semester hour. *Graduate:* $390/semester hour. *Application Fee:* $50. *Other Costs:* comprehensive fee: $50. *Credit by:* semester.

Financial Aid: Federal Stafford Loan, Federal PLUS Loan, Federal Pell Grant, Federal SEOG, VA, scholarship program.

Accreditation: Southern Association of Colleges and Schools.

Description: Founded in 1967, Southern Christian University provides educational opportunities through the (1) School of Leadership and Human Services, (2) School of Religion, and (3) Turner School of Theology. The purpose of the School of Leadership and Human Services is to prepare students to provide services for the well-being of individuals, families, and society. This purpose will be accomplished by interdis-ciplinary learning and clinical training with core courses and specialized knowledge and skills in majors such as counseling, family therapy, business, and human communications. The purpose of the School of Religion is to provide biblical instruction and practical training on the undergraduate level for Christian ministers and religious workers. The purpose of the Turner School of Theology is to educate qualified persons to be effective Christian ministers, church leaders, teachers, and scholars who will use their gifts and knowledge in proclaiming the gospel, strengthening the church, and serving humanity. To accomplish this purpose, the school prepares students for the ministerial and teaching professions and for effective voluntary Christian service through both academic and practical studies on the graduate level. Southern Christian University makes use of technology-based delivery systems as well as traditional educational methods to avail its programs to students who cannot come to campus. Students can take advantage of Southern Christian University's offerings anywhere there is Internet access.

Southern Illinois University, Carbondale

Mailcode 6705
Carbondale, IL 62901-6705

Phone: (618) 453-5659
Fax: (618) 453-5668

Division(s): Office of Distance Education/Division of Continuing Education
Web Site(s): http://www.dce.siu.edu/siuconnected.html
E-mail: ilpdce@siu.edu

Graduate Degree Programs: Workforce Education and Development degree in Distance Learning (under development).

Class Titles: General Agriculture, Biology, Engineering, Medical Terminology, Journalism, Telecommunications, Information Systems Technology, Drivers Education, Recreation Women's' Studies, Marketing, Philosophy, Political Science, Rehabilitation, History of Religion, Journalism Law, Distance Education.

Teaching Methods: *Computers:* Internet, real-time chat, electronic classroom, e-mail, CD-ROM. *TV:* videotape, satellite broadcasting, PBS. *Other:* audiotapes, fax, correspondence, independent study, individual study.

Credits Granted for: none.

Admission Requirements: *Undergraduate:* Admission application and fee, GED or High School diploma. *Graduate:* Admission application and fee.

On-Campus Requirements: None.

Tuition and Fees: *Undergraduate:* $170 per credit for online. $103.40 for independent study. *Graduate:* $203 per credit. *Credit by:* semester.

Financial Aid: Federal Stafford Loan, Federal Perkins Loan, Federal PLUS Loan, Federal Pell Grant, Federal Work-Study, VA, state programs for residents of Illinois. Please note that different financial aid packages may or may not pay for all the course charges.

Accreditation: North Central Association of Colleges and Schools.

Description: Distance Education at Southern Illinois University, Carbondale (SIUC) (1869) extends the intellectual and service mission beyond the physical boundaries of the campus to the regional, state, national, and global communities by offering departmental programs and courses for academic credit through distance education. It is the intention of SIUC to provide a culturally diverse offering of credit courses through distance learning systems that include synchronous and asynchronous delivery methods. The Distance Education initiative at SIUC started in 1981 with the Individualized Learning Program in the Division of Continuing Education. It was expanded to include two-way interactive video in 1994 and more recently in 1999 with a focus on web-based delivery.

Southern Illinois University, Edwardsville

Campus Box 1084	Phone: (618) 650-3210
Edwardsville, IL 62026-1084	Fax: (618) 650-2629

Division(s): Office of Continuing Education
Web Site(s): http://www.siue.edu/CE/
E-mail: coned@siue.edu

Undergraduate Degree Programs:
Bachelor of Science in Nursing

Teaching Methods: *Computers:* Internet, e-mail, LISTSERV. *TV:* real-time interactive compressed video and audio—closed consortium network, videotape. *Other:* fax, independent study.

Credits Granted for: examination (CLEP, DANTES) Advanced Placement.

Admission Requirements: *Undergraduate:* For a recent high school graduate, completed application 3 weeks prior to term, official transcripts, certified high school graduating rank, ACT (preferred) or SAT. The SIUE Undergraduate Catalog online at http://www.admis.siue.edu/97-99catalog/index.html) outlines additional requirements including high school courses and admission of nontraditional and international students. *Graduate:* Application deadline for classified (degree-seeking) students is one month prior to term; unclassified deadline is 5 working days. Degree program applicants must be accepted by the Graduate School and by the academic unit offering the program. All students must submit official transcripts of bachelor's degree and all graduate work. Other requirements, including admission tests, test scores, grades, interviews, etc., vary according to program (send for SIUE's Graduate Catalog, or view online at www.siue.edu/GRADUATE/catalog.html).

On-Campus Requirements: Distance learning classes meet in specially equipped classrooms at off-campus sites (usually community colleges) in southern Illinois.

Tuition and Fees: *Undergraduate:* $92/credit plus an off-campus delivery fee of $72/course. *Graduate:* $105.65/credit plus an off-campus delivery fee of $72/course. *Application Fee:* Undergraduate $0, Graduate $25 (additional application fee for MBA program $35). *Software:* varies. *Other Costs:* course-specific fees vary. *Credit by:* semester.

Financial Aid: Federal Stafford Loan, Federal Perkins Loan, Federal PLUS Loan, Federal Pell Grant, Federal Work-Study, VA, Illinois resident programs, various institutional scholarships.

Accreditation: North Central Association of Colleges and Schools, National League for Nursing.

Description: Southern Illinois University, Edwardsville, established in 1957, is located 18 miles from downtown St. Louis on a 2,660-acre campus. SIUE is a major, public university, offering a broad choice of degrees and programs ranging from career-oriented fields to the more traditional, liberal arts. Students have an opportunity to interact with outstanding teachers and scholars, as well as with other students from all parts of the U.S. and the world. They enjoy the excellent facilities of a new and growing campus, including extensive research laboratories, specialized equipment for professional preparation, and comfortable, spacious classrooms. In addition, academic services help students meet the demands of university life. Through its participation in regional, higher education consortia, SIUE utilizes the facilities of a dedicated, real-time, interactive, audio/video instructional network to deliver instruction at off-campus sites in southern Illinois.

Southern Methodist University, School of Engineering

PO Box 750335	Phone: (214) 768-3232
Dallas, TX 75275-0335	Fax: (214) 768-3778

Division(s): Distance Education
Web Site(s): http://www.engr.smu.edu
E-mail: sdye@engr.smu.edu

Graduate Degree Programs:

Master of Science in:
- Telecommunications
- Software Engineering
- Engineering Management
- Systems Engineering
- Civil Engineering
- Environmental Engineering
- Environmental Systems Management
- Manufacturing Systems Management
- Electrical Engineering
- Mechanical Engineering
- Computer Science
- Operations Research

Certificate Programs: Telecommunications.

Teaching Methods: *TV:* videotape, satellite broadcasting. *Other:* None.

Credits Granted for: Up to 6 transfer credits of previous graduate study.

Admission Requirements: *Graduate:* appropriate bachelor's degree; 3.0 GPA; GRE for Computer Science, Electrical Engineering, Mechanical Engineering; Civil Engineering and Environmental Engineering. *Certificate:* 60 semester hours with 2.0 GPA; 3 years of related work experience; courses in differential/integral calculus, physics, or electronics; programming, preferably in Assembly language.

On-Campus Requirements: None.

Tuition and Fees: *Graduate:* $777/credit, $2,331/course. *Application Fee:* $50. *Credit by:* semester.

Financial Aid: Call Financial Aid Office (800) 323-0672.

Accreditation: Southern Association of Colleges and Schools.

Description: Southern Methodist University was founded in 1911, and its School of Engineering has been a national pioneer in graduate distance education for more than 30 years. SMU'S School of Engineering offers its distance master's programs nationally and internationally via videotape and, in north Texas, via closed-circuit TV. The Master of Science in Telecommunications is available through the National Technological University satellite network. The School of Engineering offers Master of Science programs in several professional areas and in traditional engineering disciplines.

Southern New Hampshire University

2500 North River Road
Manchester, NH 03106-1045

Phone: (603) 645-9766
Fax: (603) 645-9706

Division(s): Distance Education
Web Site(s): http://de.snhu.edu/ or http://www.snhu.edu/
E-mail: de@snhu.edu

Undergraduate Degree Programs:

Business Administration
International Business
Marketing
Accounting/Finance
CIS/IT
Economics
Psychology
Social Science
Technical Management
English Language and Literature
Liberal Arts
Humanities

Graduate Degree Programs:

Masters in Business Administration (MBA)
Masters in Business Education (MBE)
Graduate Certificate in International Business (an MS in International Business is planned for Sept 2001—please contact the DE office for information).

Certificate Programs: Accounting, Computer Programming, Human Resource Management.

Class Titles: See projected schedule for year on Web site at http://de.snhu.edu/. Click on courses, then projected schedule.

Teaching Methods: 100% Internet based using Blackboard Coursoinfo software. No proctored examinations at the undergraduate level. There may be a need for a proctored comprehensive examination upon completion of course requirements for the MBA. No need to visit the main campus.

Credits Granted for: experiential learning, portfolio assessment, examination (CLEP, ACT-PEP, DANTES). Please consult with the DE advisor.

Admission Requirements: *Undergraduate:* equal opportunity institution. Distance Education has open enrollment policy. Must maintain GPA standard. Residency requirement is 30 semester hours through SNHU, including 12 from the major for the bachelor's, and 9 from the major for the associate; final 24 hours must be through SNHU. Exceptions made for active duty military personnel and dependents. Transfer credits are accepted. See the SNHU catalog for further details, and for graduate admissions requirements.

On-Campus Requirements: None.

Tuition and Fees: Subject to change, but $215/semester hour for undergraduate classes, and $440/semester hour for graduate courses, for the 2001–2002 academic year. As of this printing, SNHU has no fees for application or transcript evaluation and remains a no-fee institution.

Financial Aid: Federal Stafford Loan, Federal Perkins Loan, Federal PLUS Loan, Federal Pell Grant, Federal Work-Study, VA, Tuition Assistance, Federal and New Hampshire resident programs, vocational rehabilitation programs, etc. Contact our financial aid office for more details at (603) 645-9645.

Accreditation: New England Association of Schools and Colleges, Association of Collegiate Business Schools and Programs, New England Postsecondary Education Commission.

Description: Established in 1932, Southern New Hampshire University is a private, nonprofit coeducational institution. The main campus is on nearly 300 acres situated along the banks of the Merrimack River in Manchester New Hampshire. SNHU offers certificates and programs in business, liberal arts, and hospitality, with degrees beginning at the associate's level and continuing to the PhD. The SNHU Distance Education (DE) program offers certificates and degrees up to the MBA, and is one of the largest and fastest-growing programs in New England, is both regionally and nationally accredited, and is a leader in asynchronous learning and 100% Internet-based instruction. Total enrollments were 7,000 for the 2000–2001 academic year, which represented 40% growth from the previous year. Undergraduate terms are 8 weeks in length and there are 6 terms in an academic year. Graduate terms are 12 weeks in length with 4 terms offered in an academic year. SNHU is a Serviceman's Opportunity College.

Southern Oregon University

1250 Siskiyou Boulevard	Phone: (541) 552-6331
Ashland, OR 97520	Fax: (541) 552-6047

Division(s): Extended Campus Programs
Web Site(s): http://www.sou.edu/ecp/distlearn
E-mail: huftill@sou.edu

Undergraduate Degree Programs:
Bachelor of Science in:
    Business, Degree Completion (Medford, Grants Pass)
    Nursing (Oregon Health Sciences, Southern Oregon)
    Interdisciplinary Social Science, Human Services (Medford, Ashland)

Graduate Degree Programs:
Master of Science in Education
Master of Science in Management (Medford, Ashland)

Certificate Programs: Oregon Standard Teacher's License.

Teaching Methods: *Computers:* web-based course work. *TV:* Many courses are delivered via 2-way interactive satellite broadcasts to sites in Gold Beach, Grants Pass, Lakeview, Medford, Klamath Falls, Roseburg in Southern Oregon. *Other:* None.

Credits Granted for: professional association seminars/workshops—preapproved, CLEP, IB, some military experience.

Admission Requirements: *Undergraduate:* application. *Graduate:* undergraduate degree. *Certificate:* Contact university for details.

On-Campus Requirements: One visit for some courses. Master's in Education completion courses during summer.

Tuition and Fees: *Undergraduate:* $270/3-credit course. *Graduate:* $585/3-credit class. *Software:* varies. *Other Costs:* Internet Service Provider, nonresident tuition for full load. *Credit by:* quarter.

Financial Aid: Federal Stafford Loan, Federal Perkins Loan, Federal PLUS Loan, Federal Pell Grant, Federal Work-Study, VA.

Accreditation: Northwest Association of Schools and Colleges.

Description: Founded in 1869, Southern Oregon University is one of eight institutions in the Oregon University System. In 1956 it transitioned from a teacher education institution to a regional liberal arts college. Then in 1997 it became Southern Oregon University to reflect its role as a regional multipurpose institution serving the state through instruction, research, and public service. The university began distance learning in 1984 through regional public broadcasting and PBS video courses. In 1991 SOU received a Title III grant that funded a 2-way interactive video system at sites throughout southwestern Oregon. As technology advances, so does SOU's multimodality outreach via 2-way video, cable, web-based course work, and CD-ROM.

Southern Polytechnic State University

1100 South Marietta Parkway	Phone: (770) 528-4287
Marietta, GA 30060	Fax: (770) 528-3576

Division(s): Extended University's Center for Instructional Technology
Web Site(s): http://www.spsu.edu
E-mail: dramsey@spsu.edu

Graduate Degree Programs:
Master's in Quality Assurance

Teaching Methods: *Computers:* Internet, real-time chat, electronic classroom, e-mail, newsgroup, LISTSERV.

Admission Requirements: *Graduate:* GRE score, 4-year degree.

On-Campus Requirements: MSQA requires 2 sessions on campus.

Tuition and Fees: *Graduate:* Determined by residency and number of credit hours. *Application Fee:* $20. *Credit by:* semester.

Financial Aid: Federal Stafford Loan, Federal Perkins Loan, Federal PLUS Loan, Federal Pell Grant, Federal Work-Study, VA, Georgia resident programs.

Accreditation: Southern Association of Colleges and Schools.

Description: Southern Polytechnic State University (1948) provides the residents of Georgia with university-level education in technology, engineering technology, arts and sciences, architecture, management, and related fields. SPSU is a senior institution in the University System of Georgia. The school began providing distance learning opportunities in 1995.

Southern Utah University

351 West Center Street	Phone: (435) 586-7850
Cedar City, UT 84720	Fax: (435) 865-8087

Division(s): Continuing Education
Web Site(s): http://www.suu.edu
E-mail: workman@suu.edu

Undergraduate Degree Programs:
Contact Southern Utah University for more information

Teaching Methods: *Computers:* Internet, real-time chat, e-mail, LISTSERV *Other:* fax, correspondence, independent study, individual study, learning contracts.

Credits Granted for: examination (CLEP, ACT-PEP, DANTES, GRE).

Admission Requirements: *Undergraduate:* application, official high school and/or college transcripts, ACT/SAT scores. For transfer students, 2.25 GPA. See online information at web site.

On-Campus Requirements: All online classes are self-contained.

Tuition and Fees: *Undergraduate:* $92/credit. *Graduate:* $96/credit. *Doctoral:* $96/credit. *Application Fee:* $30. *Software:* To be established. *Credit by:* semester.

Financial Aid: Federal Pell Grant, Federal Work-Study, VA, Utah resident programs.

Accreditation: Northwest Association of Schools and Colleges.

Southwest Missouri State University

901 South National Avenue	Phone: (417) 836-4128
Springfield, MO 65804-0089	Fax: (417) 836-6016

Division(s): Academic Outreach
Web Site(s): http://ce.smsu.edu
http://smsuonline.smsu.edu
http://ccpe.smsu.edu
http://www.mscis.smsu.edu
E-mail: dianagarland@smsu.edu

Graduate Degree Programs:
Master of Administrative Studies
Master of Business Administration
Master of Science in Elementary Education
Master of Science in Computer Information Systems
(Internet Based program)

Certificate Programs: a variety of Professional Development Certificates for nonacademic credit

Class Titles: *Undergraduate:* Anthropology, Astronomy, Biology, Chemistry, Communications, Consumer/Family Studies, Economics, Finance/General Business, Health Care Management, History, Media, Middle School Education Management, Music, Mythology, Nursing, Physics, Political Science, Reading, Religious Studies, Spanish, Substance Abuse, Technology, Theater, Vocational Education. *Graduate:* Accounting, Communications, Computer Information Systems, Early Childhood Education, Educational Administration, Elementary Education, Marketing Management, Reading, Religious Studies, Secondary Education.

Teaching Methods: *Computers:* Internet, real-time chat, electronic classroom. *TV:* videotape, cable program, satellite broadcasting, interactive video. *Other:* videoconferencing, audioconferencing, audiotapes, fax.

Credits Granted for: examination (CLEP, ACT-PEP, DANTES, GRE).

Admission Requirements: *Undergraduate:* call Admissions at (800) 492-7900 for current policy and for special limited-hour policies for nondegree-seeking undergraduate, transfer, and adult students. *Graduate:* contact Graduate College at (417) 836-5335 for details and catalog. Students with bachelor's degree not wishing to pursue additional degree may be admitted in limited-hour postbaccalaureate status. *Doctoral:* for information on statewide cooperative EdD in Educational Leadership, call Educational Administration at

(417) 836-5392. *Certificate:* variable by program. Contact The Center for Continuing and Professional Education at (417) 836-6660 or Academic Outreach at (888) 879-7678 for information.

On-Campus Requirements: A one-week on-campus session is required for the MS in CIS program each semester for 4 semesters; contact mscis@smsu.edu or http://www.mscis.smsu.edu for more information.

Tuition and Fees: *Undergraduate:* $111/credit. *Graduate:* $127/credit. *Internet.* $111–$365/credit. *Software:* $15 undergraduate, $25 graduate. *Other Costs:* vary by program. *Credit by:* semester.

Financial Aid: Federal Stafford Loan, Federal Perkins Loan, Federal PLUS Loan, Federal Pell Grant, Federal Work-Study, VA, Missouri resident programs.

Accreditation: North Central Association of Colleges and Schools.

Description: Southwest Missouri State University (1905) is a state-supported, comprehensive institution. SMSU first offered distance learning courses in 1974. In 1999–2000, it offered 140 courses at a distance.

Southwest Tennessee Community College

5983 Macon Cove	Phone: (901) 333-4681
Memphis, TN 38134	Fax: (901) 333-4377

Division(s): Office of Distance Learning
Web Site(s): http://www.stcc.cc.tn.us
E-mail: wpayne@stcc.cc.tn.us

Undergraduate Degree Programs:
Associate of Applied Science in Professional Studies with a concentration in Information Technologies
Associate of Arts in General Studies (University Parallel Program)
Associate of Science in General Studies (University Parallel Program)

Class Titles: Contact school or check web site for details.

Teaching Methods: *Computers:* Internet, real-time chat, electronic classroom, e-mail, CD-ROM, newsgroup, LISTSERV. *TV:* videotape, cable program, satellite broadcasting, PBS.

Admission Requirements: Contact school.

On-Campus Requirements: None.

Tuition and Fees: *Undergraduate:* $79/credit in-state, $247/credit out-of-state. *Application Fee:* $5 nonrefundable. *Credit by:* semester.

Financial Aid: Federal Stafford Loan, Federal Perkins Loan, Federal PLUS Loan, Federal Pell Grant, Federal Work-Study, VA, state programs for residents of Tennessee.

Accreditation: Southern Association of Colleges and Schools.

Description: Southwest Tennessee Community College (2000) draws on the legacies of 2 colleges, Shelby State Community College and State Technical Institute at Memphis, which were consolidated July 1, 2000. The college was authorized when House Bill Number 1742 was passed by the General Assembly on May 28, 1999, and approved by the Governor on June 17, 1999.

Southwest Texas State University

601 University Drive	Phone: (512) 245-2322
San Marcos, TX 78666-4616	Fax: (512) 245-8934

Division(s): Office of Correspondence and Extension Studies
Web Site(s): http://www.ideal.swt.edu/correspondence
E-mail: corrstudy@swt.edu

Class Titles: Art, Biology, Career/Technology Education, English, Geography, Health Information Management, History, Mathematics, Music, Philosophy, Political Science, Psychology, Sociology, Spanish, Theater Arts.

Teaching Methods: *Computers:* Internet, e-mail. *TV:* videotape. *Other:* audiotapes, fax, correspondence.

Admission Requirements: *Undergraduate:* Completion time is 45 days to 9 months, with one extension up to 3 more months. Some courses have prerequisites. *Graduate:* same as undergraduate.

On-Campus Requirements: None.

Tuition and Fees: *Undergraduate:* $63/credit. *Graduate:* $95/credit. *Other Costs:* $25 administrative fee/course. Variable for services such as course extensions, transfers, drops, and required textbooks. *Credit by:* semester.

Financial Aid: Federal Stafford Loan, Federal Perkins Loan, Federal PLUS Loan, Federal Pell Grant, Federal Work-Study, VA, Texas resident programs.

Accreditation: Southern Association of Colleges and Schools.

Description: Southwest Texas State University (1903) is a comprehensive, public university committed to providing an intellectually stimulating and socially diverse climate for its students, faculty, and staff. SWT offers effective undergraduate and master's-level instruction dedicated to teaching, advancing knowledge and artistic expression, and serving as a resource for the surrounding regions. The Office of

Correspondence and Extension Studies began in 1953 and helps students reach their educational goals regardless of time, place, or other constraints preventing them from attending on-campus classes. Courses are delivered to distance learners in a variety of formats determined by content and learner resources.

Southwest Wisconsin Technical College

1800 Bronson Boulevard	Phone: (608) 822-3262
Fennimore, WI 53809	Fax: (608) 822-6019

Division(s): Center for Learning Innovation
E-mail: sallen@southwest.tec.wi.us

Undergraduate Degree Programs:
Associate Degree in Culinary Management
One-Year Technical Diploma in Medical Transcription

Class Titles: Written Communication, Introduction to Psychology and Sociology, Economics, Mathematics (General Math, Algebra, Trigonometry); Culinary Management courses: Managing Culinary Staff; Managing Quality in Food Service; Managing Culinary Department Finances, Advanced Nutritional Therapy, Professional Development for Dietary Managers; Medical Transcription Courses: Medical Typing/Transcription, Office Software, Basic Health and Medical Terminology, Pharmacology for Medical Transcriptionists, Body Structure and Function, Advanced Medical Transcription Courses, Technical Communication for Medical Transcription.

Teaching Methods: *Computers:* Internet, electronic classroom, e-mail, CD-ROM. *TV:* videotape, cable program, satellite broadcasting, PBS. *Other:* audiotapes, fax, correspondence, independent study.

Credits Granted for: experiential learning, portfolio assessment, examination (CLEP, ACT-PEP, DANTES, GRE).

Admission Requirements: Contact school.

On-Campus Requirements: None.

Tuition and Fees: *Undergraduate:* $64 + $1.50/credit activity fee + material fee that varies with each course. *Application Fee:* $30. *Graduation Fee:* December—$15; May—$30. *Credit by:* semester.

Financial Aid: Federal Stafford Loan, Federal Perkins Loan, Federal PLUS Loan, Federal Pell Grant, Federal Work-Study, VA.

Accreditation: North Central Association of Colleges and Schools.

Description: Southwest Wisconsin Technical College (1967) is a 2-year public college and one of 16 technical colleges in Wisconsin. Faculty and staff are devoted to customer service and excellence in education. Programs and services meet the changing needs of business, industry, and society. Because business, industry, and society are becoming more dependent on learning anywhere, anytime, Southwest Tech entered the Distance Learning area first with correspondence courses (15 years ago), then video-based courses (12 years ago), and finally with fully online courses (2 years ago).

Southwestern Adventist University

100 Hillcrest Drive	Phone: (800) 433-2240 x204
Keene, TX 76059	Fax: (817) 556-4742

Division(s): Adult Degree Program
Web Site(s): http://www.swau.edu/adp
E-mail: adp@swau.edu

Undergraduate Degree Programs:
Bachelor of Science in:
   Business Administration
   Accounting
   Computer Science
   Communication
   English
   Education
   Mathematics
   Office Administration
   Psychology
   Religion
   Social Science
   Theology
   Criminal Justice

Teaching Methods: *Computers:* Internet, real-time chat, e-mail. *TV:* videotape. *Other:* fax, correspondence, independent study, individual study.

Credits Granted for: experiential learning, portfolio assessment, extrainstitutional learning, examination (CLEP, ACT-PEP, DANTES, GRE).

Admission Requirements: *Undergraduate:* age 22, application, official high school transcript or GED if fewer than 12 transferable hours, any college transcripts, SAT/ACT scores, 2.0 GPA.

On-Campus Requirements: attend 6-day seminar offered 3 times/year.

Tuition and Fees: *Undergraduate:* $412/credit; 12–17 hours: $4,940. *Credit by:* semester.

Financial Aid: Federal Stafford Loan, Federal Perkins Loan, Federal PLUS Loan, Federal Pell Grant, VA, Texas resident programs.

Accreditation: Southern Association of Colleges and Schools.

Description: Southwestern Adventist University (1893) is a private, Christian coeducation institution with 1,200 students, 280 of whom are distance learners. The school entered distance learning in 1976.

Southwestern Assemblies of God University

1200 Sycamore St.	Phone: (972) 937-4010 x1125
Waxahachie, TX 75165	Fax: (972) 923-0488

Division(s): School of Distance Education
Web Site(s): http://www.sagu.edu
E-mail: info@sagu.edu

Undergraduate Degree Programs:
Associate of Arts in:
  Business Administration
  Bible
  Education
  English
  Foreign Language
  General Business
  General Ministries
  Media
  Music
  Psychology
  Social Science
Bachelor of Arts, or Bachelor of Science in:
  Accounting
  Biblical Studies
  Business Administration
  Children's Ministries
  Christian Education
  Church Business Administration
  Church Music
  Counseling Psychology
  Cross-Cultural Missions
  Elementary Education
  General Ministries
  Management
  Media Ministries
  Music Education
  Music—Instrumental Performance
  Music Ministries
  Music—Piano Performance
  Music—Vocal Performance
  Pastoral Ministries
  Secondary Education
  Urban Ministries
  Youth Ministries

Graduate Degree Programs:
Bible and Theology
Education—Christian School Administration
Education—Curriculum Development
Missions
Practical Theology

Certificate Programs: Biblical Studies.

Teaching Methods: Web-based courses, video and audio lectures.

Credits Granted for: experiential learning, examination (CLEP, ACT-PEP DANTES)

Admission Requirements: *Undergraduate:* age 22, ACT scores or transfer credit. *Graduate:* GRE test.

On-Campus Requirements: Courses are opened on campus where faculty meet face to face with their students.

Tuition and Fees: *Undergraduate:* $235/hour. *Graduate:* $235/hour. *Application Fee:* $35 undergraduate, $50 graduate. *Other Costs:* $30/hour general fee for less than 9 hours, $300 for 9 hours and above. $25/class with a maximum of $75 for Telecommunications/Media. *Credit by:* semester.

Financial Aid: Federal Stafford Loan, Federal Perkins Loan, Federal PLUS Loan, Federal Pell Grant, Federal Work-Study, VA, Texas resident programs.

Accreditation: Southern Association of Colleges and Schools, Accrediting Association of Bible Colleges.

Description: Southwestern Assemblies of God University (1927) is a church-based institution of higher learning, self-described as a "Bible University for Theological and Professional Studies." SAGU's parent body is the Assemblies of God. The school resulted from a merger of institutes in the first half of the 20th century and formerly included a high school and a junior college. It now offers AA, BA, BS, and MS degrees. SAGU established its distance education program in 1984.

Southwestern Baptist Theological Seminary

2001 W. Seminary Drive	Phone: (817) 923-1921
Ft. Worth, TX 76122	Fax: (817) 921-8763

Division(s): Distance Learning
Web Site(s): http://swbts.edu
E-mail: gww@swbts.edu

Undergraduate Degree Programs:
Diploma and Advanced Diploma in Theology and Education

Graduate Degree Programs:
Master's Degrees in:
    Divinity
    Education
    Music

Postgraduate Degree Programs:
Doctor of Ministry
Doctor of Philosophy in:
    Theology
    Education
    Music

Certificate Programs: Lay Theological Studies.

Class Titles: Contact school or check web sites for details.

Teaching Methods: *Computers:* Internet, real-time chat, electronic classroom, e-mail, CD-ROM, *TV:* videotape. *Other:* videoconferencing, independent study, individual study, learning contracts.

Credits Granted for: experiential learning, portfolio assessment, extrainstitutional learning (PONSI, corporate or professional association seminars/workshops), examination (CLEP, ACT-PEP, DANTES, GRE).

Admission Requirements: *Undergraduate:* 26 years of age and no bachelor's degree. *Graduate:* bachelor's degree from an accredited university or college. *Postgraduate:* Master's degree, GRE or MAT, entrance exams.

On-Campus Requirements: equivalent of 1 year on the main campus, can take up to one-third of degree online.

Tuition and Fees: *Undergraduate:* $90 on campus; $125 off campus/credit. *Graduate:* $90 on campus; $125 off campus/credit. *Postgraduate:* $1,450/semester. *Application Fees:* $35. *Graduation Fee:* $135/$220. *Other Costs:* online courses: $175/credit hour. All tuition and fees are for Southern Baptist students; non-Southern Baptist are double. *Credit by:* semester.

Accreditation: Association of Theological Schools and Southern Association of Colleges and Schools.

Description: The mission of Southwestern Baptist Theological Seminary (1908) is to provide theological education for individuals engaging in Christian ministry. We are a Southern Baptist institution that receives part of our financial support for the Southern Baptist Convention. Twenty-five years ago several off-campus sites were established. In 1998 we began offering courses online.

Southwestern Indian Polytechnic Institute (SIPI)

9169 Coors Road NW	Phone: (505) 346-2335
Albuquerque, NM 87184	Fax: (505) 346-2343

Division(s): Special Programs
Web Site(s): http://www.sipi.bia.edu
E-mail: nscala@sipi.bia.edu

Undergraduate Degree Programs:
Early Childhood Education

Class Titles: Contact school or check web site for details.

Teaching Methods: *TV:* satellite broadcasting. *Other:* videoconferencing.

Admission Requirements: *Undergraduate:* open enrollment; Native Americans only.

On-Campus Requirements: None.

Tuition and Fees: *Undergraduate:* No tuition charged. *Credit by:* quarter.

Financial Aid: Federal Pell Grant, Federal Work Study, VA.

Accreditation: North Central Association of Colleges and Schools.

Description: Satellite delivery selected to reach remote tribal sites in New Mexico and Colorado.

Southwestern Michigan College

58900 Cherry Grove Road	Phone: (616) 782-1369
Dowagiac, MI 49047	Fax: (616) 782-8414

Division(s): Community Services and Development
Web Site(s): http://www.smc.cc.mi.us
E-mail: isheffer@smc.cc.mi.us

Undergraduate Degree Programs:
Associate of Arts
Associate of Science

Class Titles: Business, Sociology, Human Communications, Psychology.

Teaching Methods: *Computers:* Internet, real-time chat, e-mail. *TV:* videotape, satellite broadcasting, PBS.

Credits Granted for: examination (CLEP, ACT-PEP, DANTES).

Admission Requirements: *Undergraduate:* application; e-mail gglynn@smc.cc.mi.us. *Certificate:* see undergraduate.

On-Campus Requirements: orientation.

Tuition and Fees: *Undergraduate:* $50/credit in-state. *Other Costs:* $5/credit technology fee, $5/credit registration fee. *Credit by:* semester.

Financial Aid: Federal Stafford Loan, Federal Perkins Loan, Federal PLUS Loan, Federal Pell Grant, Federal Work-Study, VA, Michigan resident programs.

Accreditation: North Central Association of Colleges and Schools.

Description: Southwestern Michigan College (1964) is a public, 2-year community college located on a 240-acre, tree-studded campus that showcases Michigan's 4 seasons. SMC offers affordable one- and two-year degrees in business, nursing, technology, and transfer programs. In addition, Ferris State University and Western Michigan University operate an extension site at the college, allowing students to earn a bachelor's degree in business management, business administration, computer information systems, or nursing, as well as elementary education, with all classes held on the SMC campuses in Dowagiac and Niles. SMC students come from the Michigan area, all over the U.S., and many foreign countries. Cultural experiences include the SMC Museum, the Starlight Series, and the Art Gallery. Distance learning began in 1995 through a grant from the W.K. Kellogg Foundation. Southwestern Michigan College: "Excellence with a Personal Touch."

Southwestern Oklahoma State University

100 Campus Drive	Phone: (580) 774-3149
Weatherford, OK 73096	Fax: (580) 774-7180

Division(s): Distance Learning Department
Web Site(s): http://www.swosu.edu
E-mail: price1@swosu.edu

Undergraduate Degree Programs:
Associate in General Studies

Graduate Degree Programs:
Masters in Education—Administration
Master in Business Administration

Teaching Methods: *Computers:* Internet, electronic classroom, e-mail, CD-ROM. *TV:* cable program, PBS. *Other:* videoconferencing, fax.

Credits Granted for: experiential learning, portfolio assessment, extrainstitutional learning (PONSI, corporate or professional association seminars/workshops), examination (CLEP, ACT-PEP, DANTES, GRE).

Tuition and Fees: *Undergraduate:* $70.15/credit. *Graduate:* $88.35/credit. *Application Fee:* $15. *Software:* $5/credit hour. *Credit by:* semester.

Financial Aid: Federal Stafford Loan, Federal Perkins Loan, Federal PLUS Loan, Federal Pell Grant, Federal Work-Study, VA, state programs for residents of Oklahoma.

Accreditation: North Central Association of Colleges and Schools.

Description: Southwestern Oklahoma State University (1901) celebrated its 100th birthday in 2001. The university offers courses in the School of Business, School of Education, School of Arts and Sciences, School of Health Sciences, and Graduate School. Southwestern began offering Distance Learning courses in 1972.

Southwestern Oregon Community College

1988 Newmark Avenue	Phone: (541) 888-7339
Coos Bay, OR 97420	Fax: (541) 888-7247

Division(s): Student Services
Web Site(s): http://www.southwestern.cc.or.us
E-mail: jocobock@southwestern.cc.or.us

Class Titles: Writing, Math, Prior Learning Resume, History, Sociology, Psychology, Library Skills, Hospitality/Management, Computer Information Systems, Lifetime Wellness, Personal Health, Nutrition, General Science, Physical Education, Human Development/Family Studies, Human Services.

Teaching Methods: *Computers:* Internet, e-mail.

Credits Granted for: credit by examination (CLEP, ACT-PEP, DANTES, GRE); Challenge.

Admission Requirements: *Undergraduate:* open enrollment; 18 years of age. *Certificate:* contact school.

On-Campus Requirements: some instructors require students to test on campus.

Tuition and Fees: *Undergraduate:* $38/credit. *Application Fee:* $25. *Graduation Fee:* $20. *Other Costs:* $6/credit technical fee; $8 activity fee. *Credit by:* quarter.

Financial Aid: institutional grants and loans, Federal Pell Grant, Federal Work-Study, VA, Oregon resident programs.

Accreditation: Northwest Association of Colleges and Schools.

Description: Southwestern Oregon Community College (1961) is located within 2 miles of the Pacific Ocean in an area of scenic beauty and mild climate. The 153-acre institution lies completely within the city of Coos Bay and is bordered on the east and north by the city of North Bend. Southwestern Oregon Community College was formed in a

May 1961 tax district election. It included Coos and western Douglas Counties. On July 1, 1995, Curry County joined the College District. The district now encompasses 3,648 square miles with a population of more than 92,000. The college is the only public postsecondary institution in the region. Enrollment has grown from 266 to 13,000 students. Staff size has grown from 15 to 70 full-time faculty and from 11 to 275 part-time instructors. Cultural and athletic events at the college attract 20,000 men, women and children each year. Throughout the college's years, a comprehensive instructional program has evolved. Instructional offerings include 2-year transfer programs, one- and two-year professional-technical programs, short-course occupational programs, adult basic education, high school diploma program, and adult enrichment courses.

Spokane Falls Community College

| 3410 West Fort Wright Drive | Phone: (509) 533-3216 |
| Spokane, WA 99224 | Fax: (509) 533-3049 |

Division(s): Distance Education
Web Site(s): http://www.sfcc.spokane.cc.wa.us
E-mail: distancelearning@sfcc.spokane.cc.wa.us

Undergraduate Degree Programs:
Associate of Arts

Teaching Methods: *Computers:* Internet, electronic classroom, e-mail, CD-ROM. *TV:* videotape, cable program. satellite broadcasting, PBS. *Other:* videoconferencing, audioconferencing, audiotapes, fax, correspondence.

Admission Requirements: *Undergraduate:* high school diploma or GED; must take ASSET or COMPASS exam.

On-Campus Requirements: There are a limited number of on-campus meetings for telecourses in the state.

Tuition and Fees: *Undergraduate:* $57.76/credit resident, $744/quarter out-of-state. *Application Fee:* $10. *Technology fee:* $3/credit. *Credit by:* quarter.

Financial Aid: Federal Stafford Loan, Federal PLUS Loan, Federal Pell Grant, Federal Work-Study, VA, Washington resident programs.

Accreditation: Northwest Association of Schools and Colleges.

Description: Located in northwest Spokane on a bluff overlooking the Spokane River, Spokane Falls Community College (1967) occupies the site of Fort Wright, a one-time U.S. Army installation whose history dates back to the late 1800s. The 113-acre campus, notable for its attractive brick buildings and hundreds of evergreen and deciduous trees, draws students from a wide geographic area. SFCC, Spokane

Community College, and the Institute for Extended Learning make up Washington Community College District 17, the second largest community college district in the state. The district serves more than 4,360 students each year, covering a 12,300-square-mile service area in northeastern Washington.

Spoon River College

| 23235 North County Highway 22 | Phone: (309) 647-4645 |
| Canton, IL 61520 | Fax: (309) 649-6235 |

Division(s): Academic Services
Web Site(s): www.spoonrivercollege.net
E-mail: info@src.cc.il.us

Undergraduate Degree Programs:
AA degree available online in cooperation with Western Illinois Educational Consortium.

Certificate Programs:
Associate of Arts
Associate of Applied Sciences
Associate of General Studies
Associate Degree Nursing
Associate of Science

Class Titles: Composition, Health Science, Math, Art, Biology, Education, Religion, Philosophy, English.

Teaching Methods: *Computers:* electronic classroom, CD-ROM, online. *TV:* videotape, satellite broadcasting. *Other:* two-way audio/video.

Credits Granted for: examination (CLEP, department proficiency).

Admission Requirements: *Undergraduate:* high school diploma or GED certificate. *Certificate:* Open admissions.

On-Campus Requirements: 15 credit hours from Spoon River College.

Tuition and Fees: *Undergraduate:* $57/credit. *Credit by:* semester.

Financial Aid: Federal Stafford Loan, Federal Perkins Loan, Federal PLUS Loan, Federal Pell Grant, Federal Work-Study, VA, Illinois resident programs, institutional scholarships and grants.

Accreditation: North Central Association of Colleges and Schools.

Description: Spoon River College (1959) is a multifaceted community college dedicated to providing students with a quality education. Students have a variety of educational goals, and SRC is positioned to meet the needs of all these students by providing the first 2 years of college and preprofessional courses in 30 college majors, 30 career and technical programs, and continuing education. Spoon River serves 4,000 credit students per year in a 1,400-square-mile area including Fulton, McDonough, Mason, and Schuyler counties. SRC is a member of the Western Illinois Educational Consortium and began providing distance learning in 1994. SRC graduates who transfer to other colleges and universities traditionally achieve higher GPAs than students who begin their college careers at other transfer institutions. The college also participates in the Illinois Articulation Initiative, a statewide agreement that allows transfer of the completed Illinois General Education Core Curriculum between participating institutions.

Spring Arbor University

106 E. Main Street	Phone: (800) 968-9103
Spring Arbor, MI 49283	Fax: (517) 750-6602

Division(s): School of Adult Studies
Web Site(s): http://arboronline.org
E-mail: jnemecek@arbor.edu

Undergraduate Degree Programs:
Management and Organizational Development
Family Life Education
Management of Health Services
Nursing
Elementary Education

Graduate Degree Programs:
Master of Arts in Organizational Management

Certificate Programs: Endorsement in Criminal Justice (for the Management and Organizational Development degree).

Class Titles: Contact school or check web site for details.

Teaching Methods: *Computers:* Internet, electronic classroom, e-mail, CD-ROM. *TV:* videotape, satellite broadcasting. *Other:* fax, correspondence, independent study, individual study, learning contracts.

Credits Granted for: experiential learning, portfolio assessment, extrainstitutional learning (PONSI, corporate or professional association seminars/workshops), examination (CLEP, ACT-PEP, DANTES, GRE).

Admission Requirements: *Undergraduate:* 60 semester hours completed for degree completion programs. *Graduate:* GPA of 3.0 in the undergraduate degree, letters of reference.

On-Campus Requirements: None for online. Yes for accelerated degree completion.

Tuition and Fees: *Undergraduate:* $190/credit for online classes; other programs vary in cost. *Graduate:* $240/credit. *Application Fees:* $35. *Software:* free. *Graduation Fee:* $40. *Other Costs:* books. *Credit by:* semester.

Financial Aid: Federal Stafford Loan, Federal Perkins Loan, Federal PLUS Loan, Federal Pell Grant, Federal Work-Study, VA, state programs for residents of Michigan.

Accreditation: North Central Association of Colleges and Schools.

Description: Spring Arbor University (1873) is an evangelical, Christian liberal art university. The university was a pioneer in Distance Education programs for the adult learner and has expanded its offerings to include traditional students. Spring Arbor University is known for the excellence of its programs, many of which are used by colleges and universities throughout the country.

Springfield College in Illinois

1500 N. 5th Street	Phone: (217) 525-1420
Springfield, IL 62704	Fax: (217) 525-1497

Devision(s): Biology, English
Web Site(s): http://www.sci.edu
E-mail: matheis@sci.edu

Undergraduate Degree Programs: Contact school.

Graduate Degree Programs: Contact school.

Class Titles: Biology, English.

Teaching Methods: *Computers:* Internet, real-time chat, electronic classroom, e-mail, LISTSERV. *TV:* videotape, PBS. *Other:* fax, correspondence, independent study, individual study, learning contacts.

Credits Granted for: experiential learning, portfolio assessment, extrainstitutional learning (PONSI, corporate or professional association seminars/workshop), examination (CLEP, ACT-PEP, DANTES, GRE).

Admission Requirements: *Graduate:* entrance exam.

On-Campus Requirements: None.

Tuition and Fees: *Undergraduate:* $270/credit for part-time, $125/credit for audit. *Application Fee:* $15. *Graduation Fee:* $75. *Other Costs:* student service fee, student activity fee. *Credit by:* semester.

Financial Aid: Federal Stafford Loan, Federal Perkins Loan, Federal PLUS Loan, Federal Pell Grant, Federal Work-Study, state programs for residents of Illinois.

Accreditation: North Central Association of Colleges and Schools.

Description: The mission of Springfield College in Illinois (1929) is to provide students the best liberal arts education in the Ursuline tradition of a nurturing faith-based environment.

We prepare students for a life of learning, leadership, and service in a diverse world. The college's philosophy is rooted in 5 centuries of the Ursuline tradition. Springfield College is a junior college and began offering Distance Learning classes in 2000.

Springfield Technical Community College

| One Armory Square | Phone: (413) 755-4089 |
| Springfield, MA 01105 | Fax: (413) 755-6008 |

Division(s): School of Continuing Education
Web Site(s): http://stcc.mass.edu/
E-mail: dbellucci@stcc.mass.edu

Undergraduate Degree Programs:
General Studies
Liberal Arts
Associate's Degree

Class Titles: Contact the school or check web site for details.

Teaching Methods: *Computers:* Internet, real-time chat, electronic classroom, e-mail, CD-ROM, LISTSERV. *Other:* videoconferencing.

Admission Requirements: open enrollment.

Tuition and Fees: *Undergraduate:* Tuition: $62/credit. *Other Costs:* general education fee: $14/credit; Technology Fee: $50/semester, Registration: $25/semester. *Credit by:* semester.

Financial Aid: Federal Stafford Loan, Federal Perkins Loan, Federal PLUS Loan, Federal Pell Grant, Federal Work-Study, VA, state programs for residents of Massachusetts.

Accreditation: New England Association of Schools and Colleges.

Description: Springfield Technical Community College (1967) is the most comprehensive institution in the Massachusetts community college system. STCC offers 39 associate degree programs with 31 options and 26 certificate programs to over 7,000 students in day and evening divisions. The college has a long-standing commitment to provide educational programs of the highest quality. Our major strength lies in our ability to attract faculty and staff committed to the goals and objectives of the college and dedicated to responding to the needs of our students through personalized attention. The college's faculty combine a high degree of theoretical knowledge with practical experience in their field. Our staff is dedicated to making your college experience with us a rewarding and enjoyable experience. STCC began offering Internet courses in 1998. A student doesn't need to come on campus to participate in an Internet course. Our Internet courses provide learning, anywhere, anytime. We work hard to ensure that our Distance courses are top quality and offer content equivalent to our on-campus courses.

State Center Community College District

| PO Box 1910 | Phone: (209) 683-3940 |
| Oakhurst, CA 93644 | Fax: (209) 683-4193 |

Web Site(s): http://www.scccd.com
E-mail: richard.hoffman@scccd.com

Class Titles: Health Science, Cultural Geography, Office Technology (Legal/Medical), Linguistics, Natural Resources, Child Development, Criminal Justice, Accounting, Art Appreciation, English, Psychology, Philosophy, Chemistry, Guidance Studies, Marketing, Computer Science.

Teaching Methods: *Computer:* Internet. *Other:* audioconferencing, videoconferencing, 2-way, interactive, live.

Admission Requirements: *Undergraduate:* open admission.

On-Campus Requirements: None.

Tuition and Fees: *Undergraduate:* $11/unit. *Other Costs:* $11/semester health fee. *Credit by:* semester.

Financial Aid: Federal Stafford Loan, Federal Perkins Loan, Federal PLUS Loan, Federal Pell Grant, Federal Work-Study, VA, California resident programs.

Accreditation: Western Association of Schools and Colleges.

Description: The State Center Community College District (1963) provides day, evening, and Saturday classes. Operated on an 18-week semester system, the college offers a fall and spring term as well as 4/6/8/12-week summer sessions. The district operates 8 satellite locations.

State University of New York at Buffalo

| 128 Parker Hall | Phone: (716) 829-3131 |
| Buffalo, NY 14214-3007 | Fax: (716) 829-2475 |

Division(s): Millard Fillmore College
Web Site(s): http://www.mfc.buffalo.edu
E-mail: mfc-inquire@buffalo.edu

Undergraduate Degree Programs:
Bachelor of Science in Nursing

Graduate Degree Programs:
Master of Science in Engineering in:
    Aerospace/Aeronautical

Civil
Electrical
Mechanical
Industrial
Master of Science in Nursing

Certificate Programs: Computing and Network Management; Civil, Structural, and Environmental Engineering; Electrical and Computer Engineering/Controls, Communications, and Software; Mechanical and Aerospace Engineering—Computer-Aided Design.

Class Titles: Computing, English, Nutrition, Media Study, Psychology.

Teaching Methods: *Computers:* Internet, threaded discussions, sychronous chat, group learning, streaming media, real-time chat, electronic classroom, e-mail, CD-ROM, newsgroup, LISTSERV. *TV:* videotape, cable program, interactive video classrooms, IP video classrooms. *Other:* videoconferencing.

Credits Granted for: experiential learning, portfolio assessment, extrainstitutional learning, examination (CLEP, ACT-PEP, DANTES, GRE), program-specific.

Admission Requirements: *Undergraduate:* variable—see online catalog(s). *Graduate:* BA, variable—see online catalog(s). *Certificate:* variable—see online catalog(s).

On-Campus Requirements: None.

Tuition and Fees: *Undergraduate:* $137/credit in-state, $346/credit out-of-state. *Graduate:* $213/credit in-state, $351/credit out-of-state. *Application Fee:* $30–$35. *Other Costs:* variable. *Credit by:* semester.

Financial Aid: Federal Stafford Loan, Federal Perkins Loan, Federal PLUS Loan, Federal Pell Grant, Federal Work-Study, VA, New York resident programs.

Accreditation: Middle States Association of Colleges and Schools.

Description: The University of Buffalo (1846) is New York's premier public center for graduate and professional education and the state's largest and most comprehensive public university. As the only public member in New York and New England of the prestigious Association of American Universities, the University at Buffalo stands in the first rank among the nation's research-intensive public universities. The university was a private institution from 1846 until 1962; during that time, 11 of its 12 professional schools were founded. After merging with the State University of New York in 1962, the already mature University at Buffalo was a direct beneficiary of New York's aggressive investment in public higher education and grew in size and ambition at a remarkable pace. This private-public heritage has endowed the

University at Buffalo with a special character. The University at Buffalo first began offering distance learning courses in 1994. Currently, courses are delivered through telecourses, synchronous (interactive video), and asynchronous (Web-based). Noncredit, undergraduate, and graduate degree programs will be expanded over the next few years. Millard Fillmore College, the continuing education and evening division of the university, is the point-of-contact for UB's distance learning programs.

State University of New York at New Paltz

75 South Manheim Boulevard, Suite 9 New Paltz, NY 12561-2443	Phone: (845) 257-2900 Fax: (845) 257-2899

Division(s): Continuing and Professional Education
Web Site(s): http://www.newpaltz.edu/continuing_ed/
E-mail: chandlec@newpaltz.edu

Class Titles: English Courses: Practical Grammar, Analysis and Interpretation of Literature, Freshman Comp II, Shakespeare, Creative Writing. History Courses: U.S. History to 1865, Modern Europe 1500–Present. Geography Courses: World Geography. Political Science Courses: Introduction to Law, Comparative Urban Politics. Psychology Courses: Abnormal Psychology, Psychology of Adolescence and Adults, Clinical Psychology, Personality and Psychotherapy. Communication Courses: Electronic Media Management and Economics, Conflict Management Computer Courses: Computers and Applications. Education Courses: Social and Philosophical Foundations of Education, Theoretical Foundations of Reading, Model Teaching. Science Courses: Astronomy. Anthropology Courses: Race, Ethnicity and Inequalities.

Teaching Methods: *Computers:* Internet, real-time chat, electronic classroom, e-mail, CD-ROM, newsgrpup, LISTSERV. *TV:* videotape, cable program, satellite broadcasting, PBS. *Other:* radio broadcast, videoconferencing, audioconferencing, audiographics, audiotapes, fax, correspondence, independent study, individual study, learning contracts.

Credits Granted for: experiential learning, extrainstitutional learning, portfolio assessment, examination (CLEP, ACT-PEP, DANTES, GRE).

Admission Requirements: Entrance requirements differ for undergraduate vs graduate; entrance as a freshman vs entering as a transfer student with credits. Different departments have their own entrance requirements, i.e.: GPA, preliminary entrance exams, and so on.

On-Campus Requirements: For undergraduates, the student must take at least 30 credits at New Paltz campus. May vary according to departmental major requirements. There is no requirement that all courses be "on campus."

May vary according to specific department's major/minor requirements.

Tuition and Fees: *Undergraduate:* $137/credit resident, $346/credit out-of-state. *Graduate:* $213/credit resident, $351/credit out-of-state. *Application Fee:* $30 (undergraduate application). *Software:* $60. *Other Costs:* for full-time students, additional fees total $527, for part-time students, per credit fees include: $85/credit university fee, $5/credit infirmary fee, $6.40/credit student athletic fee, $7.50/credit student activity fee. *Credit by:* semester.

Financial Aid: Federal Stafford Loan, Federal Perkins Loan, Federal PLUS Loan, Federal Pell Grant, Federal Work-Study, VA, New York resident programs.

Accreditation: Middle States Association of Colleges and Schools.

Description: SUNY New Paltz (1828) began in the field of Distance Learning by participating in a Sloan Foundation grant awarded to the State University of New York in 1995. Since that time we have seen our online course offerings expand, especially in the summer sessions. We offer several online courses in a variety of areas. Online instruction affords both instructor and student the opportunity to learn in new ways, and we look forward to increased growth in this area.

State University of New York at Oswego

43 Swetman Hall	**Phone: (315) 341-2270**
Oswego, NY 13126	**Fax: (315) 341-3078**

Division(s): Division of Continuing Education
Web Site(s): http://www.oswego.edu
E-mail: ced@oswego.edu

Class Titles: Advanced Topics in Psychology: Human Factors, Broadcast Journalism, Broadcast Sales, Broadcasting and Cable, Broadcasting Newswriting, Current Issues in Gerontology, Current Topics: Action Research, Current Topics: Including Students with Special Needs, Death and Dying: A Cross-Cultural Perspective, Discrimination in the Workplace: A Legal Perspective, Drug Studies and Student Protection Strategies for Educators and Counselors, E-Commerce, Employment Law, Environmental Science, Evaluation of Instruction, Foundations of Communication, History of Eastern Asia, China, and Japan, Inst. Improvement through Student Assessment, International Business, Introduction to Labor Economics, Introduction to Theater, Introduction to Vocational-Technical Education, Laboratory Organization and Management, Leadership Skills for Managers, Mass Media and the Law, Materials Management, Media and Society, Media Economics, Money and Banking, Multimedia and the Internet for Educators, New Communications and Information Technologies, Principles of Macroeconomics, Principles of Microeconomics, Public Sector Accounting, Seminar in Local (Regional) and Social History, Serving Special Needs Learners, Sociology of Aging, Survey of Public Relations, Telecommunications, The Eastern Religious Tradition, The Fundamentals of Marketing, Tools for Computing, Vocational Curriculum Development, What Managers Do.

Teaching Methods: *Computers:* Internet, electronic classroom, e-mail. *Other:* videoconferencing, independent study, individual study, learning contracts.

Credits Granted for: experiential learning, portfolio assessment, extrainstitutional learning, examination (CLEP, ACT-PEP, GRE).

Admission Requirements: *Undergraduate:* high school diploma. *Graduate:* acceptance by Dean of Graduate Studies. *Certificate:* acceptance by Program Coordinator.

On-Campus Requirements: Must have a minimum of 30 hours of State University of New York, Oswego credit; 122 hours total credit required for undergraduate degree.

Tuition and Fees: *Undergraduate:* $137/credit. *Graduate:* $213/credit. *Application Fee:* $30. *Other Costs:* $273 fee/term undergraduate, $191 graduate. *Credit by:* semester.

Financial Aid: Federal Stafford Loan, Federal Perkins Loan, Federal PLUS Loan, Federal Pell Grant, Federal Work-Study, VA, New York resident programs.

Accreditation: Middle States Association of Colleges and Schools.

Description: While maintaining its high standards as a former teachers' college, the State University of New York, College at Oswego (1861) broadened its academic perspective in 1962 when it became one of the colleges of arts and science in the State University system. Collectively these colleges are now called the University Colleges of the State University of New York. SUNY Oswego first offered distance learning courses over cable TV in 1995, adding ISDN-based videoconferencing in 1996 and Internet courses in 1997. Oswego's bachelor of arts degree (BA) is now available completely online to holders of 2-year degrees in a variety of electronic media fields.

State University of New York at Stony Brook

N 215 SBS Building	**Phone: (631) 632-7896**
Stony Brook, NY 11794-4310	**Fax: (631) 632-7872**

Division(s): Center for Distance Learning
Web Site(s): http://www.sunysb.edu/spd/CDL.htm
E-mail: eep@notes.cc.sunysb.edu

Graduate Degree Programs:
Master of Arts in Liberal Studies

Class Titles: Contact school or check web site for details.

Teaching Methods: *Computers:* Internet, electronic classroom, e-mail.

Admission Requirements: bachelor's degree, 2.75 GPA.

On-Campus Requirements: None.

Tuition and Fees: $213/credit (in-state). *Application Fee:* $50. *Software:* $85/semester for licensing and hosting. *Other Costs:* miscellaneous university fees totaling $38. *Credit by:* semester.

Financial Aid: Contact school.

Accreditation: Middle States Association of Colleges and Schools.

Description: Stony Brook University (1967) is a Type I Research University and is part of the State University of New York system. Its School of Professional Development (SPD) offers part-time graduate and noncredit courses for busy professionals. SPD has been offering online courses since 1996 and currently offers more than 100 sections per year.

State University of New York College at Brockport

350 New Campus Drive	Phone: (716) 395-5724
Brockport, NY 14420	Fax: (716) 395-5542

Division(s): Special Sessions and Programs
Web Site(s): http://www.brockport.edu
E-mail: sln@brockport.edu or telecourses@brockport.edu

Undergraduate Degree Programs: Contact school.

Graduate Degree Programs: Contact school.

Class Titles: Public Administration, Honors, Computational Science, Business, Health Science.

Teaching Methods: *Computers:* Internet, electronic classroom, e-mail, CD-ROM, LISTSERV. *TV:* videotape, cable program, satellite broadcasting, PBS.

Admission Requirements: *Undergraduate: Freshman Admissions:* freshman admission is competitive, emphasis is placed on the rigor of the high school academic program, high school average, regents exam scores, SAT or ACT scores, and class rank. Other information that may be considered includes letters of recommendation, teacher evaluations, essays, and school/community activities. Applicants should have a B average in a solid college preparatory program, a combined SAT score of at least 1,000, or a composite

ACT of 21, and rank in the top half of their graduating class. *Transfer Admissions:* a minimum GPA of 2.25 is required for consideration of admission, the mean GPA for transfer applicants is 3.0. Official transcripts from all colleges attended are required. Additionally, although not required for admission, official high school transcripts or GED score reports are required prior to enrollment for financial aid purposes. Criminal Justice, elementary and secondary education, nursing, and social work require a minimum GPA of 2.5. *Graduate:* baccalaureate degree from a regionally accredited institution. Other requirements vary by program.

On-Campus Requirements: None.

Tuition and Fees: *Undergraduate:* $137/credit. *Graduate:* $213/credit. *Other Costs:* fees vary. *Credit by:* semester.

Financial Aid: Federal Stafford Loan, Federal Perkins Loan, Federal Pell Grant, Federal Work-Study, VA, state programs for residents of New York State.

Accreditation: Middle States Association of Colleges and Schools.

Description: At SUNY Brockport (1835), we have identified student success as our primary mission, and we work together with students to develop their greatest abilities in their chosen field. More than 8,500 students enrolled each year find peers eager to engage in discussion of the new ideas and new challenges they are exploring. With access to the latest in computing technology, students can extend the horizons of such discussions to include disciplinary colleagues around the world. Working with our world-class faculty, students learn to apply their expanded knowledge base and research on questions that intrigue them.

State University of New York, College at Cortland

P.O. Box 2000	Phone: (607) 753-5942
Cortland, NY 13045	Fax: (607) 753-5985

Division(s): Information Resources
Web Site(s): http://www.cortland.edu/ir/dlupdate.htm
E-mail: registrar@em.cortland.edu

Undergraduate Degree Programs: Contact school.

Graduate Degree Programs: Contact school.

Certificate Programs: Contact school.

Class Titles: School Business Management, Education Law, School Curriculum, School Personnel, Public School Finance, Foundations, Supervision, School Principal, Administration of Special Education, Elementary School Social Studies, Discipline and Classroom Behavior, Reading Teaching and

Reading Program, Health Care Ethics, Beginning Arabic I, Intermediate Arabic I, Music in the U.S., African American Music, History and Philosophy of Physical Education and Sports, Social and Psychological Aspects of Physical Activity, Utopias, History of Modern Philosophy, Knowledge and Reality, Topics—Environmental Ethics, Utopias, Age of Analysis, Individual Philosophers—Berkeley and Locke, Hume and Kant, Self, Mind and Soul, Puzzle of Free Will, Media and Politics, Middle East Politics, Health Policy, Current Issues: Welfare, Discrimination Law, The Community, Gerontology for Education, Academic Writing II, Technology in Administration, Seminar in Educational Administration, Planning, Introduction to Language Study, Introduction to Writing Fiction, Online Creative Writing, Online Fiction Writing, Grammar for Teachers, Social and Psychological Aspects of Physical Activity, La Practique de L'écriture, Civilization on the Internet, Russian Studies: American-Russian Dialog, Social Psychological Aspects of Physical Education, Behavior in Sport, History of Sport and Physical Education, Graduate Readings in Physical Education, Adv. Educational Psychology, Administration of Therapeutic Recreation.

Teaching Methods: *Computers:* Internet, electronic classroom, e-mail, CD-ROM. *TV:* videotape.

Credit Granted for: examination (CLEP).

Admission Requirements: *Undergraduate:* see http://www. cortland.edu/admissions/adm.html or institution catalog. *Graduate:* see http://www.cortland.edu/admissions/adm.html or institution catalog. *Postgraduate:* see http://www. cortland.edu/admissions/adm.html or institution catalog. *Certificate:* see http://www.cortland.edu/admissions/adm. html or institution catalog.

Tuition and Fees: *Undergraduate:* $137/credit. *Graduate:* $213/credit. *Application Fee:* $50. *Other Costs:* approximately $170. *Credit by:* semester.

Financial Aid: Federal Stafford Loan, Federal Perkins Loan, Federal PLUS Loan, Federal Pell Grant, Federal Work-Study.

Accreditation: Middle States Association of Colleges and Secondary Schools.

Description: SUNY/Cortland (1868) offers programs leading to the award of bachelor's and master's degrees in both the arts and sciences, and in professional studies. SUNY/Cortland is a moderate-sized institution, and is a charter member of the State University System.

State University of New York College at Old Westbury

Box 210 **Phone: (516) 876-3000**
Old Westbury, NY 11568-0210

Division(s): Academic Affairs
Web Site(s): http://www.oldwestbury.edu
E-mail: bevere@oldwestbury.edu

Undergraduate Degree Programs: Contact school.

Certificate Programs: Contact school.

Class Titles: Management and Society, World History II: Western Civilization, Islamic Cultures, Sociology of Communications and Media. Additional classes in development.

Teaching Methods: *Computers:* Internet, e-mail, CD-ROM.

Credits Granted for: experiential learning, portfolio assessment, extrainstitutional learning (PONSI), examination (CLEP, ACT-PEP, DANTES, GRE).

Admission Requirements: *Undergraduate:* 80 high school average and a combined score of 1,000 on SATs or 22 on ACTs for freshmen. *Transfer Students Admissions:* GPA of at least 2.0 (higher for teacher education and school of business) and an official college transcript (if transferring less than 24 credits, high school transcript also required).

On-Campus Requirements: None.

Tuition and Fees: *Undergraduate:* FT students (12 credits or more): $1,700/semester for New York residents/ $4,150/semester for out-of-state residents. PT students (less than 12 credits): $137/credit for New York residents/ $346/credit for out-of-state residents. *Application Fee:* $30. *Technology Fee:* $50/semester for FT students/$4/credit for PT students. *Other Costs: College Fee:* $12.50/semester for FT students/$.85/credit for PT students. *Student Government Activity Fee:* $60/semester for FT students/$40/semester for PT students. *Intercollegiate Athletic Fee:* $100/semester for FT students/$50/semester for PT students. *Health Service Fee:* $70/semester for FT students/$6/credit for PT students. *Credit by:* semester.

Financial Aid: Grants: Federal Pell, Federal Supplemental Educational Opportunity Grant, Federal College Work Study Program, Tuition Assistance Program, Aid for Part-Time Study, Educational Opportunity Program. Loans: Federal Perkins Loan, Federal Stafford Loan (Subsidized and/or unsubsidized), Federal Parent Loan for Undergraduate Students (PLUS) Scholarships: Several scholarships are available to new and continuing students.

Accreditation: Middle States Association of Colleges and Schools.

Description: Founded in 1965 by the State University of New York Board of Trustees, the College at Old Westbury began in 1968 at Planting Fields, the former Coe Estate and arboretum located in Oyster Bay, New York. In 1971 the college moved to its present Old Westbury site—the estate formerly owned by philanthropist F. Ambrose Clark. Located on 605 acres on Long Island's historic North Shore, the college offers a peaceful learning environment, just 22 miles from midtown Manhattan and a 20-minute drive from Jones Beach. SUNY College at Old Westbury's 13 academic departments offer a total of 40 registered degree programs, awarding the Bachelor of Arts, Bachelor of Science, and Bachelor of Professional Studies degrees, as well as a certificate program in Spanish. The college is the only campus of SUNY in the New York metropolitan area offering a state-accredited Bachelor's degree in Accounting. SUNY College at Old Westbury began offering Distance Learning courses through the SUNY Learning Network in 1999. Courses are offered via the Internet and students participate by accessing the course web site at times of their own choosing periodically each week. The college is planning to expand its offering of Distance Learning courses.

State University of New York College of Technology at Canton

FH 100, SUNY Canton,	
24 Cornell Drive (credit)	**Phone: (315) 386-7042 (credit),**
NN105, SUNY Canton,	**(315) 386-7102 (noncredit)**
34 Cornell Drive (noncredit)	**Fax: (315) 379-3819 (credit),**
Canton, NY 13617	**(315) 386-7928 (noncredit)**

Division(s): Registrar's Office (credit), Center for Extended Studies (noncredit)
Web Site(s): http://canton.edu
E-mail: porter@canton.edu (credit), petryd@canton.edu (noncredit)

Undergraduate Degree Programs:
Accounting
Air Conditioning Engineering Technology
Automotive
Business Administration
Business Economics
Civil Engineering Technology
Computer Information Systems
Construction Engineering Technology
Construction Technology Management
Criminal Investigation
Criminal Justice
Early Childhood
Electrical Engineering Technology
Engineering Science
Human Services
Individual Studies
Liberal Arts and Sciences
Manufacturing Technology
Mechanical Engineering Technology
Medical Laboratory Technology
Mortuary Science
Nursing
Occupation Therapy Assistant
Physical Therapy Assistant
Recreational Leadership
Veterinary Science Technology
Wireless Communications
Apprentice Training Industrial Trades

Certificate Programs: Paralegal, MSCE Certification, various Web Design certificates.

Class Titles: *credit:* various Earth Sciences, Veterinary Technology, other online courses; *noncredit:* Computer skills (Windows, Word, Excel, etc.), Internet skills training (Web Pages, Web Graphics, JavaScript, etc.), SAT/ACT Preparation, GRE preparation, LSAT preparation, small-business courses, basic supervision courses, project management, customer service, total quality, business applications, production/inventory management, logistics, manufacturing, purchasing; professional education: professional computer skills (MSCE certification, etc.), accredited continuing education for: physicians, dentists, pharmacists, other medical professions, real estate, insurance, home inspection, funeral directors.

Teaching Methods: *Computers:* Internet, real-time chat, electronic classroom, e-mail. *TV:* videotape, cable program, satellite broadcasting. *Other:* videoconferencing, audioconferencing, audiographics, independent study, correspondence.

Admission Requirements: *Undergraduate:* high school graduate. Holders of General Equivalency Diplomas will be required to take a placement exam. Additional criteria for nontraditional students: work experience, special skills, or unusual circumstances. SAT/ACT not required. *Certificate:* same as undergraduate requirements.

On-Campus Requirements: 15 credit hours residency for degree. No requirements for noncredit courses.

Tuition and Fees: *Undergraduate:* $99 to $135/credit. *Other Costs:* $19.70/credit hour for degree students. *Credit by:* semester.

Financial Aid: Federal Stafford Loan, Federal Perkins Loan, Federal PLUS Loan, Federal Pell Grant, Federal Work-Study, VA, New York resident programs; financial aid is not available for noncredit programs.

Accreditation: Middle States Association of Colleges and Schools, Technology Accreditation Commission of the

Accreditation Board for Engineering and Technology, American Board of Funeral Service Education, American Veterinary Medicine Association, National Accrediting Agency for Clinical Laboratory Services, Nation League of Nursing, Commission on Accreditation in Physical Therapy Education.

Description: SUNY Canton (1906) is one of the 64 campuses that comprise the State University of New York. SUNY Canton currently offers over 150 Distance Education courses. Our offerings include everything from basic computer skills courses to certification courses for computer professionals, and personal enrichment courses through to continuing education for professionals (insurance, real estate salespersons and brokers, home inspectors, physicians, dentists, pharmacists, and other medical professionals).

State University of New York Downstate Medical Center

| 450 Clarkson Avenue | Phone: (718) 270-2446 |
| Brooklyn, NY 11203 | Fax: (718) 270-7592 |

Web Site(s): http://www.downstate.edu
E-mail: hflax@downstate.edu

Undergraduate Degree Programs: Contact school.

Graduate Degree Programs:
Midwifery
Nursing

Certificate Programs: Midwifery.

Class Titles: Contact school or check web site for details.

Teaching Methods: *Computers:* Internet, real-time chat, electronic classroom, e-mail, CD-ROM, newsgroup, LISTSERV. *TV:* videotape, cable program, satellite broadcasting. *Other:* videoconferencing, audioconferencing, audiotapes, fax, correspondence, independent study, individual study, learning contracts.

Credits Granted for: portfolio assessment, examination (CLEP, ACT-PEP, DANTES, GRE).

Admission Requirements: Contact school.

On-Campus Requirements: Course orientation sessions.

Tuition and Fees: *Undergraduate:* $137/credit. *Graduate:* $213/credit. *Application Fees:* $30 (undergraduate); $35 (graduate). *Software:* $100 (Student Technology Fee). *Graduation Fee:* $40. *Other Costs:* see College Bulletin. *Credit by:* semester.

Financial Aid: Federal Stafford Loan, Federal Perkins Loan, Federal PLUS Loan, Federal Pell Grant, Federal Work-Study, VA, state programs for residents of New York.

Accreditation: Middle States Association of Colleges and Secondary Schools and respective professional accrediting bodies.

Description: At SUNY Downstate Medical Center, we trace our roots back to 1860, when a school of medicine was founded at the Long Island College Hospital. The new college's faculty revolutionized medical education in this country by bringing the teaching of medicine to the hospital bedside, thus rejecting the idea that physicians should be trained exclusively in university lecture halls. Today, SUNY Downstate is one of the nation's leading urban medical centers comprising a College of Medicine, College of Health Related Professions, College of Nursing, School of Graduate Studies, and University Hospital of Brooklyn. The quality of our education, research, and patient care programs was confirmed with the awarding of the Nobel Prize in Medicine to Dr. Robert Furchgott, a member of our School of Graduate Studies faculty since 1956. More physicians who practice medicine in New York City received their training at our College of Medicine than at any other medical center in the country. Nationally, our medical school ranks seventh in the number of graduates who are now engaged in academic medicine. Our College of Health Related Professions and College of Nursing also play a unique role in the borough and the city. We have the oldest midwifery program in the country, and we recently made history again by establishing a joint program between the 2 colleges that train midwives who are not nurses. The College of Nursing is particularly proud of its role in educating minority students. SUNY Downstate Medical Center enters the new century with a renewed dedication to serving the people of Brooklyn through its three-fold mission of education, research, and patient care.

State University of New York Institute of Technology at Utica/Rome

| PO Box 3050 | Phone: (315) 792-7500 |
| Utica, NY 13504 | Fax: (315) 792-7837 |

Division(s): Schools of Management/School of Arts and Sciences/School of Nursing/School of ISET
Web Site(s): http://www.sunyit.edu
E-mail: admissions@sunyit.edu

Graduate Degree Programs:
Master of Science in Accountancy
Master of Science in Health Sciences Administration

Class Titles: Health Services Management, Communications, Accounting, Management, Information Systems, Nursing, Human Resource Management, Business, Finance, Computer Science, Tax, Health Information Management, Advanced Technology.

Teaching Methods: *Computers:* Internet, electronic classroom (in progress), e-mail, newsgroup, LISTSERV. *Other:* fax, correspondence, independent study, individual study, learning contracts.

Credits Granted for: extrainstitutional learning, examination (CLEP).

Admission Requirements: *Undergraduate:* minimum 2.5 GPA, offer only junior and senior level courses. *Graduate:* 3.0+ GPA undergraduate, GMAT exam, completed application (students without an undergraduate degree in Business, Accounting for MS Accountancy should call for more information).

On-Campus Requirements: None for Accountancy, 1–3 days for Health Services Administration.

Tuition and Fees: *Undergraduate:* New York State: $137/credit, out-of-state: $346/credit. *Graduate:* New York State: $213/credit, out-of-state: $351/credit. *Application Fee:* $30 undergraduate, $50 graduate. *Other Costs:* miscellaneous fees. *Credit by:* semester.

Financial Aid: Federal Stafford Loan, Federal Perkins Loan, Federal PLUS Loan, Federal Pell Grant, Federal Work-Study, VA, New York resident programs.

Accreditation: Middle States Association of Colleges and Schools.

Description: SUNY Institute of Technology at Utica/Rome (1966) has the best of both worlds: the intimacy, personalized instruction, and hands-on access to state-of-the-art equipment of a small college, and the many advantages of belonging to the world's largest public system of higher education—the State University of New York. In an increasingly complex world of technological advancement, SUNY Utica/Rome is an acknowledged leader in the realm of technical communication and access to the World Wide Web. The Institute of Technology is one of *Yahoo! Internet Life* magazine's "100 Most Wired Campuses," boasting a higher rating than such institutions as Syracuse, Georgetown, Clemson, and Baylor. In addition to its technological excellence, SUNY Utica/Rome's broad curriculum also emphasizes the humanities, communications, math, and science. Historically an all-transfer and graduate institution, SUNY Utica/Rome will begin admission of freshmen in select degree programs in fall 2003. Located on a beautifully landscaped 800-acre campus, all buildings are contemporary in design. Construction of a $14 million library complex is underway, with completion scheduled for fall 2002. Activities abound on campus, with student government, special interest clubs, academic organizations, and performing arts groups.

State University of West Georgia

Honors House, 1600 Maple Street　　　Phone: (770) 836-4647
Carrollton, GA 30118　　　　　　　　　Fax: (770) 836-4666

Division(s): Distance Education Center
Web Site(s): http://www.westga.edu/~distance
E-mail: distance@westga.edu

Certificate Programs: Distance Education

Class Titles: Graduate courses in Research, Media, Technology, English to Speakers of Other Languages, Public Administration, Business Administration, Nursing, Counseling/Educational Psychology.

Teaching Methods: *Computers:* Internet, real-time chat, electronic classroom, e-mail, CD-ROM, LISTSERV. *TV:* videotape. *Other:* videoconferencing.

Credits Granted for: examination (CLEP, ACT-PEP, DANTES, GRE).

Admission Requirements: *Undergraduate:* SAT or ACT, high school GPA, college preparatory curriculum. *Graduate:* bachelor's degree, appropriate admission test, 3 letters of recommendation. *Certificate:* see master's degree; see graduate.

On-Campus Requirements: varies among courses.

Tuition and Fees: *Undergraduate:* $840/12 hours or more if resident; if nonresident, add tuition of $2,231. *Graduate:* $617/12 hours or more if resident; if nonresident, add tuition of $1,640. *Doctoral:* see graduate. *Application Fee:* $15. *Other Costs:* $60 undergraduate, $40 graduate health fee; $135 undergraduate, $90 graduate athletic fee; $9 undergraduate, $6 graduate transportation fee. *Credit by:* semester.

Financial Aid: Federal Stafford Loan, Federal Perkins Loan, Federal PLUS Loan, Federal Pell Grant, Federal Work-Study, VA, Georgia resident programs

Accreditation: National Council for Accreditation of Teacher Education, American Assembly of Collegiate Schools of Business, National League for Nursing, National Association of Schools of Music, National Association of Schools of Public Affairs and Administration, American Chemical Society Consortium for Diversified Psychology Programs.

Description: The State University of West Georgia (1933) originated as the 4th District Agricultural and Mechanical School. In 1956, the institution was authorized to confer the BS degree in Education, making it a 4-year, senior college in the University System of Georgia. During the following years, the college became one of the fastest-growing institutions of higher learning in the South, maturing into a university in 1996. The Distance Learning program began in 1995 following the passing of the Distance Learning and Telemedicine Act of 1992 by the Georgia legislature.

Stephens College

1200 East Broadway
Columbia, MO 65215

Phone: (800) 388-7579
(573) 876-7225
Fax: (573) 876-7237

Division(s): School of Graduate and Continuing Education
Web Site(s): http://www.stephens.edu/gce
E-mail: sce@stephens.edu

Undergraduate Degree Programs:
Bachelor of Arts in:
    Business Administration
    English
    Law Philosophy and Rhetoric (pre-law)
    Psychology
Bachelor of Science in:
    Early Childhood Education
    Elementary Education
    Health Care (and second area)
    Health Science (and second area)
    Health Information Management

Graduate Degree Programs:
Master of Business Administration with emphasis in:
    Management
    Entrepreneurial Studies
    Clinical Information Systems Management

Certificate Programs: Health Information Administration, Elementary Education, Early Childhood Education.

Teaching Methods: *Computers:* Internet, e-mail, CD-ROM, newsgroup, LISTSERV. *Other:* fax, correspondence, independent study, individual study, learning contracts.

Credits Granted for: experiential learning, portfolio assessment, extrainstitutional learning, examination (CLEP, ACT-PEP, DANTES, GRE).

Admission Requirements: *Undergraduate:* age 23, high school diploma or GED, personal essay, college transcripts, Liberal Studies Seminar. *Graduate:* accredited bachelor's degree, 3.0 GPA, GMAT, 3 letters of recommendation, essay, interview. *Certificate:* bachelor's degree, personal essay, college transcripts.

On-Campus Requirements: Liberal Studies Seminar for undergraduate students, offered in 7-day or double-weekend format, worth 3.0 Humanities credits.

Tuition and Fees: *Undergraduate:* $670/course, $515/course Missouri residents. *Graduate:* $237/credit. *Application Fee:* $50 undergraduate, $25 graduate. *Other Costs:* Internet/e-mail access, $5 transcript requests. *Credit by:* semester.

Financial Aid: Federal Stafford Loan, Federal Perkins Loan, Federal PLUS Loan, Federal Pell Grant, Federal Work-Study, VA, Missouri resident programs.

Accreditation: North Central Association of Colleges and Schools.

Description: Stephens College began offering traditional courses in 1833. Its School of Graduate and Continuing Education offers programs designed to address the content and logistics needs of nontraditional students. The staff is attuned to the complications of maintaining jobs, handling family responsibilities, and completing degrees, because many teachers have been nontraditional students themselves. With a curriculum that emphasizes concerns of women and ethnic minorities, the program also strives to promote and enhance personal and professional development, personal empowerment, and leadership skills.

Strayer University

8382F Terminal Road
Lorton, VA 22099

Phone: (703) 339-5136
(703) 339-1850
Fax: (703) 339-1852

Division(s): Strayer Online
Web Site(s): http://www.strayer.edu/online
E-mail: dk@strayer.edu

Undergraduate Degree Programs:
Associate of Arts in:
    Acquisition and Contract Management
    Accounting
    Business Administration
    Computer Information Systems
    Computer Networking
    Economics
    Marketing
    General Studies
Bachelor of Science in:
    Computer Networking
    International Business
    Accounting
    Business Administration
    Computer Information Systems
    Economics

Graduate Degree Programs:
Master of Science in:
    Business Administration
    Information Systems
    Professional Accounting
    Computer Technology

Certificate Programs: Computer Information Systems Diploma.

Class Titles: 200 courses, including Business, Organizational Behavior, Management, International Business Environment, Business Ethics, Human Resource Management, Business Policy, Financial Management, Business Law, Computer

Information Systems, Microcomputer Applications in Business, Computer Programming Design, Using/ Programming Access, UNIX Operating System, Networking, Data Communication Technologies, Computer Architectures, Distributed Communication Systems, Computer Operating Systems, Systems Analysis/Design, Software Engineering, Database Management Systems, Management Information Systems, Accounting, Managerial Accounting.

Teaching Methods: *Computers:* Internet, real-time chat, electronic classroom. *Other:* None.

Credits Granted for: experiential learning, portfolio assessment, extrainstitutional learning, examination (CLEP, ACT-PEP, DANTES, GRE).

Admission Requirements: *Undergraduate:* high school graduate or GED, placement tests. *Graduate:* accredited bachelor's degree. *Certificate:* see undergraduate.

On-Campus Requirements: None.

Tuition and Fees: *Undergraduate:* $220.50/credit full-time, $231/credit part-time. *Graduate:* $294/credit. *Credit by:* quarter (4.5 credits/course).

Financial Aid: Federal Stafford Loan, Federal Perkins Loan, Federal PLUS Loan, Federal Pell Grant, Federal Work-Study, VA, Strayer University Education Loan Program.

Accreditation: Middle States Association of Colleges and Universities.

Description: Strayer University, founded in 1892, offers undergraduate and graduate degree programs to 12,000 students at 17 campuses in Washington, DC, Virginia, and Maryland. Strayer also provides distance learning through Internet online courses. The university attracts working students by offering computer and business programs, convenient campus locations, online courses, and an experienced teaching faculty. A pilot program for online courses (Strayer Online) began in 1996, and a year later all programs received online approval. Online courses are available as both synchronous and asynchronous.

Suffolk County Community College

533 College Road   Phone: (631) 451-4656
Selden, NY 11784   Fax: (631) 451-4681

Division(s): Office of Academic Affairs/Central Administration
Web Site(s): http://www.sunysuffolk.edu
E-mail: cosciad@sunysuffolk.edu

Class Titles: English, History, Business, Psychology, Health/Nutrition, Geology, Sociology, Science, Fine Arts, Women's Studies.

Teaching Methods: *Computers:* Internet, electronic classroom. *TV:* videotape, cable program, PBS. *Other:* independent study, contract learning.

Credits Granted for: experiential learning, portfolio assessment, examination (CLEP, ACT-PEP, DANTES, GRE).

Admission Requirements: *Undergraduate:* may be prerequisites for upper-level courses. *Certificate:* may be prerequisites for upper-level courses.

On-Campus Requirements: for telecourses, 5 required on-campus sessions (7 for lab courses).

Tuition and Fees: *Undergraduate:* $99/credit for county residents; $196/credit for nonresidents. *Application Fee:* $30. *Other Costs:* $40 fee. *Credit by:* semester.

Financial Aid: Federal Stafford Loan, Federal Pell Grant, Federal Work-Study, VA, New York resident programs.

Accreditation: Middle States Association of Colleges and Schools.

Description: Suffolk County Community College (1959) is a 3-campus community college of more than 20,000 students located in Suffolk County, Long Island, New York. The college has been offering telecourses via cable TV or through video-cassette loans for more than 10 years. It is presently offering its first 40 Web-based courses. It will offer its first 20 synchronous courses among the 3 campuses soon.

Suffolk University

8 Ashburton Place, S-1142   Phone: (617) 573-8334
Boston, MA 02108-2770   Fax: (617) 723-0139

Division(s): Online Programs
Web Site(s): http://www.suffolkemba.org/
E-mail: cmaher@suffolk.edu (or) suffolkemba@suffolk.edu

Undergraduate Degree Programs: Contact school.

Graduate Degree Programs:
Masters in Business Administration

Certificate Programs: Advanced Professionals Certificate (APC).

Class Titles: Contact school or check web site for details.

Teaching Methods: *Computers:* Internet, real-time chat, electronic classroom, e-mail, CD-ROM, document sharing, threaded discussions, webliography and webcasting. *Other:* videoconferencing, audioconferencing, audiographics, fax, correspondence, independent study, individual study.

Admission Requirements: *Undergraduate:* placement testing, transfer credits, SAT and TOEFL *Graduate:* GMAT, TOEFL, undergraduate degree. *Certificate:* advanced degree requirement for APC (Advanced Professional Certificate).

On-Campus Requirements: None.

Tuition and Fees: *Undergraduate:* $437/credit hour. *Graduate:* $649/credit hour. *Application Fee:* $50. *Software:* $120 technology fee/3-credit course. *Other Costs:* $100 for admission acceptance fee. *Credit by:* semester.

Financial Aid: Federal Stafford Loan, Federal Perkins Loan, Federal PLUS Loan, Federal Pell Grant, Federal Supplemental Educational Opportunity Grant, Federal Work-Study, VA, state programs for residents of Massachusetts. Additionally, fellowships, scholarships and grant monies may be awarded to qualified candidates.

Accreditation: AACSB International (The Association to Advance Collegiate Schools of Business), The New England Association of Schools and Colleges, and The National Association of Schools of Public Affairs and Administration.

Description: New England's first online MBA, the eMBA program at Suffolk University (1906) was founded with a mission to provide a quality education at an affordable cost for students of all ages and backgrounds. The eMBA Program at Suffolk University continues the long-standing tradition of opening doors to education for a new group of people who could not otherwise take advantage of graduate study in the past. Suffolk's online format allows students to take classes anytime, anywhere, and provides many career-oriented professionals with busy lives the opportunity to earn a quality, accredited MBA. The integrated MBA program will prepare you for the challenges you will face as a business leader of the 21st century in a convenient and flexible learning environment. The eMBA Program is based on the principles of access, excellence, and innovation. It is the result of research and experience of a dedicated faculty team of curriculum and content specialists at Suffolk University and technology experts at eCollege. The online eMBA program captures the full value of the Suffolk MBA by providing an integrated core, global perspective, and real-life business applications. The online MBA maintains the same standards demanded from on-campus students. Full-time faculty members who are over 93% Ph.D.-qualified—one of the highest ratios in the country—teach Suffolk's online eMBA program.

Sul Ross State University

Alpine, TX 79832	Phone: (915) 837-8368
	Fax: (915) 837-8382

Division(s): School of Arts and Sciences
Web Site(s): http://www.sulross.edu
E-mail: bglasrud@sulross.edu
rcullins@sulross.edu

Class Titles: Contact school.

Teaching Methods: *Computers:* Internet, electronic classroom, e-mail. *TV:* videotape. *Other:* audioconferencing, videoconferencing, fax, independent study, individual study.

Credits Granted for: portfolio assessment, examination (CLEP, ACT-PEP, DANTES, GRE).

Admission Requirements: *Undergraduate:* contact school.

On-Campus Requirements: None.

Tuition and Fees: *Undergraduate:* $248/3-credit course. *Graduate:* same as undergraduate. *Credit by:* semester.

Financial Aid: Federal Stafford Loan, Federal Perkins Loan, Federal PLUS Loan, Federal Pell Grant, Federal Work-Study, VA, Texas resident programs.

Accreditation: Southern Association of Colleges and Schools.

Description: Sul Ross State University (1917) is a comprehensive regional institution of higher education in west Texas. SRSU is a Hispanic-serving institution committed to excellence in teaching, to a "student centered" philosophy, and to serving the needs of the broad community. Set in the midst of a vast, sparsely populated region, the university offers distance learning courses to serve the needs of the remote peoples of this area.

Sullivan County Community College

122 College Road	Phone: (845) 434-5750 × 4355
Loch Sheldrake, NY 12759-5151	Fax: (845) 434-4806

Division(s): Vice President for Academic and Student Affairs
Web Site(s): http://www.sullivan.suny.edu
E-mail: jwatson@sullivan.suny.edu

Undergraduate Degree Programs:
Associate in:
   Arts
   Science
   Applied Science
   Occupational Studies

Certificate Programs: Accounting Clerk, Computer Operator, Early Childhood, Food Service, Office Technology/Word Processing.

Class Titles: Contact school or check web site for details.

Teaching Methods: *Computers:* Internet, real-time chat, electronic classroom, e-mail, CD-ROM, newsgroup, LISTSERV. *TV:* videotape, cable program, satellite broadcasting, PBS. *Other:* radio broadcast, videoconferencing, audioconferencing, audiographics, audiotapes, fax, correspondence, independent study, individual study, learning contracts.

Credits Granted for: CLEP, College Proficiency Exam of SUNY, Advanced Placement Program (given senior year of high school), college-constructed exams (subject exams).

Admission Requirements: *Undergraduate:* high school graduate, GED, passing an Ability to Benefit exam. *Certificate:* high school graduate, GED, passing an Ability to Benefit exam.

On-Campus Requirements: half of the program of study must be completed at SCCC.

Tuition and Fees: *Undergraduate:* Sullivan County and other New York State residents with a Certificate of Residence $2,500; New York State residents without a valid Certificate of Residence $3,700; out-of-state residents $3,700. *Application Fees:* SUNY Application $30, SCCC none. *Graduation Fee:* $25. *Other Costs:* books and supplies, fees, room and board, personal expenses. *Credit by:* semester.

Financial Aid: Federal Stafford Loan, Federal Perkins Loan, Federal PLUS Loan, Federal Pell Grant, Federal Work-Study, VA, state programs for residents of New York State.

Accreditation: Middle State Commission on Higher Education.

Description: Founded in 1963, SCCC offers a cosmopolitan education in a rural setting located in the Catskill Mountains of New York.

Sussex County Community College

1 College Hill	Phone: (973) 300-2136
Newton, NJ 07860	Fax: (973) 300-2277

Division(s): Academic Affairs
Web Site(s): http://www.Sussex.cc.nj.us
E-mail: Thomasi@Sussex.cc.nj.us

Undergraduate Degree Programs:
Associate of Arts
Associate of Science

Certificate Programs: Legal Assistant.

Teaching Methods: *Computers:* Internet, e-mail. *TV:* videotape, cable program. *Other:* fax, correspondence, independent study, individual study, learning contracts.

Credits Granted for: portfolio assessment, examination (CLEP, ACT-PEP, DANTES, GRE).

Admission Requirements: *Undergraduate:* open access. *Certificate:* open access.

On-Campus Requirements: To get a degree, students have to take courses on campus in addition to distance education courses.

Tuition and Fees: *Undergraduate:* $68/credit. *Credit by:* semester.

Financial Aid: Federal Stafford Loan, Federal Perkins Loan, Federal PLUS Loan, Federal Pell Grant, Federal Work-Study, VA, New Jersey resident programs.

Accreditation: Middle States Association of Colleges and Schools.

Description: Sussex County Community College (1982) is an open-access, exit-standard, 2-year public institution.

Syracuse University

700 University Avenue	Phone: (315) 443-3480
Syracuse, NY 13244	(800) 442-0501 (USA only)
	Fax: (315) 443-4174

Division(s): Continuing Education
Web Site(s): http://www.suce.syr.edu/ISDP
http://www.suce.syr.edu/ONLINE
E-mail: suisdp@syr.edu

Undergraduate Degree Programs:
Associate of Arts in Liberal Studies
Bachelor of Arts in Liberal Studies

Graduate Degree Programs:
Master of Arts in Advertising Design or Illustration
Master of Business Administration
Master of Library Science
Master of Science in:
    Communications Management
    Engineering Management
    Information Resources Management
    Nursing
    Telecommunications and Network Management
Master of Social Science

Class Titles: Writing, Philosophy, Psychology, Speech, Biology, Engineering, Political Science, English, Religion.

Teaching Methods: *Computers:* Internet, electronic classroom, e-mail, LISTSERV. *Other:* videoconferencing, fax, correspondence, independent study.

Credits Granted for: portfolio assessment, extrainstitutional learning, examination (CLEP, ACT-PEP, DANTES, GRE) undergraduate only.

Admission Requirements: *Undergraduate:* Associate/ Bachelor in Liberal Studies—TOEFL of 550; high school degree; 2.5 GPA for transfer students; January, May, or August admission. *Graduate:* program-specific; contact school.

On-Campus Requirements: 2–4 weeks/year in residence on campus or at other sites for degree programs. Selection of individual online courses: no campus requirement.

Tuition and Fees: *Undergraduate:* $336/credit. *Graduate:* $647/credit. *Application Fee:* $40. *Other Costs:* room and board (approximately $50–$100/day), books (approximately $35/credit course), Internet costs (vary). *Credit by:* semester.

Financial Aid: Federal Stafford Loan, Federal Perkins Loan, Federal Pell Grant, Federal Work-Study, Unsubsidized Federal Stafford Loan, UC Institutional Graduate Tuition Award.

Accreditation: Middle States Association of Colleges and Schools, Association of American Universities.

Description: Syracuse University (1870) is a major private research university in central New York State, with 14,500 residential and 5,000 part-time, adult students. The institution is organized into 13 schools and colleges, each offering a variety of bachelor's, master's, and doctoral degrees. Syracuse has excellent research facilities, including sophisticated computer networks and a library with more than 2.4 million volumes. The university is ranked by *U.S. News and World Report* as one of the top 50 universities in the U.S. and is one of few universities selected for membership in the prestigious Association of American Universities. In 1966 the university pioneered its nontraditional Independent Study Degree program, one of the three oldest external degree programs in the U.S. Offered through 9 of the university's academic units, the programs reflect the university's response to the demands for creative educational techniques in a constantly changing society.

Tacoma Community College

6501 S. 19th St.	Phone: (253) 460-3958
Tacoma, WA 98466	Fax: (253) 566-6077

Division(s): Distance Learning
Web Site(s):
http://www.tacoma.ctc.edu/inst_dept/distancelearning
E-mail: aduckwor@tcc.ctc.edu

Undergraduate Degree Programs:
Associate Degree

Class Titles: Anthropology, Art, Computer User, English, Human Services, Health Technology, Math, Music, Physical Education, Political Science, Psychology and Sociology.

Teaching Methods: *Computers:* Internet, real-time chat, electronic classroom, e-mail, CD-ROM. *TV:* videotape, cable program, satellite broadcasting, PBS. *Other:* videoconferencing, independent study.

Credits Granted for: experiential learning, portfolio assessment, extrainstitutional learning (PONSI, corporate or pro-

fessional association seminars/workshops), examination (CLEP, ACT-PEP, DANTES, GRE).

Admission Requirements: *Undergraduate:* GED, high school diploma, or Running Start Program.

On-Campus Requirements: None.

Tuition and Fees: *Undergraduate:* $58.05/credit. *Credit by:* quarter.

Financial Aid: Federal Stafford Loan, Federal Perkins Loan, Federal PLUS Loan, Federal Pell Grant, Federal Work-Study, VA, state programs for residents of Washington.

Accreditation: Northwest Accreditation Association of Schools and Colleges.

Description: Tacoma Community College (1965) traces its roots to 1962, when residents of the Tacoma-Pierce County area elected to fund and build a local community college. The Tacoma School District No. 10 Board of Directors applied for authorization to build the college in 1961 and received approval in 1963 from the Washington State Board of Education. The college opened in the fall of 1965 and was dedicated February 16, 1968. Tacoma Community College is a comprehensive state-supported school serving more than 650,000 residents of the Tacoma-Pierce County areas of western Washington. The Tacoma Community College district includes all of Tacoma and the Pierce County portion of the Olympic Peninsula. Tacoma Community College began offering Distance Learning programs in the mid-1970s, starting with telecourses. In 1999 online courses came into being and we now offer more than 20 online courses and continue to grow every year.

Taft College

29 Emmons Park Drive	Phone: (805) 763-7700
Taft, CA 93268	(866) 464-9229
	Fax: (805) 763-7705

Division(s): Instruction
Web Site(s): http://www.taft.cc.ca.us
E-mail: lsnowden@taft.org

Undergraduate Degree Program:
Associate of Arts

Class Titles: Computer Sciences, English, History, Humanities, Criminal Justice/Corrections, Early Childhood Education, Information Competency, Math, Psychology, Sociology, plus general education courses.

Teaching Methods: *Computers:* Internet, electronic classroom, e-mail, CD-ROM. *TV:* videotape. *Other:* independent study.

Admission Requirements: community college; see catalog.

On-Campus Requirements: None.

Tuition and Fees: *Undergraduate:* $11/unit; nonresident $134/unit; see catalog for additional information. *Credit by:* semester.

Financial Aid: Federal Pell Grant, Federal Work-Study, VA, California resident programs.

Accreditation: Western Association of Schools and Colleges.

Description: Taft College (1922) is nestled among rolling hills at the southern edge of oil- and agriculturally rich San Joaquin Valley. Although one of the smallest campuses in the California Community College System, Taft College has an academic program and low fee structure that attracts students from many states and nations. Taft offers quality education, small class size, individual attention, outstanding staff, fine facilities, and a warm friendly atmosphere.

Tarleton State University

Box T-0810	Phone: (254) 968-9050
Stephenville, TX 76402	Fax: (254) 968-9540

Division(s): Center for Instructional Technology and Distance Learning
Web Site(s): http://online.tarleton.edu
E-mail: jkwheeler@tarleton.edu

Class Titles: classes vary. Call for catalog or check web site at http://www.tarleton.edu/catalog/.

Teaching Methods: *Computers:* Internet, real-time chat, electronic classroom, e-mail, newsgroup, LISTSERV. *Other:* videoconferencing, independent study, individual study, web CT.

Admission Requirements: *Undergraduate:* request catalog for details. *Graduate:* request catalog for details.

On-Campus Requirements: state-mandated requirements. Contact school for complete information.

Tuition and Fees: *Undergraduate:* $64/credit, $144 minimum, $278/credit nonresident. Check catalog for current information and full details. *Graduate:* $74/credit, $144 minimum, $278/credit nonresident. *Other Costs:* $12.50/credit student services fee, $25/credit web-based delivery. *Credit by:* semester.

Financial Aid: Federal Stafford Loan, Federal Perkins Loan, Federal PLUS Loan, Federal Pell Grant, Federal Work-Study, VA, Texas resident programs, departmental and other grants and scholarships.

Accreditation: Southern Association of Colleges and Schools.

Description: Tarleton State University (1899) offers a wide variety of major programs in agriculture, business administration, and teacher education. Other strong degree programs exist for allied health and community services, the fine arts, social sciences, physical and biological sciences, humanities, mathematics, and technology. The university functions as an educational, scientific, and cultural center for the Crosstimbers region of Texas through its 3-fold mission of teaching, research, and service. Instruction by interactive videoconferencing began in the spring of 1992. Internet courses began in the fall of 1998.

Tarrant County College District

5301 Campus Drive	Phone: (817) 515-4532
Fort Worth, TX 76119	Fax: (817) 515-4400

Division(s): Center for Distance Learning
Web Site(s): http://dl.tccd.net
E-mail: velma.kudson@dl.tccd.net

Undergraduate Degree Programs:
Associate of Arts in Liberal Arts

Teaching Methods: *Computers:* Internet, real-time chat, e-mail, CD-ROM. *TV:* videotape, cable program, satellite broadcasting, PBS. *Other:* None.

Credits Granted for: examination (CLEP, ACT-PEP, DANTES, GRE).

Admission Requirements: *Undergraduate:* Official, accredited, high school graduation or GED; college transfers; or individual approval. Plus, mandatory Texas Academic Skills Program competency test in reading, writing, and math. Any deficiencies necessitate appropriate remediation. TASP exemptions for students with 3 college credits prior to the fall, 1989 semester; students from specific private or out-of-state institutions; senior citizens; certain noncitizens; students with accredited baccalaureate degrees or higher; and for students with board-established ACT, SAT, or TAAS scores. Call Registrar's Office for details: (817) 515-5293.

On-Campus Requirements: Yes, for some courses that require laboratory experiences, such as Biology and Geology. In addition, all courses offer on-campus orientation sessions and some courses offer enrichment seminars throughout the semester.

Tuition and Fees: *Undergraduate:* $28/semester hour with a $100 minimum, $12/semester hour out-of-district, $140/semester hour with a $200 minimum out-of-state; $140/semester hour with a $200 minimum nonresident alien. *Processing/Evaluation Fee:* $10, $30 foreign processing/

evaluation fee. *Other Costs:* Facilities Use Fee: $6/semester hour, $24 laboratory fee, $2 student services fee, other fees may apply such as returned check fee, graduation fee, transcript fee. *Credit by:* semester.

Financial Aid: Federal Stafford Loan, Federal PLUS Loan, Federal Pell Grant, Federal Work-Study, VA, Texas resident programs, Federal SEOG, Federal SSIG, State Work-Study, institutional scholarships, and short term loans.

Accreditation: Southern Association of Colleges and Schools and approved by the Texas Higher Education Coordinating Board and the Texas Education Agency. Memberships are also held in the Texas Association of Community Colleges, Association of Texas Colleges and Universities, Southern Association of Community Colleges and the American Association of Community Colleges.

Description: Tarrant County College District (1966) is a comprehensive community college dedicated to providing quality education to the people of Tarrant County. Distance learning began in 1973 with Instructional TV and has since expanded to include Internet/computer delivered instruction. The full-time faculty are dedicated to providing positive learning experiences for students, who may contact instructors by phone or e-mail. Included in the 80 Internet/CDI and 30 ITV courses offered in the standard semester are accounting, business, information technology, English, math, government, history, psychology, sociology, biology, geology, music, office occupations, speech, Spanish, French, economics, and religion.

Taylor University World Wide Campus

1025 West Rudisill Boulevard	Phone: (800) 845-3149
Fort Wayne, IN 46807-2197	(219) 744-8750
	Fax: (219) 456-2118

Division(s): College of Lifelong Learning
Web Site(s): http://wwcampus.tayloru.edu
E-mail: wwcampus@tayloru.edu

Undergraduate Degree Programs:
Associate of Arts in:
 Biblical Studies
 Liberal Arts (General Studies)
 Justice Administration (Public Policy concentration)
 Justice Administration (Ministry concentration)

Certificate Programs: Christian Worker, Justice and Ministry.

Class Titles: Over 130 individual course titles are available in African-American Studies, Biblical Languages, Biblical Studies, Business; Economics, Christian Education, Church History, Communication Arts, Conflict Management, Criminal Justice, Education, English, Fine Arts, History, Humanities, Inter-area Studies, Literature, Mathematics, Missions,

Natural Science, Pastoral Ministries, Philosophy, Political Science, Psychology, Religion, Social Sciences, Social Work, Theology, Youth Ministry. We also offer independent study for courses not listed in our catalog. See our catalog at *wwcampus.tayloru.edu* for detailed course listings.

Teaching Methods: *Computers:* Internet, electronic classroom, e-mail. *Other:* correspondence, independent study, mentored learning agreements.

Credits Granted for: portfolio assessment, examination (CLEP, ACT-PEP, DANTES, GRE).

Admission Requirements: *Undergraduate:* application form, high school diploma, GED or equivalent; personal reference; signed Code of Conduct statement; college transcripts (if applicable). No requirements if nondegree-seeking.

On-Campus Requirements: Justice and Ministries Certificate and Associate of Arts degree in Justice Administration (Ministry Concentration) require 2 one-week intensive summer sessions on the Fort Wayne, Indiana campus (this requirement may be waived with petition).

Tuition and Fees: *Undergraduate:* $149/credit, correspondence; study; $169 online study, mentored learning, independent study. *Application Fee:* $35 degree-seeking only. *Other Costs:* One-time $15 New Student Fee if nondegree-seeking student; $50 Course Development Fee guarantees independent study course delivery within 21 days. *Credit by:* semester.

Accreditation: North Central Association of Colleges and Schools.

Description: Taylor University (1846) is an evangelical, independent, interdenominational, Christian, liberal arts college where faith and learning are integrated. Taylor has a rural campus in Upland, Indiana, an urban campus in Fort Wayne, and a virtual campus known as the World Wide Campus. Under the direction of the College of Adult and Lifelong Learning, Taylor University's World Wide Campus provides undergraduate-level, credit courses through alternate delivery systems to a wide variety of individuals by offering a current, Christ-centered curriculum in liberal arts and professional disciplines. Since 1938, the World Wide Campus (known previously as the Fort Wayne Bible College Institute of Correspondence Studies) has provided distance learning opportunities to more than 35,000 students.

Technical College of the Lowcountry

921 Ribaut Road	Phone: (843) 525-8204
Beaufort, SC 29902	Fax: (843) 525-8330

Division(s): Instruction
Web Site(s): http://www.tconline.org
E-mail: fseitz@tcl.tec.sc.us

Class Titles: Teleclasses/Internet courses support certificates, diplomas, and degrees in Business, Criminal Justice, Office System Technology, Paralegal (Legal Assistant), Pharmacy Technician (MTC), Medical Records Coder (MTC), and the Transfer Program (Associate of Arts/Associate of Science). Classes include Business, Accounting, Criminal Justice, Paralegal, Office Systems Technology, Pharmacy Technician (MTC), Medical Records Coder (MTC), English, Mathematics, History, Government.

Teaching Methods: *Computers:* Internet, e-mail (support for teleclasses). *TV:* videotape, satellite broadcasting. *Other:* videoconferencing (ISDN).

Credits Granted for: experiential learning, portfolio assessment, examination (CLEP, DANTES).

Admission Requirements: *Undergraduate:* open admission. *Certificate:* open admission.

On-Campus Requirements: None.

Tuition and Fees: *Undergraduate:* $71/credit in-state, $155/credit out-of-state, $155/credit international. *Application Fee:* $20. *Credit by:* semester.

Financial Aid: Federal Stafford Loan, Federal Perkins Loan, Federal PLUS Loan, Federal Pell Grant, Federal Work-Study, VA, South Carolina resident programs.

Accreditation: Southern Association for Colleges and Schools.

Description: Technical College of the Lowcountry traces its roots to the Mather School, which began in 1868 to educate the daughters of newly freed slaves. Today it is one of 16 technical and comprehensive 2-year colleges of the South Carolina Technical College System. To better serve the needs of its 2,858 square-mile rural service area of small towns and sea islands, TCL began its distance learning program in 1996 with help from a USDE Title III grant. Teleclasses are offered via the SCETV 32-channel digital satellite system and via ISDN teleconferencing. TCL also receives teleclasses from other institutions, including graduate courses from Clemson University. Shared programs include Pharmacy Technician and Medical Records Coder. The Pharmacy Technician program is supported by a state-of-the art laboratory at the H. Mungin Center. Most teleclasses originate on the Beaufort Campus.

Télé-université, Université du Québec

2600 Boulevard Laurier
Tour de la Cité, 7th Level
Sainte-Foy, PQ G1V 4V9

Phone: (418) 657-2262
Fax: (418) 657-2094

Division(s): Anne Marrec
Web Site(s): http://www.teluq.uquebec.ca
E-mail: INFO@teluq.uquebec.ca

Undergraduate Degree Programs:
Contact school for complete listing.

Graduate Degree Programs:
Contact school for complete listing.

Teaching Methods: *Computers:* Internet, e-mail, CD-ROM, newsgroup. *TV:* videotape, cable program. *Other:* videoconferencing, audioconferencing, individual study.

Credits Granted for: experiential learning, portfolio assessment, extrainstitutional learning, examination (CLEP, ACT-PEP, DANTES, GRE).

Admission Requirements: *Undergraduate:* age 21.

On-Campus Requirements: None.

Tuition and Fees: *Undergraduate:* $56 (Canadian). *Graduate:* $56 (Canadian). *Credit by:* semester.

Accreditation: Association of Universities and Colleges of Canada.

Description: Télé-université (1972) is the only French language university in North America that offers educational training entirely at a distance. It was founded in 1972, and is a Université du Québec School of Higher Learning. Télé-université's mandate is to provide university education using the distance education mode, as well as carry out research. Programs and courses are made available to Canadian citizens as well as to foreign students directly or though local universities. Télé-université admits more than 10,000 students per year. Since its creation, it has awarded 12,000 degrees. Registered students receive their course materials by mail or via a telematic medium. Pedagogic support is provided through telephone or telematic tutoring. A variety of communications media and technologies are used as part of the courseware; these include print, audiovisuals, multimedia, telematics, teleconferencing, videoconferencing, and the Information Superhighway. The university offers programs and courses in Administration, Communications, Computer Science, Languages, General and Applied Sciences, Social Sciences and Humanities, broken down as follows: 2 Bachelor of Arts degrees, 19 certificates, 17 short programs, more than 200 courses that make up the different programs.

It also offers graduate programs. Two diplomas are currently available: the Diploma in Distance Education and the Diploma in Business Financing. Two other programs are in preparation—a master's degree in distance education and a doctorate in cognitive computing. Some programs are developed with the collaboration of other universities. For the 1995–1996 year, Tele-universite received about $3 million in research grants, of which more than half went to the LICEF Research Center (a laboratory for cognitive computing applied to training environments). The center focuses mainly on integrating information and communication technologies in the distance education setting, using multimedia, hypermedia, and the virtual classroom for teaching purposes.

Teachers College, Columbia University

525 West 120th Street, Box 132　　　Phone: (888) 633-6933
New York, NY 10027-6696　　　　　　Fax: (212) 678-3291

Division(s): The Distance Learning Project, The Center for Educational Outreach and Innovation
Web Site(s): http://dlp.tc.columbia.edu
E-mail: dlp@columbia.edu

Graduate Degree Programs:
The Distance Learning Project at Teachers College, Columbia University, offers an Intensive Masters Program (IMP) that is available partly online. The program contains 4 separate concentrations in:

　　Multimedia Development
　　Telecommunications and Global Issues
　　Teaching and Learning with Technology
　　Technology Leadership

　　The Multimedia Development concentration earns an MA degree in Instructional Technology and Media. The other concentrations lead to an MA degree in Computing and Education. The Intensive Masters Program (IMP) in educational technology is offered by the Program in Computing, Communications and Technology Education and is designed by the Center for Technology and School Change (CTSC) at Teachers College, Columbia University. The purpose of CTSC is to help schools integrate technology successfully into their curricula, to study issues in student and school use of technology, and to develop technology tools and products for education. The Intensive Masters Program currently requires two 4-week residencies at Teachers College during July.

Certificate Programs: The Distance Learning Project at Teachers College, Columbia University offers certificate programs in: Teaching and Learning with Technology, and Designing Interactive Multimedia Instruction. The Certificate in Teaching and Learning with Technology is offered jointly through the Program in Communication, Computing and Technology in Education, and the Center for Educational Outreach and Innovation at Teachers College, Columbia University. The objective of this program is to provide professional development in the integration of technology into the classroom for K-12 teachers, technology coordinators, principals, superintendents, and other educational professionals. The program includes a combination of essential hands-on and theoretical work, and is designed to make use of new technologies. The courses for the certificate can be taken on a credit or noncredit basis. The Certificate in Designing Interactive Multimedia Instruction is offered jointly through the Program in Communication, Computing, and Technology in Education and the Center for Educational Outreach and Innovation at Teachers College, Columbia University. The objective of this program is to provide professional development in the design of interactive multimedia for teachers, other school personnel, curriculum developers, software designers, publishing professionals, media specialists, and other educational professionals. The courses for the certificate can be taken on a credit or noncredit basis.

Class Titles: Certificate Course Offerings: Telecommunications, Distance Learning, and Collaborative Interchange; Hypermedia and Education; Instructional Design of Educational Technology; Computers, Problem Solving, and Cooperative Learning; Independent Study in Communication, Computing, and Instructional Technology. General Course Offerings: Sociology of Classrooms; Theories of Human Cognition and Learning; Probability and Statistical Inference; Applied Regression Analysis; Introduction to Computers, Language, and Literacy; Computers and the Uses of Information in Education; Cognition and Computers; Intelligent Computer-Assisted Instruction; Television and the Development of Youth; Leading and Sustaining Web-Based Learning; Staff Development and Training; Fostering Transformative Learning. Workshop Offerings: Publishing on the Web as an Educational Activity; Integrating Web Publishing into the Classroom Curriculum; Designing Educational Activities Using the Internet.

Teaching Methods: *Computers:* Internet, real-time chat, electronic classroom, e-mail, CD-ROM, newsgroup, LISTSERV. *TV:* videotape, cable program, satellite broadcasting, PBS. *Other:* videoconferencing, audioconferencing, audiographics, independent study, individual study.

Credits Granted for: successful completion of all course requirements.

Admission Requirements: *Graduate:* proof of baccalaureate (photocopy of your diploma or transcript showing award of degree) or teacher's license/certification. *Certificate:* proof of baccalaureate (photocopy of your diploma or transcript showing award of degree) or teacher's license/certification.

On-Campus Requirements: Only the Intensive Master's Program has a campus residency requirement. Students enrolled in the Intensive Master's Program register for a combination of online courses during the academic school year and course work at Teachers College during the summer semester. Students enrolled in a Certificate Program can complete all course work online.

Tuition and Fees: *Graduate:* For the 2001–2002 academic year, tuition for all online courses is $740/credit. Most of the online courses we offer are 3 credits. *Application Fees:* There is a $50 application fee for first-time applicants. *Software:* Some courses have specific software requirements but most require only Internet access. *Other Costs:* Courses that are taken on a noncredit basis vary in rate from $195–$795/course. *Credit by:* semester.

Financial Aid: Federal Stafford Loan, Federal Perkins Loan, Federal PLUS Loan, Federal Pell Grant, Federal Work-Study, is available for students enrolled in a degree program at Teachers College.

Accreditation: The New York State Board of Education accredits all programs of study.

Description: The Distance Learning Project at Teachers College, Columbia University (1997) is engaging learners from across the United States and around the world, utilizing the latest advances in technology, to promote and provoke a spirited exchange of global views to improve, inform, and reform the state of education. Teachers College has both anticipated and acted on critical developments that paved the way for progress in all of education. This ability to foresee societal needs has led to fields of study that now are considered standard. Today, the Distance Learning Project is keeping Teachers College in the vanguard with powerful learning opportunities, flexible formats, and superb learner support to address contemporary postgraduate concerns. The Distance Learning Project has been proud to offer a range of professional development opportunities to individuals, school districts, and other organizations through online learning. These experiences build upon the rich and varied strengths of the college in providing education in and out of the classroom and across the lifespan. For complete program information please visit our website at http://dlp.tc.columbia.edu.

Teikyo Post University

800 Country Club Rd.	**Phone: (203) 596-4670**
Waterbury, CT 06723	**Fax: (203) 596-4618**

Division(s): Accelerated Degree Programs
Web Site(s): http://www.teikyopost.edu/, For online programs: http://www.tpuonline.com/
E-mail: online@teikyopost.edu

Undergraduate Degree Programs:
Associate in Science: Early Childhood Education and Management

Bachelor of Science in:
Criminal Justice
Integrated Business
International Business Administration
Management
Management Information Systems

Certificate Programs: Early Childhood Administration, Early Childhood Education, International Business Administration, and Legal Assistant.

Class Titles: Contact school or check web site for details.

Teaching Methods: *Computers:* instructor-led asynchronous Internet courses.

Credits Granted for: Life/Work Experience (CLWEP) via portfolio assessment, examination (CLEP, DANTES, institutional exam).

Admission Requirements: *Undergraduate:* because the Accelerated Degree Program is designed for mature students who can handle the pace and workload of an 8-week term, prospective students are expected to have no less than 3 years work experience before applying to the degree program. Acceptance to the Accelerated Degree Program does not require entrance exams or application essays. The only requirements for admission are a high school diploma (or GED) and the desire to learn.

On-Campus Requirements: None.

Tuition and Fees: *Undergraduate:* $325/credit. *Application Fee:* $40. *Software:* current version of MS Office and Internet access. *Graduation Fee:* $75. *Credit by:* although our system is "by semester," the semesters in the Accelerated Degree Program are broken up into 2 categories—8-week accelerated and 14-week "modules." There are 6 eight-week modules and 3 fourteen-week modules per academic year.

Financial Aid: University-funded aid programs, Connecticut Independent College Grant Program, Federal Pell Grants, Supplemental Educational Opportunity Grants, Federal Stafford Loans, Federal PLUS Loans.

Accreditation: New England Association of Schools and Colleges.

Description: Teikyo Post founded in 1890 as Post College, is a small business and liberal arts university located in Waterbury, Connecticut. Teikyo Post is known for its international focus as exemplified by its curriculum and cultural diversity. Teikyo Post University (TPU) began offering full online degree programs in 1998. TPU Online offers 7 degree programs completely online and 4 certificate programs. TPU Online programs are known for their commitment, quality, and flexibility.

Temple Baptist Seminary

1815 Union Avenue	Phone: (423) 493-4221
Chattanooga, TN 37404	(800) 553-4050 x4221
	Fax: (423) 493-4471

Division(s): Seminary Office

Graduate Degree Programs:
Master of:
Ministry
Arts in Biblical Studies
Religious Education

Doctoral Degree Programs:
Doctor of Ministry

Certificate Programs: Biblical Studies.

Teaching Methods: *TV:* videotape. *Other:* audiotapes, independent study, individual study.

Credits Granted for: examination, institutionally developed/course.

Admission Requirements: *Graduate:* bachelor's degree of 120 hours, 3 recommendations, application. *Doctoral:* for Doctor of Ministry: Master of Divinity or equivalent, 3.0 GPA, active in ministry. *Certificate:* 2 years of college and 2 years of ministry.

On-Campus Requirements: minimum of one modular class in all degrees except for Master of Ministry and Certificate of Biblical Studies. These degrees can be done entirely through distance learning.

Tuition and Fees: $170/credit hour. *Application Fee:* $35–$50. *Other Costs:* registration fee $25–$50/semester, student activity fee $15/semester, comprehensive fee $50–$100/semester, audiotapes $80/course, videotapes $130/course. *Credit by:* semester.

Financial Aid: VA.

Accreditation: Transnational Association of Christian Colleges and Schools.

Description: Temple Baptist Seminary (1948) is a ministry of Highland Park Baptist Church, an independent Baptist Church. From the outset, the seminary has been committed to upholding the biblical faith historically believed by fundamental Baptists. In addition, there has been a strong emphasis upon Bible teaching, Christian education, evangelism, and ministry endeavor. With the theme of "Preparing for Leadership," Temple Baptist Seminary continues to expand its efforts to equip church leaders and laypersons for the work of the ministry. In recent years, a program of fall, winter, and summer modular classes has been initiated. That program has become very popular with resident and out-of-town students. In 1993, snow during a modular week prevented many students from attending. The class was taped for those who had looked forward to coming. From that beginning, modular classes have been taped for use in the External Studies program.

Temple University

1301 Cecil B. Moore Avenue	
665 Ritter Annex Bldg. (004-00)	Phone: (215) 204-3943
Philadelphia, PA 19122	Fax: (215) 204-2666

Division(s): OnLine Learning Program
Web Site(s): http://oll.temple.edu
E-mail: online@temple.edu

Undergraduate Degree Programs:
Organizational Studies (under development)

Graduate Degree Programs:
School of Business and Management (under development)

Certificate Programs: Podiatry School.

Class Titles: Contact school or check web site for details.

Teaching Methods: *Computers:* Internet, real-time chat, electronic classroom, e-mail, CD-ROM, newsgroup, LISTSERV.

Admission Requirements: *Undergraduate* and *Graduate:* student must have completed the prerequisites for the course. Contact the school for details. *Certificate:* student must have completed the prerequisites for the course. Contact the school for details.

On-Campus Requirements: One or more face-to-face meetings can be scheduled depending on the course selected.

Tuition and Fees: *Undergraduate:* $397/credit (nonresident PA), $253 PA resident. *Graduate:* $484/credit (nonresident PA), $352 PA resident. *Application Fee:* $35 for undergraduate students. No application fee for Continuing Education Students. *Software:* only if required for the course. *Credit by:* semester.

Financial Aid: FFEL Subsidized Stafford Loans, FFEL Unsubsidized Stafford Loans, FFEL PLUS Loans, Federal Perkins Loans, Federal Nursing Loans.

Accreditation: Middle States Association of Colleges and Schools.

Description: Temple University, of the Commonwealth System of Higher Education (1888), is a comprehensive public research university with more than 29,000 students. It has a distinguished faculty in 16 schools and colleges, including schools of Law, Medicine, Podiatry, and Dentistry, and a renowned Health Sciences Center. Temple is one of Pennsylvania's 3 public research universities, along with the

University of Pittsburgh and Penn State University. Temple University is the 39th largest university in the United States, and it is the largest provider of professional education (law, dentistry, medicine, pharmacy, and podiatric medicine) in the country. In 1995 the OnLine Learning Program was created to allow new forms of interactions between teachers and students and the course content. Two forms of Distance Education were adopted: online and videoconferencing. The videoconferencing technology allows students to participate synchronously in classroom presentations and discussions. Online technologies are constantly being implemented to allow students and faculty to interact via text, audio, LISTSERVS, video and to benefit from asynchronous and synchronous communication modes. Currently, Temple University offers more than 100 online/videoconferencing courses.

Tennessee State University

330 Tenth Avenue N
Nashville, TN 37203

Phone: (615) 963-7004
Fax: (615) 963-7007

Division(s): Center for Extended Education
Web Site(s): http://www.tnstate.edu
E-mail: klooney@tnstate.edu

Class Titles: Psychology, Education, English, History, Nursing, Art, Public Administration, Sociology.

Teaching Methods: *Computers:* Internet, e-mail, LISTSERV. *TV:* videotape, satellite broadcasting, PBS. *Other:* videoconferencing.

Credits Granted for: examination (CLEP, ACT-PEP, DANTES, GRE).

Admission Requirements: *Undergraduate:* see TSU Web page at www.tnstate.edu.

On-Campus Requirements: see TSU catalog at www.tnstate.edu.

Tuition and Fees: *Undergraduate:* $163/credit in-state, $433 out-of-state. *Graduate:* $247/credit in-state, $517 out-of-state. *Application Fee:* $15 undergraduate, $25 graduate. *Other Costs:* $12/credit technology fee. *Credit by:* semester.

Financial Aid: Federal Stafford Loan, Federal Perkins Loan, Federal PLUS Loan, Federal Pell Grant, Federal Work-Study, VA.

Accreditation: Southern Association of Colleges and Schools.

Description: Tennessee State University, an 1890 land-grant institution, is a major state-supported, urban and comprehensive university. This unique combination of characteristics differentiates the university from all others in the state

and distinctively shapes its instructional, research, and public service programs. In carrying out its diverse mission, the university serves the City of Nashville and Middle Tennessee, the state, the nation, and the international community. TSU provides instructional programs, state-wide cooperative extension services, cooperative agricultural research, and food and agricultural programs of an international dimension. As a comprehensive institution, TSU provides programming in agriculture, allied health, arts and sciences, business, education, engineering and technology. The institution is broadly comprehensive at the baccalaureate and master's levels. As a major urban institution located in the capital city, TSU provides both degree and nondegree programs (day, evening, weekend, and at off-campus sites) that are appropriate and accessible to a working urban population.

Tennessee Technological University

5 William L. Jones Drive
PO Box 5073, TTU
Cookeville, TN 38505-0001

Phone: (931) 372-3394
Fax: (931) 372-3499

Division(s): Interdisciplinary Studies and Extended Education
Web Site(s): http://www.tntech.edu
E-mail: selkins@tntech.edu

Class Titles: Accounting, Algebra, Chemistry, Education, English, History, Industrial Technology, Nursing.

Teaching Methods: *Computers:* Internet, e-mail, CD-ROM. *TV:* videotape, cable program, satellite broadcasting, PBS, compressed video, full-motion video. *Other:* videoconferencing, fax.

Credits Granted for: examination (CLEP, ACT-PEP, DANTES, GRE), educational experience in the Armed Forces.

Admission Requirements: *Undergraduate:* age 16, physical examination, high school graduate or GED, 2.35 high school GPA, ACT composite of 19, and assessment tests. *Graduate:* accredited bachelor's or master's, exam score (GRE, AMAT, MAT, etc.), recommendation letter.

On-Campus Requirements: None.

Tuition and Fees: *Undergraduate:* $97/hour resident, $243/hour out-of-state. *Graduate:* $157. *Application Fee:* $25 graduate, $15 undergraduate. *Other Costs:* $10/hour technology access fee. *Credit by:* semester.

Financial Aid: Federal Stafford Loan, Federal Perkins Loan, Federal Pell Grant, Federal Work-Study, VA, Tennessee resident programs, Tennessee student assistant awards.

Accreditation: Southern Association of Colleges and Schools.

Description: Tennessee Technological University (1915) originally opened its doors to students at the high school and junior-college levels. By 1929 the first class of 4-year graduates received BS degrees. In 1949 the administrative structure was expanded into 5 schools consisting of Arts/Sciences, Agriculture/Home Economics, Business Administration, Education, and Engineering. The Specialist in Education was authorized in 1970, the Doctor of Philosophy in 1971, the MBA in 1976, and the BS in Nursing and Bachelor of Fine Arts in 1980. The BS in Technical Communication and the Bachelor of Music were added in 1986 and 1994, respectively. The first distance learning courses were offered through telecourse delivery in 1980. Interactive TV became available in 1992, and Web courses were added to distance learning delivery in 1998. The Regents Online Degree Program is available beginning Fall 2001.

Tennessee Temple University

1815 Union Avenue	Phone: (800) 533-4050 (ext. 4288)
Chattanooga, TN 37404	(423) 493-4288
	Fax: (423) 493-4486

Division(s): School of External Studies
Web Site(s): http://www.tntemple.edu
E-mail: external@mail.tntemple.edu

Undergraduate Degree Programs:
Associate of Arts in Biblical Studies
Bachelor of Science in Biblical Studies

Class Titles: Biology; Creative Writing; Developmental and Child Psychology; English Composition; English Language and Literature; Family and Marriage Counseling; History; Family Studies; Liberal Arts, General Studies, and Humanities; Mathematics; Middle Eastern Languages and Literature; Philosophy and Religion; Political Science; Psychology; Social Sciences; Theological Studies; Missions; History.

Teaching Methods: audiotapes, fax, correspondence, independent study, individual study.

Credits Granted for: portfolio assessment, corporate or professional association seminars/workshops, examination (CLEP, ACT-PEP, DANTES, GRE).

Admission Requirements: *Undergraduate:* high school diploma or equivalent, high school transcript, college transcripts, essay or personal statement, letters of recommendation, $25 application fee, statement of faith in Christ.

On-Campus Requirements: Students must take a speech course and a basic computer course on campus or transfer them from another school.

Tuition and Fees: *Undergraduate:* $85/credit hour plus mandatory fees of $115/course; $285 for a 2-hour course, $370 for a 3-hour course, including materials. Costs may vary by course delivery options. *Application Fee:* $25. *Credit by:* semester.

Financial Aid: Not available right now to distance education students. Approved for training of veterans.

Accreditation: American Association of Bible Colleges, Transnational Association of Christian Colleges and Schools (TRACS).

Description: Tennessee Temple University (1946) began as the higher education ministry of Highland Park Baptist Church. The school has alumni worldwide as missionaries, preachers, school teachers, and business and professional people. Included are an academy, Bible school (2-year), university, and seminary.

Terra State Community College

2830 Napoleon Road	Phone: (419) 334-8400
Fremont, OH 43420	Fax: (419) 334-9035

Division(s): Educational Catalyst Center
Web Site(s): http://www.terra.cc.oh.us/
E-mail: cmichael@terra.cc.oh.us
(online registration form provided on Web site)

Class Titles: Accounting I, Introduction to CAD, CAD Designer, CAD Mechanical, Computer Fundamentals, College Composition I, College Composition II, Tech Writing for Business and Industry, Shakespeare on Film, Local History, Business Law, Intermediate Algebra I, Intermediate Algebra II, Intermediate Geometry and Trigonometry, Number Bases, College Algebra, General Psychology, Effective Teams and Processes, Music Fundamentals, Introduction to Humanities.

Teaching Methods: *Computers:* Internet, Web-based assignments, Web-board, real-time chat, e-mail, CD-ROM. *TV:* videotapes. *Other:* fax, phone, correspondence.

Credits Granted for: experiential learning.

Admission Requirements: *Undergraduate:* high school transcript or GED certificate. Applicants with previous college work should also submit official college transcripts to Terra's Records Office. Students currently in the senior year of high school, age 16 or older, are eligible to earn college credit by taking day or evening courses, with written approval from their high school counselor or principal. International students are welcomed at Terra. Because the entrance requirements are based on state and federal regulations that sometimes change, international students seeking admission to Terra Community College should contact the Admissions Office for the latest information. Prerequisites: check the online college catalog for course prerequisites. Restrictions: the distance learning courses are completed during the quarter.

On-Campus Requirements: The on-campus requirements vary with each Distance Learning course. These requirements may include that exams be taken on campus, that a student must attend an orientation session, or that a student must attend a certain number of on-campus classes.

Tuition and Fees: *Undergraduate:* Terra's online catalog provides a section on fees. To access this section, type http://www.terra.cc.oh.us/catalog.html. The section includes 2 tables for tuition fees: in-state and out of state. *Other Costs:* $25 security deposit for videos that are checked out to the student. *Credit by:* quarter.

Financial Aid: Federal Stafford Loan, Federal Perkins Loan, Federal PLUS Loan, Federal Pell Grant, Federal Work-Study, VA, Ohio resident programs.

Accreditation: North Central Association of Colleges and Schools.

Description: The mission of Terra College (1968) is to provide the opportunity for quality learning experiences. To support this mission, Terra, formerly a technical college for 26 years, became a state community college in 1994. Terra was then able to grant the Associate of Arts and Associate of Science degrees, as well as the Associate Degree in Applied Business and the Associate Degree in Applied Science. The college is accredited by the North Central Association of Colleges and Schools and holds memberships in many professional and service associations. To meet the students' educational needs, Terra began offering video-based distance learning courses in 1995. Just as the number of Distance Learning course offerings continues to increase, so does the use of different delivery media. Terra currently offers online courses, as well as courses that incorporate any combination of the above-mentioned teaching methods.

Texas A&M University, Commerce

PO Box 3011
Commerce, TX 75429

Phone: (903) 886-5511
Fax: (903) 886-5991

Division(s): Instructional Technology and Distance Education
Web Site(s): http://www.tamu-commerce.edu/ntep/
E-mail: online@tamu-commerce.edu

Class Titles: Accounting, Biology, Chemistry, Computer Science, Counseling, Early Childhood Education, Economics, Educational Administration, Educational Technology, Elementary Education, English, Finance, Business, Health Education, Health/Physical Education, History, Journalism, Management, Marketing, Math, Physics, Psychology, Reading, Recreation, Secondary/Higher Education, Sociology, Special Education, Technology.

Teaching Methods: *Computers:* Internet, real-time chat, electronic classroom, e-mail, CD-ROM, newsgroup, LISTSERV. *Other:* videoconferencing, audioconferencing, audiographics, audiotapes, fax, correspondence, independent study, individual study, learning contracts.

Credits Granted for: examination (CLEP), ACT/SAT subject assessments, Advanced Placement passing scores.

Admission Requirements: *Undergraduate:* application, ACT or SAT scores, transcripts. *Graduate:* application, transcripts, GRE or other. *Doctoral:* application, transcripts, GRE or other. *Certificate:* application, transcripts.

On-Campus Requirements: some for most degree programs.

Tuition and Fees: *Undergraduate:* $303/3 credits Texas resident, $1,151/12 credits resident, $960/3 credits nonresident, $3,683/12 credits nonresident. *Graduate:* $399/3 credits resident, $1,439/12 credits resident, $1,032.50/3 credits nonresident, $3,971/12 credits nonresident. *Doctoral:* same as graduate. *Software:* variable. *Credit by:* semester.

Financial Aid: Federal Stafford Loan, Federal Perkins Loan, Federal PLUS Loan, Federal Pell Grant, Federal Work-Study, VA, Texas resident programs.

Accreditation: Southern Association of Colleges and Schools.

Description: Texas A&M University, Commerce (1889) became part of the Texas A&M System in 1996. The first distance learning video classes were offered in 1993 using a compressed video system connecting 3 sites. In 1995 a full-motion fiber optic system became operational, linking the university with 11 rural schools in northeast Texas. Currently, the university has access to over 95 school districts. The university began offering web-based courses in the fall of 1998. Currently, over 60 undergraduate and graduate courses are available. The university plans to offer undergraduate and graduate degrees via web-based delivery. A&M-Commerce was one of the first universities in the state to have all student services available online.

Texas Tech University

15th Street and Akron Avenue	**Phone: (800) 692-6877 (A)**
Box 42191 (A)	**(806) 742-2352 (A)**
Box 43091 (B)	**(806) 742-2501 (B)**
Box 43103 (C)	**(800) 528-5583 (C)**
Box 41162 (D)	**(806) 742-3077 (D)**
Box 42131 (E)	**(806) 742-2816 (E)**
	Fax: (806) 742-7277 (A)
	(806) 742-0989 (B)
	(806) 742-3493 (C)
	(806) 742-0125 (D)
	(806) 742-2880 (E)

Division(s): Extended Studies (A)
Department of English (B)
College of Engineering (C)
Department of Education, Nutrition, Restaurant/Hotel and Institutional Management (D)
Department of Agricultural Education and Communications (E)

Web Site(s): http://www.dce.ttu.edu (A)
http://www.english.ttu.edu/distance_ed/grad_MATConline.asp (B)
http://aln.coe.ttu.edu (C)
http://www.hs.ttu.edu/ceo (D)
http://www.casnr.ttu.edu/ (E)

E-mail: distlearn@ttu.edu (A)
Carolyn.Rude@ttu.edu (B)
Brent.Guinn@coe.ttu.edu (C)
tdodd@hs.ttu.edu (D)
matt.baker@ttu.edu (E)

Undergraduate Degree Programs:
Bachelor of General Studies External Degree (A)

Graduate Degree Programs:
Master of Arts in Technical Communication (B)
Master of Engineering (C)
Master of Science in Petroleum Engineering (C)
Master of Science in Software Engineering (C)
Master of Science in Restaurant/Hotel and Institutional Management (D)

Postgraduate Programs: College of Agricultural Sciences and Natural Resources (joint program between Texas Tech University & Texas A&M)—Doctor of Education in Agricultural Education (E).

Certificate Programs: Contact Extended Studies for a current listing.

Class Titles: Accounting; Agricultural and Applied Economics; Architecture; Business Administration; Economics; General Education; Educational and Instructional Psychology; Educational Psychology and Leadership; Engineering; English; Food and Nutrition; History; Human Development and Family Studies; Information System and Quantitative Sciences; Language; Marketing; Mass Communications; Mathematics; Music; Plant and Soil Science; Political Science; Psychology; Restaurant, Hotel and Institutional Management; Sociology, Anthropology, and Social Work, Technical Communication.

Teaching Methods: *Computers:* Internet, real-time chat, electronic classroom, e-mail, VCD-ROM, newsgroup, LISTSERV. *TV:* videotape, satellite broadcasting. *Other:* videoconferencing, audioconferencing, audiotapes, fax, correspondence, independent study.

Admission Requirements: *Undergraduate:* application, transcripts, SAT or ACT; other information may be required depending upon the degree program. *Graduate:* application, transcripts, appropriate bachelor's degree, GRE; other information may be required depending upon the degree program. *Postgraduate:* application, transcripts, appropriate degree, GRE; other information may be required depending upon the degree program. *Certificate:* dependent on specific program.

On-Campus Requirements: Dependent on the degree program.

Tuition and Fees: Tuition and fees vary by program. Contact the respective college/department to obtain specific information. *Credit by:* semester.

Financial Aid: Contact the Financial Aid Office (806-742-3681) for information on financial aid opportunities.

Accreditation: Southern Association of Colleges and Schools.

Description: Texas Tech University is a state-supported university accredited by the Commission on Colleges of the Southern Association of Colleges and Schools to award bachelor's, master's, and doctoral degrees. Created by legislative action in 1923, Texas Tech University is a 4-year research university composed of 8 colleges and 2 schools (Agricultural Sciences and Natural Resources, Architecture, Arts and Sciences, Business Administration, Education, Engineering, Honors, Human Sciences, the Graduate School, and the School of Law).

Texas Tech University has offered courses at a distance since 1927. While the bulk of the course work historically has been print-based, Texas Tech University is actively developing courses and degree offerings for delivery via new technologies. Offering flexibility and convenience, programs provide quality course work comparable to traditional on-campus courses, Texas Tech University now offers 8-degree programs at a distance.

Thomas College

180 West River Road	**Phone: (207) 859-1102**
Waterville, ME 04901	**Fax: (207) 859-1114**

Division(s): Continuing Education
Web Site(s): http://www.thomas.edu
E-mail: CED@Thomas.edu

Graduate Degree Programs:
Master of Science in Computer Technology Education

Teaching Methods: *Computers:* Internet, real-time chat, electronic classroom, e-mail, CD-ROM, newsgroup, LISTSERV. *Other:* None.

Admission Requirements: *Graduate:* Contact school.

On-Campus Requirements: None.

Tuition and Fees: *Graduate:* $510/class. *Software:* $100/year. *Credit by:* trimester.

Financial Aid: Federal Stafford Loan, Federal Perkins Loan, Federal PLUS Loan, Federal Pell Grant, Federal Work-Study, VA, Maine resident programs.

Accreditation: New England Association of Schools and Colleges.

Description: Thomas College (1893) gives students a remarkably well-balanced blend of those skills that will be required in society and in the business world of the 21st century, combined with something far more important: the ability to learn new skills and acquire new knowledge. Thomas' graduates are lifelong learners and are thus well-prepared for a future shaped by people who take this approach to work and to life.

Thomas Edison State College

101 West State Street	Phone: (888) 442-8372
Trenton, NJ 08608-1176	Fax: (609) 984-8447

Division(s): Office of Admissions
Web Site(s): http://www.tesc.edu
E-mail: info@tesc.edu

Undergraduate Degree Programs:
Associate of Arts
Associate in Applied Science
Associate of Applied Science in Radiologic Technology
Associate of Science in:
    Management
    Natural Sciences and Mathematics
    Public and Social Services
    Applied Science and Technology
Bachelor of Arts
Bachelor of Science in:
    Business Administration
    Applied Science and Technology
    Human Services
    Nursing
    Health Sciences

Graduate Degree Programs:
Master of Science in Management
Master of Arts in Professional Studies

Certificate Programs: Accounting, Administrative Office Management, Computer Aided Design, Computer Science, Electronics, Finance, Labor Studies, Marketing, Human Resources Management, Operations Management, Public Administration, Computer Information Systems, E-Commerce.

Class Titles: refer to catalog and/or registration bulletin.

Teaching Methods: *Computers:* Internet, e-mail electronic classroom. *TV:* videotape, PBS. *Other:* independent study, individual study, audiotapes, fax.

Credits Granted for: experiential learning, portfolio assessment, extrainstitutional learning (ACE College Credit Recommendation Service, corporate or professional association seminars/workshops), examination (CLEP, ACT-PEP, DANTES, TECEP), transfer credits.

Admission Requirements: *Undergraduate:* age 21 student must live or work in New Jersey for BS in Nursing. *Graduate:* age 21, bachelor's degree in any discipline and/or 3–5 years of managerial/supervisory experience. No GRE or GMAT required.

On-Campus Requirements: Two weekend residencies for Master of Science in Management degree.

Tuition and Fees: *Undergraduate:* Tuition is payment for all costs directly associated with the academic delivery of a Thomas Edison State College education to registered students. Fees are designated as payment for administrative services associated with other activities in support of that educational process and for materials used by students for courses and other activities undertaken by them. At Thomas Edison State College, we offer one annual tuition plan, the Comprehensive Tuition Plan, for students who want access to all components of the tuition package and who are enrolling at the beginning of the academic year. For those students who are enrolling at other times of the year or those who have determined that their particular situation is one where only components of the Comprehensive Tuition Plan are required, we offer the Enrolled Options Plan. A complete listing of tuition and fees is included in the college's information packet available by calling (888) 442-8372 or by visiting the college's web site at www.tesc.edu. *Graduate:* Tuition is $298/semester hour in 2001–02. Fees and tuition are specified in the Graduate Studies Prospectus and Application. Books and materials are estimated at $200–$300/ semester. *Application Fee:* $75. *Credit by:* semester for DIAL courses.

Financial Aid: Federal Stafford Loan, Federal PLUS Loan, Federal Pell Grant, VA, New Jersey State Tuition Assistance Grants (TAG), New Jersey Garden State Scholarships, employer tuition-aid.

Accreditation: Middle States Association of Colleges and Schools.

Description: Thomas Edison State College (1972) is a worldwide community of adult learners. One of New Jersey's 12 senior public institutions of higher education, Thomas Edison State College provides adults from every state and 79 other countries with unparalleled flexibility and many ways to complete a quality degree. Originally founded to provide distance education exclusively to adults, this world-renowned institution offers 15 associate, bachelor's, and master's degrees in more than 100 areas. The college's convenient programs enable adult learners to pursue their educational goals while attending to the challenges and priorities of adult life. Named one of the nation's Top 20 Cyber-Universities by *Forbes Magazine*, this public college is a national leader in the assessment of adult learning and a pioneer in the use of educational technologies. Thomas Edison State College offers a distinguished academic program for the self-motivated adult learner.

Thomas Jefferson University: College of Health Professions

30 South 9th Street	Phone: (215) 503-7937
Philadelphia, PA 19107-5233	Fax: (215) 503-0376

Division(s): Department of Nursing and Graduate Program
Web Site(s): http://jeffline.tju.edu or http://jeffline.tju.edu/CWIS/CHP/(College of Health Professions)
E-mail: Mary.Schaal@mail.tju.edu

Undergraduate Degree Programs:
Nursing Baccalaureate Degree RN-BSN—First course via Distance fall 2001 and will expand in following semesters (see Description section).

Graduate Degree Programs:
Nursing Master of Science Degree—presently only core courses via Distance (see Description Section).

Class Titles: Contact school or web site for details.

Teaching Methods: *Computers:* Internet, electronic classroom, e-mail, LISTSERV, CD-ROM, OVID Web. *TV:* videotape. *Other:* audioconferencing, audiographics, audiotapes, fax, correspondence, independent study, individual study, learning contracts.

Credits Granted for: experiential learning (RN-BSN program), portfolio assessment.

Admission Requirements: *Undergraduate:* completion of lower-division requirements. If no prior U.S. course work and English as second language, TOEFL scores. *Graduate:* college transcripts, GREs, or MATs, and personal statement with professional goals. *Postgraduate:* college transcripts,

résumé, and personal statement with professional goals.

On-Campus Requirements: Only for those courses not currently available via Distance.

Tuition and Fees: *Undergraduate:* $630/credit. *Graduate:* $685/credit. *Postgraduate:* $685/credit. *Application Fees:* $45, undergraduate, $40, graduate. *Graduation Fee:* $50. *Other Costs:* $100 portfolio review for portfolio fees; $50/credit for challenge exams. *Credit by:* semester.

Financial Aid: Federal Stafford Loan, Federal Perkins Loan, Federal PLUS Loan, Federal Pell Grant, Federal Work-Study, VA, state programs for residents or any state grant program for which a student is eligible.

Accreditation: Middle States Association of Colleges and Schools, American Association of Colleges of Nursing's Commission on Collegiate Nursing Education.

Description: The College of Health Professions was established July 1, 1969 as the College of Allied Health Sciences; the college, renamed the College of Health Professionals in December, 1996. The Thomas Jefferson University—College of Health Professions, Department of Nursing began the development of the first Distance course in 1997 and offered its first Distance course in the fall of 1998 and from there has focused on expanding it to the nursing graduate core course via Distance. The graduate nursing clinical courses are currently in the initial phases of development, so please call or e-mail for further details. Presently, we are in the process of implementing Distance courses to the RN-BSN degree. The first course will be going live in fall 2001 and will continue to expand the course offerings over the following semesters.

Tidewater Community College

121 College Place	Phone: (757) 822-1061
Norfolk, VA 23510	Fax: (757) 822-1060

Division(s): Dean, Academic and Student Affairs
Web Site(s): http://www.tc.cc.va.us/
E-mail: tcswags@tc.cc.va.us

Class Titles: Astronomy, Meteorology, Psychology, English Composition, Mythology in Literature/Arts, Technology/Liberal Arts. American History, Economics, Accounting, Administration of Justice, Business, Geography, Engineering, Information Systems Technology, Mathematics, Music, Sociology.

Teaching Methods: *Computers:* Internet, real-time chat, electronic classroom, e-mail, CD-ROM, newsgroup, LISTSERV. *TV:* videotape, cable program, PBS. *Other:* Compressed video within the state of Virginia.

Credits Granted for: experiential learning, portfolio assessment, examination (CLEP, ACT-PEP, DANTES, GRE).

Admission Requirements: *Undergraduate:* open admission. Must be age 18 or show ability to benefit.

On-Campus Requirements: Online computer-based courses are via computer, compressed video courses meet in a classroom at one of Virginia's 23 community colleges, and telecourses meet on campus at least twice/semester.

Tuition and Fees: *Undergraduate:* $55/credit. *Credit by:* semester.

Financial Aid: Federal Stafford Loan, Federal PLUS Loan, Federal Pell Grant, Federal Work-Study, VA, Virginia resident programs.

Accreditation: Southern Association of Colleges and Schools.

Description: Tidewater Community College (1968) is a comprehensive community college that offers both transfer and occupational/technical programs and courses. The college offers distance education courses through three formats: (1) telecourses, (2) compressed video within Virginia, and (3) online, computer-based courses.

Tiffin University

| 155 Miami Street | Phone: (866) TU-WIRED |
| Tiffin, OH 44883 | Fax: (419) 443-5011 |

Division(s): Tiffin Online
Web Site(s): http://www.tiffin-global.org and www.tiffin.edu
E-mail: onlineed@tiffin.edu

Graduate Degree Programs:
Master of Business Administration
Master of Criminal Justice

Class Titles: Contact the school or check web site for details.

Teaching Methods: *Computers:* Internet, real-time chat, electronic classroom, e-mail.

Credits Granted for: experiential learning, portfolio assessment, extrainstitutional learning (PONSI, corporate or professional association seminars/workshops), examination (CLEP, ACT-PEP, DANTES, GRE).

Admission Requirements: *Graduate:* two original copies of undergraduate transcripts and personal history statement.

On-Campus Requirements: Weekend residency to begin both MBA and MCJ; no on-campus time after that.

Tuition and Fees: *Graduate:* $475/credit. *Application Fee:* $50. *Other Costs:* One-time $300 residency fee. *Credit by:* Master of Business Administration is by 7-week term; there are 2 terms/semester. Master of Criminal Justice is by semester.

Financial Aid: Federal Stafford Loan, Federal Perkins Loan, Federal PLUS Loan, Federal Pell Grant, Federal Work-Study, VA).

Accreditation: North Central Association of Colleges and Schools, Association of Business Schools and Programs.

Description: Tiffin University (1888) was established as a business university. During the last 2 decades, the university has grown and transformed to offer nationally accredited graduate and undergraduate degrees in business and criminal justice and a distinctive liberal studies degree. Recent campus development during the last decade includes construction of several new residence halls, a new and expanded student center, athletic facilities, and a new dining hall and auditorium. In addition to the growth at Tiffin, graduate and undergraduate programs of the university are offered at centers in Lorraine, Lima, and Cleveland, Ohio. The current enrollment at Tiffin University is 1,500 full-time students. The university began its online MBA in August 2000. Since then it has started 2 additional online MBA cohorts—one in January 2001 and one in May 2001. This summer we have 75 full-time students in our online MBA and with the addition of our online MCJ in the fall of 2001, we expect to have well over 150 full-time students pursuing graduate degrees online by the end of 2001.

Tompkins Cortland Community College

170 North Street, P.O. Box 139	Phone: (607) 844-8211(AA)/
Dryden, NY 13053-0139	(607) 844-6586 (noncredit)
	Fax: (607) 844-9665

Division(s): Academic Affairs/Noncredit: Business Development and Training Center
Web Site(s): http://www.tc3.edu
E-mail: howde@sunytccc.edu (AA)/hubbarm@sunytccc.edu (noncredit)

Undergraduate Degree Programs:
Paralegal
Hotel and Restaurant Management
Chemical Dependency Counseling

Class Titles: Principles of Accounting, Business Communications, Foundations of Business, International Business, Business Law, Applied Management Seminar, Advanced Databases, Web Page Design, Computer Information Systems, Food Service and Preparation, Hospitality Law, Hospitality Accounting, Hospitality Marketing, Food and Labor Cost Control, Word Processing, Spreadsheets, Databases, Presentation Software, Business Math, Academic Writing, Approaches to Literature, Scriptwriting, Report Writing, Fundamentals of interpersonal Communication, Literature for Children, College Study Skills, English for

Speakers of Other Languages, Computer Programming, Elementary Mathematical Methods, Alcohol/Substance Abuse Counseling, Field Work, Family Counseling and Chemical Dependency, Chemical Dependency Prevention, Personal Health, Drug Studies, Alcohol and Alcoholism, Paralegalism, Legal Research and Drafting, Family Law, Wills, Trusts and Estates, Litigation/Civil Procedure, Real Estate, Bankruptcy, Collections and Foreclosures, Internship and Seminar, Criminal Law and Procedures, Psychology of Personal Growth, Psychology, Social Psychology, Developmental Psychology: The Child, Developmental Psychology: The Adolescent, Abnormal Psychology, Baseball in American Culture, Human Sexuality, Sociology, The American Community, Contemporary Social Problems, Juvenile Delinquency, Hospitality Industry, Food Service and Preparation, Rooms Division Management, Consumer Nutrition, Therapeutic Recreation, Consumer Health Issues, Criminology, Computer courses in MS Office, Web Design, Pagemaker, Jafa, A+ Certification, Digital Photography, and others.

Teaching Methods: *Computers:* Internet, real-time chat, electronic classroom, e-mail, CD-ROM, newsgroup. online through Education to Go. *TV:* videotape, cable program, satellite broadcasting, PBS. *Other:* radio broadcast, video-conferencing, audioconferencing, audiotapes, fax, correspondence, independent study, individual study, learning contracts.

Credits Granted for: experiential learning, extra-institutional learning (PONSI, corporate or professional association seminars/workshops), examination (CLEP, ACT-PEP, DANTES, Excelsior College).

Admission Requirements: *Undergraduate:* GED, high school diploma. *Certificate:* none.

On-Campus Requirements: None.

Tuition and Fees: *Undergraduate:* $102 per credit in state, $204 per credit for out of state. *Application Fees:* $15. *Software:* $5/part-time, $60/full-time. *Other Costs:* $9 for ID card, Web Course Fee: $10, in lieu of technology fee for web-based courses. Noncredit: Varies with course, usually $99 per course. *Credit by:* Semester.

Financial Aid: Federal Stafford Loan, Federal Perkins Loan, Federal PLUS Loan, Federal Pell Grant, Federal Work-Study, VA, state programs for residents of New York, TAP.

Accreditation: New York State Education Department and the Middle States Association.

Description: Tompkins Cortland is a college of the State University of New York (SUNY). Our curriculum prepares students for careers in the global marketplace, particularly in business administration, accounting, hotel and restaurant management, travel and tourism, engineering science, com-munications, electronics, and computer information systems. Many of our 31 degree programs prepare students for transfer for a 4-year college or university. The college began working with Distance Learning in 1997 through the SUNY Learning Network. The SUNY Learning Network (SLN) was established as a partnership of campuses and SUNY's Office of Advanced Learning and Information Services and offered the first courses in Fall 1995. Student course registrations exceeded the 20,000 mark in the 2000–2001 academic year, making it one of the three largest online programs in the country. Tompkins Cortland Community College is currently the fourth largest enroller of distance learning courses through the SUNY Learning Network.

Towson University

8000 York Road
Towson, MD 21252

Phone: (410) 704-3534
Fax: (410) 704-2032

Division(s): Extended Learning
Web Site(s): http://www.towson.edu
http://pages.towson.edu/cep/
E-mail: mweber@towson.edu

Class Titles: Contact school.

Teaching Methods: *Computers:* Internet, e-mail. *TV:* video-tape. *Other:* videoconferencing, fax, independent study, individual study.

Credits Granted for: experiential learning, extrainstitutional learning, examination (CLEP, ACT-PEP, DANTES, GRE).

Admission Requirements: *Undergraduate:* contact school.

On-Campus Requirements: None.

Tuition and Fees: *Undergraduate:* $156/credit in-state, $384/credit out-of-state. *Graduate:* $211/credit in-state, $435/credit out-of-state. *Other Costs:* $51/credit undergraduate university fee, $52/credit graduate university fee. *Credit by:* semester.

Financial Aid: Federal Stafford Loan, Federal Perkins Loan, Federal PLUS Loan, Federal Pell Grant, Federal Work-Study, VA.

Accreditation: Middle States Association of Colleges and Schools.

Description: The institution known today as Towson University (1866) has undergone a number of changes in name and status. The university's 320-acre campus, home of the institution since 1915, boasts an impressive blend of traditional and modern architecture. With the original mission of preparing teachers for Maryland's public school system, Towson's new status recognizes its development and growth into a metropolitan university. Contrasting with its first class of 11 students, the university today enrolls 10,000 full-time and 2,800 part-time undergraduates, plus 2,000 graduate students. Thirty academic departments offer 40 majors and 60 concentrations leading to bachelor's degrees. The departments are grouped into 6 subdivisions: the colleges of Liberal Arts, Natural and Mathematical Sciences, Fine Arts and Communication, Education, Health Professions, and Business and Economics. In addition, the Graduate School offers 26 master's degree programs.

Treasure Valley Community College

650 College Boulevard
Ontario, OR 97914

Phone: (541) 881-8822
Fax: (541) 881-2717

Division(s): Continuing/Distance Education
Web Site(s): http://www.tvcc.cc
E-mail: djwilson@tvcc.cc

Undergraduate Degree Programs: Contact school.

Class Titles: Business, General Biology, Medical Terminology, Math, General Psychology, General Sociology, and computer programming databases courses.

Teaching Methods: *Computers:* Internet, real-time chat, e-mail, LISTSERV. *TV:* videotape, cable program, satellite broadcasting, PBS. *Other:* videoconferencing, audioconferencing, audiotapes, fax, correspondcence, independent study, individual study.

Credits Granted for: examination (CLEP, ACT-PEP, DANTES, GRE).

Admission Requirements: *Undergraduate:* 18 years old, but subject to waiver.

On-Campus Requirements: Not unless lab time is required.

Tuition and Fees: *Undergraduate:* $44/credit in-state, $55/credit out of state, $100/credit for international students. *Application Fee:* $20. *Credit by:* quarter.

Financial Aid: Federal Stafford Loan, Federal Perkins Loan, Federal PLUS Loan, Federal Pell Grant, Federal Work-Study, VA, state programs for residents of Oregon.

Accreditation: Northwest Association of Schools and Colleges.

Description: Treasure Valley Community College (1962) was founded as part of the Oregon Community College system. During the past 10 years TVCC has developed a variety of delivery methods for Distance Education courses, such as online and Internet instruction, videotaped courses, telecourses, interactive televised programs, cable broadcasts, correspondence, and audioconferencing. Working in conjunction with the Distance Education Department, Telemedia

Services provides for both the audio and visual needs of the campus and the technical delivery and connection with students who may be bound by distance, travel constraints, family, or work responsibilities. KMBA-TV the college's 24 hour-a-day UHF television station provides residents with televised programming of athletic events, local and community news, and instructional classes and courses.

Trinity Lutheran Seminary

2199 East Main Street
Columbus, OH 43209-2334

Phone: (614) 235-4136
Fax: (614) 238-0263

Division(s): Office of the Academic Dean and Office of Continuing Education
Web Site(s): http://www.trinity.capital.edu
E-mail: registrar@trinity.capital.edu

Graduate Degree Programs:
Master of Divinity (MDIV)
Master of Arts in:
    Church Music (MACM)
    Lay Ministry (MALM)
    Master of Theological Studies (MTS)
    Master of Sacred Theology (STM)

Certificate Programs: Lay Ministry.

Class Titles: Almost all courses may be taken as "Special Student Status." Special students may receive credit for the course, but are not eligible for financial aid or housing.

Teaching Methods: *Computers:* Internet. *TV:* videotape. *Other:* videoconferencing.

Admission Requirements: *Graduate:* requirements include Bachelor of Arts or its equivalent, minimum 2.5 cumulative GPA in undergraduate program, and ecclesiastical endorsement for some degrees. Materials required for application: application including autobiographcial essay; $25 application fee; letters of recommendation; academic transcripts.

On-Campus Requirements: Consult catalog for details.

Tuition and Fees: *Graduate:* contact Director of Financial Aid for updated information. *Application Fee:* $25. *Credit by:* quarters, plus one interim each year. Trinity also offers a summer session in June.

Financial Aid: Federal Stafford Loan, Federal Work-Study.

Accreditation: Association of Theological Schools in the United States and Canada; also, North Central Association of Colleges and Universities.

Description: Predecessor schools were founded in 1830 and 1906. Trinity consolidated in 1978 to become the first consolidated seminary of the Evangelical Lutheran Church in

America. In 1830 the German Theological Seminary of the Ohio Synod, later known as the Evangelical Lutheran Theological Seminary, was founded to meet the need for educating pastors in the Ohio region. In 1845 the English Synod of Ohio founded Wittenberg College in Springfield, Ohio. In 1906 the theological department was named Hamma Divinity School. In 1964 Hamma received a large measure of autonomy within the Wittenberg structure and was renamed Hamma School of Theology. In 1850 the Joint Synod of Ohio founded Capital University. From that time until 1959 the Evangelical Lutheran Theological Seminary was a part of Capital. In 1959 the seminary was separated from Capital, becoming an independent institution of the American Lutheran Church. As the American Lutheran Church and the Lutheran Church in America came to work closely together in theological education in the 1960s and 1970s, it became apparent that there should only be one Lutheran seminary in Ohio. In 1974 the decision was made that Hamma and ELGS should consolidate even before merger by the national churches. Trinity Lutheran Seminary opened its doors on September 1, 1978. As a seminary of the Evangelical Lutheran Church in America, Trinity stands essentially for what its predecessor schools stood for—commitment to the gospel of Jesus Christ, to educational excellence, and to thorough preparation for Christian service. Recently, Trinity has delved into the field of Distance Learning with programs in Cleveland, Ohio, and Detroit, Michigan, at the Ecumenical Theological Seminary. The seminary is just now beginning to develop classes for online use. If you desire specific information, please contact the admissions office, the academic dean's office, or the continuing education office at Trinity Lutheran Seminary.

Triton College

2000 5th Avenue	Phone: (708) 456-0300 x3868
River Grove, IL 60171	Fax: (708) 583-3121

Division(s): Arts and Sciences
Web Site(s): http://www.triton.cc.il.us
E-mail: bscism@triton.cc.il.us

Class Titles: Graphic Design I/Graphic Design II/Environmental Biology/Microeconomics/Educational Psychology/History of the US to 1877/The Popular Arts/Humanities in Western Culture/Introduction to Philosophy/Ethics/Intro to Psychology/Freshman Rhetoric and Composition I/Freshman Rhetoric and Composition II/Intro to Sociology/Principles of Effective Speaking/Intro to Theater/Spanish and Latin American Lit/Contemporary Society.

Teaching Methods: *Computers:* online.

Credits Granted for: experiential learning, portfolio assessment, examination (CLEP, ACT-PEP, DANTES, GRE).

Admission Requirements: *Undergraduate:* high school graduate or GED.

On-Campus Requirements: Some classes may require on-campus labs (for example: Speech, Environmental Biology). Check the Triton College web site for more information.

Tuition and Fees: *Undergraduate:* $48/credit. *Other Costs:* $5/credit Student Fees ($60 max), $5 part-time or $10 full-time Registration Fee Auxiliary Fee: $1/course. Technology Fee: $40/semester (full-time)/$20/semester (part-time). *Credit by:* semester.

Financial Aid: Federal Stafford Loan, Federal Perkins Loan, Federal PLUS Loan, Federal Pell Grant, Federal Work-Study, VA, Illinois resident programs.

Accreditation: North Central Association of Colleges and Schools.

Description: Triton College (1964) is a comprehensive community college that serves the near-western suburbs of Chicago. Triton is recognized for its attractive 100-acre campus, its diverse and innovative programs, and its quality faculty. Currently, the college enrolls more than 18,000 students each semester and offers more than 150 degree and certificate programs. Triton offers a growing number of courses on the Internet. Tuition/fees for all online courses are charged as in-district providing for the enrolling student a very reasonable and affordable educational opportunity. Participation in the Illinois Community Colleges Online (ILCCO) will enable the college to offer complete degree and certificate completion. Check the Triton College web site for more information and details.

Troy State University—Florida Region

PO Box 2829	Phone: (850) 301-2151
Fort Walton Beach, FL 32548	Fax: (850) 301-2179

Division(s): Distance and Partnership Programs
Web Site(s): http://www.tsufl.edu/distancelearning
E-mail: distlearn@tsufl.edu

Undergraduate Degree Programs:
Associate of Science in General Education
Associate of Science in Business Administration
Bachelor of Applied Science in Resource Management
Bachelor of Science in Management
Bachelor or Science in Computer Science

Class Titles: Principles of Accounting, Cultural Anthropology, Criminal Justice, Principles of Macroeconomics, English Composition, Western Civilization, U.S. Diplomatic History, French Revolution/Napoleonic Period, Contemporary Europe, Legal Environment, Principles of Management/Organization

Behavior, Principles of Marketing, College Algebra, Math for General Studies, Music in Individual Development, American National Government, Contemporary American Foreign Policy, American Political Processes, Survey of International Relations, Business Statistics, Sociology for General Studies, Race/Ethnic Relations, Family Relations, Social Foundations of American Education, Contemporary Europe, Survey of Business Concepts, Survey of Public Administration, Organizational Behavior, Latin America in World Affairs.

Teaching Methods: *Computers:* Internet, real-time chat, electronic classroom, e-mail, CD-ROM, Blackboard.

Credits Granted for: experiential learning, portfolio assessment, examination (CLEP, ACT-PEP, DANTES, GRE), military experience as outlined in ACE.

Admission Requirements: *Undergraduate:* open admission policy. Contact school for details.

On-Campus Requirements: No traditional classroom attendance is required for our Distance Learning courses. Most courses, however, do require 1–2 proctored exams. The student is responsible for selecting an acceptable proctor who can be verified in their area.

Tuition and Fees: *Undergraduate:* $130/credit. *Other Costs:* $55 admissions fee. *Credit by:* We award credit by the 10-week term. We run 5 terms in an academic year.

Financial Aid: Federal Stafford Loan, Federal Perkins Loan, Federal PLUS Loan, Federal Pell Grant, Federal Work-Study, VA, state programs for residents of Florida.

Accreditation: Southern Association of Colleges and Schools.

Description: Troy State University Florida Region Distance Learning (1887) is designed to support students both locally and around the globe. We use emerging technologies coupled with traditional methodology to create an optimal learning environment: The Virtual Classroom. Students enjoy the flexibility of Distance Learning course work whether they are stay-at-home parents, shift workers, active duty military, or have heavy travel schedules. Please visit our web site at www.tsufl.edu/distancelearning to find out how Troy State University Florida Region Distance Learning can help you to meet your educational goals.

Troy State University

304 Wallace Hall	Phone: (334) 670-3976
Troy, AL 36082	Fax: (334) 670-5679

Division(s): Distance Learning Center
Web Site(s): http://www.tsulearn.net
E-mail: tsulearn@trojan.troyst.edu

Graduate Degree Programs:
Master of Science in:
  Criminal Justice
  International Relations
  Master of Public Administration
Master of Science in:
  Human Resources Management
  Management

Class Titles: Contact school or check web site for details.

Teaching Methods: *Computers:* Internet, real-time chat, e-mail.

Credits Granted for: other accredited institutions and PME.

Admission Requirements: GRE, MAT, GMAT, or TOEFL (international students only), official copy of all transcripts from institutions previously attended.

On-Campus Requirements: None.

Tuition and Fees: $750/course. *Application Fee:* $20. *Graduation Fee:* $35. *Other Costs:* $5 for transcripts. *Credit by:* semester hour system.

Financial Aid: Federal Stafford Loan, Federal Perkins Loan, Federal PLUS Loan, Federal Pell Grant, Federal Work-Study, VA, GI Bill, and tuition assistance.

Accreditation: Commission on Colleges of the Southern Association of Colleges and Schools.

Description: Since its founding in 1887, Troy State University has been recognized for the quality of its academic programs and its focus on the individual student. The university is dedicated to the preparation of students in a variety of fields in the arts and sciences, fine arts, business, communication, applied science, nursing, and allied health sciences, as well as to its historic role in the preparation of teachers. The administrators, faculty, staff, and students of the university, through a system of shared governance, are committed to excellence in education. A major commitment exists to provide undergraduate and graduate education for the national and international community, especially for mature students, not only by traditional means of delivery but also by technological means.

Troy State University Montgomery

PO Drawer 4419	Phone: (800) 355-8786 (TSUM) x553
Rosa Parks Library and	(334) 241-9553
Museum, Room 310	Fax: (334) 241-5465
Montgomery, AL 36103-4419	

Division(s): Distance Learning and Extended Academic Services
Web Site(s): http://www.tsum.edu/DL/
E-mail: edp@tsum.edu

Undergraduate Degree Programs:
Associate of Science in General Education with Academic Concentrations in:
- Business
- Child Care
- History
- Political Science
- Psychology
- Social Science

Bachelor of Science in Professional Studies
Bachelor of Arts in Professional Studies with Academic Concentrations in:
- Resource Management (Business)
- English
- History
- Political Science
- Psychology
- Social Science

Class Titles: over 90 courses offered; visit Web site at http://www.tsum.edu/DL/learningcontracts/index.htm.

Teaching Methods: *Computers:* Internet, real-time chat, electronic classroom, e-mail, *TV:* videotape, live-into-cable, PBS. *Other:* learning contracts.

Credits Granted for: portfolio assessment, extrainstitutional learning, examination (CLEP, AP, DANTES, Regents, ACE—Military Transcripts (AARTS, SMARTS, CCAF).

Admission Requirements: *Undergraduate:* high school graduate or GED.

On-Campus Requirements: None.

Tuition and Fees: *Undergraduate:* $117/SH credit/$351/3SH course (Effective fall 2001, no out-of-state tuition charge). *DL Fee:* $15 (in-state), $30 (out-of-state). *Annual Participation Fee:* $100 after first year. *Graduation Fee:* $50. *Other Costs:* textbooks vary with course. *Application Fee:* $70. *Credit by:* semester.

Financial Aid: Federal Stafford Loan, Federal Perkins Loan, Federal Plus Loan, Federal Pell Grant, Federal Work-Study, VA, Military Tuition Assistance Programs, State Rehab. Programs, and Employer Reimbursement Programs.

Accreditation: Southern Association of Colleges and Schools.

Description: Troy State University, Montgomery (1887), a public, coeducational institution, is dedicated to providing excellence in traditional and nontraditional educational opportunities for mature students of all races and ethnic backgrounds. The university's uniqueness centers on its status as Alabama's only university devoted exclusively to the education of mature students. The typical student is a working adult with family and community responsibilities. The integration of military personnel into its regular programs is evidence of the university's strong commitment to meeting the needs of military as well as civilian learners.

Truckee Meadows Community College

7000 Dandini Boulevard
Reno, NV 89512-3999

Phone: (775) 673-7814
Fax: (775) 673-7176

Division(s): Distance Education
Web Site(s): http://www.tmcc.edu
E-mail: e-learning@tmcc.edu

Class Titles: Anthropology, Auto, Biology, Technology, Criminal Justice, Literature, Humans and The Environment, U.S. Involvement/Vietnam, Health Occupations, Film and Literature, Mathematics, Medical Terminology, American Government, Psychology, Sociology, Real Estate, Accounting, Art Appreciation, Astronomy, Business Mathematics, Information Systems, CCNA, Microeconomics, Composition, Communications, Firefighter Safety, US History, Algebra, Pre-Calculus, Physics, Human Sexuality, Child Psychology, Abnormal Psychology, Music Appreciation.

Teaching Methods: *Computers:* Internet, e-mail. *TV:* videotape, cable program, PBS. *Other:* videoconferencing, fax, self-paced study, individual study.

Credits Granted for: experiential learning, portfolio assessment, examination (CLEP, DANTES), extrainstitutional learning.

Admission Requirements: *Undergraduate:* open-door policy, age 18, high school graduate or equivalent, U.S. citizens or immigrants. High school students, international students, and nonimmigrants may also be eligible. Admission to Health Science Programs: The health science programs include Dental Assisting, Nursing, Paramedic and Radiologic Technology. Admission to any of these programs is limited and requires special procedures. To be admitted into English classes or Math 096 or higher, students must have taken the course prerequisites within the last 3 years with a minimum grade of C, or have qualifying scores on the CPT. The ACT or SAT scores will also be accepted. TMCC will accept credit from a variety of training and educational programs toward an associate degree and/or certificate of achievement. The maximum number of credits allowed for transfer from all sources is 45 credits per degree. The maximum number of credits possible in each category is: (1) advanced standing from other colleges and universities: 45 credits total, (2) advanced standing from credit by examination: 30 credits, (3) advanced standing from nontraditional sources: 15 credits. for more information, contact: TMCC Admissions and Records at (775) 673-7042 or visit our Web site: http://www.tmcc.edu

On-Campus Requirements: May involve selected labs for science.

Tuition and Fees: *Undergraduate:* $48/credit Nevada residents, $60/credit if student lives in neighboring county in California; $70/credit for less than 7 credits plus $2,145/semester out-of-state, $48/credit for 7 or more credits plus $2,145/semester out-of-state. *Application Fee:* $10. *Software:* varies. *Credit by:* semester.

Financial Aid: Federal Stafford Loan, Federal Perkins Loan, Federal PLUS Loan, Federal Pell Grant, Federal Work-Study, VA, Nevada resident programs.

Accreditation: Northwest Association of Schools and Colleges.

Description: Truckee Meadows Community College (1971), an institution of the University and Community College System of Nevada, is located in Reno, Nevada. TMCC recently celebrated its 30th anniversary and has experienced strong growth in enrollments and program offerings. Currently, 12,000 students are served, with the campus offering classes and degrees in 40 career fields as well as a full university transfer associate degree program. TMCC's Distance Education program is in its fifth year and offers credit instruction in several formats including: Interactive TV, Cablecast courses, Going the Distance with PBS/Channel 5 and Internet instruction.

Tulsa Community College

| 909 South Boston Avenue | Phone: (918) 595-7143 |
| Tulsa, OK 74119 | Fax: (918) 595-7306 |

Division(s): Office of Distance Learning
Web Site(s): http://www.tulsa.cc.ok.us/dl
E-mail: rdomingu@tulsa.cc.ok.us

Undergraduate Degree Programs:
Associate in Liberal Arts

Certificate Programs: various.

Teaching Methods: *Computers:* Internet, e-mail, CD-ROM, LISTSERV. *TV:* videotape, cable program, PBS. *Other:* videoconferencing.

Credits Granted for: examination (CLEP, APP, PEP).

Admission Requirements: *Undergraduate:* Demonstrated proficiency in English, math, and science. ACT scores, CPT scores, and college transcripts can be used to demonstrate proficiency. *Certificate:* Demonstrated proficiency in English, math, and science.

On-Campus Requirements: None.

Tuition and Fees: *Undergraduate:* $56/credit hour in-state, $131/credit hour out-of-state. *Application Fee:* $15. *Other Costs:* Lab fees vary. *Credit by:* semester.

Financial Aid: Available for persons who qualify, through grants, scholarships, loans and part-time employment, from federal, state, institutional, and private sources.

Accreditation: North Central Association of Colleges and Schools, Oklahoma State Regents for Higher Education.

Description: Tulsa Junior College (1970) became Tulsa Community College in May, 1996. Although TCC has only served Tulsa and the surrounding communities since 1970, the college has established a tradition of offering students a personal approach to a practical and useful higher education. When the college first opened its doors, initial enrollment was 2,800 students. Since that time, TCC has provided quality educational services to 300,000 persons. TCC Distance Learning now offers up to 30 telecourses, several Interactive TV courses, and 25 Internet courses each semester.

Tyler Junior College

| East 5th Street | Phone: (903) 510-2200 |
| Tyler, TX 75711 | Fax: (903) 510-2634 |

Division(s): Academic Dean's Office
Web Site(s): http://www.tyler.cc.tx.us
E-mail: klew@tjc.tyler.cc.tx.us

Class Titles: Biology, Environmental Science, Business, Chemistry, Computers, Macro/Micro Economics, Composition/Rhetoric, American Government, American State Government, U.S. History, Psychology, Sociology, Spanish, Speech Communication, Financial Accounting, Managerial Accounting, Art Appreciation, Design, Drawing, Accounting, Legal Environment in Business, Computer Literacy, Computer Programming: QUICK BASIC, PASCAL, C, COBOL, Business Computer Applications, DOS/Windows, Spreadsheet Concepts, Computer Programming Logic, Networking, Software Applications, Data Structures, Object Oriented Programming, Data Base Concepts, Current Computer Science Topics, Creative Writing, World Literature, Legal Ethics, Algebra, Astronomy, Wildlife Management, Survey of New Testament, Criminal Justice, Crime in America, Agriculture Economics/Finance, Health Professions, TASP Math Review, Trigonometry, Precalculus, Calculus with Analytic Geometry, Medical Terminology, Emergency Medical Service Professions.

Teaching Methods: *Computers:* Internet, electronic classroom, CD-ROM. *TV:* videotape, cable program, satellite, PBS. *Other:* videoconferencing, audiotapes, independent study, individual study.

Credits Granted for: examination (CLEP, ACT-PEP, DANTES, GRE).

Admission Requirements: *Undergraduate:* high school graduate or GED, TASP required before class placement.

On-Campus Requirements: None.

Tuition and Fees: *Undergraduate:* contact school for all tuition and fee information. *Credit by:* semester.

Financial Aid: Federal Stafford Loan, Federal PLUS Loan, Federal Pell Grant, Federal Work-Study, VA, Texas resident programs.

Accreditation: Southern Association of Colleges and Schools.

Description: Tyler Junior College (1926) is the largest single-campus community college in the state of Texas, enrolling approximately 8,000 students in credit instruction each fall. Tyler Junior College is a comprehensive community college committed to meeting the needs of East Texas by providing excellence in an environment which broadens the mind, challenges the spirit, and maximizes human potential.

UC Raymond Walters College

9555 Plainfield Road	Phone: (513) 745-5776
Cincinnati, OH 45236-1096	Fax: (513) 745-8315

Division(s): Outreach and Continuing Education
Web Site(s): http://www.rwc.uc.edu/adm/oce
E-mail: susan.kemper@uc.edu

Class Titles: Economics, English Composition, Small Business Management, Sales, Sociology of Family, Chemistry, Health, Physics, Nutrition, Library Technology, Electronic Media Technology, Office Administration Technology (various Microcomputer Software Applications).

Teaching Methods: *Computers:* Internet, Blackboard, real-time chat, e-mail, CD-ROM, LISTSERV. *TV:* videotape, PBS. *Other:* fax, independent study, individual study.

Credits Granted for: experiential learning, portfolio assessment in selected departments, extrainstitutional learning, examination (CLEP, ACT-PEP, DANTES, GRE).

Admission Requirements: *Undergraduate:* high school transcript/GED, placement exam if seeking degree. *Certificate:* varies.

On-Campus Requirements: A couple of sessions for most classes.

Tuition and Fees: *Undergraduate:* $100/credit. *Application Fee:* $30. *Software:* $5.58 (optional). *Other Costs:* $50 matriculation. *Credit by:* quarter.

Financial Aid: Federal Stafford Loan, Federal Perkins Loan, Federal PLUS Loan, Federal Pell Grant, Federal Work-Study, VA, Ohio residents (OIG).

Accreditation: North Central Association of Colleges and Schools.

Description: Since its founding in 1967, UC Raymond Walters College has strived to provide high quality general education to create informed citizenry who can think critically, communicate effectively, and solve problems. The college provides lifelong learning opportunities for job preparation and mobility, the pursuit of higher education, and personal enrichment. To maintain quality, the college engages in comprehensive assessment of its programs, courses, and services.

UCLA Extension

10995 LeConte Avenue, Suite 714	Phone: (310) 825-2648
Los Angeles, CA 90024	Fax: (310) 267-4793

Division(s): Distance Learning Programs
Web Site(s): http://www.unex.ucla.edu
E-mail: dstlrng@unex.ucla.edu or enroll@unex.ucla.edu

Certificate Programs: College Counseling, Technical Communications, Online Teaching, General Business Studies, CTC Cross-Cultural Language and Academic Development, Teaching English as a Foreign Language, Teaching English to Speakers of Other Languages.

Class Titles: Architecture, Area/Ethnic/Cultural Studies, American Studies, Asian Studies, Biological/Life Sciences, Business, Accounting, Business Administration/Management, Business Communications, Finance, Hospitality Services Management, Human Resources Management, International Business, Investments/Securities, Management Information Systems, Marketing, Organizational Behavior Studies, Real Estate, Journalism, Public Relations, Computer/Information Sciences, Computer Programming, Information Sciences/Systems, Education, Continuing Education, Curriculum/Instruction, Instructional Media, Special Education, Student Counseling, Teacher Education, Engineering, Creative Writing, English as Second Language, Composition, Technical Writing, Foreign Languages/Literature: European, Spanish Language/Literature, Health/Physical Education/Fitness, Health Professions/Related Sciences, Math, Algebra, Philosophy/Religion, Ethics, Physical Sciences, Astronomy/Astrophysics, Psychology, Cognitive Psychology, Counseling Psychology, Social Sciences, Economics, Visual/Performing Arts, Design, Film Studies.

Teaching Methods: *Computers:* Internet, real-time chat, virtual classrooms, audio. *Other:* videoconferencing.

Admission Requirements: *Undergraduate:* open admissions or specific to degree. *Graduate:* same as undergraduate. *Certificate:* TOEFL score, BA degree-specific to each certificate.

On-Campus Requirements: prerequisites specific to each program.

Tuition and Fees: *Application Fee:* already built into the course fees. *Other Costs:* graduate courses carry individual course fees, vary for text/materials; contact school for course fee information. *Credit by:* quarter.

Financial Aid: Federal Stafford Loan, Federal Perkins Loan, Federal PLUS Loan, Federal Pell Grant, Federal Work-Study, VA, California resident programs, Life Long Learning Taxpayer Relief Program.

Accreditation: Western Association of Schools and Colleges.

Description: UCLA Extension (1917) is the nation's—and probably the world's—largest urban, single-campus, continuing higher education program, enrolling 110,000 annually. The particular province of extension—continuing higher education—advances the interconnected assigned missions of the University of California. These are: to conduct and disseminate basic research; to provide instruction to the bachelor's, master's, and doctoral levels; and to be of public service. To find innovative ways to reach our primarily adult student population, a new platform evolved—education through distance learning. From the first pioneering steps in 1996 to the present, UCLA Extension has enjoyed substantial growth, presently offering nearly 800 courses to 8,000 students annually. The implications of this growth were best described by Chancellor Camesale: "Knowledge is exploding at an ever-increasing pace, but so too are the capabilities of the new information technology systems. I have no doubt that we are in the midst of a true technological revolution in this domain—one that will change fundamentally the ways in which universities carry out their missions."

Ulster County Community College

Cottekill Road	Phone: (914) 687-5040
Stone Ridge, NY 12484	Fax: (914) 687-5083

Division(s): Vice President of Academic Affairs
Web Site(s): http://www.sunyulster.edu
E-mail: makowskp@synyulster.edu

Undergraduate Degree Program:
Associate in Science in Individual Studies—Liberal Arts

Class Titles: Environmental Biology, Interpreting Statistics, Latin America 21st Century, Library Information Literacy, English, French and Spanish, Psychology, Sociology, History, Criminal Justice.

Teaching Methods: *Computers:* Internet, real-time chat, electronic classroom, e-mail, CD-ROM. *TV:* videotape, cable program, satellite. *Other:* correspondence, independent study, individual study.

Credits Granted for: experiential learning, portfolio assessment, extrainstitutional learning, examination (CLEP, ACT-PEP, DANTES, GRE).

Admission Requirements: *Undergraduate:* open admission. *Graduate:* open admission. *Doctoral:* open admission. *Certificate:* open admission.

On-Campus Requirements: None.

Tuition and Fees: *Undergraduate:* $89/credit in-state, $178/credit out-of-state. *Other Costs:* $200/credit cost enrollment fee, subject to change. *Credit by:* Semester.

Financial Aid: Federal Stafford Loan, Federal Perkins Loan, Federal PLUS Loan, Federal Pell Grant, Federal Work-Study, VA, New York resident programs.

Accreditation: The Commission of Higher Education of the Middle States Association.

Description: Ulster County Community College (1962) has grown rapidly. It began its first academic year in September 1963. Classes were held at a temporary campus in the historic Ulster Academy building made available through the corporation of the Board of Education of Kingston City Schools Consolidated. Two years later, 48 students received their degrees at the college's first graduation. The college has now conferred in excess of 11,000 degrees. Ulster County Community College began offering Internet courses through the SUNY Learning Network in 1996. Ulster plans to offer an Associate in Science Degree in individual states pending approval of the State Education Department and the Commission for the Middle States Association.

Umpqua Community College

P.O. Box 967	Phone: (541) 440-4600 x727
Roseburg, OR 97470	Fax: (541) 440-4612

Division(s): Counseling
Web Site(s): http://www.umpqua.cc.or.us/distance_ed/disted.htm
E-mail: binghac@umpqua.cc.or.us

Undergraduate Degree Programs:
Associate of Arts Oregon Transfer Degree

Class Titles: Math, Writing, Social Sciences, Humanities, Computer Skills.

Teaching Methods: *Computers:* Internet, e-mail. *TV:* videotape, cable program, satellite broadcasting, PBS.

Credits Granted for: examination (CLEP, ACT-PEP, DANTES, GRE).

Admission Requirements: *Undergraduate:* those who may be admitted: graduates of accredited secondary schools, GED Certificate holders, or Adult high school diploma holders, non-high school graduates over 18 and whose high school class has graduated, 16- or 17-year-olds who are not required to attend high school, Junior or senior level high school students with approval from their high school officials.

On-Campus Requirements: None.

Tuition and Fees: *Undergraduate:* $39/credit. *Software:* $35. *Other Costs:* $6/credit for tuition equalization. *Credit by:* quarter.

Financial Aid: Federal Stafford Loan, Federal Perkins Loan, Federal Pell Grant, Federal Work-Study, VA.

Accreditation: Northwest Association of Schools and Colleges, Oregon State Board of Education.

Description: Umpqua Community College (1965) is a member of an Oregon and Southwest Washington consortium of community colleges. The Department of Community Colleges and Workforce Development Distributed Learning and Technology oversees the program whereby all colleges of the consortium may "host" any Distance Learning course provided by any other member of the consortium.

Union County College

1033 Springfield Avenue	Phone: (908) 709-7518
Cranford, NJ 07016	Fax: (908) 709-7131

Division(s): Office of the Registrar—Distance Education
Web Site(s): http://www.ucc.edu
E-mail: kane@ucc.edu

Undergraduate Degree Programs:
Associate of Applied Science in:
  Administrative Support/Information Technology
  Business Management
  Liberal Studies/Exploring Science and Arts

Certificate Programs: Contact the Office of Professional Certification.

Class Titles: Contact school or visit web site for details.

Teaching Methods: *Computers:* Internet, real-time chat, e-mail, CD-ROM, newsgroup, LISTSERV. *TV:* videotape, cable program, satellite broadcasting, PBS. *Other:* independent study, individual study.

Credits Granted for: experiential learning, examination (CLEP, Advanced Placement Exams, Challenge Exams).

Admission Requirements: *Undergraduate:* open to all high school graduates, those holding high school equivalency certificates, or those persons 18 years of age or older.

On-Campus Requirements: None.

Tuition and Fees: *Undergraduate:* full-time for one academic year: $2,049 in-district and $3,717 out-of-district. *Application Fee:* $25. *Graduation Fee:* $60. *Other Costs:* required Fee: $381. *Credit by:* semester.

Financial Aid: Federal Stafford Loan, Federal PLUS Loan, Federal Pell Grant, Federal Work-Study, state programs for residents of New Jersey.

Accreditation: Commission on Higher Education of the Middle States Association of Colleges and Schools.

Description: As the oldest community college in New Jersey, Union County College (1933) has been serving both career-minded and transfer-oriented students for the majority of the 20th century. For 65 years, UCC has maintained its commitment to scholarship by providing a solid liberal arts foundation while, at the same time, developing new programs and courses that meet the challenges of a rapidly developing society. As it looks to the future, Union County College is focused on ensuring that its programs and facilities are equipped to prepare the student for the intellectual and technological demands of the 21st century. All students enrolled in credit courses are offered their own college e-mail accounts through which they can communicate with UCC's outstanding faculty, fellow students, and the vast world of knowledge and information available through the World Wide Web. Distance Learning opportunities that have been in place at UCC since 1985, such as telecourses and online computer courses, are increasing with each semester.

Union Institute

440 East McMillan Street	Phone: (513) 861-6400
Cincinnati, OH 45206	(800) 486-3116
	Fax: (513) 861-9026

Division(s): College of Undergraduate Studies, Center for Distance Learning
Web Site(s): http://tui.edu
E-mail: tmott@tui.edu

Undergraduate Degree Programs:
Bachelor of Arts
Bachelor of Science

Teaching Methods: *Computers:* Internet, real-time chat, e-mail, newsgroup. *Other:* audioconferencing, fax, correspondence, independent study, individual study, learning contracts.

Credits Granted for: experiential learning, examination (CLEP, ACT-PEP, DANTES), transfer credit from other regionally accredited colleges.

Admission Requirements: *Undergraduate:* college-level learning ability, interview with faculty advisor, application essay, 2 letters of recommendation, official college transcripts (if applicable).

On-Campus Requirements: None.

Tuition and Fees: *Undergraduate:* $272/credit. *Application Fee:* $50. *Credit by:* semester.

Financial Aid: Federal Stafford Loan, Federal Perkins Loan, Federal PLUS Loan, Federal Pell Grant, Federal Work-Study, VA (some states), Ohio, Florida, California (possibly others) resident programs.

Accreditation: North Central Association of Colleges and Schools.

Description: The Union Institute was founded in 1964 to provide educational opportunities to working adults through innovative and flexible delivery systems. The undergraduate distance learning program originated in 1993 to expand access to the College of Undergraduate Studies' bachelor's program to adult learners located throughout the country.

Union University

1050 Union University Drive	Phone: (731) 661-5370
Jackson, TN 38305	Fax: (731) 661-5101

Division(s): Academic Center
Web Site(s): http://www.uu.edu
E-mail: smyatt@uu.edu

Undergraduate Degree Programs: Contact school.

Class Titles: Christian Studies, Physical Science.

Teaching Methods: *Computer:* Internet, real-time chat, electronic classroom, e-mail. *Other:* independent study, individual study.

Credits Granted for: experiential learning, portfolio assessment, examination (CLEP, DANTES).

Admission Requirements: *Undergraduate:* 22 ACT or 2.50 GPA on college transcript.

Tuition and Fees: *Undergraduate:* $450/credit. *Credit by:* semester.

Financial Aid: Federal Stafford Loan, Federal Perkins Loan, Federal PLUS Loan, Federal Pell Grant, Federal Work-Study, VA, state programs for residents of Tennessee.

Accreditation: Southern Association of Colleges and Schools.

Description: Union University (1823), a private liberal arts Christian university in Jackson, Tennessee, was chartered by the legislature in 1825, making it the earliest school whose roots are linked with what later became the Southern Baptist Convention. The mission of Union University, a higher education institution of the Tennessee Baptist Convention, is to provide quality undergraduate and graduate education to students of qualified preparation and good character. Union University began offering online courses in fall 1999 delivered entirely via the Internet, at http://www.UnionUonline.org, using a combination of communications tools including audio, video, e-mail, virtual classrooms, and more.

United States Sports Academy

One Academy Drive	Phone: (800) 223-2668
Daphne, AL 36526	(334) 626-3303
	Fax: (334) 621-1149

Division(s): Distance Learning
Web Site(s): http://www.ussa.edu
E-mail: academy@ussa.edu

Graduate Degree Programs:
Master of Sport Science in:
    Sport Management
    Sport Medicine
    Sport Coaching
    Health and Fitness Management
    Recreation Management
    Dual majors available

Certificate Programs: Sport Coaching, Sport Management, Sports Medicine, Exercise Physiology, Sport Conditioning, Bodybuilding, Personal Training, Travel and Tourism.

Teaching Methods: Web-based instruction, e-mail, telephone, audiotapes, fax, correspondence, independent study. On-going enrollment for Distance Learning.

Admission Requirements: *Graduate:* application; 3.0 undergraduate GPA; 800 GRE, 27 MAT, or 400 GMAT scores; 3 recommendation letters; written personal statement of goals, résumé.

On-Campus Requirements: comprehensive examination at conclusion of course requirements and mentorship requirements. Offered at end of each semester.

Tuition and Fees: *Undergraduate:* $220/course (4 CEUs). *Graduate:* $350/credit hour (3 credits/class). *Application Fee:* $50. *Other Costs:* $100 one-time computer fee. *Credit by:* semester.

Financial Aid: Federal Stafford Loans available.

Accreditation: Southern Association of Colleges and Schools.

Description: The United States Sports Academy has been in service since 1972, providing training for the sport professional with a sports specific curriculum. The role of the academy in higher education is to prepare men and women for sport professions in the areas of sport management, sports medicine, and sport coaching.

University College of Cape Breton

PO Box 5300	Phone: (902) 563-1423
Sydney, NS, Canada B1P 6L2	Fax: (902) 563-1449

Division(s): Extension and Community Affairs
Web Site(s): http://www.uccb.ns.ca
E-mail: jpino@uccb.ns.ca

Undergraduate Degree Programs:
Bachelor of Arts Community Studies
Bachelor of Technology Environmental Studies (postdiploma)
Bachelor or Technology (Environmental Health) Post CIPHI Certification
Bachelor of Technology (Manufacturing) Post Diploma

Graduate Degree Programs:
Diploma in Education (Curriculum)
Certificate in Education (Technology)

Certificate Programs: Public Administration

Class Titles: Business Administration, Economics, Education, English, Environmental Studies, Problem-Centered Studies, Political Science, Psychology Environmental Health, Manufacturing.

Teaching Methods: *Computers:* Internet, electronic classroom, e-mail, LISTSERV. *Other:* videoconferencing, audiographics, correspondence, independent study.

Credits Granted for: experiential learning, portfolio assessment, extrainstitutional learning.

Admission Requirements: *Undergraduate:* High school graduates with 60% overall average, OR approved transfers, OR "nontraditional learners" out of high school for 2 years who have completed Grade 10 and are age 20. Admission is subject to space and program restrictions, and specific programs may have additional requirements. *Graduate:* undergraduate degree.

On-Campus Requirements: None.

Tuition and Fees: *Undergraduate:* $447/3 credits, $894/6 credits. *Graduate:* $986/6 credits, $493/3 credits. *Application Fee:* $35. *Other Costs:* $75/course Distance Fees. Transfer credit/PLA application fee: $50. *Credit by:* semester.

Accreditation: Association of Universities and Colleges of Canada, Association of Canadian Community Colleges, Association of Atlantic Universities, Associate Member of the Association of Commonwealth Universities.

Description: Located near Sydney on beautiful Cape Breton Island, the University College of Cape Breton (1974) is Canada's first university college. UCCB offers an innovative blend of degree, diploma, and certificate programs. The college also supports community economic development and applied research and provides technical assistance to business and industry. Its mission is to ensure continued emphasis on, and commitment to, meaningful, relevant, and accessible programs that build upon a unique blend of educational traditions. For many years, UCCB has enjoyed a reputation for providing flexible credit and noncredit distance learning opportunities. The school's network of electronic, audiographic classrooms facilitates course delivery throughout Nova Scotia. Correspondence courses began in 1996, and Web-delivered courses recently added to the broad range of options available to students studying at a distance.

University College of the Cariboo

900 College Drive	Phone: (250) 371-5667
Kamloops, BC, Canada V2C 5N3	Fax: (250) 371-5771

Division(s): Distance Education in the Sciences and Health Sciences
Web Site(s): http://www.cariboo.bc.ca/schs/dist_ed.htm
E-mail: daly@cariboo.bc.ca

Undergraduate Degree Programs:
Bachelor of Health Science (Respiratory Therapy)

Certificate Programs: Anesthesia Assistant, Cardiovascular Perfusion, Animal Welfare, Medical Laboratory Assistant, Asthma Educator, Polysomnography Program.

Class Titles: Animal Welfare, Animal Care, Safety in Workplace, Workplace Hazardous Management, Information Systems, Electrocardiogram Analysis, Medical Terminology, Applied Science, Anatomy/Physiology, Laboratory Procedures, Blood Gas Analysis, Veterinary Hospital Safety, Pathophysiology, Pharmacology, Forest Ecology, Respiratory Therapy Procedures, Anesthesia Technology, Neonatology, Hemodynamic/Physiological Monitoring, Emergency Cardiac Care, Asthma Educators, Elementary Science Teacher, Principles of Polysomnography.

Teaching Methods: *Computers:* Internet, real-time chat, electronic classroom, e-mail, CD-ROM, LISTSERV, newsgroup. *TV:* interactive TV, videotape, satellite broadcasting, PBS. *Other:* radio broadcast, videoconferencing, audioconferencing, audiotapes, fax, correspondence, independent study, individual study, learning contracts.

Admission Requirements: *Certificate:* diploma in Allied Health.

On-Campus Requirements: Anesthesia and Cardiovascular Perfusion have clinical practicums.

Tuition and Fees: *Undergraduate:* $150–$350 Canadian/course. *Other Costs:* Participants are responsible for all computer hardware/software costs. *Credit by:* semester.

Accreditation: Association of Universities and Colleges of Canada.

Description: University College of the Cariboo (1970) has offered distance learning opportunities for more than a decade to thousands of professional students across the country and, indeed, around the world. We note with pride that UCC has been recognized by the League of Innovation in Community Colleges as having one of the 20 best distance learning programs in North America. Distance learning students are able to take immediate advantage of UCC's extensive experience and services. We have completion rates in our Health Science distance education programs hovering around the 80% mark. We attribute our high completion rate to several critical factors: type of program, target audience, quality of contact between learner and facilitator, and ongoing evaluation.

University College of the University of Maine System

46 University Drive	**Phone: (207) 621-3408**
Augusta, ME 04330	**Fax: (207) 621-3420**

Division(s): Education Services
Web Site(s): http://www.learn.maine.edu
E-mail: teleservice@maine.edu

Undergraduate Degree Programs:
Associate of Art in Liberal Arts (UMA)
Associate of Art in Social Services (UMA)
Associate of Science in:
    Liberal Studies (UMA)
    Business Administration (UMA)
    Library and Information Technology (UMA)
    Education (KVTC)
    Law Enforcement Technology (SMTC)
Bachelor of Art in Behavioral Sciences (UMM)
Bachelor of Science in:
    Business Administration (UMA)
    Mental Health and Human Services (UMA)
Bachelor of University Studies (UM)
Registered Nursing to Bachelor of Science Nursing (UM, UMFK, USM)

Graduate Degree Programs:
Master of Art in Liberal Studies (UM)

Master of Science in Health Policy and Management (USM)
Adult Education (USM)
    Counseling with a concentration in Rehabilitation Counseling (USM)

Certificate Programs: *Undergraduate:* Early Childhood, Gerontology, Liberal Arts, Library and Information Technology, MHRT II, Substance Abuse Rehabilitation, Classical Studies, Maine Studies. *Graduate:* Health Policy and Management, Community Planning and Development, Nonprofit Management, Mental Health Rehabilitation Technician III, Child and Family Services.
    Degree programs available in Maine only; Internet courses available everywhere.

Class Titles: Contact school.

Teaching Methods: *Computers:* Internet. *TV:* videotape, satellite broadcasting. *Other:* audioconferencing, videoconferencing, audiographics, audiotapes, fax, correspondence, independent study, individual study, learning contracts.

Credits Granted for: experiential learning, portfolio assessment, extrainstitutional learning, examination (CLEP, ACT-PEP, DANTES, GRE).

Admission Requirements: *Undergraduate:* contact individual campus. *Graduate:* contact individual campus. *Certificate:* contact individual campus.

On-Campus Requirements: attendance at Maine center/site for ITV courses. Most online courses have none.

Tuition and Fees: *Undergraduate:* contact individual campus. *Graduate:* contact individual campus. *Credit by:* semester.

Financial Aid: Federal Stafford Loan, Federal Perkins Loan, Federal PLUS Loan, Federal Pell Grant, Federal Work-Study, VA, Maine resident programs.

Accreditation: UMS universities are accredited by the New England Association of Schools and Colleges.

Description: Distance Learning initiative (USM), begun in 1989, serves 3,000 students each semester through 100 courses from 31 degree and certificate programs at the associate, bachelor's, and master's levels. The University of Maine System. UNET was one of the nation's first to implement distance learning to geographically dispersed rural students. In 1989 it delivered its courses via interactive TV. Today, faculty use a variety of technology, based on course content and learning objectives, to deliver distance courses. Interactive TV courses are available only in Maine, while Internet classes may be accessed from students' homes or at dozens of convenient sites in-state. Also, UC's Teleservice Center allows students to register, add or drop courses, receive assistance with institutional forms, obtain referral to appropriate support services, and request information about the institution and its services.

University of Action Learning (UAL)

1650 38th Street, Suite 205W
Boulder, CO 80301

Phone: (303) 442-6907
Fax: (303) 442-6815

Division(s): Entire University
Web Site(s): http://www.u-a-l.org
E-mail: kim@u-a-l.org

Undergraduate Degree Programs: Bachelor:
Management
Administration
Professional Studies

Graduate Degree Programs:
Master of Business Administration
Master of Health Care Administration
Science and Management

Certificate Programs: *Bachelor of Arts:* Certificates in Office Administration, Business Administration, Quality Management, Marketing Human Resource Management. *Master of Arts:* Certificates in Long-Term Care, Health Care Services, Human Resource Management, Facility Management, Executive Leadership, Organization and Management, Strategic Human Resource Management.

Class Titles: Contact school or check web site for details.

Teaching Methods: *Computers:* Internet, real-time chat, electronic classroom, e-mail, CD-ROM, newsgroup, LISTSERV.

Credits Granted for: experiential learning, portfolio assessment.

Admission Requirements: *Undergraduate:* must be working full time in management or professional capacity. *Graduate:* must be working full time in management or professional capacity. *Certificate:* must be working full time in management or professional capacity.

Tuition and Fees: *Undergraduate:* $500/3 credits. *Graduate:* $250/credit. *Graduation Fee:* $750. *Credit by:* open.

Financial Aid: Scholarship opportunities available.

Accreditation: DETC; State of Colorado Commission on higher education.

Description: The University of Action Learning (1999) is dedicated to providing Internet Resourced Undergraduate and Graduate programs. Our mission is to play an innovative and progressive role in the lifelong development of professional practicing managers, supervisors, and leaders globally. Our program focuses on work-based projects targeting personal career as well as corporate company objectives. Associates (students) work with a group of professional peers and receive the support of tutors, advisers, and facilitators. UAL offers a range of programs including individual course offerings through bachelor's and master's degrees. Courses are designed for continuing professional development on an individual, in-company, and organizational basis. Faculty members are the heart of the UAL learning programs, whether in face-to-face workshops or Cyber Sets. Tutors work to facilitate Action Learning with groups of forward-thinking professionals.

University of Akron

Akron, OH 44325

Phone: (330) 972-5144
Fax: (330) 972-5636

Division(s): Office of Provost
Web Site(s): http://www.uakron.edu/distance
E-mail: distance@uakron.edu

Graduate Degree Programs:
Master of Education
Master of Social Work

Class Titles:
C&T
Principles of Emergency Management
Emergency Response and Prep Plan
English
English Comp I Honors
Geography and Planning
Intro to Geography—Honors
Modern Languages
Beginning German
German Conversation and Composition
Beginning Japanese I
Physics
Descriptive Astronomy
Political Science
State Politics
Campaign Management I
College of Business
Advanced Accounting
Taxation II
International Business
School of Music
Exploring Music: Bach to Rock
School of Communication
Intro. to Public Speaking
Intro. to Public Speaking Honors
School of Social Work
Fundamentals of Research I
HBSE: Small Social Systems
Social Welfare Policy I
SW Pract with Small Social Systems
Fundamentals Research I
Social Welfare Policy I
Psychopathology and Social Work

Advanced Pract with Small Social Sys I
Dynamics of Racism and Discrimination
Pract: Family & Child
Adv Practice with Small Soc Syst I
Community Org and Planning
Com Econ Sys & Soc Pol An
College of Nursing
Inquiry I
Public Health Concepts
Social and Behavioral Science in Public Health
Pathophysiological Concepts
Health Services Admin in Public Health
Environmental Health Science in Public Health
Theoretical Basic for Nursing
Policy Issues in Nursing
Nursing Research/RN Only
Center for Economic Education
W: Tech Entrepreneurship
Continuing Education—Graduate Outreach
Developmental Reading
Administration of Pupil Services
Eval in Ed Organizations
School/Community Relations
Contemporary Issues in Reading Instruction
Philosophies of Education
Tech Integration Frameworks for Success
Adapting Math Science for Stud Inclusive Set
Using Ethics Educ for Educ Tech
Working Parents of Children with Disabilities
Motivating Reluctant Reader
Prep Ohio Grad Tes
Grant Writing
Utilizing Clout in Columbus Educators
Building Positive Outcomes for Diverse Student
Crisis Intervention
Counseling and Special Education
Career Planning
MSW Program

Teaching Methods: *Computers:* Internet, real-time chat, threaded discussion, electronic classroom, e-mail, CD/DVD-ROM, newsgroup, LISTSERV. *TV:* videotape, cable program. *Other:* radio broadcast, audioconferencing, videoconferencing, multimedia, fax.

Credits Granted for: examination (CLEP).

Admission Requirements: *Undergraduate:* high school diploma or equivalent, pass state competency exam. *Graduate:* 2.75 GPA. *Doctoral:* 2.0 GPA. *Certificate:* 2.0 GPA.

On-Campus Requirements: optional—dependent on program.

Tuition and Fees: *Undergraduate:* $181/credit resident, $387/credit nonresident. *Graduate:* $218/credit resident,

$387/credit nonresident. *Doctoral:* same as graduate. *Application Fee:* $25. *Credit by:* semester.

Financial Aid: Federal Stafford Loan, Federal Perkins Loan, Federal PLUS Loan, Federal Pell Grant, Federal Work-Study, VA, Ohio resident programs.

Accreditation: Higher Learning Commission of North Central Association of Colleges and Schools.

Description: The University of Akron (1870) has an open-admission policy for its 9 degree-granting colleges. Degrees are offered from the associate level through the PhD. Two modes of delivery are offered through on-line classes and electronic classes through Distance Learning network.

The University of Akron— Wayne College

1901 Smucker Road	Phone: (330) 972-8975
Orrville, OH 44667	Fax: (330) 684-8989

Division(s): Computing Services
Web Site(s): http://www.wayne.uakron.edu
E-mail: WayneAdmissions@uakron.edu

Undergraduate Degree Programs: Contact school.

Certificate Programs: varies.

Class Titles: Windows 9x, Spreadsheet Software, Database Applications, C++ Programming, Java programming, Physics for Environmental Technicians.

Teaching Methods: *Computers:* Internet, real-time chat, electronic classroom, e-mail, CD-ROM, newsgroup, LISTSERV.

Admission Requirements: *Undergraduate:* must be admitted as a student in good standing at The University of Akron. http://www.uakron.edu/registrar.

On-Campus Requirements: Depends on the course and the instructor.

Tuition and Fees: *Undergraduate:* $133.20/credit. *Credit by:* semester.

Financial Aid: Federal Stafford Loan, Federal Perkins Loan, Federal PLUS Pell Grant, Federal Work-Study, VA, state programs for residents of Ohio.

Accreditation: North Central Accreditation of Colleges and Schools.

Description: Wayne College (1972) is a regional campus of The University of Akron, located in the rural community of Orrville, Ohio.

University of Alabama

127 Martha Parham West
PO Box 870388
Tuscaloosa, AL 35487-0388

Phone: (205) 348-9278
(800) 452-5971
Fax: (205) 348-0249

Division(s): College of Continuing Studies, Division of Distance Education
Web Site(s): http://bama.disted.ua.edu
E-mail: disted@ccs.ua.edu

Graduate Degree Programs:
Master of Science in:
    Aerospace Engineering
    Electrical and Computer Engineering
    Mechanical Engineering
    Engineering
    Engineering Management and Nursing Care Management

Certificate Programs: Criminal Justice, Computer Studies.

Class Titles: *Undergraduate credit through written correspondence:* Astronomy, Athletic Coaching, Biology, Chemical Engineering, Classics, Computer Science, Consumer Science, Counselor Education, Criminal Justice, Economics, Finance, Geography, German, Health Education, History, Human Development/Family Studies, Human Nutrition/Hospitality Management, Journalism, Library Studies, Management, Mass Communication, Math, Music Academics, Philosophy, Physics, Political Science, Psychology, Religious Studies, Sociology, Spanish, Statistics, Telecommunication/Film, Theater. *Undergraduate credit via online computer:* American Studies, Athletic Coaching, Athletic Training, Biology, Computer Science, Consumer Science, Counselor Education, Criminal Justice, Economics, Computer and Applied Technology, Health Education, Human Development and Family Studies, Human Nutrition and Hospitality Management, Nursing, Philosophy, Political Science, Psychology, Statistics, and Telecommunications and Film. *Undergraduate/graduate credit by videotape:* Engineering, Nursing, Commerce/Business Administration, Human Environmental Sciences, and College of Education. *Undergraduate/graduate credit through videoconferencing, including:* Education, Nursing, Material Science, Engineering, Communications, Law, Library Studies, Math, Business. *Noncredit courses through written correspondence:* Bail Bonding, Citizenship.

Teaching Methods: *Computers:* Internet, real-time chat, electronic classroom, e-mail, CD-ROM, newsgroup, LISTSERV. *TV:* videotape, satellite broadcasting. *Other:* radio broadcast, videoconferencing, audiotapes, fax, written correspondence, independent study.

Admission Requirements: *Undergraduate:* varies. *Graduate:* University of Alabama Graduate School admittance. *Doctoral:* varies. *Certificate:* no restrictions.

On-Campus Requirements: None.

Tuition and Fees: *Undergraduate:* varies. *Graduate:* varies. *Doctoral:* varies. *Application Fee:* varies. *Software:* varies. *Other Costs:* varies. *Credit by:* semester.

Financial Aid: Federal Stafford Loan, Federal Perkins Loan, Federal PLUS Loan, Federal Pell Grant, Federal Work-Study, VA, Alabama resident programs.

Accreditation: Southern Association of Schools and Colleges, appropriate accreditation agencies for individual academic divisions.

Description: Established in 1831, the University of Alabama is a dynamic center of learning, rich with diverse opportunities for people of varied interests. Roughly one-third of its 19,000 students come from outside the state, and the university has a growing international enrollment with students representing 80 countries. Though a traditionally residential campus, the university reaches out through Distance Education to meet the educational needs of citizens of the state, nation, and globe. UA offers distance learning in a variety of formats, including written correspondence, videotape, live videoconferencing, satellite, and the Internet. The University of Alabama Division of Distance Education extends its academic resources to people who seek college credit toward a degree but who cannot attend classes on campus.

University of Alaska Southeast, Juneau Campus

11120 Glacier Highway
Novatney Building, Rm. 103
Juneau, AK 99801

Phone: (907) 465-6409
Fax: (907) 465-6549

Division(s): Distance Academic Programs
Web Site(s): http://www.uas.alaska.edu/distance/
E-mail: Distance.Ed@uas.alaska.edu

Undergraduate Degree Programs:
Offered only within the State of Alaska except where noted:
Associate of Applied Science in:
    Business Administration
    Early Childhood Education
    Computer Information & Office Systems
Bachelor of Business Administration with emphasis in:
    Accounting
    General Business
    Management
Bachelor of Liberal Arts with emphasis in:
    General Studies

Graduate Degree Programs:
Master of Arts in Teaching with emphasis in:
    Elementary Education
    Early Childhood Education

Master of Education with emphasis in:
Early Childhood Education (also available outside Alaska)
Educational Technology (also available outside Alaska)
Master of Public Administration (also available in Whitehorse, Yukon Territory, Canada

Certificate Programs: Accounting Technician, Computer Information and Office Systems in: Administrative Office Support, Advanced Computer Programming, Computer Applications, Computer Programming, Desktop Publishing and Graphics, Medical Office Specialist, Web Publishing; Early Childhood Education, Small Business Management; Teaching Credentials: Elementary Education, Early Childhood Education; Teaching Endorsements: Early Childhood Education, Educational Technology (also available outside Alaska), Reading.

Class Titles: (Not associated with degree programs): Alaska Studies*, Bald Eagles of Alaska's Coastal Rain Forest, Brown Bears of Southeast Alaska, Humpback and Killer Whales of the Northeast Pacific Coast, Multicultural Education*.
*meets the Department of Education requirement for teacher certification.

Teaching Methods: *Computers:* Internet, electronic classroom, e-mail, CD-ROM, LISTSERV. *TV:* audiotape, videotape, satellite broadcasting. *Other:* audioconferencing, audiotapes, fax, correspondence. Classes use UAS Online course management system.

Credits Granted for: examination (CLEP, DANTES, or local credit by examination).

Admission Requirements: *Undergraduate:* high school diploma with minimum GPA of 2.0 or a GED. *Graduate:* in general, a bachelor's degree appropriate to the intended master's degree from an accredited institution with a GPA of 3.0. Final determination by the program faculty. *Certificate:* As above.

On-Campus Requirements: The Early Childhood Education programs require 2 weeks of summer on-campus courses.

Tuition and Fees: Tuition rates listed are for Alaskan residents: *Lower Division courses* (100–200): $79/credit. Distance fee/lower division course: $40. *Upper Division courses* (300–400): $90/credit. *Graduate Level courses* (600): $178/credit. Distance fee/upper division or graduate course: $75. *Application Fee:* for all levels: $35. *Credit by:* semester.

Financial Aid: *Grants:* Bureau of Indian Affairs, Federal Pell Grant, Federal Supplemental Educational Opportunity Grant; *Scholarships:* UAS and University of Alaska Foundation; *Loans:* Federal Stafford Loans, Alaska Student Loan Program Veteran's Assistance.

Accreditation: Northwest Association of Schools and Colleges.

Description: The University of Alaska Southeast is a regional university with campuses in Juneau, Ketchikan, and Sitka. The University of Alaska Southeast's Juneau campus is located in Alaska's capital city. Juneau-Douglas Community College (1956) and the Southeastern Senior College (1972) were merged in 1980 to form the current campus. The institution has a long and successful history of distance education delivery.

University of Alaska Southeast, Sitka Campus

1332 Seward Avenue   Phone: (907) 747-6653
Sitka, AK 99835   Fax: (907) 747-3552

Division(s): Distance Education Office
Web Site(s): http://www.uas-sitka.net
E-mail: tydist@alaska.edu

Undergraduate Degree Programs:
Associate of Arts
Associate of Applied Science in:
Computer Information Office Systems
Early Childhood Education
Environmental Technology
Health Information Management
Human Services Technology
Microcomputer Support Specialist

Certificate Programs: Health Information Management, Early Childhood Education, Human Service Technology, Environmental Technology, Microcomputer Support Specialist, Administrative Office Support, Computer Application, Desktop Publishing Graphics, Medical Office Procedures, Web Publishing, Networking Essentials.

Teaching Methods: *Computers:* Internet, e-mail, CD-ROM, LISTSERV. *TV:* videotape, cable program, satellite broadcasting, PBS. *Other:* radio broadcast, audioconferencing, videoconferencing, audiotapes, fax, correspondence, individual study, learning contracts.

Credits Granted for: experiential learning, portfolio assessment, extrainstitutional learning, examination (CLEP, ACT-PEP, DANTES, GRE).

Admission Requirements: *Undergraduate:* high school diploma or GED.

On-Campus Requirements: None.

Tuition and Fees: *Undergraduate:* $79/credit. Upper Level: $90/credit. *Graduate:* $178/credit. *Application Fee:* $35. *Other Costs:* $40–$75/course Distance Fee, plus additional audio conference charges for some classes. *Credit by:* semester.

Financial Aid: Federal Stafford Loan, Federal Perkins Loan, Federal PLUS Loan, Federal Pell Grant, Federal Work-Study, VA, Alaska resident programs.

Accreditation: Northwest Association of Schools and Colleges.

Description: The Sitka campus, founded as Sitka Community College in 1962, shares Sitka's heritage of being the former capital of Russian America. Sitka is rich in history and a popular tourist attraction. Mount Edgecumbe, known as Alaska's Mount Fuji, dominates the horizon across the water from the city. The Sitka campus awards certificates of completion and associate degrees. Since restructuring to include the Juneau and Ketchikan campuses, the Sitka campus has assumed administrative responsibility for the university's outreach programs. In addition, the Sitka campus and Sheldon Jackson College share cross-registration and Sheldon's library.

University of Arizona

PO Box 210158	
888 North Euclid Avenue	Phone: (520) 626-2079
Tucson, AZ 85721-0158	Fax: (520) 621-2099

Division(s): Extended University
Web Site(s): http://www.eu.arizona.edu/dist
E-mail: pshack@u.arizona.edu

Graduate Degree Programs:
Master of Engineering
Master of Arts in Information Resources and Library Science
Master of Science in Optical Sciences

Certificate Programs: Professional Graduate Certificate in Systems Engineering; Professional Graduate Certificate in Reliability and Quality Engineering.

Class Titles: Mechanical Engineering, Electrical and Computer Engineering, Optical Sciences, Systems and Industrial Engineering.

Teaching Methods: *Computers:* Internet, e-mail, CD-ROM. *TV:* videotape, *Other:* None.

Credits Granted for: examination (GRE), transfer credit from other accredited universities and colleges.

Admission Requirements: *Graduate:* bachelor's degree in relevant field. *Certificate:* bachelor's degree in relevant field.

On-Campus Requirements: For completion of Master of Arts in Information Resources and Library Science and for Master of Science in Optical Sciences, student must take at least 12 units on campus. For other programs offered, there is no on-campus requirement.

Tuition and Fees: *Graduate:* vary by program. *Application Fee:* $15/course. *Other Costs:* varies by program and course delivery method. *Credit by:* semester.

Accreditation: North Central Association of Colleges and Schools.

Description: Since 1972 the University of Arizona has been committed to delivering courses using distance technologies to those students who desire the highest quality education but cannot come to campus. Distance courses incorporating the latest research findings and technological developments are taught by top faculty members. Students can choose the courses and formats that best meet their needs. UA offers classes on videotape and also over the Internet. Students can work toward a Tri-University Master of Engineering, selecting courses from UA, Arizona State University, and Northern Arizona University and complete that degree completely at a distance. Professional Graduate Certificates in Systems Engineering and Reliability and Quality Engineering can also be completed. In addition, students can take distance courses to be applied toward master's degrees in engineering fields and in information resources and library sciences before coming to campus to fulfill the departmental residency requirement.

University of Baltimore

1420 North Charles Street	Phone: (877) ApplyUB
Baltimore, MD 21201-5779	(410) 837-4777
	Fax: (410) 837-4793

Division(s): Admissions Office
Web Site(s): http://www.ubalt.edu
E-mail: admissions@ubmail.ubalt.edu

Undergraduate Degree Programs:
Bachelor of Science in Business Administration

Graduate Degree Programs:
Master of Business Administration

Class Titles: Business, Communications Design, Criminal Justice, Government/Public Policy.

Teaching Methods: *Computers:* Internet, real-time chat, electronic classroom, e-mail, LISTSERV. *TV:* interactive video classroom. *Other:* individual study.

Credits Granted for: examination (ACT-PEP, DANTES, GRE).

Admission Requirements: *Undergraduate:* 56 credits and minimum 2.0 GPA, now accepting limited number of students with sophomore status (24+ credits) meeting specified GPA levels. *Graduate:* some programs may require GMAT or GRE, contact school for more information.

On-Campus Requirements: for courses taught in interactive video classroom.

Tuition and Fees: *Undergraduate:* $169 resident, $491 out-of-state *Graduate:* $294 resident, $438 out-of-state. *Application Fee:* $20 for undergraduate, $30 for graduate. *Other Costs:* $30/credit fee undergraduate and graduate. *Credit by:* semester.

Financial Aid: Federal Stafford Loan, Federal Perkins Loan, Federal PLUS Loan, Federal Pell Grant, Federal Work-Study, VA, Maryland resident programs, Merit Scholarships, special scholarships, student employment, emergency loans.

Accreditation: Middle States Association of Colleges and Secondary Schools, Maryland State Board of Education, American Assembly of Collegiate Schools of Business, National Association of Schools of Public Affairs and Administration, American Bar Association.

Description: The University of Baltimore (1925) holds a unique role in Maryland's higher education system as the state's only upper-division university, offering junior and senior years of bachelor study as well as distinct graduate programs in business, law, and liberal arts. As of fall 1998, UB is authorized to admit a limited number of qualified sophomores. The university's emphasis on professional education attracts students with strong career objectives. Courses in Communication Design, Criminal Justice, Government/Public Policy, and Business have been offered via interactive video classroom to sites around Maryland since 1994. Beginning in January 1999, the University of Baltimore started its Web MBA, a fully online Master of Business Administration, taught by faculty of UB's Merrick School of Business, an AACSB-accredited program provider. A unique model, emphasizing student cohorts enrolled in 2 courses in 10-week sessions across the academic year, allows students to complete their MBA, conveniently and with collegial support, in 2 years.

University of Bridgeport

126 Park Avenue	Phone: (203) 576-4851
Bridgeport, CT 06601	Fax: (203) 576-4852

Division(s): Distance Education
Web Site(s): http://www.bridgeport.edu
E-mail: gmichael@cse.bridgeport.edu

Graduate Degree Programs:
Master of Science in Human Nutrition

Certificate Programs: International Finance, Computer Science.

Teaching Methods: *Computers:* Internet, real-time chat, electronic classroom, e-mail, CD-ROM, newsgroup. *Other:* None.

Admission Requirements: *Graduate:* undergraduate degree.

On-Campus Requirements: None.

Tuition and Fees: *Graduate:* $419/credit. *Application Fee:* $40. *Credit by:* semester.

Financial Aid: Federal Stafford Loan

Accreditation: New England Association of Schools and Colleges.

Description: The University of Bridgeport, founded in 1927, is an independent, nonsectarian, comprehensive university offering a variety of undergraduate, graduate, and professional degree programs through its several colleges and schools. The university's mission is to teach, search for new knowledge, and discover solutions to social and natural problems. To this end, it offers a high-quality, central liberal arts experience with accredited scientific, technical, business, legal, professional, and liberal arts programs, as well as lifelong learning opportunities. UB's distance learning program is committed to the larger social mission of worldwide education. The program began in 1997 with 8 courses in the Master's of Science in Human Nutrition program. This convenient online program allows students to communicate with instructors and classmates from the convenience of home or office with just a computer, modem, and Internet access. Students have access to many online tools, including e-mail, newsgroups, class conferences, informal chat rooms, textbooks, and specially produced software. Distance learning students also have access to the traditional student resources of the library, counselors, registration, and financial aid through the school's Virtual Campus.

University of British Columbia

2329 West Mall, Room 1170	Phone: (604) 822-6565 or 6500
Vancouver, BC Canada V6T 1Z4	(800) 754-1811
	Fax: (604) 822-8636

Division(s): Distance Education and Technology, Continuing Studies
Web Site(s): http://det.ubc.ca
E-mail: det@cstudies.ubc.ca

Certificate Programs: Technology-Based Distributed Learning (see web site at http://itesm.cstudies.ubc.ca/info/), Post-Graduate Certificate in Rehabilitation (see web site at http://rhsc.det.ubc.ca).

Class Titles: Credit courses toward degrees are offered through 12 faculties: Agricultural Sciences, Applied Sciences, Arts, Commerce, Dentistry, Education, Forestry, Law,

Medicine, Pharmaceutical Sciences, Science. Graduate studies are offered presently in Education, Watershed Management and Rehabilitation Science. More graduate programs in the areas of social work and forestry are under development.

Teaching Methods: *Computers:* Internet, electronic classroom, e-mail, CD-ROM. *TV:* videotape, cable program: Knowledge Network. *Other:* audioconferencing, videoconferencing, audiotapes, fax, correspondence, independent study, individual study.

Credits Granted for: variable according to the academic program and policies administered by the UBC Registrar's Office; phone (604) 822-5544 for details.

Admission Requirements: *Undergraduate:* variable; call (604) 822-5544. *Graduate:* variable; call (604) 822-5544 or contact UBC Registrar's office. *Doctoral:* variable; call (604) 822-5544 or contact Distance Education and Technology. *Certificate:* variable; call (604) 822-5544, http://students.ubc.ca.

On-Campus Requirements: Usually UBC's distance education programs do not require on-campus class and lab work, but students should check with their appropriate faculty adviser for exceptions.

Tuition and Fees: *Undergraduate:* $77/credit. *Graduate:* There is no per-credit rate, graduate students pay via lump sum payments. *Doctoral:* Fees vary according to the academic program. *Application Fee:* $45. *Credit by:* semester.

Financial Aid: UBC's endowment fund endows undergraduate scholarships, undergraduate and graduate bursaries, and graduate fellowships. Please call the Awards and Financial Aid office at (604) 822-5111 for more information.

Accreditation: Association of Universities and Colleges of Canada, Provincial Legislation: Universities Act.

Description: The University of British Columbia (1915) is one of the largest universities in Canada and is recognized as a global center of research and learning. Under Continuing Studies at UBC, Distance Education and Technology (DE&T) develops and delivers programs, courses, and learning materials for individuals and clients who require cost-effective, quality education delivered in flexible formats. Faculty and off-campus organizations pool their expertise to develop interdisciplinary programs on local, national, and international levels. In this way, DE&T serves learners unable to attend the UBC campus regularly. Since 1949, UBC distance programs have focused on the needs of lifelong learners wishing to complete degrees, update their knowledge and skills, or change careers. DE&T serves these learners in collaboration with all 12 UBC faculties and the various program areas of Continuing Studies.

University of Calgary

2500 University Drive NW/
3330 Hospital Drive, NW (CME)
Calgary, AB, Canada T2N 1N4

Phone: (403) 220-7364
(403) 220-4249 (CME)
Fax: (403) 282-0730
(403) 270-2330 (CME)

Division(s): Learning Technologies and Digital Media/ Continuing Medical Education and Professional Development (CME)
Web Site(s): http://www.ucalgary.ca/commons/
http://www.cme.ucalgary.ca (CME)
E-mail: carruthe@ucalgary.ca
jrooke@ucalgary.ca (CME)

Undergraduate Degree Programs:
Bachelor of Nursing Post Diploma
Bachelor of Community Rehabilitation
Bachelor of Accounting Science

Graduate Degree Programs:
Master of Continuing Education
Master of Education in Community Rehabilitation
Master of Education with specializations in:
    Adult, Community, and Higher Education
    Curriculum, Teaching, and Learning
    Educational Technology
    Educational Leadership

Certificate Programs: Adult Learning, Teacher Assistant, General Management.

Teaching Methods: *Computers:* Internet, real-time chat, electronic classroom, e-mail, CD-ROM, newsgroup, LISTSERV. *TV:* videotape, satellite broadcasting. *Other:* audioconferencing, videoconferencing, fax, independent study, learning contracts.

Credits Granted for: extrainstitutional learning, examination (CLEP, ACT-PEP, DANTES, GRE), Mainpro M1 study credits given for hours attended.

Admission Requirements: vary per program.

On-Campus Requirements: One graduate program has a 3-week on-site requirement, none for CME.

Tuition and Fees: vary per program. *CME:* $600 for September–May sessions (34 total, weekly sessions). *Credit by:* semester. For CME, credit is yearly. Certificate of attendance and Mainpro M1 credit given in June of each year based on weekly sessions attended.

Financial Aid: Provincial Federal Student Loan Program.

Accreditation: Association of Universities and Colleges of Canada, Committee on Accreditation of Canadian Medical Schools (CACMS), and by reciprocity through the

Accreditation Council for Continuing Medical Education (ACCME) of the United States to sponsor continuing medical education for physicians.

Description: The University of Calgary (1966) shares the youth and energy of the city and province with which it has grown. Combining the best of long-established university traditions with Calgary's entrepreneurial spirit, the U of C offers a dynamic learning experience and the opportunity to study with leading academic explorers. The institution is the most research-intensive university in Alberta and among the top 10 in Canada.

University of California at Davis

1333 Research Park Drive	Phone: (530) 757-8654
Davis, CA 95616	Fax: (530) 754-5094

Division(s): UC Davis Extension
Web Site(s): http://universityextension.ucdavis.edu/distance-learning
E-mail: questions@unexmail.ucdavis.edu

Undergraduate Degree Programs: Contact school.

Certificate Programs: Specialized Studies Program in Computer Programming, Certificate Program in Information Systems Analysis, Foundation Certificate Examination Preparation Program—Brewing Science.

Class Titles: Adobe PhotoShop, Applied Sensory Evaluation, C Language Projects, Command Line in the Windows Environment, Data Communications, Data Modeling, Database Design, Development and Management, Essentials of Computer Technology, Foundation Certificate Examination Preparation Program—Brewing Science, Functional Design for the Web, Internet Architecture and Services, Introduction to Winemaking for Distance Learners, Java Programming, JavaScripting, Layout Design for the Web, Logical Analysis and Problem Solving for Programming, Microsoft Access, Network Technologies and Architectures, Object-Oriented Requirements Analysis, Object-Oriented Design, Project Management, Programming, Spanish, SQL: Concepts and Syntax, Survey of Web/Database Connectivity Tools, Systems Analysis, Systems Design, UNIX, Visual Basic 6, Web Animation With FLASH, Web/Database Connectivity Using Active Server Pages, Web Page Creation and Authoring, Wine Production for Distance Learners, XML.

Teaching Methods: *Computers:* Internet, electronic classroom, e-mail, CD-ROM. *TV:* videotape.

Admission Requirements: *Undergraduate:* some courses have prerequisites that must be met before enrolling. *Certificate:* some courses have prerequisites that must be met before enrolling. Contact school or check web site.

On-Campus Requirements: None.

Tuition and Fees: *Undergraduate:* $252/credit. *Application Fee:* $45 for certificate program. *Credit by:* quarter.

Financial Aid: UC Davis Extension is an approved training institution for: Citibank, Educational Resource Institute (TERI), and Microsoft 2000.

Accreditation: Western Association of Schools and Colleges.

Description: UC Davis Extension (1960) is the continuing education arm of the University of California at Davis. Extension first offered Distance Learning courses in 1987. UC Davis Extension currently offers more than 70 college- and professional-level courses as well as 3 certificate programs at a distance. Courses follow a variety of formats including self-paced and synchronous with most courses being conducted entirely online. Other delivery methods include videotape and CD-ROM. UC Davis Extension offers a wide variety of subject areas via Distance Learning including: information technology, writing, winemaking, Spanish, and brewing.

University of California at Riverside

1200 University Avenue	Phone: (909) 787-4105
Riverside, CA 92507	Fax: (909) 787-7273

Division(s): Student and Instructional Support Services
Web Site(s): http://www.ucrextension.net
E-mail: register@ucx.ucr.edu or ucrxonline@ucx.ucr.edu

Certificate Programs: Contact school or see web site.

Class Titles: Each quarter several courses are offered online. Please see our web site for details.

Teaching Methods: *Computers:* Internet, real-time chat, electronic classroom, e-mail. *Other:* independent study, live video, and audiostreaming (Rotor Program).

Admission Requirements: Contact school or see web site.

Tuition and Fees: Contact school or see web site. *Credit by:* quarter.

Accreditation: Western Association of Schools and Colleges.

Description: University of California (1960), Riverside Extension and Summer Sessions, is the continuing education branch of the University of California at Riverside. Extension focuses on meeting educational needs for career advancement, career changes, teacher training, and the cultural interests of the adult population. UCR Extension is open to all people—with or without a baccalaureate degree—who are interested in lifelong learning. Extension offers hundreds of courses each quarter and over 60 certificate programs. In the last few years, UCR Extension began offering some courses online. We anticipate the number of online course offerings will increase.

University of California Extension

2000 Center Street, Suite 400	Phone: (510) 642-4124
Berkeley, CA 94704	Fax: (510) 643-9271

Division(s): Center for Media and Independent Learning
Web Site(s): http://learn.berkeley.edu
E-mail: askcmil@uclink4.berkeley.edu

Certificate Programs: Business Administration, Marketing, E-Commerce, Project Management, International Business, Java Programming, Business Intelligence and Data Warehousing, Computer Information Systems.

Class Titles: Ancient Egyptian Art, Drawing, Publication Design, Graphic Design, Art of Film, History of Film, Screenwriting, Classics of Children's Literature, Multicultural Literature, Women Writers, Shakespeare, English Language, Mystery Fiction, English Novel, U.S. Fiction, Writing, Business Writing Review, ESL Grammar/Composition, Grammar for Editors, Composition/Literature, Technical Writing, Editorial Workshop, Writing/Revising Short Story, Developing the Novel, Popular Forms of Fiction, Marketing/Publishing Fiction, Nonfiction Writing, Creative Nonfiction, Writing the Memoir, Poetry Writing, World Civilization: Neolithic Age–Renaissance, World Civilization: 1500–Present, U.S. History, Cultural Diversity in U.S., Cyberculture Studies, Chinese, French, Italian, Spanish, Music Appreciation, Musics of World, History of Western Philosophy, History of Buddhist Philosophy, Comparative Philosophy, World Religions, Financial Accounting, Managerial Accounting, Accounting, Cost Accounting, Auditing, Governmental Accounting, Business Law, Investment Management, Finance, Human Resources, International Business, Cultural Diversity within Organization, International Marketing, Information Resource Management, Business Organization/Management, Project Management, Quality Management, Cultural Diversity/New Business Opportunities, Marketing, Marketing Research, Consumer Buying Behavior, Advertising, Direct Marketing, Database Marketing, Public Relations, Real Estate, Information Systems, Database Management Systems, Systems Analysis/Design, Geographic Information Systems, Information Resource Management, Online Searching/Electronic Research, ATML, XML, UNIX System, Programming: BASIC XII/PASCAL/C/C++/Java, Data Communications/Networks, Digital Telecommunications, Computer Networks, E-Commerce Business and Technology, E-Commerce Systems, E-Commerce Marketing, Business Engineering for E-Commerce, Modern Plague: HIV/AIDS, HMOs/Managed Care, Women's Health, Algebra, Precalculus, Calculus, Math for Electronics, Statistics, Astronomy, Physics, Biology, Biology of Cancer, Human Physiology, Molecular Cell Biology, Genetics, Immunology, Marine Biology, Plant Life in California, Chemistry, Organic Chemistry, Biochemistry, Environmental Issues, U.S. Environmental/Cultural History, Earthquakes, Physical Geology, Geology of California, Hazardous Materials Management, Perspectives on the Adult Learner, Instructional Strategies for Adult Learners, Mainstreaming Disabled Students, Developing Internet-based Instruction, Designing Web Pages for Classroom and Online Instruction, Poetry of Self: Writer Within, Managing Stress/Conflict in Workplace, Managing Major Life Changes, Physical Anthropology, Social/Cultural Anthropology, Exploring Contemporary Culture through Film, Economics (macro/micro), U.S. Politics, Psychology, Critical Thinking, Abnormal Psychology, Adolescence, Sociology, Crime/Society.

Teaching Methods: *Computers:* Internet, real-time chat, electronic classroom, e-mail. *Other:* audiotapes, fax, correspondence, independent study.

Admission Requirements: *Undergraduate:* Course completion in one year for independent study courses; 6 months for online courses. *Certificate:* 4 year completion.

On-Campus Requirements: None.

Tuition and Fees: *Undergraduate:* approximately $475/course. *Application Fee:* $60 certificate programs. *Other Costs:* $50 Online Resource Fee/online course. *Credit by:* semester.

Financial Aid: VA.

Accreditation: Western Association of Schools and Colleges.

Description: The University of California is one of the largest and most acclaimed institutions of higher education in the world. The Center for Media and Independent Learning is the distance learning division of University of California Extension, the continuing education arm of UC. CMIL was established more than 85 years ago to expand university resources throughout the community, state, and nation. CMIL offers more than 200 college and professional courses at a distance, including more than 120 courses online.

University of California Irvine Extension

Distance Learning Center	
PO Box 6050	Phone: (949) 824-7614
Irvine, CA 92616-6050	Fax: (949) 824-2090

Division(s): Engineering and Information Technologies
Web Site(s): http://www.unex.uci.edu
E-mail: unex-online@uci.edu

Certificate Programs: Internet marketing.

Class Titles: Fundamentals of Data Communications and Networks, cdmaOne, the Standard for Wireless Spread Spectrum Communications, Fundamentals of Digital Communications. For CDMA Wireless Systems, RF Engineering for CDMA Wireless Communications Systems, CDMA 2000, Network Design Including TCP/IP, Introduction to Visual Basic, Introduction to C++ Programming, Java Programming for Professionals, Beyond HTML: Fundamentals of Scripting for the Web, Concepts of Relational Database Management Systems, Introduction to Active Server Pages (ASP), Intermediate Active Server Pages (ASP), XML applications Development Intermediate MS Windows Programming using Visual Basic, Project Management, Project Risk Management, Capital Markets, The Investment Process, Pre-MBA Mathematics, Pre-MBA Economics, Pre-MBA Accounting, Pre-MBA Statistics, Internet Marketing, Fundamentals of Data Communications, Human Factors and Team Dynamics for Quality Management, Digital Telecommunications, Creating Web Sites with HTML.

Teaching Methods: *Computers:* Internet, real-time chat, electronic classroom, e-mail. *Other:* None.

Credits Granted for: experiential learning, extrainstitutional learning (corporate or professional association seminars/workshops), examination (SAT, GMAT, GRE).

Admission Requirements: open enrollment.

On-Campus Requirements: Open enrollment; some courses, about 25%, are partially face-to-face.

Tuition and Fees: Vary from $399 to 575. *Credit by:* quarter.

Financial Aid: Citibank Assist Student Loan Program.

Accreditation: Western Association of Schools and Colleges, National University Continuing Education Association.

Description: UC Irvine Extension (1963) is the continuing education branch of the University of California, Irvine. For more than 30 years, we have offered quality continuing education courses taught by UCI faculty members and industry experts from business and the professions. All classes are open to the public. There is no lengthy application process, and a college degree is not required for most courses. We currently offer more than 1,800 courses in 40 certificate programs and specialized studies each year. Classes are located on the UC Irvine campus, at the UCI Learning Center in Orange, California. Most courses are offered at night and on weekends. We currently offer 3 online courses in Windows programming. New courses are developed each quarter to meet the changing needs of professionals.

University of Central Florida

12424 Research Parkway, Suite 256	Phone: (407) 207-4910
Orlando, FL 32826	Fax: (407) 207-4911

Division(s): Center for Distributed Learning
Web Site(s): http://distrib.ucf.edu
E-mail: distrib@mail.ucf.edu

Undergraduate Degree Programs:
Bachelor of Science in:
  Vocational Education and Industry Training (from the College of Education)
  Health Services Administration (from the College of Health and Public Affairs)
RN to BSN in Nursing (from the College of Health and Public Affairs)
Bachelor of Arts or Bachelor of Science in Liberal Studies (from the College of Arts and Sciences)
BSET-Bachelor of Science in Engineering Technology

Graduate Degree Programs:
Master of Arts of Master of Education in:
  Vocational Education and Industry Training (from the College of Education)
  Educational Media (from the College of Education)
Master of Science in:
  Forensic Science (from the Chemistry Department, College of Arts and Sciences)

Certificate Programs: All are graduate certificates: Industrial Engineering and Management Systems from the College of Engineering and Computer Science; Mechanical, Materials, and Aerospace Engineering from the College of Engineering and Computer Science; Community College Faculty and Administrators from the College of Education; Professional Writing from the College of Arts and Sciences; Nonprofit Management from the College of Health and Public Affairs.

Class Titles: Classes are available in many areas; individual titles vary widely from semester to semester. Contact school or check web site.

Teaching Methods: *Computers:* Internet, real-time chat, electronic classroom (WebCT), e-mail, CD-ROM, newsgroup, LISTSERV. *TV:* videotape. *Other:* radio broadcast, videoconferencing.

Admission Requirements: *Undergraduate:* varies. *Graduate:* varies, generally a bachelor's degree, with GPA of 3.0, GRE of 1000, or GMA of 450. See http://graduate.ucf.edu/ *Postgraduate:* see http://graduate.ucf.edu/ *Certificate:* varies according to program.

On-Campus Requirements: all UCF distributed learning courses are considered to be resident credit, regardless of the location of the student. Interactive TV courses are available only at branch campuses and learning centers in the state of Florida. At the option of each instructor, some of our web-based courses do require occasional attendance for orientation and/or exams. Special arrangements can sometimes be made for students at a distance. Contact the specific instructor of the course or program you are interested in for more details.

Tuition and Fees: *Undergraduate:* $75.98/320.57 *Graduate:* $152.45/531.21. *Application Fee:* $25. *Credit by:* semester.

Financial Aid: Federal Stafford Loan, Federal Perkins Loan, Federal PLUS Loan, Federal Pell Grant, Federal Work-Study, VA, state programs for residents of Florida.

Accreditation: Southern Association of Colleges and Schools.

Description: The University of Central Florida (1963) is a major metropolitan research university whose mission is to deliver a comprehensive program of teaching, research, and service. UCF opened in the fall of 1968. Its original name, Florida Technological University, was changed by the Florida Legislature on December 6, 1978. UCF proudly identifies with its geographic region while striving for national and international excellence in selected programs of teaching and research. UCF delivers courses and programs over the Internet and via videotape to meet the diverse needs of a growing student population and to fulfill the general university mission. All such courses and materials are developed by UCF faculty to maximize the distance learner's achievement of course objectives. All courses provide full university credit, and are subject to standard campus tuition charges and UCF policies.

University of Central Oklahoma

100 North University, Box 192	Phone: (405) 974-5395
Edmond, OK 73034	Fax: (405) 974-3835

Division(s): Information Technology Consulting
Web Site(s): http://www.ucok.edu/Cyber
http://libweb.ucok.edu:10020/Cyber
E-mail: smartin@ucok.edu

Undergraduate Degree Programs:
Bachelor of Arts in Criminal Justice

Graduate Degree Programs:
Master of Arts in Criminal Justice

Class Titles: Psychology of Grief, Administration of Justice, Women Artists, Vocational Student Organizations, Methods of Teaching Occupational/Technical Education, History of Teaching Occupational/Technical Education, Instructional Development, Art History, Survey of Art History, Medical Terminology, Business, Business Statistics, Legal Aspects of Business Environment, Personal Finance, Business Finance, Financial Statement Analysis, Salesmanship, Marketing, Marketing Research, Sales Management, Organic Chemistry, Economics (macro/micro), Educational Psychology, Child Psychology, Adolescent Psychology, Grammar, Composition, Human Geography, American National Government, State/Local Government, Wellness/Positive Life, Oklahoma History, Nutrition, College Algebra for Business, College Algebra, Math/Analysis for Business, Math for Elementary Teachers, History of Mathematics, Sociology, Social Problems, Social Psychology, Juvenile Delinquency, Minorities/American Society, Sociology/Health/Medicine, Family, Criminology, Organizational Behavior, Human Behavior/Sociological Environment, Sociological Theory, Police Administration/Organization, Police Community Relations, Innovations of Corrections/Penology, Administration of Correctional Institutions.

Teaching Methods: *Computers:* Internet, e-mail, LISTSERV. *TV:* TV transmission, videotape, One-Net Fiber Optics System. *Other:* fax, correspondence, videoconferencing, telephone, interactive TV, videocassette, audioconferencing.

Credits Granted for: experiential learning, portfolio assessment, extrainstitutional learning, examination (CLEP, ACT-PEP, DANTES, GRE).

Admission Requirements: *Undergraduate:* high school diploma, transcripts, ACT, application fee. *Graduate:* bachelor's degree in Criminal Justice or related field, college transcripts, application fee.

On-Campus Requirements: Undergraduate Criminal Justice program: 2 6-hour visits (beginning and end of program). Graduate Criminal Justice program: same as undergraduate plus comprehensive exam.

Tuition and Fees: *Undergraduate:* $47/credit in-state, $87/credit out-of-state. *Graduate:* $62/credit in-state, $102/credit out-of-state. *Application Fee:* $15. *Credit by:* semester.

Financial Aid: Federal Stafford Loan, Federal Perkins Loan, Federal PLUS Loan, Federal Pell Grant, Federal Work-Study, VA, Oklahoma resident programs.

Accreditation: North Central Association of Colleges and Schools.

Description: Educating students to succeed in life is the primary mission of the University of Central Oklahoma (1890). UCO adheres to the philosophy that education is the key that allows us to fulfill our potential and to be of service to others. However, it also believes in one other very important concept—that everyone should have access to the benefits of higher education without going broke in the process.

University of Cincinnati

PO Box 210019
Cincinnati, OH 45221-0019

Phone: (513) 556-9154
Fax: (513) 556-6380

Division(s): College of Evening and Continuing Education
Web Site(s): http://www.uc.edu/
http://www.cece/
E-mail: melody.clark@uc.edu

Undergraduate Degree Programs:
Bachelor of Science in Addiction Studies
Bachelor of Science in Fire Science Administration—College of Applied Science
Associate of Arts Early Childhood Education

Class Titles: Social Sciences, Business/Management, Humanities.

Teaching Methods: *Computers:* Internet, electronic classroom, e-mail, CD-ROM. *TV:* videotape, cable program, satellite broadcasting, PBS. *Other:* videoconferencing, audiotapes, fax, correspondence, independent study, individual study, learning contracts.

Credits Granted for: experiential learning, portfolio assessment, examination (CLEP, ACT-PEP, DANTES, GRE).

On-Campus Requirements: yes for telecourses (individual courses), no for fire science and nursing.

Tuition and Fees: *Undergraduate:* $162/credit resident, $410/credit out-of-state. *Graduate:* $228/credit resident, $424/credit out-of-state. *Application Fee:* $30. *Credit by:* quarter.

Financial Aid: Federal Stafford Loan, Federal Perkins Loan, Federal PLUS Loan, Federal Pell Grant, Federal Work-Study, VA, Ohio resident programs.

Accreditation: North Central Association of Colleges and Schools.

Description: The University of Cincinnati (1819) traces its origins to Cincinnati College and the Medical College of Ohio. Located on 5 campuses, the university today serves 34,000 students through 17 colleges and divisions offering 450 degree programs from the associate to the doctoral level. The University of Cincinnati has established a continuing reputation for excellence in graduate and undergraduate education, cultural services, and basic and applied research. Since its founding, UC has been the source of many contributions to society, including the oral polio vaccine, the first program of cooperative education, the first electronic organ, the first safe antiknock gasoline, and the first antihistamine. The College of Evening and Continuing Education has offered telecourses for 20 years.

University of Colorado at Boulder

435 UCB
Boulder, CO 80309-0435

Phone: (303) 492-6331
Fax: (303) 492-5987

Division(s): Center for Advanced Training in Engineering and Computer Science (CATECS)
Web Site(s): http://www.colorado.edu/CATECS/
E-mail: catecs-info@colorado.edu

Graduate Degree Programs:
Master of Science in:
   Aerospace Engineering
   Electrical and Computer Engineering
   Telecommunications
Master of Engineering in:
   Aerospace Engineering
   Computer Science
   Electrical and Computer Engineering
   Engineering Management
   Telecommunications

Certificate Programs: Engineering Management.

Class Titles: Any of the 150 CATECS classes may be taken without degree program admission.

Teaching Methods: *Computers:* Internet, e-mail, LISTSERV. *TV:* videotape, ITFS (microwave). *Other:* videoconferencing, fax, correspondence, independent study, individual study.

Admission Requirements: *Graduate:* accredited bachelor's degree in engineering or technical science, 3.0 GPA, possibly GRE. Most departments allow completion time of 4 years for MS degree, 6 years for Master of Engineering. *Certificate:* For Engineering Management, 2 years of professional experience, undergraduate degree, 3.0 GPA, demonstrated writing proficiency.

On-Campus Requirements: defense of final thesis/project for some programs.

Tuition and Fees: *Graduate:* $400/credit. *Application Fee:* $40. *Software:* varies. *Other Costs:* textbooks. *Credit by:* semester.

Financial Aid: Contact Financial Aid Office (303) 492-5091.

Accreditation: North Central Association of Colleges and Schools, Accreditation Board for Engineering and Technology.

Description: For 18 years, the School of Engineering and Applied Science at the University of Colorado (1876) has been a leader in graduate distance learning courses. The Center for Advanced Training in Engineering and Computer Science allows professionals to continue their education or pursue degrees at the work site via live transmission; videotape; or the web. Courses given in previous semesters are available for rent or purchase on videotape through the CATECS Tape Library. Created in 1983 in response to the needs of business, industry, and government leaders, CATECS enrolls 1,600 annually from 250 job sites worldwide. Students pursuing master's degrees or professional development receive the best of both worlds through CATECS: the convenience of distance education and University of Colorado academic quality.

University of Colorado at Colorado Springs

1420 Austin Bluffs Parkway	Phone: (719) 262-3408
Colorado Springs, CO 80918	Fax: (719) 262-3100

Division(s): College of Business and the Graduate School of Business Administration
Web Site(s): http://web.uccs.edu/business/dmamain.htm
E-mail: busadvsr@mail.uccs.edu

Graduate Degree Programs:
Masters of Business Administration

Certificate Programs: Finance and Information Systems.

Teaching Methods: *Computers:* Internet, electronic classroom, e-mail, CD-ROM. *TV:* videotape.

Credits Granted for: examination (CLEP, ACT-PEP, DANTES, GRE).

Admission Requirements: *Graduate:* application, official transcripts, GMAT or GRE, résumé, TOEFL if international student.

On-Campus Requirements: None.

Tuition and Fees: *Graduate:* $400/credit. *Application Fee:* $75. *Other Costs:* $35 technology fee per course.

Financial Aid: VA.

Accreditation: AACSB International—The Association to Advance Collegiate Schools of Business.

Description: The University of Colorado at Colorado Springs (1965) is part of the University of Colorado system. Approximately 7,000 students are enrolled in 5 colleges. The university provides the full range of academic programs from bachelor's degrees to doctoral degrees. The College of Business was one of the first academic units to award degrees from the University of Colorado at Colorado Springs. Graduate and undergraduate business programs have earned accreditation from AACSB International—The Association to Advance Collegiate Schools of Business. The Graduate School of Business Administration initiated its Distance MBA program in fall 1996, and enrollments have been growing steadily ever since. Students may pursue areas of emphasis

in Finance, Management, or Information Systems in addition to a general MBA degree. Distance MBA students earn the same degree and receive the same diploma as on-campus students and are eligible to participate in all MBA activities, including Commencement.

University of Colorado at Denver

1250 14th Street Ste. 720	Phone: (303) 556-6505
Denver, CO 80217	Fax: (303) 556-6530

Division(s): CU Online
Web Site(s): http://www.cudenver.edu/cuonline/barron
E-mail: inquiry@cuonline.edu

Undergraduate Degree Programs:
Bachelor of Arts in Sociology

Graduate Degree Programs:
Master's Degrees in:
 Business Administration
 Engineering in Engineering Management
 Engineering in Geographic Information Systems
 Public Administration

Class Titles: Arts and Media, Business, Engineering, Liberal Arts and Sciences, Architecture and Planning, Arts and Media, Business, Education, Engineering, Liberal Arts and Sciences, Public Affairs.

Teaching Methods: *Computers:* Internet, real-time chat, electronic classroom, e-mail, CD-ROM, newsgroup, LISTSERV. *TV:* videotape, cable program, satellite broadcasting, PBS. *Other:* radio broadcast, videoconferencing, audioconferencing, audiographics, audiotapes, fax, correspondence, independent study, individual study, learning contracts.

Admission Requirements: *Undergraduate:* please see web site for details.

On-Campus Requirements: CU Online offers fully online courses that do not require any "on-campus" time. In addition CU Online offers hybrid courses that require a percentage of "on-campus" time.

Tuition and Fees: *Undergraduate:* $130–$183/credit. *Graduate:* $190–$250/credit. *Other Costs:* $100 course fee that is added to each online course; $4 fee for technology resources; $10 fee for the student information system. *Credit by:* semester.

Financial Aid: see web site for information.

Accreditation: North Central Association of Colleges and Schools.

Description: CU Online (1996) is the virtual campus of the University of Colorado at Denver. We have been offering fully accredited online versions of our campus-based courses and degree programs since 1996. CU Online offers core curriculum and elective courses in a variety of disciplines, all the same high-quality courses taught throughout the University of Colorado system. Over 200 courses are offered each year with new ones added every semester. CU Online courses are perfect for students who, because of time and/or distance, may not be able to take traditional on-campus courses.

University of Connecticut, College of Continuing Studies

One Bishop Circle, U4056-T	Phone: (860) 486-1080
Storrs, CT 06269-4056	Fax: (860) 486-0756

Division(s): Distance Education and Technology Services
Web Site(s): http://www.continuingstudies.uconn.edu/online-courses/de.html
E-mail: ccsonline@access.ced.uconn.edu

Graduate Degree Programs: Master's in Humanitarian Studies. Please contact us for additional information as we continue to expand our online offerings.

Certificate Programs: Occupational Safety and Health Certificate Program Information Technology Nepalese and Tibetan Studies Humanitarian Studies (Graduate). Please contact us for additional information as we continue to expand our online offerings.

Class Titles: Contact school or check web site for details.

Teaching Methods: *Computers:* Internet, includes: real-time chat, e-mail, and CD-ROM.

Admission Requirements: *Graduate:* Humanitarian Studies, Bachelor's Degree.

On-Campus Requirements: None.

Tuition and Fees: *Undergraduate:* 3-credit course—$681. *Graduate:* 3-credit course—$1,091. *Other Costs:* $33 for infrastructure fee. *Credit by:* semester.

Financial Aid: Federal Stafford Loan, Federal Perkins Loan, Federal PLUS Loan, Federal Pell Grant, Federal Work-Study, VA, state programs for residents of Connecticut.

Accreditation: New England Association of Schools and Colleges.

Description: The University of Connecticut (1881) is a Research I institution and was ranked the top public university in New England by *U.S. News and World Report*, America's Best Colleges in 2000. We are a land-grant, sea-grant, and space-grant Consortium College with an annual enrollment of approximately 16,700 undergraduate and 6,700 graduate/professional students.

University of Dallas Graduate School of Management

1845 East Northgate Drive	Phone: (800) 832-5622
Irving, TX 75062-4736	Fax: (972) 721-4009

Division(s): Graduate Admissions and The Center for Distance Learning
Web Site(s): http://gsmweb.udallas.edu
E-mail: kmccoy@gsm.udallas.edu

Graduate Degree Programs:
Master of Business Administration
Master of Management

Certificate Programs: Business Management, Health Services Management—Financial, Health Services Management—General, Marketing Management, E-Commerce Management, Information Technology Management, Telecommunications Management, Corporate Financial Management, Investment Management, and International Financial Management.

Teaching Methods: *Computers:* Internet, real-time chat, CD-ROM, electronic classroom, e-mail. *TV:* videotape, satellite broadcasting. *Other:* independent study, experiential learning, portfolio assessment, extrainstitutional learning.

Admission Requirements: *Graduate:* 3.0 cumulative undergraduate GPA (on a 4.0 scale), 5 years professional experience (typically after graduation), professional résumé, GMAT (of no less than a 400), 2 letters of recommendation. *Certificate:* Equivalent of a 4-year U.S. bachelor's degree, official transcript from degree-awarding institution, 2–3 years professional experience, professional résumé, 1 letter of recommendation.

On-Campus Requirements: None.

Tuition and Fees: *Graduate:* $423/credit. *Application Fee:* $50. *Graduation Fee:* $100. *Other Costs:* $30. Student Service Fee. *Credit by:* semester.

Financial Aid: Federal Stafford Loan, Federal Perkins Loan, Federal PLUS Loan, Federal Pell Grant, Federal Work-Study, VA, Texas resident programs.

Accreditation: Southern Association of Colleges and Schools third-year candidate for AACSB accreditation.

Description: The University of Dallas was founded in 1956 as an independent Catholic university dedicated to excellence in its educational programs. The Graduate School of Management (GSM) is one of the university's main components. GSM was founded in 1966 with a distinctive mission: to create a pragmatic MBA program accessible to individuals who are already professionally employed. Over 75% of GSM students work full-time. Students represent over 60 countries and all of the United States. The UD main campus is in Irving, Texas. GSM classes are also taught at campuses in Plano, Texas, Richardson, Texas, and Fort Worth, Texas, and through Internet mobile learning programs. GSM's on-line courses are taught in an asynchronous distance learning mode. Students interact with the professor and other students via the Internet at times convenient to each person. Students and professors do not have to be online at the same time; however, classes are designed to follow a 13-week trimester schedule, during which each week is considered a major learning module. Through on-going implementation of Internet MBA classes, GSM is able to offer a complete IMBA program that is conveniently accessible to the student 24 hours a day, 7 days a week.

University of Delaware

217 John M. Clayton Hall   Phone: (800) 597-1444
Newark, DE 19716-7410   Fax: (302) 831-3292

Division(s): UD Online Distance Learning
Web Site(s): http://www.udel.edu/ce/udonline
E-mail: continuing-ed@udel.edu

Undergraduate Degree Programs:
Bachelor of Science in:
  Nursing
  Hotel, Restaurant, and Institutional Management

Graduate Degree Programs:
Master of Science in:
  Mechanical Engineering
  Electrical Engineering
  Nursing

Certificate Programs: E-Commerce Certificate Programs, Graduate Certificate Program in Composite Materials, Dietetic Internship Program.

Class Titles: See the following web site for semester course listings: http://www.udel.edu/ce/udonline

Teaching Methods: *Computers:* electronic classroom, e-mail, CD-ROM. *TV:* videotape. *Other:* audioconferencing, fax, correspondence.

Credits Granted for: It is recommended that an applicant speak with an academic advisor in order to determine eligibility for potential credit awarded.

Admission Requirements: *Undergraduate:* for admission into a degree program, an admissions committee considers all academic credentials, including high school and any previous college work. Students transferring from other schools are generally required to have a minimum GPA of 2.5 for admission.

On-Campus Requirements: For the Baccalaureate for the Registered Nurse (BRN) major, 10 of 13 required nursing courses are offered in Distance Learning format. Students must enroll in 3 one-credit weekend courses held on the Newark, Delaware, campus. The Master of Science in Nursing with a concentration in health services administration is delivered entirely on the Internet, except for 1 two-day seminar that takes place on the Newark, Delaware, campus. For more information, visit http://www.udel.edu/DSP/page4.html. The Bachelor of Science in Hotel, Restaurant, and Institutional Management core courses as well as most of the required liberal arts and business courses are available in Distance Learning format, except for a required one-week management institute on the Newark, Delaware, campus. For more information, visit http://www.udel.edu/ce/hrimwelc.shtml.

Tuition and Fees: *Undergraduate:* students registering at official UD Online Distance Learning work sites or community colleges may register as site participants and pay $217/credit hour (undergraduate); $630/credit hour (graduate). Individual/non-site participants pay the resident (undergraduate, $188/credit hour; graduate, $251/credit hour) or nonresident tuition rate, (undergraduate, $553/credit hour; graduate, $737/credit hour) tuition plus a $90 fee/videotaped course. Tuition and fees are subject to change. For current information on noncredit costs, credit fees, and tuition visit http://www.udel.edu/ce/udonline/. *Credit by:* semester.

Financial Aid: The Financial Aid Office administers grants and scholarships, which do not have to be repaid; low-interest loans, and student employment. Need-based financial aid packages may include: Federal Pell Grant, Federal Supplemental Educational Opportunity Grant, Federal Perkins Loan, and Federal Direct Loan. The Federal Direct Parents Loan Program is also available. Delaware residents may also be eligible for need-based funding through General Fund Scholarships and Delaware Right to Education Scholarships. Students must be matriculated and carry at least 6 credit hours per semester.

Accreditation: Middle States Association of Colleges and Schools.

Description: A private university with public support, the University of Delaware (1751) is a land-grant, sea-grant, space-grant, and urban-grant institution with a rich 250-year history. Our main campus is located in Newark, Delaware, a suburban community situated between Philadelphia and Baltimore. The university has been fully accredited by the Middle States Association of Colleges and Schools since 1921. There are more than 21,000 students enrolled at the university as undergraduate, graduate, or continuing education students. The university's UD Online Distance Learning System, developed in 1988, supports more than 2,700 registrations a year in undergraduate and graduate courses involving 28 academic departments and 5 degree programs. In 1996 the United States Distance Learning Association gave the university its Most Outstanding Achievement in Higher Education rating for "extraordinary achievements through Distance Education." UD Online offers a way for busy professionals to continue their education on a schedule tailored to their needs.

University of Denver

2211 South Josephine Street
Denver, CO 80208   Phone: (303) 871-2000

Division(s): University College
Web Site(s): http://www.du.edu
http://du.edu
E-mail: http://www.learning.du.edu;
mailto: learning-du@du.edu

Graduate Degree Programs:
Masters of Telecommunications
Masters of Environmental Policy Management
Masters of Computer Information Systems
Masters of Applied Communication
Masters of Liberal Studies
Masters of Technology Management
Masters of Public Health

Certificate Programs: Geographic Information Systems, Modern Languages, American Indian Studies, Internet and Web Design, Database Administration, Network Analysis and Design, Ecotourism Management, Global Affairs, Project Management, Electronic Commerce, Telecommunications, Internet Telecommunications Systems, New and Emerging Telecommunications Technologies.

Teaching Methods: *Computers:* Internet, real-time chat, electronic classroom, e-mail, CD-ROM, newsgroup, LISTSERV. *Other:* videoconferencing, audioconferencing, audiographics, fax, correspondence, independent study, individual study.

Credits Granted for: Prior graduate work (transfer).

Admission Requirements: *Graduate:* acceptable GPA from accredited undergraduate institution, 2 letters of recommendation; no GRE or GMAT required.

On-Campus Requirements: None.

Tuition and Fees: *Graduate:* $325/credit. *Application Fee:* $25. *Software:* varies by program. *Credit by:* quarter

Financial Aid: Federal Stafford Loan, Federal Perkins Loan, Federal PLUS Loan, Federal Pell Grant, Federal Work-Study, VA.

Accreditation: North Central Association of Colleges and Schools.

Description: The University of Denver (1864) is the oldest independent institution of higher education in the Rocky Mountain West. More than 8,500 students from 50 states and 90 countries are enrolled. The student body is evenly divided into undergraduate, traditional graduate, and adult continuing education students. The University College specializes in adult education that is career oriented, industry specific, and immediately applicable in the workplace. Courses, degrees, and certificates have been offered by the UC via distance education since 1996. The UC tailors its programs to adult learners and has separate registration, finance, and advising functions dedicated to its adult student body.

University of Findlay

1000 North Main St.   Phone: (800) 558-9060 x 6933
Findlay, OH 45840   Fax: (419) 424-5517

Division(s): Adult and Continuing Education Office
Web Site(s): http://gcampus.findlay.edu
E-mail: simons@mail.findlay.edu or riffle@mail.findlay.edu

Undergraduate Degree Programs: All degree completion:
Bachelor of Science in:
    Business Management
    Criminal Justice
    Technical Communications
    Environmental Safety and Health Management

Graduate Degree Programs: Entire degree online:
Master of Business Administration (MBA)
Master of Science in Environmental Management

Class Titles: Technical Communication, Hispanic/Latino Influences in the U.S., Sociology, Statistics, Calculus, Oceanus, Communications for Technology, Power and the Social Sciences, Chemistry, Organic Chemistry, Global Perspectives on Gender, General Education courses: Technical Writing, Math, Sociology, Humanities, Biology, Technology Management; a few courses in the Master of Arts in Education Program, Technology Block.

Teaching Methods: *Computers:* Internet, real-time chat, electronic classroom, e-mail, CD-ROM. *TV:* cable program. *Other:* videoconferencing, independent study.

Credits Granted for: some experiential learning, portfolio assessment, examination (CLEP, ACT-PEP, DANTES, GRE).

Admission Requirements: *Undergraduate:* application (no fee), all official transcripts, degree completion program is for working adults.

On-Campus Requirements: none.

Tuition and Fees: *Undergraduate:* $220 per credit plus a $10/per class technology fee. General Undergraduate (NOT

Degree Completion): $372 pre credit plus $50 general service fee. *Graduate:* MBA $356 per credit. Master of Science in Environmental Management $365 per credit. Master of Education $286 per credit. *Credit by:* semester.

Financial Aid: Federal Stafford Loan, Federal Perkins Loan, Federal Pell Grant, VA, state programs for residents of Ohio, state-based Ohio Instructional Grant.

Accreditation: Ohio Board of Regents, North Central Association.

Description: The University of Findlay was founded as Findlay College in 1882 by the Churches of God, General Conference, and the citizens of the City of Findlay. The institution is the only university affiliated with the Churches of God, and it acknowledges, preserves, and honors its Judeo-Christian heritage. The institution offers undergraduate associate and bachelor degree programs, which strive to blend liberal arts and professional education within an ethical context to prepare individuals for lives of productive service. The University of Findlay seeks to meet the needs of the professional/practitioner by providing innovative master's degree programs and resources.

University of Florida

2209 NW 13 Street	Phone: (352) 392-2037
Gainesville, FL 32611	Fax: (352) 392-6950

Division(s): Distance, Continuing, and Executive Education
Web Site(s): http://www.fcd.ufl.edu
E-mail: csessum@doce.ufl.edu

Undergraduate Degree Programs:
Fire and Emergency Services

Graduate Degree Programs:
Agriculture
Business Administration
Engineering
Executive Master's in Health Administration
Forensic Toxicology
International Construction Management
Master of Health Science Degree in Occupational Therapy

Certificate Programs: Forensic Toxicology.

Class Titles: See http://www.correspondencestudy.ufl.edu/college.asp

Teaching Methods: *Computers:* Internet, real-time chat, electronic classroom, e-mail, CD-ROM, newsgroup, LISTSERV. *TV:* videotape, cable program, satellite broadcasting, PBS. *Other:* radio broadcast, videoconferencing, audioconferencing, audiographics, audiotapes, fax, correspondence, independent study, individual study, learning contracts.

Credits Granted for: experiential learning, portfolio assessment, extrainstitutional learning (PONSI, corporate or professional association seminars/workshops), examination (CLEP, ACT-PEP, DANTES, GRE).

Admission Requirements: Contact school.

On-Campus Requirements: depends on the specific course. See www.fcd.ufl.edu

Tuition and Fees: *Undergraduate:* in-state $75.20/credit, out-of-state: $319.79/credit *Graduate:* in-state: $151.67/credit, out-of-state: $530.43/credit *Application Fees:* see specific program for details *Software:* see specific program for details *Graduation Fee:* see specific program for details. *Other Costs:* see specific program for details. *Credit by:* semester.

Financial Aid: Federal Stafford Loan, Federal Perkins Loan, Federal PLUS Loan, Federal Pell Grant, Federal Work-Study, VA, state programs for residents of Florida.

Accreditation: Southern Association of Colleges and Schools.

Description: The University of Florida (1853) is a major, public, comprehensive, land-grant, research university. The state's oldest, largest, and most comprehensive university, Florida is among the nation's most academically diverse public universities. Florida has a long history of established programs in international education, research, and service. It is one of only 17 public, land-grant universities that belongs to the Association of American Universities.

University of Guelph

160 Johnston Hall	Phone: (519) 767-5000
Guelph, ON, Canada N1G 2W1	Fax: (519) 824-1112

Division(s): Office of Open Learning
Web Site(s): http://www.open.uoguelph.ca
E-mail: info@open.uoguelph.ca

Undergraduate Degree Programs:
Bachelor of Arts

Graduate Degree Programs:
Masters in Business Administration in:
    Hospitality and Tourism
    Agriculture

Certificate Programs: Food Science, Hospitality Studies.

Class Titles: Plants/Human Use, Economics (macro/micro), English Writers, Human Development, French, Geology, Science/Society Since 1500, History of Cultural Form, Music, Nutrition/Society, Physics, World Politics, Behaviour, Dynamics of Behaviour, Spanish, Humans in Natural World, Calculus (nondegree), Cell Biology, Personal/Financial

Management, Biology of Plant Pests, Apiculture, Contemporary Cinema, Economic Growth/Environmental Quality, Business Economics, Couple/Family Relationships, Human Sexuality, Exceptional Child in Family, Infant Development, Food Science, Food Processing, British Isles—1066–1603, Canadian Business Management, 5,000 Days, Meteorology, History of Jazz, Family/Community Nutrition, Philosophy of Environment, Canadian Government, Social Psychology, Personality, Soil Science, Environmental Stewardship, Statistics for Business Decisions, Aquatic Environments, Nature Interpretation, Finance, Equity Markets, Communication, Technology, Adolescent Development, German for Professionals, Celtic Britain/Ireland to 1066, Witchcraft/Popular Culture: Scotland 1560–1700, Celtic Britain/Ireland Since 1603, Scotland in Age of Immigration, Beyond 5,000 Days, Planning Recreation/ Tourism, Disease, Environmental Policy Formation/Administration, Occupational Health Psychology, Psychological Measurement, Industrial-Organizational Psychology, Psychology of Death/Dying, Mental Retardation, Soil/Water Conservation/Reclamation, Forest Ecology (graduate).

Teaching Methods: *Computers:* Internet, real-time chat, electronic classroom, e-mail, CD-ROM, newsgroup, LISTSERV. *TV:* videotape. *Other:* audiotapes, fax, correspondence, independent study, individual study.

Credits Granted for: experiential learning, portfolio assessment, extrainstitutional learning (PONSI, corporate, or professional association seminars/workshops), examination (CLEP, ACT-PEP, DANTES, GRE).

Admission Requirements: Please contact the Office of Open Learning regarding admission requirements for specific courses, certificate, and degree programs.

On-Campus Requirements: Some graduate programs may require a minimal residency program. Please contact the Office of Open Learning for more information.

Tuition and Fees: Please contact the Office of Open Learning for current tuition fees. *Credit by:* 3-semester system.

Financial Aid: Federal Stafford Loan, Federal Perkins Loan, Federal PLUS Loan, Federal Pell Grant, Federal Work-Study, VA, Ontario resident programs.

Accreditation: Association of Universities and Colleges of Canada.

Description: University of Guelph roots go back to the 1964 union of Ontario Agricultural College, Ontario Veterinary College, and MacDonald Institute in this historic city of 95,000 people, 60 miles west of Toronto and 75 miles northwest of Niagara Falls. This union now includes physical and biological sciences, arts, social sciences, and family and consumer studies. Also, the school's 100 years of tradition and

its progressive outlook to the future make it one of Canada's leading research institutions. The Office of Open Learning continues the university's long tradition of outreach, offering short courses, workshops, seminars, conferences, and degree-credit distance education courses. Distance courses serve nondegree and degree students, who generally complete courses on-campus and via distance.

University of Hawaii System

2532 Correa Road	Phone: (808) 956-5023
Honolulu, HI 96822	Fax: (808) 956-9966

Division(s): Distributed Learning and User Services
Web Site(s): http://www2.hawaii.edu/dlit
E-mail: cua@hawaii.edu

Undergraduate Degree Programs:
Associate of Arts
Bachelor of Arts in:
    Business Administration
    Information and Computer Science
    Liberal Studies
Bachelor of Science in:
    Nursing

Graduate Degree Programs:
Master of Arts in:
    Graduate Educational Administration
    Music Education
Master of Science in:
    Information and Computer Science
    Nursing
Master of Business Administration

Postgraduate Degree Programs:
Professional Diploma in Education (PDE)

Certificate Programs: Database Management (undergraduate), Telecommunications and Information Resource Management (graduate).

Teaching Methods: *Computers:* Internet, real-time chat, electronic classroom, e-mail, CD-ROM, newsgroup, LISTSERV. *TV:* videotape, cable program, satellite broadcasting. *Other:* radio broadcast, videoconferencing, audioconferencing, audiographics, audiotapes, fax, independent study, individual study.

Credits Granted for: experiential learning, portfolio assessment, extrainstitutional learning (PONSI, corporate or professional association seminars/workshops), examination (CLEP, ACT-PEP, DANTES, GRE).

Admission Requirements: *Undergraduate:* Must be age 18 for AA degree; for BS/BA programs must be 18 years of age with appropriate entrance exam. *Graduate:* accredited bachelor's degree, appropriate graduate exams.

On-Campus Requirements: None.

Tuition and Fees: see http://www.hawaii.edu/tuition/ for tuition schedules of the 10 campuses of the University of Hawaii System

Financial Aid: Federal Stafford Loan, Federal Perkins Loan, Federal PLUS Loan, Federal Pell Grant, Federal Work-Study, VA, Hawaii resident programs.

Accreditation: Western Association of Schools and Colleges.

Description: The University of Hawaii (UH) is a post-secondary education system and comprises 3 university campuses, 7 community college campuses, an employment training center, and 5 education centers distributed throughout the 50th state. In addition to the flagship campus at of the University of Hawaii at Manoa, the UH system also includes the 3,000-student University of Hawaii at Hilo on the island of Hawaii and the smaller University of Hawaii—West Oahu on the leeward side of Oahu. The UH Community College system has 4 campuses on Oahu and one each on Maui, Kauai, and Hawaii, making college classes accessible and affordable and easing the transition from high school to college for many students. The education centers are located in the more remote areas of the state, and support the rural communities via distance education. The UH is fully accredited by the Western Association of Schools and Colleges. The mission of the University of Hawaii system is to provide quality college and university education and training; create knowledge through research and scholarship; provide service through extension, technical assistance, and training; contribute to the cultural heritage of the community; and respond to state needs. The campuses, organized under one board, differentially emphasize instruction, research, and service. The system's special distinction is found in its Hawaiian, Asian, and Pacific orientation and international leadership role. Common values bind the system together: aloha; academic freedom and intellectual vigor; institutional integrity and service; quality and opportunity; diversity, fairness, and equity; collaboration and respect; and accountability and fiscal integrity.

University of Houston

4242 South Mason Road	Phone: (281) 395-2800
Katy, TX 77450	Fax: (281) 395-2629

Division(s): Educational Technology and Outreach
Web Site(s): http://www.uh.edu/uhdistance
E-mail: DEAdvisor@uh.edu

Undergraduate Degree Programs:
Bachelor of Arts in:
   English
   History
   Psychology
Bachelor of Science in:
   Psychology
   Hotel and Restaurant Management
   Mechanical Technology (computer drafting design)
   Industrial Technology (technology leadership and supervision)

Graduate Degree Programs:
Master of Hospitality Management
Master of Science in Occupational Technology (Training and Development)
Master of Science in Computer Science
Master of Education, Reading Specialist Certificate
Master of Education, Reading and Language Arts
Master of Electrical Engineering (Computer/Electronics)
Master of Industrial Engineering (Engineering Management)

Certificate Programs: Curriculum and Instruction-Information Processing Technologies. Curriculum and Instruction-Master of Education in Reading, Language Arts, and Literature Education.

Teaching Methods: *Computers:* Internet, real-time chat, electronic classroom, e-mail, CD-ROM, newsgroup, LISTSERV. *TV:* videotape, cable program, PBS, interactive TV. *Other:* face-to-face, videoconferencing.

Admission Requirements: *Undergraduate:* application, application fee, official high school/college transcripts TASP, SAT, or ACT. *Graduate:* graduate application, reference letters, official test scores (requirements vary/program), 2 official transcripts from each institution; refer to Graduate and Professional Studies catalog or consult major department before applying. *Certificate:* see undergraduate and graduate admission requirements.

On-Campus Requirements: None.

Tuition and Fees: *Undergraduate:* $401/3 hours residents, $1,046/3 hours nonresidents. *Graduate:* $521/3 hours residents, $1,166/3 hours nonresidents. *Application Fee:* $40 for undergraduates, varies by college for graduates. *Other Costs:* off-campus electronic course fee: $140/class with a class cap. *Credit by:* semester.

Financial Aid: General financial and programs through the University of Houston include the Texas Public Education Grant, Texas Public Educational State Student Incentive Grant, Federal Pell Grant, Federal Supplemental Educational Opportunity Grant, Federal Perkins Student Loan, Hinson-Hazlewood College Student Loan, Federal Stafford Student Loan, Federal Parent Loan Program, and other loan and scholarship opportunities based on merit or need. In 1999–2000, approximately 50% of all University of Houston students received some form of financial assistance.

Accreditation: Southern Association of Colleges and Schools, Middle States Association of Colleges and Schools, New England Association of Schools and Colleges, North Central Association of Colleges and Schools, Northwest Association of Schools and Colleges, Western Association of Schools and Colleges.

Description: University of Houston (1927) began distance education in 1980 with 2 off-campus institutes, adding live, closed-circuit, televised classes in 1984. UH began delivering complete distance degrees in 1993. Students may now complete their degrees at neighborhood sites, in the workplace, or at home. UH Distance Education delivers selected degree programs and courses to students via TV (cable and PBS), live videoconferencing, videotape, online to 4 off-campus sites and to 13 community colleges. The university offers more upper-division, resident, credit courses and degree programs and has higher enrollment than any other upper-level institution in Texas. UH DE offers 85 junior, senior, and graduate credit courses each semester enabling students to complete degrees in 13 fields. This translates to 6,500 enrollments annually, with numbers growing every semester. In 1996 the University Continuing Education Association honored UH with an award for Outstanding Distance Education Credit Program in the nation. UH DE also received the 1997 UCEA awards for Outstanding Instructor and Outstanding Promotional Video, plus a 1998 Innovative Distance Education award and 2 Outstanding Faculty awards.

University of Idaho Engineering Outreach

University of Idaho	Phone: (208) 885-6373
P.O. Box 441014	(800) 824-2889
Moscow, ID 83844-1014	Fax: (208) 885-9249

Division(s): Engineering Outreach
Web Site(s): http://www.uidaho.edu/evo/
E-mail: outreach@uidaho.edu

Graduate Degree Programs:
Master's Degree in:
  Biological and Agricultural Engineering with an emphasis in Water Resources and Management Agricultural Engineering
  Civil Engineering
  Computer Engineering
  Electrical Engineering
  Engineering Management
  Environmental Science
  Geological Engineering
  Mechanical Engineering
  Psychology with an emphasis in Human Factors
  Teaching Mathematics

Postgraduate Degree Programs:
Ph.D. in:
  Computer Science
  Electrical Engineering

Certificate Programs: Structural Engineering, Secure and Dependable Computing Systems, Character Education, Communication Systems, Power System Protection and Relaying, Applied Geotechnics, Advanced Materials Design, HVAC Systems.

Teaching Methods: *Computers:* Internet, real-time chat, e-mail, CD-ROM, LISTSERV. *TV:* videotape; satellite broadcasting. *Other:* videoconferencing, fax.

Admission Requirements: *Graduate:* some programs require GRE scores or a degree from an ABET-accredited engineering program; all require TOEFL score greater than 550 for students from a non-English-speaking country; see web site for complete details. *Certificate:* undergraduate degree required; see web site for complete details.

On-Campus Requirements: One meeting at the end of the degree to take a comprehensive exam or defend a thesis or dissertation.

Tuition and Fees: *Graduate:* $410/credit. *Application Fee:* $35 for graduate students. *Software:* varies depending on class. *Graduation Fee:* $15. *Other Costs:* books, return postage for videotapes. *Credit by:* semester.

Financial Aid: Federal Stafford Loan, Federal Perkins Loan, Federal PLUS Loan, Federal Pell Grant, Federal Work-Study, VA, Idaho resident programs.

Accreditation: Northwest Association of Schools and Colleges.

Description: The University of Idaho (1890), located in Moscow, Idaho, is the state's land-grant institution with a combined mission of teaching, research, and outreach. The university enrolls more than 13,000 students. Liberal arts and sciences, offered through the College of Letters and Science, are at the heart of the university's educational programs, with primary areas of statewide responsibility in agriculture, architecture, engineering, natural resources, foreign languages, and law. The Engineering Outreach program was founded in 1975 to provide Distance Learning opportunities in Engineering. The program has grown into one of the top providers of graduate off-campus engineering degree programs, delivering more than 100 courses each semester in 11 disciplines to more than 400 students in locations around the country and around the world. More than 200 students have received graduate degrees through Engineering Outreach.

University of Illinois at Springfield

4900 Shepherd Road
Springfield, IL 62794-9243

Phone: (217) 206-7317
(800) 252-8533
Fax: (217) 206-7539

Division(s): Office of Technology-Enhanced Learning
Web Site(s): http://online.uis.edu
E-mail: schroeder.ray@uis.edu

Undergraduate Degree Programs:
Liberal Studies

Graduate Degree Programs:
Master of Science in Management Information Systems
Master of Arts in Master Teaching and Leadership Degree
    Concentration

Certificate Programs: Career Specialist Studies

Class Titles: Accountancy, Business Administration, Chemistry, Communication, Computer Science, English, History, Human Development, Liberal Studies Colloquia, Mathematical Sciences, Psychology, Public Administration, Public Affairs Colloquia, Sociology.

Teaching Methods: *Computers:* Internet, real-time chat, electronic classroom, e-mail, CD-ROM, newsgroup, LISTSERV. *TV:* videotape, cable program, satellite broadcasting, PBS. *Other:* videoconferencing, fax, correspondence, independent study, individual study, learning contracts, audio conferencing, audiographics, audiotapes.

Credits Granted for: experiential learning, portfolio assessment.

Admission Requirements: *Undergraduate:* accredited 45 semester hours, 2.0 GPA. *Graduate:* accredited bachelor's degree, 2.5 GPA.

On-Campus Requirements: None.

Tuition and Fees: *Undergraduate:* $95.75/credit residents, $287.25/credit nonresidents. *Graduate:* $107.25/credit residents, $323.25/credit nonresidents. *Graduation Fee:* $20 for bachelor degree, $25 for graduate degree. *Other Costs:* $15 for Technology Fee. *Credit by:* semester.

Financial Aid: Federal Stafford Loan, Federal Perkins Loan, Federal PLUS Loan, Federal Pell Grant, Federal Work-Study, VA, Illinois resident programs.

Accreditation: Commission of Institutions of Higher Education of the North Central Association.

Description: The University of Illinois at Springfield (1970) is the newest of the University of Illinois campuses. Formerly known as Sangamon State University, the campus joined the University of Illinois as part of a statewide reorganization of public higher education in 1995. Throughout its 29-year history, the campus has consistently stressed practical experience, professional development, and excellent teaching as the most effective means to enlighten students' minds and to give them the skills that will prepare them for the next century. UIS Online is a part of the University of Illinois Online initiative, which provides leadership, coordination, and financial support in the areas of Internet-based education and public service. The U of I Online offers online learning opportunities, complete degree and certificate programs, to place-bound and time-restricted citizens in Illinois, the United States, and around the world. The U of I Online currently offers 150 classes with an enrollment of over 5,000 students.

University of Illinois, Urbana-Champaign

302 East John Street, Suite 1406
Champaign, IL 61820

Phone: (800) 252-1360 x31321
Fax: (217) 333-8524

Division(s): Guided Individual Study and Division of Academic Outreach
Web Site(s): http://www.outreach.uiuc.edu/gis
http://www.outreach.uiuc.edu
E-mail: GISinfo@mail.conted.uiuc.edu

Graduate Degree Programs:
Master of Science in:
    General Engineering
    Electrical Engineering
    Mechanical Engineering
    Human Resource Development
    Curriculum, Technology, and Educational Reform
    Library and Information Science

Certificate Programs: French Translation, Financial Engineering.

Class Titles: Please contact school.

Teaching Methods: *Computers:* Internet, CD-Rom, e-mail. *TV:* videotape. *Other:* print-based correspondence course.

Credits Granted for: examination (CLEP).

Admission Requirements: *Graduate:* contact school for details at www.outreach.uiuc.edu.

On-Campus Requirements: For the master's degree in Library and Information Science there are periodic on-campus sessions.

Tuition and Fees: Refer to www.outreach.uiuc.edu *Credit by:* open system with rolling enrollment period; semester hours of credit for undergraduates. Semester hours and graduate units (one unit plus 4 semester hours) for graduates.

Financial Aid: VA, University Personnel.

Accreditation: North Central Association of Colleges and Schools.

Description: Since its founding in 1867, the University of Illinois at Urbana-Champaign (UIUC) has earned a reputation of international stature. As a land-grant institution, it serves 36,000 full-time students by providing undergraduate and graduate education in more than 150 fields of study. In addition, another 75,000 Illinois residents participate in conferences, institutes, credit and noncredit courses, and workshops each year. These nontraditional programs are offered statewide and nationally at public and corporate sites. The university's more significant resource is its talented and highly respected faculty, which includes Nobel laureates and Pulitzer Prize winners. The campus's academic resources are among the finest in the world.

University of Kansas

| Continuing Education Building | Phone: (785) 864-4440 |
| Lawrence, KS 66045-2606 | Fax: (785) 864-7895 |

Division(s): Continuing Education
Web Site(s): http://www.kuce.org
E-mail: enroll@ku.edu

Class Titles: Black Experience in Americas, American Society, General Anthropology, Fundamentals of Physical Anthropology, Cultural Anthropology, Myth/Legend/Folk Belief in East Asia, Fundamentals of Physical Anthropology, Meteorology, Unusual Weather, Sign Variations/Research, Principles of Biology, Principles of Human Physiology, Human Sexuality, Greek/Roman Mythology, Word Power: Greek/Latin Elements in English, Organizational Communication, Loving Relationships, Economics, Composition, Composition/Literature, Composition/Literature: Literature of Sports, Fiction, Poetry, American Literature, Recent Popular Literature, Shakespeare, Writing Fiction, Grammar/Usage for Composition, Business Writing, Technical Writing, Literature for Children, Directed Study: Willa Cather, Directed Study: Ernest Hemingway, Kansas Literature, Principles of Environmental Studies, French for Reading Knowledge, Principles of Physical Geography, Human Geography, History of Earth, German, World History, History of U.S. through Civil War, History of U.S. after Civil War, America/World War II, Hitler/Nazi Germany, Imperial Russia/Soviet Union, History of American Indian, History of Kansas, Art History, Impressionism, Principles of Environmental Design/Family, Child Behavior/Development, Principles of Nutrition/Health in Development, Marriage/Family Relationships, Adult Development/Aging, Children/TV, Western Civilization, Latin, Latin Reading/Grammar, Virgil's Aeneid, Math, Algebra, Trigonometry, Precalculus Mathematics, Mathematics for Elementary Teachers, Calculus, Statistics, Philosophy, Reason/Argument, U.S. Politics, Comparative Politics, Public Administration, U.S. Government/Politics, General Psychology, Statistics in Psychological Research, Cognitive Psychology, Child Psychology, Social Psychology, Brain/Behavior, Mind, Psychology/Law, Psychology of Adolescence, Psychology of Families, Living Religions of West, Understanding Bible, Elements of Sociology, Social Problems/American Values, Sociology of Families, Principles of Sociology, Sociology of Sex Roles, Sociology of Aging, Spanish Reading, Spanish, Survey of Communication Disorders, History of American Sound Film, Coaching of Basketball, Personal/Community Health, Principles of Health/Nutrition, Communicable/Degenerative Diseases, Drugs in Society, Environmental Health, Career/Life Planning: Decision Making for College Students, Principles of Human Learning, Psychology/Education of Exceptional Children/Youth, Design/Delivery of Instruction Using Educational Communications, Managing Behavior Problems: Concepts/Applications, Curriculum Development for Exceptional Children/Youth, Teaching Reading in Content Areas, Teaching Literature for Young Adults (Grades 7–12), Foundations of Education, Foundations of Curriculum/Instruction, History/Philosophy of Education, Curriculum Planning for Educational Settings, Jazz, Mainstreaming/Inclusion in Music Education, Managing Stress: Principles/Techniques for Coping/Prevention/Wellness. Options for High School Students: Career Planning, Project Self-Discovery, Short Story for Reluctant Readers.

Teaching Methods: *Computers:* Internet, real-time chat, electronic classroom, e-mail, CD-ROM, newsgroup, LISTSERV. *TV:* videotape. *Other:* correspondence, independent study.

Admission Requirements: *Undergraduate:* contact school. *Graduate:* contact school.

On-Campus Requirements: None.

Tuition and Fees: *Undergraduate:* $91/credit. *Graduate:* $132/credit. *Other Costs:* $45 for materials, handling and postage; $15–$45 audio/video user fees. *Credit by:* semester.

Financial Aid: Federal Stafford Loan, Federal Pell Grant, VA, Kansas resident programs.

Accreditation: North Central Association of Colleges and Schools.

Description: The University of Kansas (1865) has been involved in distance education since 1891. The university is the premier research institution in Kansas and serves a wide variety of educational and professional groups.

University of La Verne

1950 3rd Street
La Verne, CA 91750

Phone: (800) 695-4858 x5301
Fax: (909) 981-8695

Division(s): ULV On-Line
Web Site(s): http://www.ulv.edu/dlc/dlc.html
E-mail: harrisoa@ulv.edu

Class Titles: Biology, Chemistry, Core General Education, Education, English, History, Humanities, Political Science, Psychology.

Teaching Methods: *Computers:* Internet, real-time chat, e-mail, LISTSERV. *TV:* videotape. *Other:* audiotapes, fax, correspondence, independent study, individual study.

Credits Granted for: experiential learning, portfolio assessment, extrainstitutional learning, examination (CLEP, ACT-PEP, DANTES, GRE).

Admission Requirements: *Undergraduate:* 2.0 GPA. *Graduate:* accredited bachelor's degree, 2.5 GPA in last 60 undergraduate semester hours, 3 positive references, demonstrated graduate writing ability.

On-Campus Requirements: Not for the individual courses currently being offered, except for one lab session in Biology.

Tuition and Fees: *Undergraduate:* $330/credit plus lab fees in certain lab courses. *Graduate:* $405/credit. *Application Fee:* $40. *Other Costs:* $10/course for academic services (library). *Credit by:* semester.

Financial Aid: Federal Stafford Loan, Federal Perkins Loan, Federal PLUS Loan, Federal Pell Grant, VA, California resident programs. These are available for matriculated students only.

Accreditation: Western Association of Schools and Colleges.

Description: University of La Verne (1891) is an independent, nonsectarian university with a strong liberal arts curriculum and recognized professional programs in business, communications, counseling, education, educational management, health services management, law, and public administration. It offers bachelor's and master's degrees in several fields and doctoral degrees in organizational leadership, law, psychology, and public administration. In 1969 the university began offering programs off its central campus; currently it has campuses or centers in Alaska; Athens, Greece; and at several locations in California. Building upon this solid foundation, La Verne began offering undergraduate general education, graduate business, and graduate professional courses over the Internet in 1996 and is preparing to offer its first Web-based degree programs in 1998.

University of Louisiana at Monroe

101 University Avenue
Monroe, LA 71209

Phone: (318) 342-1030
Fax: (318) 342-1049

Division(s): Continuing Education
Web Site(s): http://www.ulm.edu
E-mail: cetownsend@ulm.edu or ceupshaw@ulm.edu

Undergraduate Degree Programs:
Associate Degree in General Studies/College of Liberal Arts

Teaching Methods: *Computers:* Internet, real-time chat, electronic classroom, e-mail, CD-ROM, LISTSERV. *TV:* videotape, cable program, satellite broadcasting, PBS. *Other:* videoconferencing, audiotapes, fax, compressed video.

Credits Granted for: extrainstitutional learning, examination (CLEP, ACT-PEP, DANTES, GRE).

Admission Requirements: *Undergraduate:* open-admissions, accredited high school diploma, ACT score of 17 or higher. See web site at http://www.ulm.edu.

On-Campus Requirements: depends on the course and the instructor. Arrangements can generally be made at an off-campus site.

Tuition and Fees: *Undergraduate:* $80/credit. *Graduate:* $80/credit. *Doctoral:* $80/credit. *Application Fee:* $15. *Software:* $15. *Other Costs:* $40 distance education fee. *Credit by:* semester.

Financial Aid: Federal Stafford Loan, Federal Perkins Loan, Federal PLUS Loan, Federal Pell Grant, Federal Work-Study, VA, Louisiana resident programs (TOPS).

Accreditation: Southern Association of Colleges and Schools.

Description: The University of Louisiana at Monroe (1932) entered distance education in 1983 with LPB and PBS.

University of Louisville

First and Brandeis Streets
School of Education
Louisville, KY 40292

Phone: (502) 852-6421
Fax: (502) 852-3976

Division(s): Special Education
Web Site(s): http://www.louisville.edu/edu/edsp/distance/
E-mail: denzil.edge@louisville.edu

Graduate Degree Programs:
Master of Education in:
    Special Education
    Visual Impairment

Certificate Programs: Special Education for Teachers, Visual Impairment for Teachers.

Class Titles: Mental Retardation, Moderate/Severe Learning Disabilities, Autism, Assistive Technology, Inclusion, Visual Impairment.

Teaching Methods: *Computers:* video-streaming, Internet, real-time chat, electronic classroom, e-mail, LISTSERV. *TV:* videotape, satellite broadcasting. *Other:* audioconferencing, videoconferencing, audiographics, audiotapes, fax, correspondence, independent study, individual study, learning contracts.

Credits Granted for: transfer credits.

Admission Requirements: *Graduate:* BA, GRE, transcripts. *Certificate:* BA, transcripts.

On-Campus Requirements: The Program in Visual Impairment requires student teaching which is offered at the Kentucky School for the Blind during the summer. Special arrangements may be made at an institution near the student.

Tuition and Fees: *Graduate:* $235/credit Kentucky residents, $642/credit out-of-state. *Application Fee:* $25. *Other Costs:* books. *Credit by:* semester.

Financial Aid: Kentucky resident programs, other state programs; check with your Director of Special Education in your school district.

Accreditation: Southern Association of Colleges and Schools, National Council Accreditation of Teacher Education.

Description: The University of Louisville (1798) is a state institution originally established as Jefferson Seminary. Several years ago, in response to a critical shortage of teachers in visual impairment, the Department of Special Education developed a distance learning program. Since that time, the Distance Education Program has won 3 national awards from the U.S. Distance Learning Association for the Best Distance Learning Programs in the Nation in Higher Education. We currently offer 20 courses and enroll over 600 students annually. UL is committed to offering its distance students the same quality of education and access to resources as students studying on campus.

University of Maine

110 Chadbourne
Orono, ME 04469-5713

Phone: (207) 581-4090
Fax: (207) 581-3141

Division(s): Division of Lifelong Learning
Web Site(s): http://www.ume.maine.edu/ced/ced/
http://www.ume.maine.edu/ced/de/
E-mail: help@umit.maine.edu

Undergraduate Degree Programs:
Bachelor of University Studies

Graduate Degree Programs:
Master of Arts in Liberal Studies

Certificate Programs: Maine Studies, Classical Studies, Child and Family Studies, Information Systems.

Class Titles: Anthropology, Astronomy, Animal Physiology, Molecular Genetics, Accounting, Human Development, Human Sexuality, Interdisciplinary Studies, Geotechnical Engineering, Greek Literature, Latin, Mythology, Disability Studies, The Literature of Stephen King, Food Science and Nutrition, Higher Education and the Law, Nursing, Peace Studies, Political Science, Electric Power Systems, Survey Engineering, Technology and Society, Womens Studies.

Teaching Methods: *Computers:* Internet, real-time chat, electronic classroom, e-mail, CD-ROM, newsgroup, LISTSERV. *TV:* videotape, interactive TV. *Other:* audioconferencing, videoconferencing, audiographics, streaming multimedia on Intranet.

Credits Granted for: examination (CLEP, ACT-PEP, DANTES).

Admission Requirements: *Undergraduate:* high school diploma. *Graduate:* bachelors degree. *Postgraduate:* prerequisite courses as required by program. *Certificate:* prerequisite courses as required by program.

On-Campus Requirements: None, but may be necessary for Master of Arts in Liberal Studies depending upon area of concentration.

Tuition and Fees: *Undergraduate:* $135/credit. *Graduate:* $203/credit. *Postgraduate:* $203/credit. *Credit by:* semester.

Financial Aid: Federal Stafford Loan, Federal Perkins Loan, Federal PLUS Loan, Federal Pell Grant, Federal Work-Study, VA, scholarships, and university grants.

Accreditation: New England Association of Schools and Colleges.

Description: The University of Maine was established under the provisions of the Morrill Act, approved by President Abraham Lincoln in 1862. By 1871 curricula included Agriculture, Civil Engineering, Mechanical Engineering, and electives. From these courses gradually developed Colleges of Life Sciences and Agriculture, Engineering and Science, and Arts and Sciences, School of Education was established in 1930 and received college status in 1958. School of Business Administration formed in 1958 and was granted college status in 1965. The first master's degree was conferred in 1881; the first doctor's degree in 1960. Since 1923 there has been a separate graduate school. In 1980 the university was given Sea Grant College status by the federal government under provisions of the National Sea Grant College

Program Act. In 1988 the University began offering distance education courses on interactive television and online to centers and sites throughout the state of Maine, and in 1997 began offering courses worldwide through multiple and hybrid Internet and Intranet technologies.

sciences, teacher education, and recreation management prepares graduates to succeed in their chosen fields, to dedicate themselves to lifelong learning, and to become responsible citizens.

University of Maine, Machias

9 O'Brien Avenue	Phone: (207) 255-1200
Machias, ME 04654	Fax: (207) 255-8464

Division(s): Behavioral Science
Web Site(s): http://www.umm.maine.edu/BEX
E-mail: speabody@acad.umm.maine.edu

Undergraduate Degree Programs:
Behavioral Science External Degree Program

Class Titles: Behavioral Science in Information Age, Psychological Models, Sociocultural Models, Research Methods/Design, Ethical Dimensions. Course descriptions at http://www.umm.maine.edu/BEX/Courses. All students design an individualized concentration.

Teaching Methods: *Computers:* Internet, electronic classroom, e-mail, newsgroup, LISTSERV. *Other:* independent study, individual study, learning contracts, internships.

Credits Granted for: experiential learning, portfolio assessment (maximum credits: 3).

Admission Requirements: *Undergraduate:* AA, AS, or 45 accredited hours.

On-Campus Requirements: None.

Tuition and Fees: *Undergraduate:* $105/credit. *Application Fee:* $25. *Other Costs:* $6/credit student activity fee. *Credit by:* semester.

Financial Aid: Federal Stafford Loan, Federal Perkins Loan, Federal PLUS Loan, Federal Pell Grant, Federal Work-Study, VA, Maine resident programs.

Accreditation: New England Association of Schools and Colleges.

Description: The Behavioral Science External Degree Program is a BA completion program offered by the University of Maine at Machias to students who have an associate degree or 45 credits. Inaugurated in 1995, this program is flexible and responsive to the needs of students in the twenty-first century. It is designed to prepare students to embark on a wide variety of career paths and further education in psychology, social work, and so on. UMM is the easternmost university in the U.S. and is a public undergraduate institution chartered in 1909. UMM's personal approach in its excellent programs in liberal arts, natural and behavioral

University of Manitoba

188 Continuing Education Complex	Phone: (204) 474-8012
Winnipeg, MB, Canada R3T 2N2	Fax: (204) 474-7661

Division(s): Distance Education Program
Web Site(s): http://www.umanitoba.ca/distance
E-mail: stusvcs_ced@umanitoba.ca

Undergraduate Degree Programs:
Bachelor of Arts
Bachelor of Social Work
Baccalaureate Program for Registered Nurses

Certificate Programs: Adult and Continuing Education, Post-Baccalaureate in Education, Prairie Horticulture, Manitoba Municipal Administrators.

Class Titles: Anthropology, Biology, Classics, Computer Science, Economics, Education, English, French, General Agriculture, Geography, German and Slavic Studies, Geological Sciences, History, Interdisciplinary Studies, Mathematics, Microbiology, Native Studies, Nursing, Philosophy, Physical Education, Political Studies, Psychology, Religion, Sociology, Spanish, Statistics, Social Work.

Teaching Methods: *Independent Study Program:* Print-based course materials; courses may require audiotapes and/or videotapes; interaction with instructors and classmates using e-mail, chat, or discussion groups; assignment submission by mail, fax, or optional online assignment submission; online checking of assignment grades. *Group-Based Study:* Flexibility of studying independently with scheduled audio-conference sessions between students in various communities and the instructor; courses may require audiotapes and/or videotapes; courses offer same online services as Independent Study courses. *Net-Based Study:* Students access a course web site to read course material and participate in discussions; online assignment submission; interaction with instructors and classmates using e-mail, chat, or discussion groups. *Campus Manitoba:* Courses use a variety of technologies including virtual classroom software; Internet and Web components; students gather at various locations throughout the province and take courses from any of the three Manitoba universities.

Credits Granted for: Possible transfer of credit(s); contact the Distance Education Student Support Staff at 1-888-216-7011, ext. 8028 or de_advisor@umanitoba.ca.

Admission Requirements: *Undergraduate:* variable; please consult Distance Education Program Guide for details. *Certificate:* variable. Please consult Distance Education Program Guide for details.

On-Campus Requirements: None.

Tuition and Fees: *Undergraduate:* $115–$141/credit hour, depending on the course. *Application Fee: Application Fee:* $35 Canadian citizens/permanent residents; $60 international students. *Other Costs:* textbooks; long-distance telephone charges for group-based study courses. *Credit by:* semester.

Financial Aid: Canada Student Loans.

Accreditation: The University of Manitoba is a member of the Association of Commonwealth Universities and of the Association of Universities and Colleges of Canada.

Description: The University of Manitoba is the province's largest postsecondary institution, the only one that is research-intensive, and the only one that offers medical and doctoral degrees. More than 22,000 students, and 4,000 teaching and support staff combine to make the University of Manitoba a vibrant community committed to teaching, learning, and the search for new knowledge. The University of Manitoba was established in 1877 to confer degrees on students graduating from its 3 founding colleges. It was the first university to be established in western Canada. In 1900, the University of Manitoba Act was amended so that it could begin teaching in its own right. In 1929, the University of Manitoba moved from its downtown Winnipeg location to its present permanent location at the south end of the city of Winnipeg. The Distance Education Program was established around that same time and now offers complete degree programs, as well as over 100 degree credit courses.

University of Maryland, Baltimore County

1000 Hilltop Circle	Phone: (410) 455-2336
Baltimore, MD 21250	Fax: (410) 455-1115

Division(s): Division of Professional Education and Training
Web Site(s): http://http://continuinged.umbc.edu/index.cfm, http://www.ifsm.umbc.edu/
E-mail: connect@umbc.edu

Graduate Degree Programs:
Master of Science:
    Information Systems
    Management Studies in Emergency Health Services
Master of Arts:
    Instructional Systems Development-Training Systems

Certificate Programs: Distance Education, Biochemical Regulatory Engineering.

Class Titles: Instructional Design, Emergency Health Services, Information Systems, Biochemical Regulatory Engineering.

Teaching Methods: *Computers:* Internet, real-time chat, electronic classroom, e-mail, CD-ROM, newsgroup, LISTSERV.

Admission Requirements: *Graduate:* Bachelor's degree, 3.0 GPA. (Slightly lower GPA may be accepted by some programs.) Graduate Record Examination taken within past 5 years; minimum score varies by program. TOEFL score of 550 (written) or 213 (computerized) for those whose native language is not English. (Exception made for those who have earned a postsecondary degree in U.S.) *Certificate:* Bachelor's degree, 3.0 GPA. (Slightly lower GPA may be accepted by some programs.)

On-Campus Requirements: None.

Tuition and Fees: *Graduate:* $292/credit in-state, $480/credit out-of-state. *Application Fee:* $45. *Diploma Fee:* $110. *Other Costs:* $58/credit hour mandatory fee. *Credit by:* semester.

Financial Aid: Federal Stafford Loan, Federal Perkins Loan, Federal PLUS Loan, Federal Pell Grant, Federal Work-Study, VA, Maryland resident programs.

Accreditation: Middle States Association of Colleges and Schools.

Description: The University of Maryland, Baltimore County (1966) is a medium-sized, selective, public research university that attracts high-achieving students to its undergraduate and graduate programs in the liberal arts and sciences and engineering. The College of Arts & Sciences and the College of Engineering degree programs include 30 majors, 34 minors, 24 areas of concentration, 11 preprofessional and allied health programs, and 7 certificate programs. The Graduate School offers 26 master's degrees and 20 doctoral programs.

    UMBC has been offering online courses since 1997. These courses are delivered exclusively over the Internet, allowing students the flexibility and convenience of learning whenever and wherever it fits within their schedule. Since 1997, the online courses/programs have shown a steady increase in enrollment; from 1999–2000 alone, enrollments increased 46%. The university is committed to the continued development of quality online educational programs.

    UMBC offers several unique online programs. The Management Studies in Emergency Health Services, the first online program offered at UMBC, is the only accredited program of its kind in the United States. This program emphasizes the most current systems design and management methods employed by high performance EHS systems.

    In the spring 2001, UMBC joined in partnership with the United States Open University, an affiliate of the Open

University (one of the oldest providers of distance learning) to offer a Masters of Science in Information Systems. Developed by leading faculty in the area of information systems, the curriculum is designed to provide the learner with the most up-to-date developments in the field of information systems. With courses offered year round, students can complete this degree in less than 2 years. More recently, the university has introduced an online Master's in Instructional Systems Development, a field that is receiving a lot of attention with the growth of distance and e-learning programs for education and corporate training. The program focuses on systematic analysis, development, evaluation, and management of training and education activities. Through project-based learning, the student gains expertise in the instructional design process and the utilization of technology.

University of Maryland, University College

3501 University Blvd East	Phone: (800) 283-6832
Adelphi, MD 20783	Fax: (301) 985-7977 (undergrad)
	(240) 582-2575 (graduate)

Division(s): Undergraduate or Graduate Enrollment
Web Site(s): http://www.umuc.edu/distance
E-mail: umucinfo@umuc.edu

Undergraduate Degree Programs:
Accounting
Business Administration
Communication Studies
Computer and Information Science
Computer Studies
English
Fire Science
Humanities
Management Studies
Environmental Management
Human Resource Management
Information Systems Management
Legal Studies
Marketing
Psychology
Social Science

Graduate Degree Programs:
Master of Arts in Teaching
Master of Business Administration
Master of Distance Education
Master of Education
Master of International Management
Master of Science in:
  Computer Systems Management
  Accounting and Financial Management
  Biotechnology Studies

Electronic Commerce
Information Technology
Telecommunications Management
Technology Management
Management
Environmental Management

Certificate Programs: The following undergraduate certificate programs are available: Accounting—Introductory, Accounting—Advanced, Database Management, E-Commerce Management, Environmental and Occupational Health and Safety Management, Human Resource Management, Internet Technologies, Management Foundations, Object-Oriented Design and Programming, Paralegal Studies, Public Fire-Protection Management and Administration, Systems Approach to Fire Safety, Technology and Management, Visual Basic Programming, Web Programming, Workplace Spanish.

More than 30 graduate certificates are available in the following areas: Accounting and Financial Management, Distance Education, Electronic Commerce, General Management, Information and Telecommunication Studies, International Management, Software Engineering, Technology and Environmental Management.

Class Titles: Any distance course may be taken once student is admitted.

Teaching Methods: *Computers*: Internet, electronic classroom. Online courses are asynchronous, meaning that students can participate in courses at times convenient to them. *TV:* Closed circuit within Maryland (undergraduate courses only). *Other:* supporting technologies include videotapes, audiotapes, CD-ROM, e-mail, and cable TV programs.

Credits Granted for: experiential learning portfolio assessment, extrainstitutional learning (PONSI, Cooperative Education on-the-job learning), standardized examination (advanced placement, CLEP, DANTES, Excelsior College Testing Program), course-challenge examination (undergraduate students only).

Admission Requirements: *Undergraduate:* diploma from regionally accredited high school or equivalent (total score of 225 on GED, no score below 40 on any of the five tests). If you are not a U.S. citizen or have any foreign education, visit www.umuc.edu/ugp for requirements. *Graduate:* bachelor's degree from a regionally accredited college/university or equivalent and an overall undergraduate GPA of at least 3.0 (students with at least a 2.5 GPA can apply for provisional status). Visit www.umuc.edu/grad to find out specific requirements for individual graduate degree programs and for foreign-educated students. *Certificate:* see admissions requirements for undergraduate and graduate students.

On-Campus Requirements: None.

Tuition and Fees: *Undergraduate:* $197/credit in-state, $364/credit out-of-state. *Graduate:* $301/credit in-state,

$494/credit out-of-state (except for online MBA and executive programs). *Application Fee:* $30 undergraduate, $50 graduate. *Other Costs: Active-Duty Military:* $148/credit for undergraduate; $301/credit for graduate. *Graduation Fee:* $50. *Credit by:* semester.

Financial Aid: Federal Direct Stafford Loan, Federal Direct PLUS Loan, Federal Perkins Loan, Federal Pell Grant, Federal Supplemental Educational Opportunity Grants, Federal Work-Study, institutional grants, private and institutional scholarships, VA, Maryland resident programs.

Accreditation: Middle States Association of Colleges and Schools.

Description: UMUC (1947) specializes in providing high-quality educational opportunities to busy adult students. Currently, more than 70,000 men and women on 6 continents pursue their educational goals through UMUC. One of 11 degree-granting institutions of the University System of Maryland, UMUC became an early leader in distance education and has won many awards for innovations in that area. In fall 2000, *Forbes* named UMUC's distance education Web page "Best of the Web" in higher education, saying "This school understands Web classes better than any other." More than 50 percent of our students today are enrolled in courses that do not require on-site attendance. Technology serves as their link to the university. UMUC's online education programs offer a unique and flexible way to complete the degree or certificate you need to achieve your educational, career, and personal goals. You can participate in these programs when and where it's most convenient for you.

University of Massachusetts, Amherst

113 Marcus Hall, PO Box 35115	Phone: (413) 545-0063
Amherst, MA 01003-5115	Fax: (413) 545-1227

Division(s): Video Instructional Program
Web Site(s): http://www.ecs.umass.edu/vip/
E-mail: vip@vip.ecs.umass.edu

Graduate Degree Programs:
Master of Science in:
  Computer Science
  Electrical and Computer Engineering
  Engineering Management

Doctoral Degree Programs:
Students may begin a PhD in Electrical and Computer Engineering, or Engineering Management; however, at least one year's academic residency is required.

Class Titles: Chemical Engineering, Math.

Teaching Methods: *Computers:* Internet, e-mail. *TV:* videotape, satellite broadcasting, National Technological University. *Other:* audioconferencing, videoconferencing, fax, correspondence, independent study.

Admission Requirements: *Undergraduate:* completed application and fees, 2.75 GPA, accredited bachelor's degree, all official college transcripts, 2 letters of recommendation, general GRE. *Graduate:* same as undergraduate.

On-Campus Requirements: None.

Tuition and Fees: *Graduate:* $1,400/3-credit course for domestic U.S. students, $1,600/3-credit course for international students. *Application Fee:* $20/semester. *Software:* $15–$45. *Other Costs:* international shipping. *Credit by:* semester.

Financial Aid: For financial aid information contact Financial Aid Services at the University of Massachusetts, phone (413) 545-0801. Federal Stafford Loan, Federal Perkins Loan, Federal PLUS Loan, Federal Pell Grant, Federal Work-Study, Massachusetts resident programs.

Accreditation: New England Association of Schools and Colleges.

Description: The College of Engineering at the University of Massachusetts, Amherst (1863), in conjunction with industry partners, developed the Video Instructional Program in 1974. As a distance learning facility, the VIP addresses continuing education and advanced degree needs. The VIP videotapes and broadcasts courses as they are taught by resident, graduate, faculty members before an on-campus, student audience. The videotapes are then delivered to VIP students across the country and the world—the quality of a university education without the sacrifice in time.

University of Massachusetts, Boston

100 Morrissey Boulevard	Phone: (617) 287-7925
Boston, MA 02125	Fax: (617) 287-7297

Division(s): Division of Corporate, Continuing and Distance Education
Web Site(s): http://www.conted.umb.edu/dl
E-mail: kitty.galaitsis@umb.edu (questions)
candice.chrysostom@umb.edu (registration)

Undergraduate Degree Programs: Contact school.

Graduate Degree Programs: Contact school.

Certificate Programs: Communications Studies, Instructional Design, Education Reform: Adapting Curriculum Frameworks for All Learners, Technical Writing, Fundamentals of Computing Program, Integrated Marketing Communications.

Class Titles: Courses in Sociology, Criminal Justice, IT, Counseling and School Psychology, Music, Education, Computer Science, Communication, English, Political Science, Nursing and Management via the Internet, Biology and Geography via ITV.

Teaching Methods: *Computers:* Internet, real-time chat, electronic classroom, e-mail. *TV:* ITV.

Credits Granted for: Courses are either 3-credit undergraduate or 3-credit graduate courses.

Admission Requirements: *Undergraduate:* no admissions requirement unless student becomes degree candidate at the University of Massachusetts Boston. Continuing Education division does not offer degrees. *Graduate:* so far online courses are open enrollment but some courses may require college transcript and departmental approval for enrollment. *Certificate:* 2 courses in certificate may be taken without matriculation.

On-Campus Requirements: web courses ask that students attend 2 on-campus classes if possible or do other work assigned by professor online. Class may be question and answer or course orientation, not necessarily lecture.

Tuition and Fees: *Undergraduate:* $650 total price. *Graduate:* $695 total price. *Application Fee:* $45. *Credit by:* semester.

Financial Aid: Federal Stafford Loan, Federal Perkins Loan, Federal PLUS Loan, Federal Pell Grant, Federal Work-Study, VA, state programs for residents of Massachusetts. Financial Aid is only for matriculating UMass students.

Accreditation: New England Association of Schools and Colleges.

Description: The University of Massachusetts Boston (1964) was the second branch of the University of Massachusetts to be founded, following the landgrant University of Massachusetts Amherst. In 1982 Boston State College became part of the University of Massachusetts Boston. UMass Boston is a regional state university. Its particular strengths lie in its depth and breadth of liberal arts programs, its strong faculty, its urban specialties, and its public policy programs. It is a commuter school with no dormitory space at this time. Corporate, Continuing and Distance Education offered web-based courses for the first time in summer 2001 although ITV courses have been offered for over 10 years. CCDE web-based courses are part of the University of Massachusetts online effort that will include courses from all branches of the University (Amherst, Lowell, Dartmouth, and Boston). See web site mentioned above.

University of Massachusetts, Lowell

One University Avenue
Lowell, MA 01854

Phone: (800) 480-3190
Fax: (978) 934-3043

Division(s): Continuing Studies
Web Site(s): http://cybered.uml.edu
http://continuinged.uml.edu
E-mail: Continuing_Education@uml.edu

Undergraduate Degree Programs:
Associate's Degree in Information Technology
Bachelor's Degree in:
Information Technology
Information Technology: Business Minor
Liberal Arts

Graduate Degree Programs:
Master's Degree in Educational Administration

Certificate Programs: *Undergraduate:* Contemporary Communications, Multimedia Applications, UNIX, Fundamentals of Information Technology, Intranet Development, and Data/Telecommunications. *Graduate:* Clinical Pathology, and Photonics and Optoelectronics.

Class Titles: American Cinema, Business Writing, C Programming, C++ Programming, Dynamic HTML, Psychology, Data Structures, Perl, Sociology, UNIX, Java Programming, JavaScript, Math, Purchasing Materials, Relational Database Concepts, TCP/IP Programming, Network Architecture, Technical/Scientific Communication, UNIX Shell Programming, Visual Basic, Writing for Interactive Media.

Teaching Methods: *Computers:* Internet, e-mail, live chat, streaming media and discussion forums.

Credits Granted for: examination (CLEP, DANTES, GRE), transfer credit.

Admission Requirements: *Undergraduate:* high school graduate or equivalent; applications for all programs are accepted on a rolling admissions basis. *Graduate:* see web site.

On-Campus Requirements: None.

Tuition and Fees: *Undergraduate:* $660/3-credit course. *Graduate:* $1,200/3-credit general course, $400/3-credit Educational Administration course. *Credit by:* semester.

Financial Aid: depends on matriculation status of student; see Continuing Studies Web site (http://Continuing_Education@uml.edu).

Accreditation: New England Association of Schools and Colleges, Accreditation Board for Engineering Technology, American Association of Colleges and School of Business.

Description: The University of Massachusetts Lowell (1895) is a comprehensive university committed to providing students with the education and skills they need for continued success throughout their lives. Specializing in applied science and technology, the university conducts research and outreach activities that add great value to the northeast region. The Division of Continuing Studies at UMass Lowell is one of the largest continuing education operations in New England. Our focus in developing Distance Learning programs is to ensure a quality, interactive experience for our students, increasing their access to science and technology education.

University of Memphis

382 Administration Building	**Phone: (901) 678-2197**
Memphis, TN 38152-3370	**Fax: (901) 678-0848**

Division(s): Extended Programs
Web Site(s): http://www.extended.memphis.edu.html
E-mail: jsipes@memphis.edu

Regents Online Degree Program:
Bachelor of Science in:
   Professional Studies
   Information Technology
   Organizational Leadership
Bachelor of Science in Interdisciplinary Studies

Graduate Degree Programs:
Master's courses in Journalism, Journalism Administration, and Education

Class Titles: Anthropology, Communication, Consumer Science, Geology, Geography, Journalism, Math, Sociology, English, Health/Fitness, Criminal Justice, Psychology, Nursing.

Teaching Methods: *Computers:* Internet, real-time chat, electronic classroom, e-mail, newsgroup, LISTSERV. *TV:* videotape, cable program, PBS. *Other:* videoconferencing, independent study.

Credits Granted for: experiential learning, portfolio assessment, examination (CLEP, ACT-PEP, DANTES, GRE).

Admission Requirements: *Undergraduate:* high school diploma or GED, ACT/SAT. *Graduate:* bachelor's degree, entrance exam (GRE, GMAT, MAT).

On-Campus Requirements: None.

Tuition and Fees: *Undergraduate:* $165/credit, residents; $443/credit, nonresidents. *Graduate:* $234/credit, residents; $512/credit, nonresidents. Regents Online Degree Program: $150/credit, resident; $428/credit, nonresident. College of Business junior/senior-level courses, $10/credit; graduate level courses, $20/credit. *Application Fee:* $15 undergraduate, $25 graduate, $50 graduate international. *Other Costs:* $75–$200/course for books, software, video rental, etc. *Credit by:* semester.

Financial Aid: Federal Pell Grant, Federal Supplemental Educational Opportunity Grant, Federal PLUS Loan, Federal Perkins Loan, Federal Direct Loan Program (subsidized and unsubsidized), Federal Work-Study, VA, Tennessee resident programs.

Accreditation: Southern Association of Colleges and Schools.

Description: From the opening of its doors as a normal school for training teachers to its present status as one of Tennessee's 2 comprehensive universities, the University of Memphis (1912) has been thrust forward by the growth of Memphis and the Mid-South. The metropolitan and regional requirements for more highly trained university graduates have, of necessity, caused the university to expand all its offerings and to enhance its delivery methods to include distance learning options.

University of Michigan/Flint

303 Kearsley Street	**Phone: (810) 762-3123**
Flint, Michigan 48502	

Division(s): Distance Learning Program
Web Site(s): http://online.umflint.edu
E-mail: tmsteven@umflint.edu

Undergraduate Degree Programs:
Nursing

Graduate Degree Programs:
Master of Business Administration

Class Titles: Computer Science, Economics, Art, Africana Studies, Communication, Business.

Teaching Methods: *Computers:* Internet, real-time chat, electronic classroom, e-mail.

Credits Granted for: examination (CLEP, ACT-PEP, DANTES, GRE).

Admission Requirements: *Undergraduate* and *Graduate:* same as those of the on-campus programs.

On-Campus Requirements: The MBA program requires 3 days (Friday/Saturday)/semester.

Tuition and Fees: *Undergraduate* and *Graduate:* same as the on-campus tuition plus $43/credit hour (please see www.flint.umich.edu). *Application Fees:* $30. *Other Costs:* for online courses $43/credit hour additional. *Credit by:* semester.

Financial Aid: Federal Stafford Loan, Federal Perkins Loan, Federal PLUS Loan, Federal Pell Grant, Federal Work-Study, VA, state programs for residents of Michigan.

Accreditation: North Central Association of Colleges and Schools, American Assembly of Collegiate Schools of Business, and others.

Description: UM/Flint was established in 1956, online programs began in 2000. We are one of 3 physical campuses of the University of Michigan system, and we are committed to the highest standards of teaching, learning, scholarship, and creative endeavors. Our new online program is one of the many ways the University of Michigan demonstrates its commitment to the needs of a diverse student population. As the profile of learners continues to evolve, the University of Michigan offers unique, creative, and challenging educational opportunities to students here and abroad. We are pleased to offer this new online format. Today, the University of Michigan/Flint campus offers more than 60 undergraduate and 8 master's programs in liberal arts and sciences, as well as in preprofessional and professional fields. Our online course offerings are expected to expand rapidly. The University of Michigan/Flint is accredited by the North Central Association of Colleges and Schools and many of our programs are accredited by discipline-specific agencies. All faculty teaching online and in the classroom are committed to quality education and provide a supportive environment for our students. Our highest commitment is to educate all students in an environment that emphasizes literacy, critical thinking, and humanistic and scientific inquiry, while guiding the development of thoughtful and productive citizens and leaders.

University of Minnesota—Crookston

216 Selvig Hall
2900 University Avenue
Crookston, MN 56716

Phone: (218) 281-8681
Fax: (218) 281-8040

Division(s): Center for Adult Learning
Web Site(s): http://www.crk.umn.edu/cal
E-mail: cal@mail.crk.umn.edu

Undergraduate Degree Programs:
Bachelor of Applied Health
Bachelor of Manufacturing

Certificate Programs: Hotel, Restaurant, and Institutional Management; Applied Ethics.

Class Titles: Composition, Microeconomics, Nutrition, Menu Design, Global Tourism, Hospitality Marketing/Sales/Law, Healthcare Management/Policy, Computers/Information Technology, College Algebra/Calculus/Statistics, Management/Marketing, Philosophy/Ethics, Biology/Physics, Psychology, Sociology, Public Speaking.

Teaching Methods: *Computers:* Internet, real-time chat, electronic classroom, e-mail, CD-ROM, newsgroup, LISTSERV. *Other:* videoconferencing, independent study, individual study.

Credits Granted for: experiential learning, portfolio assessment, extrainstitutional learning, examination (CLEP, DANTES, ACT-PEP, GRE).

Admission Requirements: *Undergraduate:* None.

On-Campus Requirements: None.

Tuition and Fees: *Undergraduate: Undergraduate:* varies per program. Please inquire. *Application Fee:* $25 for degree programs only. *Other Costs:* $7.50/credit UM fee. *Credit by:* semester.

Financial Aid: Federal Direct Stafford Loan, Federal Perkins Loan, Federal PLUS Loan, Federal Pell Grant, Federal Work-Study, VA, Minnesota resident programs, Minnesota Child Care, Self-loan from Minnesota, SAOG, Minnesota Work-Study.

Accreditation: North Central Association of Colleges and Schools.

Description: The University of Minnesota, Crookston (1966) has embraced the demands of life in the Information Age society by developing a unique technology-rich interactive living and learning community in 1993, earning it the reputation across the country as the "Thinkpad" University. UMC's primary focus on polytechnic education, a balance of theory and practical application, incorporates a curriculum that is learner-driven, interactive, supported with technology, and involves collaboration between students, faculty, and employers. UMC's curriculum is transfer-friendly. UMC's size (approximately 1,200 full-time students and 1,600 part-time students) and friendly, personalized learning approach allows students to connect with and learn from others more effectively. Computer and Internet tools provide connections with more people, places, and information than ever before. Participating in our active learning environment equips students with enhanced career and life skills. As you can see, we really do help students connect with people, technology, and careers.

University of Minnesota—Morris

225 Community Services Building
600 East 4th Street
Morris, MN 56267

Phone: (320) 589-6450
Fax: (320) 589-1661

Division(s): Continuing Education
Web Site(s): http://genedweb.mrs.umn.edu
E-mail: genedweb@mrs.umn.edu

Undergraduate Degree Programs: Contact school.

Class Titles: American Government and Politics, World Politics, College Writing, Introduction to Statistics, Drugs and Human Behavior, Comparative Education.

Teaching Methods: *Computers:* Internet, real-time chat, electronic classroom, e-mail, CD-ROM, newsgroup, LISTSERV.

Admission Requirements: *Undergraduate:* Contact school.

On-Campus Requirements: None.

Tuition and Fees: *Undergraduate:* $167.71/credit. *Credit by:* semester.

Accreditation: North Central Association of Colleges and Schools.

Description: The University of Minnesota—Morris (UMM) (1959) is an undergraduate liberal arts campus of the University of Minnesota. Today, UMM offers courses leading to a bachelor's degree in 27 disciplines, as well as course work in 21 preprofessional programs. One of the nation's few public liberal arts colleges, UMM's mission is highly distinctive as an academically rigorous, public undergraduate liberal arts college. The mission of the University of Minnesota—Morris is to be a small, selective, undergraduate, residential liberal arts college of the University of Minnesota, sharing in its state-wide mission of teaching, research, and outreach. As UMM strives to be the best public liberal arts college in America, its strength as a liberal arts institution comes primarily from 3 factors: a focused, narrowly defined mission that provides a rigorous liberal arts program; a select, intellectually gifted student body; and a faculty dedicated to teaching, to personal contact with students, and to research often involving student participation. The Distance Learning program, GenEdWeb, has been in existence since 1997.

Graduate Degree Programs:
Master of Science in:
 Computer Engineering
 Computer/Information Sciences
 Electrical Engineering
 Mechanical Engineering
 Public Health

Class Titles: Many of the courses in the above degree programs may be taken on an individual basis.

Teaching Methods: *Computers:* Internet/classroom, real-time chat, electronic classroom, e-mail, LISTSERV. *TV:* videotape, satellite broadcasting, interactive television classroom. *Other:* correspondence, independent study, individual study.

Credits Granted for: classroom study, some experiential learning by arrangement with instructor/department.

Admission Requirements: *Undergraduate:* contact school for information. *Graduate:* contact school for information.

On-Campus Requirements: None.

Tuition and Fees: *Undergraduate:* $179.70/credit. *Graduate:* Departmental Masters: $233.75/credit, Graduate School: $488.60 and up/credit, dependent upon school of enrollment. $9/credit University Fee, $45–$125 UMR Technology Fee. Tuition and fees are subject to change. *Credit by:* semester.

Financial Aid: available through the University of Minnesota Twin Cities campus.

Accreditation: North Central Association of Colleges and Schools, Accrediting Board for Engineering and Technology.

Description: The University of Minnesota Rochester (1966) extends the educational resources of the University of Minnesota to southeastern Minnesota. Our recent $9 million investment in distributed learning technology will enhance and increase our distance learning opportunities.

University of Minnesota—Rochester

855 30th Avenue SE Rochester, MN 55904	Phone: (507) 280-2828 (800) 947-0117 Fax: (507) 280-2839

Web Site(s): http://www.r.umn.edu
E-mail: bbesonen@mail.cee.umn.edu

Undergraduate Degree Programs:
Bachelor of Applied Science in:
 Manufacturing Technology
 Network Administration
Bachelor of Arts or Bachelor of Science in self-designed area
 of study through the Program for Individualized Learning
 (PIL)

University of Minneapolis— Twin Cities

150 Wesbrook Hall, 77 Pleasant St SE Minneapolis, MN 55455	Phone: (612) 624-4000 or (800) 234-6564 Fax: (612) 625-1511

Division(s): College of Continuing Education
Web Site(s): http://www.idl.umn.edu, http://www.cce.umn.edu/idl
E-mail: indstudy@tc.umn.edu or adv@cce.umn.edu

Class Titles: Historical Perspectives and Contemporary Business, Small Group Behavior and Teamwork, Managing Organizational Relationships, Communicating for Results, Accessing and Using Information, Skills for Decision Making,

Leadership in a Global and Diverse Workplace, Planning and Implementation at the Business Unit Level, Project Management in Practice, Operations in Manufacturing, Management and Human Resource Practices, Entrepreneurship, Introduction to Financial Reporting, Introduction to African Literature, Issues in Sustainable Agriculture, American Indian History: Pre-contact to 1830, American Indian History: Since 1830, Understanding Cultures, Human Origins, Art of India, Biocatalysis and Biodegradation, General Biology, Genetics, Cell Biology, Greek and Roman Mythology, Introduction to Child Psychology, Introductory Child Psychology for Social Sciences, Infant Development, Adolescent Psychology, Social and Personality Development, Principles of Microeconomics, Principles of Macroeconomics, Money and Banking, Ecology and Society, Preparation for University Writing, University Writing and Critical Reading, Advanced Expository Writing, Introduction to American Literature, Introduction to Multicultural American Literature, Textual Interpretation, Analysis, and Investigation, Historical Survey of British Literature I, Historical Survey of British Literature II, Survey of American Literatures and Cultures I, Survey of American Literatures and Cultures II, Shakespeare, Studies in Narrative: Science Fiction and Fantasy, Women Writers: Modern Women Writers, Women Writers: Nineteenth Century Fiction, Topics in Rhetoric, Composition, and Language: Origins of English Words, Introduction to Editing, Intermediate Fiction Writing, Intermediate Poetry Writing, Topics in Creative Writing: Journaling into Fiction, Literary Aspects of Journalism, Counseling Procedures, Beginning Finnish I, Beginning Finnish II, Finance Fundamentals, Corporate Finance, Reading French, Beginning French I, Beginning French II, Principles of Nutrition, Sexuality and Gender in Families and Close Relationships, Introductory Algebra, Intermediate Algebra, Solar System Astrology, Stellar Astrology, Principles of Chemistry, Law in Society, Literatures of the United States, Reading Short Stories, Statistics, Introduction to Business and Society, Principles of Small Business Operations, Accounting Fundamentals I, Introduction to Microcomputer Applications, African-American Literature, Asian-American Literature, Genetics, Introduction to Geology, Introduction to Earth History, Earth Systems Science for Teachers, U.S. and Canada, Russia and Environs, Latin America, Beginning German I, Beginning German II, World History, World History: The Age of Global Contact, U.S. History: 1880 to Present, The Civil War and Reconstruction, United States in the 20th Century Since 1945, Master Gardener Core Course: Horticulture for Home and Garden, Humanities in the West IV, Humanities in the West V, Introduction to Mass Communication, The Media in American History and Law: Case Studies, Magazine Writing, Communication and Public Opinion, History of Journalism, Literary Aspects of Journalism, Beginning Latin I, Beginning Latin II, Trigonometry, Short Calculus, Intensive Precalculus,

Calculus I, Calculus II, Multivariable Calculus, Fundamentals of Management, Principles of Marketing, Fundamentals of Music, The Avant-Garde, Beginning Norwegian I, Beginning Norwegian II, Life Span, Growth, and Development I, Life Span, Growth, and Development II, Introduction to Logic, Introduction to Philosophy, Introduction to Ethics, Physical World, Elementary Physics, Basic Physics I, Basic Physics II, Modern Physics, Orientation to Occupational Therapy, Introduction to Psychology, Introduction to Biological Psychology, Introduction to Personality, Introduction to Abnormal Psychology, Directed Study: Stress Management, Fundamentals of Alcohol and Drug Abuse, Dying and Death in Contemporary Society: Implications for Intervention, Accessing Information through Electronic Media, Technical and Professional Writing, Message Design: Theory and Practice I, Beginning Russian I, Beginning Russian II, The Expressionist Film in Scandinavia, Beginning Spanish I, Beginning Spanish II, Intermediate Spanish I, Intermediate Spanish II, Social Work with Involuntary Clients, Communication in Human Organizations, Beginning Swedish I, Beginning Swedish II, Intermediate Swedish I, Intermediate Swedish II, Introduction to Theatre, Gender and Global Politics.

Teaching Methods: *Computers:* Internet, e-mail, CD-ROM, LISTSERV. *TV:* Videotape. *Other:* Audiotapes, fax, correspondence, independent study, individual study, learning contracts.

Admission Requirements: *Undergraduate:* University admission not required to take IDL courses. *Graduate:* University admission not required to take IDL courses. Department permission required to earn graduate credit. *Postgraduate:* University admission not required to take IDL courses. Department permission required to earn graduate credit. *Certificate:* University admission not required to take IDL courses.

On-Campus Requirements: None.

Tuition and Fees: *Undergraduate:* $163 per credit. *Graduate:* $443.25 per credit. *Postgraduate:* Varies by department. *Application Fees:* none. *Software:* Varies by course when applicable. *Other Costs:* Course and material fee (excluding text/audio/video/cd rom): $54. *Credit by:* semester.

Financial Aid: Federal Pell Grant; Ford Federal Direct Subsidized, Unsubsidized and PLUS Loans; Federal Work-Study; and Minnesota resident programs for students admitted to a University of Minnesota, Twin Cities degree or eligible certificate program and enrolled in term-based telecommunications courses. College of Continuing Education scholarships and grants (Minnesota residents only), VA, Department of Vocational Rehabilitation, and employer assistance for telecommunications and correspondence courses (requirements vary by program; some may exclude extended term courses).

Accreditation: North Central Association of Colleges and Schools.

Description: The University of Minnesota (1851) is regarded as one of the finest public land-grant universities in the country. It is also among the largest, with 4 campuses and more than 40,000 students enrolled. The College of Continuing Education was established in 1913. The mission of the college is to provide high-quality continuing education and lifelong learning opportunities for professional development, personal enrichment, career transitions, and academic growth.

University of Mississippi

E.F. Yerby Conference Center
University Avenue at Grove Loop
PO Box 879
University, MS 38677
Phone: (662) 915-7282
Fax: (662) 915-5138

Division(s): Continuing Studies
Web Site(s): http://umdl.olemiss.edu
http://www.olemiss.edu
E-mail: umdl@olemiss.edu

Class Titles: Management, Marketing, Finance, Education, Paralegal, Law, Engineering, English, Philosophy, Political Science, Economics, Health Safety, History, Theater, Chemistry, French, German, Portuguese, Spanish.

Teaching Methods: *Computers:* Internet, e-mail. *Other:* videoconferencing, correspondence, independent study.

Admission Requirements: *Undergraduate:* contact Institute for Continuing Studies, e-mail credit@ics.olemiss.edu

On-Campus Requirements: None.

Tuition and Fees: *Undergraduate:* $151/credit in-state. *Graduate:* $201.50/credit in-state. *Doctoral:* $201.50/credit in-state. *Credit by:* semester.

Financial Aid: Federal Stafford Loan, Federal Perkins Loan, Federal PLUS Loan, Federal Pell Grant, Federal Work-Study, VA, Mississippi resident programs.

Accreditation: Southern Association of Colleges and Schools.

Description: The University of Mississippi (1848) offers more than 100 programs that lead to careers in engineering, business, telecommunications, politics, journalism, pharmacy, law, medicine, teaching, and more. The university also has outstanding pre-med, pre-law, and pre-pharmacy programs. A long-standing support system helps ensure success for Ole Miss students.

University of Missouri, Columbia

102 Whitten Hall
Columbia, MO 65211-6300
Phone: 1-800-545-2604
(573) 882-3598
Fax: (573) 884-5371

Division(s): MU Direct: Continuing and Distance Education
Web Site(s): http://MUdirect.missouri.edu/mu/bgdl.htm
E-mail: MUdirect@missouri.edu

Undergraduate Degree Programs:
Bachelor of Health Sciences in:
    Respiratory Therapy
    Bachelor of Health
    Radiologic Sciences
    Bachelor of Science in Nursing

Graduate Degree Programs:
Master of Arts in Journalism—Media Management
Master of Education in:
    Educational Technology Focus
    Gifted Education Focus
    Literacy Focus
    Social Studies Focus
Executive Master's Program in Health Services Management
Master of Science in:
    Health Informatics
    Nursing—Mental Health Nurse Practitioner
    Nursing—Pediatric Nurse Practitioner
    Nursing—Public Health or School Health

Certificate Programs: Labor Studies, Computed Tomography, Magnetic Resonance Imaging, Rural Real Estate Appraisal (pre-certification course work).

Class Titles: Personal Property Valuation, Machinery and Equipment Valuation, Medical Terminology, Grant Proposal Writing and courses leading to Missouri teacher certification in gifted education, initial principal and library media.

Teaching Methods: *Computers:* online, real-time chat, e-mail. *Other:* interactive television, independent study, clinical experiences (nursing).

Admission Requirements: *Undergraduate:* admission requirements vary by program. *Graduate:* admission requirements vary by program. *Certificate:* admission requirements vary by program.

On-Campus Requirements: Some programs require limited on-campus visits.

Tuition and Fees: *Undergraduate:* $141.50–$189/credit. *Graduate:* $188–$450/credit. *Application Fee:* $25. *Software:* varies. *Graduation Fee:* none. *Other Costs:* program-specific costs may apply. *Credit by:* semester.

Financial Aid: Federal Direct Loan, Federal PLUS Loan, Pell Grant.

Accreditation: North Central Association of Colleges and Schools.

Description: Founded in 1839 as the first public university west of the Mississippi, the University of Missouri/Columbia is a comprehensive land-grant campus, providing undergraduate, graduate, and professional education. It is cited in several publications as one of the nation's best values in higher education. The university's 20 schools and colleges serve more than 23,000 residential students and more than 1,500 Distance students. Departments offer interactive online degrees, certificates, and courses through MU Direct: Continuing and Distance Education. Credit and noncredit online programs are available at the undergraduate and graduate levels in agriculture, education, the allied health professions, health services management and informatics, journalism, and nursing. Courses, usually conducted within a semester timeframe, allow students to interact with faculty and classmates while "attending" class virtually at their convenience—anytime, day or night. Students have online access to course offerings, advising and registration, library services, textbook purchasing, and other academic resources.

University of Missouri, Kansas City

301 Fine Arts Building
5015 Holmes
Kansas City, MO 64110

Phone: (816) 235-1096
Fax: (816) 235-1170

Division(s): Interactive Video Network
Web Site(s): http://www.umkc.edu/is/mts
E-mail: brennemant@umkc.edu

Undergraduate Degree Programs:
Bachelor of Science in Nursing

Graduate Degree Programs:
Master of Science in Nursing

Teaching Methods: *Computers:* Internet, real-time chat, electronic classroom, e-mail. *TV:* videotape, cable program, satellite broadcasting. *Other:* radio broadcast, audioconferencing, videoconferencing.

Admission Requirements: *Undergraduate:* department-specific.

On-Campus Requirements: None.

Tuition and Fees: *Undergraduate:* contact school. *Graduate:* contact school. *Credit by:* semester.

Financial Aid: Federal Stafford Loan, Federal Perkins Loan, Federal PLUS Loan, Federal Pell Grant, Federal Work-Study, VA, Missouri resident programs.

Accreditation: North Central Association of Colleges and Schools.

Description: The fundamental purpose of the University of Missouri, Kansas City (1933) is to provide enlightened and able graduates who have the potential to provide leadership in the economic, social, and cultural development of the state and nation. The university has well-defined admission requirements that ensure a high probability of academic success for its students. The university is committed to the principles of academic freedom, equal opportunity, diversity, and to protecting the search for truth and its open expression.

University of Montana, Missoula

32 Campus Drive
Missoula, MT 59812

Phone: (406) 243-2900
Fax: (406) 243-2047

Division(s): Continuing Education
Web Site(s): http://www.umt.edu/ccesp/
E-mail: http://www.umt.edu/registrar/homepage.html

Undergraduate Degree Programs:
Bachelor of Arts in Liberal Studies

Graduate Degree Programs:
Master of Business Administration
Master of Education
Master of Educational Leadership

Doctoral Degree Programs:
Doctorate of Education
Pharmacy Doctorate (PharmD)

Class Titles: extensive list in areas of Business, Education, Forestry, Pharmacy, etc.; contact Registrar for details.

Teaching Methods: *Computers:* Internet, real-time chat, electronic classroom, e-mail, CD-ROM, newsgroup, LISTSERV. *TV:* videotape, cable program, satellite broadcasting, PBS. *Other:* radio broadcast, audioconferencing, videoconferencing, audiographics, audiotapes, fax, correspondence, independent study, individual study, learning contracts.

Credits Granted for: examination (CLEP, ACT-PEP, DANTES, GRE).

Admission Requirements: *Undergraduate:* some restrictions as to location within Montana. *Graduate:* some restrictions as to location within Montana.

On-Campus Requirements: some programs require a limited residency.

Tuition and Fees: *Undergraduate:* $175–$250/credit. *Graduate:* $175–$275/credit. *Application Fee:* $30. *Software:* varies. *Other Costs:* program specific. *Credit by:* semester.

Financial Aid: Federal Stafford Loan, Federal Perkins Loan, Federal PLUS Loan, Federal Pell Grant, Federal Work-Study, VA, Montana resident programs.

Accreditation: Northwest Association of Schools and Colleges.

Description: The University of Montana (1893) is a comprehensive, graduate level one institution of 12,000 students in a community of 80,000. Comprehensive undergraduate and graduate programs include professional schools of business, fine arts, forestry, journalism, pharmacy, law, and education. Master's degrees are granted in more than 20 fields and doctoral degrees in 12 fields. Additionally, a College of Technology, located in Missoula, is part of the University of Montana, Missoula.

The University of Montana, Western

710 South Atlantic Street   **Phone: (406) 683-7537**
Dillon, MT 59725   **Fax: (406) 683-7493**

Division(s): Outreach
Web Site(s): http://www.umwestern.edu
E-mail: v_lansing@umwestern.edu

Class Titles: *Extension courses (one credit each):* Behavior is Language: Strategies for Managing Disruptive Behavior, Behavior is Language: More Strategies for Managing Disruptive Behavior, Classroom Collaboration Using Internet, Learning Basic Internet Skills. *3-credit courses:* Young Adult Literature via Internet, Children's Literature, Philosophy, Psychology, Exceptional Child, Introduction to Creative and Performing Arts, Health Education Libraries and Curriculum, Acquisition and Organization of Library Materials, Library Administration.

Teaching Methods: *Computers:* Internet, electronic classroom, e-mail, LISTSERV. *Other:* None.

On-Campus Requirements: None.

Tuition and Fees: *Undergraduate:* $90/extension credit; 3-credit course: $360 resident degree student, $1,030 nonresident degree student. *Other Costs:* Distance learning fees or software fees. *Credit by:* semester.

Financial Aid: Federal Stafford Loan, Federal Perkins Loan, Federal PLUS Loan, Federal Pell Grant, Federal Work-Study, VA, Montana resident programs.

Accreditation: Northwest Association of Schools and Colleges, National Council for the Accreditation of Teacher Education.

Description: The University of Montana—Western was founded in 1893. It is located in Dillon, Montana, a town of 5,000 situated in the beautiful Beaverhead Valley.

University of Nebraska, Lincoln

33rd and Holdrege Streets   **Phone: (402) 472-4321**
Lincoln, NE 68583-9800   **Fax: (402) 472-4317**

Division(s): Continuing Studies
Web Site(s): http://www.unl.edu/conted
E-mail: unldde1@unl.edu

Graduate Degree Programs:
Master of Arts:
     Educational Administration (Higher Education)
     Journalism and Mass Communication
Master of Business Administration
Master of Agriculture
Master of Science in:
     Entomology
     Industrial and Management Systems Engineering
     Manufacturing Systems Engineering
     Interdepartmental Human Resources and Family Sciences
     Textiles, Clothing, and Design
     Master of Education (Curriculum and Instruction K–12) and (Educational Administration K–12 or Higher Education)

Doctoral Degree Programs:
Doctorate in Administration, Curriculum, and Instruction (Cohort Recruitment and Admission) (K–12 Specialization: Educational Leadership or Teaching, Curriculum and Instruction)
Doctorate in Administration, Curriculum and Instruction (Specialization: Educational Leadership and Higher Education)

Certificate Programs: Educational Technology (K–12 instructional technology training).

Class Titles: Accounting, Agricultural Law, Natural Resources and Environmental Law, Water and Natural Resources Law, Art History, Ecology, Broadcasting, Broadcast Writing, Scientific Greek/Latin, Teaching Social Studies in Elementary School, Economics (micro/macro), Statistics, International Economics, Composition, 20th-Century Fiction, Shakespeare, Business Writing, Human Development/Family, Insurance, Finance, Real Estate Principles/Practices, Real Estate Finance, Economic Geography, Human Geography, Physical Geography, Geography of U.S., Health, Western Civilization, Latin American History, East Asian History, American History, History of Middle Ages, History of Early Modern Europe, Nebraska History, Engineering Economy, Elementary Quantitative Methods, Operations/Resource Management, Personnel/ Human Resource Management, International Management, Business Policies/Strategies, Marketing, Geometry, Algebra, Trigonometry, Calculus, Pathophysiology,

Evaluating Nursing Research, Nutrition, Logic/Critical Thinking, Modern Logic, Philosophy of Religion, Elementary Physics, Calculus-based Physics, American Government, Contemporary Foreign Governments, International Relations, Public Administration, Psychology, Psychosocial Aspects of Alcoholism, Real Estate Management, Real Estate Investments, Real Estate Appraisal, Sociology, Social Problems, Sociology of Crime, Marriage/ Family, Technical Writing, Computer Science, Electrical Engineering, courses from College of Agriculture/Natural Resources, courses from Special Education.

Teaching Methods: *Computers:* Internet, real-time chat, electronic classroom, e-mail, CD-ROM, newsgroup, LISTSERV. *TV:* videotape, cable program, satellite broadcasting. *Other:* audioconferencing, videoconferencing, audiographics, audiotapes, fax, correspondence, independent study, individual study.

Credits Granted for: experiential learning, portfolio assessment, extrainstitutional learning, examination (CLEP, ACT-PEP, DANTES, GRE). See a UNL academic advisor.

Admission Requirements: *Undergraduate:* independent study courses: prerequisites are listed with courses; students have one year to complete a semester course, with a one-year extension possible. *Graduate:* application, 2 copies of all official transcripts (including bachelor's degree completion), 6-year completion limit, GMAT for MBA, TOEFL for international students. *Doctoral:* GRE for doctoral program in Curriculum and Instruction.

On-Campus Requirements: Doctoral Programs require 2–10 week summer sessions on campus at UNL.

Tuition and Fees: *Undergraduate:* $115/credit independent study, $116.75/credit nursing courses for all other distance education courses: $101.25/credit, technology fee $5/credit, registration fee $15/term, delivery and service fee for nonresident students $65/credit. *Graduate:* $134.50/credit independent study; for all other distance education courses $134/credit, technology fee $5/credit, registration fee $15/term, delivery and service fee for nonresident students $65/credit. *Doctoral:* tuition and fees same as for graduate. *Application Fee:* $35 Graduate Studies. *Other Costs:* $23 shipping and handling, $50 extension for independent study courses, vary for books, special library resource requests (interlibrary loans, etc.). Engineering and MBA distance education courses, $125/credit. *Graduate:* $110/credit independent study, $219/credit Engineering and MBA distance education courses, $164/credit all other distance education courses. *Doctoral:* $164/credit Doctoral Programs through Teachers College. *Credit by:* semester.

Financial Aid: Federal Stafford Loan, Federal Perkins Loan, Federal PLUS Loan, Federal Pell Grant, Federal Work-Study, VA, Nebraska resident programs. Contact UNL Financial Aid Office, restrictions apply.

Accreditation: North Central Association of Colleges and Schools.

Description: The Lincoln campus of the University of Nebraska (1869) is the state's land-grant university and the only comprehensive university in Nebraska. Through its 3 primary missions of teaching, research, and outreach, the University of Nebraska has been recognized by the state legislature as the primary research and doctoral-degree granting institution in the state. NU is one of a select group of research universities that holds membership in the American Association of Universities (1909), and is classified as a Research I University by the Carnegie Foundation. The University of Nebraska boasts 22 Rhodes Scholars and 2 Nobel laureates among its alumni. The university began offering courses at a distance in 1909 and currently uses almost every distance instructional technology available. The mission of the Division of Continuing Studies is to extend the resources of the university to promote lifelong learning. Each year we serve 87,000 people with our programs that reach people in all 93 counties of Nebraska, all 50 states, and 135 countries.

University of Nevada, Reno

PO Box 14429   Phone: (775) 784-4652
Reno, NV 89507   Fax: (775) 784-1280

Division(s): Correspondence Study
Web Site(s): http://www.dce.unr.edu/istudy/
E-mail: istudy@scs.unr.edu

Class Titles: Over 150 undergraduate, graduate, and high school correspondence classes.

Teaching Methods: *Computers:* Internet, e-mail, CD-ROM. *TV:* videotape. *Other:* audiotapes, fax, correspondence, independent study.

Credits Granted for: examination (CLEP).

Admission Requirements: *Undergraduate:* age 15+. *Graduate:* graduate status.

On-Campus Requirements: None.

Tuition and Fees: *Undergraduate:* $86/credit. *Graduate:* $108/credit. *Application Fee:* $40 graduate. *Other Costs:* books, materials, handling. *Credit by:* semester.

Financial Aid: VA, DANTES.

Accreditation: Northwest Association of Schools and Colleges.

Description: The University of Nevada was founded in 1867 and has offered Correspondence Study to Nevada and the world since 1944. In addition to its 150+ classes from high school to graduate level, the university is developing many new Internet courses. UNR wants to put you in a class all your own!

University of New Brunswick

Continuing Education Centre
6 Duffie Drive
Fredericton, NB, Canada E3A 5A3

Phone: (506) 453-4646
Fax: (506) 453-3572

Division(s): College of Extended Learning
Web Site(s): http://www.unb.ca/coned/
E-mail: coned@unb.ca

Class Titles: Applied Mechanics, Electrical Engineering, Economics (micro), English–Prose Narrative, Technology Management in Entrepreneurial Environment. Available inside Canada: Human Physiology for Nurses, Pathophysiology, Shakespeare/His Contemporaries, Survey of English Literature–Beginnings to Late 18th Century, Survey of English Literature–Romantics, Development of Western Thought, Elementary Statistical Techniques, Quality Management, Politics, History of Psychology. *Noncredit:* Effective Writing. Courses under revision as of July 2001.

Teaching Methods: *Computers:* Internet, e-mail, CD-ROM, newsgroup, LISTSERV. *TV:* satellite broadcasting. *Other:* audioconferencing, videoconferencing, audiographics, audiotapes, correspondence, independent study, individual study.

Admission Requirements: Courses are available to all interested individuals. To obtain credit toward UNB degree or certificate, applicants must meet entrance requirements for specified program.

On-Campus Requirements: None.

Tuition and Fees: *Undergraduate:* $394.50/3-credit course plus $8 student fee and $40 technology fee. *Software:* varies; see http://www.unb.ca/web/coned/de/ocrsof.html. *Other Costs:* varies; see http://www.unb.ca/web/coned/de/ocrsof.html. *Credit by:* semester.

Financial Aid: limited to Canadian citizens and landed immigrants only.

Accreditation: Association of Universities and Colleges of Canada.

Description: The University of New Brunswick (1785) values academic success. *Maclean's* 1997 Annual Ranking of Canada's Universities gave UNB "top marks for going the distance" with its students. It is the only university in New Brunswick that puts student success and achievement first.

UNB strives to be known for its excellence in teaching by providing students with the highest possible quality instruction, library and laboratory resources appropriate for both undergraduate and graduate learning, and an environment conducive to the development of the whole person.

University of New England

797 Stevens Avenue
Portland, ME 04103

Phone: (207) 797-7261 x4360
Fax: (207) 878-2434

Division(s): Distance Learning
Web Site(s): http://www.uneonline.org
E-mail: cags@mailbox.une.edu

Certificate Programs: Certificate of Graduate Study in Educational Leadership. Students who do not wish to seek the Certificate of Advanced Graduate Study may enroll in an individual course. Students may take up to 2 courses as a nonmatriculate. To enroll, an abbreviated online application is all that is required. This admission form enables students to enroll in a single course without formal admission to the University of New England.

Class Titles: Math: Teaching for Understanding (K-6) (pending approval), Improving Reading in the Content Areas, Using the Internet to Enhance Teaching and Learning, Teaching Reading in the Elementary Grades, Assessment to Improve Student Learning, Managing Behavior in the Diverse Classroom, Helping Students Become Self-Directed Learners, Learning Differences: Effective Teaching with Learning Styles and Multiple Intelligences, Building Your Repertoire of Teaching Strategies, Including Students with Special Needs in the Regular Classroom, Motivating Today's Learner, Teaching Students to Get Along, Strategies for Preventing Conflict and Violence, Succeeding with Difficult Students, The High-Performing Teacher, How to Get Parents on Your Side, Assertive Discipline and Beyond.

Teaching Methods: *Computers:* Internet, realtime chat, electronic classroom, e-mail, threaded discussion.

Credits Granted for: transfer of a maximum of 2 post master's credit courses.

Admission Requirements: *Postgraduate Certificate:* Admission criteria for Advanced Degree Candidacy are: Master's degree from an accredited institution, minimum of 3 years teaching and/or administrative experience, submission of officials scores from the Graduate Record Exam (GRE), administered by the Educational Testing Service, or the Miller Analogies Test (MAT), administered by the Psychological Corporation, current employment in an educational setting, or have ready access to one, ability to pursue rigorous, online graduate study, interest in continuing professional development, and a role in educational leadership, and potential to improve practice through application of new knowledge and skills.

On-Campus Requirements: Highlighting the Educational Leadership program is the residential required seminar, which brings together all of the students in the program for an intensive session offered each summer for one week. Students will enjoy the summer session on the University of New England's beautiful seaside campus in southern Maine, or other convenient regional locations throughout the U.S.

Tuition and Fees: *Postgraduate:* $300 per credit. *Application Fee:* $40. *Other Costs:* $150 for technology fee. *Credit by:* semester.

Financial Aid: Federal Stafford Loans, Federal Pell Grant, VA.

Accreditation: New England Association of Schools and Colleges.

Description: The University of New England is an independent university with a mission to educate men and women to advance the quality of human life and the environment. The university was created in 1978 in Biddeford. Maine, by combining St. Francis College and the New England College of Osteopathic Medicine. In 1996, the university merged with Westbrook College, a small liberal arts college in Portland, Maine, giving UNE two distinctive campuses. The university now recognizes Westbrook College's 1831 charter date as the University of New England's founding date.

Degree candidates in Educational Leadership join other graduate students at the university continuing their professional education in osteopathic medicine, human services, health and life sciences, management, and education. The online Educational Leadership program builds on a successful distance-learning model—the Master's Degree in Education for experienced teachers has hundreds of students enrolled throughout the country.

Designed and developed for working professionals who aspire to administrative and leadership roles in an educational environment, the Certificate of Advanced Graduate Study in Educational Leadership provides an innovative and convenient program of study, leading to a post-master's professional credential. The part-time online program offers the self-directed, motivated adult learner the needed flexibility to accommodate a busy lifestyle while pursuing career goals.

Courses in Educational Leadership are offered online, so study is convenient and accessible. Students may opt to study at home or in their school environment, wherever they have access to the Internet. With technical support from the university's instructional technology partner, *eCollege.com*, students quickly become adept with the technology, which is simple and easy to use. There are many opportunities for interaction with faculty mentors and other students using Internet tools developed and adapted specifically for online learners, including: threaded discussions, online class sessions, and an electronic bulletin board designed for communication from a faculty mentor to the students. Highlighting the program is the one-week residential Integration Seminar, which brings together all of the students in the program for an intensive session offered each summer.

The curriculum is designed to apply as broadly as possible to requirements throughout the country; however, it is the responsibility of the candidate to confirm what course content is needed in the state in which certification is sought.

University of New Hampshire

6 Garrison Avenue   Phone: (603) 862-1938
Durham, NH 03824   Fax: (603) 862-1113

Division(s): Continuing Education
Web Site(s): http://www.learn.unh.edu
E-mail: learn.dce@unh.edu

Certificate Programs: Industrial Statistics (graduate credit), Real Estate Recertification, Surveying/Land Use Planning (both noncredit).

Class Titles: Design and Analysis of Industrial Experiments, Design of Experiments II, Statistical Methods for Quality Improvement, Statistical Methods for Researchers, Advanced Heat Transfer, Nutritional Biochemistry, Microcomputer Technology, Manufacturing Tooling/Processes, Land Records (noncredit), Real Estate Salespersons/Brokers Recertification (noncredit) and more.

Teaching Methods: *Computers:* Internet, real-time chat, electronic classroom, e-mail, CD-ROM, LISTSERV. *TV:* videotape, T1 compressed video. *Other:* videoconferencing, fax, independent study, individual study, learning contracts.

Credits Granted for: extrainstitutional learning, examination (CLEP, ACT-PEP, DANTES, GRE).

Admission Requirements: *Graduate:* program-specific, accredited college degree.

On-Campus Requirements: None.

Tuition and Fees: *Undergraduate:* $184/credit. *Graduate:* $214/credit. *Application Fee:* $40. *Other Costs:* $15 registration, special course fees where applicable. *Credit by:* semester.

Financial Aid: Federal Stafford Loan, Federal Perkins Loan, Federal PLUS Loan, Federal Pell Grant, Federal Work-Study, VA, New Hampshire resident programs.

Accreditation: New England Association of Schools and Colleges.

Description: The University of New Hampshire's (1866) community includes more than 12,000 undergraduate and graduate students as well as nearly 1,000 full- and part-time faculty. In its 135th year, UNH is committed to excellence in education and to supporting the best in scholarship and research while also contributing to economic opportunity and the quality of life in New Hampshire.

University of New Mexico

1634 University Boulevard NE	Phone: 1-800-345-1807
Albuquerque, NM 87131	or (505) 277-7490
	Fax: (505) 277-8590

Division(s): Extended University
Web Site(s): http://e-unm.unm.edu/
E-mail: bambij@unm.edu

Undergraduate Degree Programs:
Registered Nurse/Bachelor of Science in Nursing
Bachelor of Undgergraduate Studies

Graduate Degree Programs:
Master of Science in:
    Nursing Administration
    Public Administration

Postgraduate Degree Programs: Contact school.

Certificate Programs: Radiopharmacology, Substance Abuse.

Class Titles: We offer a large variety of classes through various teaching methods. Here are the major categories: Anthropology, Curriculum, and Instruction in Multicultural Education, Economics, Education—Health, Educational Leadership, Electronical and Computer Engineering, Electronical and Mechanical Engineering, English, Family Studies, History, Mathematics, Nursing, Philosophy, Physics and Astronomy, Political Science, Psychology, Public Administration, Sociology, Spanish, and Statistics.

Teaching Methods: *Computers:* Internet, real-time chat, electronic classroom, e-mail, CD-ROM. *TV:* videotape, satellite broadcasting (EDEN = Electronic Distance Education Network), ITV (Instructional TV). *Other:* videoconferencing, correspondence, independent study, traditional face-to-face by traveling faculty.

Admission Requirements: *Undergraduate:* must be admitted into the University of New Mexico. *Graduate:* must be admitted into the University of New Mexico. *Postgraduate:* must be admitted into the University of New Mexico. *Certificate:* no prerequisites or special admissions.

On-Campus Requirements: The Nursing degree completion program requires a clinical internship.

Tuition and Fees: *Undergraduate:* $126.10/credit hour in-state tuition; $476/credit hour, out-of-state tuition. *Graduate:* $139.20/credit hour in-state tuition; $490.70/credit hour, out-of-state tuition. *Postgraduate:* $139.20/credit hour in-state tuition; $490.70/credit hour, out-of-state tuition. *Application Fees:* $20; $30 fee for late registration. *Other Costs:* fully Online Courses, $100 delivery fee; ITV Courses, $350/3-credit hour delivery fee, $150/1-credit hour delivery fee. *Correspondence Courses:* $136.50/credit hour; Senior Citizen rate: $5/credit hour (can register for up to 6 credit hours). *Credit by:* semester.

Financial Aid: Federal Stafford Loan, Federal Perkins Loan, Federal PLUS Loan, Federal Pell Grant, Federal and State Work-Study, VA, New Mexico Lottery Success Scholarship, Health Profession's Nursing Loan, Health Profession's Pharmacy Loans, Robert Wood Foundation Loan.

Accreditation: North Central Association of Colleges and Secondary Schools.

Description: As UNM (1889) celebrated its 100th birthday in 1989, the school's Distance Education mission was sustained primarily by traveling faculty and correspondence courses. Branch campuses stretched and solidified the reach of those initiatives and technology expanded options in 1986 to include instructional television. This development was quickly followed by video-conference classes. Now, at the opening of the 21st century, "Extended University" formally coordinates UNM's Distance Education programs and brings coherence to the application of current and emerging technologies to instruction. Extended University is committed to facilitating access to education. Toward this purpose, the convenience and flexibility of the Internet is being actively explored. UNM has entered the arena of web-based courses modestly, with the objective of working toward entire programs in critical need areas. Nursing represents the first achievement in this effort. In addition to serving as a focal point for instruction, Extended University is developing comprehensive online support services.

University of New Orleans Metropolitan College

Education Building, Room 122	
University of New Orleans	Phone: (504) 280-7100
New Orleans, LA 70148	Fax: (504) 280-7317

Division(s): Metropolitan College
Web Site(s): http://metrocollege.uno.edu
E-mail: metrocollege@uno.edu

Certificate Programs: Clinical Supervision, Computer Training, Medical Transcription, and more.

Class Titles: Personal Enrichment, Academic Preparation, Personal Development, Career Assessment, Ethics/International Politics, Conflict/Diplomacy.

Teaching Methods: *Computers:* Internet, real-time chat, electronic classroom, e-mail, CD-ROM, newsgroup, LISTSERV. *TV:* videotape, cable program, satellite broadcasting, PBS. *Other:* radio broadcast, audioconferencing, videoconferencing, audiographics, audiotapes, fax, correspondence, independent study, individual study, learning contracts.

Admission Requirements: *Undergraduate:* students need not supply previous transcripts or test scores, and up to 30 semester hours earned in this nondegree status may apply towards a degree later from the University of New Orleans. *Graduate:* students who have a bachelor's and do not wish to pursue a graduate degree from the University of New Orleans may apply for admissions to the Metropolitan College as a nondegree seeking student. A student may apply up to 20 semester hours earned. *Doctoral:* same as graduate.

On-Campus Requirements: Tests will be proctored by an administrator at your host institution.

Tuition and Fees: *Undergraduate:* approximately $1,181 for full-time students, contact school for details. *Graduate:* contact school for details. *Application Fee:* $20 admission application fee for first-time students. *Other Costs:* $30 non-refundable late registration fee, $17 extended payment plan option, $40 international student fee, $45 off-campus registration fee (except for graduate students), $5/credit ($75 max.) technology fee, $10–$100 special fees depending on course *Credit by:* semester.

Financial Aid: Federal Stafford Loan, Federal Perkins Loan, Federal PLUS Loan, Federal Pell Grant, Federal Work-Study, VA, Louisiana resident programs.

Accreditation: Southern Association of Colleges and Schools.

Description: The University of New Orleans (1958) provides its undergraduate students equality of access to educational opportunities, and seeks to nurture in them scholarship, academic excellence, the ability to work productively with others, and qualities of leadership.

The University of North Carolina at Charlotte

9201 University City Boulevard	Phone: (704) 547-2424
Charlotte, NC 28223	Fax: (704) 547-3158

Division(s): Continuing Education, Summer Programs and Extension
Web Site(s): http://www.uncc.edu/disted/
E-mail: distanced@email.uncc.edu

Undergraduate Degree Programs:
Bachelor of Science in:
    Engineering Technology: Electrical Fire Safety
    Nursing

Certificate Programs: Special Education.

Teaching Methods: *Computers:* Internet, real-time chat, electronic classroom, e-mail, CD-ROM, newsgroup, LISTSERV. *TV:* videotape, cable program, satellite broadcasting, PBS. *Other:* audioconferencing, videoconferencing, audiotapes, fax.

Credits Granted for: examination (CLEP, ACT-PEP, DANTES, GRE).

Admission Requirements: *Undergraduate:* BEST—*Engineering Technology, Electrical Engineering:* The Engineering Technology Program at UNC Charlotte is limited to the junior and senior years. An associate in applied science degree in an appropriate field is required for admission. Your overall grade point average upon admission to the university must be at least 2.2 (based on the 4.0 system) on all courses taken at the technical institute or community college. The total maximum transfer credit from a 2-year college is 96 quarter hours or 64 semester hours. *BEST—Engineering Technology, Fire Safety:* The Engineering Technology Program at UNC Charlotte is limited to the junior and senior years. An associate in applied science degree in fire protection is required for admission. Your overall grade point average upon admission to the university must be at least 2.2 (based on the 4.0 system) on all courses taken at the technical institute or community college. *BSN—RN/BSN Completion Program:* Students must meet the following admission requirements: Current unencumbered license as a Registered Nurse in North Carolina, a cumulative GPA of 2.5 or higher in all postsecondary course work, a minimum of C in all nursing prerequisites, completion of all nursing prerequisites by the end of the semester preceding the semester for which application is made. *Graduate:* bachelor's degree, 2.75 GPA, official transcripts, GRE/GMAT/MAT. Students can be admitted for individual courses for licensure.

On-Campus Requirements: Special Education classes are held at 3 community college sites in Dallas, Albemarle and Statesville, NC. Students attend classes at the UNC Charlotte campus during summer.

Tuition and Fees: *Undergraduate:* $125 tuition and fees for 3 hours of credit as a NC resident in 2001 spring semester. *Graduate:* $186 tuition and fees for 3 hours of credit as a state resident for 2001 spring semester. *Application Fee:* $35. *Credit by:* semester.

Financial Aid: Federal Stafford Loan, Federal Perkins Loan, Federal PLUS Loan, Federal Pell Grant, Federal Work-Study, VA, North Carolina resident programs.

Accreditation: Southern Association of Colleges and Schools.

Description: The University of North Carolina at Charlotte (1945) subsumes the College of Arts and Sciences and 5 professional colleges: Architecture, Business Administration, Education, Engineering, and Nursing and Health Professions. Enrollment has passed 15,800 and is expected to reach 25,000 within the next 12 years. Located in the 33rd-largest city, UNC Charlotte serves one of the nation's most dynamic regions, with 5,500,000 people in a 100-mile radius. UNC Charlotte participates in 2 statewide, interactive-video networks that "broadcast" courses from the Charlotte campus to other institutions of higher education, community colleges, high schools, hospitals, and other sites throughout the state. Distance education will soon include a major portion of a master's degree in Special Education and a bachelor's completion program in Engineering Technology.

University of North Carolina, Chapel Hill

CB# 1020 The Friday Center	Phone: (800) 862-5669
Chapel Hill, NC 27599-1020	(919) 962-1134
	Fax: (919) 962-5549

Division(s): Friday Center for Continuing Education
Web Site(s): http://www.fridaycenter.unc.edu/
E-mail: stuserv@unc.edu

Class Titles: Accounting, African Studies, Anthropology, Art, Biology, Business, Chemistry, Classics, Computer Science, Drama, Economics, Education, English, Environmental Sciences, French, Geography, Health Administration, History, Hospitality Management, Interdisciplinary Studies, Italian, Journalism, Latin, Library Science, Marine Science, Math, Music, Nursing, Nutrition, Philosophy, Physics, Planning, Political Science, Psychology, Recreation Administration, Religious Studies, Russian, Sociology, Spanish, Statistics.

Teaching Methods: *Computers:* Internet, e-mail, CD-ROM, LISTSERV, asynchronous discussion forum. *TV:* videotape. *Other:* audiotapes, correspondence.

On-Campus Requirements: None.

Tuition and Fees: *Undergraduate:* $63/credit for in-state residents; $130/credit for out-of-state. *Credit by:* semester.

Financial Aid: not specifically for distance education students. Requests are handled on individual basis.

Accreditation: Southern Association of Colleges and Schools.

Description: University of North Carolina-Chapel Hill (1793) is a major teaching and research institution that consistently receives high rankings for the quality of its instruction. The university's 14 colleges and schools provide instruction in 100 fields. The Friday Center for Continuing Education is the current name of the organization previously known as the

Division of Continuing Education, which was established in 1913 and has offered correspondence courses since that year. Online courses were added in 1997. Since the mid-1970s, UNC-Chapel Hill has provided administrative support for all UNC campuses offering correspondence courses. Since the mid-1970s, UNC-Chapel Hill has provided administrative support for all University of North Carolina campuses offering correspondence courses.

University of North Dakota

| Box 9021 | Phone: (701) 777-2661 |
| Grand Forks, ND 58202 | Fax: (701) 777-4282 |

Division(s): Continuing Education
Web Site(s): http://www.und.nodak.edu/dept/conted/learn.htm
E-mail: diane_kinney@mail.und.nodak.edu

Undergraduate Degree Programs:
Bachelor of Business Administration in Management
Corporate Engineering Degree Program with a Bachelor of
  Science in:
    Electrical Engineering
    Mechanical Engineering
    Chemical Engineering
Bachelor of Science in Occupational Therapy

Graduate Degree Programs:
Master of Business Administration
Master of Education in:
    Elementary Education
    General Studies
    Education Leadership
Master of Public Administration
Master of Social Work
Master of Science with specialties in:
    Rural Health Nursing
    Space Studies
    Medical Technician

Class Titles: Accounting, Anthropology, Art, Chemical Engineering, Communications, Economics, English, Fine Arts, French, Geography, Geology, Grant Writing, History, Humanities, Information Systems, Management, Mathematics, Medical Terminology, Music, Nutrition and Dietetics, Occupational Therapy, Psychology, Religion, Sociology, Spanish, and Teaching and Learning.

Teaching Methods: *TV:* videoconferencing, interactive video network system within North Dakota, Internet. *Other:* correspondence.

Credits Granted for: examination (CLEP, ACT/PEP, DANTES, GRE).

Admission Requirements: *Undergraduate:* contact admissions office. *Graduate:* contact admissions office. *Doctoral:* contact admissions office.

On-Campus Requirements: distant students do not have residency requirements.

Tuition and Fees: *Undergraduate:* $85/credit, correspondence, and Internet courses. *Graduate:* contact school. *Credit by:* semester.

Financial Aid: Federal Stafford Loan, Federal Perkins Loan, Federal PLUS Loan, Federal Pell Grant, Federal Work-Study, VA, North Dakota resident programs.

Accreditation: North Central Association of Colleges and Schools.

Description: The University of North Dakota (1883) existed 6 years before North Dakota became a state. Unlike most state institutions of higher education west of the Mississippi, UND did not begin as an agricultural school or a teachers college. Organized initially as a College of Arts and Sciences, with a Normal School for the education of teachers, UND soon evolved into a full-fledged multipurpose university. The instruction of graduate students (the first master's degree was awarded in 1895) and the conducting of research were underway before the end of the 19th century. Depressions, drought, wars, and financial crises have more than once threatened UND's future, but the university has been able to withstand these challenges and to prosper as an institution of national caliber. The master's degree in Space Studies is available internationally via the Internet and videotapes.

University of Northern Iowa

124 SHC	**Phone: (800) 772-1746**
Cedar Falls, IA 50614-0223	**Fax: (319) 273-2872**

Division(s): Continuing Education
Web Site(s): http://www.uni.edu/contined/gcs
E-mail: contined@uni.edu

Undergraduate Degree Programs:
Bachelor of Liberal Studies

Class Titles: A variety of undergraduate and graduate-level courses in Business, Communication Studies, Family/Consumer Sciences, Education, Social Sciences, Humanities, and Fine Arts.

Teaching Methods: *Computers:* Internet, e-mail, CD-ROM. *TV:* videotape, PBS. *Other:* videoconferencing, correspondence, independent study. Primarily a print-based correspondence study program.

Credits Granted for: examination (Credit by Examination, ACE military).

Admission Requirements: *Undergraduate:* for BLS, 62 transferable, semester credits, college transcripts, 2.0 GPA.

On-Campus Requirements: None.

Tuition and Fees: *Undergraduate:* $99/credit (correspondence study courses). *Graduate:* $99/credit (correspondence study courses). *Application Fee:* $20 to apply for admission to Bachelor of Liberal Studies. *Other Costs:* $13 enrollment fee for each course. *Credit by:* semester.

Financial Aid: VA.

Accreditation: North Central Association of Colleges and Schools.

Description: The University of Northern Iowa (1876) has a long and distinguished history of distance education. As early as 1914 college credit courses were offered off-campus to provide opportunities for teachers, most of whom did not have bachelor's degrees. While traditional methods of on-site, off-campus teaching and print-based correspondence study will continue, an increasing number of courses and programs will be offered via the World Wide Web and the Iowa Communications Network.

University of Northwestern Ohio

1441 North Cable Road	**Phone: (419) 998-3120**
Lima, OH 45805	**Fax: (419) 229-6926**

Division(s): Admissions
Web Site(s): http://www.unoh.edu
E-mail: rmorris@unoh.edu

Undergraduate Degree Programs:
Associate of Applied Business in:
    Business Administration
    Marketing
    Automotive Management
    Accounting
    Agribusiness Marketing/Management Technology
    Business Computer Applications
    Medical Office Assistant Technology
    Travel Management
Bachelor degrees (approval pending)

Certificate Programs: Agribusiness Management, Retail Merchandising, Travel/Tourism, Medical Office Assistant.

Teaching Methods: *Computers:* Internet, e-mail. *Other:* individual study, learning contracts.

Credits Granted for: experiential learning, portfolio assessment.

Admission Requirements: *Undergraduate:* high school diploma. *Certificate:* same as undergraduate.

On-Campus Requirements: None.

Tuition and Fees: *Undergraduate:* $170/credit. *Application Fee:* $50. *Graduation Fee:* $30. *Credit by:* quarter.

Financial Aid: Federal Stafford Loan, Federal PLUS Loan, Federal Pell Grant, Federal Work-Study, VA, Ohio resident programs.

Accreditation: North Central Association of Colleges and Schools.

Description: Founded in 1920, University of Northwestern Ohio is a private, coeducational, not-for-profit institution that began offering distance learning in 1993. The Ohio Board of Regents authorizes the college to grant associate degrees and diplomas in applied science in the Technological Division and applied business in the Business Division. UNOH's enrollment averages 1,800 with approximately 982 students living in residence halls. Students can enjoy an on-campus gymnasium, baseball diamond, restaurant, student lounges, and picnic areas.

University of Notre Dame

| 126 College of Business Administration | Phone: (800) 631-3622 |
| Notre Dame, IN 46556 | Fax: (219) 631-6783 |

Division(s): Executive Programs
Web Site(s): http://www.nd.edu/~execprog/
E-mail: Rita.A.Gong.1@nd.edu

Graduate Degree Programs:
Executive Master of Business Administration

Certificate Programs: Executive Management, Supervisory Development (plus some custom programs).

Teaching Methods: *TV:* videoconferencing. *Other:* None.

Admission Requirements: *Graduate:* 5 years of meaningful management responsibilities, undergraduate degree or GMAT, registrar's transcript of previously completed college level education.

On-Campus Requirements: August 6-day residency.

Tuition and Fees: *Graduate:* $24,900/year. *Application Fee:* $50. *Credit by:* semester.

Accreditation: North Central Association of Colleges and Schools, American Assembly of Collegiate Schools of Business.

Description: Founded by a Catholic priest in 1842, the University of Notre Dame has enjoyed constant and planned growth as an institution of higher education. Its programs have successfully combined moral, ethical, and spiritual considerations with educating students to meet the requirements of contemporary industrial, commercial, social, and technological systems. Recognition of its quality, through the success of its graduates and the esteem of alumni, has generated worldwide respect for the Notre Dame degree. The College of Business Administration traces its origin to 1913, when 6 students enrolled in a series of commercial courses. The Executive MBA program began in 1982 and launched its distance education program in 1995. Its videoconferencing classrooms are equipped with tracking cameras, wireless microphones, large display monitors, and many other multimedia devices for instruction and presentation. Live, 2-way, interactive videoconferencing is offered to remote sites in Indianapolis, Toledo, and in Hoffman Estates, Illinois.

University of Oklahoma

| 1600 South Jenkins, Room 101 | Phone: (405) 325-1921 |
| Norman, OK 73071 | Fax: (405) 325-7687 |

Division(s): Center for Independent Study and Distance Learning
Web Site(s): http://isd.ou.edu
E-mail: isd@ou.edu

Class Titles: Accounting, Anthropology, Astronomy, Business, Chemistry, Chinese, Classical Culture, Drama, Economics, Education, Engineering, English, Finance, French, Geography, Geology, German, Greek, Health/Sport Sciences, History, Human Relations, Japanese, Journalism/Mass Communication, Latin, Library/Information Studies, Management, Marketing, Math, Music, Philosophy, Political Science, Psychology, Russian, Sociology, Spanish.

Teaching Methods: *Computers:* Internet, real-time chat, electronic classroom, e-mail, CD-ROM, newsgroup, LISTSERV. *Other:* videotape, audiotapes, correspondence.

Credits Granted for: Check with OU Admissions and Records Office.

Admission Requirements: *Graduate:* check with Admissions Office. *Doctoral:* check with Admissions Office. *Certificate:* check with Admissions Office.

On-Campus Requirements: None.

Tuition and Fees: *Undergraduate:* $79/credit. *Other Costs:* $7 records fee, variable materials fee, book/kits fee. *Credit by:* semester.

Accreditation: North Central Association of Colleges and Schools, Commission on Colleges and Universities.

Description: The University of Oklahoma (1890) was established 17 years before Oklahoma became a state. Today the university is a major national research university that serves the educational, cultural, and economic needs of the state, region, and nation. The university's 25,400 students are enrolled in 19 colleges. In addition, a wide variety of courses and programs are offered through the College of Continuing Education.

University of Oregon

975 High Street, Suite 110	Phone: (541) 346-4231
Eugene, OR 97401	Fax: (541) 346-3545

Division(s): Continuing Education
Web Site(s): http://de.uoregon.edu
E-mail: dasst@continue.uoregon.edu

Undergraduate Degree Programs:
Applied Information Management

Class Titles: Astronomy, Arts & Administration (multicultural), Economics, Geology, Linguistics, Physics, Political Science.

Teaching Methods: *Computers:* Internet, e-mail. LISTSERV.

Admission Requirements: *Undergraduate:* all courses must be completed within the quarter term structure. *Graduate:* courses must be completed within the specified length of time for the class.

On-Campus Requirements: None.

Tuition and Fees: *Undergraduate:* varies based on course, student status, and total course load. *Graduate:* varies based on course, student status, and total course load. *Credit by:* quarter.

Financial Aid: Federal Stafford Loan, Federal Perkins Loan, Federal PLUS Loan, Federal Pell Grant, Federal Work-Study, VA. Available only to full-time admitted students.

Accreditation: Association of American Universities, Northwest Association of Schools and Colleges.

Description: The University of Oregon (1876) is a comprehensive research university that serves its students and the people of Oregon, the nation, and the world through the creation and transfer of knowledge in the liberal arts, the natural and social sciences, and the professions. It is the Association of American Universities' flagship institution of the Oregon University System. Distance Education courses were first offered in 1996, and additional offerings are being developed each year.

University of Pennsylvania

4001 Spruce Street	Phone: 215-573-9100
Philadelphia, PA 19104	Fax: 215-573-5742

Division(s): School of Dental Medicine
Web Site(s): http://www.intelihealth.com
E-mail: wendymc@pobox.upenn.edu

Class Titles: Pediatric Dentistry, Oral Surgery, Pharmacology, Periodontics and Prosthetics, Basic and Advanced Restorative Dentistry, Implantology, Radiology, Pathology, Oral Medicine, Dental Ethics.

Teaching Methods: *Computers:* Internet.

Admission Requirements: Certificates: $25/CEU credit.

Tuition and Fees: Contact school.

Accreditation: Middle States Association of Colleges and Schools.

Description: The University of Pennsylvania School of Dental Medicine (SDM) is a private Ivy League institution that ranks among the nation's leaders in oral health education, research, and patient care. Beginning in 2001, SDM will offer online professional continuing education programs for the dental community. Courses will be offered by the SDM faculty, leaders in their fields of specialty, as reflected in their extensive publications, invited lectures and sponsored research activities.

University of Pennsylvania School of Arts and Sciences

3440 Market Street, Suite 100	Phone: (215) 898-7326
Philadelphia, PA 19104-3335	Fax: (215) 573-2053

Division(s): College of General Studies—PennAdvance
Web Site(s): http://www.advance.upenn.edu
E-mail: advance@sas.upenn.edu

Undergraduate Degree Programs: Contact school.

Graduate Degree Programs: Contact school.

Postgraduate Degree Programs: Contact school.

Class Titles: Mathematics, Biology, Anthropology, Environmental Studies, Poetry, Writing, Economics, Psychology, Art History, Theater Arts.

Teaching Methods: *Computers:* Internet, real-time chat, electronic classroom, e-mail, LISTSERV, threaded discussion. *TV:* videotape. *Other:* live streaming video, prerecorded video, audio-narrated slide shows, conference telephone.

Credits Granted for: A transcript reflecting the grade and credit earned may be obtained by students who successfully complete a course.

Admission Requirements: *Undergraduate:* application form, college transcript, letter of recommendation; current Penn students and alumni may register; others must apply. *Graduate:* application form, college transcript, letter of recommendation; current Penn students and alumni may register; others must apply. *Postgraduate:* application form, college transcript, letter of recommendation; current Penn students and alumni may register; others must apply.

On-Campus Requirements: None.

Tuition and Fees: *Undergraduate:* $1,005/course unit. *Graduate:* $3,260/course unit. *Postgraduate:* $1,005/course unit. *Application Fees:* $55. *Other Costs:* $100 (approximately) for textbooks. *Credit by:* semester.

Financial Aid: Financial aid is not available at this time.

Accreditation: Middle States Association of Colleges and Schools.

Description: Since 1998, PennAdvance has given qualified students of many ages and backgrounds an opportunity to take a Penn course and earn credit on a Penn transcript, without setting foot on campus. This interactive Distance Learning opportunity features liberal arts courses taught by some of Penn's most distinguished faculty members. Courses are completely Internet-based, with live lectures, office hours, discussions, and other materials and communication modes available on the course web site. Participants include alumni and current university students, adult students from around the world, and academically talented high school juniors and seniors.

University of Phoenix Online

3157 E. Elwood Street
Phoenix, AZ 85034

Phone: (602) 387-7000
(800) 366-9699
Fax: (602) 387-6440

Division(s): University of Phoenix Online
Web Site(s): http://online.uophx.edu
E-mail: larry.etherington@apollograp.edu

Undergraduate Degree Programs:
Bachelor of Science in:
    Business/Accounting
    Business/Administration
    E-Business
    Management and Marketing
    Information Technology
    Management
    Nursing

Graduate Degree Programs:
Master of Arts in Education with majors in Curriculum and Instruction, Curriculum and Technology, E-Education
Master of Arts in Organizational Management
Master of Business Administration (BA) with majors in Accounting, E-Business, Global Management, Health Care Management, and Technology Management
Master of Science in Nursing
Master of Science in Computer Information Systems

Doctoral Degree Program:
Doctor of Management in Organizational Leadership

Class Titles: Accounting, Business, Business Law, Communications, College Math, Corporate Finance, Computers/Information Processing, Computer/Information Technology, Economics, E-Business, Finance, History, Humanities, Management, Marketing, Philosophy, Psychology, Program Management, Program Concepts, Science, Sociology, Statistics.

Teaching Methods: *Computers:* Internet, electronic classroom, conferencing, e-mail, CD-ROM, real-time chat, newsgroup, LISTSERV.

Credits Granted for: experiential learning, portfolio assessment, extrainstitutional learning (PONSI, corporate or professional association seminars/workshops), examination (CLEP, ACT-PEP, DANTES, GRE).

Admission Requirements: *Undergraduate:* high school diploma or equivalent, age 23, current employment or access to organizational environment that allows for distance learning. *Graduate:* undergraduate degree from an accredited college; employed or have access to an organizational environment that allows for distance learning; minimum GPA: 2.5 or 3 years of significant equivalent work experience.

Tuition and Fees: *Undergraduate:* $400/credit. *Graduate:* $495/credit. *Application Fee:* $85. *Software:* $102. *Other:* Courses are offered year around. Students are awarded "semester" college credit for course work taken.

Financial Aid: Federal Stafford Loan, Federal Perkins Loan, Federal PLUS Loan, Federal Pell Grant, Federal Work-Study, VA, state programs for residents of Arizona; cash options (pay for one course at a time).

Accreditation: University of Phoenix is accredited by Higher Learning Commission (HLC), a member of the North Central Association. The Bachelor of Science in Nursing and Master of Science in Nursing is accredited by the National League for Nursing Accrediting Commission.

Description: Busy professionals can earn their bachelor's or master's degree with maximum efficiency—via the Internet. At University of Phoenix Online, there's no commuting, no schedule conflicts, and no wasted effort. You simply click into class whenever and wherever you choose—and complete your degree in just 2 to 3 years.

At University of Phoenix Online, you learn from the most qualified instructors in the world, not just your local area. In addition to holding a master's or doctoral degree, our instructors hold high-level positions within their field, so they can provide valuable real-world insights. Our programs are also continually updated to reflect the knowledge and skills that are in greatest demand.

Established in 1976, University of Phoenix was designed specifically for working professionals. Today, we're the nation's largest private accredited university, and a recognized leader in online education. We offer state-of-the-industry degree programs in: Business, E-Business, Management, IT, Education, and Nursing. Our programs qualify for most employer reimbursement programs. Financing options are available. Credits can be awarded for work experience.

University of Regina

Room 211, College Building	Phone: (306) 585-5803
Regina, SK, Canada S4S 0A2	Fax: (306) 585-5779

Division(s): Centre for Continuing Education
Web Site(s): http://www.uregina.ca
E-mail: offcamp@uregina.ca

Class Titles: Administration, Astronomy, Biology, Cree, English, French, Geology, Human Justice, Psychology, Religious Studies, Women's Studies, Social Work.

Teaching Methods: *Computers:* Web-based. *TV:* satellite broadcasting. *Other:* videoconferencing, audioconferencing.

Admission Requirements: *Undergraduate:* Saskatchewan Grade 12 standing or equivalent with specified averages in designated courses. Those age 21 without regular admission requirements may be admitted to the University Entrance Program. *Graduate:* 4-year degree with an average of 70% in undergraduate work. *Doctoral:* master's degree or equivalent. *Certificate:* same as undergraduate.

On-Campus Requirements: traditionally instructed labs for biology courses.

Tuition and Fees: *Undergraduate:* $110/credit. *Graduate:* $110/credit. *Doctoral:* $110/credit. *Application Fee:* $60. *Other Costs:* $38 (0–8 credits) service fees, $9–$17/credit course fees. *Credit by:* semester.

Financial Aid: Canada Student Loans

Accreditation: Association of Universities and Colleges of Canada.

Description: The University of Regina (1974) is a dynamic institution with a heritage going back 27 years. It has a reputation for innovative academic programming and continually seeks to provide new, nontraditional programs in response to public demand. The university is recognized as a national leader in the areas of aboriginal education, cooperative work/study education, teacher training, the fine arts, systems engineering, journalism, computer science, and training for human service careers. Centre for Continuing Education

extends learning opportunities off campus through traditional face-to-face courses and distance education. Distance education courses are primarily offered through satellite broadcast (one-way video and 2-way audio) on the Saskatchewan Communication Training Network. Other modes of delivery for distance education courses include: Internet-based courses, computer-mediated conferencing, audioconferencing, and videoconferencing.

University of Rhode Island

Campus 80 Washington Street	Phone: (401) 277-5050
Providence, RI 02903	or 277-5160
	Fax: (401) 277-5060 or 277-5168

Division(s): Special Programs Office/Providence Campus; and the Academic Programs Office/Providence
Web Site(s): http://www.uri.edu/prov/dised.html
E-mail: nardone@uri.edu, ferszt@uri.edu, petronio@uri.edu

Undergraduate Degree Programs:
Contact school.

Graduate Degree Programs:
Contact school.

Class Titles: Art History, Communication Studies, Writing, Psychology, English, Human Development, Library Science, Management Science, Nursing.

Teaching Methods: *Computers:* web-based. *TV:* videoconferencing.

Credits Granted for: portfolio assessment, (CLEP).

Admission Requirements: Contact school for details.

Tuition and Fees: *Undergraduate:* $145/496/credit. *Graduate:* $202/577/credit. *Credit by:* semester.

Accreditation: New England Association of Schools and Colleges.

Description: The University of Rhode Island (1888) is the principal public research and graduate institution in the State of Rhode Island with responsibilities for expanding knowledge, for transmitting it, and for fostering its application. Its status as a land-grant, sea-grant, and urban-grant institution highlights its traditions of natural resource, marine, and urban-related research. The university is committed to providing strong undergraduate programs to promote students' ethical development and capabilities as critical and independent thinkers. To meet student and societal needs, it offers undergraduate professional education programs in a wide range of disciplines. Graduate programs provide rigorous advanced study and research opportunities for personal and professional development. With undergraduate and graduate programs in the liberal arts and sciences and focus programs in the areas of marine and environmental studies; health; children, families, and communities; and enterprise and advanced technology, the university strives to meet the rapidly changing needs of the state.

University of Saint Augustine for Health Sciences

1 University Boulevard	Phone: (800) 241-1027
St. Augustine, FL 32086	(904) 826-0084
	Fax: (904) 826-0085

Web Site(s): http://www.usa.edu
E-mail: info@usa.edu

Graduate Degree Programs:
Postprofessional Master of Health Science

Doctoral Degree Programs:
Doctor of Physical Therapy
Doctor of Health Science

Certificate Programs: Manual Therapy, Primary Care, Sports Physical Therapy.

Teaching Methods: *TV:* videotapes. *Other:* On-line Telematica Platform replacing pen and paper. CD-Rom, printed study guides, resident instruction. Graduate credit earned through the combination of attending seminars for clinical hands-on instruction and successfully completing home study courses.

Credits Granted for: experiential learning, portfolio assessment, extrainstitutional learning, examination, by petition and review.

Admission Requirements: *Doctor of Physical Therapy:* Physical therapists who hold either a bachelor's, master's degree, college transcripts; *Master of Health Science:* Therapists with a first professional bachelor's, master's or DPT degree, licensed in the U.S., college transcripts, GRE report; *Doctor of Health Science:* Therapists with a postprofessional (advanced) master's degree, licensed in the U.S., college transcripts, GRE report. Continuing Professional Education seminars: open to all appropriately licensed physical therapists. International/foreign students considered for all university programs.

On-Campus Requirements: Master of Health Science students spend 1–2 weeks, on-campus, academic residencies. Doctor of Health Science students attend on-campus Entry Colloquium (5 days), Medical Ethics (5 days), and Behavioral Psychology (5 days).

Tuition and Fees: *Graduate:* contact school for more information. *Credit by:* semester.

Financial Aid: Postprofessional division programs: TERI Continuing Education Loan, Key Bank Loan, DANTES; post-

professional scholarships: Stanley G. Paris Commonwealth Scholarship and Faculty Development Scholarship.

Accreditation: The Master of Health Science Degree is accredited by the Distance Education and Training Council (DETC). Licensure: The Florida State Board of Independent Colleges and Universities (SBICU), Florida Department of Education, Tallahassee, Florida, license the University of St. Augustine for Health Sciences to offer its degree programs. This licensure includes the postprofessional Doctor of Physical Therapy, Master of Health Science, and Doctor of Health Science.

Description: The University of St. Augustine for Health Sciences (1966) has taught continuing professional distance education to physical therapists since its founding. The university offers appropriately licensed health care professionals seminars and clinical certifications in 3 areas. In addition, the university offers physical therapists the postprofessional Doctor of Physical Therapy degree and physical and occupational therapists the Master of Health Science and the Doctor of Health Science degrees. These distance programs are designed to assist therapists in improving their clinical skills through seminars and home study courses that require minimal time away from home and practice. The university offers 2 campus-based first professional degrees—Master of Occupational Therapy and Master of Physical Therapy—for those interested in becoming occupational or physical therapists.

University of Saint Francis

2701 Spring Street	Phone: (219) 434-3100
Fort Wayne, IN 46808	

Division(s): Division of Adult Learning and University Assessment
Web Site(s): http://www.sf.edu, http://www.sf.edu/nursing/, http://www.sf.edu/weekend/
E-mail: admiss@sf.edu

Undergraduate Degree Programs:
Web-based Bachelor of Science in Nursing for Registered Nurses (RN to BSN)

Graduate Degree Programs: Contact school.

Class Titles: Nursing, English Composition, Literature, Speech, Religion, Art.

Teaching Methods: *Computers:* Internet, real-time chat, electronic classroom, e-mail, CD-ROM, newsgroup, LISTSERV. *Other:* videoconferencing, audioconferencing, correspondence, independent study.

Credits Granted for: experiential learning, portfolio assessment, examination (CLEP, ACT-PEP, DANTES).

Admission Requirements: *Undergraduate:* traditional students (up to age 24): graduate from an accredited high school, rank in upper half of high school graduation class, have a 2 grade point average on 4 scale, earn a Scholastic Aptitude Test (SAT) score of 920 or above or American College Test (ACT) composite score of 19 or above. Students who do not graduate from high school must have completed the General Educational Development (GED) tests, with a composite score of at least 50 and no subscore below 40. Adult students (over 25 years of age and Weekend College): graduate from an accredited high school, have a 2 grade point average on 4 scale. Students who do not graduate from high school must have completed the General Educational Development (GED) tests, with a composite score of at least 50 and no subscore below 40 *Graduate:* bachelor's degree from a regionally accredited institution in the United States. (Foreign credentials will be evaluated by off-campus specialists.) They must have an undergraduate grade point average of at least 2.50 on a 4 point scale, file with the Office of Admissions an Application for Admission, and have official transcripts from all previous postsecondary study. They must fulfill additional requirements as outlined by specific degree programs.

On-Campus Requirements: None.

Tuition and Fees: *Undergraduate:* $410/credit or Block rate from 12–17 credit hours, $6,550. *Graduate:* $430/credit. *Application Fees:* $20. *Software:* $10/credit hour. *Graduation Fee:* $75. *Other Costs:* semester fee: up to $115 (varies by credit hours taken). *Credit by:* semester.

Financial Aid: Federal Stafford Loan, Federal Perkins Loan, Federal PLUS Loan, Federal Pell Grant, Federal Work-Study, VA, state programs for residents of Indiana, University of Saint Francis needs based grant for full-time students, Academic Grants (President's Scholarship), Distinctive Awards (Science Scholarships, Excellence Scholarships), Special Awards (Child of Alumni Grant and Multiple Family Member Discount).

Accreditation: North Central Association of Colleges and Schools, Indiana State Board of Nursing, Indiana State Department of Education, the Council of Social Work Education, the National League for Nursing, the National Council for Accreditation of Teacher Education, and the Commission on Collegiate Nursing Education.

Description: The University of Saint Francis (1890) exists to serve students by facilitating learning and personal and professional development in an environment permeated by Franciscan values. Founded by the Sisters of Saint Francis of Perpetual Adoration, the university is a Catholic, coeducational institution of higher education in the liberal arts tradition, offering undergraduate and graduate programs designed to meet the needs of a diverse student body. USF entered into Distance Education in 1994 with videoconferencing and added web-based courses in fall 2000. USF offers a web-based Bachelor of Science in Nursing program for registered nurses as well as computer-assisted courses for the Master of Science in Nursing program. The university offers more than 20 academic majors in its traditional on-campus environment.

University of Sarasota

5250 17th Street
Sarasota, FL 34235

Phone: (941) 379-0404
(800) 331-5995
Fax: (941) 379-9464

Division(s): Admissions
Web Site(s): http://www.sarasota.edu
E-mail: univsar@compuserve.com

Graduate Degree Programs:
Master of Arts in:
    Mental Health Counseling
    Guidance Counseling
    Counseling Psychology
Master of Business Administration (MBA)
MBA with a concentration in International Business

Doctoral Degree Programs:
Educational Specialist in:
    Educational Leadership
    Curriculum/Instruction
    School Counseling
Doctor of Education in:
    Educational Leadership
    Curriculum/Instruction
    Organizational Leadership
    Counseling Psychology
    Pastoral Community Counseling
Doctor of Business Administration (DBA)
DBA with a concentration in:
    Management
    Marketing
    Accounting

Certificate Programs: Professional Graduate Business (Human Resource); International Trade, Marketing, Finance; Healthcare Administration, NAFTA I, NAFTA II.

Teaching Methods: *Computers:* Internet, e-mail. *TV:* videotape. *Other:* fax, correspondence, independent study.

Credits Granted for: transfer credit from another college.

Admission Requirements: *Graduate:* accredited bachelor's degree, previous and sustained 3.0 GPA, possible interview, personal statement of professional and educational goals, online and e-mail access, program completion within 4 years, TOEFL of 500 (173 computer-based) for applicants whose native language is not English. *Doctoral:* EdS: accredited master's degree, previous and sustained 3.0 GPA, possible interview, personal statement of professional and educational goals, 3 current professional recommendations, online and e-mail access, TOEFL of 550 (213 computer-based) for all applicants whose native language is not English. For EdS in School Counseling ONLY: Teaching experience in either a public or private K–12 school, program completion within 3 years. Doctorates: accredited master's degree, possible interview, résumé, 3 current professional recommendations, personal statement of professional and educational goals, program completion within 7 years (within 5 years for Pastoral Community Counseling), TOEFL of 550 (213 computer-based) for applicants whose native language is not English. *Certificate:* Advanced Graduate Business Certificates: admission as a student-at-large and must meet all requirements for Doctor of Business Administration program. Professional and Basic Graduate Business Certificates: admission as a student-at-large and must meet all requirements for MBA program.

On-Campus Requirements: Doctor of Education/Doctor of Business Administration on-campus requirement is 8 courses (24 credits). Educational Specialist on-campus requirement is 5 courses (15 credits). Master of Arts/Master of Business Administration on-campus requirement is 6 courses (18 credits).

Tuition and Fees: *Graduate:* $353/credit. *Application Fee:* $50. *Software:* $11/course. *Credit by:* semester.

Financial Aid: Federal Stafford Loan

Accreditation: Southern Association of Colleges and Schools.

Description: University of Sarasota (1969) was established to serve the graduate educational needs of adult working professionals. As relevant technologies emerged, they were incorporated into the university's flexible delivery systems. The state of Florida granted licensure to the university in 1976 to offer the Doctorate in Education (EdD). Two years later, the state authorized the university to offer the Master of Arts in Education (MAEd). In 1980, the university received additional approval to offer the Master of Business Administration (MBA). In 1990, the university was accredited by the Commission on Colleges of the Southern Association of Colleges and Schools to offer master's and doctoral degrees. In 1994, the Doctor of Business Administration (DBA) program was established. The university has also gained approval to award bachelor's and educational specialist degrees.

University of Saskatchewan

Room 326 Kirk Hall
117 Science Place
Saskatoon, SK, Canada S7N 5C8

Phone: (306) 966-5563
Fax: (306) 966-5590

Division(s): Extension Credit Studies
Web Site(s): http://www.extension.usask.ca
E-mail: extcred@usask.ca

Certificate Programs: Education and Arts and Science courses, including Adult and Continuing Education, Agriculture, Prairie Horticulture, Teaching English as a Second Language.

Class Titles: Most first-year degree courses.

Teaching Methods: *Computers:* Internet, e-mail, CD-ROM, LISTSERV. *TV:* videotape, satellite broadcasting. *Other:* audioconferencing, audiotapes, fax, correspondence, independent study, individual study, learning contracts.

Credits Granted for: portfolio assessment.

Admission Requirements: *Undergraduate:* high school diploma/matriculation. *Certificate:* high school diploma/matriculation or equivalent.

On-Campus Requirements: None.

Tuition and Fees: *Undergraduate:* $100–125/credit, $100–$115/equivalent credit unit for certificate programs. *Application Fee:* $50 for ACE Certificate. *Other Costs:* $50 admission, Course materials: $10–$55 (texts not included). *Credit by:* term (3/year).

Financial Aid: part-time student loans (federal/provincial).

Accreditation: Association of Universities and Colleges of Canada.

Description: Since 1907 the University of Saskatchewan has provided a blend of liberal, professional, and applied education and research. In 1929 the university first delivered correspondence courses. Distance education courses today still use print-based material but also may incorporate audio, video, satellite, or computer technologies.

University of South Carolina

915 Gregg Street
Columbia, SC 29208

Phone: (800) 922-2577
Fax: (803) 777-6264

Division(s): Distance Education and Instructional Support
Web Site(s): http://www.sc.edu/deis/student.services
E-mail: question@gwm.sc.edu

Graduate Degree Programs:
Master of Science in:
Engineering
Business
Communication Disorders
Library and Information Science

Class Titles: Astronomy, Library Science, Education, English, French, History, Marine Science, Nursing, Anthropology, Social Work, Business Administration, Journalism, Engineering, Health.

Teaching Methods: *Computers:* Internet, real-time chat, electronic classroom, e-mail, CD-ROM, LISTSERV. *TV:* videotape, satellite broadcasting, audioconferencing, videoconferencing, audiotapes. *Other:* correspondence, independent study, individual study, learning contracts.

Credits Granted for: examination (CLEP, ACT-PEP, DANTES, GRE).

Admission Requirements: *Undergraduate:* call Distance Education and Instructional Support. *Graduate:* call Distance Education and Instructional Support.

On-Campus Requirements: some sessions for some departments; department-specific.

Tuition and Fees: *Undergraduate:* $178/credit. *Graduate:* $209/credit. *Application Fee:* $40 graduate, $35 undergraduate. *Other Costs:* $4/credit technology fee. *Credit by:* semester.

Financial Aid: Federal Stafford Loan, Federal Perkins Loan, Federal PLUS Loan, Federal Pell Grant, Federal Work-Study, VA, South Carolina resident programs.

Accreditation: Southern Association of Colleges and Schools.

Description: The University of South Carolina (1801) was the first higher education institution funded entirely by a state. Faculty included Francis Lieber, author of Civil Liberty and Self Government, scientists John and Joseph LeConte, and chemist William Eller, who produced the first daguerreotype in the U.S. The voluntary enlistment of all students in the Army of the Confederacy forced the college to close during the Civil War. It was rechartered to offer "the largest and best work in education that time and place and conditions render possible." In addition to the Columbia campus, there are two 4-year campuses and five 2-year regional campuses, with a total enrollment of 37,000. While correspondence study has been offered at USC for more than 70 years, the university's commitment to televised instruction began in 1969 through the state's closed-circuit system. Today the distance education program, utilizing satellite, video/audiocassettes, and correspondence study, is a vital part of the university's commitment to providing alternative educational opportunities to students.

University of Southern California School of Engineering

Olin Hall of Engineering, Room 108
School of Engineering, MC 1455
Los Angeles, CA 90089-1455

Phone: (213) 740-0115
Fax: (213) 749-3289

Division(s): Distance Education Network for the School of Engineering
Web Site(s): http://www.den.usc.edu

E-mail: jecks@usc.edu

Graduate Degree Programs:
Master of Science in:
Aerospace Engineering (Astronautics)
Computer Science
Computer Engineering
Electrical Engineering
Systems Architecting and Engineering

Certificate Programs: Aerospace Engineering (specialization in Astronautics), Software Engineering, Systems Engineering.

Teaching Methods: *Computers:* webcasting. *TV:* microwave and satellite broadcasting. *Other:* e-mail, newsgroup, videoconferencing.

Credits Granted for: Regular credit courses only.

Admission Requirements: *Graduate:* Accredited bachelor's degree, GRE, undergraduate GPA of 3.0. Students must be employed at DEN member company.

On-Campus Requirements: None. Students view course lectures via webcast at their computer or via broadcast to a classroom at their company site.

Tuition and Fees: *Undergraduate:* $844/credit. *Graduate:* $867/credit. *Application Fee:* $55. *Other Costs:* DEN Surcharge, varies by company site. *Credit by:* semester.

Financial Aid: Most companies reimburse 100%.

Accreditation: Western Association of Schools and Colleges.

Description: The USC School of Engineering (1906) seeks to provide undergraduate and graduate engineering degree programs for qualified students; to extend the frontiers of engineering knowledge by encouraging and assisting faculty to pursue and publish research; to stimulate and encourage in its students those qualities of scholarship, leadership, and character that mark the true academic and professional engineer; to serve the industrial community of Southern California in providing for the continuing education of engineering and scientific personnel; and to provide professional engineering leadership in solving community, regional, national, and global problems.

University of Southern Colorado

2200 Bonforte Boulevard   **Phone: (1-877) USC-WOLF (option #3)**
Pueblo, CO 81001-4901   **(719) 549-2316**
                                                          Fax: (719) 549-2438

Division(s): Continuing Education
Web Site(s): http://coned.uscolo.edu
E-mail: coned@uscolo.edu

Undergraduate Degree Programs:
Bachelor of Science in:
    Social Science
    Sociology
    Sociology/Criminology

Certificate Programs: Legal Investigation, Victim Advocacy, Legal Secretary, Paralegal.

Class Titles: Art, Biology, Business Administration, Chemistry, Economics, Education, English, Geography, Geology, History, Management, Marketing, Nursing, Political Science, Psychology, Social Science, Sociology, Social Work, Women's Studies.

Teaching Methods: *Computers:* Internet, e-mail. *TV:* videotape, telecourse broadcasting. *Other:* audiotapes, fax, correspondence, independent study.

Credits Granted for: experiential learning, CLEP, DANTES, military, transfer credit.

Admission Requirements: *Undergraduate:* ACT, high school transcripts if fewer than 30 semester college credits.

On-Campus Requirements: must complete 30 semester credits through independent study or telecourses.

Tuition and Fees: *Undergraduate:* $85/credit. *Application Fee:* $135. *Other Costs:* $75 videotapes (if course requires). *Credit by:* semester.

Financial Aid: Company- and military-sponsored assistance, DANTES.

Accreditation: North Central Association of Colleges and Schools.

Description: The University of Southern Colorado has served the changing needs of students for more than 60 years. USC's 275-acre campus crowns the north end of a historically and culturally rich city of 100,000 in the colorful Pikes Peak region. USC's 4,000 students from the state, nation, and several foreign countries represent a diversity of age groups and backgrounds. The institution's mission includes emphasizing career-oriented, technological, and applied programs while maintaining strong liberal arts programs; engaging in basic and applied research for the benefit of society; and functioning as the major educational resource for cultural, industrial, and economic growth in southeastern Colorado.

University of Southern Indiana

8600 University Boulevard   **Phone: (800) 813-4238**
Evansville, IN 47712   **Fax: (812) 465-7131**

Division(s): Distance Education
Web Site(s): http://www.usi.edu/distance
E-mail: distance@usi.edu

Undergraduate Degree Programs:
Associate of Science in Communications
Bachelor of Science in Nursing (completion degree)
Bachelor of Science in Health Services (completion degree)

Graduate Degree Programs:
Master of Science and Nursing
Master of Health Administration

Class Titles: Business, Advertising, Public Relations, Radio/TV, Theater, Mass Media, Mass Communications Law, Journalism, Education, English, Mythology, Humanities, Nursing, Political Science, Psychology, Art, Biology, Dental Assisting, Dental Hygiene, Gerontology, Health Professions, Liberal Arts, Nutrition, Organizational Communication, Radiologic Technology, Reading Power, Social Work.

Teaching Methods: *Computers:* Internet, real-time chat, electronic classroom, e-mail, CD-ROM, *TV:* videotape, cable program, satellite broadcasting, *Other:* videoconferencing.

Credits Granted for: examination (CLEP, ACT-PEP, DANTES, GRE).

Admission Requirements: *Undergraduate:* SAT or ACT (no specific score required), application, official high school and college (if any) transcripts. *Graduate:* graduation with a bachelor's degree (minimum cumulative GPA 2.5) from a college or university accredited by the North Central Association of Colleges and Schools or a comparable association; a minimum GPA of 3.0 in all courses taken at the graduate level of all schools attended; an undergraduate record that provides adequate preparation to begin graduate study; and satisfactory performance on any exams required by the graduate program. *Certificate:* must be a health professional.

On-Campus Requirements: None.

Tuition and Fees: *Undergraduate:* $102.75/credit state resident, $251.50/credit nonresident. *Graduate:* $151.25/credit state resident, $303.50/credit nonresident. *Application Fee:* $25. *Graduation Fee:* 7 or more credit hours: $62/semester. Fewer than 7 credit hours: $31/semester. *Other Costs:* $30/course or Distance Education fee. *Credit by:* semester.

Financial Aid: Federal Stafford Loan, Federal Perkins Loan, Federal PLUS Loan, Federal Pell Grant, Federal Work-Study, VA, Indiana resident programs. Students can contact the Student Financial Assistance office at (812) 464-1767 for details.

Accreditation: North Central Association of Colleges and Schools.

Description: The University of Southern Indiana (1965) is a general, multipurpose, public-supported, coeducational institution of higher education offering programs of instruction, research, and service. The 70 undergraduate programs offered through the university's 5 schools are grounded in a liberal arts and science foundation. Programs are available in Business, Education and Human Services, Liberal Arts, Nursing and Health Professions, and Science and Engineering Technology. Master's degrees are conferred in Business Administration, Industrial Management, Liberal Studies, Education, Accountancy, Nursing, Social Work, and Health Administration. Noncredit courses, business training programs, certificate programs, continuing education, and programs for K-12 teachers and students are available. Through all its programs, the university seeks to serve the academic, cultural, and career needs of the student body. As a public institution, it counsels and assists business, industry, and social, educational, governmental, and health agencies. As a university, it seeks to support education, social and economic growth, and civic and cultural awareness in southwestern Indiana, devoting itself primarily to preparing students to live wisely. USI's Learning Network enables Indiana students to enroll in distance courses that fit their time or travel needs. Courses may be delivered by videotape, CD-ROM, electronic mail, TV, or other media. Some courses meet at learning centers in Evansville or locations throughout Indiana.

University of St. Francis

500 Wilcox Street	Phone: (815) 740-3400
Joliet, IL 60435	(800) 735-7500
	Fax: (815) 740-5032

Division(s): College of Health Arts, Graduate and Professional Studies
Web Site(s): http://www.stfrancis.edu
E-mail: admissions@stfrancis.edu

Undergraduate Degree Programs:
Bachelor of Science in:
    Health Arts (degree completion program for registered nurses, radiologic technologists, respiratory therapists and dental hygienists)

Professional Arts (degree completion program)
Nursing Fast Track (for A.D.N. or diploma graduates)

Graduate Degree Programs:
M.B.A.
Master of Science in:
    Health Services Administration
    Management
    Continuing Education and Training Management
    Continuing Education and Training Technology

Teaching Methods: *Computers:* Internet, electronic classroom, e-mail real-time chat, CD-ROM, newsgroup, LISTSERV., Web CT. *Other:* independent study, faculty-directed study, correspondence.

Credits Granted for: experiential learning, portfolio assessment, extrainstitutional learning, examination (CLEP, ACT-PEP, DANTES, GRE).

Admission Requirements: *Undergraduate:* Transfer—cumulative grade point average of 2.0 from all previous college course work; eligibility for continued enrollment at last postsecondary institution attended; graduation from a recognized high school or satisfactory completion of the GED; demonstration of college-ready proficiency in mathematics and English. Health Arts—professional registration in the United States; graduation from a diploma or associate degree program in nursing or radiologic technology or an associate degree program in dental hygiene, respiratory therapy, or another qualified health profession. *Graduate:* bachelor's degree with a minimum 2.75 grade point average on a 4.0 scale from a regionally accredited college or university; acceptance by the Graduate Admissions Committee based on all official postsecondary transcripts and 2 letters of recommendation; computer competencies; specific program admissions requirements.

On-Campus Requirements: None.

Tuition and Fees: *Undergraduate:* full-time tuition and fees (12–18 hours)—$14,990; part-time (1–11 hours)/credit hour—$440. Health Arts/credit hour—$260. BSN Fast Track/credit hour—$315. *Graduate:* Health Services Administration, Management, Continuing Education and Training Management, Continuing Education and Training Technology—$340. MBA—$440. *Application Fee:* $25. *Graduation Fee:* $50. *Other Costs:* Online course fee—$70–150. Portfolio assessment—various. *Credit by:* semester.

Financial Aid: Federal Stafford Loan, Federal Perkins Loan, Federal PLUS Loan, Federal Pell Grant, Federal Work-Study, VA, Illinois resident programs.

Accreditation: North Central Association of Colleges and Schools.

Description: A national leader in providing Distance Learning opportunities, the University of St. Francis (1920) offers more than 60 areas of undergraduate study in arts and sciences, nursing, business, education, and computer science as well as 9 graduate programs in business, education, and health care. USF began its Distance Learning programming in 1972 and now serves students at sites and through online learning nationwide. USF has 1,300 students at its main campus in Joliet, Ill. and serves some 3,000 students at off-campus sites or online. A Catholic, Franciscan institution, the university is committed to academic excellence built upon strong liberal arts and academic foundations.

University of South Dakota

414 East Clark Street   Phone: (800) 233-7937
Vermillion, SD 57069   (605) 677-6926
     Fax: (605) 677-6118

Division(s): Continuing Education Center
Web Site(s): http://usd.edu/swes
E-mail: rjpeters@usd.edu

Undergraduate Degree Programs:
Associate of Arts in General Studies

Graduate Degree Programs:
Master of Arts in Adult and Continuing Education for LERN members
Master of Science in Technology for Education and Training

Postgraduate Degree Programs:
The Education Specialist Degree (EdS) in Technology for Education and Training

Class Titles: Accounting Principles; Alcohol and Drug Abuse Studies; Adult and Higher Education; Art; Human Biology; Classical Mythology; Criminal Justice; Educational Administration; English; Earth Science with Lab; Health; History; Mass Communication; Mathematics; Nursing; Political Science; Sociology; Speech Communication; Statistics; Theatre; Technology for Education and Training.

Teaching Methods: *Computers:* Internet, real-time chat, electronic classroom, e-mail, CD-ROM, newsgroup, LISTSERV. *TV:* videotape, cable program, satellite broadcasting, PBS. *Other:* videoconferencing, audioconferencing, audiotapes, fax, correspondence, independent study, learning contracts.

Credits Granted for: experiential learning, portfolio assessment, extrainstitutional learning (PONSI, Military), examination (CLEP, ACT-PEP, DANTES, GRE, LSAT, MCAT, MPRE).

Admission Requirements: *Undergraduate:* degree-seeking students complete an application ($20 fee) or non-degree-seeking students complete the special student application. Degree-seeking students, under 21 years or age, must satisfy general admission requirements of the university (http://usd.edu/admissions). Applicants who are 21 years of age or older and have graduated from high school or have successfully completed the GED will be admitted in good standing. *Graduate:* degree-seeking students are required to complete an official application (nonrefundable $35 fee), 3 letters of recommendation, any applicable standardized test score reports, and 2 official transcripts of all previous academic work (http://usd.edu/admissions). Non-degree-seeking students must have a bachelor's degree from a regionally accredited university or college and complete a Special Student Graduate Application. *Postgraduate:* students complete the application requirements of the graduate school and the college or school offering the program (http://usd.edu/admissions).

On-Campus Requirements: None, if the degree has been approved for off-campus or Distance Delivery.

Tuition and Fees: *Undergraduate:* $142.25/credit. *Graduate:* $181.60/credit. *Postgraduate:* $181.60/credit. *Application Fees:* $20 undergraduate; $35 graduate. *Other Costs:* $5 transcript fee; $13 thesis binding per copy. *Credit by:* semester.

Financial Aid: Federal Stafford Loan, Federal Perkins Loan, Federal PLUS Loan, Federal Pell Grant, Federal Work-Study, VA, state programs for residents of South Dakota (http://usd.edu/admissions).

Accreditation: Higher Learning Commission and North Central Association.

Description: The University of South Dakota (1862), the state's comprehensive, flagship university is committed to excellence in education, research, and service. Individual schools and departments have earned additional accreditation from appropriate professional organizations. The university has been recognized by *U.S. News and World Report* for its academic excellence and affordable cost. In 1997 USD was ranked in the top 100 list of the most wired colleges and universities in America by Yahoo! Internet Life. The Center for Continuing Education has been delivering education to Distance Learners since 1918 with the offering of Correspondence Study. In 1967 the Center was approved as Statewide Educational Services to "bring the academic resources of the university to the citizens of South Dakota, the region, and beyond." Learning is available by Correspondence Study, Internet, Telecourses, the South Dakota Distance Learning Network, and face-to-face at 5 locations.

University of Southern Mississippi

2901 Hardy Street
Hattiesburg, MS 39401

Phone: (601) 266-4186
Fax: (601) 266-5839

Division(s): Department of Continuing Education and Distance Learning
Web Site(s): http://www.cice.usm.edu/ce/
E-mail: distance.learning@usm.edu

Undergraduate Degree Programs: Contact school.

Graduate Degree Programs: Contact school.

Postgraduate Degree Programs: Contact school.

Certificate Programs: Geographic Information.

Class Titles: 21st Century Cartography, Administration Supervision of Programs for Exceptional Children, Advanced Methods in Behavioral Management for Individuals with Disabilities, Advanced Spatial Analysis, Anatomy and Physiology of the Hearing Mechanisms, Applications Program Development, Applied Calculus for the Business and Social Sciences, Biostatistics, Business Operating Systems, Calculus with Analytic Geometry, College Algebra, Composition, Computer Application in Geography, Concepts of Physical Fitness, Construction Organization, Construction Project Management, Criminology, Data Communications, Developing Student Centered Curriculum, Education and Psychology of Exceptional Children, Educational Research, Electric Circuits, Emerging Digital Technology, Epidemiology, Ethics, Evolution, Experimental Food, Families of the Developmentally Disabled, Fiction Writing, Finite, Mathematics and Introduction to Calculus, Foundations of Instructional Technology, Geographic Information System, Geography of the United States and Canada, Governing Agencies for Competitive Athletics, History of Biology, Human Embryology, Instruction and Programming for Individuals with Emotional and Behavioral Disorders, Instructional Leadership, International Management, Intervention and Transitional Policies for Secondary Students with Mild/Moderate Disabilities, Anthropology, Business Computer Concepts, Business Database, Business Spreadsheets, Business System Topics, Criminal Justice, Database, Economics, Financial Accounting, Geography, Information Systems, Logic, Philosophy, Phonetics, Professional Studies, Religion, Sociology, Sport Administration, Business Computer Concepts, Literature of the South, Living in the Environment, Management for Organizations, Managing Geographic Information, Medical Terminology, Multimedia Authoring for Performance Improvement Software, Nursing Health Assessment, Nursing Research, Nutrition, Organic Polymer Chemistry, Pathophysiology/Pharmacology, Pharmacotherapeutics in Health Care, Planning and Public Policy Formation, Poetry Writing, Policy and Governance in Sports, Marketing, Real Estate Law, Real Estate Principles, Research Techniques, Criminal Justice, Service Systems Planning and Control, Social and Professional Development, Specialized Studies in Developmental Disabilities, The Enjoyment of Music, The Family, The Legal Environment of Business, The Life of Jesus, The Psychology and Education of Individuals with Emotional and Behavioral Disorders, Virology, Writing, Zoogeography.

Teaching Methods: *Computers:* Internet, real-time chat, electronic classroom, e-mail, LISTSERV. *Other:* videoconferencing, telephone, correspondence, independent study.

Credits Granted for: examination (CLEP, DANTES), military education.

Admission Requirements: *Undergraduate:* unconditional freshman admission to the University of Southern Mississippi is based on completion of a required core of high school course work, grade point average (based on academic core), class rank, and ACT or SAT scores. Students not meeting unconditional standards may be considered for admission to the summer developmental program through an interview and screening process. Students planning to enter the University of Southern Mississippi as nontraditional students must be at least 21 years of age, hold a high school diploma or its equivalent, and meet acceptable grade point average requirements on transfer work. The University of Southern Mississippi does not discriminate on grounds of age, sex, race, color, religion, or national origin. These provisions also apply to disabled individuals pursuant to current federal and state regulations subject to reasonable standards of admission and employment. All inquiries concerning admission requirements should be directed to the Office of Admissions at (601) 266-5000. Undergraduate admission policies are available at http://www.registrar.usm.edu/catalogs2001/undergraduate/. Non-degree-seeking, undergraduate, Distance Learning students located off-campus do not have to be formally admitted to the university to enroll in Distance Learning courses. However, they must submit an application, which is available at http://www-dept.usm.edu/~cice/online/application.html. *Graduate:* admission for graduate studies at the University of Southern Mississippi results from evaluations of qualitative and quantitative information. All applicants must provide a completed application form, records of previous academic achievements (official transcripts), letters of recommendation, and scores from appropriate examinations. Departments and colleges may require additional criteria. All inquiries concerning graduate admission requirements should be directed to the Graduate School at (601) 266-4369. Graduate admission policies are available at http://www.registrar.usm.edu/catalogs2001/graduate/. Non-degree-seeking, graduate students may be admitted for one semester with proof of an undergraduate degree. *Postgraduate:* see graduate admission requirements. *Certificate:* admission requirements for certificate programs at the University of Southern Mississippi are unique to each program. Inquiries should be directed to the program's academic department.

Tuition and Fees: *Undergraduate:* $143/semester hour. *Graduate:* $190/semester hour; $25 out-of-state graduate application fee. *Other Costs:* $25 for international admissions. *Credit by:* semester.

Financial Aid: Federal Stafford Loan, Federal Perkins Loan, Chester P. Freeman Loan Fund, Federal Pell Grant, Federal Supplemental Educational Opportunity Grants, Federal Work-Study Program, Student Employment, Military Scholarships and Programs, VA, state programs for residents of Mississippi, university scholarships.

Accreditation: Southern Association of Colleges and Schools.

Description: The University of Southern Mississippi (USM) (1910) was established as a teachers' college and has grown to be a comprehensive public university recognized for an array of excellent programs that aim for national distinction. Its programs are fully accredited by more than 30 national accrediting agencies. The university offers 90 bachelor's degree programs, 61 master's degree programs, two specialist's degree programs, and 19 doctoral degree programs. The university seeks to educate students who will be well trained in their chosen profession, whose critical thinking skills and respect for learning will foster lifelong learning, and who recognize their obligation to contribute to society. Distance Learning has been an integral part of this process since 1913 when Independent Study through correspondence was introduced. Since then, Distance Learning at USM has grown to include interactive video, telephone conferencing, and web-based learning.

The University of Tennessee, Knoxville

1534 White Avenue	**Phone: (800) 670-8657**
Knoxville, TN 37996-1525	**(423) 974-5134**
	Fax: (865) 974-4684

Division(s): Distance Education and Independent Study
Web Site(s): http://www.anywhere.tennessee.edu
E-mail: disteducation@utk.edu

Graduate Degree Programs:
Master of Science in:
    Information Sciences
    Engineering Management
    Nuclear Engineering
Physician's Executive MBA

Certificate Programs:
Graduate Certificates in Applied Statistics, Nuclear Criticality Safety.

Class Titles: *Undergraduate correspondence:* Accounting, Agricultural Economics, Anthropology, Business Man-

agement, Chemistry, Child/Family Studies, Criminal Justice, Curriculum/Instruction, Economics, Education, English, French, Geography, German, Health, History, Library Service, Math, Nutrition, Philosophy, Political Science, Psychology, Religious Studies, Safety, Sociology, Spanish. *Graduate videotape:* Civil Engineering, Environmental Engineering, Biosystems Engineering, Rehabilitation and Deafness. *Graduate via Internet:* Astronomy, Engineering Science, Forestry, Wildlife and Fisheries.

Teaching Methods: *Computers:* e-mail, Internet, real-time chat, voice-over-IP, CD-ROM, LISTSERV. *TV:* videotape, *Other:* correspondence, audiotapes, fax, independent study, individual study.

Admission Requirements: *Undergraduate:* GPA. *Graduate:* GRE (by program). *Certificate:* same as graduate for graduate certificates.

On-Campus Requirements: Some programs may require brief residential periods.

Tuition and Fees: *Undergraduate:* $118/credit (correspondence); $135/credit in-state; $449/credit out-of-state. *Graduate:* $208/credit in-state; $627/credit out-of-state. *Application Fee:* $25 (undergraduate); $35 (graduate). *Graduation Fee:* $30 (graduate). *Other Costs:* possible multimedia materials (audio/videotapes, disks, CD-ROMS); $100 videotape access fee for videotape courses. *Credit by:* semester.

Financial Aid: VA, Federal Stafford Loan, Federal Perkins Loan, Federal PLUS Loan, Federal Pell Grant, SLM Financial Coroporation Loans (Sallie Mae).

Accreditation: Southern Association of Colleges and Schools.

Description: Founded in 1794, the University of Tennessee is the official land-grant institution for the state. UT Knoxville is the state's oldest, largest, and most comprehensive institution, offering 300 degree programs to its 25,000 students. The university entered distance education in 1923 with correspondence courses, and has offered technology-delivered courses (TV, videotape, Internet).

University of Tennessee Space Institute

411 B.H. Goethert Parkway	**Phone: (931) 393-7293 (EM)/**
Tullahoma, TN 37388	**(931) 393-7408 (AS)**
	Fax: (931) 393-7201 (EM)/
	(931) 393-7409 (AS)

Division(s): Engineering Management/Aviation Systems
Web Site(s): http://www.utsi.edu/em (EM)
http://www.utsi.edu/AvSys (AS)
E-mail: psmith@utsi.edu (EM)/bharbin@utsi.edu (AS)

Graduate Degree Programs:
Industrial Engineering
Engineering Management
Aviation Systems

Teaching Methods: *Computers:* Internet (web assisted), electronic classroom, e-mail. *TV:* videotape. *Other:* videoconferencing, audioconferencing, audiographics, fax.

Credits Granted for: graduate courses from other universities maximum of 9 semester hours (approved by department). The University of Tennessee does not accept transfer credit from foreign institutions. Proficiency exams may be taken for up to 1/3 of the course work. Aviation Systems also accepts up to 17 hours of transfer credit for graduates of either the U.S. Air Force Test Pilot School or the U.S. Naval Test Pilot School.

Admission Requirements: *Graduate:* EM: Students must graduate from an ABET accredited undergraduate engineering curriculum, GRE, 2 years engineering experience or fully employed in an engineering position at the time of application, undergraduate engineering economy, and undergraduate statistics for engineers. AS: Students must have a B.S. degree from an accredited college or university; a minimum cumulative GPA of 2.7 out of a possible 4.0; or a 3.0 during the senior year of undergraduated study. Time limit for M.S. is 6 years.

On-Campus Requirements: Students are required to present a capstone project, thesis or non-thesis project on campus.

Tuition and Fees: *Undergraduate: Graduate:* $192 per credit hour (in state), $545 per credit hour (out of state). *Application Fees:* $35.00. *Graduation Fee:* $30. *Other Costs:* $100.00 for off campus access fee. *Credit by:* semester.

Financial Aid: VA.

Accreditation: Southern Association of Schools and Colleges.

Description: The University of Tennessee Space Institute (UTSI) is a part of the graduate school of the University of Tennessee, Knoxville. It is located in Tullahoma, adjacent to the USAF Arnold Engineering and Development Center. Through Distance Learning, UTSI has built a strong reputation for its flexibility toward students who have commitments that prevent them from being in the classroom. Classes are videotaped live and distributed to off-campus sites allowing students instant access to the exact same lectures, materials, exams, and such, as students attending class on campus. The UT Engineering Management Program was developed in 1983. The program has been designed to develop the knowledge, skills, and attitudes needed by engineers to be successful in middle and upper management positions in technical organizations. This distance learning program is designed to be flexible with the working engineer. Taping live class sessions enables students to make up sessions missed because of business/military obligations. The UTSI Aviation Systems Program was developed in 1971 for students who are interested in advancement in aviation research and testing in a wide variety of aviation disciplines. Current emphasis includes flight testing, aircraft design, safety, and air traffic control. Distance learning began in 1987 to accommodate the full-time employee who wanted to pursue an advanced degree.

University of Texas, Austin

3001 Lake Austin Boulevard	Phone: (512) 232-5000
Austin, TX 78703	(800) 252-4723
	Fax: (512) 475-7933

Division(s): Continuing and Extended Education, Distance Education Center.
Web Site(s): http://www.utexas.edu/cee/dec
E-mail: dec@utexas.edu

Certificate Programs: Purchasing Management

Class Titles: The DEC college curriculum covers 30 fields of study in upper and lower division courses including substantial writing component courses. All courses are aligned with on-campus curriculum and are developed and taught by instructors who are approved by UT Austin department chairs. Specific content areas include anthropology, art history, business, curriculum and instruction, economics, educational psychology, English, government, history, kinesiology and health education, philosophy, psychology, radio/television/film production, social work, sociology, visual arts studies, and women's studies. Science and language courses include astronomy, geography, mathematics, nursing, nutrition, physics, zoology, Czech, French, German, Latin, and Spanish.

Teaching Methods: *Computers:* Internet, electronic classroom, real-time chat, e-mail, CD-ROM, LISTSERV, newsgroup, bulletin boards, diskette. *TV:* videotape. *Other:* audioconferencing, videoconferencing, audiotapes, fax, correspondence, independent study, individual study, telephony, learning contracts.

Admission Requirements: *Undergraduate:* enrollment is open to all persons. UT admission is not required. Students taking a DEC course should contact their university advisor to confirm that credit acquired through the DEC will transfer as the appropriate course. Earned college credit is recorded on an UT Austin transcript. Nonexempt, degree-seeking students entering Texas public colleges and universities are required by law to take the Texas Academic Skills Program test.

On-Campus Requirements: None.

Tuition and Fees: Tuition fees for printed courses vary, depending on the course. However, in most cases, tuition for a paper college course is $83/credit hour. There is an additional nonrefundable enrollment fee of $20. Other fees may be applicable if the course includes additional resources, such as Internet components, faxed lesson options, tapes, proctoring, reexamination, and supplemental study materials. Call the Student Services office for prices of online courses. *Credit by:* semester.

Financial Aid: For college students completing courses in traditional semester time frames, financial aid is available. Financial aid also is administered through governmental agencies to military personnel, veterans, and persons with specific, identified disabilities. Federal financial programs usually require that students be enrolled in programs leading to a degree, a certificate, or some other educational credential in order to be considered for assistance.

Accreditation: Southern Association of Colleges and Schools; high school courses approved by the Texas Education Agency.

Description: The University of Texas at Austin was founded in 1883 on 40 acres near the state capitol. As the academic flagship of the University of Texas System, UT Austin enrolls more than 49,000 students annually. It is home to students from every county in Texas, all 50 states, and about 120 foreign countries. It has the distinction of awarding more doctorate degrees than any other university in the nation. For 90 years, Continuing and Extended Education has been providing UT Austin resources to the citizens of Texas. In 1909 the first offerings through the Distance Education Center (DEC) were college courses, but today the offerings also include middle and high school courses as well as programs for professional and personal development. In the year 2000 the DEC served more than 24,000 students from across the nation and the world.

University of Toledo

SeaGate Campus
401 Jefferson Avenue   Phone: (419) 321-5130
Toledo, OH 43604-1005   Fax: (419) 321-5147

Division(s): Distance Learning
Web Site(s): http://www.dl.utoledo.edu/
E-mail: Janet.Green@utoledo.edu

Undergraduate Degree Programs:
Associate Degree in Business Management Technology
Adult Liberal Studies Program (Bachelor)
Bachelor of Science in Engineering

Graduate Degree Programs:
Master of Liberal Studies
Master of Science in Engineering

Certificate Programs: *Noncredit:* The Nutrition Program, Fundamentals of Safety On-Line Course, and Maintenance Management Certificate. *Credit:* Business Management Technology.

Class Titles: a wide variety of courses and expanding, including English, Economics, History, Philosophy, Psychology, Sociology, Political Science, Medical Terminology, Africana Studies Program, Chemistry, Nutrition, Physics, Legal Assisting Program, Leadership Skills, Special Education, Criminal Law Practice, Information Systems, Accounting, Management, Finance, Mathematics, and Statistics.

Teaching Methods: *Computers:* Internet, real-time chat, electronic classroom, e-mail, CD-ROM, LISTSERV. *TV:* videotape, cable program, PBS. *Other:* videoconferencing, fax.

Credits Granted for: portfolio assessment, corporate or professional association seminars/workshops, examination (CLEP, ACT-PEP, DANTES, GRE).

Admission Requirements: *Undergraduate, Graduate, and Doctoral:* contact Janet Green at (419) 321-5130. *Noncredit Certificate:* contact Continuing Education, (419) 321-5139.

On-Campus Requirements: None.

Tuition and Fees: *Undergraduate:* $159.48/credit in-state. *Graduate:* $246.12/credit in-state. *Doctoral:* $246.12/credit in-state—Law College. *Credit by:* semester.

Financial Aid: Federal Stafford Loan, Federal Perkins Loan, Federal PLUS Loan, Federal Pell Grant, Federal Work-Study, VA, Ohio resident programs.

Accreditation: North Central Association of Colleges and Schools.

Description: The University of Toledo's (1872) Division of Distance Learning's mission is to promote learning without time or space barriers to encourage outreach and lifelong-learning. UT's Division of Distance Learning facilitates innovative delivery of high-quality, university instruction to meet the educational needs of students, whatever their location. Distance Learning offers a variety of state-of-the-art technologies to deliver credit and noncredit education taught by skilled, enthusiastic faculty.

University of Vermont

460 South Prospect Street   Phone: (800) 639-3210
Burlington, VT 05401-3534   Fax: (802) 656-1347

Division(s): Continuing Education, Distance Learning Network
Web Site(s): http://learn.uvm.edu
E-mail: learn@ced.uvm.edu

Undergraduate Degree Programs:
RN-BS-MS in Nursing

Graduate Degree Programs:
Master of Social Work
Master of Educational Leadership
Master of Science Nursing Completer Program
Master of Public Administration

Certificate Programs: Gerontology, School Library Media Studies.

Class Titles: Online courses through CyberSummer are offered at both the undergraduate and graduate levels in: Anthropology, Business Administration, Communications Sciences, Computer Science, Economics, Education, English, History, Mathematics, Physics, Sociology, Speech, Statistics.

Teaching Methods: *Computers:* Internet, CD-ROM, electronic classroom, real-time chat, e-mail, LISTSERV. *TV:* videotape, satellite broadcasting, cable program, PBS. *Other:* videoconferencing.

Credits Granted for: examination (CLEP).

Admission Requirements: *Undergraduate:* high school graduation or GED, official high school transcripts, SAT I/ACT. The following are also considered: overall academic performance, class rank, standardized test scores, and essays. Contact department for high school classes required and program specifics. *Graduate:* accredited bachelor's degree and GRE scores. Completion limits: 3 years for full-time, 5 years for part-time. Accelerated programs available for some areas. Contact department for program specifics.

On-Campus Requirements: None.

Tuition and Fees: *Undergraduate:* $281/credit for non-degree students taking Distance Learning courses. *Graduate:* $281/credit for Distance Learning courses. *Postgraduate:* $281/credit for Distance Learning courses. *Credit by:* semester hour.

Financial Aid: State grants are need-based grants available through your State Department of Education. Vermont residents should contact the Vermont Student Assistance Corp.

Accreditation: New England Association of Schools and Colleges.

Description: The University of Vermont (1791) was chartered the same year Vermont became the 14th state in the union and has a long and well-established reputation for excellence. The campus is located in the state's largest city, Burlington. The university blends the academic heritage of private institution with its service mission in the land grant tradition. To extend its outreach obligations, the university established its Distance Learning Network within the Division of Continuing Education in 1995. The network extends individual courses and entire academic programs and support services to students nationally through the use of various interactive media.

In addition, Advanced Placement courses for high school students and extensive professional development programs for health care professionals, public sector managers, and higher education administrators and leaders are offered through the Network.

University of Victoria

PO Box 3030 STN CSC	Phone: (250) 721-8454
Victoria, BC Canada V8W 3N6	Fax: (250) 721-8774

Division(s): Distance Education Services, Division of Continuing Studies
Web Site(s): http://www.distance.uvic.ca
E-mail: distance@uvcs.uvic.ca

Undergraduate Degree Programs:
Bachelor of Arts in Child and Youth Care
Bachelor of Science in Nursing
Bachelor of Social Work
Diploma Program in:
    Cultural Conservation
    Public Sector Management
    Local Government Management
    Restoration of Natural Systems

Certificate Programs: Certificate in Computer-Based Information Systems, Business Administration, Adult and Continuing Education, Environmental and Occupational Health, Restoration of Natural Systems.

Class Titles: Contact school or check web site for details.

Teaching Methods: *Computers:* Internet, real-time chat, e-mail, CD-ROM, newsgroup, LISTSERV. *TV:* videotape. *Other:* audioconferencing, audiotapes, correspondence, independent study.

Admission Requirements: *Undergraduate:* details presented by program area: http://www.distance.uvic.ca/degree.htm and http://www.distance.uvic.ca/diploma.htm. *Certificate:* details presented by program area: http://www.distance.uvic.ca/certs.htm.

On-Campus Requirements: None.

Tuition and Fees: *Undergraduate:* see individual program areas for information. *Credit by:* see individual program areas for information.

Accreditation: Association of Universities and Colleges of Canada.

Description: The University of Victoria (1963), one of Canada's leading universities, has earned a reputation for innovation and engagement in the critical issues of our times. UVic serves more than 17,500 students and is widely recognized for its interdisciplinary research initiatives, the nontraditional approach of its professional schools, its extensive cooperative education programs, its pioneering work in Distance Education, and its support for innovative teaching. The University of Victoria has been a leader in Distance Learning in Canada for more than 25 years and has specialized in the development and delivery of programs of professional education. Through the Division of Continuing Studies and the Faculty of Human and Social Development, the university has pioneered a number of different approaches to the delivery of these programs using telecommunications technologies to encourage student-to-student, and student-to-instructor interactions.

University of Virginia

104 Midmont Lane	Phone: (434) 982-5254
Charlottesville, VA 22903	Fax: (434) 982-5270

Division(s): School of Continuing and Professional Studies
Web Site(s): http://uvace.virginia.edu
E-mail: jpayne@virginia.edu

Graduate Degree Programs:
Master of Science in Engineering

Certificate Programs: Procurement and Contracts Management, Web Content Development, Information Technology, E-Commerce Technology Leadership.

Class Titles: For a complete listing of undergraduate and graduate level courses for certificate programs, please visit web sites. sds3e@virginia.edu or tekla@virginia.edu or jsterling@virginia.edu

Teaching Methods: *Other:* videoconferencing.

Admission Requirements: *Graduate:* contact Televised Graduate Engineering Program Office, (804) 924-4051 [or call collect: (804) 924-4075].

On-Campus Requirements: courses are synchronously delivered and require attendance at remote sites.

Tuition and Fees: *Graduate:* (for all sites except Northern Virginia) $267/credit ($801/course) in-state, $516/credit ($1548/course) out-of-state; (for Northern Virginia Center) $272/credit ($816/course) in-state, $524/credit ($1572/course) out-of-state. Registrants at the Northern Virginia Center in Falls Church also pay an additional "Facilities Fee" of $10/credit. NOTE: Students must register for classes before the third class session. There are no refunds after tuition is paid. Students may drop without academic penalty at any time up to the final exam by submitting written notice explaining reasons for request. *Credit by:* semester.

Accreditation: Southern Association of Colleges and Schools, member of Association of American Universities.

Description: The leading universities in the Commonwealth of Virginia have combined to make master's degrees in several engineering disciplines easily available to qualified engineers. At the center of the system is the graduate engineering program of the University of Virginia (1819). This nationally ranked university televises regular master's courses via Net. Work.Virginia from a special classroom on campus to sites in Virginia as well as out-of-state. The classes are received live, and students are able to participate fully in all classroom discussions. Classes are scheduled in late afternoon and early evening hours. This program is directed by Dr. George L. Cahen, Jr. The administrator of the program is Rita F. Kostoff. The University of Virginia and Virginia Polytechnic Institute and State University, in cooperation with Virginia Commonwealth University, Old Dominion University, and George Mason University, deliver televised graduate engineering courses to areas in the Commonwealth of Virginia, as well as some out-of-state sites. Beginning in fall 1998, lectures will be delivered via an asynchronous transfer mode on Net.Work.Virginia within the state and via videoconferencing equipment to out-of-state sites. This means that classes are 2-way video and 2-way audio. It should be noted that on-grounds students at the University of Virginia also take these courses in the studio classroom as they are delivered to the off-site campuses. The primary intent is to provide engineers and other qualified individuals with strong backgrounds in the sciences an opportunity to pursue a program in graduate studies leading to a master's degree in engineering. However, courses may also be taken on a nondegree, continuing education basis. This effort is in response to one of the State Council of Higher Education's objectives to expand technical education opportunities for Virginians.

University of Washington

5001-25th NE	Phone: (206) 543-2320
Seattle, WA 98105	(800) 543-2320 x4
	Fax: (206) 685-9359

Division(s): UW Educational Outreach Program Support Services
Web Site(s): http://www.outreach.washington.edu
E-mail: distance@u.washington.edu

Undergraduate Degree Programs:
90 distance learning credits may count toward undergraduate degrees.

Certificate Programs: *Credit:* Graduate Public Health Practice; Gerontology; School Library Media Specialist; Teaching, Learning and Technology; Facility Management; Computing & Software Systems (seven certificates that can lead to a B.S.); Construction Management; Creative Writing; Curriculum Integration in Action; Brain Research in Education: *Noncredit:* C Programming; C++ Programming; Java

2 Enterprise Programming; Fiction Writing, Nonfiction Writing; Project Management; Data Resource Management, Internet Programming; Distance Learning Design and Development; E-Commerce Management; Embedded and Real-Time Systems Programming, Object-Oriented Analysis and Design Using UML; Small Business Webmaster; Web Technology Essentials.

Class Titles: 110 undergraduate courses in Humanities, Social Sciences, Physical Sciences, Business.

Teaching Methods: *Computers:* Internet, real-time chat, electronic classroom, e-mail, CD-ROM, newsgroup, LISTSERV. *TV:* videotape, cable program. *Other:* radio broadcast, videoconferencing, audiographics audiotapes, fax, print, correspondence, independent study, individual study, learning contracts.

Admission Requirements: *Undergraduate:* math/accounting courses may have some. *Certificate:* varies.

On-Campus Requirements: None for most course work.

Tuition and Fees: *Undergraduate:* $128/credit. *Graduate:* $282/credit. *Application Fee:* $45 certificate programs. *Credit by:* quarter.

Financial Aid: Federal Stafford Loan, Federal Perkins Loan, Federal PLUS Loan, Federal Pell Grant, Federal Work-Study, VA state programs for residents of Washington.

Accreditation: Northwest Association of Schools and Colleges.

Description: Established in 1912, University of Washington Distance Learning offers a broad range of courses and educational programs that extend the university's resources worldwide. Courses are delivered by print, video, or computer and typically consist of assigned texts, study guides, assignments, and exams. Formal university admission is not required for Distance Learning enrollment. Up to 90 Distance Learning credits may apply to a bachelor's degree, and grades are recorded on official University of Washington transcripts.

University of Waterloo

200 University Avenue West	**Phone: (519) 888-4050**
Waterloo, ON, Canada N2L 3G1	**Fax: (519) 746-6393**

Division(s): Distance and Continuing Education Office
Web Site(s): http://dce.uwaterloo.ca/
E-mail: distance@uwaterloo.ca

Undergraduate Degree Programs:
Bachelor of Arts
Bachelor of Science
Bachelor of Environmental Studies

Graduate Degree Programs:
Master of Applied Science, Management of Technology Program. Available by distance education is the Faculty of Engineering's graduate Management of Technology degree program, designed to help engineers and scientists who deal with technology management in their jobs. Information regarding this master's level degree is available at http://motdinfo.uwaterloo.ca/

Certificate Programs: Classical Studies, French Civilization and Culture, General Social Work, Social Work (Child Abuse).

Class Titles: Accounting, Actuarial Science, Anthropology, Applied Mathematics, Biology, Canadian Studies, Chemistry, Classical Studies, Combinatorics/Optimization, Computer Science, Croatian, Dance, Dutch, Earth Sciences, Economics, English, Environmental Studies, French, Geography, German, Gerontology, Greek, Health Studies, History, Interdisciplinary Social Science, Jewish Studies, Kinesiology, Latin, Management Sciences, Mathematics, Native Studies, Peace/Conflict Studies, Philosophy, Physics, Planning, Polish, Psychology, Religious Studies, Russian, Science, Social Work, Sociology, Spanish, Statistics, Studies in Personality/Religion, Women's Studies.

Teaching Methods: *Computers:* Internet, conferencing, software, e-mail, CD-ROM. *TV:* videotape. *Other:* audiotapes, print material, correspondence, textbooks, assignments, supervised examination.

Admission Requirements: *Undergraduate:* Since the University of Waterloo is located in the Province of Ontario, minimum admission requirements are given in terms of the Ontario Secondary School curriculum. Admission requirements are the same for distance study as for on-campus study. As a minimum you must have your Ontario Secondary School Diploma (or equivalent) with an overall average of 70% on 6 Ontario Academic Course (OAC) credits. Please note that some UW Plans and Programs have additional admission requirements. As an example, 30 half-credit courses are required to complete a general bachelor of arts degree. Each half-credit course operates over an approximate 13-week term. There are 3 terms per year—fall, winter, spring. If you do not have the minimum requirements for admission and have been away from formal education for some time, you may apply as a mature student. The official language of instruction at the University of Waterloo is English. There is an English language requirement for applicants whose first language is not English. This language requirement does not apply to bilingual francophone Canadians. *Graduate:* For information about the Master of Applied Science, Management of Technology program, please refer to http://motdinfo.uwaterloo.ca/ *Postgraduate:* not applicable. *Certificate:* same as for undergraduate degree programs.

On-Campus Requirements: None.

Tuition and Fees: *Undergraduate:* Tuition for the 2001/2002 academic year is $453 CDN/course for Canadian citizens and permanent residents for most programs. Tuition for non-Canadian students is $995 CDN for each undergraduate distance course. *Graduate:* refer to http://motdinfo.uwaterloo.ca/ *Application Fee:* $50 *Other Costs:* There are various costs associated with course materials; some are refundable when materials are returned.

Financial Aid: available for Canadian citizens/permanent residents. Other students should investigate their eligibility.

Accreditation: Association of Universities and Colleges of Canada and of Association of Commonwealth Universities.

Description: In just over 40 years, UW has distinguished itself as one of the best universities in Canada boasting strong teaching and research programs in Applied Health Sciences, Arts, Engineering, Environmental Studies, Mathematics, and Science. Since its founding in 1957, more than 100,000 men and women from 120 countries have graduated from UW. For 9 years in a row, UW has been ranked best overall, most innovative, and best source of leaders of tomorrow by opinion leaders across the country in Maclean's survey of Canadian universities. First offering distance education courses in 1968, UW now has one of the largest distance education programs in Canada, with over 250 courses spanning more than 45 subject areas. You can earn a degree, a certificate, or a diploma entirely by distance education. Course materials are delivered through a variety of media: audio- and videotape, print, learning tools such as lab kits, rock sample kits, and an increasing number of courses taught entirely online or with an online component.

University of Winnipeg

| 515 Portage Avenue | Phone: (204) 786-9849 |
| Winnipeg, MB, Canada R3B 2E9 | Fax: (204) 783-3116 |

Division(s): Center for Distributed/Distance Learning
Web Site(s): http://www.uwinnipeg.ca/academic
E-mail: d.frederickson@uwinnipeg.ca

Undergraduate Degree Programs:
Bachelor of Arts
Bachelor of Science
Bachelor of Education
Bachelor of Theology

Graduate Degree Programs:
Master of Arts
Master of Public Administration
Master of Divinity
Master of Marriage and Family Therapy
Master of Sacred Theology

Teaching Methods: *Computers:* Internet, real-time chat, electronic classroom, e-mail (for northern students only). *TV:* cable program (urban Winnipeg and selected rural communities). *Other:* None.

Credits Granted for: experiential learning, portfolio assessment (both under consideration).

Admission Requirements: *Undergraduate:* completion of university-track secondary program or mature status.

On-Campus Requirements: courses needed to complete degree.

Tuition and Fees: *Undergraduate:* $330/3 credits plus incidental fees. *Application Fee:* $35. *Other Costs:* varies for textbooks, etc. *Credit by:* semester.

Accreditation: Association of Universities and Colleges of Canada.

Description: The University of Winnipeg (1871) is a liberal arts undergraduate institution offering some master's programs. The university views both excellence and accessibility as important goals and values academic freedom, self-governance, and community service. The Centre for Learning Technologies has been offering limited distance education opportunities to northern students for 10 years via live satellite, teleconference and now real-time Internet-based computer programs; and in the last 5 years to urban Winnipeg and southern rural community students via cable TV.

University of Wisconsin, Eau Claire

| 105 Garfield Avenue | Phone: (715) 836-6006 |
| Eau Claire, WI 54701 | Fax: (715) 836-6001 |

Division(s): Media Development Center
Web Site(s): http://www.uwec.edu
E-mail: scleidd@uwec.edu

Undergraduate Degree Programs:
Collaborative Nursing

Teaching Methods: *Computers:* classroom computers, Internet, e-mail, CD-ROM, PowerPoint. *TV:* videotape, cable program, satellite broadcasting, PBS, NTU, PBS/ALSS, 2-way distance education networks, laser disk players, slide-to-video converters. *Other:* audioconferencing, videoconferencing, audiographics, audiotapes, fax, correspondence, independent study, individual study, ITFS.

Credits Granted for: examination (CLEP, DANTES), AP, 1B, some military experience.

Admission Requirements: *Undergraduate:* accredited high school diploma or equivalent, upper 50% of class OR 110 composite SAT I (22 on ACT). *Graduate:* college transcript, letter of recommendation, interview, essay, GMAT, GRE, 2.75 GPA, additional requirements per specific program.

On-Campus Requirements: None.

Tuition and Fees: *Undergraduate:* $145/credit residents, $489/credit nonresidents. *Graduate:* $249/credit residents, $795/credit nonresidents. *Application Fee:* $35. *Credit by:* semester.

Financial Aid: Federal Stafford Loan, Federal Perkins Loan, Federal PLUS Loan, Federal Pell Grant, Federal Work-Study, VA, Wisconsin resident programs.

Accreditation: North Central Association of Colleges and Schools.

Description: University of Wisconsin, Eau Claire, which celebrated its 75th anniversary in 1991, is one of the nation's leading regional public universities offering the opportunities of a larger school and the personal attention and academic distinction of a private college. Its innovative baccalaureate program combines liberal arts and sciences with practical training for 21st-century careers. In 1986 the UW-Eau Claire School of Nursing established an off-campus, distance education, baccalaureate program in cooperation with Saint Joseph's Hospital. In 1992 UW-Eau Claire and LacCourte Oreilles Ojibwa Community College collaborated on a Bachelor of Science in Nursing degree for Native American students. Nursing faculty and administrators from UW in Eau Claire, Green Bay, Madison, Milwaukee, and Oshkosh agreed in 1995 to develop a collaborative program for registered nurses. The most common distance technologies include audiographic conferencing and full-motion, 2-way video. In 2000 business faculty and administrators from UW in Eau Claire, LaCrosse, Oshkosh, and Parkside began offering the MBA Internet Foundation Program, a graduate-level program that enables students to complete MBA prerequisite courses offered via web-based courseware.

University of Wisconsin/Milwaukee

| 161 West Wisconsin Avenue #6000 | Phone: (414) 227-3398 |
| Milwaukee, WI 53203 | Fax: (414) 227-3396 |

Division(s): Distance Learning and Instructional Support
Web Site(s): http://www.uwm.edu/UniversityOutreach/deuwm
E-mail: nanm@uwm.edu

Graduate Degree Programs:
Master of Library and Information Science
Ph.D. in Nursing.

Certificate Programs: State and Local Taxation, Internet Technology, Child Care Center Management.

Class Titles: Library Science, Nursing, Business, Education, Child Care, Foreign Language, Communication.

Teaching Methods: *Computers:* Internet, real-time chat, electronic classroom, e-mail, LISTSERV. *TV:* cable program, satellite broadcasting, PBS. *Other:* videoconferencing, audioconferencing, audiographics, fax, correspondence.

Credits Granted for: varies by department.

Admission Requirements: *Undergraduate:* for more detailed information see: http://www.uwm.edu/UWM/Student/UGBulletin/Admission.html. *Certificate:* graduation from a recognized high school; or a high school equivalency certificate or diploma based on the General Educational Development (GED) exam, or a Wisconsin High School Equivalency exam. All new freshman applicants who are Wisconsin residents and under age 21 as of September 1 of the fall term in which they intend to enroll must submit ACT scores prior to final admission to the university. (Out-of-state applicants may submit SAT scores.) Additional testing and a personal interview may be required. Some UWM schools and colleges have additional requirements and recommendations. Normally, students with an overall C (2.0 GPA on a 4.0 scale) average on 12 or more attempted credits at a previous accredited institution(s) shall be admissible to UWM. If students do not wish to enter a specific school they may be admitted as non-degree candidates or special students. The following materials are required for application processing: (1) a completed and signed application form and (2) a $28 state-required application fee, and a $25 processing fee (if non-U.S. academic credentials are submitted). These are nonrefundable fees and are not applicable to any other university fee or bill. Fees are subject to change; (3) original or officially certified copies of all grade reports for all secondary and higher school studies, as well as original or officially certified copies of all academic diplomas, certificates, and national or other major examination results. Official records must be submitted in the native language and must be accompanied by an official English translation. Notarized copies will not be accepted. Official records should be sent to OISP Admissions directly from the institution; (4) concrete evidence of the applicant's ability in the English language. Testimonial letters are not sufficient. Most applicants must take the Test of English as a Foreign Language (TOEFL).

On-Campus Requirements: None.

Tuition and Fees: *Undergraduate:* for in-state tuition requirements see the Department of Enrollment Services at: http://des.uwm.edu/Dept/undergrad/resident.html. *Graduate:* see specific program information at http://www.uwm.edu/Dept/ Grad_Sch/Services/. *Credit by:* semester.

Financial Aid: Federal Stafford Loan, Federal Perkins Loan, Federal PLUS Loan, Federal Pell Grant, Federal Work-Study, VA, Wisconsin resident programs. For more information see: http://www.uwm.edu/Dept/FINAID/.

Accreditation: North Central Association of Colleges and Schools.

Description: The University of Wisconsin/Milwaukee (1956) traces its origin to the Milwaukee State Normal School, which was founded in 1885 and subsequently became Wisconsin State College. Its establishment in 1956 came with the merger of Wisconsin State College and the University of Wisconsin Extension Division in Milwaukee, to become University of Wisconsin/Milwaukee. The University of Wisconsin/Milwaukee is Wisconsin's premier urban university located in the economic and cultural heart of the state. Distance Learning delivers instruction to students at locations and times convenient for them. To accomplish this, the University of Wisconsin/Milwaukee faculty, staff, and students may use a variety of technologies such as satellite, ITFS, broadcast TV, computers, telephone, and compressed video. Each University of Wisconsin/Milwaukee school or college has an appointed Distance Education Liaison (DEL) who is the primary contact for instructors considering using these instructional technologies. Contact your dean's office for the name of your DEL representative.

University of Wisconsin-Platteville

1 University Plaza	Phone: 1-800-362-5460
Platteville, WI 53818	Fax: (608) 342-1071

Division(s): Distance Learning Center
Web Site(s): http://www.uwplatt.edu/~disted
E-mail: disted@uwplatt.edu

Undergraduate Degree Programs:
Bachelor of Science in Business Administration

Graduate Degree Programs:
Master of Science in:
  Project Management
  Criminal Justice
  Master of Engineering

Certificate Programs: Project Management, Human Resource Management, Leadership and Human Performance, International Business, Customized Certificate Options, Occupational Safety and Health, Criminal Justice Graduate Diploma.

Class Titles: Contact school or check web site for details.

Teaching Methods: *Computers:* Internet, real-time chat, e-mail, LISTSERV. *TV:* videotape, satellite broadcasting. *Other:* videoconferencing, audioconferencing, audiotapes, fax, correspondence, independent study, individual study.

Credits Granted for: experiential learning, portfolio assessment, extrainstitutional learning (PONSI, corporate or professional association seminars/workshops), examination (CLEP, ACT-PEP, DANTES, GRE).

Admission Requirements: *Undergraduate:* high school degree or equivalent; *Graduate:* undergraduate degree (some in specific fields).

On-Campus Requirements: No on-campus visits are required for online and correspondence programs.

Tuition and Fees: *Undergraduate:* $225/credit for online; $109 in-state; $368 out-of-state/credit for correspondence. *Graduate:* $500/credit for online; $245 in-state; $700 out-of-state for correspondence. *Application Fees:* $35 undergraduate; $45 graduate. *Graduation Fee:* $25 undergraduate; $35 graduate. *Other Costs:* textbooks approximately $75–$100/course, administrative fees: $130 annually. *Credited by:* semester.

Financial Aid: Federal Stafford Loan, Federal Perkins Loan, Federal Pell Grant, VA, state programs for residents of Wisconsin.

Accreditation: North Central Association of Colleges and Schools.

Description: The University of Wisconsin/ Platteville is one of 12 comprehensive institutions that is part of the UW system (1866, university; first Distance program, 1979; first online program, 1999). We began our work in Distance Education with the development of the Extended Degree Program in Business Administration in 1979. We have since added numerous individual courses and certificate programs that are available via the Internet and interactive television. In 1999 we added the first of our 3 graduate programs available online.

University of Wisconsin/Stevens Point

2100 Main Street	Phone: (715) 346-3838
Stevens Point, WI 54481	(800) 898-9472
	Fax: (715) 346-4641

Division(s): Extension Credit Outreach
Web Site(s): http://www.uwsp.edu/extension
E-mail: uwspext@uwsp.edu

Graduate Degree Programs:
Master of Science in Education

Certificate Programs: Technology and Leadership (all online credit classes).

Teaching Methods: *Computers:* Internet, e-mail, real-time chat, electronic classroom, CD-ROM, newsgroup. LISTSERV. *TV:* videotape, cable program, satellite broadcasting, PBS. *Other:* audioconferencing, videoconferencing, audiographics, audiotapes, fax, correspondence.

Credits Granted for: experiential learning, portfolio assessment, extra-institutional learning (PONS, corporate or professional association seminars/workshops), examination (CLEP, ACT-PEP, DANTES, GRE).

Admission Requirements: *Undergraduate:* ACT. *Graduate:* GRE.

On-Campus Requirements: None.

Tuition and Fees: *Undergraduate:* $112.25/credit in-state, $389/credit nonresident. *Graduate:* $209/credit in-state, $617/credit nonresident. *Application Fee:* $40 for Technology and Leadership certificate program. *Other Costs:* $50/class for certain distance education courses. *Credit by:* semester.

Financial Aid: Federal Stafford Loan, Federal Perkins Loan, Federal PLUS Loan, Federal Pell Grant, Federal Work-Study, VA, Wisconsin resident programs.

Accreditation: North Central Association of Colleges and Schools.

Description: University of Wisconsin at Stevens Point (1894) has a long and proud academic tradition. Since opening its doors as a teacher training school to 300 students, the university has undergone several name changes and expanded its programs. It is now one of 13 units in the University of Wisconsin System, with 8,400 undergraduate and graduate students. Nearly 80% of the 600 full- and part-time teaching staff have doctorate or equivalent degrees. Distance Learning efforts started with ITFS and cable; moved to statewide public TV wrap-around audioconferencing; and now include Internet classes.

University of Wisconsin/Stout

140 Vocational Rehabilitation Building	Phone: (715) 232-2693
Menomonie, WI 54751-0790	Fax: (715) 232-3385

Division(s): Stout Solutions, Continuing Education
Web Site(s): http://oce.uwstout.edu
http://www.uwstout.edu
E-mail: whites@uwstout.edu

Undergraduate Degree Programs:
Bachelor of Science in Industrial Management

Graduate Degree Programs:
Master of Science in Hospitality/Tourism with Global Concentration

Postgraduate Degree Programs:
Ph.D. in Technology Management

Certificate Programs: Hospitality Management.

Class Titles: Accounting, Media Technology, Education, Human Development, Vocational Rehabilitation; Vocational, Technical and Adult Education, Hospitality/Tourism, Nutrition, English, Physics, Technology, Risk Control, Training and Development.

Teaching Methods: *Computers:* Internet, real-time chat, electronic classroom, e-mail, asynchronous, CD-ROM, newsgroup, LISTSERV. *TV:* videotape, cable program, satellite broadcasting, PBS. *Other:* radio broadcast, videoconferencing, audioconferencing, audiographics, audiotapes, fax, correspondence, independent study, individual study, learning contracts.

Credits Granted for: experiential learning, portfolio assessment, extrainstitutional learning (PONSI, corporate or professional association seminars/workshops), examination (CLEP, ACT-PEP, DANTES, GRE).

Admission Requirements: Contact school.

On-Campus Requirements: None.

Tuition and Fees: *Undergraduate:* $137.40/credit for Wisconsin resident, $175.48 for out-of-state, $140.40 for MN reciprocity. *Graduate:* $246.74/credit for Wisconsin resident and MN reciprocity, $288.28 for out-of-state. *Postgraduate:* same as graduate credit listed above. *Application Fees:* $35 for undergraduate admissions fee and $45 for graduate admissions fee when applying for an entire degree; no fees when just registering for a Distance Education course other than tuition. *Credit by:* semester.

Financial Aid: Federal Stafford Loan, Federal Perkins Loan, Federal PLUS Loan, Federal Pell Grant, Federal Work-Study, VA, state programs for residents of Wisconsin.

Accreditation: North Central Association of Schools and Colleges.

Description: UW/Stout (1891) is one of 13 publicly supported universities in the University of Wisconsin System. It was founded as a private institution by James H. Stout and is located in scenic western Wisconsin in Menomonie. UW/Stout has gained a position of national leadership in its specialized areas. UW/Stout is characterized by a distinctive array of programs leading to professional careers focused on the needs of society. It has offered courses via Distance Education since the 1980s.

University of Wyoming Outreach School

P.O. Box 3274	Phone: (307) 766-4300
Laramie, WY 82071-3274	800-448-7801
	Fax: (307) 766-3445

Division(s): Division of Outreach Credit Programs
Web Site(s): http://outreach.uwyo.edu and http://online.uwyo.edu
E-mail: outreach@uwyo.edu

Undergraduate Degree Programs:
Business Administration
Criminal Justice
Family and Consumer Sciences (Professional Child Development Option)
Psychology
RN/BSN Completion Program
Social Science (distributed major)

Graduate Degree Programs:
MBA (Master of Business Administration)
Master Arts in:
    Education (Adult and Post-Secondary Education)
    Education (Instructional Technology)
    Education (Teaching and Learning)
    Education (Special Education)
    Kinesiology and Health
    MPA (Master of Public Administration)
    Nursing (Nurse Educator Option)
    Nursing (Community Health Clinical Specialist)
    Master of Social Work
    Masters in Speech-Language Pathology

Certificate Programs: Land Surveying, Real Estate Certification, Family and Consumer Sciences (Early Childhood Program Director's Certificate).

Class Titles: Contact school or check web site for details.

Teaching Methods: *Computers:* Internet, real-time chat, e-mail, threaded discussions, document sharing, CD-ROM. *TV:* videotape, compressed video, videoconferencing. *Other:* audio teleconferencing, audiotapes, fax, correspondence, independent study.

Credits Granted for: portfolio assessment, examination (CLEP, ACT-PEP, CEEB-APP, DANTES, GRE).

Admission Requirements: *Undergraduate:* To qualify for assured admission to the University of Wyoming, high school graduates who are first-time college students or college transfers with fewer than 30 transferable semester credit hours, must meet the following minimum admission requirements: Graduates of a Wyoming high school: cumulative high school grade point average of 2.75 or above based on a 4.0 grading scale. Graduate from a non-Wyoming high school: cumulative high school grade point average of 3.0 or above, or a 2.75 and an ACT score of at least 20 or a SAT score of at least 960. Graduates with fewer than 30 transferable college credit hours: cumulative transferable college GPA must be at least 2.0 home schooled: must meet the same grade point average as other high school graduates. Please contact the Admissions office for a Home School Credit Evaluation Form. The home school instructor should complete the form. Completion of at least 13 high school units in the following pre-college curriculum (English/Communication/Language Arts, Mathematics, Science, Cultural Context Electives. Outreach undergraduate students are assessed tuition at

a resident rate with a delivery fee. *Non-degree-seeking students:* complete and submit a non-degree student application. Transcripts and test scores are not required for non-degree status. Non-degree students may enroll in a maximum of 7 credit hours/semester (maximum of 2 courses). Only 12 credit hours taken in this status may be used toward a UW degree. Students admitted as non-degree are assessed tuition and fees at the same tuition as degree-seeking students. *Graduate:* UW graduate application (with nonrefundable application fee). One set of official transcripts sent directly to UW Graduate School, 4-year bachelor's degree from an institution with an acceptable accreditation, 3.0 overall GPA. Official Graduate Record Examination with a score of at least 900 (197 on computerized test) on combined verbal and quantitative sections is preferred. Applicants for the Master of Business Administration program must submit scores from the Graduate Management Admission Test (GMAT) rather than the GRE, 3 letters of recommendation. Write or call the respective academic department for questions concerning application status or degree program requirements. Outreach graduate students are assessed tuition at a resident rate with a delivery fee. *Enrichment, non-degree-seeking/Graduate:* do not have to supply transcripts. Only 12 credit hours taken in enrichment (non-degree) status may apply toward a graduate degree. Enrichment graduate students deciding to pursue a degree must apply to and be accepted by the UW Graduate School.

On-Campus Requirements: No on-campus study is required for online courses and online degree programs. Other Distance Education courses and degree programs not offered through online learning require some on-campus study. Some degree programs are delivered through Distance Education only within the state of Wyoming and are delivered to off-campus sites throughout the state.

Tuition and Fees: *Undergraduate:* $96.50/credit. *Graduate:* $160.85/credit. *Social Work:* $349.70/credit. Land Surveying Certificate Program: $175/credit. MBA Program: $206.75/credit. *Application Fees:* $30 undergraduate/$40 graduate. *Graduation Fee:* $12.50. *Other Costs:* $10/credit (nonrefundable) delivery fee for core courses and core degree programs. (No delivery fee is charged for courses in the Land Surveying Certificate Program and MBA program), $40/credit (nonrefundable) delivery fee for online courses and online degree programs (minimum of $80). *Credit by:* semester.

Financial Aid: Federal Stafford Loan, Federal Perkins Loan, Federal PLUS Loan, Federal Pell Grant, Federal Work-Study, Federal SEOG, VA, state programs for residents of Wyoming, Wyoming National Guard Tuition assistance, more than 850 scholarship programs.

Accreditation: North Central Association of Colleges and Schools Commission and Institutions of Higher Education and accreditation for individual degree programs.

Description: In 1892, University of Wyoming (1886) President Albinus Alonzo Johnson saw extension as the "missionary spirit of the church applied to education." UW's extension program was the first of its kind west of the Missouri River to offer correspondence courses. Since that time, the University of Wyoming has offered extension classes as part of its effort to help remove the obstacles to learning presented by geography, and to meet the needs of site-bound adult learners. During the early years of extension, the railroad played a major role in transporting instructors, exhibits, and demonstration equipment to Wyoming communities. In 1926 UW began using the airplane to fly instructors to teach classes. Instructional technology entered the scene in 1984, providing alternative methods of course delivery such as audioteleconferencing. In the 1990s the first interactive video telecourse was offered through compressed video and the first Internet class was delivered via Online UW, the university's virtual campus. Now, in its 109th year of Distance Education, the UW Outreach School continues the tradition of extending the intellectual resources of the university to the state of Wyoming and beyond.

University System of Georgia Independent Study

Georgia Center for Continuing Education
Suite 193
University of Georgia
Athens, GA 30602-3603

Phone: (706) 542-3243
(800) 877-3243
Fax: (706) 542-6635

Division(s): USGIS courses are offered by academic departments located at senior institutions of higher education within the University System of Georgia. Faculty of the academic departments develop the courses offered and grade lessons submitted by students to satisfy requirements of the courses. The office of University System of Georgia Independent Study is located at the University of Georgia Center for Continuing Education.

Web Site(s): http://www.gactr.uga.edu/usgis/
E-mail: usgis@arches.uga.edu

Class Titles: Agribusiness Management, Principles of Accounting, Taxation, Anthropology, Art Appreciation, Ecology, Development Within Family, Child Development, Development of Interpersonal Relationships, Family, Greek Culture, Classical Mythology, Medical Terminology, Turfgrass Management, Ecological Bases of Environmental Issues, Environment/Humans, Ecology, Principles of Macroeconomics, Principles of Microeconomics, Economic Development of U.S., Economics of Human Resources, Career/Life Planning, Foundations of Education, English Composition, English Lit: Beginnings—1700, English Lit: 1700—Present, Writing for Business, American Literature, 19th Century Brit Lit: Romantics, Medieval Literature, Modern Southern Literature, Prose: Modern Novel, People of

Paradox: American Colonial Voices, African American Literature, Children's Literature, Learning/Development in Education, Child/Adolescent Development for Education, Human Nutrition/Food, French, Outdoor Recreation/Environmental Awareness, German, Human Geography, Physical Geography, Physical Geography Lab, Economic Geography, Meteorology, Earth Processes/Environments, General Physical Geology/Lab, American History to 1865, American History Since 1865, History of Western Society to 1500, History of Western Society Since 1500, History of Georgia, Vietnam War, Horticultural Science, Fruit Crops, Effects of Drug Use/Abuse, Newswriting/Reporting, Journalism in Secondary Schools, Latin, Golden Age Latin Literature, Vergil's Aeneid, Ovid, Management of Organizations and Individuals, Integrated Resource Management, Human Resource Management, Mathematical Modeling, College Algebra, Trigonometry, Precalculus, Calculus, Statistics, Marketing, Retailing, Philosophy, Logic/Critical Thinking, Ethics, Symbolic Logic, American Government, Political Parties/Elections, Public Administration, Criminal Justice Administration, Presidency, Environmental Policy, Politics of Middle East, Politics of Modern Africa, Contemporary American Foreign Policy, Psychology, Psychology of Adjustment, Psychology in Work Place, Abnormal Psychology, Psychology of Sex/Sexual Deviations, Social/Personality Development, Theories of Personality, Outdoor Rec/Environmental Awareness, Judaism/Christianity/Islam, Religions of India/China/Japan, West Religious Thought, World Religions, Sociology, Social Problems, Personality/Social Structure, Sociology of Occupations, Spanish, Oral Decision Making, Persuasion, Women's Studies.

Teaching Methods: *Computers:* Web courses (e-mail, bulletin boards), electronic course guides, e-mail lesson submission courses. *Other:* audiotapes, independent study (all available as correspondence-based courses via postal service and fax).

Credits Granted for: course completion including final exam at an official college/university test site. Some courses include a midterm exam.

Admission Requirements: *Undergraduate:* USGIS registration does not constitute college/university admission and, therefore, does not necessitate admission tests, high school/college transcripts, or college/university enrollment (except for high school and home-school students). Registration and catalog available online (http://www.gactr.uga.edu/usgis/).

On-Campus Requirements: None.

Tuition and Fees: *Undergraduate:* $110/semester credit. *Other Costs:* $30 drop/add fee plus $10/lesson submitted for grading prior to drop/add (eligible for drop/add within 53

calendars of registration); $60 extension fee to extend the course for an additional 3 months if the extension fee is received prior to the course expiration date. Air mail costs will apply to international registrations. $30 course guide or e-guide replacement fee. Textbooks and instructional materials: USGIS has an agreement with MBS Direct Textbooks and Materials to stock materials used in our courses. You may order from MBS Direct via the Internet at http://direct.mbs-book.com/uga.htm or by phone at 800-325-3252. You may also order by mail using the order form provided by USGIS. An instructional materials order form may be found in the catalog and in all student packets. *Credit by:* semester.

Financial Aid: Eligibility to receive financial aid or scholarships must be cleared with the financial aid office of the student's institution prior to registration for an independent study course. Students receiving financial aid (e.g., loans, grants, tuition reimbursements, or scholarships) must pay tuition fees in full at the time of registration.

Accreditation: Southern Association of Colleges and Schools.

Description: University System of Georgia Independent Study's (1932) mission is to increase access to higher education by transcending barriers of geography and time while meeting the highest academic standards, encouraging academic rigor, and requiring equivalent levels of student achievements regardless of delivery format. USGIS permits students to register at any time and take several courses simultaneously with up to a year for course completion. Academic credit is recorded permanently in the University of Georgia Registrar's Office and, with institutional approval, may be transferable.

University Without Walls— Skidmore College

815 North Broadway	Phone: (518) 580-5450
Saratoga Springs, NY 12866	Toll-free (866) 310-6444
	Fax: (518) 580-5449

Division(s): University Without Walls
Web Site(s): http://www.skidmore.edu/uww
E-mail: uww@skidmore.edu

Undergraduate Degree Programs:
Individualized studies in many disciplines/fields

Class Titles:
America in the Sixties
Controversies over Evolution
People's Century
Love in Art and Idea
Comparative Human Rights
Growing Up in Literature
Nation, State, and Market
World Prehistory
History of Harlem
Expository Writing
Human Ecology
History of Information Technology
Men in Literature
Land/Human Interaction
Finance Statistics
Cultural Anthropology
Jazz: A Multicultural Expression
Statistics
Biology of the Mind
Representations of the Holocaust
Nonprofit Management
The Future of the Adirondack Park
Poetics and Poetry Writing
Criminal Law and Procedure
Jazz
Making Sense of the Modern Economy
Marketing
Psychology of Intimacy
In Search of Human Origins
Computers, Ethics, and Society
Business Policy
Strategic Thinking
The Islamic Spectrum: from Fundamentalism to Modernism
Women, Religion, and Spirituality
Mozart
Working with People
Nation, State, & Market
Divorce and Family Change
Imagining the Past
Obsessions and Addictions
Therapeutic and Systematic Change
American Folklore & Folklife
Writing the Memoir
Women & the Law
From Fiction to Film
Social Interaction
The Adirondacks in Black & White
Marketing Nonprofit Programs & Services
Faith & Science
Crime & Punishment in America
Western Religious Ethics

Teaching Methods: *Computers:* Internet, real-time chat, electronic classroom, e-mail. *Other:* fax, correspondence, independent study, individual study, internships.

Credits Granted for: experiential learning, portfolio assessment, extrainstitutional learning, examination (CLEP, ACT-PEP, DANTES, GRE).

On-Campus Requirements: None.

Tuition and Fees: *Undergraduate:* $3,800 first year annual fee; subsequent years are $3,200. UWW online and evening seminar courses are $500. Independent Study $500. *Other Costs:* $600 for final project assessment. *Credit by:* semester.

Financial Aid: Federal Stafford Loan, Federal PLUS Loan, Federal Pell Grant, VA, New York resident programs, VESID.

Accreditation: Middle States Association of Colleges and Schools.

Description: Founded in 1971 as one of several nontraditional special programs at Skidmore, University without Walls has been a pioneer in providing a flexible, nonresidential external degree option for adult learners, many of whom balance education with work and family. UWW degree programs are individually constructed to fit the experience and learning options available to its 250 students. Typically, UWW students enroll having earned the equivalent of about 60 college credits elsewhere, in addition to credit for life experiences, employment, internships, and/or volunteer work. In close consultation with their faculty advisors, UWW students map out individually tailored plans to complete their degrees.

Upper Iowa University

608 Washington (EDP)/	Phone: (563) 425-5283 (EDP)
603 Washington, Box 1857 (Online)	(800) 773-9298 (Online)
PO Box 1861	Fax: (563) 563-5353 (EDP)
Fayette, IA 52142	(563) 425-5771 (Online)

Division(s): External Degree Program/Online
Web Site(s): http://www.uiu.edu/ (EDP) and http://www.uiu.edu (Online)
E-mail: extdegree@uiu.edu (EDP) and online@uiu.edu (Online)

Undergraduate Degree Programs:
Associate of Arts
Associate of Business
Bachelor of Science

Graduate Degree Programs:
Master of Business Administration

Class Titles: Art, Accounting Principles, Marketing Principles, Management Principles, Economics (Macro/Micro), Management Information Systems, Business Ethics, Business Law, Sales Management, Financial Accounting, Federal Taxation, Corporate Financial Management, Consumer Behavior, Human Resources Management, Supervision, Advertising, Entrepreneurship/Small Business Management, Training/Development, Business Communication, Marketing Management, Compensation/Benefits Management, Complex Organizations, Personnel Selection/Evaluation, Labor Relations, Managerial Cost Accounting, International Marketing, Auditing, Production/Operations Management, Financial Accounting, Accounting for Not-for-Profit Organizations, Auditing, Contemporary Topics in Management, Marketing Research, Strategic Management, Economics of International Business, Environmental Biology, General Physical Science, Computer Applications, Interpersonal Communications, Composition, Literature, American Civilization, American History, American Economic History, College Mathematics, Elementary Statistics, Quantitative Methods, Statistics, Public Administration, Cases in Public Administration, Public Budgeting Process, Administrative Law, U.S. Government, State/Local Government, American Constitution Law, General Psychology, Human Services, Substance Abuse, Abnormal Psychology, Research Methods, Social Welfare Programs/Policies, Industrial Psychology, Issues/Ethics in Helping Professions, Social Problems, Diverse Cultures in America.

Teaching Methods: *Computers:* Internet, real-time chat, electronic classroom, e-mail, CD-ROM, newsgroup, LISTSERV. *TV:* videotape. *Other:* fax, correspondence, independent study, individual study.

Credits Granted for: experiential learning, portfolio assessment, extra-institutional learning, examination (CLEP, ACT-PEP, DANTES).

Admission Requirements: *Undergraduate:* high school graduate, GED. *Graduate:* bachelor's degree, 2.5 GPA.

On-Campus Requirements: None.

Tuition and Fees: *Undergraduate:* $155/credit (EDP), $216 (Online). *Graduate:* $290 (Online). *Application Fee:* $35 (EDP), $50 (Online). *Graduation Fee:* $60 (Online). *Other Costs:* $60/semester hour experiential learning credit. *Credit by:* semester.

Financial Aid: Federal Stafford Loan, Federal Pell Grant, VA.

Accreditation: North Central Association of Colleges and Schools, Higher Learning Commission.

Description: Upper Iowa University (1857) was established in Fayette. Numerous off-campus centers now serve working adults in civilian and military communities. In addition to completing degrees, External Degree and Online courses may supplement degrees at on-site locations, helping students pursuing degrees at other institutions or seeking personal/professional development. UIU's External Degree Program, established in 1973, was one of the country's first independent study degree completion programs. Through progressive transfer policies, students may combine Bachelor of Science experience with majors in Accounting,

Business, Human Resources Management, Public Administration (also with Law Enforcement and Fire Science emphases), Management, Social Science, Marketing, and Human Services, and Technology and Information Management. With undergraduate programs in Accounting, Management, Marketing, and Technology and Information Management, and a Master of Business Administration, UIU's Online program offers a convenient, affordable way for students to complete their degree. Students may use toll-free numbers to register, seek advising, and order textbooks, and qualified staff provide individualized instruction for independent study courses. Some courses have video supplements, and students may submit assignments via e-mail, fax, or regular mail. Students may enroll in one of 6 terms throughout the year at any time, with a 6-month initial enrollment period and two 3-month extensions. With no minimum completion time for courses, the program is self-paced and flexible. Courses run on 8-week terms.

Urbana University

| 579 College Way | Phone: (937) 484-1303 |
| Urbana, OH 43078 | Fax: (937) 484-1322 |

Division(s): Education
Web Site(s): www.urbana.edu
E-mail: alumni@urbana.edu

Undergraduate Degree Programs: Contact school.

Class Titles: Johnny Appleseed Workshop.

Teaching Methods: *Computers:* Internet, E-mail.

Credits Granted for: Experiential Learning.

Admission Requirements: *Undergraduate:* must be a student from an accredited institution. *Graduate:* must be a graduate at an accredited institution.

On-Campus Requirements: None.

Tuition and Fees: *Undergraduate:* $240/credit hour. *Graduate:* $240/credit hour. *Credit by:* semester.

Financial Aid: Federal Stafford Loan, Federal Perkins Loan, Federal PLUS Loan, Federal Pell Grant, Federal Work-Study, VA, state programs for residents of Ohio.

Accreditation: Ohio Board of Regents, North Central Association of Colleges and Schools.

Description: Serving a regional education role in West Central Ohio, Urbana University (1850) is a 4-year private undergraduate institution, with a graduate program in education. The mission of Urbana University is to offer an exemplary liberal arts education in a small-college environment, emphasizing individual attention, excellence in instruction, career-oriented programs, and affirmation of moral and ethical values. It emphasizes career development in education, social services, business, and the liberal arts. In addition to the educational offerings, the university also supports men's and women's sports, music and theater, clubs, cultural, social and leadership groups, and many other personal development and entertainment opportunities. In 1850 Urbana University was founded on land that John Chapman, the legendary Johnny Appleseed, encouraged to be donated for a university, starting a more than century-old relationship between Johnny Appleseed, the Chapman family, and Urbana University. As part of the "new beginnings," Urbana University has begun to share with others its legacy with Johnny Appleseed. Urbana University entered Distance Learning in the summer of 2000.

Utah State University

3080 Old Main Hill	Phone: (800) 233-2137
Logan, UT 84322-3080	(435) 797-2137
	Fax: (435) 797-1399

Division(s): Independent and Distance Education
Web Site(s): http://extension.usu.edu
http://online.usu.edu
E-mail: de-info@ext.usu.edu

Undergraduate Degree Programs:
Associate of Arts/Science
Bachelor of:
 Accounting
 Business Administration

Graduate Degree Programs:
Master of:
 English, Technical Writing
 Rehabilitation Counselor
We have many more degree programs that will be added online soon.
Please call to find out which degree programs have been added.

Class Titles: We offer many classes in a variety of areas. Please see our web site for more information.

Teaching Methods: *Computers:* online. *TV:* videotape, satellite broadcasting to Utah students only. *Other:* videostreaming, correspondence, independent study.

Credits Granted for: portfolio assessment, extrainstitutional learning, examination.

Admission Requirements: *Undergraduate:* new applicants: application and fees, high school transcript, and ACT (preferred) or SAT. Former students (returning after one or more semesters): must reapply plus $10 fee. Contact school for more information.

On-Campus Requirements: None.

Tuition and Fees: *Undergraduate:* $110/credit. *Graduate:* $200/credit. Tuition may vary for videostreamed classes. *Credit by:* semester.

Financial Aid: Federal Stafford Loan, Federal Perkins Loan, Federal PLUS Loan, Federal Pell Grant, Federal Work-Study, VA, Utah resident programs, alternative loans.

Accreditation: Northwest Association of Schools and Colleges.

Description: Utah State University (1888) integrates teaching, research, extension, and service to meet its unique role as Utah's land grant university. USU provides high-quality undergraduate and graduate instruction, excellent general education, and specialized academic and professional degree programs. The university's distance education program traces its beginnings to 1911 when correspondence study served the needs of off-campus students who could enroll for the modest sum of $2. Today, Independent Study, with 3,500 enrollments in 140 courses, remains the backbone of USU's distance education programs. Bachelor's and master's degrees are offered to students unable to attend USU because of time, distance, work, or family constraints. USU's new digital satellite broadcast system provides full-motion video and 2-way audio to each of its receiver sites.

Valley City State University

101 College Street	Phone: (701) 845-7302
Valley City, ND 58072	Fax: (701) 845-7121

Division(s): Interactive Active Video Coordinator
Web Site(s): http://vcsu.nodak.edu
E-mail: Jan_Drake@mail.vcsu.nodak.edu

Class Titles: Federal Tax, Sociology, Gerontology, Women in U.S. History, Spanish, Auditing, Geography of Europe.

Teaching Methods: *Computers:* Internet, chat, electronic classroom, e-mail, CD-ROM, LISTSERV. *TV:* videotape. *Other:* videoconferencing, fax, correspondence, independent study, individual study, learning contracts.

Credits Granted for: experiential learning, portfolio assessment, extrainstitutional learning, examination (CLEP, ACT-PEP).

Admission Requirements: *Undergraduate:* ACT for high school graduates from 1993; 4 English, 3 math, 3 science, and 3 social science high school classes; verification of measles or immunization if born after 1954; GED of 45.

On-Campus Requirements: None.

Tuition and Fees: *Undergraduate:* $76/credit. *Application Fee:* $25. *Other Costs:* $4/credit technology fee, $36/credit notebook computer fee. *Credit by:* semester.

Financial Aid: Federal Stafford Loan, Federal Perkins Loan, Federal PLUS Loan, Federal Pell Grant, Federal Work-Study, VA, North Dakota resident programs.

Accreditation: North Central Association of Colleges and Schools, National Council for Accreditation of Teacher Education "Exemplary Practices."

Description: Valley City State University (1888) is a small liberal arts college located in the heart of the Sheyenne River Valley. About 50% of its 1,000 students live on campus. The school's distance education, offered through the Outreach Campus, has evolved into an interactive video program available throughout the state, with plans for future expansion.

Ventura College

4667 Telegraph Road	Phone: (805) 654-6455
Ventura, CA 93003	Fax: (805) 654-6466

Division(s): Student Development
Web Site(s): www.ventura.cc.ca.us
E-mail: lmacconnaire@vcccd.net

Undergraduate Degree Programs:
Associate of Arts, General Liberal Arts/Sciences
Associate of Science

Certificate Programs: Yes.

Teaching Methods: *Computers:* Internet, e-mail, videotape, cable program, satellite broadcasting, PBS. *Other:* None.

Admission Requirements: *Undergraduate:* high school graduate or GED, age 18, high school students with permission. *Certificate:* Same.

On-Campus Requirements: For our TV classes, students meet on campus with the instructor at least 4 times/semester, 3 hours each time.

Tuition and Fees: *Undergraduate:* $11/unit. $12/unit starting fall 1998 *Application Fee:* residents $0, nonresidents $13/unit. *Other Costs:* nonresident tuition is $117/unit, health fee $10, parking (optional) $30/semester. *Credit by:* semester.

Financial Aid: Federal Perkins Loan, Federal Pell Grant, Federal Work-Study.

Accreditation: Western Association of Schools and Colleges.

Description: Ventura College (1925) traces its beginnings back to the early 1900s when a junior college department was added to Ventura Union High School. Between the years of 1929–1955, Ventura evolved to its present configuration of offering the freshman and sophomore years of college education. In 1955 the college was moved from the high school to its present 112-acre hillside campus a few miles from sandy beaches. Current enrollment is 11,000 day, evening, and off-campus students. Ventura is part of a 3-college district providing educational opportunities for all of Ventura County. The college has been offering distance learning classes for 15 years and is presently exploring developing courses to be offered over the Internet.

Vermont College of Norwich University

36 College Street
Montpelier, VT 05602

Phone: (800) 336-6794
Fax: (802) 828-8855

Web Site(s): http://www.norwich.edu/vermontcollege
E-mail: vcadmis@norwich.edu

Undergraduate Degree Programs:
Adult Degree Program, New College

Graduate Degree Programs:
Master of Arts
Master of Education
Master of Fine Arts in:
    Visual Art
    Writing (poetry, fiction, nonfiction)
    Writing for Children

Certificate Programs: Advanced graduate studies in education and integrated studies.

Class Titles: Postgraduate semester or one-year intensive study in the MFA in Writing programs.

Teaching Methods: *Computers:* Internet, electronic classroom, real-time chat, e-mail. *Other:* audiotapes, fax, correspondence, independent study, individual study, learning contracts.

Credits Granted for: experiential learning, portfolio assessment, extrainstitutional learning, examination (CLEP, ACT-PEP, DANTES, GRE).

Admission Requirements: *Undergraduate:* high school diploma, letters of recommendation. *Graduate:* accredited bachelor's degree.

On-Campus Requirements: 2 residencies each year that vary in length from 9–12 days; weekend options in ADP and the graduate program meet one weekend each month; online option also available in the graduate program.

Tuition and Fees: *Adult Degree Program:* $4,663/semester (cycle option), $4,490/semester (weekend option). *New College:* $4,663/semester. *Graduate Program:* $5,000/semester (colloquium fee: $250). *MFA in Visual Art:* $5,643/semester (residency room and board: $495). *MFA in Writing and Writing for Children:* $4,968/semester (residency room and board: $605). *Certificate of Advanced Graduate Study:* $5,543/semester. *Master of Education:* $7,401/year (residency room and board: $1,155/year).

Financial Aid: Federal Stafford Loan, Federal Perkins Loan, Federal PLUS Loan, Federal Pell Grant, Federal Work-Study, VA, Vermont resident programs.

Accreditation: New England Association of Schools and Colleges.

Description: Norwich University's (1819) Vermont College programs are the oldest brief-residency adult degree programs in the U.S., having been in existence since 1963. Based on the progressive education philosophy of John Dewey and employing the mentoring model used by Oxford and other European universities, these programs put the student's learning first. Each individual designs his or her own study in collaboration with a faculty mentor. Residencies bring students together in cohesive learning communities; directed, independent study during 6-month semesters focuses on the particular needs of each student.

Victor Valley College

18422 Bear Valley Road
Victorville, CA 92392-5849

Phone: (760) 245-4271
Fax: (760) 245-4279

Division(s): Educational Services
Web Site(s): http://www.vvconline.com

Undergraduate Degree Programs:
Associate Degree in:
    Business Administration/Management
    Business Real Estate
    Child Development
    Computer Information Systems
    Liberal Studies

Certificate Programs: Business Administration/ Management, Business Real Estate, Child Development, Computer Information Systems, Liberal Studies.

Teaching Methods: *Computers:* Internet, real-time chat, electronic classroom, e-mail, CD-ROM, newsgroup, LISTSERV. *Other:* videoconferencing, audioconferencing, audiographics, audiotapes, fax, correspondence, independent study, individual study, learning contracts.

Credits Granted for: experiential learning.

Admission Requirements: *Undergraduate:* No restrictions.

On-Campus Requirements: None.

Tuition and Fees: *Undergraduate:* $11/credit for residents. *Credit by:* semester.

Financial Aid: Federal Stafford Loan, Federal Perkins Loan, Federal PLUS Loan, Federal Pell Grant, Federal Work-Study, VA, state programs for residents of California.

Accreditation: Western Association of Schools and Colleges.

Description: Victor Valley College is part of the State of California community college system. Located in the beautiful Victor Valley, the college is one of the leaders in online distance learning. The college is currently offering 70 classes that will lead to an associate degree and certificates in the areas of general education, business administration, real estate, child development, computer information systems, and liberal studies.

Virginia Commonwealth University Medical College of Virginia Campus

1008 East Clay Street
PO Box 980203
Richmond, VA 23298-0203

Phone: (804) 828-0719
Fax: (804) 828-1894

Division(s): Department of Health Administration
Web Site(s): http://www.had.vcu.edu
E-mail: shavasy@hsc.vcu.edu

Graduate Degree Programs:
Master of Science in Health Administration (Executive Program)

Teaching Methods: *Computers:* Internet, e-mail, CD-ROM, newsgroup, streaming audio. *TV:* videotape. *Other:* audioconferencing, audiotapes, fax, correspondence, independent study, individual study, learning contracts, focus on asynchronous learning.

Admission Requirements: *Graduate:* 5 years of health care experience—preferably administrative—and an undergraduate degree from accredited college, GRE/GMAT (may be waived for advanced degrees), 2.75 GPA.

On-Campus Requirements: 6 on-campus sessions, 7 days each.

Tuition and Fees: *Undergraduate:* $3,911/semester in-state and academic common market participants, $7,948 out-of-state. *Application Fee:* $30. *Software:* $169. *Other Costs:* multimedia computer/Internet access, travel/lodging for on-campus sessions, books. *Credit by:* semester.

Financial Aid: Scholarship, grant, and loan programs.

Accreditation: Southern Association of Colleges and Schools, Accrediting Commission on Education for Health Services Administration.

Description: The Master of Science Health Administration can be completed in 22 months by U.S. residents working full-time. It is designed for physicians and other clinicians, mid-level managers, and health care executives seeking graduate education in management. The Department of Health Administration at VCU enjoys a strong national reputation. It also offers preparation leading to the Master of Health Administration and Doctor of Philosophy degrees. The department conducts major research, outreach, service, and consultation programs. The MCV campus has a 1,058-bed teaching hospital and 5 schools of clinical and basic sciences. More than 1,700 alumni provide an extensive professional development and career placement network.

Virginia Commonwealth University

West Hospital
1200 East Broad Street
Richmond, VA 23219

Phone: (804) 282-7247
Fax: (804) 828-8656

Division(s): School of Allied Health Professions
Web Site(s): http://views.vcu.edu/sahp/phd/
E-mail: mlwhite@hsc.vcu.edu

Graduate Degree Programs:
Master of Science in Health Administration (Executive Program)

Doctoral Degree Programs:
Doctorate in Health Related Sciences

Teaching Methods: *Computers:* Internet, real-time chat, electronic classroom, e-mail, CD-ROM, newsgroup, LISTSERV. *TV:* videotape. *Other:* audioconferencing, videoconferencing, audiographics, audiotapes, fax, correspondence, independent study.

Admission Requirements: *Graduate:* GRE or GMAT, 5 years of progressive work experience and related undergraduate degree from an accredited college. *Doctoral:* GRE or MAT, related master's degree.

On-Campus Requirements: One week at beginning and end of semester.

Tuition and Fees: *Graduate:* $274/credit in-state; $723/credit out-of-state. *Doctoral:* same as graduate. *Application Fee:* $30. *Software:* $300–$350. *Other Costs:* $1,326 master's program fee, $1,750 ($200/credit hour) doctoral program fee; travel, subsistence, lodging for on-campus sessions. *Credit by:* semester.

Financial Aid: Federal Stafford Loan, Federal Perkins Loan, Federal PLUS Loan, Federal Pell Grant, Federal Work-Study, VA, Virginia resident programs.

Accreditation: Southern Association of Colleges and Schools.

Description: VCU was founded in 1838 as the medical department of Hampden-Sydney College, becoming the Medical College of Virginia in 1854. In 1960, the General Assembly merged MCV with the Richmond Professional Institute, founded in 1917, to create Virginia Commonwealth University. VCU is the major urban university in the state and is classified as a Carnegie Foundation Research University I institution. The university is a public state-supported institution with 24,000 undergraduate, graduate, and health professional students. VCU's administration understands the critical role of distance learning for the next century. Distance learning began at VCU in 1988 with the Master of Science in Health Administration program. In the fall of 1998, the university began its new doctoral program in Health Related Sciences, an interdisciplinary, distance learning, Internet-based program.

Virginia Polytechnic Institute and State University

| Old Security Building (0445) | Phone: (540) 231-4199 |
| Blacksburg, VA 24061-0445 | Fax: (540) 231-5922 |

Division(s): The Office of Distance and Distributed Learning
Web Site(s): http://www.vt.edu
http://www.vto.vt.edu
http://www.iddl.vt.edu
E-mail: vtwebreg@vt.edu

Graduate Degree Programs:
Master of Science in:
  Business Administration
  Information Technology
  Civil Engineering
  Electrical Engineering
  Industrial/Systems Engineering
  Systems Engineering
Master of Arts in:
  Career and Technical Education
  Health/Physical Education
  Instructional Technology
  Political Science
MBA Business Administration

Certificate Programs: Career and Technical Education License, Computer Engineering, Information Policy and Society Studies, Networking, Software Development, Administration of Community-Based Services for Older Adults (graduate).

Class Titles: Biology, Communications, Computer Science, English, Entomology, Geography, Math, Political Science, Sociology, Spanish, Family/Child Development.

Teaching Methods: *Computers:* Internet, real-time chat, electronic classroom, e-mail, CD-ROM, newsgroup, LISTSERV. *TV:* videotape, cable program, satellite broadcasting. *Other:* videoconferencing, audiographics.

Admission Requirements: *Undergraduate:* see web site (http://www.vt.edu). *Graduate:* see web site (http://www.rgs.vt.edu). *Doctoral:* see web site (http://www.vt.edu). *Certificate:* see web site (http://www.vt.edu).

On-Campus Requirements: variable.

Tuition and Fees: *Undergraduate:* in-state: $849/3 credit course, out-of-state: $1,452. *Graduate:* in-state: $725/3 credit course, out-of-state: $1,227. *Application Fee:* $45. *Credit by:* semester.

Financial Aid: Federal Direct Stafford Loan, Federal Direct Perkins Loan, Federal Direct PLUS Loan, Federal Pell Grant, Federal Work-Study, Virginia Guaranteed Assistance Program (VGAP-VA), Commonwealth Award (VA Grant), College Scholarship Assistance Program (CSAP-VA and federal funds combined).

Accreditation: Southern Association of Colleges and Schools.

Description: Virginia Polytechnic Institute and State University (1872), a land grant university dedicated to instruction, research, and outreach, offers more than 200 degree programs and is the largest university in Virginia. It is also one of the nation's leading research institutions. Virginia Tech is a model for the development and use of sophisticated instructional technologies in the classroom. The 26,000 students (on and off campus) are enrolled in one of 7 undergraduate colleges, the Graduate School, or the Virginia-Maryland Regional College of Veterinary Medicine. Virginia Tech has been actively involved in distance learning since 1983 when it began offering televised graduate engineering courses via satellite. Currently Virginia Tech offers 8 master's degree programs, one certificate, and numerous individual courses through a variety of distance learning technologies.

Viterbo University

| 815 South Ninth Street | Phone: (608) 796-3088 |
| LaCrosse, WI 54601 | Fax: (608) 796-3050 |

Division(s): School of Extended Learning
Web Site(s): http://www.viterbo.edu
E-mail: taposey@viterbo.edu

Undergraduate Degree Programs:
Registered Nurse to Bachelor of Science in Nursing (RN to BSN)

Class Titles: Contact school or check web site for details.

Teaching Methods: *Computers:* e-mail. *TV:* PBS. *Other:* audiotapes, fax, correspondence, independent study, individual study learning contracts.

Credits Granted for: experiential learning, portfolio assessment, extrainstitutional learning (PONSI, corporate or professional association seminars/workshops), examination (CLEP, ACT-PEP, DANTES, GRE).

Admission Requirements: *Undergraduate:* must be licensed Registered Nurse with 2-year associate degree or 3-year diploma degree.

On-Campus Requirements: classes are held one day/week during the day at the chosen site location; you must travel to home campus (LaCrosse) for a one-day computer class during your education.

Tuition and Fees: *Undergraduate:* $265/credit. *Application Fees:* $15. *Graduation Fee:* $100. *Other Costs:* $5/credit resource fee; books. *Credit by:* semester.

Financial Aid: Federal Stafford Loan, Federal Pell Grant, VA, state programs for residents of Wisconsin.

Accreditation: National League for Nursing.

Description: Viterbo University (1890) is a Catholic, Franciscan institution that embraces persons of all faiths and offers professional and preprofessional education within a liberal arts experience. It had its antecedents in the early academic endeavors of the Franciscan Sisters of Perpetual Education. The school was named for the Italian town from which its patron saint, Rose of Viterbo, lived. The founding Franciscan sisters were among the first to train skilled and competent nurses for the area's frontier infirmaries and earliest hospitals. Today, the Viterbo School of Nursing keeps pace with the changing currents in modern health care, and the changing faces of nurses and nursing. The RN to BSN program allows working nurses with busy schedules to earn their degree in 3 years or less, attending class one day per week, in one of 10 sites throughout Wisconsin. Faculty and advisors are on-site, bringing their expertise to classrooms where students interact and learn from them and from their classmates, other nursing professionals.

Volunteer State Community College

1480 Nashville Pike	Phone: (615) 230-5145
Gallatin, TN 37066	Fax: (615) 451-5843

Division(s): Distance Learning
Web Site(s): http://www.vscc.cc.tn.us
E-mail: Skip.Sparkman@vscc.cc.tn.us

Undergraduate Degree Programs: Contact school.

Class Titles: Accounting, Drugs and Solutions, Medical Terms, Astronomy, Biology, Business, Business Law, Chemistry, Microcomputer Literacy, Visual Basic, Microcomputer Spreadsheets, Microcomputer Databases, Speech Communication, Public Speaking, Basic Math, Economics, English Composition, Intro. to Theater and Film, French, Geography, Physical Geology, Personal Health, Nutrition, History, Basic Sanitation, Hospitality Supervision, Legal Assisting, Geometry, College Algebra, Calculus, Management, Physical Education Walking, Political Science, Intro. to Natural Science, Psychology, Industrial Psychology, Child Psychology, Sociology, Spanish.

Teaching Methods: *Computers:* Internet, real-time chat, electronic classroom, e-mail, CD-ROM, newsgroup. *TV:* videotape, cable program. *Other:* videoconferencing.

Credits Granted for: experiential learning, portfolio assessment, extrainstitutional learning (PONSI, corporate or professional association seminars/workshops), examination (CLEP, ACT-PEP, DANTES, GRE).

Admission Requirements: Contact school for details.

Tuition and Fees: *Undergraduate:* $56/credit. *Credit by:* semester.

Financial Aid: Federal Stafford Loan, Federal Perkins Loan, Federal PLUS Loan, Federal Pell Grant, Federal Work-Study, VA, state programs for residents of Tennessee.

Accreditation: Southern Association of Colleges and Schools.

Description: Volunteer State Community College (1970) is a public 2-year community college in Gallatin, Tennessee, serving a 12-county region. Volunteer State is accredited by the Commission on Colleges of the Southern Association of Colleges and Schools and holds membership in the American Association of Community and Junior Colleges and the Tennessee College Association. The college grants associate degrees and certificates of credit and is committed to excellence in disseminating knowledge and skills necessary in achieving lifelong goals: Providing undergraduate, technical, and continuing education: Providing community services and promoting cultural and economic development: and preparing a diverse student population for successful careers, university transfer public service programs, and meaningful civic participation. Volunteer State encourages students to think critically and creatively, communicate clearly, to develop leadership and ethical standards, and compete effectively in the global community.

Walden University

155 Fifth Avenue S
Minneapolis, MN 55401

Phone: (866) 4WALDEN
Fax: (612) 338-5092

Division(s): Academic Affairs
Web Site(s): http://www.waldenu.edu
E-mail: info@waldenu.edu

Graduate Degree Programs:
Master of Science in:
Education
Psychology
Public Health

Doctoral Degree Programs:
Doctorate in:
Psychology
Applied Management and Decision Sciences
Education
Health Services
Human Services

Certificate Programs: Professional Postdoctoral Psychology.

Teaching Methods: *Computers:* Internet, real-time chat, electronic classroom, e-mail, CD-ROM, newsgroup, LIST-SERV. *TV:* videotape, cable program, satellite broadcasting, PBS. *Other:* audioconferencing, videoconferencing, audiotapes, fax, correspondence, independent study, individual study, learning contracts.

Admission Requirements: bachelor's and/or master's degree from a regionally accredited institution; 2–3 years' relevant work experience.

On-Campus Requirements: Doctoral programs require academic residencies, face-to-face sessions held throughout the year at numerous locations around the United States. Some master's programs have certain courses and specializations with residency requirements. Doctoral students must complete a new student orientation and 2-week summer session residency.

Tuition and Fees: *Graduate:* Ph.D. in Education, Health Services, Human Services, Applied Management, and Decision Sciences $3,355/quarter. Ph.D. in Professional Psychology $320/credit hour. M.S. in Education (Quarter Based Program) $240/quarter credit hour. M.S. in Education (Semester Based Program) $250/semester credit hour. M.S. in Public Health $310/quarter credit hour. M.S. in Psychology $320/quarter credit hour.

Financial Aid: Federal Stafford Loan, VA. Financial assistance is also available through group enrollment discounts, spousal assistance, and in the form of Higher Education Professional Development Fellowships.

Accreditation: North Central Association of Colleges and Schools.

Description: Walden University (1970) provides high-quality distance graduate education. Students have considerable flexibility in shaping their course of study, enabling them to apply what they learn directly to their professions. Walden students engage in self-directed research, and they schedule classes in consultation with their faculty mentor, or in interaction with other residency students, using today's technology. MS degrees in Psychology and Education can be completed in as little as 18 months and are delivered completely online. Most doctoral students earn their PhD within 3 years in Management, Psychology, Education, Health Services, and Human Services. Currently the university enrolls 1,200 students from all 50 states and 20 foreign countries, and one-third of the students are from minority groups. Walden has 2 office locations: The Office of Academic Affairs in Minneapolis, Minnesota, and the Office of Administration and Finance in Bonita Springs, Florida.

Walla Walla College

204 S. College Avenue
College Place, WA 99324

Phone: (509) 527-2520
Fax: (509) 527-2253

Division(s): Director of Distance Education
Web Site(s): http://you.wwc.edu/
E-mail: bullda@wwc.edu

Undergraduate Degree Programs: Contact school.

Graduate Degree Programs: Contact school.

Class Titles: Teaching Culturally Diverse Students, Web Page Design/Construction, Personal Computing, Software Applications, Computer Literacy, MS Word, MS Excel, MS Access, MS PowerPoint, Corel WordPerfect, StarOffice, Screenwriting, History of Adventism, Comparative Theories of Social Work Practice.

Teaching Methods: *Computers:* Internet, real-time chat, electronic classroom, e-mail, CD-ROM. *TV:* videotape. *Other:* videoconferencing, audioconferencing, audiographics, audiotapes, fax, correspondence, independent study, individual study, learning contracts.

Credits Granted for: examination (CLEP, ACT-PEP, DANTES, GRE).

Admission Requirements: *Undergraduate:* see catalog for degree requirements at http://www.wwc.edu/. *Graduate:* see catalog for degree requirements at http://www.wwc.edu/.

On-Campus Requirements: residency requirements for graduation (final 3 quarters of study).

Tuition and Fees: *Undergraduate:* $381/credit. *Graduate:* $381/credit. *Application Fees:* $30 undergraduate, $40 graduate. *Software:* required for some Distance courses. *Credit by:* quarter.

Financial Aid: Federal Stafford Loan, Federal Perkins Loan, Federal PLUS Loan, Federal Pell Grant, Federal Work-Study, VA.

Accreditation: Northwest Association of Schools and Colleges.

Description: Walla Walla College (1892) is a center of higher learning founded and supported by the Seventh-day Adventist Church. The college is committed to quality Christian education in the Seventh-day Adventist tradition. The Distance Learning opportunities at WWC are designed to serve the adult learner who would otherwise be unable to attend courses on campus.

Walla Walla Community College

500 Tausick Way	Phone: (509) 527-4583
Walla Walla, WA 99362	Fax: (509) 527-4325

Division(s): Distance Learning
Web Site(s): http://www.wallawalla.cc
E-mail: distance.learning@wallawalla.cc

Undergraduate Degree Programs:
Associates of Arts
Associates of Science

Certificate Programs: Advanced Office Skills, Administrative Assistant (medical, financial, legal and executive), Bookkeeper, Business Software Specialist, Office Aide, Office Assistant, Phlebotomy, Word Processing, and MOUS.

Teaching Methods: Online, Web enhanced, ITV (interactive television), correspondence, independent study, telecourses.

Credits Granted for: examination (course challenge, CLEP).

Admission Requirements: *Undergraduate:* open to all students, ASSET placement tests for English and math for all degree-seeking students, additional fees for out-of-state students. *Certificate:* same as undergraduate.

On-Campus Requirements: None.

Tuition and Fees: *Undergraduate:* $62.70/credit Washington resident, $62.70/credit Oregon and Idaho residents up to 6 credits. Oregon and Idaho residents taking over 6 credits pay $89.30/credit. *Application Fee:* $40. *Other Costs:* $3/credit (maximum of 10 credits) technology fees. *Credit by:* quarter.

Financial Aid: Federal Stafford Loan, Federal Perkins Loan, Federal PLUS Loan, Federal Pell Grant, Federal Work-Study, VA, Washington resident programs.

Accreditation: Northwest Association of Schools and Colleges.

Description: Walla Walla Community College (1967) serves a 4-county region of southeastern Washington State that is largely rural and diverse. In spite of having a service area 150 miles wide and 80 miles long, WWCC is proud to maintain one of the highest service levels per capita among the community and technical colleges in the state. Distance learning is the focus and a priority as a means to continue offering college, continuing, and community education opportunities to our district and beyond. WWCC is proud of its partnerships with John Deere, Cisco Systems, and Microsoft, Eastern Washington University, and Washington State University, and is looking to distance learning to extend these partnerships and create new ones in turf management, irrigation technology, agriculture, computer science, and the sciences.

Washington State University

Van Doren 104/PO Box 645220	Phone: (509) 335-3557
Pullman, WA 99163-5220	(800) 222-4978
	Fax: (509) 335-4850

Division(s): Extended University Services
Web Site(s): http://www.distance.wsu.edu
E-mail: ddpsvc@wsu.edu

Undergraduate Degree Programs:
Bachelor of Arts in:
    Social Sciences
    Human Development
    Business Administration
    Criminal Justice
Bachelor of Science in:
    Agriculture

Certificate Programs: Professional Writing

Teaching Methods: *Computers:* Internet, real-time chat, electronic classroom, e-mail, CD-ROM, LISTSERV. *TV:* videotape, cable program, satellite broadcasting, PBS. *Other:* radio broadcast, videoconferencing, audioconferencing, audiographics, audiotapes, fax, correspondence, independent study, individual study, learning contracts.

Credits Granted for: examination (CLEP, ACT-PEP, DANTES, GRE).

Admission Requirements: *Undergraduate:* Must have 27 semester (40 quarter) accredited, transferable, college credits with a 2.0 GPA. *Graduate:* bachelor's degree from a fully accredited academic institution. All courses with an x after their number (flexible enrollment courses) may be taken at any time and one does not have to apply to the university in order to register for them. Students interested in semester-based courses may apply to Washington State University as a "nondegree seeking student." This process only takes a few days.

On-Campus Requirements: None.

Tuition and Fees: *Undergraduate:* Flexible enrollment courses: $130/credit hour. Semester based courses: Washington residents: $183/credit hour (2 credit minimum). Nonresidents: $274/credit hour (2 credit minimum). Please note: Tuition costs are set in the fall of each academic year. *Graduate:* Flexible enrollment: $130/credit hour; Semester based: Washington resident: $283/credit hour (2 credit minimum). Nonresident: $425/credit hour (2 credit minimum). *Application Fee:* $35. *Software:* varies with courses. *Graduation Fee:* $30.85 graduation application fee. Distance Degree students are welcomed and encouraged to come to campus and walk in graduation. Cap and gown fee for those who choose to walk: $25.99. *Other Costs:* Additional charges for textbooks, audiotapes, and/or videotapes and required course guides vary by course; $40 course charge for foreign mailing. *Credit by:* semester.

Financial Aid: Federal Stafford Loan, Federal Perkins Loan, Federal PLUS Loan, Federal Pell Grant, Federal Work-Study, VA, Washington resident programs.

Accreditation: Northwest Association of Schools and Colleges.

Description: Washington State University is a land grant institution established in the 1890s, dedicated to the preparation of students for productive lives and professional careers, to basic and applied research in various fields, and to the dissemination of knowledge. The WSU system is comprised of 4 campuses, with the main campus in Pullman, Washington serving 18,000 students. Branch campuses in Spokane, Tri-cities (Richland, Pasco, and Kennewick), and Vancouver, along with the 10 WSU Learning Centers in various statewide locations, provide interested individuals with an opportunity to partake in the longstanding tradition of educational excellence provided by Washington State University. Established in 1992 as a means of providing laid-off timber workers with an opportunity to earn a degree at a distance, WSU's Distance Degree Programs (DDP) has grown by approximately 20% per year. From one degree offered at 4 sites to 50 students, DDP now offers 5 bachelor's and one master's degree completely at a distance. DDP is used in the distance degree delivery industry as a model of outstanding student services.

Washington University

Campus Box 1064, One Brookings Drive	Phone: (314) 935-6700
St. Louis, MO 63130-4899	Fax: (314) 935-4847

Division(s): University College (evening division of Arts and Sciences)
Web Site(s): http://www.artsci.wustl.edu/~ucollege/
E-mail: ehrlich@artsci.wustl.edu

Undergraduate Degree Programs: Contact school.

Graduate Degree Programs: Contact school.

Certificate Programs: Contact school.

Class Titles: Applied Statistics Online.

Teaching Methods: *Computers:* Internet, real-time chat, electronic classroom, e-mail, CD-ROM, newsgroup, LISTSERV.

Credits Granted for: examination (CLEP, ACT-PEP, DANTES, GRE).

Admission Requirements: *Undergraduate:* high school diploma or equivalent, application, and essay. *Graduate:* bachelor's degree, application, and essay. *Certificate:* high school diploma or equivalent for undergraduate certificates, bachelor's degree for advanced certificates, application, and essay.

Tuition and Fees: *Undergraduate:* $295/credit. *Application Fee:* $30 application fee for degree study. *Credit by:* semester.

Financial Aid: Federal Stafford Loan, Federal Perkins Loan, Federal PLUS Loan, Federal Pell Grant, Federal Work-Study, VA, state programs for residents of Missouri.

Accreditation: North Central Association of Colleges and Secondary Schools.

Description: University College (1931), formally established in 1931, is the evening division of Arts and Sciences at Washington University in St. Louis, which was founded in 1853. We offer 15 undergraduate and 6 graduate degree programs, as well as 8 certificate programs. Students may pursue their studies on a credit or noncredit basis, and complement their courses with a variety of professional development workshops, lecture series, and symposia. Historically offering courses and programs rich in the liberal arts, University College also continues a rich tradition of interdisciplinary curricula, including management studies, health care, communication, and information technology. During the next several years, we plan to offer additional Distance Learning courses fully online as well as others that include web-based components.

Washington University School of Medicine

Campus Box 8063, 660 S. Euclid Avenue	Phone: (314) 362-6891
St. Louis, MO 63110-1093	Fax: (314) 362-1087

Division(s): Continuing Medical Education
Web Site(s): http://cme.wustl.edu
E-mail: cme@msnotes.wustl.edu

Postgraduate Degree Programs:
Washington University designates this educational activity for a maximum of (to be determined) hours in Category 1 credit

toward the AMA Physicians' Recognition Award. Each physician should claim only those hours of credit that he or she actually spent in the educational activity.

Class Titles: Contact school or check web site for details.

Teaching Methods: *Computers:* Internet, real-time chat, electronic classroom, e-mail, CD-ROM, newsgroup, LISTSERV. *TV:* satellite broadcasting. *Other:* videoconferencing, audioconferencing, audiotapes, fax, correspondence, independent study, individual study, learning contracts.

Credits Granted for: seminars/workshops.

Admission Requirements: Contact school for details.

On-Campus Requirements: None.

Tuition and Fees: *Postgraduate:* fee is $15/credit hour. *Credit by:* hour.

Accreditation: Accreditation Council for Continuing Medical Education to provide continuing medical education for physicians.

Description: Washington University School of Medicine was founded in 1891; Accreditation Council for Continuing Medical Education was founded in 1981. Washington University School of Medicine holds a rich history of success in research, education, and patient care, earning it a reputation as one of the premier medical schools in the world. Since its founding in 1891, the school has trained nearly 6,000 physicians and has contributed ground-breaking discoveries in many areas of medical research. Continuing Medical Education (CME) at Washington University School of Medicine (WUSM) is responsible for providing high-quality CME activities to academic, community, and alumni physicians necessary to fulfill their educational requirements for license renewal. CME-Online.wustl.edu became available in June, 2000. It was designed and implemented to meet the educational needs of physicians through the utilization of the Internet. Specific goals have been developed to ensure high quality and easily accessible activities.

Waubonsee Community College

Route 47 at Waubonsee Drive	Phone: (630) 466-5711
Sugar Grove, IL 60554	Fax: (630) 466-9691

Division(s): Program Development and Alternative Learning
Web Site(s): http://www.wcc.cc.il.us
Registration Information: http://www.wcc.cc.il.us/schedules/4ways.html
Counseling and Advising: http://www.wcc.cc.il.us/directory/counseling.html
Distance Learning Contact/Online support: http://www.wcc.cc.il.us/onlinecourses/

Undergraduate Degree Programs: Contact school.

Class Titles: *Online Courses:* Financial Accounting, Managerial Accounting, Medical Terms for Health Occupations, Art Appreciation, Introduction to Biology Introduction to Business, C++ Programming Business Information Systems, Introduction to Java, Networking Essentials, UNIX Operating System, Introduction to Criminal Justice, Criminal Law, Foundations of Early Childhood Education, Introduction to Economics Principles of Economics—Macroeconomics, Principles of Economics—Microeconomics, English Review, Freshman English I, Freshman English II, British Literature from 1800, Masterpieces of British Literature, World Literature Survey of Earth Science, ESL Online—Intermediate I, Principles of Finance, American History to 1877, Basic Substance Abuse and Treatment, Principles of Management, Human Resources Management, Elementary Algebra, Intermediate Algebra, Basic Statistics, College Algebra, Introduction to American Government, Introduction to Psychology, Orientation to Deafness, Introduction to American Deaf Culture, Introduction to Sociology, Theatre in America: A Reflection of Race and Ethnicity, Web Server Programming.

Teaching Methods: *Computers:* Internet, real-time chat, electronic classroom, e-mail, CD-ROM, newsgroup, LISTSERV. All are provided within our online courses. *TV:* videotape, cable program, satellite broadcasting, PBS. *Other:* radio broadcast, videoconferencing, audioconferencing, audiographics, audiotapes, fax, correspondence, independent study, individual study, learning contracts. The following courses are structured to be both TV videotaped and satellite broadcast: Introduction to Astronomy, Introduction to Biology, Introduction to Business, Principles of Economics—Microeconomics, Principles of Economics—Macroeconomics, Oceanus, World Regional Geography, Personal Wellness, European Civilization Since 1648, American History Since 1877, Survey of the Humanities, Principles of Management, Challenge and Change in Life/Career Planning, Introduction to World Religions (Telecourse only), Introduction to American Government, Introduction to Psychology, Child Psychology, Abnormal Psychology, Introduction to Sociology, Marriage and the Family, Elementary Spanish I, Elementary Spanish II.

Credits Granted for: experiential learning, portfolio assessment, extrainstitutional learning (PONSI, corporate or professional association seminars/workshops), examination (CLEP, ACT-PEP, DANTES, GRE).

Admission Requirements: *Undergraduate:* Waubonsee Community College welcomes all who can benefit from the courses and programs offered. Full-time registrants are required to fill out an application and take full assessment for appropriate course placement. *Application Processing Fee:* $10. Part-time special students may take up to 11 credit hours per semester and no application is required. For greater detail on registering for classes, visit our web page at www.wcc.cc.il.us.

On-Campus Requirements: Many of our online classes do not require students to be on campus. However, depending on the course, proctor examinations may be required either at our location or at a location nearest the student. To find out more about our course requirements, link to our online courses page at http://www.wcc.cc.il.us/onlinecourses/.

Tuition and Fees: *Undergraduate:* $47/credit hour. Out-of-state tuition: $130/credit hour. *Application Fee:* $10. *Software:* $30 online lab fee. *Credit by:* credit hour.

Financial Aid: Federal Stafford Loan, Federal Perkins Loan, Federal PLUS Loan, Federal Pell Grant, Federal Work-Study, VA, state programs for residents of Illinois.

Accreditation: Waubonsee Community College is accredited by the Commission on Institutions of Higher Education of North Central Association of Colleges and Schools and is recognized by federal and state agencies administering financial aid.

Description: Waubonsee Community College (1966) is a public, comprehensive community college, organized as mandated by the Illinois Community College Act, to provide education and training services for individuals within district 516. The area encompasses approximately 600 square miles and has an assessed valuation of more than $2.7 billion. Waubonsee opened its doors for classes in September 1967, with an initial enrollment of 1,603 students: 403 full time and 1,200 part time. The college has grown steadily, currently serving over 10,000 students each semester. Delivery of instruction across the district has expanded through Distance Learning and the Waubonsee Telecommunications Instructional Consortium. As a result of our success, in 1993 the college was named the state's only Center for Distance Learning, highlighting Waubonsee's role in Illinois' initiative to provide enhanced learning opportunities using interactive technology. Being the number one leader in Distance Education, Waubonsee will continue to be at the forefront providing innovative education that will include quality, service, value, and accessibility to all our students.

Waukesha County Technical College

800 Main Street	Phone: (262) 691-5594
Pewaukee, WI 53072	Fax: (262) 691-5047

Division(s): Business Occupations Division
Web Site(s): http://www.wctonline.com
E-mail: lrevoy@waukesha.tec.wi.us

Undergraduate Degree Programs:
Associate Degree in:
    Real Estate Brokerage

Property Management
Financial Planning

Certificate Programs: Wisconsin Residential Appraisal Certification, Wisconsin General Appraisal Certification.

Teaching Methods: *Computers:* Internet, real-time chat, electronic classroom, e-mail. *TV:* videotape, cable program.

Credits Granted for: experiential learning, portfolio assessment, extrainstitutional learning, examination (CLEP, ACT-PEP, DANTES, GRE).

Admission Requirements: *Undergraduate:* Asset test.

On-Campus Requirements: None.

Tuition and Fees: *Undergraduate:* $64/credit. *Application Fee:* $30. *Other Costs:* Internet access. *Credit by:* semester.

Financial Aid: Federal Stafford Loan, Federal PLUS Loan, Federal Pell Grant, Federal Work-Study, VA, Wisconsin resident programs, various scholarships.

Accreditation: North Central Association of Colleges and Schools.

Description: Waukesha County Technical College (1923) has extensive Distance Learning opportunities via the Internet and television/video. In addition to the full Associate of Applied Science degrees mentioned above, more than 50 individual courses are offered each semester. WCTC has more than 40 degree and diploma programs, and serves more than 33,000 students annually.

Wayne County Community College

801 West Fort Street	Phone: (313) 496-2602
Detroit, MI 48226	Fax: (313) 496-8718

Division(s): Distance Learning
Web Site(s): http://www.wccc.edu
E-mail: AdePetri@wccc.edu

Undergraduate Degree Programs:
Associate of Arts
Associate of General Studies

Class Titles: Anthropology, English, Humanities, Sociology, Psychology, Geology, Geography, Business, Management, Marketing, Computer/Information Systems, Political Science, History, Philosophy.

Teaching Methods: *TV:* videotape, cable program, PBS, Interactive TV (ITV). *Other:* E-Learning.

Credits Granted for: experiential learning, examination (CLEP, ACT-PEP, DANTES, GRE).

Admission Requirements: *Undergraduate:* age 18.

On-Campus Requirements: Telecourse requires attendance at 4–6 on-campus sessions for each course. ITV is on campus.

Tuition and Fees: *Undergraduate:* $54 in-district, $70/other MI residents, $89/out-of-state. *Application Fee:* $10. *Other Costs:* $20 one-time testing fee, $25/registration fee, $2/credit activity fee. *Credit by:* semester.

Financial Aid: Federal Stafford Loan, Federal Pell Grant, Federal Work-Study, VA, Michigan resident programs, Michigan Adult Part-time Grant, Michigan College Work-Study, Michigan Educational Opportunity Grant, Michigan Tuition Incentive Program.

Accreditation: North Central Association of Colleges and Schools.

Description: Wayne County Community College District (1967) first offered courses in rented facilities throughout Wayne County. Today the district is comprised of 5 comprehensive campuses. Three telecourses were first offered in the fall of 1978. Since that time, the distance learning program has expanded to include 30 telecourses, allowing students to complete Associate of Arts or Associate of General Studies degrees exclusively through telecourse instruction. Interactive TV courses were introduced in the winter of 1997 and are offered at 2 of our 5 campuses. Satellite downlink capabilities are also available at one of our campuses.

Weber State University

4005 University Circle	**Phone: (800) 848-7770 x6785**
Ogden, UT 84408-4005	**(801) 626-6785**
	Fax: (801) 626-8035

Division(s): Office of Distance Learning
Web Site(s): http://www.weber.edu/dist-learn
E-mail: dist-learn@weber.edu

Undergraduate Degree Programs:
Associate of Science in:
  Respiratory Therapy
  General Studies
  Criminal Justice
Associate of Applied Science in:
  Respiratory Therapy
  Clinical Laboratory Science
  Health Information Technology
Bachelor of Science in:
  Health Services Administration
  Health Promotion
  Health Information Management

  Clinical Laboratory Science
  Health Information Technology
  Radiologic Sciences
  Respiratory Therapy

Certificate Programs: Radiologic Sciences, Respiratory Therapy, Health Information Technology, APICS—Production Inventory Management.

Class Titles: Survey of Accounting, Anthropology, Plants in Human Affairs, Business/Society, Chemistry, Human Development, Mass Communication, Mass Media/Society, Criminal Justice, Writing, Blueprint Reading, Developmental Writing, Technical Writing, Creative Writing, Literature, Personal Finance, Meteorology, Gerontology, Healthy Lifestyles, Human Sexuality, Nutrition, Medical Terminology, Biomedical Core Lecture/Lab, Biomedical Principles: Certificate of Completion for Paramedics, Pathophysiology, World History to 1500 c.e., World History: 1500 c.e. to Present, American Civilizations, U.S. Diplomatic History, 20th-Century U.S. Since 1945, Far Eastern History, Middle Eastern History, History of Africa, History of Utah, 20th-Century Europe, Design for Living, Intermediate Algebra, Organizational Behavior/Management, Music, Diet Therapy, Philosophy, Fitness for Life, American National Government, International Politics, Public Administration, Psychology, Psychology of Adjustment, Interpersonal Relationships, Biopsychology, Conditioning/Learning, Theories of Personality, Social Psychology, General Psychology, Counseling Theories, Selling Techniques, Retail Merchandising/Buying Methods, Distribution Principles, Fashion Merchandising, Credit/Collection Methods, Advertising Methods, Customer Service Techniques, Ethical Sales/Service, Principles of Supervision, Principles of Sociology, Social Problems.

Teaching Methods: *Computers:* Internet, real-time chat, e-mail, CD-ROM. *TV:* videotape. *Other:* videoconferencing, audiotapes, fax, correspondence, independent study, individual study, learning contracts.

Credits Granted for: extrainstitutional learning, examination (CLEP, ACT-PEP, DANTES, GRE).

Admission Requirements: *Undergraduate:* high school graduation or GED; ACT, SAT, or placement test. ARRT certification for bachelor's or certificate in Radiologic Science. Clinical Laboratory Science students must be working clinical laboratory technician.

On-Campus Requirements: None.

Tuition and Fees: *Undergraduate:* Correspondence: $99/semester credit. For online class tuition information see web site. *Application Fee:* $30 ($45 international). $10 more for degree- or certificate-seeking students. *Other Costs:* books. *Credit by:* semester.

Financial Aid: Federal Stafford Loan, Federal Perkins Loan, Federal PLUS Loan, Federal Pell Grant, Federal Work-Study, VA.

Accreditation: Northwest Association of Schools and Colleges.

Description: Weber State University was founded in 1889 and is situated in the foothills of the Wasatch Mountains overlooking Ogden. With a current student body of 16,000, Weber is recognized as a metropolitan university providing programs for students with varied interests and educational goals. Continuing Education developed the distance learning program for people who cannot attend regularly scheduled university courses. Through this self-paced, individualized program, students can meet degree requirements, enhance their professional skills, and achieve their personal goals. Weber State is committed to offering its students quality courses through correspondence, providing excellent customer service, and developing lasting relationships among students, faculty, and staff.

West Hills Community College

300 Cherry Lane	Phone: (800) 266-1114
Coalinga, CA 93210	Fax: (559) 935-2633

Division(s): Learning Resources
Web Site(s): http://www.westhills.com
E-mail: helpdesk@westhillscollege.com

Class Titles: Health, Computer Information Systems, Geography, Math, Psychology, Business, History, English, Political Science, Sociology, Administration of Justice, Economics, Social Science, Sociology.

Teaching Methods: *Computers:* Internet, e-mail, real-time chat, electronic classroom, CD-ROM. *TV:* videotape, cable program, satellite broadcasting, PBS. *Other:* videoconferencing.

Admission Requirements: *Undergraduate:* 18 years of age or high school graduate. *Certificate:* 18 years of age or high school graduate.

On-Campus Requirements: None.

Tuition and Fees: *Undergraduate:* $11/credit. *Credit by:* semester.

Financial Aid: Federal Stafford Loan, Federal Perkins Loan, Federal PLUS Loan, Federal Pell Grant, Federal Work-Study, VA, California resident programs.

Accreditation: Western Association of Schools and Colleges.

Description: West Hills Community College (1932) is committed to serving Distance Learning students. Online course offerings are expanding each semester and online student

services are as well. You can apply and register for classes online at www.westhillscollege.com.

West Los Angeles College

9000 Overland Drive	Phone: (310) 287-4200
Culver City, CA 90230	Fax: (310) 841-0396

Division(s): Distance Learning Program
Web Site(s): http://www.wlac.cc.ca
E-mail: ichone@wmail.wlac.cc.ca.us

Undergraduate Degree Programs:
Associate of Arts
Associate of Science

Certificate Programs: Administration of Justice, Dental Assistance and Travel.

Class Titles: Administration of Justice, Child Development, Cooperative Education, Dental Hygiene, English, Learning Skills, Multimedia, Music, Personal Development, Political Science, Travel.

Teaching Methods: *Computers:* Internet, real-time chat, electronic classroom, e-mail, threaded discussion. *Other:* classes taught via videoconferencing and by satellite.

Credits Granted for: transfer of credit earned through another accredited college's Credit by Examination Program and Directed Studies (guided independent studies).

Admission Requirements: *Undergraduate:* any student who will profit from the instruction; minors must have parental or high school counselor permission. *Certificate:* administration of Justice, Dental Assistance, and Travel.

On-Campus Requirements: None.

Tuition and Fees: *Undergraduate:* $11/unit for California residents, $134/unit for nonresidents. *Application Fees:* no Application, Enrollment, or Capital Improvement fees for California residents, $11/unit Enrollment Fee and $9 per unit Capital Improvements Fee for nonresidents. *Other Costs:* $1/semester Student Representation Fee and $8 (summer semester) or $11 (spring and fall semesters) Health Fee for all students. *Credit by:* semester.

Financial Aid: Federal Stafford Loan, Federal Perkins Loan, Federal Pell Grant, Federal Work-Study, Cal Grant.

Accreditation: Accreditation Commission for Community and Junior Colleges.

Description: West Los Angeles College (1969) is a fully accredited, 2-year college serving more than 11,000 students in Los Angeles offering a comprehensive variety of academic programs leading to an associate degree and completion of the first 2 years toward baccalaureate degree. Academic programs include the Distance Learning Program, the Transfer Alliance (Honors) Program, the Program for Accelerated College Education, and Weekend College. Vocational programs include Aircraft Maintenance Technology, Dental Hygiene, Travel and Tourism, Business, Child Development, Computer Science, Art, Computer Design, and Public Safety, including law enforcement and corrections as well as fire science and emergency medical training. West Los Angeles College began offering courses via videoconferencing in 1999. In 2000, in addition to courses offered via videoconferencing, courses were offered both online and via satellite. West Los Angeles College continues to offer courses via videoconferencing and by satellite and will offer 20 online courses in spring 2002. Online certificate programs in Administration of Justice, Dental Assistance, and Travel are currently being developed.

West Shore Community College

| 3000 N Stiles Rd | Phone: (231) 845-6211 x3106 |
| Scottville, MI 49454-0277 | Fax: (231) 845-0207 |

Division(s): Distance Learning
Web Site(s): http://www.westshore.cc.mi.us
E-mail: pldavidson@westshore.cc.mi.us

Undergraduate Degree Programs:
Associate's in Criminal Justice (does not include Police certification)

Class Titles: Introduction to Business, Small Business Management, Principles of Management, Principles of Retailing, Advertising, Principles of Marketing, Keyboarding, Intermediate Algebra, English Composition I and II, General Geology, General Biology I and II, Introduction to Shakespeare, Principles of Sociology, Introduction to Criminal Investigation (January 2002), Introduction to Criminal Justice (January 2002), Police Administration (January 2002), Juvenile Offender (January 2002), Evidence and Criminal Process (January 2002), Criminal Law (January 2002), Police Operations (January 2002), Introduction to Security (January 2002).

Teaching Methods: *Computers:* Internet, real-time chat, electronic classroom, e-mail, CD-ROM, newsgroup, LISTSERV. *TV:* videotape, cable program, satellite broadcasting, PBS. *Other:* radio broadcast, videoconferencing, audioconferencing, audiographics, audiotapes, fax, correspondence, independent study, individual study, learning contracts.

Credits Granted for: experiential learning, portfolio assessment, extrainstitutional learning (PONSI, corporate or professional association seminars/workshops), examination (CLEP, ACT-PEP, DANTES, GRE).

Admission Requirements: Contact school for details.

On-Campus Requirements: None; may have to take proctored exams.

Tuition and Fees: *Undergraduate:* $54.50/credit in-district, $84.75/credit out-of-district, $106/credit out-of-state. *Application Fee:* $15. *Other Costs:* $30 technology fee, $20/online class, $5 student services fee; may be other course specific fees. *Credit by:* semester.

Financial Aid: Federal Stafford Loan, Federal Perkins Loan, Federal PLUS Loan, Federal Pell Grant, Federal Work-Study, VA, state programs for residents of Michigan.

Accreditation: North Central Association of Colleges and Schools.

Description: West Shore Community College (1967), through visionary and principled leadership and team empowerment, pursues excellence by delivering high-quality, affordable educational services with student learning as its highest priority. We have been offering online courses since 1998.

West Valley College

| 14000 Fruitvale Avenue | Phone: (408) 741-2065 |
| Saratoga, CA 95070 | Fax: (408) 741-2134 |

Division(s): Instructional Development/Distance Learning
Web Site(s): http://www.westvalley.edu/wvc/dl/DL.HomePage
E-mail: steve_peltz@westvalley.edu

Undergraduate Degree Programs:
Associate of Arts
Associate of Science

Certificate Programs: 66 different programs across the curriculum.

Class Titles: Anthropology, Art Appreciation, Astronomy, Biology, Business Law, Management, Sales, General Business, Marketing, Page Layout, Child Growth/Development, English Composition, French, Spanish, Geology, Health, Nutrition, Physical Fitness, Film Studies, Digital Photography, Oceanography, Political Science, History, Sociology, Web Authoring.

Teaching Methods: *Computers:* Internet, real-time chat, electronic classroom, e-mail, CD-ROM, newsgroup, LISTSERV. *TV:* videotape, cable program, PBS. *Other:* videoconferencing, audiotapes, fax, correspondence, independent study, individual study, learning contracts.

Credits Granted for: extrainstitutional learning, Advanced Placement Program (CEEB), examination (CLEP), Military credit, credit for Certified Professional Secretary rating.

Admission Requirements: *Undergraduate:* Application, high school graduate or age 18 and can profit from instruction, including those who have passed the High School Proficiency Exam or GED. Student must declare a classification: new, continuing, returning (former), new transfer, international, or nonresident. Residency is specifically defined in the college catalog.

On-Campus Requirements: None.

Tuition and Fees: *Undergraduate:* $11/credit California resident, $145/credit out-of-state, $150/credit international. *Application Fee:* $50 for international students. *Other Costs:* $17/semester assorted basic fees. *Credit by:* semester.

Financial Aid: Federal Stafford Loan, Federal Perkins Loan, Federal PLUS Loan, Federal Pell Grant, Federal Work-Study, VA, California resident programs.

Accreditation: Western Association of Schools and Colleges.

Description: West Valley College (1963) is a public community college open to those seeking advanced educational opportunities. Our primary purpose is to facilitate successful learning. We are committed to educating the individual and fostering the economic development of the communities we serve. WVC provides students with opportunities to participate in a wide spectrum of educational experiences designed to fulfill their academic and career needs, enrich the quality of their lives, and develop job skills and other competencies necessary to function and succeed in contemporary society. We have offered distance learning courses for 22 years.

Westark College

5210 Grand	**Phone: (501) 788-7015**
Fort Smith, AR 72903	**Fax: (501) 788-7923**

Division(s): Director, Distance Learning
Web Site(s): http://creative.westark.edu (distance learning), http://www.westark.edu (college web site)
E-mail: advise@westark.edu

Undergraduate Degree Programs:
Associate of Arts (under development)

Class Titles: Microbiology, Integrated PC Application, Computers and Their Applications, Microcomputer Applications, Economics, English I and II, Technical Composition, World Literature I and II, American Literature, Geography, U.S. History, Medical Terminology, Humanities Through the Arts, Keyboarding, Office Procedures, Philosophy, General Psychology, Biological Science (Spring 2002), Chemistry I (Spring 2002), College Algebra (Fall 2001).

Teaching Methods: *Computers:* Internet, real-time chat, electronic classroom, e-mail, CD-ROM, newsgroup, LISTSERV. *TV:* videotape, cable program, satellite broadcasting, PBS.

Other: radio broadcast, videoconferencing, audioconferencing, audiographics, audiotapes, fax, correspondence, independent study, individual study, learning contracts.

Credits Granted for: examination (CLEP, ACT-PEP, DANTES, GRE).

Admission Requirements: *Undergraduate:* students should contact admissions at (501) 788-7120 or visit the web site at www.westark.edu for admissions information.

On-Campus Requirements: Most courses are delivered fully online. Some courses require on-campus labs.

Tuition and Fees: *Undergraduate:* $41/credit (in-district), $52/credit (out-of-district), $102/credit (out-of-state). *Software:* $10. *Other Costs:* Activity Fee: $10. *Credit by:* semester.

Financial Aid: Federal Stafford Loan, Federal Perkins Loan, Federal PLUS Loan, Federal Pell Grant, Federal Work-Study, VA, state programs for residents of Arkansas.

Accreditation: North Central Association of Colleges and Schools.

Description: Westark College (1928), with its University Center and Business and Industrial Institute, is a hybrid college with multifaceted learning opportunities, from single courses of instruction to certificate, 2-year degree programs, and selected bachelor's degrees, ranging in length from a few days to 3 years, offered at times and places convenient to our students and clients. Westark College developed web-based classes in response to the busy lifestyles of our students. The college continues to develop new and exciting alternative delivery methods, as telecommunications technology continues to improve. Students should visit the college web site www.westark.edu for updated courses listings and other information.

Westchester Community College

75 Grasslands Road AD-207	**Phone: (914) 785-6658**
Valhalla, NY 10595	**Fax: (914) 785-6129**

Division(s): Academic Affairs
Web Site(s): http://www.sunywcc.edu
E-mail: lucinda.fleming@sunywcc.edu

Class Titles: Art, Economics (Macro/Micro), World Geography, Western Civilization: Rome–1648, 20th Century U.S. History, American Government/Issues, American Politics/Policies, Psychology, Abnormal Psychology, Developmental Psychology, Sociology, Marriage/ Family, Criminalistics, State/Local Government, Criminal Justice Systems, Telecom, Electrical Circuits, Computer Applications.

Teaching Methods: *Computers:* Internet, real-time chat, electronic classroom, e-mail, CD-ROM, newsgroup, LISTSERV. *TV:* videotape, cable program, satellite broadcasting, PBS. *Other:* videoconferencing.

Admission Requirements: *Undergraduate:* open-enrollment. *Certificate:* open-enrollment.

On-Campus Requirements: depends on the course.

Tuition and Fees: *Undergraduate:* $98/credit in-county, $98/credit out-of-county with certificate of residency, $245/credit out-of-county, out-of-state. *Other Costs:* tuition and fees subject to change. *Credit by:* semester.

Financial Aid: Federal Stafford Loan, Federal Perkins Loan, Federal PLUS Loan, Federal Pell Grant, Federal Work-Study, VA, New York resident programs.

Accreditation: Middle States Association of Colleges and Schools.

Description: In the academic year 1996–97, Westchester Community College (1946) celebrated 50 years of excellence. It enrolls 11,000 full-time and part-time credit students each semester as well as 8,500 noncredit students. Westchester Community College offers distance learning courses as regular credit courses and through the State of New York Learning Network.

Western Baptist College

5000 Deer Park Drive S Salem, OR 97301-9392	Phone: (503) 375-7590 (800) 764-1383 Fax: (503) 375-7583

Division(s): Adult Studies, Biblical Studies
Web Site(s): asd@wbc.edu
E-mail: rtaylor@wbc.edu

Undergraduate Degree Programs:
Management and Communications

Class Titles: Global Perspectives, Bible Study Methods, Human Genetics, Infectious Diseases, Mental Health Track, Budgeting/Financial Planning Track.

Teaching Methods: *Computers:* Internet, real-time chat, electronic classroom, e-mail. *Other:* audioconferencing, fax, correspondence, independent study, individual study, learning contracts.

Credits Granted for: experiential learning, portfolio assessment, life-learning papers, extrainstitutional learning, Professional Schools and Training, examination (CLEP, DANTES, American Council of Education).

Admission Requirements: *Undergraduate:* 62 transferable semester hours that satisfy lower-division requirements, basic computer literacy, writing sample, professional and church references.

On-Campus Requirements: For the management and communication and family studies degree completion program, a 3-day orientation at the school is required. For individual courses, there is no residency requirement.

Tuition and Fees: *Undergraduate:* $280/credit. *Other Costs:* $100 class reservation deposit, $40 late applicant processing fee. *Credit by:* semester.

Financial Aid: Federal Stafford Loan, Federal Perkins Loan, Federal Pell Grant, VA, Oregon resident programs.

Accreditation: Northwest Association of Schools and Colleges.

Description: Western Baptist College (1935) has existed in Salem for the past 32 years as a Christian college offering majors in liberal arts and professional studies. The school originated in Phoenix, Arizona, as a Bible institute. In 1991 Western began offering alternatively formatted, adult degree programs (one night per week) and, building on the success of campus-based programs, expanded into modified (limited residency) distance programs in 1993. Western plans to continue expanding nontraditional, educational opportunities for its wide constituency of Christian young adults and midcareer professionals.

Western Illinois University

1 University Circle Macomb, IL 61455	Phone: (309) 298-2496 Fax: (309) 298-2226

Division(s): School of Extended and Continuing Education
Web Site(s): http://www.wiu.edu/users/misece/
E-mail: robbie_morelli@ccmail.wiu.edu

Undergraduate Degree Programs:
Board of Trustees Bachelor of Arts Degree Program

Graduate Degree Programs: Contact school.

Class Titles: Contact school or check web site for details.

Teaching Methods: *Computers:* Internet, real-time chat, electronic classroom, e-mail, CD-ROM, newsgroup, LISTSERV. *TV:* videotape, PBS. *Other:* correspondence, independent study.

Credits Granted for: experiential learning, portfolio assessment, examination (CLEP, ACT-PEP, DANTES, GRE).

Admission Requirements: *Undergraduate:* high school diploma or GED. *Graduate:* bachelor's degree.

On-Campus Requirements: None.

Tuition and Fees: *Undergraduate:* $99.40/credit. *Graduate:* $108.15/credit. *Other Costs:* $7 for transcript fee. *Credit by:* semester.

Financial Aid: VA, Illinois Veterans Grants, and others depending on course load.

Accreditation: North Central Association of Colleges and Schools.

Description: Western Illinois University (1899) offers programs of study at the undergraduate and graduate levels for traditional students, transfer students, international students, and adults who want to continue their education. Classes are delivered through the traditional classroom setting; through Distance Learning options including independent study, and World Wide Web courses; through travel study; and through weekend courses.

Western Iowa Tech Community College

4647 Stone Ave., P.O. Box 5199	Phone: (712) 274-6400
Sioux City, IA 51102-5199	Fax: (712) 274-6412

Division(s): Distance and Global Education
Web Site(s): http://www.witcc.com
E-mail: dunne@witcc.com

Undergraduate Degree Programs:
Associate of Arts

Graduate Degree Programs: Contact school.

Class Titles: Contact school or check web site for details.

Teaching Methods: *Computers:* Internet, real-time chat, electronic classroom, e-mail, CD-ROM. *TV:* videotape, satellite broadcasting, PBS. *Other:* videoconferencing via the Iowa Communications Network, correspondence, independent study.

Credits Granted for: experiential learning, portfolio assessment, extrainstitutional learning (PONSI, corporate or professional association seminars/workshops), examination (CLEP, ACT-PEP, DANTES, GRE).

Admission Requirements: *Undergraduate:* to register for classes, a student must submit a completed application for admission, pay a nonrefundable $10 processing fee, and submit an official high school transcript showing receipt of a high school diploma, or submit official documentation that a GED has been received. Students who do not have a high school diploma or GED must be tested for ability to benefit. Admission to the college does not guarantee admission into programs or courses. Students must have no outstanding financial or other obligations to the college, and must complete assessment testing unless waived. Applicants must be in good academic standing and cannot have been dismissed from the college for conduct reasons.

On-Campus Requirements: None.

Tuition and Fees: *Undergraduate:* $85/credit. *Application Fees:* $10. *Credit by:* semester.

Financial Aid: Federal Stafford Loan, Federal PLUS Loan, Federal Pell Grant, Federal Work-Study, VA, Iowa Vocational-Technical Tuition Grant, Iowa State Scholarship, Iowa Grant.

Accreditation: North Central Association of Colleges and Schools.

Description: Western Iowa Tech Community College (1966) is a publicly supported college serving the Iowa counties of Cherokee, Crawford, Ida, Monona, Plymouth, and Woodbury, which have a combined population of about 180,000. The first classes began on January 27, 1967, when Western Iowa Tech accepted responsibility for 2 technical and one vocational postsecondary programs then operated by the Sioux City Community Schools. When the college received permission to offer a 2-year Associate of Arts degree at the Sioux City campus, the college curriculum became comprehensive, serving both full- and part-time students. These programs, offered by the Liberal Arts and Transfer Education division, represent one of the fastest growing areas of the college. However, growth is occurring in the vocational technical area of the college as well. The college has been involved in Distance Education since the mid-1980s, when it began offering public television-based telecourses for credit. Since then the college has also become a primary user of the Iowa Communications Network, a state-owned fiber optic network that carries classes on 2-way interactive TV. One year ago WITCC also became a member of the Iowa Community College Online Consortium, enabling it to offer a full roster of liberal arts and business courses online. The college also offers the full menu of noncredit online courses available through Education To Go.

Western Nevada Community College

160 Campus Way	Phone: (775) 423-7565
Fallon, NV 89406	Fax: (775) 423-8029

Division(s): Off Campus Programs
Web Site(s): http://www.wncc.nevada.edu
E-mail: scharman@wncc.nevada.edu

Class Titles: Computer Information Systems, Music Appreciation, Math, Art Appreciation, Biology.

Teaching Methods: *Computers:* Internet, real-time chat, electronic classroom, e-mail, CD-ROM. *TV:* videotape, cable program, satellite broadcasting, PBS. *Other:* videoconferencing, fax, individual study compressed video (interactive video)– geographically sensitive to Nevada.

Credits Granted for: extrainstitutional learning, examination (CLEP, ACT-PEP, DANTES, GRE).

Admission Requirements: *Undergraduate:* age 15 or older and have a high school diploma or GED. *Certificate:* same as undergraduate.

On-Campus Requirements: None.

Tuition and Fees: *Undergraduate:* $40/credit. *Application Fee:* $5. *Other Costs:* $15/credit for interactive video classes, $20/class for Internet and telecourses. *Credit by:* Semester.

Financial Aid: Federal Stafford Loan, Federal PLUS Loan, Federal Pell Grant, Federal Work-Study, VA, Nevada Residency Grant.

Accreditation: Northwest Association of Schools and Colleges.

Description: Western Nevada Community College (1971) is one of 4 community colleges in the state of Nevada. WNCC is governed by the University and Community College System of Nevada Board of Regents. The main campus is located in Carson City, with satellite campuses in Fallon and Gardnerville/Minden. The 19,971 square mile service area is spotted with 7 other instructional centers in Yerington, Hawthorne, Lovelock, Fernley, Virginia City, South Lake Tahoe, and Dayton. The college first began its distance education efforts in 1993 when, with a grant from the Nevada Rural Hospital Project, it started its 2-year Registered Nursing program via interactive video. Since that humble beginning, WNCC now offers more than 18 classes per semester via interactive video joining as many as 9 interactive video classrooms with college courses. In the fall of 1998, the college will begin its first efforts in Internet "online" courses and telecourse "public access" courses. In the spring 1998 semester, more than 400 students registered for distance education courses through Western Nevada Community College.

Western New England College

1219 Wilbraham Road	Phone: (413) 782-1249
Springfield, MA 01119	Fax: (413) 782-1779

Division(s): Continuing Education
Web Site(s): http://www.wnec.edu/CE or http://www.online.wnec.edu/
E-mail: CE@ wnec.edu

Undergraduate Degree Programs:
Bachelor's in Business Administration (BBA)

Graduate Degree Programs: Contact school.

Class Titles: Undergraduate courses have included the following (not every course is available every semester): Computer Information Systems, English (Business Communications), Criminal Justice, Humanities/Cultures courses, Marketing, Psychology (Intro and Learning), Sociology (several electives). Graduate courses have included the following: Accounting, Computer Information Systems, Management (Organizational Theory, Human Resource Management), Marketing.

Teaching Methods: *Computers:* Internet, real-time chat, electronic classroom, e-mail, CD-ROM, newsgroup, LISTSERV. *Other:* fax, correspondence, independent study.

Credits Granted for: experiential learning, portfolio assessment (to be developed), extrainstitutional learning when ACE recognized (PONSI, corporate or professional association).

Admission Requirements: *Undergraduate:* proof of high school graduation; minimum 2.0 GPA; there may be additional requirements depending on the degree. *Graduate:* all require undergraduate degree from an accredited college. School of Business MBA and MS programs require GMATs (GREs and LSATs also accepted) along with foundation requirements; Master of Science in Criminal Justice Administration (MSCJA) offered through the off-campus programs requires in-service law enforcement background; GREs and minimum 2.8 undergraduate GPA required for School of Arts and Sciences Master's in Public administration (MPA) program. *Certificate:* postgraduate certificates available in business and engineering.

On-Campus Requirements: None.

Tuition and Fees: *Undergraduate:* $188/credit. *Graduate:* $357/credit. *Application Fee:* $30. *Software:* additional charges may apply. *Credit by:* semester.

Financial Aid: Federal Stafford Loan, Federal Perkins Loan, Federal PLUS Loan, Federal Pell Grant, Federal Work-Study, VA, state programs for residents of Massachusetts.

Accreditation: New England Association of Schools and Colleges, School of Business is in candidacy for accreditation by American Assembly of Collegiate Schools of Business, Bachelor of Science in Engineering programs area accredited by Accreditation Board for Engineering and Technology.

Description: Western New England College (1919) has been involved in Distance Education for the past 4 years. The college employs a user-friendly, homegrown software program known as Manhattan to provide Distance Learning opportunities to students. Manhattan was developed by Steve Narmontas, Manager of the College's Educational Technology Center in 1997. The software has been receiving excellent reviews not only on campus but nationally and internationally as well. It was recently released for public use over the Internet and has been downloaded for free by hundreds of users.

Western Oklahoma State College

2801 North Main	Phone: (580) 477-7914
Altus OK 73521	Fax: (580) 477-7861

Division(s): Distance Learning
Web Site(s): http://western.cc.ok.us (main menu)
E-mail: ietv@western.cc.ok.us

Undergraduate Degree Programs:
Associate of Arts—Liberal Arts

Class Titles: Primarily general education courses.

Teaching Methods: *Computers:* Internet, real-time chat, electronic classroom, e-mail. *TV:* videotape, cable program. *Other:* videoconferencing (we call it Interactive Television).

Credits Granted for: experiential learning, extrainstitutional learning (PONSI, corporate or professional association (selected) examination CLEP, ACT-PEP, DANTES, GRE). Extra institutional learning is limited to 30 semester hours.

Admission Requirements: *Undergraduate:* any individual who has graduated from an accredited high school or obtained a GED, and has met high school curricular requirements listed in the catalog, and has participated in American College Testing (ACT) or similar acceptable test battery is eligible for admission. The GED recipient's high school class must have graduated to be eligible for admission. *Certificate:* same as for undergraduate.

On-Campus Requirements: It is not required, but students may wish to take classes that are not offered by Distance Learning.

Tuition and Fees: *Undergraduate:* $45/credit. *Application Fee:* $15. *Software:* variable. *Graduation Fee:* $10. *Other Costs:* $4/semester Student ID fee, $7.50/semester hour for telecourses (videotape-based). There is a developmental fee of $13/semester hour for all "0" level courses. In addition, lab fees apply for appropriate lab courses. *Credit by:* semester.

Financial Aid: Federal Stafford Loan, Federal Perkins Loan, Federal PLUS Loan, Federal Pell Grant, Federal Work-Study, VA, state programs for residents of Oklahoma.

Accreditation: Higher Learning Commission; member North Central Association of Colleges and Schools.

Description: Western Oklahoma State College (1926) is a comprehensive 2-year college serving primarily southwest Oklahoma. Established as Altus Junior College it is the oldest municipal 2-year college in Oklahoma. Altus Junior College became a state junior college in 1970, built a new campus in 1971, and in 1974 became a state community college and assumed the name Western Oklahoma State College. On campus, Western offers Associate of Science, Associate of Arts, Associate of Applied Science degrees, and a Certificate of Mastery—Child Development Assistant. Two-way Interactive Television courses began in 1998 with broadcasts to 3 high school sites. Western currently broadcasts to multiple high school receive sites as well as several technology centers and a university within the state. Western currently has limited online courses, but has several in development. Telecourses during fall and spring semesters are broadcast by the Oklahoma Educational Television Authority. Western Oklahoma State College is committed to expanding its Distance Learning course offerings.

Western Oregon University

345 North Monmouth Avenue	Phone: (503) 838-8483
Monmouth, OR 97361	Fax: (503) 838-8473

Division(s): Extended Programs
Web Site(s): http://www.wou.edu/provost/extprogram/
E-mail: extend@wou.edu

Undergraduate Degree Programs:
Bachelor of Arts/Bachelor of Science in Fire Services Administration

Graduate Degree Programs:
Master of Arts in Teaching
Master of Science in Special Education

Class Titles: Courses not associated with a degree program are in Writing, Psychology, Anthropology, Education.

Teaching Methods: *Computers:* Internet, real-time chat, electronic classroom, e-mail, CD-ROM, newsgroup, LISTSERV. *TV:* videotape, IP video broadcasting, PBS. *Other:* videoconferencing, fax, correspondence, independent study, individual study.

Credits Granted for: examination.

Admission Requirements: *Undergraduate:* call Admissions. *Graduate:* call Admissions.

On-Campus Requirements: varies by courses within programs.

Tuition and Fees: *Undergraduate:* $90/credit. *Graduate:* $154/credit. *Application Fee:* TBA. *Software:* TBA. *Other Costs:* TBA. *Credit by:* quarter.

Financial Aid: Federal Stafford Loan, Federal Perkins Loan, Federal PLUS Loan, Federal Pell Grant, Federal Work-Study, VA, Oregon resident programs.

Accreditation: Northwest Association of Schools and Colleges, National Council on Accreditation of Teacher

Education, American Association of Colleges for Teacher Education, National Association of Schools of Music, Council on Rehabilitation Education, Council on Education of the Deaf, Oregon Teacher Standards and Practices Commission.

Description: With a tradition of excellence since its founding, Western Oregon University (1856) is a comprehensive liberal arts institution offering a variety of programs leading to bachelor's and master's degrees and as a leading institution in teacher preparation. WOU provides a comprehensive higher education experience including teaching and research activities, personal growth and cultural opportunities, and public service. Campus-based outreach and continuing education programs prepare students to make personal and professional contributions to the economy, culture, and society of Oregon, the nation, and the world. Responding to the challenges Oregonians face in career changes, life transitions, and in adapting to new technologies, WOU provides a multitude of lifelong learning and professional growth opportunities. Distance education has been integral to WOU since the mid-1970s via videotape-based learning, correspondence study, and, most recently, Internet-based courses.

Western Seminary

5511 SE Hawthorne Boulevard	Phone: (800) 547-4546
Portland, OR 97215	Fax: (503) 239-4216

Division(s): Center for Lifelong Learning
Web Site(s): http://www.westernseminary.edu
E-mail: cll@westernseminary.edu
jlraible@westernseminary.edu

Graduate Degree Programs:
Master of Arts
Master of Christian Leadership
Master of Divinity

Doctoral Degree Programs:
Doctor of Ministry
Doctor of Missiology

Certificate Programs: Theological Studies, Biblical Studies, Church Ministries, Diploma in Theological Studies, Diploma in Ministerial Studies, Pastoral Care to Women (advanced certificate).

Class Titles: Biblical Literature, Theology, Church History, New Testament Greek.

Teaching Methods: *Computers:* Internet, real-time chat, electronic classroom, CD-ROM, e-mail. *TV:* videotape. *Other:* audiotapes, correspondence, fax, independent study, individual study.

Credits Granted for: examination.

Admission Requirements: *Graduate:* accredited bachelor's degree, 2.5 GPA for MDiv, 3.0 for MA. *Doctoral:* 3.0 GPA, accredited MDiv or equivalent.

On-Campus Requirements: Up to one-half of an M.A. degree or two-thirds of an M.Div degree may be earned through external study; the remainder must be completed at one of our campuses (Portland, Oregon or northern California sites at San Jose or Sacramento).

Tuition and Fees: *Graduate:* $260/credit. *Application Fee:* $30. *Credit by:* semester.

Financial Aid: Federal Stafford Loan, Federal Perkins Loan, Federal PLUS Loan, Federal Work-Study, VA, Oregon resident programs.

Accreditation: Northwest Association of Schools and Colleges, Association of Theological Schools.

Description: Western Seminary (1927) is a transdenominational graduate school of ministry with branch campuses in San Jose and Sacramento. Our mission statement accurately describes Western as "nurturing for the church godly leaders who are committed to, and competent for, the redemptive purpose of Christ throughout the world." Western is a convictionist institution and believes in the inerrancy of the Scriptures in the original autographs. The seminary has students from 30 major denominations and from many nations of the world studying for ministry. The distance education program began in 1981 and has traditionally served students with video and audio courses. Western is now moving aggressively into online, Internet-mediated courses to increase student interaction with their instructors.

Western University of Health Sciences

309 East Second Street	Phone: (909) 469-5523
Pomona, CA 91766-1854	Fax: (909) 469-5521

Division(s): College of Graduate Nursing
Web Site(s): http://www.westernu.edu
E-mail: sdouville@westernu.edu

Graduate Degree Programs:
Master of Science in Nursing/Family Nurse Practitioner

Certificate Program: Family Nurse Practitioner.

Teaching Methods: *Computers:* Internet, discussion boards, e-mail. *TV:* videotape. *Other:* independent study, correspondence, individual study learning contracts.

Admission Requirements: *Graduate:* Bachelor of Science in Nursing or a Related Field, GPA of 3.0 Overall in the last 60

Semester Units, Registered Nurse (RN) Licensure and 1 Year Experience as an RN, Statistics Course, Pathophysiology Course, Completed Application, 3 letters of reference, résumé, personal statement, application fee, official transcripts, and personal computer. *Certificate:* contact school.

On-Campus Requirements: Students will attend 2 on-campus orientation sessions and 6 on-campus seminar weekends (Friday, Saturday, and Sunday) each year.

Tuition and Fees: *Graduate:* $400–$450/credit. *Application Fee:* $60. *Software:* personal computer with Internet access and Microsoft Office Suite. *Other Costs:* approximately $2,000 for textbooks and medical equipment. *Credit by:* semester.

Financial Aid: Federal Stafford Loan, Federal Perkins Loan, Federal Work-Study, VA.

Accreditation: Western Association of Schools and Colleges. Board of Registered Nursing.

Description: Western University (1977) is a graduate university of medical sciences that educates health professionals to practice and teach with excellence and compassion. Western University's Master of Science in Nursing/Family Nurse Practitioner program provides comprehensive preparation for baccalaureate-prepared nurses who are looking for career mobility in today's healthcare environment. Full-time students can complete the program in 2 years. Part-time tracks are also available. The College of Graduate Nursing also offers a FNP-Only and a MSN-Only program. Having been nationally recognized as the first web-based FNP program, the college offers maximum scheduling and pacing flexibility for self-directed adult-learners. All courses are offered over the Internet and students attend 6 intensive weekend seminars each year at the Pomona, California campus. The University is WASC-accredited and the program is Board of Registered Nursing-approved. The College of Graduate Nursing has received preliminary approval by the Commission on Collegiate Nursing Education (CCNE) and expects to be accredited in Fall 2001.

Western Washington University

516 High Street	**Phone: (360) 650-3650**
Bellingham, WA 98225-5293	**Fax: (360) 650-6858**

Division(s): Extended Education and Summer Programs
Web Site(s): http://www.ac.wwu.edu/~extended/ilearn.html
E-mail: ilearn@cc.wwu.edu

Undergraduate Degree Programs:
Bachelor of Arts in Human Services

Certificate Programs: MCSE Windows 2000 and Oracle Foundations/Administration/Architecture.

Class Titles: Professional development for educators, counselors and human service professionals. Undergraduate courses in Anthropology, Canadian-American Studies, East Asian Studies, Economics, Education, English, Environmental Studies, Finance, French, History, Human Services, Liberal Studies, Linguistics, Mathematics, Music, Psychology, Sociology, Teaching English as a Second Language, Women Studies.

Teaching Methods: *Computers:* Internet, real-time chat, electronic classroom, e-mail, CD-ROM, LISTSERV. *TV:* videotape, satellite broadcasting. *Other:* videoconferencing, audiotapes, fax, correspondence, independent study, individual study, learning contracts.

Admission Requirements: *Undergraduate:* B.A. in Human Services requires a transferable Associate of Art degree or 90 credits that include general university requirements and a miniumum transferrable 2.50 GPA. Other WWU Admissions requirements may apply. *Certificate:* open to all.

On-Campus Requirements: None.

Tuition and Fees: *Undergraduate:* Correspondence courses $80/credit. Human Services degree classes $137/credit, other fees apply. *Application Fee:* for degree program. *Credit by:* quarter.

Financial Aid: Federal Stafford Loan, Federal Perkins Loan, Federal PLUS Loan, Federal Pell Grant, Federal Work-Study, VA, Washington resident programs. Available for degree program only; not available for correspondence courses or certificate programs.

Accreditation: Northwest Association of Schools and Colleges, National Council for Accreditation of Teacher Education.

Description: Western Washington University (1899) is part of the higher education system of the state of Washington. Western began as a state college for teachers and is recognized as a regional university offering quality undergraduate education. Western has offered distance education since 1906 when many teachers could not make the journey by horseback to town. Today, WWU offers one online degree, a selection of courses for teachers seeking professional development, as well as over 80 correspondence courses.

Western Wyoming Community College

2500 College Drive	**Phone: (307) 382-1600**
Rock Springs, WY 82901	**Fax: (307) 382-1812**

Division(s): Extended Education
Web Site(s): http://www.wwcc.cc.wy.us
E-mail: wwcc@wwcc.cc.wy.us

Certificate Programs: Middle School Certification, state of Wyoming.

Class Titles: Freshmen English, Technical Writing, Accounting, Economics, Sociology, History, MS Word, Access, Excel, Powerpoint, Statistics, Philosophy, Medical Terminology, Business.

Teaching Methods: *Computers:* Internet, real-time chat, electronic classroom, e-mail, CD-ROM, bulletin boards. *TV:* videotape.

Credits Granted for: Challenge examinations and CLEP.

Admission Requirements: *Undergraduate:* 16 years of age, GED, or high school diploma.

On-Campus Requirements: None.

Tuition and Fees: *Undergraduate:* $58/credit. *Other Costs:* $18 for course fee for Distance courses. *Credit by:* semester.

Financial Aid: Federal Stafford Loan, Federal Perkins Loan, Federal PLUS Loan, Federal Pell Grant, Federal Work-Study, VA, state programs for residents of Wyoming.

Accreditation: The Higher Learning Commission (formerly North Central Association).

Description: Western Wyoming Community College (1959) is a 2-year public institution that prides itself on its focus on quality instruction that leads to student success. Western has developed Distance courses based on high expectations and strong interactivity—student-to-student interaction as well as student-to-instructor. In addition to the course's content, our courses strive to challenge students' problem solving abilities, communication skills, and ability to retrieve and apply relevant information.

Westlawn Institute of Marine Technology

733 Summer Street
Stamford, CT 06901

Phone: (203) 359-0500
Fax: (203) 359-2466

Division(s): School of Yacht Design
Web Site(s): http://westlawn.org
E-mail: westlawn@aol.com

Certificate Programs: Yacht Design/Yacht Design Lite.

Teaching Methods: *Computers:* Internet, e-mail *Other:* fax, independent study, individual study.

Admission Requirements: *Undergraduate:* high school or equivalent, 2 years of math (algebra, trigonometry).

On-Campus Requirements: None.

Tuition and Fees: *Undergraduate:* Four modules at $199 per module. *Software:* approximately $400.

Accreditation: Distance Education and Training Council.

Description: Westlawn (1930) is the leading yacht design correspondence course in the world. In this course, topics such as hydrostatics, resistance, hull lines, arrangements, fiberglass and aluminum construction, systems, and equipment are studied to provide the student with a sound understanding of production yacht design. Westlawn graduates and advanced students are working within the production boat industry as designers and design department heads. Other graduates are employed with independent design firms. Refer to the Westlawn Internet site for more information on the courses offered.

Westmoreland County Community College

400 Armbrust Road
Youngwood, PA 15697

Phone: (724) 925-4000
(724) 836-1600
Fax: (724) 925-1150

Division(s): Learning Resources
Web Site(s): http://www.westmoreland.cc.pa.us
E-mail: stubbsms@westmoreland.cc.pa.us

Undergraduate Degree Programs:
Associate of Arts
Associate of Applied Science

Certificate Programs: available in a number of programs, contact school for more information.

Class Titles: Allied Health, Anthropology, Art, Banking/ Finance, Biology, Business, Computer Technology, Criminal Justice, Early Childhood Education, Earth Science, Economics, English, Environmental Science, Fire Science, Food Service, French, Geography, Geology, Health/Physical Education, History, Human Services, Humanities, Legal Assisting, Mathematics, Multimedia Technology, Philosophy, Physics, Political Science, Psychology, Real Estate, Sociology, Speech Communication.

Teaching Methods: *Computers:* Internet, real-time chat, electronic classroom, e-mail. *TV:* videotape. *Other:* videoconferencing, independent study.

Credits Granted for: experiential learning, portfolio assessment, extrainstitutional learning, examination (CLEP, ACT-PEP, DANTES, GRE).

Admission Requirements: *Undergraduate:* age 18; high school graduate or GED.

On-Campus Requirements: None.

Tuition and Fees: *Undergraduate:* $46/credit Westmoreland County residents, double for out-of-county, triple for out-of-state. *Credit by:* semester.

Financial Aid: Federal Stafford Loan, Federal Perkins Loan, Federal PLUS Loan, Federal Pell Grant, Federal Work-Study, VA, Pennsylvania state programs.

Accreditation: Middle States Association of Colleges and Schools.

Description: Westmoreland County Community College (1970) began telecourses in 1987, interactive videoconferencing in 1996, and online courses in 1998.

Whatcom Community College

237 West Kellogg Road	Phone: (360) 676-2170 x3371
Bellingham, WA 98226	Fax: (360) 676-2171

Division(s): Extended Learning
Web Site(s): http://www.whatcom.ctc.edu
E-mail: chagman@whatcom.ctc.edu

Undergraduate Degree Programs:
Associate of Arts

Class Titles: Math, Science, Social Science, Fine Arts, Humanities.

Teaching Methods: *Computers:* Internet, electronic classroom. *TV:* videotape. *Other:* learning contracts.

Credits Granted for: experiential learning, portfolio assessment, extrainstitutional learning, examination (CLEP, ACT-PEP, DANTES, GRE).

Admission Requirements: *Undergraduate:* assessment tests for math and English, high school degree or GED.

On-Campus Requirements: None.

Tuition and Fees: *Undergraduate:* $50/credit resident, $192/credit nonresident. *Other Costs:* $52/online course. *Credit by:* quarter.

Financial Aid: Federal Stafford Loan, Federal Perkins Loan, Federal PLUS Loan, Federal Pell Grant, Federal Work-Study, VA, Washington resident programs.

Accreditation: Northwest Association of Schools and Colleges.

Description: Whatcom Community College (1967) is a comprehensive community college, part of the Washington Community and Technical College System. In fall of 1998 WCC enrolled 6,000 students, with 200 in various distance education classes. WCC is a charter member of Washington

Online, a consortium of Washington Community Colleges which offers an AA degree via the Internet. In the fall of 1998 WAOL offered 9 classes, 2 of which were offered by Whatcom faculty. 106 students enrolled for WAOL classes through WCC.

Wheaton College Graduate School

501 College Avenue	Phone: (630) 752-5944
Wheaton, IL 60187	Fax: (630) 752-5935

Division(s): Distance Learning
Web Site(s): http://www.wheaton.edu/distancelearning/
E-mail: distance.learning@wheaton.edu

Graduate Degree Programs:
Master of Arts in:
   Theology
   Missions and Intercultural Studies
   up to 16 semester hours of Distance Learning may be taken in these special GradLink programs.

Certificate Programs: Certificate of Advanced Biblical Studies (graduate level).

Class Titles: Contact school or check web site for details.

Teaching Methods: *Computers:* Internet, real-time chat, electronic classroom, e-mail, CD-ROM, newsgroup, LISTSERV. *Other:* radio broadcast, videoconferencing, audioconferencing, audiographics, audiotapes, fax, correspondence, independent study, individual study, learning contracts.

Admission Requirements: *Graduate:* bachelor's degree from a regionally accredited college with a 2.75 grade point (on a 4.0 scale), facility in the reading, writing, speaking, and listening of English to adequately complete graduate work, undergraduate liberal arts studies recommended. Each department maintains additional requirements. *Certificate:* same.

On-Campus Requirements: Certificate of Advanced Biblical Studies can be earned entirely at a distance. GradLink Master of Arts in Theology: 16 of 36 hours may be earned at a distance. GradLink Master of Arts in Missions/Intercultural Studies: 16 of 40 hours may be earned at a distance.

Tuition and Fees: *Graduate:* $273/hour for Certificate and GradLink students. *Application Fee:* $30. *Credit by:* semester.

Accreditation: North Central Association of Colleges and Schools.

Description: Wheaton College (1860) exists to help build the church and improve society worldwide by promoting the development of whole and effective Christians through excellence in programs of Christian higher education. Since the mid-1970s, Distance Learning has assisted incoming graduate students in fulfilling Bible Proficiency requirements and helped others to get a head start on their graduate school programs. The Certificate of Advanced Biblical Studies represents our first program that can be earned entirely at a distance. It is designed for people who desire advanced training in biblical and theological study that will deepen their personal Christian growth and service for Christ and his Kingdom. The program provides professional development opportunities for pastors, teachers, missionaries, and other Christian workers. It also offers a way for those working in other vocations and disciplines to attain a biblical and theological foundation necessary for the deep integration of faith, learning, and living.

Wichita State University

1845 Fairmount	Phone: (316) 978-3575
Wichita, KS 67260-0057	Fax: (316) 978-3560

Division(s): Media Resources Center
Web Site(s):
http://www.mrc.twsu.edu/mrc/telecourse/index.asp
E-mail: Telecourses: morriss@mrc.twsu.edu
Web-based Courses: Gibson@mrc.twsu.edu

Undergraduate Degree Programs: Contact school.

Graduate Degree Programs: Contact school.

Postgraduate Degree Programs: Contact school.

Certificate Programs: Contact school.

Class Titles: Accounting, Anthropology, Communications, Economics, English, Ethnic Studies, Finance, Geology, Gerontology, History, Management, Astronomy, Psychology, Sociology, Nursing, Human Resources, Math.

Teaching Methods: *Computers:* Internet, real-time chat, electronic classroom, e-mail, CD-ROM, newsgroup, LISTSERV. *TV:* videotape, cable program. *Other:* videoconferencing.

Credits Granted for: examination (CLEP).

Admission Requirements: *Undergraduate:* see www.wichita.edu for admission information. *Graduate:* see www.wichita.edu for admission information. *Postgraduate:* See www.wichita.edu for admission information. *Certificate:* See www.wichita.edu for admission information.

On-Campus Requirements: Telecourses generally require 5–8 on-campus meetings/semester. Some Web courses have a face-to-face component.

Tuition and Fees: *Undergraduate:* $94.10/credit—resident, $320/CH nonresident. *Graduate:* $128.35/credit resident, $368.35/CH nonresident. *Application Fees:* UG—$25 domestic, $50 international. *Other Costs:* $12/CH for Mediated instruction. *Credit by:* semester.

Financial Aid: Federal Stafford Loan, Federal Perkins Loan, Federal Pell Grant, Federal Work-Study, VA.

Accreditation: North Central Association of Colleges and Schools.

Description: Wichita State University (1895) was founded as Fairmount College. Shortly after the turn of the century, it transitioned to a municipal university, the University of Wichita, and remained such until the 1960s. In 1964 WU was absorbed into the state system, becoming Wichita State University. WSU is a metropolitan university with 6 colleges (Liberal Arts, Fine Arts, Education, Business, Engineering, and Heath Professions) and a graduate school. The existing telecourse program began in 1982.

Widener University

One University Place, KLC 137-A	Phone: (610) 499-4282
Chester, PA 19013	Fax: (610) 499-4369

Division(s): University College
Web Site(s): http://www.widener.edu
E-mail: uc.distance@widener.edu

Undergraduate Degree Programs:
Associate in Science in Allied Health
Bachelor of Science in Allied Health

Certificate Programs: Certificate in Applied Supervision.

Class Titles: Contact school or check web site for details.

Teaching Methods: *Computers:* Internet, WebStudy (commercial course management software), electronic classroom, e-mail, CD-ROM, LISTSERV. *Other:* independent study, directed study.

Credits Granted for: experiential learning, portfolio assessment, extrainstitutional learning (PONSI, corporate or professional association seminars/workshops), examination (CLEP, ACT-PEP, DANTES, GRE), hospital-based allied health training.

Admission Requirements: *Undergraduate:* high school diploma for all; college courses or hospital-based training in allied health field. *Certificate:* minimum 30 college credits and equivalent of English 101 for Certificate in Applied Supervision.

On-Campus Requirements: None.

Tuition and Fees: *Undergraduate:* $330/credit for 2001–2002 academic year. *Other Costs:* $10, new student fee. *Credit by:* semester.

Financial Aid: Federal Stafford Loan, Federal Perkins Loan, Federal PLUS Loan, Federal Pell Grant, Federal Work-Study,

VA, state programs for residents of Pennsylvania and Delaware, and Pennsylvania work-study program.

Accreditation: Middle States Association of Colleges and Schools. Member, Association for Continuing Higher Education.

Description: Widener University (1821) is a private, non-profit, comprehensive teaching institution of 8 schools and colleges in suburban Philadelphia that offer liberal arts and sciences, professional and preprofessional curricula leading to associate's, baccalaureate, master's, or doctoral degrees. University College, which began in 1980, serves adult students through undergraduate evening, weekend, and Distance programs. Online, telecourse, and a computer-based course can be selected by students as an alternative to campus-based courses. University College entered the field of Distance Learning nearly 5 years ago and, beginning in the fall of 2001, will offer an Associate's or Baccalaureate Degree in Allied Health completely online as well as a certificate in applied supervision. Many students supplement their campus-based program with a variety of Distance Learning courses.

Wilfrid Laurier University

75 University Avenue W	Phone: (519) 884-1970
Waterloo, Ontario, Canada N2L 3C5	Fax: (519) 884-0181

Division(s): Part-time, Distance and Continuing Education
Web Site(s): http://www.wlu.ca/pts
E-mail: distance@wlu.ca

Undergraduate Degree Programs:
Sociology
Geography

Class Titles: general fields of Anthropology, Biology, Business, Canadian Studies, Economics, Fine Arts, French, German, History, Philosophy, Political Science, Psychology, Religion/Culture, Science, Social Welfare, Sociology, Spanish.

Teaching Methods: *Computers:* Internet, real-time chat, electronic classroom, e-mail, CD-ROM, newsgroup. *Other:* audiotapes, fax.

Credits Granted for: 1. From fully accredited universities, subject to the guidelines, a credit-for-credit transfer will be allowed wherever possible. If an equivalent course is not available at Laurier, we will attempt to award an unspecified elective credit. 2. Colleges of Applied Arts and Technology (CAATs) or equivalent—2-year or 3-year diploma programs: may be granted up to 5.0 transfer credits (usually unspecified elective credits, subject to the factors noted above). 3. For

other postsecondary institutions see the Undergraduate Calendar or contact the Admissions Office for details.

Admission Requirements: *Undergraduate:* The normal requirements for admission to Ontario universities is completion of the Ontario Secondary School Diploma with 6 Ontario Academic Credits (OSSD/six OACs) or the former Ontario Grade 13 diploma or equivalent. However, you may qualify for admission as a mature student if you have no post-secondary academic background and comply with either of the following conditions: OSSD, Ontario Grade 12 or equivalent standing, and at least 2 years of work experience prior to the first day of classes for the session to which you are applying, or age 21 and at least 2 years of work experience prior to the first day of classes for the session to which you are applying. In considering your application, we may request that you submit a letter outlining why you feel you will be successful at the university, your current career ambitions, and your work experience since you last attended school. *Certificate:* age 21, worked for 2 years.

On-Campus Requirements: None.

Tuition and Fees: *Undergraduate:* $886/credit. *Application Fee:* $30. *Credit by:* semester.

Financial Aid: OSAP (Ontario Study Assistance Program). All students who are residents of Ontario, Canadian citizens, or permanent residents of Canada, whose parents reside and work in Ontario, may apply for financial aid under this program. To receive assistance, students must establish need under the terms of the program and be enrolled at Wilfrid Laurier University. An award under this program will be made to the extent of established need in loan funds only. Application forms are available from the Student Awards Office, Wilfrid Laurier University.

Ontario Work Study Program. Students who are experiencing financial difficulties and who wish to work on a part-time basis may be eligible for assistance under this program. Students must be registered as full-time students at Wilfrid Laurier University, and qualify to receive funding through OSAP. Application forms are available in the Student Awards Office, Wilfrid Laurier University.

Accreditation: Association of Universities and Colleges of Canada.

Description: Two synods of the Lutheran Church founded Wilfrid Laurier University in 1911 as the Evangelical Lutheran Seminary of Canada. Today, WLU grants bachelor's, master's, and doctoral degrees through 5 faculties and one school in arts, science, music, business, and economics, graduate studies, and social work. The university has a total enrollment of 7,377 with 97% of students coming from Ontario.

Wilfrid Laurier entered into distance learning (known as Telecollege) in 1978 with 2 courses. Today, with the facilitation of Web technology, Distance Education offers over 80 courses.

Williston State College

PO Box 1326	Phone: (710) 774-4200
Williston, ND 58802	Fax: (710) 774-4275(DE)/
	(710) 774-4201(WTCE)

Division(s): Distance Education/Workforce Training and Continuing Education
Web Site(s): http://www.wsc.nodak.edu
E-mail: Jan_Solem@wsc.nocak.edu (ED)/ Deanette_Piesik@ wsc.nodak.edu (WTCE)

Undergraduate Degree Programs:
Associate of Arts
Associate of Science

Certificate Programs: Medical Transcription

Teaching Methods: *Computers:* Internet, real-time chat, electronic classroom, e-mail, CD-ROM, LISTSERV. *TV:* videotape, videoconferencing, audioconferencing, audiotapes, fax, correspondence.

Credits Granted for: examination (CLEP).

On-Campus Requirements: none.

Tuition and Fees: *Undergraduate:* $80.00 per credit. Each correspondence class is a different price. For instance, Beginning Medical Terminology is $275.00. The student pays for the class, no other fee. *Application Fees:* $25. *Software:* none. *Graduation Fee:* none. *Other Costs:* $25/credit access fee for distance education classes. *Credit by:* semester.

Financial Aid: Federal Stafford Loan, Federal Perkins Loan, Federal PLUS Loan, Federal Pell Grant, Federal Work-Study, VA, state programs for residents of North Dakota.

Accreditation: North Central Association of Colleges and Schools.

Description: Williston State College (1967) was established as a branch campus of the University of North Dakota in Grand Forks. Its name was University of North Dakota-Williston until 1999 when the North Dakota State Legislature created a separate status and renamed the campus Williston State College. WSC offers students transfer courses through the AA and AS degrees and vocational programs through the AAS degree, certificate programs, certificates of completions and diplomas. Vocational programs include practical nursing, physical therapy assistant, massage therapy, medical transcription, automotive, diesel, computer science and technician, and medical office. WSC became involved with online courses in 2000. It will continue to increase its offerings in

courses and programs via online, videoconferencing, and correspondence.

Winthrop University

Thurmond Building	Phone: (803) 323-2409
Rock Hill, SC 29733	Fax: (803) 323-2539

Division(s): College of Business Administration
Web Site(s): http://www.cba.winthrop.edu/programs/grad-prog.htm
E-mail: hagerp@mail.winthrop.edu

Graduate Degree Programs:
Master of Business Administration
Master of Business Administration, Accounting

Teaching Methods: *Computers:* Internet, real-time chat, electronic classroom, e-mail, LISTSERV. *TV:* videotape, satellite broadcasting. *Other:* videoconferencing, audiotapes, fax, correspondence, independent study.

Credits Granted for: examination (CLEP).

Admission Requirements: *Graduate:* undergraduate degree and Graduate Management Admission Test.

On-Campus Requirements: No, however, will transfer only 12 hours from another institution.

Tuition and Fees: *Graduate:* $189/credit in-state, $356/ credit out-of-state. *Application Fee:* $35. *Other Costs:* Books. *Credit by:* semester.

Financial Aid: Federal Stafford Loan, Federal Perkins Loan, Federal PLUS Loan, Federal Pell Grant, Federal Work-Study, VA, South Carolina resident programs.

Accreditation: American Assembly of Collegiate Schools of Business.

Description: Winthrop University (1886) is a comprehensive teaching university committed to being a model of excellence in higher education. Winthrop's distinctive mission is to offer challenging academic programs of national caliber to its 5,500 high-achieving, culturally diverse, socially responsible students in a contemporary physical environment of exceptional beauty and historic character only 20 miles south of Charlotte. In keeping with a technology emphasis, Winthrop began distance education in 1994. With seating for 40, the school's state-of-the-art distance learning facility is equipped for fully interactive, 2-way video and audio (utilizing T1 transmission), and more services are in development. It delivers MBA courses to Coastal Carolina University and dual-credit courses to 3 local high schools.

Wisconsin Indianhead Technical College

505 Pine Ridge Drive   Phone: (715) 468-2815
Shell Lake, WI 54871   Fax: (715) 468-2819

Division(s): Instructional Services
Web Site(s): http://witc.tec.wi.us/online
E-mail: bczyscon@witc.tec.wi.us
acharbon@witc.tec.wi.us
dhelleru@witc.tec.wi.us
enowak@witc.tec.wi.us

Undergraduate Degree Program: Computer Information Systems—Programmer Analyst (Associate Degree).

Class Titles: many in areas of Computers, Child Care, Medical Transcription, Business, Accounting, Finance.

Teaching Methods: *Computers:* Internet, electronic classroom, e-mail, CD-ROM, LISTSERV. *TV:* videotape. *Other:* videoconferencing, audioconferencing, audiotapes, fax, correspondence, independent study, individual study.

Credits Granted for: experiential learning, portfolio assessment, extrainstitutional learning, examination (CLEP, ACT-PEP, DANTES, GRE).

Admission Requirements: *Undergraduate:* ASSET or COMPASS assessment, counselor interview, in-state/out-of-state tuition, ability to benefit. *Certificate:* same as undergraduate.

On-Campus Requirements: None.

Tuition and Fees: *Undergraduate:* $70.70/credit. *Application Fee:* $30. *Credit by:* semester.

Financial Aid: Federal Stafford Loan, Federal Perkins Loan, Federal PLUS Loan, Federal Pell Grant, Federal Work-Study, VA, Wisconsin resident programs.

Accreditation: North Central Association of Colleges and Schools.

Description: Wisconsin Indianhead Technical College (1912) is a public postsecondary educational institution that serves the communities of the college district and their residents by providing comprehensive educational programming and support services for meaningful career preparation and personal effectiveness. As a dynamic organization dedicated to lifelong learning, WITC seeks to improve the quality of life for individuals and enhance the economic potential of their communities. One of 16 districts in the Wisconsin Technical College System, WITC began serving northwest Wisconsin 89 years ago in Superior, and now has campuses in Ashland (since 1920), New Richmond (since 1967), and Rice Lake (since 1941). The administrative office is located in Shell Lake (since 1973).

Wittenberg University

P.O. Box 720   Phone: (937) 327-7012
Springfield, OH 45501-0720   or (800) 677-7558
      Fax: (937) 327-7014

Division(s): School of Community Education
Web Site(s): http://www.wittenberg.edu/
E-mail: emoore@wittenberg.edu

Undergraduate Degree Programs:
Bachelor of Arts with major concentrations in Health Care Leadership and Organizational Leadership

Certificate Programs: Health Care Leadership and Organizational Leadership.

Class Titles: Contact school or check web site for details.

Teaching Methods: *Computers:* Internet, real-time chat, electronic classroom, e-mail, CD-ROM, newsgroup, LISTSERV. *TV:* videotape, cable program, satellite broadcasting, PBS. *Other:* radio broadcast, videoconferencing, audioconferencing, audiographics, audiotapes, fax, correspondence, independent study, individual study, learning contracts.

Credits Granted for: experiential learning, extrainstitutional learning (PONSI, corporate or professional association seminars/workshops).

Admission Requirements: *Undergraduate:* age 23, transfer with GPA of 3.0+. *Certificate:* 23, transfer with GPA of 3.0+.

On-Campus Requirements: Typically 5–8 meetings within a 16-week course.

Tuition and Fees: *Undergraduate:* $266/credit hour. *Application Fee:* $40. *Other Costs:* $42 registration fee/term. *Credit by:* semester.

Financial Aid: Federal Stafford Loan, Federal Plus Loan, Federal Pell Grant, VA, State programs for residents of Ohio: Ohio Instructional Grant and Ohio Student Choice Grant. Adult Access Award: Wittenberg-funded grant up to $58/credit.

Accreditation: North Central Association of Colleges and Schools.

Description: In its recent evolution, Wittenberg (1848) has become a selective, largely residential undergraduate school committed to a challenging version of the liberal arts and sciences and carefully chosen career programs. It has also maintained a small adult program under the direction of the School of Community Education (SCE). About half the adult constituency enrolls in the evening/weekend program while the other half enrolls in various portions of the day program. To more effectively serve the former group, SCE is initiating a new format, @witt/@home, that combines limited classroom meetings and interactive online activities. The format follows the model of the best "limited residency" programs and presumes the enrollment of students who are both capable and highly motivated. Three courses are being adapted for the fall 2001 semester, and the remaining core courses in the Health Care and Organizational Leadership concentrations are to be adapted within 2 years.

Worcester Polytechnic Institute

| 100 Institute Road | Phone: (508) 831-5220 |
| Worcester, MA 01609 | Fax: (508) 831-5881 |

Division(s): Advanced Distance Learning Network
Web Site(s): http://www.wpi.edu/academics/ADLN
E-mail: adln@wpi.edu

Graduate Degree Programs:
Civil and Environmental Engineering
Fire Protection Engineering
Management (MBA)

Certificate Programs: customized graduate certificates in Management, Fire Protection Engineering, Civil and Environmental Engineering, and Wireless Communications.

Class Titles: All classes offered through ADLN may be taken individually. Subject areas include topics in Environmental Engineering, many of which highlight water resources; Fire Protection Engineering; Project Management for Engineers, Accounting, Finance, various topics in Marketing and Economics, various courses in Managing Technological Organizations, Operations, Entrepreneurship, Project Management, Wireless Networks.

Teaching Methods: *Computers:* Internet, real-time chat, electronic classroom, e-mail, CD-ROM, newsgroup, LISTSERV. *TV:* videotape. *Other:* videoconferencing, fax, correspondence, independent study, individual study.

Credits Granted for: examination for some MBA courses (internally prepared exam).

Admission Requirements: *Graduate:* GMAT for MBA, TOEFL, letters of recommendation, statement of purpose, official transcripts. *Postgraduate:* TOEFL, official transcripts. *Certificate:* TOEFL, official transcripts; MBA also requires GMAT and letters of recommendations.

On-Campus Requirements: None.

Tuition and Fees: *Graduate:* $752/credit for FY01. *Application Fee:* $60. *Other Costs:* possible shipping fees for students outside continental U.S. *Credit by:* semester.

Financial Aid: Loans possible for half- or full-time students.

Accreditation: New England Association of Schools and Colleges.

Description: Worcester Polytechnic Institute, the nation's third-oldest private university of engineering, science, and management, has been a pioneer in technological higher education since its founding in 1865. Its mission is to educate talented men and women for careers of professional practice, civic contribution, and leadership. WPI awarded its first advanced degree in 1893. Since then, the university has earned a reputation for excellence in technological education, for practical application to marketplace challenges, and for a faculty of renowned academicians and industry experts who are practitioners in their fields. Today, most departments offer master's and doctoral programs and support leading-edge research in a broad range of fields. In 1979 WPI's commitment to lifelong learning prompted the creation of the Advanced Distance Learning Network. ADLN programs empower working professionals to grow in their chosen fields without making repeated trips to the WPI campus in Worcester, Massachusetts.

York Technical College

| 452 South Anderson Road | Phone: (803) 981-7044 |
| Rock Hill, SC 29730 | Fax: (803) 981-7193 |

Division(s): Distance Learning
Web Site(s): http://www.yorktech.com
E-mail: mcbride@yorktech.com

Certificate Programs: Entrepreneurial, Accounting Clerk.

Class Titles: Accounting, History, Sociology, Psychology, English, Math, Business, Economics, Office Systems.

Teaching Methods: *Computers:* Internet, real-time chat, electronic classroom, e-mail, CD-ROM. *TV:* videotape, cable program, live 2-way interactive ATM, T1 classes. *Other:* independent study, textbased telecourses.

Credits Granted for: experiential learning, examination (CLEP).

Admission Requirements: *Undergraduate:* age 18, admissions application, $10 nonreturnable fee, admissions test or placement test, interview with admissions counselor, admission into a program. *Certificate:* same as undergraduate.

On-Campus Requirements: 25% of the credit hours need to be completed with York Technical College classes.

Tuition and Fees: *Undergraduate:* $51/credit in-county, $61/credit out-of-county, $209/credit out-of-state. *Application Fee:* $10. *Credit by:* semester.

Financial Aid: Federal Stafford Loan, Federal Perkins Loan, Federal PLUS Loan, Federal Pell Grant, Federal Work-Study, VA, South Carolina resident programs.

Accreditation: Southern Association of Colleges and Schools.

Description: York Technical College (1964) opened as a Technical Education Center with 60 students enrolled in 7 programs housed in one building. The college's enrollment has grown in the past 3 decades to 3,600 credit-students in 50 programs. In 1974 York County Technical Education Center became York Technical College.

York University, Atkinson College

4700 Keele Street	Phone: (416) 736-5831
Toronto, ON, Canada M3J 1P3	Fax: (416) 736-5439

Division(s): Centre for Distance Education
Web Site(s): http://www.atkinson.yorku.ca (see Internet and Correspondence link for detailed information about our Distance Education program, courses and how it works.)
E-mail: akade@yorku.ca

Undergraduate Degree Programs:
Bachelor of Administrative Studies
Bachelor of Arts (Public Service Studies)
Bachelor of Science

Teaching Methods: *Computers:* Internet, real-time chat, electronic classroom, e-mail, CD-ROM, newsgroup, LISTSERV, videotape, audiotapes, fax, correspondence, independent study, individual study, learning contracts.

Credits Granted for: None.

Admission Requirements: *Undergraduate:* see Admissions web site: http://www.yorku.ca/admissio/index.asp

On-Campus Requirements: None.

Tuition and Fees: see Registrar's web site at: http://registrar.yorku.ca. Courses start fall, winter, and summer.

Financial Aid: See web site for financial aid: http://www.yorku.ca/osfc/ index/shtm/

Accreditation: Association of Universities and Colleges of Canada, International Association of Universities, Association of Commonwealth Universities.

Description: Atkinson was founded in 1962 to meet the needs of adult, part-time students. Today, it is the second largest Faculty at York University, offering a wide variety of degree and certificate programs in professional studies and the liberal arts. While courses are primarily offered in the late afternoon, evenings, and weekends, Atkinson students enjoy the flexibility of combining day courses, distance courses (via the Internet and correspondence), and off-campus classes into their academic schedule. With over 130 full-time faculty and 150 part-time instructors, Atkinson maintains a proud tradition of offering students excellent and innovative academic programs, flexibility and choice. Atkinson now offers even more choice as to how, where, and when students can pursue university studies. Widely acknowledged for the breadth of its program and course offerings in the humanities and social, natural, and applied sciences, Atkinson is also acclaimed for developing and delivering professional programs that respond to real issues.

Whether your goal is personal development or professional advancement, Atkinson has the experience, the resources, and the commitment to make your university learning experience a rewarding and successful one.

Yuba Community College

2088 North Beale Road	Phone: (530) 741-6757
Marysville, CA 95901	Fax: (530) 741-6824

Division(s): Learning Resources
Web Site(s): http://yubalib.yuba.cc.ca.us
E-mail: jobryan@yuba.cc.ca.us

Undergraduate Degree Programs:
Associate of Arts
Transfer Program

Certificate Programs: Management Series.

Teaching Methods: *Computers:* Internet, real-time chat, electronic classroom, e-mail, CD-ROM, newsgroup, LISTSERV, online courses. *TV:* videotape, cable program, satellite broadcasting, PBS, ITFS. *Other:* radio broadcast, videoconferencing, audioconferencing, audiographics, audiotapes, fax, correspondence, independent study, individual study, learning contracts.

Credits Granted for: experiential learning, portfolio assessment, extra-institutional learning (PONSI, corporate or professional association seminars/workshops), examination (CLEP, ACT-PEP, DANTES, GRE).

Admission Requirements: *Undergraduate:* Yuba College does not restrict admission to residents of the District, nor does it restrict the privilege of District residents to attend any other community college. Nonresident students are accepted on the same basis as California resident students, except that state law requires a tuition charge.

On-Campus Requirements: None.

Tuition and Fees: *Undergraduate:* $11/credit. *Housing:* applications must be accompanied by a $100 deposit; $75 will be held as a security deposit, and the remaining $25 is a nonrefundable application and processing fee. The total annual cost for room and board is $4,595. With the 25% In-Lieu discount, the total annual cost is $3,446. The payment for room and board may be made in 2 equal installments. The installment for the fall semester is due August 1; the installment for the spring semester is due January 1. *Student Services Fee:* $6/semester. *Parking Decals:* $20/semester. *Nonresident Tuition:* $142/unit in addition to enrollment fee. *Foreign Student Tuition:* $150/unit in addition to enrollment fee. *Credit by:* semester.

Financial Aid: Federal Stafford Loan, Federal SEOG (Supplemental Educational Opportunity Grant), BIA (Bureau of Indian Affairs) Grant, E.O.P.S. (Extended Opportunity Program and Services) Grant Program, CARE (Cooperative Agency Resources and Education) Grant, CAL GRANTS B & C, Federal Pell Grant, Federal Stafford Loan, Federal Work-Study, and Sawtell Grant.

Accreditation: Western Association of Schools and Colleges, Accrediting Commission for Community and Junior Colleges.

Description: Yuba College is an institution of higher education that prepares students to meet the intellectual, occupational, and technological challenges of a complex world. Since 1927 the primary mission of Yuba College has been to provide rigorous, high-quality degree and certificate curricula in lower division arts and sciences and in vocational and occupational fields. Yuba has offered distance education courses since 1974 and today delivers 100 hours/week of degree-bound and certificate courses.

Appendix

Information about the following institutions reached us too late to be included in the main body of this book.

Anoka-Ramsey Community College Coon Rapids Campus

11200 Mississippi Boulevard NW	Phone: (612) 427-2600
Coon Rapids, MN 55433	Fax: (612) 422-3341

Division(s): Education Services–Instruction
Web Site(s): http://www.an.cc.mn.us

Undergraduate Degree Programs:
Associate in Arts
Associate in Science
Associate in Applied Science

Certificate Programs: Business-related.

Class Titles: Business, Accounting, Marketing, Management, Economics, Geography.

Teaching Methods: *Computers:* Internet, real-time chat, electronic classroom, e-mail, newsgroup, LISTSERV. *Other:* independent study.

Credits Granted for: experiential learning, examination (CLEP, ACT-PEP).

Admission Requirements: *Undergraduate:* application and fees, assessment tests.

On-Campus Requirements: Faculty determine on-campus meetings—up to 3.

Tuition and Fees: *Undergraduate:* $78/credit. *Application Fee:* $20. *Other Costs:* $3 transcripts. *Credit by:* semester.

Financial Aid: Federal Stafford Loan, Federal Perkins Loan, Federal PLUS Loan, Federal Pell Grant, Federal Work-Study, VA, Minnesota resident programs.

Accreditation: North Central Association of Colleges and Schools, Association of Collegiate Business Schools and Programs.

Description: Anoka-Ramsey Community College, Coon Rapids Campus (1965), a multicampus college just north of Minneapolis/St. Paul, offers associate degrees in transfer and career areas and certificates through its business program and its continuing education department. In 1978, this publicly supported institution added its Cambridge campus about 35 miles away. More than 8,500 students of all ages and backgrounds enroll in transfer and career programs each semester at the 2 campuses. Another 4,000 participate annually in continuing education and community service activities. Appropriate Anoka-Ramsey credits are transferable to all Minnesota colleges and universities and are accepted by out-of-state schools as well. Distance learning through Internet classes began 2 years ago and has grown to 6 offerings/semester in 1998.

Avila College

11901 Wornall Road	Phone: (816) 501-3737
Kansas City, MO 64145	Fax: (816) 941-4550

Division(s): Avila Advantage
Web Site(s): http://www.avila.edu
E-mail: advantage@mail.avila.edu

Undergraduate Degree Programs:
Business Administration
Psychology
Health Care Services

Certificate Programs: Customer Service and other programs available through the Avila Resource Group.

Teaching Methods: *Computers:* Internet, electronic classroom, e-mail, CD-ROM, newsgroup, LISTSERV. *TV:* videotape, cable program, satellite broadcasting, PBS. *Other:* radio broadcast, videoconferencing, audioconferencing, audiographics, audiotapes, fax, correspondence, independent study, individual study, learning contracts.

Credits Granted for: experiential learning, portfolio assessment, extra-institutional learning (PONSI, corporate or professional association seminars/workshops), examination (CLEP, ACT-PEP, DANTES, GRE).

Admission Requirements: *Undergraduate:* 23 yrs. of age or three years of full time work experience *Certificate:* Case by case.

On-Campus Requirements: None.

Tuition and Fees: *Undergraduate:* $293 per credit. *Other Costs:* variable for books. *Credit by:* semester.

Financial Aid: Federal Stafford Loan, Federal Perkins Loan, Federal PLUS Loan, Federal Pell Grant, Federal Work-Study, VA.

Accreditation: Commission on Institutes of Higher Education of the North Central Association of Colleges and Schools.

Description: Founded by the Sisters of Saint Joseph (1916), who opened the first private high school for young women in

Kansas City, Saint Teresa's Academy in 1866, the academy administration chartered the first private college for women in Kansas City, the Saint Teresa College. Now known as Avila College, it is a value-based community of learning, Catholic and co-educational. The Avila Advantage program was founded in 1997 as a degree-completion program and entered the field of distance learning as a response to the need of its adult students in 1999.

Bryn Athyn College of the New Church

2895 College Drive	Phone: (215) 938-2453
Bryn Athyn, PA 19009	Fax: (215) 938-2658

Web Site(s): http://www.newchurch.edu/college
E-mail: chebert@newchurch.edu

Class Titles: Perspectives on the Decalogue.

Teaching Methods: *Computers:* Internet, e-mail. *Other:* fax, correspondence, independent study, individual study.

Admission Requirements: *Undergraduate:* high school graduate or GED.

On-Campus Requirements: None.

Tuition and Fees: contact school. *Credit by:* semester.

Accreditation: Middle States Association of Colleges and Schools.

Description: Bryn Athyn College (1877) is one of four schools that comprise The Academy of the New Church, an institution chartered by the governor of Pennsylvania in 1877. In 1989, the Academy was relocated from Cherry Street in Philadelphia to its present site in the borough of Bryn Athyn, 15 miles north of the city center.

Central Baptist Theological Seminary

741 North 31st Street	Phone: (913) 371–5313
Kansas City, KS 66102-3964	Fax: (913) 371-8110

Division(s): Academic
Web Site(s): http://www.cbts.edu
E-mail: rejohnson@cbts.edu

Undergraduate Degree Programs:
Diploma in Theological Studies

Graduate Degree Programs:
Master of Divinity
Master of Arts in Religious Studies

Teaching Methods: *Computers:* Internet, e-mail. *TV:* videotape. *Other:* videoconferencing, audioconferencing, audio-graphics, audiotapes, fax, correspondence, independent study, individual study, learning contracts.

Credits Granted for: extrainstitutional learning (preapproved workshops).

Admission Requirements: *Undergraduate:* 2.3 undergraduate GPA, must matriculate within 2 years of admission. *Graduate:* accredited bachelor's degree, 2.3 GPA for undergraduate and graduate work, must matriculate within 2 years of admission.

On-Campus Requirements: yes, required opening and closing intensives are held on campus for each distance learning class. In addition, only 25% of the total hours for any degree program may be taken off campus.

Tuition and Fees: *Undergraduate:* $185/credit part-time, $1850 full-time tuition flat rate. *Graduate:* same as undergraduate. *Application Fee:* $30-MDiv., MA, diploma; $20-special, audit, continuing education. *Other Costs:* $66 audit or continuing education; $75/semester registration; $600 one-year internship; $305 summer internship; $455 military chaplain internship; $100 for 1st semester MDiv. assessment, $25 following completion of 30 hours, $100 following completion of 60 hours; $25 MA, diploma and special student assessment; $45 electronic telecommunication (nonresident LDL only); $55/6-hr unit of CPE. *Credit by:* semester.

Financial Aid: Federal Stafford Loan; VA; scholarships—Presidential, Honor, Tuition, and Matching Funds; American Indian students are guaranteed full tuition grants; special tuition rate for couples; 50% tuition discount for children of alumni/alumnae; spouses of degree program students may audit courses for $10/semester hour.

Accreditation: Association of Theological Schools in the U.S. and Canada, North Central Association of Colleges and Schools.

Description: Central Baptist Theological Seminary (1901) was chartered to offer professional graduate training for ministers and laypeople, without regard for race, color, national origin, gender, age, or disability. Initially a cooperative effort between Northern and Southern Baptists, the school now enjoys a longstanding covenant relationship with the American Baptist Churches in the U.S. The new Cooperative Baptist Fellowship, for which the seminary has expressed full support, is also well represented among our faculty, staff, students, and board of directors. Indeed, Baptists of every kind make up more than half of the student body, with the rest drawn from Christian denominations of similar theology and heritage. The distance learning program began in 1989 and has evolved into one of the few distance education programs serving graduate theological education in America. It has offered 23 courses since that time by using videotaped lectures and telephone conference calls linking on-campus students and students at remote locations—for up to 24 participants per class. In the fall of 1995, an Internet dimension was added, allowing students with e-mail capabilities to converse with other students and professors.

Concordia University, St. Paul

275 N. Syndicate Street	**Phone: (800) 333–1180**
St. Paul, MN 55104	**(800) 211-3370**
	Fax: (651) 603-6144

Division(s): College of Graduate and Continuing Studies, School of Human Services and School of Accelerated Learning
Web Site(s): http://www.cshs.csp.edu
E-mail: csal@csp.edu

Undergraduate Degree Programs:
Bachelor of Arts in:
  Marketing
  School Age Care
  Criminal Justice
  Youth Development
  Management of Human Services Organizations
  Child Development
Fast Track (34 General Education Credits)

Graduate Degree Programs:
Master of Arts in Education:
  Early Childhood
  School-Age Care
  Youth Development
Master of Arts in Human Services:
  Family Studies
  Leadership

Certificate Programs: School-Age Care, Early Childhood.

Class Titles: Anthropology, Sociology, Psychology, History, Computer, Math, English, Child Development, Leadership, Human Development.

Teaching Methods: *Computers:* Internet, real-time chat, electronic classroom, e-mail, CD-ROM, asynchronous discussion group. *TV:* videotape. *Other:* textbooks, handouts, audiotapes, independent study.

Credits Granted for: experiential learning, examination (CLEP).

Admission Requirements: *Undergraduate:* 50 credits transferred, 2 reference letters, resume, 4-day residency for distance ed. *Graduate:* accredited baccalaureate degree, 4-day residency for distance ed, portfolio, 2 reference letters. *Certificate:* high school diploma.

On-Campus Requirements: A 4-day residency is required at the beginning of the program.

Tuition and Fees: *Undergraduate:* $228/credit. *Graduate:* $264/credit. *Application Fee:* $25. *Graduation Fee:* $100. *Credit by:* semester.

Financial Aid: Federal Stafford Loan, Federal Perkins Loan, VA.

Accreditation: North Central Association of Colleges and Schools.

Description: Founded in 1893, Concordia University is a private, liberal arts university owned and operated by the Lutheran Church-Missouri Synod. Since 1994, The Concordia School of Human Services has offered several programs. All of the programs are offered by distance education and all are designed for working adults. The distance education program begins with a 4-day residency at the Concordia University campus in St. Paul, Minnesota. At the residency, students learn the technology they will be using, and begin their first class. They will meet the instructors and will have a chance to ask questions about specific courses. Students will also meet the department staff and learn the support services that are available. Finally, the residency is a time to meet the other members of the cohort. The distance education cohorts are very interactive; there is a great deal of communication that goes back and forth between learners and between learners and professors. The distance education process relies heavily on e-mail. Like the traditional "on-campus" cohorts, the distance education process is reading and writing intensive. The mission of the School of Human Services is to create and deliver outstanding education programs that will prepare professionals for enlightened care—facilitating their continued growth and development in fields that serve children, youth, and adults.

New Hampshire Community Technical College, Claremont

One College Drive	**Phone: (603) 542-7744**
Claremont, NH 03743	**Fax: (603) 543-1844**

Division(s): Division of Continuing Education
Web Site(s): http://www.claremont.tec.nh.us/
E-mail: ckusselow@tec.nh.us

Undergraduate Degree Programs:
Associate of Arts

Class Titles: General education classes.

Teaching Methods: *Computers:* Internet, real-time chat, electronic classroom, e-mail. *TV:* videotape, cable program, satellite broadcasting, PBS. *Other:* fax, correspondence, independent study, individual study, learning contracts.

Credits Granted for: examination (CLEP).

Admission Requirements: *Undergraduate:* high school degree or GED.

On-Campus Requirements: None.

Tuition and Fees: *Undergraduate:* $120/credit. *Application Fee:* $10. *Other Costs:* $3 per credit administrative fee. *Credit by:* semester.

Financial Aid: Federal Stafford Loan, Federal Perkins Loan, Federal PLUS Loan, Federal Pell Grant, Federal Work-Study, VA, state programs for residents of New Hampshire.

Accreditation: The New England Association of Schools and Colleges.

Description: The New Hampshire Community Technical College at Claremont and Nashua (1968) provides affordable study opportunities that answer the needs of a diverse student population and address the needs/demands of the region. The college offers open access to academic, technical, professional, and enrichment courses, preparing students for responsible citizenship and for employment. The college provides leadership in higher education, including school-to-work partnerships and transfer opportunities to other postsecondary institutions. The college also provides technological training for regional industry and business through the expertise of its faculty and staff. New Hampshire Community Technical College began offering distance learning classes in 1999.

Northeastern University

360 Huntington Avenue, 328 C.P.	Phone: (617) 373-5620
Boston, MA 02115	Fax: (617) 373-5625

Division(s): Network Northeastern
Web Site(s): http://www.neu.edu/network-nu
E-mail: L.Alosso@neu.edu

Graduate Degree Programs:
Master of Science in:
    Electrical and Computer Engineering
    Computer Science
    Information Systems

Certificate Programs: UNIX/C++, Webmaster Technology and Internet Technologies (online).

Class Titles: Algebra, Calculus, Physics.

Teaching Methods: *Computers:* Internet, real-time chat, electronic classroom, e-mail, CD-ROM, newsgroup, LISTSERV. *TV:* videotape, cable program, satellite broadcasting, PBS. *Other:* radio broadcast, audioconferencing, videoconferencing, audiographics, audiotapes, fax, correspondence, independent study, individual study, learning contracts.

Credits Granted for: experiential learning, portfolio assessment, association seminars/workshops, examination (CLEP, ACT-PEP, DANTES, GRE).

Admission Requirements: *Undergraduate:* open enrollment. *Graduate:* GRE in some cases.

On-Campus Requirements: None.

Tuition and Fees: *Undergraduate:* $250/credit. *Graduate:* $535/credit. *Application Fee:* $50. *Credit by:* quarter.

Financial Aid: Federal Stafford Loan, Federal Perkins Loan, Federal PLUS Loan, Federal Pell Grant, Federal Work-Study, VA, Massachusetts resident programs.

Accreditation: Accreditation Board for Engineering and Technology.

Description: Northeastern University (1898) is located in the heart of Boston and is a practice-oriented, student-centered, urban university dedicated to high-quality teaching and research.

University of Alaska, Fairbanks

PO Box 756700	Phone: (907) 474-5353
Fairbanks, AK 99775	Fax: (907) 474-5402

Division(s): Distance Education and Independent Learning
Web Site(s): http://www.dist-ed.uaf.edu
E-mail: distance@uaf.edu

Undergraduate Degree Programs:
Associate of Arts
Associate of Applied Science in:
    Community Health
    Early Childhood Development
    Human Service Technology
    Microcomputer Support Specialist
Bachelor of Arts in Rural Development
Bachelor of Arts in Social Work

Certificate Programs: Community Health, Early Childhood Development, Microcomputer Support Specialist.

Teaching Methods: *Computers:* Internet, e-mail, CD-ROM. *TV:* videotape, satellite broadcasting, PBS. *Other:* radio broadcast, audioconferencing, videoconferencing, audiographics, audiotapes, fax, correspondence, independent study, individual study, learning contracts.

Credits Granted for: experiential learning, portfolio assessment, extrainstitutional learning, examination (CLEP, ACT-PEP, DANTES, GRE).

Admission Requirements: *Undergraduate:* age 18, high school diploma/GED, SAT/ACT.

On-Campus Requirements: None.

Tuition and Fees: *Undergraduate:* $77/credit lower division, $90/credit upper division. *Graduate:* $100/credit 500-level. *Doctoral:* $178/credit 600-level. *Application Fee:* $35. *Other Costs:* $20/course service/handling, average $75/course materials. *Credit by:* semester.

Financial Aid: Federal Stafford Loan, Federal Perkins Loan, Federal PLUS Loan, Federal Pell Grant, VA, Alaska resident programs.

Accreditation: Northwest Association of Schools and Colleges.

Description: In 1922, just 20 years after the discovery of gold in the heart of the Alaskan wilderness, the Alaska Agricultural College and School of Mines opened with 6 faculty members and 6 students. Today UAF has branches in Bethel, Dillingham, Kotzebue, Nome, and the Interior/Aleutians, in addition to the main campus in Fairbanks. UAF is the state's land-, sea-, and space-grant institution. Its College of Rural Alaska has the primary responsibility for Alaska Native education and study, and UAF remains the state's only university offering doctoral degrees. UAF's colleges and schools offer 70 fields of study and a variety of technical and vocational programs. The university developed a correspondence study program in the late 1950s, then created its Center for Distance Education and Independent Learning in 1987. The center supports 200 distance-delivered courses for certificate, degree, and master's programs, and the Independent Learning Program serves 3,400 students worldwide each year.

University of Missouri

136 Clark Hall
Columbia, MO 65211-4200

Phone: (800) 609-3727
(573) 882-2491
Fax: (573) 882-6808

Division(s): Distance and Independent Study
Web Site(s): http://indepstudy.ext.missouri.edu
E-mail: cdis@missouri.edu

Class Titles: Abnormal Psychology, Accounting, Programs for Children/Families, Adolescent Psychology, Affective Development of Gifted Students, African-American Literature, Aging, America Since 1865, American Government, American Health Care, American Literary Masterpieces, American Literature, Analytic Geometry/Calculus, Animal Behavior, Applied Nutrition, Art Activities in Elementary School, Home Horticulture, Career Planning, Child Development, Child Psychology, Mythology, Algebra, Computer Application, Corrections, Cosmic Evolution/Astronomy, Fiction Writing, Poetry Writing, French, German, Russian, Spanish, Statistics, Engineering Mechanics: Dynamics, Engineering Mechanics: Statics, Environmental Psychology, Ethics/Professions, Exposition/Argumentation, Finite Math, Formal Logic, Educational/Psychological Measurement, Logic/Scientific Method, Philosophy, Management, Anthropology, Psychology, Geography of Missouri, Geometric Concepts, History of Missouri, History of Modern Europe, History of American South, Horse Production, Human Resource Management, Insects in Environment, Latin, Intercultural Communication, BASIC, Educational Statistics, Folklore, Mental Retardation/Severe Handicaps, Philosophy, Political Science, Sociology, Special Education, Special Education for Regular Educators, Meteorology, Issue/Trends in Reading Instruction, Learning/Instruction, Literature of New Testament, Literature of Old Testament, Logic/Language, Major Questions in Philosophy, Making of Modern Britain, Mathematical Logic, Money/Banking/Monetary Theory, Multicultural Study of Children/Families, Music Appreciation, Number Systems/Applications, Organizational Theory, Personal/Family Finance, Physical Geography, Physical Geology, Politics of Third World, Geology, Marketing, Psychology of Sensation/Perception, Public Administration, Regions/ Nations of World, Revolutionary America 1754–1789, Rights of Offender, Rural Sociology, Secondary School Curriculum, Teaching Reading Comprehension, Social Inequalities, Social Psychology, Symbolic Logic, Surface Water Management, Teaching of Reading, Teaching Reading in Content Areas, British Literature to 1784, Technical Writing, Rural Sociology, Introduction to Programming Using C++, Microeconomics, Macroeconomics, International Trade, Community College, Cultural Anthropology, World Literatures, US History—1940 to Present, Business Law, Calculus, Care/Prevention of Athletic Injuries, Peace Studies, Neuroscience. Special Topics: Changing World/Changing Classroom: Dealing with Critical Situation in School, New Approach to Discipline: Democratic Classroom, Cooperative Classroom Management, Coping with Student Problems in Classroom—Dealing in Discipline, Developing Personal System of Discipline, Educating Gifted, Preventing School Failure, Shakespeare, Teaching Students Optimism, Teaching Tolerance to Students, Working with Students at Risk; Topics: American Poetry, Experiencing American Cultures in Contemporary Novel, Gothic Fiction, Shakespeare, Twilight of Sioux, War in Vietnam/the U.S., Women in Popular Culture, Helping Students/Teachers Deal with Bullies/School Violence, Helping Students/Teachers Deal with Stress/Anger, Special Topics in Educational Leadership, Teachers and the Law.

Teaching Methods: *Computers:* Online, e-mail. *TV:* videotape. *Other:* audiotapes, print study guide, independent study.

Admission Requirements: *Undergraduate:* Students may enroll in Independent Study courses anytime, with 9 months' completion time, but enrollment does not constitute university admission. *Graduate:* same as undergraduate.

On-Campus Requirements: None.

Tuition and Fees: *Undergraduate:* $142/credit. *Graduate:* $179/credit. *Other Costs:* $15 handling/enrollment. *Credit by:* semester.

Accreditation: North Central Association of Colleges and Secondary Schools.

Description: The University of Missouri Center for Distance and Independent Study was established in 1911. Today it is one of the nation's largest distance learning programs, with 18,000 annual enrollments. The center has earned a solid reputation based on providing quality courses and superior service to its students worldwide. Current efforts are focused on utilizing the latest technology in all program areas. By accessing the web site, students can get up-to-date course information, enroll in courses, request exams, and submit lessons for courses. In addition, the center offers a number of online courses; all lessons and instructions for these courses are online.

The University of Pennsylvania, School of Dental Medicine

| 4001 Spruce Street | Phone: (215) 573-9100 |
| Philadelphia, PA 19104 | Fax: (215) 573-5742 |

Division(s): School of Dental Medicine
Web Site(s): http://www.intellihealth.com
E-mail: wendymc@pobox.upenn.edu

Class Titles: Pediatric Dentistry, Oral Surgery, Pharmacology, Periodontics and Prosthetics, Basic and Advanced Restorative Dentistry, Implantology, Radiology, Pathology, Oral Medicine, Dental Ethics.

Teaching Methods: *Computers:* Internet

Admission Requirements: None.

On-Campus Requirements: None.

Tuition and Fees: *Undergraduate:* $25 per CEU credit.

Accreditation: Middle States Association of Schools and Colleges.

Description: The University of Pennsylvania School of Dental Medicine (SDM) is a private Ivy League institution that ranks among the nation's leaders in oral health education, research, and patient care. Beginning in 2001, SDM began offering online professional continuing education programs for the dental community. Courses are offered by the SDM faculty, leaders in their fields of specialty, as reflected in their extensive publications, invited lectures, and sponsored research activities.

University of Texas of the Permian Basin

| 4901 East University | Phone: (915) 552-2870 |
| Odessa, TX 79762 | Fax: (915) 552-2871 |

Division(s): REACH Distance Learning Program Center
Web Site(s): http://www.utpb.edu/reach/
E-mail: REACH@utpb.edu

Certificate Programs: Early Childhood Endorsement.

Class Titles: Accounting, Art, Computer Science, Criminology, Criminal Justice Administration, Education, English, Finance, History, Kinesiology, Management, Marketing, Math, Theater, Psychology, Political Science, Sociology.

Teaching Methods: *Computers:* Internet, real-time chat, e-mail, CD-ROM. *Other:* videoconferencing.

Credits Granted for: examination (CLEP, AP).

Admission Requirements: *Undergraduate:* high school diploma, SAT/ACT score (sliding scale), specific list of high school courses. *Graduate:* undergraduate degree, GRE, minimum GPA.

On-Campus Requirements: None.

Tuition and Fees: *Undergraduate:* $100/credit Texas resident, $300/credit nonresident. *Graduate:* $193/credit Texas resident, $373/credit nonresident. *Other Costs:* $70, any number of hours. *Credit by:* semester.

Financial Aid: Federal Stafford Loan, Federal Perkins Loan, Federal PLUS Loan, Federal Pell Grant, Federal Work-Study, VA, Texas resident programs, various scholarships.

Accreditation: Southern Association of Colleges and Schools.

Description: University of Texas of the Permian Basin (1973) is a comprehensive university serving a mostly nonresidential student body in a vast area of western Texas. Some UTPB students commute from communities as far as 100 miles from the main campus. The university offers undergraduate and master's degrees in a variety of disciplines. For the first 18 years of its existence, UTPB was an upper-division and graduate-only institution. The first lower-division students entered in the fall of 1991. UTPB began its distance learning program in 1996, sharing courses via an interactive (compressed) video network linking UT System components and area community colleges. Web-based courses were offered for the first time in the spring of 1998. Although many distance courses are offered, no full degree programs are currently available through distance learning.

University of Utah

1901 East South Campus Drive
Annex Room 1215
Salt Lake City, UT 84112-9364

Phone: (801) 581-8801
(800) 467-8839
Fax: (801) 581-6267

Division(s): ULEARN
Web Site(s): http://ulearn.utah.edu
E-mail: ulearn@aoce.utah.edu

Certificate Program: Geographic Information Systems for Professionals.

Class Titles: Anthropology, Art, Art History, Bioengineering, Biology, Chemistry, Communication Disorders, Economics, Educational Studies (Teaching and Learning), English, Ethnic Studies, Film, Finance, Foods and Nutrition, Geography, Gerontology, History, Mathematics, Meteorology, Music, Performing Arts, Physics, Political Science, Psychology, Special Education.

Teaching Methods: *Computers:* Internet, real-time chat, electronic classroom, e-mail, CD-ROM, newsgroup, LISTSERV. *TV:* videotape, PBS. *Other:* audiotapes, fax, correspondence, independent study, learning contracts.

Admission Requirements: *Undergraduate:* Enrollment does not constitute admission. High school students must be 18 years old and provide written permission from a parent or guardian and high school principal.

On-Campus Requirements: None.

Tuition and Fees: *Undergraduate:* $95/credit. *Other Costs:* Course manual and textbook costs. Some classes have a video licensing fee. *Credit by:* semester.

Financial Aid: Most financial aid, loans, and grant monies may be applied to semester term-specific courses but not for open-enrollment courses.

Accreditation: Northwest Association of Schools and Colleges.

Description: The University of Utah has been the flagship institution of higher education in the Intermountain West since its founding in 1850. As a public urban research and teaching institution, the U of U allows students to pursue academic disciplines on the undergraduate and graduate levels. ULEARN (the distance education department at the university) extends the university's resources to a diverse student population that requires creative course delivery. ULEARN serves approximately 6,000 students annually in open-enrollment and term-specific courses. The courses fulfill many general education requirements, with a cluster of courses specifically designed for teacher recertification.

University of Windsor

401 Sunset Avenue
Windsor, ON, Canada N9V 3P4

Phone: (519) 561-1414
Fax: (519) 971-3623

Division(s): Flexible Learning
Web Site(s): http://www.uwindsor.ca/flexible
E-mail: askme@uwindsor.ca

Undergraduate Degree Programs:
Bachelor of Arts in Liberal and Professional Studies
Bachelor of Commerce for University Graduates
Bachelor of Business Studies, Accounting Track
Bachelor of Commerce for University Graduates
Bachelor of Science, General Science for Medical Laboratory Technician

Certificate Programs: Business Administration

Teaching Methods: The University of Windsor offers a flexible approach to learning. You can take daytime or evening courses, or you can study by distance education at your kitchen table or at your office computer during lunch hour. Home study employs course guides, online materials, textbooks, software, audiotapes, videotapes, and Internet connection. Support services available by telephone or e-mail include Windsor's online library catalog and computer services help desk. Students are encouraged to form study groups, either face to face or online. Many courses offer opportunities to correspond with professors and fellow students through the Web. Professors are available for consultation in person, over the telephone, or through e-mail.

Admission Requirements: To enroll in a distance education course, applicants must be a student of the university. Applicants should complete a University of Windsor application form and submit it with the requested supporting documents to the Office of the Registrar at least two months prior to the start date of the course in which they wish to enroll. The part-time (3 or fewer courses per semester) application fee is $25. Applicants who have credits from college or university and wish to have them transferred to a program at the University of Windsor must submit official transcripts, course descriptions, and pay a $40 evaluation fee. *Ontario Secondary School:* Completion of six OAC subjects with a minimum of 50%, including OAC English. *Mature Student:* Minimum of 21 years of age, Canadian citizens, have grade 12 standing or equivalent, away from formal education for two calendar years. *Transfer Student:* Transcript of record from each institution previously attended. *USA Student:* Graduation from an accredited high school with a cumulative GPA of 2.75 or higher. Transfers from a college or university must produce transcripts. *International (non-USA):* Official secondary school documents. Transfers from accredited universities must produce transcripts and original course descriptions. TOEFL. Notarized English translations necessary if documents are not in English. *Letter of Permission:* Students of another university who wish to enroll at the

University of Windsor, with the intention of transferring courses back to their home university, will be allowed to register upon receipt of a letter of permission issued by the home university.

On-Campus Requirements: None.

Tuition and Fees: *Undergraduate:* C$385.80 to C$400 per course (Canadian students), C$943 to C$1,227 per course (international non-USA students), US$393 per course (USA students). *Application Fee:* $25. *Other Costs:* Distance education fee. *Credit by:* semester.

Financial Aid: provincial (OSAP) and Canada student loans, bursaries.

Accreditation: Association of Universities and Colleges of Canada.

Description: In 1963 the new, nondenominational University of Windsor (1857) inherited Assumption College, an educational complex developed since 1870 by the Basilian Fathers (the Congregation of St. Basil) and expanded to independent university status in 1953. This unprecedented transition from a historically Roman Catholic university to a nondenominational institution began in 1956 with the affiliation of Essex College, the first provincially-assisted public institution of higher education. During 1963–1964, affiliation agreements were also made with Holy Redeemer College, Canterbury College, and the new Iona College (United Church of Canada). UW assumed control of the campus in 1963 and soon became a member of the International Association of Universities. Distance education courses were first offered in 1989.

University of Wisconsin, Whitewater

800 West Main Street	Phone: (262) 472-1945 (MBA)
Whitewater, WI 53190	(262) 472-5247 (Other)
	Fax: (262) 472-4863 (MBA)
	(262) 472-5210 (Other)

Divisions: College of Business and Economics (MBA) or Continuing Education (other programs)
Web Sites: http://academics.uww.edu/business/onlinemba/
http://www.uww.edu/conteduc/credit.htm
E-mail: zahnd@mail.uww.edu (MBA)
gibbsk@mail.uww.edu (other programs)

Graduate Degree Programs:
Online Master of Business Administration

Class Titles: (vary by semester) *Online MBA:* Accounting Foundations, Profit Planning and Control, Business and Professional Communication, Business Technologies, Business Telecommunications, Managerial Economics, Statistics Foundations, Economic Foundations, Advanced International Economics, Financial Management, The Legal Environment of Business, Multinational Business Finance, Financial Markets, Portfolio Theory and Practice, Operations Management, Introduction to Computer-based Information Systems, Management of Technology, Building Effective Organizations, Seminar in Human Resource Management, Current Issues in Compensation and Benefits, Training and Development, Management and Labor Relations, Social Responsibility of Business, Strategic Management of Human Resources, Strategic Management Planning, International Management, Business Policy, Marketing, Advanced Statistical Methods, Operations Research, Seminar in Methodology of Business Research, Buyer Behavior, International Business (Marketing), Product Innovation and Pricing, Corporate Marketing Planning.

Teaching Methods: *Computers, Online MBA:* LearningSpace, Lotus Notes, Internet, instructional CD, e-mail. *Other:* textbook, audioconferencing.

Credits Granted for: examination.

Admission Requirements: *Graduate:* bachelor's degree, 2.75 GPA, GMAT composite score of 1,000, TOEFL: 550, 7 years to complete.

On-Campus Requirements: None.

Tuition and Fees: *Graduate:* Current resident and nonresident graduate business fees for online courses will apply. Contact *zahnd@mail.uww.edu* for specific information. *Application Fee:* $45. *Credit by:* semester.

Financial Aid: Federal Stafford Loan, Federal Perkins Loan, Federal PLUS Loan, Federal Pell Grant, Federal Work-Study, Supplemental Educational Opportunity Grant, Indian Grant (state and federal), VA, Wisconsin resident programs: Talent Incentive Program, Lawton Retention Grant for Minority Students, Division of Vocational Rehabilitation, Wisconsin Handicapped Program.

Accreditation: American Assembly of Collegiate Schools of Business.

Description: The University of Wisconsin, Whitewater (1868), a public institution, is part of a 26-campus university system. UW-Whitewater is committed to the goal of achieving Excellence for the 21st Century where faculty teaching is the first and foremost responsibility of every faculty member. UW-Whitewater enrolls 10,500 students and offers 45 undergraduate and 16 graduate degree programs in the Colleges of Arts and Communication, Business and Economics, Education, and Letters and Sciences. The Whitewater campus is nationally recognized for serving disabled students. UW-Whitewater ranked in the first tier among 123 Midwestern comprehensive colleges and universities in the *1999 College Guide of America's Best Colleges,* published by *U.S. News and World Report* magazine. UW-Whitewater entered the field of distance education 2 decades ago when it began offering teacher education courses over the statewide Educational Teleconference Network and the SEEN network (audio and freeze frame video images). In the past 3 years, a number of interactive video courses have been offered in the areas of foreign languages, women's studies, and school business management and, more recently, the online MBA has been launched.

VanderCook College of Music

3140 S. Federal Street	Phone: (312) 225-6288
Chicago, IL 60616	Fax: (312) 225-5211

Division(s): MECA Office
Web Site(s): http://www.vandercook.edu
E-mail: rrhodes@vandercook.edu

Class Titles: Web Page Design.

Teaching Methods: *Computers:* Internet, real-time chat, electronic classroom, e-mail.

Admission Requirements: *Graduate:* a degree in music or a music-related discipline.

On-Campus Requirements: None.

Tuition and Fees: *Graduate:* $175 per credit. *Credit by:* semester.

Accreditation: North Central Association of Schools and Colleges, National Association of Schools of Music.

Description: Established in 1909, VanderCook College of Music is the only independent college in the country dedicated exclusively to educating music teachers. At the moment, our distance learning opportunities consist of a single course, but that may change. There are no plans, however, to offer any degree programs entirely or mostly through distance learning.

Wayne State College

1111 Main Street	Phone: (402) 375-7217
Wayne, NE 68787	Fax: (402) 375-7204

Division(s): Office of Continuing Education
Web Site(s): http://www.wsc.edu
E-mail: extcampus@wsc.edu

Undergraduate Degree Programs:
Bachelor of Arts
Bachelor of Science

Graduate Degree Programs:
Master of Business Administration
Master of Science in Education
Education Specialist in School Administration

Class Titles: Business, English, Biology, Math, Chemistry, Education, Wellness, Political Science, Criminal Justice, Sociology, History, Geography, Vocational Education, Industrial Technology, German, Spanish, Literature, Communication.

Teaching Methods: *Computers:* Internet, electronic classroom, e-mail, CD-ROM, LISTSERV. *TV:* satellite broadcasting. *Other:* audioconferencing, videoconferencing, independent study, individual study, learning contracts.

Credits Granted for: extrainstitutional learning, examination (CLEP, ACT-PEP, DANTES, GRE).

Admission Requirements: *Undergraduate:* open-admission, high school diploma or GED, ACT test scores preferred, high school transcripts as proof of graduation, and a one-time admission fee must accompany admission application. Nebraska resident status determined by length of time in state (more than 6 months) or may be obtained by special authorization—contact Admissions Office. *Graduate:* open-admission, undergraduate transcripts for all degree-seeking graduate students, GMAT or GRE scores and references for degree programs, and a one-time application fee must accompany application for graduate admission (fee waived if paid as an undergraduate). Nebraska resident status determined by length of time in state (more than 6 months) or may be obtained by special authorization—contact Admissions Office.

On-Campus Requirements: None.

Tuition and Fees: *Undergraduate:* $70/credit resident, $140/credit nonresident. *Graduate:* $88/credit resident, $176/credit nonresident. *Application Fee:* $20. *Graduation Fee:* $30 undergraduate, $50 graduate. *Other Costs:* $28/credit hour. *Credit by:* semester.

Financial Aid: Federal Stafford Loan, Federal Perkins Loan, Federal PLUS Loan, Federal Pell Grant, Federal Work-Study, VA, Nebraska resident programs.

Accreditation: North Central Association of Colleges and Schools, National Council for Accreditation of Teacher Education.

Description: Wayne State College (1891) is a regional, public, 4-year college located in northeast Nebraska. Students can major in 31 programs, with an average of 50% majoring in arts and sciences, 30% in education, and 20% in business. WSC is part of a three-school state college system geographically positioned to serve rural Nebraska. The three colleges, supported by the Nebraska Educational TV system and the University of Nebraska, have joined together to provide distance learning programming across the system and to isolated rural communities. The Nebraska state college system has been producing satellite-based and videoconferencing-based programming for most of the past decade. The system has recently added Internet-based course work to supplement the other programs and add flexibility for the nontraditional students across the region.

Index by State and Province

Index by On-Campus Requirements

Some degree and certificate programs require that students take certain classes or seminars in a traditional classroom setting either on the university's campus or in an off-campus location. If you live a long distance from the campus, this on-campus time requirement becomes a very important part of your decision-making process. The amount of time required on campus varies by school, program, and class. For example, some schools require time on campus for certain types of degree programs and not for others. Attendance might be necessary only for examinations or orientations. Always check with the individual college or university about its on-campus requirements, and remember that attendance requirements are sometimes negotiable.

The following colleges and universities have some type of on-campus requirement:

Index by Fields of Study
Undergraduate Degree Programs

(A) = Associate Degree
(B) = Bachelor's Degree
(M) = Minor
(MS) = Major
(R) = Registered Nurse
(V) = Vocational

ACCOUNTING
(see also Business)
Alaska Pacific University, 99
Caldwell College (B), 140
Champlain College (A), 158
City University (B), 162
Concordia University, Austin (A), 185
DeSales University, 203
Graceland University (B), 247
Harcourt, Learning Direct (A), 252
Indiana College Network (A), 264
Inter-American University of Puerto Rico (A), 268
Ivy Tech State College, 272
Keiser College (A), 281
Lake Superior State University (B), 287
Linfield College (B), 298
Marywood University (B), 310
Northampton Community College (A), 349
Northwest Missouri State University (B) (completion), 354
Northwest Technical College (A), 354
Saint Mary-of-the-Woods College (A, B), 399
Southern New Hampshire University, 425
Southwestern Adventist University (B), 429
Southwestern Assemblies of God University (B), 430
State University of New York College of Technology at Canton, 440
Strayer University (A, B), 443
University of Calgary (B), 479
University of Maryland, University College, 499
University of Northwestern Ohio (A), 515
University of Windsor (B), 579
Utah State University (B), 542

ACQUISITION AND CONTRACT MANAGEMENT
Strayer University (A), 443

ADDICTION STUDIES
(see Chemical Dependency Studies/Counseling)

ADMINISTRATION
(see also under specific categories: Business, Business Administration, Health Administration, Public Administration, etc.)
University of Action Learning, 473

Industrial Relations and Human Resources
Athabasca University (B), 116

Management
Athabasca University (B), 116

Organization
Athabasca University (B), 116

ADMINISTRATIVE OFFICE TECHNOLOGY
Ivy Tech State College, 272

ADMINISTRATIVE SUPPORT/INFORMATION TECHNOLOGY
Union County College (A), 469

ADOLESCENT TO YOUNG ADULT LICENSE
Cincinnati Bible College and Seminary (B), 161

ADULT DEGREE PROGRAM
Prescott College, 377
Vermont College of Norwich University, 544

ADULT LIBERAL STUDIES PROGRAM
University of Toledo (B), 530

AERONAUTICS
(see Professional Aeronautics)

AGRICULTURE
Community Colleges of Colorado Online (A), 184
University of Northwestern Ohio (A), 515
Washington State University (B), 549

AIR CONDITIONING ENGINEERING TECHNOLOGY
State University of New York College of Technology at Canton, 440

AIRWAY SCIENCES
Management
Inter-American University of Puerto Rico (B), 268

Electronic Systems
Inter-American University of Puerto Rico (B), 268

Computer Sciences
Inter-American University of Puerto Rico (B), 268

Aircraft Management
Inter-American University of Puerto Rico (B), 268

ALLIED HEALTH
(see Health Sciences)

AMERICAN INDIAN STUDIES
Fort Peck Community College (A), 228

AMERICAN MILITARY HISTORY
American Military University (B), 108

ANIMAL SCIENCES AND INDUSTRY
Kansas State University (B), 280

ANTHROPOLOGY
Athabasca University (B), 116

APPLIED ARTS, UNSPECIFIED
Casper College (A), 151

APPLIED BUSINESS
Edison Community College (Ohio) (A), 214
Fort Peck Community College (B, Completion), 228
Owens Community College (A), 365
University of Northwestern Ohio (A), 515

APPLIED COMPUTING
Rochester Institute of Technology (B), 387

APPLIED HEALTH
University of Minnesota, Crookston (B), 503

APPLIED MANAGEMENT
Everglades College (B), 218
Hamilton College (A), 251

APPLIED NUTRITION
American Academy of Nutrition (A), 103

APPLIED SCIENCE AND TECHNOLOGY
(Occupational Training Programs)
Richland Community College (A), 384
Thomas Edison State College (A, B), 458

APPLIED SCIENCE, UNSPECIFIED
Angelina College (A), 111
Anoka-Ramsey Community College Coon Rapids Campus (A), 573
Carl Sandburg College (A), 149
Casper College (A), 151
Central Community College (A), 152
Coconino Community College (A), 168
College of DuPage (A), 170
Columbia State Community College (A), 179
County College of Morris (A), 190
Cumberland County College (A), 192
Dickinson State University (A), 204
Dutchess Community College (A), 208
East Central Community College (A), 210
East Central College (A), 210
Edison Community College (Ohio) (A), 214
Florida Community College at Jacksonville (A), 224
Fond du Lac Tribal and Community College (A), 226
Grays Harbor College (A), 249
Harper College (A), 254
Herkimer County Community College (A), 257
Kansas City, Kansas Community College (A), 280

DIETETIC FOOD SYSTEMS MANAGEMENT
Penn State University (A), 371

DIETETICS
Eastern Michigan University (B), 212
Kansas State University (B), 280

DIGITAL COMMUNICATION
Franklin University (A) (completion), 230

DIGITAL DESIGN
Sessions.edu, 412

DIGITAL MEDIA COMMUNICATION
Saint Mary-of-the-Woods College (B), 399

DISASTER AND EMERGENCY MANAGEMENT
Rochester Institute of Technology (B), 387

DRAFTING/DESIGN TECHNOLOGY
Ivy Tech State College, 272

DROIT ET JUSTICE
Laurentian University (B), 292

DRUG AND ALCOHOL ABUSE
Oklahoma State University (A), 360
Oklahoma State University, Oklahoma City (A), 361

EARLY CHILDHOOD
State University of New York College of Technology at
Canton, 440

EARLY CHILDHOOD DEVELOPMENT
University of Alaska, Fairbanks (A),

EARLY CHILDHOOD EDUCATION
California College for Health Sciences (A), 141
Central Piedmont Community College (A), 154
Cincinnati Bible College and Seminary (A), 161
Fort Peck Community College (A), 228
Parkland College (A), 368
Saint Mary-of-the-Woods College (A), 399
Stephens College (B), 443
University of Alaska Southeast, Juneau Campus (A), 475
University of Alaska Southeast, Sitka Campus (A), 476
University of Cincinnati (A), 484

EARLY CHILDHOOD TEACHER EDUCATION
Cincinnati Bible College and Seminary (B), 161

ECONOMICS
Foothill College (A), 226
Southern New Hampshire University, 425
Strayer University (A, B), 443

EDUCATION
(see also Vocational Education and Industry Training)
Allegany College of Maryland (A), 101
Bergen Community College (A), 127
Carl Sandburg College, 149
Central Washington University, 154
Fort Peck Community College (A), 228
Goddard College (B), 241
Lakehead University (B), 288
Northwest Indian College (A, B), 352
Saint Mary-of-the-Woods College (B), 399
Southwestern Adventist University (B), 429
Southwestern Assemblies of God University (A), 430
Troy State University, Florida Region (A), 464
University College of the University of Maine System
(A), 472
University of Winnipeg (B), 534

Early Childhood
Bethany College (A, B), 128
Concordia University, Austin (A), 185
Lake Region State College (A), 287
Northwest Indian College (A), 352
Ohio University Eastern, 359
Saint Mary-of-the-Woods College (B), 399
Southwestern Indian Polytechnic Institute, 431
Teikyo Post University (A), 451

Elementary
Concordia University, Austin (A), 185
Saint Mary-of-the-Woods College (B), 399
Spring Arbor University, 434

K-8
Alaska Pacific University, 99

Middle Childhood
Ohio University Eastern, 359

Secondary
Concordia University, Austin (A), 185
Saint Mary-of-the-Woods College (B), 399

EDUCATIONAL TECHNOLOGY
Sacred Heart University, 392

EEG/EEG TECHNOLOGY
California College for Health Sciences (A), 141

ELECTIVE STUDIES
Community Psychology Major
Saint Cloud State University, 394

ELECTRIC POWER TECHNOLOGY
Bismarck State College (A), 128

ELECTRICAL ENGINEERING
Inter-American University of Puerto Rico (B), 268
University of North Dakota (B), 514

ELECTRICAL ENGINEERING AND TECHNOLOGY
Harcourt, Learning Direct (A), 252

ELECTRICAL ENGINEERING TECHNOLOGY
State University of New York College of Technology at
Canton, 440

**ELECTRICAL/MECHANICAL ENGINEERING
TECHNOLOGY**
Rochester Institute of Technology (B), 387

ELECTRICAL TRANSMISSION SYSTEMS TECHNOLOGY
Bismarck State College (A), 128

ELECTRICIAN
The University of North Carolina at Charlotte (B), 513

**ELECTRONIC BUSINESS (e-BUSINESS), ELECTRONIC
COMMERCE (e-COMMERCE)**
(see also Business)
Bellevue University (completion), 126
Champlain College (A), 158
Cleveland Institute of Electronics (A and B), 166
Everglades College (B), 218
Friends University, 231
Keiser College (A), 281
Rochester Institute of Technology (B), 387

ELECTRONICS
Technology Major
Aims Community College (A), 99

Fort Peck Community College (A), 228
Harcourt, Learning Direct (A), 252

Biomedical Major
Aims Community College (A), 99

ELECTRONICS ENGINEERING TECHNOLOGY
Grantham College of Engineering (A, B), 248

ELECTRONICS TECHNOLOGY
Indiana College Network (B), 264

ELEMENTARY EDUCATION
California State University, Fullerton (B), 144
Fort Peck Community College (B), 228
Graceland University (B), 247
Oral Roberts University (B), 363
Parkland College (A), 368
Southeast Missouri State University, 420
Southwestern Assemblies of God University (B), 430
Stephens College (B), 443

ELEMENTARY TEACHER EDUCATION LICENSE
Cincinnati Bible College and Seminary (B), 161

ELEMENTARY TEACHER PREPARATION
Mountain State University (A), 330

EMERGENCY MANAGEMENT AND PLANNING
Red Rocks Community College (A), 380

EMERGENCY MEDICAL SERVICES
American College of Prehospital Medicine (A, B), 105

EMERGENCY MEDICAL SERVICES TECHNOLOGY
Lima Technical College, 297

EMERGENCY STUDIES
Management Major
Community Colleges of Colorado Online (A), 184

ENGINEERING
California National University for Advanced Studies (B),
142
Northern Virginia Community College (A), 351
University of Toledo (B), 530

Manufacturing
Michigan Technological University (B), 317

Mechanical Design
Michigan Technological University (B), 317

ENGINEERING MANAGEMENT
Lake Superior State University (B), 287

ENGINEERING SCIENCE
Richland Community College (A), 384
State University of New York College of Technology at
Canton, 440

ENGINEERING SCIENCE AND TECHNOLOGY
College of DuPage (A), 170
South Suburban College, 419
University of Central Florida (B), 482

ENGINEERING TECHNOLOGY(IES)
North Central State College (A), 345
The University of North Carolina at Charlotte (B), 513

ENGLISH
(see also English minor concentration under Arts,
Unspecified; English under Secondary Education)

GLOBAL BUSINESS MANAGEMENT
Bellevue University (completion), 126

GLOBAL STUDIES
National University (B), 335

GOVERNMENTAL ADMINISTRATION
(see also Criminal Justice)
Public Management
Christopher Newport University (B), 160

International Studies
Christopher Newport University (B), 160

GRAPHIC DESIGN
Sessions.edu, 412

HAZARDOUS MATERIAL
Barton County Community College (A), 123
Fort Peck Community College (A), 228

HOME HEALTH AIDE
California College for Health Sciences (V), 141

HEALTH SCIENCES
(see also Nursing)

Accredited Record Technician (ART) Progression Program
College of Saint Scholastica, 172

Allied Health
California College for Health Sciences (A), 141
Greenville Technical College (A), 250
Northwest Indian College (A), 352
Widener University (A and B), 565

Clinical Management and Leadership
George Washington University (B), 237

Clinical Research Administration
George Washington University (B), 237

Community Health
Indiana College Network (B), 264
University of Alaska, Fairbanks (A),

Community Health Services
Ohio University Eastern, 359

Emergency Health Services Management
George Washington University (B), 237

Health Arts and Science(s)
Lower Columbia College (A), 300
Goddard College (B), 241

Health Care
Avila College,
Stephens College (B), 443

Health Care Administration/Management
Athabasca University (B), 116
Baker College Center for Graduate Studies and Baker College On-Line (B), 120
Bellevue University (completion), 126
Columbia International University, 178
Franklin University (A) (completion), 230
Mountain State University (B), 330
Saint Joseph's College of Maine, 396

Health Care Business
Clarkson College (B), 165

Health Care Leadership
Wittenberg University, 568

Health Information Administration/Management
Dakota State University, 195
Stephens College (B), 443
Weber State University (B), 553

Health Information Technology
Central Piedmont Community College (A), 154
Marylhurst University (A), 309
Pitt Community College, 375
Weber State University (A, B), 553

Health Promotion
Weber State University (B), 553

Health Science(s)
North Central State College (A), 345
Stephens College (B), 443
Thomas Edison State College (B), 458

Health Services
Indiana College Network (B), 264
University of Southern Indiana (B) (completion), 525

Health Services Administration/Management
Weber State University (B), 553
California College for Health Sciences (B), 141
Canadian School of Management (B), 147
Keiser College (A), 281
Ohio University Eastern, 359
Spring Arbor University, 434
University of Central Florida (B), 482

Long Term Care Administration
Saint Joseph's College of Maine, 396

Medical Informatics
Mountain State University (B), 330

Physical Therapy
Allegany College of Maryland (A), 101
Open Learning Agency (B), 362

Radiologic Major
Allegany College of Maryland (A), 101
University of Missouri, Columbia (B), 506

Radiologic Science
Weber State University (B), 553
Saint Joseph's College of Mainez (degree completion), 396

Radiologic Technology
Allegany College of Maryland (A), 101
Southeast Community College, 420
Thomas Edison State College (A), 458

Respiratory Care
California College for Health Sciences (B), 141
Saint Joseph's College of Maine (degree completion), 396

Respiratory Therapy
Allegany College of Maryland (A), 101
California College for Health Sciences (A), 141
J. Sargeant Reynolds Community College, 273
Open Learning Agency (B), 362

University of Missouri, Columbia (B), 506
Weber State University (A, B), 553

HIGH SCHOOL
Hadley School for the Blind, 251
Lock Haven University of Pennsylvania, 298
Oral Roberts University (B), 363

General Education Degree
Citrus Community College, 161
Concordia University (Minnesota), 186
Edison Community College (Florida), 213

HEALTH SYSTEMS ADMINISTRATION MANAGEMENT
Rochester Institute of Technology (B), 387

HISTORY
(see also History minor concentration under Arts, Unspecified)
Athabasca University (B), 116
Bergen Community College (A), 127
Caldwell College (B), 140
California State University, Stanislaus (B), 145
Concordia University, Austin (A), 185
Foothill College (A), 226
Laurentian University (B), 292
Parkland College (A), 368
Queen's University, 380
Troy State University Montgomery (A, B), 464
University of Houston (B), 491

HISTORY OF POLITICAL SCIENCE/PRE-LAW
Saint Mary-of-the-Woods College (B), 399

HISTOTECHNOLOGY
Indiana College Network (A), 264

HORTICULTURE/AGRIBUSINESS
Southeast Missouri State University, 420

HOSPITALITY MANAGEMENT
Allegany College of Maryland (A), 101
Harcourt, Learning Direct (A), 252
New York Institute of Technology, 342
Northwest Indian College (A), 352

HOTEL AND RESTAURANT MANAGEMENT
Tompkins Cortland Community College, 460
University of Delaware (B), 487
University of Houston (B), 491

HOTEL, RESTAURANT, AND INSTITUTIONAL MANAGEMENT
Penn State University (A), 371

HUMAN DEVELOPMENT
(see also Child Development)
Pacific Oaks College (B), 366
Penn State University (A), 371
Southern Christian University (B), 422
Washington State University (B), 549

HUMAN RESOURCE DEVELOPMENT/MANAGEMENT
Baker College Center for Graduate Studies and Baker College On-Line (B), 120
Indiana College Network (B), 264
Saint Mary-of-the-Woods College (B), 399
University of Maryland, University College, 499

HUMAN SCIENCE(S)
Athabasca University (B), 116
Thomas Edison State College (B), 458

Franklin University (A) (subsequent), 230
Lock Haven University of Pennsylvania (A), 298
Teikyo Post University (B), 451

MANAGEMENT/MARKETING
(see also Business)
Bucks County Community College (A), 137

MANAGEMENT OF HEALTH SERVICES
Ottawa University, Kansas City (B), 364

MANAGEMENT OF HUMAN RESOURCES
Bellevue University (completion), 126

MANAGEMENT OF HUMAN SERVICES
 ORGANIZATIONS
Concordia University, St. Paul (B), 575

MANAGEMENT OF TECHNICAL OPERATIONS
Embry-Riddle Aeronautical University, 216

MANAGEMENT STUDIES
University of Maryland, University College, 499

MANUFACTURING
University of Minnesota, Crookston (B), 503

MANUFACTURING MANAGEMENT TECHNOLOGY
Rochester Institute of Technology (B), 387

MANUFACTURING TECHNOLOGY
State University of New York College of Technology at
 Canton, 440
University of Minnesota, Rochester Center (B),
 504

MARITIME STUDIES
Memorial University of Newfoundland (B), 313

MARKETING
(see also Business)
American Military University (B), 108
Bergen Community College (A), 127
Concordia University (Minnesota) (B), 186
Concordia University, St. Paul (B), 575
Mountain State University (A, B), 330
Saint Mary-of-the-Woods College (B), 399
Southern New Hampshire University, 425
Strayer University (A), 443
University of Maryland, University College, 499
University of Northwestern Ohio (A), 515

MARKETING AND MANAGEMENT
Caldwell College (B), 140

MARKETING, NEW MEDIA
Sessions.edu, 412

MASS COMMUNICATIONS
Advertising/Public Relations
Parkland College (A), 368

Integrated
Parkland College (A), 368

Journalism
Parkland College (A), 368

MASS COMMUNICATIONS AND JOURNALISM
City University (B), 162

MASSAGE, THERAPEUTIC
Allegany College of Maryland (A), 101

MATHEMATICS
Inter-American University of Puerto Rico (B), 268
Saint Mary-of-the-Woods College (B), 399
Southwestern Adventist University (B), 429

MECHANICAL ENGINEERING
(see also Electrical/Mechanical Engineering Technology)
Inter-American University of Puerto Rico (B), 268
University of North Dakota (B), 514

MECHANICAL ENGINEERING TECHNOLOGY
Harcourt, Learning Direct (A), 252
State University of New York College of Technology at
 Canton, 440

MECHANICAL TECHNOLOGY
Indiana College Network (B), 264
Rochester Institute of Technology (B), 387

Computer Drafting Designer
University of Houston (B), 491

MEDIA
Bellevue Community College (A), 125
Southwestern Assemblies of God University (A), 430

MEDICAL ASSISTING
California College for Health Sciences (V), 141
Mountain State University (A), 330

MEDICAL IMAGING (RADIOGRAPHERS)
Clarkson College (B), 164

MEDICAL LABORATORY TECHNOLOGY
Allegany College of Maryland (A), 101
City University (A), 162
State University of New York College of Technology at
 Canton, 440

MEDICAL OFFICE ASSISTANT TECHNOLOGY
University of Northwestern Ohio (A), 515

MEDICAL OFFICE TECHNOLOGY
City University (A), 162

MEDICAL TRANSCRIPTION
California College for Health Sciences (A), 141
Southwest Wisconsin Technical College (One-Year
 Technical Diploma), 429

MENTAL HEALTH AND HUMAN SERVICES
University College of the University of Maine System
 (B), 472

MEXICAN AMERICAN STUDIES
Concordia University, Austin (A), 185

MICROBIOLOGY
(see Biology)

MICROCOMPUTER AND NETWORK TECHNOLOGY
Northwest Technical College (A), 354

MICROCOMPUTER DATABASE SPECIALIST
Lansing Community College (A), 291

MICROCOMPUTER SUPPORT SPECIALIST
University of Alaska, Fairbanks (A),
University of Alaska Southeast, Sitka Campus (A),
 476

MIDDLE CHILDHOOD LICENSE
Cincinnati Bible College and Seminary (B), 161

MILITARY
Barton County Community College (A), 123

MILITARY MANAGEMENT
American Military University (B), 108

MORTGAGE LENDING
Aims Community College (A), 99

MORTUARY SCIENCE
State University of New York College of Technology at
 Canton, 440

MULTIDISCIPLINARY STUDIES
Caldwell College (B), 140
Liberty University (B), 296

MULTIMEDIA
College of Lake County (A), 170
Sessions.edu, 412

MUSIC
(see also under Religious Studies)
Cincinnati Bible College and Seminary (B), 161
Marylhurst University, 309
Oakland University (B), 357
South Suburban College, 419
Southwestern Assemblies of God University (A), 430

Instrumental Performance
Southwestern Assemblies of God University (B), 430

Jazz Studies
Open Learning Agency (B), 362

Music Education
Cincinnati Bible College and Seminary (B), 161
Southwestern Assemblies of God University (B), 430

Music Performance
Open Learning Agency (B), 362

Music Therapy
Open Learning Agency (B), 362

Piano Performance
Southwestern Assemblies of God University (B), 430

Vocal Performance
Southwestern Assemblies of God University (B), 430

NATIVE AMERICAN STUDIES
Northwest Indian College (A), 352

NATIVE STUDIES
Laurentian University (B), 292

NATURAL SCIENCES AND MATHEMATICS
Thomas Edison State College (A), 458

NETWORK ADMINISTRATION
University of Minnesota, Rochester Center (B), 504

NEW MEDIA
College Misericordia (B), 169

NOT-FOR-PROFIT STUDIES/ADMINISTRATION
Saint Mary-of-the-Woods College (B), 399

NURSING
Allegany College of Maryland (A), 101
Athabasca University (post RN), 116
Brenau University (RN, B), 134

Index by Fields of Study
Graduate Degree Programs

Southwestern Baptist Theological Seminary, 430
Trinity Lutheran Seminary, 462
University of Winnipeg, 534
Western Seminary, 561

EARLY CHILDHOOD TEACHER EDUCATION
Cincinnati Bible College and Seminary, 161

EARTH LITERACY
Saint Mary-of-the-Woods College, 399

ECONOMICS, APPLIED
(see Applied Economics)

EDUCATION
(see also Instructional Technology and Media;
   Computing and Education)
Antioch University McGregor, 112
Atlantic Union College, 117
Baker University, 120
Capella University, 148
Central Methodist College, 152
Concordia University, Austin, 185
Goddard College, 241
Hebrew College, 256
Indiana Wesleyan University, 267
Liberty University, 296
Loyola College, Maryland, 301
Michigan State University, 316
New Mexico State University, 340
Olivet Nazarene University, 362
Saint Joseph's College of Maine, 396
Southern Oregon University, 426
University of Akron, 473
University of Maryland, University College, 499
University of Montana, Missoula, 507
University of New England, 510
University of Wisconsin, Stevens Point, 536
Vermont College of Norwich University, 544
Walden University, 548
Wayne State College, 580

Adult and Post-Secondary
University of Wyoming Outreach School, 537
University of Calgary, 479

Alternative Education
Lock Haven University of Pennsylvania, 298

Art
East Carolina University, 209

Christian School Administration
Oral Roberts University, 363
Southwestern Assemblies of God University, 430

Christian School Curriculum
Oral Roberts University, 363

Christian School Postsecondary Administration
Oral Roberts University, 363

Christian School Program
Regent University, 381

Christian School Teaching
Oral Roberts University, 363

*Corporate Training and Knowledge Management
   Major*
Jones International University, 277

Curriculum
University College of Cape Breton, 471

Curriculum and Instruction
City University, 162
Lock Haven University of Pennsylvania, 298
University of Phoenix Online, 518

Curriculum and Instruction K-12
University of Nebraska, Lincoln, 508

Curriculum and Technology
University of Phoenix Online, 518

Curriculum Development
Southwestern Assemblies of God University, 430

Curriculum, Teaching and Learning
University of Calgary, 479

e-Education
University of Phoenix Online, 518

Early Childhood Education
Brenau University, 134
Concordia University, St. Paul, 574
Oral Roberts University, 363
University of Alaska Southeast, Juneau Campus,
   475

Educational Administration and Supervision
Indiana College Network, 264

Educational Administration Higher Education
University of Nebraska, Lincoln, 508

Educational Administration K-12
University of Nebraska, Lincoln, 508

Educational Leadership
University of Calgary, 479

Educational Technology
University of Alaska Southeast, Juneau Campus, 475
University of Calgary, 479

Elementary Education
Indiana College Network, 264

Generalist Major
Jones International University, 277

Gifted Education Focus
University of Missouri, Columbia, 506

Global Leadership and Administration Major
Jones International University, 277

Guidance and Counseling
City University, 162

Individualized Degree
Regent University, 381

Information technology
Memorial University of Newfoundland, 313

Instructional Technology
University of Wyoming Outreach School, 537

Language Education
Indiana College Network, 264

Learning Development
Fort Peck Community College, 228

Library and Resource Management Major
Jones International University, 277

Literacy Education
Mount St. Vincent University, 329

Literary Focus
University of Missouri, Columbia, 506

Master Educator Program
Regent University, 381

Public School Administration
Oral Roberts University, 363

Reading and Language Arts
University of Houston, 491

Reading and Literacy
City University, 162

Reading Specialist Certificate
University of Houston, 491

Research and Assessment Major
Jones International University, 277

School Age Care
Concordia University, St. Paul, 574

School Based Security and Community Policing
Regent University, 381

Social Studies Focus
University of Missouri, Columbia, 506

Special Education
East Carolina University, 209
Indiana College Network, 264
University of Louisville, 495

Special Education Generalist Major
Jones International University, 277

Teaching and Learning
University of Wyoming Outreach School, 537

Teaching English as a Second Language
Oral Roberts University, 363

Teaching with Certification
Oral Roberts University, 363

Technology
University College of Cape Breton, 471

Technology and Design Major
Jones International University, 277

TESOL
Regent University, 381

Visual Impairment
University of Louisville, 495

Youth Development
Concordia University, St. Paul, 574

EDUCATION ADMINISTRATION/MANAGEMENT
Concordia University, Wisconsin, 187

North Dakota State University, 346
Southwestern Oklahoma State University, 432
University of Hawaii System, 490

EDUCATION, CONTEMPLATIVE
Naropa University, 333

EDUCATION COUNSELING
Concordia University, Wisconsin, 187

EDUCATION, RELIGIOUS
(see Religious Education)

EDUCATION IN SCHOOL AGE CARE
Concordia University (Minnesota), 186

EDUCATION IN e-LEARNING
Jones International University, 277

EDUCATION SPECIALIST
School Administration
Wayne State College, 580

EDUCATION TECHNOLOGY
California State University, Bakersfield, 142

EDUCATION VIA DISTANCE LEARNING
The College of Saint Catherine, 171
Cumberland University, 193
Southern Illinois University, Carbondale, 423

EDUCATION, YOUTH DEVELOPMENT
Concordia University (Minnesota), 186

EDUCATIONAL ADMINISTRATION
California State University, Bakersfield, 142
National University, 335
Southeast Missouri State University, 420
University of Massachusetts, Lowell, 501

Higher Education
University of Nebraska, Lincoln, 508

EDUCATIONAL ADMINISTRATION AND SUPERVISION
Seton Hall University, 412

EDUCATIONAL COUNSELING
Southeast Missouri State University, 420

EDUCATIONAL LEADERSHIP
Marylhurst University, 309
University of North Dakota, 514
University of Montana, Missoula, 507
University of Vermont, 530

EDUCATIONAL MEDIA
Saint Cloud State University, 394
University of Central Florida, 482

EDUCATIONAL TECHNOLOGY
Boise State University, 131
Cleveland State University, 166
Connecticut State University System, 187
George Washington University, 237
National University, 335
University of Missouri, Columbia, 506
University of South Dakota, 523

EDUCATIONAL TECHNOLOGY AND INSTRUCTIONAL DESIGN
Michigan State University, 316

EDUCATIONAL TECHNOLOGY LEADERSHIP
George Washington University, 237

ELECTRIC POWER ENGINEERING
Rensselaer Polytechnic Institute, 382

ELECTRICAL AND COMPUTER ENGINEERING
Auburn University, 118
Georgia Institute of Technology, 238
Indiana College Network, 264
Kansas State University, 280
Northeastern University, 576
Oklahoma State University, 360
University of Alabama, 475
University of Colorado at Boulder, 484
University of Massachusetts, Amherst, 500

ELECTRICAL ENGINEERING
Bradley University, 133
California State University, Northridge, 144
Colorado State University, 176
Iowa State University, 270
National Technological University, 334
Southern Methodist University, School of Engineering, 424
State University of New York at Buffalo, 435
University of Delaware, 487
University of Idaho, Engineering Outreach, 492
University of Illinois, Urbana-Champaign, 493
University of Minnesota, Rochester Center, 504
University of Southern California School of Engineering, 524
Virginia Polytechnic Institute and State University, 546

Computer/Electronics
University of Houston, 491

Microelectronics
Rensselaer Polytechnic Institute, 382

ELECTRONIC COMMERCE
(see also Internet Business)
Capella University, 148
National University, 335
University of Maryland, University College, 499

ELEMENTARY EDUCATION
Newman University, 343
Southwest Missouri State University, 427
University of North Dakota, 514

ELEMENTARY TEACHER EDUCATION LICENSE
Cincinnati Bible College and Seminary, 161

ENERGY MANAGEMENT
New York Institute of Technology, 342

ENGINEERING
Arizona State University, 113
California National University for Advanced Studies, 142
Florida Atlantic University, 223
Kettering University, 283
New Mexico State University, 340
Purdue University, 379
Texas Tech University, 457
University of Alabama, 475
University of Arizona, 477
The University of Florida, 489
University of Nebraska, Lincoln, 508
University of South Carolina, 522
University of Toledo, 530
University of Virginia, 532
University of Wisconsin, Platteville, 536

Electrical Engineering Major
Arizona State University, 113

ENGINEERING AND TECHNOLOGY MANAGEMENT
Oklahoma State University, 360

ENGINEERING MANAGEMENT
Colorado State University, 176
Eastern Michigan University, 212
Kansas State University, 280
Metropolitan Community College, 315
National Technological University, 334
The New Jersey Institute of Technology, 339
Southern Methodist University, School of Engineering, 424
Syracuse University, 446
The University of Tennessee, Knoxville, 528
University of Tennessee Space Institute, 528
University of Colorado at Boulder, 484
University of Massachusetts, Amherst, 500
University of Colorado at Denver, 485
University of Alabama, 475
University of Idaho, Engineering Outreach, 492

ENGINEERING SCIENCE
Management of Technology concentration
Rensselaer Polytechnic Institute, 382

Manufacturing Systems Engineering concentration
Rensselaer Polytechnic Institute, 382

Microelectronics Manufacturing Engineering concentration
Rensselaer Polytechnic Institute, 382

ENGLISH
Utah State University, 542

Technical and Professional Communication
East Carolina University, 209

ENGLISH AS A SECOND LANGUAGE
Newman University, 343

ENTOMOLOGY
University of Nebraska, Lincoln, 508

ENVIRONMENT POLICY MANAGEMENT
University of Denver, 488

ENVIRONMENTAL AND TECHNOLOGICAL STUDIES
Saint Cloud State University, 394

ENVIRONMENTAL ENGINEERING
Colorado State University, 176
Georgia Institute of Technology, 238
Southern Methodist University, School of Engineering, 424

ENVIRONMENTAL, HEALTH AND SAFETY MANAGEMENT
Rochester Institute of Technology, 387

ENVIRONMENTAL MANAGEMENT
The University of Findlay, 488
University of Maryland, University College, 499

ENVIRONMENTAL SCIENCE
Oklahoma State University, 360
University of Idaho, Engineering Outreach, 492

ENVIRONMENTAL SCIENCE MANAGEMENT
Duquesne University, 207

Index by Fields of Study
Doctoral Degree Progams

Index by Fields of Study
Certificate and
Diploma Programs

CHILD DEVELOPMENT
(see Human Development)

CHIROPRACTIC TECHNICIAN
Highline Community College, 258

CHRISTIAN
(see Religious Studies)

CIVIL, STRUCTURAL, AND ENVIRONMENTAL ENGINEERING
State University of New York at Buffalo, 435
Worcester Polytechnic Institute, 569

CIVIL WAR
Carroll College, 149

CLASSICAL STUDIES
University College of the University of Maine System, 472
University of Maine, 496
University of Waterloo, 533

CLERICAL
(see also specifics under Computer Science; Law/Justice; Health Administration)
Coconino Community College, 168

Administrative Office Assistant
University of Alaska Southeast, Juneau Campus, 475

Word Processing
Highline Community College, 258
Sullivan County Community College, 445
Walla Walla Community College, 549

CLINICAL BIOETHICS
Cleveland State University, 166

CLINICAL PATHOLOGY
University of Massachusetts, Lowell, 501

CLINICAL RESEARCH ADMINISTRATION
George Washington University, 237

CLINICAL SUPERVISION
University of New Orleans Metropolitan College, 512

COACH MAINTENANCE
South Suburban College, 419

CODING
Midland College, 319

COLLEGE BASIC EDUCATION/CAREER PREPARATION
Open Learning Agency, 362

COMMERCIAL PERFORMANCE
Columbia State Community College, 179

COMMUNICATION SYSTEMS
University of Idaho, Engineering Outreach, 492

COMMUNICATIONS
Capella University, 148
Jones International University, 277
University of Massachusetts, Boston, 500
University of Massachusetts, Lowell, 501

Communications Technology Management
Capella University, 148

Data Communications
Rochester Institute of Technology, 387

COMMUNITY AND ECONOMIC DEVELOPMENT
Penn State University, 371

COMMUNITY HEALTH
University of Alaska, Fairbanks, 576

COMMUNITY HEALTH EDUCATION
California College for Health Sciences, 141
Saint Cloud State University, 394

COMMUNITY PLANNING AND DEVELOPMENT
University College of the University of Maine System, 472

COMPLETION
Casper College, 151

COMPOSITE MATERIALS
University of Delaware, 487

COMPUTER SCIENCE
(see also Internet; Intranet Development; Microsoft; Telecommunications)
Acadia University, 97
Allegany College of Maryland, 101
Bunker Hill Community College, 137
Laval University, 293
Loyola University Chicago, 302
National Technological University, 334
Rensselaer Polytechnic Institute, 382
Thomas Edison State College, 458
University of Alabama, 475
University of Bridgeport, 478

Client-Server Specialist
Highline Community College, 258

Computer Aided Design (CAD)
Michigan State University, 316
South Suburban College, 419
Thomas Edison State College, 458

Computer and Information Sciences
Diablo Valley College, 204
Dixie State College of Utah, 205
Knowledge Systems Institute, 285

Computer Application
Edison Community College (Florida), 213
University of Alaska Southeast, Juneau Campus, 475

Computer Graphics and Data Visualization
(see also Graphics and Multimedia)
Midland College, 319
Rensselaer Polytechnic Institute, 382

Computer Hardware Support
Diablo Valley College, 204

Computer Operator
Fort Peck Community College, 228
Sullivan County Community College, 445

Computer Skills for Managers
College of San Mateo, 172

Computer Software
Coconino Community College, 168
Pitt Community College, 375
University of Washington, 532

Computer Systems
Kentucky Community and Technical College System, 283
Montgomery County Community College, 326

Computer Training
University of New Orleans Metropolitan College, 512

Computing
Athabasca University, 116
State University of New York at Buffalo, 435
University of Massachusetts, Boston, 500
University of Washington, 532

Data/Database
Connecticut State University System, 187
Loyola University Chicago, 302
Palo Alto College, 366
Rensselaer Polytechnic Institute, 382
University of California Extension, 481
University of Denver, 488
University of Maryland, University College, 499
University of Washington, 532

Desktop Publishing and Graphics
University of Alaska Southeast, Juneau Campus, 475

Information Systems
Athabasca University, 116
Cerro Coso Community College, 156
Linfield College, 298
Strayer University, 443
Thomas Edison State College, 458
University of California Extension, 481
Victor Valley College, 544

Microcomputer Hardware Support
Diablo Valley College, 204

Microcomputer Database Specialist
Lansing Community College, 291

Microcomputer Information Specialist
Highline Community College, 258

Microcomputer Maintenance And Service Technician
Grays Harbor College, 249

Microcomputer Software Specialist
Fond du Lac Tribal and Community College, 226

Microcomputer Support Specialist
University of Alaska, Fairbanks, 576
University of Alaska Southeast, Sitka Campus, 476

Microcomputers
Skagit Valley College, 416

Networking/Networks
Burlington County College, 138
Capella University, 148
Community Colleges of Colorado Online, 184
East Carolina University, 209
Edison Community College (Florida), 213
Fort Hays State University, 227
Grays Harbor College, 249
Highline Community College, 258
Kentucky Community and Technical College System, 283
Loyola University Chicago, 302
The New Jersey Institute of Technology, 339
Rensselaer Polytechnic Institute, 382
Rio Salado College, 385

Rochester Institute of Technology, 387
Santa Barbara City College, 406
State University of New York at Buffalo, 435
University of Alaska Southeast, Sitka Campus, 476
University of Denver, 488

Personal Computer Specialist
Palo Alto College, 366
Lifetime Career Schools, 296
Anne Arundel Community College, 111

Programming
Carroll College, 149
City University, 162
Edison Community College (Florida), 213
Mott Community College, 328
Rio Salado College, 385
Northwest Indian College, 352
Southern New Hampshire University, 425
University of Alaska Southeast, Juneau Campus, 475
University of California Extension, 481
University of Washington, 532

Software Development/Management
Champlain College, 158
Dalhousie University, 195
Grays Harbor College, 249
Rensselaer Polytechnic Institute, 382
Sinclair Community College, 415
University of Maryland, University College, 499
University of Southern California School of Engineering, 524

Specialized Studies Program
University of California at Davis, 480

System Analysis
Rio Salado College, 385

UNIX
University of Massachusetts, Lowell, 501

Visual Basic Programming
University of Maryland, University College, 499

CONFLICT AND CULTURE
(see also Negotiation and Conflict Resolution)
Marylhurst University, 309

CONSTRUCTION
Antioch University McGregor, 112
Coconino Community College, 168
Diablo Valley College, 204
Fort Peck Community College, 228
Midland College, 319
Northwest Indian College, 352
South Suburban College, 419
University of Washington, 532

CONVERGENT TECHNOLOGIES
Community Colleges of Colorado Online, 184

CORPORATE FINANCIAL MANAGEMENT
University of Dallas Graduate School of Management, 486

CORPORATE RECORDS
South Suburban College, 419

CORRECTIONS
American Military University, 108
Grays Harbor College, 249
Indiana College Network, 264

COUNSELING
Aids Counseling
Albertus Magnus College, 100

Career Counseling
American Military University, 108

College Counseling
UCLA Extension, 467

Counseling Psychology
Capella University, 148

Counseling Women
Athabasca University, 116

Counselor Education and Supervision
Capella University, 148

Professional Counseling
Capella University, 148

COURT REPORTING
South Suburban College, 419

CREATIVE EXPRESSIONS
Institute of Transpersonal Psychology, 268

CRIMINOLOGY
(see also Law/Justice)
Bunker Hill Community College, 137
Capella University, 148
Edison Community College (Florida), 213
Grays Harbor College, 249
Memorial University of Newfoundland, 313
Spring Arbor University, 434
Saint Joseph's College of Maine, 396
University of Alabama, 475
University of Wisconsin, Platteville, 536

CTC CROSS-CULTURAL LANGUAGE AND ACADEMIC DEVELOPMENT
National University, 335
UCLA Extension, 467

CULTURE
(see Conflict and Culture)
Cultural Conservation
University of Victoria, 531

CURRICULUM AND INSTRUCTION
(see also Education)
Information Processing Technologies
University of Houston, 491

Master of Education in Reading, Language Arts, and Literature Education
University of Houston, 491

Curriculum Integration in Action
University of Washington, 532

CUSTOMER SERVICE
Avila College, 573
Burlington County College, 138
Columbia State Community College, 179
Fond du Lac Tribal and Community College, 226
Palo Alto College, 366
Rio Salado College, 385

Customer Relationship Management
Penn State University, 371

CUSTOMIZED CERTIFICATE OPTIONS
University of Wisconsin, Platteville, 536

DANCE STUDIO MANAGEMENT
Columbia State Community College, 179

DENTAL
Edison Community College (Florida), 213
West Los Angeles College, 554

Dental Assisting
Diablo Valley College, 204
Highline Community College, 258
Monroe Community College, 322
Open Learning Agency, 362

Dental Hygiene
Diablo Valley College, 204

Dental Laboratory Technology
Diablo Valley College, 204

DESKTOP PUBLISHING GRAPHICS
University of Alaska Southeast, Sitka Campus, 476

DIESEL MECHANIC
Dixie State College of Utah, 205

DIGITAL OFFICE
Penn State University, 371

DIGITAL SIGNAL PROCESSING
Indiana College Network, 264
Purdue University, 379

DISABILITY MANAGEMENT
Dalhousie University, 195

DISASTER
(see Emergency)

DISTRIBUTION/LOGISTICS
Lima Technical College, 297

DIVERSITY STUDIES
Capella University, 148

DIVING, HARVEST
Northwest Indian College, 352

DOCUMENT IMAGING SPECIALIST
Northwest Indian College, 352

DOLL REPAIR
Lifetime Career Schools, 296

DRAFTING/DESIGN
Coconino Community College, 168
Diablo Valley College, 204
Highline Community College, 258

Mechanical Drafting
Diablo Valley College, 204

DRIVER EDUCATION
Indiana College Network, 264

Accelerated Commercial Drivers License Preparation
National Training, Incorporated, National Truck Drivers School, National Heavy Equipment Operator School, 335

Commercial Drivers License Preparation
National Training, Incorporated, National Truck Drivers School, National Heavy Equipment Operator School, 335

Commercial Drivers License Prepared Truckers Program
National Training, Incorporated, National Truck Drivers School, National Heavy Equipment Operator School, 335

Truck Driving/Heavy Equipment Operator
Fort Peck Community College, 228

DRUG AND ALCOHOL
(see Addiction)

ECOPSYCHOLOGY
Naropa University, 333

ECOTOURISM MANAGEMENT
University of Denver, 488

EDUCATION
(see also Curriculum and Instruction; Paraprofessional Education; TESOL)
Capella University, 148
Fort Hays State University, 227
Kansas City, Kansas Community College, 280
University of Manitoba, 497
University of Massachusetts, Boston, 500
Vermont College of Norwich University, 544

Adult Education
Capella University, 148
Open Learning Agency, 362
University of Calgary, 479
University of Manitoba, 497
University of Victoria, 531

Brain Research in Education
University of Washington, 532

California Teacher Credential
City University, 162

Community College Faculty And Administrators
University of Central Florida, 482

Distance Education
Capella University, 148
George Washington University, 237
Indiana College Network, 264
Indiana University, 265
State University of West Georgia, 442
University of Maryland, Baltimore County, 498
University of Maryland, University College, 499
University of Washington, 532

Distance Education Technology
Athabasca University, 116

Early Childhood Education
Central Piedmont Community College, 154
Coconino Community College, 168
Columbia State Community College, 179
Concordia University (Minnesota), 186
Concordia University, St. Paul, 574
Highline Community College, 258
Northwest Indian College, 352
San Joaquin Delta College, 403
Stephens College, 443
Sullivan County Community College, 445

Teikyo Post University, 451
University College of the University of Maine System, 472
University of Alaska Southeast, Sitka Campus, 476
University of Alaska Southeast, Juneau Campus, 475
University of Wyoming Outreach School, 537

Early Childhood Education
University of Alaska Southeast, Juneau Campus, 475
University of Texas of the Permian Basin, 578

Early Childhood Special Education
Emporia State University, 217
Pacific Oaks College, 366

Educational Administration
Capella University, 148
Indiana College Network, 264

Educational Technology
Boise State University, 131
Harvard University Extension School, 254
Jones International University, 277
Michigan State University, 316
National University, 335
Penn State University, 371
Saint Cloud State University, 394
San Jose City College, 404
Teachers College, Columbia University, 449
University of Alaska Southeast, Juneau Campus, 475
University of Nebraska, Lincoln, 508

Electronic Learning (E-learning)
Roosevelt University, 390

Elementary Education
California State University, Bakersfield, 142
Stephens College, 443
University of Alaska Southeast, Juneau Campus, 475

Inclusive Education
Athabasca University, 116

Middle School
Western Wyoming Community College, 562

Multiple Subject Teaching Credential
National University, 335

Online Teaching
Capella University, 148
UCLA Extension, 467

Oregon Standard Teacher's License
Southern Oregon University, 426

Paraeducation
Northwest Indian College, 352

Postsecondary Teaching
Colorado State University, 176

Professional Clear Teaching Credential
California State University, Bakersfield, 142

Reading Endorsement
North Georgia College and State University, 347
University of Alaska Southeast, Juneau Campus, 475

Special Education
Central Missouri State University, 153
Gonzaga University, 243

Highline Community College, 258
Kansas City, Kansas Community College, 280
San Jose State University, 404
University of Calgary, 479
University of Louisville, 495
The University of North Carolina at Charlotte, 513

Substitute Teacher
California State University, Bakersfield, 142

Teacher Aide/Assistant
South Suburban College, 419

Teaching and Training Online
Capella University, 148

Teaching English as a Second Language
Emporia State University, 217
UCLA Extension, 467

Teaching, Learning And Technology
University of Washington, 532

Tele-Learning
East Carolina University, 209

TESOL
Regent University, 381

Virtual Reality in Education
East Carolina University, 209

ELECTRIC POWER ENGINEERING/TECHNOLOGY
Bismarck State College, 128
Rensselaer Polytechnic Institute, 382

ELECTRICAL AND COMPUTER ENGINEERING/ CONTROLS, COMMUNICATIONS, AND SOFTWARE
State University of New York at Buffalo, 435

ELECTRICAL CONSTRUCTION WIRING TRAINING
Coconino Community College, 168

ELECTRICAL TRANSMISSION SYSTEMS TECHNOLOGY
Bismarck State College, 128

ELECTRONIC SERVICE TECHNOLOGY
Diablo Valley College, 204

ELECTRONIC TECHNOLOGY
Diablo Valley College, 204

ELECTRONICS
Thomas Edison State College, 458

Electronics Computer Technology
Cleveland Institute of Electronics, 166

Electronics Engineering/Technology
Columbia State Community College, 179
Midland College, 319
South Suburban College, 419

EMBEDDED AND REAL-TIME SYSTEMS PROGRAMMING
University of Washington, 532

EMERGENCY SCIENCES
Disaster and Emergency Management
Rochester Institute of Technology, 387

Emergency Health Services Management
Dalhousie University, 195

Index by Fields of Study
Individual Classes

Please note that the colleges and universities responding to the survey were asked to provide listings of representative classes, so this listing is not exhaustive. Some schools requested that prospective students call for a complete listing of available classes. Therefore, you should not eliminate a school from consideration just because its name does not appear under a category in which you are interested. Check the school's web site or call for a current catalog.

Emporia State University, 217
Fort Hays State University, 227
George Washington University, 237
Grand Canyon University, 247
Hebrew College, 256
Marshall University, 307
Marygrove College, 309
Montana State University, Northern, 324
New Jersey City University, 338
Olivet Nazarene University, 362
San Diego State University, 403
San Jose City College, 404
San Jose State University, 404
Texas A&M University, Commerce, 456
University of California Extension, 481
The University of Findlay, 488
University of Louisville, 495
University of South Dakota, 523
University of Southern Mississippi, 526

EDUCATIONAL LEADERSHIP
Andrews University, 110
George Washington University, 237
Jamestown Community College, 274
Marshall University, 307
Pacific Oaks College, 366

EDUCATIONAL RESEARCH
George Washington University, 237
Marshall University, 307
Pacific Oaks College, 366
Saint Cloud State University, 394
San Jose State University, 404
University of Southern Mississippi, 526

ELECTRIC UTILITY TECHNOLOGY
North Central State College, 345

ELECTRICAL CIRCUITS
Westchester Community College, 556

ELECTRICAL ENGINEERING
(see Engineering, Electrical)

ELECTRICAL MAINTENANCE
North Central State College, 345

ELECTRICITY
Delaware Technical and Community College, 201
University of Southern Mississippi, 526

ELECTRONIC DEVICES
Kellogg Community College, 282

ELECTRONIC INFORMATION
Central Missouri State University, 153

ELECTRONIC MEDIA
State University of New York at New Paltz, 436
Palo Alto College, 366
UC Raymond Walters College, 467
University of Minnesota, Twin Cities, 504

ELECTRONICS
(see also Automotive Electricity/Electronics)
Cleveland Institute of Electronics, 166
Cuesta College, 192
Joliet Junior College, 277

ELECTRONICS ENGINEERING
Edison Community College (Florida), 213
Houston Community College, 262
The University of New Mexico, 512

EMBRYOLOGY
(see also Child and Human Development)
University of Southern Mississippi, 526

EMERGENCY
(see also Crisis and Disaster Management)

Emergency Care
University College of the Cariboo, 471

Emergency Communications
Renton Technical College, 383

Emergency Health Services
University of Maryland, Baltimore County, 498

Emergency Management
Jacksonville State University, 273
Saint Petersburg Junior College, 400
University of Akron, 473

Emergency Medical Leadership
Saint Petersburg Junior College, 400

Emergency Medical Service Professions
Tyler Junior College, 466

Emergency Medical Services Technology
Edison Community College (Florida), 213

Emergency Medical Technician (EMT) And Paramedic
Alvin Community College, 103
Cuesta College, 192
Dodge City Community College, 205
Weber State University, 553

Emergency Technical Applications
Saint Petersburg Junior College, 400

ENGINEERING
(see also Biochemical Regulatory Engineering;
    Bioengineering; Biology, Biology and Life Sciences
    for Biosystems Engineering; Computer Sciences,
    Computer Engineering; Computer Sciences,
    Software Engineering; Electronics Engineering;
    Environment, Environmental Engineering; Industrial
    Engineering; Manufacturing Engineering
    Technology)
Bluefield State College, 131
Cleveland State University, 166
Edison Community College (Florida), 213
Frostburg State University, 232
Jamestown Community College, 274
Marshall University, 307
Massachusetts Institute of Technology, 310
Montana Tech of the University of Montana, 324
Montgomery County Community College, 326
North Carolina State University, 344
North Dakota State University, 346
Open Learning Agency, 362
Southern Illinois University, Carbondale, 423
Syracuse University, 446
Texas Tech University, 457
Tidewater Community College, 459
UCLA Extension, 467
University of Alabama, 475
University of Colorado at Denver, 485
University of Mississippi, 506
University of Missouri, 577
University of Nebraska, Lincoln, 508
University of Oklahoma, 516
University of South Carolina, 522
The University of Tennessee, Knoxville, 528

University of Toledo, 530
Worcester Polytechnic Institute, 569

Chemical Engineering
University of Alabama, 475
University of Massachusetts, Amherst, 500

Electrical Engineering
Bluefield State College, 131
Bradley University, 133
North Central State College, 345
University of Minnesota, Rochester Center, 504
University of Nebraska, Lincoln, 508
University of New Brunswick, 510

Electrical and Computer Engineering
University of Arizona, 477

Engineering, Civil/Land Surveying
Edison Community College (Florida), 213
Lake Superior College, 287
The University of Tennessee, Knoxville, 528
Worcester Polytechnic Institute, 569

Mechanical Engineering
Bradley University, 133
North Central State College, 345
San Jose State University, 404
University of Arizona, 477
University of Minnesota, Rochester Center, 504
The University of New Mexico, 512

ENGINEERING GRAPHICS
Southern Arkansas University Tech, 422

ENGINEERING/TECH
Montana Tech of the University of Montana, 324

ENGLISH
(includes Developmental English)
Adams State College, 97
Allan Hancock College, 101
Alvin Community College, 103
American Academy of Nutrition, 103
American River College, 108
Arcadia University, 113
Athabasca University, 116
Austin Community College, 118
Barstow College, 122
Beaufort County Community College, 125
Bellevue Community College, 125
Bismarck State College, 128
Back Hills State University, 130
Bluefield State College, 131
Borough of Manhattan Community College, 132
Butte Community College, 139
Cabrillo Community College, 140
Calhoun State Community College, 141
California College for Health Sciences, 141
California State University, Stanislaus, 145
Carroll Community College, 150
Chadron State College, 157
Charter Oak State College, 159
Chesapeake College, 160
Christopher Newport University, 160
Cleveland State University, 166
Coastline Community College, 167
College of the Canyons, 174
College of the Sequoias, 174
College of the Siskiyous, 174
Columbia Union College, 180
Community College of Rhode Island, 182
Community College of Southern Nevada, 183

FARM/RANCH MANAGEMENT
(see also Agriculture)

FASHION DESIGN AND MERCHANDISING
(see also Textiles)

FILM STUDIES
(see also Mass Media; Radio and Television;
    Screen/Scriptwriting)

FINANCE
(see also Fund Raising; Financial Management and
    Services; Financial Planning; Personal Finance)

Corporate Finance

International Finance

Personal Finance

FINANCIAL MANAGEMENT/SERVICES

FINANCIAL PLANNING

FINANCING, HEALTHCARE
(see Health Sciences, Health Care Financing)

FINE ARTS

FINNISH LANGUAGE
(see Languages, Finnish)

FIRE SCIENCE AND TECHNOLOGY

Abnormal Psychology

Adolescent Psychology

Applied Psychology

Child Psychology

REFRIGERATION/HEAT/AIR CONDITIONING
Danville Community College, 198
Monroe Community College, 322
North Central State College, 345
Palomar Community College, 367

REGULATORY AFFAIRS
San Diego State University, 403

REHABILITATION
(see also Occupational Therapy)
Southern Illinois University, Carbondale, 423
State University of New York, College at Cortland, 438
University of British Columbia, 478
The University of Tennessee, Knoxville, 528

RELIGIONS OF INDIA/CHINA/JAPAN
University System of Georgia Independent Study, 539

RELIGIOUS STUDIES
(see also Buddhist Studies; Islam; Jewish Studies;
    Philosophy; Religions of India/China/Japan)
Assemblies of God Theological Seminary, 115
Athabasca University, 116
Bakersfield College, 121
Bergen Community College, 127
Bryn Athyn College of the New Church, 574
California State University, Fullerton, 144
California State University, Stanislaus, 145
Central Methodist College, 152
Chadron State College, 157
Christopher Newport University, 160
College of Saint Scholastica, 171
Columbia International University, 178
Columbia Union College, 180
Concordia University, Austin, 185
De Anza College, 200
Delaware County Community College, 200
Drury University, 206
Duquesne University, 207
Eastern Kentucky University, 211
Gordon-Conwell Theological Seminary, 244
Governors State University, 245
Grace University, 246
Grand Rapids Baptist Seminary, 248
Indiana University, 265
Indiana Wesleyan University, 267
Jefferson College, 274
Judson College, 278
Las Positas College, 292
Lutheran Theological Seminary at Philadelphia, 304
Middle Tennessee State University, 318
Naropa University, 333
Notre Dame College, 356
Ohio University Eastern, 359
Peralta Community College District: Alameda, Laney,
    Merritt, and Vista Colleges, 372
Portland State University, 376
Queen's University, 380
The Richard Stockton College of New Jersey, 384
Saint Francis Xavier University, 395
Saint Gregory's University, 395
Seminary Extension, 411
Southwest Missouri State University, 427
Spoon River College, 433
State University of New York at Oswego, 437
Syracuse University, 446
Taylor University World Wide Campus, 449
Tennessee Temple University, 455
Trinity Lutheran Seminary, 462
Tyler Junior College, 466
UCLA Extension, 467
Union University, 470
University of Alabama, 475

University of California Extension, 481
University of Kansas, 494
University of Manitoba, 497
University of Missouri, 577
University of North Carolina, Chapel Hill, 514
University of Regina, 519
University of Saint Francis, 520
University of Southern Mississippi, 526
The University of Tennessee, Knoxville, 528
University of Waterloo, 533
University System of Georgia Independent Study, 539
University Without Walls—Skidmore College, 540
Western Seminary, 561
Wilfrid Laurier University, 566

Adventism
Walla Walla College, 548

Biblical Counseling
Columbia International University, 178
Grace University, 246

Biblical Literature
Hebrew College, 256
Indiana Wesleyan University, 267
Western Seminary, 561

Christian Ethics
Columbia International University, 178
Gordon-Conwell Theological Seminary, 244
University Without Walls—Skidmore College, 540

Christian Evidences
Columbia International University, 178

Church History
Assemblies of God Theological Seminary, 115
Concordia University, Austin, 185
Gordon-Conwell Theological Seminary, 244
Grace University, 246
Grand Rapids Baptist Seminary, 248
Judson College, 278
Saint Gregory's University, 395
Southern Illinois University, Carbondale, 423
Taylor University World Wide Campus, 449
Western Seminary, 561

Church Leadership/Administration
Gordon-Conwell Theological Seminary, 244
Grand Rapids Baptist Seminary, 248

Communication in Congregation
Lutheran Theological Seminary at Philadelphia, 304

Evangelism
Lutheran Theological Seminary at Philadelphia, 304

Ministry
Columbia International University, 178
Gordon-Conwell Theological Seminary, 244
Grand Rapids Baptist Seminary, 248
Hope International University, 261
Notre Dame College, 356

Pastoral Care/Counseling
Gordon-Conwell Theological Seminary, 244
Hope International University, 261

Pastoral Ministries
Hope International University, 261
Seminary Extension, 411
Taylor University World Wide Campus, 449

Religious Education
Seminary Extension, 411

Stewardship
Lutheran Theological Seminary at Philadelphia, 304

Theology
Columbia International University, 178
Columbia Union College, 180
Concordia University (Illinois), 184
Franciscan University of Steubenville, 230
Gordon-Conwell Theological Seminary, 244
Grand Rapids Baptist Seminary, 248
Hope International University, 261
Lutheran Theological Seminary at Philadelphia, 304
Saint Gregory's University, 395
Seminary Extension, 411
Taylor University World Wide Campus, 449
Tennessee Temple University, 455
Western Seminary, 561

Youth Ministry
Taylor University World Wide Campus, 449

REPORTING
(see also Journalism; Newswriting; Radio and
    Television)
Clackamas Community College, 163

RESEARCH METHODOLOGIES
(includes Business Research Methods; see also
    Education; Educational Research; Internet
    Research; Nursing Research; Operations Research)
Acadia University, 97
American Graduate University, 105
Arcadia University, 113
Brevard Community College, 134
Broome Community College, 135
Cabrillo Community College, 140
California State University, Stanislaus, 145
Columbia Basin College, 177
Columbus State Community College, 181
Emporia State University, 217
Metropolitan Community College, 315
Minnesota State University, Moorhead, 320
The New School, 341
Olivet Nazarene University, 362
Pierce College, 373
San Jose City College, 404
Sandhills Community College, 405
State University of New York at Oswego, 437
University of Maine, Machias, 497
University of New Hampshire, 511
University of Southern Mississippi, 526
University of Wisconsin, Whitewater, 579
Upper Iowa University, 541

RESOURCE MANAGEMENT
Florida State University, 224
University System of Georgia Independent Study, 539

RETAILING
Contra Costa College, 188
Genesee Community College, 237
Lima Technical College, 297
Monroe Community College, 322
Saginaw Valley State University, 393
University System of Georgia Independent Study, 539
Weber State University, 553
West Shore Community College, 555

RISK CONTROL
University of Wisconsin, Stout, 537

RISK MANAGEMENT
(see Project Risk Management; Safety Sciences)

RUSSIAN LANGUAGE
(see Languages, Russian)